América Central y el Caribe
Estados Unidos
Golfo de México
Océano Atlántico
N
W
E
S
Estrecho de la Florida
Islas Bahamas
Canal de Yucatán
La Habana
Matanzas
Pinar del Río
Cienfuegos
Cuba
Camagüey
Guantánamo
Santiago de Cuba
Rep. Dominicana
Haití
Puerto Príncipe
Santo Domingo
Mayagüez
Puerto Rico
San Juan
Ponce
Jamaica
Kingston
México
Belice
Belmopan
Guatemala
Chichicastenango
Quezaltenango
Antigua
Guatemala
Honduras
Copán
Tegucigalpa
San Salvador
El Salvador
Nicaragua
Managua
Mar Caribe
Islas Vírgenes
(EE.UU & Br.)
Antigua
Antillas Menores
Guadalupe
Dominica
Martinica
Sta. Lucía
San Vicente
Barbados
Granada
Tobago
Puerto España
Trinidad
Aruba
Bonaire
Curaçao
Puntarenas
Puerto Limón
San José
Costa Rica
Canal de Panamá
Colón
Panamá
Panamá
Islas de San Blas
Colombia
Venezuela
Océano Pacífico

Instructor's Annotated Edition

VISTAS

Introducción a la lengua española

José A. Blanco

Mary Ann Dellinger
University of Phoenix

Philip Donley
Austin Community College

María Isabel García
Boston University

• • •

Elaine K. Horwitz
Senior Consulting Editor
University of Texas

VISTA HIGHER LEARNING

Boston, Massachusetts • Auburn, California

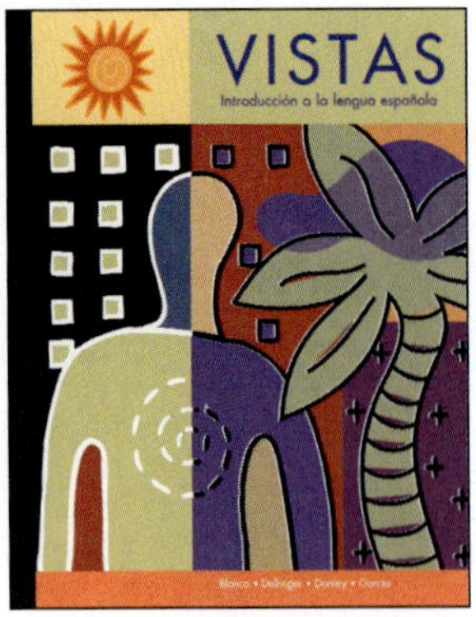

Award-winning cover Illustrator **José Ortega** was born in Ecuador and studied at New York's prestigious School of Visual Arts. His work has appeared in magazines and advertisements throughout the world.

Publisher: José A. Blanco

Editorial Director of College Publishing: Denise St. Jean

Director of Manufacturing: Stephen Pekich

Director of Production & Design: Peter O'Faherty

Staff Editors: María Cinta Aparisi, Pamela Mishkin, Gustavo Cinci, Sonny Regelman, Mark Porter, Daniella Tourgeman, Abby Smuckler

Contributing Writers: Sharon Alexander, Karin Fajardo, Ana M. Fores, Gregory Garretson, Jane Ann Johnson, Norah L. Jones, Ralph Kite, Susan Lake, Ann Morrill, Isabel Picado, Beatriz Pojman, Teresa Shu, Marcia Tugendhat

Art Director: Linda Jurras

Design Team: Suzanne Korschun, Martin Beveridge, Barbara Gazley, Susan Prentiss, Ianka de la Rosa

Photographer: Martin Bernetti

Production Team: Ted Cantrell, Eric Murphy, Janet Spicer, Holly Kersey, Greg Moutafis, Oscar Díez

Student Text ISBN 1-931100-00-4
Instructor's Annotated Edition ISBN 1-931100-01-2

Library of Congress Card Number: 00-109094

1 2 3 4 5 6 7 8 9 VH 05 04 03 02 01

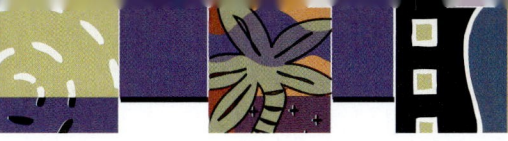

Instructor's Annotated Edition

Table of Contents

The **VISTAS** Story

Vista Higher Learning, the publisher of **VISTAS,** was founded with one mission: to raise the teaching of Spanish to a higher level. Years of experience working with textbook publishers convinced us that more could be done to offer you superior tools and to give your students a more profound learning experience. Along the way, we questioned everything about the way textbooks support the teaching of introductory college Spanish.

The result is **VISTAS: Introducción a la lengua española,** a textbook and coordinated package of ancillaries that look different and *are* different. We took a fresh look at introductory college Spanish and, with our authors and senior consulting editor, created an alternative program built completely around your and your students' needs.

We welcome you to **VISTAS,** and we hope that you and your students will enjoy using it. And please contact us with your questions, comments, and reactions.

Vista Higher Learning
13620 Lincoln Way, Suite 325
Auburn, CA 95603
TEL: 530-888-1111 / 800-618-7375
FAX: 530-888-1191
www.vistahigherlearning.com

Getting to Know VISTAS

Vibrant and original, **VISTAS** takes a fresh, student-friendly approach to introductory Spanish aimed at making students' learning and instructors' teaching easier, more enjoyable, and more successful. At the same time, **VISTAS** takes a communicative approach to language learning. It develops students' speaking, listening, reading, and writing skills so that they will be able to express their own ideas and interact with others meaningfully and for real-life purposes. It emphasizes frequently used vocabulary, and it presents grammar as a tool for effective communication. And because cultural knowledge is an integral part of both language learning and successful communication, **VISTAS** introduces students to the everyday lives of Spanish speakers, as well as the twenty-one countries of the Spanish-speaking world.

While other introductory college Spanish programs are based on these same pedagogical principles, **VISTAS** offers several additional features that make it truly different.

- **VISTAS** is the first introductory college Spanish textbook to incorporate graphic design—page layout, use of colors, typefaces, and other graphic elements—as an integral part of the learning process. To enhance learning and make navigation easy, lesson sections appear either completely on one page or on spreads of two facing pages. The textbook pages themselves are also visually dramatic, with an array of photos, drawings, realia, charts, graphs, diagrams, and word lists, all designed for both pedagogical impact and visual appeal.
- **VISTAS** offers student sidebars with on-the-spot linguistic, cultural, or language-learning information, as well as **Recursos** boxes containing on-page correlations of student supplements, to increase students' comfort level and to save them time.
- **VISTAS** integrates video with the student textbook in a distinct, more cohesive way in each lesson's three-page **Fotonovela** section and through the incorporation of video stills in **Estructura** explanations.
- **VISTAS** offers a unique four-part practice sequence for virtually every grammar point. It moves from form-focused **¡Inténtalo!** exercises to directed, yet meaningful, **Práctica** exercises to communicative, interactive **Comunicación** activities, and lastly to cumulative, open-ended **Síntesis** activities.

> To learn more about **VISTAS** and its ancillaries, please jump ahead in this Instructor's Annotated Edition to page i, where you will find the beginning of the front matter of the Student Textbook. The remainder of these introductory pages to your Instructor's Annotated Edition (pages IAE-6 – IAE-16) assume that you have familiarized yourself with that front matter. In particular, you will find it helpful to look over these sections: Introduction (p. iii), **VISTAS**-At-A-Glance (pages xiv–xxv), Video Program (pages xxvi–xxvii), and Ancillaries (pages xxviii–xxix).

Getting to Know Your Instructor's Annotated Edition

VISTAS offers you the most comprehensive and thoroughly developed Instructor's Annotated Edition (IAE) ever written for introductory college Spanish. The same size as the student edition, the IAE features slightly reduced student–text pages overprinted with answers to all exercises with discrete responses. Surrounding side and bottom panels place a wealth of teaching resources at your fingertips. The annotations were written to complement and support varied teaching styles, to extend the already rich contents of the student textbook, and to save you time in class preparation and course management.

Because the **VISTAS** IAE is a new kind of teaching resource, this section is designed as a quick orientation to the principal types of instructor annotations you will find in it. As you familiarize yourself with them, it is important to know that the annotations are suggestions only. Any Spanish questions, sentences, models or simulated instructor-student exchanges are not meant to be prescriptive or limiting. You are encouraged to view these suggested "scripts" as flexible points of departure that will help you achieve your instructional goals.

On the Lesson Opening Page

- **Lesson Goals** A list of the lexical, grammatical, and cultural goals of the lesson, including language-learning strategies and skill-building techniques
- **Lesson Preview** Questions on the full-page photograph for use in jump-starting the lesson
- **Instructional Resources** A correlation, including page references, to all student and instructor supplements available to reinforce the lesson

In the Side Panels

- **Section Goals** A list of the goals of the corresponding section
- **Instructional Resources** A correlation, including page references, to all ancillaries
- **Before Presenting** A suggestion for leading into the corresponding section before working with the on-page material. These typically end with a study or written **Assignment** which will help students to prepare for the next class.
- **Present** Tips for introducing and working with the on-page materials
- **Expand** Expansions and variations on exercises and activities
- **Suggestion** Teaching suggestions for specific exercises, sections, or subsections
- **Warm-up** Ideas for quick ways to start classes or activities by recycling language or ideas
- **Possible Response** Answers based on known vocabulary, grammar, and language functions that students might produce for the final activity of each **Reacciona a la fotonovela** section
- **Assignment** Study and/or homework assignments based on the student text and the Student Activities Manual
- **Close** Suggestions for wrapping up a specific section
- **Video Synopsis** Summaries in the **Fotonovela** sections that recap the video module

- **Script** Printed transcripts of the audio recordings on the Student Cassette/CD for the first **Práctica** exercise in each **Contextos** section and the **Estrategia** and **Ahora escucha** features in each **Escuchar** section
- **Writing Sample** Samples of writing that students might produce in Spanish in response to the writing task in each **Escritura** section, based on language students have studied up to that point
- **Section-specific Annotations** Suggestions for presenting, expanding, varying, and reinforcing individual instructional elements. Throughout the side panels, these are anchored by numbers or titles of the corresponding student text pages.
- **Successful Language Learning** Tips and strategies to enhance students' language-learning experience
- **The Affective Dimension** Suggestions for managing and/or reducing students' language-learning anxieties

In the *Teaching Options* Boxes

- **Extra Practice, Pairs, Small Groups, and Large Groups** Additional exercises and activities over and above those already in the student textbook
- **Game** Games that practice the language of the lesson section and/or recycle previously learned language
- **TPR** Total Physical Response activities that engage students physically in learning Spanish
- **Enfoque cultural** Additional cultural information related to the **Enfoque cultural** in **Fotonovela**
- **Variación léxica** Extra information related to the **Variación léxica** in **Contextos** and/or the Spanish-speaking countries in **Panorama**
- **Worth Noting** More detailed information about an interesting aspect of the history, geography, culture, or people of the Spanish-speaking countries in **Panorama**
- **Heritage Speakers** Suggestions and activities tailored to heritage speakers, who in many colleges and universities nationwide are enrolled in the same introductory courses as non-heritage speakers
- **Video** Techniques and activities for using the **VISTAS** video program with **Fotonovela** and other lesson sections
- **Proofreading Activity** Activities exclusive to the **Escritura** sections that guide students in the development of good proofreading skills. Each item contains two errors related to a structure taught in the lesson's **Estructura** section or, in Lessons 10–18, a spelling rule taught in **Ortografía.**
- **Evaluation** Suggested rubrics in **Escritura** and **Proyecto** for grading students' writing efforts and oral presentations

Please check our WWW sites (www.vistasonline.com and www.vistahigherlearning.com) periodically for program updates and additional teaching support.

Language Teaching as Dialogue:

How the Language Textbook Can Foster and Reinforce a Positive Orientation to Language Learning

Elaine K. Horwitz
The University of Texas at Austin

I have never before been involved with a set of textbook materials for the language classroom. Frankly, I have always felt that the textbook was less important than a good language teacher and that a good teacher could be successful with almost any set of materials. My research with language learners, however, has caused me to change my mind somewhat. While good language teachers can and should adapt language teaching materials to their personal teaching philosophies and the needs and goals of their particular students, for language learners, the textbook is the omnipresent symbol of their language course. Learners transport their book back and forth to classes and fervently hope it will prepare them adequately for exams and the other trials of language classes.

It seems to me, therefore, that we should demand more of our language textbooks. In addition to being a clear and lively presenter and explainer of the target language, the language textbook should help students learn *how* to approach language learning. When students are doing homework or preparing for tests, they are alone with their textbooks, and their books should guide them to effective learning practices.

Many students do not know how to approach learning a language and/or have misconceptions about language learning that interfere with their effectiveness as learners. As experienced language teachers know, students often arrive in language classes with many preconceived—and often erroneous—notions about how languages should be learned and taught. They come with beliefs about how languages should be studied, how difficult it is to learn a particular language, who has foreign language aptitude, and why anyone should want to learn the language. Some of these beliefs can be helpful, while others can be truly counterproductive. In fact, the word *myth* best describes some learner beliefs. For example, in a study of college-level beginning language learners in the United States (exactly the kind who will use this textbook), over one-third of the students thought that they could become fluent in a foreign language if they studied that language for one hour a day for two years or less. This belief represents a great underestimate of the actual amount of time required to learn a language and probably leads to great frustration in students when they find that they are far from fluent after two years of study.

In addition, substantial numbers of the students I have studied believe that learning a second language primarily involves learning vocabulary words or grammatical rules, beliefs that clash substantially with proficiency-oriented language instruction. Perhaps of even greater concern, many students feel that it is important never to make a mistake when speaking a foreign language because mistakes can lead to permanent errors. With unrealistic beliefs such as these, it is unlikely that students will adopt effective language learning strategies without significant support from both their language teacher and their textbook.

The language textbook can also help address issues of foreign language anxiety. I believe that many people are anxious when learning and speaking another language because they cannot express their true thoughts in that language; therefore, they do not feel like themselves when communicating in it. Several studies have found that many people who are anxious about learning a language are not generally anxious about other things. In some ways, I think that foreign language anxiety is like the discomfort we feel when we wear ill-fitting or disliked clothing, or have a bad haircut. We know that we usually look better—more like ourselves—, but we also know that the people we meet only see us as we are at that moment. Sadly, language ability is not nearly as easily changed as clothing, and we must live with our inability to express ourselves to our own satisfaction every time we use the foreign language.

Although anxiety has been associated with several subject matters that are studied in schools—most notably math and science—educators have not recognized the potential for anxiety in foreign language learning until recently. Many students report that they feel particularly uncomfortable when they are in foreign language classes. In fact, surveys indicate that up to one-third of American foreign language students feel moderately to highly anxious about language study. Physical symptoms of foreign language anxiety can include heart-pounding or palpitations, sweating, trembling, fast breathing, and general feelings of unease. Anxiety can also have more subtle effects such as difficulties in concentrating or focusing attention. Some students even say that being in a language class is the one of the worst things they have ever done. One American student offered this remarkable comment about her classes: "I feel like my French teacher is some kind of Martian death ray, and I never know when he is going to point at me." Of course, all difficulties in language learning are not due to anxiety or unrealistic beliefs about language learning, but too many language learners experience anxiety, and language teachers should do whatever they can to reduce these feelings.

In recent years, language teachers have been encouraged to help their students develop more effective language learning strategies. It seems to me, however, that since students often approach language learning with unrealistic beliefs and find their language classes anxiety-provoking, many students will not be ready to adopt the language learning strategies that their teachers suggest. Simply mentioning excellent strategies to students will not be sufficient to increase their effectiveness as language learners. Thus, I believe that a continuous dialogue between students and teachers about language learning should be established in all language classes. We need to talk to students about realistic expectations for language learning. How can we expect them to participate in communicative activities if they think that they should never guess or make a mistake in the foreign language or if the very thought of speaking in Spanish publicly makes their hearts race and their hands sweat? We also need to listen to their thoughts and experiences so that we can address their concerns.

In order to start this dialogue, I suggest that we open our classes to discussions of the shared human experience of language learning before we plan lessons around less personally relevant, but common classroom topics such as the world economy. Students should be encouraged to talk about their own concerns and fears about learning another language. To counter students' unrealistic expectations about language learning, it can be helpful for teachers to tell their students about their own experiences as language learners. Knowing that their teacher, an obviously successful language learner, took many years to learn Spanish (or English), often made errors, and sometimes felt (or even still feels) anxious using it can make students more comfortable with their own limitations and encourage them to talk about their own feelings and experiences. Many students are relieved to learn that they are not the only ones experiencing anxiety about learning and using a foreign language, and will likely find these discussions anxiety-reducing.

Language textbooks can and should be an integral part of the language-learning dialogue. VISTAS was designed to help foster this dialogue by offering features that establish clear communication between students and their textbook. The textbook contains student sidebars that include immediately relevant information about culture (**Nota cultural**), everyday language usage (**¡Lengua viva!**), grammatical points (**¡Atención!**), and cross-references to previously learned or closely related information (**Consúltalo**). **Ayuda** sidebars offer specific grammatical and vocabulary reminders related to a particular activity, while **Consejos** sidebars suggest pertinent language learning strategies. The **Adelante** sections are based on a process approach, providing students with step-by-step support as they develop their reading, writing, listening, and speaking skills. Also included in the **Adelante** sections are **Estrategia** boxes that contain both concrete strategies for building language skills and activities to guide students in applying them. Very importantly, in VISTAS, students encounter a highly structured design in which all lesson sections are color-coded for easy reference and appear either completely on one page or on spreads of two facing pages. From the beginning, the design was conceived as a learning tool in its own right that, through its very consistency and visual interest, would enhance students' learning and increase their comfort level with their language learning materials.

The VISTAS Instructor's Annotated Edition also plays an important role in the language learning dialogue. It is chock-full of wonderful annotations aimed at acquainting teachers with the student textbook and exploiting it for maximum benefit in the classroom. Of particular relevance are the *Successful Language Learning* tips that offer learning strategies to help teachers enhance their students' learning experiences and *The Affective Dimension* annotations, which provide suggestions for managing and/or reducing students' language learning anxieties. Clearly, VISTAS not only recognizes students' feelings of foreign language anxiety, but also addresses them explicitly.

The ultimate goal of language learning is communicating personally meaningful and conversationally appropriate messages, but, in doing so, students encounter unfamiliar syntactic, semantic, and phonological systems. Moreover, language learners must deal with the stress and ambiguities of communicating within the parameters of an unfamiliar culture. This is a truly demanding and ego-involving endeavor, yet most language learners receive very little guidance on how to negotiate this complicated process. VISTAS, however, acknowledges the feelings and perspectives of language learners by talking to them about the exciting human experience of learning another language as they progress through their studies. I sincerely hope that you and your students will come to see VISTAS as a true partner in the teaching and learning of Spanish.

General Teaching Considerations

Orienting Students to the Student Textbook

Because **VISTAS** treats interior and graphic design as an integral part of students' language-learning experience, you may want to take a few minutes to orient students to the student textbook. Have them flip through one lesson, and point out that all lessons are organized exactly the same way. Let them know that, because of this, they can be confident that they will always know "where they are" in their textbook. Emphasize that sections are self-contained, occupying either a full page or a spread of two facing pages, thereby eliminating "bad breaks" and the need to flip back and forth to do activities or to work with explanatory material. Call students' attention to the use of color to highlight key information in elements such as charts, diagrams, word lists, exercise **modelos**, and activity titles. Also point out how the major sections of each lesson are color-coded for easy navigation: red for **Contextos**, purple for **Fotonovela**, blue for **Estructura**, green for **Adelante**, orange for **Panorama**, and gold for **Vocabulario.**

Flexible Lesson Organization

VISTAS uses a flexible lesson organization designed to meet the needs of diverse teaching styles, institutions, and instructional goals. For example, you can begin with the lesson opening page and progress sequentially through a lesson. If you do not want to devote class time to grammar, you can assign the **Estructura** explanations for outside study, freeing up class time for other purposes like developing oral communication skills; building listening, reading, or writing skills; learning more about the Spanish-speaking world; or working with the video program. You might decide to work extensively with the **Adelante** and **Panorama** sections in order to focus on students' reading, writing, listening, and oral presentation skills; as well as their knowledge of the Spanish-speaking world. On the other hand, you might prefer to skip these sections entirely, dipping into them periodically in response to your students' interests as the opportunity arises. If you plan on using the **VISTAS** Testing Program, however, be aware that its tests and exams check language presented in **Contextos, Estructura,** and the **Expresiones útiles** boxes of **Fotonovela.**

Identifying Active Vocabulary

All words and expressions taught in the illustrations and **Más vocabulario** lists in **Contextos** are considered active, testable vocabulary. Any items in the **Variación léxica** boxes, however, are intended for receptive learning and are presented for enrichment only. The words and expressions in the **Expresiones útiles** boxes in **Fotonovela,** as well as words in charts, word lists, and sample sentences in **Estructura** are also part of the active vocabulary load. At the end of each lesson, **Vocabulario** provides a convenient one-page summary of the items students should know and that may appear on tests and exams. You will want to point this out to students. You might also tell them that an easy way to study from **Vocabulario** is to cover up the Spanish half of each section, leaving only the English equivalents exposed. They can then quiz themselves on the Spanish items. To focus on the English equivalents of the Spanish entries, they simply reverse this process.

Creating and Using a Picture File

Because many language instructors find picture files useful, some of the annotations in the **VISTAS** IAE advise using one to extend or vary practice of selected vocabulary groups or grammatical points. One of the easiest ways to assemble a picture file is to get into the habit of looking for dramatic photographs or drawings as you flip through magazines. Another way is to ask students to bring in illustrations that appeal to them and that they would like to talk about. These materials can be mounted on posterboard, laminated, and filed in a box. The pictures can be arranged in various ways—by theme (for example, the family, clothing, or pastimes), by grammatical topic (preterite vs. imperfect, descriptive adjectives, or the present subjunctive), or by the lesson of the textbook in use.

NATIONAL communication cultures STANDARDS

VISTAS and the *Standards for Foreign Language Learning*

Since 1982, when the *ACTFL Proficiency Guidelines* were first published, that seminal document and its subsequent revisions have influenced the teaching of modern languages in the United States. **VISTAS** was written with the concerns and philosophy of the *ACTFL Proficiency Guidelines* in mind, incorporating a proficiency-oriented approach from its planning stages.

VISTAS' pedagogy was also informed from its inception by the *Standards for Foreign Language Learning in the 21st Century.* First published in 1996 under the auspices of the National Standards in Foreign Language Education Project, the Standards are organized into five goal areas, often called the Five Cs: Communication, Cultures, Connections, Comparisons, and Communities.

Since **VISTAS** takes a communicative approach to the teaching and learning of Spanish, the Communication goal is central to the student text. For example, the diverse formats used in **Comunicación** and **Síntesis** activities—pair work, small group work, class circulation, information gap, task-based, and so forth— engage students in communicative exchanges, providing and obtaining information, and expressing feelings and emotions. The **Proyecto** sections guide students in presenting information, concepts, and ideas to their classmates on a variety of topics *and* in varied ways—oral, written, recorded, and videotaped.

The Cultures goal is most evident in the lessons' **Enfoque cultural** boxes and **Panorama** sections, but **VISTAS** also weaves culture into virtually every page, exposing students to the multiple facets of practices, products, and perspectives of the Spanish-speaking world. In keeping with the Connections goal, students can connect with other disciplines such as geography, history, fine arts, and science in the **Panorama** sections; they can acquire information and recognize distinctive cultural viewpoints in the non-literary and literary texts of the **Lectura** sections. The **Estructura** sections, with their clear explanations and special *Compare & Contrast* sections, reflect the Comparisons goal, while the Communities goal is particularly visible in the **Recursos para la investigación** boxes of the **Proyecto** sections. Students can work toward the Connections and Communities goal when they do the **Panorama** sections' **Conexión Internet** activities, as well as the activities and information on the **VISTAS** Web site. In addition, special Standards icons appear on the student text pages of your IAE to call out sections that have a particularly strong relationship with the Standards. All in all, these are just a few examples of how **VISTAS** was written with the Standards firmly in mind. You will find many more as you work with the student textbook and its ancillaries.

General Suggestions for Using the VISTAS Video

The **Fotonovela** section in each of the student textbook's eighteen lessons and the **VISTAS** video were created as interlocking pieces. All photos in **Fotonovela** are actual video stills from the corresponding video module, while the printed conversations are abbreviated versions of the video module's dramatic segment. Both the **Fotonovela** conversations and their expanded video versions represent comprehensible input at the discourse level; they were purposely written to use language from the corresponding lesson's **Contextos** and **Estructura** sections. Thus, as of **Lección 2**, they recycle known language, preview grammar points students will study later in the lesson, and, in keeping with the concept of "i + 1," contain a small amount of unknown language.

Because the **Fotonovela** sections and the **VISTAS** video are so closely connected, you may use them in many different ways. For instance, you can use **Fotonovela** as an advance organizer, presenting it before showing the video module. You can also show the video module first and follow up with **Fotonovela.** You can even use **Fotonovela** as a stand-alone, video-independent section.

Depending on your teaching preferences and campus facilities, you might decide to show all video modules in class or to assign them solely for viewing outside of the classroom. You could begin by showing the first one or two modules in class to familiarize yourself and students with the characters, storyline, style, "flashbacks," and **Resumen** sections. After that, you could work in class only with **Fotonovela** and have students view the remaining video modules outside of class. No matter which approach you choose, students have ample materials to support viewing the video independently and processing it in a meaningful way. For each video module, there are **Reacciona a la fotonovela** activities in the **Fotonovela** section of the corresponding textbook lesson and video activities in the Student Activities Manual.

You might also want to use the **VISTAS** video in class when working with the **Estructura** sections. You could play the parts of the dramatic episode that correspond to the video stills in the grammar explanations or show chunks of the episode and ask students to identify certain grammar points.

You could also focus on the video's **Resumen** sections. In these, one of the main video characters recaps the dramatic episode by reminiscing about its key events. These reminiscences, which emphasize the lesson's active vocabulary and grammatical points, take the form of footage pulled out of the dramatic episode and repeated in black and white images. The main character who "hosts" each **Resumen** begins and ends the section with a few lines that do not appear in the live segment. These sentences provide a new, often humorous setting for the host character's reminiscences, as well as additional opportunities for students to process language they have been studying within the context of the video storyline.

In class, you could play the parts of the **Resumen** section that exemplify individual grammar points as you progress through each **Estructura** section. You could also wait until you complete an **Estructura** section and review it by showing the corresponding **Resumen** section in its entirety.

Course Planning

The entire **VISTAS** program was developed with an eye to flexibility and ease of use in a wide variety of course configurations. **VISTAS** can be used in courses taught on a semester or quarter system, and in courses that complete the book in two, three, or four semesters. Here are some sample course plans that illustrate how **VISTAS** can be used in a variety of academic situations. You should, of course, feel free to organize your courses in the way that best suits your students' needs and your instructional objectives.

Two-Semester System

The following chart illustrates how the **VISTAS** program can be completed in a two-semester course. This division of material allows the present tense, the present progressive tense, and the preterite to be presented in the first semester; the second semester focuses on the imperfect tense, the subjunctive, and the perfect tenses.

Semester 1	Semester 2
Lecciones 1–9	Lecciones 10–18

Three-Semester System

This chart shows how **VISTAS** can be used in a three-semester course. The lessons are equally divided among the three semesters, allowing students to absorb the material at a steady pace.

Semester 1	Semester 2	Semester 3
Lecciones 1–6	Lecciones 7–12	Lecciones 13–18

Four-Semester System

The following chart shows one way to configure the **VISTAS** materials for a four-semester course of study. This arrangement allots only four lessons to the first and fourth semesters; this gives students time to get their bearings in the first semester and and permits extra time for review in the fourth semester.

Semester 1	Semester 2	Semester 3	Semester 4
Lecciones 1–4	Lecciones 5–9	Lecciones 10–14	Lecciones 15–18

Quarter System

In the following chart, the **VISTAS** materials are organized in three balanced segments for use in the quarter system, allowing ample time for learning and review in each quarter.

First Quarter	Second Quarter	Third Quarter
Lecciones 1–6	Lecciones 7–12	Lecciones 13–18

Lesson Planning

VISTAS has been carefully planned to meet your instructional needs, whether you teach on a semester or quarter system and whether you plan to use the textbook for two, three, or four semesters or over three quarters. Vocabulary presentations and grammar topics have been methodically designed for maximum instructional flexibility. This sample lesson plan for **Lección 1** illustrates how **VISTAS** can be used in a two-semester program with five contact hours per week.

NOTE: This lesson plan deals with order of presentation rather than specific instructional techniques and suggestions, which are presented in detail in the annotations of the **VISTAS** IAE. In addition, it is important to note that the **Panorama** section in **Lección 1** can be presented at any point during the lesson.

Sample Lesson Plan for Lección 1

Day 1

1. Introduce yourself and present the course syllabus.
2. Present the **Lección 1** objectives.
3. Preview the **Contextos** section; present the **Contextos** vocabulary.
4. Work through the **Práctica** activities with the class; have students read over the **Comunicación** activities for the next class.
5. Preview the **Fotonovela** and the **Expresiones útiles**.
6. Have students read through the **Fotonovela** and prepare the first **Reacciona a la fotonovela** activity for the next class.

Day 2

1. Review **Contextos** vocabulary; have the class do the **Comunicación** activities.
2. Present the **Fotonovela** and **Expresiones útiles**.
3. Do the first **Reacciona a la fotonovela** activity with the class.
4. Have your students do the next three **Reacciona a la fotonovela** activities.
5. Preview the **Pronunciación** section and **Estructura 1.1**.
6. Have students read **Estructura 1.1** and prepare the **Inténtalo** and **Práctica** activities for the next class.

Day 3

1. Review the **Expresiones útiles**.
2. Go over the **Pronunciación** section with the class and work through the corresponding activities.
3. Present **Estructura 1.1**.
4. Work through the **Inténtalo** and **Práctica** activities with the class.
5. Have your students do the **Comunicación** activity in class.
6. Preview **Estructura 1.2**.
7. Have students read **Estructura 1.2** and prepare the **Inténtalo** and **Práctica** activities for the next class.

Day 4

1. Review **Estructura 1.1.**
2. Present **Estructura 1.2** and work through the **Inténtalo** and **Práctica** activities with the class.
3. Have your students do the **Comunicación** activities during class.
4. Preview **Estructura 1.3.**
5. Have your students read **Estructura 1.3** and prepare the **Inténtalo** and **Práctica** activities for the next class.

Day 5

1. Review **Estructura 1.2.**
2. Present **Estructura 1.3** and work through the **Inténtalo** and **Práctica** activities with the class.
3. Have your students do the **Comunicación** activities during class.
4. Preview **Estructura 1.4.**
5. Have your students read **Estructura 1.4** and prepare the **Inténtalo** and **Práctica** activities for the next class.

Day 6

1. Quickly review **Estructura 1.3.**
2. Present **Estructura 1.4** and work through the **Inténtalo** and **Práctica** activities with the class.
3. Have your students do the **Comunicación** activities and the **Síntesis** activity.
4. Assign material from the **Adelante** section as desired for integrated practice and review.

Day 7

1. Go over assigned material from the **Adelante** section.
2. Review **Lección 1** with the class.
3. Have your students prepare to take **Prueba A** or **Prueba B** for **Lección 1** during the next class session.

Day 8

1. Administer **Prueba A** or **Prueba B** for **Lección 1.**
2. Preview the **Lección 2** objectives.
3. Have your students read the **Contextos** section and prepare the **Práctica** activities for the next class.

The lesson plan presented here is not prescriptive. You should feel free to present lesson materials as you see fit, tailoring them to your own teaching preferences and to your students' learning styles. You may, for example, want to allow extra time for concepts students find challenging. You may want to allot less time to topics they comprehend without difficulty or to group topics together when making assignments. Based on your students' needs, you may want to omit certain topics or activities altogether. If you have fewer than five contact hours per semester or are on a quarter system, you will find the **VISTAS** program very flexible: simply pick and choose from its array of instructional resources and sequence them in the way that makes the most sense for your program.

VISTAS

Introducción a la lengua española

José A. Blanco

Mary Ann Dellinger
University of Phoenix

Philip Donley
Austin Community College

María Isabel García
Boston University

•••

Elaine K. Horwitz
Senior Consulting Editor
University of Texas

VISTA
HIGHER LEARNING

Boston, Massachusetts • Auburn, California

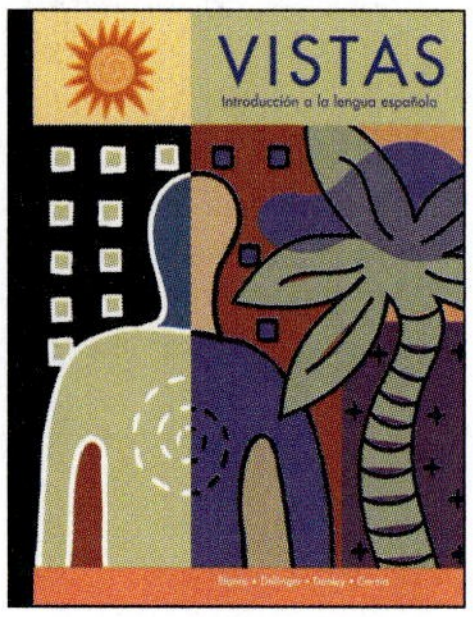

Award-winning cover Illustrator, **José Ortega** was born in Ecuador and studied at New York's prestigious School of Visual Arts. His work has appeared in magazines and advertisements throughout the world.

Publisher: José A. Blanco

Editorial Director of College Publishing: Denise St. Jean

Director of Manufacturing: Stephen Pekich

Director of Production & Design: Peter O'Faherty

Staff Editors: María Cinta Aparisi, Pamela Mishkin, Gustavo Cinci, Sonny Regelman, Mark Porter, Daniella Tourgeman

Contributing Writers: Sharon Alexander, Karin Fajardo, Ana M. Fores, Gregory Garretson, Jane Ann Johnson, Norah L. Jones, Ralph Kite, Susan Lake, Ann Morrill, Isabel Picado, Beatriz Pojman, Teresa Shu, Marcia Tugendhat

Art Director: Linda Jurras

Design Team: Suzanne Korschun, Martin Beveridge, Barbara Gazley, Susan Prentiss, Ianka de la Rosa

Photographer: Martin Bernetti

Production Team: Ted Cantrell, Eric Murphy, Janet Spicer, Holly Kersey, Greg Moutafis, Oscar Díez

Student Text ISBN 1-931100-00-4
Instructor's Annotated Edition ISBN 1-931100-01-2

Library of Congress Card Number: 00-109093

1 2 3 4 5 6 7 8 9 VH 05 04 03 02 01

Introduction

Welcome to **VISTAS**, your gateway to the Spanish language and to the vibrant, diverse cultures of the Spanish-speaking world.

VISTAS is a new introductory Spanish program written with you, the student, in mind. The driving force behind **VISTAS** was the desire to create the most student-friendly program available to college students taking introductory Spanish. In light of this, here are some of the elements you will encounter:

- Practical, high-frequency vocabulary that will allow you to communicate in everyday situations
- Clear, comprehensive grammar explanations with special features that make it easier to learn and to use
- Ample guided, focused practice to make you comfortable with the vocabulary and grammar you are learning and to give you a solid foundation for communication
- An emphasis on communicative interactions with a classmate, small groups, the full class and your instructor
- Careful development of reading, writing, and listening skills incorporating learning strategies and a process approach
- Integration of the culture of the everyday lives of Spanish speakers and coverage of the entire Spanish-speaking world
- A complete set of print and technology ancillaries to help you learn Spanish more easily

In addition, **VISTAS** offers some elements that set it apart from other college-level introductory Spanish textbooks:

- A different and more cohesive way of integrating video with the student textbook
- Student annotations with handy point-of-use information on virtually every page
- An abundance of drawings, photos, charts, and graphs, all designed to help you learn
- A highly structured, easy-to-navigate design and organization

VISTAS has eighteen lessons, each of which is organized exactly the same way. To familiarize yourself with the organization of the text, turn the page and take the at-a-glance tour.

table of contents

estructura	adelante	panorama

estructura	adelante	panorama

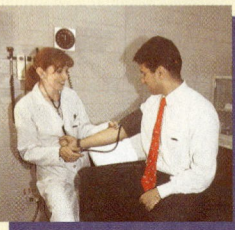

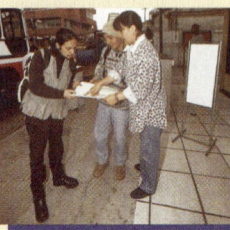

estructura	adelante	panorama

contextos | fotonovela

Lección 17
Un festival de arte

Lección 18
Las actualidades

Consulta (Reference)

estructura	adelante	panorama

Lesson Openers
outline the content and features of each lesson

Hola, ¿qué tal?

1

Communicative Goals

You will learn how to:

- Greet people in Spanish
- Say goodbye
- Identify yourself and others
- Talk about the time of day

contextos

pages 2-5

- Words and phrases related to greetings and leave-takings
- Terms to identify yourself and others
- Expressions of courtesy

fotonovela

pages 6-9

Mrs. Ramos, from the travel agency Ecuatur, greets the students and hands out their travel papers. Don Francisco, the driver, introduces himself and asks the students to board the bus.

estructura

pages 10-25

- Nouns and articles
- Numbers 0-30
- Present tense of the verb **ser**
- Telling time

adelante

pages 26-31

Lectura: Read a telephone list.
Escritura: Create an address list in Spanish.
Escuchar: Listen to a conversation in a bus station.
Proyecto: Research the influence of Hispanic culture in a U.S. city.

panorama

pages 32-33

Featured Country: United States

- Cities and states with the largest Hispanic populations
- Influence of Hispanic culture in the U.S.

Contextos
presents vocabulary in meaningful contexts

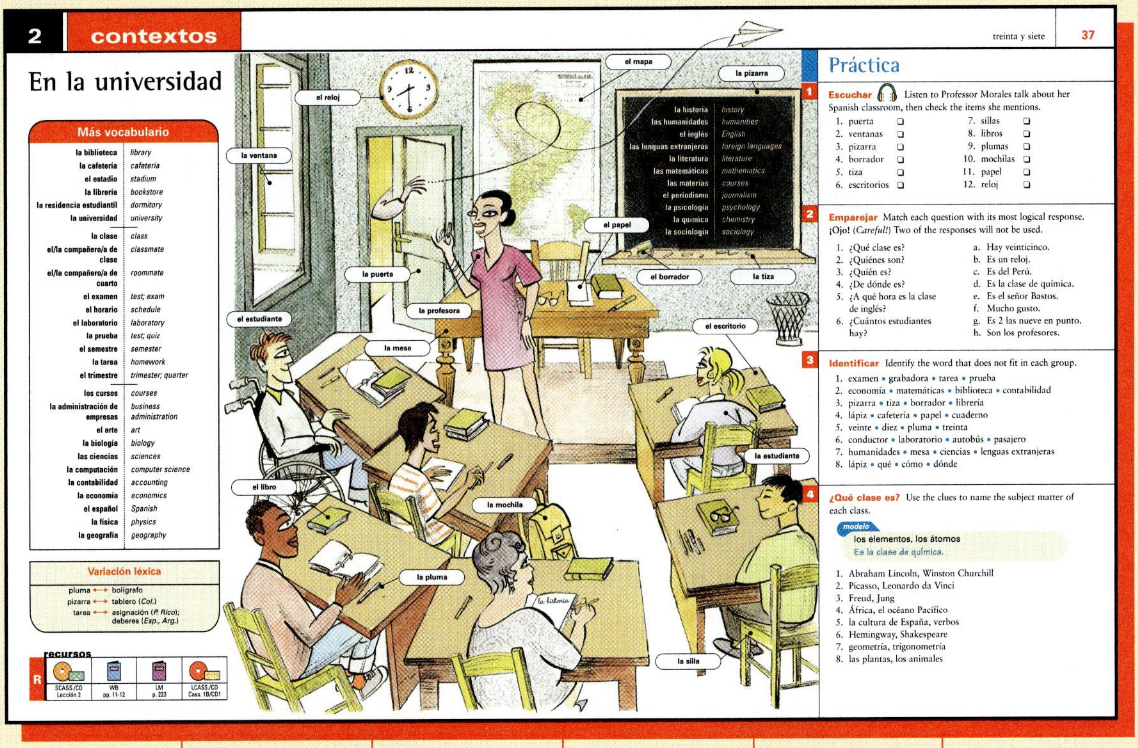

2 contextos

En la universidad

Más vocabulario

la biblioteca	*library*
la cafetería	*cafeteria*
el estadio	*stadium*
la librería	*bookstore*
la residencia estudiantil	*dormitory*
la universidad	*university*
la clase	*class*
el/la compañero/a de clase	*classmate*
el/la compañero/a de cuarto	*roommate*
el examen	*test; exam*
el horario	*schedule*
el laboratorio	*laboratory*
la prueba	*test; quiz*
el semestre	*semester*
la tarea	*homework*
el trimestre	*trimester; quarter*
los cursos	*courses*
la administración de empresas	*business administration*
el arte	*art*
la biología	*biology*
las ciencias	*sciences*
la computación	*computer science*
la contabilidad	*accounting*
la economía	*economics*
el español	*Spanish*
la física	*physics*
la geografía	*geography*

Variación léxica

pluma ⟷ bolígrafo
pizarra ⟷ tablero (*Col.*)
tarea ⟷ asignación (*P. Rico*); deberes (*Esp., Arg.*)

recursos

R | SCASS./CD Lección 2 | WB pp. 11-12 | LM p. 223 | LCASS./CD Cass. 1B/CD1

Práctica

1 Escuchar Listen to Professor Morales talk about her Spanish classroom, then check the items she mentions.

1. puerta ❑
2. ventanas ❑
3. pizarra ❑
4. borrador ❑
5. tiza ❑
6. escritorios ❑
7. sillas ❑
8. libros ❑
9. plumas ❑
10. mochilas ❑
11. papel ❑
12. reloj ❑

2 Emparejar Match each question with its most logical response. ¡Ojo! (*Careful!*) Two of the responses will not be used.

1. ¿Qué clase es?
2. ¿Quiénes son?
3. ¿Quién es?
4. ¿De dónde es?
5. ¿A qué hora es la clase de inglés?
6. ¿Cuántos estudiantes hay?

a. Hay veinticinco.
b. Es un reloj.
c. Es del Perú.
d. Es la clase de química.
e. Es el señor Bastos.
f. Mucho gusto.
g. Es 2 las nueve en punto.
h. Son los profesores.

3 Identificar Identify the word that does not fit in each group.

1. examen • grabadora • tarea • prueba
2. economía • matemáticas • biblioteca • contabilidad
3. pizarra • tiza • borrador • librería
4. lápiz • cafetería • papel • cuaderno
5. veinte • diez • pluma • treinta
6. conductor • laboratorio • autobús • pasajero
7. humanidades • mesa • ciencias • lenguas extranjeras
8. lápiz • qué • cómo • dónde

4 ¿Qué clase es? Use the clues to name the subject matter of each class.

modelo
los elementos, los átomos
Es la clase de química.

1. Abraham Lincoln, Winston Churchill
2. Picasso, Leonardo da Vinci
3. Freud, Jung
4. África, el océano Pacífico
5. la cultura de España, verbos
6. Hemingway, Shakespeare
7. geometría, trigonometría
8. las plantas, los animales

Más vocabulario boxes call out other important theme-related vocabulary in easy-to-reference Spanish-English lists.

Illustrations High-frequency vocabulary is introduced through expansive, full-color illustrations.

Práctica This section always begins with a listening exercise and continues with activities that practice the new vocabulary in meaningful contexts.

Variación léxica presents alternate words and expressions used throughout the Spanish-speaking world.

Recursos boxes let you know exactly what ancillaries you can use to reinforce or expand on the section.

Contextos

practices vocabulary in a variety of formats

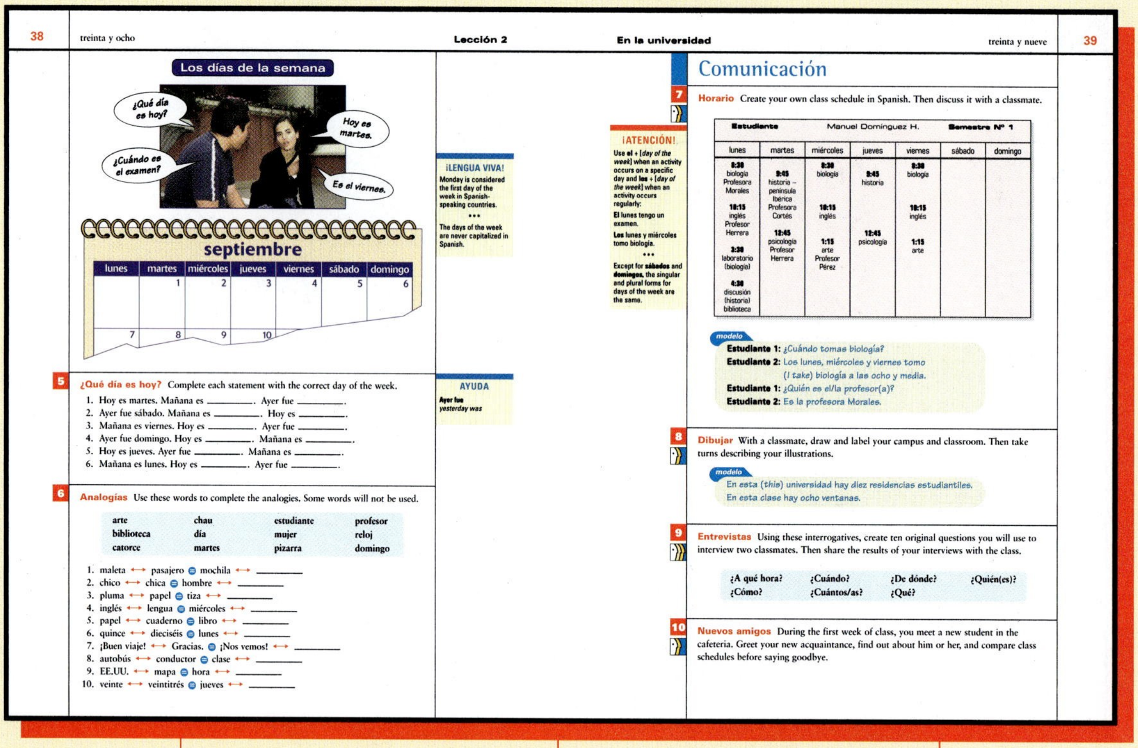

Los días de la semana

¿Qué día es hoy?
Hoy es martes.
¿Cuándo es el examen?
Es el viernes.

septiembre

lunes	martes	miércoles	jueves	viernes	sábado	domingo
	1	2	3	4	5	6
7	8	9	10			

¡LENGUA VIVA!
Monday is considered the first day of the week in Spanish-speaking countries.
• • •
The days of the week are never capitalized in Spanish.

5 ¿Qué día es hoy? Complete each statement with the correct day of the week.

1. Hoy es martes. Mañana es ________. Ayer fue ________.
2. Ayer fue sábado. Mañana es ________. Hoy es ________.
3. Mañana es viernes. Hoy es ________. Ayer fue ________.
4. Ayer fue domingo. Hoy es ________. Mañana es ________.
5. Hoy es jueves. Ayer fue ________. Mañana es ________.
6. Mañana es lunes. Hoy es ________. Ayer fue ________.

AYUDA
Ayer fue *yesterday was*

6 Analogías Use these words to complete the analogies. Some words will not be used.

arte	chau	estudiante	profesor
biblioteca	día	mujer	reloj
catorce	martes	pizarra	domingo

1. maleta ↔ pasajero = mochila ↔ ________
2. chico ↔ chica = hombre ↔ ________
3. pluma ↔ papel = tiza ↔ ________
4. inglés ↔ lengua = miércoles ↔ ________
5. papel ↔ cuaderno = libro ↔ ________
6. quince ↔ dieciséis = lunes ↔ ________
7. ¡Buen viaje! ↔ Gracias. = ¡Nos vemos! ↔ ________
8. autobús ↔ conductor = clase ↔ ________
9. EE.UU. ↔ mapa = hora ↔ ________
10. veinte ↔ veintitrés = jueves ↔ ________

Comunicación

¡ATENCIÓN!
Use **el** + [*day of the week*] when an activity occurs on a specific day and **los** + [*day of the week*] when an activity occurs regularly:
El lunes tengo un examen.
Los lunes y miércoles tomo biología.
• • •
Except for **sábados** and **domingos**, the singular and plural forms for days of the week are the same.

7 Horario Create your own class schedule in Spanish. Then discuss it with a classmate.

Estudiante	Manuel Domínguez H.			Semestre Nº 1		
lunes	martes	miércoles	jueves	viernes	sábado	domingo
8:30 biología Profesora Morales **10:15** inglés Profesor Herrera **3:30** laboratorio (biología) **4:30** discusión (historia) biblioteca	**9:45** historia – península Ibérica Profesora Cortés **12:45** psicología Profesor Herrera	**8:30** biología **10:15** inglés **1:15** arte Profesor Pérez	**9:45** historia **12:45** psicología	**8:30** biología **10:15** inglés **1:15** arte		

modelo
Estudiante 1: ¿Cuándo tomas biología?
Estudiante 2: Los lunes, miércoles y viernes tomo (*I take*) biología a las ocho y media.
Estudiante 1: ¿Quién es el/la profesor(a)?
Estudiante 2: Es la profesora Morales.

8 Dibujar With a classmate, draw and label your campus and classroom. Then take turns describing your illustrations.

modelo
En esta (*this*) universidad hay diez residencias estudiantiles.
En esta clase hay ocho ventanas.

9 Entrevistas Using these interrogatives, create ten original questions you will use to interview two classmates. Then share the results of your interviews with the class.

¿A qué hora?	¿Cuándo?	¿De dónde?	¿Quién(es)?
¿Cómo?	¿Cuántos/as?	¿Qué?	

10 Nuevos amigos During the first week of class, you meet a new student in the cafeteria. Greet your new acquaintance, find out about him or her, and compare class schedules before saying goodbye.

Práctica exercises reinforce the vocabulary through varied and engaging formats.

Student Sidebars provide handy, on-the-spot information that helps you complete the activities.

Comunicación activities get you using the vocabulary creatively in interactions with a partner, a small group, or the entire class.

Fotonovela
tells the story of four students traveling in Ecuador

4 fotonovela

ciento nueve 109

¡Vamos al parque!

Los estudiantes pasean por la ciudad y hablan de sus pasatiempos.

PERSONAJES

DON FRANCISCO

JAVIER

INÉS

ÁLEX

MAITE

JOVEN

1 DON FRANCISCO Son las tres. Tienen una hora libre. Pueden explorar la ciudad, si quieren. Tenemos que ir a las cabañas a las cuatro.

2 JAVIER Inés, ¿quieres ir a pasear por la ciudad?
INÉS Sí, vamos.

3 ÁLEX ¿Por qué no vamos al parque, Maite? Podemos hablar y tomar el sol.
MAITE ¡Buena idea! Hace mucho sol hoy. También quiero escribir unas postales.

4 MAITE ¿Eres aficionado a los deportes, Álex?
ÁLEX Sí, me gusta mucho el fútbol. Me gusta también nadar, correr e ir de excursión a las montañas.
MAITE Yo también corro mucho.

5 ÁLEX Oye, Maite, ¿por qué no jugamos al fútbol con él?
MAITE Mmm... no quiero. Voy a terminar de escribir unas postales.

6 ÁLEX ¡Maite!
MAITE ¡Dios mío!

7 JOVEN Mil perdones. Lo siento muchísimo.
MAITE ¡No es nada! Estoy bien.

8 ÁLEX Ya son las dos y treinta. Debemos regresar al autobús, ¿no?
MAITE Tienes razón.
ÁLEX Oye, Maite, ¿qué vas a hacer esta noche?
MAITE No tengo planes. ¿Por qué?

9 ÁLEX Eh, este... a veces salgo a correr por la noche. ¿Quieres venir a correr conmigo?
MAITE Sí, vamos. ¿A qué hora?
ÁLEX ¿A las seis?
MAITE Perfecto.

10 DON FRANCISCO Esta noche van a correr. ¡Y yo no tengo energía para pasear!

Enfoque cultural El fútbol

Soccer, or **fútbol,** is the most popular spectator sport and the most widely-played team game in the world. It is also the most popular sport in the Spanish-speaking world. People of all ages can be seen playing soccer in public parks and streets, and each country has a professional league with its own stars. Gabriel Batistuta from Argentina, Marcelo Salas from Chile, and Hugo Sánchez from Mexico are among the most famous contemporary Hispanic soccer players.

recursos
R VIDEO Lección 4 | VM pp. 333-334

Expresiones útiles

Making invitations
- **¿Por qué no vamos al parque?** *Why don't we go to the park?*
- **¡Buena idea!** *Good idea!*
- **¿Por qué no jugamos al fútbol?** *Why don't we play soccer?*
- **Mmm... no quiero.** *Hmm... I don't want to.*
- **Lo siento, pero no puedo.** *I'm sorry, but I can't.*
- **¿Quieres ir a pasear por la ciudad conmigo?** *Do you want to walk around the city with me?*
- **Sí, vamos.** *Yes, let's go.*
- **Sí, si tenemos tiempo.** *Yes, if we have time.*

Making plans
- **¿Qué vas a hacer esta noche?** *What are you going to do tonight?*
- **No tengo planes.** *I don't have any plans.*
- **Voy a terminar de escribir unas postales.** *I'm going to finish writing some postcards.*

Talking about pastimes
- **¿Eres aficionado/a a los deportes?** *Are you a sports fan?*
- **Sí, me gustan todos los deportes.** *Yes, I like all sports.*
- **Sí, me gusta mucho el fútbol.** *Yes, I like soccer a lot.*
- **Me gusta también nadar, correr e ir de excursión a las montañas.** *I also like to swim, run, and go hiking in the mountains.*
- **Yo también corro mucho.** *I also run a lot.*

Apologizing
- **Mil perdones./Lo siento muchísimo.** *I'm so sorry.*

Personajes The photo-based conversations take place among a cast of recurring characters—four college students on vacation in Ecuador and the bus driver who accompanies them.

VISTAS Video The **Fotonovela** episode appears in the VISTAS Video Program. To learn more about the video, turn to pages xxvi and xxvii in this at-a-glance tour.

Dialogues use vocabulary from **Contextos** and introduce in a comprehensible way examples of the grammar points you will study in the **Estructura** section.

Enfoque cultural provides detailed cultural information on a topic related to the **Fotonovela** conversation.

Expresiones útiles organizes new, active words and expressions by language function so you can focus on using them for real-life, practical purposes.

Pronunciación & Ortografía
present the rules of Spanish pronunciation and spelling

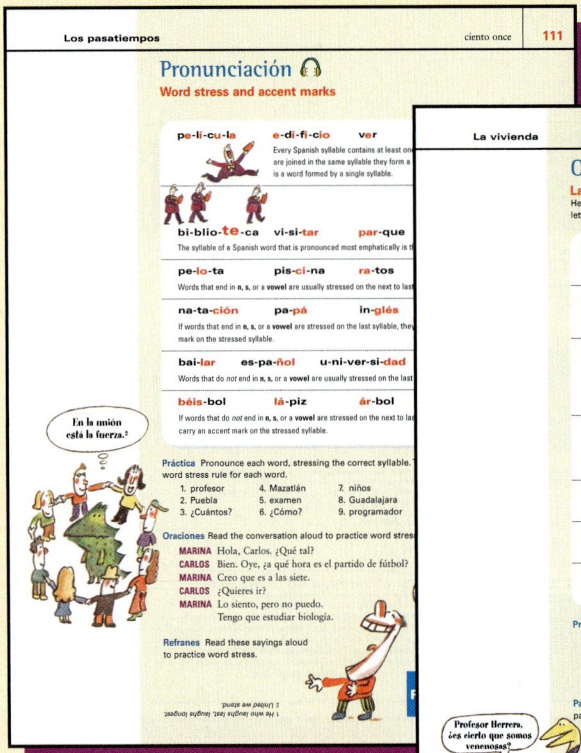
Los pasatiempos | ciento once | 111

Pronunciación

Word stress and accent marks

pe-lí-cu-la e-di-fi-cio ver

Every Spanish syllable contains at least on
are joined in the same syllable they form a
is a word formed by a single syllable.

bi-blio-te-ca vi-si-tar par-que

The syllable of a Spanish word that is pronounced most emphatically is t

pe-lo-ta pis-ci-na ra-tos

Words that end in **n**, **s**, or a **vowel** are usually stressed on the next to last

na-ta-ción pa-pá in-glés

If words that end in **n**, **s**, or a **vowel** are stressed on the last syllable, they
mark on the stressed syllable.

bai-lar es-pa-ñol u-ni-ver-si-dad

Words that do *not* end in **n**, **s**, or a **vowel** are usually stressed on the last

béis-bol lá-piz ár-bol

If words that do *not* end in **n**, **s**, or a **vowel** are stressed on the next to las
carry an accent mark on the stressed syllable.

En la unión
está la fuerza.[2]

Práctica Pronounce each word, stressing the correct syllable.
word stress rule for each word.

1. profesor
2. Puebla
3. ¿Cuántos?
4. Mazatlán
5. examen
6. ¿Cómo?
7. niños
8. Guadalajara
9. programador

Oraciones Read the conversation aloud to practice word stres

MARINA Hola, Carlos. ¿Qué tal?
CARLOS Bien. Oye, ¿a qué hora es el partido de fútbol?
MARINA Creo que es a las siete.
CARLOS ¿Quieres ir?
MARINA Lo siento, pero no puedo.
Tengo que estudiar biología.

Refranes Read these sayings aloud
to practice word stress.

1 He who laughs last, laughs longest.
2 United we stand.

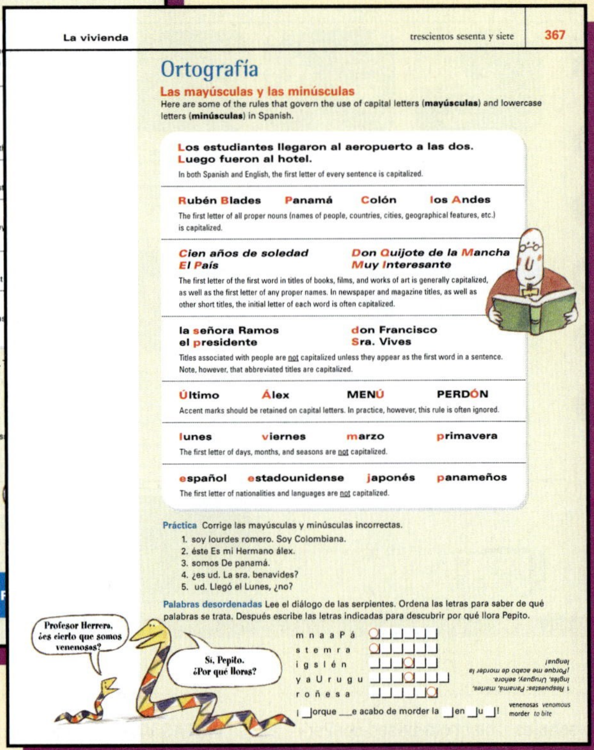
La vivienda | trescientos sesenta y siete | 367

Ortografía

Las mayúsculas y las minúsculas

Here are some of the rules that govern the use of capital letters (**mayúsculas**) and lowercase letters (**minúsculas**) in Spanish.

**Los estudiantes llegaron al aeropuerto a las dos.
Luego fueron al hotel.**

In both Spanish and English, the first letter of every sentence is capitalized.

Rubén Blades **Panamá** **Colón** **los Andes**

The first letter of all proper nouns (names of people, countries, cities, geographical features, etc.) is capitalized.

Cien años de soledad ***Don Quijote de la Mancha***
El País ***Muy Interesante***

The first letter of the first word in titles of books, films, and works of art is generally capitalized, as well as the first letter of any proper names. In newspaper and magazine titles, as well as other short titles, the initial letter of each word is often capitalized.

la señora Ramos **don Francisco**
el presidente **Sra. Vives**

Titles associated with people are not capitalized unless they appear as the first word in a sentence. Note, however, that abbreviated titles are capitalized.

Último **Álex** **MENÚ** **PERDÓN**

Accent marks should be retained on capital letters. In practice, however, this rule is often ignored.

lunes **viernes** **marzo** **primavera**

The first letter of days, months, and seasons are not capitalized.

español **estadounidense** **japonés** **panameños**

The first letter of nationalities and languages are not capitalized.

Práctica Corrige las mayúsculas y minúsculas incorrectas.

1. soy lourdes romero. Soy Colombiana.
2. éste Es mi Hermano álex.
3. somos De panamá.
4. ¿es ud. La sra. benavides?
5. ud. Llegó el Lunes, ¿no?

Palabras desordenadas Lee el diálogo de las serpientes. Ordena las letras para saber de qué palabras se trata. Después escribe las letras indicadas para descubrir por qué llora Pepito.

Profesor Herrera,
¿es cierto que somos
venenosas?
Sí, Pepito.
¿Por qué lloras?

m n a a P á
s t e m r a
i g s l é n
y a U r u g u
r o ñ e s a

¡__orque __e acabo de morder la __en__u__!

venenosas *venomous*
morder *to bite*

1 Respuestas: Panamá, martes, inglés, Uruguay, señora. ¡Porque me acabo de morder la lengua!

Pronunciación explains the sounds and pronunciation of Spanish in Lessons 1–9.

Ortografía focuses on topics related to Spanish spelling in Lessons 10–18.

Estructura
presents Spanish grammar in a graphic-intensive format

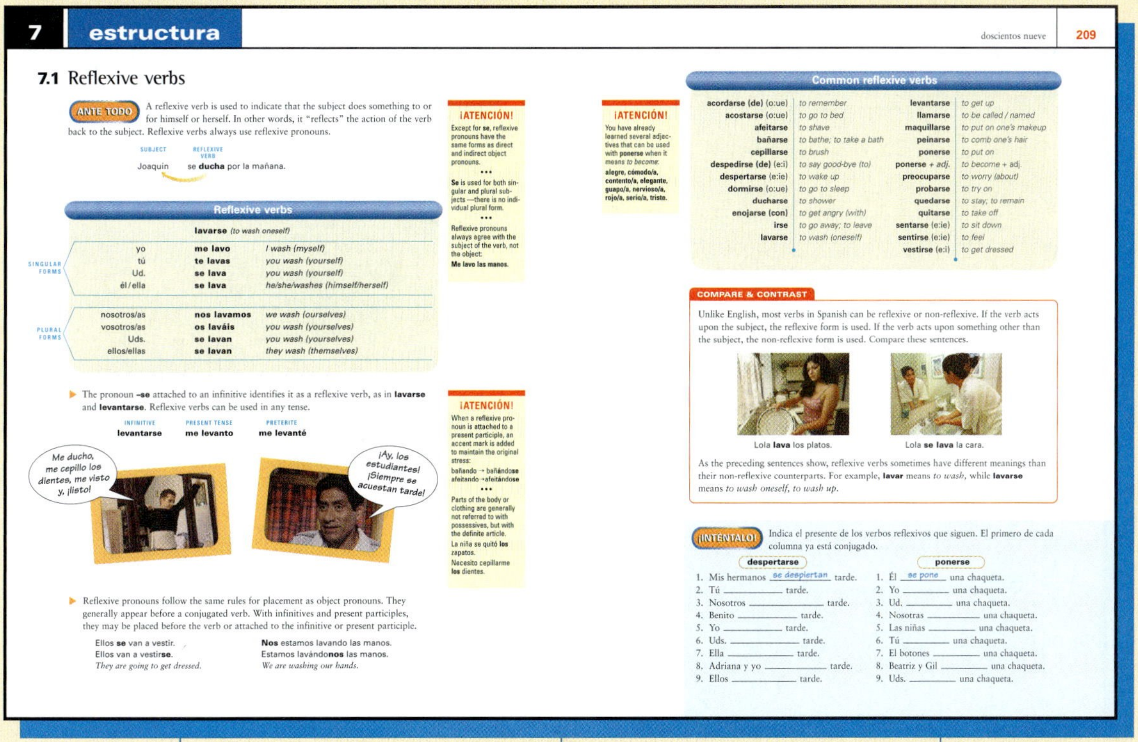

7 **estructura**

doscientos nueve 209

7.1 Reflexive verbs

ANTE TODO A reflexive verb is used to indicate that the subject does something to or for himself or herself. In other words, it "reflects" the action of the verb back to the subject. Reflexive verbs always use reflexive pronouns.

SUBJECT: Joaquín — REFLEXIVE VERB: se **ducha** por la mañana.

Reflexive verbs

		lavarse *(to wash oneself)*	
SINGULAR FORMS	yo	**me lavo**	*I wash (myself)*
	tú	**te lavas**	*you wash (yourself)*
	Ud.	**se lava**	*you wash (yourself)*
	él / ella	**se lava**	*he/she/washes (himself/herself)*
PLURAL FORMS	nosotros/as	**nos lavamos**	*we wash (ourselves)*
	vosotros/as	**os laváis**	*you wash (yourselves)*
	Uds.	**se lavan**	*you wash (yourselves)*
	ellos/ellas	**se lavan**	*they wash (themselves)*

¡ATENCIÓN! Except for **se**, reflexive pronouns have the same forms as direct and indirect object pronouns. • • • **Se** is used for both singular and plural subjects —there is no individual plural form. • • • Reflexive pronouns always agree with the subject of the verb, not the object: **Me lavo las manos.**

▶ The pronoun **-se** attached to an infinitive identifies it as a reflexive verb, as in **lavarse** and **levantarse**. Reflexive verbs can be used in any tense.

INFINITIVE	PRESENT TENSE	PRETERITE
levantarse	**me levanto**	**me levanté**

Me ducho, me cepillo los dientes, me visto y, ¡listo!
¡Ay, los estudiantes! ¡Siempre se acuestan tarde!

¡ATENCIÓN! When a reflexive pronoun is attached to a present participle, an accent mark is added to maintain the original stress: bañando → bañándo**se** afeitando → afeitándo**se** • • • Parts of the body or clothing are generally not referred to with possessives, but with the definite article. La niña se quitó **los** zapatos. Necesito cepillarme **los** dientes.

▶ Reflexive pronouns follow the same rules for placement as object pronouns. They generally appear before a conjugated verb. With infinitives and present participles, they may be placed before the verb or attached to the infinitive or present participle.

Ellos **se** van a vestir.
Ellos van a vestir**se**.
They are going to get dressed.

Nos estamos lavando las manos.
Estamos lavándo**nos** las manos.
We are washing our hands.

¡ATENCIÓN! You have already learned several adjectives that can be used with **ponerse** when it means *to become*: **alegre, cómodo/a, contento/a, elegante, guapo/a, nervioso/a, rojo/a, serio/a, triste.**

Common reflexive verbs

acordarse (de) (o:ue)	*to remember*	**levantarse**	*to get up*
acostarse (o:ue)	*to go to bed*	**llamarse**	*to be called / named*
afeitarse	*to shave*	**maquillarse**	*to put on one's makeup*
bañarse	*to bathe; to take a bath*	**peinarse**	*to comb one's hair*
cepillarse	*to brush*	**ponerse**	*to put on*
despedirse (de) (e:i)	*to say good-bye (to)*	**ponerse** + *adj.*	*to become* + adj.
despertarse (e:ie)	*to wake up*	**preocuparse**	*to worry (about)*
dormirse (o:ue)	*to go to sleep*	**probarse**	*to try on*
ducharse	*to shower*	**quedarse**	*to stay; to remain*
enojarse (con)	*to get angry (with)*	**quitarse**	*to take off*
irse	*to go away; to leave*	**sentarse** (e:ie)	*to sit down*
lavarse	*to wash (oneself)*	**sentirse** (e:ie)	*to feel*
		vestirse (e:i)	*to get dressed*

COMPARE & CONTRAST

Unlike English, most verbs in Spanish can be reflexive or non-reflexive. If the verb acts upon the subject, the reflexive form is used. If the verb acts upon something other than the subject, the non-reflexive form is used. Compare these sentences.

Lola **lava** los platos.

Lola **se lava** la cara.

As the preceding sentences show, reflexive verbs sometimes have different meanings than their non-reflexive counterparts. For example, **lavar** means *to wash*, while **lavarse** means *to wash oneself, to wash up*.

¡INTÉNTALO! Indica el presente de los verbos reflexivos que siguen. El primero de cada columna ya está conjugado.

despertarse
1. Mis hermanos se despiertan tarde.
2. Tú ________ tarde.
3. Nosotros ________ tarde.
4. Benito ________ tarde.
5. Yo ________ tarde.
6. Uds. ________ tarde.
7. Ella ________ tarde.
8. Adriana y yo ________ tarde.
9. Ellos ________ tarde.

ponerse
1. Él se pone una chaqueta.
2. Yo ________ una chaqueta.
3. Ud. ________ una chaqueta.
4. Nosotras ________ una chaqueta.
5. Las niñas ________ una chaqueta.
6. Tú ________ una chaqueta.
7. El botones ________ una chaqueta.
8. Beatriz y Gil ________ una chaqueta.
9. Uds. ________ una chaqueta.

Ante todo eases you into the grammar with definitions of grammatical terms and reminders about what you already know of English grammar or have learned in earlier lessons.

Compare & contrast homes in on aspects of grammar that native speakers of English could find difficult, clarifying similarities and differences between Spanish and English.

Diagrams To clarify concepts, clear and easy-to-grasp grammar explanations are reinforced by diagrams that colorfully present sample words, phrases, and sentences.

Charts To help you learn, colorful, easy-to-use charts call out key grammatical structures and forms, as well as important related vocabulary.

Student sidebars provide you with on-the-spot linguistic, cultural, or language-learning information directly related to the materials in front of you.

¡Inténtalo! exercises offer an easy first step in your practice of each new grammar point. They get you working with the grammar right away in simple, easy-to-understand formats.

Estructura

provides directed and communicative practice

148 ciento cuarenta y ocho **Lección 5** **Las vacaciones** ciento cuarenta y nueve 149

Práctica

1 **Completar** Alfredo's Spanish class is preparing to travel to Puerto Rico. Use the present progressive of the verb in parentheses to complete Alfredo's description of what everyone is doing.

1. Yo __________ (investigar) el estado político de la isla (*island*).
2. La esposa del profesor __________ (hacer) las maletas.
3. Marta y José Luis __________ (buscar) información sobre San Juan en el Internet.
4. Enrique y yo __________ (leer) un correo electrónico de nuestro amigo puertorriqueño.
5. Javier __________ (aprender) mucho sobre la cultura puertorriqueña.
6. Y tú __________ (practicar) tu español, ¿verdad?

2 **¿Qué están haciendo?** María and her friends are vacationing at a resort in San Juan, Puerto Rico. Complete her description of what everyone is doing right now.

1. Yo 2. Javier 3. Alejandro y Rebeca
4. Celia y yo 5. Samuel 6. Lorenzo

3 **Personajes famosos** Say what these celebrities are doing right now, using the cues provided.

modelo
Serena Williams está jugando al tenis ahora mismo.

John Grisham	Mikhail Baryshnikov	bailar	hablar
Celine Dion	Picabo Street	cantar	hacer
Steven Spielberg	Regis Philbin	correr	jugar
Venus Williams	??	escribir	??
Tiger Woods	??	esquiar	??

AYUDA
John Grisham - **novelas**
Celine Dion - **canciones**
Steven Spielberg - **cine**
Venus Williams - **tenis**
Tiger Woods - **golf**
Mikhail Baryshnikov - **ballet**
Picabo Street - **esquí**
Regis Philbin - **televisión**

Comunicación

4 **Un amigo preguntón** You have a friend who calls you at all hours to see what you're doing. What do you tell him/her if he/she calls you at the following times?

¡LENGUA VIVA!
In Spain and Latin America, time is often given based on the 24-hour clock. For example, 3:00 p.m. is said 15:00h.

modelo
8:00 a.m.
Estoy desayunando.

1. 5:00 a.m. 2. 9:30 a.m. 3. 11:00 a.m. 4. 12:00 p.m.
5. 2:00 p.m. 6. 5:00 p.m. 7. 9:00 p.m. 8. 2:30 a.m.

5 **Describir** Work with a partner and use the present progressive to describe what's going on in this beach scene.

6 **Conversar** Imagine that you and a classmate are each babysitting a group of children. One of you has great kids; the other's kids are mischievous. You're on the phone, telling each other what the children are doing at this very moment. Be creative, and be prepared to share some of your sentences with the class.

Síntesis

7 **¿Qué están haciendo?** With two other classmates, create at least three sentences about what these people are doing right now in these places. Also, say how they feel and what they are going to do.

modelo
Uds. están en la clase de español.
Estamos hablando con los otros estudiantes.
Estamos practicando los verbos.
No estamos aburridos/as.
Vamos a tener un examen mañana.

1. Tres amigas están de vacaciones.
2. Un padre y su hijo están en el parque.
3. Tú y tus compañeros/as están en la playa.
4. Una familia está en el centro.
5. El/la profesor(a) está en la biblioteca.
6. Unos jóvenes están en un estadio.

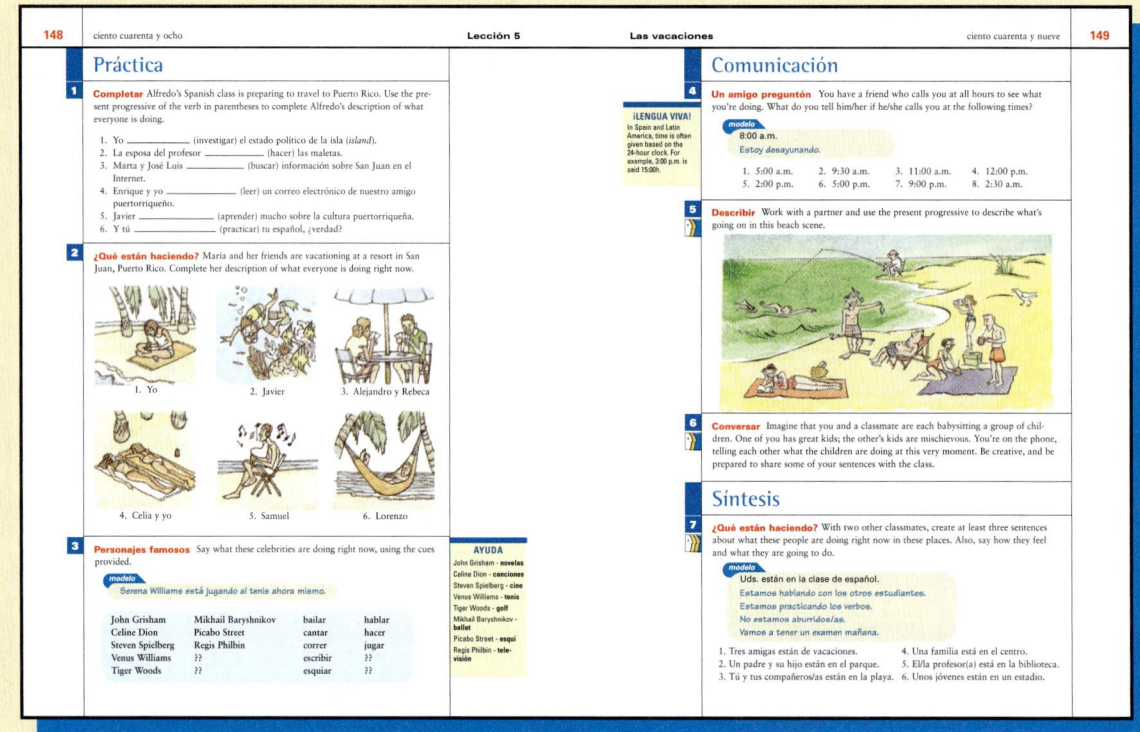

Práctica exercises provide a wide range of guided, yet meaningful exercises that weave current and previously learned vocabulary together with the current grammar point.

Comunicación offers opportunities for creative expression using the lesson's grammar and vocabulary. These take place with a partner, in small groups, or with the whole class.

Síntesis integrates the current grammar point with previously learned points, providing built-in, consistent review and recycling as you progress through the text.

Adelante

Lectura develops reading skills in the context of the lesson theme

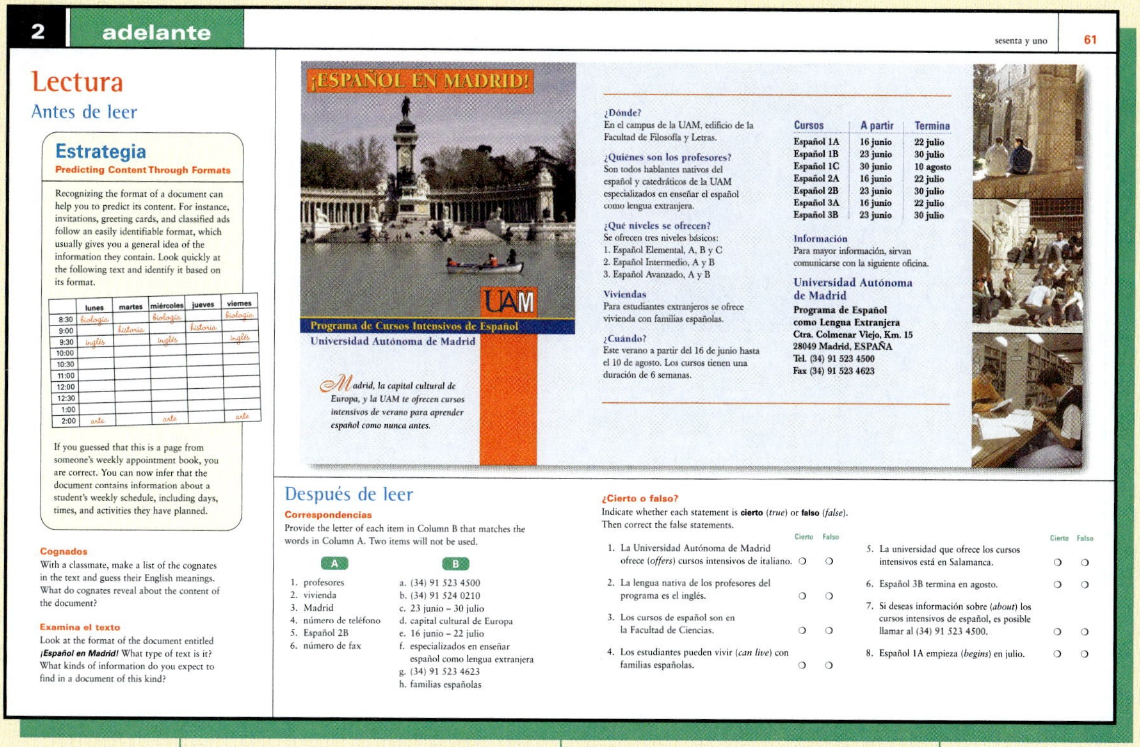

2 adelante

sesenta y uno 61

Lectura

Antes de leer

Estrategia

Predicting Content Through Formats

Recognizing the format of a document can help you to predict its content. For instance, invitations, greeting cards, and classified ads follow an easily identifiable format, which usually gives you a general idea of the information they contain. Look quickly at the following text and identify it based on its format.

	lunes	martes	miércoles	jueves	viernes
8:30	biología		biología		biología
9:00		historia		historia	
9:30	inglés		inglés		inglés
10:00					
10:30					
11:00					
12:00					
12:30					
1:00					
2:00	arte		arte		arte

If you guessed that this is a page from someone's weekly appointment book, you are correct. You can now infer that the document contains information about a student's weekly schedule, including days, times, and activities they have planned.

Cognados

With a classmate, make a list of the cognates in the text and guess their English meanings. What do cognates reveal about the content of the document?

Examina el texto

Look at the format of the document entitled ***¡Español en Madrid!*** What type of text is it? What kinds of information do you expect to find in a document of this kind?

¡ESPAÑOL EN MADRID!

UAM

Programa de Cursos Intensivos de Español

Universidad Autónoma de Madrid

Madrid, la capital cultural de Europa, y la UAM te ofrecen cursos intensivos de verano para aprender español como nunca antes.

¿Dónde?
En el campus de la UAM, edificio de la Facultad de Filosofía y Letras.

¿Quiénes son los profesores?
Son todos hablantes nativos del español y catedráticos de la UAM especializados en enseñar el español como lengua extranjera.

¿Qué niveles se ofrecen?
Se ofrecen tres niveles básicos:
1. Español Elemental, A, B y C
2. Español Intermedio, A y B
3. Español Avanzado, A y B

Viviendas
Para estudiantes extranjeros se ofrece vivienda con familias españolas.

¿Cuándo?
Este verano a partir del 16 de junio hasta el 10 de agosto. Los cursos tienen una duración de 6 semanas.

Cursos	A partir	Termina
Español 1A	16 junio	22 julio
Español 1B	23 junio	30 julio
Español 1C	30 junio	10 agosto
Español 2A	16 junio	22 julio
Español 2B	23 junio	30 julio
Español 3A	16 junio	22 julio
Español 3B	23 junio	30 julio

Información
Para mayor información, sirvan comunicarse con la siguiente oficina.

Universidad Autónoma de Madrid
Programa de Español como Lengua Extranjera
Ctra. Colmenar Viejo, Km. 15
28049 Madrid, ESPAÑA
Tel. (34) 91 523 4500
Fax (34) 91 523 4623

Después de leer

Correspondencias

Provide the letter of each item in Column B that matches the words in Column A. Two items will not be used.

A	B
1. profesores	a. (34) 91 523 4500
2. vivienda	b. (34) 91 524 0210
3. Madrid	c. 23 junio – 30 julio
4. número de teléfono	d. capital cultural de Europa
5. Español 2B	e. 16 junio – 22 julio
6. número de fax	f. especializados en enseñar español como lengua extranjera
	g. (34) 91 523 4623
	h. familias españolas

¿Cierto o falso?

Indicate whether each statement is **cierto** (*true*) or **falso** (*false*). Then correct the false statements.

	Cierto	Falso
1. La Universidad Autónoma de Madrid ofrece (*offers*) cursos intensivos de italiano.	❍	❍
2. La lengua nativa de los profesores del programa es el inglés.	❍	❍
3. Los cursos de español son en la Facultad de Ciencias.	❍	❍
4. Los estudiantes pueden vivir (*can live*) con familias españolas.	❍	❍
5. La universidad que ofrece los cursos intensivos está en Salamanca.	❍	❍
6. Español 3B termina en agosto.	❍	❍
7. Si deseas información sobre (*about*) los cursos intensivos de español, es posible llamar al (34) 91 523 4500.	❍	❍
8. Español 1A empieza (*begins*) en julio.	❍	❍

Antes de leer presents valuable reading strategies and pre-reading activities that strengthen your reading abilities in Spanish.

Readings are specifically related to the lesson theme and recycle vocabulary and grammar you have learned.

Después de leer Includes post-reading exercises that review and check your comprehension of the reading.

Adelante

Escritura develops writing skills in the context of the lesson theme

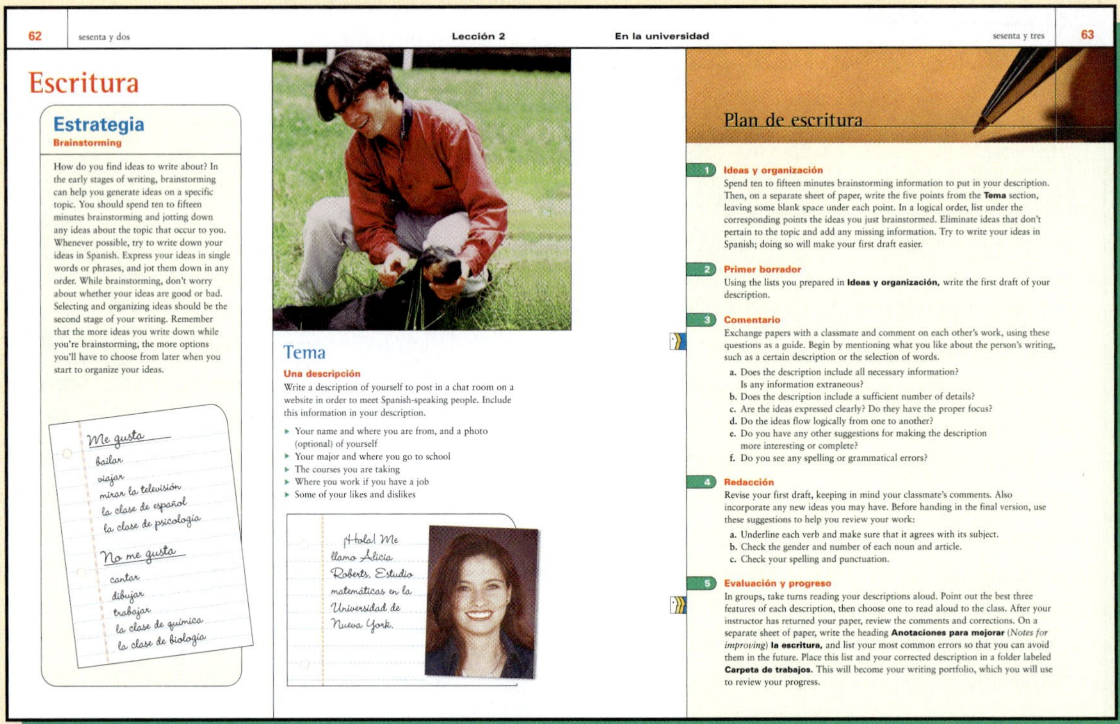

62 sesenta y dos — Lección 2 — En la universidad — sesenta y tres 63

Escritura

Estrategia

Brainstorming

How do you find ideas to write about? In the early stages of writing, brainstorming can help you generate ideas on a specific topic. You should spend ten to fifteen minutes brainstorming and jotting down any ideas about the topic that occur to you. Whenever possible, try to write down your ideas in Spanish. Express your ideas in single words or phrases, and jot them down in any order. While brainstorming, don't worry about whether your ideas are good or bad. Selecting and organizing ideas should be the second stage of your writing. Remember that the more ideas you write down while you're brainstorming, the more options you'll have to choose from later when you start to organize your ideas.

Me gusta
bailar
viajar
mirar la televisión
la clase de español
la clase de psicología

No me gusta
cantar
dibujar
trabajar
la clase de química
la clase de biología

Tema

Una descripción

Write a description of yourself to post in a chat room on a website in order to meet Spanish-speaking people. Include this information in your description.

- Your name and where you are from, and a photo (optional) of yourself
- Your major and where you go to school
- The courses you are taking
- Where you work if you have a job
- Some of your likes and dislikes

¡Hola! Me llamo Alicia Roberts. Estudio matemáticas en la Universidad de Nueva York.

Plan de escritura

1 Ideas y organización

Spend ten to fifteen minutes brainstorming information to put in your description. Then, on a separate sheet of paper, write the five points from the **Tema** section, leaving some blank space under each point. In a logical order, list under the corresponding points the ideas you just brainstormed. Eliminate ideas that don't pertain to the topic and add any missing information. Try to write your ideas in Spanish; doing so will make your first draft easier.

2 Primer borrador

Using the lists you prepared in **Ideas y organización,** write the first draft of your description.

3 Comentario

Exchange papers with a classmate and comment on each other's work, using these questions as a guide. Begin by mentioning what you like about the person's writing, such as a certain description or the selection of words.

a. Does the description include all necessary information? Is any information extraneous?
b. Does the description include a sufficient number of details?
c. Are the ideas expressed clearly? Do they have the proper focus?
d. Do the ideas flow logically from one to another?
e. Do you have any other suggestions for making the description more interesting or complete?
f. Do you see any spelling or grammatical errors?

4 Redacción

Revise your first draft, keeping in mind your classmate's comments. Also incorporate any new ideas you may have. Before handing in the final version, use these suggestions to help you review your work:

a. Underline each verb and make sure that it agrees with its subject.
b. Check the gender and number of each noun and article.
c. Check your spelling and punctuation.

5 Evaluación y progreso

In groups, take turns reading your descriptions aloud. Point out the best three features of each description, then choose one to read aloud to the class. After your instructor has returned your paper, review the comments and corrections. On a separate sheet of paper, write the heading **Anotaciones para mejorar** (*Notes for improving*) **la escritura,** and list your most common errors so that you can avoid them in the future. Place this list and your corrected description in a folder labeled **Carpeta de trabajos.** This will become your writing portfolio, which you will use to review your progress.

Estrategia provides strategies that help you prepare for the writing task presented in the next section.

Tema describes the writing topic and includes suggestions for approaching it.

Plan de escritura takes you step-by-step through the writing process, including planning, creating a first draft, peer review, and checking your work.

Adelante

Escuchar & Proyecto provide more listening practice and a task-based project

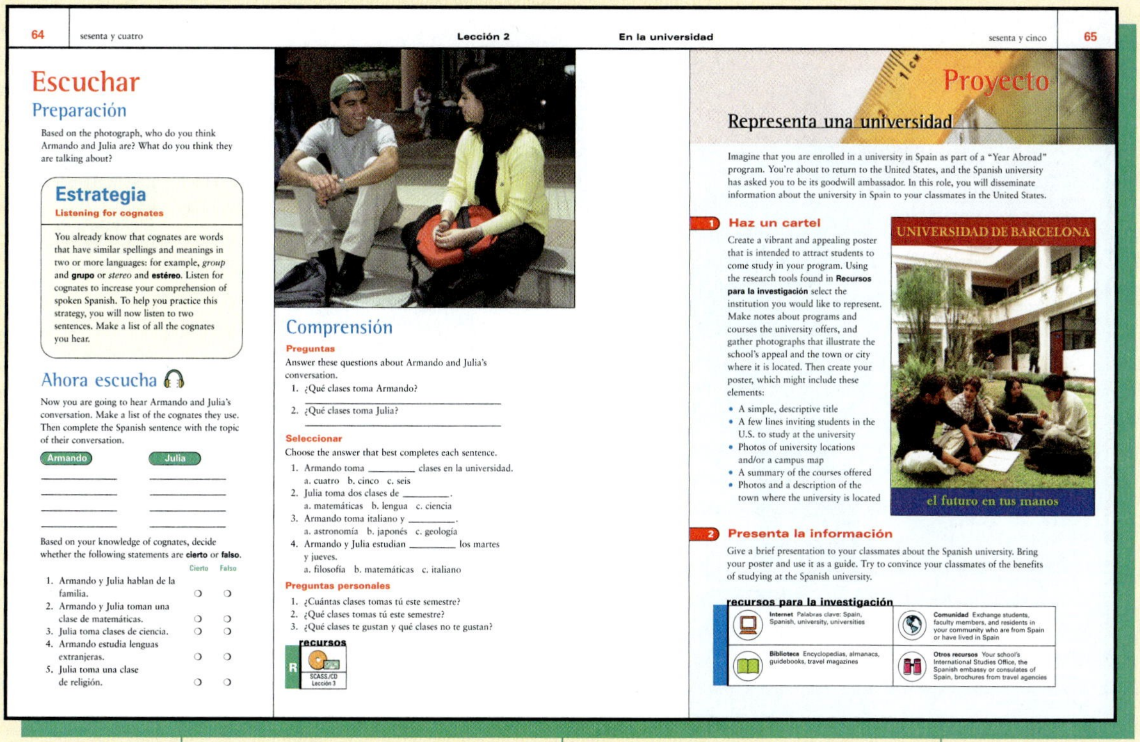

64 sesenta y cuatro Lección 2 En la universidad sesenta y cinco 65

Escuchar

Preparación

Based on the photograph, who do you think Armando and Julia are? What do you think they are talking about?

Estrategia

Listening for cognates

You already know that cognates are words that have similar spellings and meanings in two or more languages: for example, *group* and **grupo** or *stereo* and **estéreo**. Listen for cognates to increase your comprehension of spoken Spanish. To help you practice this strategy, you will now listen to two sentences. Make a list of all the cognates you hear.

Ahora escucha

Now you are going to hear Armando and Julia's conversation. Make a list of the cognates they use. Then complete the Spanish sentence with the topic of their conversation.

Armando | Julia

Based on your knowledge of cognates, decide whether the following statements are **cierto** or **falso**.

	Cierto	Falso
1. Armando y Julia hablan de la familia.	○	○
2. Armando y Julia toman una clase de matemáticas.	○	○
3. Julia toma clases de ciencia.	○	○
4. Armando estudia lenguas extranjeras.	○	○
5. Julia toma una clase de religión.	○	○

Comprensión

Preguntas

Answer these questions about Armando and Julia's conversation.

1. ¿Qué clases toma Armando?
2. ¿Qué clases toma Julia?

Seleccionar

Choose the answer that best completes each sentence.

1. Armando toma ________ clases en la universidad.
   a. cuatro b. cinco c. seis
2. Julia toma dos clases de ________.
   a. matemáticas b. lengua c. ciencia
3. Armando toma italiano y ________.
   a. astronomía b. japonés c. geología
4. Armando y Julia estudian ________ los martes y jueves.
   a. filosofía b. matemáticas c. italiano

Preguntas personales

1. ¿Cuántas clases tomas tú este semestre?
2. ¿Qué clases tomas tú este semestre?
3. ¿Qué clases te gustan y qué clases no te gustan?

recursos R SCASS/CD Lección 2

Proyecto

Representa una universidad

Imagine that you are enrolled in a university in Spain as part of a "Year Abroad" program. You're about to return to the United States, and the Spanish university has asked you to be its goodwill ambassador. In this role, you will disseminate information about the university in Spain to your classmates in the United States.

1 Haz un cartel

Create a vibrant and appealing poster that is intended to attract students to come study in your program. Using the research tools found in **Recursos para la investigación** select the institution you would like to represent. Make notes about programs and courses the university offers, and gather photographs that illustrate the school's appeal and the town or city where it is located. Then create your poster, which might include these elements:

- A simple, descriptive title
- A few lines inviting students in the U.S. to study at the university
- Photos of university locations and/or a campus map
- A summary of the courses offered
- Photos and a description of the town where the university is located

UNIVERSIDAD DE BARCELONA

el futuro en tus manos

2 Presenta la información

Give a brief presentation to your classmates about the Spanish university. Bring your poster and use it as a guide. Try to convince your classmates of the benefits of studying at the Spanish university.

recursos para la investigación

Internet Palabras clave: Spain, Spanish, university, universities	**Comunidad** Exchange students, faculty members, and residents in your community who are from Spain or have lived in Spain
Biblioteca Encyclopedias, almanacs, guidebooks, travel magazines	**Otros recursos** Your school's International Studies Office, the Spanish embassy or consulates of Spain, brochures from travel agencies

Escuchar presents a recorded conversation or narration to develop your listening skills in Spanish. **Preparación** and **Estrategia** prepare you for the listening passage.

Ahora escucha tracks you through the passage, and **Comprensión** checks your understanding of what you heard.

Proyecto gets you involved in a project by researching and creating a tangible product such as a brochure, a radio broadcast, or a Web page.

Recursos para la investigación points you toward research sources on the Web, in the library, and in your community.

Panorama

presents the nations of the Spanish-speaking world

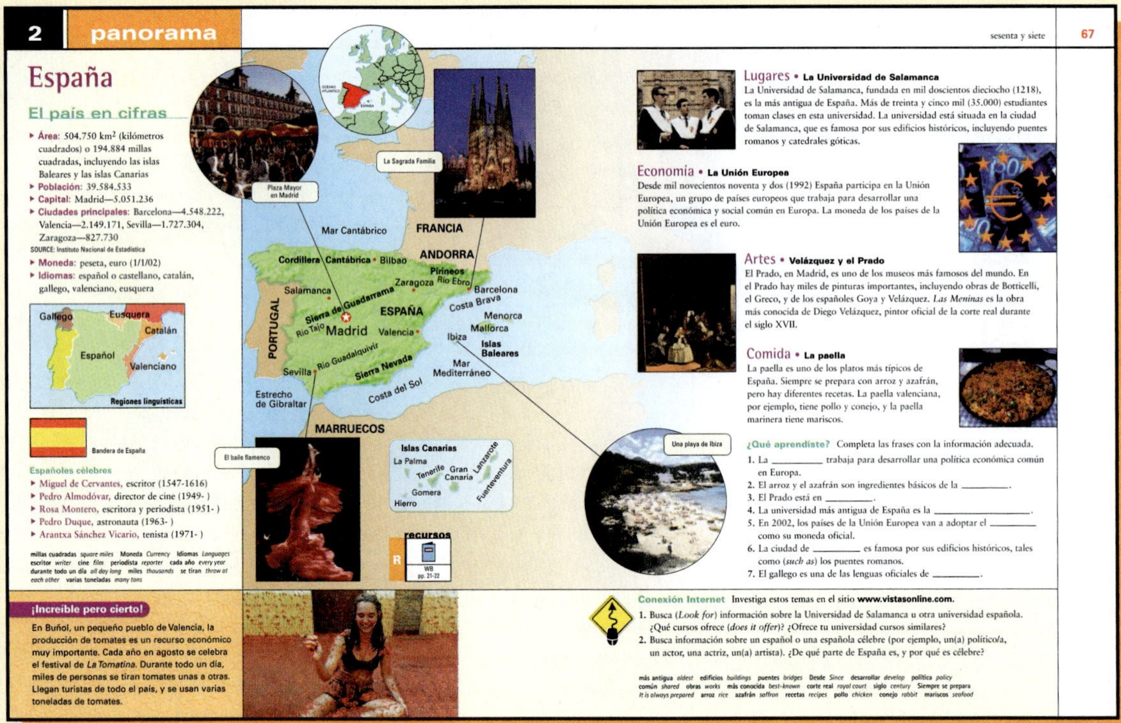
2 panorama

sesenta y siete 67

España

El país en cifras

- Área: 504.750 km² (kilómetros cuadrados) o 194.884 millas cuadradas, incluyendo las islas Baleares y las islas Canarias
- Población: 39.584.533
- Capital: Madrid—5.051.236
- Ciudades principales: Barcelona—4.548.222, Valencia—2.149.171, Sevilla—1.727.304, Zaragoza—827.730

SOURCE: Instituto Nacional de Estadística

- Moneda: peseta, euro (1/1/02)
- Idiomas: español o castellano, catalán, gallego, valenciano, euskera

Regiones lingüísticas

Bandera de España

Españoles célebres

- Miguel de Cervantes, escritor (1547-1616)
- Pedro Almodóvar, director de cine (1949-)
- Rosa Montero, escritora y periodista (1951-)
- Pedro Duque, astronauta (1963-)
- Arantxa Sánchez Vicario, tenista (1971-)

recursos WB pp. 21-22

¡Increíble pero cierto!

En Buñol, un pequeño pueblo de Valencia, la producción de tomates es un recurso económico muy importante. Cada año en agosto se celebra el festival de *La Tomatina*. Durante todo un día, miles de personas se tiran tomates unas a otras. Llegan turistas de todo el país, y se usan varias toneladas de tomates.

Lugares • La Universidad de Salamanca

La Universidad de Salamanca, fundada en mil doscientos dieciocho (1218), es la más antigua de España. Más de treinta y cinco mil (35.000) estudiantes toman clases en esta universidad. La universidad está situada en la ciudad de Salamanca, que es famosa por sus edificios históricos, incluyendo puentes romanos y catedrales góticas.

Economía • La Unión Europea

Desde mil novecientos noventa y dos (1992) España participa en la Unión Europea, un grupo de países europeos que trabaja para desarrollar una política económica y social común en Europa. La moneda de los países de la Unión Europea es el euro.

Artes • Velázquez y el Prado

El Prado, en Madrid, es uno de los museos más famosos del mundo. En el Prado hay miles de pinturas importantes, incluyendo obras de Botticelli, el Greco, y de los españoles Goya y Velázquez. *Las Meninas* es la obra más conocida de Diego Velázquez, pintor oficial de la corte real durante el siglo XVII.

Comida • La paella

La paella es uno de los platos más típicos de España. Siempre se prepara con arroz y azafrán, pero hay diferentes recetas. La paella valenciana, por ejemplo, tiene pollo y conejo, y la paella marinera tiene mariscos.

¿Qué aprendiste? Completa las frases con la información adecuada.

1. La ________ trabaja para desarrollar una política económica común en Europa.
2. El arroz y el azafrán son ingredientes básicos de la ________.
3. El Prado está en ________.
4. La universidad más antigua de España es la ________.
5. En 2002, los países de la Unión Europea van a adoptar el ________ como su moneda oficial.
6. La ciudad de ________ es famosa por sus edificios históricos, tales como (*such as*) los puentes romanos.
7. El gallego es una de las lenguas oficiales de ________.

Conexión Internet Investiga estos temas en el sitio www.vistasonline.com.

1. Busca (*Look for*) información sobre la Universidad de Salamanca u otra universidad española. ¿Qué cursos ofrece (*does it offer*)? ¿Ofrece tu universidad cursos similares?
2. Busca información sobre un español o una española célebre (por ejemplo, un(a) político/a, un actor, una actriz, un(a) artista). ¿De qué parte de España es, y por qué es célebre?

El país en cifras presents interesting, key facts about the featured country.

Maps point out major cities, rivers, and geographical features and situate the country in the context of its immediate surroundings and the world.

Readings A series of brief paragraphs explores facets of the country's culture such as history, places, fine arts, literature, and aspects of everyday life.

¡Increíble pero cierto! highlights an intriguing fact about the country or its people.

Conexión Internet offers Internet activities on the VISTAS Web Site for additional avenues of discovery.

Vocabulario
summarizes all the active vocabulary of the lesson

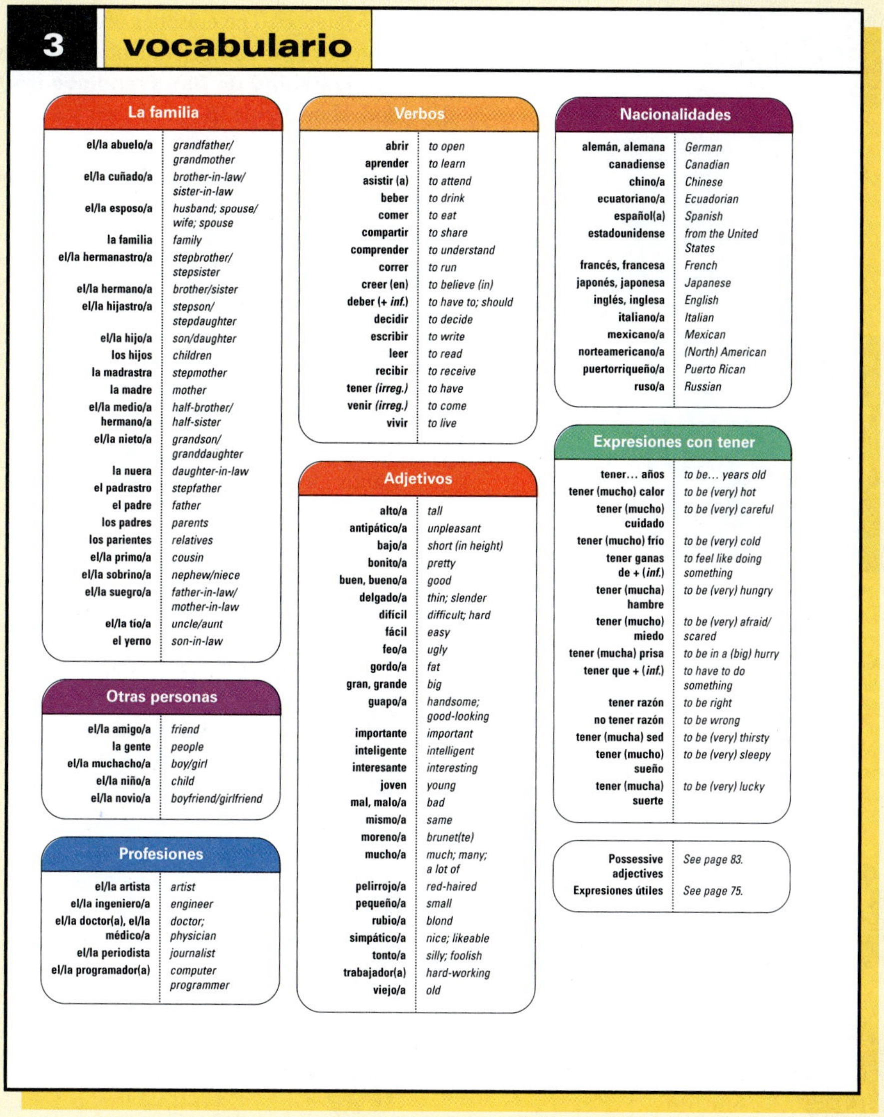

3 vocabulario

La familia

el/la abuelo/a	grandfather/ grandmother
el/la cuñado/a	brother-in-law/ sister-in-law
el/la esposo/a	husband; spouse/ wife; spouse
la familia	family
el/la hermanastro/a	stepbrother/ stepsister
el/la hermano/a	brother/sister
el/la hijastro/a	stepson/ stepdaughter
el/la hijo/a	son/daughter
los hijos	children
la madrastra	stepmother
la madre	mother
el/la medio/a hermano/a	half-brother/ half-sister
el/la nieto/a	grandson/ granddaughter
la nuera	daughter-in-law
el padrastro	stepfather
el padre	father
los padres	parents
los parientes	relatives
el/la primo/a	cousin
el/la sobrino/a	nephew/niece
el/la suegro/a	father-in-law/ mother-in-law
el/la tío/a	uncle/aunt
el yerno	son-in-law

Otras personas

el/la amigo/a	friend
la gente	people
el/la muchacho/a	boy/girl
el/la niño/a	child
el/la novio/a	boyfriend/girlfriend

Profesiones

el/la artista	artist
el/la ingeniero/a	engineer
el/la doctor(a), el/la médico/a	doctor; physician
el/la periodista	journalist
el/la programador(a)	computer programmer

Verbos

abrir	to open
aprender	to learn
asistir (a)	to attend
beber	to drink
comer	to eat
compartir	to share
comprender	to understand
correr	to run
creer (en)	to believe (in)
deber (+ *inf.*)	to have to; should
decidir	to decide
escribir	to write
leer	to read
recibir	to receive
tener (*irreg.*)	to have
venir (*irreg.*)	to come
vivir	to live

Adjetivos

alto/a	tall
antipático/a	unpleasant
bajo/a	short (in height)
bonito/a	pretty
buen, bueno/a	good
delgado/a	thin; slender
difícil	difficult; hard
fácil	easy
feo/a	ugly
gordo/a	fat
gran, grande	big
guapo/a	handsome; good-looking
importante	important
inteligente	intelligent
interesante	interesting
joven	young
mal, malo/a	bad
mismo/a	same
moreno/a	brunet(te)
mucho/a	much; many; a lot of
pelirrojo/a	red-haired
pequeño/a	small
rubio/a	blond
simpático/a	nice; likeable
tonto/a	silly; foolish
trabajador(a)	hard-working
viejo/a	old

Nacionalidades

alemán, alemana	German
canadiense	Canadian
chino/a	Chinese
ecuatoriano/a	Ecuadorian
español(a)	Spanish
estadounidense	from the United States
francés, francesa	French
japonés, japonesa	Japanese
inglés, inglesa	English
italiano/a	Italian
mexicano/a	Mexican
norteamericano/a	(North) American
puertorriqueño/a	Puerto Rican
ruso/a	Russian

Expresiones con tener

tener… años	to be… years old
tener (mucho) calor	to be (very) hot
tener (mucho) cuidado	to be (very) careful
tener (mucho) frío	to be (very) cold
tener ganas de + (*inf.*)	to feel like doing something
tener (mucha) hambre	to be (very) hungry
tener (mucho) miedo	to be (very) afraid/ scared
tener (mucha) prisa	to be in a (big) hurry
tener que + (*inf.*)	to have to do something
tener razón	to be right
no tener razón	to be wrong
tener (mucha) sed	to be (very) thirsty
tener (mucho) sueño	to be (very) sleepy
tener (mucha) suerte	to be (very) lucky

Possessive adjectives	See page 83.
Expresiones útiles	See page 75.

Video program

Fully integrated with your textbook, the **VISTAS** video contains eighteen episodes, one for each lesson of the text. The episodes present the adventures of four college students who are studying at the **Universidad de San Francisco** in Quito, Ecuador. They decide to spend their vacation break on a bus tour of the Ecuadorian countryside with the ultimate goal of hiking up a volcano. The video, shot in various locations in Ecuador, tells their story and the story of don Francisco, the tour bus driver who accompanies them.

The **Fotonovela** section in each textbook lesson is actually an abbreviated version of the dramatic episode featured in the video. Therefore, each **Fotonovela** section can be done before you see the corresponding video episode, after it, or as a section that stands alone in its own right.

The Cast

Here are the main characters you will meet when you watch the **VISTAS** video:

From Ecuador,
Inés Ayala Loor

From Spain,
María Teresa (Maite) Fuentes de Alba

From México,
Alejandro (Álex) Morales Paredes

From Puerto Rico,
Javier Gómez Lozano

And, also from Ecuador,
don Francisco Castillo Moreno

As you watch each video episode, you will first see a live segment in which the characters interact using vocabulary and grammar you are studying. As the video progresses, the live segments carefully combine new vocabulary and grammar with previously taught language. You will then see a **Resumen** section in which one of the main video characters recaps the live segment, emphasizing the grammar and vocabulary you are studying within the context of the episodes key events.

In addition, in most of the video episodes, there are brief pauses to allow the characters to reminisce about their home country. These flashbacks—montages of real-life images shot in Spain, México, Puerto Rico, and various parts of Ecuador—connect the theme of the video to everyday life in various parts of the Spanish-speaking world.

Student Ancillaries

Student Cassette/CD

Provided free-of-charge with each copy of **VISTAS**, the Student Cassette/CD contains the audio recordings that accompany the following materials in each lesson of the student textbook: the first **Práctica** exercise of each **Contextos** section, the **Pronunciación** exercises (Lessons 1–9 only), and the **Estrategia** and **Ahora escucha** activities in each **Escuchar** section.

Student Activities Manual

The Student Activities Manual contains workbook and laboratory activities that reinforce the vocabulary, grammar, and language functions presented in each lesson of the student textbook. The final section provides pre-viewing, viewing, and post-viewing video activities to be used in conjunction with the **VISTAS** video program. An answer key rounds out the manual.

Lab Cassettes/CDs

The Lab Cassettes/CDs contain the recordings that are used in conjunction with the laboratory activities of the Student Activities Manual.

Pocket Dictionary/Language Guide

The Pocket Dictionary/Language Guide is provided free-of-charge with each copy of **VISTAS**. It is designed to be a portable reference tool in which you can quickly look up Spanish words and expressions and summaries of grammatical concepts.

Video Program

This text-specific video provides dramatic vignettes, cultural footage, and unique summary features, all of which are fully integrated with each lesson of the **VISTAS** student textbook.

CD-ROM

This state-of-the-art, dual-platform CD-ROM provides highly interactive and visually captivating multimedia materials that focus on the grammar and vocabulary of each lesson of your textbook and incorporates selected ancillaries such as the video program and the Web site.

Web Site (vistasonline.com)

The **VISTAS** Web site offers a wide range of on-line resources for you and your instructor that directly correlate to your textbook and go beyond it. Here are some examples of the types of materials you will find: research materials related to the **Proyecto** sections, activities tied to the **Panorama** sections, other lesson-related activities, links to sites throughout the Spanish-speaking world, preparations for tests and exams, and interactive maps of the Spanish-speaking countries.

Instructor Ancillaries

In addition to the student ancillaries, all of which are available to the instructor, the following supplementary materials are also available. They were specially created to increase teaching options and to provide even more ways for students to learn and to practice using Spanish.

Instructor's Annotated Edition

Your Instructor's Annotated Edition contains a wealth of teaching information designed to support teaching in the classroom and to save instructors time in preparation and course management. With the same dimensions as the student text, this unique, innovative component shows reduced versions of the pages of the student text on which the answers to exercises and activities with discrete answers are conveniently overprinted. The student pages are surrounded by side and bottom panels containing abundant instructional information. Annotations include, but are not limited to, warm-ups, variations, expansions, additional exercises, tips for heritage speakers, on-page correlations of available ancillaries, and the text of the tapescript recorded on the Student Cassette/CD.

Instructor's Resource Manual

Your Instructor's Resource Manual offers a variety of materials that reinforce and expand on the lessons in the student text. The **Hojas de actividades** are reproducible charts, grids, and handouts correlated to the textbook's pair, small group, class circulation, and information gap activities. **Vocabulario adicional** sheets contain reproducible supplementary vocabulary lists related to the themes of selected textbook lessons. The answers to the **¡Inténtalo!** and **Práctica** exercises in the student textbook are also included.

Testing Program

The Testing Program contains two versions of the following tests and examinations: a test for each of the textbook's 18 lessons, semester examinations for Lessons 1–9 and Lessons 10–18, and quarter examinations for Lessons 1–6, Lessons 7–12, and Lessons 13–18. All tests and examinations include sections on listening comprehension, vocabulary, grammar, and communication. Listening scripts, an answer key, and suggestions for oral tests are also provided.

Tapescript/Videoscript

The Tapescript/Videoscript video program contains the complete written transcripts of the audio tracks of the Lab Cassettes/CDs, the Student Cassette/CD, and the **VISTAS** video program.

Overhead Transparencies

The Overhead Transparencies consist of the maps of the countries of the Spanish-speaking world, the **Contextos** vocabulary drawings, and other selected illustrations from the student text.

acknowledgments

On the behalf of its authors and editors, Vista Higher Learning expresses its sincere appreciation to the many college professors nationwide who contributed their ideas and suggestions to the **VISTAS** program. We are grateful to the members of the Spanish-teaching community who participated in the focus groups held at the program's initial stages. We are also indebted to the teaching professionals who reviewed manuscript and class tested **VISTAS** materials. Their insights and detailed comments were invaluable to the final product.

Focus Group Participants

Helga Barkemeyer
Montclair State University, NJ

Kathy P. Barton
Indiana University of Pennsylvania

Christine Bennett
College of Notre Dame, CA

Mara-Lee Bierman
Rockland County Community College, NY

Arthur Brady
Mercy College, NY

Elizabeth C. Calvera
Virginia Polytechnic Institute and State University

Richard P. Castillo
College of San Mateo, CA

William Chace
Hunter College, NY

Robert Chávez
West Valley College, CA

María Costa
California State University at Los Angeles

Frances Diccicco
Bucks County Community College, PA

Ronna Feit
Nassau County Community College, NY

Judith Gale
Pace University, NY

Javier Gallvan
Rancho Santiago College, CA

Susan C. Giráldez
University of the Pacific, CA

Jacquelyn W. Green
City College of San Francisco, CA

Josef Hellebrandt
Santa Clara University, CA

Librada Hernández
Los Angeles Valley College, CA

Steven Hess
Long Island University, NY

Juergen Kempff
University of California at Irvine

Denis Murphy
College of New Jersey

José Ramón Núñez
Long Beach City College, CA

Tyrone Parker
Catonsville Community College, MD

Bernardo García Pondavenes
Laney College, CA

Carmen I. Román
University of Maryland

Tony Ruiz
Gavilan Community College, CA

Monica F. Sasscer
Northern Virginia Community College

Lynn Sekelick
George Mason University, VA

Billy Bussell Thompson
Hofstra University, NY

Mercedes A. Thompson
El Camino College, CA

Elizabeth Turner
Dutchess County College, NY

J. Francisco Zermeño
Chabot College, CA

Class Testing Participants

Pat Brady
Tidewater Community College, VA

José Carmona
Daytona Beach Community College, FL

Richard K. Curry
Texas A&M University, TX

Marcella Fierro
Mesa Community College, AZ

Carmen Forner
Community College of Southern Nevada, NV

Maricarmen Gracia
Modesto Junior College, CA

Jorge Gracia
De Anza College, CA

Josef Hellebrandt
Santa Clara University, CA

Tania Hering
Alabama A&M University, AL

Shelly A. Moorman
University of St. Thomas, MN

Claire L. Reetz
Florida Community College at Jacksonville, FL

Monica Rivas
Mission College, CA

Joaquín Rodríguez-Barberá
Sam Houston State University, TX

Rosa Salinas Samelson
Palo Alto College, TX

José Alejandro Sandoval Erosa
Des Moines Area Community College, IA

Roy L. Tanner
Truman State University, MO

Evelyn F. Trujillo
Florida A&M University, FL

Fausto G. Vergara
Houston Community College, TX

Reviewers

Luz María Álvarez
Johnson County Community College, KS

Pilar B. Ara
Pasadena City College, CA

Enrica J. Ardemagni
Indiana University-Purdue University Indianapolis

Barbara Ávila-Shah
State University of New York at Buffalo

Helga Barkemeyer
Montclair State University, NJ

Clementina L. Bassi
Santa Fe Community College, FL

Kevin E. Beard
Richland College, TX

Nuria Bustamante
Los Angeles Community College, CA

Jeremy W. Cole
University of Kansas

Richard K. Curry
Texas A & M University (10)

William O. Deaver, Jr.
Armstrong Atlantic State University, GA

Octavio Delasuaree
William Paterson College, NJ

Humberto Delgado-Jenkins
Georgia Perimeter College

John J. Deveny, Jr.
Oklahoma State University

Susana Durán
Gulf Coast Community College, FL

Ronna S. Feit
Nassau Community College, NY

José A. Feliciano-Butler
University of South Florida

Marcella Fierro
Mesa Community College, AZ

John L. Finan
William Rainey Harper College, IL

Melissa Anne Fitch
University of Arizona

Ken Fleak
University of South Carolina

Marianne Franco
Modesto College, CA

Kathleen Gallivan
West Virginia University

Barbara N. Gantt
Northern Arizona University

David Ross Gerling
Sam Houston State University, TX

Yolanda L. González
Valencia Community College, FL

Jorge Gracia
De Anza College, CA

Jacquelyn W. Green
City College of San Francisco, CA

Margaret B. Haas
Kent State University, OH

Ellen Haynes
University of Colorado

Eda Henao
Borough of Manhattan Community College, NY

Steven Konopacki
Palm Beach Community College, FL

Roxana Levin
St. Petersburg Junior College, FL

María Helena López
Okaloosa-Walton Community College, FL

Melina L. Lozano
Madison Area Technical College, WI

Nelson I. Madera
Tallahassee Community College, FL

Verónica Mejía Noguer
Chaffey College, CA

Alfonso Millet
Oakland Community College, MI

James E. Palmer
Tarrant County College (Northeast Campus), TX

Monserrat Piera
Temple University, PA

Alcibiades Policarpo
Sam Houston State University, TX

Claire L. Reetz
Florida Community College at Jacksonville

Duane Rhoades
University of Wyoming

Charisse Richarz
Blinn College, TX

Karen L. Robinson
University of Nebraska at Omaha

Joaquín Rodríguez-Barberá
Sam Houston State University, TX

Paul Roggendorff
The University of Kentucky

Carmen I. Román
University of Maryland

Dora Marrón Romero
Broward Community College (North Campus), FL

S. Louise Roswell
Monroe Community College, NY

Rosa Salinas Samelson
Palo Alto College, TX

Vernon C. Smith
Rio Salado College, AZ

Jorge W. Suazo
Georgia Southern University

Roy L. Tanner
Truman State University, MO

Lourdes María Torres
De Paul University, IL

Ana Torres-Smith
Florida State University

Edith Valladares
Central Piedmont Community College, NC

Mayela Vallejos-Ramírez
University of Nebraska-Lincoln

Fausto G. Vergara
Houston Community Collge, TX

Virginia Vigil, deceased
Austin Community College, TX

Nancy Virumbrales
Waubsonsee Community College, IL

Alicia J. von Lehe
Santa Fe Community College, FL

Gloria Yampey-Jörg
Houston Community College Central Campus, TX

Gerald P. Young
Indian River Community College, FL

Additional Acknowledgments

We are especially grateful to our Senior Consulting Editor, Professor Elaine Horwitz, for her critical reading of the manuscript and her contributions to the student sidebars and the Instructor's Annotated Edition.

We also would like to express our gratitude to the entire staff of Vista Higher Learning that worked on the project for the last three years. Without the hard work and tenacity of these individuals, **VISTAS** would have never seen the light. In alphabetical order they are:

María Cinta Aparisi
Martin Beveridge
Ted Cantrell
Gustavo Cinci
Ianka De La Rosa
Linda Jurras
Holly Kersey
Suzanne Korschun
Pam Mishkin
Greg Moutafis
Eric Murphy
Peter O'Faherty
Stephen Pekich
Mark Porter
Sonny Regelman
Janet Spicer
Denise St. Jean
Daniella Tourgeman
Bruce Zimmerli

Hola, ¿qué tal?

1

Communicative Goals

You will learn how to:

- **Greet people in Spanish**
- **Say goodbye**
- **Identify yourself and others**
- **Talk about the time of day**

contextos

pages 2-5

- Words and phrases related to greetings and leave-takings
- Terms to identify yourself and others
- Expressions of courtesy

fotonovela

pages 6-9

Mrs. Ramos, from the travel agency Ecuatur, greets the students and hands out their travel papers. Don Francisco, the driver, introduces himself and asks the students to board the bus.

estructura

pages 10-25

- Nouns and articles
- Numbers 0-30
- Present tense of the verb **ser**
- Telling time

adelante

pages 26-31

Lectura: Read a telephone list.
Escritura: Create an address list in Spanish.
Escuchar: Listen to a conversation in a bus station.
Proyecto: Research the influence of Hispanic culture in a U.S. city.

panorama

pages 32-33

Featured Country: United States

- Cities and states with the largest Hispanic populations
- Influence of Hispanic culture in the U.S.

Lesson Goals

In **Lesson 1** students will be introduced to the following:

- terms for greetings and leave-takings
- identifying where one is from
- expressions of courtesy
- nouns and articles (definite and indefinite)
- numbers 0–30
- present tense of **ser**
- telling time
- recognizing cognates
- reading a telephone list rich in cognates
- writing a telephone/address list in Spanish
- the strategy of listening for known vocabulary
- how Hispanic cultures have influenced United States cities
- cultural and demographic information about Hispanics in the United States

Lesson Preview

Have students look at the photo. Ask: What do you think the young women are doing? Say: It is common in Hispanic cultures for friends to greet each other with a kiss (or two) on the cheek. Ask: How do you greet your friends?

INSTRUCTIONAL RESOURCES

Student Activities Manual: Workbook, 1–10
Student Activities Manual: Lab Manual, 217–222
Student Activities Manual: Video Activities, 327–328
Instructor's Resource Manual: Answer Keys
Instructor's Resource Manual: Vocabulario adicional, 51–52
Tapescript/Videoscript
Overhead Transparencies, 9–12
Student Cassette/CD
Lab Cassette/CD
Video Program
CD-ROM
Website: **www.vistasonline.com**
Testing Program: Prueba A, Prueba B

Section goals

In **Contextos**, students will learn and practice:
- basic greetings
- introductions
- courtesy expressions

Instructional Resources
Student Activities Manual: Workbook, 1–2; Lab Manual, 217
Transparencies 9–10
Student Cassette/CD
Vocabulario adicional 51–52

Note: You may wish to begin course work by teaching *Expresiones útiles para la clase*, **Vocabulario adicional 51** in the **Instructor's Resource Manual.**

Before Presenting Contextos Write a few greetings, farewells, and courtesy expressions on the board, explain their meaning, and model their pronunciation. Go around the class greeting students, making introductions, and encouraging responses.
Assignment Have students study **Contextos** and read through the activities on pages 3–4 as homework.

Present Circulate around the room conducting brief conversations based on the vocabulary in **Contextos**. Engage as many students as you can. Use the occasion to get to know your students and help them get to know one another. Have students open to pages 2–3 or project **Transparency 9** and ask them to identify which conversations seem to be exchanges between friends and which seem more formal. Overlay **Transparency 10** or use the printed text to draw attention to the use of **Ud.** vs. **tú** in these conversations. Explain situations in which each form is appropriate.

Successful Language Learning Encourage your students to make flash cards to help them memorize new vocabulary words.

1 contextos

Hola, ¿qué tal?

Más vocabulario

Buenos días.	*Good morning.*
Buenas noches.	*Good evening; Good night.*
Hasta la vista.	*See you later.*
Hasta pronto.	*See you soon.*
¿Cómo se llama usted?	*What's your name?*
Le presento a...	(formal) *I would like to introduce (name) to you.*
Te presento a...	(familiar) *I would like to introduce (name) to you.*
¿Cómo estás?	*How are you?*
No muy bien.	*Not very well.*
¿Qué pasa?	*What's happening?; What's going on?*
Por favor	*Please*
De nada.	*You're welcome.*
No hay de qué.	*You're welcome.*
Lo siento.	*I'm sorry.*
Muchas gracias.	*Thank you very much; Thanks a lot.*

Variación léxica

Items are presented for recognition purposes only.

Buenos días. ⟷ Buenas.
De nada. ⟷ A la orden.
Lo siento. ⟷ Perdón.
¿Qué tal? ⟷ ¿Qué hubo? (*Col.*)

recursos

R	SCASS./CD Lección 1	WB pp. 1-2	LM p. 217	LCASS./CD Cass. 1A/CD1

ELENA Patricia, éste es el señor Perales.
PATRICIA Encantada.
SEÑOR PERALES Igualmente. ¿De dónde es usted, señorita?
PATRICIA Soy de México. ¿Y usted?
SEÑOR PERALES De Puerto Rico.

TOMÁS ¿Qué tal, Alberto?
ALBERTO Regular. ¿Y tú?
TOMÁS Bien. ¿Qué hay de nuevo?
ALBERTO Nada.

SEÑOR VARGAS Buenas tardes, señora Wong. ¿Cómo está usted?
SEÑORA WONG Muy bien, gracias. ¿Y usted, señor Vargas?
SEÑOR VARGAS Bien, gracias.
SEÑORA WONG Hasta mañana, señor Vargas. Saludos a la señora Vargas.
SEÑOR VARGAS Adiós.

TEACHING OPTIONS

Variación léxica Point out that **Buenas, Chévere,** and **¿Qué hubo?** (often pronounced **¿Quihubo?**) are all coloquial. You may add that another common equivalent of **¿Qué tal?** is **¿Cómo te va?**.
Extra Practice Bring family photos or magazine photos in which people are shown greeting each other. Ask groups to write dialogue captions for each photo. Remind the class to use formal and informal expressions as appropriate.

Small Groups Have small groups role-play an original conversation in which older adults, children, and college-age people interact. Verify that the groups are using formal and informal expressions as appropriate. Have a few groups present their conversations to the class.
Extra Practice Double task when you take roll. After calling a name, greet that student and ask a question related to the day's lesson. Roll can thus serve as a class warm-up.

BERTA Hasta luego, Tere.
TERESA Chau, Berta. Nos vemos mañana.
CARMEN Buenas tardes. Me llamo Carmen. ¿Cómo te llamas tú?
ANTONIO Buenas tardes. Me llamo Antonio. Mucho gusto.
CARMEN El gusto es mío. ¿De dónde eres?
ANTONIO Soy de los Estados Unidos, de California.

Práctica

1 Escuchar Listen to each question or statement, then choose the correct response.

1. a. Muy bien, gracias. b. Me llamo Graciela. b
2. a. Lo siento. b. Mucho gusto. b
3. a. Soy de Puerto Rico. b. No muy bien. a
4. a. No hay de qué. b. Regular. a
5. a. Mucho gusto. b. Hasta pronto. b
6. a. Nada. b. Igualmente. a
7. a. Me llamo Guillermo Montero. b. Muy bien, gracias. b
8. a. Buenas tardes. ¿Cómo estás? b. El gusto es mío. a
9. a. Saludos a la Sra. Ramírez. b. Encantada. b
10. a. Adiós. b. Regular. b

2 Escoger For each expression, write another word or phrase that expresses a similar idea.

modelo
¿Cómo estás?
¿Qué tal?

1. De nada. No hay de qué.
2. Encantado. Mucho gusto.
3. Adiós. Chau o Hasta luego/mañana/pronto.
4. Te presento a Antonio. Este es Antonio
5. ¿Cómo estás? ¿Qué tal?
6. Mucho gusto. El gusto es mío.

3 Ordenar Work with a classmate to put this scrambled conversation in order. Then act it out.

—Muy bien, gracias. Soy Rosabel.
—Soy del Ecuador. ¿Y tú?
—Mucho gusto, Rosabel.
—Hola. Me llamo Carlos. ¿Cómo estás?
—Soy de Argentina.
—Igualmente. ¿De dónde eres, Carlos?

CARLOS Hola. Me llamo Carlos. ¿Cómo estás?
ROSABEL Muy bien, gracias. Soy Rosabel.
CARLOS Mucho gusto, Rosabel.
ROSABEL Igualmente. ¿De dónde eres, Carlos?
CARLOS Soy del Ecuador. ¿Y tú?
ROSABEL Soy de Argentina.

1 Warm-up Before students listen to the tape, ask them to read the possible answers provided for each item and jot down the questions or statements they think would elicit those responses. After they have listened to the tape and completed the activity, go over the answers with the whole class and confirm students' predictions.

1 Tapescript 1. ¿Cómo te llamas? 2. Te presento a Juan Pablo. 3. ¿De dónde es Ud.? 4. Muchas gracias. 5. Nos vemos. 6. ¿Qué pasa? 7. ¿Cómo está Ud.? 8. Buenas tardes, Sr. Fernández. 9. Susana, éste es el Sr. Ramírez. 10. ¿Qué tal?

2 Present/Expand Pronounce the expressions in **Modelo**. Ask volunteers to supply the similar expression. After they have finished, have students provide the question or statement that would elicit each item in this activity. Ex: 1. **—Gracias. —De nada.**

3 Present When they have finished, ask for a volunteer pair to read its conversation to the whole class. Verify that the order is correct.

3 Expand Have students in small groups each write a conversation based on the vocabulary and expressions on pages 2–3. Then ask the groups to rewrite their conversations, scrambling the order of the exchanges. When they have prepared a clean copy, groups should trade scrambled conversations and put the one they receive in logical order. Close by having groups verify the correct order of the conversations they wrote.

TEACHING OPTIONS

Game Divide the class into two groups. Create original statements and questions based on the **Más vocabulario** and the illustrated conversations. Indicate one group member at a time, alternating between groups. The indicated group member should respond to your statement or question. Each correct response wins the group a point. The group with the most points at the end of the game wins.

Heritage Speakers Have Spanish speakers mention other greetings and expressions of courtesy that are used in their countries of origin or that they know about. Ask them to tell where in the Spanish-speaking world the expressions are used. Write them on the board. Ask volunteers to use these expressions in a conversation.

4 Warm-up/Present Briefly circulate in the classroom, conducting conversations with individual students to activate their knowledge of greetings and courtesy expressions from pages 2–3. Assign pairs to do the activity. When they have finished, review their responses with the whole class.

4 Expand Have pairs or small groups create conversations that include the expressions used in Activity 4. Ask volunteers to present their conversations to the class.

Suggestion Discuss the titles of respect described in **¡Lengua viva!** Have students locate examples of the titles in Activity 5 or in the illustrated conversations on pages 2–3. Then have them create short sentences in which they use the titles with people they know.

5 Present Discuss the **Modelo** with the whole class before assigning the activity to pairs.

5 Expand Have eight pairs of students role-play one of the corrected mini-conversations. Ask them to substitute their own names and personal information where possible. Encourage other pairs as well to say their corrections to the second half of each conversation.

5 Expand Write a few sentences following the pattern of those in this activity and use them as a dictation. Read each sentence twice, pausing after the second time to allow students to write.

5 Expand Have volunteers write each conversation on the board. Work together as a class to identify and explain any errors.

4 Completar Work with a partner to complete these exchanges.

modelo

Estudiante 1: ¿Cómo estás?
Estudiante 2: Muy bien, gracias.

1. **Persona 1:** Buenos días.
   Persona 2: Buenos días. ¿Qué tal?
2. **Persona 1:** ¿Cómo te llamas?
   Persona 2: Me llamo Carmen Sánchez.
3. **Persona 1:** ¿De dónde eres?
   Persona 2: De México.
4. **Persona 1:** Te presento a Marisol.
   Persona 2: Encantado/a.
5. **Persona 1:** Gracias.
   Persona 2: De nada.
6. **Persona 1:** ¿Qué tal?
   Persona 2: Regular
7. **Persona 1:** ¿Qué pasa?
   Persona 2:: Nada.
8. **Persona 1:** ¡Hasta la vista!
   Persona 2: Answers will vary.

5 Cambiar Work with a partner and correct the second part of each conversation to make it logical. Answers will vary.

modelo

Estudiante 1: ¿Qué tal?
Estudiante 2: ~~No hay de qué.~~ Bien. ¿Y tú?

1. **Estudiante 1:** Hasta mañana, señora Ramírez. Saludos al señor Ramírez.
   Estudiante 2: *Muy bien, gracias.*
2. **Estudiante 1:** ¿Qué hay de nuevo, Alberto?
   Estudiante 2: *Sí, me llamo Alberto. ¿Cómo te llamas tú?*
3. **Estudiante 1:** Gracias, Tomás.
   Estudiante 2: *Regular. ¿Y tú?*
4. **Estudiante 1:** Miguel, ésta es la señorita Perales.
   Estudiante 2: *No hay de qué, señorita.*
5. **Estudiante 1:** ¿De dónde eres, Antonio?
   Estudiante 2: *Muy bien, gracias. ¿Y tú?*
6. **Estudiante 1:** ¿Cómo se llama usted?
   Estudiante 2: *El gusto es mío.*
7. **Estudiante 1:** ¿Qué pasa?
   Estudiante 2: *El gusto es mío.*
8. **Estudiante 1:** Buenas tardes, señor. ¿Cómo está usted?
   Estudiante 2: *Soy de Puerto Rico.*

¡LENGUA VIVA!

Titles of Respect
The titles **señor, señora,** and **señorita** are abbreviated **Sr., Sra.** and **Srta.** Note that these abbreviations are capitalized.

There is no Spanish equivalent for the English title *Ms.;* women are addressed as **señora** or **señorita.**

TEACHING OPTIONS

Extra practice Read some phrases to the class and ask if the class would use them with a another student of the same age or with an older person. Ex.: 1. **Te presento a Luis.** (student) 2. **Muchas gracias, señor.** (older person) 3. **¿Cómo estás?** (student) 4. **Buenos días, Dr. Soto.** (older person) 5. **¿De dónde es Ud., señora?** (older person) 6. **Chau, Teresa.** (student) **¿Cómo se llama Ud.?** (older person) **No hay de qué, señor Perales.** (older person)

Game Prepare a series of response statements using language in **Contextos**. Divide the class into two groups and invite students to guess the question or statement that would have elicited each of your response statements. Read a statement at a time. The team to correctly guess the question or statement first wins the point. Ex: **Me llamo Lupe Torres Garza. (¿Cómo se llama Ud.? / ¿Cómo te llamas?)** The team with the most correct guesses wins.

NATIONAL communication STANDARDS

Comunicación

6 **Diálogos** With a partner, complete and act out these conversations. Answers will vary.

Conversación 1
—Hola. Me llamo Teresa. ¿Cómo te llamas tú?
—________________________________
—Soy de Puerto Rico. ¿Y tú?
—________________________________

Conversación 2
—________________________________
—Muy bien. gracias. ¿Y usted, señora López?
—________________________________
—Hasta luego, señora. Saludos al señor López.
—________________________________

Conversación 3
—________________________________
—Regular. ¿Y tú?
—________________________________
—Nada.

7 **Conversaciones** This is the first day of class. Write four conversations based on what the people in this scene would say. Answers will vary.

8 **Situaciones** Work with two classmates to write and act out these situations. Answers will vary.

1. On your way out of class on the first day of school, you strike up a conversation with the two students who were sitting next to you. You find out each student's name and where he or she is from before you say goodbye and go to your next class.
2. At the next class you meet up with a friend and find out how he or she is doing. As you are talking, your friend Elena enters. Introduce her to your friend.
3. As you're leaving the bookstore, you meet your parents' friends Mrs. Sánchez and Mr. Rodríguez. You greet them and ask how each person is. As you say goodbye, you send greetings to Mrs. Rodríguez.
4. Make up and act out a real-life situation that you and your classmates can imagine yourselves in.

6 Suggestion Students will need about five minutes to complete the activity.

6 Expand Have the class work in small groups to write a few mini-conversations modeled on those in this activity. Then ask them to copy the dialogues, omitting a few exchanges. Each group should exchange its mini-conversations with another group, which will fill in the blanks.

6 Expand Have students rephrase **Conversaciones 1** and **3** in the formal register and **Conversación 2** in the informal register.

7 Warm-up Have students brainstorm who the people in the illustration are and what they are talking about. Tell students to look for clues in the people's names, ages, clothing, and their locations in the classroom. Ask students which groups would be speaking to each other in the **Ud.** form, and which would be using the **tú** form.

8 The Affective Dimension Point out that if students rehearse the situations a few times, they will feel more comfortable with the material and less anxious when they are asked to present it before the class.

8 Suggestion Have each group pick a situation to prepare and perform. Tell groups not to memorize the conversations, but to recreate them.

Assignment Have students do the activities in **Student Activities Manual: Workbook**, pages 1–2.

Note: At this point you may want to present *Otros países*, **Vocabulario adicional 52**, in the **Instructor's Resource Manual**.

TEACHING OPTIONS

Extra Practice Have students circulate around the classroom and conduct unrehearsed mini-conversations in Spanish with other students, using the words and expressions that they have learned on pages 2–3. As students are carrying out the activity, circulate around the room yourself, monitoring your students' work and offering assistance if requested.

Heritage Speakers Ask Spanish speakers to role-play some of the conversations and situations in **Comunicación**, page 5, modeling correct pronunciation and intonation for the class. Remind students that there are regional differences in the way English is pronounced, and that the same is true of Spanish. Help clarify unfamiliar vocabulary as necessary.

Section Goals

In **Fotonovela** students will:

- receive comprehensible input from free-flowing discourse
- learn functional phrases that preview lesson grammatical structures

Instructional Resources
Student Activities Manual: Video Activities 327–328
Video Program (Start: 00:02:18)

Video Synopsis Don Francisco, the bus driver, and Sra. Ramos, a representative of Ecuatur, meet the four travelers at the university. Sra. Ramos passes out travel documents. Inés and Maite introduce themselves, as do Javier and Álex. The travelers board the bus.

Before Presenting Fotonovela Have students cover the Spanish captions and guess the plot of this **Fotonovela** episode based only on the video stills. Record their predictions.

Assignment Have students study **Fotonovela** and **Expresiones útiles** as homework.

Warm-up Quickly review the predictions made in the previous class. Ask the class to point out any discrepancies between their predictions and what actually occurred in the **Fotonovela** episode.

Present Pronounce each item in **Expresiones útiles** and have the class repeat after you. Point out that all the entries on the list are new active vocabulary except for **¿Cómo se llama usted?; Yo soy don Francisco, el conductor**; and **¿Cómo te llamas?** Review the **Expresiones útiles** by using them in short conversations with individual students.

Continued on page 7.

¡Todos a bordo!

NATIONAL communication cultures STANDARDS

Los cuatro estudiantes, don Francisco y la Sra. Ramos se reúnen (*meet*) en la universidad.

PERSONAJES

DON FRANCISCO

SRA. RAMOS

ÁLEX

JAVIER

INÉS

MAITE

1

SRA. RAMOS Buenos días, chicos. Yo soy Isabel Ramos de la agencia Ecuatur.

DON FRANCISCO Y yo soy don Francisco, el conductor.

2

SRA. RAMOS Bueno, ¿quién es María Teresa Fuentes de Alba?

MAITE ¡Soy yo!

SRA. RAMOS Ah, bien. Aquí tienes los documentos de viaje.

MAITE Gracias.

3

SRA. RAMOS ¿Javier Gómez Lozano?

JAVIER Aquí... soy yo.

6

JAVIER ¿Qué tal? Me llamo Javier.

ÁLEX Mucho gusto, Javier. Yo soy Álex. ¿De dónde eres?

JAVIER De Puerto Rico. ¿Y tú?

ÁLEX Yo soy de México.

7

DON FRANCISCO Bueno, chicos, ¡todos a bordo!

8

INÉS Con permiso.

recursos

R	VIDEO Lección 1	VM pp. 327-328

TEACHING OPTIONS

Video Tips General suggestions for using video clips in the classroom can be found on page IAE-13 of the **Instructor's Annotated Edition**.

¡Todos a bordo! Play the **¡Todos a bordo!** segment of this video module once and ask the class to write down the basic greetings they hear. Play this segment a second time and ask the class to make a list of all the expressions the characters use to identify themselves. Then play the **¡Todos a bordo!** segment for a third time, asking the class to write down all the courtesy expressions they hear, including ways to say "pleased to meet you" and "excuse me."

SRA. RAMOS Y tú eres Inés Ayala Loor, ¿verdad?

INÉS Sí, yo soy Inés.

SRA. RAMOS Y tú eres Alejandro Morales Paredes, ¿no?

ÁLEX Sí, señora.

INÉS Hola. Soy Inés.

MAITE Encantada. Yo me llamo Maite. ¿De dónde eres?

INÉS Soy del Ecuador, de Portoviejo. ¿Y tú?

MAITE De España. Soy de Madrid, la capital. Oye, ¿qué hora es?

INÉS Son las diez y tres minutos.

ÁLEX Perdón.

DON FRANCISCO ¿Y los otros?

SRA. RAMOS Son todos.

DON FRANCISCO Está bien.

Enfoque cultural Saludos y presentaciones

In the Hispanic world, it is customary for men and women to shake hands when meeting someone for the first time and when saying hello and goodbye to people they already know. Men greet female friends and family members with a brief kiss, and they greet males they know well with an **abrazo**—a quick hug and pat on the back. Women of all ages frequently greet good friends, family members, and other loved ones with a brief kiss on one or both cheeks.

Expresiones útiles

Identifying yourself and others

▶ **¿Cómo se llama usted?**
What's your name?
▷ **Yo soy don Francisco, el conductor.**
I'm don Francisco, the driver.

▶ **¿Cómo te llamas?**
What's your name?
▷ **Me llamo Javier.**
My name is Javier.

▶ **¿Quién es... ?**
Who is... ?
▷ **Aquí... soy yo.**
Here... that's me.

▶ **Tú eres... , ¿verdad?/¿no?**
You are ..., right?/no?
▷ **Sí, señora.**
Yes, ma'am.

Saying what time it is

▶ **¿Qué hora es?**
What time is it?
▷ **Es la una.**
It's one o'clock.
▷ **Son las dos.**
It's two o'clock.
▷ **Son las diez y tres minutos.**
It's 10:03.

Saying "excuse me"

▷ **Con permiso.**
Pardon me; Excuse me. (to request permission)
▷ **Perdón.**
Pardon me; Excuse me. (to get someone's attention or to ask forgiveness)

When starting a trip

▷ **¡Todos a bordo!**
All aboard!
▷ **¡Buen viaje!**
Have a good trip!

Getting a friend's attention

▷ **Oye...**
Listen...

TEACHING OPTIONS

Enfoque cultural Point out to the class that greeting friends, family members, and loved ones with a kiss on one or both cheeks is not unique to the Spanish-speaking world; this custom is common in many European countries and in other parts of the world.
Mention also that the concept of an appropriate personal space as it is understood in the United States differs from that of the Hispanic world. Linguists have determined that in the United States friends and acquaintances generally stand or sit at least 18 inches apart while chatting. In Hispanic cultures, however, 18 inches would probably seem like an excessive distance between friends who are having a conversation. It is not considered unusual for casual acquaintances to stand or sit closer to each other.

Have students volunteer to read individual parts of the **Fotonovela** episode aloud. Then have students get together in groups of six to act out the episode. Have one or two groups present the episode to the class. See ideas for using the video in **Teaching Options**, page 6.

Comprehension Check Check comprehension of the **Fotonovela** episode by doing Activity 1, **¿Cierto o falso?**, page 8, orally with the whole class.

Suggestion In the video-still captions, in **Expresiones útiles**, and as they occur in conversation with your students, draw attention to the following: subject pronouns **yo**, **tú**, and **Ud.**; the singular and plural forms **es** and **son**, derived from the verb **ser**; the singular and plural definite articles **la** and **las**; and time-telling expressions. Point out that the singular forms **es** and **la** are used with one o'clock and that the plural forms **son** and **las** are used with two o'clock, three o'clock, and so forth. Tell your students that they will learn more about these concepts in the upcoming **Estructura** section.

Successful Language Learning Tell your students that their conversational skills will grow more quickly if they learn each lesson's **Expresiones útiles.** This feature is designed to teach phrases that will be useful in conversation, and it will also help the students understand key phrases in each **Fotonovela**.

Assignment Have students prepare activities 2–4 in **Reacciona a la fotonovela**, page 8, as homework.

Reacciona a la fotonovela

1 **¿Cierto o falso?** Indicate if each statement is **cierto** or **falso**. Then correct the false statements.

	Cierto	Falso	
1. Javier y Álex son pasajeros (*passengers*).	✓	❍	
2. Javier Gómez Lozano es el conductor.	❍	✓	Don Francisco es el conductor.
3. Inés Ayala Loor es de la agencia Ecuatur.	❍	✓	Isabel Ramos es de la agencia Ecuatur.
4. Inés es del Ecuador.	✓	❍	
5. Maite es de España.	✓	❍	
6. Javier es de Puerto Rico.	✓	❍	
7. Álex es del Ecuador.	❍	✓	Álex es de México.

2 **Identificar** Indicate which person would make each statement. One name will be used twice.

1. Yo soy de México. ¿De dónde eres tú? Álex
2. ¡Atención! ¡Todos a bordo! Don Francisco
3. ¿Yo? Soy de la capital de España. Maite
4. Y yo soy del Ecuador. Inés
5. ¿Qué hora es, Inés? Maite
6. Yo soy de Puerto Rico. ¿Y tú? Javier

3 **Completar** Complete this slightly altered version of the conversation that Inés and Maite had.

INÉS Hola. ¿Cómo te __llamas__?
MAITE Me llamo Maite. ¿Y __tú__?
INÉS Inés. Mucho __gusto__.
MAITE __El__ gusto es mío.
INÉS ¿De __dónde__ eres?
MAITE __De__ España. ¿Y __tú__?
INÉS Del __Ecuador__.

4 **Conversar** Imagine that you are chatting with a traveler you just met at the airport. With a partner, prepare a conversation using these cues.

Estudiante 1	Estudiante 2
Say "good afternoon" to your partner and ask for his or her name.	→ Say hello and what your name is. Then ask what your partner's name is.
Say what your name is and that you are glad to meet your partner.	→ Say that the pleasure is yours.
Ask how your partner is.	→ Say that you're doing well, thank you.
Ask where your partner is from.	→ Say where you're from.
Wish your partner a good trip.	→ Say thank you and goodbye.

¡LENGUA VIVA!
In Spanish-speaking countries, **don** and **doña** are used with men's and women's first names to show respect: **don Francisco, doña Rita.** Note that these words are not capitalized.

NATIONAL communication STANDARDS

Reacciona a la fotonovela

1 Expand Give these true-false statements to the class as items 8–10: **8. Maite es de la capital de España. (Cierto) 9. Son las tres y diez minutos. (Falso. Son las diez y tres minutos.) 10. Inés es de Quito, la capital del Ecuador. (Falso. Inés es de Portoviejo.)**

2 Expand Tell students to add Sra. Ramos to the list of possible answers. Then give these statements to the class as items 7–8: **7. ¿Quién es Inés Ayala Loor? (Sra. Ramos) 8. Hola, chicos. Yo soy el conductor. (don Francisco)**

Suggestion Go over **¡Lengua viva!** with students. Point out that the travelers might call the representative of Ecuatur **Sra. Ramos**. Ask the class what else the travelers could call her. **(doña Isabel)**

3 Warm-up/Present Have students quickly review the conversation between Carmen and Antonio on page 3. Then go over the activity by asking volunteers to take the roles of Maite and Inés.

4 Possible Response
S1: Buenas tardes. ¿Cómo te llamas?
S2: Hola. Me llamo Felipe. Y tú, ¿cómo te llamas?
S1: Me llamo Denisa. Mucho gusto.
S2: El gusto es mío.
S1: ¿Cómo estás?
S2: Bien, gracias.
S1: ¿De dónde eres?
S2: Soy de Venezuela.
S1: ¡Buen viaje!
S2: Gracias. ¡Adiós!

The Affective Dimension Point out that many people feel a bit nervous about speaking in front of a group. Encourage your students to think of anxious feelings as extra energy that will help them accomplish their goals.

TEACHING OPTIONS

Pairs Ask students to work in pairs to ad-lib the exchanges between don Francisco and Sra. Ramos, between Inés and Maite, and between Álex and Javier. Tell them to get the general meaning across using vocabulary and expressions they know, and assure them that they don't have to stick to the original exchanges word for word. Ask volunteers to present each exchange in front of the class.

Extra Practice Choose four or five lines of the **Fotonovela** episode to use as a dictation. Read the lines twice slowly to give students an opportunity to write. Then read them again at normal speed to allow students to correct any errors or fill in any gaps. You may have students correct their own work by checking it against the **Fotonovela** text.

NATIONAL STANDARDS comparisons

Pronunciación

The Spanish alphabet

The Spanish alphabet consisted of 30 letters until 1994, when the **Real Academia Española** (Royal Spanish Academy) removed **ch (che)** and **ll (elle)**. You may still see **ch** and **ll** listed as separate letters in reference works printed before 1994. Two Spanish letters, **ñ (eñe)** and **rr (erre)**, don't appear in the English alphabet. The letters **k (ka)** and **w (doble ve)** are used only in words of foreign origin.

Letra	Nombre(s)	Ejemplos	Letra	Nombre(s)	Ejemplos
a	a	**a**diós	**ñ**	eñe	ma**ñ**ana
b	be	**b**ien, pro**b**lema	**o**	o	**o**nce
c	ce	**c**osa, **c**ero	**p**	pe	**p**rofesor
d	de	**d**iario, na**d**a	**q**	cu	**q**ué
e	e	**e**studiante	**r**	ere	**r**egular, seño**r**a
f	efe	**f**oto	**rr**	erre	ca**rr**o
g	ge	**g**racias, **G**erardo, re**g**ular	**s**	ese	**s**eñor
h	hache	**h**ola	**t**	te	**t**ú
i	i	**i**gualmente	**u**	u	**u**sted
j	jota	**J**avier	**v**	ve	**v**ista, nue**v**o
k	ka, ca	**k**ilómetro	**w**	doble ve	***w**alkman*
l	ele	**l**ápiz	**x**	equis	e**x**istir, Mé**x**ico
m	eme	**m**apa	**y**	i griega, ye	**y**o
n	ene	**n**acionalidad	**z**	zeta, ceta	**z**ona

Práctica Spell these words aloud in Spanish.

1. nada
2. maleta
3. quince
4. muy
5. hombre
6. por favor
7. San Fernando
8. Estados Unidos
9. Puerto Rico
10. España
11. Javier
12. Ecuador
13. Maite
14. gracias
15. Nueva York

Oraciones Repeat these sentences after your instructor, then spell each word aloud.

1. Hola. Me llamo Anita Amores. Soy del Ecuador.
2. Somos seis en mi familia.
3. Tengo dos hermanos y una hermana.
4. Mi papá es del Ecuador y mi mamá es de España.

Refranes Read these sayings aloud after your instructor.

Ver es creer.[1]
En boca cerrada no entran moscas.[2]

1 Seeing is believing.
2 Silence is golden.

recursos

R	SCASS./CD Lección 1	LM p. 218	LCASS./CD Cass. 1A/CD1

TEACHING OPTIONS

Extra practice Do a dictation activity in which you spell out a list of words in Spanish to the class. Spell each word twice to allow students sufficient time to write. After you have finished, write your list on the board or project it on a transparency and have your students check their work.

Extra Practice Here are four more **refranes** to use for practicing the alphabet: **De tal palo, tal astilla** (*A chip off the old block*); **Los ojos son el espejo del alma** (*The eyes are the mirror of the soul*); **El rayo nunca cae dos veces en el mismo lugar** (*Lightning never strikes twice in the same place*); **No dejes para mañana lo que puedas hacer hoy** (*Don't put off until tomorrow what you can do today*).

Section Goals

In **Pronunciación** students will be introduced to:

- the Spanish alphabet and how it contrasts with the English alphabet
- the names of the letters

Instructional Resources
Student Activities Manual: Lab Manual, 218
Student Cassette/CD

Note: The first two exercises in this section, **The Spanish Alphabet** and **Práctica**, are recorded on the **Student Cassette/CD**. The English introductory paragraph and the last two exercises, **Oraciones** and **Refranes**, are not.

Present

- Pronounce the letters of the Spanish alphabet and have your students repeat them.
- Draw attention to any posters, signs, or maps in the classroom. Point out individual letters in words and ask the class to identify them in Spanish.
- Write on the board the Hispanic abbreviations of several famous organizations. Ex: **ONU**, **OPEP**, **UNAM**. Have students spell out the abbreviations in Spanish. Tell the class what each abbreviation stands for. Ex: **ONU** = **Organización de Naciones Unidas** (*United Nations, UN*), **OPEP** = **Organización de Países Exportadores de Petróleo** (*Organization of Petroleum-Exporting Countries, OPEC*)
- Write the names of some famous Hispanics on the board and have the class spell the names in Spanish.
- Have students spell out their own names in Spanish.

Práctica/Oraciones/Refranes Model the pronunciation of each word or sentence, having students repeat after you.

1.1 Nouns and articles

Spanish nouns

ANTE TODO A noun is a word used to identify people, animals, places, things, or ideas. Unlike English, all Spanish nouns, even those that refer to non-living things, have gender; that is, they are considered either masculine or feminine. As in English, nouns in Spanish also have number, meaning that they are either singular or plural.

Nouns that refer to living things

Masculine nouns		Feminine nouns	
el hombre	*the man*	**la mujer**	*the woman*
ending in –o		**ending in –a**	
el chico	*the boy*	**la chica**	*the girl*
el pasajero	*the (male) passenger*	**la pasajera**	*the (female) passenger*
ending in –or		**ending in –ora**	
el conductor	*the (male) driver*	**la conductora**	*the (female) driver*
el profesor	*the (male) teacher*	**la profesora**	*the (female) teacher*
ending in –ista		**ending in –ista**	
el turista	*the (male) tourist*	**la turista**	*the (female) tourist*

- As shown above, nouns that refer to males, like **el hombre**, are generally masculine, while nouns that refer to females, like **la mujer**, are generally feminine.

- Many nouns that refer to male beings end in **–o** or **–or**. Their corresponding feminine forms end in **–a** and **–ora**, respectively.

el conductor

la profesora

- The masculine and feminine forms of nouns that end in **–ista** are the same, so gender is indicated by the article **el** (masculine) or **la** (feminine). Some other nouns have identical masculine and feminine forms.

el joven *the youth; the young man*	**la** joven *the youth; the young woman*
el estudiante *the (male) student*	**la** estudiante *the (female) student*

CONSEJOS

Profesor(a) and **turista** are *cognates*—words that share similar spellings and meanings in Spanish and English. Recognizing cognates will help you determine the meaning of many Spanish words. Beware, however, of "false" cognates, words that have similar spellings in Spanish and English but different meanings:

el conductor *driver*

el director *orchestra conductor*

Section Goals

In **Estructura 1.1** students will be introduced to:
- gender nouns
- definite and indefinite articles

Instructional Resources
Student Activities Manual: Workbook, 3; Lab Manual, 219

Before Presenting Estructura 1.1
Write these nouns from **Fotonovela** on the board: **conductor, agencia, documentos, universidades**. Ask volunteers to tell what each means. Point out the different endings of the words and introduce the concept of gender in Spanish. Explain what a noun is and give examples of people (**chicos**), places (**universidad**), things (**documentos**), and ideas (**nacionalidad**). Ask volunteers to point out which of these nouns are singular and which are plural and why.
Assignment Have students study **Estructura 1.1** and prepare the exercises on pages 12–13 (through Activity 2) as homework.

Nouns that refer to living things
Present
- Work through the discussion of nouns and singular definite articles point by point, writing examples on the board. Test comprehension as you proceed by asking volunteers to supply the correct definite article for nouns you suggest.
- Point out that while nouns for male beings generally are masculine, likewise for feminine nouns, grammatical gender doesn't necessarily reflect the actual gender of the being referred to.
- Point out patterns of noun endings **–o, –a; –or, –ora**. Stress that **–ista** can refer to males or females and give additional examples: **el/la artista, el/la dentista**, and so forth.

TEACHING OPTIONS

Extra Practice Write 10 singular nouns on the board. Make sure the nouns represent a mix of the different types of noun endings taught so far. In a rapid-response drill, call on random students to give the appropriate gender. For **–ista** words, accept either masculine or feminine, but be sure to clarify that both are used. You may also do this as a completely oral drill by not writing the words on the board.

Game Divide the class into groups of three to four students. Using your picture file, point to various objects or people and say the Spanish noun without saying the article. Call on groups to indicate the object or person's gender. The members of the group have 10 seconds to confer on the correct answer. Give a point for each correct answer. Deduct a point for each incorrect answer. The group with the most points at the end wins.

Nouns that refer to non-living things

Masculine nouns		Feminine nouns	
ending in –o		**ending in –a**	
el cuaderno	*the notebook*	**la cosa**	*the thing*
el diario	*the diary*	**la escuela**	*the school*
el diccionario	*the dictionary*	**la grabadora**	*the tape recorder*
el número	*the number*	**la palabra**	*the word*
ending in –ma		**ending in –ción**	
el problema	*the problem*	**la lección**	*the lesson*
el programa	*the program*	**la conversación**	*the conversation*
ending in –s		**ending in –dad**	
el autobús	*the bus*	**la nacionalidad**	*the nationality*
el país	*the country*	**la comunidad**	*the community*

CONSEJOS

Since **la fotografía** is feminine, so is its shortened form, **la foto,** even though it ends in **–o.**

- As shown above, certain noun endings are strongly associated with a specific gender, so you can use them to determine if a noun is masculine or feminine.
- Because the gender of nouns that refer to non-living things cannot be determined by foolproof rules, you should memorize the gender of each noun you learn. It is helpful to memorize each noun with its corresponding article, **el** for masculine and **la** for feminine.
- Another reason to memorize the gender of every noun is that there are common exceptions to the rules of gender. For example, **el mapa** (*map*) and **el día** (*day*) end in **–a,** but are masculine. **La mano** (*hand*) ends in **-o,** but is feminine.

Plural of nouns

¡ATENCIÓN!

When a singular noun has an accent mark on the last syllable, the accent is dropped from the plural form:
la lección → **las lecciones**
el autobús → **los autobuses**
You will learn more about accent marks in Lesson 4, **Pronunciación**, p. 111.

- In Spanish, nouns that end in a vowel form the plural by adding **-s.** Nouns that end in a consonant add **-es**. Nouns that end in **-z** change the **-z** to **-c**, then add **-es**.

el chic**o** → los chic**os**	la nacionalida**d** → las nacionalida**des**
el diari**o** → los diari**os**	el paí**s** → los paí**ses**
la palabr**a** → las palabr**as**	el profeso**r** → los profeso**res**
el problem**a** → los problem**as**	el lápi**z** → los lápi**ces**

- You use the masculine plural form of the noun to refer to a group that includes both males and females.

1 pasajer**o** + 2 pasajer**as** = 3 pasajer**os**

2 chic**os** + 2 chic**as** = 4 chic**os**

TEACHING OPTIONS

TPR Assign a different definite article to each of four students. Then line up ten students, each of whom is assigned a noun. Include a mix of masculine, feminine, singular, and plural nouns. Say one of the nouns (without the article), and that student must step forward. The student assigned the corresponding article has five seconds to join the noun student. After all ten nouns have been identified, reassign articles to different students for maximum participation.

Game Divide the class into two teams, A and B. Indicate one team member at a time, alternating between the teams. Give a singular noun to the member of team A. He or she must repeat it, preceeded by the correct definite article. The corresponding member of team B must correctly say the word's plural and definite article. Give a point per correct answer. Deduct a point for each wrong answer. The team with the most points at the end of play wins.

Nouns that refer to non-living things
Present/Expand Work through the list of nouns, modeling their pronunciation. Point out patterns of gender, including word endings **–ma**, **-ción**, and **–dad**. Either written on the board or orally, give cognate nouns with these endings and ask students to indicate the gender. Ex: **diagrama**, **acción**, **personalidad**, and so forth. Be sure to point out common exceptions to gender agreement rules for **el mapa**, **el día**, and **la mano**.

Plural of nouns
Present/Expand Work through the explanation and examples of the first point. Stress the addition of **–s** to nouns that end in vowels and **–es** to nouns that end in consonants. Write 8–10 nouns on the board and ask volunteers to give the plural forms, along with the appropriate articles.

Expand For the second point, stress that even if a group contains 100 women and one man, the masculine plural form and article are used. Point to three male students and ask if the group is **los** or **las estudiantes** (**los**). Next, point to three female students and ask the same question (**las**). Then indicate a mixed group of males and females and ask for the correct term to refer to them (**los estudiantes**).

¡Atención!
Present Point out that these words lose the written accent in the plural form in order to keep the stress on the same syllable as in the singular noun.

The Affective Dimension
Tell your students that many people feel anxious when learning grammar. Tell them that grammar will seem less intimidating if they think of it as a description of how the language works instead of a list of strict rules.

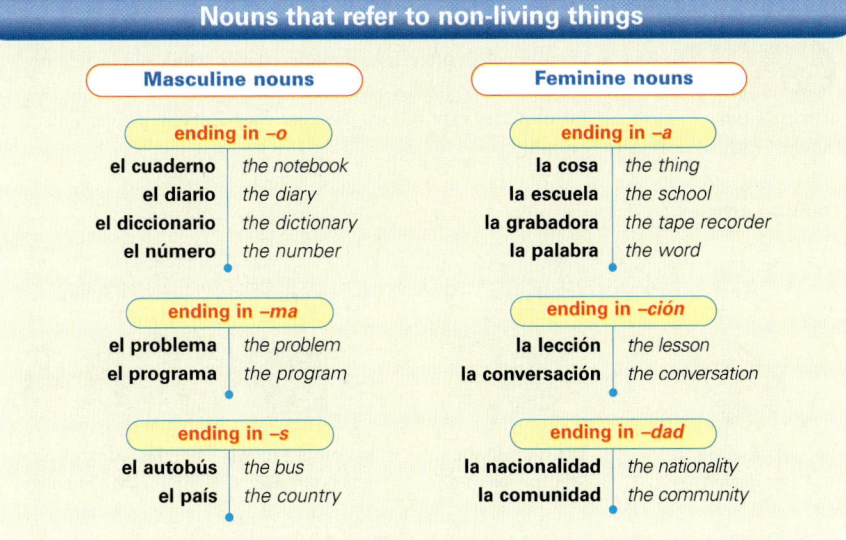

Spanish articles
Present Work through the discussion of definite and indefinite articles point by point. Make sure students know the difference between definite and indefinite articles and when they are appropriately used.

¡Lengua viva!
Suggestion You may wish to point out that the masculine singular article is used with words like these in order to avoid awkward pronunciation: **la agua, la hacha**, and so forth. This is why the feminine plural article is used when these words appear in the plural.

Expand After working through each grammar point, practice and consolidate it by doing the following exercises:
Definite articles
¿El, la, los o las? 1. hombre (el) 2. computadora (la) 3. profesor (el) 4. universidades (las) 5. turistas (los) 6. diccionario (el) 7. problema (el) 8. mujeres (las)
Indefinite articles
¿Un, una, unos o unas? 1. pasajeros (unos) 2. chico (un) 3. escuela (una) 4. lecciones (unas) 5. autobuses (unos) 6. maleta (una) 7. programas (unos) 8. cosa (una)

Expand Do a pair of conversion activities. Students respond with the article and the noun: **Definido → Indefinido. 1. los turistas (unos turistas) 2. la computadora (una computadora) 3. el hombre (un hombre) 4. las mujeres (unas mujeres) 5. el programa (un programa) 6. el hacha (un hacha) Indefinido → Definido. 1. unas lecciones (las lecciones) 2. una maleta (la maleta) 3. unos lápices (los lápices) 4. unas pasajeras (las pasajeras) 5. un diario (el diario) 6. una foto (la foto)**

Close Consolidate by doing **¡Inténtalo!** with the whole class.

Spanish articles

ANTE TODO As you know, English often uses definite articles (**the**) and indefinite articles (**a, an**) before nouns. Spanish also has definite and indefinite articles. Unlike English, Spanish articles vary in form because they agree in gender and number with the nouns they modify.

Definite articles

Masculine		Feminine	
SINGULAR	PLURAL	SINGULAR	PLURAL

el diccionario *the dictionary*	**los** diccionarios *the dictionaries*	**la** computadora *the computer*	**las** computadoras *the computers*

▶ Spanish has four forms that are equivalent to the English definite article *the*. You use definite articles to refer to specific nouns.

¡LENGUA VIVA!
Feminine singular nouns that begin with **a-** or **ha-** require the masculine articles **el** and **un**. This is done in order to avoid repetition of the **a** sound:
el agua *water*
las aguas *waters*
un hacha *ax*
unas hachas *axes*

Indefinite articles

Masculine		Feminine	
SINGULAR	PLURAL	SINGULAR	PLURAL
			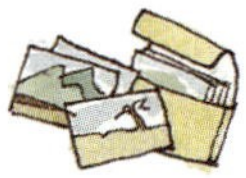
un pasajero *a (one) passenger*	**unos** pasajeros *some passengers*	**una** fotografía *a (one) photograph*	**unas** fotografías *some photographs*

▶ Spanish has four forms that are equivalent to the English indefinite article, which according to context may mean *a*, *an*, or *some*. You use indefinite articles to refer to unspecified persons or things.

¡INTÉNTALO! Provide a definite article for each noun in the first column and an indefinite article for each noun in the second column. The first item has been done for you.

¿el, la, los o las?	¿un, una, unos o unas?
1. ___la___ chica	1. ___un___ autobús
2. ___el___ chico	2. ___unas___ escuelas
3. ___la___ maleta	3. ___una___ computadora
4. ___los___ cuadernos	4. ___unos___ hombres
5. ___el___ lápiz	5. ___una___ señora
6. ___las___ mujeres	6. ___unos___ lápices

TEACHING OPTIONS

Extra Practice Hold up or point to objects whose names students are familiar with (**diccionario, lápiz, computadora, foto[grafía]**, and so forth). Ask random students to indicate the appropriate definite article and the noun. Include a mix of singular and plural nouns. Do the same exercise but subsitute indefinite articles for definite articles.

Pairs Have pairs of students write down a mix of 10 singular and plural nouns, *without their articles*. Have them exchange their list with another pair. Each pair then has to write down the appropriate definite or indefinite article to accompany each item. You will assign which group is to concentrate on definite articles and which is to concentrate on indefinite articles. After pairs have finished, have them return the lists and verify the correctness of the articles.

Práctica

1 **¿Singular o plural?** If the word is singular, make it plural. If it is plural, make it singular.

1. el número los números
2. un diario unos diarios
3. la estudiante las estudiantes
4. el conductor los conductores
5. el país los países
6. las cosas la cosa
7. unos turistas un turista
8. las nacionalidades la nacionalidad
9. unas computadoras una computadora
10. los problemas el problema
11. una fotografía unas fotografías
12. los profesores el profesor
13. unas señoritas una señorita
14. el hombre los hombres
15. la grabadora las grabadoras
16. la señora las señoras

2 **Identificar** For each drawing, provide the noun with its corresponding definite and indefinite articles.

modelo

las maletas, unas maletas

1. la computadora, una computadora

2. los cuadernos, unos cuadernos

3. las mujeres, unas mujeres

4. el chico, un chico

5. la escuela, una escuela

6. las fotos, unas fotos

7. los autobuses, unos autobuses

8. el diario, un diario

Comunicación

NATIONAL communication STANDARDS

3 **Charadas** In groups, play a game of charades. Individually, think of two nouns for each charade, for example, a boy using a computer (**un chico; una computadora**). The first person to guess correctly acts out the next charade.

1 Expand Reverse the activity by reading the on-page answers and having students convert the singular to plural and vice versa. Make sure they close their books before beginning this activity. You may also want to give the nouns in random order.

2 Expand Bring in photos or magazine pictures that illustrate items whose names students know. Have them respond to the photos and pictures the same way as they did in the activity.

3 Present Explain the basic rules of charades relevant to what they know at this point: (1) the student acting out the charade may not speak and (2) he or she may show the number of syllables by extending that number of fingers and tapping them on the other arm.

3 Expand Instead of having students work in groups, you may want to split the class into two groups with volunteers from each group acting out the charades. Give a point to each team for correctly guessing the charade. Deduct a point for incorrect guesses. The team with the most points at the end wins.

Assignment Have students prepare activities in **Student Activities Manual: Workbook**, page 3.

TEACHING OPTIONS

Video Show the video again to give students more input on singular and plural nouns and their articles. With their books closed, students write down every noun and article that they hear. After viewing the video, ask volunteers to list the nouns and articles they came up with. Explain that the **las** when telling time refers to **las horas** (Ex: **Son las cinco** = **Son las cinco horas**). Can they name all the nouns that appeared in the video?

Extra Practice Slowly read a short passage from a novel, story, or poem written in Spanish, preferably one with a great number of nouns and articles. As a listening exercise, students write down every noun and article they hear, even unfamiliar ones (the articles may cue when nouns appear). See if students can get most of them, even the ones they're unfamiliar with.

1.2 Numbers 0–30

NATIONAL comparisons STANDARDS

Los números 0 a 30

0	cero				
1	uno	**11**	once	**21**	veintiuno
2	dos	**12**	doce	**22**	veintidós
3	tres	**13**	trece	**23**	veintitrés
4	cuatro	**14**	catorce	**24**	veinticuatro
5	cinco	**15**	quince	**25**	veinticinco
6	seis	**16**	dieciséis	**26**	veintiséis
7	siete	**17**	diecisiete	**27**	veintisiete
8	ocho	**18**	dieciocho	**28**	veintiocho
9	nueve	**19**	diecinueve	**29**	veintinueve
10	diez	**20**	veinte	**30**	treinta

- The number **uno** (*one*) and numbers ending in **-uno**, such as **veintiuno**, have more than one form. Before masculine nouns, **uno** shortens to **un**. Before feminine nouns, **uno** changes to **una**.

  un hombre → veinti**ún** hombres **una** mujer → veinti**una** mujeres

- To ask *how many* people or things there are, use **cuántos** before masculine nouns and **cuántas** before feminine nouns.

- The Spanish equivalent of both *there is* and *there are* is **hay**. Use **¿Hay...?** to ask *Is there...?* or *Are there...?* Use **no hay** to express *there is not* or *there are not*.

—¿Cuántos estudiantes **hay**?
How many students are there?

—Hay tres estudiantes en la foto.
There are three students in the photo.

—¿**Hay** chicas en la fotografía?
Are there girls in the picture?

—**Hay** cuatro chicos, y **no hay** chicas.
There are four guys, and there are no girls.

¡ATENCIÓN!

The numbers sixteen through nineteen can also be written as three words: **diez y seis, diez y siete...**

•••

The forms **uno** and **veintiuno** are used when counting (**uno, dos, tres...veinte, veintiuno, veintidós...**) and when the number *follows* a noun, even if the noun is feminine: **la lección uno**

¡INTÉNTALO!

Provide the Spanish words for these numbers.

1. **7** siete	6. **15** quince	11. **30** treinta	16. **10** diez
2. **16** dieciséis	7. **21** veintiuno	12. **4** cuatro	17. **2** dos
3. **29** veintinueve	8. **9** nueve	13. **12** doce	18. **5** cinco
4. **1** uno	9. **23** veintitrés	14. **28** veintiocho	19. **22** veintidós
5. **0** cero	10. **11** once	15. **14** catorce	20. **13** trece

Section Goals

In **Estructura 1.2** students will be introduced to:
- numbers 0–30
- the verb form **hay**

Instructional Resources
Student Activities Manual: Workbook, 4; Lab Manual, 220

Before Presenting Estructura 1.2
- Introduce numbers by asking students how many of them can count to 10 in Spanish (some will know how to do so). Hold up varying numbers of fingers on your hands and ask students to shout out the corresponding number in Spanish.
- Next, walk up and down the rows of students and assign each a number. Ask them to remember which number they've been assigned. When finished, have the student assigned **uno** recite his or her number aloud, then **dos, tres,** and so forth. Help anyone who struggles with his or her number.

Assignment Have students study **Estructura 1.2** and prepare the exercises on page 15 as homework.

Present
- Go through the numbers 0–30, modeling the pronunciation of each. Write individual numbers on the board and call on students at random to say the number.
- Emphasize the variable forms of **uno** and **veintiuno**, giving examples of each. Ex: **veintiún profesores, veintiuna profesoras.**
- Combine the second and third points, asking questions of individual students. Ex: _____, **¿cuántos estudiantes hay en la clase? Sí, hay quince estudiantes en la clase,** and so forth.

Expand Consolidate entire section by doing **¡Inténtalo!** with the whole class.

TEACHING OPTIONS

TPR Assign 10 students a number from 0–30 and line them up in front of the class. Call out one of the numbers at random, and the student assigned that number is to take a step forward. When two students have stepped forward, ask them to repeat their numbers. Then ask individuals to add (Say: **Suma**) or subtract (Say: **Resta**) the two numbers. The volunteer should say the complete number sentence as he or she does so.

Game Hand out Bingo cards with B-I-N-G-O across the top of five columns. The 25 squares underneath will contain random numbers. From a hat, draw letters and numbers and call them out in Spanish. The first student that can fill in a number in each one of the lettered columns yells "**¡Bingo!**" and wins.

Práctica

1 **Contar** Following the pattern, provide the missing numbers in Spanish.

1. 1, 3, 5, .., 29   7, 9, 11, 13, 15, 17, 19, 21, 23, 25, 27
2. 2, 4, 6, .., 30   8, 10, 12, 14, 16, 18, 20, 22, 24, 26, 28
3. 3, 6, 9, .., 30   12, 15, 18, 21, 24, 27
4. 30, 28, 26, .., 0   24, 22, 20, 18, 16, 14, 12, 10, 8, 6, 4, 2
5. 30, 25, 20, .., 0   15, 10, 5
6. 28, 24, 20, .., 0   16, 12, 8, 4

2 **Resolver** Solve these math problems with a partner.

AYUDA
+ → **más**
– → **menos**
= → **es/son**

modelo
5 + 3 =
Estudiante 1: *cinco más tres son…*
Estudiante 2: *ocho*

1. **2 + 15 =** Dos más quince son diecisiete.
2. **20 – 1 =** Veinte menos uno son diecinueve.
3. **5 + 7 =** Cinco más siete son doce.
4. **18 + 12 =** Dieciocho más doce son treinta.
5. **3 + 22 =** Tres más veintidós son veinticinco.
6. **6 – 3 =** Seis menos tres son tres.
7. **11 + 12 =** Once más doce son veintitrés.
8. **7 – 7 =** Siete menos siete son cero.
9. **8 + 5 =** Ocho más cinco son trece.
10. **23 – 14 =** Veintitrés menos catorce son nueve.

3 **¿Cuántos hay?** How many persons or things are there in these drawings?

modelo
Hay cuatro maletas.

1. Hay veinte lápices.

2. Hay un hombre.

3. Hay veinticinco chicos.

4. Hay una conductora.

5. Hay cuatro fotos.

6. Hay treinta cuadermos.

7. Hay seis turistas.

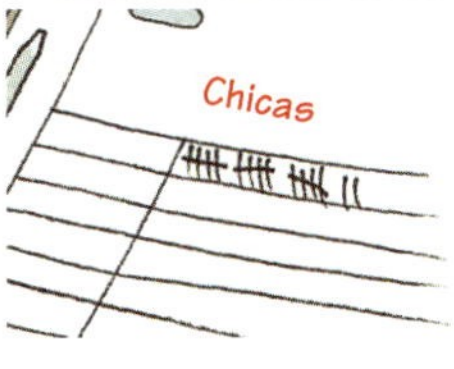

8. Hay diecisiete chicas.

TEACHING OPTIONS

TPR Give ten students a card that contains a number from 0–30 (you may want to assign numbers in fives to simplify the activity). The card must be visible to the other students. Then call out simple math problems (addition, subtraction) involving the assigned numbers. When the first two numbers are called, each student steps forward. The student whose assigned number completes the math problem then has five seconds to join them.

Extra Practice Ask questions about the university and the town or city in which it's located. Ex: **¿Cuántos profesores hay en el departamento de español? ¿Cuántas universidades hay en ____? ¿Cuántas pizzerías hay en ___?** and so forth. Encourage students to guess the number. If a number exceeds 30, write that number on the board and model its pronunciation.

1 Present Before beginning the activity, make sure students know each pattern to be followed: odds (**los números impares**), evens (**los números pares**), count by threes (**contar de tres en tres**), and so forth.

1 Expand Ask the class a more difficult problem, that of giving the pattern of prime numbers (**los números primos**) up to 30. Explain that a prime number is any number that can only be divided by itself and 1. You may wish to begin the pattern in English first. Prime numbers to 30 are: 1, 2, 3, 5, 7, 11, 13, 17, 19, 23, 29.

2 Present/Expand Point out the **Ayuda** sidebar and give the terms necessary to orally complete the math problems. Model pronunciation of the number sentence in **Modelo**. Make the model sentence a subtraction problem: **cinco menos tres son… (dos)**.

2 Expand Do simple multiplication problems. Introduce the phrase **(multiplicado) por**. Ex: **cinco multiplicado por cinco son… (veinticinco)** or **cinco por cinco son… (veinticinco)**.

3 Present Have students read directions and model sentence. Cue student responses by asking the questions related to the drawings. Ex: **¿Cuántos lápices hay? (Hay veinte lápices.)** and so forth.

3 Expand Hold up or point to classroom objects and ask how many there are. Since students won't know the names of many of the items, a simple number will suffice or **hay** and then the number. Ex: —**¿Cuántos bolígrafos hay aquí? —(Hay) Dos.**

Comunicación
4 Present Read directions aloud and facilitate activity by asking questions yourself. You may want to assign questions to individual students or to have students call out the answers at random.

4 Expand For items 3, 4, 7, and 9, ask students **¿Cuántos/as hay?** If there are no examples of the item listed, students should say **No hay ____**.

4 Expand After completing the activity, call on individual students to give rapid responses to the same items. Mix up the order of items to make the activity more challenging. See if the students can remember the number of items from the first time through the activity.

5 Present Have students read the directions and look at the drawing for a minute. Remind students that they will be forming sentences with **hay** and a number. Give them four minutes to do the activity. You may also wish for them to write out their answers.

5 Expand After pairs have finished analyzing the drawing, call on individual students to respond. Convert the statements into questions in Spanish. Ask: **¿Cuántos chicos hay? ¿Cuántas mujeres hay?** and so forth.

Assignment Have students prepare activities in **Student Activities Manual: Workbook**, page 4.

Comunicación

NATIONAL communication STANDARDS

4 **En la clase** With a classmate, take turns asking and answering these questions about your classroom.

1. ¿Cuántos estudiantes hay?
2. ¿Cuántos profesores hay?
3. ¿Hay una computadora?
4. ¿Hay una maleta?
5. ¿Cuántos mapas hay?
6. ¿Cuántos lápices hay?
7. ¿Hay cuadernos?
8. ¿Cuántas grabadoras hay?
9. ¿Hay hombres?
10. ¿Cuántas mujeres hay?

5 **Preguntas** With a classmate, take turns asking and answering questions about the drawing. Talk about: Answers will vary.

1. How many children there are
2. How many women there are
3. If there are some photographs
4. If there is a boy
5. How many notebooks there are
6. If there is a bus
7. If there are tourists
8. How many pencils there are
9. If there is a man
10. How many computers there are

TEACHING OPTIONS

Pairs Have each student draw a scene similar to the one on page 16. Of course, stick figures are perfectly acceptable! Give them three minutes to draw the scene. Then pairs of students take turn describing what is in the other's picture. Encourage students to include multiple numbers of particular items (**cuadernos**, **maletas**, **lápices**, and so forth).

Pairs Divide students into pairs. Give half of the pairs magazine pictures that contain images of words that are familiar to them or that are close cognates. Give the other half descriptions of those pictures, including **hay** in the description. Ex: **En esta foto hay dos mujeres, un chico y una chica.** Pairs walk around the room to match the descriptions with the corresponding pictures.

1.3 Present tense of the verb **ser** (*to be*)

NATIONAL STANDARDS comparisons

Subject pronouns

ANTE TODO In order to use verbs, you will need to learn about subject pronouns. A subject pronoun replaces the name or title of a person or thing and acts as the subject of a verb. In both Spanish and English, subject pronouns are divided into three groups: first person, second person, and third person.

Subject pronouns

	SINGULAR		PLURAL	
FIRST PERSON	**yo**	*I*	**nosotros**	*we* (masculine)
			nosotras	*we* (feminine)
SECOND PERSON	**tú**	*you* (familiar)	**vosotros**	*you* (masc., fam.)
			vosotras	*you* (fem., fam.)
THIRD PERSON	**usted (Ud.)**	*you* (formal)	**ustedes (Uds.)**	*you* (form.)
	él	*he*	**ellos**	*they* (masc.)
	ella	*she*	**ellas**	*they* (fem.)

¡LENGUA VIVA!
In Latin America, **ustedes** is used as the plural for both **tú** and **usted**. In Spain, however, **vosotros** and **vosotras** are used as the plural of **tú**, and **ustedes** is used only as the plural of **usted**.

• • •

Usted and **ustedes** are abbreviated as **Ud.** and **Uds.**, or occasionally as **Vd.** and **Vds.**

- Spanish has two subject pronouns that mean *you* (singular). Use **tú** when addressing a friend, a family member, or a child you know well. Use **usted** to address a person with whom you have a formal or more distant relationship, such as a superior at work, a professor, or an older person.

- The masculine plural forms **nosotros**, **vosotros**, and **ellos** refer to a group of males or to a group of males and females. The feminine plural forms **nosotras**, **vosotras**, and **ellas** can refer only to groups made up exclusively of females.

nosotros, vosotros, ellos

nosotros, vosotros, ellos

nosotras, vosotras, ellas

- There is no Spanish equivalent of the English subject pronoun *it*. Generally it is not expressed in Spanish.

Es un problema.	Es una computadora.
It's a problem.	*It's a computer.*

Section Goals
In **Estructura 1.3** students will be introduced to:
- subject pronouns
- present tense of the verb **ser**
- using **ser** to identify, to indicate possession, to describe origin, and to talk about professions or occupations

Instructional Resources
Student Activities Manual: Workbook, 5–6; Lab Manual, 221

Before Presenting Estructura 1.3
Introduce subject pronouns and forms of the verb **ser** before giving their meaning. Point to yourself and say: **Yo soy profesor(a)**. Then walk up to a student and say: **Tú eres…** Correct student response should be **estudiante**. Once the pattern has been established, include other subject pronouns and forms of **ser** while indicating other students. Ex: **Él es…, Ella es…, Ellos son…** and so forth.
Assignment Have students study **Estructura 1.3** and prepare the activities on page 20 as homework.

Subject pronouns
Present
- Work through the entire presentation, including the chart of subject pronouns.
- Remind students of familiar and formal forms of address they learned in **Contextos.**
- You may want to point out that while **Ud.** and **Uds.** are part of the second person *you*, they use third person forms.
- Point out that **nosotros/as** and **vosotros/as** are the only subject pronouns that indicate gender.
- While the **vosotros/as** forms are listed in verb paradigms in **Vistas,** they will not be actively practiced. Depending on your usage, you may want to incorporate these forms into your presentations and the activities.

TEACHING OPTIONS

Extra Practice Explain that students are to give subject pronouns based on your (the instructor's) point of view. Ex: Point to yourself (**yo**), a female student (**ella**), everyone in the class (**nosotros**), and so forth.
Extra Practice Ask students to indicate whether the following people would be addressed as **tú** or **Ud.** Ex: a roommate, a best friend's grandfather, a doctor, a neighbor's child, and so forth.

Heritage Speakers Ask heritage speakers how they address elder members of their family such as parents, grandparents, aunts and uncles—whether they use **tú** or **Ud.** Also ask them if they use **vosotros/as** or not (they typically won't unless they or their family are from Spain).

The present tense of *ser*
Present Work through the explanation and the forms of **ser** in the chart. Emphasize that **es** is used for **Ud.**, **él**, and **ella**, and that **son** is used for **Uds.**, **ellos**, and **ellas**. Context or the use of subject pronouns or names will determine whom is being addressed or talked about.

Uses of *ser*
Present
- Explain that **ser** is used to identify people and things. At this point there is no need to explain that **estar** also means *to be*; it will be introduced in **Lesson 2**.
- Explain the meaning of **¿quién?** and ask questions about who students in the class are. Ex: ____, **¿quién es ella? Sí, es** ____. **¿Quién soy yo? Sí, soy el profesor/la profesora** ____. and so forth. Introduce **¿qué?** and ask questions about items in the class. Ex: **¿Qué es esto? Sí, es un mapa.** and so forth.
- Point out the construction of **ser** + **de** to indicate possession. Stress that there is no *'s* in Spanish. (Direct students to the second part of the **¡Atención!** sidebar.) Walk around the class and pick up objects belonging to students and ask questions. Ex: **¿De quién es este cuaderno? Sí, es de** ____. **¿De quién son estos libros? Sí, son de** ____. and so forth.

¡Atención!
Present Introduce contraction **de** + **el** = **del**. Emphasize that **de** and other definite articles do not make contractions and support with examples. Ex: **Soy del estado de** ____. **No soy de la nación de** ____. and so forth. Also use examples of possession to illustrate the contraction. Ex: **¿Es este mapa del presidente de la universidad?** and so forth.

The present tense of *ser*

ANTE TODO In **Contextos** and **Fotonovela**, you have already used several forms of the present tense of **ser** (*to be*) to identify yourself and others and to talk about where you and others are from. **Ser** is an irregular verb, which means its forms don't follow the regular patterns that most verbs follow. You need to memorize the forms, which appear in the following chart.

The present tense of *ser*

		ser (*to be*)	
SINGULAR FORMS	yo	**soy**	*I am*
	tú	**eres**	*you are* (fam.)
	Ud./él/ella	**es**	*you are* (form.); *he/she is*
PLURAL FORMS	nosotros/as	**somos**	*we are*
	vosotros/as	**sois**	*you are* (fam.)
	Uds./ellos/ellas	**son**	*you are* (form.); *they are*

Uses of *ser*

▶ To identify people and things

—¿Quién **es** él?
Who is he?

—**Es** Javier Gómez Lozano.
He's Javier Gómez Lozano.

—¿Qué **es**?
What is it?

—**Es** un mapa de España.
It's a map of Spain.

▶ To express possession, with the preposition **de**

—¿**De** quién **es**?
Whose is it?

—**Es** el diario **de** Maite.
It's Maite's diary.

—**Es** la computadora **de** Álex.
It's Alex's computer.

—¿**De** quiénes **son**?
Whose are they?

—**Son** los lápices **de** la chica.
They are the girl's pencils.

—**Son** las maletas **del** chico.
They are the boy's suitcases.

¡ATENCIÓN!
When **de** is followed by the article **el**, the two combine to form the contraction **del**.
De does *not* contract with **la**, **las**, or **los**.
• • •
There is no Spanish equivalent of the English construction [*noun*] +'s (*Maite's*). In its place, Spanish uses [*noun*] + **de** + [*owner*]: **el diario de Maite**.

TEACHING OPTIONS

Extra Practice As a rapid response drill, call out subject pronouns and have students respond with the correct form of **ser**. Ex: **tú** (**eres**), **Uds.** (**son**), and so forth. Reverse the drill by starting with forms of **ser**. Students must give the subject pronouns. Accept multiple answers for **es** and **son**.

TPR Take a small beanbag or rubber ball and toss it to individual students for them to catch. When a student catches the ball, call on another student to indicate whose ball it is. Ex: **Es de** ____. Take two beanbags or balls and toss them to different students to elicit the response **Son de** ____ **y** ____.

LENGUA VIVA

Some geographic locations can be referred to either with or without a definite article:

Soy de Ecuador./Soy del Ecuador.

•••

Sometimes a definite article is a part of a proper name, as in **El Salvador, El Paso,** and **Los Ángeles.** In these cases, **de** and **el** do not contract:

Soy de El Salvador.

▶ To express origin, with the preposition **de**

¿De dónde eres?
Yo soy de México.

¿De dónde eres?
Yo soy de España.

—¿**De** dónde **es** Javier?
Where is Javier from?

—Es **de** Puerto Rico.
He's from Puerto Rico.

—¿**De** dónde **es** Inés?
Where is Inés from?

—**Es del** Ecuador.
She's from Ecuador.

¡ATENCIÓN!

Unlike English, Spanish does not use the indefinite article (**un, una**) after **ser** when referring to professions unless accompanied by an adjective or other description:

Marta es profesora.
Marta es una profesora excelente.

You will learn more about adjectives in Lesson 3, pp. 78-85.

▶ To express profession or occupation

Don Francisco **es conductor**.
Don Francisco is a driver.

Yo **soy estudiante**.
I am a student.

Somos Peru
AeroPeru

¡INTÉNTALO! Provide the correct subject pronouns in Column 1, and the correct present forms of **ser** in Column 2. The first item has been done for you.

1. Gabriel	él	es
2. Juan y yo (*m.*)	nosotros	somos
3. Óscar y Flora	ellos	son
4. Adriana	ella	es
5. las turistas	ellas	son
6. el chico	él	es
7. los conductores	ellos	son
8. el señor y la señora Ruiz	ellos	son

Present

- Explain **ser** + **de** to express origin. Start practicing this construction by indicating where you are from. Ex: **Soy de** ____. You may also want to further practice and contrast **de** + **el**. Ex: **Soy del estado de** ____**/de la región (de)** ____. Introduce **¿de dónde?** and ask students where they are from. Ex: ____, **¿de dónde eres?** After student answers, ask another student: ____, **¿de dónde es** ____**? Sí, es de** ____. and so forth.
- Explain the use of **ser** to describe professions or occupations. Say: **Yo soy profesor(a) de español.** ____, **¿qué eres tú?** Response: **Soy estudiante.** Say: **Sí, eres estudiante** and so forth. If students want to name occupations or professions, give them the vocabulary item necessary. Ask others to repeat the occupations or professions their classmates give. Ex: ____ **es recepcionista.**
- Point out that the definite articles **un** and **una** are not used in these constructions with **ser** and professions: **Él es arquitecto. Somos artistas.** You may want to point out that the indefinite article is used when describing professions and people (**Él es un arquitecto excelente.**), but there is no specific need to go into that discussion at this point.

Expand Consolidate entire section by doing **¡Inténtalo!** with the whole class.

TEACHING OPTIONS

Extra Practice Write cognates on the board and ask students to identify the professions of famous people. Ex: **actor/actriz, presidente, artista, pianista**, and so forth. Ask: **¿Qué es Brad Pitt?** (**Es actor.**) **¿Quién es presidente?** (____ **es presidente.**) and so forth.

Pairs Have pairs of students interview each other. Write on the board the questions they should ask. Include: **¿Quién eres?, ¿De dónde eres?, ¿Qué eres?** (occupation or profession). After students interview each other, call on students to report the information they gathered from their partner. Students begin by saying: **Él/Ella es...**

1 Warm-up Quickly review subject pronouns by pointing at various people in the class and asking students to identify what subject pronoun they would use to talk *about* them. Also review **tú** and **Ud.**, asking students which pronoun they would use in a formal situation and which they would use in an informal situation.

1 Expand Once students have identified the correct subject pronouns, ask them to give the appropriate form of **ser** they would use when addressing each person and when talking about each person.

2 Present Have students read directions as you model pronunciation of the model sentences. Before beginning the activity, you may wish to identify the people and the country each comes from. (The point of the activity is to use the question structures and **ser** correctly.) If not, have students look over the **Ayuda** sidebar for phrases they can use with their partner.

2 Expand Give names of additional well-known Hispanics and ask students to tell where they are from. Have students give the country names in English if they don't know the Spanish equivalent. Ex: **¿De dónde es Gloria Estefan? (Es de Cuba.)**

3 Present Have students read directions as you model pronunciation of the model sentences. Inform students that they can answer the second part of the question (**¿De quién es?**) with any answer they wish. Make sure students take turns asking and answering questions.

3 Expand Call on individal students to give answers to the questions you ask: **¿Qué es? and ¿De quién es?**

Práctica

1 **Pronombres** What subject pronouns would you use to a) talk to these people directly and b) talk about them?

1. una chica tú, ella
2. el presidente de México Ud./ él
3. tres chicas y un chico Uds., ellos
4. un estudiante tú, él
5. la señora Ochoa Ud., ella
6. dos profesoras Uds., ellas

2 **Identidad y origen** With a partner, take turns asking and answering questions about these people: **¿Quién es?/¿Quiénes son?** and **¿De dónde es?/¿De dónde son?**

modelo

Estudiante 1: *¿Quién es?*
Estudiante 2: *Es Ricky Martin.*
Estudiante 1: *¿De dónde es?*
Estudiante 2: *Es de Puerto Rico.*

1. Enrique Iglesias
E1: ¿Quién es? E2: Es Enrique Iglesias. E1: ¿De dónde es? E2: Es de España.
2. Sammy Sosa
E2: ¿Quién es? E1: Es Sammy Sosa. E2: ¿De dónde es? E1: Es de la República Dominicana.
3. Rebecca Lobo y Robert Rodríguez E1: ¿Quiénes son? E2: Son Rebecca Lobo y Robert Rodríguez. E1: ¿De dónde son? E2: Son de los Estados Unidos.
4. Laura Esquivel y Salma Hayek E2: ¿Quiénes son? E1: Son Laura Esquivel y Salma Hayek. E2: ¿De dónde son? E1: Son de México.
5. Gabriel García Márquez
E1: ¿Quién es? E2: Es Gabriel García Márquez. E1: ¿De dónde es? E2: Es de Colombia.
6. Antonio Banderas y Sergio García E2: ¿Quiénes son? E1: Son Antonio Banderas y Sergio García. E2: ¿De dónde son? E1: Son de España.
7. Edward James Olmos y Jimmy Smits E1: ¿Quiénes son? E2: Son Edward James Olmos y Jimmy Smits. E1: ¿De dónde son? E2: Son de los Estados Unidos.
8. Octavio Paz E2: ¿Quién es? E1: Es Octavio Paz. E1: ¿De dónde es? E1: Es de México.

AYUDA
No sé.
I don't know.
No estoy seguro/a
I'm not sure.
Es de..., ¿no?
He/she is from..., right?

3 **¿Qué es?** Ask your partner what each object is and to whom it belongs.

modelo

Estudiante 1: *¿Qué es?*
Estudiante 2: *Es una grabadora.*
Estudiante 1: *¿De quién es?*
Estudiante 2: *Es del profesor.*

1. E1: ¿Qué es? E2: Es una maleta. E1: ¿De quién es? E2: Es de la Sra. Valdés.

2. E1: ¿Qué es? E2: Es un cuaderno. E1: ¿De quién es? E2: Es de Gregorio.

3. E1: ¿Qué es? E2: Es una computadora. E1: ¿De quién es? E2: Es de Rafael.

4. E1: ¿Qué es? E2: Es un diario. E1: ¿De quién es? E2: Es de Marisa.

TEACHING OPTIONS

Video Replay the video segment, having students focus on subject pronouns and the verb **ser**. Ask them to copy down as many examples of sentences that use forms of **ser** as they can. Stop the video where appropriate to ask comprehension questions on what the characters said.

Heritage Speakers Encourage Spanish speakers to briefly describe themselves and their family. Make sure they use the cognates **familia**, **mamá**, and **papá**. Call on students to report the information given. Ex: **Francisco es de la Florida. La mamá de Francisco es de España. Ella es profesora. El papá de Francisco es de Cuba. Él es dentista.**

NATIONAL communication STANDARDS

Comunicación

4 **En la oficina** Using the items in the word bank, ask your partner questions about this businessman's office. Be imaginative in your responses. Answers will vary.

¿Quién?	¿De dónde?	¿Cuántos?
¿Qué?	¿De quién?	¿Cuántas?

5 **¿Quién es?** In small groups, take turns pretending to be individuals or groups from Spain, Mexico, Puerto Rico, Cuba, or the United States who are famous for their work in the following professions. The others will ask questions using the verb **ser** until they guess the identity of each person or group. Answers will vary.

actor *actor*	deportista *athlete*	escritor(a) *writer*
actriz *actress*	cantante *singer*	músico/a *musician*

modelo

Estudiante 3: ¿Eres de los Estados Unidos?
Estudiante 1: Sí.
Estudiante 2: ¿Eres hombre?
Estudiante 1: No. Soy mujer.
Estudiante 3: ¿Eres escritora?
Estudiante 1: No. Soy actriz.
Estudiante 2: ¿Eres Rita Moreno?
Estudiante 1: ¡Sí! ¡Sí!

NOTA CULTURAL

Rita Moreno, a Puerto Rican actress, is the only female performer to have won all four prestigious entertainment awards: the Oscar, the Emmy, the Grammy, and the Tony. She played Anita in *West Side Story,* a role for which she won an Oscar.

4 Present Take a few moments to point out the objects in the drawing, asking students to name what they are.

4 Suggestion If students ask, explain that the abbreviation **S.A.** in the drawing stands for **sociedad anónima** and is equivalent to English ***Inc.*** (***Incorporated***).

4 Expand Ask volunteers to make true-false statements about the drawing. Classmates have to indicate whether the statements are true or false and correct false statements. Ex: **Hay dos grabadoras. (Falso. Hay una grabadora.)**

5 Warm-up/Present Have students read directions while you answer any questions they may have about the activity. If students do not know the names of many Hispanic celebrities, brainstorm a list of names in the categories suggested. Then with two other students, model pronunciation of the model conversation. Draw students' attention to the sidebar **Nota cultural**.

5 Expand Ask student volunteers to answer questions about the famous person they chose. Have classmates other than those in their group ask them questions similar to those in the activity.

Assignment Have students prepare activities in **Student Activities Manual: Workbook**, pages 5–6.

TEACHING OPTIONS

Small Groups Bring in personal photos or magazine pictures that show people. In groups of three to four, students invent stories about the people: who they are, where they're from, what they do. Circulate around the room and assist with unfamiliar vocabulary as necessary, but encourage students to use terms they already know.

Game Hand out individual strips of paper with names of famous people on them. There should be several duplicates of each name. Then give descriptions of one of the famous people (**Es de ____, Es** [profession]), including cognate adjectives if you wish (**inteligente**, **pesimista**, and so forth). The first person to stand and indicate that the name they have is the one you're describing (**¡Yo lo tengo!**) wins that round.

Section Goals

In **Estructura 1.4** students will be introduced to:
- asking and telling time
- times of day

Instructional Resources
Student Activities Manual: Workbook, 7–8; Lab Manual, 222
Transparency 11

Before Presenting Estructura 1.4 To prepare students for telling time, review **es** and **son** and their meanings and the numbers to 30.

Assignment Have students study **Estructura 1.4** and prepare the **actividades** on pages 23–24 as homework.

Present/Expand
- Introduce **es la una** and **son las dos (tres, cuatro...)**. Remind students that **las** in time constructions refers to **las horas**. Introduce **y cinco (diez, veinte...)**, **y quince/cuarto**, and **y treinta/media**.
- Project **Transparency 11**, use a paper plate clock, or any other clock where you can quickly move the hands to different positions and display a number of different times for students to identify. Ask: **¿Qué hora es?** Spend about three minutes on this or work until students are relatively comfortable with expressing the time in Spanish.

1.4 Telling time

ANTE TODO In both English and Spanish, the verb *to be* (**ser**) and numbers are used to tell time.

- To ask what time it is, use **¿Qué hora es?** When telling time, use **es + la** with **una** and **son + las** with all other hours.

Es la una.

Son las dos.

Son las seis.

- As in English, you express time from the hour to the half-hour in Spanish by adding minutes.

Son las cuatro **y cinco.**

Son las once **y veinte.**

- You may use either **y cuarto** or **y quince** to express fifteen minutes or quarter past the hour. For thirty minutes or half past the hour, you may use either **y media** or **y treinta**.

Es la una **y cuarto.**

Son las doce **y media.**

Son las nueve **y quince.**

Son las siete **y treinta.**

TEACHING OPTIONS

Extra Practice Draw a large clock face on the board with its numbers but without its hands. Say a time and ask a volunteer to come up to the board to draw the hands so they indicate that time. The rest of the class verifies whether their classmate has written the correct time or not. Continue until several volunteers have participated.

Pairs In pairs, students take turns telling each other what time their classes are this semester/quarter. (Present: **Tengo una clase a las...**) For each time given, the other student draws a clock face with the corresponding time. The first student verifies whether this is the correct time or not. (Note: If you implement this activity before presenting the material on page 23, ask students to round off class times to the nearest hour or half hour.)

▶ You express time from the half-hour to the hour in Spanish by subtracting minutes or a portion of an hour from the next hour.

Es la una menos **cuarto.**

Son las tres menos **quince.**

Son las ocho **menos veinte.**

Son las tres **menos diez.**

▶ Here are some useful words and phrases associated with telling time:

¿A qué hora es la clase de biología?
(At) what time is biology class?

La clase es **a la una/a las dos**.
The class is at 1 o'clock/at two o'clock.

Son las ocho **en punto**.
It's 8 o'clock on the dot/sharp.

Son las nueve **de la mañana**.
It's 9 a.m. (in the morning).

Es **el mediodía**.
It's noon.

Son las cuatro y cuarto **de la tarde**.
It's 4:15 p.m. (in the afternoon).

Es **la medianoche**.
It's midnight.

Son las diez y media **de la noche**.
It's 10:30 p.m. (at night).

LENGUA VIVA

Other useful expressions for telling time:

Son las doce (del día).
It is twelve o'clock (pm).

Son las doce (de la noche).
It is twelve o'clock (am).

•••

Es la... or **Son las...** are used to tell time.
Es a la(s)... is used to indicate *at what time* a particular event takes place:

Son las dos.
It's two o'clock.

Mi clase es a las dos.
My class is at two o'clock.

Oye, ¿qué hora es?
Son las diez y tres minutos.

Oiga, ¿qué hora es?
Son las diez.

¡INTÉNTALO! Practice telling time by completing these sentences. The first item has been done for you.

1. (1:00 a.m.) Es la ___una___ de la mañana.
2. (2:50 a.m.) Son las tres ___menos___ diez de la mañana.
3. (4:15 p.m.) Son las cuatro y ___cuarto/quince___ de la tarde.
4. (8:30 p.m.) Son las ocho y ___media/treinta___ de la noche.
5. (9:15 a.m.) Son las nueve y quince de la ___mañana___.
6. (12:00 p.m.) Es el ___mediodía___.
7. (6:00 a.m.) Son las seis de la ___mañana___.
8. (4:05 p.m.) Son las cuatro y cinco de la ___tarde___.
9. (12:00 a.m.) Es la ___medianoche___.
10. (3:45 a.m.) Son las cuatro menos ___cuarto/quince___ de la mañana.
11. (9:55 p.m.) Son las ___diez___ menos cinco de la noche.

Present
- Introduce **menos diez (cuarto, veinte...)** and explain this method of telling time in Spanish. It typically takes students longer to master this aspect of telling time due to the forward hour and minute subtraction. Spend about five minutes with your moveable-hands clock and ask students to indicate the times given.
- Review **¿Qué hora es?** and introduce **¿A qué hora?** and make sure students know the difference between each. Ask a few questions to clarify. Ex: **¿Qué hora es en este momento? ¿A qué hora es la clase de español?**
- Go over **en punto, mediodía, medianoche.** Explain that **medio/a** means half in Spanish.
- Go over **de la mañana/tarde/noche.** Ask students what time it is now, giving the correct time of day as well.

¡Lengua viva!
Present Introduce the Spanish equivalents for noon (**las doce del día**) and midnight (**las doce de la noche**).

Suggestion You may wish to explain that Hispanics tend to view times of day differently than English speakers do. In many countries, only after someone has eaten lunch does one say **Buenas tardes**. Similarly with the evening, Hispanics tend to view 6:00 and even 7:00 as **de la tarde**, not **de la noche**.

Expand Consolidate entire section by doing **¡Inténtalo!** with the whole class.

TEACHING OPTIONS

Extra Practice Hand out slips of paper with clock faces depicting certain times on them to half of the class. Hand out the corresponding times written out in Spanish to the other half of the class. Students must find their partner. To increase difficulty, include duplicates of each time with **de la mañana** or **de la tarde/noche** on the written-out times and a sun or a moon on the clock faces so that students find only one partner.

Heritage Speakers Ask Spanish speakers if they generally tell time as presented in the text or if they use different constructions. Some ways Hispanics use time constructions include (1) forgoing **menos** and using a number from 31–59 and (2) asking the question **¿Qué horas son?** Stress, however, that the constructions presented in the text are the ones students should focus on.

1 Present After students have put the times in order, go over the answers quickly in class.

1 Expand Have students draw clock faces showing the times presented in the activity. Then they exchange their drawings with a partner to verify accuracy.

2 Present Model the pronunciation of the two ways of saying 4:15 in the model sentence. Point out that some of the clocks and watches also indicate the part of day (morning, afternoon, or evening) as well as the hour. Have students include this information in their responses.

2 Expand At random, give times shown in activity. Students must give the number of the clock or watch described. Ex: **Es la una de la mañana. (Es el número 2.)**

3 Present Working with a student, read the **Modelo** to model the activity for the whole class.

3 Expand Have partners switch roles and ask and answer the questions again. Alternatively, have each student who asked questions the first time pair up with a student from another pair who answered questions. The new pair then switches roles.

3 Expand Have students come up with three original items to ask their partner, based on the items in the activity. The partner should respond with actual times. Ex: **—¿A qué hora es el programa Friends? —Es a las ocho.**

Práctica

1 Ordenar Put these times in order, from the earliest to the latest.

a. Son las dos de la tarde. 4
b. Son las once de la mañana. 2
c. Son las siete y media de la noche. 6
d. Son las seis menos cuarto de la tarde. 5
e. Son las dos menos diez de la tarde. 3
f. Son las ocho y veintidós de la mañana. 1

2 ¿Qué hora es? Give the times shown on each clock or watch.

modelo

Son las cuatro y cuarto/quince de la tarde.

1. Son las doce y media.

2. Es la una de la mañana.

3. Son las cinco y cuarto.

4. Son las ocho y diez.

5. Son las cinco y media/treinta.

6. Son las once menos cuarto/quince.

7. Son las dos y doce de la tarde.

8. Son las siete y cinco.

9. Son las cuatro menos cinco.

10. Son las doce menos veinticinco de la noche.

3 ¿A qué hora? Ask your partner at what time these events take place. Your partner will answer according to the cues provided.

modelo

la clase de matemáticas (2:30 p.m.)
Estudiante 1: ¿A qué hora es la clase de matemáticas?
Estudiante 2: Es a las dos y media de la tarde.

1. el programa *Las cuatro amigas* (*11:30 a.m.*)
2. el drama *La casa de Bernarda Alba* (*7:00 p.m.*)
3. el programa *Las computadoras* (*8:30 a.m.*)
4. la clase de español (*10:30 a.m.*)
5. la clase de biología (*9:40 a.m. sharp*)
6. la clase de historia (*10:50 a.m.*)
7. el partido (*game*) de béisbol (*5:15 p.m.*)
8. el partido de tenis (*12:45 p.m. sharp*)
9. el partido de baloncesto (*basketball*) (*7:45 p.m.*)
10. la fiesta (*8:30 p.m.*)

1. E1: ¿A qué hora es el programa *Las cuatro amigas*? E2: Es a las once y media/treinta de la mañana.
2. E1: ¿A qué hora es el drama *La casa de Bernada Alba*? E2: Es a las siete de la noche.
3. E1: ¿A qué hora es el programa *Las computadoras*? E2: Es a las ocho y media/treinta de la mañana.
4. E1: ¿A qué hora es la clase de español? E2: Es a las diez y media/treinta de la mañana.
5. E1: ¿A qué hora es la clase de biología? E2: Es a las diez menos veinte de la noche en punto.
6. E1: ¿A qué hora es la clase de historia? E2: Es a las once menos diez de la mañana.
7. E1: ¿A qué hora es el partido de béisbol? E2: Es a las cinco y cuarto de la tarde.
8. E1: ¿A qué hora es el partido de tenis? E2: Es a la una menos cuarto de la tarde en punto.
9. E1: ¿A qué hora es el partido de baloncesto? E2: Es a las ocho menos cuarto de la noche.
10. E1: ¿A qué hora es la fiesta? E2: Es a las ocho y media/treinta de la noche.

NOTA CULTURAL

La casa de Bernarda Alba is a famous play by Spanish poet and playwright **Federico García Lorca** (1898-1936). Lorca was one of the most famous writers of the 20th century, and was a close friend of Spain's most talented artists, including the painter Salvador Dalí and the filmmaker Luis Buñuel.

TEACHING OPTIONS

Pairs Have students work with a partner to create an original conversation similar to the one in Activity 3. They should do at least the following in their conversation: (1) greet each other appropriately, (2) ask for the time, (3) ask what time a particular class is, (4) say good-bye. Have pairs present their conversations in front of the rest of the class.

Extra Practice Give certain times of the day and ask students whether those times are typical times to be awake for **un médico, un estudiante**, or **los dos** (*both*). Ex: **Son las cinco menos cuarto de la mañana. (un médico) Es la medianoche. (un estudiante)**

NATIONAL communication STANDARDS

Comunicación

4 **En la televisión** With a partner, take turns asking and answering questions about these television listings. Answers will vary.

modelo

Estudiante 1: *¿A qué hora es Las computadoras?*
Estudiante 2: *Es a las nueve en punto de la noche.*

TV Hoy – Programación

11:00 am Telenovela: *Cuatro viajeros y un autobús*
12:00 pm Película: *El cóndor* (drama)
2:00 pm Telenovela: *Dos mujeres y dos hombres*
3:00 pm Programa juvenil: *Fiesta*
3.30 pm Telenovela: *¡Sí, sí, sí!*
4:00 pm Telenovela: *El diario de la Sra. González*
5:00 pm Telenovela: *Tres mujeres*
6:00 pm Noticias
7:00 pm Especial musical: *Música folklórica de México*
7:30 pm La naturaleza: *Jardín secreto*
8:00 pm Noticiero: *Veinticuatro horas*
9:00 pm Documental: *Las computadoras*

NOTA CULTURAL

Telenovelas are the Latin American version of soap operas, but they differ from North American soaps in many ways. Many **telenovelas** are prime-time shows enjoyed by a large segment of the population. They seldom run for more than one season and they are sometimes based on famous novels.

5 **Preguntas** With a partner, answer these questions based on your own knowledge. Some answers will vary.

1. Son las tres de la tarde en Nueva York. ¿Qué hora es en Los Ángeles? Es el mediodía./ Son las doce.
2. Son las ocho y media en Chicago. ¿Qué hora es en Miami? Son las nueve y media.
3. Son las dos menos cinco en San Francisco. ¿Qué hora es en San Antonio? Son las cuatro menos cinco.
4. ¿A qué hora es el programa *60 Minutes*? 7:00 P.M. Eastern Time
5. ¿A qué hora es el programa *Today Show*? 7:00 A.M. Eastern Time

6 Using the questions in the previous activity as a model, make up four questions of your own. Then, get together with a classmate and take turns asking and answering each other's questions.

NATIONAL communication STANDARDS

Síntesis

7 **Situación** With two classmates, play the roles of university journalism students and a visiting literature professor (**profesor(a) de literatura**) from Venezuela whom they are interviewing. The students arrive early for the interview, introduce themselves, and find out about each other. When the professor arrives, the students ask what his/her name is, where he/she is from, what time his/her literature class is, and how many students are in the class. The professor asks a few questions to find out about the students. The professor ends the interview by looking at the clock and saying that the class begins in five minutes. The students say thank you and goodbye. Answers will vary.

4 Present Model pronunciation of the **Modelo** with a student.

4 Suggestion Before beginning the activity, have students look over the schedue and point out cognates they see and predict their meanings. Help them with the meanings of other programming categories: **novela** (short for **telenovela**) = *soap opera*; **película** = *movie*; **programa juvenil** = *children's program*; **noticias/ noticiero** = *news*; **documental** = *documentary*.

4 Expand Ask students questions about what time some popular TV programs are shown. Ex: **—¿A qué hora es el programa "Will y Grace"? —Es a las ocho.**

5 Warm-up Remind students that there are 4 time zones in the continental United States, and that when it is noon in the Eastern Time Zone, it is three hours earlier in the Pacific Time Zone.

7 Present

- Point out that this activity synthesizes everything they have learned in this chapter: greetings and leave-takings, nouns and articles, numbers 0–30 and **hay**, the verb **ser**, and telling time. Spend a few moments reviewing these topics.
- Read through the directions with students, answering any questions they may have. Explain that you will be the visiting literature professor and that the questions they ask of you should be in the **Ud.** form. They can, however, address each other as **tú**.
- Give students a few minutes to jot down the questions they will ask you before embarking on the interview.

Assignment Have students prepare activities in **Student Activities Manual: Workbook**, pages 7–8.

TEACHING OPTIONS

Small Groups Have small groups of students prepare skits. Groups can choose any situation they wish, provided that they use material presented in the **Contextos** and **Estructura** sections. Possible situations include: meeting to go on an excursion (as in **Fotonovela**), meeting in between classes, introducing friends to professors, and so forth.

Heritage Speakers Have heritage speakers prepare brief interviews of their classmates, which they then give. They should use vocabulary and structures presented in **Lesson 1**. Then they report their findings to the class.
Heritage Speakers Ask heritage speakers what **novelas** are currently featured on Spanish-language television in your area and if they watch them regularly. Ask them the channel (**canal**) and time when they are shown.

Lectura

Antes de leer

Estrategia

Recognizing cognates

As you learned earlier in this lesson, cognates are words that share similar meanings and spellings in two or more languages. When reading in Spanish, it's helpful to look for cognates and use them to guess the meaning of what you're reading. But watch out for false cognates. For example, **librería** means *bookstore,* not *library,* and **embarazada** means *pregnant,* not *embarrassed.* Look at this list of Spanish words, paying special attention to prefixes and suffixes. Can you guess the meaning of each word?

importante	oportunidad
farmacia	cultura
inteligente	activo
dentista	sociología
decisión	espectacular
televisión	restaurante
médico	policía

Examinar el texto

Glance quickly at the reading selection and guess what type of document it is. Explain your answer.

Cognados

Read the document and make a list of the cognates you find. Guess their English equivalents, then compare your answers with those of a classmate.

Teléfonos importantes

Policía
Médico
Dentista
Pediatra
Farmacia
Banco Central
Aerolíneas Nacionales
Cine Metro
Hora/Temperatura
Profesora Salgado (universidad)
Felipe (oficina)
Gimnasio Gente Activa
Restaurante Roma
Supermercado Famoso
Librería El Inteligente

TEACHING OPTIONS

Heritage Speakers Ask Spanish speakers to model reading and writing the numbers in **Teléfonos importantes**, and to discuss how digits are grouped and punctuated (periods instead of hyphens). For example, 732.5722 may be pronounced by a combination of tens, **siete, treinta y dos, cincuenta y siete, veintidós**, or hundreds and tens, **setecientos treinta y dos, cincuenta y siete, veintidós**.

Extra Practice Write some of these Spanish words on the board and have students name the English cognate: **democracia, actor, eficiente, nacionalidad, diferencia, guitarrista, artista, doctora, dificultad, exploración**. Then write on the board some of these words with less obvious cognates: **ciudad, cafetería, ciencia, población, número, signo, remedio**. Where students do not recognize the correspondence, clarify it for them.

Section Goals

In **Lectura** students will:
- learn to recognize cognates
- use suffixes to recognize cognates
- read a telephone list rich in cognates

Antes de leer
Introduce the strategy. Tell students that cognates are words in one language that have identical or similar counterparts in another language. True cognates are close in meaning, so recognizing Spanish words that are cognates of English words can help you read Spanish. Have students look at the list of cognates in the **Estrategia** box. Write some of the common suffix correspondences between Spanish and English cognates on the board: **-ción/-sión** = -tion/-sion (**decisión, nación**); **-ante/-ente** = -ant/-ent (**importante, inteligente, elegante**); **-ia/-ía** = -y (**farmacia, sociología, historia**); **-dad** = -ty (**oportunidad, universidad**).

The Affective Dimension
Tell your students that reading in Spanish will be less anxiety-provoking if they follow the advice in the **Estrategia** sections, which are designed to reinforce and improve reading comprehension skills.

Examinar el texto
Ask students to tell you what type of text **Teléfonos importantes** is and how they can tell. (It's a list and it contains names and telephone numbers.)

Cognados
Ask students to mention any cognates they see in the phone list. Discuss the cognates and explain any discrepancies with the list of corresponding suffixes given above. Ex: **policía** = police, *not* policy

Assignment Have students read **Teléfonos importantes** and do the activities in **Después de leer** as homework.

54.11.11

54.36.92

54.87.11

53.14.57

54.03.06

54.90.83

54.87.40

53.45.96

53.24.81

54.15.33

54.84.99

54.36.04

53.75.44

54.77.23

54.66.04

Después de leer

¿Cierto o falso?

Indicate whether each statement is **cierto** or **falso.** Then correct the false statements.

1. There is a child in this household.
   Cierto
2. To renew a prescription you would dial 54.90.83.
   Falso. To renew a prescription you would dial 54.03.06.
3. If you wanted the exact time and information about weather you'd dial 53.24.81.
   Cierto
4. Felipe probably works outdoors.
   Falso. Felipe works in an office.
5. This household probably orders a lot of Chinese food.
   Falso. They probably order a lot of Italian food.
6. If you had a toothache, you would dial 54.87.11.
   Cierto
7. You would dial 54.87.40 to make a flight reservation.
   Cierto
8. To find out if a best-selling book was in stock, you would dial 54.66.04.
   Cierto
9. If you needed information about aerobics classes, you would dial 54.15.33.
   Falso. If you needed information about aerobics classes you would call Gimnasio Gente Activa at 54.36.04.
10. You would call **Cine Metro** to find out what time a movie starts.
    Cierto

Hacer una lista

Make your own list of phone numbers like the one shown in this reading. Include emergency phone numbers as well as frequently called numbers. Use as many cognates from the reading as you can.

Después de leer

¿Cierto o falso?

Suggestion Go over Items 1–10 orally with the whole class. If students have trouble inferring the answer to any question, help them identify the cognate or provide additional corresponding context clues.

Suggestion This activity is also appropriate for pairs of students to do in class if you have not assigned it to be done as homework. Ask students to work with a partner to use cognates and context clues to determine whether each statement is **cierto** or **falso**. When pairs are finished, go over the answers with the whole class.

Hacer una lista

Suggestion With the whole class, brainstorm possible categories of phone numbers they may wish to include in their lists. Begin an idea map on the board or overhead projector, jotting down the students' responses in Spanish, explaining unfamiliar vocabulary as necessary.

Expand You may wish to have students include e-mail addresses (**direcciones electrónicas**) in their lists.

Suggestion Encourage students to record false cognates (**falsos amigos**) as well as cognates and other words they learn in **Lectura** in their portfolios (**carpeta de trabajos**).

TEACHING OPTIONS

Variación léxica The first thing a Spanish-speaker says upon answering the telephone may reveal where in the Spanish-speaking world that person is from. A telephone call in Mexico is likely answered **¿Bueno?**. In other parts of the Spanish-speaking world you may hear the greetings **Diga, Dígame, Oígame**, and even **Aló**.

Small Groups In groups of three, have students read aloud entries from their lists. The listeners should copy down the items they hear. Have group members switch roles so each has a chance to read. Have groups compare and contrast their lists.

Heritage Speakers Ask Spanish speakers to share phone etiquette they may know, such as answering the phone or the equivalents of "Is ____ there?" (**¿Está ____?**); "Speaking," (**Soy yo.** or **Al habla.**) and identifying oneself, "This is ____." (**Habla ____.** or **Soy ____.**)

Section Goals

In **Escritura** students will:

- learn to write a telephone/address list in Spanish
- integrate lesson vocabulary, including cognates, and structures

Tema

Present Introduce students to standard headings (**Nombre, Teléfono, Dirección electrónica**) used in a telephone/address list. Students may wish to add notes pertaining to home (**número de casa**) or office (**número de oficina**) telephone numbers, fax numbers (**número de fax**), or office hours (**horas de oficina**). Encourage them to use their imagination in adding categories and making their annotations.

Suggestion Tell students that to find electronic resources for students of Spanish, they may enter the key words *Spanish Language* into an Internet search engine.

Estrategia

Present Have students create their telephone/address lists in Spanish. Special annotations are likely to include items for which students do not have structures or vocabulary.

Some students may find it helpful to brainstorm what headings or additional notes they wish to include for each type of entry, creating a type of template that they can reuse.

The Affective Dimension

Tell the class that they will feel less anxious about writing in a foreign language if they follow the step-by-step advice in the **Estrategia, Tema,** and **Plan de escritura** sections.

Assignment Have students prepare **Ideas y organización** and **Primer borrador** as homework.

Escritura

Estrategia

Writing in Spanish

Why do we write? All writing has a purpose. For example, we may write a poem to reveal our innermost feelings, a letter to impart information, or an essay to persuade others to accept a point of view. Proficient writers are not born, however. Writing requires time, thought, effort, and a lot of practice. Here are some tips to help you write more effectively in Spanish.

DO

- Try to write your ideas in Spanish
- Use the grammar and vocabulary that you know
- Use your textbook for examples of style, format, and expression in Spanish
- Use your imagination and creativity
- Put yourself in your reader's place to determine if your writing is interesting

AVOID

- Translating your ideas from English to Spanish
- Simply repeating what is in the textbook or on a web page
- Using a dictionary until you have learned how to use foreign language dictionaries

Tema

Hacer una lista

Create a telephone/address list that includes important names, numbers, and websites that will be helpful to you in your study of Spanish. Make whatever entries you can in Spanish without using a dictionary. You might want to include this information:

- The names, phone numbers, and e-mail addresses of at least four classmates
- Your professor's name, e-mail address, and office hours
- Three phone numbers and e-mail addresses of campus offices or locations related to your study of Spanish
- Five electronic resources for students of Spanish, such as chat rooms, international keypal sites, and sites dedicated to the study of Spanish as a second language

Nombre Sally (la chica de Indiana)
Teléfono 655-8888
Dirección electrónica sally@uru.edu

Nombre Profesor José Ramón Casas
Teléfono 655-8090
Dirección electrónica jrcasas@uru.edu
Horas de oficina 12 a 12:30

Nombre Biblioteca 655-7000
Dirección electrónica library@uru.edu

TEACHING OPTIONS

Proofreading Activity Copy onto the board or a transparency the following items containing mistakes as a proofreading activity to do with the whole class.

1. **Telefonos importants**
2. **Direccion electrónico**
3. **Hora de oficina: 12 a 2**
4. **Nombre: David (amiga de Jaime)**
5. **Teléfon (del oficina) 407-2925**

Spanish Characters on the Word Processor

	Macintosh	PC (Windows)
á Á, etc.	*alt* + *e* then *a* or *A*, etc.	*ctrl* + ' then *a* or *A*, etc.
ñ Ñ	*alt* + *n* then *n* or *N*	*ctrl* + ~ then *n* or *N*
ü Ü	*alt* + *u* then *u* or *U*	*ctrl* + : then *u* or *U*
¿	*alt* + *shift* + ?	*ctrl* + *alt* + ?
¡	*alt* + !	*ctrl* + *alt* + !

Plan de escritura

1 Ideas y organización

Begin by making a list of all your campus resources, including your professor, campus facilities, and your classmates. Then spend some time exploring web resources and jotting down the addresses of several sites. Choose various types of web pages; they shouldn't all be keypal sites or chat rooms.

2 Primer borrador

Using the lists you prepared in **Ideas y organización,** write a first draft of the new section for your telephone/address book.

3 Comentario

Exchange first drafts with a classmate and comment on each other's work using the questions below as a guide. Begin by mentioning what you like best about his or her telephone/address book, such as the organization of the entries, or a resource you didn't know about.

a. Is all the required information included and logically organized?
b. Are the websites included pertinent to Spanish students?
c. Do the entries appear in Spanish whenever possible?
d. Do you have any suggestions for additional or different entries in Spanish?
e. Are there any spelling or grammatical errors?

4 Redacción

Revise your first draft, keeping in mind your classmate's comments. Also incorporate any new ideas or information you may have. Before handing in the final version, use these suggestions to help you review your work:

a. Be sure you have included as much Spanish as possible.
b. Check for errors in spelling and punctuation.

5 Evaluación y progreso

Share your final draft with three classmates. Note the addresses of campus resources or websites mentioned on your classmates' lists; you might want to add them to your list. After your instructor has returned your paper, keep your list on hand with your other study aids.

EVALUATION: Lista

Criteria	Scale
Content	1 2 3 4 5
Organization	1 2 3 4 5
Accuracy	1 2 3 4 5
Creativity	1 2 3 4 5

Scoring	
Excellent	18–20 points
Good	14–17 points
Satisfactory	10–13 points
Unsatisfactory	< 10 points

Comentario
Present Go over guide questions a–e with the whole class so peer readers understand their task. Then have pairs of students exchange lists. Allow five minutes for reading and comments. Allow five minutes for discussing comments.
Assignment Have students read **Redacción** as homework. Ask them to rewrite their drafts incorporating the peer comments and following the directions in **Redacción**. Tell them to prepare a clean copy of their final draft to hand in.

Evaluación y progreso
Give the class five minutes to exchange and read the final drafts of their lists. Then have students hand them in to you.

Writing Sample Here is an example of a well-organized and annotated telephone/address list.

Números de urgencia
Policía 677-1000
Bomberos 677-1100
Hospital 677-2000

La universidad
Teléfono 677-3000
Sitio en el Internet: www.uru.edu

Profesores
Nombre Profesora Julia Gil (literatura)
Teléfono 677-3434
Dirección electrónica jgil@uru.edu
Horas de oficina 10:30 a 12:00

Nombre Profesor Juan José Alarcón (español comercial)
Teléfono 677-3437
Dirección electrónica jjalarcon@uru.edu
Horas de oficina 12:00 a 2:00

Biblioteca
Teléfono 677-3400

Café Alegre
Teléfono 677-3450

Section Goals

In **Escuchar** students will:

- listen to sentences containing familiar and unfamiliar vocabulary
- learn the strategy of listening for known vocabulary
- answer questions based on the content of a recorded conversation

Instructional Resource
Student Cassette/CD

Preparación
Warm-up Have students look at the photo and describe what they see. Guide them to guess where they think Dr. Cavazos and Srta. Martínez are and what they are talking about.

Estrategia
Script **Creo que hay... este... treinta pasajeros en el autobús que va a Guayaquil.**

The Affective Dimension
Tell your students that many people feel nervous about their ability to comprehend what they hear in a foreign language. Tell them that they will probably feel less anxious if they follow the advice for increasing listening comprehension in the **Estrategia** sections.

Assignment Have students do the activities in **Ahora escucha** and **Comprensión** as homework. Verify the responses to **Ahora escucha** with the whole class and go over **Identificar** and **¿Cierto o falso?** by reading each question aloud and calling on different students to answer.

Ahora escucha
Script
Dr. Cavazos: Buenos días, señorita.
Srta. Martínez: Buenos días, señor. ¿En qué le puedo servir?
Dr. Cavazos: Yo soy el doctor Alejandro Cavazos. Voy a Quito. Aquí tiene mi boleto. Deseo facturar mis maletas.
Srta. Martínez: ¿Alejandro Cavazos? ¿C-A-V-A-Z-O-S?
Dr. Cavazos: Sí, señorita.
Srta. Martínez: ¿Un viaje de ida y vuelta a Quito?
Dr. Cavazos: Sí.
Srta. Martínez: ¿Cuántas maletas tiene usted? ¿Tres?
Dr. Cavazos: Dos.
Srta. Martínez: Bueno, aquí tiene usted su boleto.
Dr. Cavazos: Muchas gracias, señorita.
Srta. Martínez: No hay de qué, doctor Cavazos. ¡Buen viaje!
Dr. Cavazos: Gracias. ¡Adiós!

Escuchar

NATIONAL communication STANDARDS

Preparación

Based on the photograph, what do you think Dr. Cavazos and Srta. Martínez are talking about? How would you get the gist of their conversation, based on what you know about Spanish?

Estrategia

Listening for words you know

You can get the gist of a conversation by listening for words and phrases you already know. To help you practice this strategy, listen to the following sentence and make a list of the words you have already learned.

Ahora escucha

Now you are going to hear Dr. Cavazos's conversation with Srta. Martínez. List the familiar words and phrases each person says.

Dr. Cavazos	Srta. Martínez
1. ________	9. ________
2. ________	10. ________
3. ________	11. ________
4. ________	12. ________
5. ________	13. ________
6. ________	14. ________
7. ________	15. ________
8. ________	16. ________

With a classmate, use your lists of familiar words as a guide to come up with a summary of what happened in the conversation.

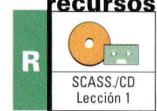

recursos
R SCASS./CD Lección 1

Comprensión

Identificar

Who would say the following things, Dr. Cavazos or Srta. Martínez?

1. Me llamo... Dr. Cavazos
2. De nada. Srta. Martínez
3. Gracias. Muchas gracias. Dr. Cavazos
4. Aquí tiene usted los documentos de viaje, señor. Srta. Martínez
5. Ud. tiene tres maletas, ¿no? Srta. Martínez
6. Tengo dos maletas. Dr. Cavazos
7. Hola, señor. Srta. Martínez
8. ¿Viaja Ud. a Buenos Aires? Srta. Martínez

Contestar

1. Does this scene take place in the morning, afternoon, or evening? How do you know? The scene takes place in the morning, as indicated by **Buenos días.**
2. How many suitcases does Dr. Cavazos have? two
3. Using the words you already know to determine the context, what might the following words and expressions mean?
   - boleto
   - pasaporte
   - un viaje de ida y vuelta
   - ¡Buen viaje!

NATIONAL STANDARDS communication cultures

NATIONAL STANDARDS connections communities

Proyecto

Describe una ciudad

Imagine that you are a journalist reporting on the influence of Hispanic cultures on cities in the United States. You have been asked to present a report to a Spanish class, focusing on one American city.

1 Prepara una presentación

Prepare a brief presentation about how Hispanic cultures have influenced a city in the United States. Using the research tools in **Recursos para la investigación,** choose a city and take notes about how it has been affected by Hispanic cultures. Your presentation might include these elements:

- A description of the city, its location, its history, and its population
- Explanations of how the city has been influenced by Hispanic cultures: for example, its cuisine, arts, politics, and architecture
- Descriptions and photos of famous people, places, and things in the city that are related to Hispanic cultures

2 Presenta la información

Using an outline and your photos, tell the class about the city you chose and how it reflects the influence of Hispanic cultures. Make your presentation vivid so that your classmates will want to learn more about Hispanic cultures in the United States. Use as much Spanish as possible in your presentation, especially to greet the class, to introduce youself, to say where you are from, and to state that you are a journalist (**Soy periodista**).

ciudad *city* Palabras clave *keywords* Biblioteca *library* Otros recursos *other resources*

recursos para la investigación

Internet Palabras clave: United States, city, cities, Hispanic influence(s)	**Comunidad** Faculty members and residents of your community who have lived in the city you chose
Biblioteca Almanacs, encyclopedias, history books, maps, newspapers	**Otros recursos** Brochures from travel agencies

Section Goals

In **Proyecto** students will:
- learn about how Hispanic cultures have influenced a city in the United States
- use Spanish as they research and interact with the wider world
- incorporate Spanish in an oral presentation

Before Assigning Proyecto

Students will need approximately a week to complete the project, so at the beginning of that time period, have them open their books to page 31 and glance over **Proyecto**. Explain that they are going to use their research skills to prepare a brief presentation in which they describe how Hispanic cultures have influenced an American city (**ciudad estadounidense**).

Assignment Have students read page 31 and follow directions in **Prepara una presentación** to plan their presentation.

Prepara una presentación

Suggestions
- If they choose a city they live in or visit, students may seek information from Hispanic members of the community, the Hispanic Chapter of the Chamber of Commerce, or other Hispanic organizations.
- Students' presentations will be more interesting if they incorporate visual aids such as posters and brochures, or integrate music or audio recordings.

Presenta la información

Suggestions
- To prepare, students may practice before a small group of friends who can critique the presentation or before a mirror.
- You may wish to do a few presentations at a time until all students have had a chance to present.

EVALUATION: Descripción

Criteria	Scale
Content	1 2 3 4
Comprehensibility	1 2 3 4
Organization	1 2 3 4
Accuracy	1 2 3 4
Creativity	1 2 3 4

Scoring	
Excellent	18–20 points
Good	14–17 points
Satisfactory	10–13 points
Unsatisfactory	< 10 points

Section Goals

In **Panorama** students will read statistics and cultural information about Hispanics in the United States.

Instructional Resources
Student Activities Manual: Workbook, 9–10
Transparency 12

Estados Unidos
Before Presenting Panorama Have students look at the map of the United States or project **Transparency 12**. Have volunteers read aloud the labeled cities and geographic features. Model Spanish pronunciation of names as necessary. Give students a minute to jot down as many names of places and geographic features with Hispanic origins as they can think of. Then ask volunteers to share their lists with the class. Write the names they mention on the board and model their pronunciation. Ex: **Alamosa está en Colorado.** Finally, have students look at the items in **El país en cifras** and identify the kind of information contained there. **Assignment** Have students read **Panorama** and write out the completed sentences in **¿Qué aprendiste?**, page 33, as homework.

Present Ask volunteers to read the bulleted headings in **El país en cifras**. Pause to point out cognates and clarify unfamiliar words. Explain that numerals in Spanish have a comma where English speakers would expect a decimal point (**4,3%**) and have a period where English speakers would expect a comma (**31.360.000**). Explain that **EE.UU.** is the abbreviation of **Estados Unidos**, the doubling of the initial letters indicating the plural. Model the pronunciation of **Florida** (accent on the second syllable) and point out that it is often used with an article (**la Florida**) by Spanish speakers.

Continued on page 33.

Estados Unidos

Influencia de la cultura hispánica

NATIONAL STANDARDS connections cultures

El país en cifras

- **Población de origen hispano:** 31.360.000
- **País de origen de hispanos en EE.UU.:**

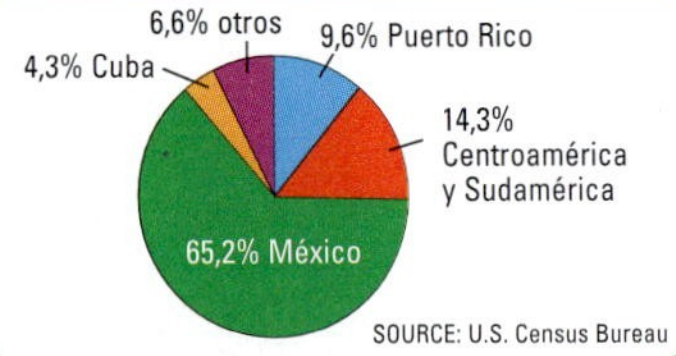

- **Estados con la mayor población hispana:**

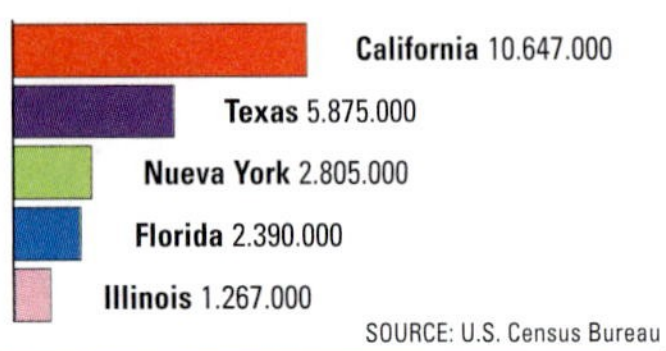

- **Ciudades de mayor población hispana:**

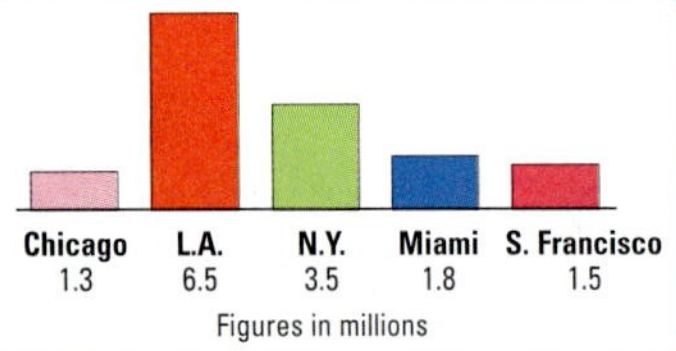

- **Estados con nombres españoles**

Nombre	Significado
Arizona	zona árida (*arid zone*)
California	tierra cálida (*warm land*)
Nevada	tormenta de nieve (*snowstorm*)
Colorado	de color rojo (*of reddish color*)
Montana	montaña (*mountain*)
Florida	tierra de flores (*land of flowers*)
Texas (Tejas)	tejas de color rojo (*red roof tiles*)

mayor *biggest* van a ser *are going to be* más grande *largest* será *will be* se duplicará *will double*

Mission District, en San Francisco

Tito Puente (1925-2000), músico

El Álamo, en San Antonio, Texas

recursos
R | WB pp. 21-22 | vistasonline.com

¡Increíble pero cierto!

Se estima que en el año 2015 los hispanos van a ser el grupo minoritario más grande de los Estados Unidos. La población hispana de EE.UU. será de 46.704.000. En 10 años el número de hispanos se duplicará en los estados de California, Texas, Nueva York, Florida e Illinois.

SOURCE: U.S. Census Bureau

TEACHING OPTIONS

Heritage Speakers Ask class members of Hispanic ancestry to describe for the whole class the Hispanic celebrations that are held in the region where they come from. Ask them to tell the date when the celebration takes place, the event it commemorates, and some of the particulars of the celebration. Possible celebrations: **Cinco de Mayo, Día de la Raza, Día de los Muertos, Fiesta de San Juan, Carnaval**

Game Divide the class into groups of five students. Give groups five minutes to brainstorm place names (cities, states, lakes, rivers, montain ranges, and so forth) in the United States that have Spanish origins. One member of the group should take down the names in a numbered list. After five minutes, go over the names with the whole class, confirming the accuracy of each name. The team with the greatest number wins.

Comida • La comida mexicana

La comida mexicana es muy popular en los Estados Unidos. Los tacos, las enchiladas, los burritos y los frijoles, entre otros, son platos mexicanos que frecuentemente forman parte de las comidas de muchos norteamericanos. También son populares las variaciones estadounidenses de la comida mexicana... el tex-mex y el cali-mex.

Lugares • La Pequeña Habana

Una de las joyas de la Florida es la Pequeña Habana, un barrio de Miami donde viven muchos cubanoamericanos. En todas sus calles se encuentran las costumbres de la cultura cubana, los aromas y sabores de su comida y la música salsa. La Pequeña Habana es un verdadero trozo de Cuba en los Estados Unidos.

Costumbres • Desfile puertorriqueño

Cada junio desde mil novecientos cincuenta y uno (1951), mucha gente de origen puertorriqueño celebra su orgullo latino con un desfile en la ciudad de Nueva York. El desfile es un gran espectáculo con carrozas y música salsa, flamenco y hip-hop. Muchos espectadores participan llevando la bandera de Puerto Rico en su ropa o pintándose los colores de la bandera en la cara.

¿Qué aprendiste? Completa las frases con la información adecuada (*appropriate*).

1. Hay 31.360.000 personas de origen hispano en los Estados Unidos.
2. Los cuatro estados con las poblaciones hispanas más grandes son (en orden) California, Texas, Nueva York y Florida.
3. Los burritos y las enchiladas son platos mexicanos.
4. El tex-mex y el cali-mex son variaciones de la comida mexicana.
5. La Pequeña Habana es un barrio de Miami.
6. En Miami hay muchas personas de origen cubano.
7. Cado junio se celebra en Nueva York un gran desfile para personas de origen puertorriqueño.
8. El estado de Nueva York tiene una gran población puertorriqueña.

Una partida de ajedrez en un parque de Miami

Conexión Internet Investiga estos temas en el sitio **www.vistasonline.com.**

1. Haz (*Make*) una lista de seis hispanoamericanos célebres: dos mexicoamericanos, dos puertorriqueños y dos cubanoamericanos. Explica (*Explain*) por qué (*why*) son célebres.
2. Escoge (*Choose*) seis lugares en los Estados Unidos con nombres hispanos y busca información sobre el origen y el significado (*meaning*) de cada nombre.

Comida *Food* entre otros *among others* platos *dishes* También *Also* Lugares *Places* La Pequeña Habana *Little Havana* joyas *jewels* barrio *neighborhood* viven *live* todas sus calles *all of its streets* se encuentran *are found* costumbres *customs* sabores *flavors* verdadero trozo *true slice* Desfile *parade* Cada junio desde *Each June since* gente *people* orgullo *pride* ciudad *city* con carrozas *with floats* llevando *wearing* bandera *flag* ropa *clothing* pintándose *painting* cara *face*

Ask volunteers to read sentences from **¡Increíble pero cierto!, Comida, Lugares**, and **Costumbres**. Model pronunciation as necessary and pause to point out cognates and clarify unfamiliar words.

¡Increíble, pero cierto! Don't expect students to produce numbers greater than 30 at this point. Explain phrases such as **se estima** and **grupo minoritario**.

La comida mexicana Have students look at illustrated cookbooks or recipes to identify the ingredients and variations of the dishes mentioned in the paragraph.

La pequeña Habana Many large cities in the United States have neighborhoods where people of Hispanic origin predominate. Encourage students to speak of neighborhoods they are familiar with.

Desfile puertorriqueño The Puerto Rican Parade takes place on the weekend nearest the feast day of St. John the Baptist (San Juan Bautista), the patron of San Juan, capital of Puerto Rico.

¿Qué aprendiste? Go over the questions and answers with the whole class, modeling the pronunciation of unfamiliar words.

Assignment Have students prepare the activites in **Student Activities Manual: Workbook**, pages 9–10.

Conexión Internet Students will find information about well-known Hispanics in the United States and about American communities with Spanish names at **www.vistasonline.com**, as well as links to other Spanish-related sites.

TEACHING OPTIONS

Variación Léxica Hispanic groups in the United States refer to themselves with various names. The most common of these terms, **hispano** and **latino**, refer to all people who come from Hispanic backgrounds, whatever the country of origin of their ancestors. **Puertorriqueño, cubanoamericano**, and **mexicoamericano** refer to Hispanics whose ancestors came from Puerto Rico, Cuba, and Mexico, respectively. Many Mexican Americans also refer to themselves as **chicanos**. This word has stronger socio-political connotations than **mexicoamericano**. Use of the word **chicano** implies identification with Mexican Americans' struggle for civil rights and equal opportunity in the United States. It also suggests an appreciation of the indigenous aspects which are an important part of Mexican and Mexican-American culture.

1 vocabulario

Saludos

Hola.	*Hello; Hi.*
Buenos días.	*Good morning.*
Buenas tardes.	*Good afternoon.*
Buenas noches.	*Good evening; Good night.*

Despedidas

Adiós.	*Good-bye.*
Nos vemos.	*See you.*
Hasta luego.	*See you later.*
Hasta la vista.	*See you later.*
Hasta pronto.	*See you soon.*
Hasta mañana.	*See you tomorrow.*
Saludos a...	*Greetings to …*
Chau.	*Bye.*

¿Cómo está?

¿Cómo está usted?	*How are you?* (form.)
¿Cómo estás?	*How are you?* (fam.)
¿Qué hay de nuevo?	*What's new?; What's happening?*
¿Qué pasa?	*What's going on?*
¿Qué tal?	*How are you?; How is it going?*
(Muy) bien, gracias.	*(Very) well, thanks.*
Nada.	*Nothing.*
No muy bien.	*Not very well.*
Regular.	*So, so; OK.*

¿A qué hora?

¿A qué hora...?	*(At) what time …?*
¿Qué hora es?	*What time is it?*
Es la una.	*It's one o'clock.*
Son las...	*It's … o'clock.*
la medianoche	*midnight*
el mediodía	*noon*
de la mañana	*in the morning; A.M.*
de la noche	*in the evening; at night; P.M.*
de la tarde	*in the afternoon; in the early evening; P.M.*
en punto	*on the dot; exactly; sharp*
menos cuarto, menos quince	*quarter to*
y cuarto/y quince	*quarter after*
y media/y treinta	*thirty (minutes past the hour)*

Presentaciones

¿Cómo se llama usted?	*What's your name?* (form.)
¿Cómo te llamas (tú)?	*What's your name?* (fam.)
Me llamo...	*My name is …*
¿Y tú?	*And you?* (fam.)
¿Y Ud.?	*And you?* (form.)
Mucho gusto.	*Pleased to meet you.*
El gusto es mío.	*The pleasure is mine.*
Encantado/a.	*Delighted; Pleased to meet you.*
Igualmente.	*Likewise.*
Éste/ésta es...	*This is …*
Le presento a...	*I would like to introduce you to…* (form.)
Te presento a...	*I would like to introduce to you…* (fam.)

Expresiones de cortesía

Con permiso.	*Pardon me; Excuse me.*
De nada.	*You're welcome.*
Lo siento.	*I'm sorry.*
(Muchas) gracias.	*Thank you (very much); Thanks (a lot).*
No hay de qué.	*You're welcome.*
Perdón.	*Pardon me; Excuse me.*

Títulos

señor (Sr.)	*Mr.; sir*
señora (Sra.)	*Mrs.; ma'am*
señorita (Srta.)	*Miss*

Países

Ecuador	*Ecuador*
España	*Spain*
Estados Unidos (EE.UU.; E.U.)	*United States*
México	*Mexico*
Puerto Rico	*Puerto Rico*

Verbos

ser	*to be*

Sustantivos

el autobús	*bus*
la capital	*capital city*
la chica	*girl*
el chico	*boy*
la computadora	*computer*
el/la conductor(a)	*chauffeur; driver*
la cosa	*thing*
el cuaderno	*notebook*
el día	*day*
el diario	*diary*
el diccionario	*dictionary*
la escuela	*school*
el/la estudiante	*student*
la foto(grafía)	*photograph*
el hombre	*man*
la grabadora	*tape recorder*
el/la joven	*youth; young person*
el lápiz	*pencil*
la maleta	*suitcase*
la mano	*hand*
el mapa	*map*
la mujer	*woman*
la nacionalidad	*nationality*
el número	*number*
el país	*country*
la palabra	*word*
el/la pasajero(a)	*passenger*
el problema	*problem*
el/la profesor(a)	*teacher*
el programa	*program*
el/la turista	*tourist*

¿De dónde es?

¿De dónde es Ud.?	*Where are you from?* (form.)
¿De dónde eres?	*Where are you from?* (fam.)
Soy de...	*I'm from …*

Palabras adicionales

¿cuánto(s)/a(s)?	*how many?*
¿de quién...?	*whose …?* (sing.)
¿de quiénes...?	*whose …?* (plural)
(no) hay	*there is (not); there are (not)*

Los números 0 a 30	*See page 14.*
Expresiones útiles	*See page 7.*

En la universidad

2

Communicative Goals

You will learn how to:

- Talk about your classes and school life
- Discuss everyday activities
- Ask questions in Spanish
- Describe the location of people and things

contextos

fotonovela

estructura

adelante

panorama

Lesson Goals

In **Lesson 2** students will be introduced to the following:

- classroom- and university-related words
- names of academic courses and fields of study
- class schedules
- days of the week
- present tense of regular **-ar** verbs
- forming negative sentences
- forming questions
- the present tense of **estar**
- prepositions of location
- numbers 31–100
- using text formats to predict content
- brainstorming and organizing ideas for writing
- writing descriptions of themselves
- listening for cognates
- creating a poster for a "Year Abroad" program in Spain
- cultural and historical information about Spain

Lesson Preview

Have students look at the photo. Say: **Es una foto de dos jóvenes en la universidad.** Then ask: **¿Qué son los jóvenes? (Son estudiantes.) ¿Qué tiene el chico en la mano?**

INSTRUCTIONAL RESOURCES

Student Activities Manual: Workbook, 11–22
Student Activities Manual: Lab Manual, 223–228
Student Activities Manual: Video Activities, 329–330
Instructor's Resource Manual: Hojas de actividades, 3–4
Instructor's Resource Manual: Answer Keys
Instructor's Resource Manual: Vocabulario adicional, 53
Tapescript/Videoscript
Overhead Transparencies, 7–8, 13–15

Student Cassette/CD
Lab Cassette/CD
Video Program
CD-ROM
Website: **www.vistasonline.com**
Testing Program: Prueba A, Prueba B

Section Goals

In **Contextos**, students will learn and practice:
- names for people, places, and things at the university
- names of academic courses

Instructional Resources
Student Activities Manual: Workbook, 11–12; Lab Manual, 223
Transparency 13
Student Cassette/CD
Vocabulario adicional 53

Before Presenting Contextos Introduce vocabulary for classroom objects such as **mesa, libro, pluma, lápiz, papel,** and so forth. Hold up or point to an object and say: **Es un lápiz.** Indicate a student and ask **Y tú ____, ¿tienes un lápiz?**, explaining the meaning of **tienes**, if necessary. Follow the same procedure with other objects. Alternate questions containing **¿Tienes... ?** with questions that include **¿Hay/No hay... ?** and **¿Cuántos/as... ?**
Assignment Have students study **Contextos** and do the exercises in **Práctica** on pages 37–38 as homework.

Present Write **¿Qué es esto?** on the board and explain that it means *What is this?* Then, using either objects in the classroom or projecting **Transparency 13**, point to items and ask questions such as: **¿Qué es esto? ¿Es una mesa? ¿Es un reloj?** Vary the format of questions by asking questions such as: **¿Qué hay en el escritorio? ¿Qué hay en la mesa? ¿Cuántas tizas hay en la pizarra? ¿Hay una pluma en el escritorio de ____?** Continue until you have introduced all the active vocabulary.

Then draw the attention of the class to the teacher's desk and to individual students' desks on the transparency. Ask: **¿Qué hay en el escritorio? ¿Qué hay en la mesa de la profesora?**

2 contextos

En la universidad

Más vocabulario

la biblioteca	*library*
la cafetería	*cafeteria*
el estadio	*stadium*
la librería	*bookstore*
la residencia estudiantil	*dormitory*
la universidad	*university*
la clase	*class*
el/la compañero/a de clase	*classmate*
el/la compañero/a de cuarto	*roommate*
el examen	*test; exam*
el horario	*schedule*
el laboratorio	*laboratory*
la prueba	*test; quiz*
el semestre	*semester*
la tarea	*homework*
el trimestre	*trimester; quarter*
los cursos	*courses*
la administración de empresas	*business administration*
el arte	*art*
la biología	*biology*
las ciencias	*sciences*
la computación	*computer science*
la contabilidad	*accounting*
la economía	*economics*
el español	*Spanish*
la física	*physics*
la geografía	*geography*

Variación léxica

pluma ↔ bolígrafo
pizarra ↔ tablero (*Col.*)
tarea ↔ asignación (*P. Rico*); deberes (*Esp., Arg.*)

recursos

R	SCASS./CD Lección 2	WB pp. 11-12	LM p. 223	LCASS./CD Cass. 1B/CD1

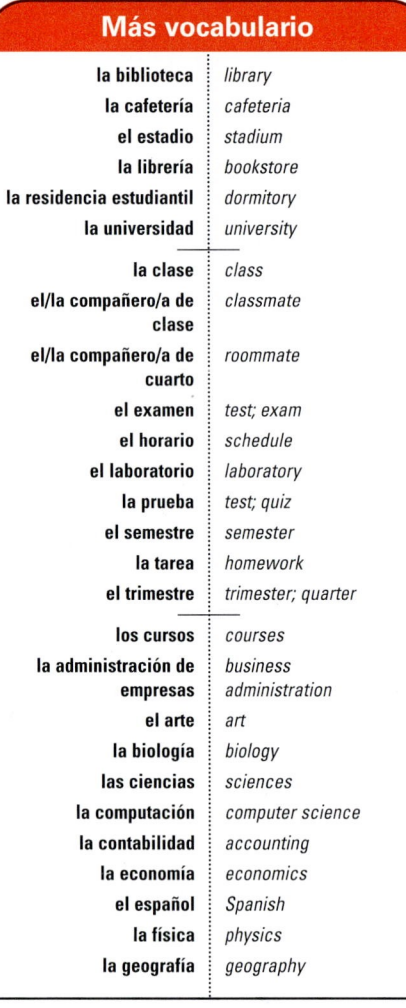

TEACHING OPTIONS

Variación léxica Ask Spanish speakers to tell the class any other terms they use to talk about people, places, or things at the university. Ask them to tell where these terms are used. Possible responses: **el boli, la ciudad universitaria, el profe, el catedrático, la facultad, el profesorado, la asignatura, el gimnasio, el pizarrón, el salón de clases, el aula, el pupitre, el giz**

Game Divide the class into teams. Then, in English, read aloud the name of an academic course and ask one of the teams to provide the Spanish equivalent. If the team provides the correct term, it gets a point. If not, the second team gets a chance at the same item. Alternate asking questions of the two teams until you have read all the course names. The team that has the most points at the end of the game wins.

Práctica

1 Escuchar Listen to Professor Morales talk about her Spanish classroom, then check the items she mentions.

1.	puerta	☑	7.	sillas	☐
2.	ventanas	☑	8.	libros	☑
3.	pizarra	☑	9.	plumas	☑
4.	borrador	☐	10.	mochilas	☐
5.	tiza	☑	11.	papel	☑
6.	escritorios	☑	12.	reloj	☑

2 Emparejar Match each question with its most logical response. **¡Ojo!** (*Careful!*) Two of the responses will not be used.

1. ¿Qué clase es? d
2. ¿Quiénes son? h
3. ¿Quién es? e
4. ¿De dónde es? c
5. ¿A qué hora es la clase de inglés? g
6. ¿Cuántos estudiantes hay? a

a. Hay veinticinco.
b. Es un reloj.
c. Es del Perú.
d. Es la clase de química.
e. Es el señor Bastos.
f. Mucho gusto.
g. Es a las nueve en punto.
h. Son los profesores.

3 Identificar Identify the word that does not fit in each group.

1. examen • grabadora • tarea • prueba grabadora
2. economía • matemáticas • biblioteca • contabilidad biblioteca
3. pizarra • tiza • borrador • librería librería
4. lápiz • cafetería • papel • cuaderno cafetería
5. veinte • diez • pluma • treinta pluma
6. conductor • laboratorio • autobús • pasajero laboratorio
7. humanidades • mesa • ciencias • lenguas extranjeras mesa
8. lápiz • qué • cómo • dónde lápiz

4 ¿Qué clase es? Use the clues to name the subject matter of each class.

modelo
los elementos, los átomos
Es la clase de química.

1. Abraham Lincoln, Winston Churchill Es la clase de historia.
2. Picasso, Leonardo da Vinci Es la clase de arte.
3. Freud, Jung Es la clase de psicología.
4. África, el océano Pacífico Es la clase de geografía.
5. la cultura de España, verbos Es la clase de español.
6. Hemingway, Shakespeare Es la clase de literatura.
7. geometría, trigonometría Es la clase de matemáticas.
8. las plantas, los animales Es la clase de biología.

TEACHING OPTIONS

Extra Practice Ask students what phrases or vocabulary words they associate with items such as the following: 1. **la pizarra** (ex: **la tiza, el borrador**), 2. **la residencia estudiantil** (ex. **el compañero de cuarto, la compañera de cuarto, el/la estudiante**), 3. **el reloj** (ex: **¿Qué hora es? Son las… Es la…**), 4. **la biblioteca** (ex: **los libros, los exámenes, las materias**).

Extra Practice On the board, write **¿Qué clases tomas?** and **Tomo…** . Explain the meaning of these phrases and ask your students to circulate around the classroom and imagine that they are meeting their classmates for the first time. Tell them to introduce themselves, find out where each person is from, and what classes he or she is taking this semester. After a few minutes, you can follow up by asking individual students about what their classmates are taking.

1 Present Go over the tapescript with the class so that students can check their answers. **Tapescript** ¿Qué hay en mi clase de español? ¡Muchas cosas! Hay una puerta y cinco ventanas. Hay una pizarra con tiza. Hay muchos escritorios para los estudiantes. En los escritorios de los estudiantes hay libros y plumas. En la mesa de la profesora hay papel. Hay un mapa y un reloj en la clase también.

2 Present/Expand With the whole class, ask each question and indicate a student to answer. Items **b** and **f** were not used. Ask the class to come up with questions or statements that would elicit these items as responses. Possible answers: **b (¿Qué es?), f (Me llamo ____.)**

3 Present/Expand Read each item aloud. Then read the following as items 9 and 10: **9. pluma, lápiz, silla, tiza (silla); 10. ventana, estudiante, profesor, compañera de cuarto (ventana).**

3 Present Ask a volunteer to read the model aloud. Then read each item and ask volunteers to answer.

4 Expand Have the class brainstorm a list of famous people that they would associate with the following fields: **periodismo** (ex: Dan Rather, Barbara Walters), **computación** (ex: Bill Gates, Michael Dell), **humanidades** (ex: Maya Angelou, Sandra Cisneros). Then have the class guess the field associated with each of the following people: Albert Einstein (**física**), Charles Darwin (**biología**), Alan Greenspan (**economía**).

Note: At this point you may want to present *Otras materias*, **Vocabulario adicional 53**, in the **Instructor's Resource Manual.**

Present Write the following questions and answers on the board, explaining their meaning as you do so:
—¿Qué día es hoy?
—Hoy es ____.
—¿Qué día es mañana?
—Mañana es ____.
—¿Cuándo es la prueba?
—Es el ____.
—¿Cuándo es la clase de español?
—Es los ____, ____ y ____. Explain that **el viernes** means *on Friday* and that **los lunes, miércoles y viernes** means *on Mondays, Wednesdays, and Fridays.* Then ask students a few questions based on the material on the board. Ex: **¿Cuándo es la clase de historia? ¿Cuándo es la prueba de español? ¿Qué día es hoy? ¿Qué día es mañana?**

Suggestion Tell students that Monday, rather than Sunday, is traditionally the first day of the week in the Spanish-speaking world and usually appears as such on calendars, such as the one on page 38.

5 Expand Ask the class questions such as: **Mañana es viernes... ¿qué día fue ayer? (miércoles); Ayer fue domingo... ¿qué día es mañana? (martes)**

6 Warm-up Have the class review the list of **sustantivos** on page 34 and the numbers 0–30 on page 14 before doing this activity.

Los días de la semana

septiembre

lunes	martes	miércoles	jueves	viernes	sábado	domingo
	1	2	3	4	5	6
7	8	9	10			

¡LENGUA VIVA!
Monday is considered the first day of the week in Spanish-speaking countries.
•••
The days of the week are never capitalized in Spanish.

5 **¿Qué día es hoy?** Complete each statement with the correct day of the week.

1. Hoy es martes. Mañana es miércoles. Ayer fue lunes.
2. Ayer fue sábado. Mañana es lunes. Hoy es domingo.
3. Mañana es viernes. Hoy es jueves. Ayer fue miércoles.
4. Ayer fue domingo. Hoy es lunes. Mañana es martes.
5. Hoy es jueves. Ayer fue miércoles. Mañana es viernes.
6. Mañana es lunes. Hoy es domingo. Ayer fue sábado.

AYUDA
Ayer fue *yesterday was*

6 **Analogías** Use these words to complete the analogies. Some words will not be used.

arte	chau	estudiante	profesor
biblioteca	día	mujer	reloj
catorce	martes	pizarra	domingo

1. maleta ⟷ pasajero ⊜ mochila ⟷ estudiante
2. chico ⟷ chica ⊜ hombre ⟷ mujer
3. pluma ⟷ papel ⊜ tiza ⟷ pizarra
4. inglés ⟷ lengua ⊜ miércoles ⟷ día
5. papel ⟷ cuaderno ⊜ libro ⟷ biblioteca
6. quince ⟷ dieciséis ⊜ lunes ⟷ martes
7. ¡Buen viaje! ⟷ Gracias. ⊜ ¡Nos vemos! ⟷ Chau.
8. autobús ⟷ conductor ⊜ clase ⟷ profesor
9. EE.UU. ⟷ mapa ⊜ hora ⟷ reloj
10. veinte ⟷ veintitrés ⊜ jueves ⟷ domingo

TEACHING OPTIONS

Heritage Speakers Have Spanish speakers prepare a day-planner for the upcoming week. Tell them to list each day of the week and the things they expect to do each day, including classes, homework, tests, appointments, and social events. Tell them to include the time each activity takes place. Have them exchange their day-planners with a partner and check each other's work for errors.

Game Have the class play a chain-forming game in which the first student says a word in Spanish (e.g., **estudiante**). The next student has to think of a word that begins with the last letter of the first person's word (e.g., **español**). If a student can't think of a word, he or she is out of the game and it's the next student's turn. The last student left in the game is the winner.

¡ATENCIÓN!

Use **el** + [*day of the week*] when an activity occurs on a specific day and **los** + [*day of the week*] when an activity occurs regularly:

El lunes tengo un examen.

Los lunes y miércoles tomo biología.

• • •

Except for **sábados** and **domingos,** the singular and plural forms for days of the week are the same.

Comunicación

NATIONAL communication STANDARDS

7 **Horario** Create your own class schedule in Spanish. Then discuss it with a classmate. Answers will vary.

Estudiante		Manuel Domínguez H.			**Semestre Nº 1**	
lunes	martes	miércoles	jueves	viernes	sábado	domingo
8:30 biología Profesora Morales **10:15** inglés Profesor Herrera **3:30** laboratorio (biología) **4:30** discusión (historia) biblioteca	**9:45** historia – península Ibérica Profesora Cortés **12:45** psicología Profesor Herrera	**8:30** biología **10:15** inglés **1:15** arte Profesor Pérez	**9:45** historia **12:45** psicología	**8:30** biología **10:15** inglés **1:15** arte		

modelo

Estudiante 1: ¿Cuándo tomas biología?
Estudiante 2: Los lunes, miércoles y viernes tomo (*I take*) biología a las ocho y media.
Estudiante 1: ¿Quién es el/la profesor(a)?
Estudiante 2: Es la profesora Morales.

8 **Dibujar** With a classmate, draw and label your campus and classroom. Then take turns describing your illustrations. Answers will vary.

modelo

En esta (*this*) universidad hay diez residencias estudiantiles.
En esta clase hay ocho ventanas.

9 **Entrevistas** Using these interrogatives, create ten original questions you will use to interview two classmates. Then share the results of your interviews with the class. Answers will vary.

¿A qué hora?	¿Cuándo?	¿De dónde?	¿Quién(es)?
¿Cómo?	¿Cuántos/as?	¿Qué?	

10 **Nuevos amigos** During the first week of class, you meet a new student in the cafeteria. Greet your new acquaintance, find out about him or her, and compare class schedules before saying goodbye. Answers will vary.

TEACHING OPTIONS

Groups Have students do Activity 10 in groups, imagining that they are going to meet several new students in the cafeteria and find out about them. Have the groups prepare and present this activity as a skit in front of the class. Give the groups time to prepare and rehearse their skit, and tell them that they will be presenting it without a script or any other kind of notes.

Game Teach the class the word **con** (with). Then have your students write down a few simple sentences that describe their course schedules. Ex: **Los lunes, miércoles y viernes tomo español con la profesora Dávalos. Los martes y jueves tomo arte con el profesor Casas.** Then collect the descriptions and read them to the class. The class should try to guess who wrote each description.

7 Present Ask the whole class a few questions about Manuel Dominguez's schedule. Ex: **¿Qué clases toma Manuel? ¿Quién es la profesora?** Then tell students to model their own schedules on Manuel's. Tell them to follow the Hispanic tradition of listing **lunes** as the first day of the week.

7 Expand Tell students to exchange schedules with a different classmate than the one with whom they did Activity 7. Then have them repeat the activity with the schedule they have received, asking and answering questions in the third person this time. Ex: **—¿Qué clases toma ____? —Los viernes y jueves ____ toma geografía.**

8 Expand Ask volunteers to describe their illustrations to the class.

Successful Language Learning Remind the class that errors are a natural part of language learning. Point out that they shouldn't expect themselves to produce error-free Spanish at this level of study. Emphasize that their spoken and written Spanish will improve if they make the effort to practice.

9 Present Tell students to first write out their questions on strips of paper or index cards. They should then arrange them in a logical order before interviewing their classmates.

10 Warm-up Quickly review basic greetings, courtesy expressions, and introductions taught in the **Lesson 1 Contextos**, pages 2–3. Then have pairs of students complete the activity.

Assignment Have students do the activities in **Student Activities Manual: Workbook**, pages 11–12.

Section goals

In **Fotonovela** students will:

- receive comprehensible input from free-flowing discourse
- learn functional phrases that preview lesson grammatical structures

Instructional Resources
Student Activities Manual: Video Activities 329–330
Video Program (Start: 00:06:10)

Video Synopsis While Álex writes an e-mail, Maite pretends to be a radio reporter and asks Inés and Javier a few questions about school. Álex is shocked that Javier doesn't like computers.

Before Presenting Fotonovela Have students cover the **Expresiones útiles** with a sheet of paper. Then have them scan the captions under the video stills in **Fotonovela** and find two phrases about classes and two phrases that express likes and dislikes. Have volunteers read aloud one of the phrases they found.

Assignment Have students study **Fotonovela** and **Expresiones útiles** as homework.

Warm-up Ask a few basic questions that use the **Expresiones útiles. Ex: ¿Qué clases tomas? ¿Te gusta la clase de _____?**

Present Read the following mini-dialogues aloud. Have students tell you whether each one is about classes, likes and dislikes, or location.

1. **—¿Dónde está la Srta. Ayala?**
—Está cerca de la ventana. (location)
2. **—¿Tomas inglés?**
--No, tomo geografía. (classes)
3. **—¿Te gustan los libros?**
—Sí, me gustan muchísimo. (likes and dislikes)

Continued on page 42

¿Qué clases tomas?

NATIONAL STANDARDS communication cultures

Maite, Inés, Javier y Álex hablan de las clases.

PERSONAJES

MAITE

INÉS

ÁLEX

JAVIER

ÁLEX Hola, Ricardo... Aquí estamos en la Mitad del Mundo. ¿Qué tal las clases en la UNAM?

MAITE Es exactamente como las fotos en los libros de geografía.

INÉS ¡Sí! ¿También tomas tú geografía?

MAITE Yo no. Yo tomo inglés y literatura. También tomo una clase de periodismo.

MAITE Muy buenos días. María Teresa Fuentes, de Radio Andina FM 93. Hoy estoy con estudiantes de la Universidad San Francisco de Quito. ¡A ver! La señorita que está cerca de la ventana... ¿Cómo te llamas y de dónde eres?

MAITE ¿En qué clase hay más chicos?

INÉS Bueno, eh... en la clase de historia.

MAITE ¿Y más chicas?

INÉS En la de sociología hay más chicas, casi un ochenta y cinco por ciento.

MAITE Y tú, joven, ¿cómo te llamas y de dónde eres?

JAVIER Me llamo Javier Gómez y soy de San Juan, Puerto Rico.

MAITE ¿Tomas muchas clases este semestre?

JAVIER Sí, tomo tres: historia y arte los lunes, miércoles y viernes y computación los martes y jueves.

MAITE ¿Te gustan las computadoras, Javier?

JAVIER No me gustan nada. Me gusta mucho más el arte... y sobre todo me gusta dibujar.

ÁLEX ¿Cómo que no? ¿No te gustan las computadoras?

recursos

R	VIDEO Lección 2	VM pp. 329-330

TEACHING OPTIONS

Video Tips General suggestions for using video clips in the classroom can be found on page IAE-13 of the **Instructor's Annotated Edition**.

¿Qué clases tomas? Play the **¿Qué clases tomas?** segment of this video module and have students give you a "play-by-play" description of the action. Write their descriptions on the board. After playing this segment of the video module, give the class a moment to read the descriptions you have written on the board. Then play the **¿Qué clases tomas?** segment a second time so students can add more details to the descriptions on the board, if necessary, or simply consolidate information. Finally, discuss the material on the board with the class and call attention to any incorrect information. Through discussion, help your students prepare a brief plot summary.

INÉS Hola. Me llamo Inés Ayala Loor y soy del Ecuador... de Portoviejo.

MAITE Encantada. ¿Qué clases tomas en la universidad?

INÉS Tomo geografía, inglés, historia, sociología y arte.

MAITE Tomas muchas clases, ¿no?

INÉS Pues sí, me gusta estudiar mucho.

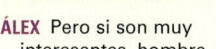

ÁLEX Pero si son muy interesantes, hombre.

JAVIER Sí, ¡muy interesantes!

Enfoque cultural La vida universitaria

Universities in Spanish-speaking countries differ from those in the United States. In most cases students enroll in programs that prepare them for a specific career, rather than choosing a major. The courses for these programs are standardized within each country, so students take few elective courses. The classes themselves are also taught differently. Most are conducted as lectures that meet one or two times weekly. Grades are often based on a scale of one to ten, where five is passing.

Expresiones útiles

Talking about classes

▶ **¿Qué tal las clases en la UNAM?**
How are classes going at UNAM?

▶ **¿También tomas tú geografía?**
Are you also taking geography?

▷ **No, tomo inglés y literatura.**
No, I'm taking English and literature.

▶ **Tomas muchas clases, ¿no?**
You're taking lots of classes, aren't you?

▷ **Pues sí.** *Well, yes.*

▶ **¿En qué clase hay más chicos?**
In which class are there more guys?

▷ **En la clase de historia.**
In history class.

Talking about likes/dislikes

▶ **¿Te gusta estudiar?**
Do you like to study?

▷ **Sí, me gusta mucho. Pero también me gusta mirar la televisión.**
Yes, I like it a lot. But I also like to watch television.

▶ **¿Te gusta la clase de sociología?**
Do you like sociology class?

▷ **Sí, me gusta muchísimo.**
Yes, I like it very much.

▶ **¿Te gustan las computadoras?**
Do you like computers?

▷ **No, no me gustan nada.**
No, I don't like them at all.

Talking about location

▷ **Aquí estamos en...**
Here we are at/in...

▶ **¿Dónde está la señorita?**
Where is the young woman?

▷ **Está cerca de la ventana.**
She's near the window.

Expressing hesitation

▷ **A ver...**
Let's see...

▷ **Bueno...**
Well...

Model pronunciation by reading a few lines from **Fotonovela** aloud, having students repeat after each line. Then have the class read through the entire **Fotonovela**, with volunteers playing the parts of Álex, Maite, Inés, and Javier. See ideas for using the video in **Teaching Options**, page 40.

Comprehension Check Check comprehension of the **Fotonovela** episode by doing Activity 1, **Escoger**, page 42, orally with the whole class.

Suggestion Illustrating points with examples from **Expresiones útiles**, point out that **tomo** and **tomas** are present-tense forms of the verb **tomar** (to take), a regular **-ar** verb whose forms they will learn in this lesson. Also mention that **está** and **estamos** are present-tense forms of **estar** (to be), a verb used to express location and well-being. Then explain that questions can be formed by adding the tag-word **¿no?** to a statement. Finally, explain that **¿qué?** and **¿dónde?** are question words, which are very useful when asking for specific information. Point out that question words have a written accent. Ask the class what question words they remember from Lesson 1 (**¿cómo?**; **¿quién?**). Tell students that they will learn more about all these concepts in the upcoming **Estructura** section.

Assignment Have students do activities 2–4 in **Reacciona a la fotonovela**, page 42, as homework.

TEACHING OPTIONS

Enfoque cultural **¿Qué clases tomas?** Draw students' attention to the first segment of the **Fotonovela**. Point out that when Álex asks how classes are going at the **UNAM**, he's referring to the **Universidad Nacional Autónoma de México**, located in Mexico City. The **UNAM** was founded in 1551. The university is a center of teaching and research in many disciplines, including accounting, architecture, medicine, philosophy and letters, psychology, and zoology.

In addition to being an educational center, the university is famous for its spectacular architecture. The front exterior wall of the library, for example, features a monumental mosaic by Juan O'Gorman. Other buildings are adorned with murals by other important Mexican artists such as Diego Rivera and David Alfaro Siqueiros.

Reacciona a la fotonovela

1 Warm-up Quickly review with the whole class the names of courses, pages 36–37, and the days of the week, page 38, before doing this activity.

2 Expand Give these statements to the class as items 9–12: **9. Hay muchos chicos en mi clase de historia. (Inés) 10. Tomo tres clases... computación, historia y arte. (Javier) 11. Yo tomo tres clases... inglés, literatura y periodismo. (Maite) 12. ¿Yo? Soy de la capital de Puerto Rico. (Javier)**

3 Present/Expand Point out to the class that one of the answers in the word bank will not be used. After your students complete this activity, have them write a sentence that includes the unused word (**sociología**).

4 Possible response
S1: Buenos días.
S2: Hola.
S1: Me llamo Sonia. Y tú, ¿cómo te llamas?
S2: Me llamo José. Mucho gusto.
S1: El gusto es mío. ¿De dónde eres?
S2: Soy de México. ¿Y tú?
S1: Soy de España. Oye, ¿qué clases tomas?
S2: Historia, inglés, literatura y computación.
S1: ¿Te gusta la clase de literatura?
S2: Sí, me gusta muchísimo.
S1: ¿Qué clases no te gustan?
S2: Bueno, no me gusta nada la clase de computación.

4 Expand Ask volunteers to present their conversation in front of the class.

The Affective Dimension Reassure students who seem anxious about speaking that perfect pronunciation isn't necessary for communication and that their pronunciation will improve with practice.

Reacciona a la fotonovela

1 Escoger Choose the answer that best completes each sentence.

1. Maite toma (*is taking*) __c__ en la universidad.
   a. geografía, inglés y periodismo b. inglés, periodismo y geografía
   c. periodismo, inglés y literatura
2. Inés toma sociología, geografía, __a__.
   a. inglés, historia y arte b. periodismo, computación y arte
   c. historia, literatura y biología
3. Javier toma __b__ clases este semestre.
   a. cuatro b. tres c. dos
4. Javier toma historia y __c__ los __c__.
   a. computación; martes y jueves b. arte; lunes, martes y miércoles
   c. arte; lunes, miércoles y viernes

2 Identificar Indicate which person would make each statement. The names may be used more than once.

1. Sí, me gusta estudiar. Inés
2. ¡Hola! ¿Te gustan las clases en la UNAM? Álex
3. ¿La clase de periodismo? Sí, me gusta mucho. Maite
4. Hay más chicas en la clase de sociología. Inés
5. Buenos días. Yo soy de Radio Andina FM 93. Maite
6. ¡Uf! ¡No me gustan las computadoras! Javier
7. Las computadoras son muy interesantes. Me gustan muchísimo. Álex
8. Me gusta dibujar en la clase de arte. Javier

INÉS

JAVIER

MAITE

ÁLEX

NOTA CULTURAL

Álex is a student at **la UNAM,** or **Universidad Nacional Autónoma de México** (*National Autonomous University of Mexico*). Founded in 1551, it is now the largest university in the world, with an annual enrollment of 280,000 students.

3 Completar These sentences are similar to things said in the **Fotonovela.** Complete each sentence with the correct word(s).

la sociología	el arte	la Universidad San Francisco de Quito
la clase de historia	geografía	la Mitad del Mundo

1. Maite, Javier, Inés y yo estamos en... la Mitad del Mundo
2. Hay fotos impresionantes de la Mitad del Mundo en los libros de... geografía
3. Me llamo María Teresa Fuentes. Estoy aquí con estudiantes de... la Universidad San Francisco de Quito
4. Hay muchos chicos en... la clase de historia
5. No me gustan las computadoras. Me gusta más... el arte

NOTA CULTURAL

In the **Fotonovela,** Álex, Maite, Javier, and Inés visit **la Mitad del Mundo** (*Center of the World*), a monument north of Quito, Ecuador. It marks the line at which the equator divides the Earth's northern and southern hemispheres.

4 Conversar Prepare a conversation in which you greet a classmate, introduce yourself, and find out where he/she is from. Find out if he or she likes to study, how many classes he/she is taking this semester, and which classes he/she likes and doesn't like.
Answers will vary.

NATIONAL communication STANDARDS

TEACHING OPTIONS

Small Groups Have your students work in small groups to create a skit in which a radio reporter asks local university students where they are from, what classes they are taking, and which classes they like. Encourage your students to use the phrases in **Expresiones útiles** as much as possible. Have one or two groups present their skit to the class.

Extra practice Have your students close their books and complete these statements with information from the **Fotonovela**. You may present the sentences orally or write them on the board. **1. Hoy estoy con dos _____ de la Universidad San Francisco de Quito. (estudiantes); 2. ¿En qué _____ hay más chicos? (clase); 3. ¿_____ te llamas y de _____ eres? (Cómo; dónde)**

NATIONAL STANDARDS comparisons

Pronunciación

Spanish vowels

a **e** **i** **o** **u**

Spanish vowels are never silent; they are always pronounced in a short, crisp way without the glide sounds used in English.

Álex **clase** **nada** **encantada**

The letter **a** is pronounced like the *a* in *father*, but shorter.

el **ene** **mesa** **elefante**

The letter **e** is pronounced like the *e* in *they*, but shorter.

Inés **chica** **tiza** **señorita**

The letter **i** sounds like the *ee* in *beet*, but shorter.

hola **con** **libro** **don Francisco**

The letter **o** is pronounced like the *o* in *tone*, but shorter.

uno **regular** **saludos** **gusto**

The letter **u** sounds like the *oo* in *room*, but shorter.

Práctica Practice the vowels by saying the names of these places in Spain.

1. Madrid
2. Alicante
3. Tenerife
4. Toledo
5. Barcelona
6. Granada
7. Burgos
8. La Coruña

Oraciones Read the sentences aloud, focusing on the vowels.

1. Hola. Me llamo Ramiro Morgado.
2. Estudio arte en la Universidad de Salamanca.
3. Tomo también literatura y contabilidad.
4. Ay, tengo clase en cinco minutos. ¡Nos vemos!

Refranes Practice the vowels by reading these sayings aloud.

Del dicho al hecho hay un gran trecho.[1]
Cada loco con su tema.[2]

[1] Easier said than done.
[2] To each his own.

recursos

R	SCASS./CD Lección 2	LM p. 224	LCASS./CD Cass. 1B/CD1

TEACHING OPTIONS

Extra practice Supply the class with the names of more places in Spain. Have your students spell each name aloud in Spanish, then ask them to pronounce each one. Avoid names that contain diphthongs. Ex: **Sevilla, Salamanca, Santander, Albacete, Gerona, Lugo, Badajoz, Tarragona, Logroño, Valladolid, Orense, Pamplona, Bilbao.**

Small Groups Have the class turn to the **Fotonovela**, pages 40–41. Have students work in groups of four to read all or part of the **Fotonovela** aloud, focusing on the correct pronunciation of the vowels. Circulate among the groups. and model the correct pronunciation and intonation of words and phrases as needed.

Section Goals

In **Pronunciación** students will be introduced to the Spanish vowels and how they are pronounced.

Instructional Resources
Student Activities Manual: Lab Manual, 224
Student Cassette/CD
Note: The exercises in this section are recorded on the Student Cassette/CD. The explanation and sample words are not.

Present

- Point out that the drawings above the vowels on page 43 indicate the approximate position of the mouth where the vowels are pronounced.
- Draw students' attention to the five vowels listed under the drawings. Model the pronunciation of each vowel. Have students watch the shape of your mouth as you pronounce each vowel and then repeat the vowel after you. Then go through the example words for each vowel, as directed below.
- Write **Álex, clase, nada,** and **encantada** on the board. Pronounce each word and have the class repeat it after you.
- Write **el, ene, mesa,** and **elefante** on the board. Pronounce each word and have the class repeat.
- Pronounce the words **Inés, chica, tiza,** and **señorita** and have students write them on the board.
- Follow the same procedure with the words **hola, con, libro,** and **don Francisco.**
- Write **uno, regular, saludos,** and **gusto** on the board. Have the class repeat each word after you.

Práctica/Oraciones/ Refranes Model the pronunciation of each word or sentence, having students repeat after you.

2 estructura

2.1 The present tense of regular –ar verbs

NATIONAL STANDARDS comparisons

ANTE TODO In order to talk about activities, you need to use verbs. Verbs express actions or states of being. In English and Spanish, the infinitive is the base form of the verb. In English, the infinitive is preceded by the word *to*: *to study, to be*. The infinitive in Spanish is a one-word form and can be recognized by its endings: **-ar, -er,** or **-ir.** In this lesson, you will learn the forms of **-ar** verbs.

–ar verb		*–er* verb		*–ir* verb	
estudiar	*to study*	**comer**	*to eat*	**escribir**	*to write*

Present tense of *estudiar*

		estudiar *(to study)*	
SINGULAR FORMS	yo	estudi**o**	*I study*
	tú	estudi**as**	*you* (fam.) *study*
	Ud./él/ella	estudi**a**	*you* (form.) *study; he/she studies*
PLURAL FORMS	nosotros/as	estudi**amos**	*we study*
	vosotros/as	estudi**áis**	*you* (fam.) *study*
	Uds./ellos/ellas	estudi**an**	*you* (form.)/*they study*

¿Tomas muchas clases este semestre?

Sí, tomo tres.

▶ To create the forms of most regular verbs in Spanish, you drop the infinitive endings (**-ar, -er, -ir**). You then add to the stem the endings that correspond to the different subject pronouns. The following diagram will help you visualize the process by which verb forms are created.

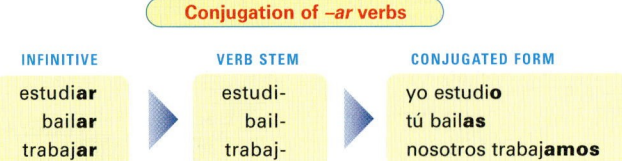

Conjugation of *–ar* verbs

INFINITIVE		VERB STEM		CONJUGATED FORM
estudi**ar**	▶	estudi-	▶	yo estudi**o**
bail**ar**		bail-		tú bail**as**
trabaj**ar**		trabaj-		nosotros trabaj**amos**

Section Goals
In **Estructura 2.1** students will learn:
- the present tense of regular **–ar** verbs
- the formation of negative sentences

Instructional Resources
Student Activities Manual: Workbook, 13–14; Lab Manual, 225

Before Presenting Estructura 2.1 Point out that students have been using verbs and verb constructions since the first day of Spanish instruction: **¿Cómo te llamas?, hay, ser,** and so forth. Write these sentences from **Fotonovela** on the board: **¿Qué clases tomas?** and **Yo tomo inglés.** Ask volunteers to tell what they mean. Ask a student: **¿Qué clases tomas?** Model student answer as **Yo tomo...** Then ask another student to verify information. Ask: **¿Qué clases toma ____? Sí, toma ____.**
Assignment Have students study **Estructura 2.1** and prepare the activities on pages 46–47 (except Activity 1) as homework.

The present tense of regular *–ar* verbs
Present Work through the discussion of verbs in **Ante todo** and explain what an infinitive is.

Present tense of *estudiar*
Present
- Work through the verb endings presented in the chart. Explain that because the verb endings mark the person speaking or spoken about, subject pronouns are usually optional in Spanish.
- Work through explanation of verb stems and endings, writing the meanings of **estudiar, bailar,** and **trabajar** on the board.

Suggestion Remember that **vosotros/as** forms will not be actively practiced in ***Vistas***. You may wish to include **vosotros/as** forms.

TEACHING OPTIONS

Extra Practice Do a pattern practice drill. Write an infinitive (**estudiar, bailar,** or **trabajar**) on the board and ask individual students to provide conjugations for the different subject pronouns and/or names you suggest. Reverse activity by saying a conjugated form and asking students to give the appropriate subject pronoun.

Extra Practice Ask questions, using the verbs **estudiar, bailar,** and **trabajar**. Students should answer in complete sentences. Ask additional questions to get more information. Ex: **—____, ¿trabajas? —Sí, trabajo. —¿Dónde trabajas? —Trabajo en ____. • —¿Quién baila los sábados? —Yo bailo los sábados. —Baila el merengue? • —¿Estudian Uds. mucho? —¿Quién estudia más? —¿Cuántas horas estudias los lunes? ¿los sábados?**

Common –ar verbs

bailar	*to dance*	**hablar**	*to talk; to speak*
buscar	*to look for*	**llegar**	*to arrive*
caminar	*to walk*	**llevar**	*to carry*
cantar	*to sing*	**mirar**	*to look (at); to watch*
comprar	*to buy*	**necesitar**	*to need*
contestar	*to answer*	**practicar**	*to practice*
conversar	*to converse*	**preguntar**	*to ask (a question)*
descansar	*to rest*	**preparar**	*to prepare*
desear	*to want; to wish*	**regresar**	*to return*
dibujar	*to draw*	**terminar**	*to end; to finish*
enseñar	*to teach*	**tomar**	*to take; to drink*
escuchar	*to listen (to)*	**trabajar**	*to work*
esperar	*to wait (for); to hope*	**viajar**	*to travel*
estudiar	*to study*		

COMPARE & CONTRAST

Compare the verbs in the English sentences to the verb in the Spanish equivalent.

Paco **trabaja** en la cafetería.

1. *Paco works in the cafeteria.*
2. *Paco is working in the cafeteria.*
3. *Paco does work in the cafeteria.*

English uses three sets of forms to talk about the present: 1) the simple present (*Paco works*), 2) the present progressive (*Paco is working*), and 3) the emphatic present (*Paco does work*). In Spanish, the simple present can be used in all three cases.

In both Spanish and English, the present tense is also sometimes used to express future action.

Marina **viaja** a Madrid mañana.

1. *Marina travels to Madrid tomorrow.*
2. *Marina will travel to Madrid tomorrow.*

▶ In Spanish, as in English, when two verbs are used together with no change of subject, the second verb is generally in the infinitive.

Deseo hablar con don Francisco.
I want to speak with don Francisco.

Necesitamos comprar cuadernos
We need to buy notebooks.

▶ To make a sentence negative in Spanish, the word **no** is placed before the conjugated verb. In this case, **no** means *not*.

Ellos **no** miran la televisión.
They don't watch television.

Alicia **no** desea bailar ahora.
Alicia doesn't want to dance now.

TEACHING OPTIONS

Heritage Speakers Ask heritage speakers to come up with original sentences about the current semester/quarter that are true for them: what they study, if/where they work, television programs they like to watch, and any other activity that uses a verb found in this section. Ask comprehension questions of the rest of the class to verify the information.

Pairs Ask students to work with a partner to come up with 10 original sentences, using verbs presented in this section. Point out that students may also use many of the vocabulary words from **Contextos** with these verbs. Pairs then share their sentences with the rest of the class to find out how many original sentences can the class come up with?

Common *–ar* verbs
Present Model pronunciation of each infinitive, having students repeat it after you. Then model the **yo** form of several verbs, creating simple sentences about yourself. Additionally, create sentences using **Me gusta...** and several infinitives. Finally, ask students if they like to do some of the activities listed Ex: **¿Te gusta bailar?** If students don't like to do a certain activity, they should answer negatively. Ex: **No me gusta bailar.** Ask other students to verify whether their classmates do certain activities or not. Ex: **¿____ baila mucho? No, ____ no baila.** and so forth.

Compare & Contrast
Present Work through the explanation in the box. Explain that the simple present tense in Spanish is the equivalent of the three present tense forms of English. Model sentences and give a few additional examples, asking students for the three possible equivalents in English.

Present/Expand
- Work through explanation of a conjugated verb followed by an infinitive, writing additional examples on the board. Model additional sentences with **Me gusta..., ¿Te gusta... ?,** and **Espero...** and infinitives.
- Model negative sentences, writing additional ones on the board. Explain that, when answering questions negatively, **no** must be used twice. To practice this, ask questions of students that will most likely result in negative answers. Ex: **—____, ¿bailas el tango? —No, no bailo el tango.**

Present
- Point out the lack of subject pronouns and the use of the double **no** in the photo captions.
- Model clarification/contrast sentences as well as those that show emphasis. Give a few additional statements in which you contrast and emphasize. Use **sí** to give further emphasis. Ex: —____, **¿te gusta bailar? —No, no me gusta bailar.** —____ **no baila. Yo sí bailo.**
- Point out the position of subjects and subject pronouns with regard to the verbs in positive and negative sentences. You may also want to point out and contrast Spanish and English regarding the position of subjects and subject pronouns in questions. Ex: **¿Dónde trabaja Maite?** contrasted with *Where does Maite work?* (This is formally presented in **Estructura 2.2.**)

Expand Have students open to **Fotonovela** on pages 40–41. Ask brief questions about the characters using verbs from this lesson. Ex: **¿Qué clases toma Maite? ¿Dónde trabaja ella? ¿Qué estudia Javier?** and so forth.

Close Consolidate entire section by doing **¡Inténtalo!** with the whole class.

¿Hablas español?
No, no hablo español.

Note that no subject pronouns were used in the Spanish conversation depicted above. Spanish speakers often omit them because the verb endings indicate who the subject is. In Spanish, subject pronouns are used for emphasis, clarification, or contrast, as in the examples below.

Clarification/Contrast

—¿Qué enseñan **ellos**?
What do they teach?

—**Ella** enseña arte y **él** enseña física.
She teaches art, and he teaches physics.

Emphasis

—¿Quién desea trabajar hoy?
Who wants to work today?

—**Yo** no deseo trabajar hoy.
I don't want to work today.

¡ATENCIÓN!

The Spanish verbs **buscar, escuchar, esperar,** and **mirar** do not need to be followed by prepositions as they do in English.

Busco la tarea.
I'm looking for the homework.

Escucho la música.
I'm listening to the music.

Espero las noticias.
I'm waiting for the news.

Miro la pizarra.
I'm looking at the blackboard.

¡INTÉNTALO! Provide the present tense forms of these verbs. The first items have been done for you.

hablar

1. Yo ___hablo___ español.
2. Ellos ___hablan___ español.
3. Inés ___habla___ español.
4. Nosotras ___hablamos___ español.
5. Tú ___hablas___ español.
6. Los estudiantes ___hablan___ español.
7. Ud. ___habla___ español.
8. Javier y yo ___hablamos___ español.

trabajar

1. Uds. ___trabajan___ mucho.
2. Juanita y yo ___trabajamos___ mucho.
3. Nuestra profesora ___trabaja___ mucho.
4. Tú ___trabajas___ mucho.
5. Yo ___trabajo___ mucho.
6. Las chicas ___trabajan___ mucho.
7. Él ___trabaja___ mucho.
8. Tú y Álex ___trabajan___ mucho.

desear

1. Ud. ___desea___ viajar.
2. Yo ___deseo___ viajar.
3. Nosotros ___deseamos___ viajar.
4. Lourdes y Luz ___desean___ viajar.
5. Tú ___deseas___ viajar.
6. Ella ___desea___ viajar.
7. Marco y yo ___deseamos___ viajar.
8. Uds. ___desean___ viajar.

TEACHING OPTIONS

Video Show the video again to give students additional input containing verbs and verb forms. Stop the video where appropriate to discuss how certain verbs were used and to ask comprehension questions.

Game Divide the class into two teams. Indicate one team member at a time, alternating between teams. Give a verb in its infinitive form and name a subject pronoun that the team member should give. Give a point per correct answer. Deduct a point for each wrong answer. The team with the most points at the end of play wins.

Práctica

1 **Me gusta...** Get together with a classmate and take turns asking each other if you like these activities.

¿Te gusta...? *Do you like...?* **Sí, me gusta...** *Yes, I like...*

bailar	escuchar música rock	trabajar
cantar	mirar la televisión	viajar
dibujar	practicar el español	estudiar

modelo

tomar el autobús

Estudiante 1: *¿Te gusta tomar el autobús?*

Estudiante 2: *Sí, me gusta tomar el autobús. / No, no me gusta tomar el autobús.*

AYUDA

Spanish **no** translates to both *no* and *not* in English. In negative answers to questions, you will need to use **no** twice:

¿Estudias geografía?

No, no estudio geografía.

2 **Completar** Complete the conversation with the appropriate forms of the verbs. Then act it out with a partner.

JUAN ¡Hola, Linda! ¿Qué tal las clases?

LINDA Bien. __Tomo__ (tomar) tres clases... química, biología y computación. Y tú, ¿cuántas clases __tomas__ (tomar)?

JUAN __Tomo__ (tomar) cuatro... sociología, biología, arte y literatura. Yo __tomo__ (tomar) biología a las cuatro con el doctor Cárdenas. ¿Y tú?

LINDA Lily, Alberto y yo __tomamos__ (tomar) biología a las diez, con la profesora Garza.

JUAN ¿__Estudian__ (estudiar) ustedes mucho?

LINDA Sí, porque hay muchos exámenes. Alberto y yo __estudiamos__ (estudiar) dos horas juntos todos los días (*together every day*).

JUAN ¿Lily no __estudia__ (estudiar) con ustedes?

LINDA Shhh... no... ella __estudia__ (estudiar) con su novio (*boyfriend*), Arturo.

3 **Oraciones** Form sentences using the words provided. Remember to conjugate the verbs and add any other necessary words.

1. Uds. / practicar/ vocabulario Uds. practican el vocabulario.
2. (Yo) desear / practicar / verbos / hoy Deseo practicar los verbos hoy.
3. ¿Preparar (tú) / tarea? ¿Preparas la tarea?
4. Clase de español / terminar / once La clase de español termina a las once.
5. ¿Qué / buscar / Uds.? ¿Qué buscan Uds.?
6. (Nosotros) buscar / pluma Buscamos una pluma.
7. (Yo) comprar / computadora Compro una computadora.
8. Mi (*My*) compañera de cuarto desear / regresar / lunes
   Mi compañera de cuarto regresa el lunes.
9. Ella / bailar / y / cantar / muy bien Ella baila y canta muy bien.
10. Jóvenes / desear / descansar / ahora Los jóvenes desean descansar ahora.

1 Warm-up Before beginning activity, give a two–three minute oral rapid-response drill. Give infinitives and call on students to give the conjugated form for the subjects you name.

1 Present With a student, model pronunciation of sample questions and model responses.

1 Suggestion If students ask about the definite article in **practicar el español,** explain the definite article is generally used with the names of languages except after the verbs **hablar, escribir,** and the preposition **en.**

1 Expand Ask questions of students at random and have them answer as they did with their partner.

2 Expand Go over the answers quickly in class, then ask several pairs of students to read the dialogue before the class.

3 Present Explain that these items are known as "dehydrated" sentences. Point out to students that they will need to conjugate the verbs and add missing articles and other words to complete dehydrated sentences. Tell them that subject pronouns in parentheses are not included in the completed sentences. Model completion of the first sentence for the class. Ask volunteers to give complete sentences orally.

3 Expand Ask questions that involve the people and items from the activity. Students answer in complete sentences. Ex: **—¿Quiénes practican el vocabulario? —Nosotros practicamos el vocabulario.**

TEACHING OPTIONS

Pairs Have individual students write five dehydrated sentences and exchange them with a partner who will complete them. After pairs have completed their sentences, ask volunteers to share some of their dehydrated sentences. Write them on the board and have the whole class "rehydrate" them.

Listening Comprehension Prepare short descriptions of five easily recognizable people. Write their names on the board in random order. Then read your descriptions, having students match the description to the appropriate name. Ex: **Ella canta, baila y viaja mucho. (Jennifer López)**

4 Present/Expand Model pronunciation of the model sentence. Encourage students to offer additional descriptions of activities seen in the drawings and to give an additional description based on the picture. Ex: **La profesora habla en clase. Hay números y letras en la pizarra y un libro en la mesa.**

4 Expand Ask volunteers to share their descriptions of the drawings.

5 Present Remind students of the basic rules of charades.

5 Expand Instead of having students working in groups, you may want to split the class into two teams with volunteers from each team acting out the charades. Give a point to a team for correctly guessing the charade. Deduct a point for incorrect guesses. The team with the most points at the end of play wins.

6 Present Point out that, in addition to practicing **–ar** verbs, this activity recycles and reviews material from **Lección 1**: greetings, leave-takings, and telling time. Give students several minutes to plan their conversation before they begin speaking.

6 Expand Have pairs of students present their conversations in front of the class.

Assignment Have students do activities in **Student Activities Manual: Workbook**, pages 13–14.

Comunicación

4 **Describir** With a partner, describe what you see in the pictures using the given verbs. Answers will vary.

modelo

enseñar

La profesora enseña química.

1. caminar, hablar, llevar

2. buscar, descansar, estudiar

3. dibujar, cantar, escuchar

4. llevar, tomar, viajar

5 **Charadas** In groups of three students, play a game of charades using the verbs in the word bank. For example, if someone is studying, you say "**Estudias.**" The first person to guess correctly acts out the next charade. Answers will vary.

mirar	conversar	enseñar	caminar	preguntar
bailar	dibujar	descansar	escuchar	cantar

Síntesis

6 **Conversación** Get together with a classmate and pretend that you are friends who have not seen each other on campus for a few days. Have a conversation in which you catch up on things. Mention how you're feeling, what classes you're taking, what days and times you have classes, and what classes you like and don't like. Answers will vary.

TEACHING OPTIONS

Extra Practice Have students write a description of themselves made up of activities they like or don't like to do, using sentences containing **me gusta...** and **no me gusta...** . Collect the descriptions and read a few of them to the class. Have the class guess who wrote each description.

Game Play **Concentración**. Write an infinitive from this lesson on each of eight cards. On another eight cards, draw or paste a picture that illustrates the action of each infinitive. Place the cards face-down in four rows of four. Play with even-numbered groups of students. In pairs, students select two cards. If the two cards match, the pair keeps them. If the cards don't match, students replace them in their original position. The pair with the most cards at the end wins.

2.2 Forming questions in Spanish

ANTE TODO There are three basic ways to ask questions in Spanish. Can you guess what they are by looking at the photos and photo captions on this page?

¿Dibujas mucho?
Las computadoras son muy interesantes, ¿no?
¿También tomas tú geografía?

CONSEJOS

With a partner, take turns saying the example statements and questions on this page out loud. With books closed, your partner should guess whether you are making a statement or asking a question. Make sure to raise the pitch of your voice at the end of the questions. Then take turns making up statements of your own and turning them into questions, using all three of the methods described on this page.

- One way to form a question is to raise the pitch of your voice at the end of a declarative sentence. When writing any question in Spanish, be sure to use an upside down question mark (**¿**) at the beginning and a regular question mark (**?**) at the end of the sentence.

Statement	Question
Uds. trabajan los sábados. *You work on Saturdays.*	¿Uds. trabajan los sábados? *Do you work on Saturdays?*
Miguel busca un mapa. *Miguel is looking for a map.*	¿Miguel busca un mapa? *Is Miguel looking for a map?*

- As in English, you can form a question by inverting the order of the subject and the verb of a declarative statement. The subject may even be placed at the end of the sentence.

Statement	Question
SUBJECT VERB **Uds. trabajan** los sábados. *You work on Saturdays.*	VERB SUBJECT ¿**Trabajan Uds.** los sábados? *Do you work on Saturdays?*
SUBJECT VERB **Carlota regresa** a las seis. *Carlota returns at six.*	VERB SUBJECT ¿**Regresa** a las seis **Carlota**? *Does Carlota return at six?*

- Questions can also be formed by adding the tags **¿no?** or **¿verdad?** at the end of a statement.

Statement	Question
Uds. trabajan los sábados. *You work on Saturdays.*	Uds. trabajan los sábados, **¿verdad?** *You work on Saturdays, right?*
Carlota regresa a las seis. *Carlota returns at six.*	Carlota regresa a las seis, **¿no?** *Carlota returns at six, doesn't she?*

TEACHING OPTIONS

Extra Practice/Pairs Write 8–10 statements on the board. Have students convert the statements into questions by inverting subject/verb order. Students can work in pairs to write their questions. When they have finished, ask volunteers to present ther questions to the class. Model rising intonation and inverting subject/verb order in the questions. Have the class pronounce the questions after you.

Extra Practice Using the same 8–10 statements on the board from the activity above, ask students to say them aloud using tag questions. Add a few negative statements to the statements on the board so that students will have to use **¿verdad?** as a tag question.

Section Goals

In **Estructura 2.2** students will be introduced to:
- forming questions in Spanish
- rising and falling intonation in questions and statements
- tag questions
- interrogative words

Instructional Resources
Student Activities Manual: Workbook, 15–16; Lab Manual, 226
Hoja de actividades 3

Before Presenting Estructura 2.2 Review questions that students already know, such as: **¿Cómo te llamas? ¿Qué clases tomas?** Ask students to suggest others. Tell them they will now learn three ways of forming questions in Spanish.
Assignment Have students study **Estructura 2.2** and prepare the activities on pages 50–51 (except Activity 2) as homework.

Forming questions in Spanish
Present
- Model the pronunciation and intonation of the questions in the photo captions.
- Model the pronunciation of each example statement and question. Point out that this type of question signals a yes-no response.
- Explain that a more common way to form questions in Spanish is to invert the order of the subject and verb. Model pronunciation of the example sentences and give a few more.
- Point out the use of tag questions. Explain that **¿no?** can only be used when the first part of the sentence does not include a negative statement. Use **¿verdad?** when a negative statement is given. Ex: **No trabajan hoy, ¿verdad?**
- Draw attention to the Spanish inverted question mark. Clarify that it does not necessarily appear at the beginning of the sentence.

Question words

Interrogative words

¿Cómo?	*How?*	**¿Adónde?**	*Where (to)?*
¿Cuál?, ¿Cuáles?	*Which?; Which one(s)?*	**¿De dónde?**	*From where?*
¿Cuándo?	*When?*	**¿Por qué?**	*Why?*
¿Qué?	*What?; Which?*	**¿Cuánto/a?**	*How much?*
¿Dónde?	*Where?*	**¿Cuántos/as?**	*How many?*
		¿Quién?, ¿Quiénes?	*Who?*

▸ To ask a question that requires more than a simple *yes* or *no* answer, an interrogative word is used.

¿**Cuál** de ellos estudia en la biblioteca?
Which of them studies in the library?

¿**Cuándo** descansan Uds.?
When do you rest?

¿**Cuántos** estudiantes hablan español?
How many students speak Spanish?

¿**Dónde** trabaja Ricardo?
Where does Ricardo work?

¿**Qué** clases tomas?
What classes are you taking?

¿**Adónde** caminamos?
Where are we walking?

¿**De dónde** son Álex y Javier?
Where are Alex and Javier from?

¿**Por qué** necesitas hablar con ella?
Why do you need to talk to her?

¿**Quién** enseña la clase de arte?
Who teaches the art class?

¿**Cuánta** tarea hay?
How much homework is there?

▸ When pronouncing this type of question, the pitch of your voice falls at the end of the sentence.

¿**Cómo** llegas a clase?
How do you get to class?

¿**Por qué** necesitas estudiar?
Why do you need to study?

CONSÚLTALO

¿Qué? and ¿cuál(es)? You will learn more about the difference between **qué** and **cuál** in Lesson 9, section 2.4, p. 280.

¡INTÉNTALO! Make questions out of these statements. Use intonation in column 1 and the tag **¿no?** in column 2. The first item has been done for you.

Statement	Intonation	Tag questions
1. Hablas inglés.	¿Hablas inglés?	Hablas inglés, ¿no?
2. Trabajamos mañana.	¿Trabajamos mañana?	Trabajamos mañana, ¿no?
3. Uds. desean bailar.	¿Ustedes desean bailar?	Ustedes desean bailar, ¿no?
4. Raúl estudia mucho.	¿Raúl estudia mucho?	Raúl estudia mucho, ¿no?
5. Enseño a las nueve.	¿Enseño a las nueve?	Enseño a las nueve, ¿no?
6. Luz mira la televisión.	¿Luz mira la televisión?	Luz mira la televisión, ¿no?
7. Los chicos descansan.	¿Los chicos descansan?	Los chicos descansan, ¿no?
8. Él prepara la prueba.	¿Él prepara la prueba?	Él prepara la prueba, ¿no?
9. Tomamos el autobús.	¿Tomamos el autobús?	Tomamos el autobús, ¿no?
10. Necesito una pluma.	¿Necesito una pluma?	Necesito una pluma, ¿no?

Question Words: Interrogative Words
Present/Expand

- Model pronunciation of interrogative words, asking questions using each one. Ex: **¿Cómo estás? ¿Cuál es tu clase favorita?** and so forth.
- Draw attention to written accent marks on interrogative words.
- Point out that while **¿qué?** and **¿cuál?** both mean what? or which?, they are not used interchangeably in Spanish. The question **¿qué?** generally precedes a noun while **¿cuál?** is typically used with a verb. Compare and contrast the following: **¿Qué clase te gusta? ¿Cuál es tu clase favorita?** Write similar questions on the board but leave out the interrogative word. Ask students to tell whether **¿qué?** or **¿cuál?** is used for each.
- Point out plurals for **¿cuáles?** and **¿quiénes?** and give examples for each.
- Explain that the answer to the question **¿por qué?** is **porque**.
- Point out singular/plural and masculine/feminine variants for **¿cuánto/a?** and **¿cuántos/as?** Explain their use. Ex: **¿Cuánta tarea hay? ¿Cuántos libros hay?**
- Model pronunciation of example sentences, asking similar questions of students. Ex: ____, **¿dónde trabajas?** Ask other students for verification of their classmates' answers. Ex: ____ **trabaja en** ____.
- Emphasize that falling intonation when using interrogative words signals an information response. Model pronunciation, asking students to repeat after you.

Close Consolidate entire section by doing **¡Inténtalo!** with the whole class.

TEACHING OPTIONS

Video Show the video again to give students more input on forming questions and interrogative words. Stop the video where appropriate to discuss how certain questions, including tag questions, are formed. Have students focus on characters' rising and falling intonation in questions and statements.

Heritage Speakers Ask Spanish speakers to give original statements and questions at random. Have the rest of the class determine whether each sentence is a statement or a question.

Pairs Give pairs of students five minutes to write original questions using as many interrogative words as they can. Can any group come up with questions using all interrogative words?

Práctica

1 **Preguntas** Change these sentences into questions by inverting the word order.

modelo

Ernesto habla con el señor Gómez.
¿Habla Ernesto con el señor Gómez? / ¿Habla con el señor Gómez Ernesto?

1. La profesora prepara la prueba.
   ¿Prepara la profesora la prueba? / ¿Prepara la prueba la profesora?
2. Sandra y yo necesitamos estudiar.
   ¿Necesitamos Sandra y yo estudiar? / ¿Necesitamos estudiar Sandra y yo?
3. Los chicos practican el vocabulario.
   ¿Practican los chicos el vocabulario? / ¿Practican el vocabulario los chicos?
4. Jaime termina la tarea.
   ¿Termina Jaime la tarea? / ¿Termina la tarea Jaime?
5. Tú escuchas la radio. ¿Escuchas tú la radio? / ¿Escuchas la radio tú?

2 **El escritorio** Get together with a partner and take turns asking questions about each other's desks. Answers will vary.

modelo

Estudiante 1: *Hay un libro en el escritorio, ¿verdad?*
Estudiante 2: *No, no hay un libro en el escritorio.*

Estudiante 1: *¿Cuántos cuadernos hay en el escritorio?*
Estudiante 2: *Hay un cuaderno en el escritorio.*

3 **Completar** Irene and Manolo are chatting in the library. Complete their conversation with the appropriate questions. Answers will vary.

AYUDA

Notice the difference between **¿por qué?**, which is written as two words and has an accent, and **porque**, which is written as one word:

¿por qué? *why?*
porque *because*

IRENE Hola, Manolo. ¿Cómo estás?/¿Qué tal?
MANOLO Bien, gracias. ¿Y tú?
IRENE Muy bien. ¿Qué hora es?
MANOLO Son las nueve.
IRENE ¿Qué estudias?
MANOLO Estudio historia.
IRENE ¿Por qué?
MANOLO Porque hay un examen mañana.
IRENE ¿Te gusta la clase?
MANOLO Sí, me gusta mucho la clase.
IRENE ¿Quién enseña la clase?
MANOLO El profesor Padilla enseña la clase.
IRENE ¿Tomas psicología este semestre?
MANOLO No, no tomo psicología este semestre.
IRENE ¿A qué hora regresas a la residencia?
MANOLO Regreso a la residencia a las once.
IRENE ¿Deseas tomar una soda?
MANOLO No, no deseo tomar una soda. ¡Deseo estudiar!

1 Present Model the pronunciation of the model statement and questions. Ask students to give both ways of forming questions for each item. Explain that the last element in a question is in the emphatic position, thus **¿Habla Ernesto con el Sr. Gómez?** and **¿Habla con el Sr. Gómez Ernesto?** have different emphases. You may wish students to do this activity with a partner, having them take turns making the statements and converting them into questions.

1 Expand Have students add tag questions to the statements. Then have them convert the statements into negative sentences and add the tag question **¿verdad?**

2 Present Model pronunciation of the model conversation with a student.

2 Expand Have pairs talk about what is in or on other items and places. Suggestions: **la mochila, la clase, la pizarra**.

3 Warm-up To prepare students for the activity, have them brainstorm possible topics of conversation between two students in the library.

3 Present You may wish to have students do this in pairs, taking turns asking and answering the questions.

3 Expand Have pairs of students create a similar conversation, replacing the answers with items that are true for them. Then ask volunteer pairs to present their conversations to the class.

TEACHING OPTIONS

Heritage Speakers/Pairs Ask students in the class to interview heritage speakers, whether in the class or outside. Students should prepare questions about who the person is, if/where he or she works and when, what he or she studies and why, and so forth. Have students present to the rest of the class the information they gather in the interviews.

Large Groups Divide the class into two groups. To each member of one group give a strip of paper with a question on it. Ex: **¿Cuántos estudiantes hay en la clase?** To each member of the other group give an answer. Ex: **Hay treinta estudiantes en la clase.** Have students find their partner. When you write the questions and answers, be careful that each question has only one possible answer.

4 Present This is the first activity in which the **Hojas de actividades** are used. Explain to students that they can use the **Hojas** to complete the corresponding activities.

4 Present Explain that this is a signature-search activity. Students must actively approach their classmates and ask them the questions they created from the **Categorías** column. When they find someone who answers a question affirmatively, that student signs his or her name in the **Nombres** column.

4 Expand Ask students who some of the people who signed their names next to particular activities are. Then ask that student questions to expand on the information given. Ex: **¿Quién estudia computación? Ah, ¿sí? ____ estudia computación. ¿Dónde estudias computación, ____? ¿Quién es el profesor/la profesora?** and so forth.

5 Present Explain to students that they must give their answers in the form of a question, usually beginning with **¿qué?** or **¿quién(es)?** Model pronunciation of the model conversations with another student.

5 Expand You may wish to play this with the entire class, selecting a few students to play the contestants and to "buzz in" their answers.

6 Warm-up/Suggestion Brainstorm ideas by calling on students to suggest interview questions and by writing them on the board. You may wish to have students prepare their interview questions as homework in preparation for an in-class interview session.

Assignment Have students do activities in **Student Activities Manual: Workbook,** pages 15–16.

Comunicación

NATIONAL communication STANDARDS

4 **Encuesta** Your instructor will give you a worksheet. Change the categories in the first column into questions, then use them to survey your classmates. Find at least one person for each category. Be prepared to report the results of your survey to the class.
Answers will vary.

Categorías	Nombres
1. Estudiar computación	
2. Tomar una clase de psicología	
3. Dibujar bien	
4. Cantar bien	
5. Escuchar música clásica	
6. Escuchar jazz	
7. Hablar mucho en clase	
8. Desear viajar a España	

5 **Un juego** (*A game*) In groups of four or five, play a game of *Jeopardy.*® Each person has to write two clues. Then take turns reading the clues and guessing the question. The person who guesses correctly reads the next clue. Answers will vary.

Es algo que...	Es un lugar donde...	Es una persona que...
It's something that...	*It's a place where...*	*It's a person that...*

modelo

Estudiante 1: Es un lugar donde estudiamos.
Estudiante 2: ¿Qué es la biblioteca?

Estudiante 1: Es algo que escuchamos.
Estudiante 2: ¿Qué es la música?

Estudiante 1: Es un actor de España.
Estudiante 2: ¿Quién es Antonio Banderas?

NOTA CULTURAL

Pedro Almodóvar is an award-winning film director from Spain. His films are full of both humor and melodrama, and their controversial subject matter has often sparked great debate. His 1999 film **Todo sobre mi madre** (*All About My Mother*) received an Oscar for Best Foreign Film and Best Director at the Cannes Film Festival.

Síntesis

NATIONAL communication STANDARDS

6 **Entrevista** Imagine that you are a reporter for the school newspaper. Write five questions about student life at your school and use them to interview two classmates. Be prepared to report your findings to the class. Answers will vary.

TEACHING OPTIONS

Extra Practice Have students go back to the **Fotonovela** on pages 40–41 and write as many questions as they can about what they see in the photos. Ask volunteers to share their questions as you write them on the board. Then call on individual students to answer the questions.

Listening Comprehension Prepare 6–8 questions. Write their answers, but not the questions, on the board in random order. Then read your questions, having students match the question to the appropriate answer. Ex: **¿Cuándo es la clase de español? (Es los lunes, miércoles y viernes.)**

2.3 The present tense of estar

NATIONAL comparisons STANDARDS

CONSÚLTALO

Present tense of ser
To review forms of **ser**, see Lesson 1, section 1.3, p. 17.

ANTE TODO In Lesson 1 you learned how to conjugate and use the ver **ser** (*to be*). You will now learn a second verb which means *to be*, the verb **estar**. Although **estar** ends in **–ar**, it does not follow the pattern of regular **–ar** verbs. The **yo** form (**estoy**) is irregular. Also, all forms but the **yo** and **nosotros/as** forms have an accented **á**.

Present tense of *estar*

estar (*to be*)

SINGULAR FORMS	yo	est**oy**	*I am*
	tú	est**ás**	*you* (fam.) *are*
	Ud./él/ella	est**á**	*you* (form.) *are; he/she is*
PLURAL FORMS	nosotros/as	est**amos**	*we are*
	vosotros/as	est**áis**	*you* (fam.) *are*
	Uds./ellos/ellas	est**án**	*you* (form.)/*they are*

Hola, Ricardo... Aquí estamos en la Mitad del Mundo.

María está en la biblioteca.

COMPARE & CONTRAST

In the following chart, compare the uses of the verb **estar** to those of the verb **ser**.

Uses of *estar*

Location
Estoy en el Ecuador.
I am in Ecuador.

Inés **está** al lado de Javier.
Inés is next to Javier.

Health
Álex **está** enfermo hoy.
Álex is sick today.

Well-being
—¿Cómo **estás**, Maite?
How are you, Maite?

—**Estoy** muy bien, gracias.
I'm very well, thank you.

Uses of *ser*

Identity
Hola, **soy** Maite.
Hello, I'm Maite.

Occupation
Soy estudiante.
I'm a student.

Origins
—¿**Eres** de España?
Are you from Spain?

—Sí, **soy** de España.
Yes, I'm from Spain.

Time-telling
Son las cuatro.
It's four o'clock.

TEACHING OPTIONS

Extra Practice Give statements in English and have students say if they would use **ser** or **estar** in each. Ex: *I'm at home.* (**estar**) *I'm a student.* (**ser**) *I'm tired.* (**estar**) *I'm glad.* (**estar**) *I'm generous.* (**ser**) and so forth.
Extra Practice Ask students where certain people are or probably are at this moment. Ex: **¿Dónde estás? (Estoy en la clase.) ¿Dónde está el presidente? (Está en Washington, D.C.)** and so forth.

Heritage Speakers Ask heritage speakers whether they know of any instances where either **ser** or **estar** may be used. (They may point out more advanced uses, such as with certain adjectives: **Es aburrido**. vs. **Está aburrido**.) This may help to compare and contrast inherent vs. temporary conditions and qualities.

Section Goals

In **Estructura 2.3** students will be introduced to:
- the present tense of **estar**
- contrasts between **ser** and **estar**
- prepositions of location used with **estar**

Instructional Resources
Student Activities Manual: Workbook, 17–18; Lab Manual, 227

Before Presenting Estructura 2.3 Draw students' attention to the fact that they have been using two Spanish verbs that mean *to be*, **ser** and **estar**, since **Lesson 1**. Ex: **¿De dónde eres, Maite? ¿Cómo estás, Maite?** Ask students to suggest other questions with **ser** or **estar** that they can think of. Explain that they have used **ser** to express peoples' origins and to tell time, and **estar** to express peoples' temporary conditions. Tell them that they are now going to learn all the present-tense forms and some other uses of **estar**, an irregular verb.
Assignment Have students study **Estructura 2.3** and prepare the exercises on pages 54–55 (except **Práctica 3**) for the next class.

The present tense of *estar*
Present With their books closed, ask students to give you the paradigm for the present tense of **estar**. Write it on the board and point out the written accents on all forms except those for **yo** and **nosotros/as**.

Compare & Contrast
Present
- Discuss the three uses of **estar** described here.
- Emphasize that the principal distinction between **estar** and **ser** is that **estar** is used to express temporary conditions (**Álex está enfermo hoy**) and **ser** is used to express inherent qualities (**Álex es inteligente**).

Prepositions of location
Present
- Explain that prepositions of location indicate where one thing or person is in relation to another thing or person: *near, far, on, between, below,* and so forth. Another way to describe a preposition of location is to say that it is just about anywhere a small animal can go, such as *under, over, through, behind,* and so forth.
- Model pronunciation of each preposition and have students repeat after you.
- Read through the explanation and examples of **estar** with prepositions of location, modeling displayed sentences. Point out that **estar** in these instances indicates presence or existence in a place.
- Ask volunteers to read each of the captions for the video stills.

Expand Take a book or other object and place it in various locations in relation to your or another student's desk as you ask individual students about its location. Ex: (placing it on top of your desk) **¿Dónde está el libro? ¿Está cerca o lejos del escritorio de ____? ¿Qué está al lado/a la izquierda del libro?** Work through various locations, eliciting all of the prepositions of location.

Expand Spend about five minutes asking where different students are in relation to each other. Ex: ____, **¿dónde está ____? Sí, está al lado (a la derecha/izquierda, delante, detrás) de ____.**

Close Consolidate entire section by doing **¡Inténtalo!** with the whole class.

Prepositions of location

al lado de	*next to; beside*	**delante de**	*in front of*
a la derecha de	*to the right of*	**detrás de**	*behind*
a la izquierda de	*to the left of*	**encima de**	*on top of*
en	*in; on*	**entre**	*between; among*
cerca de	*near*	**lejos de**	*far from*
con	*with*	**sobre**	*on; over*
debajo de	*below*		

▶ **Estar** is often used with certain prepositions to describe the location of a person or an object.

La clase **está al lado de** la biblioteca.
The class is next to the library.

Los libros **están encima del** escritorio.
The books are on top of the desk.

El laboratorio **está cerca de** la clase.
The lab is near the classroom.

Maribel está **delante de** José.
Maribel is in front of José.

El estadio no **está lejos de** la librería.
The stadium isn't far from the bookstore.

Estamos **entre** amigos.
We're among friends.

Hay muchos estudiantes **en** la clase.
There are a lot of students in the class.

El libro está **sobre** la mesa.
The book is on the table.

¡A ver! La señorita que está cerca de la ventana...

Aquí estoy con cuatro estudiantes de la universidad... ¡Qué aventura!

¡INTÉNTALO! Provide the present tense forms of estar. The first item has been done for you.

1. Uds. ___*están*___ en la clase.
2. José ___está___ en la biblioteca.
3. Yo ___estoy___ en el estadio.
4. Nosotras ___estamos___ en la cafetería.
5. Tú ___estás___ en el laboratorio.
6. Elena ___está___ en la librería.
7. Ellas ___están___ en la clase.
8. Ana y yo ___estamos___ en la clase.
9. Ud. ___está___ en la biblioteca.
10. Javier y Maribel ___están___ en el estadio.
11. Nosotros ___estamos___ en la cafetería.
12. Yo ___estoy___ en el laboratorio.
13. Carmen y María ___están___ en la librería.
14. Tú ___estás___ en la clase.

TEACHING OPTIONS

Extra Practice Name well-known campus buildings and ask students to identify where they are in relation to other buildings. Model sample sentences so students will know how to answer. You may wish to write **la Facultad de** on the board and explain its meaning. Ex: **—¿Dónde está la biblioteca? —Está al lado de la Facultad de Química y detrás de la librería.**

TPR One student starts with a small beanbag or rubber ball. You call out another student identified only by his or her location with reference to other students. Ex: **Es la persona a la derecha de ____.** The student with the beanbag or ball has to throw it to the student identified. The latter student must then throw the object to the next person you identify, and so forth.

Práctica

1 **Completar** Complete this phone conversation between Daniela and her mother with the appropriate forms of **ser** or **estar**.

MAMÁ Hola, Daniela. ¿Cómo __estás__?
DANIELA Hola, mamá. __Estoy__ bien. ¿Dónde __está__ papá? ¡Ya (*already*) __son__ las ocho de la noche!
MAMÁ No __está__ aquí. __Está__ en la oficina.
DANIELA Y Andrés y Margarita, ¿dónde __están__ ellos?
MAMÁ __Están__ en el Restaurante García con Martín.
DANIELA ¿Quién __es__ Martín?
MAMÁ __Es__ un compañero de clase. __Es__ de México.
DANIELA Ah. Y el restaurante García, ¿dónde __está__?
MAMÁ __Está__ cerca de la Plaza Mayor, en San Modesto.
DANIELA Gracias, mamá. Voy (*I'm going*) al restaurante. ¡Hasta pronto!

2 **Escoger** Choose the preposition that best completes each sentence.

1. La pluma está (encima de / detrás de) la mesa. encima de
2. La ventana está (a la izquierda de / debajo de) la puerta. a la izquierda de
3. La pizarra está (debajo de / delante de) los estudiantes. delante de
4. Las sillas están (encima de / detrás de) los escritorios. detrás de
5. Los estudiantes llevan los libros (en / sobre) la mochila. en
6. La biblioteca está (sobre / al lado de) la residencia estudiantil. al lado de
7. España está (cerca de / lejos de) Puerto Rico. lejos de
8. Cuba está (cerca de / lejos de) los Estados Unidos. cerca de
9. Felipe trabaja (con / en) Ricardo en la cafetería. con

3 **¿Dónde está...?** Imagine that you are in the school bookstore and can't find various items. Ask the clerk (your partner) where the items in the drawing are located. Then switch roles. Answers will vary.

modelo

Estudiante 1: ¿Dónde están los diccionarios?
Estudiante 2: Los diccionarios están debajo de los libros de literatura.

1 Warm-up Before beginning the activity, quickly review the uses of **ser** and **estar** as well as the conjugations of each verb.

1 Present Go over the answers with the whole class, indicating individual students to read each sentence. Ask students to explain why they chose **ser** or **estar** in each case.

1 Expand Ask two volunteers to present the conversation to the class.

2 Present Go over the activity orally, converting each statement into an either/or question. Ex: **¿La pluma está encima de o detrás de la mesa?** With their books closed, students should answer with complete sentences.

2 Expand Rework items 1 through 6, asking questions about items in the classroom or places at the university. You may need to point to or identify an item or person if more than one answer is possible. Ex: **¿Qué está encima de la mesa aquí** (point)? **¿Dónde está la** (point) **ventana?** and so forth.

3 Warm-up Quickly have volunteers name the objects they see in the illustration.

3 Present With a student, model the pronunciation of the model conversation.

3 Expand Assign one student the role of clerk (**vendedor(a)**) and another the role of customer (**cliente**). Then name one of the items in the drawing and ask the participants to create a conversation as in the activity. Switch students and roles for maximum class participation.

TEACHING OPTIONS

Extra Practice Use a large world map (one with Spanish labels is best) to ask students where countries and cities are in relationship to each other on the map. Ex: **¿Bolivia está a la derecha del Brasil? Uruguay está más cerca de Chile o del Ecuador? ¿Qué país está entre Colombia y Costa Rica? Está Puerto Rico a la izquierda o a la derecha de la República Dominicana?**

Small Groups Have each group member think of a country or well-known location on campus and describe it with progressively more specific statements. After each statement, the other group members guess what country or location it is. Ex: **Es un país. Está en Europa. Esta cerca de España. Está a la izquierda de Suiza y Italia. Es Francia.**

4 Present Have students read directions as you model pronunciation of the model conversation.

4 Expand After students have worked through the items, ask the same questions of selected individuals. Then expand on students' answers by asking additional questions. Ex: **—¿Dónde estás los lunes a las diez de la mañana? —Estoy en la clase de español. —¿Dónde está la clase de español?** and so forth.

5 Present Give students a minute to look over the drawing and to familiarize themselves with the names and locations of the buildings. Read the directions aloud and model the conversation with another student.

5 Expand Make copies of your university's campus map and distribute them to the class. Ask questions about where particular buildings are. Give yourself a starting point so that you can ask questions with **cerca de** and **lejos de**. Ex: **Estoy en la biblioteca. ¿Está lejos la librería?**

6 Present Give students a total of 10 minutes to conduct the interviews (about 3 minutes per student in each group). Have them jot down notes about their partners' answers.

6 Expand Call on students to relate to the whole class the information obtained in the interviews.

Assignment Have students do activities in **Student Activities Manual: Workbook,** pages 17–18.

Comunicación

4 **¿Dónde estás...?** Get together with a partner and take turns asking each other where you are at these times. Answers will vary.

modelo

lunes / 10:00 a.m.
Estudiante 1: ¿Dónde estás los lunes a las diez de la mañana?
Estudiante 2: Estoy en la clase de español.

1. sábado / 6:00 a.m.
2. miércoles / 9:15 a.m.
3. lunes / 11:10 a.m.
4. jueves / 12:30 a.m.
5. viernes / 2:25 p.m.
6. martes / 3:50 p.m.
7. jueves / 5:45 p.m.
8. miércoles / 8:20 p.m.

5 **La ciudad universitaria** Imagine you are an exchange student at a Spanish university. Tell a classmate which buildings you are looking for and ask if they are near or far away. Your classmate will respond according to the campus map. Answers will vary.

modelo

Estudiante 1: ¿La Facultad (*School*) de Medicina está lejos?
Estudiante 2: No, está cerca. Está a la izquierda de la Facultad de Administración de Empresas.

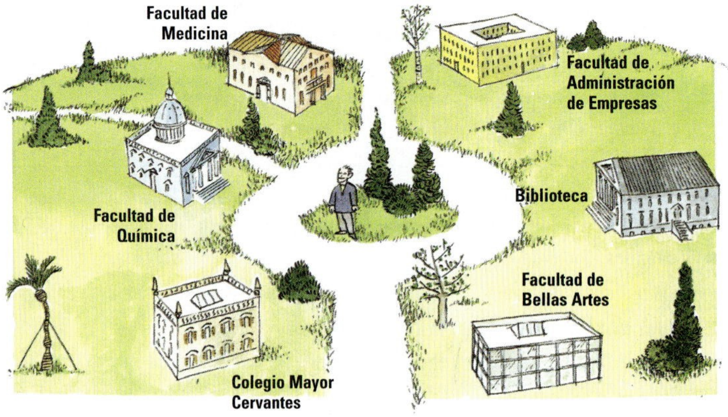

¡LENGUA VIVA!

La Facultad de Filosofía y Letras includes departments, such as language, literature, philosophy, history, and linguistics. Fine Arts can be studied in **la Facultad de Bellas Artes.** In Spain the Business School is sometimes called **la Facultad de Ciencias Empresariales. Residencias estudiantiles** are referred to in Spain as **colegios mayores.**

Síntesis

6 **Entrevista** Use these questions to interview two classmates. Then switch roles. Answers will vary.

1. ¿Cómo estás?
2. ¿Dónde estamos ahora?
3. ¿Dónde está tu (*your*) compañero/a de cuarto ahora?
4. ¿Cuántos estudiantes hay en la clase de español?
5. ¿Quiénes no están en la clase hoy?
6. ¿A qué hora termina la clase hoy?
7. ¿Estudias mucho?
8. ¿Cuántas horas estudias para (*for*) una prueba?

TEACHING OPTIONS

Video Show the video again to give students more input containing **estar** and prepositions of location. Stop the video where appropriate to discuss how **estar** and prepositions of location were used and to ask comprehension questions.

Game Divide the class into two teams. Select a student from the first team to choose an item in the classroom and to write it down. Call on five students from the other team one at a time to ask questions in Spanish about where this item is. The first student can respond only with **sí, no, caliente** (*hot*), or **frío** (*cold*). If a team guesses the item within five tries, award it a point. If not, give the other team a point. The team with the most points wins.

2.4 Numbers 31-100

NATIONAL STANDARDS comparisons

Los números 31 – 100

31	treinta y uno	**37**	treinta y siete	**50**	cincuenta
32	treinta y dos	**38**	treinta y ocho	**60**	sesenta
33	treinta y tres	**39**	treinta y nueve	**70**	setenta
34	treinta y cuatro	**40**	cuarenta	**80**	ochenta
35	treinta y cinco	**41**	cuarenta y uno	**90**	noventa
36	treinta y seis	**42**	cuarenta y dos	**100**	cien, ciento
			(and so on)		

▶ The word **y** is used in most numbers from **31** through **99**. Also, beginning with **31**, most numbers are written as three words.

Hay **ochenta y cinco** exámenes.
There are eighty-five exams.

Hay **cuarenta y dos** estudiantes.
There are forty-two students.

¿En qué clase hay más chicas?

En la de sociología... casi un ochenta y cinco por ciento.

▶ With numbers that end in **uno** (31, 41, etc.), **uno** becomes **un** before a masculine noun and **una** before a feminine noun.

Hay **treinta y un** chicos.
There are thirty-one guys.

Hay **treinta y una** chicas.
There are thirty-one girls.

▶ **Cien** is used before nouns and in counting. The words **un**, **una**, and **uno** are never used before **cien** in Spanish. **Ciento** is used for numbers over one hundred.

¿Cuántos libros hay? **Cientos.**
How many books are there? Hundreds.

Hay **cien** libros y **cien** sillas.
There are one hundred books and one hundred chairs.

¡INTÉNTALO! Provide the words for these numbers.

1. **56** cincuenta y seis
2. **31** treinta y uno
3. **84** ochenta y cuatro
4. **99** noventa y nueve
5. **43** cuarenta y tres
6. **68** sesenta y ocho
7. **72** setenta y dos
8. **35** treinta y cinco
9. **87** ochenta y siete
10. **59** cincuenta y nueve
11. **100** cien
12. **61** sesenta y uno
13. **96** noventa y seis
14. **74** setenta y cuatro
15. **42** cuarenta y dos

TEACHING OPTIONS

Extra Practice Do simple math problems (addition and subtraction) with numbers to 100. Include numbers 0–30 as well, for a well-balanced review. Remind students that **más** = plus, **menos** = minus, and **es** = equals.

Extra Practice Write the beginning of a series of numbers on the board and have students continue the sequence. Ex: **5, 10, 15,...** or **3, 6, 9, 12,...**

Heritage Speakers Ask heritage speakers to give the house or apartment number where they live (they don't have to give the street name). Ask them to give the addresses in tens (**1471 = catorce setenta y uno**). Have volunteers write the numbers they say on the board.

Section Goals

In **Estructura 2.4**, students will be introduced to numbers 31–100.

Instructional Resources
Student Activities Manual: Workbook, 19–20; Lab Manual, 228
Hoja de actividades 4

Before Presenting Estructura 2.4 Review 0–30, having the class count with you. When you reach 30, if students recognize the pattern, signal individual students to count each of the numbers through 39. Count 40 yourself, writing **cuarenta** on the board, and signal students to continue counting through 49. Follow the same procedure to 100.

Assignment Have students study **Estructura 2.4** and prepare **¡Inténtalo!** and **Práctica 1**, pages 57–58, for the next class.

Numbers 31–100
Present

- Model pronunciation of numbers 31–100. Write on the board numbers not included in the chart: 56, 68, 72, and so forth. Ask students to say the number in Spanish.
- Emphasize that from 31 to 99, numbers are written as three words (**treinta y nueve**).
- Work through the explanation of **uno** and its change into **un** and **una**, reminding students that they learned this in **Lesson 1** with **uno** and **veintiuno**.
- Numbers 101 and greater are presented in **Lesson 5**. If students ask about numbers greater than 100, simply continue the counting sequence (**ciento uno, ciento dos**, and so forth), but it is unnecessary to go into number and adjective agreement of hundreds at this point.

Close Consolidate entire section by doing **¡Inténtalo!** with the whole class.

1 Present Go over the activity with the whole class, signalling individual students to read each pair of scores (**puntos**).

1 Expand In pairs, have each student write three additional basketball scores and dictate them to his or her partner. The partner writes them down.

2 Present Model the pronunciation of the mini-dialogue with a volunteer. Have each student within a pair work through at least four numbers, then switch roles.

2 Suggestions
- Point out that when giving telephone numbers, the definite article **el** is used to refer to **el número: Es el noventa y uno,...** Make sure students get used to hearing and giving numbers in that way.
- If students ask, explain the use of two surnames in the Spanish-speaking world. (This is covered in **Lesson 3**.)

2 Expand Ask students at random to give phone numbers you select from the phone book page in the text.

2 Expand Give actual phone numbers (yours, the department's, the bookstore's, and so forth) as a dictation.

3 Present Read the directions aloud. Emphasize how numbers in addresses are generally written in Spanish. Model pronunciation of model sentences with a student. Have each student within a pair work through at least four addresses, then switch roles.

3 Expand Have students dictate their own address as it would be written in the Spanish-speaking world. Ask a volunteer to write down the dictation on the board.

Práctica

1 Baloncesto Provide these basketball scores in Spanish.

1. Ohio State 76, Michigan 65 setenta y seis, sesenta y cinco
2. Florida 92, Florida State 84 noventa y dos, ochenta y cuatro
3. Stanford 58, UCLA 49 cincuenta y ocho, cuarenta y nueve
4. Purdue 81, Indiana 78 ochenta y uno, setenta y ocho
5. Princeton 67, Harvard 55 sesenta y siete, cincuenta y cinco
6. Duke 100, Virginia 91 cien, noventa y uno
7. Kansas 95, Colorado 53 noventa y cinco, cincuenta y tres
8. Texas 79, Oklahoma 47 setenta y nueve, cuarenta y siete
9. Army 86, Navy 71 ochenta y seis, setenta y uno
10. Kentucky 98, Tennessee 74 noventa y ocho, setenta y cuatro

NOTA CULTURAL

Basketball (called **baloncesto** or **básquetbol**) is also a popular sport in many Spanish-speaking countries. Spain, Puerto Rico, Argentina, and Mexico, for example, have national leagues and champion teams often go on to international competitions.

2 Números de teléfono Imagine that you are a telephone operator in Spain. Give the appropriate phone numbers when callers ask for them. Answers will vary.

modelo

Estudiante 1: *¿Cuál es el número de teléfono de José Morales Ballesteros, por favor?*
Estudiante 2: *Es el noventa y uno, noventa y cuatro, cuatro, sesenta y seis, sesenta y dos.*

122 MOR

Morales Ballesteros, José	Venerable Centenares, 22	(91) **944-6662**
Morales Benito, Francisco	Plaza Ahorro, 16	(91) **773-1216**
Morales Borrego, Flora	Mayor, 51	(91) **634-3211**
Morales Calvo, Emilio	Villafuerte, 49	(91) **472-2350**
Morales Campos, María Josefa	Toledo, 35	(91) **419-7660**
Morales Cid, Pedro	Rosal, 98	(91) **773-1382**
Morales Conde, Ángel	Alameda, 67	(91) **944-3915**
Morales Crespo, José Pascual	Fernando de la Peña, 13	(91) **634-7148**
Morales de la Iglesia, Juliana	Buenavista, 80	(91) **834-5238**
Morales Fraile, María Rosa	Plaza March, 74	(91) **834-3371**

NOTA CULTURAL

In Spanish-speaking countries, the number of digits in phone numbers may vary from four to seven; they are often said in pairs. In the past, telephones were not as common as they are today, and smaller towns didn't need many digits in their phone numbers.

3 Direcciones With a partner, practice requesting people's addresses using the list of phone numbers in Activity 2. Note that in Spanish address numbers are usually written after the name of the street. Answers will vary.

modelo

Estudiante 1: *¿Cuál es la dirección (address) de José Morales?*
Estudiante 2: *Es Venerable Centenares, número veintidós.*

TEACHING OPTIONS

Heritage Speakers Ask heritage speakers if they or their parents (uncles, grandparents, great-grandparents, and so forth) use or used both surnames in their daily life. To students who answer affirmatively, ask them to give both of their surnames.

Game Ask for two volunteers and station them at opposite ends of the board so neither one can see what the other is writing. Give a number from 0–100 for them to write on the board. If both students are correct, continue to give numbers until one writes an incorrect number. The winner continues on to play against another student, and so forth.

communication NATIONAL STANDARDS

Comunicación

4

Precios (*Prices*) With a partner, take turns asking how much the items in the ad cost.

modelo

Estudiante 1: Deseo comprar papel.
¿Cuánto cuesta (How much does it cost)?
Estudiante 2: Un paquete cuesta (it costs) cuatro dólares y cuarenta y un centavos.

AYUDA AL INSTANTE

una caja de *a box of*
un paquete de *a package of*

...

Note that in Spanish, a comma is used in place of a decimal period, which is the standard in the U.S.

U.S.	Spanish
$4.95	$4,95
$12.50	$12,50

Conversely, Spanish uses a period instead of a comma to indicate thousands.

U.S.	Spanish
1,500	1.500
50,000	50.000

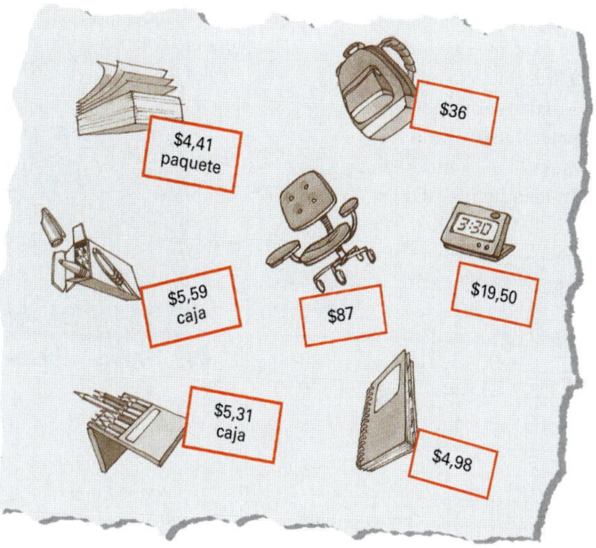

5

Entrevista Find out the telephone numbers and e-mail addresses of four classmates.

Answers will vary.

modelo

Estudiante 1: ¿Cuál es tu (your) número de teléfono?
Estudiante 2: Es el 6-35-19-51.
Estudiante 1: ¿Y tu dirección de correo electrónico?
Estudiante 2: Es jota-Smith-arroba-pe-ele-punto-e-de-u. (jsmith@pl.edu)

AYUDA

arroba @
punto *dot* (.)

communication NATIONAL STANDARDS

Síntesis

6

¿A cuánta distancia...? Your instructor will give you and a partner incomplete charts that indicate the distances between Madrid and various locations. Fill in the missing information on your chart by asking your partner questions. Answers will vary.

modelo

Estudiante 1: ¿A qué distancia está Arganda del Rey?
Estudiante 2: Está a veintisiete kilómetros de Madrid.

4 Present With a volunteer, model the mini-dialogue. Explain the phrase **¿cuánto cuesta...?** Present **dólares** and **centavos**. Emphasize **cuarenta y un centavos**, and so forth.

4 Expand Ask students how much they think common items cost. Suggested items: **un disco compacto, un video,** and so forth.

5 Present
- Model pronunciation of **arroba** and **punto**. Give your own e-mail address as an example, writing it on the board as you pronounce it.
- Point out that **el correo electrónico** means e-mail.

5 Suggestion Explain that the information given in this activity provides students with a way to contact their classmates for study sessions, missed homework, and so forth. If they are reluctant to reveal their personal information, ask them to invent a phone number and e-mail address.

5 Expand Ask volunteers to share their phone numbers and e-mail addresses. Other students write the dictation on the board.

6 Present
- Distribute **Hoja de actividades 4**. Explain that this type of activity is called an information-gap activity. In it each partner has information that the other needs, and the way to get this information is by asking the partner questions.
- Point out and model phrase **está a** [distance] **de...** to express distance.

6 Close Go over answers with the whole class.

Assignment Have students do activities in **Student Activities Manual: Workbook,** pages 19–20.

TEACHING OPTIONS

Small Groups In groups of three or four, have students think of a city or town within a 100-mile radius of your university city or town. They need to figure out how many miles away it is and what other cities or towns are nearby (**está cerca de...**). Then they get together with another group and read their descriptions. The other group has to guess which city or town is being described.

TPR Assign 10 students a number from 0–100 and line them up in front of the class. Call out a number at random, and that student is to take a step forward. When two students have stepped forward, ask them to repeat their numbers. Then ask volunteers to add or subtract the two numbers given. Make sure the resulting sum is not greater than 100.

Section Goals

In **Lectura** students will:
- learn to use text formats to predict content
- read documents in Spanish

Antes de leer

Introduce the strategy. Point out that many documents have easily identifiable formats that can help readers predict content. Have students look at the document in the **Estrategia** box and ask them to name the recognizable elements:
- days of the week
- time
- classes

Ask what kind of document it is. (a student's weekly schedule)

Cognados

Have pairs of students scan **¡Español en Madrid!** for cognates and guess their meanings. Discuss cognates such as the following with the whole class: **cursos intensivos, ofrecen, campus, especializados, elemental, intermedio, avanzado, duración, termina, junio, julio, información, comunicarse**

Examinar el texto

Ask students what type of information is contained in **¡Español, en Madrid!** (It's a brochure for a summer intensive Spanish language program.) Discuss elements of the recognizable format that helped them predict the content, such as headings, list of courses, course schedule with dates.

Assignment Have students read **¡Español en Madrid!** and prepare the exercises in **Después de leer** as homework.

Lectura

Antes de leer

Estrategia

Predicting Content Through Formats

Recognizing the format of a document can help you to predict its content. For instance, invitations, greeting cards, and classified ads follow an easily identifiable format, which usually gives you a general idea of the information they contain. Look quickly at the following text and identify it based on its format.

	lunes	martes	miércoles	jueves	viernes
8:30	biología		biología		biología
9:00		historia		historia	
9:30	inglés		inglés		inglés
10:00					
10:30					
11:00					
12:00					
12:30					
1:00					
2:00	arte		arte		arte

If you guessed that this is a page from someone's weekly appointment book, you are correct. You can now infer that the document contains information about a student's weekly schedule, including days, times, and activities they have planned.

Cognados

With a classmate, make a list of the cognates in the text and guess their English meanings. What do cognates reveal about the content of the document?

Examina el texto

Look at the format of the document entitled ***¡Español en Madrid!*** What type of text is it? What kinds of information do you expect to find in a document of this kind?

¡ESPAÑOL EN MADRID!
UAM
Programa de Cursos Intensivos de Español
Universidad Autónoma de Madrid
Madrid, la capital cultural de Europa, y la UAM te ofrecen cursos intensivos de verano para aprender español como nunca antes.

Después de leer

Correspondencias

Provide the letter of each item in Column B that matches the words in Column A. Two items will not be used.

A

1. profesores f
2. vivienda h
3. Madrid d
4. número de teléfono a
5. Español 2B c
6. número de fax g

B

a. (34) 91 523 4500
b. (34) 91 524 0210
c. 23 junio – 30 julio
d. capital cultural de Europa
e. 16 junio – 22 julio
f. especializados en enseñar español como lengua extranjera
g. (34) 91 523 4623
h. familias españolas

TEACHING OPTIONS

Extra Practice Have students write as homework a weekly schedule (**horario semanal**) of a friend or family member. Ask them to label the days of the week in Spanish and add notes for that person's appointments and activities as well. In class, ask students questions about the schedules they wrote. Ex: **¿Qué clase toma _____ hoy? ¿Trabaja _____ mañaña? ¿Cuántos días trabaja _____esta semana?**

Heritage Speakers Ask Spanish speakers who have attended a university or institution of higher education in the Spanish-speaking world to describe what their schedule there was like, comparing and contrasting it with their schedule now. Invite them to make other comparisons between American institutions of higher education and those in the Spanish-speaking world.

¿Dónde?
En el campus de la UAM, edificio de la Facultad de Filosofía y Letras.

¿Quiénes son los profesores?
Son todos hablantes nativos del español y catedráticos de la UAM especializados en enseñar el español como lengua extranjera.

¿Qué niveles se ofrecen?
Se ofrecen tres niveles básicos:
1. Español Elemental, A, B y C
2. Español Intermedio, A y B
3. Español Avanzado, A y B

Viviendas
Para estudiantes extranjeros se ofrece vivienda con familias españolas.

¿Cuándo?
Este verano a partir del 16 de junio hasta el 10 de agosto. Los cursos tienen una duración de 6 semanas.

Cursos	A partir	Termina
Español 1A	16 junio	22 julio
Español 1B	23 junio	30 julio
Español 1C	30 junio	10 agosto
Español 2A	16 junio	22 julio
Español 2B	23 junio	30 julio
Español 3A	16 junio	22 julio
Español 3B	23 junio	30 julio

Información
Para mayor información, sirvan comunicarse con la siguiente oficina.

Universidad Autónoma de Madrid
Programa de Español como Lengua Extranjera
Ctra. Colmenar Viejo, Km. 15
28049 Madrid, ESPAÑA
Tel. (34) 91 523 4500
Fax (34) 91 523 4623

¿Cierto o falso?

Indicate whether each statement is **cierto** (*true*) or **falso** (*false*). Then correct the false statements.

	Cierto	Falso
1. La Universidad Autónoma de Madrid ofrece (*offers*) cursos intensivos de italiano. *Ofrece cursos intensivos de español.*	❍	✓
2. La lengua nativa de los profesores del programa es el inglés. *La lengua nativa de los profesores es el español.*	❍	✓
3. Los cursos de español son en la Facultad de Ciencias. *Son en el edificio de la Facultad de Filosofía y Letras.*	❍	✓
4. Los estudiantes pueden vivir (*can live*) con familias españolas.	✓	❍
5. La universidad que ofrece los cursos intensivos está en Salamanca. *Está en Madrid.*	❍	✓
6. Español 3B termina en agosto. *Termina en julio.*	❍	✓
7. Si deseas información sobre (*about*) los cursos intensivos de español, es posible llamar al (34) 91 523 4500.	✓	❍
8. Español 1A empieza (*begins*) en julio. *Empieza en junio.*	❍	✓

TEACHING OPTIONS

Variación lexica Explain that in Spanish dates are usually written in the order of day/month/year rather than month/day/year, as they are in the United States. Someone from Mexico with a birthdate of July 5, 1980, therefore, would write his or her birthdate as 5/7/80. To avoid confusion, the month is often written with a roman numeral, 5/VII/80.

Paired Work Provide students with magazines and newspapers in Spanish. Have pairs of students work together to look for documents in Spanish with easily recognizable formats, such as classified ads or advertisements in periodicals or on the Internet. Ask them to use cognates and other context clues to predict the content. Then have partners present their examples and findings to the class. Help them with unfamiliar words and phrases.

Después de leer

Correspondencias

Suggestion You may either go over the answers with the whole class or assign pairs of students to work together to check each other's answers. If students have difficulty matching any pair of items, encourage them to refer to the document to find the answer.

¿Cierto o falso?

Suggestion Go over items 1–8 orally, asking individuals whether each statement is **cierto** or **falso**. Have students correct false statements.

Expand Continue the activity with true/false statements such as these. **1. El campus de la UAM está en la Ciudad de México. (Falso; está en Madrid.) 2. Los cursos terminan en junio. (Falso; terminan en julio y agosto.) 3. Hay un curso de español intermedio. (Falso; hay dos cursos.) 4. Los cursos se ofrecen en el verano. (Cierto) 5. Hay una residencia estudiantil para los estudiantes extranjeros en el campus. (Falso; los estudiantes extranjeros viven con familias españolas.) 6. Hay un número en la universidad para más información. (Cierto) 7. Todos los profesors son hablantes nativos. (Cierto) 8. Los cursos tienen una duración de 12 semanas. (Falso; tienen una duración de 6 semanas.)**

Section Goals
In **Escritura** students will:
- brainstorm, or organize their ideas for writing
- write a description of themselves
- incorporate vocabulary and structures from **Lesson 2**

Tema
Present Copy on the board the brief chat-room description for Alicia Roberts on page 62, leaving blanks instead of the name, major, and university or institution name. At the end, add the sentences **Me gusta** _____ and **No me gusta** _____. Model completing the description orally with your own information and then ask volunteers to complete it with their own information.

Estrategia
Present Discuss information students might want to include in a self-description, recording their suggestions on the board in Spanish. Quickly review structures students will include in their writing, such as **me gusta** and **no me gusta** as well as the first person singular of several verbs, for example: **soy, estoy, tomo, asisto, trabajo, estudio**.

Assignment Have students prepare **Ideas y organización** and **Primer borrador**, page 63, for the next class.

Escritura

Estrategia
Brainstorming

How do you find ideas to write about? In the early stages of writing, brainstorming can help you generate ideas on a specific topic. You should spend ten to fifteen minutes brainstorming and jotting down any ideas about the topic that occur to you. Whenever possible, try to write down your ideas in Spanish. Express your ideas in single words or phrases, and jot them down in any order. While brainstorming, don't worry about whether your ideas are good or bad. Selecting and organizing ideas should be the second stage of your writing. Remember that the more ideas you write down while you're brainstorming, the more options you'll have to choose from later when you start to organize your ideas.

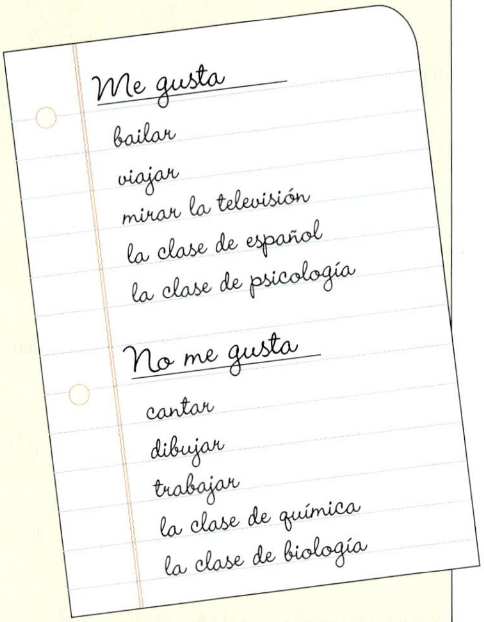

Tema
Una descripción

Write a description of yourself to post in a chat room on a website in order to meet Spanish-speaking people. Include this information in your description.

- Your name and where you are from, and a photo (optional) of yourself
- Your major and where you go to school
- The courses you are taking
- Where you work if you have a job
- Some of your likes and dislikes

TEACHING OPTIONS

Proofreading Activity Copy the following sentences containing mistakes onto the board or a transparency as a proofreading activity to do with the whole class.

1. **¡Hola! Me llama Roberto García y estoy estudiante de lenguas extranjeras.**
2. **La biblioteca es al lado de la Facultad de Medicina, ¿sí?**
3. **Hay treintiún centavos acima de la mesa.**
4. **Sara, necesitas a esudiar más, si deseas a tomar la clase de psicología.**
5. **¿Te no gustas la clase de química, Carlos?**
6. **Los estudiantes escuchar la música rock en español sobre la mesa, ¿verdad?**
7. **¿Porque necesitas ciento dólares, Francisco?**
8. **¿Adónde son las tres chicas de España?**
9. **La residencia es no lejos del gimnasio.**

Plan de escritura

1 Ideas y organización

Spend ten to fifteen minutes brainstorming information to put in your description. Then, on a separate sheet of paper, write the five points from the **Tema** section, leaving some blank space under each point. In a logical order, list under the corresponding points the ideas you just brainstormed. Eliminate ideas that don't pertain to the topic and add any missing information. Try to write your ideas in Spanish; doing so will make your first draft easier.

2 Primer borrador

Using the lists you prepared in **Ideas y organización,** write the first draft of your description.

3 Comentario

Exchange papers with a classmate and comment on each other's work, using these questions as a guide. Begin by mentioning what you like about the person's writing, such as a certain description or the selection of words.

a. Does the description include all necessary information? Is any information extraneous?
b. Does the description include a sufficient number of details?
c. Are the ideas expressed clearly? Do they have the proper focus?
d. Do the ideas flow logically from one to another?
e. Do you have any other suggestions for making the description more interesting or complete?
f. Do you see any spelling or grammatical errors?

4 Redacción

Revise your first draft, keeping in mind your classmate's comments. Also incorporate any new ideas you may have. Before handing in the final version, use these suggestions to help you review your work:

a. Underline each verb and make sure that it agrees with its subject.
b. Check the gender and number of each noun and article.
c. Check your spelling and punctuation.

5 Evaluación y progreso

In groups, take turns reading your descriptions aloud. Point out the best three features of each description, then choose one to read aloud to the class. After your instructor has returned your paper, review the comments and corrections. On a separate sheet of paper, write the heading **Anotaciones para mejorar** (*Notes for improving*) **la escritura,** and list your most common errors so that you can avoid them in the future. Place this list and your corrected description in a folder labeled **Carpeta de trabajos.** This will become your writing portfolio, which you will use to review your progress.

Comentario

Present Go over questions a-f with the whole class so peer readers understand their task. Then have pairs of students exchange descriptions. Allow five minutes for reading and comments. Allow five minutes for discussing comments.

Assignment Have students read **Redacción** as homework. Ask them to rewrite their drafts incorporating the peer comments and following the directions in **Redacción.** Tell them to prepare a clean copy of their final draft to hand in.

Evaluación y progreso

Divide class into groups of five or six students each and give the groups approximately a minute for each student to read his or her description. Then ask one member of each group to read his or her description for the class. Afterward, have students hand in their papers to you.

Writing Sample

Here is a sample self-description that would constitute superior writing achievement.

¡Muy buenos días! Soy José Miguel Gutiérrez. Soy de Nogales, Arizona. Soy estudiante de computación en la Universidad de Arizona. Tomo cuatro clases este semestre. Tomo clases de computación, matemáticas, inglés, y español. Me gusta estudiar, leer y trabajar, pero también me gusta bailar y cantar. También trabajo en la biblioteca. Trabajo los sábados de las ocho a las doce de la mañana.

EVALUATION: Descripción

Criteria	Scale
Content	1 2 3 4 5
Organization	1 2 3 4 5
Use of vocabulary	1 2 3 4 5
Grammatical accuracy	1 2 3 4 5

Scoring	
Excellent	18–20 points
Good	14–17 points
Satisfactory	10–13 points
Unsatisfactory	< 10 points

Section Goals

In **Escuchar** students will:
- listen for cognates in a short paragraph
- answer questions based on the content of a recorded conversation

Instructional Resource
Student Cassette/CD

Preparación
Warm-up Invite students to look at the photo and describe what they see. Guide them to guess where they think Armando and Julia are and what they are talking about.

Estrategia
Script
1. **La democracia es una forma de gobierno.**
2. **A mí me gustan los conciertos, las obras de teatro y la danza.**

Assignment Have students do the activities in **Ahora escucha** and **Comprensión** as homework. Verify the responses to **Ahora escucha** with the whole class. Go over **Preguntas** orally. Ask volunteers to read each completed statement in **Seleccionar.** Ask the questions in **Preguntas personales** of several volunteers.

Ahora escucha
Script
Armando: ¡Hola, Julia! ¿Cómo estás?
Julia: Bien. ¿Y tú, Armando?
Armando: Bien, gracias. ¿Qué tal tus clases?
Julia: Van bien.
Armando: ¿Tomas biología?
Julia: Este semestre no. Pero sí tomo astronomía y geología... los lunes, miercoles y viernes.
Armando: ¿Sólo dos? ¿Qué otras clases tomas?
Julia: Italiano y cálculo, los martes y jueves. ¿Y tú?
Armando: Los lunes, miércoles y viernes tomo antropología, filosofía y japonés. Los martes y jueves tomo italiano y cálculo.
Julia: ¿A qué hora es tu clase de italiano?
Armando: A las nueve, con la profesora Menotti.
Julia: Yo también tomo italiano los martes y jueves con la profesora Menotti, pero a las once.

Escuchar

National communication Standards

Preparación

Based on the photograph, who do you think Armando and Julia are? What do you think they are talking about?

Estrategia
Listening for cognates

You already know that cognates are words that have similar spellings and meanings in two or more languages: for example, *group* and **grupo** or *stereo* and **estéreo.** Listen for cognates to increase your comprehension of spoken Spanish. To help you practice this strategy, you will now listen to two sentences. Make a list of all the cognates you hear.

Ahora escucha

Now you are going to hear Armando and Julia's conversation. Make a list of the cognates they use. Then complete the Spanish sentence with the topic of their conversation.

Armando	Julia
clases, biología	semestre, astronomía
antropología, filosofía	geología, italiano
japonés, italiano	cálculo, clase
cálculo, profesora	italiano, profesora

Based on your knowledge of cognates, decide whether the following statements are **cierto** or **falso.**

	Cierto	Falso
1. Armando y Julia hablan de la familia.	○	✓
2. Armando y Julia toman una clase de matemáticas.	✓	○
3. Julia toma clases de ciencia.	✓	○
4. Armando estudia lenguas extranjeras.	✓	○
5. Julia toma una clase de religión.	○	✓

Comprensión

Preguntas

Answer these questions about Armando and Julia's conversation.

1. ¿Qué clases toma Armando?
   Toma antropología, filosofía, japonés, italiano, y cálculo.
2. ¿Qué clases toma Julia?
   Toma astronomía, geología, italiano, y cálculo.

Seleccionar

Choose the answer that best completes each sentence.

1. Armando toma ___b___ clases en la universidad.
   a. cuatro b. cinco c. seis
2. Julia toma dos clases de ___c___.
   a. matemáticas b. lengua c. ciencia
3. Armando toma italiano y ___b___.
   a. astronomía b. japonés c. geología
4. Armando y Julia estudian ___c___ los martes y jueves.
   a. filosofía b. matemáticas c. italiano

Preguntas personales Answers will vary.

1. ¿Cuántas clases tomas tú este semestre?
2. ¿Qué clases tomas tú este semestre?
3. ¿Qué clases te gustan y qué clases no te gustan?

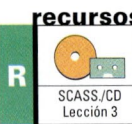

recursos
R — SCASS./CD Lección 3

NATIONAL STANDARDS communication cultures connections communities

Proyecto

Representa a una universidad

Imagine that you are enrolled in a university in Spain as part of a "Year Abroad" program. You're about to return to the United States, and the Spanish university has asked you to be its goodwill ambassador. In this role, you will disseminate information about the university in Spain to your classmates in the United States.

1 Haz un cartel

Create a vibrant and appealing poster that is intended to attract students to come study in your program. Using the research tools found in **Recursos para la investigación** select the institution you would like to represent. Make notes about programs and courses the university offers, and gather photographs that illustrate the school's appeal and the town or city where it is located. Then create your poster, which might include these elements:

- A simple, descriptive title
- A few lines inviting students in the U.S. to study at the university
- Photos of university locations and/or a campus map
- A summary of the courses offered
- Photos and a description of the town where the university is located

2 Presenta la información

Give a brief presentation to your classmates about the Spanish university. Bring your poster and use it as a guide. Try to convince your classmates of the benefits of studying at the Spanish university.

recursos para la investigación

Internet Palabras clave: Spain, Spanish, university, universities	**Comunidad** Exchange students, faculty members, and residents in your community who are from Spain or have lived in Spain
Biblioteca Encyclopedias, almanacs, guidebooks, travel magazines	**Otros recursos** Your school's International Studies Office, the Spanish embassy or consulates of Spain, brochures from travel agencies

EVALUATION: Cartel

Criteria	Scale
Content	1 2 3 4
Comprehensibility	1 2 3 4
Organization	1 2 3 4
Accuracy	1 2 3 4
Visual Appeal	1 2 3 4

Scoring	
Excellent	18–20 points
Good	14–17 points
Satisfactory	10–13 points
Unsatisfactory	< 10 points

Section Goals

In **Proyecto** students will:
- create a poster for a "Year Abroad" program in Spain
- use Spanish as they research and interact with the wider world
- incorporate Spanish in an oral presentation

Before Assigning Proyecto

Students will need approximately a week to complete the project, so at the beginning of that time period, have them open their books to page 65 and glance over **Proyecto**. Explain that they are going to use their research skills to create a poster (**cartel**) that tells about a "Year Abroad" program at a university in Spain.

Haz un cartel Suggestions

- Information on the Internet about Spanish universities will usually appear in Spanish. Tell students to use their knowledge of cognates and the formats of web pages to unlock the meaning of what they find. Sometimes an English translation of all or parts of a web page is available by clicking an icon (frequently a British flag). Encourage students to try to decipher as much as the Spanish page as they can before looking at the translation.
- Remind students to search in both Spanish and English for key words or phrases. Possible Spanish key words: **universidades españoles, estudiantes extranjeros, programa internacional, estudio internacional**

Presenta la información Suggestions

- You may wish to do a few presentations at a time until all students have had a chance to present.
- Display posters around the classroom after students have given their presentations.

España

connections cultures NATIONAL STANDARDS

El país en cifras

- **Área:** 504.750 km^2 (kilómetros cuadrados) o 194.884 millas cuadradas, incluyendo las islas Baleares y las islas Canarias
- **Población:** 39.584.533
- **Capital:** Madrid—5.051.236
- **Ciudades principales:** Barcelona—4.548.222, Valencia—2.149.171, Sevilla—1.727.304, Zaragoza—827.730

SOURCE: Instituto Nacional de Estadística

- **Moneda:** peseta, euro (1/1/02)
- **Idiomas:** español o castellano, catalán, gallego, valenciano, eusquera

Bandera de España

Españoles célebres

- **Miguel de Cervantes,** escritor (1547-1616)
- **Pedro Almodóvar,** director de cine (1949-)
- **Rosa Montero,** escritora y periodista (1951-)
- **Pedro Duque,** astronauta (1963-)
- **Arantxa Sánchez Vicario,** tenista (1971-)

millas cuadradas *square miles* Moneda *Currency* Idiomas *Languages* escritor *writer* cine *film* periodista *reporter* cada año *every year* durante todo un día *all day long* miles *thousands* se tiran *throw at each other* varias toneladas *many tons*

Plaza Mayor en Madrid

La Sagrada Familia

El baile flamenco

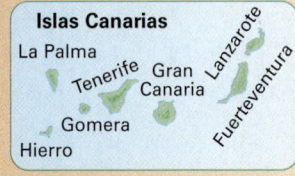

recursos

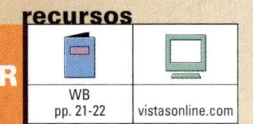

R | WB pp. 21-22 | vistasonline.com

¡Increíble pero cierto!

En Buñol, un pequeño pueblo de Valencia, la producción de tomates es un recurso económico muy importante. Cada año en agosto se celebra el festival de *La Tomatina*. Durante todo un día, miles de personas se tiran tomates unas a otras. Llegan turistas de todo el país, y se usan varias toneladas de tomates.

Section Goals

In **Panorama**, students will receive comprehensible input by reading about the culture and economy of Spain.

Instructional Resources
Student Activities Manual: Workbook, 21–22
Transparencies 7, 8, 15

España

Before Presenting Panorama Have students scan **El país en cifras.** Project **Transparency 15** or have students use the map in their books to find the localities mentioned. Then have the class look at the call-out photos. Ask volunteers to read the captions and translate them. Encourage students to share anything they might know about the subjects of the photos. **Assignment** Have students read **Panorama** and write out the completed sentences in **¿Qué aprendiste?**, page 67, as homework.

Present Ask volunteers to read aloud the items in **El país en cifras**. Model the pronunciation of numbers and dates. After **Idiomas** has been read, associate the regional languages with the larger map by asking questions such as: **¿Hablan catalán cerca de la Costa del Sol? ¿Qué idioma hablan en Madrid? ¿Eusquera es el idioma de Bilbao?** Point out that the names of languages may be capitalized as labels on maps, but are not capitalized when they appear in running text.

Increíble pero cierto In addition to festivals related to economic and agricultural resources, Spain has many festivals rooted in its deep Catholic tradition. Among the most famous is **Semana Santa** (Holy Week) which is celebrated annually in Seville with great reverence and pageantry.

TEACHING OPTIONS

Heritage Speaker The paella, the national dish of Spain, is the ancestor of the popular Latin American dish, **arroz con pollo**. Ask heritage speakers if they know of any dishes traditional in their families that have their roots in Spanish cuisine. Invite them to describe the dish to the class.

Variación léxica Tell students that they may also see the word **eusquera** spelled **euskera** and **euskara**. The letter **k** is used in Spanish only in words of foreign origin. **Euskera,** or **euskara,** is the name of the Basque language in Basque, a language that linguists believe is unrelated to any other known language. **Euskera** is sometimes spelled **eusquera**, following the principles of Spanish orthography. The Spanish name for Basque is **vascuence** or **vasco**.

Lugares • La Universidad de Salamanca

La Universidad de Salamanca, fundada en mil doscientos dieciocho (1218), es la más antigua de España. Más de treinta y cinco mil (35.000) estudiantes toman clases en esta universidad. La universidad está situada en la ciudad de Salamanca, que es famosa por sus edificios históricos, incluyendo puentes romanos y catedrales góticas.

Economía • La Unión Europea

Desde mil novecientos noventa y dos (1992) España participa en la Unión Europea, un grupo de países europeos que trabaja para desarrollar una política económica y social común en Europa. La moneda de los países de la Unión Europea es el euro.

Artes • Velázquez y el Prado

El Prado, en Madrid, es uno de los museos más famosos del mundo. En el Prado hay miles de pinturas importantes, incluyendo obras de Botticelli, el Greco, y de los españoles Goya y Velázquez. *Las Meninas* es la obra más conocida de Diego Velázquez, pintor oficial de la corte real durante el siglo XVII.

Comida • La paella

La paella es uno de los platos más típicos de España. Siempre se prepara con arroz y azafrán, pero hay diferentes recetas. La paella valenciana, por ejemplo, tiene pollo y conejo, y la paella marinera tiene mariscos.

Una playa de Ibiza

¿Qué aprendiste? Completa las frases con la información adecuada.

1. La Unión Europea trabaja para desarrollar una política económica común en Europa.
2. El arroz y el azafrán son ingredientes básicos de la paella.
3. El Prado está en Madrid.
4. La universidad más antigua de España es la Universidad de Salamanca.
5. En 2002, los países de la Unión Europea van a adoptar el euro como su moneda oficial.
6. La ciudad de Salamanca es famosa por sus edificios históricos, tales como (*such as*) los puentes romanos.
7. El gallego es una de las lenguas oficiales de España.

Conexión Internet Investiga estos temas en el sitio **www.vistasonline.com.**

1. Busca (*Look for*) información sobre la Universidad de Salamanca u otra universidad española. ¿Qué cursos ofrece (*does it offer*)? ¿Ofrece tu universidad cursos similares?
2. Busca información sobre un español o una española célebre (por ejemplo, un(a) político/a, un actor, una actriz, un(a) artista). ¿De qué parte de España es, y por qué es célebre?

más antigua *oldest* edificios *buildings* puentes *bridges* Desde *Since* desarrollar *develop* política *policy* común *shared* obras *works* más conocida *best-known* corte real *royal court* siglo *century* Siempre se prepara *It is always prepared* arroz *rice* azafrán *saffron* recetas *recipes* pollo *chicken* conejo *rabbit* mariscos *seafood*

TEACHING OPTIONS

Variación léxica Regional culture and languages have remained strong in Spain despite efforts made in the past to surpress them in the name of national unity. The language that has come to be called *Spanish*, **español,** is the language of the region of north central Spain called **Castilla**. Because Spain was unified under the social and political dominance of the Kingdom of Castille at the end of the Middle Ages, the language of Castille, **castellano**, became the principal language of government, business and literature. Even today one is as likely to hear Spanish referred to by Spanish speakers as **castellano** as **español**. Efforts to suppress the regional languages, though often harsh, were ineffective, and after the death of the dictator Francisco Franco and the devolution of power to regional governing bodies, the languages of Spain were given co-official status with Spanish in the regions where they are spoken.

La Universidad de Salamanca The University of Salamanca hosts many programs for foreign students, and your university foreign-study office may have brochures. One of the oldest univesities in Europe, Salamanca is famous for its medieval buildings and student musical societies called **tunas**.

La Unión Europea Students can use the Internet, a newspaper, or a bank to learn the current exchange rate for both pesetas and euros on the international market.

Velázquez y el Prado Point out **la infanta Margarita**, the royal princess, with her attendants. The name **Las meninas** comes from the Portuguese word for "girls" used to refer to royal attendants. Reflected in the mirror are Margarita's parents, los reyes **Felipe IV y Mariana de Asturias.** Have students find Velázquez himself, standing paintbrush in hand, before an enormous canvas. You may wish to ask students to research the identity of the man in the doorway.

La paella Partners can role-play a restaurant scene: the customer asks the waiter/waitress about the ingredients in the paella, then chooses **paella valenciana** or **paella marinera.**

¿Qué aprendiste? Go over the questions and answers with students, making sure everyone understands unfamiliar words and what the correct answers are.

Conexión Internet Students will find information about the University of Salamanca and famous Spaniards at **www.vistasonline.com,** as well as links to other sites that can help them in their research.

2 vocabulario

La clase y la universidad

el borrador	*eraser*
la clase	*class*
el/la compañero/a de clase	*classmate*
el/la compañero/a de cuarto	*roommate*
el escritorio	*desk*
el libro	*book*
la mesa	*table*
la mochila	*backpack*
el papel	*paper*
la pizarra	*blackboard*
la pluma	*pen*
la puerta	*door*
el reloj	*clock; watch*
la silla	*seat*
la tiza	*chalk*
la ventana	*window*
la biblioteca	*library*
la cafetería	*cafeteria*
el estadio	*stadium*
el laboratorio	*laboratory*
la librería	*bookstore*
la residencia estudiantil	*dormitory*
la universidad	*university; college*
el curso, la materia	*course*
el examen	*test; exam*
el horario	*schedule*
la prueba	*test; quiz*
el semestre	*semester*
la tarea	*homework*
el trimestre	*trimester; quarter*

Los días de la semana

¿Cuándo?	*When*
¿Qué día es hoy?	*What day is it?*
Hoy es…	*Today is …*
la semana	*week*
lunes	*Monday*
martes	*Tuesday*
miércoles	*Wednesday*
jueves	*Thursday*
viernes	*Friday*
sábado	*Saturday*
domingo	*Sunday*

Las materias

la administración de empresas	*business administration*
el arte	*art*
la biología	*biology*
las ciencias	*sciences*
la computación	*computer science*
la contabilidad	*accounting*
la economía	*economics*
el español	*Spanish*
la física	*physics*
la geografía	*geography*
la historia	*history*
las humanidades	*humanities*
el inglés	*English*
las lenguas extranjeras	*foreign languages*
la literatura	*literature*
las matemáticas	*mathematics*
el periodismo	*journalism*
la psicología	*psychology*
la química	*chemistry*
la sociología	*sociology*

Preposiciones

al lado de	*beside*
a la derecha de	*to the right of*
a la izquierda de	*to the left of*
en	*in; on*
cerca de	*near*
con	*with*
debajo de	*below; under*
delante de	*in front of*
detrás de	*behind*
encima de	*on top of*
entre	*between; among*
lejos de	*far from*
sobre	*on; over*

Verbos

bailar	*to dance*
buscar	*to look for*
caminar	*to walk*
cantar	*to sing*
comprar	*to buy*
contestar	*to answer*
conversar	*to converse, to chat*
descansar	*to rest*
desear	*to wish; to desire*
dibujar	*to draw*
enseñar	*to teach*
escuchar la radio/música	*to listen (to) the radio/music*
esperar	*to wait (for); to hope*
estar *(irreg.)*	*to be*
estudiar	*to study*
hablar	*to talk; to speak*
llegar	*to arrive*
llevar	*to carry*
mirar (la) televisión	*to watch television*
necesitar	*to need*
practicar	*to practice*
preguntar	*to ask (a question)*
preparar	*to prepare*
regresar	*to return*
terminar	*to end; to finish*
tomar	*to take; to drink*
trabajar	*to work*
viajar	*to travel*

Palabras adicionales

¿adónde?	*(to) where?*
ahora	*now*
¿cuál?, ¿cuáles?	*which?; which one(s)?*
¿por qué?	*why?*
porque	*because*

Los números 31-100	*See page 57.*
Expresiones útiles	*See page 41.*

La familia

3

Communicative Goals

You will learn how to:

- Talk about your family and friends
- Describe people and things
- Express ownership

contextos

pages 70-73

- Words and phrases related to the family
- Terms to identify people
- Some professions and occupations

fotonovela

pages 74-77

On their way to Otavalo, Maite, Inés, Álex, and Javier talk about their families. Don Francisco observes the growing friendship between the four students.

estructura

pages 78-93

- Descriptive adjectives
- Possessive adjectives
- Present tense of regular **–er** and **–ir** verbs
- Present tense of **tener** and **venir**

adelante

pages 94-99

Lectura: Read a brief article about the family.
Escritura: Write a letter to a friend.
Escuchar: Listen to a conversation between friends.
Proyecto: Create a family tree.

panorama

pages 100-101

Featured country: Ecuador

- The Galápagos Islands
- Hiking the Andes
- The world's highest volcano
- The art of Osvaldo Guayasamín

Lesson Goals

In **Lesson 3** students will be introduced to the following:

- terms for family relationships
- names of various professions
- descriptive adjectives
- possessive adjectives
- the present tense of common regular **-er** and **-ir** verbs
- the present tense of **tener** and **venir**
- context clues to unlock meaning of unfamiliar words
- using idea maps when writing
- how to write a friendly letter
- strategies for asking clarification in oral communication
- researching and creating a Spanish family tree
- cultural and historical information about Ecuador

Lesson Preview

Have students look at the photo. Say: **Es una foto de una familia. Es una familia ecuatoriana.** Then ask: **¿Quién es el papá? ¿Quién es la mamá? ¿Cuántos hijos tiene la familia?**

INSTRUCTIONAL RESOURCES

Student Activities Manual: Workbook, 23–34
Student Activities Manual: Lab Manual, 229–234
Student Activities Manual: Video Activities, 331–332
Instructor's Resource Manual: Hojas de actividades, 5
Instructor's Resource Manual: Answer Keys
Instructor's Resource Manual: Vocabulario adicional, 54
Tapescript/Videoscript
Overhead Transparencies, 16–18

Student Cassette/CD
Lab Cassette/CD
Video Program
CD-ROM
Website: **www.vistasonline.com**
Testing Program: Prueba A, Prueba B

Section Goals

In **Contextos**, students will learn and practice
- terms for family relationships
- names of professions

Instructional Resources
Student Activities Manual: Workbook, 23–24; Lab Manual, 229
Transparencies 16–17
Student Cassette/CD

Before Presenting Contextos Introduce active lesson vocabulary. Beginning in English, ask volunteers about their families. Ask: Who has a brother? Write **hermano** on the board and explain that it means brother. To the student who answers, ask: **¿Cómo se llama tu hermano?** After the student has answered, ask another student **¿Cómo se llama el hermano de ____?** Respond: **Sí, su hermano se llama ____.** Next switch to **hermana** and follow the same procedure. Work your way through various family relationships.

Assignment Have students study **Contextos** and do the exercises on pages 71–72 as homework.

Present Give students two minutes to review the family tree (**árbol genealógico**) on pages 70–71. Then project **Transparency 16.** Point out that the family tree is drawn from the point of view of José Miguel Pérez Santoro. Have students refer to the family tree to answer your questions about it. Ex: **¿Cómo se llama la madre de Víctor? ¿Es Socorro González la abuela de Carmen? ¿Héctor Manuel es el primo o el nieto de José Miguel?** and so forth.

Close Discuss the pattern of Hispanic last names (**apellidos**). If your name follows this pattern, you may wish to use it as an example. Then ask volunteers to say what their names would be following this pattern.

La familia

La familia de José Miguel Pérez Santoro

Más vocabulario

la familia	*family*
el/la hermanastro/a	*stepbrother/stepsister*
el/la hijastro/a	*stepson/stepdaughter*
la madrastra	*stepmother*
el medio hermano/ la media hermana	*half-brother/ half-sister*
el padrastro	*stepfather*
los parientes	*relatives*
el/la cuñado/a	*brother-in-law/ sister-in-law*
la nuera	*daughter-in-law*
el/la suegro/a	*father-in-law/ mother-in-law*
el yerno	*son-in-law*
el/la amigo/a	*friend*
la gente	*people*
el/la muchacho/a	*boy/girl*
el/la niño/a	*child*
el/la novio/a	*boyfriend/girlfriend*
el/la artista	*artist*
el/la ingeniero/a	*engineer*
el/la doctor(a), el/la médico(a)	*doctor; physician*
el/la periodista	*journalist*
el/la programador(a)	*computer programmer*

Variación léxica

madre ⟷ mamá, mami (*colloquial*)
padre ⟷ papá, papi (*colloquial*)
muchacho/a ⟷ chico/a

¡LENGUA VIVA!

Middle names and last names are used differently in Spanish than in English:
- It is common to go by both first name and middle name, such as **José Miguel**.
- Spanish speakers have two last names: first the father's, then the mother's (the first last name of each parent).
- Wives sometimes replace their second last name with their husband's first last name, preceded by **de: Mirta Santoro de Pérez.**

recursos

R				
	SCASS./CD Lección 3	WB pp. 23-24	LM p. 229	LCASS./CD Cass. 2A/CD2

TEACHING OPTIONS

Extra Practice Draw your own family tree on a transparency or the board and label it with names. Ask students questions about it. Ex: **¿Es ____ mi tío o mi abuelo? ¿Cómo se llama mi madre? ____ es el primo de ____, ¿verdad? ¿____ es el sobrino o el hermano de ____? ¿Quién es el cuñado de ____?** Help them identify the relationships between members. Then invite them to ask you questions.

Variación léxica Ask Spanish speakers to tell the class any other terms they use to refer to members of their families. These may include terms of endearment. Ask them to tell where these terms are used. Possible responses: **nene/nena, guagua, m'hijo/m'hija, chamaco/chamaca, chaval/chavala, cielo, cariño, corazón.**

Práctica

1 **Escuchar** Listen to each statement made by José Miguel Pérez Santoro, then indicate whether it is **cierto** or **falso,** based on his family tree.

	Cierto	Falso		Cierto	Falso
1.	✓	❍	6.	✓	❍
2.	✓	❍	7.	✓	❍
3.	❍	✓	8.	❍	✓
4.	✓	❍	9.	❍	✓
5.	❍	✓	10.	✓	❍

2 **Emparejar** Provide the letter of the phrase that matches each description. Two items will not be used.

1. Es un hombre que programa las computadoras. c
2. Son los padres de mi esposo. e
3. Son los hijos de mis (*my*) tíos. h
4. Es una mujer que trabaja en un hospital. a
5. Es el hijo de mi madrastra y el hijastro de mi padre. b
6. Es el esposo de mi hija. l
7. Es el hijo de mi hermana. k
8. Es un hombre que dibuja y pinta mucho. i
9. Es una mujer que da (*gives*) clases en la universidad. j
10. Es un hombre que trabaja con planos (*blueprints*). d

a. Es una médica.
b. Es mi hermanastro.
c. Es un programador.
d. Es un ingeniero.
e. Son mis suegros.
f. Es mi novio.
g. Es mi padrastro.
h. Son mis primos.
i. Es un artista.
j. Es una profesora.
k. Es mi sobrino.
l. Es mi yerno.

3 **Completar** Complete these sentences with the correct family terms.

1. La madre de mi madre es mi abuela.
2. La hija de mi tío es mi prima.
3. El hijo de mi hermana es mi sobrino.
4. La esposa de mi hermano es mi cuñada.
5. La hermana de mi padre es mi tía.
6. Mi madre y mi padre son mis padres.
7. El hijo de mi padre pero no de mi madre es mi medio hermano.
8. Mi hija es la nieta de mi padre.
9. Mi esposa es la nuera de mis padres.
10. El hijo de mi esposo no es hijo mío; es mi hijastro.
11. El esposo de mi hija es mi yerno.
12. Mi hermanastra es la hija de mi padrastro pero no de mi madre.
13. El padre de mi madre es mi abuelo.
14. Los padres de mi esposa son mis suegros.

1 Present Help students check their answers by reading each statement in the tapescript to the whole class and asking volunteers to say whether the statement is true or false. Have students correct the false statements by referring to José Miguel's family tree.
Tapescript 1. Beatriz Alicia es mi hermana. 2. Rubén es el abuelo de Víctor Miguel. 3. Silvia es mi sobrina. 4. Mirta y Rubén son los tíos de Héctor Manuel. 5. Anita es mi prima. 6. Ernesto es el hermano de mi madre. 7. Soy el tío de Anita. 8. Víctor Miguel es mi nieto. 9. Carmen, Beatriz Alicia y Marina son los nietos de Juan y Socorro. 10. El hijo de Juan y Socorrro es el tío de Beatriz Alicia.
Student Cassette/CD

The Affective Dimension Assure students that it isn't necessary to understand every word they hear. They may feel less anxious if they listen for general meaning.

2 Present Model the activity by reading statement 1 to the class and asking **Un hombre que programa las computadoras, ¿qué es?** Guide them to see that the correct response is **c. Es un programador.**

2 Expand After students finish, ask each one to provide a complete sentence combining elements from the numbered and lettered lists. Ex. **Un programador es un hombre que programa las computadoras. Los padres de mi esposo son mis suegros. Mis primos son los hijos de mis tíos.**

3 Expand Write five sentences following the pattern of those in the activity and use them as a dictation. Read each sentence twice, pausing after the second time for students to write.

TEACHING OPTIONS

Small Groups Have groups of three interview each other about their families, one conducting the interview, one answering, and one taking notes. At three-minute intervals have students switch roles until each has had each role. As a whole class, ask random students questions about the families of other members of their group of three.

Game Have students state the relationship between people on José Miguel's family tree; their classmates will guess which person on the family tree they are describing. Ex. **Es la hermana de Ernesto y su padre es Juan. (Mirta) Hector Manuel es su hermano y Beatriz Alicia es su prima. (Carmen o Silvia)** Take turns until each member of the class or group has had a chance to state a relationship.

4 Warm-up To start the activity, have groups of three students, working together, look at each photo and brainstorm what is going on in each one.

4 Present After groups have decided what is happening in the photos, have them write out the completed sentences on a sheet of paper. If necessary, have them review **Contextos**, pages 70–71. When they are finished, go over the answers with the whole class. Model the pronunciation of each sentence as you work through the activity.

4 Expand Bring to class family-related photos that can be shown on an overhead projector. Prepare a fill-in-the-blank sentence for each. Project the photos, talk about them, and ask volunteers to complete the sentences.

4 Expand Have students work in pairs to convert each item into a yes-no question. Ex: **¿Son novios Héctor y Lupita? (Sí.) ¿Es médica Irene? (No, es programadora.)** Have students take turns answering the questions.

4 Expand Ask the class questions about the photos and captions. Ex: **¿Quién es artista? (Elena Vargas Soto es artista.) ¿Quiénes juegan al fútbol? (Los dos hermanos juegan al fútbol.) ¿Trabaja Irene? (Sí, es programadora.)** Explain unfamiliar vocabulary as necessary.

4 **Escoger** Complete the description of each photo using words you have learned in **Contextos.** Some answers will vary.

1. La familia de Sara es muy grande.

2. Héctor y Lupita son novios.

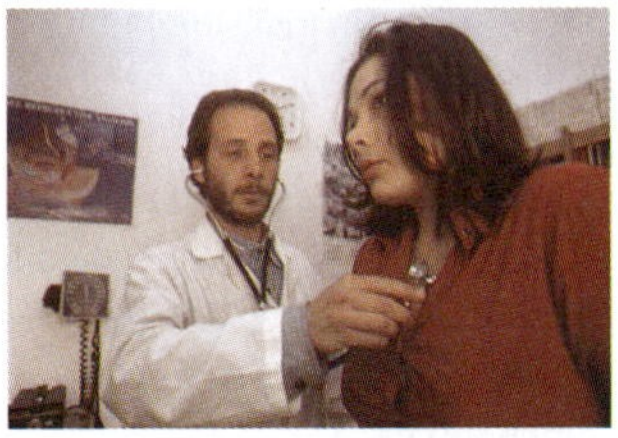

3. Alberto Díaz es médico.

4. Elena Vargas Soto es artista.

5. Los dos hermanos juegan al fútbol.

6. Don Manuel es el abuelo de Martín.

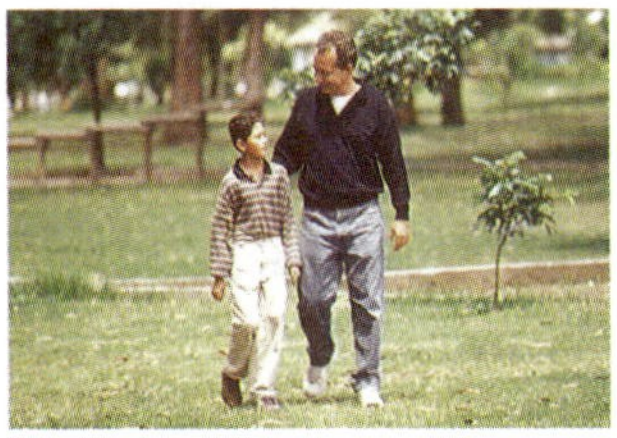

7. Rubén camina con su hijo/padre.

8. Irene es programadora.

TEACHING OPTIONS

Extra Practice Ask students to bring in a family-related photo of their own and have them write a fill-in-the-blank sentence to go with it. Working in pairs, have them brainstorm what is happening in each other's photo and complete the sentence.

Pairs Have pairs of students work together to create another sentence for each of the photos on page 72. Ask one student to write sentences for the first four photos and the other student write sentences for the remainder. When both have finished, ask them to exchange their sentences and correct their partner's work.

NATIONAL communication STANDARDS

Comunicación

5

Una familia With a classmate, identify the members in the family tree by asking questions about how each family member is related to Graciela Vargas García.

modelo

Estudiante 1: ¿Quién es Beatriz Pardo de Vargas?
Estudiante 2: Es la abuela de Graciela.

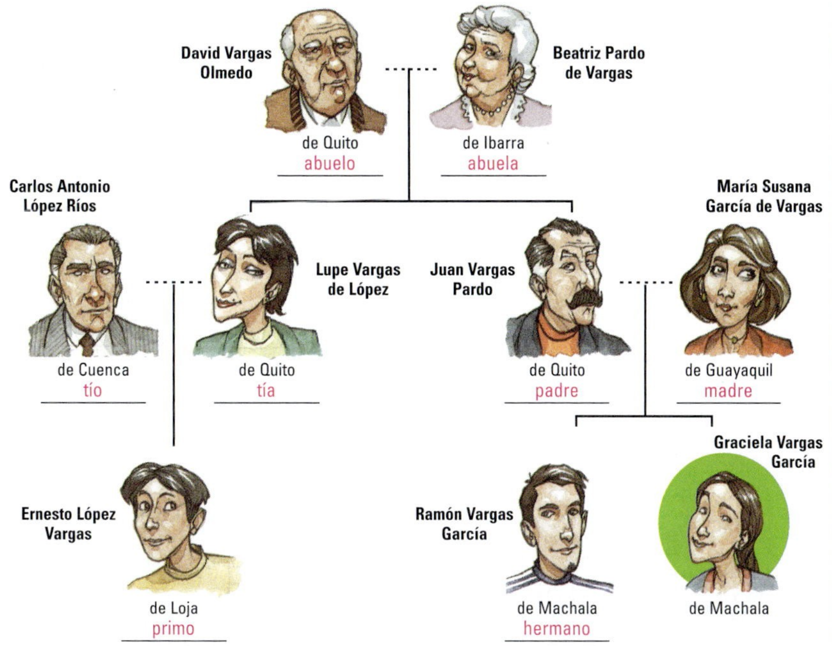

Now take turns asking each other these questions.

1. ¿Cómo se llama el primo de Graciela? Se llama Ernesto López Vargas.
2. ¿Cómo se llama la hija de David y de Beatriz? Se llama Lupe Vargas de López.
3. ¿De dónde es María Susana? Es de Guayaquil.
4. ¿De dónde son Ramón y Graciela? Son de Machala.
5. ¿Cómo se llama el yerno de David y de Beatriz? Se llama Carlos Antonio López Ríos.
6. ¿De dónde es Carlos Antonio? Es de Cuenca.
7. ¿De dónde es Ernesto? Es de Loja.
8. ¿Cómo se llama el sobrino de Lupe? Se llama Ramón Vargas García.

6

Preguntas personales With a classmate, take turns asking each other the following questions. Answers will vary.

1. ¿Cuántas personas hay en tu familia?
2. ¿Cómo se llaman tus padres? ¿De dónde son? ¿Dónde trabajan?
3. ¿Cuántos hermanos tienes? ¿Cómo se llaman? ¿Dónde estudian o trabajan?
4. ¿Cuántos primos tienes? ¿Cuántos son niños y cuántos son adultos? ¿Hay más (*more*) chicos o más chicas en tu familia?
5. ¿Eres tío/a? ¿Cómo se llaman tus sobrinos/as? ¿Dónde estudian o trabajan?
6. ¿Quién es tu pariente favorito?
7. ¿Tienes novio/a? ¿Tienes esposo/a? ¿Cómo se llama?

CONSÚLTALO

Panorama Cities and towns where family members are from can be seen on, p.100.

AYUDA

tengo *I have*
tienes *you have*
tu *your* (sing.)
tus *your* (plural)
mi *my* (sing.)
mis *my* (plural)

5 Warm-up Ask students to determine from whose point of view the family tree is composed. **(Graciela Vargas García)**

5 Present You may project **Transparency 17** to do this activity.

5 Expand Model the pronunciation of the Ecuadorian cities mentioned. Ask students to locate each on the map of Ecuador, page 100. Ask students to say what they can tell about each city from the map. Help them with unfamiliar terms. Ex: **Guayaquil y Machala son ciudades de la costa del Pacífico. Quito, Loja y Cuenca son ciudades de la cordillera de los Andes. Quito es la capital del Ecuador.**

6 Present With the whole class, ask volunteers the questions. Then ask other students questions about the answers their classmates give.

6 Expand After modeling the activity with the whole class, have students circulate around the classroom asking their classmates these questions.

6 Expand Have pairs of students ask each other these questions, writing down the answers. After they have finished, working with the whole class, ask students questions about their partner's answers. Ex: ____, **¿cuántas personas hay en la familia de ____? ____, ¿cómo se llaman los padres de ____? ¿De dónde son ellos? ____, ¿cuántos hermanos tiene ____?**

Assignment Have students do the activities in **Student Activities Manual: Workbook,** pages 23–24.

TEACHING OPTIONS

Extra Practice Ask students to draw their own family tree as homework. Have them label each position on the tree with the appropriate Spanish family term and the name of their family member. In class ask students questions about the families. Ex: **¿Cómo se llama su prima? ¿Cómo es ella? ¿Ella es estudiante? ¿Cómo se llama su madre? ¿Quién es su cuñado?**

TPR Make a family tree using the whole class. Have each student write down the family designation you assign him or her on a note card or sheet of paper, then arrange students as in a family tree, with each one displaying his or her note card. Then, ask questions about relationships. Ex: **Quién es la madre de ____? ¿Cómo se llama el tío de ____?**

¿Es grande tu familia?

NATIONAL communication cultures STANDARDS

Los chicos hablan de sus familias en el autobús.

PERSONAJES

MAITE

INÉS

DON FRANCISCO

ÁLEX

JAVIER

MAITE Inés, ¿tienes una familia grande?

INÉS Pues, sí... mis papás, mis abuelos, cuatro hermanas y muchos tíos y primos.

INÉS Sólo tengo un hermano mayor, Pablo. Su esposa, Francesca, es médica. No es ecuatoriana, es italiana. Sus papás viven en Roma, creo. Vienen de visita cada año. Ah... y Pablo es periodista.

MAITE ¡Qué interesante!

INÉS ¿Y tú, Javier? ¿Tienes hermanos?

JAVIER No, pero aquí tengo unas fotos de mi familia.

INÉS ¡Ah! ¡Qué bien! ¡A ver!

INÉS ¿Y cómo es él?

JAVIER Es muy simpático. Él es viejo pero es un hombre muy trabajador.

MAITE Oye, Javier, ¿qué dibujas?

JAVIER ¿Eh? ¿Quién? ¿Yo? ¡Nada!

MAITE ¡Venga! ¡No seas tonto!

MAITE Jaaavieeer... Oye, pero ¡qué bien dibujas!

JAVIER Este... pues... ¡Sí! ¡Gracias!

recursos

R	VIDEO Lección 3	VM pp. 331-332

Section Goals

In **Fotonovela** students will:

- receive comprehensible input from free-flowing discourse
- learn functional phrases for talking about their families

Instructional Resources
Student Activities Manual: Video Activities 331–332
Video Program (Start: 00:12:14)

Video Synopsis The bus trip continues. Maite, Inés, and Javier talk about their families. As they talk, Javier secretly sketches Inés. When Maite discovers what he is drawing, both he and Inés are embarrassed. Behind the wheel, Don Francisco wonders what is happening.

Before Presenting Fotonovela Ask students to read the title, glance at the video stills, and predict what they think the episode will be about. Record the predictions. **Assignment** Have students study **Fotonovela** and **Expresiones útiles** as homework.

Warm-up Quickly review the predictions made in the preceding class and confirm the correct one, asking a few questions that guide students in summarizing this episode.

Present Work through the **Expresiones útiles** by asking students about their families using the active vocabulary in **Expresiones útiles.** As you do, respond to the content of the student responses and ask other students questions that get them to repeat information about their classmates. Ex: ____, **¿tienes una familia grande? (No.) ¿Cuántos hermanos tienes? (Sólo una hermana.) ¿Tienes una hermana mayor o menor? (Tengo un hermano mayor.)**

Continued on page 75.

TEACHING OPTIONS

Video Tips General suggestions for using video clips in the classroom can be found on page IAE-13 of the **Instructor's Annotated Edition.**

¿Es grande tu familia? As an advance organizer before viewing the **¿Es grande tu familia?** segment of this video module, ask students to brainstorm a list of things that they think might happen in an episode in which the characters find out about each other's families. Then play the video segment once without sound and have the class create a plot summary based on visual clues. Afterward, show the video segment with sound and have the class correct any mistaken guesses and fill in any gaps in the plot summary they created.

4

JAVIER ¡Aquí están!

INÉS ¡Qué alto es tu papá! Y tu mamá, ¡qué bonita!

5

JAVIER Mira, aquí estoy yo. Y éste es mi abuelo. Es el padre de mi mamá.

INÉS ¿Cuántos años tiene tu abuelo?

JAVIER Noventa y dos.

9

MAITE Álex, mira, ¿te gusta?

ÁLEX Sí, mucho. ¡Es muy bonito!

10

DON FRANCISCO Epa, ¿qué pasa con Inés y Javier?

Enfoque cultural La familia hispana

It is difficult to generalize about families in any culture, not just among Spanish speakers. There are many kinds of Hispanic families—large and small, close-knit and distant, loving and contentious. Traditionally, however, the family is one of the most important social institutions for Spanish speakers. Extended families, consisting of nuclear families and grandparents, aunts, and uncles, may reside in the same dwelling. Unmarried children often may live with their parents while attending college or working full-time.

Expresiones útiles

Talking about your family

- ▶ **¿Tienes una familia grande?**
  Do you have a large family?
- ▷ **Sí… mis papás, mis abuelos, cuatro hermanas y muchos tíos.**
  Yes, my parents, my grandparents, four sisters, and many (aunts and) uncles.
- ▷ **Sólo tengo un hermano mayor/menor.**
  I only have one older/younger brother.
- ▶ **¿Tienes hermanos?**
  Do you have siblings (brothers or sisters)?
- ▷ **No, soy hijo único.**
  No, I'm an only (male) child.
- ▷ **Su esposa, Francesca, es médica.**
  His wife, Francesca, is a doctor.
- ▷ **No es ecuatoriana, es italiana.**
  She's not Ecuadorian; she's Italian.
- ▷ **Pablo es periodista.**
  Pablo is a journalist.
- ▷ **Es el padre de mi mamá.**
  He is my mother's father.

Describing people

- ▷ **¡Qué alto es tu papá!**
  How tall your father is!
- ▷ **Y tu mamá, ¡qué bonita!**
  And your mother, how pretty!
- ▶ **¿Cómo es tu abuelo?**
  What is your grandfather like?
- ▷ **Es simpático.**
  He's nice.
- ▷ **Es viejo.**
  He's old.
- ▷ **Es un hombre muy trabajador.**
  He's a very hard-working man.

Saying how old people are

- ▶ **¿Cuántos años tienes?**
  How old are you?
- ▶ **¿Cuántos años tiene tu abuelo?**
  How old is your grandfather?
- ▷ **Noventa y dos.**
  Ninety-two.

To another student: **¿Cuántos hermanos tiene ____? (Sólo tiene una hermana.) ¿Es la hermana de ____ mayor o menor que él? (Es mayor.)**

After you have worked through **Expresiones útiles**, ask students to read the **Fotonovela** conversation in groups of five. Give groups time to assign roles and practice reading their parts. Ask one or two groups to present the script to the rest of the class. (See ideas for using the video in **Teaching Options**, page 74.)

Comprehension Check Have students close their books while you play the video episode. Then check comprehension of main ideas by doing Activity 1 **¿Cierto o falso?**, page 76, orally with the whole class.

Suggestion Draw attention to the masculine, feminine, singular, and plural forms of descriptive adjectives and the present tense of **tener** in the video-still captions, **Expresiones útiles**, and as they occur in your conversation with the students. Point out that this material will be formally presented in the upcoming **Estructura**. Correct students' mistakes with these forms when they ask for correction, but do not expect students to be able to produce the forms correctly at this time.

Assignment Have students do activities 2–4 in **Reacciona a la fotonovela**, page 76, as homework.

TEACHING OPTIONS

Enfoque cultural The influence of Hispanic families frequently extends beyond the household. In the entertainment business, for instance, it is not unusual to find children following in the footsteps of their famous parents. Though theatrical families are not unheard of in the United States or Great Britain, the phenomenon of children reaping the benefits of a parent's fame and connections is probably more frequent in the Spanish-speaking world.

Students may recognize some of these stars of popular music whose parents were/are stars: Enrique Iglesias (Julio Iglesias), Christian Castro (Verónica Castro), Alejandro Fernández (Vicente Fernández).

Reaccciona a la fotonovela

1 Suggestion Have students glance over **Fotonovela** before answering the questions. Go over the questions orally, asking volunteers to answer and to correct false statements.

1 Expand Continue the activity with true/false statements such as these. **El padre de Javier es alto. (Cierto) Javier tiene tres hermanos. (Falso; Javier no tiene hermanos.) Javier tiene unas fotos de su familia. (Cierto) Inés es italiana. (Falso; Inés es del Ecuador.)**

2 Expand Álex is the only student not associated with a statement. Ask the class to look at **Fotonovela** and **Expresiones útiles** on pages 74–75 and invent a statement for him. Remind students not to use his exact words. Ex: **¡Qué bonito! ¡Me gusta mucho!**

3 Expand Have students create sentences using the adjectives **americana** and **bonito**. You may preview the concept of gender agreement by having them also create sentences with **americano** and **bonita**.

4 Possible Response
S1: ¿Cuántos años tienes?
S2: Tengo veintiún años. Y ¿cuántos años tienes tú?
S1: Yo también tengo veintiún años.
S2: ¿Tienes una familia grande o pequeña?
S1: Mi familia es pequeña. Yo soy hija única. ¿Es grande tu familia?
S2: Sí, tengo una hermana y dos hermanos. En total somos cuatro hijos.
S1: ¿Cuántos años tienen tus hermanos?
S2: Mi hermano mayor tiene veintitrés años. Mi hermana tiene veintidós y mi hermano menor tiene sólo dieciocho años.
S1: Y ¿cómo son tus padres?
S2: Son muy buenos… ¡y trabajadores!

Reacciona a la fotonovela

1 **¿Cierto o falso?** Indicate whether each sentence is **cierto** or **falso.** Correct the false statements.

	Cierto	Falso	
1. Inés tiene una familia grande.	✓	○	
2. El hermano de Inés es médico.	○	✓	Es periodista.
3. Francesca es de Italia.	✓	○	
4. Javier tiene cuatro hermanos.	○	✓	Javier no tiene hermanos.
5. El abuelo de Javier tiene ochenta años.	○	✓	Tiene noventa y dos años.
6. Javier habla del padre de su (*his*) padre.	○	✓	Javier habla del padre de su madre.

2 **Identificar** Indicate which person would make each statement. The names may be used more than once. **¡Ojo!** One name will not be used.

1. ¡Tengo una familia grande! ¡Tengo un hermano, cuatro hermanas y muchos primos! Inés
2. Mi abuelo tiene mucha energía. Trabaja mucho. Javier
3. ¿Es tu mamá? ¡Es muy bonita! Inés
4. Oye, chico… ¿qué dibujas? Maite
5. ¿Fotos de mi familia? ¡Tengo muchas! Javier
6. Mmm… Inés y Javier… ¿qué pasa con ellos? don Francisco
7. ¡Dibujas muy bien! Eres un artista excelente. Maite
8. Mmm… ¿Yo? ¡No dibujo nada! Javier

3 **Completar** These sentences are based on the **Fotonovela.** Complete each sentence with the correct word from the box. Two words won't be used.

simpático	italiana	Roma	americana
esposa	primos	hermanos	gente

1. Tengo cuatro hermanas y muchos tíos y ___primos___.
2. La esposa de mi hermano no es ecuatoriana, es ___italiana___.
3. ¿Cómo es mi abuelo? Es muy ___simpático___.
4. Soy hijo único. No tengo ___hermanos___.
5. Los papás de Francesca viven (*live*) en ___Roma___.
6. Francesca es la ___esposa___ de Pablo.

4 **Conversar** With a partner, use these questions to talk about your families.

1. ¿Cuántos años tienes?
2. ¿Tienes una familia grande?
3. ¿Tienes hermanos o hermanas?
4. ¿Cuántos años tiene tu abuelo (tu hermana, tu primo, etc.)?
5. ¿Cómo son tus padres?

AYUDA
Yo tengo… años.
Mi abuelo tiene… años.

NATIONAL communication STANDARDS

TEACHING OPTIONS

Extra Practice Ask volunteers to ad-lib the **Fotonovela** episode for the class. Assure them that it is not necessary to memorize the **Fotonovela** or stick strictly to its content. They should try to get the general meaning across with the vocabulary and expressions they know, and they should also feel free to be creative. Give them time to prepare.

Variación léxica Clarify that in Spanish the adjective **americano/a** applies to all inhabitants of North and South America, not just citizens of the United States. In Spanish, residents of the United States are usually referred to with the adjective **norteamericano/a** or, more formally, with the adjective **estadounidense**.

Pronunciación

Diphthongs and linking

hermano **niña** **cuñado**

In Spanish, **a**, **e**, and **o** are considered strong vowels. The weak vowels are **i** and **u**.

ruido **parientes** **periodista**

A diphthong is a combination of two weak vowels or of a strong vowel and a weak vowel. Diphthongs are pronounced as a single syllable.

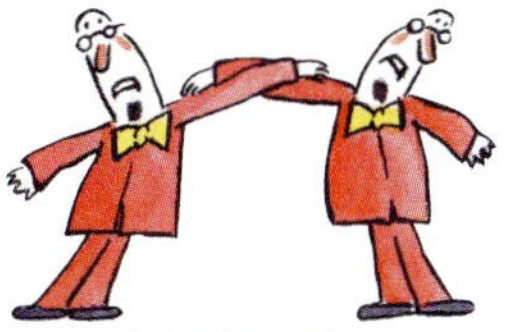

la abuela

mi hijo **una clase excelente**

Two identical vowel sounds that appear together are pronounced like one long vowel.

con Natalia **sus sobrinos** **las sillas**

Two identical consonants together sound like a single consonant.

es ingeniera **mis abuelos** **sus hijos**

A consonant at the end of a word is linked with the vowel at the beginning of the next word.

mi hermano **su esposa** **nuestro amigo**

A vowel at the end of a word is linked with the vowel at the beginning of the next word.

Práctica Say these words aloud, focusing on the diphthongs.

1. historia
2. nieto
3. parientes
4. novia
5. residencia
6. prueba
7. puerta
8. ciencias
9. lenguas
10. estudiar
11. izquierda
12. ecuatoriano

Oraciones Read these sentences aloud to practice diphthongs and linking words.

1. Hola. Me llamo Anita Amaral. Soy del Ecuador.
2. Somos seis en mi familia.
3. Tengo dos hermanos y una hermana.
4. Mi papá es del Ecuador y mi mamá es de España.

Refranes Read these sayings aloud to practice diphthongs and linking sounds.

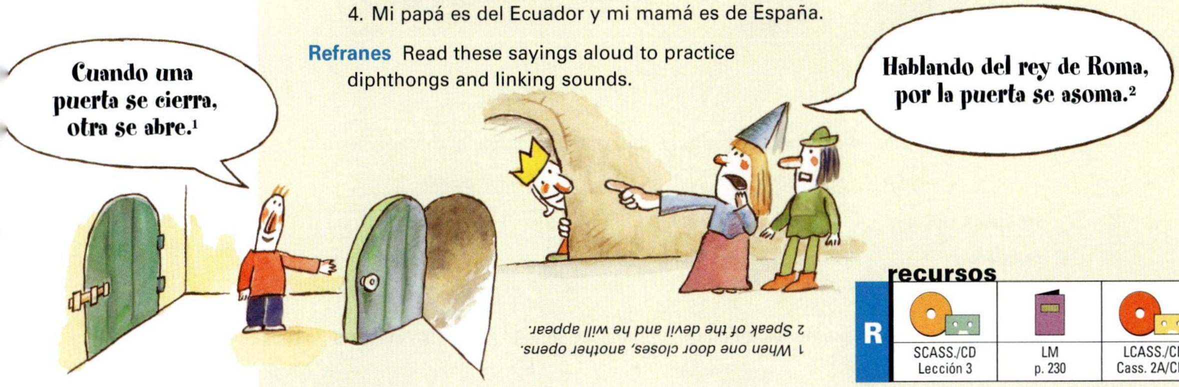
Cuando una puerta se cierra, otra se abre.[1]
Hablando del rey de Roma, por la puerta se asoma.[2]

1 When one door closes, another opens.
2 Speak of the devil and he will appear.

recursos

R	SCASS./CD Lección 3	LM p. 230	LCASS./CD Cass. 2A/CD2

Section Goals

In **Pronunciación** students will be introduced to
- the strong and weak vowels
- common diphthongs
- linking in pronunciation

Instructional Resources
Student Activities Manual: Lab Manual, 230
Student Cassette/CD

Present
- Write **hermano, niña,** and **cuñado** on the board, pronounce them, and have students repeat. Ask students to identify the strong and weak vowels.
- Pronounce **ruido, parientes** and **periodista**, have students repeat them, and identify the diphthong in each word. Point out that the strong vowels (**a, e, o**) do not combine with each other to form diphthongs. When two strong vowels come together, they are in different syllables.
- Pronounce **la abuela, mi hijo,** and **una clase excelente** and ask volunteers to write them on the board. Correct any errors. Point out that the letter **h** is silent; thus, a word that begins with **h** begins with a vowel sound.
- Follow the same procedure with **mi hermano** and **su esposa**. Point out that the resulting linked vowels form a diphthong and are pronounced as one syllable.
- Follow the same procedure with **Es ingeniera** and **mis abuelos**. You may want to introduce linking involving the other final consonants. (**l, n, r, z**) Ex: **Son hermanos. El hermano mayor está aquí. ¿Cuál es tu hermana?**

Práctica/Oraciones/Refranes Model the pronunciation of each word or sentence, having students repeat after you.

TEACHING OPTIONS

Heritage Speakers Ask Spanish speakers if they know of other **refranes**. Write each **refrán** on the board and have the student who volunteered it explain what it means. Ex: **A quien Dios no le dio hijos, el diablo le da sobrinos.** • **Más sabe el diablo por viejo que por diablo.**

Extra Practice Here are additional sentences to use for extra practice with diphthongs and linking. **Los estudiantes extranjeros hablan inglés. Mi abuela Ana tiene ochenta años. Juan y Enrique son medio hermanos. ¿Tu esposa aprende una lengua extranjera? Tengo un examen en la clase de español hoy.**

Section Goals

In **Estructura 3.1**, students will learn:
- forms, agreement, and position of adjectives ending in **–o/–a, –e,** or a consonant
- high-frequency descriptive adjectives and some adjectives of nationality

Instructional Resources *Student Activities Manual: Workbook, 25–26; Lab Manual, 231; Vocabulario adicional 54*

Before Presenting Estructura 3.1 Write these adjectives on the board: **ecuatoriana, alto, bonito, viejo, trabajador**. Ask volunteers to tell what each means and say whether it is masculine or feminine. Model one of the adjectives in a sentence and ask volunteers to use the others in sentences. Correct any agreement errors. Tell students they are now going to learn a number of common adjectives.
Assignment Have students study **Estructura 3.1** and prepare the exercises on page 81 as homework.

Present Work through the discussion of adjective forms point by point, writing examples on the board. Test comprehension as you proceed by asking volunteers to supply the correct form of adjectives for nouns you suggest. Remind students that grammatical gender doesn't necessarily reflect the actual gender.

Suggestion After you have presented the forms of adjectives ending in **–o**, consolidate by doing the first column of **¡Inténtalo!** on page 80. After you have presented adjectives ending in **–e** or a consonant, use sentences following the same pattern to consolidate.

3.1 Descriptive adjectives

NATIONAL STANDARDS comparisons

ANTE TODO Adjectives are words that describe people, places, and things. In Spanish, descriptive adjectives are often used with the verb **ser** to point out the characteristics or qualities of nouns or pronouns, such as nationality, size, color, shape, personality, and appearance.

NOUN	ADJECTIVE	PRONOUN	ADJECTIVE
El abuelo de Maite es **alto.**		**Él** es muy **simpático** también.	

Forms and agreement of adjectives

COMPARE & CONTRAST

In English, the forms of descriptive adjectives do not change to reflect the gender (masculine/feminine) and number (singular/plural) of the noun or pronoun they describe.

*Juan is **nice**.* *Elena is **nice**.* *They are **nice**.*

In Spanish, the forms of descriptive adjectives agree in gender and/or number with the nouns or pronouns they describe.

Juan es simpátic**o**. Elena es simpátic**a**. Ellos son simpátic**os**.

▶ Adjectives that end in **–o** have four different forms. The feminine singular is formed by changing the **–o** to **–a.** The plural is formed by adding **–s** to the singular forms.

Masculine SINGULAR	Masculine PLURAL	Feminine SINGULAR	Feminine PLURAL
el muchach**o** alt**o**	los muchach**os** alt**os**	la muchach**a** alt**a**	las muchach**as** alt**as**

Mi abuelo es muy simpático.

¡Qué alto es tu papá! Y tu mamá, ¡qué bonita!

▶ Adjectives that end in **–e** or a consonant have the same masculine and feminine forms.

Masculine SINGULAR	Masculine PLURAL	Feminine SINGULAR	Feminine PLURAL
el muchacho inteligent**e**	los muchachos inteligent**es**	la muchacha inteligent**e**	las muchachas inteligent**es**
el examen difíci**l**	los exámenes difíci**les**	la clase difíci**l**	las clases difíci**les**

TEACHING OPTIONS

Extra Practice Have pairs of students write sentences using adjectives such as **inteligente, alto, joven**, and so forth. When they have finished, ask volunteers to dictate their sentences to you to write on the board. After you have written a sentence and corrected any errors, ask volunteers to suggest a sentence that uses the antonym of the adjective.

Heritage Speakers Have Spanish speakers create short dialogues in which they use as many of the descriptive adjectives as they can. Ask them to read their dialogues to the class. Dialogues may also be assigned to pairs of Spanish speakers.

▶ Adjectives that end in **–or** are variable in both gender and number.

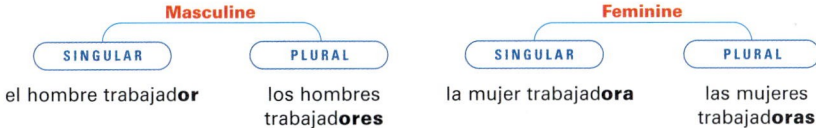

Masculine		Feminine	
SINGULAR	PLURAL	SINGULAR	PLURAL
el hombre trabajad**or**	los hombres trabajad**ores**	la mujer trabajad**ora**	las mujeres trabajad**oras**

▶ Adjectives that refer to nouns of different genders use the masculine plural form.

Manuel es alt**o**. Lola es alt**a**. Manuel y Lola son alt**os**.

Common adjectives

alto/a	*tall*	**gordo/a**	*fat*	**moreno/a**	*brunet(te)*
antipático/a	*unpleasant*	**grande**	*big; large*	**mucho/a**	*much; many; a lot of*
bajo/a	*short (in height)*	**guapo/a**	*handsome; good-looking*	**pelirrojo/a**	*red-haired*
bonito/a	*pretty*	**importante**	*important*	**pequeño/a**	*small*
bueno/a	*good*	**inteligente**	*intelligent*	**rubio/a**	*blond*
delgado/a	*thin; slender*	**interesante**	*interesting*	**simpático/a**	*nice; likeable*
difícil	*hard; difficult*	**joven**	*young*	**tonto/a**	*silly; foolish*
fácil	*easy*	**malo/a**	*bad*	**trabajador(a)**	*hard-working*
feo/a	*ugly*	**mismo/a**	*same*	**viejo/a**	*old*

Adjectives of nationality

▶ Adjectives of nationality are formed like other descriptive adjectives. Adjectives of nationality that end in **–o** form the feminine by changing the **–o** to **–a.**

chin**o** → chin**a** mexican**o** → mexican**a**

The plural is formed by adding an **–s** to the masculine or feminine form.

chin**o** → chin**os** mexican**a** → mexican**as**

▶ Adjectives of nationality that end in **–e** have only two forms, singular and plural.

canadiense → canadiense**s** estadounidense → estadounidense**s**

▶ Adjectives of nationality that end in a consonant form the feminine by adding **–a.**

alemá**n** → alema**na** españo**l** → españo**la**
japoné**s** → japone**sa** inglé**s** → ingle**sa**

¡ATENCIÓN!

Unlike in English, Spanish adjectives of nationality are **not** capitalized. Proper names of countries, however, are capitalized.

México **Canadá**
China **Perú**

Note that adjectives of nationality which carry an accent mark on the last syllable, drop it in the feminine and plural forms.

inglés → inglesa
alemán → alemanes

Some adjectives of nationality

alemán, alemana	*German*	**japonés, japonesa**	*Japanese*
canadiense	*Canadian*	**inglés, inglesa**	*English*
chino/a	*Chinese*	**italiano/a**	*Italian*
ecuatoriano/a	*Ecuadorian*	**mexicano/a**	*Mexican*
español(a)	*Spanish*	**norteamericano/a**	*(North) American*
estadounidense	*from the United States*	**puertorriqueño/a**	*Puerto Rican*
francés, francesa	*French*	**ruso/a**	*Russian*

TEACHING OPTIONS

Extra Practice Write on the board the Spanish country name corresponding to each adjective of nationality that students have learned. Practice the adjectives by indicating a student, saying the country, and having the student come up with the corresponding adjective.

Heritage Speakers Ask Spanish speakers to tell what countries their families have come from. Ask: **¿De dónde es tu familia? (de Cuba) ¿Tu familia es cubana? (Sí.)**

Game Divide the class into two teams. Indicate one team member at a time, alternating between teams. Give a certain form of an adjective and name another form which the team member should give. Ex: **ecuatorianos;** feminine singular (**ecuatoriana**). Give a point per correct answer. Deduct a point for each wrong answer. The team with the most points at the end of play wins.

Common adjectives

Present Use your picture file and the names of celebrities to teach descriptive adjectives in semantic pairs. Use either/or questions, yes/no questions, or a combination. Ex: **¿Michael Jordan es alto o bajo? (Es alto.) ¿Cindy Crawford es fea? (No, es bonita.) ¿Los candidatos son inteligentes o tontos? (Son inteligentes.)**

Some adjectives of nationality

Present Use your picture file and the names of celebrities to practice adjectives of nationality. Ex: **Tony Blair, ¿es canadiense? (No, es inglés.) Madeleine Albright, ¿es francesa? (No, es norteamericana.)**

Point out that adjectives with an accent mark on the last syllable are spelled without it when they add another syllable to form the feminine or the plural. Ex: **irlandés, irlandesa, irlandeses, irlandesas.**

Point out that adjectives of nationality can be used as nouns as well as adjectives. Ex: **La chica ecuatoriana es guapa. La ecuatoriana es guapa.** Like adjectives, nouns of nationality are not capitalized in Spanish.

Expand Add the nationalities of students and celebrities not on the list. When you introduce another nationality, write one of its forms on the board and ask what the other forms would be. Ex: **¿Los chicos del grupo *The Cardigans* son suecos? (Sí, son suecos.) ¿Cuales son las formas singulares de *suecos*?**

Note: At this point you may want to present *Más adjetivos de nacionalidad*, **Vocabulario adicional 54,** in the **Instructor's Resource Manual.**

Present After describing each grammar point, practice and consolidate it by asking questions like the following, which students should answer with complete sentences.

Descriptive adjectives **¿Tienes amigos inteligentes? ¿Tienes amigas guapas? ¿Tomas clases difíciles? ¿Tienes compañeros trabajadores? ¿Tienes profesores simpáticos o antipáticos?**

Adjectives of quantity **¿Cuántos hermanos tienes? ¿Cuántas personas hay en la clase de español? ¿Cuántos amigos españoles tienes? ¿Cuántas materias estudias?**

Bueno/a** and **malo/a **¿Tus amigos son buenos estudiantes? ¿Tienes un buen diccionario? ¿Hoy es un mal día? ¿Tu novio es una persona mala?**

Grande **¿Vives en una residencia grande o pequeña? ¿Estudias en una universidad grande o pequeña?**

Suggestion To practice the meanings of **grande**, ask: **¿Cómo se dice en inglés?: una gran ciudad, una ciudad grande, una gran universidad, una universidad grande,** and so forth. Then ask: **¿Cómo se dice en español?:** a big man, a great man, a great book, a big book, and so forth.

Close Have students open to **Fotonovela**, pages 74–75. Ask short questions about the characters using adjectives from this lesson. Have students answer with complete sentences. Ex: **¿Son estadounidenses los cuatro estudiantes? ¿Es simpático o antipático el conductor? ¿Las dos muchachas son altas?**

Position of adjectives

▶ Descriptive adjectives and adjectives of nationality generally follow the nouns they modify.

El chico **rubio** es de España.
The blond boy is from Spain.

La mujer **española** habla inglés.
The Spanish woman speaks English.

▶ Unlike descriptive adjectives, adjectives of quantity are placed before the modified noun.

Hay **muchos** libros en la biblioteca.
There are many books in the library.

Hablo con **dos** turistas puertorriqueños.
I am talking with two Puerto Rican tourists.

▶ **Bueno/a** and **malo/a** can be placed before or after a noun. When placed before a masculine singular noun, the forms are shortened: **bueno → buen; malo → mal.**

Joaquín es un **buen** amigo.
Joaquín es un amigo **bueno.** → *Joaquín is a good friend.*

Hoy es un **mal** día.
Hoy es un día **malo.** → *Today is a bad day.*

▶ When **grande** appears before a singular noun, it is shortened to **gran,** and the meaning of the word changes: **gran** = *great* and **grande** = *big, large.*

Nelson Mandela es un **gran** hombre.
Nelson Mandela is a great man.

La familia de Inés es **grande**.
Inés' family is large.

¡LENGUA VIVA!
Like **bueno** and **grande, santo** is also shortened before masculine nouns (unless they begin with **To-** or **Do-**): **San Francisco, San José, Santo Tomás. Santa** is used with the names of female saints: **Santa Bárbara, Santa Clara.**

¡INTÉNTALO! Provide the appropriate forms of the adjectives. The first item in each column has been done for you.

1. Eres simpático.
2. Yolanda es simpática.
3. Nosotros somos simpáticos.
4. Dolores y Pilar son simpáticas.
5. Diego es simpático.
6. Tomás y yo somos simpáticos.
7. Ellas son simpáticas.
8. La médica es simpática.
9. Los niños son simpáticos.
10. Él es simpático.

1. Soy español.
2. Ángela es española.
3. Los turistas son españoles.
4. Nosotros somos españoles.
5. El periodista es español.
6. Ellos son españoles.
7. Clara y Bárbara son españolas.
8. Ella es española.
9. Rafael y yo somos españoles.
10. Luis es español.

TEACHING OPTIONS

Video Show the video again to give students more input with descriptive adjectives. Stop the video where appropriate to discuss how certain adjectives were used.
Game Give pairs of students three minutes to jot down as many cities as they can that have **san, santo,** or **santa** as part of the name. After three minutes, go through the names with the whole class. The pair with the most names wins.

Extra Practice To reinforce adjective agreement, create sentences that follow the pattern of the sentences in **Inténtalo**. Say the sentence, have students repeat it, then say a different subject, varying the gender and number. Have students then say the sentence with the new subject, changing adjectives and verbs as necessary.

Práctica

1 **Emparejar** Find the words in column B that are the opposite of the words in column A. One word in B will not be used, and another will be used twice.

A		B
1. guapo	d	a. delgado
2. moreno	f	b. pequeño
3. alto	h	c. malo
4. gordo	a	d. feo
5. joven	e	e. viejo
6. grande	b	f. rubio
7. simpático	g	g. antipático
8. bonito	d	h. bajo

2 **Completar** Indicate the nationalities of the following people by selecting the correct adjectives and changing their forms when necessary.

1. Una persona de Ecuador es ecuatoriana.
2. Carlos Fuentes es un gran escritor (*writer*) de México; es mexicano.
3. Los habitantes de Vancouver son canadienses.
4. Armani es un diseñador de moda (*fashion designer*) italiano.
5. Catherine Deneuve es una actriz francesa.
6. Tony Blair y Margaret Thatcher son ingleses.
7. Steffi Graf y Boris Becker son alemanes.
8. Los habitantes de Puerto Rico son puertorriqueños.

NOTA CULTURAL
Carlos Fuentes (1928–) is one of Mexico's best known living writers. His novel, **La muerte** (death) **de Artemio Cruz**, explores the psyche of a Mexican revolutionary.

3 **Describir** Look at the drawing and describe each family member using as many adjectives as possible. Some answers will vary.

1. Susana Romero Barcos es alta, delgada, rubia.
2. Tomás Romero Barcos es pelirrojo, inteligente.
3. Los dos hermanos son jóvenes.
4. Josefina Barcos de Romero es alta, delgada, bonita, rubia.
5. Carlos Romero Sandoval es bajo, gordo, pelirrojo.
6. Alberto Romero Pereda es viejo, bajo.
7. Tomás y su (*his*) padre son bajos, pelirrojos.
8. Susana y su (*her*) madre son altas, delgadas, rubias.

1 Expand Ask volunteers to create oral sentences describing famous people, using an adjective from column A and its opposite from B. Ex: **Tom Cruise no es gordo, es delgado. Cristina Saralegui no es morena, es rubia. Jack Lemmon no es joven, es viejo.**

2 Expand Give pairs of students four minutes to write four more statements modeled on the activity sentences. Have them leave a space where the adjectives of nationality should go. Ask each pair to exchange its sentences with another. Each pair will fill in the adjectives of nationality in the statements it receives.

3 Warm-up Before beginning the activity, have students work in pairs to brainstorm as many adjectives as they can for each person in the drawing.

3 Expand Have students say what each person in the drawing is not. Ex: **Susana Romero Barcos no es vieja y gorda. Tomás Romero Barcos no es bajo y moreno.**

3 Expand Have students ask each other questions about the family relationships shown in the illustration. Ex: **—¿Tomás Romero Barcos es el hijo de Alberto Romero Pereda? —No, Tomás es el hijo de Carlos Romero Sandoval.**

TEACHING OPTIONS

Extra Practice Have students write short descriptions of themselves. Tell them to mention where they are from and what they are studying, as well as describing their personalities and what they look like. Collect the descriptions and read a few of them to the class. Have the class guess who wrote each description.

Extra Practice Prepare short descriptions of five easily recognizable people. Write their names on the board in random order. Then read your descriptions as a dictation, having students copy your description and match the description to the appropriate name.
Ex: **Ella es joven, morena, atlética e inteligente. (Serena Williams)**

4 Present Model the activity for the class before assigning it to pairs.

4 Expand Go over a few of the items. Have volunteers give a description. Encourage the rest of the class to react. Expand the activity by adding plural items. Ex: **¿Cómo son los muchachos del grupo *The Cardigans*?**

4 Expand Have small groups brainstorm a list of famous people, places, and things not in the activity. Ask them to include some plural items. Then ask the groups to exchange lists and describe the people, places, and things on the lists they receive.

5 Warm-up Have students divide a sheet of paper into two columns, labeling one **Yo** and the other **Mi novio/a ideal** or **Mi esposo/a ideal**. Have them brainstorm Spanish adjectives for each column. Ask them to rank each adjective in the second column in terms of its importance to them.

5 Expand Ask small groups to write a personal ad describing a fictional person and his or her ideal mate. Have groups exchange and respond to each other's ads.

6 Present Model the activity with the whole class before having groups work together. Give a clue (Ex: **Es alto y guapo**) and encourage students to guess, beginning their guesses with **¿Quién es ____?** If they guess incorrectly, give progressively more specific clues. Ex: **Es un hombre inteligente y importante. No es muy joven. Le gusta mucho hablar. Es de Arkansas. (Bill Clinton)**

Assignment Have students do activities in **Student Activities Manual: Workbook**, pages 25–26.

Comunicación

4 **¿Cómo es?** With a partner, take turns describing each item on the list. Tell your partner whether you agree (**Estoy de acuerdo.**) or disagree (**No estoy de acuerdo.**) with the descriptions. Answers will vary.

modelo

San Francisco
Estudiante 1: *San Francisco es una ciudad muy bonita.*
Estudiante 2: *No estoy de acuerdo. Es muy fea.*

1. Nueva York
2. Ben Affleck
3. Madonna
4. El presidente de los Estados Unidos
5. Steven Spielberg
6. La primera dama (*first lady*) de los Estados Unidos
7. El/La profesor(a) de español
8. Los Ángeles
9. Mi universidad
10. Mi clase de español

AYUDA

Here are some tips to help you complete the descriptions:

- **Ben Affleck es actor de cine.**
- **Madonna es cantante y actriz.**
- **Steven Spielberg es director de cine.**

5 **Anuncio personal** Write a personal ad that describes yourself and your ideal boyfriend, girlfriend, or mate. Then compare your ad with a classmate's. How are you similar and how are you different? Are you looking for the same things in a boyfriend, girlfriend, or mate? Answers will vary.

SOY ALTA, morena y bonita. Soy ecuatoriana, de Quito, Ecuador. Estudio arte en la universidad. Busco un chico similar. Mi novio ideal es alto, moreno, inteligente y muy simpático.

Síntesis

6 **¿Quién es?** Working in groups, take turns describing a favorite famous person. The description may include physical appearance, personality traits, nationality, profession, and any other information you know. As you give your description, other group members will try to guess who you are describing. Answers will vary.

TEACHING OPTIONS

Heritage Speakers Ask Spanish speakers to write descriptions of their extended families. Ask them to share their finished descriptions with the rest of the class. Encourage them to illustrate the descriptions with a few family photos, if they are available, or with photocopies of photos.

Extra Practice Have students collect several interesting pictures of people from magazines or newspapers. Have them prepare a description of one of the pictures ahead of time. Invite them to show the pictures to the class and then give their descriptions orally. The class will guess which of the pictures is being described.

3.2 Possessive adjectives

NATIONAL comparisons STANDARDS

ANTE TODO Possessive adjectives, like descriptive adjectives, are words that are used to qualify people, places, or things. Possessive adjectives express the quality of ownership or possession.

Forms of possessive adjectives

SINGULAR FORMS	PLURAL FORMS	
mi	**mis**	*my*
tu	**tus**	*your* (fam.)
su	**sus**	*his, her, its, your* (form.)
nuestro/a	**nuestros/as**	*our*
vuestro/a	**vuestros/as**	*your* (fam.)
su	**sus**	*their, its, your* (form.)

COMPARE & CONTRAST

In English, possessive adjectives are invariable; that is, they do not agree in gender and number with the nouns they modify. Spanish possessive adjectives, however, do agree in number with the nouns they modify.

my cousin	*my cousins*	*my aunt*	*my aunts*
mi primo	**mis** primos	**mi** tía	**mis** tías

The forms **nuestro** and **vuestro** agree in both gender and number with the nouns they modify.

nuestr**o** prim**o** — nuestr**os** prim**os** — nuestr**a** tí**a** — nuestr**as** tí**as**

CONSEJOS
Look at the context, focusing on nouns and pronouns, to help you determine the meaning of **su(s)**.

▶ Possessive adjectives are always placed before the nouns they modify.

—¿Está **tu novio** aquí?
Is your boyfriend here?

—No, **mi novio** está en la biblioteca.
No, my boyfriend is in the library.

▶ Because **su** and **sus** have multiple meanings (*your, his, her, their, its*), you can avoid confusion by using this construction instead: [*article*] + [*noun*] + **de** + [*subject pronoun*].

sus parientes ◀
- los parientes **de él/ella** — *his/her relatives*
- los parientes **de Ud./Uds.** — *your relatives*
- los parientes **de ellos/ellas** — *their relatives*

¡INTÉNTALO! Provide the appropriate form of each possessive adjective. The first item in each column has been done for you.

1. Es ___mi___ (*my*) libro.
2. ___Mi___ (*My*) familia es ecuatoriana.
3. ___Tu___ (*Your*, fam.) esposo es italiano.
4. ___Nuestro___ (*Our*) profesor es español.
5. Es ___su___ (*her*) reloj.
6. Es ___tu___ (*your*, fam.) mochila.
7. Es ___su___ (*your*, form.) maleta.
8. ___Su___ (*Their*) sobrina es alemana.

1. ___Sus___ (*Her*) primos son franceses.
2. ___Nuestros___ (*Our*) primos son canadienses.
3. Son ___sus___ (*their*) lápices.
4. ___Sus___ (*Their*) nietos son japoneses.
5. Son ___nuestras___ (*our*) plumas.
6. Son ___mis___ (*my*) papeles.
7. ___Mis___ (*My*) amigas son inglesas.
8. Son ___sus___ (*his*) cuadernos.

TEACHING OPTIONS

Video Replay the video segment, having students focus on possessive adjectives. Ask them to write down each one they hear, with the noun it modifies. Afterward, ask the class to describe the families of Inés and Javier. Remind them to use definite articles and **de** if necessary to avoid confusion with the possessive **su**.

Small Groups Give small groups three minutes to brainstorm how many words they can associate with the phrases **es nuestro país, nuestro estado, nuestra universidad, nuestra clase de español** and so forth. Have them model their responses on **En nuestra clase hay** ____ and **Nuestro país es** ____. Have the groups share their associations with the rest of the class.

Lesson Goals

In **Estructura 3.2** students will be introduced to:
- possessive adjectives
- ways of clarifying **su(s)** when referent is ambiguous

Instructional Resources
Student Activities Manual: Workbook, 27–28, Lab Manual, 232

Before Presenting Estructura 3.2
Introduce the concept of possessive adjectives. Ask volunteers questions, such as: **¿Es simpática tu madre? ¿Cómo es tu profesor(a) favorito/a?** Point out the possessive adjectives in the questions and responses. Explain to students that they are now going to learn the other possessives.
Assignment Have students study **Estructura 3.2** and prepare the exercises on pages 83–84 (except **Práctica 3**) as homework.

Present List the possessive adjectives on the board. Use each with a noun to illustrate agreement. Point out that all possessive adjectives agree in number with the noun they modify but that only **nuestro/a** and **vuestro/a** show gender. Then associate each possessive with the corresponding subject pronoun. Point out that **tú** (subject) has an accent mark; **tu** (possessive) does not. Afterward, ask students to give the plural or singular of possessive adjectives with nouns. Say: **Da el plural: mi profesor, nuestra libro,** and so forth. Say: **Da el singular: mis manos, nuestras abuelas.**

Present Write **su familia** and **sus amigos** on the board and ask the class to tell you the possible meanings. Write them down. Then ask for volunteers to supply the equivalent clarifying phrases.

Close Do **¡Inténtalo!** orally with the whole class.

1 Expand Have students replace the nouns in the predicate with nouns of a different number and gender. Then have them say each new sentence, changing the possessives as necessary.

1 Expand Have students use interrogative words (**¿Qué? ¿Quién? ¿Cuándo?**) to write the questions that would elicit the statements in items 1–6 and 8. Ex: **¿Qué busca Marta? ¿Quiénes necesitan terminar su tarea?** Then have students respond to the question in item 7. Ex: **Sí, busco mi maleta. No, busco mi cuaderno.**

2 Present Read the **Modelo** aloud and point out the transformation before doing the activity orally with the whole class.

2 Expand Replace the subject pronouns in parentheses with others and have the class provide new answers. Then have groups of students provide new nouns and the corresponding answers.

2 Expand Give the class sentences such as **Es su libro** and have volunteers rephrase them with **su(s)** or a clarifying prepositional phrase.

3 Warm-up Before doing the activity, quickly review **estar** by writing the present-tense forms on the board.

3 Present Read the **Modelo**. Remind students that **estar** is used to indicate location.

3 Expand Ask questions about objects that are in the classroom. Ex: **¿Dónde está mi escritorio? ¿Dónde está la tiza? ¿Dónde está el libro de Rafael? ¿Dónde están las plumas de Carlos? ¿Dónde está tu cuaderno? ¿Dónde están los libros de Anita? ¿Dónde están tus lápices?**

Práctica

1 Completar Complete each sentence with the correct possessive adjective. Use the subject of each sentence as a guide.

modelo
Ana busca __su__ (su, tu, nuestro) libro de español.

1. Marta busca __su__ (sus, tus, su) libro de psicología.
2. Los estudiantes necesitan terminar __su__ (nuestro, mi, su) tarea.
3. Carlos y yo llegamos a __nuestro__ (nuestro, tu, su) apartamento a las nueve.
4. Marta y Susana hablan con __sus__ (nuestras, sus, tus) amigos del Ecuador.
5. Los lunes y los martes regreso a __mi__ (mi, su, nuestro) casa a las ocho.
6. Tú estudias con __tu__ (su, sus, tu) amiga Rafaela, ¿no?
7. ¿Busca Ud. __su__ (tu, nuestro, su) maleta?
8. Mi hermano trabaja con __nuestro__ (sus, tu, nuestro) tío.

2 Clarificar Clarify each sentence with a prepositional phrase. Follow the model.

modelo
Su hermana es muy bonita. (ella)
La hermana de ella es muy bonita.

1. Su casa es muy grande. (ellos) La casa de ellos es muy grande.
2. ¿Cómo se llama su hermano? (ellas) ¿Cómo se llama el hermano de ellas?
3. Es su computadora. (ella) Es la computadora de ella.
4. Sus abuelos son muy simpáticos. (él) Los abuelos de él son muy simpáticos.
5. Maribel es su prima. (ella) Maribel es la prima de ella.
6. Son sus libros. (ellos) Son los libros de ellos.

3 ¿Dónde está? With a partner, imagine that you can't remember where you put some of the belongings you see in the pictures. Your partner will help you by reminding you where your things are. Take turns playing each role. Answers will vary.

modelo
Estudiante 1: ¿Dónde está mi mochila?
Estudiante 2: Tu mochila está en el escritorio.

1.

2.

3.

4.

5.

6.

TEACHING OPTIONS

Extra Practice Ask students a few questions about the members of their immediate and extended families. Ex: **¿Cómo son tus padres? ¿Cómo se llama tu tío favorito? ¿Es el hermano de tu madre o de tu padre? ¿Tienes muchos primos? ¿Cómo se llaman tus primos? ¿De dónde son tus abuelos? ¿Hablas mucho con tus abuelos?**

Heritage Speakers Ask Spanish speakers to write a paragraph about a favorite relative. Ask them to include the characteristics that make that relative their favorite. Have them explain what they have learned from their relative.

NATIONAL communication STANDARDS

Comunicación

4

Describir Get together with a partner and describe the people and places on the list. Answers will vary.

modelo

La biblioteca de tu universidad

La biblioteca de nuestra universidad es muy grande. Hay muchos libros en la biblioteca. Mis amigos y yo estudiamos en la biblioteca.

1. Tu profesor favorito
2. Tu profesora favorita
3. Tu clase de español
4. La librería de tu universidad
5. Tus padres
6. Tus abuelos
7. Tu mejor (*best*) amigo
8. Tu mejor amiga
9. Tu universidad
10. Tu país de origen

5

Una familia Working with two classmates, imagine that you are an elderly couple showing a photograph of your son's family to a friend. Look at the photograph and take turns describing it as the friend asks questions. After you've acted out the situation once, switch roles. Answers will vary.

NATIONAL communication STANDARDS

Síntesis

6

Describe a tu familia Get together with two classmates and describe your family to them in several sentences (**Mi padre es alto y moreno. Mi madre es delgada y muy bonita. Mis hermanos son...**). They will work together to try to repeat your description (**Su padre es alto y moreno. Su madre...**). If they forget any details, they will ask you questions (**¿Es alto tu hermano?**). Alternate roles until all of you have described your families. Answers will vary.

TEACHING OPTIONS

Extra Practice Have students work in small groups to prepare a description of a famous person, such as a politician, a movie star, or a sports figure, and his or her extended family. Tell them to feel free to invent family members as necessary. Have groups present their descriptions to the rest of the class.

Heritage Speakers Ask Spanish speakers to describe their home country (**país de origen**) for the whole class. As they are giving their descriptions, ask them questions that elicit more information. Also, clarify for the class any unfamiliar words and expressions they may use.

4 Present Model the activity for the class by reading the **Modelo** and encouraging students to suggest a few other details to add. Then tell students to work in pairs, taking turns describing three or four of the items. You may revisit this activity by having the class pair up differently and having the new pairs describe items not described the first time.

5 Warm-up Quickly review the descriptive adjectives on page 79. You can do this by saying an adjective and having volunteers give its opposite (**palabra opuesta**).

5 Present Explain the activity to the class. Encourage students playing the friend to ask the couple questions about their picture. Have students playing the couple give names to the people in the photo following Hispanic naming conventions.

5 Expand Ask a couple of groups to perform the activity for the class. Encourage students to ask questions about the photo.

6 Warm-up Review the family vocabulary on pages 70–71. Say a word and ask volunteers to give the masculine or feminine form.

6 Present Explain that the class will divide into groups of three. One student will describe his or her own family (using **mi**), and then the other two will describe the first student's family to one another (using **su**) and ask for clarification as necessary (using **tu**). Before beginning, ask students to list the family members they plan to describe.

Assignment Have students do activities in **Student Activities Manual: Workbook**, pages 27–28.

3.3 Present tense of regular –er and –ir verbs

NATIONAL comparisons STANDARDS

ANTE TODO In Lesson 2, you learned how to form the present tense of regular **–ar** verbs. You also learned about the importance of verb forms, which change to show who is performing the action. The chart below contains the forms of the regular **–ar** verb **trabajar,** which is conjugated just like **hablar, enseñar, comprar, estudiar,** and other **–ar** verbs you have learned. The chart also shows the forms of an **–er** verb and an **–ir** verb.

Present tense of *–ar, –er,* and *–ir* verbs

		trabajar *(to work)*	**comer** *(to eat)*	**escribir** *(to write)*
SINGULAR FORMS	yo	trabaj**o**	com**o**	escrib**o**
	tú	trabaj**as**	com**es**	escrib**es**
	Ud./él/ella	trabaj**a**	com**e**	escrib**e**
PLURAL FORMS	nosotros/as	trabaj**amos**	com**emos**	escrib**imos**
	vosotros/as	trabaj**áis**	com**éis**	escrib**ís**
	Uds./ellos/ellas	trabaj**an**	com**en**	escrib**en**

- **–Ar, –er,** and **–ir** verbs have very similar endings. Study the preceding chart to detect the patterns that make it easier for you to learn the forms of these verbs and to use them to communicate in Spanish.

Inés y Javier comen.

Maite escribe.

- The **yo** forms of all three types of verbs end in **–o.**

yo trabaj**o**   yo com**o**   yo escrib**o**

- Except for the **yo** form, all of the verb endings for **–ar** verbs begin with **–a.**

–as	**–amos**	**–an**
–a	**–áis**	

- Except for the **yo** form, all of the verb endings for **–er** verbs begin with **–e.**

–es	**–emos**	**–en**
–e	**–éis**	

- **–Er** and **–ir** verbs have the exact same endings, except in the **nosotros/as** and **vosotros/as** forms.

nosotros: com**emos**, escrib**imos**   vosotros: com**éis**, escrib**ís**

CONSÚLTALO

Present tense of regular –ar verbs. To review the conjugation of **–ar** verbs, see Lesson 2, section 2.1, p. 44.

CONSEJOS

Here are some tips on learning Spanish verbs:
1) Learn to identify the stem of each verb, to which all endings attach.
2) Memorize the endings that go with each verb and verb tense.
3) As often as possible, practice using different forms of each verb in speech and writing.
4) Devote extra time to learning irregular verbs, such as **ser** and **estar.**

Section Goals

In **Estructura 3.3** students will learn:
- the present-tense forms of regular **–er/–ir** verbs
- some high-frequency regular **–er/–ir** verbs

Instructional Resources
Student Activities Manual: Workbook, 29–30; Lab Manual, 233
Hoja de actividades 5

Before Presenting Estructura 3.3 Quickly review the present-tense endings of **-ar** verbs. Write **trabajo** on the board and ask for the corresponding subject pronoun. (**yo**) Continue until you have the entire paradigm. Underline the endings, pointing out the characteristic vowel (**-a-**) where it appears and the personal endings. Tell students that they are now going to learn the present-tense forms of regular **-er/-ir** verbs. Explain that these endings are similar to those of **-ar** verbs. **Assignment** Have students study **Estructura 3.3** and do the exercises on pages 87–88 (except Activity 3) as homework.

Present Ask questions and make statements that use the verb **comer** to elicit all the present-tense forms. Ex: **¿Comes en la cafetería o en un restaurante? Yo no como en la cafetería. ¿Come ____ en casa o en un bar?** As you elicit responses, write just the verbs on the board until you have the complete conjugation. Do the same with **escribir.** Ex: **¿Quién escribe muchas cartas? ¿A quién escribes? ¿Escriben Uds. buenos trabajos en clase?** When you have a complete paradigm of both verbs, write the paradigm of **trabajar** alongside. Help students identify the ending that is the same in all three conjugations **yo** = (**-o**).

Continued on page 87.

TEACHING OPTIONS

Heritage Speakers Have Spanish speakers write ten true statements about themselves, their family, and people that they know using ten different **–er/-ir** verbs introduced on pages 86–87.

Game Divide the class into two teams. Announce an infinitive and a subject pronoun (Ex: **creer/yo**) and have the first member of Team A give the appropriate conjugated form of the verb. If the team member answers correctly, his or her team gets one point. If he or she does not know the answer, give the first member of Team B the same infinitive and pronoun. If he or she does not know the answer, say the correct verb form and move on to the next team member of Team A. The team with the most points at the end of play wins.

Common *-er* and *-ir* verbs

-er verbs		*-ir* verbs	
aprender	*to learn*	**abrir**	*to open*
beber	*to drink*	**asistir (a)**	*to attend*
comer	*to eat*	**compartir**	*to share*
comprender	*to understand*	**decidir**	*to decide*
correr	*to run*	**escribir**	*to write*
creer (en)	*to believe (in)*	**recibir**	*to receive*
deber (+ *inf.*)	*should; must; ought to*	**vivir**	*to live*
leer	*to read*		

Ellos **corren** en el parque.

Él **escribe** una carta.

¡INTÉNTALO! Provide the appropriate present tense forms of these verbs. The first item in each column has been done for you.

correr

1. Graciela corre.
2. Tú corres.
3. Nosotros corremos.
4. Yo corro.
5. Ellos corren.
6. Ud. corre.
7. Uds. corren.
8. La gente corre.
9. Marcos y yo corremos.

abrir

1. Ellos abren la puerta.
2. Carolina abre la maleta.
3. Yo abro las ventanas.
4. Nosotras abrimos los libros.
5. Ud. abre el cuaderno.
6. Tú abres la ventana.
7. Uds. abren las maletas.
8. Él abre el libro.
9. Los muchachos abren los cuadernos.

aprender

1. Él aprende español.
2. Uds. aprenden español.
3. Maribel y yo aprendemos inglés.
4. Tú aprendes japonés.
5. Uds. aprenden francés.
6. Mi hijo aprende chino.
7. Yo aprendo alemán.
8. Ud. aprende inglés.
9. Nosotros aprendemos italiano.

TEACHING OPTIONS

Video Play the video and have students listen for –er/–ir verbs. Have them write down those they hear. Afterward, write the verbs on the board. Ask their meanings. Have students write original sentences using each verb.

Extra Practice Have students answer questions like the following about their Spanish class. Have them answer in complete sentences. **Uds. estudian mucho para la clase de español, ¿verdad? Deben estudiar más, ¿no? Leen las lecciones, ¿no? Escriben mucho en clase, ¿verdad? Abren los libros, ¿no? Asisten al laboratorio de lenguas, ¿verdad? Comen sándwiches en la clase, ¿verdad? Beben café, ¿no? Comprenden el libro, ¿no?** Pairs may ask each other these questions by changing the verbs to the singular.

Point out the characteristic vowel (**-e-**) of **-er** verbs. Then help students see that all the present-tense endings of regular **-er/-ir** verbs are the same except for the **nosotros/as** and **vosotros/as** forms.

Close Consolidate by doing one or two of the columns of **¡Inténtalo!** on page 87.

Common *-er* and *-ir* verbs

Present Reinforce **-er/-ir** endings and introduce the verbs presented on page 87 by asking the whole class questions using those verbs. First ask a series of questions with a single verb until you have elicited all of its present-tense forms. Write the infinitive on the board when you ask the first question. Have students answer with whole sentences. Ex: **¿Aprenden Uds. historia en nuestra clase? ¿Aprendes álgebra en tu clase de matemáticas? ¿Qué aprenden ____ y ____ en su clase de computación? Aprendo mucho cuando leo, ¿verdad?** After you have elicited the complete paradigm of a few **-er/ir** verbs, ask questions using all the verbs at random.

Expand Ask questions that spin off of the photos on page 87. Ex: **¿Quiénes corren en el parque en esta foto? ¿Cuáles de Uds. corren? ¿Corren en el parque? ¿Dónde corren? ¿A quién escribe el muchacho, creen? ¿Escribe a su novia? ¿Escribe a su mamá? ¿Uds. escriben a sus mamás? ¿Escriben a sus novios(as)?**

Close Ask students to come up with a list of things they routinely do in Spanish class or in any of their other classes. Encourage them to use as many of the **-er/-ir** verbs that they have learned so far.

1 Expand Working with the whole class, come up with the questions that would elicit the statements in this activity. Ex: **¿Dónde viven tú y tu familia? ¿Cuántos libros tienes? ¿Por qué tienes muchos libros? ¿Cómo es tu hermano Alfredo? ¿Cuándo asiste Alfredo a sus clases? ¿Cuándo corren Uds.? ¿Cuánto comen tus padres? ¿Qué crees?**

1 Expand Have small groups describe the family pictured here. Ask the groups to invent each person's name, using Hispanic naming conventions, and include his or her physical description, place of origin, and the family relationship to the other people in the photo.

2 Present Model the activity by reading the **Modelo** and explaining the transformation. This activity is suitable for doing orally with the whole class. You may also have pairs work together to write the sentences. Then have six volunteers each write a sentence on the board. Go over the sentences on the board, making corrections as necessary.

2 Expand Ask pairs of students to brainstorm new subjects (changing the number or person of the originals) for the activity sentences. Have pairs exchange their six new subjects and write complete sentences for those they receive.

3 Suggestion For practice with the formal register, have students do this activity using the **Ud.** forms.

3 Expand Write these words on the board for students to add to the activity: **estudiar menos, aprender italiano, escribir más cartas, viajar a otro país, comer más.**

Práctica

1 Completar Complete Susana's sentences about her family with the correct forms of the verbs in parentheses. One of the verbs will remain in the infinitive.

1. Mi familia y yo __vivimos__ (vivir) en Guayaquil.
2. Tengo muchos libros. Me gusta __leer__ (leer).
3. Mi hermano Alfredo es muy inteligente. Alfredo __asiste__ (asistir) a clases los lunes, miércoles y viernes.
4. Los martes y jueves Alfredo y yo __corremos__ (correr).
5. Mis padres __comen__ (comer) mucho.
6. Yo __creo__ (creer) que (*that*) mis padres deben comer menos (*less*).

2 Oraciones Form complete sentences using the clues provided.

modelo

Yo / correr / amigos / lunes y miércoles

Yo corro con mis amigos los lunes y miércoles.

1. Manuela / asistir / universidad / Quito Manuela asiste a la Universidad de Quito.
2. Eugenio / abrir / puerta / ventanas Eugenio abre la puerta y las ventanas.
3. Isabel y yo / leer / biblioteca Isabel y yo leemos en la biblioteca.
4. Sofía y Roberto / aprender / hablar / español Sofía y Roberto aprenden a hablar español.
5. Tú / comer / cafetería / universidad / ¿no? Tú comes en la cafetería de la universidad, ¿no?
6. Yo / no desear / compartir / libro de español Yo no deseo compartir mi libro de español.

3 Consejos Get together with a partner and give him or her advice based on these clues. Your partner will respond by agreeing or disagreeing with your advice. Then switch roles. Answers will vary.

modelo

Correr

Estudiante 1: *Debes correr más (more).*

Estudiante 2: *Sí, debo correr más.*

No, no debo correr más. Debo correr menos (less).

1. Asistir a clase todos los días (*every day*)
2. Escribir a tu familia
3. Decidir tus cursos para el próximo (*next*) semestre
4. Beber menos café (*coffee*)
5. Leer más y mirar menos la televisión
6. Estudiar más
7. Hablar más en clase
8. Aprender a hablar japonés

TEACHING OPTIONS

Pairs Have pairs of students play the roles of interviewer and movie star. Students can review previous lesson vocabulary lists in preparation. Give pairs sufficient time to plan and practice. When all pairs have completed the activity, ask a few of them to introduce their characters and perform the interview for the whole class.

Heritage Speakers Ask Spanish speakers to brainstorm a list of five imaginary people and their problems and then write advice for them following the pattern of the **Modelo** in activity 3. You may want them to share some of their "advice" with the whole class.

Comunicación

4

Entrevista Get together with a classmate and use these questions to interview each other. Be prepared to report the results of your interviews to the class. Answers will vary.

1. ¿A qué hora comes el desayuno (*breakfast*)? ¿Comes mucho?
2. ¿Debes comer más (*more*) o menos (*less*)?
3. ¿Cuándo asistes a tus clases?
4. ¿Cuál es tu clase favorita? ¿Por qué?
5. ¿Dónde vives?
6. ¿Con quién vives?
7. ¿Qué cursos debes tomar el próximo (*next*) semestre?
8. ¿Lees el periódico (*newspaper*)? ¿Qué periódico lees y cuándo?
9. ¿Recibes muchas cartas (*letters*)? ¿De quiénes?
10. ¿Escribes poemas?

5

Encuesta Walk around the class and ask your classmates if they do (or should do) the things mentioned on the questionnaire. Try to find at least two people for each item. Be prepared to report the results of your survey to the class.
Answers will vary.

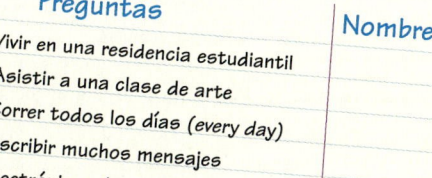

Preguntas	Nombres
1. Vivir en una residencia estudiantil	
2. Asistir a una clase de arte	
3. Correr todos los días (every day)	
4. Escribir muchos mensajes electrónicos (e-mails)	
5. Recibir muchos mensajes electrónicos	
6. Comprender tres lenguas	
7. Deber estudiar más (more)	
8. Deber leer más libros	

AYUDA
¿Qué piensas de...? *What do you think of...?*
¿Qué piensas tú? *What do you think?*
Creo que... *I think that...*
(No) me gusta(n)... *I (don't) like...*
a veces *sometimes*
muy *very*
más *more*
cosas *things*

Síntesis

6

Conversación Get together with a partner and talk about your Spanish class. Don't forget to include the following topics: Answers will vary.

- What the teacher is like
- What the students are like
- Things that happen in class
- What the homework is like
- Things you should do before the next test (**antes del próximo examen**)

4 Present Allow pairs about five minutes for the activity. Tell them that after one of them has interviewed his or her partner, they should switch roles. Remind them that, since they will present the information they learn to the class, they should take some notes.

4 Suggestion This activity is also suited to a group of three students, one of whom acts as note taker. They should switch roles at the end of each interview until all three have played all three roles.

5 Present Model one or two of the questions for the whole class. Then distribute copies of **Hoja de actividades 5** for students to fill in with their classmates' responses.

5 Suggestion The activity can also be done by pairs of students interviewing each other. Have students change the heading of the second column to **¿Sí o no?**

5 Expand With the whole class, go through the survey (**encuesta**) to find out the number of students who perform each activity. Record the results on the board as you go through the survey. Ask: **¿Quiénes viven en una residencia? ¿Cuántos son?**, and so forth.

6 Suggestion As necessary, students may review descriptive adjectives and the present tense forms of regular verbs before beginning their conversation. You may also have them brainstorm a list of words and ideas for each item.

Assignment Have students do activities in **Student Activities Manual: Workbook**, pages 29–30.

TEACHING OPTIONS

Small Groups Have small groups talk about their favorite classes and teachers. They should describe the classes and the teachers and indicate why they like them. They should also mention what days and times they attend each class. A few volunteers may present a summary of their conversation.

Extra Practice Here are five sentences containing **–er/–ir** verbs to use as a dictation. Read each twice, pausing after the second time for students to write. 1. **Mi hermana Juana y yo asistimos a la universidad de Quito.** 2. **Ella vive en la casa de mis padres y yo vivo en una residencia.** 3. **Juana es estudiante de letras y lee mucho.** 4. **Yo estudio computación y aprendo a programar computadoras.** 5. **Nuestros padres creen mucho en la educación para sus hijos.**

Section goals

In **Estructura 3.4** students will:
- learn the present tense forms of **tener** and **venir**
- learn several common expressions with **tener**

Instructional Resources
Student Activities Manual: Workbook, 31–32, Lab Manual, 234

Before Presenting Estructura 3.4 Model **tener** with the whole class by asking volunteers questions such as: **¿Tienes una familia grande? ¿Tienes hermanos? ¿Cuántos tíos tienes? ¿Cuántos tíos tiene ____? ¿Tienes muchos primos?** Point out that students have been using forms of **tener** since the beginning of the lesson. Tell them they are going to learn all of its present tense forms and some expressions with **tener**.

Assignment Have students study **Estructura 3.4** and prepare the exercises on pages 91–92.

Present
- Point out that the **yo** form of **tener** is irregular and ends in **–go**. Begin a paradigm for **tener** by writing **tengo** on the board. Ask volunteers questions that elicit **tengo** such as: **Tengo una pluma, ¿quién tiene un lápiz? Tengo un diccionario, ¿quién tiene un libro de texto?**
- Write **tienes, tiene, tienen**, in the paradigm. Point out that in the **tú**, **Ud.**, and **Uds**. forms, the **-e-** of the verb stem changes to **-ie-**. Explain that the stem vowel **-e-** in verbs frequently changes to **-ie-** when the syllable it is in is stressed. Model each of these verb forms in a complete sentence.
- Write **tenemos** in the paradigm and point out that this form is regular. Use it in a sentence.

Continued on page 91.

3.4 Present tense of **tener** and **venir**

NATIONAL STANDARDS comparisons

ANTE TODO The verbs **tener** (*to have*) and **venir** (*to come*) are among the most frequently used in Spanish. Because most of their forms are irregular, you will have to learn each one individually.

Present tense of *tener* and *venir*

		tener (*to have*)	**venir** (*to come*)
SINGULAR FORMS	yo	ten**go**	ven**go**
	tú	tien**es**	vien**es**
	Ud./él/ella	tien**e**	vien**e**
PLURAL FORMS	nosotros/as	ten**emos**	ven**imos**
	vosotros/as	ten**éis**	ven**ís**
	Uds./ellos/ellas	tien**en**	vien**en**

- The endings are the same as those of regular **–er** and **–ir** verbs, except for the **yo** forms, which are irregular: **tengo, vengo.**

- In the **tú, Ud.,** and **Uds.** forms, the **e** of the stem changes to **ie.**

INFINITIVE	VERB STEM	VERB FORM
tener →	ten- →	tú **tie**nes él/ella/Ud. **tie**ne ellos/ellas/Uds. **tie**nen
venir →	ven- →	tú **vie**nes él/ella/Ud. **vie**ne ellos/ellas/Uds. **vie**nen

CONSEJOS
Use what you already know about regular **–er** and **–ir** verbs to identify the irregularities in **tener** and **venir**:
1) Which verb forms use a regular stem? Which use an irregular stem?
2) Which verb forms use the regular endings? Which use irregular endings?

¿Tienes hermanos?

Sí, tengo cuatro hermanas y un hermano mayor.

- The **nosotros** and **vosotros** forms are the only ones which are regular. Compare them to the forms of **comer** and **escribir** that you learned on page 86.

	tener	comer	venir	escribir
nosotros/as	ten**emos**	com**emos**	ven**imos**	escrib**imos**
vosotros/as	ten**éis**	com**éis**	ven**ís**	escrib**ís**

TEACHING OPTIONS

Heritage Speakers Have Spanish speakers work in pairs to invent a short dialogue in which they use forms of **tener, venir**, and other **-ir/-er** verbs they know. Tell them their dialogues should involve the family and should include some descriptions of family members. Have pairs present their dialogues to the whole class.

Extra Practice Use sentences such as the following for further practice with the conjugation of **tener** and **venir.** First write a sentence on the board and have students say it. Then say a new subject and have students repeat the sentence, substituting the new subject and making all necessary changes. **Yo tengo una familia grande. (Ernesto y yo, Ud., Tú, Ellos) Claudia y Pilar vienen a clase de la residencia. (Nosotras, Ernesto, Uds., Tú)**

Expressions with *tener*

tener... años	*to be... years old*	**tener (mucha) prisa**	*to be in a (big) hurry*
tener (mucho) calor	*to be (very) hot*	**tener razón**	*to be right*
tener (mucho) cuidado	*to be (very) careful*	**no tener razón**	*to be wrong*
		tener (mucha) sed	*to be (very) thirsty*
tener (mucho) frío	*to be (very) cold*	**tener (mucho) sueño**	*to be (very) sleepy*
tener (mucha) hambre	*to be (very) hungry*	**tener (mucha) suerte**	*to be (very) lucky*
tener (mucho) miedo	*to be (very) afraid/ scared*		

- In certain idiomatic or set expressions in Spanish, you use the construction **tener** + [*noun*] instead of **ser** or **estar** to express *to be* + [*adjective*]. The chart above contains a list of the most common expressions with **tener.**

- To express an obligation, use **tener que** (*to have to*) + [*infinitive*].

—¿Qué **tienes que** estudiar hoy?
What do you have to study today?

—**Tengo que** estudiar biología.
I have to study biology.

- To ask people if they feel like doing something, use **tener ganas de** (*to feel like*) + [*infinitive*].

—¿**Tienes ganas de** comer?
Do you feel like eating?

—No, **tengo ganas de** dormir.
No, I feel like sleeping.

LAciudad.COM
Ud. tiene que visitarnos.

¡INTÉNTALO! Provide the appropriate forms of **tener** and **venir**. The first item in each column has been done for you.

tener

1. Ellos ___tienen___ dos hermanos.
2. Yo ___tengo___ una hermana.
3. El artista ___tiene___ tres primos.
4. Nosotros ___tenemos___ diez tíos.
5. Eva y Diana ___tienen___ un sobrino.
6. Ud. ___tiene___ cinco nietos.
7. Tú ___tienes___ dos hermanastras.
8. Uds. ___tienen___ cuatro hijos.
9. Ella ___tiene___ una hija.

venir

1. Mis padres ___vienen___ de México.
2. Tú ___vienes___ de España.
3. Nosotras ___venimos___ de Cuba.
4. Pepe ___viene___ de Italia.
5. Yo ___vengo___ de Francia.
6. Uds. ___vienen___ de Canadá.
7. Alfonso y yo___venimos___ de Portugal.
8. Ellos ___vienen___ de Alemania.
9. Ud. ___viene___ de Venezuela.

TEACHING OPTIONS

Small Groups Give groups of three students five minutes to write nine sentences, each of which uses a different expression with **tener**, including **tener que** + *infinitive* and **tener ganas de** + *infinitive*. Ask volunteers to write some of their group's best sentences on the board. Work with the whole class to read the sentences and correct any errors.

Variación léxica Point out that **tener que** + *infinitive* not only expresses obligation, but also need. **Tengo que estudiar más** can mean either *I have to (am obligated to) study more* or *I need to study more.* Another way of expressing need is with the regular **–ar** verb **necesitar** + *infinitive.* **Necesito estudiar más.** This can also be said with **deber** + *infinitive.* **Debo estudiar más.**

- Consolidate by going over column one of **¡Inténtalo!** on page 91 with the whole class.
- Follow the same procedure to present **venir.** Have students give you the **nosotros** forms of **beber** and **escribir** for comparison.
- Consolidate by going over column two of **¡Inténtalo!** on page 91 with the whole class.

Expressions with *tener*
Present

- Remind the class that Spanish uses **tener** + *noun* in many cases where English uses *to be* + *adjective.* Then model the pronunciation of each expression, writing it on the board as you pronounce it. Ask volunteers what each one means.
- Then model the use of the expressions by talking about yourself and asking students questions about themselves. **Ex: Tengo ____ años. ¿Cuántos años tengo? Y tú, ¿cuántos años tienes? Esta mañana tengo frío. ¿Tienen frío Uds.? Y tú, ____, ¿tienes frío también o tienes calor? Yo no tengo sueño esta mañana. Me gusta enseñar por la mañana. ¿Uds. tienen sueño?**
- Present **tener que** + *infinitive* and **tener ganas de** + *infinitive* together. Ask students: **¿Cómo se dice en español?** *I don't feel like eating/drinking/ writing letters,* and so forth. *I have to study/attend Spanish class/open my book,* and so forth. Then go around the class asking questions that use the expressions to individual students, having them answer in complete sentences. Ex: ____ **¿tienes que estudiar más para la clase de español?** ____ **¿tienes ganas de estudiar para el examen de matemáticas?**

Práctica

1 **Emparejar** Find the phrase in column B that matches best with the phrase in column A. One phrase in column B will not be used.

A		B
1. el Polo Norte	c	a. tener calor
2. una sauna	a	b. tener sed
3. la comida salada (*salty food*)	b	c. tener frío
4. una persona muy inteligente	d	d. tener razón
5. un abuelo	g	e. tener ganas de
6. una dieta	f	f. tener hambre
		g. tener 75 años

2 **Completar** Complete each sentence with the forms of **tener** or **venir.**

1. Manolo y Laura vienen a las ocho. Carlos __viene__ a las nueve.
2. Cristian tiene cinco hermanos, pero yo __tengo__ ocho.
3. Clara y yo no venimos a la fiesta, pero Sandra sí __viene__.
4. Tú y Ricardo tienen mucha hambre, pero yo sólo (*only*) __tengo__ sed.
5. Uds. no tienen razón; nosotros sí __tenemos__ razón.
6. Yo no vengo a clase mañana. ¿__Vienes__ tú?
7. Yo tengo que estudiar para un examen, pero mis amigos __tienen__ que trabajar.
8. Muchos estudiantes tienen miedo de los exámenes; Sandra y yo __tenemos__ miedo de los profesores.

3 **Describir** Look at the drawings and describe what people are doing using an expression with **tener.**

1. Tiene (mucha) prisa.

2. Tiene (mucho) calor.

3. Tiene veintiún años.

4. Tienen (mucha) hambre.

5. Tienen (mucho) frío.

6. Tiene (mucha) sed.

1 Present Go over the activity with the whole class, reading a statement in Column A and having volunteers give the corresponding phrase in Column B. **Tener ganas de** doesn't match any items in Column A. Help students think of a word or phrase that would match it. Ex: **comer una pizza, asistir a un concerto**

1 Expand Have pairs of students write sentences by combining elements from the two columns. Ex: **Sonia está en el Polo Norte y tiene mucho frío. José es una persona muy inteligente pero no tiene razón.**

2 Warm-up If necessary, quickly review the present tense of **tener** and **venir** with the whole class before completing this activity.

2 Suggestion This activity is also suitable for pairs or small groups.

2 Expand Have students answer questions based on the completed activity: **¿A qué hora viene Carlos? ¿Cuántos hermanos tiene Cristian? ¿Vienen Sandra y Clara a la fiesta?**

3 Warm-up Before doing this activity with the whole class, have students identify which picture is referred to in each of the following statements. (Have them answer: **La(s) persona(s) del dibujo número ____.**) Ask: **¿Quién bebe Coca-cola?** (6), **¿Quién asiste a una fiesta de cumpleaños?** (3), **¿Quiénes comen pizza?** (4), **¿Quiénes esperan el autobús?** (5), **¿Quién corre a la oficina?** (1), **¿Quién hace ejercicios en una bicicleta?** (2)

TEACHING OPTIONS

Extra Practice Create sentences with **tener** and **venir** such as these: **Paula y Luis no tienen hambre, pero yo sí ____ mucha hambre. • Mis padres vienen del Ecuador, pero mis hermanos y yo ____ de los Estados Unidos. • ¿Tienes frío, Marta? Pues, Carlos y yo ____ calor. • Enrique viene de la residencia. ¿De dónde ____ tú, Angélica? • ¿Uds. tienen que trabajar hoy? Yo no ____ que trabajar.**

TPR Assign gestures to each expression with **tener**. Ex: **tener calor**: wipe brow; **tener cuidado**: look around suspiciously; **tener frío**: wrap arms around oneself and shiver; **tener miedo**: hold hand over mouth in fear; and so forth. Have students stand. Say an expression at random (**Tienes sueño**) and point at a student who should perform the appropriate gesture. Vary by pointing to more than one student (**Uds. tienen hambre**).

Comunicación

4 **¿Sí o no?** Using complete sentences, indicate whether these statements apply to you. Answers will vary.

1. Mi padre tiene 50 años.
2. Mis amigos vienen a mi casa todos los días (*every day*).
3. Vengo a la universidad los martes.
4. Tengo hambre.
5. Tengo dos computadoras.
6. Tengo sed.
7. Tengo que estudiar los domingos.
8. Tengo una familia grande.

Now interview a classmate by transforming each statement into a question. Be prepared to report the results of your interview to the class. Answers will vary.

modelo

Estudiante 1: ¿Tiene tu padre 50 años?
Estudiante 2: No, no tiene 50 años. Tiene 65.

5 **Preguntas** Get together with a classmate and ask each other the following questions. Answers will vary.

1. ¿Tienes que estudiar hoy?
2. ¿Cuántos años tienes? ¿Y tus hermanos/as?
3. ¿Cuándo vienes a la clase de español?
4. En tu opinión, ¿quién siempre (*always*) tiene razón?
5. ¿Cuándo vienen tus amigos a tu casa, apartamento o residencia estudiantil?
6. ¿De qué tienes miedo? ¿Por qué?
7. ¿Qué tienes ganas de hacer esta noche (*tonight*)?

6 **Conversación** Working with a partner, continue the conversation between Juana and Carlos, based on the drawing. Use your imagination! Answers will vary.

modelo

Carlos: ¿No tienes ganas de comer, Juana?
Juana: No, porque tengo que...

Síntesis

7 **Minidrama** Act out this situation with a few classmates: you are taking a few friends to a reunion of your extended family. Before you go, you and your friends talk about who is coming and what each family member is like so there won't be any surprises. Answers will vary.

TEACHING OPTIONS

Small Groups Have small groups prepare skits in which one person presents his or her significant other to the extended family for the first time. The introducer should make polite introductions and tell the people he or she is introducing a few facts about each other. All the people involved should attempt to make small talk.

Game Give pairs of students five minutes to write a dialogue in which they use in a logical manner as many of the expressions with **tener** as they can. After the time is up ask pairs the number of **tener** expressions they used in their dialogues. Have the top three or four perform their dialogues before the whole class.

4 Present Give students three minutes to read and answer the eight questions. Have them rephrase any statement that does not apply to them so that it does. Ex: **Mi padre tiene 80 años. No. Mi padre tiene 45 años.** Then read the **Modelo** and make clear the transformations involved. Tell students to take notes on the interviews.

5 Suggestion This activity is also suitable to small groups. Remind groups that each member should both ask and answer all the questions. Ask volunteers to summarize their group's responses. Record these responses on the board as a survey (**encuesta**) about the class's characteristics.

6 Warm-up Have students look at the illustration and jot down all the words and phrases it suggests.

6 Present Read the **Modelo** to the whole class. Invent one more exchange between Carlos and Juana, and then give pairs five minutes to carry out the activity.

6 Expand Ask for volunteers to present their conversation to the whole class. Tell them they need not stick to an exact script.

7 Warm-up Before doing **Síntesis**, have students quickly refamiliarize themselves with the following material: family vocabulary on pages 70–71, descriptive adjectives on pages 78–80; possessive adjectives on page 83; and the forms of **tener** and **venir** on page 90.

Assignment Have students do activities in **Student Activities Manual: Workbook**, pages 31–32.

Section Goals

In **Lectura** students will:

- learn to use context clues in reading
- read context-rich selections about Hispanic families

Antes de leer

Introduce the strategy. Tell students that they can often infer the meaning of an unfamiliar Spanish word by looking at the word's context and by using their common sense. Five types of context clues are

- synonyms
- antonyms
- clarifications
- definitions
- additional details

Have students read the sentence **Ayer fui a ver a mi bisabuela, la abuela de mi mamá** from the letter in **Estrategia.** Point out that the meaning of **bisabuela** can be inferred from its similarity to the known word **abuela** and from the clarification that follows **bisabuela** in the letter.

Examinar el texto Have students read Paragraph 1 silently. Point out the phrase **salgo a pasear** and ask a volunteer to explain how the context might give clues to the meaning. Afterward, point out that **salgo** is the first-person singular present form of **salir** (to go out). Tell students they will learn all the forms of this important verb in **Lesson 4**.

Examinar el formato Guide students to see that the photos and captions reveal that the paragraphs are about several different families.

Assignment Have students read **Gente... Las familias** and prepare the exercises in **Después de leer** as homework.

Lectura

Antes de leer

Estrategia

Guessing meaning from context

As you read in Spanish, you'll often come across words you haven't learned. You can guess what they mean by looking at the surrounding words and sentences. Look at the following text and guess what **bisabuela** means, based on the context.

¡Hola, Claudia!
¿Qué hay de nuevo?
¿Sabes qué? Ayer fui a ver a mi bisabuela, la abuela de mi mamá. Tiene 85 años pero es muy independiente. Vive en un apartamento en Quito con su prima Lorena, quien también tiene 85 años.

If you guessed *great-grandmother*, you are correct, and you can conclude from this word and the format clues that this is a letter about someone's visit with his or her great-grandmother.

Examinar el texto

Quickly read through the paragraphs and find two or three words you don't know. Using the context as your guide, guess what these words mean. Then glance at the paragraphs where these words appear and try to predict what the paragraphs are about.

Examinar el formato

Look at the format of the reading. What clues do the captions, photos, and layout give you about its content?

Gente • • • Las Familias

1. Me llamo Armando y tengo setenta años pero no me considero viejo. Tengo seis nietas y un nieto. Vivo con mi hija y tengo la oportunidad de pasar mucho tiempo con ella y con mi nieto. Por las tardes salgo a pasear por el parque con mi nieto y por la noche le leo cuentos.

Armando. Tiene seis nietas y un nieto.

2. Mi prima Victoria y yo nos llevamos muy bien. Estudiamos juntas en la universidad y compartimos un apartamento. Ella es muy inteligente y me ayuda con los estudios. Además, es muy simpática y generosa. Si no tengo dinero, ¡ella me lo presta!

Diana. Vive con su prima.

3. Me llamo Ramona y soy paraguaya, aunque ahora vivo en los Estados Unidos. Tengo tres hijos, uno de nueve años, uno de doce y el mayor de quince. Es difícil a veces, pero mi esposo y yo tratamos de ayudarlos y comprenderlos siempre.

Ramona. Sus hijos son muy importantes para ella.

TEACHING OPTIONS

Heritage Speakers Ask Spanish speakers to use the paragraphs in **Gente... Las familias** as models for writing paragraphs about themselves and their families. Have them read their paragraphs to the class.

Extra Practice Use the following sentences, each of which contains an unfamiliar word or phrase, to practice using context clues. **Mi tío Daniel es maestro en una escuela secundaria; enseña ciencias. • No, mi sobrina no es antipática, ¡es un cariño! • Por favor, ¿tienes un boli o un lápiz con que escribir tu número de teléfono?**

4. Tengo mucha suerte. Aunque mis padres se divorciaron, tengo una familia muy unida. Tengo dos hermanos y dos hermanas. Me gusta hablar y salir a fiestas con ellos. Ahora tengo novio en la universidad y él no conoce a mis hermanos. ¡Espero que se lleven bien!

Ana María. Su familia es muy unida.

5. Antes quería tener hermanos pero ya no es tan importante. Saco provecho de ser hijo único: no tengo que compartir mis cosas con hermanos, no hay discusiones y, como soy nieto único también, ¡mis abuelos piensan que soy perfecto!

Fernando. Es hijo único.

6. Como soy bastante joven todavía, no tengo ni esposa ni hijos. Pero tengo un sobrino, el hijo de mi hermano, que es muy especial para mí. Se llama Benjamín y tiene diez años. Es un muchacho muy simpático. Siempre tiene hambre y por lo tanto vamos frecuentemente a comer hamburguesas. Nos gusta también ir al cine a ver películas de acción. Hablamos de todo. ¡Creo que ser tío es mejor que ser padre!

Santiago. Ser tío es divertido.

dinero *money* discusiones *arguments*

Después de leer

Emparejar

Glance at the paragraphs and see how the words and phrases in column A are used in context. Then find their definitions in column B.

A		B
1. me lo presta	d	a. the oldest
2. nos llevamos bien	h	b. movies
3. no conoce	g	c. the youngest
4. películas	b	d. loans it to me
5. mejor que	j	e. borrows it from me
6. el mayor	a	f. we see each other
		g. doesn't know
		h. we get along
		i. portraits
		j. better than

Seleccionar

Choose the sentence that best summarizes each paragraph.

1. Párrafo 1 a
   a. Me gusta mucho ser abuelo.
   b. No hablo mucho con mi nieto.
   c. No tengo nietos.
2. Párrafo 2 c
   a. Mi prima es antipática.
   b. Mi prima no es muy trabajadora.
   c. Mi prima y yo somos muy buenas amigas.
3. Párrafo 3 a
   a. Tener hijos es un gran sacrificio pero es muy bonito también.
   b. No comprendo a mis hijos.
   c. Mi esposo y yo no tenemos hijos.
4. Párrafo 4 c
   a. No hablo mucho con mis hermanos.
   b. Comparto mis cosas con mis hermanos.
   c. Mis hermanos y yo somos como (*like*) amigos.
5. Párrafo 5 a
   a. Me gusta ser hijo único.
   b. Tengo hermanos y hermanas.
   c. Vivo con mis abuelos.
6. Párrafo 6 b
   a. Mi sobrino tiene diez años.
   b. Me gusta mucho ser tío.
   c. Mi esposa y yo no tenemos hijos.

Después de leer

Emparejar

Suggestion If students have trouble inferring the meaning of any item, help them identify the corresponding context clues.
1. me lo presta (si no tengo dinero) 2. nos llevamos bien (compartimos un apartamento) 3. no conoce (ahora tengo novio en la universidad) 4. películas (cine) 5. mejor que (ser tío, ser padre)

Seleccionar

Expand You might wish to ask students these listening comprehension questions.
1. ¿Cuántos años tiene Armando? (setenta) 2. ¿Con quién vive Armando? (con su hija) 3. ¿Con quién comparte un apartamento Diana? (con Victoria) 4. ¿Cómo es Victoria? (inteligente, simpática y generosa) 5. ¿De dónde es Ramona? (Es de Paraguay.) 6. ¿En qué país vive Ramona ahora? (en los Estados Unidos) 7. ¿Cómo es la familia de Ana María? (muy unida) 8. ¿Ana María tiene un novio? (Sí, tiene un novio.) 9. ¿De qué saca provecho Fernando? (de ser hijo único) 10. ¿Qué piensan los abuelos de Fernando? (que es perfecto) 11. ¿Cómo se llama el sobrino de Santiago? (Benjamín) 12. ¿Qué siempre tiene Benjamín? (hambre)

Suggestion Encourage students to record unfamiliar words and phrases that they learn in **Lectura** in their portfolios (**carpetas**).

TEACHING OPTIONS

Pairs Have pairs of students work together to read aloud several paragraphs and write a question about each. When they have finished, ask them to exchange their questions with another pair who can work together to answer them.

Extra Practice Have partners check their work in **Emparejar** by locating in the paragraphs the words and phrases which enabled them to infer the meanings of the target words and phrases.

Extra Practice Ask students yes/no questions about the paragraphs in **Lectura**. Ex: **Armando es muy joven, pero se considera viejo.**

Section Goals

In **Escritura** students will:

- learn to write a friendly letter in Spanish
- integrate vocabulary and structures taught in **Lesson 3** and before

Tema

Present Introduce students to the common salutations (**saludos**) and closings (**despedidas**) used in friendly letters in Spanish. Point out that the salutation **Estimado/a** is more formal than **Querido/a**, which is rather familiar. Also point out that **Un abrazo** is less familiar in Spanish than its translation *a hug* would be in English.

Estrategia

Present Have students create their idea maps in Spanish. English maps are likely to include items for which students don't have structures or vocabulary.

Some students may find it helpful to create their idea maps with note cards. They can write each detail that would be contained in a circle on a separate card. This facilitates rearrangement and experiments with various organizations.

Assignment Have students prepare **Ideas y organización** and **Primer borrador** as homework.

Comentario

Present Go over each of the guide questions with the whole class so peer readers understand their task. Then have pairs of students exchange letters. Allow five minutes for reading and comments. Allow five minutes for discussing comments.

Continued on page 97.

Escritura

Estrategia

Using idea maps

How do you organize ideas for a first draft? Often, the organization of ideas represents the most challenging part of the process. Idea maps are useful for organizing pertinent information. Here is an example of an idea map you can use:

MAPA DE IDEAS

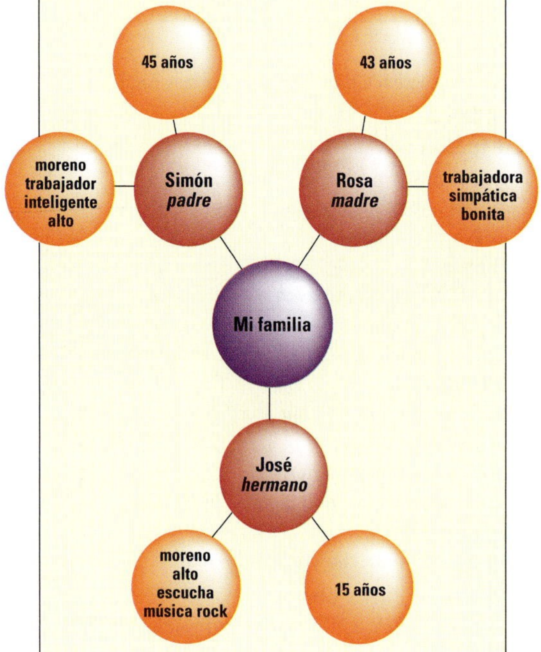

Tema

Escribir una carta

A friend you met in a chat room for Spanish speakers wants to know about your family. Using some of the verbs and adjectives you have learned in this lesson, write a brief letter describing your family or an imaginary family, including:

- Names and relationships
- Physical characteristics
- Hobbies and interests

Here are some useful expressions for letter writing in Spanish:

Salutations

Estimado/a Julio/Julia	*Dear Julio/Julia*
Querido/a Miguel/Ana María	*Dear Miguel/Ana María*

Closings

Un abrazo,	*A hug,*
Abrazos,	*Hugs,*
Cariños,	*Much love,*
¡Hasta pronto!	*See you soon!*
¡Hasta la próxima semana!	*See you next week!*

TEACHING OPTIONS

Proofreading Activity Copy as many of the following sentences containing mistakes onto the board or a transparency as you think appropriate for a proofreading activity to do with the whole class.

1. **Mis hermana Paula es una persona muy simpático y inteligente.**
2. **Ella es estudiante y asista a clases en una grande universidad.**
3. **Viva en una residencia estudiantil y lea muchos libros.**
4. **Tiene cinco clase y tiene de estudiar mucho.**
5. **A ella le gusta más tu clase de literatura inglésa.**

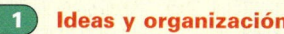

Plan de escritura

1 Ideas y organización

Create an idea map by filling out the first subsections with the names of your family members, then filling in as much information as possible about each one in Spanish.

2 Primer borrador

Using the idea map you prepared in **Ideas y organización,** write the first draft of the letter to your keypal.

3 Comentario

Exchange papers with a classmate and comment on each other's work, using the questions below as a guide. Begin by mentioning one or two points that you like about the person's letter, such as the adjectives used or the variety of **-ar, -er,** and **-ir** verbs.

a. Does the document contain all the elements of a letter?
b. Does the letter include sufficient details about each family member? Are any details extraneous?
c. Is the letter organized in a logical fashion? Does each paragraph transition logically to the next?
d. Do you have suggestions for making the letter more interesting or complete?
e. Do you see spelling or grammatical errors?

4 Redacción

Revise your first draft, keeping in mind your classmate's comments. Also incorporate any new ideas or information you may have. Before handing in the final version, review your work using these guidelines:

a. Underline each verb and make sure it agrees with the subject.
b. Check the gender and number of each article, noun, and adjective.
c. Check your spelling and punctuation.

5 Evaluación y progreso

Swap letters with a classmate. Then read the letter and point out the two things you like best about it. After your instructor returns your paper, review the comments and corrections. Note the most important issues on your **Anotaciones para mejorar la escritura** list in your **Carpeta de trabajos.**

Assignment Have students read **Redacción** for the next class. Ask them to rewrite their drafts, incorporating the peer comments and following the directions in **Redacción**. Tell them to prepare a clean copy of their final draft to hand in.

Evaluación y progreso Give the class five minutes to exchange and read the final drafts of their classmates' letters. Then have them hand them in to you.

Writing Sample Here is a sample of a letter that would constitute superior writing achievement.

Querida Pilar,

Me llamo Francisco. Tengo veintiún años. Soy alto, moreno y delgado. También soy inteligente y trabajador.

Soy de los Estados Unidos. Mis padres también son de los Estados Unidos, pero mis abuelos, los padres de mi papá, son mexicanos. Vienen de visita cada año. No tengo una familia muy grande. Tengo sólo un hermano mayor y una hermana menor, pero tengo muchos tíos y primos.

Soy estudiante en la Universidad de Texas en Austin. Me gusta mucho la clase de matemáticas.

¿Y tú, Pilar? ¿Cómo eres? ¿Qué materias estudias? ¿Te gusta la universidad? ¿Cómo es tu familia?

¡Hasta pronto!
Francisco

EVALUATION: Carta

Criteria	Scale
Appropriate salutations/closings	1 2 3 4 5
Appropriate details	1 2 3 4 5
Organization	1 2 3 4 5
Accuracy	1 2 3 4 5

Scoring	
Excellent	18–20 points
Good	14–17 points
Satisfactory	10–13 points
Unsatisfactory	< 10 points

Escuchar

Preparación

Based on the photograph, where do you think Cristina and Laura are? What do you think Laura is saying to Cristina?

Estrategia

Asking for repetition/ Replaying the recording

Sometimes it is difficult to understand what people say, especially in a noisy environment. During a conversation, you can ask someone to repeat by saying **¿Cómo?** (*What?*) or **¿Perdón?** (*Pardon me?*). In class, you can ask your teacher to repeat by saying **Repita, por favor** (*Repeat, please*). If you don't understand a recorded activity, you can simply replay it. To help you practice this strategy, you will listen to a short paragraph. Ask your professor to repeat it or replay the recording, and then summarize what you heard.

Ahora escucha

Now you are going to hear Laura and Cristina's conversation. Use **R** to indicate which adjectives describe Cristina's boyfriend, Rafael. Use **E** for adjectives that describe Laura's boyfriend, Esteban. Some adjectives will not be used.

____ **rubio**	E **interesante**
____ **feo**	____ **antipático**
R **alto**	R **inteligente**
E **trabajador**	R **moreno**
E **un poco gordo**	____ **viejo**

recursos

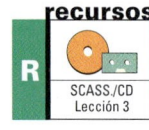

R SCASS./CD Lección 3

Comprensión

Identificar

Which person would make each statement: Cristina or Laura?

	Cristina	Laura
1. Mi novio habla sólo del fútbol y del béisbol.	✓	❍
2. Tengo un novio muy interesante y simpático.	❍	✓
3. Mi novio es alto y moreno.	✓	❍
4. Mi novio trabaja mucho.	❍	✓
5. Mi amiga no tiene buena suerte con los muchachos.	❍	✓
6. El novio de mi amiga es un poco gordo, pero guapo.	✓	❍

¿Cierto o falso?

Indicate whether each sentence is **cierto** or **falso,** then correct the false statements.

	Cierto	Falso
1. Esteban es un chico interesante y simpático.	✓	❍
2. Laura tiene mala suerte con los chicos. Cristina tiene mala suerte con los chicos.	❍	✓
3. Rafael es muy interesante. Esteban es muy interesante.	❍	✓
4. Laura y su novio hablan de muchas cosas.	✓	❍

Section Goals

In **Escuchar** students will:
- listen to and summarize a short paragraph
- learn strategies for asking for clarification in oral communication
- answer questions based on the content of a recorded conversation

Instructional Resource
Student Cassette/CD

Preparación
Warm-up Have students look at the photo and describe what they see. Guide them to guess where they think Cristina and Laura are and what they are talking about.

Estrategia
Script **La familia de María Dolores es muy grande. Tiene dos hermanos y tres hermanas. Su familia vive en España. Pero la familia de Alberto es muy pequeña. No tiene hermanos ni hermanas. Alberto y sus padres viven en el Ecuador.**

Assignment Have students do the activities in **Ahora escucha** and **Comprensión** as homework for the next class. At that time, verify the responses to **Ahora escucha** with the whole class and go over **Identificar** and **¿Cierto o falso?** by reading each question aloud and calling on different students to answer.

Ahora escucha
Script
Laura: ¿Qué hay de nuevo, Cristina?
Cristina: No mucho... sólo problemas con mi novio.
Laura: ¿Perdón?
Cristina: No hay mucho de nuevo... sólo problemas con mi novio, Rafael.
Laura: ¿Qué les pasa?
Cristina: Bueno, Rafael es alto y moreno... es muy guapo. Y es buena gente. Es inteligente también... pero es que no lo encuentro muy interesante.
Laura: ¿Cómo?
Cristina: No es muy interesante. Sólo habla del fútbol y béisbol. No me gusta hablar del fútbol las veinticuatro horas al día. No comprendo a los muchachos. ¿Cómo es tu novio, Laura?
Laura: Esteban es muy simpático. Es un poco gordo pero creo que es muy guapo. También es muy trabajador.
Cristina: ¿Es interesante?
Laura: Sí. Hablamos dos o tres horas cada día. Hablamos de muchas cosas... las clases, los amigos... de todo.
Cristina: ¡Qué bien! Siempre tengo mala suerte con los novios.

NATIONAL STANDARDS communication cultures
NATIONAL STANDARDS connections communities

Proyecto

Describe a tu familia

Imagine that you have just returned from a summer exchange program in Ecuador. Your Spanish instructor has asked you to give a short presentation about the Ecuadorian family you stayed with.

1 Haz un árbol genealógico

Create an illustrated family tree of your Ecuadorian family. Using the research tools found in **Recursos para la investigación,** collect photographs of the family members, as well as photographs and short descriptions of the cities in Ecuador where they live. Your family tree might include these elements:

- A simple, yet descriptive title
- A format that clearly shows the relationships between the family members
- Photographs of the family members
- The names of the family members, using Hispanic conventions for the way names are written
- The names and photographs of the cities where the family members live
- Three or four adjectives that describe each family member

2 Presenta la información

Using your family tree as a guide, give a brief presentation to the class about your Ecuadorian family. Make your descriptions of the family members and where they live as interesting as you can so that your classmates will want to go to Ecuador and experience the country and its people for themselves.

recursos para la investigación

Internet Palabras clave: Ecuador, Ecuadorian, cities, geography, map(s)	**Comunidad** Exchange students, faculty members, and residents in your community who are from Ecuador or have lived in Ecuador
Biblioteca Newspapers, magazines, travel magazines	**Otros recursos** Your school's International Studies Office, the Ecuadorian embassy or consulates of Ecuador, brochures from travel agencies

EVALUATION: Descripción

Criteria	Scale
Content	1 2 3 4
Comprehensibility	1 2 3 4
Organization	1 2 3 4
Accuracy	1 2 3 4
Use of visuals	1 2 3 4

Scoring	
Excellent	18–20 points
Good	14–17 points
Satisfactory	10–13 points
Unsatisfactory	< 10 points

Section Goals

In **Proyecto** students will:
- use Spanish as they carry out research and to interact with the wider world
- have the opportunity to make a presentation in Spanish
- create a family tree

Before Assigning

Proyecto Students will need approximately a week to complete the project, so at the beginning of that time period, have them read through **Proyecto**. Explain that they are going to carry out research on the cities and people of Ecuador. Tell them that they will make a family tree for an imaginary Ecuadorian family and present the family tree to the class.

Assignment Have students read page 99 and follow directions in **Haz un árbol genealógico** to create the family tree.

Haz un árbol geneológico

Suggestions
- Students may use use newspaper or magazine photos for their family tree.
- Students' family trees will be more visible if they are drawn on poster paper or projected on an overhead projector.

Presenta la información

Suggestions
- In preparation for their presentations, students may practice before a small groups of friends who can critique the presentation.
- Rather than having all presentations on the same day, set aside sufficient class time to do a few at a time until all students have had a chance to present.

Section Goals

In **Panorama**, students will receive comprehensible input by reading about the geography and culture of Ecuador.

Instructional Resources
Student Activities Manual: Workbook, 33–34
Transparency 18

Ecuador

Before Presenting Panorama Have students look at the map of Ecuador or project **Transparency 18**. Guide them in discussing details they notice. Then have them look at the call-out photos and read the captions. Help them with unfamiliar vocabulary. Encourage students to mention anything they may know about Ecuador. Next, ask them to glance at the headings of **El país en cifras**. Establish the kind of information contained in each and clarify unfamiliar words. Point out that every word in the headings has an English cognate. **Assignment** Have students read **Panorama** and write out the completed sentences in **¿Qué aprendiste?** on page 101 as homework.

Present Go through **El país en cifras**, asking volunteers to read the sections. After each section, ask other students questions about the content. Point out that where hundreds, thousands, and millions are separated by commas in English, most Spanish-speaking countries use periods. Model the pronunciation of the numbers.

Increíble pero cierto Mt. St. Helens in Washington and Cotopaxi in Ecuador are just two of a chain of volcanos that stretches along the entire Pacific coast of North and South America, from Mt. McKinley in Alaska to Monte Sarmiento in Tierra del Fuego of southern Chile.

Ecuador

NATIONAL STANDARDS connections cultures

El país en cifras

- **Área:** 283.560 km² (109.483 millas²), *incluyendo las islas Galápagos, aproximadamente el área de Colorado*
- **Población:** 13.112.000
- **Capital:** Quito — 1.892.000
- **Ciudades principales:** Guayaquil — 2.452.000, Cuenca — 247.000, Machala — 191.000, Portoviejo — 164.000

SOURCE: Population Division, UN Secretariat

- **Moneda:** sucre
- **Idiomas:** español (oficial), quichua

La lengua oficial del Ecuador es el español, pero también se hablan otras lenguas en el país. Aproximadamente unos 4.000.000 de ecuatorianos hablan lenguas indígenas; la mayoría de ellos habla quichua. El quichua es el dialecto ecuatoriano del quechua, la lengua de los incas.

Los indios del Ecuador hablan quichua.

Bandera de Ecuador

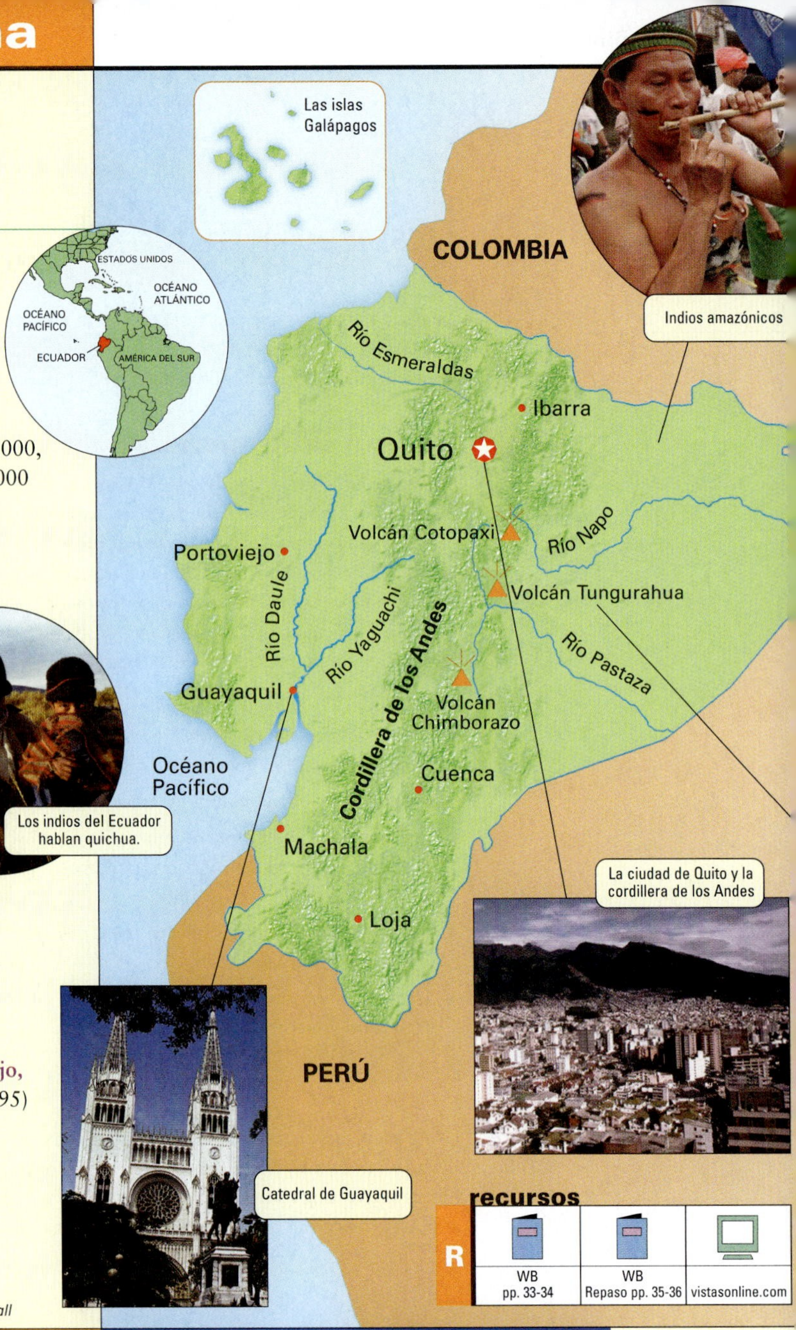

Indios amazónicos

La ciudad de Quito y la cordillera de los Andes

Ecuatorianos célebres

- Francisco Eugenio De Santa Cruz y Espejo, médico, periodista y patriota (1747-1795)
- Juan León Mera, novelista (1832-1894)
- Eduardo Kingman, pintor (1911-)
- Rosalía Arteaga, abogada, política y ex-vicepresidenta (1956-)

Catedral de Guayaquil

recursos

R	WB pp. 33-34	WB Repaso pp. 35-36	vistasonline.com

se hablan *are spoken* otras *other* mayoría *majority* abogada *lawyer* mundo *world* dos veces más alto *twice as tall*

¡Increíble pero cierto!

El volcán Cotopaxi, situado a unos 60 kilómetros al sur de Quito, es considerado el volcán activo más alto del mundo. Tiene una altura de 5.897 metros (19.340 pies). Es dos veces más alto que el volcán St. Helens (2.550 metros o 9.215 pies) en el estado de Washington.

TEACHING OPTIONS

Heritage Speakers If a Spanish speaker has visited Ecuador, ask him or her to prepare a short presentation about his or her experiences there. If possible, the presentation should be illustrated with photos and articles of the country.

Extra Practice Remind students that **km²** is the abbreviation for **kilómetros cuadrados** and that **millas²** is the abbreviation for **millas cuadradas**. Ask a volunteer to explain why **kilómetros** takes **cuadrados** and **millas** takes **cuadradas**.

Lugares • Las islas Galápagos

Muchas personas de todo el mundo visitan las islas Galápagos porque son un verdadero tesoro ecológico. En estas islas Charles Darwin estudió las especies que inspiraron sus ideas sobre la evolución. Debido a que las islas están lejos del continente, sus plantas y animales son únicos y evolucionaron de una manera diferente. Las islas son famosas por sus tortugas gigantes.

Artes • Osvaldo Guayasamín

Osvaldo Guayasamín (1919-1999) fue uno de los pintores latinoamericanos más famosos del mundo. También fue escultor y muralista. Su expresivo estilo muestra la influencia del cubismo y sus temas preferidos son la injusticia y la pobreza sufridas por los indígenas de su país.

Deportes • El *trekking*

El sistema montañoso de los Andes cruza y divide el Ecuador en dos. La Sierra, que tiene volcanes, grandes valles y una variedad increíble de plantas y animales, es un lugar perfecto para el *trekking*. Miles de turistas visitan el Ecuador todos los años para hacer *trekking* y escalar montañas.

Artesanía • Los tejidos

Los tejidos de colores vivos son característicos del Ecuador. Los indígenas, continuando una larga tradición, tejen bolsas, cinturones y tapices apreciados en todo el mundo. Cada pueblo usa colores, figuras y diseños diferentes. Los turistas pueden admirar y comprar los tejidos en tiendas y en mercados como el de Otavalo.

Explosión del volcán Tungurahua en 1999

¿Qué aprendiste? Completa las frases con la información correcta.

1. La ciudad más grande (*biggest*) del Ecuador es Guayaquil.
2. La capital del Ecuador es Quito.
3. Unos 4.000.000 de ecuatorianos hablan quichua.
4. Darwin estudió el proceso de la evolución en las islas Galápagos.
5. Dos temas del arte de Guayasamín son la pobreza y la injusticia.
6. Los tejidos de colores son característicos del país.
7. Los Andes son un lugar perfecto para el trekking.
8. El volcán Cotopaxi es el volcán activo más alto del mundo.

Conexión Internet Investiga estos temas en el sitio **www.vistasonline.com.**

1. Busca información sobre una ciudad del Ecuador. ¿Te gustaría (*would you like*) visitar la ciudad? ¿Por qué?
2. Haz una lista de tres animales o plantas que viven sólo en las islas Galápagos. ¿Dónde hay animales o plantas similares?

verdadero tesoro *true treasure* estudió *studied* inspiraron *inspired* Debido a que *Due to the fact that* evolucionaron *they evolved* tortugas *tortoises* fue *was* más *most* muestra *shows* pobreza *poverty* cruza *crosses* lugar *place* Miles *Thousands* tejidos *weavings* vivos *bright* larga *long* tejen *weave* bolsas *bags* cinturones *belts* tapices *tapestries* pueblo *town* diseños *designs* pueden *can* tiendas *stores* mercados *markets*

TEACHING OPTIONS

Variación léxica A word that the Quichua language has contributed to English is *jerky* (salted, dried meat), which comes from the Quichua word *charqui.* The Quichua-speaking peoples of the Andean highlands had perfected techniques for "freeze-drying" both vegetable tubers and meat before the first Spaniards arrived in the region. Freeze-dried potatoes, called **chuño**, are a staple in the diet of the inhabitants of the Andes.

In Ecuador and throughout the rest of South America, **charqui** is the word used to name meat preserved by drying. **Charqui** is an important component in the national cuisines of South America, and in Argentina, Uruguay, and Brazil its production is a major industry. In other parts of the Spanish-speaking world you may hear the terms **tasajo** or **carne seca** used instead of **charqui**.

Las islas Galápagos Show magazine and book articles that give an idea of the Galapagos Islands. (See *National Geographic en Español*, April 1999, pp. 2–41 as a source of dramatic photography.)

Osvaldo Guayasamín The name Guayasamín means *white bird* in Quichua. The artist took this name out of solidarity with his Inca forebears. Bring reproductions of some of Guayasamín's work to class. Show a variety of his often disturbing paintings and encourage students to talk about what the artist's social and political stance might be.

El *trekking* *Trekking* is one of several English words that have been accepted into Spanish. These words name phenomena whose popularity originated in the English-speaking world. Some words like these enter Spanish without much change: **cámping, márketing, ránking**. Others are changed to match Spanish spelling patterns, as **líder** (leader) or **mítin** (meeting).

Los tejidos Show photos and magazine pictures of Otavalo and ask students to talk about what they see.

¿Qué aprendiste? Go over the questions and answers with students, making sure everyone understands unfamiliar words and what the correct answers are.

Assignment Have students do activites in **Student Activities Manual: Workbook**, pages 33–34.

Conexión Internet Students will find information about Ecuador at **www.vistasonline.com**, as well as links to other sites that can help them in their research.

3 vocabulario

La familia

el/la abuelo/a	*grandfather/ grandmother*
el/la cuñado/a	*brother-in-law/ sister-in-law*
el/la esposo/a	*husband; spouse/ wife; spouse*
la familia	*family*
el/la hermanastro/a	*stepbrother/ stepsister*
el/la hermano/a	*brother/sister*
el/la hijastro/a	*stepson/ stepdaughter*
el/la hijo/a	*son/daughter*
los hijos	*children*
la madrastra	*stepmother*
la madre	*mother*
el/la medio/a hermano/a	*half-brother/ half-sister*
el/la nieto/a	*grandson/ granddaughter*
la nuera	*daughter-in-law*
el padrastro	*stepfather*
el padre	*father*
los padres	*parents*
los parientes	*relatives*
el/la primo/a	*cousin*
el/la sobrino/a	*nephew/niece*
el/la suegro/a	*father-in-law/ mother-in-law*
el/la tío/a	*uncle/aunt*
el yerno	*son-in-law*

Otras personas

el/la amigo/a	*friend*
la gente	*people*
el/la muchacho/a	*boy/girl*
el/la niño/a	*child*
el/la novio/a	*boyfriend/girlfriend*

Profesiones

el/la artista	*artist*
el/la ingeniero/a	*engineer*
el/la doctor(a), el/la médico/a	*doctor; physician*
el/la periodista	*journalist*
el/la programador(a)	*computer programmer*

Verbos

abrir	*to open*
aprender	*to learn*
asistir (a)	*to attend*
beber	*to drink*
comer	*to eat*
compartir	*to share*
comprender	*to understand*
correr	*to run*
creer (en)	*to believe (in)*
deber (+ *inf.*)	*to have to; should*
decidir	*to decide*
escribir	*to write*
leer	*to read*
recibir	*to receive*
tener *(irreg.)*	*to have*
venir *(irreg.)*	*to come*
vivir	*to live*

Adjetivos

alto/a	*tall*
antipático/a	*unpleasant*
bajo/a	*short (in height)*
bonito/a	*pretty*
buen, bueno/a	*good*
delgado/a	*thin; slender*
difícil	*difficult; hard*
fácil	*easy*
feo/a	*ugly*
gordo/a	*fat*
gran, grande	*big*
guapo/a	*handsome; good-looking*
importante	*important*
inteligente	*intelligent*
interesante	*interesting*
joven	*young*
mal, malo/a	*bad*
mismo/a	*same*
moreno/a	*brunet(te)*
mucho/a	*much; many; a lot of*
pelirrojo/a	*red-haired*
pequeño/a	*small*
rubio/a	*blond*
simpático/a	*nice; likeable*
tonto/a	*silly; foolish*
trabajador(a)	*hard-working*
viejo/a	*old*

Nacionalidades

alemán, alemana	*German*
canadiense	*Canadian*
chino/a	*Chinese*
ecuatoriano/a	*Ecuadorian*
español(a)	*Spanish*
estadounidense	*from the United States*
francés, francesa	*French*
japonés, japonesa	*Japanese*
inglés, inglesa	*English*
italiano/a	*Italian*
mexicano/a	*Mexican*
norteamericano/a	*(North) American*
puertorriqueño/a	*Puerto Rican*
ruso/a	*Russian*

Expresiones con tener

tener... años	*to be... years old*
tener (mucho) calor	*to be (very) hot*
tener (mucho) cuidado	*to be (very) careful*
tener (mucho) frío	*to be (very) cold*
tener ganas de + (*inf.*)	*to feel like doing something*
tener (mucha) hambre	*to be (very) hungry*
tener (mucho) miedo	*to be (very) afraid/ scared*
tener (mucha) prisa	*to be in a (big) hurry*
tener que + (*inf.*)	*to have to do something*
tener razón	*to be right*
no tener razón	*to be wrong*
tener (mucha) sed	*to be (very) thirsty*
tener (mucho) sueño	*to be (very) sleepy*
tener (mucha) suerte	*to be (very) lucky*

Possessive adjectives	*See page 83.*
Expresiones útiles	*See page 75.*

Los pasatiempos

4

Communicative Goals

You will learn how to:

- Talk about pastimes weekend activities, and sports
- Make plans and invitations
- Talk about the weather

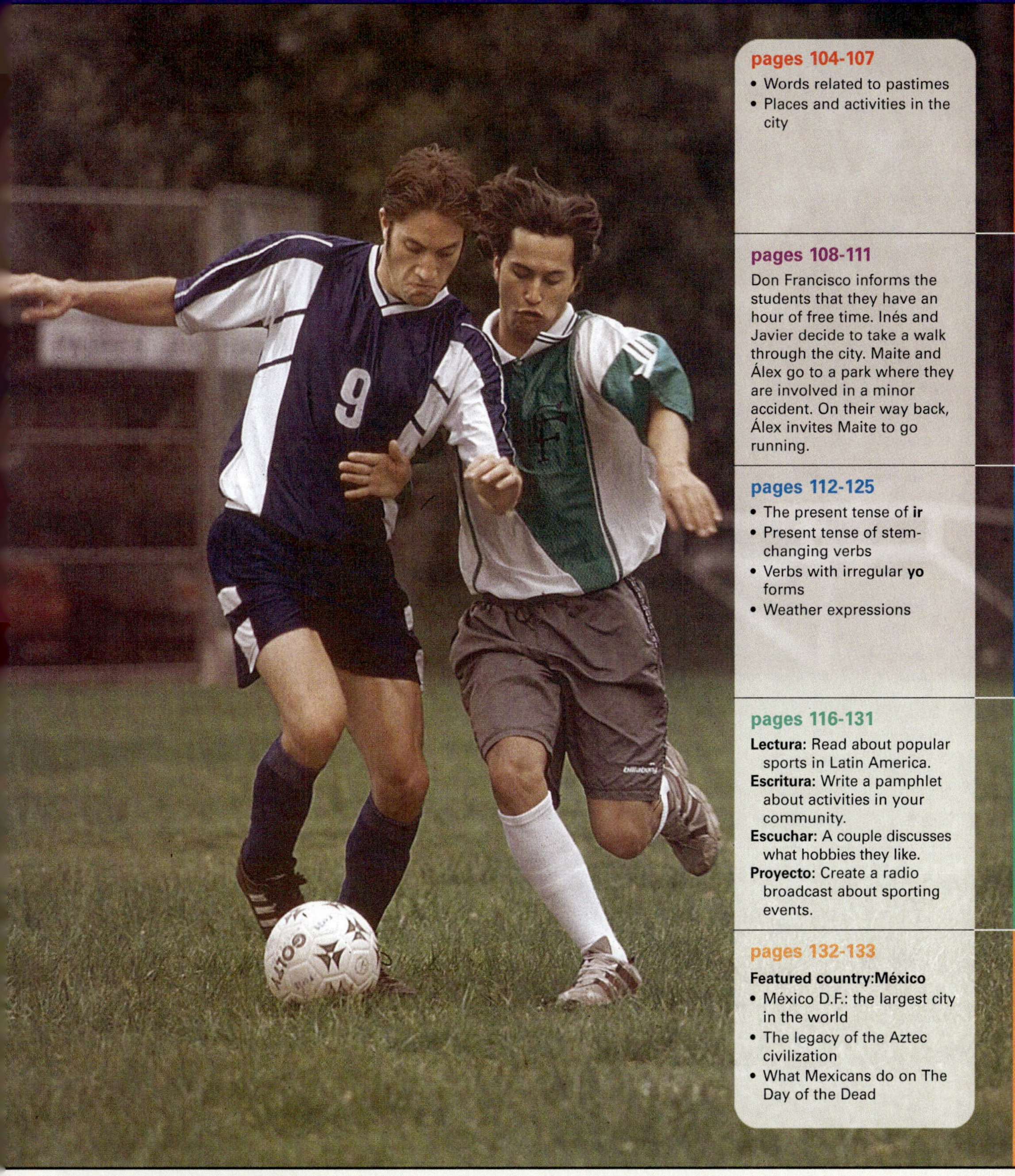

contextos

fotonovela

Don Francisco informs the students that they have an hour of free time. Inés and Javier decide to take a walk through the city. Maite and Álex go to a park where they are involved in a minor accident. On their way back, Álex invites Maite to go running.

estructura

adelante

Lectura: Read about popular sports in Latin America.
Escritura: Write a pamphlet about activities in your community.
Escuchar: A couple discusses what hobbies they like.
Proyecto: Create a radio broadcast about sporting events.

panorama

Featured country:México
- México D.F.: the largest city in the world
- The legacy of the Aztec civilization
- What Mexicans do on The Day of the Dead

Lesson Goals

In **Lesson 4** students will be introduced to the following:

- names of sports and other pastimes
- names of places in a city
- present tense of **ir**
- the contraction **al**
- **ir + a +** *infinitive*
- present tense of common stem-changing verbs
- verbs with irregular **yo** forms
- weather expressions with **hacer** and **estar**
- predicting content by surveying graphic elements
- using a Spanish-English dictionary
- writing a pamphlet that lists events
- listening for the gist
- writing and delivering a radio sports broadcast
- cultural, historical, and geographic information about Mexico

Lesson Preview

Have students look at the photo. Say: **Es una foto de dos atletas. Ellos juegan al fútbol.** Then ask: **¿Cómo son los jóvenes? ¿Juegan al fútbol o al tenis?**

INSTRUCTIONAL RESOURCES

Student Activities Manual: Workbook, 37–48
Student Activities Manual: Lab Manual, 235–240
Student Activities Manual: Video Activities, 333–334
Instructor's Resource Manual: Hojas de actividades, 6–8
Instructor's Resource Manual: Answer Keys
Tapescript/Videoscript
Overhead Transparencies, 1–2, 19–22
Student Cassette/CD
Lab Cassette/CD
Video Program
CD-ROM
Website: **www.vistasonline.com**
Testing Program: Prueba A, Prueba B

Section Goals

In **Contextos**, students will learn and practice:

- names of sports, pastimes, and other activities
- names of places in a city

Instructional Resources
Student Activities Manual: Workbook, 37-38; Lab Manual, 235
Hoja de actividades, 6
Transparencies 19–20
Student Cassette/CD

Before Presenting Contextos Introduce active lesson vocabulary. Beginning in English, ask volunteers about sports they may enjoy. Ask: **Who likes to play a sport?** Write **practicar un deporte** on the board and explain that it means *to practice, play a sport.* To a student who answers, ask: **¿Qué deportes practicas?** Offer some cognates as suggestions: **¿Practicas el béisbol? ¿el vóleibol? ¿el tenis? ¿el golf?** Offer help if student's sport is not a cognate. After the student has answered, ask another student: **¿Qué deporte practica ____?** Respond: **Sí, ____ practica ____.** Work your way through various students and various sports.

Assignment Have students study **Contextos** and prepare the activities in **Práctica** (except Activity 5) as homework.

Present Give students two minutes to review the park scene on pages 104–105. Then project **Transparency 19**. Have students refer to the scene to answer your true-false questions about it. Ex: **¿Cierto o falso? Dos hombres practican el baloncesto.** (**Cierto.**) **Una chica nada en la piscina.** (**Falso. Es un chico.**) and so forth. Next, give names of famous athletes and ask students which sport each one is associated with. Ex: **¿Qué deporte practica Tiger Woods? ¿Sammy Sosa? ¿Arantxa Sánchez-Vicario?** and so forth.

Los pasatiempos

Lee el periódico. (leer)

Visitan el monumento. (visitar)
Pasean. (pasear)
Toma el sol. (tomar)
Patina en línea. (patinar)
Nada. (nadar)

Más vocabulario

el béisbol	*baseball*
el ciclismo	*cycling*
el equipo	*team*
el esquí (acuático)	*(water) skiing*
el/la excursionista	*hiker*
el fútbol americano	*football*
el golf	*golf*
el hockey	*hockey*
el/la jugador(a)	*player*
la natación	*swimming*
el partido	*game; match*
la pelota	*ball*
la piscina	*swimming pool*
el tenis	*tennis*
el vóleibol	*volleyball*
bucear	*to scuba dive*
escalar montañas	*to climb mountains*
escribir una carta/ un mensaje electrónico/ una tarjeta (postal)	*to write a letter/ an e-mail message/ a postcard*
esquiar	*to ski*
ganar	*to win*
ir de excursión (a las montañas)	*to go on a hike (in the mountains)*
leer correo electrónico	*to read e-mail*
leer una revista	*to read a magazine*
practicar deportes (*m. pl.*)	*to play sports*
ser aficionado/a a	*to be a fan of*
deportivo/a	*sports-related*

Variación léxica

piscina ⟷ pileta (*Arg.*); alberca (*Méx.*)
baloncesto ⟷ básquetbol (*Amér. L.*)
béisbol ⟷ pelota (*P. Rico, Rep. Dom.*)

recursos

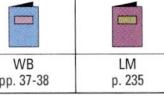

R			
SCASS./CD Lección 4	WB pp. 37-38	LM p. 235	LCASS./CD Cass. 2b/CD2

TEACHING OPTIONS

Game Have students work in pairs. Ask each to write down in Spanish his or her three favorite sports or leisure activities. In turn, each student shares his or her information with the other, who must remember what his or her partner has said without writing it down. With the whole class, ask random students to report their partner's activities. The partner confirms whether all three reported activities were correct or not.

Variación léxica Point out that many sports in Spanish are referred to by names derived from English (**básquetbol, béisbol, fútbol**), including many in **Más vocabulario: el golf, el hockey, el vóleibol**. Ask students to guess the meaning of the following activities (be sure to use Spanish pronunciation): **el footing** (*jogging*), **el cámping**, **el surf**(**ing**), **el windsurf**.

Práctica

1 Escuchar Indicate the letter of the activity in Column B that best corresponds to each statement you hear. Two items in Column B will not be used.

A	B
1. b	a. Leer correo electrónico
2. d	b. Tomar el sol
3. f	c. Pasear en bicicleta
4. c	d. Ir a un partido de fútbol americano
5. g	e. Escribir una tarjeta postal
6. h	f. Practicar muchos deportes
	g. Nadar
	h. Ir de excursión a las montañas

2 ¿Cierto o falso? Indicate whether each statement is **cierto** or **falso** based on the illustration.

	Cierto	Falso
1. Un hombre nada en la piscina.	✓	❍
2. Un hombre lee una revista.	❍	✓
3. Un chico pasea en bicicleta.	✓	❍
4. Hay un partido de baloncesto en el parque.	✓	❍
5. Dos muchachos esquían.	❍	✓
6. Dos mujeres practican el golf.	❍	✓
7. Una mujer y dos niños visitan un monumento.	✓	❍
8. Un hombre bucea.	❍	✓
9. Hay dos excursionistas.	❍	✓
10. Una mujer toma el sol.	✓	❍

3 Clasificar Classify the following words as related to **deportes, lugares** (*places*), or **personas.**

1. el hockey deportes
2. el ciclismo deportes
3. el excursionista personas
4. el esquí acuático deportes
5. la jugadora personas
6. la montaña lugares
7. la natación deportes
8. el parque lugares
9. el aficionado personas
10. la piscina lugares
11. el béisbol deportes
12. la pelota deportes

1 Present Have students check their answers by going over the tapescript questions with the whole class.

1 Tapescript 1. No me gusta nadar pero paso mucho tiempo al lado de la piscina. 2. Alicia y yo vamos al estadio a las cuatro. Creemos que nuestro equipo va a ganar. 3. Me gusta patinar en línea, esquiar y practicar el tenis. 4. El ciclismo es mi deporte favorito. 5. Me gusta mucho la natación. Paso mucho tiempo en la piscina. 6. Mi hermana es una gran excursionista.
Student Cassette/CD

2 Expand Give students three minutes to write three additional true-false sentences based on the drawing. Ask volunteers to read their sentences aloud. The rest of the class indicates whether the statements are true or false.

3 Expand Ask students to provide complete sentences based on the items. You may wish to cue them to create different responses. Ex: **—____, ¿qué es la natación? —La natación es un deporte. —¿Dónde nadan las personas? —Nadan en una piscina.**

TEACHING OPTIONS

Extra Practice Narrate a brief series of activities you want or need to do. Students have to guess the place to which you will have to go. Ex: **Necesito estudiar en un lugar tranquilo. También deseo leer una revista y uno o dos periódicos. ¿Adónde voy?** (Write on board and explain meaning of **voy.**) (**la biblioteca**)

Game Play a modified version of Twenty Questions. Ask a volunteer to think of a sport, activity, person, or place (the item must come from the vocabulary drawing or list). Other students get one chance each to ask a yes-no question until someone guesses the item correctly. Limit attempts to 10 questions per item. You may want to write some phrases on the board to cue students' questions.

4 Warm-up Project **Transparency 20** and ask brief yes-no questions to review vocabulary in **En el centro** and **Más vocabulario**. Ex: **¿Hay muchas diversiones en el centro? No tienen tiempo libre los fines de semana, ¿verdad? ¿Pasan Uds. los ratos libres en el museo?** and so forth.

4 Present/Expand Read each item aloud and ask individuals to respond with the correct answer. After each answer is given, ask a different student to verify whether the answer is correct or not, using a complete sentence. Do the first verification yourself to model possible student responses. Ex: **—Tomamos una limonada. —Es un café/restaurante. —Sí. En un café/restaurante tomamos un café.**

4 Expand Have students work in pairs to convert items into a yes-no question. Ex: **¿Tomamos una limonada en el café? (Sí.) ¿Vemos una película en el restaurante? (No.)** Have students take turns answering questions.

5 Expand After students select the correct responses in pairs, have them repeat the questions/statements and responses aloud.

5 Expand Working with the same partner, students create an original question/statement and response, modeled after those in the activity. Then have volunteers share their mini-conversation with the class.

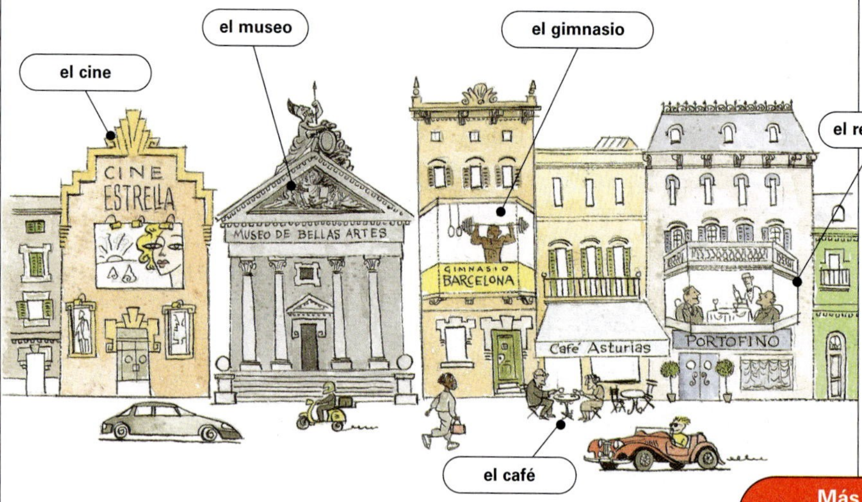

En el centro

Más vocabulario

la diversión	*fun activity; entertainment; recreation*
el fin de semana	*weekend*
el lugar	*place*
el pasatiempo	*pastime; hobby*
los ratos libres	*spare (free) time*
el tiempo libre	*free time*
pasar tiempo	*to spend time*
pasear por la ciudad/el pueblo	*to walk around the city/the town*
ver películas (*f. pl.*)	*to see movies*
favorito/a	*favorite*

4 **Identificar** Identify the place where these activities would take place.

modelo
Esquiamos.
Es una montaña.

1. Tomamos una limonada. Es un café./Es un restaurante.
2. Vemos una película. Es un cine.
3. Nadamos y tomamos el sol. Es una piscina./Es un parque.
4. Hay muchos monumentos. Es un parque./Es una ciudad.
5. Comemos tacos y fajitas. Es un restaurante.
6. Miramos pinturas (*paintings*) de Diego Rivera y Frida Kahlo. Es un museo.
7. Hay mucho tráfico. Es una ciudad./Es el centro.
8. Hacemos ejercicio. Es un gimnasio.

5 **Seleccionar** Working with a partner, select the most logical response to each statement.

1. ¿Dónde está la piscina? ¿Está cerca de aquí? d
2. ¿Hay un restaurante bueno en el centro? c
3. Me gusta visitar monumentos. a
4. ¿Qué tal, Juanita? ¿No corres hoy? e
5. ¿Te gusta ir al cine los fines de semana? b
6. ¿No te gusta practicar el béisbol? f

a. Pues, en el parque hay una estatua (*statue*) de Benito Juárez.
b. Sí, me gusta ver películas los sábados.
c. Sí, me gusta comer en el restaurante Portofino.
d. Sí, está en el parque municipal, cerca del gimnasio.
e. No, hoy no estoy bien.
f. Sí, pero me gusta más practicar el ciclismo.

AYUDA

Me gusta...
I like (to)...
No me gusta...
I don't like (to)...
¿Te gusta...?
Do you like (to)...?

• • •

Gustar becomes plural when the thing liked is plural:
Me gustan los gatos.
I like cats.
No me gustan los insectos.
I don't like insects.

• • •

Gustar and verbs like gustar For more information on **gustar**, see lesson 7, section 7.4, p. 218.

TEACHING OPTIONS

Extra Practice Give students five minutes to jot down the description of a typical weekend for them: what they do, where they go, whom they spend their time with. Circulate among the class to help out with unfamiliar vocabulary. Then have volunteers share their information with the others. The class decides whether they are representative of the "typical" student or not.

Game Play a game of continuous narration. One student begins with: **Es sábado por la mañana y voy [al café].** The next student then describes what he or she is doing there: **Estoy en el café y tomo una Coca-Cola.** Students should feel free to move the narration to other locales. You may need to write certain words and phrases on the board to aid them: **voy a/al...**, **luego**, **después**, and so forth. See how long the class can continue the narration.

Comunicación

6 **Preguntar** Ask a classmate what he or she does in the places mentioned below. Your classmate will respond using verbs from the word bank. Answers will vary.

beber	leer	patinar
correr	mirar	practicar
escalar	nadar	tomar
escribir	pasear	visitar

modelo

un pueblo interesante
Estudiante 1: ¿Qué haces (*do you do*) cuando estás en un pueblo interesante?
Estudiante 2: Paseo por el pueblo y busco lugares interesantes.

1. una biblioteca
2. un estadio
3. una ciudad grande
4. una piscina
5. las montañas
6. un parque
7. un café
8. un museo

7 **Conversación** Using the words and expressions provided, work with a partner to prepare a short conversation about your pastimes. Answers will vary.

¿a qué hora?	¿cuándo?	¿qué?
¿cómo?	¿dónde?	¿con quién(es)?

modelo

Estudiante 1: ¿Cuándo patinas en línea?
Estudiante 2: Patino en línea los domingos. Y tú, ¿patinas en línea?
Estudiante 1: No, no me gusta patinar en línea. Me gusta practicar el béisbol.

8 **Entrevista** Your instructor will give you a worksheet. Working with one or two classmates, interview each other to find how you like to spend your free time and note the responses on your worksheet. Each of you should mention at least five activities and specify where they take place. Answers will vary.

Nombre ______________

Actividades	Lugares

TEACHING OPTIONS

Extra Practice On a sheet of paper, students write down six activities they like to do. Then they circulate around the room trying to find other students who also like to do those activities (**¿Te gusta… ?**) Once a student finds someone that shares a particular activity in common, he or she asks that student to sign his or her name (**Firma aquí, por favor.**). How many signatures can each student collect?

Game On a slip of paper, each student writes down the one activity that best describes him or her without writing down his or her name. Collect the slips of paper and mix them up in a hat. Pull out each slip of paper and read the activity. The rest of the class has to guess who the student is. If a particular activity best describes more than one student, ask them to elaborate: With whom do they do the activity? Where? When? and so forth.

6 Warm-up/Present Have students read the directions. Quickly review some of the verbs listed. Ask a volunteer to read the **Modelo** with you. Make sure students understand the meaning of **¿Qué haces… ?** and that they will use the phrase throughout the activity.

6 Expand Ask additional questions and have volunteers answer. Ex: **¿Qué haces en la residencia estudiantil (el apartamento, la casa)?** Suggested places: **la casa de un amigo/una amiga, el centro de la ciudad, el gimnasio**.

7 Present Have students read the directions and the **Modelo**. Model the pronunciation of the model sentences. Have students ask and answer questions for four to five minutes.

7 Expand After students have asked and answered questions, ask volunteers to report his or her partner's activities back to the class. The partner should verify whether the information is correct or not.

8 Warm-up Ask students to indicate possible questions they may use to interview their partner(s) and write these on the board. Then distribute **Hoja de actividades 6**.

8 Expand Ask volunteers to list the information they collected, but not the student names. Write down these activities and places on the board. When you have 8–10 activities listed, ask for a show of hands to see how many students do those activities and if they do them in the same or similar places. What are the general tendencies of the class?

Assignment Have students prepare the activities in **Student Activities Manual: Workbook**, pages 37–38.

Section goals

In **Fotonovela** students will:

- receive comprehensible input from free-flowing discourse
- learn functional phrases for making invitations and plans, talking about pastimes, and apologizing

Instructional Resources
Student Activities Manual: Video Activities 333–334
Video Program (Start: 00:17:00)

Video Synopsis The travelers have an hour to explore the city before checking into the cabins. Javier and Inés decide to stroll around the city. Álex and Maite go to the park. While Maite writes postcards, Álex and a young man play soccer. A stray ball hits Maite. Álex and Maite return to the bus, and Álex invites her to go running with him that evening.

Before Presenting Fotonovela Have students quickly glance over the **Fotonovela** and make a list of the cognates they find. Ask them to guess what this **Fotonovela** episode is about, based on the cognates.

Assignment Have students study **Fotonovela** and **Expresiones útiles** as homework.

Warm-up Have students tell you a few expressions used to talk about pastimes. Then ask a few questions about pastimes. Ex: **¿Eres aficionado/a a un deporte? ¿Te gusta el fútbol?**

Present Read the **Expresiones útiles** aloud and have the class repeat. Then ask individual students a few questions. Ex: **¿Qué vas a hacer esta noche? ¿Por qué no vamos al parque?**

Continued on page 109.

¡Vamos al parque!

NATIONAL STANDARDS communication cultures

Los estudiantes pasean por la ciudad y hablan de sus pasatiempos.

PERSONAJES

DON FRANCISCO

JAVIER

INÉS

ÁLEX

MAITE

JOVEN

1

DON FRANCISCO Son las tres. Tienen una hora libre. Pueden explorar la ciudad, si quieren. Tenemos que ir a las cabañas a las cuatro.

2

JAVIER Inés, ¿quieres ir a pasear por la ciudad?

INÉS Sí, vamos.

3

ÁLEX ¿Por qué no vamos al parque, Maite? Podemos hablar y tomar el sol.

MAITE ¡Buena idea! Hace mucho sol hoy. También quiero escribir unas postales.

6

ÁLEX ¡Maite!

MAITE ¡Dios mío!

7

JOVEN Mil perdones. Lo siento muchísimo.

MAITE ¡No es nada! Estoy bien.

8

ÁLEX Ya son las dos y treinta. Debemos regresar al autobús, ¿no?

MAITE Tienes razón.

ÁLEX Oye, Maite, ¿qué vas a hacer esta noche?

MAITE No tengo planes. ¿Por qué?

recursos

R	VIDEO Lección 4	VM pp. 333-334

TEACHING OPTIONS

Video Tips General suggestions for using video clips in the classroom can be found on page IAE-13 of the **Instructor's Annotated Edition**.

¡Vamos al parque! Play the last half of the **¡Vamos al parque!** segment of this video module and have the class give you a description of what they saw. Write their observations on the board, pointing out any incorrect information. Repeat this process to allow the class to pick up more details of the plot. Then ask students to use the information they have accumulated to guess what happened at the beginning of the **¡Vamos al parque!** segment. Write their guesses on the board. Then play the entire video module and, through discussion, help the class summarize the plot.

MAITE ¿Eres aficionado a los deportes, Álex?

ÁLEX Sí, me gusta mucho el fútbol. Me gusta también nadar, correr e ir de excursión a las montañas.

MAITE Yo también corro mucho.

ÁLEX Oye, Maite, ¿por qué no jugamos al fútbol con él?

MAITE Mmm... no quiero. Voy a terminar de escribir unas postales.

ÁLEX Eh, este... a veces salgo a correr por la noche. ¿Quieres venir a correr conmigo?

MAITE Sí, vamos. ¿A qué hora?

ÁLEX ¿A las seis?

MAITE Perfecto.

DON FRANCISCO Esta noche van a correr. ¡Y yo no tengo energía para pasear!

Enfoque cultural El fútbol

Soccer, or **fútbol,** is the most popular spectator sport and the most widely-played team game in the world. It is also the most popular sport in the Spanish-speaking world. People of all ages can be seen playing soccer in public parks and streets, and each country has a professional league with its own stars. Gabriel Batistuta from Argentina, Marcelo Salas from Chile, and Hugo Sánchez from Mexico are among the most famous contemporary Hispanic soccer players.

Expresiones útiles

Making invitations

▶ **¿Por qué no vamos al parque?**
Why don't we go to the park?
▷ **¡Buena idea!**
Good idea!
▶ **¿Por qué no jugamos al fútbol?**
Why don't we play soccer?
▷ **Mmm... no quiero.**
Hmm... I don't want to.
▷ **Lo siento, pero no puedo.**
I'm sorry, but I can't.

▶ **¿Quieres ir a pasear por la ciudad conmigo?**
Do you want to walk around the city with me?
▷ **Sí, vamos.**
Yes, let's go.
▷ **Sí, si tenemos tiempo.**
Yes, if we have time.

Making plans

▶ **¿Qué vas a hacer esta noche?**
What are you going to do tonight?
▷ **No tengo planes.**
I don't have any plans.
▷ **Voy a terminar de escribir unas postales.**
I'm going to finish writing some postcards.

Talking about pastimes

▶ **¿Eres aficionado/a a los deportes?**
Are you a sports fan?
▷ **Sí, me gustan todos los deportes.**
Yes, I like all sports.
▷ **Sí, me gusta mucho el fútbol.**
Yes, I like soccer a lot.

▷ **Me gusta también nadar, correr e ir de excursión a las montañas.**
I also like to swim, run, and go hiking in the mountains.
▷ **Yo también corro mucho.**
I also run a lot.

Apologizing

▷ **Mil perdones./Lo siento muchísimo.**
I'm so sorry.

Have the class read through the entire **Fotonovela**, with volunteers playing the parts of don Francisco, Javier, Inés, Álex, Maite, and the **Joven**. Model correct pronunciation as needed. You may want to have students take turns playing the roles so that more students have the opportunity to participate. See ideas for using the video in **Teaching Options**, page 108.

Comprehension Check Check comprehension of the **Fotonovela** episode by doing Activity 1, page 110, orally with the whole class.

Suggestion Have the class look at the **Expresiones útiles**. Point out the written accents in the words **¿qué?, ¿por qué?**, and **también**. Explain that accents indicate a stressed syllable in a word (**también**) and that all question words have accent marks. Then mention that **voy, vas, va,** and **vamos** are present-tense forms of the verb **ir**. Point out that **ir a** is used with an infinitive to tell what is going to happen. Ex: **¿Qué vas a hacer? Voy a terminar de escribir unas postales.** Explain that **quiero, quieres,** and **siento** are forms of the verbs **querer** and **sentir**, which undergo a stem-vowel change from **e** to **ie** in certain forms. Tell your students that they will learn more about these concepts in the upcoming **Estructura** section.

Assignment Have students prepare activities 2–4 in **Reacciona a la fotonovela** as homework.

TEACHING OPTIONS

Enfoque cultural Tell the class that children—generally boys—in Spanish-speaking countries often take up soccer at a very early age, playing on pick-up soccer teams in their neighborhoods. Many people continue to participate as players or spectators in local soccer clubs through adulthood. Explain that nearly every town or city has its own club and that larger cities have professional clubs that may be well-known through out the nation. Team rivalries can be fierce. Mention that excitement about soccer often rises to a fever pitch every four years during the **Copa Mundial** (*World Cup*), which is the sport's international championship. At that time top-notch professional players, who may be members of teams in other countries, form national teams to compete with other national teams. Spanish-speaking countries have competed regularly in the World Cup, which was first played in Uruguay in 1930.

Reacciona a la fotonovela

1 Warm-up Have the class briefly glance over the **Fotonovela** before beginning this activity.

2 Expand Tell the class to add the **Joven** to the list of possible answers. Then give these items to the class as numbers 6, 7, and 8: **6. ¿Te gustan los deportes? (Maite) 7. ¡Ay, señorita! Lo siento mucho. (Joven) 8. Ay, no tengo mucha energía. (don Francisco)**

3 Present This activity is suitable for individual work, pair work, group work, or whole-class discussion.

3 Expand Give these questions to the class as items 6–7: **6. ¿A qué hora corren Álex y Maite esta noche? (a las seis) 7. ¿A qué hora tienen que ir a las cabañas los estudiantes? (a las cuatro)**

3 Expand Rephrase the questions as true-false statements. Have students correct the false statements. Ex: **Inés y Javier desean ir al parque. (Falso. Desean pasear por la ciudad.)**

4 Possible response
S1: ¿Eres aficionada a los deportes?
S2: Sí, me gustan mucho.
S1: ¿Te gusta el fútbol?
S2: Sí, mucho. Me gusta también nadar y correr. Oye, ¿qué vas a hacer esta noche?
S1: No tengo planes.
S2: ¿Quieres ir a correr conmigo?
S1: Lo siento pero no me gusta correr. ¿Te gusta patinar en línea? ¿Por qué no vamos al parque a patinar?
S2: ¡Buena idea!

Reacciona a la fotonovela

1 Escoger Choose the answer that best completes each sentence.

1. Inés y Javier __b__.
   a. toman el sol b. pasean por la ciudad c. corren por el parque
2. Álex desea __a__ en el parque.
   a. hablar y tomar el sol b. hablar y leer el periódico c. nadar y tomar el sol
3. A Álex le gusta nadar, __c__.
   a. jugar al fútbol b. escalar montañas c. ir de excursión y correr
4. A Maite le gusta __b__.
   a. nadar y correr b. correr y escribir postales c. correr y jugar al fútbol
5. Maite desea __c__.
   a. ir de excursión b. jugar al fútbol c. ir al parque

2 Identificar Identify the person who would make each statement.

1. No me gusta practicar el fútbol pero me gusta correr. __Maite__
2. ¿Por qué no vamos a pasear por la ciudad? __Javier__
3. ¿Por qué no exploran Uds. la ciudad? Tienen tiempo. __don Francisco__
4. ¿Por qué no corres conmigo esta noche? __Álex__
5. No voy al parque. Prefiero estar con mi amigo. __Inés__

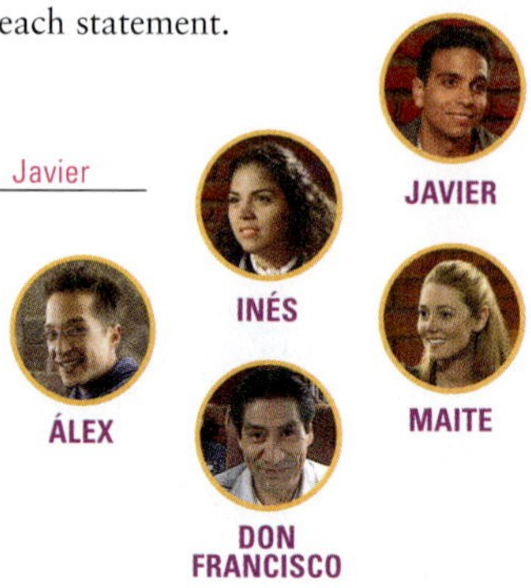

3 Preguntas Answer the questions using the information from the **Fotonovela.**

1. ¿Qué desean hacer Inés y Javier?
   Desean pasear por la ciudad.
2. ¿Qué desea hacer Álex en el parque?
   Desea jugar al fútbol.
3. ¿Qué desea hacer Maite en el parque?
   Maite desea escribir postales./Maite desea terminar de escribir unas postales.
4. ¿A qué hora regresan Maite y Álex al autobús?
   Regresan a las dos y media.
5. ¿Qué deciden hacer Maite y Álex esta noche?
   Deciden ir a correr.

4 Conversación With a partner, prepare a conversation in which you talk about pastimes and invite each other to do some activity together. Use the following expressions:
Answers will vary.

1. ¿Eres aficionado/a a...?
2. ¿Te gusta...?
3. ¿Qué vas a hacer esta noche...?
4. ¿Por qué no...?
5. ¿Quieres... conmigo?

NATIONAL communication STANDARDS

AYUDA
contigo *with you*
¿A qué hora? *(At) What time?*
¿Dónde? *Where?*
No puedo porque... *I can't because...*
Nos vemos a las siete. *See you at seven.*

TEACHING OPTIONS

Small Groups Have the class quickly glance at frames 4–9 of the **Fotonovela**. Then have students work in groups of three to ad-lib what transpires between Álex, Maite, and the **Joven**. Assure them that it is not necessary to follow the **Fotonovela** word for word. Students should be creative while getting the general meaning across with the vocabulary and expressions they know.

Extra practice Have your students close their books and complete these statements with words from the **Fotonovela. 1. _____ a terminar de escribir unas postales. (Voy) 2. ¡Mil _____! Lo siento muchísimo. (perdones) 3. Inés, ¿_____ ir a pasear por la ciudad? (quieres) 4. ¿Por qué no _____ al parque, Maite? (vamos) 5. Maite, ¿qué vas a _____ esta noche? (hacer)**

NATIONAL STANDARDS comparisons

Pronunciación

Word stress and accent marks

pe-lí-cu-la **e-di-fi-cio** **ver** **yo**

Every Spanish syllable contains at least one vowel. When two vowels are joined in the same syllable they form a **diphthong.** A **monosyllable** is a word formed by a single syllable.

bi-blio-te-ca **vi-si-tar** **par-que** **fút-bol**

The syllable of a Spanish word that is pronounced most emphatically is the "stressed" syllable.

pe-lo-ta **pis-ci-na** **ra-tos** **ha-blan**

Words that end in **n, s,** or a **vowel** are usually stressed on the next to last syllable.

na-ta-ción **pa-pá** **in-glés** **Jo-sé**

If words that end in **n, s,** or a **vowel** are stressed on the last syllable, they must carry an accent mark on the stressed syllable.

bai-lar **es-pa-ñol** **u-ni-ver-si-dad** **tra-ba-ja-dor**

Words that do *not* end in **n, s,** or a **vowel** are usually stressed on the last syllable.

béis-bol **lá-piz** **ár-bol** **Gó-mez**

If words that do *not* end in **n, s,** or a **vowel** are stressed on the next to last syllable, they must carry an accent mark on the stressed syllable.

En la unión está la fuerza.[2]

Práctica Pronounce each word, stressing the correct syllable. Then give the word stress rule for each word.

1. profesor
2. Puebla
3. ¿Cuántos?
4. Mazatlán
5. examen
6. ¿Cómo?
7. niños
8. Guadalajara
9. programador
10. México
11. están
12. geografía

Oraciones Read the conversation aloud to practice word stress.

MARINA Hola, Carlos. ¿Qué tal?
CARLOS Bien. Oye, ¿a qué hora es el partido de fútbol?
MARINA Creo que es a las siete.
CARLOS ¿Quieres ir?
MARINA Lo siento, pero no puedo. Tengo que estudiar biología.

Refranes Read these sayings aloud to practice word stress.

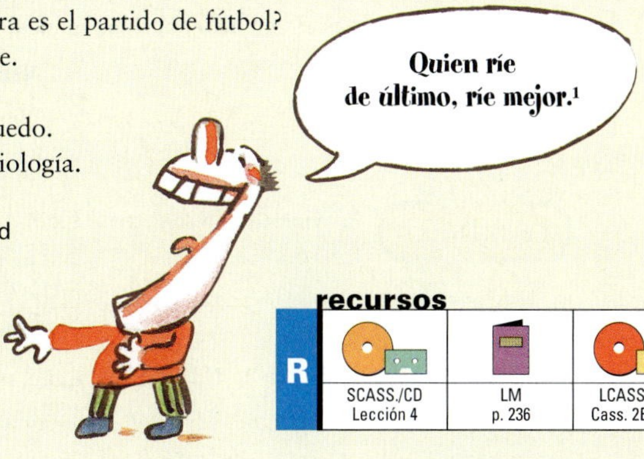
Quien ríe de último, ríe mejor.[1]

1 He who laughs last, laughs longest.
2 United we stand.

recursos

R	SCASS./CD Lección 4	LM p. 236	LCASS./CD Cass. 2B/CD2

Section Goals

In **Pronunciación** students will be introduced to
- the concept of word stress
- diphthongs and monosyllables
- accent marks

Instructional Resources
Student Activities Manual: Lab Manual, 236
Student Cassette/CD

Present
- Write **película**, **edificio**, **ver**, and **yo** on the board. Model their pronunciation. Ask the class to identify the diphthongs and the monosyllables.
- Write **biblioteca**, **visitar**, and **parque** on the board. Model their pronunciation, then ask which syllables are stressed.
- Explain that words that end in a vowel, **n**, or **s** are usually stressed on the next to last syllable. Write **pelota**, **ratos**, and **hablan** on the board and have the class pronounce them.
- Say that when words that end in **n**, **s**, or a vowel are stressed on the last syllable, they carry an accent mark. Pronounce the words **natación**, **papá**, and **inglés**, and have the class repeat.
- Point out that words that don't end in **n**, **s**, or a vowel are usually stressed on the last syllable. Write **bailar**, **español**, and **universidad** on the board and have volunteers pronounce them.
- Mention that when words that do not end in **n**, **s**, or a vowel are stressed on the next to last syllable, they carry an accent mark. Say the words **béisbol**, **lápiz**, and **árbol** and have a volunteer write them on the board.

Práctica/Oraciones/Refranes Model pronunciation having students repeat after you. Explain that **¿Cómo?** has an accent because it is a question word.

TEACHING OPTIONS

Extra practice Write on the board or an overhead transparency a list of Mexican place names, then have the class pronounce each name, paying particular attention to word stress. Ex: **Campeche, Durango, Culiacán, Tepic, Chichén Itzá, Zacatecas, Colima, Nayarit, San Luis Potosí, Sonora, Puebla, Morelos, Veracruz, Toluca, Guanajuato, Pachuca, Durango, El Tajín, Chetumal**. Model pronunciation as necessary.

Small Groups On the chalkboard, write a list of words that the class already knows. Then have the class work in small groups to come up with the word stress rule that applies to each word. Ex: **Inés, lápiz, equipo, pluma, Javier, chicas, comer, Álex, mujer, tenis, hombre, libros, papel, parque, béisbol, excursión, deportes, fútbol, pasear, esquí.**

Section Goals

In **Estructura 4.1**, students will learn:

- the present tense of **ir**
- the contraction **al**
- **ir** + **a** + *infinitive* to express future events
- **vamos a** to express *Let's . . .*

Student Activities Manual: Workbook, 39-40; Lab Manual, 237; Hoja de actividades 7

Before Presenting Estructura 4.1 Write your next day's schedule on the board, mixing infinitives with nouns. Ex: **8:00–la biblioteca; 12:00–comer**, and so forth. Explain what you are going to do using the verb **ir.** Ask volunteers questions in which you use forms of **ir** about their schedules.
Assignment Have students study **Estructura 4.1** and prepare the exercises on pages 112–113 as homework.

Present Work through the discussion of the present tense of the verb **ir**, writing the paradigm on the board as you do so. Test comprehension as you proceed by asking individuals questions about their future plans using **ir.** **Ex: ____, ¿adónde vas el sábado? ¿Cuándo vas a viajar a México, ____?** Point out the difference in usage between **dónde** and **adónde**. Ex: **¿Dónde está la casa de los Franco? ¿Adónde va José Franco?**

Suggestion After you have presented the use of **ir** to express the idea of *let's*, consolidate by asking volunteers to respond to your prompts with suggestions of things to do. Ex: **—Tengo hambre. —Vamos a la cafetería. —Quiero ver una buena película. —Vamos al cine.**

4.1 The present tense of **ir**

NATIONAL STANDARDS comparisons

ANTE TODO The verb **ir** (*to go*) is irregular in the present tense. Note that, except for the **yo** form (**voy**) and the lack of a written accent on the **vosotros** form (**vais**), the endings are the same as those for **–ar** verbs.

***ir* (to go)**

Singular forms		Plural forms	
yo	**voy**	nosotros/as	**vamos**
tú	**vas**	vosotros/as	**vais**
Ud./él/ella	**va**	Uds./ellos/ellas	**van**

▶ **Ir** is often used with the preposition **a** (*to*). If **a** is followed by the definite article **el**, they combine to form the contraction **al**. If **a** is followed by the other definite articles (**la, las, los**), there is no contraction.

a + el = al

Voy **al** parque con Juan.
I'm going to the park with Juan.

Los excursionistas van **a las** montañas.
The hikers are going to the mountains.

CONSÚLTALO

Estructura To review **de** + **el** contraction, see Lesson 1, section 1.3, pp. 18-19.

▶ The construction **ir a** + [*infinitive*] is used to talk about actions that are going to happen in the future. It is equivalent to the English *to be going to* + [*infinitive*].

Va a leer el periódico.
He is going to read the newspaper.

Van a pasear por el pueblo.
They are going to walk around town.

¡ATENCIÓN!

Remember to use **adónde** when asking a question that contains a form of the verb **ir**:
¿Adónde vas?
(To) Where are you going?

Voy a escribir unas postales.

Álex y Maite van a volver al autobús.

▶ **Vamos a** + [*infinitive*] can also express the idea of *let's (do something)*.

Vamos a ir al cine.
Let's go to the movies.

¡**Vamos** a ver!
Let's see!

¡INTÉNTALO! Provide the present tense forms of **ir**. The first item has been done for you.

1. Ellos ___van___.
2. Yo ___voy___.
3. Tu novio ___va___.
4. Adela ___va___.
5. Mi prima y yo ___vamos___.
6. Tú ___vas___.
7. Uds. ___van___.
8. Nosotros ___vamos___.
9. Ud. ___va___.
10. Nosotras ___vamos___.
11. Miguel ___va___.
12. Ellos ___van___.

TEACHING OPTIONS

TPR Invent gestures to pantomime activities mentioned in Lesson 4. Ex: **poner la televisión** (press the button on a remote control), **patinar** (skate), **nadar** (move arms as if swimming) Signal individuals to gesture appropriately as you cue activities with **Vamos a. . .** . Keep the pace brisk.
Heritage Speakers Have Spanish speakers make a list of public or commercial places where people go in their home country but do not exist in the U.S. Ex: **En nuestro país vamos a la churrería.** Have them write these names on the board and explain their meaning to the class.
Extra Practice To provide oral practice with the verb **ir**, provide prompts similar to those in **Inténtalo**. Say the subject and the verb, have students repeat it, then say a different subject, varying the gender and number. Have students then say the phrase with the new subject, changing the verb as necessary.

Práctica

1 **¿Adónde van?** Everyone in your neighborhood is dashing off to various places. Say where they are going.

1. la señora Castillo / el centro La señora Castillo va al centro.
2. las hermanas Gómez / la piscina Las hermanas Gómez van a la piscina.
3. tu tío y tu papá / el partido de fútbol Tu tío y tu papá van al partido de fútbol.
4. yo / el Museo de Arte Moderno (Yo) Voy al Museo de Arte Moderno.
5. nosotros / el restaurante Miramar (Nosotros) Vamos al restaurante Miramar.

CONSEJOS

Remember that when the subject is a pronoun (**tu, nosotros**, etc.) it can be dropped to avoid being repetitive.

2 **¿Qué van a hacer?** These sentences describe what several people are doing today. Use **ir a** + [*infinitive*] to say that they are also going to do the same activities tomorrow.

modelo

Martín y Rodolfo nadar en la piscina.
Van a nadar en la piscina mañana también.

1. Sara lee el periódico. Va a leer el periódico mañana también.
2. Yo practico deportes. Voy a practicar deportes mañana también.
3. Uds. van de excursión. Van a ir de excursión mañana también.
4. Mi hermana escribe una carta. Va a escribir una carta mañana también.
5. Tú tomas el sol. Vas a tomar el sol mañana también.
6. Paseamos con nuestros amigos. Vamos a pasear con nuestros amigos mañana también.
7. Mis amigos ven una película. Van a ver una película mañana también.

3 **Preguntas** With a partner, take turns asking and answering questions about where the people in the drawings are going.

modelo

Estudiante 1: *¿Adónde va Estela?*
Estudiante 2: *Va a la Librería Sol.*

1. Álex y Miguel ¿Adónde van Álex y Miguel? Van al parque.

2. mi amigo ¿Adónde va mi amigo? Va al gimnasio.

3. tú ¿Adónde vas? Voy al partido de tenis.

4. los estudiantes ¿Adónde van los estudiantes? Van al estadio.

5. profesora Torres ¿Adónde va la profesora Torres? Va a la Biblioteca Nacional.

6. Uds. ¿Adónde van Uds.? Vamos a la piscina.

1 Present Using pictures of people dressed for a particular activity, describe them to the class using the verb **ir** + *place*. Ex: Showing a picture of a basketball player, say: **Va al gimnasio.**

1 Suggestion Reiterate the information in **Consejos prácticos**, explaining that the personal endings on verbs make personal pronouns unnecessary except for emphasis.

1 Expand Once you have done the exercise, extend each answer with **pero** + **name/pronoun**, and have students complete the sentence. Ex: **La señora Castillo va al centro, pero el señor Castillo... (va al trabajo).**

2 Expand Use the same pictures you used for Activity 1 to describe what the people are going to do. Ex: **Va a jugar al baloncesto.**

2 Expand Have students answer questions about tomorrow's activities. Ex: **¿Qué van a hacer tus amigos mañana? ¿Qué va a hacer tu compañero/a mañana?** and so forth.

3 Expand Ask questions about the activities to be done at each place pictured in Activity 3 Ex: **¿Qué van a hacer Álex y Miguel en el parque? (Van a jugar.)**

3 Expand Have students work with a partner to write logic problems using **ir** + **a** + [*infinitive*]. Ex: **Pilar, Guadalupe, Salvador y Manuel van a hacer diferentes cosas hoy. Salvador va a nadar y Manuel va a comer, pero no en la casa. Guadalupe y Pilar van a ver una película. ¿Adónde van?** Then have pairs exchange papers and solve one another's problem.

TEACHING OPTIONS

Heritage Speakers Ask Spanish speakers to write six sentences with **ir** indicating places they go on weekends either by themselves or with friends and family. Ex: **Mi familia y yo siempre vamos a visitar a mi abuela los domingos.**

Game Divide the class into four-member teams. Each team will write a description of tomorrow's events for a well-known fictional character. Teams take turns reading and/or writing the description on the board without giving the name of the character. The other teams guess the identity of the character. Each correct guess earns a point for the team while the team that is able to fool the others receives two points. The team with the most points wins. Ex: **Mañana va a dormir de día. Va a caminar de noche. Va a buscar a una muchacha bonita. La muchacha va a tener miedo. (Es Drácula.)**

4 Present Model the activity for the whole class before assigning it to pairs.

4 Expand Have students convert the dependent clause to its negative form and create a new independent clause. Ex: **Cuando no deseo descansar, voy al gimnasio.**

5 Present Model turning the first phrase into a question. Ex: ____, **¿vas a comer en un restaurante hoy?** Then distribute copies of **Hoja de Actividades 7**. Give students five minutes to fill out the surveys.

5 Expand After collecting the surveys, ask individuals about their plans. Ex: If Wahid's name appears by **mirar la televisión**, ask: **¿Qué programa vas a mirar hoy?**

6 Warm-up Have each student use an idea map to brainstorm a trip he or she would like to take. Write **lugar** in the central circle and in surrounding circles write: **visitar, deportes, otras actividades, comida, compañeros/as.** Then ask a volunteer to model the mini-dialogue with you.

7 Warm-up Have students make two columns on a sheet of paper. The first one should be headed **El fin de semana tengo que...** and the other **El fin de semana deseo...** Give students a few minutes to brainstorm about their activities for the weekend.

Assignment Have students prepare activities in **Student Activities Manual: Workbook**, pages 39–40.

Comunicación

4 Situaciones Work with a partner and say where you and your friends go in the following situations. Answers will vary.

1. Cuando deseo descansar...
2. Cuando mi novio/a tiene que estudiar...
3. Si mis compañeros de clase necesitan practicar el español...
4. Si deseo hablar con unos amigos...
5. Cuando tengo dinero (*money*)...
6. Cuando mis amigos y yo tenemos hambre...
7. Si tengo tiempo libre...
8. Cuando mis amigos desean esquiar...
9. Si estoy de vacaciones...
10. Si quiero leer...

5 Encuesta Your instructor will give you a worksheet. Walk around the class and ask your classmates if they are going to do these activities today. Try to find at least two people for each item and note their names on the worksheet. Be prepared to report your findings to the class. Answers will vary.

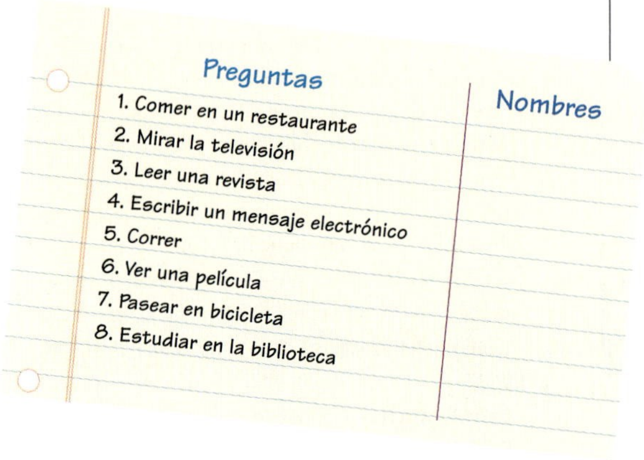

6 Entrevista Interview two classmates to find out where they are going and what they are going to do on their next vacation. Answers will vary.

modelo

Estudiante 1: ¿Adónde vas de vacaciones (for vacation)?
Estudiante 2: Voy a Guadalajara con mis amigos.
Estudiante 1: ¿Y qué van a hacer Uds. en Guadalajara?
Estudiante 2: Vamos a visitar unos monumentos y museos.

Síntesis

7 El fin de semana Create a schedule with your activities for this weekend. For each day, list at least three things you need to do and two things you will do for fun. Then tell a classmate what your weekend schedule is, and he or she will write down what you say. Switch roles to see if you have any plans in common, and then take turns inviting each other to participate in some of the activities you listed. Answers will vary.

TEACHING OPTIONS

Pairs Divide the class into pairs. Have the members of each pair take turns reading a time which you write on the board and making a suggestion of something to do. Ex: Write: **12:00** Student 1: **Son las doce en punto.** Student 2: **Vamos a la cafetería.** Write: **12:45** Student 2: **Es la una menos quince.** Student 1: **Vamos a la biblioteca**, and so forth.

Game Divide the class into groups of three. Each group has a piece of paper to write the answer on. Name a category. Ex: **lugares públicos** The first group member will write one answer and pass the paper to the next person. The paper will continue to circulate for two minutes. The group with the most words wins.

Video Show the video again to give students more input containing the verb **ir**. Stop the video where appropriate to discuss how **ir** is used to express different ideas.

4.2 Present tense of stem-changing verbs

CONSÚLTALO

The present tense of regular -ar verbs To review, see Lesson 2, section 2.1, p. 44.

•••

The present tense of regular -er and ir verbs To review, see Lesson 3, section 3.3, p. 86.

ANTE TODO Stem-changing verbs deviate from the normal pattern of regular verbs in that the stressed vowel of the stem changes when the verb is conjugated. Observe the following diagram:

Present tense of stem-changing verbs

		e ➤ ie **empezar** *(to begin)*	o ➤ ue **volver** *(to return)*	e ➤ i **pedir** *(to ask for; to request)*
SINGULAR FORMS	yo	emp**ie**zo	v**ue**lvo	p**i**do
	tú	emp**ie**zas	v**ue**lves	p**i**des
	Ud./él/ella	emp**ie**za	v**ue**lve	p**i**de
PLURAL FORMS	nosotros/as	empezamos	volvemos	pedimos
	vosotros/as	empezáis	volvéis	pedís
	Uds./ellos/ellas	emp**ie**zan	v**ue**lven	p**i**den

El joven pide perdón.

Álex empieza a enviar mensajes.

COMPARE & CONTRAST

If you compare the *endings* of the stem-changing verbs in the preceding chart with those of regular **-ar**, **-er**, and **-ir** verbs, you will see that they are the same. The difference is that stem-changing verbs have a *stem* change in all of their present tense forms *except* the **nosotros/as** and **vosotros/as** forms, which are regular.

LENGUA VIVA

As you learned on Lesson 2, **preguntar** means *to ask a question*. **Pedir** means *to ask for something*:

Ella me pregunta cuantos años tengo. *She asks me how old I am.*

Él me pide ayuda. *He asks for help.*

INFINITIVE		VERB STEM		STEM CHANGE		CONJUGATED FORM
empezar	▶	empez-	▶	emp**ie**z-	▶	empiezo
volver		volv-		v**ue**lv-		vuelvo
pedir		ped-		p**i**d-		pido

To help you identify stem-changing verbs they will appear as follows throughout the text:

empezar (e:ie), volver (o:ue), pedir (e:i)

TEACHING OPTIONS

Extra Practice Write a pattern sentence on the board, Ex: **Ella pide café**. Have students copy the model and then dictate a list of different subjects. Ex: **Maite, nosotras, don Francisco**, and so forth. Have students write down the subjects and supply the correct verb form. Ask volunteers to read their answers aloud.

Heritage Speakers Ask heritage speakers to work in pairs to conduct a mock interview with a Spanish-speaking celebrity such as **Ricky Martin, Arantxa Sánchez-Vicario, Luis Miguel**, and so forth, in which they use the verbs **empezar**, **volver**, and **pedir**. Ask them to present their interview before the class and have the class write down the forms of **empezar**, **volver**, and **pedir** that they hear.

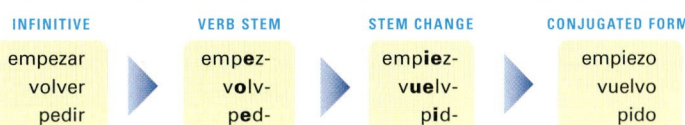

Section Goals

In **Estructura 4.2** students will be introduced to:

- present tense of stem-changing verbs
- common stem-changing verbs

Instructional Resources
Student Activities Manual: Workbook, 41–42; Lab Manual, 238; Hoja de actividades 8

Before Presenting Estructura 4.2 Take a survey of students' habits. Ask: **¿Quiénes empiezan las clases a las ocho?** and so forth. Make a chart on the board. Ask: **¿Quiénes vuelven a casa a las seis?** and so forth. Then summarize the chart. Ex: **Tú vuelves a casa a las siete, pero Amanda vuelve a las seis. Nosotros volvemos a las cinco.** Give a brief overview of the present tense of **empezar** and **volver**, emphasizing the forms in which the stem vowel changes.
Assignment Have students study **Estructura 4.2** and prepare the activities on pages 116–117 as homework.

Present tense of stem-changing verbs
Present Write **empezar, volver**, and **pedir** on the board. Then write the present-tense forms of each verb under the appropriate infinitive, in a two column paradigm, modeling the pronunciation as you do.

Suggestion Explain that an easy way to remember which persons of these verbs have stem changes is to recall that they are sometimes called boot verbs. Draw a line around the stem-changing forms in each paradigm to show the boot-like shape.

Expand Ask volunteers to answer questions using the three stem-changing verbs. Ex: **¿Qué pides en un restaurante mexicano? (Pido unas enchiladas en un restaurante mexicano.)**

Common stem-changing verbs

Present Write **e:ie, o:ue, e:i** on the board and explain that some very common verbs have these three types of stem-changes. Point out that all the verbs listed are conjugated like **empezar, volver,** or **pedir**. Model the pronunciation of the verbs and ask students a few questions using verbs of each type, having them answer in complete sentences. Ex: **¿A qué hora cierra la biblioteca? ¿Duerman los estudiantes tarde, por lo general? ¿Dónde consigues la comida cubana? ¿Qué piensan hacer este fin de semana? ¿Quién quiere comer en un restaurante esta noche?**

Reiterate that the personal endings of all the listed verbs except **seguir** and **conseguir** are the same as those of regular **-ar**, **-er**, and **-ir** verbs.

Point out the structure **jugar al** + *sport*. Practice it by asking students about the sports they play. Have them answer in complete sentences. Ex: _____, **¿te gusta jugar al fútbol? Y tú, _____, ¿juegas al fútbol? ¿Prefieres jugar al fútbol o a ver una partida en el estadio? ¿Cuántos juegan al tenis? ¿Cuál prefieres, _____, jugar al tenis o jugar al fútbol?**

Follow the same procedure with **seguir** and **conseguir**.

Suggestion Prepare "dehydrated" sentences such as these: **Maite/empezar/la lección Uds./mostrar/los trabajos Nosotros/jugar/al fútbol Tú/conseguir/libros** and write them on the board one at a time.

Close To consolidate, do **¡Inténtalo!** with the class.

Common stem-changing verbs

e:ie		o:ue		e:i	
cerrar	*to close*	**dormir**	*to sleep*	**conseguir**	*to get; to obtain*
comenzar	*to begin*	**encontrar**	*to find*	**repetir**	*to repeat*
entender	*to understand*	**mostrar**	*to show*	**seguir**	*to follow; to continue*
pensar	*to think*	**poder**	*to be able; can*		
perder	*to lose; to miss*	**recordar**	*to remember*		
preferir	*to prefer*	**volver**	*to return*		
querer	*to want; to love*				

LENGUA VIVA

The verb **perder** can mean *to lose* or *to miss*, in the sense of "to miss a train":

Siempre pierdo mis llaves.
I always lose my keys.

Es importante no perder el autobús.
It's important not to miss the bus.

▶ **Jugar**, which means to play (*a sport or game*), is the only Spanish verb in which the stem change is **u** → **ue. Jugar** is followed by **a** + [*definite article*] when the name of a sport or game is mentioned.

Oye, Maite, ¿por qué no jugamos al fútbol?

Álex y el joven juegan al fútbol.

¡ATENCIÓN!

Comenzar and **empezar** require the preposition **a** when they are followed by an infinitive:

Ana empieza a estudiar.

Comienzan a trabajar.

•••

Pensar + [*infinitive*] means *to plan* or *to intend to do something.* **Pensar en** means *to think about someone or something.*

¿Piensan ir al partido?
Are you thinking about going to the match?

Pienso mucho en mi novio.
I think about my boyfriend a lot.

▶ In addition to the stem change **e** → **i, seguir** and **conseguir** have irregular **yo** forms: **sigo, consigo.**

Sigo su plan.
I'm following their plan.

Consigo libros en el Internet.
I get books on the Internet.

¡INTÉNTALO! Provide the present tense forms of these verbs. The first item in each column has been done for you.

cerrar (e:ie)	**dormir (o:ue)**	**repetir (e: i)**
1. Uds. cierran	1. Mi abuela no duerme	1. Ellos repiten
2. Tú cierras	2. Yo no duermo	2. Teresa repite
3. Nosotras cerramos	3. Tú no duermes	3. Tú repites
4. Mi hermano cierra	4. Mis hijos no duermen	4. Raúl y yo repetimos
5. Yo cierro	5. Ud. no duerme	5. Uds. repiten
6. Ud. cierra	6. Nosotros no dormimos	6. Yo repito
7. Los chicos cierran	7. Él no duerme	7. Ana y Simón repiten
8. Ella cierra	8. Uds. no duermen	8. Ud. repite

TEACHING OPTIONS

Extra Practice For additional drills of stem-changing verbs with the whole class or with students who need extra practice, do **¡Inténtalo!** orally using other infinitives than **cerrar**, **dormir**, and **repetir**. Keep the pace rapid.

Large group Arrange all the classroom chairs in a circle and use a small ball or paper wadded into a ball for this activity. Begin by naming the infinitive of a common stem-changing verb. Then name a pronoun. Ex: **seguir/tú**. Then throw the paper ball to a student. The student catches the ball and says the appropriate form of the verb. (**sigues**) Then he or she names a different pronoun and throws the ball to a another student who must catch it and give the appropriate form of the verb. Continue until all subject pronouns have been covered, and then begin again with another infinitive.

Práctica

1 **Preferencias** With a partner, take turns asking and answering questions about what these people want to do, using the cues provided.

modelo

Guillermo: estudiar / pasear en bicicleta.
Estudiante 1: ¿Quiere estudiar Guillermo?
Estudiante 2: No, prefiere pasear en bicicleta.

1. tú: trabajar / dormir
¿Quieres trabajar? No, prefiero dormir.
2. Uds.: mirar la televisión / ir al cine
¿Quieren Uds. mirar la televisión? No, preferimos ir al cine.
3. tus amigos: ir de excursión / descansar
¿Quieren ir de excursión tus amigos? No, mis amigos prefieren descansar.
4. tú: comer en la cafetería / ir a un restaurante
¿Quieres comer en la cafetería? No, prefiero ir a un restaurante.
5. Elisa: ver una película / leer una revista
¿Quiere ver una película Elisa? No, (Elisa) prefiere leer una revista.
6. María y su hermana: tomar el sol / practicar el esquí acuático
¿Quieren tomar el sol María y su hermana? No, (María y su hermana) prefieren practicar el esquí acuático.

2 **Completar** Complete this conversation with the appropriate forms of the verbs. Then act it out with a partner.

PABLO Óscar, voy al centro ahora.
ÓSCAR ¿A qué hora ___piensas___ (pensar) volver? El partido de fútbol ___empieza___ (empezar) a las dos.
PABLO ___Vuelvo___ (Volver) a la una. ___Quiero___ (querer) ver el partido.
ÓSCAR ¿___Piensas___ (Pensar) que (*that*) nuestro equipo ___puede___ (poder) ganar?
PABLO No, ___pienso___ (pensar) que va a ___perder___ (perder). Los jugadores de Guadalajara son salvajes (*wild*) cuando ___juegan___ (jugar).

3 **Describir** Use a verb from the list to describe what these people are doing.

cerrar dormir mostrar conseguir

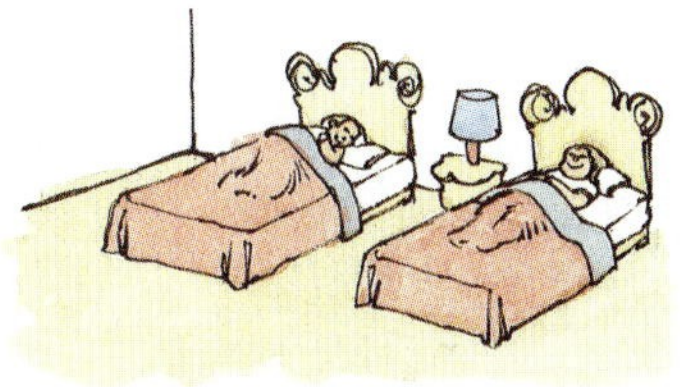
1. Las niñas Las niñas duermen.

2. Yo (Yo) Cierro la ventana.

3. Tú (Tú) Consigues una maleta.

4. Pedro Pedro muestra una foto.

1 Warm-up Model the activity by reading the **Modelo** and giving other examples in the **yo** form before assigning the activity to pairs. Ex: **¿Quiero descansar en casa? No, prefiero enseñar la clase.**

1 Expand Have students ask one another questions of their own using the same pattern. Ex: **—¿Quieres jugar al baloncesto? —No, prefiero jugar al tenis.**

2 Suggestion Go over **¡Atención!** before assigning **Actividad 2**.

2 Present Divide the class into pairs and give them three minutes to act out the conversation. Then have partners switch roles.

2 Expand Supply students with short-answer prompts based on the conversation. Ask students to give the questions that would have elicited the answers. Ex: **A las dos. (¿A qué hora empieza el partido de fútbol?) Porque no quiere perder el partido. (¿Por qué vuelve Pablo a la una?)**

2 Expand Ask questions using **pensar** + *infinitive*; **pensar en**, and **perder** (in both senses). Ex: **¿Qué piensas hacer mañana? ¿En qué piensas ahora? ¿Cuándo pierdes las cosas?**

3 Expand Use your picture file to extend this activity. Choose pictures that lend themselves to being described by the common stem-changing verbs. Have students describe what the person or persons in the picture is/are doing using stem-changing verbs.

TEACHING OPTIONS

TPR Brainstorm gestures to go with each of the stem-changing verbs. Have students pantomime the activity you mention. Tell them that only male students should respond to **él/ellos** and only females to **ella/ellas**. Everyone should respond to **nosotros**.

Game Arrange students in rows of five or six (depending on whether you use **vosotros** or not), one behind the other. The first person in the row has a piece of paper. Call out the infinitive of a stem-changing verb. The first person writes the **yo** form and passes the paper to the student behind. That student writes the **tú** form and passes the paper on. There is to be no talking. The last person in the row holds up the paper to show the team has finished. The first team to finish the conjugation correctly gets a point. Have students rotate positions in their row before calling out another verb.

Comunicación

4 **Encuesta** Your instructor will give you a worksheet. Walk around the room and ask your classmates if they play these sports. If someone plays a sport, ask where, when, and with whom he or she plays it. Note his or her name on your worksheet. Be prepared to report your findings to the class. Answers will vary.

Preguntas	Nombres	Lugares	Día(s) y hora(s)	Otros jugadores
1. el baloncesto				
2. el béisbol				
3. el fútbol				
4. el fútbol americano				
5. el golf				
6. el hockey				
7. el tenis				
8. el vóleibol				

5 **En la televisión** Read the sports listing that will be televised this weekend and choose the programs you want to watch. Compare your choices with those of a classmate and explain why you made them. Then agree on one program you will watch together on each day. Answers will vary.

sábado

13:30 NATACIÓN
1 Copa Mundial *(World Cup)* de Natación
15:00 TENIS
8 Abierto *(Open)* Mexicano de Tenis
Alejandro Hernández (México)
vs. Jacobo Díaz (España)
Semifinales
16:00 FÚTBOL NACIONAL
3 Chivas vs. Monterrey

CABLE
16:30 FÚTBOL AMERICANO PROFESIONAL
21 los Vaqueros de Dallas
vs. los Leones de Detroit
20:00 BALONCESTO PROFESIONAL
16 los Knicks de Nueva York
vs. los Toros de Chicago

domingo

13:00 GOLF
40 Audi Senior Classic
14:30 VÓLEIBOL
1 Campeonato *(Championship)* Nacional de México
16:00 BALONCESTO
3 Campeonato de Cimeba
los Correcaminos de Tampico
vs. los Santos de San Luis
Final

CABLE
15:00 ESQUÍ ALPINO
19 Eslálom
18:30 FÚTBOL INTERNACIONAL
30 Copa América: México vs. Argentina
Ronda final
20:00 PATINAJE ARTÍSTICO
16 Exhibición mundial

Síntesis

6 **Situación** Work in groups of three to role-play this situation. One of you is a tour guide in a city you know well. The other two are tourists. Using some of the verbs, nouns, and other expressions you have learned, come up with a plan for your tour of the city. Answers will vary.

CONSÚLTALO

Lectura Are your classmates' preferences in sports like those of people in Spanish-speaking countries? To find out, see pp. 126-127.

4 Warm-up/Present Model the activity for the whole class by asking questions about a well-known athlete. Ex: **¿A qué deporte juega Tiger Woods? ¿Dónde juega al golf? ¿Cuándo juega al golf? ¿Quiénes juegan a golf con él?** Write the answers on the board and point out the correspondences between the answers and the column heads in Activity 4. Distribute **Hoja de actividades 8** and have students ask their classmates questions like these .

4 Expand After tallying results on the board, ask students to graph them. Have them refer to the **Lectura** section, pages 126–127, for models.

4 Suggestion Have students respond to **Consúltalo** in writing.

5 Warm-up/Present Model the activity for the whole class by choosing two events from the program that you would watch and asking the class to react. Give pairs four or five minutes to read the list and compare their choices.

5 Expand Ask students to report the results of their choices with the class. Compare and contrast students' reasons for their choice of sports event.

6 Suggestion Refer groups to the vocabulary on page 134 for help in developing their plan.

6 Expand Station one member of each group in one part of the classroom. The other groups will circulate from one station to the other. Give stationed students one minute to explain their tourist plan to each visiting group.

Assignment Have students do activities in **Student Activities Manual: Workbook**, pages 41–42.

TEACHING OPTIONS

Small Groups Have students choose their favorite sport and work together in groups of three with other students who have chosen that same sport. Have each group write six true sentences about the sport they have chosen, using a stem-changing verb in each.

Heritage Speakers Ask Spanish speakers to describe sports preferences in their home communities, especially ones that are not widely-known in the United States, such as **jai-alai**. How do the sports preferences in their home community compare to those of the class or with those graphed in **Deportes en el mundo hispano**, pages 126–127?

4.3 Verbs with irregular **yo** forms

NATIONAL STANDARDS comparisons

ANTE TODO In Spanish, several commonly used verbs have **yo** forms that are irregular in the present tense. The other forms are generally regular.

Verbs with irregular *yo* forms

	hacer *(to do; to make)*	**poner** *(to put; to place)*	**salir** *(to leave)*	**suponer** *(to suppose)*	**traer** *(to bring)*	**oír** *(to hear)*	**ver** *(to see)*
SINGULAR FORMS	**hago**	**pongo**	**salgo**	**supongo**	**traigo**	**oigo**	**veo**
	haces	pones	sales	supones	traes	oyes	ves
	hace	pone	sale	supone	trae	oye	ve
PLURAL FORMS	hacemos	ponemos	salimos	suponemos	traemos	oímos	vemos
	hacéis	ponéis	salís	suponéis	traéis	oís	véis
	hacen	ponen	salen	suponen	traen	oyen	ven

¡ATENCIÓN!

Salir de (*to leave from*) is used when someone is leaving a place:

Hoy sale del hospital.

•••

To indicate someone's destination, you use **salir para** (*to leave for*):

Hoy sale para México.

•••

Salir con means *to leave with someone, to leave with something* or *to date someone*:

Juan sale con su papá.

Yo salgo con mi mochila.

Anita sale con Miguel.

▶ Note that the **yo** forms of **hacer, poner, salir, suponer, traer,** and **oír** end in **-go: hago, pongo, salgo, supongo, traigo,** and **oigo.**

Nunca salgo a correr, no hago ejercicio, pero sí tengo energía... ¡para leer el periódico y tomar un café!

▶ The verb **oír** is irregular in all forms except **vosotros**. Note that the **nosotros** form has an accent mark.

▶ **Poner** can mean *to turn on* when referring to household appliances.

Voy a **poner** la televisión.
I'm going to turn on the television.

Álex **pone** la radio.
Álex turns on the radio.

¡INTÉNTALO! Provide the appropriate forms of these verbs. The first item has been done for you.

1. salir	Isabel sale	Nosotros salimos	Yo salgo
2. ver	Yo veo	Uds. ven	Tú ves
3. poner	Rita y yo ponemos	Yo pongo	Los niños ponen
4. hacer	Yo hago	Tú haces	Ud. hace
5. oír	Él oye	Nosotros oímos	Yo oigo
6. traer	Éllas traen	Yo traigo	Tú traes
7. suponer	Yo supongo	Mi amigo supone	Nosotras suponemos

TEACHING OPTIONS

TPR Use the verbs with irregular **yo** forms in different sentences. Students will pantomime what you are saying. Ex: **Hago la tarea**. (Students pantomime writing their homework.) **Pongo la radio**. (turning on a radio.) **Oigo la música**. (cupping a hand over their ear.)

Game Divide the class into teams of four. Each team has a piece of paper. Call out an infinitive and a person. Ex: **traer/primera persona plural**. Each team has to compose a sentence with each person writing one part. The first team member writes a subject. Ex: **nosotras** The second writes the correct form of the verb. Ex: **traemos** The third gives a direct or indirect object. Ex: **el libro** The fourth member finishes the sentence with an adverb or a prepositional phrase. The first team to write a logical and correct sentence wins. Team members should rotate positions each time a new verb is given.

Section Goals

In **Estructura 4.3** students will learn verbs with irregular **yo** forms.

Instructional Resources
Student Activities Manual: Workbook, 43–44.

Before Presenting Estructura 4.3 Quickly review the present tense of **tener**, pointing out the **-go** ending of the **yo** form. Tell students that they are now going to learn seven very common verbs with irregular **yo** forms.

Assignment Have students study **Estructura 4.3** and prepare the exercises on pages 119–120 as homework.

Successful Language Learning Point out that students should learn the verbs with irregular **yo** forms thoroughly because these will often be used in conversation.

Present Ask questions and make statements that elicit the **yo** forms of the verbs. Ex: **¿Haces la tarea en casa o en la biblioteca? (Hago la tarea en la biblioteca.) ¿Traes un diccionario a la clase?** As you elicit responses, write just the verbs on the board until you have listed all the irregular **yo** forms.

Suggestion Go over the different uses of **salir** outlined in **¡Atención!**. Then model a second example of each usage.

Present Point out that **oír** is irregular in all forms except **nosotros** and **vosotros**. Write a model sentence on the board. Ex: **Uds. oyen el programa de radio todos los viernes**. Then change the subject, and have students give the new sentence. Ex: **tú (Tú oyes el programa de radio todos los viernes.)**

Close Consolidate by doing **¡Inténtalo!** on page 119.

1 Warm-up/Present Quickly review the new verbs with irregular **yo** forms by asking the students questions about their social habits. Ex: **¿Sales a comer en restaurantes con tus padres? ¿Ves la televisión en español? ¿Supones que una clase de matemáticas es muy difícil? ¿Haces ejercicios por la mañana?** Then, ask pairs to complete and act out the conversation, then switch roles. Give them five minutes to do the activity.

1 Expand Ask questions about the dialogue. **¿Qué hace David hoy? ¿Qué hace Diana? ¿Por qué tienen que hacer las maletas Andrés y Javier? ¿Por qué pone Ernesto la televisión?**

2 Present Model the activity by completing the **Modelo** orally. Then write another "dehydrated sentence" on the board. Ex: **ellos/?/para Guadalajara/mañana** Ask volunteers to say aloud each complete sentence.

2 Expand Change the subjects of the dehydrated sentences in the exercise and have students write the new sentences.

3 Expand Use pictures from your picture file which elicit the target verbs to extend the activity. Encourage students to add further descriptions if they can.

Close Call out different forms of the verbs studied in **Estructura 4.3**, and have volunteers say the infinitive. Ex: **oyen (oír)**.

Práctica

1 Completar Complete this conversation with the appropriate forms of the verbs. Then act it out with a partner.

ERNESTO David, ¿qué ___haces___ (hacer) hoy?
DAVID Ahora estudio biología, pero esta noche ___salgo___ (salir) con Luisa. Vamos al cine. Queremos ___ver___ (ver) la nueva (*new*) película de Almodóvar.
ERNESTO ¿Y Diana? ¿Qué ___hace___ (hacer) ella?
DAVID ___Sale___ (Salir) a comer con sus padres.
ERNESTO ¿Qué ___hacen___ (hacer) Andrés y Javier?
DAVID Tienen que ___hacer___ (hacer) las maletas. ___Salen___ (Salir) para Monterrey mañana.
ERNESTO Pues, ¿qué ___hago___ (hacer) yo?
DAVID ___Supongo___ (Suponer) que puedes estudiar o ___ver___ (ver) la televisión.
ERNESTO No quiero estudiar. Mejor, ___pongo___ (poner) la televisión. Mi programa favorito empieza en unos minutos.

2 Oraciones Form complete sentences using the cues provided and verbs you learned on page 119.

modelo
Tú / ? / libros / debajo de / escritorio
Tú pones los libros debajo del escritorio.

1. Nosotros / ? / mucha / tarea Nosotros hacemos mucha tarea.
2. ¿Tú / ? / la radio? ¿Tú oyes la radio?
3. Yo / no / ? / problema Yo no veo el problema.
4. Marta / ? / grabadora / clase Marta trae una/la grabadora a clase.
5. señores Marín / ? / su casa / siete Los señores Marín salen de/para su casa a las siete.
6. Yo / ? / que (*that*) / tú / ir / cine / ¿no? Yo supongo que tú vas al cine, ¿no?

3 Describir Use a verb from page 119 to describe what these people are doing.

1. Fernán Fernán pone la mochila en el escritorio.

2. Los aficionados Los aficionados salen del estadio.

3. Yo Yo traigo una cámara.

4. Nosotros Nosotros vemos el monumento.

5. La señora Vargas La señora Vargas no oye bien.

6. El estudiante El estudiante hace su tarea.

TEACHING OPTIONS

Pairs Have students write three sentences in each of which they use one of the target verbs from **Estructura 4.3**. Then ask them to copy their sentences onto a sheet of paper in "dehydrated" form, following the model of the sentences in Activity 2. Students exchange their sentences with a partner, who writes the complete sentences on the paper. Finally, have partners check each other's work.

Extra Practice Have students use five of the target verbs from **Estructura 4.3** to write sentences about habits or likes they have that they think are somewhat unusual. Ex: **Traigo doce bolígrafos en la mochila. Hago la tarea en un café del centro. No pongo la televisión hasta las diez de la noche.**

Comunicación

4 **Preguntas** Get together with a classmate and ask each other these questions.

Answers will vary.

1. ¿Qué traes a clase?
2. ¿Quiénes traen un diccionario a clase? ¿Por qué traen un diccionario?
3. ¿A qué hora sales de tu residencia o de tu casa por la mañana? ¿A qué hora sale tu compañero/a de cuarto o tu esposo/a?
4. ¿Dónde pones tus libros cuando regresas de clase? ¿Siempre (*Always*) pones tus cosas en su lugar?
5. ¿Pones fotos de tu familia en tu casa? ¿De quiénes son?
6. ¿Oyes la radio cuando estudias?
7. ¿Qué vas a hacer esta noche?
8. ¿Haces mucha tarea los fines de semana?
9. ¿Supones que el examen sobre la Lección 4 va a ser fácil o difícil? ¿Por qué?
10. ¿Te gusta ver deportes en la televisión o prefieres ver otros programas? ¿Cuáles?

5 **Charadas** In groups, play a game of charades. Each person should think of two phrases using the verbs **hacer, poner, salir, suponer, oír, traer,** or **ver**. The first person to guess correctly acts out the next charade. Answers will vary.

6 **Entrevista** You are doing a market research report on lifestyles. Interview a classmate to find out when he or she goes out with the following people and what they do for entertainment. Answers will vary.

- los amigos
- el/la novio/a
- el/la esposo/a
- la familia

Síntesis

7 **Situación** Ask a classmate if he or she wants to go out. He or she will accept. Then find out what activities your classmate prefers so you can decide where you want to go. Finally, negotiate the place, the day, and the time for your date with your classmate.

Answers will vary.

TEACHING OPTIONS

Pairs Have pairs of students role-play the perfect date. Students should write their script first, then present it to the class. Encourage students to use descriptive adjectives as well as the new verbs learned in **Estructura 4.3**.

Heritage Speakers Ask Spanish speakers to make an oral presentation to the class about dating customs in their home community. Remind them to use familiar vocabulary and simple sentences.

4 Warm-up Model the activity for the class by asking volunteers the first two items. Give pairs five minutes to complete the activity.

4 Expand Ask students questions about their own and their classmate's responses to the activity questions. Ex: **¿Tu compañera trae un diccionario a clase? ¿Por qué?**

4 Expand Have students write a brief summary of the information they learn.

5 Present Model the activity by doing a charade and having the class guess. Ex: **Pongo un lápiz en la mesa.** Then divide the class into groups of 5–7 students. Give groups 15 minutes to do the activity.

5 Expand Ask each group to pick out the best **charada**. Then ask the students to present them to the whole class, having the other groups guess what activities they are pantomiming.

6 Present Model the activity for the class, giving a report on your own lifestyle. Ex: **Salgo al cine con mis amigas. Me gusta comer en restaurantes con mi esposo. En familia vemos deportes en la televisión.** Remind students that a market researcher and his or her interviewee would address each other with the **Ud.** form of verbs.

7 Present Have students brainstorm the different questions to be used when inviting someone to go out. Ex: **¿Quieres salir el sábado? ¿Te gusta ir al cine?** Write the responses on the board.

Assignment Have students do the activities in **Student Activities Manual: Workbook**, pages 43–44

Section Goals

In **Estructura 4.4** students will learn:
- weather expressions with **hacer** and **estar**
- expressing hot and cold with reference to people and weather

Instructional Resources
Student Activities Manual: Workbook, 45–46; Hoja de actividades 9

Before Presenting Estructura 4.4
Introduce weather-related vocabulary by discussing the weather in your area today. Write **¿Qué tiempo hace?** on the board, explain its meaning, and point out the use of **hacer** in weather expressions. Then describe the weather outside, writing the expressions on the board. Ex: **Hoy hace sol.** (Write **Hace sol** on the board.) **Hace mucho sol. Hace calor, pero también hace un poco de viento. Por eso no hace mucho calor.** Tell students they are now going to learn other weather expressions.
Assignment Have students study **Estructura 4.4** and prepare the exercises on pages 123–124 as homework.

Present To teach weather related expressions, use pictures from your picture file that cover all the weather conditions mentioned in **Estructura 4.4**.
- Begin to describe one of the pictures using weather expressions with **hacer**. Then ask volunteers further questions that elicit the other expressions with **hacer**. Point out the use of **mucho** in these expressions and explain that it is masculine in form because **calor**, **frío**, **sol**, and **fresco** are masculine nouns.

Continued on page 123.

4.4 Weather expressions

NATIONAL comparisons STANDARDS

ANTE TODO In English, the verb *to be* is used to describe weather conditions: for example, *It's sunny*. Spanish, however, does not use **ser** or **estar** to express most weather conditions. Instead, it uses the verb **hacer**. To ask what the weather is like, use the question **¿Qué tiempo hace?**

—¿Qué tiempo **hace** hoy?
What's the weather like today?

—**Hace** buen/mal tiempo.
The weather is good/bad.

¡ATENCIÓN!
Remember that **bueno** and **malo** are shortened to **buen** and **mal** before a masculine singular noun: **buen tiempo, mal tiempo.**

Expressions with hacer

Hace (mucho) sol.
It's (very) sunny.

Hace (mucho) calor.
It's (very) hot.

Hace (mucho) viento.
It's (very) windy.

Hace (mucho) frío.
It's (very) cold.

Hace fresco.
It's cool.

- Weather expressions are frequently used with **mucho/a**, not **muy**.
- **Llover (o:ue)** (*to rain*) and **nevar (e:ie)** (*to snow*) are usually used in the third person singular form: **llueve** (*it's raining*), **nieva** (*it's snowing*).

Hoy no vamos al parque porque **llueve**.
We're not going to the park today because it's raining.

Si **nieva** hoy, voy a esquiar mañana.
If it snows today, I'm going skiing tomorrow.

TEACHING OPTIONS

Heritage Speakers Have Spanish speakers prepare and present a mid-day weather report describing the weather conditions in your area using expressions from **Estructura 4.4.**

Extra Practice Create a number of cloze sentences about the weather that require the verb forms **hace**, **hay**, and **está** to be completed. Ex: **La península de Yucatán (está) en México. (Hace) mucho calor y (hay) poca contaminación en Yucatán. No (está) muy nublado cuando (hace) sol, pero cuando (llueve) sí está nublado.**

Other weather expressions

Está (muy) nublado.
It's (very) cloudy.

Está despejado.
It's clear.

Nieva.
It's snowing.

Llueve.
It's raining.

Hay (mucha) niebla.
It's (very) foggy.

Hay (mucha) contaminación.
It's (very) smoggy.

COMPARE & CONTRAST

Calor and **frío** are conditions that can apply to both weather and people.

El niño **tiene** calor. *The child is hot.*	**Hace** calor. *It's hot.*
Tenemos frío. *We are cold.*	**Hace** frío. *It's cold.*

English uses the verb *to be* when describing either people or the weather as *hot* or *cold*. Spanish, however, uses **tener calor/frío** to refer to people and **hacer calor/frío** to refer to weather.

¡INTÉNTALO! Complete these sentences. The first item has been done for you.

1. ¿Qué tiempo ___hace___ hoy?
2. ___Hace___ fresco.
3. ___Hay___ mucha contaminación hoy.
4. Carlos ___tiene___ mucho frío.
5. ___Hace___ mal tiempo.
6. ___Está___ despejado hoy.
7. ___Hace___ mucho frío.
8. En abril ___llueve___ mucho.
9. ___Hace___ mucho viento.
10. Julia y Ana ___tienen___ calor.
11. ___Hace___ mucho sol.
12. ___Hay___ niebla.
13. ___Está___ muy nublado.
14. ___Hace___ calor.
15. Vamos a esquiar si ___nieva___.
16. ___Hace___ buen tiempo.

- Quickly review the shortened forms **buen** and **mal** and their use before the masculine noun **tiempo**.
- Next, still using pictures from your picture file, introduce **nevar**, **llover**, and weather expressions with **estar** and **hay**. Ex: **En esta foto está nublado, ¿no? ¿Creen que va a llover o no? Y en esta foto hay niebla, ¿no? ¿o hay contaminación?**
- Point out the use of **muy** with expressions that contain **estar**, and **mucha** with those that contain **hay**. Elicit that the feminine form **mucha** is used with **contaminación** and **niebla** because these are feminine nouns.
- Use pictures that include human beings to illustrate the distinction between **tener calor/frío** and **hacer calor/frío**. Ex: **En esta foto nieva. Nieva mucho, ¿no? Parece que hace mucho viento y mucho frío también. Y los jóvenes que esquían en la nieve, ¿creen que tienen frío o no? Y esta chica que sólo mira, ¿tiene frío ella?**
- Consolidate by going over **¡Inténtalo!** on page 123 orally with the whole class.

Successful Language Learning Remind your class that the weather expressions are used very frequently in conversation and that they should make a special effort to learn them.

TEACHING OPTIONS

TPR Designate a gesture to accompany each weather expression. Ex: **Hace frío** (*shiver*). **Hay contaminación** (*rub stinging eyes*). **Está nublado** (*big frown*). **Está despejado** (*big smile*). Then have the class stand. Say a weather expression and point to a student, who pantomimes the expression. Keep the pace fast. At a certain point introduce **mucho/a** and **muy** into the expressions, encouraging students to exaggerate their pantomimes.

Small Groups Bring in the weather page of a newspaper. Assign each group a different city, and have the members work together to write a description of the city's weather conditions.

1 Warm-up Quickly review weather expressions by asking students about current weather conditions around the world. Ex: **¿Hace calor en Alaska hoy? ¿Nieva en Puerto Rico? ¿Hace buen tiempo en Hawai? ¿Hay mucha contaminación en Houston? ¿Hay niebla en Londres? ¿Hace fresco en San Francisco? ¿Llueve en La Coruña?**

1 Expand Use the alternate choices in the exercise to ask students weather-related questions. Ex: **No nieva en Cancún. ¿Dónde nieva?**

2 Present Model the activity for the class before assigning it to pairs. Ask a volunteer to help you read the **Modelo** and give another example using the present conditions in your location. Give pairs ten minutes to complete the activity.

2 Suggestion Point out that the word **clima** is masculine, not feminine.

2 Expand Ask students questions that compare and contrast the weather conditions presented in Activity 2. Ex: **Cuando hace 85 grados en Buenos Aires, ¿cuántos grados hace en Tokio? Cuando llueve en Quito, ¿qué tiempo hace en la Ciudad de México?**

3 Present Model the activity, completing the first two sentences about a friend (imaginary or real). Ex: **Mi amiga se llama Regina. Cuando hace sol, Regina va a la piscina y nada. Cuando llueve, no quiere salir de la casa.**

Práctica

1

Seleccionar Choose the word or phrase that completes each sentence logically.

1. (Hace sol, Nieva) en Cancún. Hace sol
2. Durante (*During*) un tornado, (hace mucho sol, hace mucho viento). hace mucho viento
3. Mis amigos van a esquiar si (nieva, llueve). nieva
4. Tomo el sol cuando (hace calor, hay niebla). hace calor
5. Vamos a ver una película si hace (buen, mal) tiempo. mal
6. Daniel prefiere correr cuando (hay contaminación, hace fresco). hace fresco
7. Ana y José van de excursión si hace (buen, mal) tiempo. buen
8. No queremos jugar al golf si (está despejado, llueve). llueve

2

El clima With a partner, take turns asking and answering questions about the weather and temperatures in these cities. Answers will vary.

modelo

Estudiante 1: ¿Qué tiempo hace hoy en Nueva York?
Estudiante 2: Hace frío y hace viento.
Estudiante 1: ¿Cuál es la temperatura máxima?
Estudiante 2: Treinta y un grados (*degrees*).
Estudiante 1: ¿Y la temperatura mínima?
Estudiante 2: Diez grados.

3

Completar Complete these sentences with your own ideas. Answers will vary.

1. Cuando hace sol, yo...
2. Cuando llueve, mis amigos y yo...
3. Cuando hace calor, mi familia...
4. Cuando hay contaminación, la gente...
5. Cuando hace frío, yo...
6. Cuando hace mal tiempo, mis amigos...
7. Cuando nieva, muchas personas...
8. Cuando está nublado, mis amigos y yo...
9. Cuando hace fresco, mis padres...
10. Cuando está despejado, yo...

NOTA CULTURAL

Cancún, at the tip of Mexico's Yucatán Peninsula, is a popular tourist destination for foreigners and Mexicans alike. It offers beautiful beaches and excellent opportunities for snorkeling, diving, and sailing.

NOTA CULTURAL

In most Spanish-speaking countries, temperatures are given in degrees Celsius. Do you know how to convert between **grados centígrados** and **grados Farenheit**?

degrees C. × 9 ÷ 5 + 32 = degrees F.

degrees F. - 32 × 5 ÷ 9 = degrees C.

TEACHING OPTIONS

Video Replay the video segment, having students focus on weather expressions. Ask them to write down each one they hear. Have students compare their answers in pairs.

Heritage Speakers Have Spanish speakers write ten typical weather-dependent activities that they take part in when they are in their home communities. Refer them to Activity 3 as a model. When they have finished, invite them to share their summaries with the rest of the class.

Comunicación

4

Preguntas Get together with a classmate and ask each other the following questions.
Answers will vary.

1. ¿Hace buen tiempo o mal tiempo hoy?
2. ¿Qué tiempo va a hacer mañana?
3. ¿Nieva mucho en tu ciudad/pueblo?
4. ¿Dónde nieva mucho?
5. ¿Llueve mucho en tu ciudad/pueblo?
6. ¿Dónde llueve mucho?
7. ¿Hay mucha contaminación donde vives?
8. ¿Dónde hay mucha contaminación?
9. ¿Hay mucha niebla donde vives?
10. ¿Dónde hay mucha niebla?

5

Encuesta Your instructor will give you a worksheet. How does the weather affect what you do? Walk around the class and ask your classmates what they prefer or like to do in the following weather conditions. Note their responses on your worksheet. Make sure to personalize your survey by adding a few original questions of your own to the list. Be prepared to report your findings to the class.
Answers will vary.

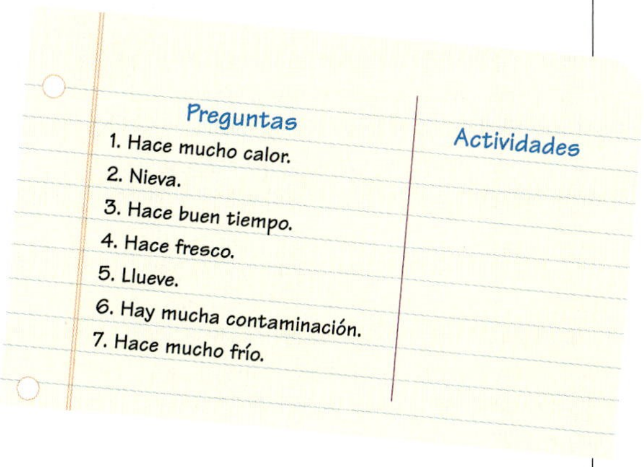
Preguntas
Actividades
1. Hace mucho calor.
2. Nieva.
3. Hace buen tiempo.
4. Hace fresco.
5. Llueve.
6. Hay mucha contaminación.
7. Hace mucho frío.

6

Pronóstico del tiempo You work for a local TV station. With a partner, write a weather forecast for today and tomorrow to be read on the morning news. In preparing your forecast, keep in mind that viewers may want to know about more than just the temperature. Consider whether it will be cloudy or clear, and whether there is any chance of precipitation. Depending on where you live, you may also want to inform your viewers about current pollution conditions. Be prepared to present your forecast to the class. Answers will vary.

Síntesis

7

Situación Act out this situation with a classmate. You are going to visit a friend who lives in another part of the country for the weekend. You call your friend to tell him or her what day and time you are planning to arrive. Then you ask about the weather so that you will know how to pack for your trip. Your friend tells you about the weather forecast, and then the two of you plan some activities for the weekend based on the weather conditions. Answers will vary.

TEACHING OPTIONS

Pairs Tell students they are part of a scientific expedition to Antarctica (**Antártica**). Have them write a letter back home about the weather conditions and their activities there. Begin the letter for them by writing **Queridos amigos** on the board.

Game Have each student draw a *Bingo* card with 25 squares (5 rows of 5). Tell them to write **GRATIS** (*free*) in the center square and the name of a different city in each of the other squares. Have them exchange cards. Call out different weather expressions. Ex: **Hace viento**. Students who think this description fits a city or cities on their board should mark the square with the weather condition. In order to win, a student must have marked five squares in a row and be able to give the weather condition for each one. Ex: **Hace mucho viento en Chicago**.

4 Present Use a picture from your picture file to model possible answers.

4 Present Pairs should take turns asking and answering questions. Give them five minutes for the activity.

5 Model Model the activity by asking volunteers activities they enjoy in hot weather. Ask: **Cuando hace calor, ¿qué haces? (Nado.)** Then distribute the copies of **Hoja de actividades 11**. Give students ten minutes to gather responses.

6 Warm-up Have students organize their forecast with an idea map. Draw the outline on the board. In the center circle write **Pronóstico del tiempo**. In surrounding circles write: **condiciones, actividades recomendadas, actividades no recomendadas, advertencias**. Model possible answers for a location in a different hemisphere.

6 Suggestion Have students surf the Internet (**navigar el Internet**) for weather reports in the Spanish-speaking world.

7 Warm-up/Present Divide the class into pairs, asking each pair to decide who will be the visitor and who will be the host/hostess. Then write the following questions on the board. Have students prepare for the activity by jotting down the answers to these questions taking the point of view the visitor or host/hostess.

- **¿Dónde vives?**
- **¿Qué tiempo hace?**
- **¿Qué actividades quieres hacer durante la visita?**

Assignment Have students do activities in **Student Activities Manual: Workbook**, pages 45–46

Section Goals

In **Lectura** students will:

- learn the strategy of predicting content by surveying the graphic elements in reading matter
- read a magazine article containing graphs and charts

Antes de leer Introduce the strategy. Tell students that they can infer a great deal of information about the content of an article by surveying the graphic elements included in it. When students survey an article for its graphic elements, they should look for such things as:

- headlines or headings
- bylines
- photos
- photo captions
- graphs and tables

Examinar el texto Then give students two minutes to take a look at the visual clues in the article and write down on a sheet of paper all the ideas the clues suggest. Have pairs of students compare their lists and discuss similarities and differences.

Contestar Ask the whole class the five questions. You might want to explain the meanings of **mundo** and **mundial** to students. 1. Pamela Aranda is the author of the article. 2. The article is about sports in the Hispanic world. 3. The data was collected in a survey of university students. 4. The most popular sports 5. Hispanic countries in world soccer championships

Assignment Have students read **Deportes en el mundo hispano** and do the activities in **Después de leer** as homework.

Lectura

NATIONAL STANDARDS communication cultures

Antes de leer

Estrategia

Predicting content from visuals

When you are reading in Spanish, be sure to look for visual clues that will orient you as to the content and purpose of what you are reading. Photos and illustrations, for example, will often give you a good idea of the main points that the reading covers. You may also encounter very helpful visuals that are used to summarize large amounts of data in a way that is easy to comprehend; these include bar graphs, pie charts, flow charts, lists of percentages, and other sorts of diagrams.

Examinar el texto

Take a quick look at the visual elements of the magazine article in order to generate a list of ideas about its content. Then compare your list with a classmate's. Are your lists the same or are they different? Discuss your lists and make any changes needed to produce a final list of ideas.

Contestar

Read the list of ideas you wrote in **Examinar el texto,** and look again at the visual elements of the magazine article. Then answer these questions:

1. Who is the woman in the photo, and what is her role?
2. What is the article about?
3. How was the data collected?
4. What is the subject of the pie chart?
5. What is the subject of the bar graph?

por Pamela Aranda

¿Cuál es el deporte más popular?

El fútbol es el deporte más popular en los países de habla hispana. Mucha gente practica este deporte y tiene un equipo de fútbol favorito. Los aficionados miran los partidos en la televisión y, a veces, van al estadio. Los jóvenes juegan al fútbol con sus amigos en parques y gimnasios. A muchos jóvenes les gusta practicar este deporte y vivir la emoción de hacer un gol con su equipo.

Según una encuesta realizada entre jóvenes universitarios de países de habla hispana, los deportes más populares son:

Deportes más populares

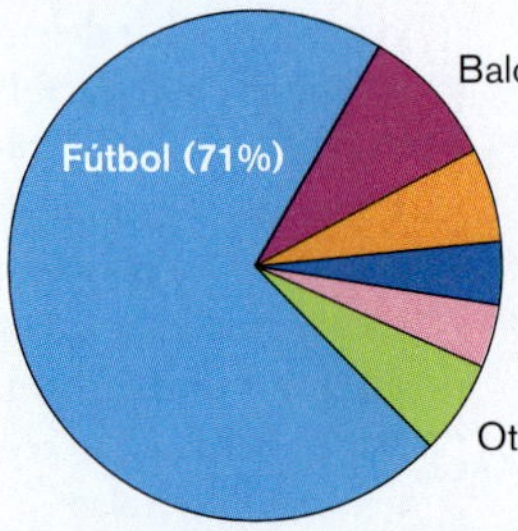

Según *According to* una encuesta *survey* atletismo *track and field*

Después de leer

Evaluación y predicción

Which of the following sports events would be most popular among the college students surveyed? Rate them from one (most popular) to five (least popular). Which would be the most popular at your college or university?

Answers will vary.

_______ 1. La Copa Mundial de Fútbol

_______ 2. Los Juegos Olímpicos

_______ 3. El torneo de tenis de Wimbledon

_______ 4. La Serie Mundial de Béisbol

_______ 5. El Tour de Francia

TEACHING OPTIONS

Variación léxica Remind students that the term **fútbol** in the Hispanic world refers to soccer. Remind them that in the English-speaking world outside of the United States and Canada, soccer is called football. The game called football in the United States is called **fútbol americano** in the Spanish-speaking world.

Extra Practice Ask questions that require students to refer to the the article. Model the use of the definite article with percentages. **¿Qué porcentaje de los jóvenes universitarios prefieren el fútbol? (el 71 por ciento) ¿Qué porcentaje prefieren el vóleibol? (el 6 por ciento) ¿Qué porcentaje de jóvenes ven 3 ó 4 partidos de fútbol por TV a la semana? (el 15 por ciento) ¿Qué porcentaje ven sólo 1 partido al mes? (el 8 por ciento)**

Deportes en el mundo hispano

El fútbol es un deporte importante y muy popular en América, Europa, Asia y África. Cada cuatro años se realiza la Copa Mundial de Fútbol. Argentina y Uruguay han ganado este campeonato más de una vez.

Países hispanos en campeonatos mundiales de fútbol (1938-1998)

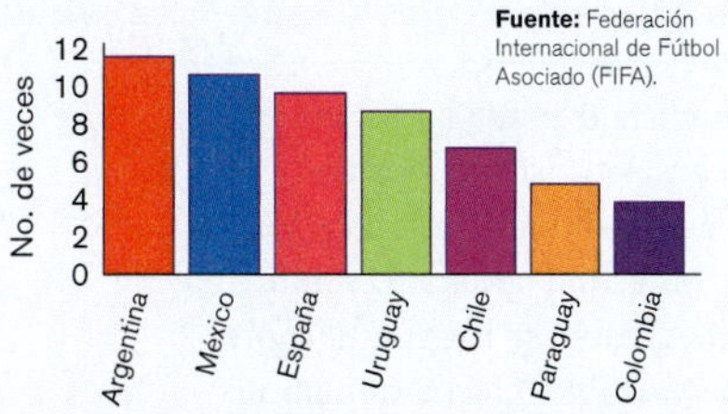

¿Cuántos partidos de fútbol ves por TV a la semana?

15%	3 o 4 veces	40%	1 vez
25%	2 veces	20%	menos de 1 vez

¿Cuántos partidos de fútbol ves por TV en el mes?

66%	más de 4 partidos	8%	1 partido
24%	2 partidos	2%	menos de 1 partido

¿Cuál es tu lugar favorito para ver el fútbol?

39%	el estadio
25%	la casa
17%	el restaurante/bar
12%	el club deportivo
5%	la cafetería de la universidad
2%	no especifica

realizarse *to occur* campeonato *championship* vez *time* más de *more than* menos de *less than*

Completar

Complete the following statements with information from the article.

1. The university cafeteria is the least popular gathering place to watch soccer matches.
2. Both playing and watching soccer are popular pastimes in the Spanish-speaking world.
3. The second most popular sport in the Spanish-speaking countries surveyed is basketball.
4. Argentina and Uruguay have won the World Cup more than once.
5. According to the graph, the country that has participated in the most World Cups is Argentina.

Preguntas

Answer these questions in Spanish.

1. ¿Te gusta el fútbol? ¿Por qué?
2. ¿Miras la Copa Mundial en la televisión?
3. ¿Qué deportes miras en la televisión?
4. En tu opinión, ¿cuáles son los tres deportes más populares en tu universidad? ¿en tu comunidad? ¿en los Estados Unidos?

TEACHING OPTIONS

Paired Work Have pairs of students work together to read the article aloud write three questions about it. After they have finished, ask students to exchange their questions with another pair who can work together to answer them. Alternatively, you might pick pairs to read their questions to the class. Ask volunteers to answer them.

Heritage Speakers Ask Spanish speakers to prepare a short presentation about soccer in their countries. Encourage them to include how popular the sport is, what the principal teams are, whether their country has participated in a World Cup, and so forth.

Peer Review Have partners check their work in **Completar** by locating the sections where the answers can be found.

Después de leer

Evaluación y predicción
Suggestion Write two headings on the board: **Entre los jóvenes del mundo hispano** and **Entre los jóvenes de nuestra universidad**. Ask students to raise their hands (**levantar la mano**) to respond to your questions about the ranking of each sporting event. Write down their reponses as you proceed. Ask: **¿Cuántos de Uds. creen que entre los jóvenes hispanos la Copa Mundial del Fútbol es el evento más popular? ¿Cuántos creen que los Juegos Olímpicos son el evento más popular?** and so forth until you have asked about each event. Then ask: **Entre los jóvenes de nuestra universidad, ¿cuántos de Uds. creen que la Copa Mundial de Fútbol es el evento más popular?** and so forth. Briefly discuss the differences indicated by student responses.

Completar
Expand You might want to ask your students these listening comprehension questions. **1. ¿Cuál es el deporte más popular en el mundo hispano? (el fútbol) 2. ¿Dónde ven los partidos de fútbol los aficionados? (en la televisión, en los estadios) 3. ¿Los jóvenes hispanos practican el fútbol o sólo lo ven de aficionados? (Practican y ven.) 4. ¿En qué países va a realizarse la próxima Copa Mundial de Fútbol? (en el Japón y en Corea) 5. Participan muchos países hispanos en campeonatos mundiales de fútbol? (sí)**

Preguntas
Suggestion Ask the whole class the questions. Ask volunteers to answer orally or to write their answers on the board.

Section Goals

In **Escritura** students will:
- write a pamphlet listing sports events in their locality
- integrate recreation-related vocabulary and structures taught in **Lesson 3**

Tema
Present Discuss the three topics students may choose to write about. Quickly list the requirements of each on the board. You may wish to introduce terms like **comité, guía de orientación, cámara de comercio** as you do so. Remind students of some of the common graphic features used in pamphlets: headings, times and places, brief descriptions of events, prices, and so forth.

Estrategia Explain to students that when they look up a translation of an English word in a Spanish-English dictionary they will frequently find more than one translation and that they must decide which translation best fits the context. This is especially the case for words that have more than one meaning in English. Ex: *bat, goal, root*. Discuss the meanings of *racket* that might be found in an entry in an Spanish-English dictionary and the usefulness of the explanatory notes and abbreviations found in dictionary entries. Tell them that a good way of checking the meaning of a Spanish translation of an English word is to look the Spanish word up in the Spanish side of the dictionary and see how it is translated into English.

Successful Language Learning Tell students that they should resist the temptation to look up every unknown word. Advise them to guess the word's meaning based on context clues first.

Assignment Have students prepare **Ideas y organización** and **Primer borrador** as homework.

Escritura

NATIONAL communication STANDARDS

Estrategia

Using a dictionary

A common mistake made by beginning language learners is to embrace the dictionary as the ultimate resource for reading, writing, and speaking. While it is true that the dictionary is a useful tool that can provide valuable information about vocabulary, using the dictionary correctly requires that you understand the elements of each entry.

If you glance at a Spanish-English dictionary, you will notice that its format is similar to that of an English dictionary. The word is listed first, usually followed by its pronunciation. Then come the definitions, organized by parts of speech. Sometimes the most frequently used definitions are listed first.

To find the best word for your needs, you should refer to the abbreviations and the explanatory notes that appear next to the entries. For example, imagine that you are writing about your pastimes. You want to write, "I want to buy a new racket for my match tomorrow," but you don't know the Spanish word for "racket." In the dictionary, you may find an entry like this:

racket s 1. alboroto; 2. raqueta (*dep.*)

The abbreviation key at the front of the dictionary says that *s* corresponds to **sustantivo** *(noun)*. Then, the first word you see is **alboroto.** The definition of **alboroto** is *noise* or *racket,* so **alboroto** is probably not the word you're looking for. The second word is **raqueta,** followed by the abbreviation *dep.*, which stands for **deportes.** This indicates that the word **raqueta** is the best choice for your needs.

Tema

Escribir un panfleto.

Choose one topic.

1. You are the head of the Homecoming Committee at your school this year. Create a pamphlet that lists events for Friday night, Saturday, and Sunday. Include a brief description of each event and its time and location. Include activities for different age groups, since some alumni will bring their families.
2. You are on the Freshman Student Orientation Committee and are in charge of creating a pamphlet for new students describing the sports offered at your school. Write the flyer and include activities for both men and women.
3. You work for the Chamber of Commerce in your community. It is your job to market your community to potential residents. Write a brief pamphlet that describes the recreational opportunities your community provides, the areas where the activities take place, and the costs, if any. Be sure to include activities that will appeal to singles as well as couples and families; you should include activities for all age groups and for both men and women.

TEACHING OPTIONS

Proofreading Activity Copy the following sentences containing errors on the board or project on a transparency as a proofreading activity to do with the whole class. Each sentence contains two errors related to spelling, grammar, vocabulary, or usage taught in this lesson. **1. Ernesto, ¿queres ir a el parque esta tarde? 2. Creo que va llover, Graciela; es muy nublado. 3. Si llove, volvimos a la residencia. 4. Vamos a ver si los muchachos jugan a fútbol. 5. ¡Ay, Ernesto! ¡Sólo pensas en el futbol! 6. ¡No es verdad! También salo para correr y ir de excursion. 7. Sí, veyo que eres un gran aficionado a los desportes. 8. Graciela, ¿nunca pensas haser un poco de ejercicio? 9. No, no haso ejercício nunca.**

Plan de escritura

1 Ideas y organización

Brainstorm the different types of activities included in the pamphlet, creating an idea map to organize them. Refer to a Spanish-English dictionary for words you don't know, but remember to consider each entry carefully before making a choice.

2 Primer borrador

Using your idea map from **Ideas y organización,** write the first draft of your pamphlet.

3 Comentario

Exchange papers with a classmate and comment on each other's work using these questions as a guide. Begin by mentioning one or two points that you like about your classmate's pamphlet, such as the activities listed for Homecoming, the description of the sports at your school, or the description of the recreational activities in your community.

a. Does the document contain all the required information?
b. Is any important information omitted? Is there any extraneous information that should be deleted?
c. Does the document include an appropriate variety of activities?
d. Is the document organized in a logical fashion?
e. Do you see errors in spelling, grammar, or word usage?
f. What other suggestions do you have for improving the document?

4 Redacción

Revise your first draft, keeping in mind your classmate's comments. Also, incorporate any new ideas or information you may have. Before handing in the final version, review your work using these guidelines:

a. Underline each verb and make sure it agrees with its subject. Double check stem-changing verbs and verbs with irregular **yo** forms.
b. Check the gender and number of each article, noun, and adjective.
c. Check your spelling and punctuation.
d. Consult your **Anotaciones para mejorar la escritura** to avoid repetition of previous errors.

5 Evaluación y progreso

Exchange papers with a new partner. Read his or her pamphlet and note any words and expressions that are new to you so that you can look them up in your dictionary later. After your instructor returns your paper, review the comments and corrections. Note the most important issues in your **Anotaciones para mejorar la escritura** in your **Carpeta.** If you have repeated a previous mistake, highlight it in your **Anotaciones.**

EVALUATION: Panfleto

Criteria	Scale
Appropriate details	1 2 3 4
Organization	1 2 3 4
Use of vocabulary	1 2 3 4
Grammatical accuracy	1 2 3 4
Mechanics	1 2 3 4

Scoring	
Excellent	18–20 points
Good	14–17 points
Satisfactory	10–13 points
Unsatisfactory	< 10 points

Comentario

Present Go over guide questions **a–f** with the whole class. Then have students exchange their pamphlets. Allow five minutes for reading and comments.

Assignment Have students read **Redacción** as homework. Ask them to rewrite their drafts, incorporating the peer comments and following the directions in **Redacción.**

Evaluación y progreso

Give the class five minutes to exchange their final drafts, read them, and copy down unfamiliar words. Then students hand their pamphlets in to you.

Writing Sample Here is a sample pamphlet that would constitute superior writing achievement.

Las diversiones de nuestra ciudad

Ud. puede encontrar la diversión que quiere en nuestra comunidad.

Estadio Sol—¿Es Ud. aficionado de fútbol? Ud. y su familia pueden ver partidos de fútbol los sábados y domingos.

Museo de Arte—¿Le gusta el arte? Ud. puede venir a ver las pinturas de los grandes artistas en nuestro museo.

El Parque Central—Es un lugar bueno para pasear, patinar, conversar con los amigos, practicar baloncesto y también tomar el sol. Toda la familia puede venir al parque o sólo Ud.

También hay restaurantes, cafés y cines en nuestra ciudad. Nuestra ciudad es un buen lugar para practicar su pasatiempo favorito.

Section Goals

In **Escuchar** students will:
- listen to and summarize a short paragraph
- learn the strategy of listening for the gist
- answer questions based on the content of a recorded conversation

Instructional Resource
Student Cassette/CD

Preparación
Warm-up Have students look at the photo and describe what they see. Guide them in saying what José and Anabela are like and guessing what their favorite pastimes might be.

Estrategia
Script **Buenas tardes y bienvenidos a la clase de español. En esta clase van a escuchar, escribir y conversar en cada clase, y ustedes también deben estudiar y practicar todos los días. Ahora encuentran el español difícil, pero cuando termine el curso van a comprender y comunicarse bien en español.**

Assignment Have students do the activities in **Ahora escucha** and **Comprensión** as homework for the next class. Verify the responses to **Ahora escucha** with the whole class and go over **Identificar** and **¿Cierto o falso?** by reading each question aloud and calling on different students to answer.

Ahora escucha
Script **José: No me gusta practicar deportes, pero sí tengo muchos pasatiempos. Me gusta mucho escribir y recibir correo electrónico. Me gusta también ir con mis amigos a mi café favorito. Siempre duermo una siesta por la tarde. A veces voy a ver un partido de béisbol. Me gusta mucho ver películas de acción pero mi novia prefiere las de romance… y por lo tanto veo muchas películas de romance.**
Anabela: Todos mis parientes dicen que soy demasiado activa. Soy aficionada a los deportes, pero también estudio mucho y necesito diversión. Aunque prefiero practicar el ciclismo, me gustan mucho la natación, el tenis, el golf... bueno, en realidad todos los deportes. No, eso no es cierto—no juego al baloncesto porque no soy alta. Para mis vacaciones quiero esquiar o escalar la montaña — depende si nieva. Suena divertido, ¿no?

Escuchar

NATIONAL communication STANDARDS

Preparación

Based on the illustration, what do you think José and Anabela are like? How might they be different from each other?

Estrategia
Listening for the gist

Listening for the general idea, or gist, can help you follow what someone is saying even if you can't hear or understand some of the words. When you listen for the gist, you simply try to capture the essence of what you hear without focusing on individual words. To help you practice this strategy, you will listen to a paragraph made up of three sentences. Jot down a brief summary of what you hear.

Ahora escucha

You will hear first José talking, then Anabela. As you listen, check off each person's favorite activities.

Pasatiempos favoritos de José

1. ___✔___ leer correo electrónico
2. ________ jugar al béisbol
3. ___✔___ ver películas de acción
4. ___✔___ ir al café
5. ___✔___ ir a partidos de béisbol
6. ________ ver películas románticas
7. ___✔___ dormir la siesta
8. ___✔___ escribir correo electrónico

Pasatiempos favoritos de Anabela

9. ___✔___ esquiar
10. ___✔___ nadar
11. ___✔___ practicar el ciclismo
12. ___✔___ jugar al golf
13. ________ jugar al baloncesto
14. ________ ir a ver partidos de tenis
15. ___✔___ escalar montañas
16. ________ estudiar

Comprensión

Preguntas

1. Who participates in more sports-related activities? Anabela
2. Who believes it's important to get enough rest? José
3. What sport does José like to watch? baseball
4. Why doesn't Anabela play basketball? Anabela says she is too short to play basketball.
5. What kind of movies does José's girlfriend prefer? She prefers romantic movies.
6. What is Anabela's favorite sport? cycling

Seleccionar

Which person do these statements best describe?

1. Le gusta practicar deportes. Anabela
2. Prefiere las películas de acción. José
3. Le gustan las computadoras. José
4. Le gusta nadar. Anabela
5. Siempre duerme una siesta por la tarde. José
6. Quiere ir de vacaciones a las montañas. Anabela

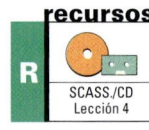

recursos
R SCASS./CD Lección 4

communication cultures connections communities

Proyecto

Presenta un reportaje

Imagine that you are a sports announcer for a large radio station in Mexico City. Your boss has asked you to deliver a new weekly broadcast, a guide to weekend sporting events.

1 Prepara el reportaje

Prepare a radio broadcast of the **Guía de eventos deportivos del fin de semana.** Using the research tools found in **Recursos para la investigación,** find out about the sports that are typically played in Mexico City. Then create your radio broadcast, which might include the following elements:

- A greeting to your listeners in which you introduce yourself and your program
- A list of the various sports events your listeners can attend or participate in
- The day and time each event is going to take place
- A brief, creative sign-off

2 Presenta la información

You may present your radio broadcast live or audiotape it so that it can be replayed for your class. You may want to greet your listeners as **radioyentes** and introduce yourself as **reportero/a** [your name]. Make your broadcast as appealing as possible so that your listeners will want to stay tuned.

recursos para la investigación

Internet Palabras clave: sports, pastimes, Mexico, Mexico City	**Comunidad** Exchange students, faculty members, and residents of your community who are from or have lived in Mexico City
Biblioteca Newspapers, sports magazines, travel magazines, travel guides	**Otros recursos** Sports programs on Spanish-language television stations

EVALUATION: Reportaje

Criteria	Scale
Use of vocabulary	1 2 3 4
Comprehensibility	1 2 3 4
Organization	1 2 3 4
Grammatical accuracy	1 2 3 4
Audience Appeal	1 2 3 4

Scoring	
Excellent	18–20 points
Good	14–17 points
Satisfactory	10–13 points
Unsatisfactory	< 10 points

Section Goals

In **Proyecto** students will:
- use Spanish to carry out research and to interact with the wider world
- write and deliver a guide to weekend sporting events
- learn about sports in Mexico City

Before Assigning Proyecto Students will need approximately a week to complete the project, so at the beginnning of that time period, have them open their books to page 131 and look over **Proyecto**. Explain that they are going to research the most popular sports played in Mexico City and deliver the radio broadcast of a guide to weekend sporting events. Encourage students to talk about the kind of things they typically hear in a broadcast guide to sporting events.

Suggestions
- Students who have not heard a Spanish language sports broadcast may need help with greetings and sign-offs. Possible greeting: **Buenas tardes, estimados radioyentes. Hoy es viernes, el ___, y su reportero es ___.** Possible sign-off: **Y por ahora, estimados radioyentes, eso es todo. Hasta el próximo viernes.**
- Remind students that they should address their radio audience with **Uds.** forms.
- Students may have the capability of editing and taping their broadcast.
- Sound effects can add to the appeal of the broadcast.
- Assign a number of broadcasts spread over several class meetings rather than having them all on the same day.

Section Goals

In **Panorama**, students will read about:
- the geography and culture of Mexico
- Mexico's relationship to the United States.

Instructional Resources
Student Activities Manual: Workbook, 47–48
Transparencies 1, 2, 22

México
Before Presenting Panorama Have students look at the map of Mexico or project **Transparencies 1** and **2**. Ask questions about the locations of cities and natural features of Mexico. Ex: **¿Dónde está la capital? (en el centro del país) ¿Dónde esta la Sierra Madre Oriental? (en el norte)** Model pronunciation of names and list words for natural features on the board: **bahía, golfo, laguna, océano, península, río, sierra.**

Assignment Have students read **Panorama** and write out the answers to the questions in **¿Qué aprendiste?** on page 133 as homework.

Present Go through **El país en cifras**, asking volunteers to read. Model reading greater numbers. Expand with questions related to section content. Ex: After **Área**, ask: **¿Qué ciudad mexicana está en la frontera con los EE.UU.? (Ciudad Juárez)** Ask students if they can name other sister cities (**ciudades hermanas**) on the Mexico-U.S. border. (Tijuana/San Diego, Calexico/Mexicali, Laredo/Nuevo Laredo, Piedras Negras/Eagle Pass, Matamoros/Brownsville). Follow the same procedure with other sections.

Increíble pero cierto Streets in the ever-expanding Mexico City are also named for bodies of water, scientists, philosophers, professions, zodiac signs, and colors.

México

NATIONAL STANDARDS connections cultures

El país en cifras

- **Área:** 1.972.550 km^2 (761.603 millas^2), casi tres veces el área de Texas.

La situación geográfica de México, al sur de los Estados Unidos, ha influido en la economía y la sociedad de los dos países. Una de las consecuencias es la emigración de la población mexicana al país vecino. Hoy día, más de 20 millones de personas de descendencia mexicana viven en los Estados Unidos.

- **Población:** 101.851.000
- **Capital:** México, D.F.—18.372.000
- **Ciudades principales:** Guadalajara—4.017.000, Monterrey—3.514.000, Puebla—2.025.000, Cancún—1.325.000, Ciudad Juárez—1.226.000

SOURCE: Population Division, UN Secretariat

- **Moneda:** peso mexicano
- **Idiomas:** español (oficial), náhuatl, idiomas mayas

La bandera de México

Mexicanos célebres

- **Benito Juárez,** héroe nacional (1806-1872)
- **Octavio Paz,** poeta (1914-1998)
- **Elena Poniatowska,** periodista y escritora (1933-)
- **Julio César Chávez,** boxeador (1962-)

casi *almost* veces *times* sur *south* ha influido en *has influenced* vecino *neighboring*

Un delfín en Baja California

El castillo de Tulum cerca de Cancún

Ruinas aztecas en México D.F.

Saltador en Acapulco

recursos

R | WB pp. 47-48 | vistasonline.com

¡Increíble pero cierto!

En la Ciudad de México cada vecindario nombra sus calles en honor a un tema especial. Un vecindario ha elegido la literatura, y tiene calles llamadas *Dickens, Dante* y *Shakespeare.* En otro está la calle del *Atún* y del *Cilantro.* Irónicamente, las calles del *Amor* y la *Felicidad* son cortas, mientras que la calle del *Trabajo* nunca termina.

TEACHING OPTIONS

Heritage Speaker Mexico is a large and diverse nation, with many regions and regional cultures. Have Spanish speakers who have visited Mexico describe the region which they visited in a short oral report to the class. Encourage them to include information about the cities, art, history, geography, customs, and cuisine of the region.

Group Many of the dishes that distinguish Mexican cuisine have their origins in native produce and pre-Hispanic practices. To these native dishes have been added elements of Spanish and French cuisines, making Mexican food, like Mexican civilization, a dynamic mix of ingredients. Have groups of students look through Mexican cookbooks to find some striking examples of Mexican cuisine, and describe them to the rest of the class.

Ciudades • México D.F.

La ciudad de México, fundada en 1525, también se llama el D.F. o Distrito Federal. La ciudad atrae a miles de inmigrantes y turistas por ser el centro cultural y económico del país. El crecimiento de la población es de los más altos del mundo. El D.F. tiene una población mayor que la de Nueva York o cualquier capital europea.

Artes • Diego Rivera y Frida Kahlo

Los pintores Diego Rivera y Frida Kahlo, casados en 1929, fueron muy importantes en la vida política de su país. Rivera, muralista, trató temas sociales e históricos. Kahlo, conocida por sus autorretratos, pintó cuadros más personales y psicológicos. Los dos se interesaron por la vida y el arte de la gente sencilla.

Historia • Los aztecas

Los aztecas dominaron en México desde el siglo XIV hasta el siglo XVI. Construyeron canales, puentes y pirámides con templos religiosos. Aunque el imperio azteca terminó cuando llegaron los conquistadores en 1519, todavía se siente su presencia. La ciudad de México está construida en el sitio de la capital azteca, Tenochtitlán, y muchos turistas visitan a ver las ruinas.

Costumbres • Día de los muertos

Algunos mexicanos creen que los espíritus de los muertos regresan a la tierra el dos de noviembre para visitar a los vivos. Muchas personas visitan el cementerio en el Día de los muertos, y algunos pasan la noche allí. También es costumbre preparar ofrendas y comer pan y dulces en forma de calaveras y de esqueletos.

¿Qué aprendiste? Responde a las preguntas (*questions*) con una frase completa.

1. ¿Qué lenguas hablan los mexicanos? Los mexicanos hablan español, náhuatl e idiomas mayas.
2. ¿Cómo es la población del D.F. en comparación a otras ciudades? La población del D.F. es mayor.
3. ¿En qué son diferentes las obras de Kahlo y Rivera? Rivera trató temas sociales e históricos. Kahlo pintó cuadros más personales y psicológicos.
4. ¿Qué construyeron los aztecas? Los aztecas construyeron muchos canales, puentes y pirámides con templos religiosos.
5. ¿En qué sitio está construida la capital de México? Está construida en el sitio de la capital azteca, Tenochtitlán.
6. ¿Cuándo celebran los mexicanos el Día de los muertos? Los mexicanos celebran el Día de los muertos el dos de noviembre.

Conexión Internet Investiga estos temas en el sitio **www.vistasonline.com**.

1. Busca información sobre dos lugares de México. ¿Te gustaría (*Would you like*) vivir allí? ¿Por qué?
2. Busca información sobre dos artistas mexicanos. ¿Cómo se llaman sus obras (*works*) más famosas?

atrae a *attracts* miles *thousands* por ser *due to being* crecimiento *growth* más altos *highest* pintores *painters* casados *married* fueron *were* vida *life* trató *treated* e *and* conocida *known* autorretratos *self-portraits* pintó *painted* cuadros *paintings* se interesaron por *were interested in* sencilla *common* dominaron *dominated* desde *from* Contruyeron *They built* puentes *bridges* Aunque *Although* imperio *empire* terminó *ended* llegaron *arrived* todavía se siente *is still felt* construida *constructed* muertos *dead* Algunos *Some* vivos *living* allí *there* ofrendas *offerings* pan *bread* dulces *sweets* calaveras *skulls*

México, D.F. Mexicans seldom refer to their capital as **Ciudad de México**, but simply as **México**, or less frequently as **la capital**.

Diego Rivera y Frida Kahlo Show students reproductions of paintings by Kahlo and Rivera. Point out the artist's distinctive styles and their typically painted specifically Mexican subjects.

Los aztecas Have students look at the image of an eagle holding a snake as the bird perches on a nopal cactus which appears on the Mexican flag. This image recalls an Aztec legend which declared that a great city would be built on the place where the nomadic Aztecs saw an eagle atop a cactus devouring a snake. That place grew into Mexico City.

Día de los muertos The traditions observed around the Day of the Dead in Mexico are the result of the convergence of indigenous and Catholic beliefs about life after death.

¿Qué aprendiste? Go over the questions and answers with the class, making sure everyone understands unfamiliar words and what the correct answers are.

Assignment Have students do activites in **Student Activities Manual: Workbook**, pages 47–48.

Conexión Internet Students will find information about Mexican cities and artists at **www.vistasonline.com**, as well as links to other sites that can help them in their research.

TEACHING OPTIONS

Variación léxica Over fifty-two Indian languages are spoken by indigenous communities in Mexico today. Not all of these languages have a written form. The speakers of Mayan languages are the most numerous non-Spanish speakers in Mexico. Náhuatl, the language of the Aztecs, is still spoken by many, and a number of Náhuatl words have entered Mexican Spanish. A few have also entered other languages. Mexican Spanish words derived from Náhuatl include **aguacate** (avocado), **guajolote** (turkey), **cacahuate** (peanut), **ejote** (green bean), **chile** (chili), and **elote** (corn). Two words Náhuatl has given to other world languages are *tomato* and *chocolate*, products native to Mexico and brought to Europe only in the sixteenth century.

Pasatiempos

bucear	*to scuba dive*
escalar montañas (*f. pl.*)	*to climb mountains*
escribir una carta	*to write a letter*
escribir un mensaje electrónico	*to write an e-mail message*
escribir una (tarjeta) postal	*to write a postcard*
esquiar	*to ski*
ganar	*to win*
ir de excursión (a las montañas)	*to go for a hike (in the mountains)*
leer correo electrónico	*to read e-mail*
leer un periódico	*to read a newspaper*
leer una revista	*to read a magazine*
nadar	*to swim*
pasar tiempo	*to spend time*
pasear	*to take a walk; to stroll*
pasear en bicicleta	*to ride a bicycle*
pasear por la ciudad/el pueblo	*to walk around the city/the town*
patinar (en línea)	*to skate (in-line)*
practicar deportes (*m. pl.*)	*to play sports*
ser aficionado/a (a)	*to be a fan (of)*
tomar el sol	*to sunbathe*
ver películas (*f. pl.*)	*to see movies*
visitar monumentos (*m. pl.*)	*to visit monuments*
la diversión	*fun activity; entertainment; recreation*
el/la excursionista	*hiker*
el fin de semana	*weekend*
el pasatiempo	*pastime*
los ratos libres	*spare (free) time*
el tiempo libre	*free time*

Deportes

el baloncesto	*basketball*
el béisbol	*baseball*
el ciclismo	*cycling*
el equipo	*team*
el esquí (acuático)	*(water) skiing*
el fútbol	*soccer*
el fútbol americano	*football*
el golf	*golf*
el hockey	*hockey*
el/la jugador(a)	*player*
la natación	*swimming*
el partido	*game; match*
la pelota	*ball*
el tenis	*tennis*
el vóleibol	*volleyball*

Verbos

cerrar (e:ie)	*to close*
comenzar (e:ie)	*to begin*
conseguir (e:i)	*to get; to obtain*
dormir (o:ue)	*to sleep*
empezar (e:ie)	*to begin*
encontrar (o:ue)	*to find*
entender (e:ie)	*to understand*
hacer	*to do; to make*
ir	*to go*
jugar (u:ue)	*to play*
mostrar (o:ue)	*to show*
oír	*to hear*
pedir (e:i)	*to ask for; to request*
pensar (e:ie)	*to think*
perder (e:ie)	*to lose*
poder (o:ue)	*to be able to; can*
poner	*to put; to place*
preferir (e:ie)	*to prefer*
querer (e:ie)	*to want; to love*
recordar (o:ue)	*to remember*
repetir	*to repeat; to go on; to continue*
salir	*to leave*
seguir (e:i)	*to follow*
suponer	*to suppose*
traer	*to bring*
ver	*to see*
volver (o:ue)	*to return*

Adjetivos

deportivo/a	*sports-related*
favorito/a	*favorite*

¿Qué tiempo hace?

¿Qué tiempo hace?	*How's the weather?; What's the weather like?*
Está despejado.	*It's clear.*
Está (muy) nublado.	*It's (very) cloudy.*
Hace buen (mal) tiempo.	*It's nice (bad) weather.*
Hace (mucho) calor.	*It's (very) hot.*
Hace fresco.	*It's cool.*
Hace (mucho) frío.	*It's (very) cold.*
Hace (mucho) sol.	*It's (very) sunny.*
Hace (mucho) viento.	*It's (very) windy.*
Hay (mucha) contaminación.	*It's (very) smoggy.*
Hay (mucha) niebla.	*It's (very) foggy.*
llover	*to rain*
Llueve.	*It's raining.*
nevar	*to snow*
Nieva.	*It's snowing.*

Lugares

el café	*café*
la casa	*house*
el centro	*downtown*
el cine	*movie theater*
el gimnasio	*gymnasium*
el lugar	*place*
el museo	*museum*
el parque (municipal)	*(municipal) park*
la piscina	*swimming pool*
el restaurante	*restaurant*

Expresiones útiles	*See page 109.*

Las vacaciones

5

Communicative Goals

You will learn how to:

- Discuss and plan a vacation
- Describe a hotel
- Talk about how you feel
- Talk about the seasons and the weather

contextos

pages 136-139

- Words related to travel and vacations
    - At a travel agency
    - At a hotel
    - At an airport
    - At the beach
- Months of the year
- Ordinal numbers

fotonovela

pages 140-143

After arriving in Otavalo, the students and don Francisco check into the hotel where they will be staying. Inés and Javier then decide to explore more of the city, while Maite and Álex decide to rest before their afternoon run.

estructura

pages 144-159

- **Estar** with conditions and emotions
- The present progressive
- Comparing **ser** and **estar**
- Direct object nouns and pronouns
- Numbers 101 and above

adelante

pages 160-165

Lectura: Read a hotel brochure from Puerto Rico.
Escritura: Write a travel brochure for a hotel.
Escuchar: Listen to a weather report.
Proyecto: Create a web page about Puerto Rico.

panorama

pages 166-167

Featured Country: Puerto Rico

- The Spanish fortress of El Morro
- The origins of "Salsa"
- U.S. – Puerto Rico relations

Lesson Goals

In **Lesson 5** students will be introduced to the following:

- terms for traveling and vacations
- seasons and months of the year
- ordinal numbers (1st–10th)
- **estar** with conditions and emotions
- adjectives for conditions and emotions
- present progressive tense of regular and irregular verbs
- comparison of the uses of **ser** and **estar**
- direct object nouns and pronouns
- personal **a**
- numbers 101 and greater
- scanning to find specific information
- making an outline
- writing a brochure for a hotel or resort
- listening for key words
- designing a travel website
- cultural, geographic, and historical information about Puerto Rico

Lesson Preview

Have students look at the photo. Ask: **¿Dónde están los jóvenes? ¿Qué hacen en la piscina? ¿Qué tiempo hace? ¿Ellos están en la universidad? ¿Están de vacaciones?**

INSTRUCTIONAL RESOURCES

Student Activities Manual: Workbook, 49–60
Student Activities Manual: Lab Manual, 241–247
Student Activities Manual: Video Activities, 335–336
Instructor's Resource Manual: Hoja de actividades, 10
Instructor's Resource Manual: Answer Keys
Tapescript/Videoscript
Overhead Transparencies, 23–27
Student Cassette/CD
Lab Cassette/CD
Video Program
CD-ROM
Website: **www.vistasonline.com**
Testing Program: Prueba A, Prueba B

Las vacaciones

Más vocabulario

la cabaña	*cabin*
la cama	*bed*
el campo	*countryside*
el equipaje	*luggage*
la estación de autobuses, del metro, de tren	*bus, subway, train station*
la habitación individual, doble	*single, double room*
la llegada	*arrival*
el paisaje	*landscape*
el pasaje (de ida y vuelta)	*(round-trip) ticket*
la pensión	*boarding house*
el piso	*floor (of a building)*
la planta baja	*ground floor*
la salida	*departure; exit*
la tienda de campaña	*tent*
acampar	*to go camping*
estar de vacaciones	*to be on vacation*
hacer las maletas	*to pack (one's suitcases)*
hacer una excursión	*to go on a hike, tour*
hacer turismo (m.)	*to go sightseeing*
hacer un viaje	*to take a trip*
ir de compras	*to go shopping*
ir de vacaciones	*to go on vacation*
ir en autobús (m.), auto(móvil) (m.), avión (m.), motocicleta (f.), taxi (m.)	*to go by bus, car, plane, motorcycle, taxi*
recorrer	*to tour an area*
turístico/a	*tourist-related*

Variación léxica

automóvil ⟷ coche (*Esp.*), carro (*Amér. L.*)
autobús ⟷ camión (*Méx.*), guagua (*P. Rico*)
motocicleta ⟷ moto (*coloquial*)

recursos

R				
	SCASS./CD Lección 5	WB pp. 49-50	LM p. 241	LCASS./CD Cass. 3A/CD3

En la agencia de viajes

En el hotel

Section Goals

In **Contextos**, students will learn and practice:

- travel- and vacation-related vocabulary
- seasons and months of the year
- ordinal numbers

Instructional Resources
Student Activities Manual: Workbook, 49–50; Lab Manual, 241
Transparencies 23–24
Student Cassette/CD
Hoja de actividades 10

Before Presenting Contextos Introduce active lesson vocabulary by discussing travel preferences. Ask: **¿A quién le gusta mucho viajar?** To a student who answers, ask: **Y ¿cómo prefieres viajar?** Introduce cognates as suggestions: **¿Te gusta viajar en auto? ¿en autobús? ¿en tren? ¿en avión?** Write each term on the board as you say it. To another student who responds, ask: **¿Adónde te gusta viajar? ¿A México? ¿A Nueva York? ¿A Tokio?** Ask other students about their classmates' statements: **¿Adónde le gusta viajar ____? Sí, le gusta viajar a ____. ¿Cómo puede ____ viajar a ____? ¿Puede viajar a ____ en tren? ¿en barco?** Cue various students to give different types of responses.

Assignment Have students study **Contextos** and do the exercises in **Práctica** as homework.

Present Give students two minutes to review the four scenes. Then project **Transparency 23**. Ask volunteers questions about the four scenes. Ex: **¿Quién trabaja en una agencia de viajes? (el/la agente de viajes) ¿Quiénes trabajan en un hotel? (el botones, el/la empleado/a)** and so forth until you have presented all the active vocabulary.

TEACHING OPTIONS

Extra Practice Ask questions about the people, places, and activities in **Contextos**. Ex: **¿Qué actividades pueden hacer los turistas en una playa? ¿Pueden nadar? ¿tomar el sol? ¿sacar fotos?** and so forth. Then expand questions to ask students what they specifically do at these places. ____, **¿qué haces tú cuando vas a la playa?** Students should respond in complete sentences.

Variación léxica Point out that these are just some of the different Spanish names for vehicles. Ask heritage speakers in class if they are familiar with other terms. While some of these terms are mutually understood in different regions (**el coche, el carro, el auto, el automóvil**), others are specific to a region and may not be understood by others (**el guagua, el camión**). Stress that the feminine article **la** is used with the abbreviation **moto**.

Saca/Toma fotos. (sacar, tomar)
BIENVENIDOS
Pasa por la aduana. (pasar)
viajero
la inspectora de aduanas

En el aeropuerto

Va de pesca. (pescar)
Monta a caballo. (montar)
Va en barco.
Juegan a las cartas. (jugar)
océano, el mar
la playa

En la playa

Práctica

Escuchar Indicate who would probably make each statement you hear. Each answer is used twice.

a. el agente de viajes
b. la inspectora de aduanas
c. un empleado del hotel

1. __a__ 3. __c__ 5. __c__
2. __a__ 4. __b__ 6. __b__

Escoger Choose the best answer for each sentence.

1. Un huésped es una persona que __b__.
   a. hace una excursión
   b. está en un hotel
   c. pesca en el mar
2. Abrimos la puerta con __a__.
   a. una llave
   b. una cabaña
   c. una llegada
3. Enrique tiene __b__ en las montañas.
   a. un pasaporte
   b. una cabaña
   c. un pasaje
4. Antes de (*Before*) ir de vacaciones hay que __c__.
   a. pescar
   b. ir en tren
   c. hacer las maletas
5. A veces (*Sometimes*) es necesario __b__ en un aeropuerto internacional.
   a. hacer turismo
   b. pasar por la aduana
   c. pescar
6. Me gusta mucho ir al campo. __a__ es increíble.
   a. El paisaje
   b. El pasaje
   c. El equipaje

Analogías Complete the analogies using the words below.

pasaporte	auto	mar	avión
huésped	botones	sacar	llegada

1. acampar → campo ⊜ pescar → mar
2. aduana → inspector ⊜ hotel → botones
3. llave → habitación ⊜ pasaje → avión
4. estudiante → libro ⊜ turista → pasaporte
5. aeropuerto → viajero ⊜ hotel → huésped
6. maleta → hacer ⊜ foto → sacar

1 Present Have students check their answers as you go over the tapescript questions with the whole class.

1 Tapescript
1. **¡Deben ir a Puerto Rico! Allí hay unas playas muy hermosas y pueden acampar.**
2. **Deben llamarme el lunes para confirmar la reservación.**
3. **Muy bien, señor… aquí tiene la llave de su habitación.**
4. **Lo siento, pero tengo que abrir sus maletas.**
5. **Su habitación está en el piso once, señora.**
6. **Necesito ver su pasaporte y sus maletas, por favor.**

Student Cassette/CD

2 Present Go over the answers quickly with the class. Ask volunteers to read the entire statement aloud.

2 Expand Ask a volunteer to help you model making statements similar to item 1. Say: **Un turista es una persona que… (va de vacaciones.)** Then ask volunteers to do the same with **un agente de viajes, un botones, un inspector de aduanas, un empleado de hotel.**

3 Present You may want to present these items aloud using the following formula: ***Acampar* tiene la misma relación con *campo* que *pescar* tiene con… (*mar*).**

3 Expand Ask volunteers to explain the relationship between each pair of words in the analogy. Ex: **El campo es un lugar donde las personas acampan. El mar es un lugar donde las personas pescan.**

TEACHING OPTIONS

Small Groups Have students work in groups of three to write a riddle about one of the people or objects in the **Contexto** illustrations. The group must come up with at least three descriptions of their subject. Then one of the group members reads the description to the class and asks **¿Quién soy?** Ex: **Soy un pequeño libro. Tengo una foto de una persona. Un viajero me necesita si quiere viajar a otro país. ¿Quién soy? (Soy un pasaporte.)**

Large Groups Split the class into two evenly-numbered groups. Hand out cards at random to the members of each group. One type of card should contain a verb or verb phrase (ex: **confirmar una reservación**). The other will contain a related noun (ex: **el agente de viajes**). The people within the groups must find their partner. Both groups can use identical cards, if you wish.

4 Warm-up To start the activity, review ordinal numbers by making 10 vertical tally marks (**tachas**) on the board. Point to each at random and ask students to give the ordinal number each represents: Ex: **Es la tercera (quinta, octava)** and so forth. Do some of the same with dots (**puntos**), eliciting masculine forms.

4 Suggestion Point out that for numbers greater than 10, ordinal numbers do exist, though Spanish speakers rarely use them. They tend to use the cardinal numbers (11, 12, 20, and so forth) instead: **Está en el piso veintiuno.**

4 Expand Ask students questions about ordinal numbers in their lives. Ex: **La clase de español, ¿en qué piso está? ¿En qué piso vives? ¿En qué piso está mi oficina?** and so forth.

5 Warm-up Review seasons and months of the year. Have students close their books while you ask questions. Ex: **¿En qué estación estamos? ¿Qué estación tiene los meses de junio, julio y agosto?** and so forth.

5 Expand After students have completed their work in pairs, ask them to provide complete sentences based on the items. Ex: **El primer mes del invierno es diciembre.** Point out that the names of the months, like the names of days, are not capitalized.

5 Expand Ask a student which month his or her birthday is in. Ask another student to then give the season the first student's birthday falls in.

Las estaciones y los meses del año

el invierno: **diciembre, enero, febrero**

la primavera: **marzo, abril, mayo**

el verano: **junio, julio, agosto**

el otoño: **septiembre, octubre, noviembre**

¡ATENCIÓN!

Primero is used to say that it's the first day of the month. Other dates use cardinal numbers.

Hoy es el primero de enero (not **el uno**).

Hoy es el nueve de octubre (*not* **el noveno**).

Primero and **tercero** are shortened to **primer** and **tercer** before a masculine noun: **el tercer piso.**

4 **El Hotel Regis** Label the floors of the hotel.

a. séptimo piso
b. sexto piso
c. quinto piso
d. cuarto piso
e. tercer piso
f. segundo piso
g. primer piso
h. planta baja

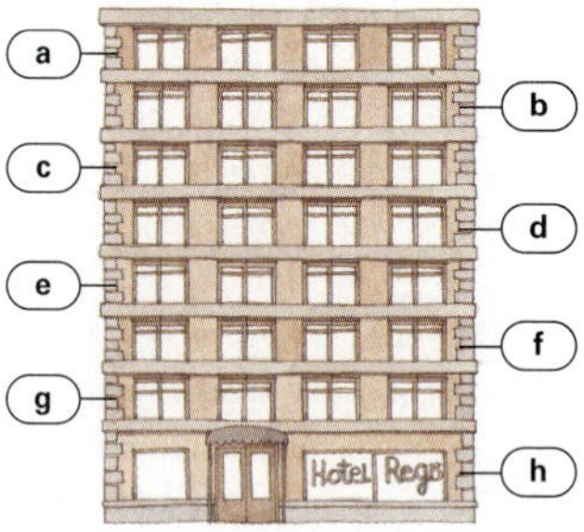

Números ordinales

primer, primero/a	*first*
segundo/a	*second*
tercer, tercero/a	*third*
cuarto/a	*fourth*
quinto/a	*fifth*
sexto/a	*sixth*
séptimo/a	*seventh*
octavo/a	*eighth*
noveno/a	*ninth*
décimo/a	*tenth*

5 **Contestar** Look at the illustration of the months and seasons on this page. Then, with a classmate, answer these questions.

modelo

Estudiante 1: *¿Cuál es el primer mes de la primavera?*
Estudiante 2: *marzo*

1. ¿Cuál es el primer mes del invierno? diciembre
2. ¿Cuál es el segundo mes de la primavera? abril
3. ¿Cuál es el tercer mes del otoño? noviembre
4. ¿Cuál es el primer mes del año? enero
5. ¿Cuál es el quinto mes del año? mayo
6. ¿Cuál es el octavo mes del año? agosto
7. ¿Cuál es el décimo mes del año? octubre
8. ¿Cuál es el segundo mes del verano? julio
9. ¿Cuál es el tercer mes del invierno? febrero
10. ¿Cuál es la cuarta estación del año? el otoño

¡ATENCIÓN!

Note that **estación** has two different meanings: *station* (bus or train) and *season* (of the year).

•••

The names of the months are not capitalized in Spanish: **enero, julio.**

TEACHING OPTIONS

Pairs Have pairs of students work together to create sentences for each of the drawings on page 138 (**Las estaciones y los meses del año**). Ask one student to write sentences for the first two drawings and the other to write sentences for the last two. When each has finished, ask them to exchange their sentences and correct their partner's work. Before beginning, you may wish to review weather expressions from **Lesson 4**.

TPR/Game Ask 10 volunteers to line up facing the class. Make sure students know the starting point and what number in line they are. At random, call out ordinal numbers. The student to which each ordinal number corresponds has until the count of three to take a step forward. If they miss it, they sit down and the order changes for the rest of the students further down the line. Who will the last student(s) standing be?

Comunicación

NATIONAL communication STANDARDS

6 **Preguntas personales** With a classmate, answer the following questions. Answers will vary.

1. ¿Cuál es la fecha de hoy? ¿Qué estación es? ¿Te gusta esta (*this*) estación? ¿Por qué? ¿Qué estación prefieres? ¿Por qué?
2. ¿Prefieres el mar o las montañas? ¿La playa o el campo? ¿Por qué?
3. Cuando estás de vacaciones, ¿qué haces? Cuando haces turismo, ¿qué te gusta hacer y ver?
4. ¿Piensas ir de vacaciones este verano? ¿Adónde quieres ir? ¿Por qué? ¿Qué deseas ver y visitar allí (*there*)? ¿Cómo vas a ir... en avión, en motocicleta...?

7 **Encuesta** Your instructor will give you a worksheet. Turn the phrases in the first column into yes/no questions, then use them to survey your classmates. Try to find at least one person who does each activity and note his or her name on your worksheet. Be prepared to share the results of your survey with the class.

Actividades	Nombres
1. Jugar bien a las cartas	______
2. Acampar en las montañas o en el desierto	______
3. Pescar en el mar	______
4. Tener miedo de viajar en avión	______
5. Viajar mucho en barco	______
6. Comer mucho en restaurantes	______
7. Hacer turismo en Puerto Rico	______
8. Montar a caballo	______
9. Llevar mucho equipaje en tus viajes	______
10. Ir en motocicleta al campo	______

8 **Mis vacaciones** Write a paragraph describing how you prepare for vacation and what you like to do on vacation. While brainstorming ideas for your paragraph, you might want to consider the following questions:

- During what month of the year or season do you like to travel?
- What resources do you use to help you plan your trip (travel agents, books, the Internet, etc.)?
- Do you spend your vacations with family? With friends?
- Do you plan vacations on the beach? In the mountains? In a favorite city or country?
- What activities do you enjoy when you're on vacation?

When you have finished writing, share your paragraph with the class. Answers will vary.

9 **Minidrama** With two or three classmates, prepare and act out a skit about people who are on vacation or are planning a vacation. The skit should take place in one of the areas mentioned below. Answers will vary.

1. Una agencia de viajes
2. Una casa
3. Un aeropuerto, una estación de tren o una estación de autobuses
4. Un hotel
5. El campo o la playa

6 Expand Ask individuals to share their answers. Ex: ____, **cuando estás de vacaciones, ¿qué haces?** Ask other students to repeat the preferences of their classmates. Ex: ____, **¿qué hace ____ cuando está de vacaciones?** Students must answer in complete sentences.

7 Present Have students glance at the list of activities to prepare for answering the questions. Remind them to ask and answer using the **tú** form of the verbs. Distribute **Hoja de actividades 10**.

7 Expand After students have finished circulating, ask them to share the names they collected. Ex: ____, **¿quién juega bien a las cartas? ¿Verdad?** ____, **¿qué te gusta jugar? ¿el póker? ¿el veintiuno?** and so forth.

8 Present/Expand Have students work in pairs or small groups to brainstorm ideas for their paragraphs. When they finish writing, you may want them to share their paragraphs with others to assist in peer editing.

8 Expand Ask for volunteers to share their paragraphs. Students can vote for the most unusual vacation.

9 Present With the whole class brainstorm a list of people and topics that may be encountered in each situation. Write the list on the board. Also set a time limit on how long the skit should be (no more than five minutes).

9 Expand Have students judge the skits in categories such as most original, funniest, most realistic, and so forth.

Assignment Have students do the activities in **Student Activities Manual: Workbook**, pages 49–50

TEACHING OPTIONS

Small Groups Bring in personal pictures or pictures from magazines that show people in travel situations: in the airport, at the beach, at a hotel, and so forth. Have groups of three to five invent stories about the people in the pictures: who they are, their family or work relationships, how they are traveling (airplane, bus, and so forth), whether they're on vacation, and so forth. Groups share their descriptions and pictures with the rest of the class.

Small Groups Have students form groups of two to four. Hand out cards that contain the name of a holiday or other annual event. The group must come up with at least three sentences to describe the holiday or occasion *without mentioning its name.* They can, however, mention the season of the year. The other groups must first guess the month in which the event takes place, then name the holiday or event itself.

Section goals

In **Fotonovela** students will:

- receive comprehensible input from free-flowing discourse
- learn functional phrases for talking to hotel personnel and describing a hotel room

Instructional Resources
Student Activities Manual: Video Activities 335–336
Video Program (Start: 00:22:28)

Video Synopsis The travelers check in at a hotel. Álex and Javier drop by the girls' cabin. Inés and Javier decide to explore the city further. Álex and Maite decide to stay behind. Maite notices that Javier and Inés spend lots of time together.

Before Presenting Fotonovela Tell the class that in this episode, the travelers arrive at a hotel and decide how to spend the rest of the day. Have the class glance over the **Fotonovela** and list words and phrases related to tourism and to making and responding to invitations.

Assignment Have students study **Fotonovela** and **Expresiones útiles** as homework.

Warm-up Ask various individuals how they are today, including the adjectives **cansado/a** and **aburrido/a**. Next write **describir** on the board. Model the pronunciation and have the class guess its meaning. Ask the class to describe the perfect hotel. Ex: **¿Quién quiere describir una habitación de hotel perfecta?**

Present Read the **Expresiones útiles** aloud and have the class repeat. Check comprehension of this active vocabulary by asking **¿Cómo se dice...?** questions. Ex: **¿Cómo se dice en español *I'm a little bit bored*?**

Continued on page 141.

Tenemos una reservación.

NATIONAL STANDARDS communication cultures

Don Francisco y los estudiantes llegan al hotel.

PERSONAJES

MAITE

INÉS

DON FRANCISCO

ÁLEX

JAVIER

EMPLEADA

BOTONES

1

EMPLEADA ¿En qué puedo servirles?

DON FRANCISCO Mire, yo soy Francisco Castillo Moreno y tenemos una reservación a mi nombre.

EMPLEADA Mmm... no veo su nombre aquí. No está.

2

DON FRANCISCO ¿Está segura, señorita? Quizás la reservación está a nombre de la agencia de viajes, Ecuatur.

EMPLEADA Pues sí, aquí está... dos habitaciones dobles y una individual, de la ciento uno a la ciento tres,... todas en las primeras cabañas.

DON FRANCISCO Gracias, señorita. Muy amable.

3

BOTONES Bueno, la habitación ciento dos... Por favor.

INÉS Oigan, yo estoy aburrida. ¿Quieren hacer algo?

JAVIER ¿Por qué no vamos a explorar la ciudad un poco más?

INÉS ¡Excelente idea! ¡Vamos!

7

MAITE No, yo no voy. Estoy cansada y quiero descansar un poco porque a las seis voy a correr con Álex.

ÁLEX Y yo quiero escribir un mensaje electrónico antes de ir a correr.

8

JAVIER Pues nosotros estamos listos, ¿verdad, Inés?

INÉS Sí, vamos.

MAITE Adiós.

INÉS & JAVIER ¡Chau!

recursos

R	VIDEO Lección 5	VM pp. 335-336

TEACHING OPTIONS

Video Tips General suggestions for using video clips in the classroom can be found on page IAE-13 of the **Instructor's Annotated Edition.**

Tenemos una reservación As a method of setting expectations before viewing the **Tenemos una reservación** segment of this video module, ask students to brainstorm a list of things that might happen in a video episode in which the characters check into a hotel and decide how to spend the rest of the day. Then play the **Tenemos una reservación** segment once without sound and have the class create a plot summary based on visual clues. Afterward, show the video segment with sound and have the class correct any mistaken guesses and fill in any gaps.

ÁLEX Hola, chicas. ¿Qué están haciendo?

MAITE Estamos descansando.

JAVIER Oigan, no están nada mal las cabañas, ¿verdad?

INÉS Y todo está muy limpio y ordenado.

ÁLEX Sí, es excelente.

MAITE Y las camas son tan cómodas.

ÁLEX Bueno, nos vemos a las seis.

MAITE Sí, hasta luego.

ÁLEX Adiós.

MAITE ¿Inés y Javier? Juntos otra vez.

Enfoque cultural El alojamiento

There are many different types of lodging **(alojamiento)** for travelers in Hispanic countries. In major cities there are traditional hotels, but a more economical choice is a youth hostel, or **albergue juvenil,** where people can stay in a large, barracks-type room for a very low fee. Another option is an inn, or **hostal,** usually a privately owned residence. A unique type of lodging in Spain is a **parador,** which is usually a converted castle, palace, or villa that has been preserved and emphasizes the culture and cuisine of the region.

Expresiones útiles

Talking to hotel personnel

- **¿En qué puedo servirles?**
  How can I help you?
- **Tenemos una reservación a mi nombre.**
  We have a reservation in my name.
- **Mmm... no veo su nombre. No está.**
  I don't see your name. It's not here.
- **¿Está seguro/a? Quizás/Tal vez está a nombre de Ecuatur.**
  Are you sure? Maybe it's in the name of Ecuatur.
- **Aquí está... dos habitaciones dobles y una individual.**
  Here it is, two double rooms and one single.
- **Aquí tienen las llaves.**
  Here are your keys.
- **Gracias, señorita. Muy amable.**
  Thank you, miss. Very kind (nice).
- **¿Dónde pongo las maletas?**
  Where do I put the suitcases?
- **Allí, encima de la cama.**
  There, on the bed.

Describing a hotel

- **No están nada mal las cabañas.**
  The cabins aren't bad at all.
- **Todo está muy limpio y ordenado.**
  Everything is very clean and orderly.
- **Es excelente/estupendo/fabuloso/fenomenal.**
  It's excellent/stupendous/fabulous/great.
- **Es increíble/magnífico/maravilloso/perfecto.**
  It's incredible/magnificent/marvelous/perfect.
- **Las camas son tan cómodas.**
  The beds are so comfortable.

Talking about how you feel

- **Estoy un poco aburrido/a/cansado/a.**
  I'm a little bored/tired.

To practice pronunciation, read a few sentences from the **Fotonovela** and have the class repeat. Then work through segments 1–3 with the whole class, asking volunteers to play each part. Finally, have students work together in groups of four to read segments 4–10 of the **Fotonovela** aloud. See ideas for using the video in **Teaching Options**, page 140.

Comprehension Check Check comprehension of the **Fotonovela** episode by doing Activity 1, **Completar**, page 142, orally with the whole class.

Suggestion Have students look at the **Expresiones útiles**. Remind the class that **estoy**, **está**, and **están** are present tense forms of the verb **estar**, which is often used with adjectives that describe conditions and emotions. Remind the class that **es** and **son** are present-tense forms of the verb **ser**, which is often used to describe the characteristics of people and things and to make generalizations. Draw students' attention to segment 4 of the **Fotonovela**. Point out that **están haciendo** and **estamos descansando** are examples of the present progressive, which is used to emphasize that an action is in progress. Tell your students that they will learn more about these concepts in the upcoming **Estructura** section.

Assignment Have students do activities 2–4 in **Reacciona a la fotonovela**, page 142, as homework.

TEACHING OPTIONS

Enfoque cultural Point out to the class that a private residence that serves as an inn is sometimes called **una pensión**. Mention also that through exchange programs (**programas de intercambio**), many students travel to Spanish-speaking countries and live with host families. Tell the class that for long-term visits, travelers often save money by renting an apartment (**apartamento** or **departamento**) and cooking for themselves. In addition, you may want to encourage students to think critically about this information by discussing which type of lodging they would prefer if they were traveling to a Spanish-speaking country, and why.

Reaccionа a la fotonovela

1 Present This activity can be done either orally or in writing. It is suitable for whole-class work, group work, or pair work.

2 Warm-up Have students glance at the video stills and skim the captions before answering the questions in this activity.

2 Expand Give these statements to the class as items 7–9: **7. Yo no voy. Necesito descansar. (Maite) 8. Ah, sí. Aquí tienen Uds. las llaves. (Empleada) 9. Bueno, aquí estamos... ésta es su habitación. (Botones)**

3 Suggestion Students may write the sentences on slips of paper that they can rearrange on their desks as they determine the correct order.

4 Possible response
S1: ¿Puede llevar mis maletas a mi habitación?
S2: Sí, señorita.
S1: El hotel es excelente. Me gusta muchísimo. Todo está muy limpio.
S2: Sí, es un hotel maravilloso. Bueno, aquí estamos... la habitación seiscientos veinte, una habitación individual en el sexto piso.
S1: ¿Está Ud. seguro? Creo que tengo la habitación número quinientos veinte.
S2: No, señorita. Ud. tiene la habitación seiscientos veinte. ¿Dónde pongo las maletas?
S1: Puede ponerlas encima de la cama. Gracias.
S2: De nada. Adiós, señorita.

Reacciona a la fotonovela

1 Completar Complete these sentences with the correct term from the word bank.

descansar	habitaciones individuales	las maletas
hacer las maletas	cansada	aburrida
las camas	la agencia de viajes	habitaciones dobles

1. La reservación para el hotel está a nombre de _la agencia de viajes_.
2. Los estudiantes tienen dos _habitaciones dobles_.
3. Maite va a _descansar_ porque está _cansada_.
4. El botones lleva _las maletas_ a las habitaciones.
5. Las habitaciones son buenas y _las camas_ son cómodas.

2 Identificar Identify the person who would make each statement.

1. Antes de correr voy a trabajar en la computadora un poco. Álex
2. Estoy aburrido. Tengo ganas de explorar la ciudad. ¿Vienes tú también? Javier
3. Lo siento mucho, señor, pero su nombre no está en la lista. Empleada
4. Creo que la reservación está a mi nombre, señorita. Don Francisco
5. Oye, el hotel es maravilloso, ¿no? Las habitaciones están muy limpias. Inés

EMPLEADA ÁLEX DON FRANCISCO JAVIER INÉS

¡ATENCIÓN!
The meaning of some adjectives, such as **aburrido**, changes depending on whether they are used with **ser** or **estar**. See section 5.3, p. 151.

3 Ordenar Place these events in correct order.

a. Las chicas descansan en su habitación. _3_
b. Javier e Inés deciden ir a explorar la ciudad. _5_
c. Don Francisco habla con la empleada del hotel. _1_
d. Javier, Maite, Inés y Álex hablan en la habitación de las chicas. _4_
e. El botones pone (*puts*) las maletas en la cama. _2_

4 Conversar With a partner use these cues to create a conversation between a bellhop and a hotel guest.

NATIONAL communication STANDARDS

Huésped	Botones
Ask the bellhop to carry your suitcases to your room.	Say "yes, sir/ma'am/miss."
Comment that the hotel is excellent and that everything is very clean.	Agree, then point out the guest's room, a single room on the sixth floor.
Ask if the bellhop is sure. You think you have room 520.	Confirm that the guest has room 620. Ask where you should put the suitcases.
Tell the bellhop to put them on the bed and thank him or her.	Say "you're welcome" and "goodbye."

TEACHING OPTIONS

Extra practice Give your students some true-false items about the **Fotonovela**. Have them correct the false items. Ex: **1. Maite quiere ir a explorar la ciudad. (Falso. Maite quiere descansar.) 2. Álex y Maite van a correr a las seis. (Cierto.) 3. Las reservaciones están a nombre de Ecuatur. (Cierto.) 4. Inés no quiere explorar la ciudad porque está cansada. (Falso. Está aburrida y quiere explorar.)**

Small groups Have students work in groups of four to prepare a skit to present to the class. In the skit two friends check into a hotel, have a bellhop carry their suitcases to their rooms, and decide what to do for the rest of the day. Have students decide what city they are visiting, describe the hotel and their rooms, and explain what activities they want to do while they are visiting the city.

NATIONAL comparisons STANDARDS

Pronunciación

Spanish b and v

bueno **vóleibol** **biblioteca** **vivir**

There is no difference in pronunciation between the Spanish letters **b** and **v**. However, each letter can be pronounced two different ways, depending on which letters appear next to them.

bonito **viajar** **tambien** **investigar**

B and **v** are pronounced like the English hard *b* when they appear either as the first letter of a word, at the beginning of a phrase, or after **m** or **n**.

deber **novio** **abril** **cerveza**

In all other positions, **b** and **v** have a softer pronunciation, which has no equivalent in English. Unlike the hard **b**, which is produced by tightly closing the lips and stopping the flow of air, the soft **b** is produced by keeping the lips slightly open.

bola **vela** **Caribe** **declive**

In both pronunciations, there is no difference in sound between **b** and **v**. The English *v* sound, produced by friction between the upper teeth and lower lip, does not exist in Spanish. Instead, the soft **b** comes from friction between the two lips.

Verónica y su esposo cantan boleros.

When **b** or **v** begins a word, its pronunciation depends on the previous word. At the beginning of a phrase or after a word that ends in **m** or **n**, it is pronounced as a hard **b**.

Benito **es de Boquerón** **pero vive** **en Victoria.**

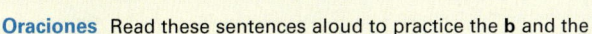

Words that begin with **b** or **v** are pronounced with a soft **b** if they appear immediately after a word that ends in a vowel or any consonant other than **m** or **n**.

Práctica Read these words aloud to practice the **b** and the **v**.

1. hablamos	4. van	7. doble	10. cabaña
2. trabajar	5. contabilidad	8. novia	11. llave
3. botones	6. bien	9. béisbol	12. invierno

No hay mal que por bien no venga.[1]

Hombre prevenido vale por dos.[2]

Oraciones Read these sentences aloud to practice the **b** and the **v**.

1. Vamos a Guaynabo en autobús.
2. Voy de vacaciones a la Isla Culebra.
3. Tengo una habitación individual en el octavo piso.
4. Víctor y Eva van en avión al Caribe.
5. La planta baja es bonita también.
6. ¿Qué vamos a ver en Bayamón?
7. Beatriz, la novia de Víctor, es de Arecibo, Puerto Rico.

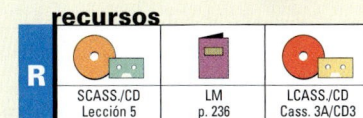

Refranes Read these sayings aloud to practice the **b** and the **v**.

1 Every cloud has a silver lining.
2 An ounce of prevention equals a pound of cure.

recursos

R			
	SCASS./CD Lección 5	LM p. 236	LCASS./CD Cass. 3A/CD3

TEACHING OPTIONS

Extra practice Write some additional proverbs on the board and have the class practice saying each one. Ex: **Más vale que sobre y no que falte.** (*Better too much than too little.*) **No sólo de pan vive el hombre.** (*Man doesn't live by bread alone.*) **A caballo regalado no se le ve el colmillo.** (*Don't look a gift horse in the mouth.*)

Small Groups Have students work in small groups and take turns reading aloud sentences from the **Fotonovela** on pages 140–141, focusing on the correct pronunciation of **b** and **v**. If a group member gets stuck on a word that contains **b** or **v**, the rest of the group should supply the rule that explains how it should be pronounced.

Section Goals

In **Pronunciación** students will be introduced to the pronunciation of **b** and **v**.

Instructional Resources
Student Activities Manual: Lab Manual, 242
Student Cassette/CD

Present

- Emphasize that **b** and **v** are pronounced alike in Spanish but that, depending on the letter's position in a word, each is pronounced two ways. Pronounce **vóleibol** and **vivir** several times, asking students to listen for the difference between the initial and medial sounds represented by **b** and **v**.
- Explain the cases in which **b** and **v** are pronounced like a hard English **b** and model the pronunciation of **bonito, viajar, también**, and **investigar**.
- Point out that before **b** or **v**, **n** is usually pronounced **m**.
- Explain that in all other positions, **b** and **v** have a softer sound. Pronounce **deber, novio, abril** and **cerveza** as students watch your lips. Then ask them to repeat after you.
- Remind the class that Spanish has no sound like the English **v**. Write **vela** and **declive** on the board and have the class pronounce them. Practice with other words with **v**: **vida, vacaciones, avión, automóvil**
- Explain that the same rules for the pronunciation of **b** and **v** in individual words pertain in connected speech. Model the pronunciation of soft **b** and **v** in **es de Boquerón** and **pero vive**, and have students repeat. Practice with other phrases: **de vacaciones, de ida y vuelta**

Práctica/Oraciones/Refranes Model pronunciation, having students repeat after you.

Section Goals

In **Estructura 5.1**, students will learn:
- to use **estar** to describe conditions and emotions
- adjectives that describe emotions and conditions

Instructional Resources *Student Activities Manual: Workbook, 51–52; Lab Manual, 243*

Before Presenting Estructura 5.1 Remind students that they have already learned to use **estar** to indicate location and describe well-being and health. Tell them that **estar** is also used to describe physical conditions and people's feelings. Then ask them to find examples of **estar** used with adjectives in **Fotonovela**. Then draw attention to the caption for video still 5 and compare the use of **estar** in the first two sentences with the use of **ser** in the third. Elicit that **estar** is used to describe the physical condition of the rooms while **ser** is used to describe the inherent state of the beds.

Assignment Have students study **Estructura 5.1** and prepare the activities on pages 144–145 as homework.

Present Model the pronunciation of the adjectives, having students repeat each, and then brainstorm corresponding gestures or expressions. Use TPR to practice the adjectives. Have the class stand and signal a student. Say: ____, **estás enojado/a.** (Student makes an angry face.) Continue signalling individuals until you have introduced most of the adjectives. Then vary the procedure by indicating more than one student. Say: ____ **y** ____, **están preocupados/as.** Keep the pace rapid, so drill seems like a game.

Close Review the answers in **¡Inténtalo!**

5.1 Estar with conditions and emotions

NATIONAL STANDARDS comparisons

ANTE TODO As you learned in Lessons 1 and 2, the verb **estar** is used to talk about how you feel and to say where people, places, and things are located. **Estar** is also used with adjectives to talk about certain emotional and physical conditions.

▶ **Estar** is used with adjectives to describe the physical condition of places and things.

La habitación **está** sucia.
The room is dirty.

La puerta **está** cerrada.
The door is closed.

▶ **Estar** is also used with adjectives to describe how people feel, both mentally and physically.

Estoy aburrida. ¿Quieren hacer algo?

No, estoy cansada.

CONSÚLTALO

The present tense of ser. To review **ser**, see Lesson 1, section 1.3, p.18.

The present tense of estar. To review **estar**, see Lesson 2, section 2.3, p. 53.

Adjectives that describe emotions and conditions

abierto/a	*open*	**contento/a**	*happy; content*	**nervioso/a**	*nervous*
aburrido/a	*bored; boring*	**desordenado/a**	*disorderly*	**ocupado/a**	*busy*
alegre	*happy; joyful*	**enamorado/a (de)**	*in love (with)*	**ordenado/a**	*orderly*
avergonzado/a	*embarrassed*	**enojado/a**	*mad, angry*	**preocupado/a (por)**	*worried (about)*
cansado/a	*tired*	**equivocado/a**	*wrong*	**seguro/a**	*sure*
cerrado/a	*closed*	**feliz**	*happy*	**sucio/a**	*dirty*
cómodo/a	*comfortable*	**limpio/a**	*clean*	**triste**	*sad*

¡INTÉNTALO! Provide the present tense forms of the verb **estar.** The first item has been done for you.

1. La biblioteca ___*está*___ cerrada los domingos por la noche.
2. Nosotros ___estamos___ muy ocupados todos los lunes.
3. Ellas ___están___ alegres porque tienen tiempo libre.
4. Javier ___está___ enamorado de Maribel.
5. Diana ___está___ enojada con su novio.
6. Yo ___estoy___ nerviosa en el avión.
7. La habitación ___está___ ordenada cuando vienen sus padres.
8. Uds. ___están___ equivocados.
9. Marina y yo ___estamos___ preocupadas por el examen.
10. Ud. ___está___ muy cansado los lunes por la mañana.

TEACHING OPTIONS

TPR Call out a sentence using an adjective and have students mime the emotion or show the condition. Ex: **Sus libros están abiertos.** (Students show their open books.) **Ustedes están alegres.** (Students act happy.) Next, call on volunteers to act out an emotion or condition and have the class tell what's going on. Ex: A student pretends to cry. (**Carlos está triste.**)

Video Show the video of the **fotonovela** again and ask comprehension questions using **estar** and adjectives expressing emotions or conditions. Ex: **¿Cómo está la cabaña? (Todo está muy limpio y ordenado.)¿Está cansado Javier? (No, no está cansado.) ¿Quíen está cansado? (Maite está cansada.)**

Práctica

AYUDA

Make sure that you have agreement between:

- Nouns and verbs in person and number
- Nouns and adjectives in gender and number

Ell**os** no est**án** enferm**os**.
They are not sick.

1 **¿Cómo están?** Complete Martín's statements about how he and other people are feeling. In the first blank, fill in the correct form of **estar**. In the second blank, fill in the adjective that best fits the context.

1. Yo <u>estoy</u> un poco <u>nervioso</u> porque tengo un examen mañana.
2. Mi hermana Patricia <u>está</u> muy <u>contenta</u> porque mañana va a hacer una excursión al campo.
3. Mis hermanos Juan y José salen de la casa a las cinco de la mañana. Por la noche, siempre <u>están</u> muy <u>cansados</u>.
4. Mi amigo Ramiro <u>está</u> <u>enamorado</u>; su novia se llama Adela.
5. Mi papá y sus colegas <u>están</u> muy <u>ocupados</u> hoy. ¡Hay mucho trabajo!
6. Patricia y yo <u>estamos</u> un poco <u>preocupados</u> por ellos porque trabajan mucho.
7. Mi amiga Mónica <u>está</u> un poco <u>triste/enojada</u> porque su novio no puede salir esta noche.
8. Nuestras clases no son muy interesantes hoy. ¿Tú <u>estás</u> <u>aburrido</u> también?

2 **Describir** Describe the following people and places. Answers will vary.

1. Anabela
Está contenta.

2. Juan y Luisa
Están enojados.

3. la habitación de Teresa
Está ordenada/limpia.

4. la habitación de César
Está desordenada/sucia.

3 **Situaciones** With a partner, talk about how you feel in these situations.
Answers will vary.

1. Cuando hace sol
2. Cuando tomas un examen
3. Cuando estás de vacaciones
4. Cuando tienes mucho trabajo
5. Cuando viajas en avión
6. Cuando estás con la familia
7. Cuando estás en la clase de español
8. Cuando ves una película con tu actor favorito

1 Present Have students read the sentence, fill in the correct form of **estar**, and decide which adjective is appropriate. Remind them that the adjective must agree in number and gender with the subject. Go over the questions orally with the whole class.

1 Expand Have students write five more sentences missing **estar** and an adjective, like those in the activity, and exchange them with a partner who completes them.

2 Warm-up/Present Before beginning the activity, ask students to brainstorm who or what they see in each item. This activity is suitable for pairs, small groups, or the whole class.

2 Expand Have students write a sentence explaining why the people feel the way they do and why the rooms are the way they are.

2 Expand Ask students to pretend they are Anabela, Juan, or Luisa and give a short oral presentation describing who they are and how they feel today.

3 Present Have partners alternate asking and answering questions until each has covered all items. Give pairs five minutes to complete the activity.

3 Expand Ask students to keep a record of their partner's responses. Take a classroom poll to see what percentage of students felt a particular way for each situation.

Assignment Have students prepare the activities in **Student Activities Manual: Workbook**, pages 51–52

TEACHING OPTIONS

Pairs Have students write a list of 4 questions using different conjugations of **estar** and 5 adjectives that have an opposite from the list on page 144. Students ask partners their questions. They respond negatively, then use the opposite adjective in an affirmative statement. Ex: **¿Está abierta la biblioteca? (No, no está abierta. Está cerrada.)**

Heritage Speakers Ask Spanish speakers to work with a partner to play with word associations. Student one calls out an adjective. Student two calls out all the words that come to mind. After partners have each taken several turns, have them choose one set of associations to include in a poem or haiku.

5.2 The present progressive

comparisons — NATIONAL STANDARDS

ANTE TODO Both Spanish and English have a present progressive tense. In both languages, it consists of the present tense of the verb *to be* and the present participle (the *-ing* form of the verb in English).

Estoy escuchando.	Carlos **está corriendo**.	Ella **está escribiendo** una carta.
I am listening.	*Carlos is running.*	*She is writing a letter.*

Hola, chicas. ¿Qué están haciendo?

Estamos descansando.

▶ The present progressive is formed with the present tense of **estar** and the present participle of the main verb.

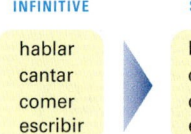

FORM OF ESTAR	+ PRESENT PARTICIPLE	FORM OF ESTAR	+ PRESENT PARTICIPLE
Estoy	**trabajando.**	**Estamos**	**comiendo.**
I am	*working.*	*We are*	*eating.*

▶ The present participle of regular **-ar**, **-er**, and **-ir** verbs is formed as follows:

INFINITIVE	STEM	ENDING	PRESENT PARTICIPLE
hablar	habl	**-ando**	habl**ando**
cantar	cant	**-ando**	cant**ando**
comer	com	**-iendo**	com**iendo**
escribir	escrib	**-iendo**	escrib**iendo**

▶ **Ir**, **poder**, and **venir** have irregular present participles (**yendo**, **pudiendo**, **viniendo**), but these verbs are rarely used in the present progressive. Several other verbs have irregular present participles that you will need to learn.

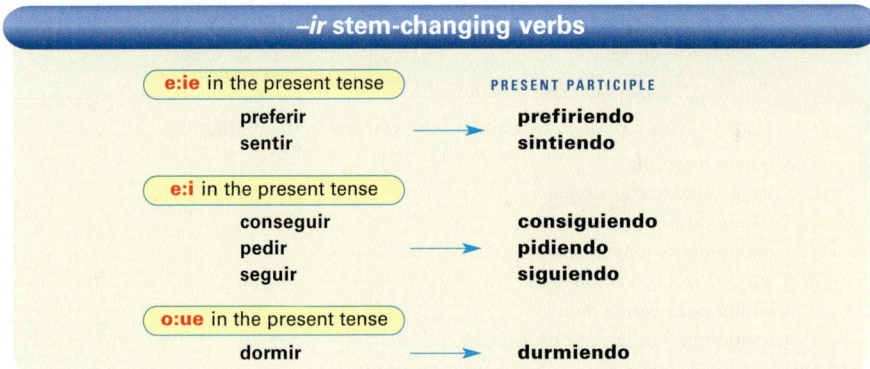

–ir stem-changing verbs

	PRESENT PARTICIPLE
e:ie in the present tense	
preferir	**prefiriendo**
sentir	**sintiendo**
e:i in the present tense	
conseguir	**consiguiendo**
pedir	**pidiendo**
seguir	**siguiendo**
o:ue in the present tense	
dormir	**durmiendo**

¡ATENCIÓN!

When the stem of an –**er** or –**ir** verb ends in a vowel, the present participle ends in –**yendo**.

leer → **le** → **leyendo**
oír → **o** → **oyendo**
traer → **tra** → **trayendo**

Section Goals

In **Estructura 5.2**, students will learn:

- the present progressive tense of regular and irregular verbs
- the present progressive tense versus the simple present tense in Spanish

Instructional Resources *Student Activities Manual: Workbook, 53; Lab Manual, 244 Transparency 25*

Before Presenting Estructura 5.2 Have students read the caption of video still 4 on page 141. Focus attention on **estar** + *present participle* to express what is going on at the moment. Point out the similarity of the structure to English. Note how the present participle is formed. Then use regular verbs to ask questions about things students are not doing to elicit the present progressive. Ex: **¿Estás comiendo una pizza? (No, no estoy comiendo una pizza.)**

Assignment Have students study **Estructura 5.2** and prepare the activities on pages 147–148 as homework.

Present Explain the formation of the present progressive of regular verbs, writing examples on the board. Then use your picture file to elicit sentences with the present progressive. Ask: **¿Qué está haciendo el hombre alto? (Está sacando fotos.)** Continue until most students have had a chance to respond. Next introduce the use of **-yendo** with **-er/-ir** verbs with stems ending in a vowel and practice it with your picture file. Finally introduce and practice **-ir** stem-changing verbs.

Note: Explain that **sentir** and **preferir** are rarely used in the present progressive.

TEACHING OPTIONS

Large Groups Divide the class into three groups. Appoint leaders and give them a list of verbs. Leaders call out a verb and a subject (**seguir/yo**), then toss a ball or a piece of paper wadded into a ball to someone in the group. That student says the appropriate present progressive form of the verb (**estoy siguiendo**) and tosses the ball back. Leaders should call out all verbs on the list and toss the ball to every member of the group.

Extra Practice Mime an action. Ask students what you are doing. Students respond using the present progressive. Ex: Pick up a newspaper and pretend to read it. Ask: ____, **¿Qué estoy haciendo? (Ud. está leyendo el periódico.) Perfecto**. Also ask leading questions that may require either affirmative or negative answers depending on what you pantomime. **Y ahora, ¿estoy lavando el coche? (No, Ud. está bebiendo café.)**

COMPARE & CONTRAST

The use of the present progressive is much more restricted in Spanish than in English. In Spanish, the present progressive is simply used to emphasize that an action is in progress at the time of speaking.

Inés **está escuchando** música latina ahora mismo.
Inés is listening to Latin music right now.

Álex y su amigo ecuatoriano todavía **están jugando** al fútbol.
Álex and his Ecuadorian friend are still playing soccer.

In English, the present progressive is often used to talk about situations and actions that occur over an extended period of time or in the future. In Spanish, the simple present tense is used instead.

Javier **estudia** computación este semestre.
Javier is studying computer science this semester.

Inés y Maite **salen** mañana para los Estados Unidos.
Inés and Maite are leaving tomorrow for the United States.

Estamos pensando en lo mismo:
su Futuro
Su asesor para ganar
FIDUCOLOMBIA
Sociedad Fiduciaria S.A.

¡INTÉNTALO! Create complete sentences by putting the verbs in the present progressive. The first item has been done for you.

1. Mis amigos / descansar en la playa Mis amigos están descansando en la playa.
2. Nosotros / practicar deportes Estamos practicando deportes.
3. Carmen / comer en casa Carmen está comiendo en casa.
4. Nuestro equipo / ganar el partido Nuestro equipo está ganando el partido.
5. Yo / leer el periódico Estoy leyendo el periódico.
6. Él / pensar en comprar una bicicleta Está pensando en comprar una bicicleta.
7. Uds. / explicar la lección Uds. están explicando la lección.
8. José y Francisco / dormir José y Francisco están durmiendo.
9. Marisa / leer correo electrónico Marisa está leyendo correo electrónico.
10. Yo / preparar sándwiches Estoy preparando sándwiches.
11. Carlos / tomar fotos Carlos está tomando fotos.
12. ¿dormir / tú? ¿Estás durmiendo?

Present Discuss each point in the **Compare and Contrast** box. Emphasize that the present progressive in Spanish is only used to describe an action in progress at the time of speaking. Point out that for this reason, the present progressive is rarely used with the verbs **ir**, **poder**, and **venir**, since they already imply an action in progress. Confirm that students undertand the distinction between the present progressive and simple present tenses in Spanish by writing the following statements on the board:
1. I'm going on vacation tomorrow.
2. She's packing her suitcase right now.
3. They are sightseeing in Madrid this week.
4. Roberto is still working.

Ask students if they would use the present or the present progressive tense in Spanish for each item. Then, ask students to translate each item. **(1. Voy de vacaciones mañana. 2. Está haciendo la maleta ahora mismo. 3. Hacen turismo en Madrid esta semana. 4. Roberto todavía está trabajando.)**

Close Go over **¡Inténtalo!** orally with the class. Then have students write the sentences out using the simple present. Call on volunteers to explain how the meaning of each sentence changes depending on whether the verb is in the present progressive or the simple present.

TEACHING OPTIONS

Pairs Have students write eight sentences in Spanish modeled after the examples in the **Compare and Contrast** box. There should be two sentences modeled after each example. Ask students to replace the verbs with blanks. Then, have students exchange their sentences with a partner for completion.

Extra Practice Ask students to find five photos from a magazine or create five drawings of people performing different activities. Have them write one sentence telling what the people in the photo/drawing are doing and one describing how they feel. Ex: **Juan está trabajando. Está cansado.**

1 Present/Expand After you have gone over the questions orally with the whole class, ask students comprehension questions that elicit the present progressive. Ex: **¿Quién está buscando información? (Marta y José están buscando información.) ¿Qué información están buscando? (Están buscando información sobre San Juan.)**

2 Warm-up Ask students questions about each drawing to elicit a description of what they see. Ex: **¿Quién está en el dibujo número 5? (Samuel está en el dibujo.) ¿Dónde está Samuel? (Está en la playa.) ¿Qué más ven en la foto? (Vemos una silla y el mar.)**

2 Expand Ask students to imagine they are creating a scrapbook of photos from a vacation in Puerto Rico. Have them pick three of the activities pictured to include in their scrapbooks. Students then draw themselves doing those activities and write a brief caption below their drawings describing where they are, what the weather is like, and what they are doing.

3 Warm-up Review the information in **Ayuda**. Ask students which verbs from the activity they would associate with the nouns listed.

3 Expand Have students choose five more celebrities and write what they are doing right now.

3 Expand Add names to the list of celebrities in the activity. Assign the identities of the celebrities to different students, then ask the class what they are doing right now. Ex: **Lisa es Venus Williams. Marta es Serena Williams. ¿Qué están haciendo ellas? (Están jugando al tenis.)**

Práctica

1 **Completar** Alfredo's Spanish class is preparing to travel to Puerto Rico. Use the present progressive of the verb in parentheses to complete Alfredo's description of what everyone is doing.

1. Yo <u>estoy investigando</u> (investigar) el estado político de la isla (*island*).
2. La esposa del profesor <u>está haciendo</u> (hacer) las maletas.
3. Marta y José Luis <u>están buscando</u> (buscar) información sobre San Juan en el Internet.
4. Enrique y yo <u>estamos leyendo</u> (leer) un correo electrónico de nuestro amigo puertorriqueño.
5. Javier <u>está aprendiendo</u> (aprender) mucho sobre la cultura puertorriqueña.
6. Y tú <u>estás practicando</u> (practicar) tu español, ¿verdad?

2 **¿Qué están haciendo?** María and her friends are vacationing at a resort in San Juan, Puerto Rico. Complete her description of what everyone is doing right now.

1. Yo
estoy escribiendo una carta.

2. Javier
está buceando en el mar.

3. Alejandro y Rebeca
están jugando a las cartas.

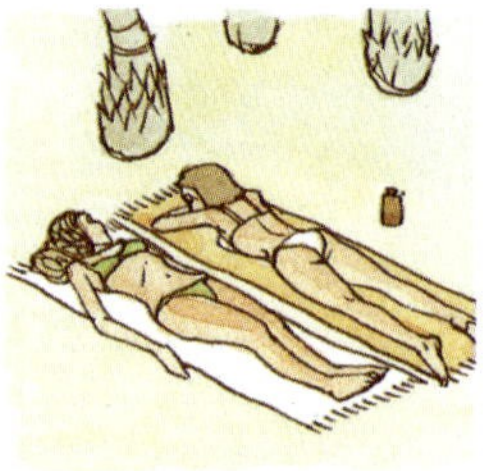

4. Celia y yo
estamos tomando el sol.

5. Samuel
está escuchando música.

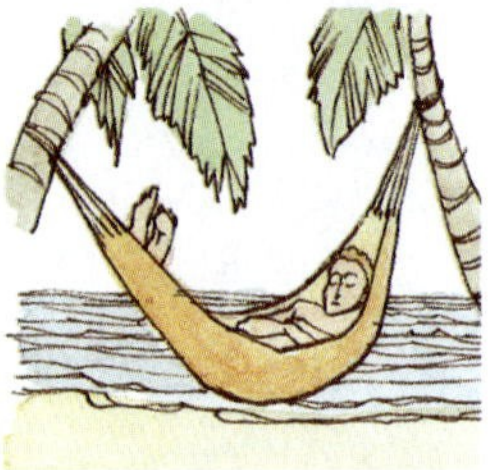

6. Lorenzo
está durmiendo.

3 **Personajes famosos** Say what these celebrities are doing right now, using the cues provided.

modelo

Serena Williams está jugando al tenis ahora mismo.

John Grisham	Mikhail Baryshnikov	bailar	hablar
Celine Dion	Picabo Street	cantar	hacer
Steven Spielberg	Regis Philbin	correr	jugar
Venus Williams	¿?	escribir	¿?
Tiger Woods	¿?	esquiar	¿?

AYUDA

John Grisham - **novelas**
Celine Dion - **canciones**
Steven Spielberg - **cine**
Venus Williams - **tenis**
Tiger Woods - **golf**
Mikhail Baryshnikov - **ballet**
Picabo Street - **esquí**
Regis Philbin - **televisión**

TEACHING OPTIONS

Heritage Speakers Have students bring in photos (photocopies or magazine illustrations will also do) from a vacation. Ask them to describe the photos to a partner. Students should explain who is in the photo, what they are doing, and where they are. After students have practiced with a partner, have them present their descriptions to the class.

Game Student one mimes an action and states what she is doing. Student two says what the first student is doing, mimes the action, then states what he is doing and mimes his action. Students continue to add actions to the chain until it breaks. A new chain begins with the student following the breakdown. After 5 minutes of play, the group of students comprising the longest chain wins.

NATIONAL communication STANDARDS

Comunicación

¡LENGUA VIVA!
In Spain and Latin America, time is often given based on the 24-hour clock. For example, 3:00 p.m. is said 15:00h.

4 **Un amigo preguntón** You have a friend who calls you at all hours to see what you're doing. What do you tell him/her if he/she calls you at the following times? Answers will vary.

modelo
8:00 a.m.
Estoy desayunando.

1. 5:00 a.m.
2. 9:30 a.m.
3. 11:00 a.m.
4. 12:00 p.m.
5. 2:00 p.m.
6. 5:00 p.m.
7. 9:00 p.m.
8. 2:30 a.m.

5 **Describir** Work with a partner and use the present progressive to describe what's going on in this beach scene. Answers will vary.

6 **Conversar** Imagine that you and a classmate are each babysitting a group of children. One of you has great kids; the other's kids are mischievous. You're on the phone, telling each other what the children are doing at this very moment. Be creative, and be prepared to share some of your sentences with the class. Answers will vary.

NATIONAL communication STANDARDS

Síntesis

7 **¿Qué están haciendo?** With two other classmates, create at least three sentences about what these people are doing right now in these places. Also, say how they feel and what they are going to do. Answers will vary.

modelo
Uds. están en la clase de español.
Estamos hablando con los otros estudiantes.
Estamos practicando los verbos.
No estamos aburridos/as.
Vamos a tener un examen mañana.

1. Tres amigas están de vacaciones.
2. Un padre y su hijo están en el parque.
3. Tú y tus compañeros/as están en la playa.
4. Una familia está en el centro.
5. El/la profesor(a) está en la biblioteca.
6. Unos jóvenes están en un estadio.

TEACHING OPTIONS

Video Show the video again, pausing after each exchange. Ask students to describe what each person in the shot is doing right at that moment.

TPR Write sentences with the present progressive on strips of paper. Call on a volunteer to pick a strip out of a hat to act out. The class tries to guess what the sentence is. Sample sentence: **Yo estoy durmiendo en la cama.**

Pairs Ask students to write five sentences using the present progressive. Students should try to make their sentences as complex as possible. Have students dictate their sentences to their partners. After both partners have finished dictating their sentences, have them exchange papers for correction.

4 Warm-up Have students outline their daily activities and what time they do them before beginning the exercise.

4 Present This activity is appropriate for pairs. Ex: Student 1: **¡Hola Andrés! Son las 8 de la mañana. ¿Qué estás haciendo?** Student 2: **Estoy desayunando.**

5 Expand Ask students to work with a partner to write a dialogue between two or more of the persons in the drawing. Dialogues should consist of at least three exchanges.

6 Warm-up Before beginning their conversation, have students brainstorm verbs that describe what children do at home.

6 Present After practicing their conversation with a partner, have students present it to the class. To make the conversation more realistic, have students call on their classmates to act as the children in the background.

7 Present Ask four volunteers to read the **Modelo** aloud. Then have each student in each group write one sentence about what the people in the six items are doing right now. Afterward the group works together to create sentences describing how the people feel and what they are going to do. When they finish, have groups exchange papers with another group for peer editing.

7 Expand Ask groups to choose an item and expand their sentences into a paragraph. Paragraphs should include the original sentences as well as information about the people and the location where the action takes place.

Assignment Have students do activities in **Student Activities Manual: Workbook**, page 53.

Section Goals

In **Estructura 5.3** students will review and compare the uses of **ser** and **estar**.

Instructional Resources
Student Activities Manual: Workbook, 54–55; Lab Manual, 245
Transparency 26

Before Presenting Estructura 5.3 Remind students that although **ser** and **estar** both mean to be, they have different purposes. Have partners brainstorm as many uses of **ser** with examples as they can. Compile a list on the board, correcting as you do so. Repeat for **estar**. Ask students where they think there might be some confusion about which verb to use.

Assignment Have students study **Estructura 5.3** and prepare the activities (except Activity 3) on pages 151–152.

Present On the board or an overhead transparency, write in a single column one example of each use of **ser** and **estar**. Ex: **1. Álex es de México.** In a second column, write in random order each of the uses of **ser** and **estar** taught so far. Ex. **g. place of origin** Call on individuals to match each example with the corresponding use. Then write sentences with **estar** and **ser** on the board, but omitting the verb. Ask students to supply the correct form of **ser** or **estar**. Ex: **Mi casa ____ lejos de aquí. (estar, location; está)** If either **ser** or **estar** could be used, ask students to explain how the meaning of the sentence would change.

The Affective Dimension If students feel anxious that Spanish has two verbs that mean *to be*, reassure them that they will soon feel more comfortable with this concept. Point out that Spanish speakers express rich shades of meaning by the way they use **ser** and **estar**.

5.3 Comparing **ser** and **estar**

NATIONAL comparisons STANDARDS

ANTE TODO You have already learned that **ser** and **estar** both mean *to be* but are used for different purposes. The following chart summarizes the key differences in usage between **ser** and **estar**.

Uses of *ser*

Nationality and place of origin	Martín **es** argentino. **Es** de Buenos Aires.
Profession or occupation	Adela **es** ingeniera. Francisco **es** médico.
Characteristics of people and things	José y Clara **son** simpáticos. El clima de Puerto Rico **es** agradable.
Generalizations	¡**Es** fabuloso viajar! **Es** difícil estudiar a la una de la mañana.
Possession	**Es** la pluma de Maite. **Son** las llaves de don Francisco.
What something is made of	La bicicleta **es** de metal. Los libros **son** de papel.
Time and date	Hoy **es** martes. **Son** las dos. Hoy **es** el primero de julio.
Where or when an event takes place	El partido **es** en el estadio Santa Fe. La conferencia **es** a la siete.

Soy Francisco Castillo Moreno. Yo soy de la agencia Ecuatur.

Su nombre no está en mi lista.

Uses of *estar*

Location or spatial relationships	El aeropuerto **está** lejos de la ciudad. Tu habitación **está** en el tercer piso.
Health	¿Cómo **estás**? **Estoy** bien, gracias.
Physical states and conditions	El profesor **está** ocupado. Las ventanas **están** abiertas.
Emotional states	Marisa **está** feliz hoy. **Estoy** muy enojado con Javier.
Certain weather expressions	**Está** lloviendo. **Está** nublado.
Ongoing actions (progressive tenses)	**Estamos** estudiando para un examen. Ana **está** leyendo una novela.

TEACHING OPTIONS

Extra Practice Call out sentences containing forms of **ser** or **estar**. Ask students to identify the use of the verb.

Heritage Speakers Ask Spanish speakers to write a postcard home about their vacation in Puerto Rico, incorporating as many of the uses of **ser** and **estar** as they can.

Game Divide the class into teams. Call out a purpose for either **ser** or **estar**. The first member of each team runs to the board and writes a sample sentence. If the sentence of the team finishing first is correct, the team gets a point. If not, check team two, and so on. Practice all purposes for each verb, making sure each team member has had at least two turns, then tally the points to see which team wins.

Ser and *estar* with adjectives

▶ With many descriptive adjectives, **ser** and **estar** can both be used.

Juan **es** delgado. *Juan is thin.*	Ana **es** feliz siempre. *Ana is always happy.*
Juan **está** más delgado hoy. *Juan is thinner today.*	Ana **está** feliz en la fiesta. *Ana is happy at the party.*

▶ In the examples above, the sentences with **ser** have a different meaning than the sentences with **estar**. The statements with **ser** are general observations about the inherent, permanent qualities of Juan and Ana. The statements with **estar** describe conditions that are temporary and changeable.

▶ Some adjectives change in meaning when used with **ser** and **estar**.

With *ser*	With *estar*
El chico **es listo**. *The boy is **smart**.*	El chico **está listo**. *The boy is **ready**.*
La profesora **es mala**. *The professor is **bad**.*	La profesora **está mala**. *The professor is **sick**.*
Jaime **es aburrido**. *Jaime is **boring**.*	Jaime **está aburrido**. *Jaime is **bored**.*
Las peras **son verdes**. *The pears are **green**.*	Las peras **están verdes**. *The pears are **not ripe**.*
El gato **es muy vivo.** *The cat is **very lively**.*	El gato **está vivo.** *The cat is **alive***
El puente **es seguro.** *The bridge is **safe***	Él no **está seguro.** *He's **not sure**.*

¡INTÉNTALO! Form complete sentences by using the correct form of **ser** or **estar**, the correct form of each adjective, and any other necessary words. The first item has been done for you.

1. Alejandra / cansado — Alejandra está cansada.
2. Ellos / guapo — Ellos son guapos.
3. Carmen / alto — Carmen es alta.
4. Yo / la clase de español — Estoy en la clase de español.
5. Película / a las once — La película es a las once.
6. Hoy / viernes — Hoy es viernes.
7. Nosotras / enojado — Nosotras estamos enojadas.
8. Antonio / médico — Antonio es médico.
9. Romeo y Julieta / enamorado — Romeo y Julieta están enamorados.
10. Libros / de Ana — Los libros son de Ana.
11. Marisa y Juan / estudiando — Marisa y Juan están estudiando.
12. Partido de baloncesto / gimnasio — El partido de baloncesto es en el gimnasio.

TEACHING OPTIONS

Extra Practice Have students write sentences illustrating the contrasting meanings of adjectives that change meaning when used with **ser** or **estar**. Have students trade sentences for peer-editing before going over them with the class.

Video Show the **fotonovela** video module again. Have students jot down every time they hear **ser** or **estar** used. Discuss each use of **ser** and **estar** in the **fotonovela**.

Pairs Tell students to imagine that they are to interview a celebrity visiting their hometown. Ask students to write questions employing at least 10 different uses of ser and estar. Next, have them interview a partner, recording his/her answers. Students should then write a summary of their interviews.

Present Discuss points one and two on this page. Emphasize that **ser** is used with permanent qualities while **estar** is used with temporary conditions. Ask students if they notice any context clues in the examples that would help them choose between **ser** and **estar**. (The words **hoy, siempre, en la fiesta** all indicate a period of time.) To further practice this point, write sentences like the following examples on the board: 1. *Pilar is worried because she has a test tomorrow.* (**Pilar está preocupada porque tiene una prueba mañana.**) 2. *The bellman is very busy right now.* (**El botones está muy ocupado ahora.**) 3. *The beach is beautiful.* (**La playa es hermosa.**) 4. *Juan is very handsome today.* (**Juan está muy guapo hoy.**) Then ask students to translate these sentences into Spanish. Finally, ask why they chose either **ser** or **estar** for their translation.

Next, review those adjectives that change in meaning depending on whether they are used with **ser** or **estar**. Ask students questions like these to practice the different meanings of the adjectives: 1. **Manuel es un muchacho muy inteligente. ¿Está listo o es listo?** 2. **No me gusta la clase de física. ¿Está aburrida o es aburrida?** 3. **No sé si Carlos tiene 50 o 51 años. ¿No estoy seguro/a o no soy seguro/a?** 4. **¿El color del taxi es verde o está verde?** 5. **El profesor no enseña muy bien. ¿Está malo o es malo?**

Close Before checking the answers to **¡Inténtalo!**, have students write down the purpose of the verb for each item, then check to make sure the purpose matches the verb they chose. Then, check the answers orally with the class.

Práctica

1 **¿Ser o estar?** They say that opposites attract. Complete the statements about Andrés and Andrea using **ser** or **estar** and any other necessary words.

modelo

Andrés ___es___ bajo pero Andrea ___es alta___.

1. Andrés ___es___ un poco gordo pero Andrea ___es delgada.___.
2. La habitación de Andrea siempre (*always*) ___está___ sucia pero la habitación de Andrés ___está limpia___.
3. Andrés siempre ___está___ contento pero Andrea siempre ___está triste___.
4. Andrea ___es___ rubia pero Andrés ___es moreno___.
5. Andrés ___es___ perezoso (*lazy*) pero Andrea ___es trabajadora___.
6. Andrea ___es___ muy seria pero Andrés ___es alegre___.
7. A pesar de todo (*in spite of everything*), Andrés y Andrea ___están___ enamorados.

2 **Completar** Complete this conversation with the appropriate forms of **ser** and **estar**.

EDUARDO ¡Hola, Ceci! ¿Cómo ___estás___?
CECILIA Hola, Eduardo. Bien, gracias. ¡Qué guapo ___estás___ hoy!
EDUARDO Gracias. ___Eres___ muy amable. Oye, ¿qué ___estás___ haciendo? ¿___Estás___ ocupada?
CECILIA No, sólo ___estoy___ escribiendo una carta a mi prima Pilar.
EDUARDO ¿De dónde ___es___ ella?
CECILIA Pilar ___es___ del Ecuador. Su papá ___es___ médico en Quito. Pero ahora Pilar y su familia ___están___ de vacaciones en Ponce, Puerto Rico.
EDUARDO Y... ¿cómo ___es___ Pilar?
CECILIA ___Es___ muy lista. Y también ___es___ alta, rubia y muy bonita.

3 **En el aeropuerto** In a small group, take turns using **ser** and **estar** to describe the following scene. Say as many things as you can. Answers will vary.

NOTA CULTURAL

Luis Muñoz Marín International Airport in San Juan, Puerto Rico, is a major transportation hub of the Caribbean. The airport connects the region with the rest of the world via flights that depart daily for the mainland U.S. and various Caribbean nations.

1 Warm-up/Present Review pairs of adjectives with opposite meanings from this lesson and Lesson 3. Then ask a volunteer to supply the missing words to the **Modelo** and explain his or her choice. Then model pronunciation of the completed sentence.

2 Warm-up Before completing the activity, ask students to point out context clues which will help them determine whether to use **ser** or **estar**. For example, the word **hoy** in line 2 of the dialogue indicates a temporary quality so a conjugation of **estar** would be used in the blank.

2 Expand Ask volunteers to perform the dialogue for the class.

2 Expand Have students work with a partner to write a continuation of the dialogue in this activity and then present it to the class.

3 Present Ask groups to choose a leader to moderate the activity, a secretary to record the group's description, and a proofreader to check that the written description is accurate. All students should take turns adding one sentence at a time to the group's description.

3 Expand Have students pick one of the individuals pictured and write a one-paragraph description of that person, employing as many different uses of **ser** and **estar** as possible.

3 Expand Ask students to continue working in their groups to make up a story about the airport scene, incorporating some elements from their descriptions.

TEACHING OPTIONS

Extra Practice Have students write a paragraph about a close friend, including the person's physical appearance, general disposition, place of birth, birthday, profession, and where the friend is now. Ask volunteers to share their paragraphs with the class.

Pairs Ask students to work with a partner to act out the following scenario. Student one is at the beach with some friends while student two is at home. Student one calls student two, trying to convince him or her to come to the beach. Students should try to employ as many uses of **ser** and **estar** in their scenario as possible. After acting out the scene once, have students switch roles.

Comunicación

4 **Describir** With a classmate, take turns describing the following people. First mention where each person is from. Then describe what each person is like, how each person is feeling, and what he or she is doing right now. Answers will vary.

modelo

tu compañero/a de cuarto

Mi compañera de cuarto es de San Juan, Puerto Rico. Es muy inteligente. Está cansada pero está estudiando en la biblioteca.

1. tu mejor (*best*) amigo/a
2. tus padres
3. tu profesor(a) favorito/a
4. tu novio/a o esposo/a
5. tu primo/a favorito/a
6. tus abuelos

5 **Adivinar** Get together with a partner and describe a few of your classmates to him or her using these questions as a guide. Don't mention the classmates' names. Can your partner guess which classmates you are describing? Answers will vary.

1. ¿Cómo es?
2. ¿Cómo está?
3. ¿De dónde es?
4. ¿Dónde está?
5. ¿Qué está haciendo?

6 **Fotos** Use **ser** and **estar** to describe what you see in the photo. Answers will vary.

Síntesis

7 **Conversación** Get together with a classmate you don't know very well and ask each other questions using **ser**, **estar**, and other verbs. Be sure to ask about these topics: Answers will vary.

- las clases
- la familia
- los amigos
- los pasatiempos

4 Present Read the **Modelo,** then divide the class into pairs. After pairs have practiced their descriptions, have them select two to present to the class.

5 Present This activity is also suitable for doing with the whole class. Assign the name of each student in the class to another student. Students circulate around the room asking the activity questions to determine the identity of the student assigned to each person. Students record the names of the students interviewed and their assigned students. After 5 minutes, see how many identities students were able to discover.

6 Warm-up To model the types of sentences students should create, ask them to listen to statements you make about the drawing and determine if they are true or false. Have students correct false statements. Ex: **Dos hombres están caminando. (cierto) Los dos hombres son altos. (falso; Un hombre es alto y un hombre es bajo.)**

7 Warm-up Have students make a list of the interrogative words they will use in their questions. Then have them list the uses of **ser** and **estar** they could use with each interrogative word.

The Affective Dimension Ask your students if they are more comfortable speaking Spanish with students they already know or students they don't know very well. Encourage them to consider pair and group activities as a cooperative venture in which group members support and encourage each other.

Assignment Have students do activities in the **Student Activities Manual: Workbook,** pages 54–55.

TEACHING OPTIONS

Heritage Speakers Have Spanish speakers write a television commercial for a vacation resort in the Spanish-speaking world. Ask them to employ as many uses of **ser** and **estar** as they can. If possible, after they've written their commercial, have them videotape it to show to the class.

TPR Call on a volunteer and whisper the name of a celebrity in his or her ear. The volunteer mimes actions, acts out characteristics, and uses props to elicit descriptions of the person. Ex: The volunteer points to the U.S. on a map. (**Es de los Estados Unidos.**) She then indicates a short man. (**Es un hombre bajo.**) She mimes riding a bicycle. (**Está paseando en bicicleta. ¿Es Lance Armstrong?**)

Section Goals

In **Estructura 5.4** students will study:
- direct object nouns
- the personal **a**
- direct object pronouns

Instructional Resources *Student Activities Manual: Workbook, 56; Lab Manual, 246*

Before Presenting Estructura 5.4 Write these sentences on the board: **—¿Quién tiene el *pasaporte*? —Juan *lo* tiene.** Underline **pasaporte** and explain that it is a direct object noun. Then underline **lo** and explain that it is the masculine singular direct object pronoun. Translate both sentences. Follow the same procedure with these sentences. **—¿Quién hace turismo? —Simón lo hace. —¿Quién tiene la llave? —Pilar la tiene. —¿Quién escribe postales? —Juan las escribe.** Explain to students that they are now going to learn the direct object pronouns in Spanish.

Assignment Have students study **Estructura 5.4** and prepare the activities on pages 155–156 as homework.

Present Review what a direct object noun is. Then discuss the use of the personal **a**. Ask individuals questions that elicit it: **¿Tienes que esperar a tu novio con frecuencia? ¿Visitas a tu abuela los fines de semana? ¿Llamas a tu padre los sábados?**

Then introduce the third person direct object pronouns one at a time, beginning with the masculine singular. Ask a series of questions to elicit each. Ask: **¿Quién ve el lápiz de Marcos? ¿Ves el libro de Daniela? ¿Quién quiere este diccionario? Escuchas al profe de matemáticas?** Prepare questions like these to elicit each direct object pronoun.

Continued on page 155.

5.4 Direct object nouns and pronouns

NATIONAL STANDARDS comparisons

SUBJECT	VERB	DIRECT OBJECT NOUN
Álex y Javier	están tomando	fotos.
Álex and Javier	*are taking*	*photos.*

- A direct object noun receives the action of the verb directly and generally follows the verb. In the example above, the direct object noun answers the question *What are Javier and Álex taking?*

- When a direct object noun in Spanish is a person or a pet, it is preceded by the word **a**. This is called the personal **a**; there is no English equivalent for this construction.

Don Francisco visita **a** la señora Ramos.	Don Francisco visita el Hotel Prado.
Don Francisco is visiting Mrs. Ramos.	*Don Francisco is visiting the Hotel Prado.*

In the first sentence above, the personal **a** is required because the direct object is a person. In the second sentence, the personal **a** is not required because the direct object is a place, not a person.

¿Dónde pongo las maletas?
Puede ponerlas encima de la cama.

Hay muchos lugares interesantes por aquí. ¿Quieren ir a verlos?

Direct object pronouns

SINGULAR		PLURAL	
me	*me*	**nos**	*us*
te	*you* (fam.)	**os**	*you* (fam.)
lo	*you* (m., form.) *him; it* (m.)	**los**	*you* (m., form.) *them* (m.)
la	*you* (f., form.) *her; it* (f.)	**las**	*you* (f., form.) *them* (f.)

- Direct object pronouns are words that replace direct object nouns. Like English, Spanish sometimes uses a direct object pronoun to avoid repeating a noun that has already been mentioned.

	DIRECT OBJECT		DIRECT OBJECT PRONOUN	
Maribel hace	las maletas.	Maribel	las	hace.
Felipe compra	el sombrero.	Felipe	lo	compra.
Vicky tiene	la llave.	Vicky	la	tiene.

¡ATENCIÓN!
In Spain and parts of Latin America, **le** and **les** are used instead of the pronouns **lo, la, los,** and **las** when referring to people:
No le veo.
I don't see him/her.

TEACHING OPTIONS

TPR Call out a series of sentences with direct object nouns, some of which have direct object nouns that require the personal **a** and some which do not. Have students raise their hands if the personal **a** is used.

Extra Practice Write 6 sentences on the board that have direct object nouns. Use two verbs in the simple present tense, two in the present progressive, and two using **ir a** + *infinitive.* Draw a line through the direct objects as students call them out. Have students state which pronoun to write to replace them. Now, draw an arrow from the pronoun to where it goes in the sentence as indicated by the students.

- In affirmative sentences, direct object pronouns generally appear before the conjugated verb. In negative sentences, the pronoun is placed between the word **no** and the verb.

Adela practica **el tenis**. Adela **lo** practica.	Adela no tiene **las llaves**. Adela **no las** tiene.
Carmen compra **los pasajes**. Carmen **los** compra	Diego no hace **las maletas**. Diego **no las** hace.

- When the verb is an infinitive construction, such as **ir a** + [*infinitive*], the direct object pronoun can be placed before the conjugated form or attached to the infinitive.

Ellos van a escribir **unas postales**.	Ellos **las** van a escribir. Ellos van a escribir**las**.
Lidia quiere ver **una película.**	Lidia **la** quiere ver. Lidia quiere ver**la**.

¡ATENCIÓN!

When a direct object pronoun is attached to the present participle, an accent mark is added to maintain the proper stress. To learn more about accents, see Lesson 4, **Pronunciación,** p. 111, Lesson 10, **Ortografía,** p. 305, and Lesson 11, **Ortografía,** p. 335.

- When the verb is in the present progressive, the direct object pronoun can be placed before the conjugated form or attached to the present participle.

Gerardo está leyendo **la lección**.	Gerardo **la** está leyendo. Gerardo está leyéndo**la**.
Toni está mirando el **partido**.	Toni **lo** está mirando. Toni está mirándo**lo.**

¡INTÉNTALO!

Change the direct object nouns into direct object pronouns and make any other necessary changes. The first item in each column has been done for you.

1. Juan tiene el pasaporte. *Juan lo tiene.*
2. Confirman la reservación. La confirman.
3. Leemos la lección. La leemos.
4. Estudio el vocabulario. Lo estudio.
5. Aprendemos las palabras. Las aprendemos.
6. Escucho al profesor. Lo escucho.
7. Escribe los párrafos. Los escribe.
8. Tengo los pasajes Los tengo.
9. Quiero un avión. Lo quiero.
10. Van a ver la película. *Van a verla./La van a ver.*
11. Quiero ver los monumentos. Quiero verlos./Los quiero ver.
12. Vamos a tomar el examen mañana. Vamos a tomarlo mañana./Lo vamos a tomar mañana.
13. ¿Cuándo vas a hacer la tarea? ¿Cuándo vas a hacerla?/¿Cuándo la vas a hacer?
14. Están explorando el pueblo. Están explorándolo./Lo están explorando.
15. Miguel está comprando los libros. Miguel está comprándolos./Miguel los está comprando.
16. Estoy leyendo las cartas de Sonia. Estoy leyéndolas./Las estoy leyendo.
17. ¡Están estudiando los verbos! Están estudiándolos./Los están estudiando.
18. No queremos escalar esa montaña. No queremos escalarla./No la queremos escalar.

TEACHING OPTIONS

Extra Practice Make a list of 20 questions requiring direct object pronouns in the answer. Arrange students in two concentric circles. Students in the center circle ask questions from the list of those in the outer circle until you say stop (**¡Paren!**). The outer circle moves one person to the right and the questions begin again. Continue for five minutes, then have the students in the outer circle ask the questions.

Pairs Have students write 10 sentences using direct object nouns. Their sentences should also include a mixture of verbs in the present progressive, simple present, and near future. Ask students to exchange their sentences with a partner, who will rewrite them using a direct object pronoun. Students should check their partners' work.

After you have practiced all third person forms, move to the first and second person. Elicit first person direct object pronouns (while practicing second person familiar direct object pronouns) by asking questions first of individual students and then of groups of students. **¿Quién te invita a bailar con frecuencia? (Mi novio me invita a bailar.) ¿Quién te pide información? (Mi compañero de cuarto me la pide.) ¿Quién te comprende? (Mi amigo me comprende.)**

Questions directed at the class as a whole can elicit first person plural direct object pronouns. **¿Quién los llama los fines de semana? (Nuestros padres nos llaman.) ¿Quién los espera después de la clase? (Los amigos nos esperan.) ¿Quiénes los busca los sábados? (Nuestros amigos nos buscan.)**

Discuss the placement of direct object pronouns in affirmative sentences and in constructions with infinitives and the present progressive. Point out the use of written accents in **¡Atención!**.

Use your picture file to practice the third person direct object pronouns with infinitives and the present progressive. Ex: **¿Quién está practicando tenis? (Pete Sampras lo está practicando. Pete Sampras está practicándolo.) ¿Quién va a mirar la televisión? (El hombre con el pelo corto la va a mirar. El hombre con el pelo corto va a mirarla.)**

Suggestion Point out that the direct object pronoun **los** refers to both masculine or mixed groups. **Las** refers only to feminine groups.

Close Check **¡Inténtalo!** orally with the whole class.

1 Warm-up/Present Begin the activity by reading the first question aloud and asking a volunteer to point out the direct object, say the corresponding direct object pronoun, and read the correct response. Confirm by rereading the item and response together as connected text. Follow the same procedure for the rest of the items.

1 Expand Repeat the activity but change the direct object noun or pronoun (varying gender and number) in each item.

2 Present Go over the instructions and read the **Modelo** with the whole class before doing the activity.

2 Expand Ask students true-false questions about who does what in the activity. Students respond orally, correcting your incorrect statements. Ex: **La Sra. Garza busca la cámara. (No, María la busca.)**

Suggestion Present the information in the **Nota cultural**. Tell students that the term for Puerto Rico's political status is **estado libre asociado**. You might add that Puerto Rico uses U.S. currency and that Puerto Ricans have U.S. citizenship, though they cannot vote in presidential elections and don't pay federal income tax.

3 Present/Expand Ask a volunteer to help you go through the **Modelo** for the whole class. After pairs have gone through the activity once, ask them to switch roles and do it again. Write on the board other activities students may include in their conversations, such as: **comprar las mapas, comprar una revista para leer en el vuelo, llamar al taxi, practicar el español**, and so forth

3 Expand Create a dictation using two or three exchanges based on the activity.

Práctica

1 Seleccionar Choose the correct response to each question.

1. ¿Tienes el libro de español? c
   a. Sí, la tengo. b. No, no los tengo. c. Sí, lo tengo.
2. ¿Me puedes llevar al partido de baloncesto? b
   a. Sí, los puedo llevar. b. Sí, te puedo llevar. c. No, no las puedo llevar.
3. El artista quiere dibujarte con tu mamá, ¿no? b
   a. Sí, quiere dibujarlos mañana. b. Sí, nos quiere dibujar mañana.
   c. Sí, quiere dibujarte mañana.
4. ¿Quién tiene las llaves de nuestra habitación? a
   a. Yo no las tengo. b. Amalia los tiene, ¿no? c. Yo la tengo.
5. ¿Quién te lleva al aeropuerto? c
   a. Yo te llevo al aeropuerto. b. Rita los lleva al aeropuerto.
   c. Mónica me lleva al aeropuerto a las seis.
6. ¿Puedes oírme? a
   a. Sí, te puedo oír bien. b. No, no los oigo. c. Sí, las oigo bien.

2 ¿Quién? The Garza family is preparing to go on a vacation to Puerto Rico. Based on the clues, answer the questions about their preparations. Be sure to use direct object pronouns in your answers.

modelo
¿Quién hace las reservaciones para el hotel? (El Sr. Garza)
El Sr. Garza las hace.

1. ¿Quién compra los pasajes para el vuelo (*flight*)? (La Sra. Garza)
   La Sra. Garza los compra.
2. ¿Quién tiene que hacer las maletas de los niños? (María)
   María tiene que hacerlas./María las tiene que hacer.
3. ¿Quiénes buscan los pasaportes? (Antonio y María)
   Antonio y María los buscan.
4. ¿Quién va a confirmar las reservaciones para el hotel? (La Sra. Garza)
   La Sra. Garza va a confirmarlas./La Sra. Garza las va a confirmar.
5. ¿Quién busca la cámara? (María)
   María la busca.
6. ¿Quién compra un mapa de Puerto Rico? (Antonio) Antonio lo compra.

NOTA CULTURAL

The Garza family needs passports to travel to Puerto Rico if they are coming from a foreign country. When traveling from the U.S. mainland, however, passports are not required, since Puerto Rico is a U.S. territory.

3 Preguntas Imagine that you and a classmate are chatting on your cell phones, trying to find out what each of you is doing to prepare for tomorrow's trip. Follow the model.
Answers will vary.

modelo
buscar tu pasaporte
Estudiante 1: *¿Estás buscando tu pasaporte?*
Estudiante 2: *No, no estoy buscándolo.*
Estudiante 1: *¿Cuándo lo vas a buscar?*
Estudiante 2: *Voy a buscarlo mañana (el lunes, a las dos, etc.).*

1. hacer tus maletas
2. buscar tu pasaje
3. confirmar tus reservaciones
4. comprar una cámara
5. preparar los documentos de viaje
6. leer el folleto (*brochure*) del hotel

¡LENGUA VIVA!

There are many Spanish words that correspond to *ticket*. **Boleto, billete,** and **pasaje** usually refer to a ticket used for travel, such as an airplane ticket. **Entrada** and **boleto** refer to a ticket to an event, such as a concert or a movie.

TEACHING OPTIONS

Pairs Have students take turns asking each other whom they know who does the following activities: **leer revistas, practicar el ciclismo, siempre ganar los partidos, visitar a sus padres durante las vacaciones, leer el periódico, escribir cartas, escuchar a sus profesores, practicar la natación.** Ex: **—¿Quién lee revistas? —Yo las leo.**

Heritage Speakers Have Spanish speakers create a dialogue between a travel agent and client. The client would like to go to Puerto Rico and wants to know what he needs for the trip, what he should to do to prepare for the trip, and what he'll be able to do once he's there. Have partners take turns playing both roles, choosing one of their role-plays to present to the class.

NATIONAL communication STANDARDS

Comunicación

4

Entrevista Interview a classmate using these questions. Be sure to use direct object pronouns in your responses. Answers will vary.

1. ¿Tienes tus llaves?
2. ¿Traes tu libro a la clase de español? ¿Y tu cuaderno?
3. ¿Estudias español todos los días?
4. ¿Visitas mucho a tus abuelos?
5. ¿Quién prepara la comida (*food*) en tu casa?
6. ¿Cuándo vas a hacer la tarea de la clase de español?
7. ¿Cuándo ves a tus amigos/as?
8. ¿Miras mucho la televisión? ¿Cuándo vas a mirar tu programa favorito?

5

En el centro Get together with a partner and take turns asking each other questions about the drawing. Use direct object pronouns whenever possible. Answers will vary.

modelo

Estudiante 1: *¿Quién está leyendo el periódico?*
Estudiante 2: *El Sr. López está leyéndolo.*

NATIONAL communication STANDARDS

Síntesis

6

Adivinanzas Play a guessing game in which you describe a person, place, or thing and your partner guesses who or what it is. Then switch roles. Each of you should give at least five descriptions. Answers will vary.

modelo

Estudiante 1: *Lo uso para (I use it to) escribir en mi cuaderno. Es amarillo y no es muy grande. ¿Qué es?*
Estudiante 2: *¿Es un lápiz?*
Estudiante 1: *¡Sí!*

4 Present Ask students to take notes on their partner's answers. After interviewing is over, have participants review their answers with a group and report a group consensus of the answers to the class.

4 Expand Have students write five more questions like the ones in the activity, then continue their interviews.

5 Warm-up Before assigning the activity, activate vocabulary by having the whole class describe what the people in the drawing are doing. Ex: **—Qué hacen el hombre y la mujer a la izquierda? —Hacen el turismo. —Y la mujer en el centro, ¿qué hace? —Saca fotos. —¿Qué más hace el jóven que está patinando? —Escucha música.** Then give students two minutes to jot down as many questions about the illustration as they can.

5 Present Give pairs four minutes to complete the activity. After one partner has asked his or her questions, the pair switches roles and the other partner asks his or her questions.

5 Expand Have students work with a partner to create a list of questions about the drawing. Then have partners ask another pair of students their questions.

6 Warm-up Before assigning the activity, review classroom objects and personal possessions with the students. Write a list of colors and their translations on the board for easy reference.

6 Expand Have pairs write five riddles like that in Activity 6. Have pairs present their riddles to other pairs to answer.

Assignment Have students prepare the activities in the **Student Activities Manual: Workbook**, page 56.

TEACHING OPTIONS

Game Play a game of "20 Preguntas" with the class. Divide the class into two teams. Think of an object in the room. Alternate calling on teams to ask questions. Once a team knows the answer, the team captain should raise her hand. If right, the team gets a point. If wrong, the team loses a point. Play until one team has earned 5 points.

Pairs Have students create five questions that include the direct object pronouns **me**, **te**, and **nos**. Then have them ask their partners the questions on their list. Ex: **—¿Quién te llama con más frecuencia? —Mi novia me llama con más frecuencia. —¿Quién nos escucha cuando hacemos preguntas en español? —El/La profesor(a) y los estudiantes nos escuchan.**

Section Goals

In **Estructura 5.5** students will learn:

- to count from 101 on
- punctuation and agreement rules pertaining to numbers

Instructional Resources
Student Activities Manual: Workbook, 57–58; Lab Manual, 247

Before Presenting Estructura 5.5 Review numbers 0–100. Ask students questions, calling for a number in the answer. Ex: **¿Cuántos estudiantes hay en la clase? ¿Cuántos años tiene... ? Ana tiene trece lápices y yo tengo cuarenta, ¿cuántos lápices tenemos?** Next, write the following on the board: **cuatrocientos estudiantes, novecientas personas, dos mil libros, once millones de viajeros**. Help students deduce the meanings of the numbers. Then, point out that forms with **ciento** agree in gender with the words they modify. Explain the objectives for this lesson.

Assignment Have students study **Estructura 5.5** and do the exercises on pages 158–159.

Present Model pronunciation of the numbers and lead students in counting. Write numbers on the board and call on individuals to read them. To practice agreement, write numbers from 101 to 999 followed by various nouns and have students read them.

Present **mil** and **millón** in a similar fashion.

Suggestion Discuss the information in **¡Lengua viva!**. Then write 5 different years on the board. Have the class read each year as a group.

Close Call out a number from **¡Inténtalo!**. Have students identify the exercise item. Then call on a volunteer to spell out the number on the board.

5.5 Numbers 101 and higher

NATIONAL STANDARDS comparisons

Numbers 101 and higher

101	ciento uno	**1.000**	mil
200	doscientos/as	**1.100**	mil cien
300	trescientos/as	**2.000**	dos mil
400	cuatrocientos/as	**5.000**	cinco mil
500	quinientos/as	**100.000**	cien mil
600	seiscientos/as	**200.000**	doscientos mil
700	setecientos/as	**550.000**	quinientos cincuenta mil
800	ochocientos/as	**1.000.000**	un millón (de)
900	novecientos/as	**8.000.000**	ocho millones (de)

▶ As shown in the preceding chart, Spanish uses a period to indicate thousands, rather than a comma as used in English.

▶ The numbers 200 through 999 agree in gender with the nouns they modify.

324 maletas
trescientas veinticuatro maletas

605 pasajeros
seiscientos cinco pasajeros

Aquí está la reservación... dos habitaciones dobles y una individual, de la ciento uno a la ciento tres.

▶ The word **mil**, which can mean *a thousand* and *one thousand*, is not usually used in the plural form. **Un millón** (*a million* or *one million*), however, has the plural form **millones** in which the accent is dropped.

1.000 aviones
mil aviones

2.000.000 de turistas
dos millones de turistas

¡LENGUA VIVA!

In Spanish, years are not expressed as pairs of 2-digit numbers as they are in English (1979, *nineteen seventy-nine*):

1776, mil setecientos setenta y seis

1945, mil novecientos cuarenta y cinco

2001, dos mil uno

¡ATENCIÓN!

When **millón** or **millones** is used before a noun, the word **de** is placed between the two:

1.000.000 de hombres = un millón de hombres

12.000.000 de aviones = doce millones de aviones

•••

See Lesson 2, section 2.4, p. 57 to review the difference between **cien** and **ciento:**

100.000 = cien mil

2.101 = dos mil ciento uno

¡INTÉNTALO! Give the Spanish equivalent of each number. The first item has been done for you.

1. **102** ciento dos
2. **935** novecientos treinta y cinco
3. **5.000.000** cinco millones
4. **2001** dos mil uno
5. **1776** mil setecientos setenta y seis
6. **345** trescientos cuarenta y cinco
7. **550.300** quinientos cincuenta mil trescientos
8. **235** doscientos treinta y cinco
9. **1999** mil novecientos noventa y nueve
10. **113** ciento trece
11. **205** doscientos cinco
12. **2105** dos mil ciento cinco
13. **17.123** diecisiete mil ciento veintitrés
14. **497** cuatrocientos noventa y siete

TEACHING OPTIONS

Game Ask students to stand up to create a number chain. The first student states the number 25. The next student says 50. Students continue the chain, using multiples of 25. If a student misses the next number in sequence, he must sit down. Continue play until only one student is left standing. If a challenge is required to break a tie, play the game with multiples of 30.

Pairs Ask students to create a list of 9 things containing both feminine and masculine items, 3 numerals in the hundreds, 3 numerals in the thousands, and 3 numerals in the millions. Once lists are completed, students read their partners' lists aloud as partners listen for the correct number and any agreement errors. Ex: **204 personas (doscientas cuatro personas)**

Práctica

1 **Completar** Complete the following sequences of numbers.

1. cincuenta, ciento cincuenta, doscientos cincuenta... mil cincuenta
trescientos cincuenta, cuatrocientos cincuenta, quinientos cincuenta, seiscientos cincuenta, setecientos cincuenta, ochocientos cincuenta, novecientos cincuenta
2. cinco mil, veinte mil, treinta y cinco mil... noventa y cinco mil
cincuenta mil, sesenta y cinco mil, ochenta mil
3. cien mil, doscientos mil, trescientos mil... un millón
cuatrocientos mil, quinientos mil, seiscientos mil, setecientos mil, ochocientos mil, novecientos mil
4. cien millones, noventa millones, ochenta millones... cero setenta millones, sesenta millones, cincuenta millones, cuarenta millones, treinta millones, veinte millones, diez millones

2 **Resolver** Read the math problems aloud and solve them.

+ más
– menos
= son/es

modelo

200 + 300 =

Doscientos más trescientos son quinientos.

1. 1000 + 753 = Mil más setecientos cincuenta y tres son mil setecientos cincuenta y tres.
2. 1.000.000 – 30.000 = Un millón menos treinta mil son novecientos setenta mil.
3. 10.000 + 555 = Diez mil más quinientos cincuenta y cinco son diez mil quinientos cincuenta y cinco.
4. 150 + 150 = Ciento cincuenta más ciento cincuenta son trescientos.
5. 100.000 + 205.000 = Cien mil más doscientos cinco mil son trescientos cinco mil.
6. 29.000 – 10.000 = Veintinueve mil menos diez mil son diecinueve mil.

3 **¿Cuándo?** Look at the timeline and tell when each of these events occurs.

1776	1861-1865	1914-1918	1939-1945	1963	1969	1997
Independencia de los EE.UU.	Guerra Civil de los EE.UU.	Primera Guerra Mundial	Segunda Guerra Mundial	El presidente Kennedy es asesinado	El hombre llega a la Luna	El *Pathfinder* llega al planeta Marte

1. La Primera Guerra Mundial termina.
2. El *Pathfinder* llega al planeta Marte.
3. La Segunda Guerra Mundial termina.
4. La Primera Guerra Mundial comienza.
5. El hombre llega a la Luna (*Moon*).
6. La Segunda Guerra Mundial comienza.

Comunicación

NATIONAL communication STANDARDS

4 **Entrevista** Work together with a classmate and use these questions to interview each other. Be prepared to report the results of your interview to the class.

1. ¿Cuántas personas hay en la clase de español?
2. ¿Cuántas personas hay en la universidad?
3. ¿Cuántas personas hay en tu ciudad?
4. ¿Cuántas personas hay en tu estado?
5. ¿Cuántas personas hay en los Estados Unidos? ¿Y cuántos hispanohablantes?
6. ¿Cuántas personas hay en el mundo (*world*)? ¿Y cuántos hispanohablantes?

¡ATENCIÓN!

Note this difference between Spanish and English:

mil millones
a billion (1,000,000,000)

un billón
a trillion (1,000,000,000,000)

TEACHING OPTIONS

Heritage Speakers Ask Spanish speakers to create a worksheet consisting of five math word problems for their classmates to complete. Have them read the problems to the class or a group of students, who, in turn, will solve the problems. They should also include an answer key to accompany their problems.

Large Groups Divide the class into groups of 10. Each person in each group is given a flashcard with a number 0–9. If one group is smaller, give the extra numbers to the group to distribute as necessary. Call out a number in which none of the digits are repeated. Students arrange themselves, showing their flashcard(s) to reflect the number you called out. Repeat with other numbers.

1 Present After students have written out their answers individually, have them answer orally without looking at their papers.

1 Expand Practice listening comprehension by having students read numbers from the activity to a partner, who writes them in numerals.

2 Warm-up Review the math information in the box. Practice a few problems using lesser numbers with the whole class before going over the activity.

2 Present Have students read the math problems aloud to a partner. Then have students spell out the problems in writing.

3 Warm-up Review the information in **¡Lengua viva!**, page 158. Practice reading the years on the timeline with the whole class.

3 Present Have students write out the years for each item in the exercise, then call on volunteers to read the answers for each item.

4 Suggestion Have students look up the data which would help them answer the questions in the **Entrevista** before they come to class.

Suggestion Discuss the information in **¡Atención!** before doing **Entrevista**. Practice the difference between billions and trillions by writing numbers on the board for students to read aloud.

4 Expand Have students create a graph illustrating the results of their interviews. They may also want to include other data regarding population figures in their community, state, the United States, or the world.

Assignment Have students do the activities in the **Student Activities Manual: Workbook**, pages 57–58.

Section Goals

In **Lectura** students will:

- learn the strategy of scanning to find specific information in reading matter
- read a brochure about eco-tourism in Puerto Rico

Antes de leer
Introduce the strategy. Explain to students that a good way to get an idea of what an article or other text is about is to scan it before reading. Scanning means running one's eyes over a text in search of specific information that can be used to infer the content of the text. Explain that scanning a text before reading it is a good way to improve Spanish reading comprehension.

The Affective Dimension
Point out to students that becoming familiar with cognates will help them feel less overwhelmed when they encounter new Spanish texts.

Examinar el texto
Do the activity orally with the whole class. Some cognates that give a clue to the content of the text are: **turismo ecológico, hotel, aire acondicionado, perfecto, Parque Nacional Foresta, Museo de Arte Nativo, Reserve, Bioesfera, Santuario**. These clues should tell a reader scanning the text that it is about a hotel promoting eco-tourism.

Preguntas
Ask the questions orally of the whole class. Possible responses: 1. travel brochure, 2. Puerto Rico, 3. Photos of beautiful tropical beaches, bays, and forests; the document is trying to attract the reader, 4. Hotel La Cabaña in Lajas, Puerto Rico; attract guests

Assignment Have students read **Turismo ecológico en Puerto Rico** and do the activities in **Después de leer** as homework.

Lectura

Antes de leer

Estrategia

Scanning

Scanning involves glancing over a document in search of specific information. For example, you can scan a document to identify its format, to find cognates, to locate visual clues about the document's content, or to find specific facts. Scanning allows you to learn a great deal about a text without having to read it word for word.

Examinar el texto

Scan the reading selection for cognates and write a few of them down.

1. ____________
2. ____________
3. ____________
4. ____________
5. ____________

Based on the cognates you found, what do you think this document is about?

____

____

Preguntas

Read the following questions. Then scan the document again to look for answers to the questions.

1. What is the format of the reading selection?
   ____
2. What country is the document about?
   ____
3. What are some of the visual cues this document provides? What do they tell you about the content of the document?
   ____
   ____
4. Who produced the document, and what do you think the document is for?
   ____
   ____

Turismo ecológico en Puerto Rico

Hotel La Cabaña

~ Lajas, Puerto Rico ~

Habitaciones

- 40 individuales
- 15 dobles
- Teléfono/TV/Cable
- Aire acondicionado
- Restaurante (Bar)
- Piscina
- Área de juegos
- Cajero automático

El hotel está situado en Playa Grande, un pequeño pueblo de pescadores del mar Caribe. Es el lugar perfecto para el viajero que viene de vacaciones. Las playas son seguras y limpias, ideales para tomar el sol, descansar, tomar fotografías y nadar. Está abierto los 365 días del año. Hay una rebaja especial para estudiantes.

DIRECCIÓN: Playa Grande 406, Lajas, PR 00667, cerca del Parque Nacional Foresta.

TEACHING OPTIONS

Heritage Speakers Ask Spanish speakers of Puerto Rican heritage who have lived on or visited the island to prepare a short presentation about the climate, geography, or people of Puerto Rico. Ask them to illustrate their presentations with photos they have taken or illustrations from magazines, if possible.

Small Groups Have five students work together to brainstorm a list what would constitute an ideal tropical vacation for them. Each student should contribute at least one idea. Opinions will vary. Ask the group to designate one student to take notes and another to present the information to the class. When each group has its list, ask the designated presenter to share the information with the rest of the class. How do the groups differ? How are they similar?

Atracciones cercanas

Playa Grande ¿Busca la playa perfecta? Playa Grande es la playa que está buscando. Usted puede ir de pesca, sacar fotos, nadar y pasear en bicicleta. Playa Grande es un paraíso para el turista que quiere practicar deportes acuáticos. El lugar es bonito e interesante y usted tiene muchas oportunidades para descansar y disfrutar en familia.

Valle Niebla Ir de excursión, tomar café, montar a caballo, caminar, acampar, hacer picnic. Más de 100 lugares para acampar.

Bahía Fosforescente Sacar fotos, pescar, salidas de noche, excursión en barco. Una maravillosa experiencia con peces fosforescentes.

Arrecifes de Coral Sacar fotos, bucear, explorar. Es un lugar único en el Caribe.

Playa Vieja Tomar el sol, pasear en bicicleta, jugar a las cartas, escuchar música. Ideal para la familia.

Parque Nacional Foresta Sacar fotos, visitar el Museo de Arte Nativo. Reserva Mundial de la Biosfera.

Santuario de las Aves Sacar fotos, observar aves, seguir rutas de excursión.

aves *birds*

Después de leer

Listas

Which of the amenities of the Hotel La Cabaña would most interest these potential guests? Explain your choices.
Answers will vary.

1. Dos padres con un hijo de seis años y una hija de ocho años.
   ____
2. Un hombre y una mujer en su luna de miel (*honeymoon*).
   ____
3. Una persona en un viaje de negocios (*business trip*).
   ____

Conversaciones

With a partner, take turns asking each other the following questions.

1. ¿Quieres visitar el Hotel La Cabaña? ¿Por qué?
2. Tienes tiempo de visitar sólo tres de las atracciones turísticas que están cerca del hotel. ¿Cuáles vas a visitar? ¿Por qué?
3. ¿Qué prefieres hacer en Valle Niebla? ¿En Playa Vieja? ¿En el Parque Nacional Foresta?

Situaciones

You have just arrived at the Hotel La Cabaña. Your classmate is the concierge. Use the phrases below to express your interests and ask him or her for suggestions about where to go.

1. montar a caballo
2. bucear
3. pasear en bicicleta
4. pescar
5. observar aves

Contestar

Answer the following questions.

1. ¿Quieres visitar el Hotel La Cabaña? Explica tu respuesta.
   ____
2. ¿Adónde quieres ir de vacaciones el verano que viene? Explica tu respuesta.
   ____

Después de leer

Listas

Present Do this activity orally with the whole class. Encourage discussion on each of the points by asking questions such as: **En su/tu opinión, ¿qué tipo de atracciones buscan los padres con hijos de seis y ocho años? ¿Qué quieren en un hotel? Y una pareja en su luna de miel, ¿qué tipo de atracciones buscan en un hotel? En su/tu opinión, ¿qué busca una persona en un viaje de negocios?**

Conversaciones

Present/Expand Give pairs five minutes to ask and answer the questions. Then, with the whole class, question various individuals about what their partner said. **¿Por qué (no) quiere ____ visitar el Hotel La Cabaña? ¿Qué atracciones quiere ver?** and so forth. As you proceed, ask other students: **Y tú, ¿quieres visitar el Parque Nacional o prefieres visitar un lugar diferente?** and so forth.

Situaciones

Warm-up Give students a couple of minutes to review **Más vocabulario** on page 136 and **Expresiones útiles** on page 141. To expand, add activities such as **sacar fotos, correr, nadar, ir de excursion.**

Contestar

Suggestion This activity is suitable for written work which may be checked with the whole class.

Expand You may wish to ask the following listening comprehension questions. **1. El Hotel La Cabaña está situado cerca de qué mar? (el mar Caribe) 2. ¿Qué playa es un paraíso para el turista? (la Playa Grande) 3. ¿Dónde puede una persona ver peces fosforescentes? (en la Bahía Fosforescente)**

TEACHING OPTIONS

Pairs Have pairs of students work together to read the brochure aloud and write three questions about it. After they have finished, ask pairs to exchange their questions with another pair that can work together to answer the questions. Alternatively, you might pick pairs to read their questions to the class. Ask volunteers to answer them.

Extra Practice To practice scanning written material to infer its content, bring in short, simple Spanish-language magazine or newspaper articles you have read. Have pairs or small groups scan the articles to determine what they are about. Have them write down all the clues that help them. When each group has come to a decision, ask it to present its findings to the class. Confirm the accuracy of the inferences.

Section Goals

In **Escritura** students will:
- write a brochure for a hotel or resort
- integrate travel-related vocabulary and structures taught in **Lesson 5**

Tema

Present Discuss the hotel or resort brochure students are to write. Go over the list of information that they might include. You might indicate a specific number of the points that should be included in the brochure. Tell students that the brochure for **Hotel La Cabaña** in **Lectura**, pages 160–161, can serve as a model for their writing. Remind them that they are writing with the purpose of attracting guests to the hotel or resort, so they should describe it in the most favorable light possible. Suggest that, as they begin to think about writing, students should brainstorm as many details as they can remember about the hotel they are going to describe. Tell them to do as much of this in Spanish as they can.

Estrategia Explain that outlines are a great way for a writer to think about what a piece writing will be like before actually expending much time and effort on writing. An outline is also a great way of keeping a writer on track while writing and helps him or her keep the whole writing project in mind as he or she is focusing attention on a specific part.

Suggestion If students write each of the individual items of their brainstorm lists on index cards, they can arrange and rearrange them into different idea maps as they plan their hotel or resort brochure.

Assignment Have students prepare **Ideas y organización** and **Primer borrador** as homework.

Escritura

Estrategia

Making an outline

When we write to share information, an outline can serve to separate topics and subtopics, providing a framework for the presentation of data. Consider the following excerpt from an outline of the tourist brochure on pages 160-161.

IV. Descripción del sitio (con foto)
- A. Playa Grande
  1. Playas seguras y limpias
  2. Ideal para tomar el sol, descansar, tomar fotografías, nadar
- B. El hotel
  1. Abierto los 365 días del año
  2. Rebaja para estudiantes universitarios

Mapa de ideas

Idea maps can be used to create outlines. The major sections of an idea map correspond to the Roman numerals in an outline. The minor idea map sections correspond to the outline's capital letters, and so on. Consider the idea map that led to the outline above.

Tema

Escribir un folleto

Write a tourist brochure for a hotel or resort you have visited. If you wish, you may write about an imaginary hotel or resort. You may want to include some of the following information in your brochure:

- The name of the hotel or resort
- Phone and fax numbers that tourists can use to make contact
- The address of a website that tourists can consult
- An e-mail address that tourists can use to request information
- A description of the exterior of the hotel or resort
- A description of the interior of the hotel or resort, including facilities and amenities
- A description of the area around the hotel or resort, including its climate
- A listing of scenic natural attractions that are near the hotel or resort
- A listing of nearby cultural attractions
- A listing of recreational activities that tourists can pursue in the vicinity of the hotel or resort
- The rates charged by the hotel or resort

TEACHING OPTIONS

Proofreading Activity Copy on the board or onto a transparency the following items containing errors as a proofreading activity to do with the whole class.

1. **¿Cuál es la fecha del primero día de inbierno?**
2. **César, tu habitación es muy sucia! ¿No lo prefieres limpia?**
3. **Maribel, ¿es buscando las llaves? Yo los tengo aquí.**
4. **Nuestras habitaciones son en el tercero piso del hotel.**
5. **Este hotel está muy viejo y las camas están muy incómodas.**
6. **La primer puerta a la izquierda está su habitación, señorita**
7. **Soy muy contento aprender sobre el ecotrismo. Voy a estudiar lo en mi clase de economía.**

Plan de escritura

1 Ideas y organización

Which aspects of your vacation spot are the most attractive to prospective guests? Jot down your ideas based on your recollections or on the "perfect getaway." Then, organize your ideas in an outline, using only Spanish words and expressions. Remember to use a dictionary as a last resort.

2 Primer borrador

Using the outline you prepared in **Ideas y organización,** write the first draft of your brochure.

3 Comentario

Exchange papers with a classmate and comment on your partner's brochure, using these questions as a guide. Begin by mentioning one or two points that you like about the person's brochure, such as the description of the hotel or the location.

a. Would the brochure influence you to visit this hotel or resort?
b. Does the brochure provide all the required information?
c. Is the brochure organized in a logical fashion?
d. Do you have any suggestions for making the brochure more exciting?
e. Do you see any spelling or grammatical errors?

4 Redacción

Revise your first draft, keeping in mind your classmate's comments. Also incorporate any new ideas or information you may have. Before handing in the final version, review your work using these guidelines:

a. Underline each verb and make sure it agrees with the subject. Double check stem-changing verbs and verbs with irregular **yo** forms.
b. Check the gender and number of each article, noun, and adjective.
c. Check your spelling and punctuation, and consult your **Anotaciones para mejorar la escritura** to avoid repetition of previous errors.

5 Evaluación y progreso

Swap brochures with a classmate. After you have read the brochure, write a response in Spanish in which you:

- Name the three aspects of the resort that appeal to you most or least.
- Formulate two questions to clarify or expand on the information contained in the brochure.
- Request a room for yourself and a companion in the near future.

After your instructor returns your paper, review the comments and corrections. Note the most important issues on your **Anotaciones para mejorar la escritura** list in your **Carpeta de trabajos.**

Comentario
Present Go over guide questions **a–e** with the whole class. Then have students exchange their brochures. Allow five minutes for reading and comments.
Assignment Have students read **Redacción** as homework. Ask them to rewrite their drafts, incorporating the peer comments and following the directions in **Redacción.**

Evaluación y progreso
Give the class five minutes to exchange their final drafts, read them, and write their responses in Spanish. Then students hand their brochures in to you.

Writing Sample
Here is a writing sample that would constitute superior achievement.

Bienvenidos al Hotel Playa Bonita
Teléfono: 617.983.9322
Fax: 617.983.9344
Internet: www.playabonita.com

El Hotel Playa Bonita está muy cerca de San Francisco de Macorís, una pequeña ciudad situada en la costa del mar Caribe.

Nuestra atracción más famosa es la Playa Bonita. En Playa Bonita Ud. puede nadar, pescar, montar a caballo, pasear en bicicleta, sacar fotos, tomar el sol o, si Ud. quiere, sólo descansar.

Nuestras habitaciones son bonitas, limpias, y muy cómodas. También tenemos cabañas más cerca del mar.

Ud. puede también ir de excursión en el cercano Parque Nacional Buena Vista. O puede visitar el Museo de Arte Nativo en San Francisco de Macorís. Sólo hay que viajar quince minutos en autobús para llegar a sus puertas.

EVALUATION: Folleto

Criteria	Scale
Appropriate details	1 2 3 4 5
Organization	1 2 3 4 5
Use of vocabulary	1 2 3 4 5
Grammatical accuracy	1 2 3 4 5

Scoring	
Excellent	18–20 points
Good	14–17 points
Satisfactory	10–13 points
Unsatisfactory	< 10 points

Section Goals

In **Escuchar** students will:
- learn the strategy of listening for key words
- listen to a short paragraph and note the key words
- answer questions based on the content of a recorded conversation

Instructional Resource
Student Cassette/CD

Preparación
Warm-up Have students look at the photo and describe what they see. Guide them in saying what Hernán Jiménez is like and what he is doing.

Estrategia
Script **Aquí está la foto de mis vacaciones en la playa. Ya lo sé; no debo pasar el tiempo tomando el sol. Es que vivo en una ciudad donde llueve casi todo el año y mis actividades favoritas son bucear, pescar en el mar y nadar.**

Assignment Have students do the activities in **Ahora escucha** and **Comprensión** as homework as homework. Verify the responses to **Ahora escucha** with the whole class and go over **Identificar** and **¿Cierto o falso?** by reading each question aloud and calling on different students to answer.

Ahora escucha
Script **Buenos días, queridos televidentes, les saluda el meteorólogo Hernán Jiménez, con el pronóstico del tiempo para nuestra bella isla.**

Hoy, 17 de octubre, a las diez de la mañana, la temperatura en Santo Domingo es de 26 grados. Hace sol con viento del este a 10 kilómetros por hora.

Escuchar

NATIONAL communication STANDARDS

Preparación

Based on the illustration, who is Hernán Jiménez, and what is he doing? What key words might you listen for to help you understand what he is saying?

Estrategia
Listening for key words

By listening for key words or phrases, you can identify the subject and main ideas of what you hear, as well as some of the details. To practice this strategy, you will now listen to a short paragraph. As you listen, jot down the key words that help you identify the subject of the paragraph and its main ideas.

Ahora escucha

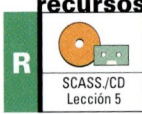

Now you are going to listen to a weather report by Hernán Jiménez. Note which phrases are correct according to the key words and phrases you hear.

Santo Domingo
1. hace sol ✔
2. va a hacer frío
3. una mañana de mal tiempo
4. va a estar nublado ✔
5. buena tarde para tomar el sol
6. buena mañana para la playa ✔

San Francisco de Macorís
1. hace frío ✔
2. hace sol
3. va a nevar
4. va a llover ✔
5. hay niebla ✔
6. buen día para excursiones

recursos
R SCASS./CD Lección 5

Comprensión

¿Cierto o falso?

Indicate whether each statement is **cierto** or **falso,** based on the weather report. Correct the false statements.

1. Según (*According to*) el meteorólogo, la temperatura en Santo Domingo es de 26 grados.
   Cierto.
2. La temperatura máxima en Santo Domingo hoy va a ser de 30 grados.
   Cierto.
3. Está lloviendo ahora en Santo Domingo.
   Falso. Hace sol.
4. En San Francisco de Macorís la temperatura mínima de hoy va a ser de 20 grados.
   Falso. La temperatura mínima va a ser de 18 grados.
5. Va a llover mucho hoy en San Francisco de Macorís.
   Cierto.

Preguntas

In Spanish, answer these questions about the weather report.

1. ¿Hace viento en Santo Domingo ahora?
   Sí, hace viento en Santo Domingo.
2. ¿Hay niebla en Santo Domingo ahora? No, no hay niebla ahora en Santo Domingo. Hay niebla en San Francisco de Macorís.
3. ¿Está nevando ahora en San Francisco de Macorís?
   No, no está nevando ahora en San Francisco de Macorís.
4. ¿Hace calor ahora en San Francisco de Macorís?
   No, hace frío.

En la tarde, va a estar un poco nublado con la posibilidad de lluvia. La temperatura máxima del día va a ser de 30 grados. Es una buena mañana para ir a la playa.

En las montañas hace bastante frío ahora y hay niebla, especialmente en el área de San Francisco de Macorís. La temperatura mínima de estas 24 horas va a ser de 18 grados. Va a llover casi todo el día. ¡No es buen día para excursiones a las montañas!

Hasta el noticiero del mediodía, me despido de ustedes. ¡Que les vaya bien!

NATIONAL STANDARDS communication cultures
NATIONAL STANDARDS connections communities

Proyecto

Crea un sitio Web

Imagine that a travel agency has hired you to develop a web page to promote a travel package to Puerto Rico. The web page is intended to market the tour and inform potential travelers about the specifics.

1 Diseña un sitio Web

Create a real or simulated website to tell potential customers about the merits of the tour. You will want to create a general home page for your site, as well as links to pages that describe the details. Use the research tools found in **Recursos para la investigación** to identify the sites the tour will visit, where the travelers will stay, and the activities they will be able to participate in. You might include the following elements:

- A home page with a general description of the tour and links to pages that supply the details
- A page describing the means of transportation
- A page describing hotels and other accomodations, including images if possible
- A page about the locations to be visited, including images if possible
- A page describing activities available to travelers, including images if possible

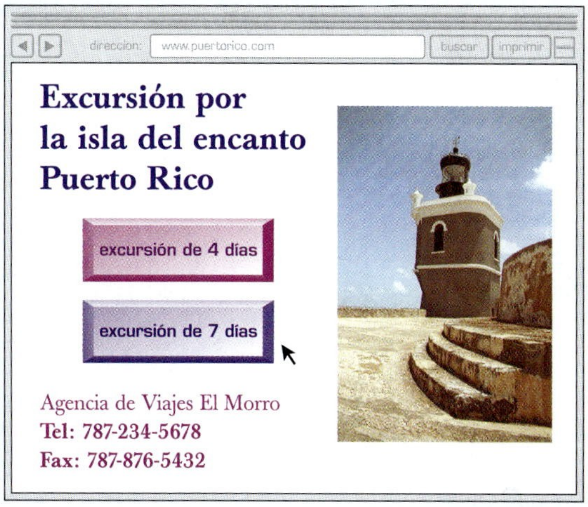

2 Presenta la información

Acting as the web page designer, present your work to the travel agency that hired you. Explain all the information that you have included and the images you have chosen. Answer any questions the agency executives may have about the website.

Crea *Create* Diseña *Design*

recursos para la investigación

Internet Palabras clave: Puerto Rico, vacations, hotels, transportation	**Comunidad** Students and faculty members who are from Puerto Rico or who have traveled to Puerto Rico
Biblioteca Guidebooks, travel magazines	**Otros recursos** Brochures from travel agencies

EVALUATION: Sitio Web

Criteria	Scale
Content	1 2 3 4
Organization	1 2 3 4
Accuracy	1 2 3 4
Creativity	1 2 3 4
Oral Presentation	1 2 3 4

Scoring	
Excellent	18–20 points
Good	14–17 points
Satisfactory	10–13 points
Unsatisfactory	< 10 points

Section Goals

In **Proyecto** students will:
- use Spanish to carry out research on travel destinations and to interact with the wider world
- design a website advertising a tour to Puerto Rico
- learn about attractions in Puerto Rico

Before Assigning Proyecto Students will need approximately a week to complete the project, so at the beginning of that time period, have them open their books to page 165 and look over **Proyecto**.

Diseña un sitio Web
Suggestions
- Students may create web page "frames" by drawing a navigation bar on the long side of a sheet of letter paper and photocopying it for each "web page" they create.
- Encourage students to come up with addresses for their websites.
- You may want to teach students some Spanish terms related to the internet, such as: **navegar la red** (surf the web), **página principal** (home page), **hacer clic** (click), **pasar a la próxima página** (go to the next page).
- Students may use photos cut from magazines or their own drawings as visuals, if they wish.

Presenta la información
Suggestions
- Presentations may be made to the whole class or to medium-sized groups. Encourage the audience to assume the roles of travel agency executives and ask questions of the website presenter.
- You may wish to set aside an entire class for presentations, or you may set aside a period of time during several classes for students to give their presentations.

Section Goals

In **Panorama**, students will read about the geography, history, and culture of Puerto Rico.

Instructional Resources
Student Activities Manual: Workbook, 59–60
Transparency 27

Puerto Rico
Before Presenting Panorama Have students look at the map of Puerto Rico or project **Transparency 27**. Model the pronunciation of the labeled features. Then look at the call-out photos and the inset map. Discuss Puerto Rico's location in respect to the U.S. mainland and the other Caribbean islands. Encourage students to describe what they see in the photos.

Assignment Have students read **Panorama** and write out the completed sentences in **¿Qué aprendiste?** on page 167 as homework.

Present Go through **El país en cifras**, asking volunteers to read the sections. After reading **Puertorriqueños célebres**, ask volunteers who are familiar with the three individuals to tell a little more about each. You might also mention novelist Rosario Ferrer, whose *House on the Lagoon* ***(La casa de la laguna)*** gives a fictional portrait of a large part of Puerto Rican history.

Increíble pero cierto The Río Camuy caves are actually a series of karstic sinkholes, formed by water sinking into and eroding limestone. Another significant cave in this system is Clara Cave, located in the Río Camuy Cave Park. The entrance of the 170-foot high cave resembles the facade of a cathedral.

Puerto Rico

El país en cifras

- **Área:** 8.959 km² (3.459 millas²) *menor que el área de Connecticut*
- **Población:** 3.930.000

Puerto Rico es una de las islas más densamente pobladas del mundo. Cerca de la mitad de la población vive en San Juan, la capital.

- **Capital:** San Juan—1.410.000

SOURCE: Population Division, UN Secretariat

- **Ciudades principales:** Arecibo—100.000, Bayamón—222.815, Fajardo—40.000, Mayagüez—100.371, Ponce—187.749
- **Moneda:** dólar estadounidense
- **Idiomas:** español (oficial); inglés (oficial)

Aproximadamente la cuarta parte de la población puertorriqueña habla inglés. Sin embargo, en las zonas turísticas este porcentaje es mucho más alto. Para documentos federales, el uso del inglés es obligatorio.

Plaza de Arecibo

Hoteles en El Condado, San Juan

Bandera de Puerto Rico

Pescadores en Mayagüez

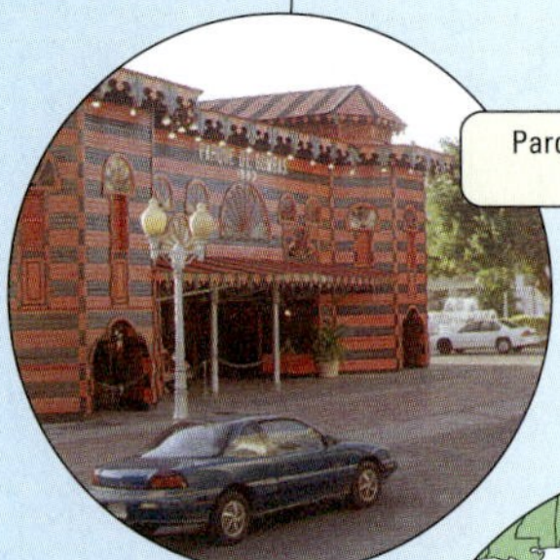
Parque de Bombas, Ponce

Puertorriqueños célebres

- **Luis Muñoz Rivera,** poeta, periodista y político (1859-1916)
- **Roberto Clemente,** beisbolista (1934-1972)
- **Luis Rafael Sánchez,** escritor (1936-)
- **Ricky Martin,** cantante y actor (1971-)

recursos
R | WB pp. 59-60 | vistasonline.com

subterráneos *underground* sistema de cuevas *cave system*

¡Increíble pero cierto!

El río *Camuy* es el tercer río subterráneo más largo del mundo y tiene el sistema de cuevas más grande en el hemisferio oeste. La *Cueva de los Tres Pueblos* es una gigantesca bóveda, tan grande que toda la fortaleza del Morro podría caber en su interior.

TEACHING OPTIONS

Heritage Speaker Encourage heritage speakers of Puerto Rican descent who have lived on the island or visited it to write a short description of their impressions. Ask them to describe people they knew or met, places they saw, and experiences they had. Ask them to think about what the most important thing they would tell a person from the mainland unfamiliar with the island would be and try to express it.

Worth Noting Baseball is a popular sport in Puerto Rico, home of the Winter League. Roberto Clemente, a player with the Pittsburgh Pirates who died tragically in a plane crash, was the first Latino to be inducted into the Baseball Hall of Fame.

Lugares • El Morro

El Morro es una fortaleza que custodiaba la bahía de San Juan entre los años 1500 y 1900. Hoy día El Morro es un museo que atrae a miles de turistas cada año. De hecho, es el sitio más fotografiado de Puerto Rico. La arquitectura de la fortaleza es impresionante. Tiene misteriosos túneles, oscuras mazmorras y vistas fabulosas de la bahía.

Artes • Salsa

La música salsa, viva y rítmica, está hecha para bailar. Este estilo musical nació en la ciudad de Nueva York de raíces puertorriqueñas y cubanas. Su nombre significa que la música es la "salsa" de las fiestas. Dos de sus músicos más famosos son Tito Puente y Willie Colón, los dos de Nueva York. Sus estrellas puertorriqueñas son Felipe Rodríguez y Héctor Lavoe. Hoy día, Puerto Rico es el centro mundial de la salsa; de hecho, el Gran Combo de Puerto Rico es una de las orquestas más famosas.

Ciencias • El Observatorio de Arecibo

El Observatorio de Arecibo tiene el radiotelescopio más grande del mundo. Gracias al telescopio los científicos pueden estudiar la atmósfera de la Tierra y la Luna, además de fenómenos celestiales como quásares y púlsares. Los científicos también escuchan emisiones de radio de otras galaxias, buscando indicios de inteligencia extraterrestre.

Historia • Relación con los Estados Unidos

Puerto Rico se hizo parte de los Estados Unidos después de la Guerra de 1898 y se hizo un estado libre asociado en 1952. Los puertorriqueños, ciudadanos estadounidenses desde 1917, tienen representación en el Congreso pero no votan en las elecciones presidenciales y no pagan impuestos federales. Hay un debate entre los puertorriqueños: ¿debe la isla seguir como estado libre asociado, hacerse un estado como los demás o hacerse independiente?

¿Qué aprendiste? Responde a las preguntas con una frase completa.

1. ¿Cuál es la moneda de Puerto Rico? La moneda de Puerto Rico es el dólar estadounidense.
2. ¿Qué idiomas se hablan (*are spoken*) en Puerto Rico? Se habla español e inglés en Puerto Rico.
3. ¿Cuál es el sitio más fotografiado de Puerto Rico? El Morro es el sitio más fotografiado de Puerto Rico.
4. ¿Cómo es la música salsa? La música salsa es viva y rítmica.
5. ¿Qué hacen los científicos en el Observatorio de Arecibo? Los científicos estudian la atmósfera de la Tierra y la Luna y escuchan emisiones de otras galaxias.

Conexión Internet Investiga estos temas en el sitio **www.vistasonline.com.**

1. Describe a dos puertorriqueños famosos. ¿Cómo son? ¿Qué hacen? ¿Dónde viven? ¿Por qué son célebres?
2. Busca información sobre lugares buenos para el ecoturismo en Puerto Rico. Luego presenta un informe a la clase.

custodiaba *guarded* bahía *bay* entre *between* Hoy día *Nowadays* atrae *attracts* cada *each* de hecho *in fact* mazmorras *dungeons* viva *lively* estilo *style* nació *was born* raíces *roots* salsa *sauce* estrellas *stars* mundial *worldwide* científicos *scientists* Tierra *Earth* Luna *Moon* además *as well as* indicios *evidence* se hizo *became* después de *after* ciudadanos *citizens* desde *since* impuestos *taxes* seguir *continue* demás *the rest*

El Morro Remind students that at the time **El Morro** was built, piracy was a major concern for Spain and its Caribbean colonies. If possible, show other photos of El Morro, San Juan Bay, and El Viejo San Juan.

Salsa With students, listen to **salsa, merengue** from the Dominican Republic, and **rumba** or **mambo** from Cuba. Encourage students to identify common elements in the music (strong percussion patterns rooted in African traditions, alternating structure of soloist and ensemble, incorporation of Western instruments and musical vocabulary, and so forth). Then, have them point out contrasts.

Ciencias The Arecibo Ionospheric Observatory has the world's most sensitive radio telescope. It can detect objects up to 13 billion light years away. The telescope dish is 1,000 feet in diameter and covers 20 acres. The dish is made of about 40,000 aluminum mesh panels.

Historia Point out that only Puerto Ricans living on the island vote in plebiscites to determine the island's political relationship to the United States.

¿Qué aprendiste? Go over the questions and answers with students, making sure everyone understands unfamiliar words and what the correct answers are.

Assignment Have students do activites in **Student Activities Manual: Workbook,** pages 59–60.

Conexión Internet Students will find information about famous Puerto Ricans and ecotourism destinations in Puerto Rico at **www.vistasonline.com**, as well as links to other sites that can help them in their research.

TEACHING OPTIONS

Variación léxica When the first Spanish colonists arrived on the island they were to name Puerto Rico, they found it inhabited by the Taíno, who called the island **Borínquen**. Puerto Ricans still use that name to refer to the island, and they frequently call themselves **borinqueños** or **boricuas**. The Puerto Rican national anthem is **"La borinqueña."** Some other Taíno words that have entered Spanish (and English) are **huracán**, **hamaca**, **canoa**, and **iguana**.

Juracán was the name of the Taíno god of the winds whose anger stirred up the great storms that periodically devastated the island. The hammock, of course, was the device the Taíno slept in, and canoes were the boats made of great hollowed-out logs with which they paddled between islands. The Taíno language also survives in many Puerto Rican place names: Arecibo, Bayamón, Guayama, Sierra de Cayey, Yauco, Coamo, and so forth.

Los viajes y las vacaciones

acampar	*to camp*
confirmar una reservación	*to confirm a reservation*
estar de vacaciones (*f. pl.*)	*to be on vacation*
hacer las maletas	*to pack (one's suitcases)*
hacer turismo (*m.*)	*to go sightseeing*
hacer un viaje	*to take a trip*
hacer una excursión	*to go on a hike; to go on a tour*
ir de compras (*f. pl.*)	*to go shopping*
ir de pesca (*f.*)	*to go fishing*
ir de vacaciones	*to go on vacation*
ir en autobús (*m.*), **auto(móvil)** (*m.*), **avión** (*m.*), **barco** (*m.*), **motocicleta** (*f.*), **taxi** (*m.*,	*to go by bus, car, plane, boat, motorcycle, taxi*
jugar a las cartas	*to play cards*
montar a caballo (*m.*)	*to ride a horse*
pasar por la aduana	*to go through customs*
pescar	*to fish*
recorrer	*to tour an area*
sacar/tomar fotos (*m. pl.*)	*to take pictures*
el/la agente de viajes	*travel agent*
el/la huésped	*guest*
el/la inspector(a) de aduanas	*customs inspector*
el/la viajero/a	*traveler*
el aeropuerto	*airport*
la agencia de viajes	*travel agency*
la cabaña	*cabin*
el campo	*countryside*
el equipaje	*luggage*
la estación de autobuses, del metro, de tren	*bus, subway, train station*
la llegada	*arrival*
el mar	*sea; ocean*
el océano	*ocean; sea*
el paisaje	*landscape; countryside*
el pasaje (de ida y vuelta)	*(round-trip) ticket*
el pasaporte	*passport*
la pensión	*boarding house*
la playa	*beach*
la salida	*departure; exit*
la tienda de campaña	*tent*
turístico/a	*touristic*

El hotel

el ascensor	*elevator*
el/la botones	*bellhop*
la cama	*bed*
el/la empleado/a	*employee*
la habitación individual, doble	*single, double room*
el hotel	*hotel*
la llave	*key*
el piso	*floor (of a building)*
la planta baja	*ground floor*

Adjetivos

abierto/a	*open*
aburrido/a	*bored; boring*
agradable	*pleasant*
alegre	*happy; joyful*
amable	*nice; friendly*
avergonzado/a	*embarrassed*
cansado/a	*tired*
cerrado/a	*closed*
cómodo/a	*comfortable*
contento/a	*happy; content*
desordenado/a	*disorderly*
enamorado/a de	*in love (with)*
enojado/a	*mad, angry*
equivocado/a	*wrong*
feliz	*happy*
limpio/a	*clean*
listo/a	*ready; smart*
nervioso/a	*nervous*
ocupado/a	*busy*
ordenado/a	*orderly*
preocupado/a (por)	*worried (about)*
seguro/a	*sure*
sucio/a	*dirty*
triste	*sad*

Los números ordinales

primer, primero/a	*first*
segundo/a	*second*
tercer, tercero/a	*third*
cuarto/a	*fourth*
quinto/a	*fifth*
sexto/a	*sixth*
séptimo/a	*seventh*
octavo/a	*eighth*
noveno/a	*ninth*
décimo/a	*tenth*

Palabras adicionales

ahora mismo	*right now*
el año	*year*
¿Cuál es la fecha (de hoy)?	*What is the date (today)?*
la estación	*season*
el mes	*month*
todavía	*yet; still*

Las estaciones y los meses del año	*See page 138.*
Los pronombres del complemento directo	*Direct object pronouns See page 154.*
Del número 101 en adelante	*Numbers 101 and higher See page 158.*
Expresiones útiles	*See page 141.*

¡De compras!

6

Communicative Goals

You will learn how to:

- **Talk about and describe clothing**
- **Express preferences in a store**
- **Negotiate and pay for items you buy**

contextos

pages 170-173
- Clothing and shopping
- Colors
- Negotiating a price and buying

fotonovela

pages 174-177
Inés and Javier explore the market in Otavalo, looking for something to buy. Inés purchases a gift for her sister. Javier must bargain for a better price in order to get what he wants.

estructura

pages 178-190
- The preterite tense of regular verbs
- Indirect object pronouns
- Demonstrative adjectives and pronouns

adelante

pages 190-195
Lectura: Read an advertisement for a sale in a store.
Escritura: Write an interview with a student.
Escuchar: Listen to a conversation between two shoppers.
Proyecto: Create a business plan for a store.

panorama

pages 196-197
Featured Country: Cuba
- The Cuban National Ballet
- Sugar cane and tobacco
- The Taíno culture
- Celia Cruz: Queen of Salsa

Lesson Goals

In **Lesson 6** students will be introduced to the following:
- terms for clothing and shopping
- colors
- preterite tense of regular verbs
- indirect object pronouns
- demonstrative adjectives and pronouns
- skimming a text
- how to report an interview
- writing a report
- listening for linguistic clues
- writing and presenting a business plan
- cultural, geographic, economic, and historical information about Cuba

Lesson Preview
Have students look at the photo. Say: **Es una foto de un mercado. La mujer es vendedora. El chico piensa comprar la camisa.** Then ask: **¿Cómo está la mujer? ¿Va a comprar la camisa el chico?**

INSTRUCTIONAL RESOURCES

Student Activities Manual: Workbook, 61–70
Student Activities Manual: Lab Manual, 249–253
Student Activities Manual: Video Activities, 337–338
Instructor's Resource Manual: Hojas de actividades, 11
Instructor's Resource Manual: Answer Keys
Tapescript/Videoscript
Overhead Transparencies, 28–30
Student Cassette/CD
Lab Cassette/CD
Video Program
CD-ROM
Website: **www.vistasonline.com**
Testing Program: Prueba A, Prueba B

Section Goals

In **Contextos**, students will learn and practice:
- clothing vocabulary
- vocabulary to use while shopping
- colors

Instructional Resources
Student Activities Manual: Workbook, 61–62; Lab Manual, 249
Transparencies 28–29
Student Cassette/CD

Before Presenting Contextos Introduce active lesson vocabulary. Ask volunteers about shopping preferences and habits. Say: **¿A quién le gusta ir de compras?** To a student who answers, ask: **¿Qué te gusta comprar? ¿Discos compactos? ¿Programas para la computadora? ¿Ropa?** (point to your own clothing) **¿Adónde vas para comprar esas cosas? ¿Cuánto dinero gastas** (pantomime reaching in your pocket and paying for something) **normalmente?** and so forth. After the student has answered, ask another student: **¿Adónde va de compras, ____? Sí, va ____. ¿Y qué compra allí? Sí, compra ____. Y tú, ¿qué te gusta comprar?** and so forth. Tell students that they are going to learn vocabulary related to shopping. **Assignment** Have students study **Contextos** and do the exercises in **Práctica** as homework.

Present Give students two minutes to review the store scene on pages 170–171 or project **Transparency 28**. Have students guess meaning of **damas** and **caballeros**. Have students refer to the scene to answer your true-false questions about it. Ex: **El hombre paga con tarjeta de crédito. (Cierto.) No venden zapatos en la tienda. (Falso.) Se puede regatear en el almacén. (Falso.)** and so forth. Use as many clothing items and verbs from **Más vocabulario** as you can in your sentences.

¡De compras!

Más vocabulario

el abrigo	*coat*
el almacén	*department store*
los calcetines	*socks*
el centro comercial	*shopping mall*
el cinturón	*belt*
las gafas (de sol), las gafas (oscuras)	*(sun)glasses*
los guantes	*gloves*
el impermeable	*raincoat*
los lentes de contacto	*contact lenses*
los lentes de sol	*sunglasses*
el mercado (al aire libre)	*(open-air) market*
el precio (fijo)	*(fixed; set) price*
la rebaja	*sale*
la ropa	*clothing; clothes*
la ropa interior	*underwear*
las sandalias	*sandals*
la tienda	*shop; store*
el vestido	*dress*
los zapatos de tenis	*tennis shoes; sneakers*
costar (o:ue)	*to cost*
gastar	*to spend (money)*
hacer juego (con)	*to match*
llevar	*to wear; to take*
regatear	*to bargain*
usar	*to wear; to use*
vender	*to sell*

Variación léxica

calcetines ⟷	medias (*Amér. L.*)
cinturón ⟷	correa (*Col., Venez.*)
gafas/lentes de sol ⟷	gafas/lentes oscuras/os, gafas/lentes negras/os
zapatos de tenis ⟷	zapatillas de deporte (*Esp.*), zapatillas (*Arg., Perú*)

recursos

R	SCASS./CD Lección 6	WB pp. 61-62	LM p. 249	LCASS./CD Cass. 3B/CD3

TEACHING OPTIONS

Small Groups In groups of three to four, students close their books and make a list of as many of the articles of clothing that appear in the store scene as they can. Then have all groups call out their lists as you write down the items on the board. Did the groups remember all of the items pictured in the drawing?

Variación léxica Point out that terms for clothing vary widely throughout the Spanish-speaking world. For the most part, Spanish speakers of different regions can mutually understand each other when talking about clothing. Other variations include **los bluejeans = los vaqueros, los jeans; zapatos de tenis = los tenis; los pantalones = el pantalón; el suéter = el pulóver, el jersey; la chaqueta = la chamarra**

Práctica

1 Escuchar Listen to Juanita and Vicente talk about what they're packing for their vacations. Indicate who is packing each item. If both are packing an item, write both names. If neither is packing an item, write an X.

1. abrigo Vicente
2. zapatos de tenis Juanita, Vicente
3. impermeable X
4. chaqueta Vicente
5. sandalias Juanita
6. bluejeans Juanita, Vicente
7. gafas de sol Vicente
8. camisetas Juanita, Vicente
9. traje de baño Juanita
10. botas Vicente
11. pantalones cortos Juanita
12. suéter Vicente

2 Completar Anita is talking about going shopping. Complete each sentence with the correct word(s), adding definite or indefinite articles when necessary.

caja	dependientas	tarjeta de crédito
vendedores	medias	centro comercial
traje de baño	par	ropa

1. Hoy voy a ir de compras al nuevo centro comercial.
2. Voy a ir a la tienda de ropa para mujeres. Siempre hay muchas rebajas y las dependientas son muy simpáticas.
3. Necesito comprarme un par de zapatos.
4. Y tengo que comprarme un traje de baño nuevo porque el sábado voy a la playa con mis amigos.
5. También voy a comprar unas medias para mi mamá.
6. Voy a pagar todo (*everything*) en la caja.
7. Pero hoy no llevo dinero. Voy a tener que usar mi tarjeta de crédito.
8. Mañana voy al mercado al aire libre. Me gusta regatear con los vendedores.

3 Escoger Choose the item in each group that does not belong.

1. gafas • ropa interior • gafas de sol • lentes de contacto ropa interior
2. camisa • camiseta • blusa • botas botas
3. bluejeans • bolsa • falda • pantalones bolsa
4. abrigo • suéter • corbata • chaqueta corbata
5. mercado • tienda • almacén • cartera cartera
6. usar • costar • gastar • regatear usar
7. botas • sandalias • zapatos • traje traje
8. vender • regatear • ropa interior • gastar ropa interior

1 Present Have students check their answers by going over the tapescript questions with the whole class.

1 Tapescript *Juanita:* **Hola. Me llamo Juanita. Mi familia y yo salimos de vacaciones mañana y estoy haciendo mis maletas. Para nuestra excursión al campo ya tengo bluejeans, camisetas y zapatos de tenis. También vamos a la playa… ¡no puedo esperar! Para ir a la playa necesito un traje de baño, pantalones cortos y sandalias. ¿Qué más necesito? Creo que es todo.** *Vicente:* **Buenos días. Soy Vicente. Estoy haciendo mis maletas porque mi familia y yo vamos a las montañas a esquiar. Los primeros dos días vamos a hacer una excursión por las montañas. Necesito zapatos de tenis, camisetas, una chaqueta y bluejeans. El tercer día vamos a esquiar. Necesito un abrigo, un suéter y botas… y gafas del sol.** *Student Cassette/CD*

1 Expand Have students share their answers by asking: **¿Qué necesita llevar Juanita? ¿Y Vicente?** Then have students indicate where these two are going: **¿Por qué necesita llevar sandalias Juanita?** and so forth.

2 Expand Go over answers in class by having students read each sentence.

3 Expand Go over answers quickly in class. After each answer, indicate why a particular item doesn't belong. Ex: **1. La ropa interior. La ropa interior no se lleva en la cara** (point). **No se usa para ver bien.** and so forth.

TEACHING OPTIONS

Extra Practice Suggest a vacation spot and then ask students at random what clothing they need to take. Make it a continuing narration whereby the next student must say all of the items of clothing that came before and add one. Ex: (you say:) **Vas a la playa. ¿Qué vas a llevar?** (S1:) **Voy a llevar un traje de baño.** (S2:) **Voy a llevar un traje de baño y lentes de sol,** and so forth.

TPR Play a game of Simon Says (**Simón dice…**). Write on the board **levántense** and **siéntense** and explain that they mean stand up and sit down, respectively. Then start by saying: **Simón dice… los que llevan bluejeans, levántense.** Students wearing blue jeans stand up and remain standing until further instruction. Work through various articles of clothing. Be sure to give instructions without saying **Simón dice…** once in awhile.

Los colores
Present Project **Transparency 29** and review the color words. Point to a drawing and say: **¿De qué color es esta camiseta? Sí, es negra.** After you go through several colors ask: **Si mezclo el rojo y el azul, qué color resulta? (el morado) Y si yo mezclo el amarillo y el rojo, ¿qué color resulta? (el anaranjado)** Then point to objects in the classroom, clothes you and students are wearing, and so forth, eliciting color words. Point out that color words are adjectives and agree with the nouns they modify.

4 Warm-up Before beginning the activity, ask several brief comprehension questions. Ex: **¿Quién lleva una camiseta roja? Sí, ____ lleva una camiseta roja. ¿Son baratos o caros los discos compactos?** and so forth.

4 Present Call on individual students by reading the first part of each item and having them give the correct response. Remind students that any opposite adjectives they give must agree in gender and number with the nouns they modify.

4 Expand Show magazine pictures of various products (cars, computers, and so forth) and ask students: **¿Es cara esta computadora o es barata? Sí, para las computadoras, es barata.** and so forth.

5 Expand Go over answers in class by having students give complete sentences. Ex: **La rosa de Texas es amarilla.**

5 Expand Point to various students in the class and ask others what color of clothing each is wearing. Ex: ____, **¿de qué color es la falda de ____? Sí, es ____.**

Los colores

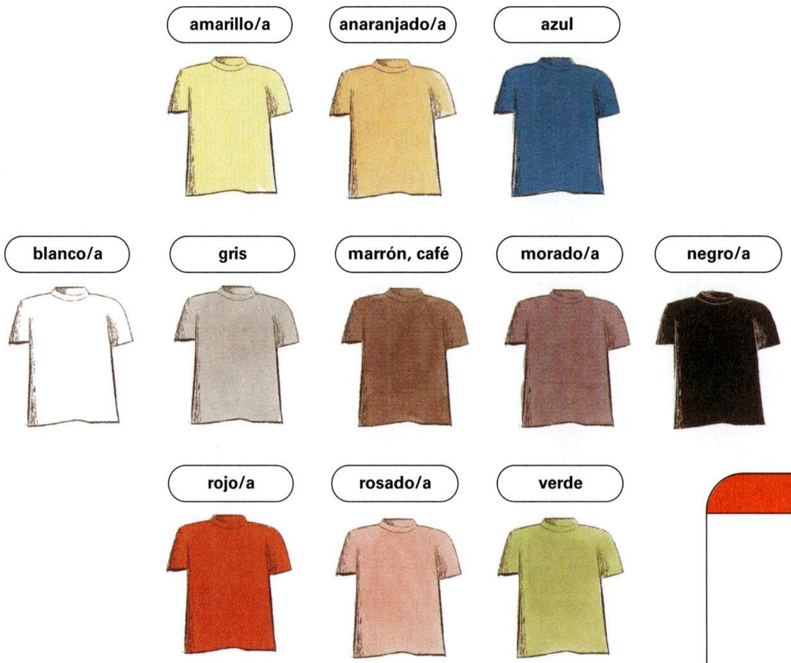

¡LENGUA VIVA!
The names of colors vary throughout the Spanish-speaking world. For example, **anaranjado/a** may be referred to as **naranja**, **morado/a** as **púrpura**, and **rojo/a** as **colorado**.

Other terms that will prove helpful include **claro** (*light*) and **oscuro** (*dark*): **azul claro, azul oscuro**

Adjetivos

barato/a	*cheap*
bueno/a	*good*
cada	*each*
caro/a	*expensive*
corto/a	*short (in length)*
elegante	*elegant*
hermoso/a	*beautiful*
largo/a	*long (in length)*
loco/a	*crazy*
nuevo/a	*new*
otro/a	*other; another*
pobre	*poor*
rico/a	*rich*

4 **Contrastes** Complete each phrase with the opposite of the underlined word.

1. una corbata barata • unas camisas... caras
2. unas sandalias malas • unos zapatos de tenis... buenos
3. un vestido corto • una falda... larga
4. un hombre muy pobre • una mujer muy... rica
5. una cartera nueva • un cinturón... viejo
6. unos trajes hermosos • unos bluejeans... feos
7. un chico que compra ropa • una chica que... ropa vende
8. unos lentes de contacto limpios • unas gafas... sucias
9. un impermeable grande • unos suéteres... pequeños
10. unos calcetines blancos • unas medias... negras

5 **Preguntas** Answer these questions with a classmate.

1. ¿De qué color es la rosa de Texas? Es amarilla.
2. ¿De qué colores es la bandera (*flag*) de los EE.UU.? Es roja, blanca y azul.
3. ¿De qué color es la casa donde vive el presidente de los EE.UU.? Es blanca.
4. ¿De qué color es el océano Atlántico? Es azul.
5. ¿De qué color es la nieve? Es blanca.
6. ¿De qué color es el café? Es marrón./Es café.
7. ¿De qué colores es el dólar de los EE.UU.? Es verde y blanco.
8. ¿De qué colores es una cebra (*zebra*)? Es negra y blanca.

TEACHING OPTIONS

Pairs In pairs, students spend a few minutes creating a physical description of a well-known TV or cartoon character. Then they read their descriptions while the rest of the class guesses who the character is. Ex: **Soy bajo y un poco gordo. Llevo pantalones cortos azules y una camiseta anaranjada. Tengo el pelo amarillo. También soy amarillo. ¿Quién soy? (Bart Simpson)**

Game Play **Concentración**. On eight cards, write descriptions of clothing, including colors (Ex: **unos pantalones negros**). On another eight cards, draw pictures that match the descriptions. Place the cards face-down in four rows of four. In pairs, students select two cards. If the two cards match, the pair keeps them. If the two cards don't match, students replace them in their original position. The pair with the most cards at the end wins.

Comunicación

CONSÚLTALO

Weather expressions
To review weather, see Lesson 4, section 4.4, p. 122.

6 **Las maletas** With a classmate, answer these questions about the drawings.

1. ¿Qué hay al lado de la maleta de Carmela?
   Hay una camiseta, unos pantalones cortos y un traje de baño al lado de la maleta.
2. ¿Qué hay en la maleta?
   Hay un sombrero y un par de sandalias en la maleta.
3. ¿De qué color son las sandalias?
   Las sandalias son rojas.
4. ¿Adónde va Carmela?
   Va a la playa.
5. ¿Qué tiempo va a hacer?
   Va a hacer sol./ Va a hacer calor.

6. ¿Qué hay al lado de la maleta de Pepe?
   Hay un par de calcetines, un par de guantes, un suéter y una chaqueta al lado de la maleta.
7. ¿Qué hay en la maleta?
   Hay dos pares de pantalones en la maleta.
8. ¿De qué color es el suéter?
   El suéter es rosado.
9. ¿Qué va a hacer Pepe?
   Va a esquiar.
10. ¿Qué tiempo va a hacer?
    Va a hacer frío./ Va a nevar.

7 **¿Adónde van?** Imagine that you are going on a vacation with two classmates. Get together with your classmates and decide where you're going. Then draw three suitcases and write in each one what clothing each person is taking. Present your drawings to the rest of the class, answering these questions. Answers will vary.

- ¿Adónde van?
- ¿Qué tiempo va a hacer allí (*there*)?
- ¿Qué van a hacer allí?
- ¿Qué hay en sus maletas?
- ¿De qué color es la ropa en sus maletas?

8 **Preferencias** Use these questions to interview a classmate. Then switch roles. Answers will vary.

1. ¿Adónde vas para (*in order to*) comprar ropa? ¿Por qué?
2. ¿Qué tipo de ropa prefieres? ¿Por qué?
3. ¿Cuáles son tus colores favoritos?
4. En tu opinión, ¿es importante comprar ropa nueva frecuentemente? ¿Por qué?
5. ¿Cuánto dinero gastas en ropa cada mes? ¿Buscas rebajas?
6. ¿Regateas cuando compras ropa? ¿Usas una tarjeta de crédito?

6 Warm-up Have pairs of students spend a minute looking at the two drawings and anticipate the kinds of questions that will be asked about each.

6 Present Point out that questions 1–5 pertain to the first drawing and that 6-10 pertain to the second drawing.

6 Expand Go over answers quickly in class by asking the questions of pairs of students and having them answer in complete sentences.

6 Expand Ask volunteers what kind of clothing they take with them when they visit the following places at the following times: **Seattle en la primavera, la Florida en el verano, Minnesota en el invierno, San Francisco en el otoño.**

7 Present You may want to assign groups and have them discuss where they are going the day before you plan to do this activity in class. Then as homework students draw what's in their suitcases.

7 Expand Have students guess where the groups are going, based on the content of the suitcases. Facilitate guessing by asking the questions listed on the page.

8 Present Have students quickly read through the questions before interviewing their partner.

8 Expand Students report the findings of their interviews to the class. Ex: ____ **va a The Gap para comprar ropa porque la ropa no es cara. Prefiere la ropa informal...**

Assignment Have students do the activities in **Student Activities Manual: Workbook,** pages 61–62.

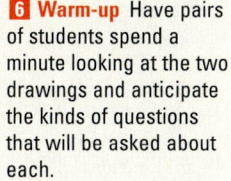

TEACHING OPTIONS

Extra Practice Students write a paragraph about the next vacation they plan to take and what clothing they plan to take with them. If students don't have a vacation planned, ask them to invent one. They should also include what kind of weather they expect at their destination and any weather-specific clothing they will need. Ask volunteers to share their paragraphs with the class.

Extra Practice Students write descriptions of the one article of clothing or complete outfit that best describes them without indicating who they are. Collect the papers and read the descriptions aloud. The rest of the class has to guess who each student is based on his or her defining article or outfit.

Section goals

In **Fotonovela** students will:

- receive comprehensible input from free-flowing discourse
- learn functional phrases involving clothing and how much things cost

Instructional Resources
Student Activities Manual: Video Activities 337–338
Video Program (Start: 00:28:03)

Video Synopsis Inés and Javier go to an open-air market. Inés browses the market and eventually buys a purse for her sister, as well as a shirt and a hat for herself. Javier buys a sweater for the hike in the mountains.

Before Presenting Fotonovela Tell the class that this **Fotonovela** episode is about shopping in an open-air market. Have them scan the **Fotonovela** captions for vocabulary related to clothing or colors.

Assignment Have students study **Fotonovela** and **Expresiones útiles** as homework.

Warm-up Bring color photographs from magazines and ask the class questions about what the people in the photographs are wearing. Ex: **¿Qué lleva la señorita? ¿De qué color es?**

Present Have students take turns reading the **Expresiones útiles** aloud. To check comprehension of this active vocabulary, point out the clothing that a few individual students are wearing and ask them some questions about it. Ex: **Me gusta esa camisa azul. ¿Es de algodón? ¿Dónde la compraste? ¿Qué talla llevas?**

Continued on page 175.

¡Qué ropa más bonita!

NATIONAL communication cultures STANDARDS

Javier e Inés van de compras al mercado.

PERSONAJES

INÉS

JAVIER

EL VENDEDOR

1

INÉS Javier, ¡qué ropa más bonita! A mí me gusta esa camisa blanca y azul. Debe ser de algodón. ¿Te gusta?

JAVIER Yo prefiero la camisa de la izquierda... la gris con rayas rojas. Hace juego con mis botas marrones.

2

INÉS Está bien, Javier. Mira, necesito comprarle un regalo a mi hermana Graciela. Acaba de empezar un nuevo trabajo...

JAVIER ¿Tal vez una bolsa?

3

VENDEDOR Esas bolsas son típicas de las montañas. ¿Le gusta?

INÉS Sí. Quiero comprarle una a mi hermana.

6

VENDEDOR Buenas tardes, joven. ¿Le puedo servir en algo?

JAVIER Sí. Voy a ir de excursión a las montañas y necesito un buen suéter.

VENDEDOR ¿Qué talla usa Ud.?

JAVIER Uso talla grande.

7

VENDEDOR Éstos son de talla grande.

JAVIER ¿Qué precio tiene ése?

VENDEDOR ¿Le gusta este suéter? Le cuesta ciento cincuenta mil sucres.

JAVIER Quiero comprarlo. Pero, señor, no soy rico. ¿Ciento veinte mil sucres?

8

VENDEDOR Bueno, para usted... sólo ciento treinta mil sucres.

JAVIER Está bien, señor.

recursos

R	VIDEO Lección 6	VM pp. 337-338

TEACHING OPTIONS

Video Tips General suggestions for using video clips in the classroom can be found on page IAE-13 of the **Instructor's Annotated Edition.**

¡Qué ropa más bonita! Photocopy the videoscript and opaque out 7–10 words with white correction fluid in order to create a master for a cloze activity. Hand out photocopies of the master to your students and have them fill in the missing words as they watch the **¡Que ropa más bonita!** segment of this video module. You may want to show the segment twice or more if your students experience difficulties with this activity. You may also want your students to share their pages in small groups and help each other fill in any gaps.

INÉS Me gusta aquélla. ¿Cuánto cuesta?

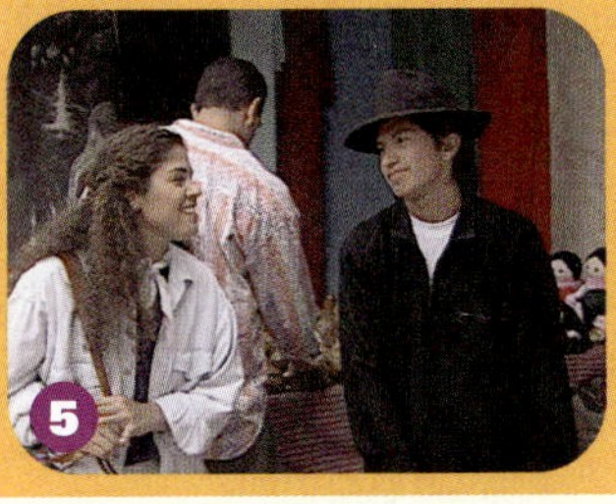

VENDEDOR Ésa cuesta ciento sesenta mil sucres. ¡Es de muy buena calidad!

INÉS Uy, demasiado cara. Quizás otro día.

JAVIER Acabo de comprarme un suéter. Y tú, ¿qué compraste?

INÉS Compré esta bolsa para mi hermana.

INÉS También compré una camisa y un sombrero. ¿Qué tal me veo?

JAVIER ¡Guapa, muy guapa!

Enfoque cultural Mercados al aire libre

Open-air markets, or **mercados al aire libre,** are an important part of the commerce and culture of many Hispanic countries. Fresh fruits and vegetables, tapestries, clothing, pottery and crafts are commonly seen among the vendors' wares. One of the most famous is the market in Otavalo, Ecuador, which has taken place every Saturday since pre-Incan times. Another popular market is **El Rastro** in Madrid, held every Sunday, where tourists can buy antiques and many other goods.

Expresiones útiles

Talking about clothing

▷ **¡Qué ropa más bonita!**
What pretty clothes!

▷ **Me gusta esta/esa camisa blanca de rayas negras.**
I like this/that white shirt with black stripes.

▷ **Está de moda.**
It's in fashion.

▷ **Debe ser de algodón/lana/seda.**
It must be cotton/wool/silk.

▷ **Es de cuadros/lunares/rayas.**
It's plaid/polka-dotted/striped.

▷ **Me gusta este/ese suéter.**
I like this/that sweater.

▷ **Es de muy buena calidad.**
It's very good quality.

▶ **¿Qué talla lleva/usa Ud.?**
What size do you wear?

▷ **Llevo/Uso talla grande.**
I wear a large.

▶ **¿Qué número calza Ud.?**
What (shoe) size do you wear?

▷ **Calzo el treinta y seis.**
I wear a size six.

Talking about how much things cost

▶ **¿Cuánto cuesta?**
How much does it cost?

▷ **Sólo cuesta noventa mil sucres.**
It only costs ninety thousand sucres.

▷ **Demasiado caro/a.**
Too expensive.

▷ **Es una ganga.**
It's a bargain.

Saying what you bought

▶ **¿Qué compró Ud./él/ella?**
What did you (form.)/he/she buy?

▷ **Compré esta bolsa para mi hermana.**
I bought this purse for my sister.

▶ **¿Qué compraste?**
What did you buy?

▷ **Acabo de comprarme un sombrero.**
I have just bought myself a hat.

Have students work in pairs to read the parts of Inés and Javier as they arrive at the market (frames 1–2), Inés bargaining with the vendor (frames 3–5), and Javier bargaining with the vendor (frames 6–8). Circulate around the classroom; model correct forms and punctuation as needed. Ask for volunteers to read their segment for the class. See ideas for using the video in **Teaching Options**, page 174.

Comprehension Check Check comprehension of the **Fotonovela** episode by doing Activity 1, **¿Cierto o falso?**, page 176, orally with the whole class.

Suggestion Have students look at the **Expresiones útiles**. Point out the verb forms **compré, compraste,** and **compró**. Tell the class that these are forms of the verb **comprar** in the preterite tense, and that the preterite is used to tell what happened in the past. Tell the class that **este, esta, ese,** and **esa** are examples of demonstrative adjectives, which are used to single out particular nouns. Also point out that the **me** in **Acabo de comprarme un sombrero** is an indirect object pronoun, used to tell for whom the hat was bought. Tell your students that they will learn more about these concepts in the upcoming **Estructura** section.

Assignment Have students do activities 2–4 in **Reacciona a la fotonovela**, page 176, as homework.

TEACHING OPTIONS

Enfoque cultural Tell the class that in many open-air markets in the Spanish-speaking world, customers are expected to engage in good-natured bargaining (**regateo**) with the sellers. Bargaining is not just a way of arriving at a price that is agreeable to both buyer and seller, it is a means of social interchange. Both participants enjoy the exchange. Point out that many stores and some open-air markets, however, charge a **precio fijo** (*fixed price*) for each item and do not allow bargaining. Also, point out to the class that consumers in Spanish-speaking countries, like their counterparts in the United States, may purchase goods in many different ways. Some prefer to visit open-air markets, small specialty shops, supermarkets, department stores, shopping centers, or malls, while others prefer the convenience of Internet shopping.

Reacciona a la fotonovela

1 Present Change the six statements in this activity to yes-no questions. Then have the class work in pairs to answer the questions.

2 Warm-up Have your students read the six statements and quickly read through the **Fotonovela** before doing this activity.

2 Expand Give these additional items to the class: **7. Pero, señor… no traigo mucho dinero. (Javier), 8. Señor, para usted… ochenta mil sucres. (vendedor), 9. Me gusta mucho esta camisa blanca de algodón. (Inés)**

3 Present This activity can be done orally or in writing. It is suitable for whole-class, group, or pair work.

4 Possible response
S1: Buenas tardes, señor. ¿Le puedo servir en algo?
S2: Buenas tardes. Necesito una camisa.
S1: ¿Qué talla usa Ud.?
S2: Uso talla mediana.
S1: Muy bien. Pues, tengo esta camisa azul y esta camisa blanca. Son de algodón y son de muy buena calidad. ¿Cuál prefiere Ud.?
S2: Prefiero la camisa blanca. ¿Cuánto cuesta?
S1: Veinte dólares.
S2: Demasiado cara. ¿Quince dólares?
S1: Bueno, para Ud., dieciocho dólares.
S2: Muy bien. ¡Gracias!

Successful Language Learning Tell your students to devote extra effort and attention to Activity 4. This activity sums up the vocabulary and functional phrases that the students have learned earlier in the lesson. In addition, this activity explores a real-life situation that travelers might encounter when visiting a Spanish-speaking country.

Reacciona a la fotonovela

1 **¿Cierto o falso?** Indicate whether each sentence is **cierto** or **falso**. Correct the false statements.

	Cierto	Falso
1. A Inés le gusta la camisa verde y amarilla. *A Inés le gusta la camisa blanca y azul.*	○	✓
2. Javier necesita comprarle un regalo a su hermana. *Inés necesita comprarle un regalo a su hermana.*	○	✓
3. Las bolsas en el mercado son típicas de las montañas.	✓	○
4. Javier busca un traje de baño. *Javier busca un suéter.*	○	✓
5. Inés compró un sombrero, un suéter y una bolsa. *Inés compró una bolsa, una camisa y un sombrero.*	○	✓
6. Javier regatea con el vendedor.	✓	○

2 **Identificar** Provide the name of the person who would make each statement. The names may be used more than once.

1. ¿Te gusta el sombrero que compré? Inés
2. Estos suéteres son de talla grande. ¿Qué talla usa Ud.? el vendedor
3. ¿Por qué no compras una bolsa para Graciela? Javier
4. Creo que mis botas hacen juego con la camisa. Javier
5. Estas bolsas son excelentes, de muy buena calidad. el vendedor
6. Creo que las blusas aquí son de algodón. Inés

INÉS

JAVIER

EL VENDEDOR

3 **Contestar** Answer the questions using the information in the **Fotonovela**.

1. Inés quiere comprarle un regalo a su hermana. ¿Por qué? *Inés quiere comprarle un regalo a su hermana porque ella acaba de empezar un nuevo trabajo.*
2. ¿Cuánto cuesta la bolsa típica de las montañas? *La bolsa típica de las montañas cuesta ciento cincuenta mil sucres.*
3. ¿Por qué necesita Javier un buen suéter? *Javier necesita un buen suéter porque va de excursión a las montañas.*
4. ¿Cuál es el precio final del suéter? *El precio final del suéter es ciento treinta mil sucres.*
5. ¿Qué compra Inés en el mercado? *Inés compra una bolsa, una camisa y un sombrero.*
6. ¿Qué talla usa Javier? *Javier usa talla grande.*

4 **Conversar** With a classmate, role-play a conversation in which the salesperson greets a customer in an open-air market and offers assistance. The customer is looking for a particular item of clothing. The salesperson and the customer discuss colors and sizes and negotiate a price. *Answers will vary.*

NATIONAL communication STANDARDS

CONSEJOS

When discussing prices, it's important to keep in mind singular and plural forms of verbs. Look carefully for the subject of the sentence:

La camisa **cuesta** diez dólares.

Las botas **cuestan** sesenta dólares.

El precio de las botas **es** sesenta dólares.

Los precios de la ropa **son** altos.

AYUDA

¿Qué desea?
What would you like?
Estoy buscando...
I'm looking for...
Prefiero el/la rojo/a.
I prefer the red one.
¿Cuánto cuesta?
How much does it cost?
Es demasiado.
It's too much.

TEACHING OPTIONS

Extra Practice Have the class answer questions about **Fotonovela**. Ex: **1. ¿Quién necesita una bolsa nueva para su trabajo? (Graciela, la hermana de Inés) 2. ¿Quién cree que las bolsas son demasiado caras? (Inés) 3. ¿De qué color son las botas de Javier? (marrones) 4. ¿Quién acaba de comprarse un suéter? (Javier)**

Small Groups Have the class work in small groups to write statements about the **Fotonovela**. Ask each group to exchange its statements with another group. Each group will then write out the question that would have elicited each statement. Ex: G1: **Graciela acaba de empezar un nuevo trabajo.** G2: **¿Quién acaba de empezar un nuevo trabajo?**

Pronunciación

The consonants d and t

¿Dónde? vender nadar verdad

Like **b** and **v**, the Spanish **d** can also have a hard sound or a soft sound, depending on which letters appear next to it.

Don dinero tienda falda

At the beginning of a phrase and after **n** or **l**, the letter **d** is pronounced with a hard sound. This sound is similar to the English *d* in *dog*, but a little softer and duller. The tongue should touch the back of the upper teeth, not the roof of the mouth.

medias verde vestido huésped

In all other positions, **d** has a soft sound. It is similar to the English *th* in *there*, but a little softer.

Don Diego no tiene el diccionario.

When **d** begins a word, its pronunciation depends on the previous word. At the beginning of a phrase or after a word that ends in **n** or **l**, it is pronounced as a hard **d**.

Doña Dolores es de la capital.

Words that begin with **d** are pronounced with a soft **d** if they appear immediately after a word that ends in a vowel or any consonant other than **n** or **l**.

traje pantalones tarjeta tienda

When pronouncing the Spanish **t**, the tongue should touch the back of the upper teeth, not the roof of the mouth. Unlike the English *t*, no air is expelled from the mouth.

Práctica Read these phrases aloud to practice the **d** and the **t**.

1. Hasta pronto.
2. De nada.
3. Mucho gusto.
4. Lo siento.
5. No hay de qué.
6. ¿De dónde es usted?
7. ¡Todos a bordo!
8. No puedo.
9. Es estupendo.
10. No tengo computadora.
11. ¿Cuándo vienen?
12. Son las tres y media.

Una tienda Read these sentences aloud to practice the **d** and the **t**.

1. Don Teodoro tiene una tienda en un almacén en La Habana.
2. Don Teodoro vende muchos trajes, vestidos y zapatos todos los días.
3. Un día un turista, Federico Machado, entra en la tienda para comprar un par de botas.
4. Federico regatea con don Teodoro y compra las botas y también un par de sandalias.

Refranes Read these sayings aloud to practice the **d** and the **t**.

En la variedad está el gusto.[1]

Aunque la mona se vista de seda, mona se queda.[2]

1 Variety is the spice of life.
2 You can't make a silk purse out of a sow's ear.

recursos

R	SCASS./CD Lección 6	LM p. 250	LCASS./CD Cass. 3B/CD3

TEACHING OPTIONS

Extra Practice Write some additional proverbs on the board and have the class practice saying each one. Ex: **De tal padre, tal hijo.** (Like father, like son.) **El que tiene tejado de cristal no tira piedras al vecino.** (People who live in glass houses shouldn't throw stones.) **Cuatro ojos ven más que dos.** (Two heads are better than one.)

Extra Practice Write on the board the names of these famous Cuban literary figures: José Martí, Julián del Casal, Gertrudis Gómez de Avellaneda, and Dulce María Loynaz. Say the names aloud and have the class repeat after you. Then ask the class to explain the pronunciation of each **d** and **t** in these names.

Section Goals

In **Pronunciación** students will be introduced to the pronunciation of the letters **d** and **t**.

Instructional Resources
Student Activities Manual: Lab Manual, 250
Student Cassette/CD

Present

- Point out that the letters around the Spanish **d** determine whether its sound is hard or soft. Pronounce **¿Dónde?, vender, nadar,** and **verdad** and have the class repeat.
- Say that **d** has a hard sound at the beginning of a phrase or after **n** or **l**. Write **don, dinero, tienda,** and **falda** on the board and have the class pronounce them.
- Explain that **d** has a soft sound in all other situations. Pronounce the words **medias, verde, vestido,** and **huésped** and have the class repeat.
- Point out that **d** at the beginning of a word has a hard sound if the preceding word ends in **n** or **l**. Read the example sentence aloud and have the class repeat.
- Say that **d** is pronounced with a soft sound at the beginning of a word in all other cases. Write the example sentence on the board and have a volunteer pronounce it.
- Explain that **t** is pronounced with the tongue at the back of the upper teeth and that no air is expelled from the mouth. Pronounce **traje, pantalones, tarjeta,** and **tienda** and have the class repeat. Then pronounce pairs of similar-sounding Spanish and English words, having students focus on the difference between the sounds of **t**: ***ti/tea; tal/tall; todo/toad; tema/tame, tela/tell***

Práctica/Oraciones/Refranes Model pronunciation, having students repeat after you.

6.1 The preterite tense of regular verbs

NATIONAL comparisons STANDARDS

ANTE TODO In order to talk about events in the past, Spanish uses two simple tenses: the preterite and the imperfect. In this lesson, you will learn how to form the preterite tense, which is used to express actions or states completed in the past.

Preterite of regular *–ar*, *–er*, and *–ir* verbs

		–ar verbs **comprar**	*–er* verbs **vender**	*–ir* verbs **escribir**
SINGULAR FORMS	yo	compr**é** *I bought*	vend**í** *I sold*	escrib**í** *I wrote*
	tú	compr**aste**	vend**iste**	escrib**iste**
	Ud./él/ella	compr**ó**	vend**ió**	escrib**ió**
PLURAL FORMS	nosotros/as	compr**amos**	vend**imos**	escrib**imos**
	vosotros/as	compr**asteis**	vend**isteis**	escrib**isteis**
	Uds./ellos/ellas	compr**aron**	vend**ieron**	escrib**ieron**

¡ATENCIÓN!
The **yo** and **Ud./él/ella** forms of all three conjugations have written accents on the last syllable to show that it is stressed.

▶ As the preceding chart shows, the endings for regular **-er** and **-ir** verbs are identical in the preterite.

¿Qué compraste?

Compré esta bolsa.

▶ Note that the **nosotros/as** forms of regular **-ar** and **-ir** verbs in the preterite are identical to the present tense forms. Context will help you determine which tense is being used.

En invierno **compramos** la ropa en la tienda de la universidad.
In the wintertime, we buy clothing at the university store.

Anoche **compramos** unos zapatos de tenis y unas sandalias.
Yesterday we bought a pair of tennis shoes and a pair of sandals.

▶ **-Ar** and **-er** verbs that have a stem change in the present tense are regular in the preterite. They do *not* have a stem change.

	PRESENT	PRETERITE
cerrar (e:ie)	Ana **cierra** la puerta.	Ana **cerró** la puerta.
volver (o:ue)	Carlitos **vuelve** a las dos.	Carlitos **volvió** a las dos.

¡ATENCIÓN!
Preterite of stem-changing verbs
-Ir verbs that have a stem change in the present tense also have a stem change in the preterite. See Lesson 8, section 8.1, p. 240.

Section Goals

In **Estructura 6.1** students will learn:

- the preterite of regular verbs
- spelling changes in the preterite for verbs ending in **-car, -gar,** and **-zar**
- words commonly used with the preterite tense

Instructional Resources
Student Activities Manual: Workbook, 63–64; Lab Manual, 251
Hoja de actividades 11

Before Presenting Estructura 6.1 Ask students to skim the video-still captions on pages 174–175. In items 9 and 10, point out **compraste** and **compré** and ask students what they mean. Guide students to see that these verbs describe actions that took place in the past. Tell students that they are now going to learn the preterite tense so that they will be able to talk in Spanish about things that happened in the past.
Assignment Have students study **Estructura 6.1** and do the exercises on pages 179–180.

Present Introduce the preterite by describing some things you did yesterday, using the first-person preterite of known regular verbs. Use adverbs that signal the preterite (page 179) with your presentation. Ex: **Ayer compré una nueva chaqueta. Bueno, entré en el almacén, y compré una de ellas. Y de repente, vi un sombrero. En aquel momento decidí comprarlo también** and so forth. Each time you introduce a preterite form, write it on the board (you will eventually have the complete paradigm) and make sure students understand that it is a past tense. After you have used several regular first-person preterites, expand by asking students questions. Ex: **Ayer compré un sombrero. Y tú, ____, ¿qué compraste ayer? (Compré un libro.)**

Continued on page 179.

TEACHING OPTIONS

Extra Practice For practice with discrimination between preterite forms, call out randomly preterite forms of regular verbs and designate individuals to call out the corresponding subject pronoun. Ex: **comimos, creyeron, llegué, leíste, comenzamos, cerré, compraste, vendió,** and so forth.

Pairs Have students tell their partners two things they did last week, two things their best friend did, and two things they did together. Each student then reports the things his or her partner said to a member of another pair and listens to what that student reports.

Small Group Give each group of five a list of verbs, including some with spelling changes. Student 1 chooses a verb from the list and gives the **yo** form. Student 2 gives the **tú** form, and so on. Students work their way down the list, alternating who begins the conjugation chain.

▶ Verbs that end in **–car**, **–gar**, and **–zar** have a spelling change in the first person singular (**yo** form) in the preterite.

bus**car**	bus**c-**	**qu-**	yo bus**qu**é
lle**gar**	lle**g-**	**gu-**	yo lle**gu**é
empe**zar**	empe**z-**	**c-**	yo empe**c**é

▶ Except for the **yo** form, all other forms of **–car**, **–gar**, and **–zar** verbs are regular in the preterite.

bus**qu**é, buscaste, buscó, buscamos, buscasteis, buscaron
lle**gu**é, llegaste, llegó, llegamos, llegasteis, llegaron
empe**c**é, empezaste, empezó, empezamos, empezasteis, empezaron

¡ATENCIÓN!

Ver is regular in the preterite. The **yo** and **Ud./él/ella** forms do not have a written accent because they are monosyllables. For more information on accents, see **Pronunciación**, p. 111, **Ortografía**, p. 305, and p. 335.

▶ Four other verbs —**creer**, **leer**, **oír**, and **ver**— have spelling changes in the preterite. The **i** of the verb endings of **creer**, **leer**, and **oír** carries an accent in the **yo, tú, nosotros/as,** and **vosotros/as** forms, and changes to **y** in the **Ud./él/ella** and **Uds./ellos/ellas** forms.

creer	cre-	creí, cre**í**ste, cre**y**ó, cre**í**mos, cre**í**steis, cre**y**eron
leer	le-	leí, le**í**ste, le**y**ó, le**í**mos, le**í**steis, le**y**eron
oír	o-	oí, o**í**ste, o**y**ó, o**í**mos, o**í**steis, o**y**eron
ver	v-	vi, viste, vio, vimos, visteis, vieron

Words commonly used with the preterite

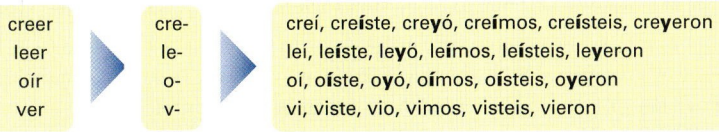

anoche	*last night*	**pasado/a** (adj.)	*last; past*
anteayer	*the day before yesterday*	**el año pasado**	*last year*
		la semana pasada	*last week*
ayer	*yesterday*	**una vez**	*once; one time*
de repente	*suddenly*	**dos veces**	*twice; two times*
desde... hasta...	*from... until...*	**ya**	*already*

Ayer llegué a París.
Yesterday I arrived in Paris.

Anoche oí un ruido extraño.
Last night I heard a strange noise.

¡INTÉNTALO! Provide the appropriate preterite forms of the verbs. The first item in each column has been done for you.

celebrar	comer	salir	comenzar
1. Elena celebró.	1. Los niños comieron.	1. Tú y yo salimos.	1. Uds. comenzaron.
2. Yo celebré.	2. Tú comiste.	2. Ella salió.	2. Nosotras comenzamos.
3. Los chicos celebraron.	3. Ud. comió.	3. Pablo y Elena salieron.	3. Yo comencé.
4. Emilio y yo celebramos.	4. Nosotros comimos.	4. Nosotros salimos.	4. Marcos comenzó.
5. Tú celebraste.	5. Yo comí.	5. Yo salí.	5. Tú comenzaste.
6. Ellos celebraron.	6. Uds. comieron.	6. Ud. salió.	6. Los clientes comenzaron.
7. Ud. celebró.	7. Carlota comió.	7. Tú saliste.	7. La vendedora comenzó.

TEACHING OPTIONS

Game Divide the class into teams of six people, arranged in rows. Call out the infinitive of a verb. The first person writes the **yo** form on a sheet of paper and passes it to the second person, who writes the **tú** form. The third writes the **él/ella/ud.** form, and so on. The sixth checks spelling. If all forms are correct, the team gets a point. Continue play, starting with a different person each time. The team with the most points after six rounds win.

Extra Practice Have students write five things they did yesterday. Ask students questions about what they did to elicit as many different conjugations as possible. Ex: **Carlos, ¿leíste el periódico ayer? ¿Quién más leyó el periódico ayer? . . . Carlos y Ana, ustedes dos leyeron el periódico ayer, ¿verdad? Clase, ¿quiénes leyeron el periódico ayer?**

Expand again by asking students about their classmates' answers. Ex: **¿Qué compró ____ ayer? (____ compró un libro.)** Follow the same procedure until you have the complete paradigms for an **-ar, -er,** and **-ir** verb on the board.

Model the pronunciation of each form. Emphasize the stress on **yo** and **Ud.** forms. Point out that endings of regular **-er** and **-ir** verbs are the same.

Help student see that although the present and preterite forms of regular verbs in the **nosotros** form are the same, there will rarely be confusion about which is meant.

Explain the spelling changes that verbs ending in **-car, -gar,** and **-zar** undergo. In the case of **-car** and **-gar**, the spelling change maintains the hard consonant sound before the **-é** of the **yo** form. The **z** of **-zar** changes because **z** never appears before **e** or **i** in Spanish. Remind students of the spelling of **lápiz/lápices.** Three other known verbs with this change are **practicar, jugar,** and **comenzar.**

Present the spelling changes in **creer, leer, oír,** and **ver.** Then practice them by asking students about things they read, heard, and saw yesterday. Ex: **¿Leíste el periódico ayer? ¿Quiénes vieron el pronóstico de tiempo? Yo oí que va a llover hoy; ¿qué oyeron Uds.?**

Suggestion Use the first three columns of **¡Inténtalo!** to consolidade after you first present the preterite of regular verbs of each conjugation. For further practice, change the infinitives.

1 Present Do the activity orally with the whole class. If any student has difficulty deciding which verb to choose, have him or her look for context clues in the sentence.

1 Expand Ask questions about Andrea's weekend. Have students answer with complete sentences. Ex: **¿Quién asistió a una reunión? ¿Qué compraron los amigos?**

2 Warm-up Before beginning the activity, have students note which verbs have spelling changes. (**oír, pagar, empezar, ver**)

2 Present Have students work through the activity in pairs. After Item 8 have them switch roles and repeat.

2 Expand Call on volunteers to write the exchanges on the board. Point out spelling changes.

2 Expand Have students redo the activity, using **Uds.** as the subject of the questions and **nosotros** in the answers.

3 Warm-up Have students work with a partner to quickly review the preterite forms of the verbs in the activity.

3 Present Divide the class into groups of four. Give students 5 minutes to see how many different sentences they can write. Have groups exchange their work with another group for peer editing. The group with the most sentences free of error wins.

3 Expand Have students rewrite their sentences using different subjects.

Práctica

1 Completar Andrea is talking about what happened last weekend. Complete each sentence by choosing the correct verb and putting it in the preterite.

1. El sábado a las diez de la mañana, la profesora Mora ___asistió___ (asistir, costar, usar) a una reunión (*meeting*) de profesores.
2. A la una, yo ___llegué___ (llegar, bucear, llevar) a la tienda con mis amigos.
3. Mis amigos y yo ___compramos___ (comprar, regatear, gastar) dos o tres cosas.
4. Yo ___compré___ (costar, comprar, escribir) unos pantalones negros y mi amigo Mateo ___compró___ (gastar, pasear, comprar) una camisa azul.
5. A las siete, mis amigos y yo ___comimos___ (llevar, vivir, comer) en un café.
6. A las nueve, Pepe ___habló___ (hablar, pasear, nadar) con su novia por teléfono.
7. La tarde del sábado, mi mamá ___escribió___ (escribir, beber, vivir) una carta a nuestros parientes en Cuba.
8. La mañana del domingo mi tía Manuela ___decidió___ (decidir, salir, escribir) vender su auto y su bicicleta.
9. A las cuatro de la tarde, mi tía ___vendió___ (beber, salir, vender) su auto a la profesora Mora y su bicicleta a su amiga Loli.

2 Preguntas Imagine that you have a pesky friend who keeps asking you questions. Respond that you already did or have just done what he/she asks.

modelo

leer la lección
Estudiante 1: ¿Leíste la lección? **Estudiante 2:** Sí, ya la leí.

1. escribir el correo electrónico
   —¿Escribiste el correo electrónico?
   —Sí, ya lo escribí.
2. lavar (*to wash*) la ropa
   —¿Lavaste la ropa?
   —Sí, ya la lavé.
3. oír las noticias (*news*)
   —¿Oíste las noticias?
   —Sí, ya las oí.
4. comer el sándwich
   —¿Comiste el sándwich?
   —Sí, ya lo comí.
5. practicar los verbos
   —¿Practicaste los verbos?
   —Sí, ya los practiqué.
6. pagar la cuenta (*bill*)
   —¿Pagaste la cuenta?
   —Sí, ya la pagué.
7. empezar la composición
   —¿Empezaste la composición?
   —Sí, ya la empecé.
8. ver la película *Titanic*
   —¿Viste la película *Titanic*?
   —Sí, ya la vi.

¡ATENCIÓN!

To say that you have just done something, use the construction **acabar** + **de** + [*infinitive*]. Note that **acabar** is used in the present tense even though the action expressed has already taken place.

José acaba de llegar.
José has just arrived.

Acabo de comprar un suéter.
I have just bought a sweater.

3 Combinar Combine words and phrases from each column to talk about things you and others did. Be sure to use the correct form of each verb. Answers will vary.

modelo

Mis amigos y yo llegamos tarde a clase una vez.

yo	ver televisión	anoche
mi compañero/a de cuarto	hablar con un(a) chico/a guapo/a	anteayer
mis amigos y yo	estudiar español	ayer
mi mejor (*best*) amigo/a	comprar ropa nueva	la semana pasada
mis padres	leer un buen libro	el año pasado
el/la profesor(a) de español	llegar tarde a clase	una vez
el presidente de los Estados Unidos	visitar Europa	dos veces
	escribir una carta	

AYUDA

pasado mañana *the day after tomorrow*
próximo/a *next*
la semana que viene *next week*
último/a *last, not past*
penúltimo/a *next to last*

TEACHING OPTIONS

Heritage Speakers Ask Spanish speakers to imagine they have just visited an open-air market for the first time. Have them write a letter to a friend describing what they saw and did in the market. Then, ask students to exchange their letters with another person who will respond to them.

TPR Have groups of three students write out three sentences that use verbs in the preterite, with a verb from a different conjugation in each sentence. After they have finished writing, have each group pantomime its sentences for the class. When someone guesses the pantomimed action, the group writes its sentence on the board.

Comunicación

4 **Encuesta** Your instructor will give you **una hoja de actividades** (*a worksheet*). Walk around the room and ask people if they did each activity listed. Try to find at least two people for each activity, and note their names on your worksheet. Be prepared to report the results of your survey to the class. Answers will vary.

modelo

comprar ropa nueva la semana pasada
Estudiante 1: ¿Compraste ropa nueva la semana pasada?
Estudiante 2: Sí, compré ropa nueva el jueves pasado.

Actividades	Nombres
1. Comprar ropa interior ayer	
2. Viajar a Europa el año pasado	
3. Ver a una persona famosa el año pasado	
4. Mirar tres programas de televisión anoche	
5. Tomar tres exámenes la semana pasada	
6. Recibir un mensaje electrónico ayer	
7. Visitar otro país el verano pasado	
8. Jugar a las cartas anoche	

5 **Las vacaciones** Imagine that you took these photos on a vacation with friends. Get together with a partner and use the pictures to tell him or her about your trip. Answers will vary.

Síntesis

6 **Conversación** Get together with a partner and have a conversation about what you did last week. Don't forget to include school activities, shopping, and pastimes. Answers will vary.

TEACHING OPTIONS

Large Group Have students create a story chain about a student who had a very bad day. Begin the story by saying **Ayer, Rigoberto pasó un día desastroso.** Call on a student at one corner of the class to continue the story by telling how Rigoberto began his day. The second person tells what happened next. Different students continue adding sentences until only one student remains. That person must conclude the story.

Extra Practice Have students make a "to do" list at the beginning of their day. Then, ask students to return to their list at the end of the day and write sentence stating which activities they completed. Ex: **limpiar mi habitación; No, no limpié mi habitación.**

4 Warm-up Explain the directions and ask volunteers to read **Modelo.** Point out that questions should be answered with complete sentences. Distribute **Hoja de actividades 11.**

4 Present To save time, have students ask one person all the questions before moving on to the next person.

4 Expand As a class, brainstorm a follow-up question for each of the original ones. Have students ask those individuals who answer the original questions affirmatively the follow-up questions and note their answers for the report. Ex: **¿Dónde compraste ropa nueva? ¿Qué países visitaste? ¿A qué persona famosa viste?**

5 Present Have students first state where they traveled and when. Then, have them identify the people in the photos, stating their names, their relationship to them, and describing their personality. Finally, students should tell what everyone did on the vacation.

5 Expand After completing the activity orally, have partners write a paragraph about their vacation, basing their account on the photos.

6 Warm-up Quickly review vocabulary for school activities, shopping, and pastimes before students begin the activity.

6 Expand Have volunteers rehearse their conversation, then present it to the class.

6 Expand Have volunteers report orally to the class what their partners did last week.

Assignment Have students do activities in **Student Activities Manual: Workbook,** pages 63–64.

6.2 Indirect object pronouns

ANTE TODO In Lesson 5, you learned that a direct object is the noun or pronoun that receives the action of the verb directly. In contrast, indirect objects are nouns or pronouns that receive the action of the verb indirectly. Note the following example:

SUBJECT	I.O. PRONOUN	VERB	DIRECT OBJECT	INDIRECT OBJECT
Roberto	**le**	prestó	cien pesos	**a Luisa.**
Roberto		*loaned*	*100 pesos*	*to Luisa.*

An indirect object is the noun or pronoun that answers the question *to whom* or *for whom* an action is done. In the preceding example, the indirect object answers this question: **¿A quién le prestó Roberto cien pesos?** *To whom did Roberto loan 100 pesos?*

Indirect object pronouns

SINGULAR		PLURAL	
me	(to, for) *me*	**nos**	(to, for) *us*
te	(to, for) *you* (fam.)	**os**	(to, for) *you* (fam.)
le	(to, for) *you* (form.) (to, for) *him; her*	**les**	(to, for) *you* (form.) (to, for) *them*

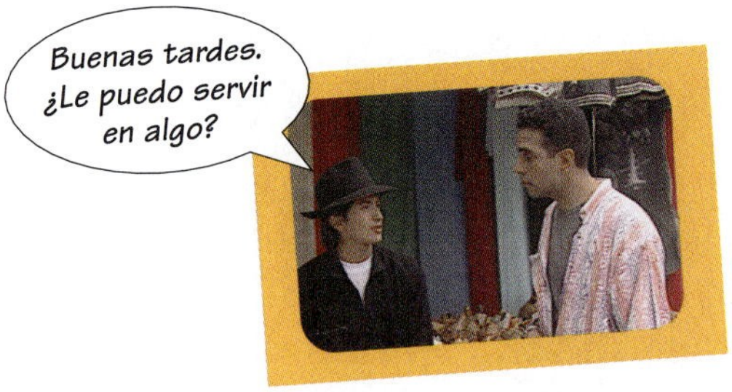

Using indirect object pronouns

- Spanish speakers commonly use both an indirect object pronoun and the indirect object noun to which it refers in the same sentence. This is done to emphasize and clarify to whom the pronoun refers.

  Ella **le** vendió la ropa a **Elena**. (I.O. PRONOUN: le; INDIRECT OBJECT: Elena)

  Les prestamos el dinero a **Inés y Álex**. (I.O. PRONOUN: Les; INDIRECT OBJECT: Inés y Álex)

- Indirect object pronouns are also used without the indirect object noun when the person for whom the action is being done is known.

  Ana **le** prestó la falda a **Elena**.
  Ana loaned her skirt to Elena.

  También **le** prestó unos bluejeans.
  She also loaned her a pair of blue jeans.

¡ATENCIÓN!
The forms of indirect object pronouns for the first and second persons (**me, te, nos, os**) are the same as the direct object pronouns.
Indirect object pronouns agree in number with the corresponding nouns, but not in gender.

¡LENGUA VIVA!
Jeans can be also be called **vaqueros, jeans,** or **mahones**.

Section Goals
In **Estructura 6.2**, students will learn:
- to identify an indirect object noun
- how to use indirect object pronouns

Instructional Resources
Student Activities Manual: Workbook, 65–66; Lab Manual, 252

Before Presenting Estructura 6.2 Remind students that a direct object is a noun or pronoun that receives the action of a verb and answers the question *what*? Tell them that in this lesson they will learn the Spanish indirect object pronouns. Write on the board: **Mi novio me escribió un mensaje electrónico.** Ask students what the direct object of the verb is. (**mensaje**) Then tell them that an indirect object is a noun or pronoun that answers the question *to or for whom or what?* Tell students that they are now going to learn the Spanish indirect object pronouns.

Assignment Have students study **Estructura 6.2** and do the exercises on pages 183-184 as homework.

Present Write the indirect object pronouns on the board. Point out that only the third-person forms (**le/les**) differ from the direct object pronouns. Ask volunteers to read aloud the video-still captions. Have them identify the indirect pronoun in each. (**le, me**) Have them identify the direct object in the second caption. (**suéter**)

Suggestion Point out that the redundant use of both an indirect object pronoun and an indirect object noun is common in Spanish and that, unlike in English, it is the indirect object noun that is optional, not the pronoun. Ex: **Ella le vendió la ropa** is possible but **Ella vendió la ropa a Elena** is less common.

TEACHING OPTIONS

Extra Practice Write sentences like these on the board: **Ana te preparó unos tacos. Pablo no me escribió. Le presté dinero a Luisa. Ayer les compramos unos regalos a los niños. María nos habló ayer.** Ask students to come to the board and underline the direct objects and circle the indirect objects. If the indirect object is implied, have them write *I* next to the sentence.

Small Groups Have Student 1 "lend" an object to Student 2 and say: **Te presto mi...** Student 2 responds: **Me prestaste tu...** Student 3 says: **Marcos le prestó a Juana su...** Groups of 3 practice until everyone has begun the chain twice. Practice plural pronouns by having two groups join together and two students "lend" something to two other students.

- Indirect object pronouns are usually placed before the conjugated form of the verb. In negative sentences the pronoun is placed between **no** and the conjugated verb.

Martín **me** compró un regalo. *Martín bought me a gift.*	Eva **no me** escribió una carta. *Eva didn't write a letter to me.*

¡ATENCIÓN!

When an indirect object pronoun is attached to a present participle, an accent mark is added to maintain the proper stress. For more information on accents, see **Pronunciación**, p. 111, **Ortografía**, p. 305, and p. 335.

- When a conjugated verb is followed by an infinitive or the present progressive, the indirect object pronoun may be placed before the conjugated verb or attached to the infinitive or present participle.

Él quiere **hablarte** en inglés. *He wants to talk to you in English.*	Él está **escribiéndole** una postal a ella. *He is writing a postcard to her.*
Él **te** quiere hablar en inglés. *He wants to talk to you in English.*	Él **le** está escribiendo una postal a ella. *He is writing a postcard to her.*

- Because the indirect object pronouns **le** and **les** have multiple meanings, Spanish-speakers often clarify to whom the pronouns refer with the preposition **a** + [*pronoun*] or **a** + [*noun*].

UNCLEAR STATEMENT	CLARIFIED STATEMENTS
Yo **le** compré un abrigo.	Yo **le** compré un abrigo **a él/ella/Ud.**
Ella **le** dio un libro.	Ella **le** dio un libro **a Juan**.

UNCLEAR STATEMENT	CLARIFIED STATEMENTS
Él **les** vendió unos sombreros.	Él **les** vendió unos sombreros **a ellos/ellas/Uds.**
Ellos **les** hablaron muy claro.	Ellos **les** hablaron muy claro **a los turistas**.

¡INTÉNTALO! Use the cues in parentheses to provide the indirect object pronoun for the sentence. The first item has been done for you.

1. Juan __le__ escribió ayer. (*to Elena*)
2. María __nos__ habló también. (*to us*)
3. Beatriz y Felipe __me__ escribieron desde Cuba. (*to me*)
4. Marta y yo __les__ compramos unos guantes. (*for them*)
5. Los vendedores __te__ vendieron ropa. (*to you, fam.*)
6. La maestra __nos__ enseñó los verbos. (*to us*)
7. Yo __le__ canté en español. (*to her*)
8. Nosotros __les__ compramos dos vestidos. (*for them*)
9. Ella __me__ escribió todos los días. (*to me*)

Rewrite the following sentences, attaching the indirect object pronoun to the end of the infinitive or present participle. Remember to add accent marks when necessary.

1. Susana te está escribiendo una carta. Susana está escribiéndote una carta.
2. Le tienes que pedir un lápiz al profesor. Tienes que pedirle un lápiz al profesor.
3. Mi novia me va a comprar una camisa. Mi novia va a comprarme una camisa.
4. Mi novio me está preparando unos tacos. Mi novio está preparándome unos tacos.
5. La mamá le va a leer un libro al niño. La mamá va a leerle un libro al niño.

Point out that the position of indirect object pronouns in a sentence, including when they appear in negative sentences, with an infinitive, or with the present progressive, is the same as that of direct object pronouns. (If a student asks about using direct and indirect object pronouns together in a sentence, say that that will be taught in Lesson 8.)

Then explain how to clarify the meanings of **le** and **les** when the referent is ambiguous. Point out that the pronouns that follow a preposition are the same as the subject pronouns except in the first and second person singular: **a mí, a ti.** Thus **a él, a ella, a Ud. a ellos, a ellas, a Uds.** would be used.

Suggestion Go over the answers to items 1–9 of **¡Inténtalo!** orally with the class. Then go back and ask students which items might require clarification (items 1, 4, 7, and 8). Ask students what they would add to each sentence in order to clarify **le** or **les**. Next, call on volunteers to write their answers to items 10–14 on the board for the other students to use as an answer key.

Close As a comprehension check, have students write answers to these questions: **1. Necesitas comprar un regalo para tu mejor amigo. ¿Qué vas a comprarle? 2. ¿A quiénes les hablaste ayer? 3. ¿Quién te presta dinero cuando lo necesitas? 4. ¿Quién les está enseñando español a ustedes?** Go over the answers orally. Be sure that students give both ways to answer questions one and four.

TEACHING OPTIONS

Video Have students read along as you replay the **Fotonovela**. Ask them to note each time an indirect object pronoun is used. Point out that the pronouns used with the verb **gustar** are indirect objects because they answer the question *to whom*? Next, have students find each use of **le** and **les** and state to whom or what the pronouns refer.

Game Have students write a sentence with an indirect object pronoun. Each word is written on a separate slip of paper, then placed in an envelope. Students trade envelopes. After putting the sentences together, students write them down. Students continue trading envelopes and writing sentences. At the end of 3 minutes, the student with the most correctly deciphered sentences wins.

1 Warm-up Have students find the indirect object in each sentence and circle it.

1 Expand Have students write four sentences about themselves modeled on those in the activity, leaving out the indirect object pronoun. Ex: **Yo ____ compré un regalo a mis padres. Mi tío ____ compró una moto a mí.**

2 Present As students complete the dialogue, have them give both possible positions for the indirect object pronoun when applicable. After students have completed the dialogue individually, call on volunteers to read the different roles.

2 Expand Ask students to work with a partner to create their own dialogues and perform them for the class. Each dialogue should consist of at least two exchanges.

3 Present Have students describe to a partner what they see in the photos. Ask them to describe not only the action, but also what the people look like physically and what they are wearing.

3 Expand Divide the class into groups of four students. Have each student pick a photo to present to his or her group as a verbal portrait. Each portrait should be a complete paragraph with an introductory sentence that sets the scene, followed by a body and conclusion. The paragraph should answer the questions *who, what, where, when,* and *why* with regard to what is seen in the photo. After everyone in the group has presented his/her photo, the group votes on the best portrait to present to the class.

Práctica

1 Completar Fill in the correct pronouns to complete Mónica's description of her family's holiday shopping.

1. Juan y yo __le__ compramos una blusa a nuestra hermana Gisela.
2. Mi tía __nos__ compró a nosotros una mesa para la casa.
3. Gisela __le__ compró dos corbatas a su novio.
4. A mi mamá yo __le__ compré un par de guantes negros.
5. A mi profesora __le__ compré dos novelas de García Márquez.
6. Juan __les__ compró un regalo a mis padres.
7. Mis padres __me__ compraron a mí un traje nuevo.
8. Y a ti, yo __te__ compré una sorpresa también. ¿Quieres verla?

2 Minidiálogos Supply the missing words in the minidialogues.

1. **NIÑOS** Mamá, ¿vas a leernos una historia (*story*)?
   MAMÁ Sí, __voy a leerles / les voy a leer__ Blanca Nieves (*Snow White*). Creo que les va a gustar.
2. **JUAN** ¿Vas a comprarles un regalo a Héctor y a Linda?
   MONA Sí, __voy a comprarles / les voy a comprar__ un viaje a Europa.
3. **ESTUDIANTES** Profesora, ¿__va a hablarnos / nos va a hablar__ en español todos los días (*every day*)?
   PROFESORA ¡Claro que (*of course*) voy a hablarles a Uds. en español! Es importante hablar en español todos los días.
4. **SARA** ¿__Estás escribiéndole / Le estás escribiendo__ una carta a Maripili?
   LAURA No, estoy escribiéndoles una carta a Alicia y Orlando. ¿Por qué?
5. **ALFREDO** Ramón, ¿__me__ puedes prestar tu bicicleta hoy?
   RAMÓN No, no te puedo prestar mi bicicleta. Lo siento, es que tienes muchos accidentes.
6. **ESPOSO** ¿Qué me vas a comprar en el centro comercial? ¿Una camisa? ¿Una corbata?
   ESPOSA ¡No __voy a comprarte / te voy a comprar__ nada!

3 Describir Describe what's happening in these photos based on the cues provided.

1. escribir / mensaje electrónico
Aléx le escribe un mensaje electrónico (a Ricardo).

2. mostrar / fotos
Javier les muestra fotos (a Inés y Maite).

3. pedir / llaves
Don Francisco le pide las llaves (a la empleada).

4. vender / suéter
El vendedor le vende un suéter (a Javier).

TEACHING OPTIONS

Heritage speakers Imagine that it's the holiday season. Ask Spanish speakers to create a radio commercial for their favorite clothing store. Commercials should tell prospective customers what they can buy, for whom, and at what price.

Pairs Ask students to write 5 questions calling for an indirect object pronoun in the answer. Students ask their partners the questions, writing down their partners' answers. Students then review the questions and answers together to ensure that they were correct.

NATIONAL communication STANDARDS

Comunicación

4 **Entrevista** Take turns with a classmate asking and answering questions using the word bank. Answers will vary.

modelo

escribir mensajes electrónicos
Estudiante 1: ¿A quién le escribes mensajes electrónicos?
Estudiante 2: Le escribo mensajes electrónicos a mi hermano.

comprar ropa	prestar dinero
escribir tarjetas postales	cantar canciones de amor (*love songs*)
escribir mensajes electrónicos	preparar comida (*food*) mexicana
pedir dinero	pedir ayuda con tus clases

5 **Entrevista** Use these questions to interview a classmate. Answers will vary.

1. ¿Te gusta escribir tarjetas postales?
2. ¿Te gusta ir de compras? ¿Adónde te gusta ir?
3. ¿Les compras regalos a tus amigos/as cuando hay rebajas?
4. ¿Me compraste un regalo de Navidad el año pasado?
5. ¿Les prestas dinero a tus amigos/as? ¿Por qué?
6. ¿Me prestas cien dólares?

6 **Situación** Money is no object, so the entire Spanish class is going on a shopping spree. In groups of three, interview each other to find out what everyone is going to buy for family and friends. Be prepared to share your findings with the rest of the class. Answers will vary.

NATIONAL communication STANDARDS

Síntesis

7 **Minidrama** With two classmates, take turns playing the roles of two shoppers and a clerk in a clothing store. The shoppers should take turns talking about the articles of clothing they are looking for, for whom they are buying the clothes, and what they bought for the same people last year. The clerk should recommend several items, based on the shoppers' descriptions. Answers will vary.

AYUDA

Other phrases (in addition to those given on page 174) that you can use are:

Me queda grande/pequeño.
It's big/small on me.

¿Tiene otro color?
Do you have another color?

¿Está en rebaja?
Is it on sale?

4 Warm-up Remind students that to ask about more than one person, they need to use **a quiénes.** Ask a volunteer to help you read the **Modelo**. Then repeat in the plural.

4 Expand Give students five minutes to work in groups of three to brainstorm as many questions as they can using different forms of the verbs listed in the word bank. Invite two groups to come to the front of the class. Each group takes a turn asking the other its questions.

5 Present/Expand Have students interview classmates they don't know very well. Each partner takes the role of interviewer and interviewee. After the interview, ask them to write a two-sentence "psychological profile" (**perfil psicológico**) based on their partner's answers.

6 Warm-up Have students brainstorm a list of questions they might use in their interviews.

6 Present Have students take turns interviewing each other. As one student interviews another, the third student takes notes. Students then work as a team to compile results to share with the class.

7 Warm-up Review the clothing vocabulary on pages 170–171, the colors and adjectives on page 172, and the **Expresiones útiles** on page 175 before beginning the activity.

7 Present Have students rehearse their mini-dramas. If possible, have them videotape their scenes or perform them for the class.

Assignment Have students do activities in **Student Activities Manual: Workbook,** pages 65–66.

TEACHING OPTIONS

Small Groups Have students write a dialogue between two friends. One friend tries to convince the other to go shopping with him/her this weekend. The other friend explains that she can't and lists all the things she is going to do this weekend. Students should try to incorporate as many different indirect object pronouns in their dialogues as possible.

Pairs Ask students to imagine they are going on an extended trip. Have them make a list of 5 things they are going to do (people they are going to write to, things they are going to buy for themselves or others, money they are going to borrow, etc.) before leaving. Ex: **Voy a comprarme unos zapatos nuevos.**

6.3 Demonstrative adjectives and pronouns

NATIONAL comparisons STANDARDS

Demonstrative adjectives

ANTE TODO In Spanish, as in English, demonstrative adjectives are words that "demonstrate" or "point out" nouns. Demonstrative adjectives precede the nouns they modify and, like other Spanish adjectives you have studied, agree with them in gender and number. Observe the following examples, then study the following chart.

esta camisa	**ese** vendedor	**aquellos** zapatos
this shirt	*that salesman*	*those shoes (over there)*

Demonstrative adjectives

Singular		Plural		
MASCULINE	FEMININE	MASCULINE	FEMININE	
este	**esta**	**estos**	**estas**	*this; these*
ese	**esa**	**esos**	**esas**	*that; those*
aquel	**aquella**	**aquellos**	**aquellas**	*that; those (over there)*

- There are three sets of demonstrative adjectives. To determine which one to use, you must establish the relationship between the speaker and the noun(s) being pointed out.

- The demonstrative adjectives **este, esta, estos,** and **estas** are used to point out nouns that are close in space and time to the speaker and the listener.

- The demonstrative adjectives **ese, esa, esos,** and **esas** are used to point out nouns that are not close in space and time to the speaker. They may, however, be close to the listener.

Section Goals
In **Estructura 6.3** students will learn to use demonstrative adjectives and pronouns.

Instructional Resources
Student Activities Manual: Workbook, 67–68; Lab Manual, 253

Before Presenting Estructura 6.3 Write **este, ese,** and **aquel** on the board and explain that they mean this, that, and that (over there). Point to the book on your desk. Say: **Este libro está en la mesa.** Point to a book on a student's desk. Say **Ese libro está encima del escritorio de** ____. Point to a book on the window ledge. Say: **Aquel libro está cerca de la ventana.** Follow the same procedure with **tiza, papeles,** and **plumas.** Tell students that these are demonstrative adjectives and that they are now going to learn how to use them and demonstrative pronouns.

Assignment
Have students study **Estructura 6.3** and do the exercises on pages 187–188 as homework.

Present Bring in items of clothing and display them. Using TPR and the clothing, present all forms of the three types of demonstrative adjectives. Ex: (Hold up a hat.) **Este sombrero es azul.** (Point to a hat farther away.) **Pero ese sombrero es verde.** (Point to a hat you have located away from both you and the class.) **Aquel sombrero es rojo.** Give special emphasis to singular and plural masculine forms, pointing out that, though the singular forms do not end in **-o**, the plural forms end in **-os**. Lead class in questions and answers that discriminate between singular and plural forms. Hold up or point to objects and have students give the plural: **este libro, esta mochila, este traje, este zapato.** Follow the same procedure to have them indicate things in the singular.

TEACHING OPTIONS

Extra Practice Hold up an item, or two items, of clothing or classroom objects. Have students write all three forms of the demonstrative pronouns that would apply. Ex: **estos zapatos, esos zapatos, aquellos zapatos.**

Pairs Refer students to **Contextos** on pages 170–171. Have students work with a partner to comment on the articles of clothing pictured. Ex: **Este suéter es bonito, ¿no? (No, ese suéter no es bonito. Es feo.)** or **Aquella camiseta es muy larga. (Sí, aquella camiseta es larga.)**

▶ The demonstrative adjectives **aquel, aquella, aquellos,** and **aquellas** are used to point out nouns that are far away in space and time from the speaker and the listener.

Aquellos chicos son mis amigos.

Demonstrative pronouns

▶ Demonstrative pronouns are identical to their corresponding demonstrative adjectives, except that they carry an accent mark on the stressed vowel.

—¿Quieres comprar **este suéter**?
Do you want to buy this sweater?

—No, no quiero **éste**. Quiero **ése**.
No, I don't want this one. I want that one.

—¿Vas a leer **estas revistas**?
Are you going to read these magazines?

—Sí, voy a leer **éstas**. También voy a leer **aquéllas**.
Yes, I'm going to read these. I'll also read those.

¡ATENCIÓN!
Eso, esto, and **aquello** do not change in gender or number and never carry an accent mark.

Demonstrative pronouns

Singular		Plural			
MASCULINE	FEMININE	MASCULINE	FEMININE	NEUTER	
éste	**ésta**	**éstos**	**éstas**	**esto**	*this (one); these*
ése	**ésa**	**ésos**	**ésas**	**eso**	*that (one); those*
aquél	**aquélla**	**aquéllos**	**aquéllas**	**aquello**	*that (one); those (over there)*

¡ATENCIÓN!
Like demonstrative adjectives, demonstrative pronouns agree in gender and number with the corresponding noun.
Este libro es de Pablito.
Éstos son de Juana.

▶ Each of the three sets of demonstrative pronouns has a neuter form: **esto, eso,** and **aquello.** These forms refer to unidentified or unspecified nouns, situations, ideas, and concepts.

—¿Qué es **esto**?
What's this?

—Es una cartera.
It's a wallet.

—¿Qué es **eso**?
What's that?

—¡**Aquello** es bonito!
That's pretty!

¡INTÉNTALO! Provide the correct form of the demonstrative adjective and demonstrative pronoun for these nouns. The first item has been done for you.

1. la falda / este *esta falda, ésta*
2. los estudiantes / este estos estudiantes, éstos
3. los países / aquel aquellos países, aquéllos
4. la ventana / ese esa ventana, ésa
5. los periodistas / ese esos periodistas, ésos
6. las empleadas / ese esas empleadas, ésas
7. el chico / aquel aquel chico, aquél
8. las sandalias / este estas sandalias, éstas
9. el autobús / ese ese autobús, ése
10. las chicas / aquel aquellas chicas, aquéllas

TEACHING OPTIONS

Small Groups Ask students to bring in fashion magazines. Have students work in groups of three to give their opinions about the clothing they see in the magazines. Students should tell which items they like and which they don't, using demonstrative adjectives and pronouns when giving their opinions.

Video Have students listen for the use of demonstrative pronouns as you replay the **Fotonovela**. Ask students to write each pronoun and the object(s) it refers to. Then, have students look at the transcript of the **Fotonovela** to see if they were correct.

Remind students that a demonstrative adjective always modifies a noun. When a demonstrative stands alone, it is a pronoun. Point out that the masculine and feminine forms of the demonstrative pronouns are the same as the demonstrative pronouns except they have an accent mark on the stressed syllable.

Then present the demonstrative pronouns by engaging students in short conversations about classroom objects and items of clothing. Ex: Pick up a student's backpack and ask him or her: **¿Es ésta mi mochila? (No, ésta es mi mochila)** Turn to another student and ask about the same backpack: **¿Es ésa mi mochila? (No, ésa es la mochila de ____.)** Point to a pencil you have placed on the windowsill. Ask: **¿Es aquél tu lápiz, ____? (No, aquél es su lápiz.)** Continue the procedure to practice all the demonstrative pronoun forms.

Explain that when demonstrative pronouns refer to a whole concept or idea or to an object that is still unknown, rather than a specific, known object, Spanish uses the neuter forms **esto, eso,** and **aquello.** Point out that the neuter forms do not have an accent. Write on the board: **¡Eso es fenomenal!, ¡Esto es terrible!, ¡Esto es horrible! ¡Esto es estupendo!** and **¿Qué es eso?** Then state situations and have students respond to them with one of the expressions. Situations: **Voy a cancelar el próximo examen. • Voy a comprar un nuevo traje totalmente morado. • La cafetería va a cerrar los lunes, miércoles y viernes. • Aquí te tengo un regalo. • Los coches están prohibidos en el cámpus.**

Close Call on volunteers to write their answers for **¡Inténtalo!** on the board.

1 Warm-up Write the first sentence in the **Modelo** on the board. Ask a volunteer to change **camisas** to singular and make other appropriate changes. Then go through each item orally with the whole class.

1 Expand Have students expand each sentence with a phrase that includes a demonstrative pronoun. Ex: **Aquellos chalecos son my elegantes, pero estos son más baratos.**

2 Present Have students underline the nouns the demonstrative pronoun will refer to, noting their gender and number. After students have filled in the blanks, go over the activity orally with the whole class. Write each demonstrative pronoun on the board so students may verify that they have placed the accent marks correctly.

3 Warm-up Review colors, classroom objects, and articles of clothing by identifying them in the classroom before beginning the activity. Ex: **Mi lápiz es amarillo. El vestido de Amy es blanco y negro.**

3 Expand Ask students to find a photo featuring different articles of clothing or to draw several articles of clothing. Have them write five statements like the **Estudiante 1** model in part one of this activity. Then, have students exchange their statements and photo/drawing with a partner to write responses like the **Estudiante 2** model.

Práctica

1 **Cambiar** Make the singular sentences plural and the plural sentences singular.

modelo

Estas camisas son blancas.
Esta camisa es blanca.

1. Aquellos chalecos son muy elegantes. Aquel chaleco es muy elegante.
2. Ese abrigo es muy caro. Esos abrigos son muy caros.
3. Estos cinturones son hermosos. Este cinturón es hermoso.
4. Esos precios son muy buenos. Ese precio es muy bueno.
5. Estas faldas son muy cortas. Esta falda es muy corta.
6. ¿Quieres ir a aquel almacén? ¿Quieres ir a aquellos almacenes?
7. Esas blusas son baratas. Esa blusa es barata.
8. Esta corbata hace juego con mi traje. Estas corbatas hacen juego con mi traje.

2 **Completar** Here are some things people might say while shopping. Complete the sentences with the correct demonstrative pronouns.

1. No me gustan esos zapatos. Voy a comprar __éstos__. (*these*)
2. ¿Vas a comprar ese traje o __éste__? (*this one*)
3. Esta guayabera es bonita pero prefiero __ésa__. (*that one*)
4. Estas corbatas rojas son muy bonitas pero __ésas__ son fabulosas. (*those*)
5. Estos cinturones cuestan demasiado. Prefiero __aquéllos__. (*those over there*)
6. ¿Te gustan esas botas o __éstas__? (*these*)
7. Esa bolsa roja es bonita pero prefiero __aquélla__. (*that one over there*)
8. No voy a comprar estas botas, voy a comprar __aquéllas__. (*those over there*)
9. ¿Prefieres estos pantalones o __ésos__? (*those*)
10. Me gusta este vestido pero voy a comprar __ése__. (*that one*)
11. Me gusta ese almacén pero __aquél__ es mejor (*better*). (*that one over there*)
12. Esa blusa es bonita pero cuesta demasiado. Voy a comprar __ésta__. (*this one*)

NOTA CULTURAL

The **guayabera** is a men's shirt typically worn in the Caribbean. Never tucked in, it is casual wear, but variations exist for more formal occasions, such as weddings, parties, or the office. See page 169 for a photo of a guayabera.

3 **Describir** With your partner, look for two items in the classroom that are one of these colors: **amarillo, azul, blanco, marrón, negro, verde, rojo.** Point them out, first using demonstrative adjectives, and then demonstrative pronouns. Answers will vary.

modelo

azul
Estudiante 1: *Esta silla es azul. Aquella mochila es azul.*
Estudiante 2: *Ésta es azul. Aquélla es azul.*

Now use demonstrative adjectives and pronouns to discuss the colors of your classmates' clothing. One of you can ask a question about an article of clothing, using the wrong color. Your partner will correct you and point out that color somewhere else in the room.

modelo

Estudiante 1: *¿Esa camisa es negra?*
Estudiante 2: *No, ésa es azul. Aquélla es negra.*

TEACHING OPTIONS

Heritage Speakers Have students role-play a scene between friends out shopping for clothes. Student 1 tries to convince the friend that the clothes she/he wants to buy are not attractive. Student 1 suggests other items of clothing, but the friend does not agree. Students should use as many demonstrative adjectives and pronouns as possible.

Game Post pictures of different versions of the same object (sedan, sports car, all-terrain vehicle) on the board. Assign each a dollar figure. Team 1 guesses the price of each object, using demonstrative adjectives and pronouns. Team 2 either agrees or guesses a higher or lower price. The team that guesses the closest price, wins. Ex: **Este carro cuesta $20.000, ése cuesta $35.000 y aquél cuesta $18.000.**

NATIONAL communication STANDARDS

Comunicación

4 **Conversación** With a classmate, use demonstrative adjectives and pronouns to ask each other questions about the people around you. Use words and expressions from the word bank and/or your own ideas. Answers will vary.

¿Cómo se llama...?	¿Cuántos años tiene(n)...?
¿Cómo es (son)...?	¿A qué hora...?
¿De quién es (son)...?	¿Cuándo...?
¿De dónde es (son)...?	¿Qué clases toma(n)...?

modelo

Estudiante 1: *¿Cómo se llama esa chica?*
Estudiante 2: *Se llama Rebeca.*
Estudiante 1: *¿A qué hora llegó aquel chico a la clase?*
Estudiante 2: *A las nueve.*

5 **En una tienda** Imagine that you and a classmate are in a small clothing store for both men and women. Study the floor plan, then have a conversation about what you see around you. Use demonstrative adjectives and pronouns as much as possible. Answers will vary.

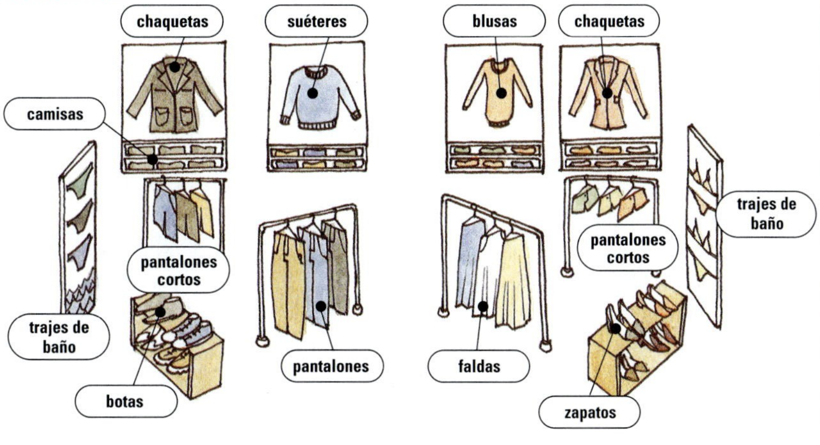

NATIONAL communication STANDARDS

Síntesis

6 **Adivinar** Using demonstrative adjectives and other words you have learned, describe people, places, and things to a group of classmates. They will guess who or what you are describing. Answers will vary.

modelo

Estudiante 1: *Este hombre es alto, guapo y muy inteligente. Llegó a la clase a las nueve.*
Estudiante 2: *¿Es el profesor?*
Estudiante 1: *¡Sí!*

TEACHING OPTIONS

Pairs Ask students to write a conversation between two people sitting at a busy sidewalk cafe in the city. They are watching the people who walk by, asking each other questions about what the passersby are doing and making comments on their clothing. Students should use as many demonstrative adjectives and pronouns as possible in their conversations. Invite several pairs to present their conversation to the whole class.

Small Groups Ask students to bring in pictures of their families, a sports team, a group of friends, and so forth. Have students take turns asking about and identifying the people in the pictures.
Ex: **—¿Quién es aquella mujer? (¿Cuál?)**
—¿Aquélla con la camiseta roja? (Es mi...)

4 Warm-up Model at least one question for each of the items in the word bank. Then, have the class brainstorm some other possible questions using interrogatives not included in the word bank.

4 Present Challenge both partners to ask a question for each item in the word bank and to ask at least one other question using an interrogative expression which is not included.

5 Warm-up Review the lesson's vocabulary and discuss what types of comments students might make to each other.

5 Expand Divide students into groups of three to role-play a scene between a salesperson and two customers. The customers should ask about the different items of clothing pictured and the salesperson will answer. They talk about how the items fit and their cost. The customers then express their preferences and decide which items to buy.

6 Present Divide the class into two teams, then divide each team into small groups. Each small group writes three different riddles. Small groups bring their riddles to the team captain, who compiles them. The captain from Team 1 reads a riddle. Team 2 guesses the answer. If Team 2 is correct, a point is awarded. If Team 2 is wrong, Team 1 gets a point. The team with the most points after all the riddles have been read wins. If there is a tie, teams must develop new riddles on the spot until the tie is broken.

Assignment Have students do activities in **Student Activities Manual: Workbook,** pages 67–68.

Section Goals

In **Lectura** students will:

- learn to skim a text
- use what they know about text format to predict a document's content
- read a text rich in cognates and recognizable format elements

Antes de leer
Introduce the strategy. Tell students that they can often predict the content of an unfamiliar document in Spanish by skimming it and looking for recognizable format elements.

Examinar el texto Have students skim the text at the top of the ad. Point out the cognate **Liquidación** and the series of percentages. Ask them to predict what type of document it is. (advertisement for a liquidation sale) Then ask students to scan the rest of the ad.

Buscar cognados Ask volunteers to point out cognates they notice: **elegante, increíbles, crédito, colores, suéteres.**

Impresiones generales Finally, ask students to sum up their general impression of the document by answering the three questions at the bottom. Guide them to see that the document is a newspaper or magazine advertisement for a liquidation sale at a clothing store that caters to women, men, young people, and children.

Assignment Have students read **¡Real liquidación en Corona!** and prepare the activities in **Después de leer** as homework.

Lectura

Antes de leer

Estrategia

Skimming

Skimming involves quickly reading through a document to absorb its general meaning. This allows you to understand the main ideas without having to read word for word. When you skim a text, you might want to look at its title and subtitles. You might also want to read the first sentence of each paragraph.

Examinar el texto

Look at the format of the reading selection. How is it organized? What does the organization of the document tell you about its content?

Buscar cognados

Scan the reading selection to locate cognates and write a few of them down. Based on the cognates, what is the reading selection about?

1. ____________
2. ____________
3. ____________
4. ____________
5. ____________
6. The reading selection is about ____________.

Impresiones generales

Now skim the reading selection to understand its general meaning. Jot down your impressions. What new information did you learn about the document by skimming it? Based on all the information you now have, answer these questions.

1. Who produced this document?
2. What is its purpose?
3. Who is its intended audience?

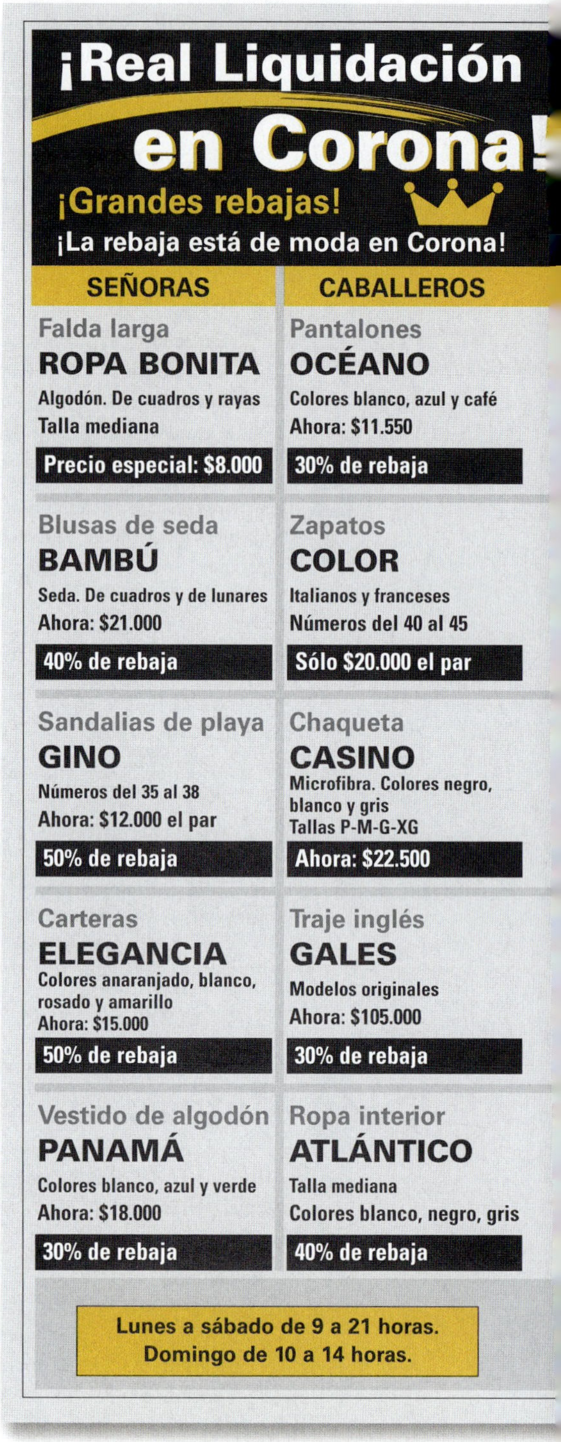
¡Real Liquidación en Corona!

¡Grandes rebajas!

¡La rebaja está de moda en Corona!

SEÑORAS	CABALLEROS
Falda larga **ROPA BONITA** Algodón. De cuadros y rayas Talla mediana Precio especial: $8.000	Pantalones **OCÉANO** Colores blanco, azul y café Ahora: $11.550 30% de rebaja
Blusas de seda **BAMBÚ** Seda. De cuadros y de lunares Ahora: $21.000 40% de rebaja	Zapatos **COLOR** Italianos y franceses Números del 40 al 45 Sólo $20.000 el par
Sandalias de playa **GINO** Números del 35 al 38 Ahora: $12.000 el par 50% de rebaja	Chaqueta **CASINO** Microfibra. Colores negro, blanco y gris Tallas P-M-G-XG Ahora: $22.500
Carteras **ELEGANCIA** Colores anaranjado, blanco, rosado y amarillo Ahora: $15.000 50% de rebaja	Traje inglés **GALES** Modelos originales Ahora: $105.000 30% de rebaja
Vestido de algodón **PANAMÁ** Colores blanco, azul y verde Ahora: $18.000 30% de rebaja	Ropa interior **ATLÁNTICO** Talla mediana Colores blanco, negro, gris 40% de rebaja

Lunes a sábado de 9 a 21 horas.
Domingo de 10 a 14 horas.

TEACHING OPTIONS

Heritage Speakers Ask Spanish speakers to create an ad for one or two items of clothing. Have them use the **¡Real Liquidación en Corona!** advertisement as a model. Have them share their ads with the class. Discuss the ads with the whole class.

Small Groups Have small groups of students work together to write a cloze paragraph about shopping for clothing, modeled on the **Completar** paragraph. Ask each group member to contribute two sentences to the paragraph. Then have the group make a clean copy, omitting several words or phrases, and writing the omitted words and phrases below the paragraph. Each group then exchanges its paragraph with another group, which, in turn, completes it. Finally, the groups that exchanged paragraphs get together to check and discuss the completed paragraphs.

¡Corona tiene las ofertas más locas del verano!

30% 40% 50%

La tienda más elegante de la ciudad con precios increíbles y con la tarjeta de crédito más conveniente del mercado.

JÓVENES	NIÑOS
Bluejeans chicos y chicas **PACOS** Americano. Tradicional Ahora: $9.000 el par **30% de rebaja**	Vestido de niña **GIRASOL** Tallas de la 2 a la 12. De cuadros y rayas Ahora: $8.625 **30% de rebaja**
Suéteres **CARAMELO** Algodón y lana. Colores blanco, gris y negro Antes: $10.500 **Ahora: $6.825**	Pantalón deportivo de niño **MILÁN** Tallas de la 4 a la 16 Ahora: $13.500 **30% de rebaja**
Lentes de contacto **VISIÓN** Americano. Colores azul, verde y morado Antes: $15.000 el par **Ahora $10.000**	Zapatos de tenis **ACUARIO** Números del 20 al 25 Ahora: $15.000 el par **30% de rebaja**
Trajes de baño chicos y chicas **SUBMARINO** Microfibra. Todas las tallas Ahora: $12.500 **50% de rebaja**	Pantalones cortos **MACARENA** Talla mediana Ahora: $15.000 **30% de rebaja**
Gafas de sol **VISIÓN** Origen canadiense Antes: $23.000 **Ahora: $14.950**	Camisetas de algodón **POLO** Antes: $15.000 Ahora: $7.500 **50% de rebaja**

Por la compra de $40.000, puede llevar un regalo gratis.

- Un hermoso cinturón de señora
- Un par de calcetines
- Una corbata de seda
- Una bolsa para la playa
- Una mochila
- Unas medias

real *royal* liquidación *clearance sale* antes *before* regalos *gifts*

Después de leer

Completar

Complete this paragraph about the reading selection with the correct forms of words from the word bank.

falda	rebaja
dinero	verano
increíble	zapato
hacer juego	pantalón
almacén	tarjeta de crédito

En este anuncio de periódico el ___almacén___ Corona anuncia la liquidación de ___verano___ con grandes ___rebajas___ en todos los departamentos. Con muy poco ___dinero___ Ud. puede equipar a toda su familia. Si no tiene dinero en efectivo (*cash*), puede utilizar su ___tarjeta de crédito___ y pagar luego. Para el caballero con gustos refinados, hay ___zapatos___ importados de París y Roma. La señora elegante puede encontrar blusas de seda que ___hacen juego___ con todo tipo de ___pantalones/faldas___ o ___faldas/pantalones___. Los precios de esta liquidación son realmente ___increíbles___.

¿Cierto o falso?

Indicate whether each statement is **cierto** or **falso**. Correct the false statements.

1. Hay ropa de algodón para jóvenes.
   Cierto.
2. La ropa interior tiene una rebaja del 30%.
   Falso. Tiene una rebaja del 40%.
3. El almacén Corona tiene un departamento de zapatos.
   Cierto.
4. Normalmente las sandalias cuestan $22.000 el par.
   Falso. Normalmente cuestan $24.000.

Preguntas

Contesta las preguntas en español.

1. Imagina que vas a ir a la tienda Corona. ¿Qué departamentos vas a visitar? ¿el departamento de ropa para señoras, el departamento de ropa para caballeros...?
2. ¿Qué vas a buscar en Corona?
3. ¿Hay tiendas similares a la tienda Corona en tu pueblo o ciudad? ¿Cómo se llaman? ¿Tienen muchas gangas?

TEACHING OPTIONS

TPR Write items of clothing on slips of paper. Divide the class into two teams. Have a member of one team draw a slip. That team member pantomimes putting on the item of clothing. The other team guesses what it is. Give points for correct answers. The team with the most points wins.

Variación léxica Ask Spanish speakers to tell the class phrases they use to ask the price of items. Ex: **¿Cuánto sale? ¿Cuánto vale? ¿Cuánto cuesta? ¿A qué precio se vende? ¿Qué precio tiene?**

Game Ask students to work in pairs to play a game of **Diez preguntas**. Partner A thinks of an item of clothing. Partner B asks questions and guesses the name of the item. Partner A keeps track of the number of questions and guesses. Allow partners to ask a total of ten questions and attempt to guess three times before moving on to the next item. The pair with the fewest questions overall wins.

Después de leer

Completar

Warm-Up/Present Have students quickly review the lesson vocabulary on pages 170–171 before they do this activity. Check responses by going over the paragraph with the whole class. Ask volunteers to read aloud each sentence, one at a time, filling in the blanks with a word from the word bank. Make sure that students understand the meaning of **dinero en efectivo** and **el caballero de gustos refinados.**

Suggestion This activity is also appropriate for small groups of students to do in class if you have not assigned it as homework. Ask groups to work together to complete each sentence in the paragraph. Check responses with the whole class.

¿Cierto o falso?

Suggestion Ask students to work together in pairs to use cognates and context clues to determine whether each statement is **cierto** or **falso**. When pairs are finished, go over the answers to Items 1–4 orally with the whole class.

Expand You may present these as Items 5–8. **5. Las camisetas Polo no tienen una rebaja grande. (Falso. Tienen una rebaja del 50%.) 6. Hay regalos gratis con compras de $40.000. (Cierto.) 7. El almacén Corona está cerrado los domingos. (Falso. El almacén Corona está abierta de 10:00 a 14:00 los domingos.) 8. Se puede conseguir lentes de contacto verdes y moradas en rebaja. (Cierto.)**

Preguntas

Suggestion Ask the questions of the whole class. Ask volunteers to answer orally or to write their answers on the board.

Section Goals

In **Escritura** students will:
- conduct an interview
- integrate vocabulary and structures taught in Lesson 6 into a written report
- report on an interview

Tema

Present Tell students that they may interview another member of their class or they may interview a Spanish-speaking student they know. Tell them that they may want to take notes as they conduct the interview, but they can also tape record it so they can check their notes and transcribe exact words later. Tell them that they should brainstorm ample questions in Spanish. They might want to work with a classmate they are not going to interview to brainstorm the questions. You may wish to introduce terms such as **entrevista, entrevistar, diálogo,** and **citas** as you present the activity.

Estrategia

Present Model how to answer questions in an interview by playing the role of an interviewee. Have students be interviewers, asking you the questions on page 192. Allow recording so students can transcribe the interview. Then choose volunteers to report orally on the interview, either transcribing the interview verbatim, summarizing it, or summarizing it and quoting you occasionally.

Assignment Have students prepare **Ideas y organización** and **Primer borrador** as homework.

Comentario

Present Go over questions **a–e** with the whole class so peer readers understand their task. Then have pairs of students exchange reports. Allow five minutes for reading and comments. Allow five minutes for discussing comments.

Continued on page 193.

Escritura

Estrategia

How to report an interview

There are several ways to prepare a written report about an interview. For example, you can transcribe the interview verbatim, you can simply summarize it, or you can summarize it but quote the speakers occasionally. In any event, the report should begin with an interesting title and a brief introduction, which may include the five W's (*what, where, when, who, why*) and the H (*how*) of the interview. The report should end with an interesting conclusion. Note that when you transcribe dialogue in Spanish, you should pay careful attention to format and punctuation.

Writing dialogue in Spanish

- If you are transcribing an interview verbatim, you can use speakers' names to indicate a change of speaker.

CARMELA ¿Qué compraste? ¿Encontraste muchas gangas?

ROBERTO Sí, muchas. Compré un suéter, una camisa y dos corbatas. Y tú, ¿qué compraste?

CARMELA Una blusa y una falda muy bonitas. ¿Cuánto costó tu camisa?

ROBERTO Sólo diez dólares. ¿Cuánto costó tu blusa?

CARMELA Veinte dólares.

- You can also use a dash (*raya*) to mark the beginning of each speaker's words.

—¿Qué compraste?
—Un suéter y una camisa muy bonitos. Y tú,¿encontraste muchas gangas?
—Sí... compré dos blusas, tres camisetas y un par de zapatos.
—¡A ver!

Tema

Escribe un informe

Write a report for the school newspaper about an interview you conducted with a student about his or her shopping habits and clothing preferences. First, brainstorm a list of interview questions. Then conduct the interview using the questions below as a guide, but feel free to ask other questions as they occur to you.

Examples of questions:

- ¿Cuándo vas de compras?
- ¿Adónde vas de compras?
- ¿Con quién vas de compras?
- ¿Qué tiendas, almacenes o centros comerciales prefieres?
- ¿Compras ropa de catálogos o por el Internet?
- ¿Prefieres comprar ropa cara o barata? ¿Por qué? ¿Te gusta buscar gangas?
- ¿Qué ropa llevas cuando vas a clase?
- ¿Qué ropa llevas cuando sales a bailar?
- ¿Qué ropa llevas cuando practicas un deporte?
- ¿Cuáles son tus colores favoritos? ¿Compras mucha ropa de esos colores?
- ¿Compras ropa para tu familia o para tus amigos/as?

TEACHING OPTIONS

Proofreading Activity Copy the following interview questions and answers containing mistakes onto the board or a transparency as a proofreading activity to do with the whole class.

1. **Este blusa me costó veinte dólores y esta veinticinco.**
2. **Luis no creó que los pantalones cuestaron sólo treinta dólares.**
3. **Ayer buscé gangas en el almacén Corona pero no encuentré nada interestante.**
4. **¿Cuál prefieres, éste sombrero elegante pero caro o aquello sombrero barato?**
5. **No compré me nada ayer pero pensé comprar un par de bluejeans hoy.**
6. **El dependiente quiere le vender los zapatos caros pero mi tío busca aquéllas en rebaja.**

Plan de escritura

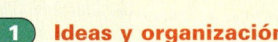

1 Ideas y organización

First, brainstorm a title for the report as well as ideas for how to introduce and present the information. Then use an idea map to help you organize your ideas, taking into account the variety of question words your interview answers. Finally, develop an outline for your report, organizing the interview questions in a logical order.

2 Primer borrador

Using your idea map and outline from **Ideas y organización,** write the rough draft of your report. Be sure that you have included an interesting introduction and conclusion.

3 Comentario

Exchange papers with a classmate and comment on each other's work using the questions below as a guide. Begin by mentioning one or two points that you like about the person's report, such as the title, the introduction, the conclusion, or the questions the interviewer asked.

a. Does the title capture your interest?
b. Are the introduction and conclusion adequate?
c. Is the report organized in a logical fashion?
d. Do you have suggestions for making the report more interesting?
e. Do you see spelling or grammatical errors?

4 Redacción

Revise your first draft, keeping in mind your classmate's comments. Also incorporate any new ideas or information you may have. Before handing in the final version, review your work using these guidelines:

a. Underline each verb and make sure that it agrees with the subject and that you have used the correct tense.
b. Check the gender and number of each article, noun, and adjective.
c. Circle the object pronouns and verify that you have used the correct form.
d. Check your spelling and punctuation, consulting your **Anotaciones para mejorar la escritura.**

5 Evaluación y progreso

Working in groups of four, share your papers. Give the title "best" or "most" to each paper on the basis of its strongest points. For example, "best use of Spanish," "most interesting questions," etc. After your instructor returns your paper, review the comments and corrections. Note the most important issues on your **Anotaciones para mejorar la escritura** list in your **carpeta.**

Assignment Have students prepare **Redacción** as homework. Ask them to rewrite their drafts incorporating the peer comments and following the directions in **Redacción**. Tell them to prepare a clean copy of their final draft to hand in.

Evaluación y progreso Give groups fifteen minutes to exchange and comment on the final drafts of their reports. Then have students hand them in to you.

Writing Sample Here is a sample report on an interview that would constitute superior writing achievement.

¡Cómo conseguir una ganga!

Roberto Álvarez habló con Gloria Becerra sobre cómo buscar las gangas. A ver cómo Gloria encuentra gangas fabulosas.

RA: Gloria, tú compras muchas cosas por precios muy bajos. ¿Cómo lo haces?
GB: Voy a los mercados al aire libre y las tiendas de centros comerciales.
RA: ¿Te gusta regatear?
GB: Sí, me gusta mucho. Y voy a las tiendas cuando hay liquidaciones. Siempre hay gangas.
RA: ¿Cómo sabes de las liquidaciones?
GB: Voy de compras muchas veces por mes. También leo el periódico y escucho la radio.
RA: Gracias, Gloria. ¿Puedo ir de compras con usted?
GB: ¡Sí, vamos!

Después de esta entrevista, el periodista salió para el centro comercial Soles con Gloria Becerra. ¡A ver las rebajas!

EVALUATION: Informe

Criteria	Scale
Content	1 2 3 4 5
Organization	1 2 3 4 5
Accuracy	1 2 3 4 5
Creativity	1 2 3 4 5

Scoring	
Excellent	18–20 points
Good	14–17 points
Satisfactory	10–13 points
Unsatisfactory	< 10 points

Section Goals
In **Escuchar** students will:
- listen for specific linguistic clues in oral sentences
- answer questions based on a recorded conversation

Instructional Resource
Student Cassette/CD

Preparación
Warm-up Ask students to look at the photo of Marisol and Alicia and predict what they are talking about.

Estrategia
Script **1. Acabamos de explorar la ciudad y encontramos unos monumentos fenomenales. 2. Estoy haciendo las maletas. 3. Carmen y Alejandro decidieron ir a un restaurante. 4. Mi familia y yo vamos a ir a la playa.**

Assignment Have students do the activities in **Ahora escucha** and **Comprensión** as homework. Verify the responses to **Ahora escucha** with the whole class and go over **¿Cierto o falso?** and **Identificar** by reading each question aloud and calling on different students to answer.

Ahora escucha
Script
Marisol: Oye, Alicia, ¿qué estás haciendo?
Alicia: Estudiando no más. ¿Qué hay de nuevo?
Marisol: Acabo de comprarme esos pantalones que andaba buscando.
Alicia: ¿Los encontraste en el centro comercial? ¿Y cuánto te costaron?
Marisol: Míralos. ¿Te gustan? En el almacén Melo tienen tremenda rebaja. Como estaban baratos me compré una blusa también. Es de cuadros pero creo que hace juego con los pantalones por el color rojo. ¿Qué piensas?
Alicia: Es de los mismos colores que la falda y la blusa que llevaste cuando fuimos al cine anoche. La verdad es que te quedan muy bien esos colores. ¿No encontraste unos zapatos y un cinturón para completar el juego?
Marisol: No lo digas ni de chiste. Mi tarjeta de crédito está que no aguanta más. Y trabajé poco la semana pasada. ¡Acabo de gastar todo el dinero para la semana!
Alicia: ¡Ay, chica! Fui al centro comercial el mes pasado y encontré unos zapatos muy, pero muy de moda. Muy caros... pero buenos. No me los compré porque no los tenían en mi número. Voy a comprarlos cuando lleguen más.... el vendedor me va a llamar.
Marisol: Ajá... ¿Y va a invitarte a salir con él?
Alicia:¡Ay! ¡No seas así! Ven, vamos al café. Te ves muy bien y no hay que gastar eso aquí.
Marisol: De acuerdo. Vamos.

Escuchar

NATIONAL communication STANDARDS

Preparación

Based on the photograph at right, what do you think Marisol has recently done? What do you think Marisol and Alicia are talking about? What else can you guess about their conversation from the visual clues in the photograph?

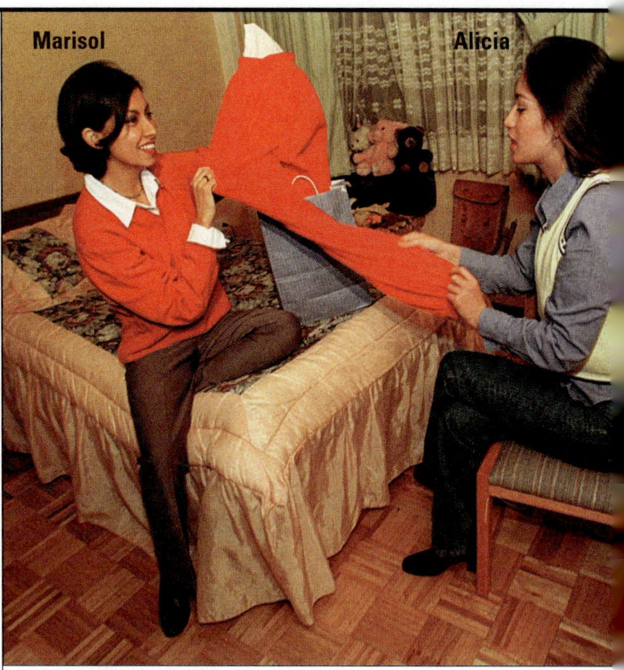

Estrategia
Listening for linguistic cues

You can enhance your listening comprehension by listening for specific linguistic cues. For example, if you listen for the endings of conjugated verbs, or for familiar constructions, such as **acabar de** + [*infinitive*] or **ir a** + [*infinitive*], you can find out whether an event already took place, is taking place now, or will take place in the future. Verb endings also give clues about who is participating in the action. To practice listening for linguistic cues, you will now listen to four sentences. As you listen, note whether each sentence refers to a past, present, or future action. Also jot down the subject of each sentence.

Ahora escucha

Now you are going to hear Marisol and Alicia's conversation. Make a list of the clothing items that each person mentions. Then put a check mark after the item if the person actually purchased it.

Marisol	Alicia
1. pantalones ✓	1. falda
2. blusa ✓	2. blusa
3. ______	3. zapatos
4. ______	4. cinturón

recursos
R SCASS./CD Lección 6

Comprensión

¿Cierto o falso?

Indicate whether each statement is **cierto** or **falso**. Then correct the false statements.

1. Marisol y Alicia acaban de ir de compras juntas (*together*). Falso. Marisol acaba de ir de compras.
2. Marisol va a comprar unos pantalones y una blusa mañana. Falso. Marisol ya los compró.
3. Marisol compró una blusa de cuadros. Cierto.
4. Alicia compró unos zapatos nuevos hoy. Falso. Alicia va a comprar unos zapatos nuevos.
5. Alicia y Marisol van a ir al café. Cierto.
6. Marisol gastó todo su dinero para la semana en ropa nueva. Cierto.

Preguntas

Discuss the following questions with a classmate. Be sure to explain your answers. Answers will vary.

1. ¿Crees que Alicia y Marisol son buenas amigas? ¿Por qué?
2. ¿Cuál de las dos estudiantes parece (*seems*) ser más ahorradora (*frugal*)? ¿Por qué?
3. ¿Crees que a Alicia le gusta la ropa que Marisol compró?
4. ¿Crees que la moda (*fashion*) es importante para Alicia? ¿Para Marisol? ¿Por qué?
5. ¿Es importante para ti estar a la moda? ¿Por qué?

communication cultures connections communities (National Standards)

Proyecto

Prepara un plan de negocios

Imagine that you are opening a store in Miami that will cater to customers of Cuban heritage. In order to get a start-up loan, you have to write and present your business plan to the bank.

1 Prepara el plan

Develop a business plan to present your idea to your banker. Using the research tools found in **Recursos para la investigación,** choose a location in Miami for your store. You should also choose the products you are going to sell and select a name that will appeal to your clientele. Your business plan might include these elements:

- The name and location of the store
- A visual presentation of your products
- The prices of your products and your expected profits
- An explanation of why you think your store will be successful

2 Presenta la información

You are meeting with your banker to summarize your business plan. Greet him or her in a formal, businesslike manner. Explain your business plan to the banker. You may want to show photographs or drawings of products and explain why the products will sell. Ask your banker for his or her reaction to your plan.

negocios *business*

recursos para la investigación

Internet Palabras clave: Miami, Cuban, stores, business	**Comunidad** Students, faculty members, and residents of your community who are of Cuban heritage or who are from Miami
Biblioteca Almanacs, newspapers, magazines	**Otros recursos** Maps of Cuba or books about Cuba that may suggest a name for the store

Section Goals

In **Proyecto** students will:

- use Spanish as they carry out research and interact with the wider world
- write and present a business plan for a store in Miami to cater to Cuban customers

Before Assigning Proyecto Students will need approximately a week to complete the project, so at the beginning of that time period, have them open their books to page 195 and glance over **Proyecto**. Explain that they are going to write a business plan (**plan de negocios)** to acquire a bank loan (**préstamo bancario**) and present the plan to the bank.

Assignment Have students read page 195 and follow directions in **Prepara el plan** to complete their business plan.

Prepara un plan de negocios

Suggestions

- Students may acquire templates for business plans from local offices of the Small Business Administration or SCORE (Service Corps of Retired Executives), or download them from www.sba.gov, www.score.org, or other business-related sites on the Internet.
- Remind students that they should address business contacts with **Uds.** forms.
- Background music such as Afro-Cuban selections can add to the appeal of the presentation.
- Students may wish to seek advice from marketing professionals in the community when thinking about a business name and a product line.
- You may wish to set aside sufficient class time to do a few presentations at a time until all students have had a chance to present.

EVALUATION: Plan de negocios

Criteria	Scale
Content	1 2 3 4
Organization	1 2 3 4
Accuracy	1 2 3 4
Oral Presentation	1 2 3 4
Creativity	1 2 3 4

Scoring	
Excellent	18–20 points
Good	14–17 points
Satisfactory	10–13 points
Unsatisfactory	< 10 points

Section Goals

In **Panorama**, students will read about the geography, culture, and economy of Cuba.

Instructional Resources
Student Activities Manual: Workbook, 69–70
Transparency 30

Cuba

Before Presenting Panorama Ask students to look at the map or project **Transparency 30.** Model the pronunciation of the labeled features. Ask volunteers read the captions on each call-out. Then discuss the call-out photos with the class.

Assignment Have students read **Panorama** and write out the anwers to the questions in **¿Qué aprendiste?** on page 197 as homework.

The Affective Dimension Some students may have strong feelings about Cuba. Ask your students to discuss their feelings.

Present Ask volunteers to read each section of **El país en cifras.** After reading about **La Habana Vieja**, if possible, show students illustrations of this part of the city. See *National Geographic en Español*, June 1999, pages 36–45 for dramatic photos.

Draw attention to the design and colors of the Cuban flag. Compare the Cuban flag to the Puerto Rican flag (page 166). Explain that Puerto Rico and Cuba, the last Spanish colonies in the western hemisphere, both gained their independence from Spain in 1898 in part through the intervention of the United States.

Increíble pero cierto Due to the patterns of evolution and adaptation common to islands, Cuba has many examples of unique flora and fauna. Students may wish to research other examples.

Cuba

NATIONAL STANDARDS connections cultures

El país en cifras

- **Área:** 110.860 km² (42.803 millas²), *aproximadamente el área de Pensilvania*
- **Población:** 11.275.000
- **Capital:** La Habana—2.278.000

La Habana Vieja fue declarada Patrimonio Cultural de la Humanidad por la UNESCO en 1982. Este distrito es uno de los lugares más fascinantes de Cuba. En La Plaza de Armas, se puede visitar el majestuoso Palacio de Capitanes Generales, que ahora es un museo. En la calle Obispo, frecuentada por el autor Ernest Hemingway, hay hermosos cafés, clubes nocturnos y tiendas elegantes.

- **Ciudades principales:** Santiago de Cuba—446.000; Camagüey—294.000; Holguín—242.000; Guantánamo—208.000

SOURCE: Population Division, UN Secrelariat

- **Moneda:** peso cubano
- **Idiomas:** español (oficial)

Bandera de Cuba

Cubanos célebres

- Carlos Finlay, doctor y científico (1833-1915)
- José Martí, poeta (1853-1895)
- Fidel Castro, primer ministro, jefe de las fuerzas armadas (1926-)
- Zoe Valdés, escritora (1959-)

fue declarada *was declared* Patrimonio *Heritage* calle *street* liviano *light* tira de chicle *stick of gum* colibrí *hummingbird* abeja *bee* sino *but* ave *bird* miden *measure* apenas *just*

Famoso cabaret El Tropicana de la Habana

Fortaleza El Morro

Playa en Santiago de Cuba

Vista aérea de campos de caña de azúcar

recursos

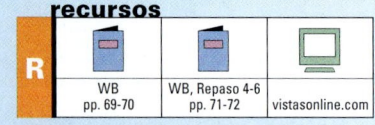

R	WB pp. 69-70	WB, Repaso 4-6 pp. 71-72	vistasonline.com

¡Increíble pero cierto!

Más corto y liviano que una tira de chicle, el colibrí abeja de Cuba no es sólo el más pequeño de las 320 especies de colibrí, sino también el ave más pequeña del mundo. Menores que muchos insectos, estas aves minúsculas miden apenas 5 centímetros y pesan sólo 1,95 gramos.

TEACHING OPTIONS

Variación léxica An item of clothing that you will see everywhere if you visit Cuba (or any of the other countries bordering the Caribbean) is the **guayabera**. A loose-fitting, short-sleeved shirt made of natural fibers, the **guayabera** is perfect for hot, humid climates. **Guayaberas** generally have large pockets and may be decorated with embroidery. They are worn open at the neck and never tucked in.

Extra Practice Introduce students to two stanzas of José Martí's poem **Versos sencillos**. Some students may recognize these as verses from the song **Guantanamera**.

Yo soy un hombre sincero
de donde crece la palma;
Y, antes de morirme, quiero
echar mis versos del alma.

Yo vengo de todas partes,
y hacia todas partes voy;
arte soy entre las artes;
en los montes montes soy.

Baile • **Ballet Nacional de Cuba**

La bailarina Alicia Alonso fundó el Ballet Nacional de Cuba en 1948, después de convertirse en una estrella internacional en el Ballet de Nueva York y en Broadway. El Ballet Nacional de Cuba es famoso en todo el mundo por su creatividad y perfección técnica.

Economía • **La caña de azúcar y el tabaco**

La caña de azúcar es el producto agrícola más cultivado de la isla y su exportación es muy importante para la economía del país. El tabaco, que se usa para fabricar los famosos cigarros cubanos, es otro cultivo de mucha importancia.

Historia • **Los taínos**

Los taínos eran una de las tres tribus indígenas que vivían en la isla cuando llegaron los españoles en el siglo XV. Los taínos también vivían en Puerto Rico, la República Dominicana, Haití, Trinidad, Jamaica y partes de las Bahamas y la Florida. Muchos taínos huyeron a las montañas para escaparse de los españoles; sus descendientes todavía viven en la región.

Música • **Celia Cruz**

La cantante Celia Cruz es considerada la reina de la música salsa. Su carrera empezó en Cuba en los años cincuenta. Aunque Cruz salió de Cuba en 1960, prefiere cantar en español. Su forma personal de cantar atrae a oyentes de todo el mundo. Cruz ganó un *Grammy* en 1990.

¿Qué aprendiste? Responde a las preguntas con una frase completa.

1. ¿Quién es el líder del gobierno de Cuba? El líder de Cuba es Fidel Castro.
2. ¿Dónde está la calle Obispo? La calle Obispo está en la Habana Vieja.
3. ¿Qué autor está asociado con la Habana Vieja? Ernest Hemingway está asociado con la Habana Vieja.
4. ¿Por qué es famoso el Ballet Nacional de Cuba? Es famoso por su creatividad y perfección técnica.
5. ¿Cuáles son los dos cultivos más importantes para la economía cubana? Los cultivos más importantes son la caña de azúcar y el tabaco.
6. ¿Qué fabrican los cubanos con el tabaco? Los cubanos fabrican cigarros.
7. ¿Cuándo empezó Celia Cruz su carrera musical? Empezó su carrera en los años cincuenta.

Conexión Internet Investiga estos temas en el sitio **www.vistasonline.com.**

1. Busca información sobre un(a) cubano/a célebre. ¿Por qué es célebre? ¿Qué hace? ¿Todavía vive en Cuba?
2. Busca información sobre una de las ciudades principales de Cuba. ¿Qué atracciones hay en esta ciudad?

estrella *star* en todo el mundo *throughout the world* caña *cane* cultivado *grown* se usa *is used* eran *were* cigarros *cigars* vivían *lived* huyeron *fled* reina *queen* Aunque *Although* atrae a oyentes *attracts listeners*

TEACHING OPTIONS

Variación léxica If you listen to Cuban music, it will not be long before you hear songs that mention beings with un-Spanish sounding names such as **Obatalá, Eleggúá,** and **Babaluayé**. These are divinities (**orichás**) of the Afro-Cuban religion which has its origins in Yoruba-speaking West Africa. Forcibly converted to Catholicism upon their arrival in Cuba, but left virtually uncatechized after that, the kidnapped Africans upon whose labor the Cuban economy was built developed a syncretized religion in which they worshiped the gods they had brought from Africa in the form of Catholic saints. Babaluayé, for instance, is worshiped as San Lázaro. Obatalá is Nuestra Señora de las Mercedes. Cuban popular music is deeply rooted in the songs and dances with which Afro-Cubans expressed their devotion to the Orichás. It is not surprising then that these gods should be so frequently invoked in this music.

Ballet Nacional de Cuba Although the **Ballet Nacional de Cuba** specializes in classical dance, Cuban popular dances (**habanera, mambo, rumba**) have gained world wide popularity. Students can interview parents or others to see what they remember about previous Cuban dance crazes.

La caña y el tabaco The collapse of the Soviet bloc and the end of subsidies that sustained its economy dealt Cuba a blow. Since 1990, Cuba has been in **el período especial en tiempo de paz**. Government planners have decided to develop tourism, formerly seen as bourgeois and corrupting, as a means of gaining badly-needed foreign currency.

Los taínos The Taínos had a deep understanding of the use of native plants for medicinal purposes. Traditional Taíno healing arts have been preserved and handed down across generations in Cuba. Today, ethnobotanists are exploring this traditional knowledge as they search for modern medical resources.

Celia Cruz Bring in some of Celia Cruz's music for students to hear. Read song titles and make predictions about songs before listening to them, then confirm and revise predictions.

¿Qué aprendiste? Go over the questions and answers with students, making sure everyone understands unfamiliar words and what the correct answers are.

Assignment Have students do activites in **Student Activities Manual: Workbook,** pages 69–70.

Conexión Internet Students will find information about Cuba at **www.vistasonline.com,** as well as links to other sites that can help them in their research.

La ropa

el abrigo	*coat*
los bluejeans	*jeans*
la blusa	*blouse*
la bolsa	*purse; bag*
la bota	*boot*
el calcetín	*sock*
la camisa	*shirt*
la camiseta	*t-shirt*
la cartera	*wallet*
la chaqueta	*jacket*
el cinturón	*belt*
la corbata	*tie*
la falda	*skirt*
las gafas (de sol), las gafas (oscuras)	*(sun)glasses*
los guantes	*gloves*
el impermeable	*raincoat*
los lentes de contacto	*contact lenses*
los lentes (de sol)	*(sun)glasses*
las medias	*pantyhose*
los pantalones	*pants*
los pantalones cortos	*shorts*
la ropa	*clothing; clothes*
la ropa interior	*underwear*
la sandalia	*sandal*
el sombrero	*hat*
el suéter	*sweater*
el traje	*suit*
el traje (de baño)	*(bathing) suit*
el vestido	*dress*
los zapatos de tenis	*(tennis) shoes, sneakers*

Los colores

el color	*color*
amarillo/a	*yellow*
anaranjado/a	*orange*
azul	*blue*
blanco/a	*white*
gris	*gray*
marrón, café	*brown*
morado/a	*purple*
negro/a	*black*
rojo/a	*red*
rosado/a	*pink*
verde	*green*

Adjetivos

barato/a	*cheap*
bueno/a	*good*
cada	*each*
caro/a	*expensive*
corto/a	*short (in length)*
elegante	*elegant*
hermoso/a	*beautiful*
largo/a	*long (in length)*
loco/a	*crazy*
nuevo/a	*new*
otro/a	*other; another*
pobre	*poor*
rico/a	*rich*

Ir de compras

el almacén	*department store*
la caja	*cash register*
el centro comercial	*shopping mall*
el/la cliente/a	*customer*
el/la dependiente/a	*clerk*
el dinero	*money*
el mercado (al aire libre)	*(open-air) market*
el par	*pair*
el precio (fijo)	*(fixed; set) price*
la rebaja	*sale*
el regalo	*gift*
la tarjeta de crédito	*credit card*
la tienda	*shop; store*
el/la vendedor(a)	*salesperson*
costar (o:ue)	*to cost*
gastar	*to spend (money)*
hacer juego (con)	*to match (with)*
llevar	*to wear*
regatear	*to bargain*
usar	*to wear; to use*
vender	*to sell*

Palabras adicionales

acabar de (+ inf.)	*to have just done something*
anoche	*last night*
anteayer	*the day before yesterday*
ayer	*yesterday*
de repente	*suddenly*
desde	*from; since*
dos veces	*twice; two times*
pasado/a (*adj.*)	*last; past*
el año pasado	*last year*
prestar	*to lend; to loan*
una vez	*once; one time*
ya	*already*

Indirect object pronouns	*See page 182.*
Demonstrative adjectives and pronouns	*See page 186.*
Expresiones útiles	*See page 175.*

La rutina diaria

7

Communicative Goals

You will learn how to:

- **Describe your daily routine**
- **Talk about personal hygiene**
- **Reassure someone**

contextos

pages 200-203

- Daily routine
- Personal hygiene
- Time expressions

fotonovela

pages 204-207

Javier and Álex talk about their plans for the following morning. Javier explains that he doesn't like to wake up early because he usually stays up late. Álex promises to wake him up after his morning run.

estructura

pages 208-221

- Reflexive verbs
- Indefinite and negative words
- Preterite of **ser** and **ir**
- **Gustar** and verbs like **gustar**

adelante

pages 222-227

Lectura: Read an entry from Maribel's diary.
Escritura: Describe someone's daily routine.
Escuchar: Listen to an interview with a famous actor.
Proyecto: Create a travel itinerary.

panorama

pages 228-229

Featured Country: Perú

- Lima: capital of Perú
- The ruins of Machu Picchu
- Llamas and alpacas
- The mysterious Nazca lines

Lesson Goals

In **Lesson 7** students will be introduced to the following:

- terms for daily routines
- reflexive verbs
- adverbs of time
- indefinite and negative words
- preterite of **ser** and **ir**
- forms of **gustar** and verbs like **gustar**
- predicting content from the title
- sequencing events
- writing a description of a place
- listening for background information
- writing a tour itinerary
- cultural, geographic, and historical information about Peru

Lesson Preview

Have students look at the photo. Say: **El joven se mira. Se peina. Then ask: ¿Qué ropa lleva el joven? ¿Adónde va él? ¿Creen que se peina todos los días?**

INSTRUCTIONAL RESOURCES

Student Activities Manual: Workbook, 73–84
Student Activities Manual: Lab Manual, 255–260
Student Activities Manual: Video Activities, 339–340
Instructor's Resource Manual: Hojas de actividades, 12–16
Instructor's Resource Manual: Answer Keys
Tapescript/Videoscript
Overhead Transparencies, 31–32
Student Cassette/CD
Lab Cassette/CD
Video Program
CD-ROM
Website: **www.vistasonline.com**
Testing Program: Prueba A, Prueba B

Section Goals

In **Contextos**, students will learn and practice:
- vocabulary to talk about daily routines
- reflexive verbs to talk about daily routines
- adverbs of time

Instructional Resources
Student Activities Manual: Workbook, 73–74; Lab Manual, 255
Transparency 31
Student Cassette/CD

Before Presenting Contextos Introduce the active lesson vocabulary. Beginning in English, ask volunteers aobut their daily routine on weekdays. Ask: Who gets up early on Mondays? Write **levantarse por la mañana** on the board and explain that it means to get up in the morning. To a student who answers ask: **¿A qué hora te levantas por la mañana?** After the student has answered ask another student: **¿A qué hora se levanta ____ por la mañana?** Respond: **Sí, se levanta a las ____.** Write **acostarse (o:ue)** on the board and explain that it means to go to bed. Follow the same procedure as you did for **levantarse**. **Assignment** Have students study **Contextos** and do the exercises in **Práctica** as homework.

Present
- Briefly explain the concept of reflexive verbs and the pronoun **se**. Reflexives will only be used in the infinitive and third person forms until **Estructura 7.1.**
- Give students two minutes to review the scenes on pages 200–201. Then project Transparency 31 and have students refer to the scenes as you ask true-false statements about them. Have them correct false statements. Ex: **En la habitación por la noche hay una chica que se peina. (Cierto.)** and so forth.

La rutina diaria

En la habitación por la mañana

Más vocabulario

el baño, el cuarto de baño	*bathroom*
el champú	*shampoo*
el despertador	*alarm clock*
el jabón	*soap*
el maquillaje	*makeup*
la rutina diaria	*daily routine*
bañarse	*to bathe; to take a bath*
cepillarse el pelo	*to brush one's hair*
dormirse	*to go to sleep; to fall asleep*
lavarse la cara	*to wash one's face*
levantarse	*to get up*
maquillarse	*to put on makeup*
antes (de)	*before*
después	*afterwards; then*
después de	*after*
durante	*during*
entonces	*then*
luego	*then*
más tarde	*later*
por la mañana	*in the morning*
por la noche	*at night*
por la tarde	*in the afternoon; in the evening*
por último	*finally*

Variación léxica

afeitarse ⟷ rasurarse *(Méx., Amér. C.)*
ducha ⟷ la regadera *(Col., Méx., Venez.)*
ducharse ⟷ bañarse *(Amér. L.)*

recursos

R			
SCASS./CD Lección 7	WB pp. 73-74	LM p. 255	LCASS./CD Cass. 4A/CD4

Por la mañana

TEACHING OPTIONS

Game This game involves two groups of pairs and an impartial judge. You mime various actions associated with a daily routine. When they think they know what the action is, students raise their hands. The judge indicates which pair was first to raise a hand. The pair then has until the count of five to indicate the action (Ex: **Ud. se lava las manos**). Give each set of groups five actions, then let new groups participate.

Variación léxica Ask heritage speakers if they use some of the additional words in **Variación léxica** and if they know of other words used to describe daily routines that are not listed. You may want to point out that other words for *bedroom* include **la alcoba, el cuarto, el dormitorio,** and **la recámara**.

En la habitación por la noche

Por la noche

Práctica

1 Escuchar Escucha las frases (*sentences*) e indica si cada frase es **cierta** o **falsa,** según el dibujo.

1. falsa
2. cierta
3. falsa
4. cierta
5. falsa
6. falsa
7. falsa
8. cierta
9. falsa
10. cierta

2 Seleccionar Selecciona las palabras que no están relacionadas con su grupo.

1. lavabo • toalla • despertador • jabón despertador
2. manos • antes de • después de • por último manos
3. acostarse • jabón • despertarse • dormirse jabón
4. espejo • lavabo • despertador • entonces entonces
5. dormirse • toalla • vestirse • levantarse toalla
6. pelo • cara • manos • durante durante
7. espejo • champú • jabón espejo
8. maquillarse • vestirse • peinarse • dientes dientes
9. baño • dormirse • despertador • acostarse baño
10. ducharse • crema de afeitar • bañarse crema de afeitar

3 Identificar Con un(a) compañero/a, identifica las cosas que cada persona necesita. Sigue el modelo. Some answers will vary.

modelo
Jorge / lavarse la cara
Estudiante 1: *¿Qué necesita Jorge para lavarse la cara?*
Estudiante 2: *Necesita jabón y una toalla.*

1. Mariana /maquillarse ¿Qué necesita Mariana para maquillarse? Necesita maquillaje.
2. Gerardo / despertarse ¿Qué necesita Gerardo para despertarse? Necesita un despertador.
3. Celia / bañarse ¿Qué necesita Celia para bañarse? Necesita jabón y una toalla.
4. Gabriel / ducharse ¿Qué necesita Gabriel para ducharse? Necesita una ducha, una toalla y jabón.
5. Roberto / afeitarse ¿Qué necesita Roberto para afeitarse? Necesita crema de afeitar.
6. Sonia / lavarse el pelo ¿Qué necesita Sonia para lavarse el pelo? Necesita champú y una toalla.
7. Vanesa / lavarse las manos ¿Qué necesita Vanesa para lavarse las manos? Necesita jabón y una toalla.
8. Manuel / vestirse ¿Qué necesita Manuel para vestirse? Necesita su ropa/una camiseta/unos pantalones/etc.
9. Simón / acostarse ¿Qué necesita Simón para acostarse? Necesita una cama.
10. Daniela / lavarse la cara ¿Qué necesita Daniela para lavarse la cara? Necesita jabón y una toalla.

TEACHING OPTIONS

Pairs Have students write out three daily routine activities without showing them to their partner. The partner asks questions that contain adverbs of time in order to figure out what the action is. Ex: **—¿Es antes de o después de ducharse? —Antes de ducharse. —¿Es *levantarse*? —Sí.**

Small Groups Hand out strips of paper with verbs used to describe daily routines written on them. Small groups of students place them in the most logical order in which the actions occur. There may be more than one correct way of ordering the daily activities.

1 Present Have students check their answers by going over the tapescript questions with the whole class.

1 Tapescript **1. Hay dos despertadores en la habitación de las chicas. 2. Un chico se pone crema de afeitar en la cara. 3. Una de las chicas se ducha. 4. Uno de los chicos se afeita. 5. Hay una toalla en la habitación de las chicas. 6. Una de las chicas se maquilla. 7. Las chicas están en el baño. 8. Uno de los chicos se cepilla los dientes en el baño. 9. Uno de las chicos se viste. 10. Una de las chicas se despierta.**
Student Cassette/CD

1 Expand Go through the answers by reading the Tapescript statements. Students should correct the false statements.

2 Expand Go over answers quickly in class. After each answer, indicate why a particular item doesn't belong. (Students haven't yet learned the passive **se**. You may want to explain it so that they can indicate why items don't belong.) Ex: **El lavabo, la toalla y el jabón se usan para lavarse. El despertador se usa para despertarse**, and so forth.

3 Present Have students read directions. With another student, model pronunciation of model sentences. You may want to do this as a whole-class activity, giving different students the opportunity to ask and answer questions.

3 Expand If done in pairs, go over answers with the whole class.

3 Expand Have students make statements about the people's actions, then ask a question. Ex: **Jorge se lava la cara. ¿Qué necesita?**

4 Warm-up Before beginning the activity, read **Nota cultural** aloud with students. If you have personal experience with this type of schedule, discuss that briefly.

4 Expand After students have completed items, go over answers quickly in class.

4 Expand Ask students if Andrés' schedule represents that of a "typical" student. Ask: **Para el estudiante típico, ¿es normal despertarse a las seis y media de la mañana? ¿A qué hora se despiertan Uds.?** and so forth.

5 Expand Have pairs of students read their descriptions aloud. Cue descriptions by asking: **En el dibujo número uno, ¿qué hace Ángel?** and so forth.

5 Expand Ask brief comprehension questions about the actions in the drawings. Ex: **¿Quién se maquilla? (Lupe) ¿Quién se cepilla el pelo? (Ángel)** and so forth.

5 Suggestion If students ask, point out that in drawing number 7, **Ángel se mira en el espejo.** Reflexive pronouns and verbs will be formally presented in **Estructura 7.1**. For now it's enough just to explain that *he's looking at himself*, hence the use of the pronoun **se**.

4 Ordenar Pon (*Put*) esta historia (*story*) en orden.

a. Se afeita después de cepillarse los dientes. 4
b. Se acuesta a las once y media de la noche. 9
c. Por último se duerme. 10
d. Después de afeitarse, sale para las clases. 5
e. Asiste a todas sus clases y vuelve a su casa. 6
f. Andrés se despierta a las seis y media de la mañana. 1
g. Después de volver a casa, come un poco. Luego estudia en su habitación. 7
h. Se viste y entonces se cepilla los dientes. 3
i. Se cepilla los dientes antes de acostarse. 8
j. Se ducha antes de vestirse. 2

NOTA CULTURAL

In some Spanish-speaking countries, it is common to return home around 2 p.m. for lunch, the largest meal of the day. The workday often ends between 6 and 8 p.m.

5 La rutina diaria Con un(a) compañero/a, mira los dibujos y describe lo que hacen Ángel y Lupe.

1.

Ángel se afeita y mira la televisión.

2.

Lupe se maquilla y escucha la radio.

3.

Ángel se ducha y canta.

4.

Lupe se baña y lee.

5.

Ángel se lava la cara con jabón.

6.

Lupe se lava el pelo con champú en la ducha.

7.

Ángel se cepilla el pelo.

8.

Lupe se cepilla los dientes.

TEACHING OPTIONS

Extra Practice Name daily routine activities and have students give a list of all the words that they associate with each activity. They can be things, places, parts of the body, and so forth. Ex: **lavarse las manos: el jabón, el cuarto de baño, el agua, la toalla,** and so forth. How many associations can the class make for each activity?

Small Groups In groups of three or four, students think of a famous person or character and describe his or her daily routine. In their descriptions, students may use names of friends or family of the famous person or character. The rest of the class has to guess who is being described.

NATIONAL communication STANDARDS

Comunicación

6 **Tu mejor (*best*) amigo/a** Contesta estas preguntas sobre la rutina diaria de tu mejor amigo/a.

1. ¿A qué hora se levanta durante la semana?
2. ¿A qué hora se levanta los fines de semana?
3. ¿Prefiere levantarse tarde o temprano?
4. ¿Se ducha por la mañana, por la tarde o por la noche?
5. ¿Se afeita todos los días (*every day*)? ¿Tiene barba (*beard*) o bigote (*moustache*)?
6. ¿Se maquilla todos los días?
7. ¿Se cepilla el pelo antes de acostarse?
8. ¿Se lava las manos antes de comer?
9. ¿Se acuesta tarde o temprano durante la semana?
10. ¿A qué hora se acuesta los fines de semana?

7 **Rutinas diarias** Trabajen en parejas (*pairs*) para describir la rutina diaria de dos o tres de estas personas. Pueden usar palabras de la lista. Answers will vary.

primero	antes de	temprano
luego	después	después de
entonces	tarde	por último
durante el día		

1. un(a) profesor(a) de la universidad
2. un(a) turista
3. un hombre o una mujer de negocios (*businessman/woman*)
4. un vigilante (*night watchman*)
5. un(a) jubilado/a (*retired person*)
6. el presidente de los Estados Unidos
7. un niño de cuatro años
8. la reina (*queen*) Sofía de España

NOTA CULTURAL

Queen Sofía of Spain, wife of King Juan Carlos, was born in Greece and is related to the oldest royal families of Europe —the Czars of Russia and Queen Victoria of England.

8 **Compañeros de cuarto** En grupos, comparen las rutinas diarias de sus compañeros/as de cuarto o de los miembros de sus familias. Answers will vary.

modelo

Estudiante 1: Mi compañera de cuarto, Sofía, se despierta muy temprano, ¡a las cinco de la mañana! Sale a correr y después se ducha. ¿Y sus compañeros de cuarto?

Estudiante 2: Yo vivo con mi hermano, Miguel, y él también se despierta muy temprano, pero lo hace para estudiar antes de ir a sus clases.

Estudiante 3: Javier, mi esposo, se despierta a las diez y cuarto. Se viste rápidamente (*quickly*) y no se ducha hasta la tarde, porque tiene clase a las once. Se acuesta muy tarde. ¿A qué hora se acuesta Sofía? ¿Y Miguel?

TEACHING OPTIONS

Small Groups In groups of three or four, students act out a brief skit. The situation: they are all roommates who are trying to get ready for their morning classes at the same time. The problem: there's only one bathroom in the house or apartment. You may wish for the class to vote for the most original or funniest skit.

Heritage Speakers Have heritage speakers write paragraphs in which they describe their daily routine when living with their family. If they're not talking about their current situation, be sure that they keep their narration in the historical present. Students then present their paragraphs orally to the class. Verify comprehension by asking other students to relate aspects of the speaker's description.

6 Present You may want to have pairs ask and answer these questions. Students may write down their answers.

6 Expand Have volunteers describe their best friend's daily routine to the rest of the class. If students wrote down their answers, have them give their descriptions in the form of a brief narration. Ex: **Mi mejor amigo ____ se levanta a las ocho durante la semana. Los fines de semana se levanta a las diez,** and so forth.

7 Warm-up Before presenting the activity, read the **Nota cultural** with the class. It pertains to Item 8.

7 Present Have pairs of students select a couple of the people listed in the activity and brainstorm daily activities for each. Then have students place them in sequential order. You may also wish for students to write out their descriptions for them to hand in later.

7 Expand Ask volunteers to read their descriptions of the people they chose. Ask other pairs who chose the same people if their descriptions are similar and how they differ.

8 Warm-up Have students read the directions. Model pronunciation of the **Modelo** with two students.

8 Expand Ask volunteers to share their descriptions with the rest of the class. Ask other students comprehension questions to verify what they heard. Ex: ____, **¿a qué hora se despierta el esposo de ____?**

Assignment Have students do the activities in **Student Activities Manual: Workbook,** pages 73–74.

Section goals

In **Fotonovela** students will:

- receive comprehensible input from free-flowing discourse
- learn functional phrases that preview lesson grammatical structures

Instructional Resources
Student Activities Manual: Video Activities 339–340
Video Program (Start: 00:34:37)

Video Synopsis Javier returns from the market and shows Álex the sweater he bought. Álex and Javier discuss the fact that they have to get up early the next day. Álex, an early riser, agrees to wake Javier up after his morning run. Don Francisco comes by to remind them that the bus will leave at 8:30 a.m. tomorrow.

Before Presenting Fotonovela Have your students skim the **Fotonovela** for the gist and write down their impressions. Ask for a few volunteers to share their impressions with the class. **Assignment** Have students study **Fotonovela** and **Expresiones útiles** as homework.

Warm-up Write the sentence **Describe tu rutina diaria** on the board and have the class guess its meaning. Then use this sentence to ask individual students to talk about their daily routines.

Present Work quickly through the **Expresiones útiles** by pronouncing each expression and having the class repeat after you. Check comprehension of this active vocabulary by asking **¿Cómo se dice...?** questions. Ex: **¿Cómo se dice** *Everything is under control?*

Continued on page 205.

¡Jamás me levanto temprano!

NATIONAL STANDARDS communication cultures

Álex y Javier hablan de sus rutinas diarias.

PERSONAJES

DON FRANCISCO

ÁLEX

JAVIER

JAVIER Hola, Álex. ¿Qué estás haciendo?

ÁLEX Nada... sólo estoy leyendo mi correo electrónico. ¿Adónde fueron?

JAVIER Inés y yo fuimos a un mercado. Fue muy divertido. Mira, compré este suéter. Me encanta. No fue barato pero es chévere, ¿no?

ÁLEX Sí, es ideal para las montañas.

JAVIER ¡Qué interesantes son los mercados al aire libre! Me gustaría volver pero ya es tarde. Oye, Álex, sabes que mañana tenemos que levantarnos temprano.

ÁLEX Ningún problema.

JAVIER ¡Increíble! ¡Álex, el superhombre!

ÁLEX Oye, Javier, ¿por qué no puedes levantarte temprano?

JAVIER Es que por la noche no quiero dormir, sino dibujar y escuchar música. Por eso es difícil despertarme por la mañana.

JAVIER El autobús no sale hasta las ocho y media. ¿Vas a levantarte mañana a las seis también?

ÁLEX No, pero tengo que levantarme a las siete menos cuarto porque voy a correr.

JAVIER Ah, ya... ¿Puedes despertarme después de correr?

ÁLEX Éste es el plan para mañana. Me levanto a las siete menos cuarto y corro por treinta minutos. Vuelvo, me ducho, me visto y a las siete y media te despierto. ¿De acuerdo?

JAVIER ¡Absolutamente ninguna objeción!

recursos

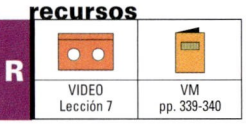

R	VIDEO Lección 7	VM pp. 339-340

TEACHING OPTIONS

Video Tips General suggestions for using video clips in the classroom can be found on page IAE-13 of the **Instructor's Annotated Edition.**

¡Jamás me levanto temprano! Play the **¡Jamás me levanto temprano!** segment of this video module for the first time and have your students jot down notes on what they see and hear. Then have them work in groups of three to compare notes and prepare a brief plot summary. Play the segment again. Have students return to their groups to refine their summaries. Finally, discuss the plot with the entire class and correct any errors of fact or sequencing.

4

JAVIER ¿Seguro? Pues yo jamás me levanto temprano. Nunca oigo el despertador cuando estoy en casa y mi mamá se enoja mucho.

ÁLEX Tranquilo, Javier. Yo tengo una solución.

5

ÁLEX Cuando estoy en casa en la ciudad de México, siempre me despierto a las seis en punto. Me ducho en cinco minutos y luego me cepillo los dientes. Después me afeito, me visto y ¡listo! ¡Me voy!

9

DON FRANCISCO Hola, chicos. Mañana salimos temprano, a las ocho y media... ni un minuto antes ni un minuto después.

ÁLEX No se preocupe, don Francisco. Todo está bajo control.

DON FRANCISCO Bueno, pues, hasta mañana.

10

DON FRANCISCO ¡Ay, los estudiantes! Siempre se acuestan tarde. ¡Qué vida!

Enfoque cultural El horario de la vida diaria

En muchos países hispanos, el horario de la vida diaria es muy diferente al de EE.UU. En estos países, muchas personas trabajan de las ocho de la mañana a las dos de la tarde. A las dos salen del trabajo para ir a almorzar (*eat lunch*). Vuelven a las cuatro y salen a las seis de la tarde. Muchos utilizan esas dos horas para almorzar en casa con sus familias y, a veces (*sometimes*), dormir una siesta. También es común que la gente cene (*eats dinner*) más tarde que en los EE.UU.

Expresiones útiles

Telling where you went

- **¿Adónde fuiste/fue Ud.?**
  Where did you go?
- **Fui a un mercado.**
  I went to a market.
- **¿Adónde fueron Uds.?**
  Where did you go?
- **Fuimos a un mercado. Fue muy divertido.**
  We went to a market.
  It was a lot of fun.

Talking about morning routine

- **(Jamás) me levanto temprano/tarde.**
  I (never) get up early/late.
- **Nunca oigo el despertador.**
  I never hear the alarm clock.
- **Es difícil/fácil despertarme.**
  It's hard/easy to wake up.
- **Cuando estoy en casa, siempre me despierto a las seis en punto.**
  When I'm home, I always wake up at six on the dot.
- **Me ducho y luego me cepillo los dientes.**
  I take a shower and then I brush my teeth.
- **Después me afeito y me visto.**
  Afterwards, I shave and get dressed.

Reassuring someone

- **Ningún problema.**
  No problem.
- **No te preocupes.**
  Don't worry.
- **Todo está bajo control.**
  Everything is under control.
- **Tranquilo.**
  Stay calm.; Be cool. (lit. Quiet.)

Additional vocabulary

- **sino**
  but (rather)

Have students volunteer to read individual parts of the **Fotonovela** episode aloud. Then have students get together in groups of three to act out the episode. Circulate around the class and model correct pronunciation as needed. Have one or two groups present the episode to the class. See ideas for using the video in **Teaching Options**, page 204.

Comprehension Check Check comprehension of the **Fotonovela** episode by doing Activity 1, **¿Cierto o falso?**, page 206, orally with the whole class.

Suggestion Have students look at the **Expresiones útiles**. Draw the class's attention to the verb forms **fui, fuiste, fue,** and **fuimos**. Explain that these are forms of the verbs **ir** and **ser** in the preterite tense. The context always makes clear which is meant. Then point out the phrases **me levanto, me despierto, me ducho, me cepillo, me afeito,** and **No te preocupes**. Tell the class that these are forms of the reflexive verbs **levantarse, despertarse, ducharse, cepillarse, afeitarse,** and **preocuparse**. Also, point out the words **siempre, nunca, jamás,** and **ningún**. Explain that **siempre** is called an indefinite word and that the other three are called negative words. Tell your students that they will learn more about all of these concepts in the **Estructura** section of Lesson 7.

Assignment Have students do activities 2–4 in **Reacciona a la fotonovela**, page 206, as homework.

TEACHING OPTIONS

Enfoque cultural The two-hour "lunch" break (2:00 p.m. to 4:00 p.m.), which includes the day's largest meal and a period of rest afterward, is observed in many Spanish-speaking countries as the **siesta**. Explain to the class that although the **siesta** is part of the daily routine of many people in Spanish-speaking countries, the observance of this tradition is not universal. For example, when Spain entered the European Union, many Spanish businesspeople began to adjust their work schedules to mirror those of their counterparts in other European countries. Ask your students to discuss the custom of the **siesta** and its impact on businesses and on individual workers. Ask them if they think the **siesta** should be incorporated into the schedules of businesses in the United States, and why.

Reacciona a la fotonovela

1 Present This activity can be done either orally or in writing. It is suitable for whole-class work, group work, or pair work. Go over the answers with the whole class.

1 Expand Give these additional items to the class: **6. Javier siempre se despierta temprano. (Falso. Álex siempre se despierta temprano.) 7. Don Francisco cree que los estudiantes siempre se acuestan temprano. (Falso. Don Francisco cree que los estudiantes siempre se acuestan tarde.)**

2 Expand Give these additional items to the class: **7. Quiero volver al mercado pero no hay tiempo. (Javier) 8. Cuando estoy en casa, siempre me despierto muy temprano. (Álex)**

3 Warm-up Have your students quickly glance over the caption to video still 8, page 205, before doing this activity.

4 Possible response
S1: ¿Prefieres levantarte temprano o tarde?
S2: Prefiero levantarme tarde… muy tarde.
S1: ¿A qué hora te levantas durante la semana?
S2: A las siete. ¿Y tú?
S1: Siempre me levanto muy temprano… a las cinco y media.
S2: Y ¿a qué hora te acuestas?
S1: Siempre me acuesto temprano, a las diez o a las once. ¿Y tú?
S2: Yo prefiero acostarme a la medianoche.

Reacciona a la fotonovela

1 **¿Cierto o falso?** Indica si las siguientes oraciones (*sentences*) son ciertas o falsas. Corrige (*Correct*) las frases falsas.

1. Álex está mirando la televisión.
   Falso. Álex está leyendo su correo electrónico.
2. El suéter que Javier acaba de comprar es caro pero es muy bonito.
   Cierto.
3. Javier cree que el mercado es aburrido y no quiere volver.
   Falso. Javier piensa que el mercado es muy interesante.
4. El autobús va a salir mañana a las siete y media en punto.
   Falso. El autobús sale mañana a las ocho y media en punto.
5. A Javier le gusta mucho dibujar y escuchar música por la noche.
   Cierto.

2 **Identificar** Identifica quién puede decir las siguientes frases. Puedes usar cada nombre más de una vez.

1. ¡Ay, los estudiantes nunca se acuestan temprano! don Francisco
2. ¿El despertador? ¡Jamás lo oigo por la mañana! Javier
3. Es fácil despertarme temprano. Y sólo necesito cinco minutos para ducharme. Álex
4. Mañana vamos a salir a las ocho y media. Javier, don Francisco
5. Acabo de ir a un mercado fabuloso. Javier
6. No te preocupes. Tenemos todo bajo control para mañana. Álex

DON FRANCISCO

JAVIER

ÁLEX

3 **Ordenar** Ordena correctamente los planes que tiene Álex para mañana.

a. Voy a vestirme. 5
b. Voy a correr por media hora. 2
c. Voy a despertar a Javier a las siete y media. 6
d. Voy a volver a la habitación. 3
e. Voy a levantarme a las siete menos cuarto. 1
f. Voy a ducharme. 4

4 **Mi rutina** En parejas (*pairs*), preparen una conversación hablando de sus rutinas en la mañana y en la noche. Indiquen a qué horas hacen las actividades más importantes.
Answers will vary.

modelo

Estudiante 1: *¿Prefieres levantarte temprano o tarde?*
Estudiante 2: *Prefiero levantarme tarde… muy tarde.*
Estudiante 1: *¿A qué hora te levantas durante la semana?*
Estudiante 2: *A las once. ¿Y tú?*

¡LENGUA VIVA!
Remember that **en punto** means *on the dot*. If the group were instead leaving at *around seven thirty*, you would say **a eso de las siete y media**

CONSÚLTALO
Telling time To review telling time in Spanish, see Lesson 1, section 1.4, p. 22.

NATIONAL communication STANDARDS

TEACHING OPTIONS

Extra practice Have your students close their books. Then use the sentences from Activity 3, in the correct order, as a dictation activity. Read each sentence twice slowly to give students an opportunity to write. Then read them again at normal speed, without pausing, to allow students to correct any errors or fill in any gaps.

Small groups Have your students get together in groups of three to discuss and compare their daily routines. Tell your students to use as many of the words and expressions they have learned so far in this lesson as they can. Then ask for a few volunteers to describe the daily routine of one of their group members.

NATIONAL comparisons STANDARDS

Pronunciación

The consonants r and rr

ropa **rutina** **rico** **Ramón**

In Spanish, **r** has a strong trilled sound at the beginning of a word. No English words have a trill, but English speakers often produce a trill when they imitate the sound of a motor.

gustar **durante** **primero** **crema**

In any other position, **r** has a weak sound similar to the English *tt* in *better* or the English *dd* in *ladder*. In contrast to English, the tongue touches the roof of the mouth behind the teeth.

pizarra **corro** **marrón** **aburrido**

The letter **rr**, which only appears between vowels, always has a strong trilled sound.

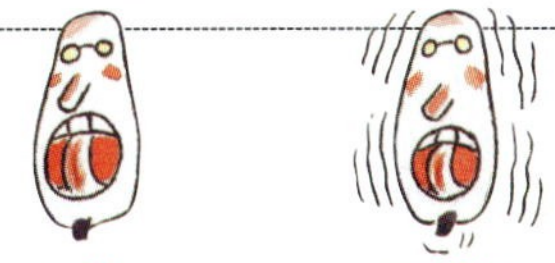

caro **carro** **pero** **perro**

Between vowels, the difference between the strong trilled **rr** and the weak **r** is very important, as a mispronunciation could lead to confusion between two different words.

Práctica Lee las palabras en voz alta, prestando (*paying*) atención a la pronunciación de la **r** y la **rr**.

1. Perú
2. Rosa
3. borrador
4. madre
5. comprar
6. favor
7. rubio
8. reloj
9. Arequipa
10. tarde
11. cerrar
12. despertador

Oraciones Lee las oraciones en voz alta, prestando atención a la pronunciación de la **r** y la **rr**.

1. Ramón Robles Ruiz es programador. Su esposa Rosaura es artista.
2. A Rosaura Robles le encanta regatear en el mercado.
3. Ramón nunca regatea... le aburre regatear.
4. Rosaura siempre compra cosas baratas.
5. Ramón no es rico pero prefiere comprar cosas muy caras.
6. ¡El martes Ramón compró un carro nuevo!

Refranes Lee en voz alta los refranes, prestando atención a la **r** y a la **rr**.

Perro que ladra no muerde.[1]

No se ganó Zamora en una hora.[2]

1 The dog's bark is worse than its bite.
2 Rome wasn't built in a day.

recursos

R	SCASS./CD Lección 7	LM p. 256	LCASS./CD Cass. 4A/CD4

Section Goals

In **Pronunciación** students will be introduced to the pronunciation of the letters **r** and **rr**.

Instructional Resources
Student Activities Manual: Lab Manual, 256
Student Cassette/CD

Present

- Explain that **r** is trilled at the beginning of a word, and that there are no words that have a trill in American English. Model the pronunciation of **ropa, rutina, rico,** and **Ramón** and have the class repeat.
- Point out that in any other position, **r** is pronounced much like the *tt* in better, with the tongue touching the roof of the mouth behind the teeth. Write the words **gustar, durante, primero,** and **crema** on the board and ask for a volunteer to pronounce each word.
- Draw attention to the fact that **rr** always has a strong strilled sound and that it only appears between vowels. Pronounce the words **pizarra, corro, marrón,** and **aburrido** and have the class repeat.
- Have your students close their books. To help students discriminate between **r** and **rr**, pronounce the minimal pairs **caro/carro** and **pero/perro**. Write each word on the board as you pronounce it. Then pronounce each pair several times in random order, pausing after each for students to say which you pronounced. Ex: **caro, carro, caro, carro, carro, carro,** and so forth.

Práctica/Oraciones/Refranes Model the pronunciation of each word or sentence, having students repeat after you.

TEACHING OPTIONS

Extra Practice Write the names of a few Peruvian cities on the board and ask for a volunteer to pronounce each name. Ex: **Huaraz, Cajamarca, Trujillo, Puerto Maldonado, Cerro de Pasco, Piura**. Then write the names of a few Peruvian literary figures on the board and repeat the process. Ex: **Ricardo Palma, Ciro Alegría, Mario Vargas Llosa, César Vallejo**.

Small Groups Have students work in small groups and take turns reading aloud sentences from the **Fotonovela** on pages 204–205, focusing on the correct pronunciation of **r** and **rr**. Circulate around the class and model the correct pronunciation of each letter as necessary.

Section Goals

In **Estructura 7.1** students will learn:
- the conjugation of reflexive verbs
- common reflexive verbs

Instructional Resources
Student Activities Manual: Workbook, 75–76; Lab Manual, 257
Hoja de actividades 12–13

Before Presenting Estructura 7.1 Model first-person singular reflexives by talking about yourself. Ex: Write **levantarse** on the board. Say: **Me levanto muy temprano. Me levanto a las cinco y media de la mañana.** Then model the second person by asking questions with a verb you have already used in the first person. Ex: **Y tú, ____, ¿a que hora te levantas? (Me levanto a las ocho.)** After a few exchanges, introduce the third person by making statements and asking questions about what a student has told you. Ex: **¡____ se levanta a las ocho! Se levanta muy tarde, ¿no? (Sí, se levanta tarde.)** Tell students they are now going to learn a number of common reflexive verbs like **levantarse**. **Assignment** Have students study **Estructura 7.1** and prepare the exercises on pages 209–210 as homework.

Present Write the paradigm of **lavarse** on the board and model its pronunciation. Clarify the possible meanings of **Se lava las manos** and **Se lavan las manos.**

Remind students of the rules for the placement of object pronuns in sentences, including sentences with infinitives and the present progressive. Draw attention to the written accent that appears on gerunds when a reflexive pronoun is attached.

Continued on page 209.

7.1 Reflexive verbs

NATIONAL STANDARDS comparisons

ANTE TODO A reflexive verb is used to indicate that the subject does something to or for himself or herself. In other words, it "reflects" the action of the verb back to the subject. Reflexive verbs always use reflexive pronouns.

SUBJECT	REFLEXIVE VERB
Joaquín	se **ducha** por la mañana.

Reflexive verbs

lavarse *(to wash oneself)*

SINGULAR FORMS	yo	**me lavo**	*I wash (myself)*
	tú	**te lavas**	*you wash (yourself)*
	Ud.	**se lava**	*you wash (yourself)*
	él / ella	**se lava**	*he/she/washes (himself/herself)*
PLURAL FORMS	nosotros/as	**nos lavamos**	*we wash (ourselves)*
	vosotros/as	**os laváis**	*you wash (yourselves)*
	Uds.	**se lavan**	*you wash (yourselves)*
	ellos/ellas	**se lavan**	*they wash (themselves)*

▶ The pronoun **–se** attached to an infinitive identifies it as a reflexive verb, as in **lavarse** and **levantarse**. Reflexive verbs can be used in any tense.

INFINITIVE	PRESENT TENSE	PRETERITE
levantarse	**me levanto**	**me levanté**

Me ducho, me cepillo los dientes, me visto y, ¡listo!

¡Ay, los estudiantes! ¡Siempre se acuestan tarde!

▶ Reflexive pronouns follow the same rules for placement as object pronouns. They generally appear before a conjugated verb. With infinitives and present participles, they may be placed before the verb or attached to the infinitive or present participle.

Ellos **se** van a vestir.
Ellos van a vestir**se**.
They are going to get dressed.

Nos estamos lavando las manos.
Estamos lavándo**nos** las manos.
We are washing our hands.

¡ATENCIÓN!

Except for **se**, reflexive pronouns have the same forms as direct and indirect object pronouns.

• • •

Se is used for both singular and plural subjects —there is no individual plural form.

• • •

Reflexive pronouns always agree with the subject of the verb, not the object:

Me lavo las manos.

¡ATENCIÓN!

When a reflexive pronoun is attached to a present participle, an accent mark is added to maintain the original stress:

bañando → bañ**á**ndo**se**
afeitando → afeit**á**ndo**se**

• • •

Parts of the body or clothing are generally not referred to with possessives, but with the definite article.

La niña se quitó **los** zapatos.

Necesito cepillarme **los** dientes.

TEACHING OPTIONS

Extra Practice To provide oral practice with reflexive verbs, create sentences that follow the pattern of the sentences in the examples. Say the sentence, have students repeat it, then say a different subject, varying the gender and number. Have students then say the sentence with the new subject, changing pronouns and verbs as necessary.

Heritage Speakers Have Spanish speakers describe daily routines in their home communities. Encourage them to use their own linguistic variation of words presented in this lesson. Ex: **regarse (e:ie)**, **pintarse**. Have Spanish speakers work together to compare and contrast activities as well as lexical variations.

Common reflexive verbs

acordarse (de) (o:ue)	*to remember*	**levantarse**	*to get up*
acostarse (o:ue)	*to go to bed*	**llamarse**	*to be called / named*
afeitarse	*to shave*	**maquillarse**	*to put on one's makeup*
bañarse	*to bathe; to take a bath*	**peinarse**	*to comb one's hair*
cepillarse	*to brush*	**ponerse**	*to put on*
despedirse (de) (e:i)	*to say good-bye (to)*	**ponerse** + *adj.*	*to become* + adj.
despertarse (e:ie)	*to wake up*	**preocuparse**	*to worry (about)*
dormirse (o:ue)	*to go to sleep*	**probarse**	*to try on*
ducharse	*to shower*	**quedarse**	*to stay; to remain*
enojarse (con)	*to get angry (with)*	**quitarse**	*to take off*
irse	*to go away; to leave*	**sentarse** (e:ie)	*to sit down*
lavarse	*to wash (oneself)*	**sentirse** (e:ie)	*to feel*
		vestirse (e:i)	*to get dressed*

¡ATENCIÓN!

You have already learned several adjectives that can be used with **ponerse** when it means *to become*: **alegre, cómodo/a, contento/a, elegante, guapo/a, nervioso/a, rojo/a, serio/a, triste.**

COMPARE & CONTRAST

Unlike English, most verbs in Spanish can be reflexive or non-reflexive. If the verb acts upon the subject, the reflexive form is used. If the verb acts upon something other than the subject, the non-reflexive form is used. Compare these sentences.

Lola **lava** los platos.

Lola **se lava** la cara.

As the preceding sentences show, reflexive verbs sometimes have different meanings than their non-reflexive counterparts. For example, **lavar** means *to wash,* while **lavarse** means *to wash oneself, to wash up.*

¡INTÉNTALO! Indica el presente de los verbos reflexivos que siguen. El primero de cada columna ya está conjugado.

despertarse

1. Mis hermanos se despiertan tarde.
2. Tú te despiertas tarde.
3. Nosotros nos despertamos tarde.
4. Benito se despierta tarde.
5. Yo me despierto tarde.
6. Uds. se despiertan tarde.
7. Ella se despierta tarde.
8. Adriana y yo nos despertamos tarde.
9. Ellos se despiertan tarde.

ponerse

1. Él se pone una chaqueta.
2. Yo me pongo una chaqueta.
3. Ud. se pone una chaqueta.
4. Nosotras nos ponemos una chaqueta.
5. Las niñas se ponen una chaqueta.
6. Tú te pones una chaqueta.
7. El botones se pone una chaqueta.
8. Beatriz y Gil se ponen una chaqueta.
9. Uds. se ponen una chaqueta.

To practice reflexive verbs in preterite and periphrastic future (**ir a** + *infinitive*) talk and ask questions about what you and your students did yesterday and plan to do tomorrow. Ex: **Ayer me levanté a las cinco y media, claro, pero el sábado me voy a levantar a las seis y media.**

Common reflexive verbs

Present Go through the list of common reflexive verbs asking students to answer closed-answer questions that use reflexive verbs. Ex: **¿Te acuerdas de tu primer día en la universidad? (Sí, me acuerdo) ¿Los niños pequeños se acuestan tarde o temprano? (Se acuestan temprano.)**

Give special attention to **irse, ponerse** (two meanings), and the discrimination of **sentarse** and **sentirse**.

Consolidate by completing **¡Inténtalo!** as a class.

Compare and Contrast

Present Compare and contrast reflexive and non-reflexive verbs by giving examples. **Me lavo cada mañana. Nunca lavo el gato. Me pongo un suéter. Pongo la radio.**

Then ask volunteers to translate sentences such as: *He wakes the children at seven. He wakes up at seven.*

Close Have students open to **Fotonovela**, pages 206–207. Ask short questions about the characters using reflexive verbs from this lesson. Have students answer with complete sentences. Ex: **¿A qué hora tienen que levantarse los estudiantes mañana? ¿Qué hace Álex después de ducharse cuando está en casa en México? ¿Por qué Javier jamás se despierta temprano?**

TEACHING OPTIONS

TPR Model gestures for a few of the reflexive verbs. Ex: **acordarse** (tap side of head), **acostarse** (lay head on folded hands) and so forth. Have students stand. Begin by practicing as a class using only the **nosotros** form, saying an expression at random (**Nos lavamos la cara.**). Then vary the verb forms and point to a student who should perform an appropriate gesture. Keep the pace rapid. Vary by pointing to more than one student (**Uds. se peinan.**).

Pairs Have students write a short account of their own daily routine. Then have pairs compare and contrast their routines using a Venn Diagram (see **Escritura 8**). Have the pair write one of their names on the left circle and one on the right circle, writing **Los/Las dos** where the circles overlap. Then have them list their activities in the appropriate location. Remember verbs under **Los/Las dos** should be in the first-person plural.

1 Warm-up Briefly review reflexive verbs by comparing and contrasting weekday and weekend routines. Ex: **¿Te levantas temprano o tarde los sábados? ¿Te acuestas temprano o tarde los domingos?**

1 Present Model the activity by doing the **Modelo** for the class. Then change the subject to form a new sentence. Ex: **Nosotros. (Nos despertamos a las cinco.)**

1 Expand To practice the formal register, pose certain situations to the students and have them tell you what you are going to do. Ex: **Acabo de comer y estoy en el cuarto de baño. (Ud. va cepillarse los dientes.) Hace frío y nieva, pero necesito salir. (Ud. va a ponerse el abrigo.) Acabo de levantarme. (Ud. va a lavarse la cara.)**

1 Suggestion Call students' attention to the **Nota cultural**. Add any anecdote from your own experience in Spanish-speaking countries.

2 Present Review reflexive and non-reflexive forms by asking general questions using both forms. Ex: **¿Dónde nos lavamos? ¿Dónde lavamos el coche? ¿Dónde nos pone la comida? ¿Cuándo nos ponemos el abrigo?**

2 Suggestion Point out the different words for car. Expand the explanation to include other meanings of **coche (coach)** and **carro (cart)**.

3 Present Ask a volunteer to describe the first picture. Ex: **El joven no se pone los zapatos. ¿Qué hace?**

3 Expand Expand the exercise with illustrations from your picture file.

Práctica

1 Nuestra rutina La familia de Blanca sigue la misma rutina todos los días. Según (*According to*) Blanca, ¿qué hacen ellos?

modelo
mamá / despertarse a las 5:00
Mamá se despierta a las cinco.

1. Roberto y yo / levantarse a las 7:00 Roberto y yo nos levantamos a las siete.
2. papá / ducharse primero y / luego afeitarse Papá se ducha primero y luego se afeita.
3. yo / lavarse la cara y / vestirse antes de tomar café Yo me lavo la cara y me visto antes de tomar café.
4. mamá / peinarse y / luego maquillarse Mamá se peina y luego se maquilla.
5. todos / sentarse a la mesa para comer Todos se sientan a la mesa para comer.
6. Roberto / cepillarse los dientes después de comer Roberto se cepilla los dientes después de comer.
7. yo / ponerse el abrigo antes de salir Yo me pongo el abrigo antes de salir.
8. nosotros / despedirse de mamá Nosotros nos despedimos de mamá.

NOTA CULTURAL

Having coffee with breakfast is as common in Spanish-speaking countries as it is in the U.S. In fact, it is not unusual for children to have a cup of **café con leche** (*coffee with milk*) with their breakfasts served before heading off to school. Coffee served in Spanish-speaking countries is generally stronger than in North America, and decaffeinated coffee is not as common.

2 Completar Selecciona el verbo apropiado y completa la frase con la forma correcta.

1. Tú __lavaste__ (lavar / lavarse) el auto ayer, ¿no?
2. Nosotros no __nos acordamos__ (acordar / acordarse) de comprar champú y jabón.
3. Anoche ellos __acostaron__ (acostar / acostarse) a los niños a las ocho.
4. Yo no __me siento__ (sentir / sentirse) bien hoy.
5. Mis amigos siempre __se visten__ (vestir / vestirse) con ropa muy cara.
6. ¿__Se probaron / Se prueban__ (probar / probarse) Uds. la ropa antes de comprarla?
7. Ud. __se preocupa / se preocupó__ (preocupar / preocuparse) mucho por su hijo, ¿no?
8. En general __me afeito__ (afeitar / afeitarse) yo mismo, pero hoy el barbero (*barber*) __me afeita / me afeitó__ (afeitar / afeitarse).

¡LENGUA VIVA!

In Spain a car is called a **coche** while in many parts of Latin America it is known as a **carro.** Although you'll be understood using any of these terms, using **auto (automóvil)** will surely get you where you want to go.

3 Describir Mira los dibujos y describe lo que estas personas hacen.

1. El joven se quita los zapatos.

2. Carmen se duerme.

3. Juan se pone la camiseta.

4. Ellos se despiden.

5. Estrella se maquilla.

6. Toni se enoja con el perro.

TEACHING OPTIONS

Game Each group of four writes the daily routine of a celebrity or cartoon character. Groups take turns reading their descriptions aloud without giving the celebrity's name. The groups that guess the subject win a point while any group able to fool the rest of the class gets two points.

Extra Practice Have students figure out the morning schedule of the Ramírez family. Say: **El Sr. Ramírez se afeita antes de Alberto, pero después de Rafael. La Sra. Ramírez es la primera a ducharse y Montse es la última. Lolita se peina cuando sale su padre del cuarto de baño y antes de entrar uno de sus hermanos. Nuria se maquilla después de Lolita, pero no inmediatamente después. (Primero se ducha la Sra. Ramírez. Después de afeita Rafael seguido por el Sr. Ramírez. Entonces se peina Lolita. Alberto se afeita y después Nuria se maquilla. Finalmente Montse se ducha.)**

Comunicación

4 **Encuesta** Tu profesor(a) va a darte (*to give you*) una hoja de actividades. Camina por la clase y pregúntales a tus compañeros cuándo sienten las emociones que se mencionan en la lista. Entrevista por los menos (*at least*) a dos personas y anota sus respuestas. Tienes que estar preparado/a para informar a la clase de los resultados de tu encuesta. Answers will vary.

Preguntas	Nombres	Ocasiones
1. Sentirse aburrido/a		
2. Sentirse avergonzado/a		
3. Sentirse cansado/a		
4. Enojarse		
5. Sentirse feliz		
6. Ponerse nervioso/a		
7. Preocuparse		
8. Sentirse triste		

5 **Charadas** En grupos, jueguen a las charadas. Cada (*Each*) persona debe pensar en dos frases con verbos reflexivos. La primera persona que adivina (*guesses*) la charada dramatiza la próxima (*next*) charada. Answers will vary.

6 **Debate** En grupos, discutan (*discuss*) este tema (*topic*): ¿Quiénes necesitan más tiempo para arreglarse (*to get ready*) antes de salir, los hombres o las mujeres? Hagan una lista de las razones (*reasons*) que tienen para defender sus ideas e informen a la clase. Answers will vary.

Síntesis

7 **Entrevista** Tu profesor(a) va a darte (*to give you*) una hoja de actividades. Completa el horario de la hoja con las actividades que hiciste (*you did*) anoche. Después de completar el horario, trabajen en parejas, comparen las actividades que hicieron y tomen notas de lo que (*what*) hizo tu compañero/a. Answers will vary.

4 Present Model the activity by giving a personal example. Ex: **Me siento nervioso cuando estoy en un avión.** Then distribute copies of **Hoja de actividades 12.**

4 Expand Ask students to suggest ways of alleviating the negative feelings listed in the **encuesta** by finishing sentences. Ex: **Cuando me siento aburrido/a... (corro.). Cuando me siento avergonzado... (pienso en cosas felices.). Cuando me siento triste... (salgo a ver una película cómica.)**

5 Present Model the activity for the students, choosing one of the feelings included in Activity 4. Ex: **Se enoja**—Clench your hands and grit your teeth.

6 Present Briefly go over some of the things men and women do to get ready to go out. Ex: **Las mujeres se maquillan. Los hombres se afeitan.** Then ask the students to indicate their opinion on the question, and divide the class into groups accordingly.

7 Present After you have distributed **Hoja de actividades 13** to the class, make sure everyone understands the instructions by modeling one or two sentences. Ex: **Anoche salí a una fiesta a las siete. Regresé a casa a la una. En la fiesta bailé, comí y hablé con mis amigos.**

7 Expand Have pairs team up in groups of four. After teams have compared their answers, have them make a pictorial representation on the board. The rest of the groups will guess the activities by the pictures.

Assignment Have students prepare the activities in **Student Activities Manual: Workbook,** pages 75–76.

TEACHING OPTIONS

Game Divide the class into groups of 3. Each member should tell his/her group about the strangest, funniest, or most exciting thing that s/he has done. The group chooses one account and writes it on a slip of paper. For each group's turn, you read the description aloud. The class has two minutes to ask group members questions to find out who did the activity. The groups that guess win 1 point; a group that is able to fool the class wins 2 points.

Extra Practice Prepare descriptions of five celebrities, using reflexives. Write their names randomly on the board. Then read the descriptions as a dictation, having students match each to a name. Ex: **Su deporte es el tenis, pero no juega en competiciones ahora. Se pone nervioso en los torneos y se enoja con frecuencia. (John McEnroe)**

Section Goals

In **Estructura 7.2** students will learn:
- high-frequency indefinite and negative words
- the placement and use of indefinite and negative words

Instructional Resources
Student Activities Manual: Workbook, 77–78; Lab Manual, 258
Hoja de actividades 14

Before presenting Estructura 7.2 Write **alguien** and **nadie** on the board and ask questions about what students are wearing today. Ex: **Hoy alguien lleva una camiseta de Puerto Rico. ¿Quién es? ¿Alguien lleva pantalones anaranjados? No, nadie los lleva.** Tell students they are now going to learn other important indefinite and negative words in Spanish. **Assignment** Have students study **Estructura 7.2** and prepare the activities on pages 213–214 as homework.

Present Use your picture file to compare and contrast indefinite and negative words. Ex: **La señora de la foto tiene algo en las manos. ¿El señor tiene algo en las manos también? No, el señor no tiene nada en las manos.** As you work through each word pair, write it on the board.

Explain the two ways of forming negative sentences in Spanish. To consolidate, ask volunteers questions about their activities since the last class and reiterate the answers using the targeted structures. Ex: **¿Quién compró algo nuevo? Sólo dos personas. Nadie más compró algo nuevo. Los otros no compraron nada nuevo. Yo no compré nada nuevo tampoco.**

7.2 Indefinite and negative words

NATIONAL comparisons STANDARDS

ANTE TODO Indefinite words refer to people and things that are not specific, for example, *someone* or *something*. Negative words deny the existence of people and things or contradict statements, for instance, *no one* or *nothing*. As the following chart shows, Spanish indefinite words have corresponding negative words, which are opposite in meaning.

Indefinite and negative words

Indefinite words		Negative words	
algo	*something; anything*	**nada**	*nothing; not anything*
alguien	*someone; somebody; anyone*	**nadie**	*no one; nobody; not anyone*
alguno/a(s), algún	*some; any*	**ninguno/a, ningún**	*no; none; not any*
o... o	*either... or*	**ni... ni**	*neither... nor*
siempre	*always*	**nunca, jamás**	*never*
también	*also; too*	**tampoco**	*neither; not either*

▶ There are two ways to form negative sentences in Spanish. You can place the negative word before the verb, or you can place **no** before the verb and the negative word after the verb.

Nadie se levantó temprano.
No one got up early.

No se levantó nadie temprano.
No one got up early.

Ellos **nunca se enojan**.
They never get angry.

Ellos **no se enojan nunca**.
They never get angry.

Yo siempre me despierto a las seis en punto. ¿Y tú?

Pues yo jamás me levanto temprano. Nunca oigo el despertador.

¡ATENCIÓN!

Before a masculine, singular noun, **alguno** and **ninguno** are shortened to **algún** and **ningún**.

—¿Tienen Uds. algún amigo peruano?
—No, no tenemos ningún amigo peruano.

• • •

Alguno/a, algunos/as are not used in the same way English uses *some* or *any*. Often, **algún** is used where *a* would be used in English. Also, in negative sentences, **ninguno** always replaces **alguno**.

▶ Because they refer to people, **alguien** and **nadie** are often used with the personal **a**. The personal **a** is also used before **alguno/a, algunos/as,** and **ninguno/a** when these words refer to people and they are the direct object of the verb.

—Perdón, señor, ¿busca Ud. **a alguien**?
—No, gracias, señorita, no busco **a nadie**.

—Tomás, ¿buscas **a alguno** de tus hermanos?
—No, mamá, no busco **a ninguno**.

TEACHING OPTIONS

Extra Practice Write sentences like the following on the board and have the students complete them with an indefinite or negative word. Ex: **Los vegeterianos no comen carne ____ (nunca). Las madres ____ se preocupan por sus hijos (siempre). En las fiestas no es sociable, ____ (ni) baila ____ (ni) habla con ____ (nadie).**

Pairs Have students practice by taking turns giving one-word indefinite and negative word prompts and having the other respond in full sentences. Ex: S1: **siempre**. S2: **Siempre mando un mensaje electrónico a mi madre por la mañana.** S1: **tampoco** S2: **Yo no me levanto temprano tampoco.**

COMPARE & CONTRAST

In English, it is incorrect to use more than one negative word in a sentence. It is correct, however, to use indefinite words with negative words, because indefinite words are considered affirmative. In Spanish, however, sentences frequently contain two or more negative words. Compare the following Spanish and English sentences.

Nunca le escribo a **nadie**.
*I **never** write to **anyone**.*

No me preocupo por **nada nunca**.
*I do **not ever** worry about **anything**.*

As the preceding sentences show, once an English sentence contains one negative word (for example, *not* or *never*), no other negative word may be used. Instead, indefinite (or affirmative) words are used. In Spanish, however, once a sentence is negative, no other affirmative (that is, indefinite) word may be used. Instead, all indefinite ideas must be expressed in the negative.

▶ Although in Spanish **pero** and **sino** both mean *but*, they are not interchangeable. **Sino** is used when the first part of a sentence is negative and the second part contradicts it. In this context, **sino** means *but rather* or *on the contrary*. In all other cases, **pero** is used to mean *but*.

Los estudiantes no se acuestan temprano **sino** tarde.
*The students don't go to bed early, **but rather** late.*

Las toallas son caras, **pero** bonitas.
*The towels are expensive, **but** beautiful.*

María no habla francés **sino** español.
*Maria doesn't speak French, **but rather** Spanish.*

José es inteligente, **pero** no saca buenas notas.
*José is intelligent, **but** doesn't get good grades.*

¡INTÉNTALO! Cambia las siguientes frases para que sean negativas. La primera frase se da como ejemplo.

1. Siempre se viste bien.
   Nunca se viste bien.
   No se viste bien nunca.
2. Alguien se ducha.
   Nadie se ducha.
   No se ducha nadie.
3. Ellas van también.
   Ellas tampoco van.
   Ellas no van tampoco.
4. Alguien se pone nervioso.
   Nadie se pone nervioso.
   No se pone nervioso nadie.
5. Tú siempre te lavas las manos.
   Tú nunca / jamás te lavas las manos.
   Tú no te lavas las manos nunca / jamás.
6. Juan se afeita también.
   Juan tampoco se afeita.
   Juan no se afeita tampoco.
7. Voy a traer algo.
   No voy a traer nada.
8. Mis amigos viven en una residencia o en casa.
   Mis amigos no viven ni en una residencia ni en casa.
9. La profesora hace algo en su escritorio.
   La profesora no hace nada en su escritorio.
10. Tú y yo vamos al mercado.
    Ni tú ni yo vamos al mercado.
11. Tienen un espejo en su casa.
    No tienen ningún espejo en su casa.
12. Algunos niños se ponen el abrigo.
    Ningún niño se pone el abrigo.

TEACHING OPTIONS

Video Show the video again to give students more input containing indefinite and negative words. Stop the video where appropriate to discuss how these words are used.

Small Groups Give small groups five minutes to write a description of **Un/a señor/a muy, pero muy antipático/a.** Tell students to use as many indefinite and negative words as possible to describe what makes this person so unpleasant.

Suggestion Work through **¡Atención!** before continuing the presentation of **alguien** and **nadie**. Point out that the forms **algún** and **ningún** appear in the same situations where **un** rather than **uno** would be used.

Remind students that **alguien** and **nadie** are used with the personal **a**. Give further examples to consolidate the information presented in **¡Atención!**. Ex: **¿Buscas a algún compañero? No, no busco a ningún compañero.**

Compare and contrast

Present Give further examples of what is correct and incorrect in both languages. Ex: It is incorrect to say *I don't never do it,* but rather *I never do it.* In Spanish, it is correct to say **Nada tengo** or **No tengo nada**. But you will not be understood by Spanish speakers if you say **No tengo algo**. Point out that there is no limit to the negative words that can be strung in a sentence. Ex: **No hablo con nadie nunca de ningún problema, ni con mi familia ni con mis amigos.**

Elicit negative responses by asking questions whose answers will clearly be negative. Ex: **¿Alguien lleva zapatos de lunares? (No, nadie lleva zapatos de lunares.) ¿Alguien tiene una moto en la mochila? (No, nadie tiene ninguna moto.)**

Give examples of **pero** and **sino** using the seating of the students. Ex: **Jessica se sienta al lado de Will, pero no al lado de Janet. No se sienta a la izquierda de Will, sino a la derecha. Janet no se sienta al lado de la ventana, pero está cerca de la puerta,** and so forth.

Close Do **¡Inténtalo!** orally with the whole class.

1 Present Model the activity by reading the **Modelo** aloud and asking for a volunteer to explain why **sino,** and not **pero,** is used. Ask another volunteer to change the model so that **pero** would be the correct choice. Ex: **El examen es mañana/ va a ser muy fácil; El examen es mañana, pero va a ser muy fácil.**

1 Expand Have pairs of students work together to create four sentences following the model of Activity 1, two of which use **sino** and two **pero**. Have pairs "dehydrate" their sentences as in the model and exchange with another pair who will write the complete sentence.

2 Warm-up Review indefinite and negative words by using them in short sentences and asking volunteers to contradict your statement. Ex: **Tengo algo en la mano. (No, Ud. no tiene nada en la mano.) Veo a alguien en la puerta. (No, Ud. no ve a nadie en la puerta.)**

2 Present Use a picture from your picture file that shows a group of people involved in a specific activity. Then talk about the picture, modeling the types of constructions required in Activity 2. Ex: **Todos trabajan en la oficina, pero sólo algunos tienen computadora. No hay ningún problema.**

2 Expand After students have dramatized the conversation in pairs, ask for volunteers to summarize the information contained therein. **Ana María no encontró ningún regalo para Eliana. Tampoco vio a ninguna amiga en el centro comercial** and so forth.

Práctica

1 ¿Pero o sino? Forma frases usando **pero** o **sino.**

modelo

el examen no es hoy / mañana
El examen no es hoy sino mañana.

1. el niño no se despertó temprano / llegó puntual
El niño no se despertó temprano, pero llegó puntual.
2. Armando y yo no vamos a la playa / al campo
Armando y yo no vamos a la playa sino al campo.
3. Alfonso es inteligente / algunas veces es antipático
Alfonso es inteligente, pero algunas veces es antipático.
4. esos señores no son ecuatorianos / peruanos
Esos señores no son ecuatorianos sino peruanos.
5. no nos acordamos de comprar champú / compramos jabón
No nos acordamos de comprar champú, pero compramos jabón.
6. Emilia no es morena / rubia
Emilia no es morena sino rubia.
7. no quiero levantarme / tengo que ir a clase
No quiero levantarme, pero tengo que ir a clase.
8. no se acostaron tarde / temprano No se acostaron tarde sino temprano.

2 Completar Completa esta conversación. Usa expresiones negativas en tus respuestas. Luego, dramatiza la conversación con un(a) compañero/a. Answers will vary.

AURELIO Ana María, ¿encontraste algún regalo para Eliana?
ANA MARÍA No, no encontré ningún regalo/nada para Eliana.
AURELIO ¿Viste a algunas amigas en el centro comercial?
ANA MARÍA No, no vi a ninguna amiga/ninguna/nadie en el centro comercial.
AURELIO ¿Me llamó alguien?
ANA MARÍA No, nadie te llamó./No, no te llamó nadie.
AURELIO ¿Quieres ir al teatro o al cine esta noche?
ANA MARÍA No, no quiero ir ni al teatro ni al cine.
AURELIO ¿No quieres salir a comer?
ANA MARÍA No, no quiero salir a comer (tampoco).
AURELIO ¿Hay algo interesante en la televisión esta noche?
ANA MARÍA No, no hay nada interesante en la televisión.
AURELIO ¿Tienes algún problema?
ANA MARÍA No, no tengo ningún problema/ninguno.

TEACHING OPTIONS

Extra Practice Have students bring pairs of realia or pairs of pictures to class, such as two different hats or two pictures of different bicycles. They will compare and contrast these. Divide the class into groups of three and have each group select a pair of realia/pictures around which they will do a role-play. Remind them to use complex sentences and that all three members must participate in the presentation to the class.

Extra Practice To provide oral practice with indefinite and negative words, create prompts that follow the pattern of the sentences in Activity 1 and Activity 2. Say the first part of the sentence, have students repeat it, then finish the sentence. Ex: **Latisha no se viste de azul hoy, sino (de verde). Norman no llegó puntualmente a clase hoy, sino (tarde)** and so forth.

Comunicación

3 **Opiniones** Completa estas frases de una manera lógica. Luego, compara tus respuestas con las respuestas de un(a) compañero/a. Answers will vary.

1. Mi habitación es ________ pero ________.
2. Mis padres no son ________ sino ________.
3. Mi compañero/a no es ________ pero ________.
4. Por la noche no me gusta ________ pero ________.
5. Un(a) profesor(a) ideal no es ________ sino ________.
6. Mis amigos no son ________ pero ________.

4 **Quejas** (*Complaints*) Con un(a) compañero/a, haz (*make*) una lista de cinco quejas comunes (*common*) que tienen los estudiantes. Usa expresiones negativas. Answers will vary.

modelo
Nadie me entiende.

Ahora hagan (*make*) una lista de cinco quejas que los padres tienen de sus hijos.

modelo
Nunca limpian sus habitaciones.

5 **Anuncios** (*Ads*) Con un(a) compañero/a, mira estos anuncios. Luego, preparen su propio (*own*) anuncio usando expresiones afirmativas o negativas. La clase va a votar para decidir cuál es el anuncio más original o creativo. Answers will vary.

¡LENGUA VIVA!
When companies decide to advertise in foreign markets, they must be very careful not to rely on literal translations, since false cognates and unintended interpretations can become real problems. For example, the Chevy Nova did not sell in Spanish-speaking countries because **No va** means "It doesn't go."

Síntesis

6 **Encuesta** Tu profesor(a) te va a dar (*to give*) una hoja de actividades para hacer una encuesta. Circula por la clase y pídeles a tus compañeros que comparen las actividades que hacen durante los días de la semana con las que hacen durante los fines de semana. Toma nota de las respuestas. Answers will vary.

3 Present Model the activity by giving some personal examples using different subjects. Ex: **Mi hijo es inteligente, pero no le gusta estudiar. Mi amiga no es norteamericana, sino española.**

4 Present Model the activity by comparing and contrasting the complaints of young children and of adults. Ex: **Nunca puedo acostarme tarde./Nunca puedo acostarme temprano.**

4 Expand Divide the class into all-male and all-female groups. Then have each group make two different lists: **Quejas que tienen los hombres de las mujeres** and **Quejas que tienen las mujeres de los hombres.** After five minutes, compare and contrast the answers and perceptions.

5 Warm-up Ask volunteers questions about the two ads. Ex: **¿Para quién son estos regalos? ¿Qué día se celebra? ¿Es más interesante el anuncio de la derecha o él de la izquierda? ¿Por qué?**

6 Present Model one or two of the questions for the whole class. Then distribute copies of **Hoja de actividades 14** and have students circulate around the classroom to fill them out.

6 Expand Have students write five sentences using the information obtained through the **encuesta**. Ex: **Nadie va a la biblioteca durante el fin de semana, pero muchos vamos durante la semana. No estudiamos los sábados, sino los domingos.**

Assignment Have students do activities in **Student Activities Manual: Workbook**, pages 77–78.

TEACHING OPTIONS

Large group Write the names of four vacation spots on four slips of paper and post them in different corners of the room. Ask students to pick their vacation preference by going to one of the corners. Then, have each group produce five reasons for their choice as well as one complaint about each of the other places.

Extra Practice Have students complete the following cloze activity using **pero, sino,** and **tampoco: Cuando la gente va de compras en los países hispanos, no van a un centro comercial, ____ (sino) a tiendas locales. No hay grandes almacenes ____ (tampoco), ____ (sino) en las capitales grandes. Los mercados al aire libre sirven como puntos de reunión** (*meeting*) **para las señoras que hacen las compras domésticas.**

Section goals
In **Estructura 7.3** students will learn the preterite of **ser** and **ir**.

Instructional Resources
Student Activities Manual: Workbook, 79; Lab Manual, 259

Before Presenting Estructura 7.3 Model the preterite tense of **ser** and **ir** with the whole class by asking volunteers to answer questions such as: **¿Fuiste al cine el sábado pasado? ¿Cómo fue la película? ¿Fueron tus amigos y tú a alguna fiesta durante el fin de semana? ¿Fue agradable la fiesta? ¿Quiénes fueron?** Point out to students that both verbs share a common conjugation in the preterite tense. Tell them they are now going to learn to use these irregular forms. **Assignment** Have students study **Estructura 7.3** and prepare the activities on pages 216–217.

Present Contrast the present and preterite of **ser** and **ir** by saying pairs of sentences. Ex: **Anteayer fue sábado. Fui al supermercado el sábado. Ayer fue domingo. No fui al supermercado ayer. ¿Fueron Uds. al partido de fútbol el sábado? ¿Fue divertido el partido?** As you do so, write the verb forms in a paradigm on the board. When you have completed the paradigm, model the pronunciation of each form. Point out that, although **ser** and **ir** have the same form in the preterite, there is rarely any confusion about which is meant because context makes that clear.

Suggestion Review the information contained in **¡Atención!** Point out that students may find these verb forms accented in older texts.

Close As a class, do both columns of **¡Inténtalo!** orally.

7.3 Preterite of **ser** and **ir**

NATIONAL comparisons STANDARDS

ANTE TODO In Lesson 6, you learned how to form the preterite tense of regular **-ar**, **-er** and **-ir** verbs. The following chart contains the preterite forms of **ir** (*to go*) and **ser** (*to be*). Since the forms are irregular, you will need to memorize them.

Preterite of *ser* and *ir*

		ser (*to be*)	**ir** (*to go*)
SINGULAR FORMS	yo	**fui**	**fui**
	tú	**fuiste**	**fuiste**
	Ud./él/ella	**fue**	**fue**
PLURAL FORMS	nosotros/as	**fuimos**	**fuimos**
	vosotros/as	**fuisteis**	**fuisteis**
	Uds./ellos/ellas	**fueron**	**fueron**

¡ATENCIÓN!
Note that, whereas regular **-er** and **-ir** verbs have accent marks in the **yo** and **Ud.** forms of the preterite, **ser** and **ir** do not.

▶ Since the preterite forms of **ser** and **ir** are identical, context clarifies which of the two verbs is being used.

Él **fue** a comprar champú y jabón.
He went to buy shampoo and soap.

—¿Cómo **fue** la película anoche?
How was the movie last night?

¿Adónde fueron Uds.?

Inés y yo fuimos a un mercado. Fue muy divertido.

¡INTÉNTALO! Completa las siguientes frases usando el pretérito de **ir** y **ser**. La primera frase de cada columna se da (*is given*) como ejemplo.

ir

1. Los viajeros __fueron__ a Perú.
2. Patricia __fue__ a Cuzco.
3. Tú __fuiste__ a Iquitos.
4. Gregorio y yo __fuimos__ a Lima.
5. Yo __fui__ a Trujillo.
6. Uds. __fueron__ a Arequipa.
7. Mi padre __fue__ a Lima.
8. Nosotras __fuimos__ a Cuzco.
9. Él __fue__ a Machu Picchu.
10. Ud. __fue__ a Nazca.

ser

1. Ud. __fue__ muy amable.
2. Yo __fui__ muy cordial.
3. Ellos __fueron__ muy simpáticos.
4. Nosotros __fuimos__ muy desagradables.
5. Ella __fue__ muy antipática.
6. Tú __fuiste__ muy chistoso.
7. Uds. __fueron__ muy cordiales.
8. La gente __fue__ muy agradable.
9. Tomás y yo __fuimos__ muy corteses.
10. Los profesores __fueron__ muy buenos.

TEACHING OPTIONS

Video Play the video segment and have students listen for preterite forms of **ser** and **ir**. Stop the video with each example to illustrate how context makes the meaning of the verb clear.

Pairs Have pairs of students solve this logic problem . **"Las vacaciones" Mis compañeros de casa, Julia, Fernando y yo fuimos de vacaciones durante el mes de julio a Puerto Rico, a Chile y a México. Julia fue en un viaje de esquí, pero Fernando y yo fuimos a lugares de sol. El viaje de Fernando fue desagradable porque hubo** (*there was*) **un huracán y fue imposible nadar en el Pacífico. Por suerte, mi viaje fue muy agradable. ¿Adónde fui? (A Puerto Rico.)**

Práctica

1 Completar Completa estas conversaciones con la forma correcta del pretérito de **ser** o **ir**. Indica el infinitivo de cada forma verbal.

Conversación 1

RAÚL ¿Adónde fueron/ir Uds. de vacaciones?
PILAR Fuimos/ir al Perú.
RAÚL ¿Cómo fue/ser el viaje?
PILAR ¡Fue/ser estupendo! Machu Picchu y el Museo de Oro son increíbles.
RAÚL ¿Fue/ser caro el viaje?
PILAR No, el precio fue/ser muy bajo, sólo costó tres mil dólares.

Conversación 2

ISABEL Tina y Vicente fueron/ser novios, ¿no?
LUCÍA Sí, pero ahora no salen. Anoche Tina fue/ir a comer con Gregorio y la semana pasada ellos fueron/ir al partido de fútbol.
ISABEL ¿Ah sí? Javier y yo fuimos/ir al partido y no los vimos.

2 Descripciones Forma frases con los siguientes elementos. Usa el pretérito.

Answers will vary.

A	B	C
yo	(no) ir	a un restaurante
tú	(no) ser	en autobús
mi compañero/a		estudiante
nosotros		a casa
mis amigos		a la playa
Uds.		dependiente/a en una tienda
		en avión

NATIONAL communication STANDARDS

Comunicación

3 Preguntas En parejas, túrnense (*take turns*) para hacerse estas preguntas.

Answers will vary.

1. ¿Adónde fuiste de vacaciones este año? ¿Con quién fuiste?
2. ¿Cómo fueron tus vacaciones?
3. ¿Fuiste de compras esta semana? ¿Adónde? ¿Qué compraste?
4. ¿Fuiste al cine la semana pasada? ¿Fueron tus amigos también?
5. ¿Qué película viste? ¿Cómo fue?
6. ¿Fuiste a la cafetería hoy? ¿A qué hora?
7. ¿Adónde fuiste durante el fin de semana? ¿Por qué?
8. ¿Quién fue tu profesor(a) favorito/a el semestre pasado? ¿Por qué?

4 Personas famosas En grupos pequeños, cada estudiante debe pensar en una persona famosa del pasado. Luego, los otros miembros del grupo tienen que hacer preguntas usando el pretérito hasta que adivinen (*they guess*) la identidad de la persona. Por ejemplo, pueden hacer preguntas acerca de (*about*) su profesión, su nacionalidad, su personalidad o su apariencia (*appearance*) física. Answers will vary.

1 Present Model this exercise by writing these cloze sentences on the board and asking volunteers to fill in the blanks. Ex: **¿Cómo ____ los guías turísticos durante tu viaje? (fueron) ¿Quién ____ con Marcela al baile? (fue)** Then ask other volunteers to indicate the infinitive. **(ser, ir)**

1 Expand Ask small groups to write four questions based on the conversations. They should not write the answers. Groups then exchange papers and answer the questions they receive. Have each group check the answers to the questions it wrote.

2 Present Ask a volunteer to model one sentence before assigning the exercise to the class. Ex: **No fui a un restaurante.** This activity is suitable for oral or written work, with the whole class or in pairs.

2 Expand Ask a volunteer to read/say one of his or her sentences. Point to another student, and call out an interrogative word in order cue a question. Ex: S1: **No fui a un restaurante.** You: **¿Adónde?** S2: **¿Adónde fuiste?**

3 Present Make sure that all students understand that they are to take turns asking questions.

4 Present Explain that this is a variation of the game "Twenty Questions." Model the activity using a famous Hispanic such as **Evita Perón.**

Assignment Have students do activities in **Student Activities Manual: Workbook**, page 79.

TEACHING OPTIONS

Pairs Have groups of students role-play a TV interview with astronauts who have just returned from a long stay on Mars. Have students review previous-lesson vocabulary lists as necessary in preparation. Give groups sufficient time to plan and practice their skits. When all groups have completed the activity, ask a few of them to perform their role-play for the whole class.

Heritage Speakers Ask Spanish-speakers to write a brief essay about their first experiences learning English. Have them read their accounts to the class, making sure to note new vocabulary on the board.

Section Goals

In **Estructura 7.4** students will learn:

- all forms of **gustar**
- other verbs that follow the pattern of **gustar**

Instructional Resources
Student Activities Manual: Workbook, 80–82; Lab Manual, 260
Hojas de actividades 15–16

Before presenting Estructura 7.4 Use realia to compare different products using the verb **gustar**. Ex: Bring in different articles of clothing, the more eccentric, the better. **Me gustan estos pantalones, pero no me gustan estos zapatos.** Then ask volunteers questions using different indirect object pronouns. Ex: **Crystal, ¿te gusta este suéter? Charlie, ¿a Crystal le gusta este suéter?**

Assignment Have students study **Estructura 7.4** and prepare the exercises on pages 219–220 as homework.

Warm-up Write the headings **Gustos** and **Disgustos** on the board. Have the class brainstorm a list of likes and dislikes among the college population including musical groups/artists, movies, clothes, hobbies, and so forth.

Present Use the lists to form statements and questions illustrating the use of the verb **gustar**. Use different indirect object pronouns and mix present and past tenses. Ex: **A los estudiantes universitarios no les gustan los Beatles. A mis amigos y yo, sí nos gustan los Beatles. A los estudiantes no les gustan las películas infantiles. Pero de niño, sí les gustaron las películas infantiles.**

Continued on page 219.

7.4 **Gustar** and verbs like **gustar**

NATIONAL STANDARDS comparisons

ANTE TODO In Lesson 2, you learned that the expressions **me gusta(n)** and **te gusta(n)** express the English concepts of *I like* and *you like*. You will now learn more about the verb **gustar** and other similar verbs. Observe the following examples.

Me gusta ese champú.
ENGLISH EQUIVALENT *I like that shampoo.*
LITERAL MEANING *That shampoo is pleasing to me.*

¿**Te gustaron** las clases?
ENGLISH EQUIVALENT *Did you like the classes?*
LITERAL MEANING *Were the classes pleasing to you?*

- As the examples show, the construction **me gusta(n)** does not have a direct equivalent in English. The literal meaning of this construction is *to be pleasing to* (*someone*), and it requires the use of an indirect object pronoun.

INDIRECT OBJECT PRONOUN		SUBJECT	SUBJECT		DIRECT OBJECT
Me	**gusta**	ese champú.	*I*	*like*	*that shampoo.*

- In the diagram above, observe how in the Spanish sentence the object being liked **(ese champú)** is really the subject of the sentence. The person who likes the object, in turn, is an indirect object because it answers the question: *To whom is the shampoo pleasing?*

¿No te gustan las computadoras?

Me gustan mucho los parques.

- The forms most commonly used with **gustar** and similar verbs are the third person (singular and plural). When the object or person being liked is singular, the singular form **(gusta)** is used. When two or more objects or persons are being liked, the plural form **(gustan)** is used. Observe the following diagram:

SINGULAR	me, te, le	gusta gustó	la película el concierto
PLURAL	nos, os, les	gustan gustaron	las papas fritas los helados

- To express what someone likes or does not like to do, **gustar** is followed by an infinitive. The singular form of **gustar** is used even if there is more than one infinitive.

No **nos gusta comer** a las nueve.
We don't like to eat at nine o'clock.

Les gusta cantar y **bailar** en las fiestas.
They like to sing and dance at parties.

TEACHING OPTIONS

Heritage Speakers Have Spanish speakers compare and contrast activities they like to do with activities their parents/grandparents like to do. Encourage them to use the verb **gustar** and others that follow the same pattern, referring them to the list of verbs on page 219.

Game Divide the class into small groups. Give a prompt including subject and object. Ex: **ella/películas de horror.** Groups will have one minute to construct a sentence using **gustar** or one of the verbs that follow the pattern of **gustar**. Then one member from each group will write the sentence on the board. Award one point to each team for every correct response.

- The construction **a** + [*pronoun*] (**a mí, a ti, a Ud., a él,** etc.) is used to clarify or to emphasize the person(s) who are pleased.

A ella le gustan las toallas verdes, pero **a él** no le gustan.
She likes green towels, but he doesn't like them.

A ti te gusta quedarte en casa, pero **a mí** no me gusta.
You like to stay at home, but I don't like to.

- The construction **a** + [*noun*] can also be used before the indirect object pronoun to clarify or to emphasize who is pleased.

A los turistas les gustó mucho Machu Picchu.
The tourists liked Machu Picchu a lot.

A Juanita le gustaron mucho los mercados al aire libre.
Juanita liked the open-air markets a lot.

- Other verbs in Spanish are used in the same way as **gustar**. Here is a list of the most common ones.

Verbs like *gustar*

aburrir	*to bore*	**importar**	*to be important to; to matter*
encantar	*to like very much; to love* (inanimate objects)	**interesar**	*to be interesting to; to interest*
faltar	*to lack; to need*	**molestar**	*to bother; to annoy*
fascinar	*to fascinate*	**quedar**	*to be left over; to fit* (clothing)

¡ATENCIÓN!

Faltar and **quedar** express how many of something someone lacks or has left:

Me falta una página.
I'm missing one page.

Nos quedan tres pesos.
We have three pesos left.

• • •

Quedar means *to fit* or *to look* (on someone):

Estos zapatos me quedan mal.
These shoes fit badly on me.

Esa camisa te queda muy bien.
That shirt looks good on you.

¡INTÉNTALO! Indica el pronombre de objeto indirecto y la forma del tiempo presente adecuados en cada frase. La primera frase de cada columna se da (*is given*) como ejemplo.

gustar

1. A él __le gusta__ viajar.
2. A mí __me gusta__ bailar.
3. A nosotras __nos gusta__ cantar.
4. A Uds. __les gusta__ leer.
5. A ti __te gusta__ correr.
6. A Elena __le gusta__ gritar.
7. A mis padres __les gusta__ beber.
8. A Ud. __le gusta__ jugar tenis.
9. A mi esposo y a mí __nos gusta__ dormir.
10. A Pinto __le gusta__ dibujar.
11. A todos __nos gusta__ opinar.
12. A Pili no __le gusta__ pensar.

encantar

1. A ellos __les encantan__ los deportes.
2. A ti __te encantan__ las películas.
3. A Ud. __le encantan__ los viajes.
4. A mí __me encantan__ las revistas.
5. A Jorge y a Luis __les encantan__ los perros.
6. A nosotros __nos encantan__ las vacaciones.
7. A Uds. __les encantan__ las fiestas.
8. A Marcela __le encantan__ los libros.
9. A mis amigos __les encantan__ los museos.
10. A ella __le encanta__ el ciclismo.
11. A Pedro __le encanta__ el limón.
12. A ti y a mí __nos encanta__ el baile.

TEACHING OPTIONS

Large group Have the class sit in a circle. One student begins by saying **Me gusta** and an activity he or she enjoys. Ex: **Me gusta correr.** Student 2 reports what student 1 said and adds his or her own favorite activity. **A Frank le gusta correr. A mí me gusta bailar.** Student 3 reports the preferences of the first two students and adds his/her own, and so forth. This activity may be used with any verb that follows the pattern of **gustar**.

Extra Practice Use this as a dictation. **1. A nuestra familia nos encanta viajar. 2. Nos gusta ir en avión, pero nos molestan los aviones pequeños. 3. A mi hijo le interesan las culturas latinoamericanas, a mi esposo le encantan los países de Asia y a mí me fascina Europa. 4. Todavía nos quedan muchos lugares por visitar, y nos falta el tiempo necesario.**

Present Compare and contrast the English verb *like* with the Spanish verb **gustar**. Point out that the subject in the English construction is the indirect object in Spanish. Likewise, the direct object in English is the subject in Spanish. Tell students that they will find this construction less difficult if they think of **gustar** as meaning *be pleasing to* rather than *like*.

Expand To consolidate, use the list generated by the students to ask questions using different forms of **gustar**. Ex: **¿Te gustan los Smashing Pumpkins? ¿Te gustó la película *Titanic*? ¿Te gusta nadar en una piscina o en el océano?** and so forth.

Explain the use of the construction **a +** *pronoun/noun* to clarify or emphasize in constructions using **gustar**.

Expand Write a model sentence on the board such as those found in the examples. Ex: **A Carlos le gusta la comida argentina.** Then change the proper name and ask volunteers to say the new sentence. Ex: **A nosotros (A nosotros nos gusta la comida argentina.)**

Point out that several other common Spanish verbs follow the pattern of **gustar**. Give examples and ask questions until you have modeled all eight verbs. Ex: **A mí me encantan las lenguas, pero me aburren las matemáticas. ¿Qué les encanta a Uds.? ¿Qué les aburre?** Then, work through the explanations given in **¡Atención!**

Close Consolidate by doing **¡Inténtalo!** as a class.

1 Warm up Review the verbs listed by asking either/or questions. Ex: **¿Te aburren las fiestas o te gustan? ¿Te interesa la música clásica o la música pop?**

1 Present Use a picture from your picture file to model the use of one of these verbs. Ex: **A la muchacha le encanta hablar por teléfono.**

1 Expand Have students describe pictures from your picture file using the target verbs.

2 Warm-up/Present If necessary, have students identify the subject in each of the first three sentences. Remind the students that the verb ending depends on the subject, not the object.

2 Suggestion This activity is also suitable for pairs. One student can do the even numbers and the other the odd numbers. Then they check one another's work.

2 Expand Have the students use the verbs found in Activity 2 to write a paragraph describing their own musical tastes. Have them use sentences 1–6 as models.

3 Present Before assigning this activity to pairs have two volunteers read the **Modelo**.

3 Expand Have each pair write two sentences about something the pair would like to do this afternoon. Ex: **Nos gustaría ir de compras.**

Práctica

1 Describir Mira los dibujos y describe lo que está pasando. Usa los siguientes verbos.

aburrir	faltar	molestar
encantar	interesar	quedar

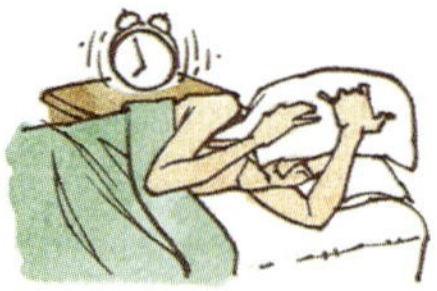

1. A Ramón le molesta el despertador.

2. A nosotros nos encanta esquiar.

3. A ti no te queda bien este vestido. A ti te queda mal/grande este vestido.

4. A Sara le interesan los libros de arte moderno.

2 Completar Completa las frases con la forma correcta del verbo entre paréntesis.

1. A Adela le gustan (gustar) las canciones (*songs*) de Enrique Iglesias.
2. A mí me gusta (gustar) más Ricky Martin.
3. A mis amigos les encanta (encantar) la música de Gloria Estefan.
4. A nosotros nos fascinan (fascinar) los grupos de pop latino.
5. Creo que a Elena le interesa (interesar) más la música clásica.
6. A mí me aburre (aburrir) esa música.
7. ¿A ti te falta (faltar) dinero para el concierto de Carlos Santana?
8. Sí. Sólo me quedan cinco dólares.

NOTA CULTURAL

Recently, Latin music has gained mainstream popularity in the U.S. thanks to entertainers like Puerto Rican-born **Ricky Martin** and Spaniard **Enrique Iglesias**. However, older artists such as **Carlos Santana** and **Gloria Estefan** started to bring Latin music into the mainstream in the 60's, 70's, and 80's.

3 Gustos Pregúntale a un(a) compañero/a si le gustaría hacer las siguientes actividades esta tarde. Answers will vary.

modelo

patinar en línea
Estudiante 1: *¿Te gustaría ir al cine esta tarde?*
Estudiante 2: *Sí, me gustaría ir al cine esta tarde./ No, no me gustaría ir al cine esta tarde.*

1. ir al centro comercial
2. ir a la piscina
3. jugar a las cartas
4. jugar al tenis
5. montar a caballo
6. pasear en bicicleta
7. ver una película
8. tomar algo en un café

TEACHING OPTIONS

Heritage Speakers Ask Spanish speakers to talk about the music they like to listen to and don't like to listen to. Ask them to explain why they like it or don't like it. Ask if some music is good for dancing and some for listening, and so forth. Have them bring in an example for the class to listen to.

Extra Practice Write sentences like these on the board. Have students copy them and draw a face (☺/☹) next to each to indicate the feelings expressed in each sentence. Ex: **Me encantan las enchiladas verdes.** (☺) **1. Me aburren las matemáticas. 2. Me fascina la ópera italiana. 3. Me falta dinero para comprar un auto. 4. Me queda pequeño el sombrero. 5. Me molestan los niños. 6. Me interesa la ecología.**

Comunicación

4 **Preguntas** En parejas, túrnense para hacer y contestar estas preguntas. Answers will vary.

1. ¿Te gusta levantarte temprano o tarde? ¿Por qué? ¿Y tu compañero/a de cuarto?
2. ¿Te gusta acostarte temprano o tarde? ¿Y tu compañero/a de cuarto?
3. ¿Te gusta bañarte o ducharte?
4. ¿Te gusta acampar o prefieres quedarte en un hotel cuando estás de vacaciones?
5. ¿Qué te gustaría hacer este verano?
6. ¿Qué te gusta más de esta universidad? ¿Qué te molesta?
7. ¿Te interesan más las ciencias o las humanidades? ¿Por qué?
8. ¿Qué cosas te molestan?

5 **Completar** Completa estas frases de una manera lógica. Answers will vary.

1. A mi novio/a le fascina(n)...
2. A mi mejor (*best*) amigo/a no le interesa(n)...
3. A mis padres les importa(n)...
4. A nosotros nos molesta(n)...
5. A mis hermanos les aburre(n)...
6. A mi compañero/a de cuarto le aburre(n)...
7. A los turistas les interesa(n)...
8. A los jugadores profesionales les encanta(n)...
9. A nuestro/a profesor(a) le molesta(n)...

6 **Encuesta** Tu profesor(a) va a darte una hoja de actividades. Camina por la clase y pregúntales a tus compañeros qué cosas o actividades les encantan, les aburren, les importan y les interesan. Entrevista por los menos a tres personas. Toma notas de sus respuestas. Toma notas de sus respuestas. Tienes que estar preparado/a para informar a la clase sobre los resultados de tu encuesta. Answers will vary.

Nombre	Le encanta(n)	Le aburre(n)	Le importa(n)	Le interesa(n)

Síntesis

7 **Situación** En grupos de tres, trabajen con la hoja de actividades que les va a dar (*to give*) su profesor(a). Una persona es el/la dependiente/a en una tienda. Las otras dos personas son los clientes que quieren comprar ropa y/o zapatos.

4 Warm-up Write on the board: **¿Te gusta la playa o te gustan las montañas? ¿Y a tu amiga? ¿Julio vive en una casa o en un apartamento?** Cite the answers given. Give another example using two different verbs. **Me gustan las montañas, pero me fascina la playa.**

5 Present This activity is suitable for oral work with the whole class. Ask several students to answer each question. Students may also write their answers and read them to the class.

6 Present Pick a cartoon character on which to model this activity. Ex: **Popeye. Le encantan las espinacas y Oliva. Le aburren Bruto y Wimpy. Le importan las personas buenas y la fuerza** (mime *strength*). **Le interesan comer las espinacas y ganar las peleas con Bruto.** Then distribute copies of **Hoja de actividades 15.**

6 Expand Ask for volunteers to present their findings to the whole class.

7 Present Distribute copies of the top half of **Hoja de actividades 16** to half the class and the bottom half to the rest before assigning the activity to groups of students. Go over the directions by using proper names of class members and a local shop. Ex: **Por ejemplo, yo soy la dependienta en** (name a local store). **Maribel y Pam son clientes. Maribel quiere comprar una falda y Pam quiere comprar una blusa.** You need to look at the **Hoja** to figure out how this activity works.

7 Expand Pair up groups and have them dramatize their **situación** for each other.

Assignment Have students do activities in **Student Activities Manual: Workbook,** pages 80–82.

TEACHING OPTIONS

Pairs Have pairs prepare short TV commercials in which they use the target verbs presented in **Estructura 7.4.** to sell a particular product. Group three pairs together so that each pair presents its skit to four other students.

Game Give groups of students five minutes to write a description of social life during a specific historical period such as the French Revolution or Prehistoric times using as many of the target verbs presented in **Estructura 7.4.** as possible. After the time is up ask groups the number of these verbs they used in their descriptions. Have the top three or four read their descriptions for the whole class, which decides which description it likes best.

Section Goals

In **Lectura** students will:

- learn the strategy of predicting content from the title
- read a diary entry in Spanish

Antes de leer Introduce the strategy. Tell students that they can often predict the content of a newspaper article from its headline. Display or make up several cognate-rich headlines from Spanish newspapers, for example: **Decenas de miles recuerdan la explosión atómica en Hiroshima; Lanzamiento de musicahoy.net, sitio para profesionales y aficionados a la música; Anuncian el descubrimiento de nueve planetas.** Ask students to predict the content of each article.

Examinar el texto/Compartir Ask students to work in pairs to give their predictions about the content of the text. Then, with the whole class, discuss how they are able to tell what the content will be by looking at the format of the text.

Cognados Ask students to identify any cognates they see in the text. Discuss how scanning the text for cognates can help you predict the content of a text.

Assignment Have students read **Un día para recordar** and prepare the activities in **Después de leer** as homework.

Lectura

Antes de leer

Estrategia

Predicting content from the title

Prediction is an invaluable strategy in reading for comprehension. We can usually predict the content of a newspaper article in English from its headline, for example. More often than not, we decide whether or not to read the article based on its headline. Predicting content from the title will help you increase your reading comprehension in Spanish.

Examinar el texto

Lee el título de la lectura y haz tres predicciones sobre el contenido. Escribe tus predicciones en una hoja de papel.

Compartir

Comparte tus ideas con un(a) compañero/a de clase.

Cognados

Haz una lista de seis cognados que encuentres en la lectura.

1. ______________________.
2. ______________________.
3. ______________________.
4. ______________________.
5. ______________________.
6. ______________________.

¿Qué te dicen los cognados sobre el tema de la lectura?

El diario de Maribel

Un día para recordar

23 de marzo de 2001

Anoche dormí por primera vez en mi nuevo apartamento. Pero dormí poco porque me despertó el radio-despertador del vecino de arriba a las 4 de la mañana. No pude volver a dormirme pero creo que él tiene el sueño muy pesado y el despertador siguió y siguió sonando más de media hora.

Me levanté a las 4:30 con los ojos rojos y sin saber qué hacer a esas horas de la mañana en un apartamento sin muebles y lleno de cajas sin abrir. Busqué mis cosas para el baño sin encontrarlas. Intenté ducharme sin jabón, tuve que cepillarme los dientes sin cepillo de dientes y me peiné con las manos. Tampoco encontré la ropa y me tuve que poner la misma ropa que usé ayer.

Maravilloso, el día se presentaba maravilloso. A las 5:00 de la mañana empecé a ordenar el apartamento. Abrí todas las cajas y entonces me di cuenta de que el televisor y la computadora se rompieron durante la mudanza. ¡Estupendo!

A las 6:00 de la mañana empezó a venir un ruido muy extraño del piso de arriba. Estuve

TEACHING OPTIONS

Extra Practice Write the following lines of dialogue from the selection on the board:

—Buenos días —me dijo—. ¿Quieres algo?

—Me equivoqué de puerta —le dije y salí corriendo.

Explain that dashes (**rayas**) and not quotation marks are used to punctuate dialogue in Spanish. Spoken words begin with a dash and a new paragraph. If other, unspoken, words follow, these are set off with a dash at the beginning if no further speech follows and with another dash if more speech follows. Have students practice punctuating the dialogue by copying out some exchanges from the video-still captions on pages 204–205. Encourage them to add explanatory phrases after direct speech, such as **dice Javier** or **responde Álex**, and so forth.

intentando identificar el ruido: ¿una cafetera exprés, algún instrumento musical desconocido para mí, el radio? Decidida, abrí la puerta, subí las escaleras y toqué la puerta, una, dos, tres veces. Miré mi reloj: 6:30. Me enojé tanto que estuve media hora tocando la puerta.

Al fin el vecino abrió la puerta. ¿Qué puedo escribir? ¿Cómo puedo describir lo que pasó entonces? Nunca en mi vida vi a un joven tan... tan, en una palabra: guapo. —Buenos días —me dijo. Yo no dije nada. —¿Quieres algo? —me preguntó. Yo no dije nada. Él sonrió y yo, en ese momento, me acordé de mi aspecto: sin lavarme, sin peinarme, sin maquillarme... —Me equivoqué de puerta —le dije y salí corriendo para mi apartamento. Con las prisas me caí y me rompí el brazo.

vecino de arriba *upstairs neighbor*
él tiene el sueño muy pesado *he's a heavy sleeper*
siguió sonando *kept on ringing* ojos *eyes* sin saber *without knowing*
muebles *furniture* lleno de cajas *full of boxes* me di cuenta *I realized*
se rompieron *broke* mudanza *move* ruido *noise*
cafetera exprés *expresso machine* desconocido *unknown* toqué *I knocked* sonrió *smiled* aspecto *appearance* Me equivoqué de *I knocked on the wrong* Con las prisas *In the rush* me caí *I fell* el brazo *arm*

Después de leer

Seleccionar

Selecciona la respuesta (*answer*) correcta.

1. ¿Quién es el/la narrador(a)? __c__.
   a. la mamá de Maribel
   b. el vecino de arriba
   c. Maribel
2. ¿Qué hace por primera vez la narradora? __b__.
   a. tiene un sueño muy pesado
   b. duerme en su nuevo apartamento
   c. duerme con los ojos rojos
3. ¿Por qué se levanta la narradora a las 4:30? __c__.
   a. porque le duelen (*hurt*) los ojos
   b. porque tiene que limpiar (*clean*) el apartamento
   c. porque el despertador del vecino de arriba no para (*doesn't stop*) de sonar
4. ¿Qué decide hacer la narradora a las seis de la mañana? ¿Por qué? __d__.
   a. lavarse los dientes / porque están sucios
   b. dar un paseo porque no puede dormir
   c. escuchar música / porque quiere molestar a los vecinos
   d. hacer una visita a su vecino / porque su apartamento es muy ruidoso (*noisy*)
5. La lectura se titula *Un día para recordar* porque la narradora __b__.
   a. se enoja con su nuevo vecino
   b. tiene un día horrible
   c. conoce (*meets*) a un chico muy guapo

Ordenar

Ordena los sucesos de la narración. Utiliza los números del 1 al 9.

El radio-despertador del vecino de arriba sigue sonando. __2__

Se da cuenta de que el televisor y la computadora están rotos (*broken*). __5__

Toca la puerta de su vecino por media hora. __7__

Se va corriendo, se cae y se rompe el brazo. __9__

Oye un ruido muy extraño que no puede identificar. __6__

Se viste con la misma ropa de ayer. __4__

La narradora no puede dormir en su nuevo apartamento. __1__

Le dice a su vecino que se equivocó de puerta. __8__

Se levanta y busca sus cosas para el baño, pero no las encuentra. __3__

Después de leer

Seleccionar

Suggestion You may have pairs of students work through this activity together before you go over the answers orally with the whole class. Ask pairs to find the correct answers to each item in the text. If pairs have difficulty answering any question, suggest one of the partners read aloud corresponding portions of the text.

Ordenar

Warm-up Ask a volunteer to summarize in Spanish, using the third-person and present tense, the first two sentences of the selection: **Maribel duerme poco la primera noche en su apartamento porque le despierta el radio-despertador de su vecino a las 4 de la mañana.** Continue having volunteers summarize events in the selection. Afterward, go over the items in **Ordenar** orally with the whole class.

TEACHING OPTIONS

Variación léxica Maribel calls her apartment **un apartamento**. Elsewhere one may hear **departamento** (Mexico) or **piso** (Spain). An apartment house may be a **casa de apartamentos** or **casa de pisos.**

Heritage Speakers Ask Spanish speakers to share what they say when answering the door in Spanish, such as asking **¿Quién es?** (Who is it?) or **¿En qué le puedo ayudar?** (How can I help you?)

Pairs Have pairs of students work together to read the selection and write two questions about each paragraph. When they have finished, have them exchange their questions with another pair who can work together to answer them.

Section Goals

In **Escritura** students will:
- learn adverbial expressions of time to clarify transitions
- write a composition with an introduction, body, and conclusion in Spanish

Tema

Present Read through the list of possible places with the students and have them choose the one in which they want to set their composition. Then go over the instructions, making sure that students understand everything. Finally, have groups of students who have chosen the same location get together and brainstorm ideas about how their daily routines would change in that place.

Estrategia

Present Discuss the importance of having an introduction (**introducción**), body (**parte principal**), and a conclusion (**conclusion**) in a narrative (**narración**). Then, with the entire class, read through the list of adverbs and adverbial phrases in the **Adverbios** box. Have volunteers create a sentence for each adverb or adverbial phrase listed.

Assignment Have students prepare **Ideas y organización** and **Primer borrador** as homework. Make clear that students should write their composition in the present tense.

Note: This is the first time students will see these instructions entirely in Spanish. Remind them that much of what they will read in Spanish in **Plan de escritura** they already have seen several times in English. Go over **Ideas y organización** and **Primer borrador** with the class. Ask students to identify cognates that help them understand the instructions.

Escritura

NATIONAL communication STANDARDS

Estrategia

Sequencing events

Paying strict attention to sequencing in a narrative will ensure that your writing flows logically from one part to the next. Of course, every composition should have an introduction, a body, and a conclusion.

The introduction presents the subject, the setting, the situation, and the people involved. The main part, or the body, describes the events and people's reactions to these events. The conclusion brings the narrative to a close.

Adverbs and adverbial phrases are sometimes used as transitions between the introduction, the body, and the conclusion. Here is a list of commonly used adverbs in Spanish:

Adverbios

además; también	*in addition; also*
al principio; en un principio	*at first*
antes (de)	*before*
después	*then*
después (de)	*after*
entonces; luego	*then*
más tarde	*later*
primero	*first*
pronto	*soon*
por fin, finalmente	*finally*
al final	*finally*

Tema

Escribe acerca de un lugar

¿Cómo cambiaría tu rutina diaria si pasaras un día en uno de estos lugares?

- una isla desierta
- el Polo Norte
- un crucero (*cruise ship*) transatlántico
- el desierto

Escribe una composición en la que describes tu rutina diaria en uno de estos lugares, o en algún otro lugar interesante de tu propia invención. Mientras planeas tu composición, considera cómo cambian algunos de los elementos más básicos de tu rutina diaria en el lugar que escogiste. Por ejemplo, ¿dónde te acuestas en el Polo Norte?, ¿cómo te duchas en el desierto?

Usa el presente de los verbos reflexivos que conoces e incluye algunos de los adverbios de esta página para organizar la secuencia de tus actividades. Piensa también en la información que debes incluir en cada sección de la narración. Por ejemplo, la introducción puede dar una descripción del lugar y de las personas que están allí, y la conclusión puede dar tus opiniones acerca del lugar y de tu vida diaria allí.

acerca de *about* cambiaría *would change* si pasaras *if you spent* tu propia *your own* escogiste *chose* dar *give*

TEACHING OPTIONS

Proofreading Activity Copy the following items containing mistakes onto the board or a transparency as a proofreading activity to do with the whole class.

1. **Por la mañana, Joaquín siempre ducha se pero no baña se nunca.**
2. **Abro el refrigerador, sino allí no encuentro algo de comer.**
3. **En la residencia nadie no se levanta o se acuesta temprano.**
4. **Anoche fuí al centro para ver una película de aventuras, pero no me gusté nada.**
5. **A Miriam no le gusta las matematicas pero sí las lenguas estranjeras.**
6. **Alfredo se fue a abrir la puerta pero no vio nadie allí.**

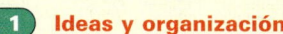

Plan de escritura

1 Ideas y organización

Utiliza adverbios para planear la secuencia de tu composición.

1. **Primero** 2. **Después** 3. **Entonces** 4. **Más tarde** 5. **Al final**

Al finalizar la secuencia de eventos, escribe unas notas sobre la introducción de tu narración. Recuerda las seis preguntas principales: **¿qué?, ¿quién?, ¿cuándo?, ¿dónde?, ¿cómo?** y **¿por qué?**.

2 Primer borrador

Utiliza tus notas de **Ideas y organización** para escribir el primer borrador.

3 Comentario

Intercambia tu composición con un(a) compañero/a. Lee su borrador y reflexiona sobre los aspectos mejor escritos, por ejemplo, los adverbios que conectan las diferentes partes de su composición. Compartan sus impresiones mutuamente. Utiliza estas preguntas para evaluar el trabajo de tu compañero/a:

a. ¿Tiene una introducción con toda la información importante?
b. ¿Es lógica la secuencia de eventos?
c. ¿Tienes sugerencias para hacer la composición más interesante?
d. ¿Notas algún error de gramática o de ortografía?

4 Redacción

Revisa el primer borrador según las indicaciones de tu compañero/a. Incorpora nuevas ideas y/o más información para ampliar tu composición y hacerla más interesante. Utiliza esta guía antes de escribir tu copia final:

a. Subraya cada verbo para comprobar la concordancia con el sujeto y el uso del tiempo correcto. ¡Cuidado con los verbos reflexivos!
b. Revisa la concordancia entre los sustantivos, los artículos y los adjetivos.
c. Comprueba el uso correcto de los pronombres.
d. Revisa la ortografía y la puntuación.

5 Evaluación y progreso

Intercambia tu composición con otro/a compañero/a. Lee su trabajo y en otra hoja de papel dibuja las escenas que describe utilizando los adverbios que introducen la narración. Tu compañero/a puede usar tus dibujos para presentar la composición a la clase. Cuando tu profesor(a) devuelva tu trabajo, anota los errores más importantes en **Anotaciones para mejorar la escritura** en tu **Carpeta de trabajos.**

Intercambia *Exchange* mejor escritos *best-written* sugerencias *suggestions* ortografía *spelling* ampliar *expand* Subraya *Underline* comprobar *check* concordancia *agreement* devuelva *returns*

Comentario
Present Go over guide questions **a-d** with the whole class so peer readers understand their task. Then have pairs of students exchange lists. Allow five minutes for reading and comments. Allow five minutes for discussing comments.
Assignment Go over **Redacción** in class, making sure everyone understands the instructions. Ask students to rewrite their drafts, incorporating peer comments and following the directions in **Redacción**. Tell them to prepare a clean copy of their final draft to hand in.

Evaluación y progreso
Give the class five minutes to exchange compositions and draw scenes. Then have students hand in their compositions to you.

Writing Sample Here is a sample composition that would constitute superior writing achievement.

En la isla más bonita
Esta isla es muy pequeña. De aquí sólo veo el océano, océano y más océano. Llegué aquí en un barco y no tengo planes para irme. Nadie vive en este lugar. Bueno, yo vivo aquí, pero yo soy la única.
Aquí me levanto cuando quiero levantarme. Como cuando quiero comer, y me acuesto cuando quiero acostarme. No tengo que asistir a las clases ni ir a trabajar. ¡Qué vida!
Cada mañana me ducho bajo una ducha especial. Como las frutas y las plantas. Camino por la isla. Cada día es una aventura. Siempre veo algo nuevo. Hoy vi unos animales estupendos.
Me gusta mucho esta isla desierta. Quiero quedarme aquí mucho tiempo. Algún día tengo que volver a mi vida, pero por ahora la vida en esta isla es ¡la vida más bonita!

EVALUATION: Descripción

Criteria	Scale
Content	1 2 3 4 5
Organization	1 2 3 4 5
Use of vocabulary	1 2 3 4 5
Grammatical accuracy	1 2 3 4 5

Scoring	
Excellent	18–20 points
Good	14–17 points
Satisfactory	10–13 points
Unsatisfactory	< 10 points

Section Goals
In **Escuchar** students will learn the strategy of listening for background information.

Instructional Resource
Student Cassette/CD

Preparación
Read the directions with the students, then have them identify the photo situation.

Estrategia
Script
¿Te puedes creer los precios de la ropa que venden en el mercado al aire libre? Tienen unos bluejeans muy buenos que cuestan 52 soles. Y claro, puedes regatear y los consigues todavía más baratos. Vi unos iguales en el centro comercial y son muchos más caros. ¡Cuestan 97 soles!

Assignment Have students do the activities in **Ahora escucha** and **Comprensión** as homework for the next class.

Ahora escucha
Script
Carolina: Buenas tardes, queridos televidentes, y bienvenidos a "Carolina al mediodía". Tenemos el gran placer de conversar hoy con Julián Larrea, un joven actor de extraordinario talento. Bienvenido, Julián. Ya sabes que tienes muchas admiradoras entre nuestro público y más que todo quieren saber los detalles de tu vida. **Julián:** Buenas, Carolina, y saludos a todos. No sé qué decirles; en realidad en mi vida hay rutina, como en la vida de todos. **Carolina:** No puede ser. Me imagino que tu vida es mucho más exótica que la mía. Bueno, para comenzar, ¿a qué hora te levantas? **Julián:** Normalmente me levanto todos los días a la misma hora, también cuando estoy de viaje filmando una película. Siempre me despierto a las 5:30. Antes de ducharme y vestirme, siempre me gusta tomar un café mientras escucho un poco de música clásica. Así medito, escribo un poco y pienso sobre el día. • **Carolina:** Cuando no estás filmando, ¿te quedas en casa durante el día? • **Julián:** Pues, en esos momentos, uso el tiempo libre para sentarme en casa a escribir. Pero sí tengo una rutina diaria de ejercicio. Corro unas 5 millas diarias y si hace mal tiempo voy al gimnasio. • **Carolina:** Veo que eres una persona activa. Te mantienes en muy buena forma. ¿Qué más nos puedes decir de tu vida? • **Julián:** Bueno, no puedo negar que me encanta viajar. ¡Y la elegancia de algunos hoteles es increíble! Estuve en un hotel en Londres que tiene una ducha del tamaño de un cuarto normal. • **Carolina:** Ya vemos que tu vida no es nada aburrida. Qué gusto hablar contigo hoy, Julián. • **Julián:** El placer es mío. Gracias por la invitación, Carolina.

Escuchar

Preparación

Según el dibujo, ¿dónde están Carolina y Julián? Piensa en lo que sabes de este tipo de situación. ¿De qué van a hablar?

Estrategia
Using background information

Once you discern the topic of a conversation, take a minute to think about what you already know about the subject. Using this background information will help you guess the meaning of unknown words or linguistic structures. To help you practice this strategy, you will now listen to a short paragraph. Jot down the subject of the paragraph, and then use your knowledge of the subject to listen for and write down the paragraph's main points.

Ahora escucha

Ahora escucha la entrevista entre Carolina y Julián, teniendo en cuenta (*taking into account*) lo que sabes sobre este tipo de situación. Elige los datos que completan correctamente cada oración.

1. Julián es __c__.
   a. político
   b. deportista profesional
   c. artista de cine
2. El público de Julián quiere saber de __b__.
   a. sus películas
   b. su vida
   c. su novia
3. Julián habla de __a__.
   a. sus viajes y sus rutinas
   b. sus parientes y sus amigos
   c. sus comidas favoritas
4. Julián __b__.
   a. se levanta y se acuesta a diferentes horas todos los días
   b. tiene una rutina diaria
   c. no quiere hablar de su vida

Comprensión

¿Cierto o falso?

Lee las oraciones y decide si pueden haber sido dichas por Julián. Indica **Cierto** o **Falso** para cada frase.

1. Es difícil despertarme; generalmente duermo hasta las diez. __Falso__
2. Pienso que mi vida no es más interesante que las vidas de Uds. __Cierto__
3. Me gusta tener tiempo para pensar y meditar. __Cierto__
4. Nunca hago mucho ejercicio; no soy una persona activa. __Falso__
5. Me fascinan las actividades tranquilas como escribir y escuchar música clásica. __Cierto__
6. Los viajes me parecen aburridos. __Falso__

Preguntas Answers will vary.

1. ¿En qué se parece Julián a otras personas de su misma profesión?
2. ¿Te parece que Julián siempre ha sido rico? ¿Por qué?
3. ¿Qué piensas de Julián como persona?

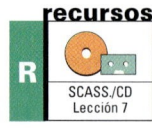

recursos
R
SCASS./CD
Lección 7

pueden haber sido dichas *could have been said* **se parece** *is like* **ha sido** *has been*

NATIONAL STANDARDS: communication, cultures, connections, communities

Proyecto

Crea un itinerario de viaje

Tú y un grupo de estudiantes están planeando un viaje a Perú para ver las famosas ruinas incas de Machu Picchu. Individualmente o en grupos, planea un itinerario de viaje, incluyendo un programa diario de actividades.

Investiga el país, la historia del imperio inca y de la ciudad antigua de Machu Picchu, y busca información práctica y turística para planear la excursión y también las costumbres y la rutina diaria de los peruanos. Considera si algunos aspectos de la rutina diaria de tu grupo van a cambiar durante el viaje. Por ejemplo, ¿cómo deben vestirse para una excursión a los Andes?

1 Prepara el itinerario

Haz un folleto para presentar el itinerario de cada día de viaje e indica la hora para cada actividad. Incluye tiempo para la rutina diaria de tu grupo: cuidado personal, comidas y tiempo libre. Considera también:

- Restaurantes y comidas
- Transporte: horarios de autobuses, trenes y aviones
- Hoteles: reservaciones, horas de facturación
- Información turística: horario de museos, de parques y de otros lugares turísticos
- Costumbres y rutinas locales
- Fotos y gráficos: elementos visuales para crear interés en el viaje
- Historia, descripciones y otra información interesante y útil para el grupo

2 Presenta la información

Usa tu folleto para presentar tu itinerario a la clase. Describe el país, la historia inca de Machu Picchu y también las actividades programadas para el viaje, mostrando fotos y respondiendo a las preguntas de tus compañeros.

recursos para la investigación

Internet Palabras clave: Perú, fotos de Machu Picchu, turismo, ciudades	**Comunidad** Estudiantes o profesores que son del Perú o que vivieron o viajaron allí, peruanos que viven en la comunidad
Biblioteca Mapas, almanaques, revistas, guías turísticas	**Otros recursos** Folletos (*Brochures*) turísticos o revistas viejas que puedes recortar (*cut up*)

programa *schedule* imperio *empire* cambiar *to change* comidas *meals* facturación *check-in*

Section Goals

In **Proyecto** students will:

- learn about Peru, its history, its geography, and its people
- use Spanish as they research and interact with the wider world
- write and present a brochure for a group tour of Peru

Before Assigning Proyecto Students will need approximately a week to complete the project, so at the beginning of that time period, have them open their books to page 227 and glance over **Proyecto**. Explain that they are going to use their research skills to prepare an itinerary for a tour of Peru that includes an excursion to Machu Picchu, the ancient city of the Incas. Tell them they will be writing a brochure that includes an itinerary, which they will present to the class. Encourage students to brainstorm what types of information they want to feature in their brochures.

Assignment Have students read page 227 and follow directions in **Prepara el itinerario** to plan their presentation.

Prepara el itinerario Suggestions

- Students may search for information on Machu Picchu on the following Internet sites, among others: www.lonelyplanet.com, www.adventuresin-peru.com, www.incatrail.com, www.travelperu.com.
- A trip from Lima to Cuzco, Peru, a starting point for most excursions to Machu Picchu, takes travelers from sea level to approximately 11,000 feet in altitude. Remind students to add information in their brochures about Peru's geography and how to dress appropriately.

EVALUATION: Itinerario

Criteria	Scale
Content	1 2 3 4
Organization	1 2 3 4
Accuracy	1 2 3 4
Visual appeal	1 2 3 4
Oral Presentation	1 2 3 4

Scoring	
Excellent	18–20 points
Good	14–17 points
Satisfactory	10–13 points
Unsatisfactory	< 10 points

Section Goals

In **Panorama**, students will read about the geography, culture, and history of Peru.

Instructional Resources
Student Activities Manual: Workbook, 83–84
Transparency 32

Perú

Before Presenting Panorama Have students look at the map of Peru or project **Transparency 32**. Ask them to find the **Río Amazonas** and the **Cordillera de los Andes**, and to speculate about the types of climate found in Peru. As a mountainous country near the equator, climate varies according to elevation and ranges from tropical to arctic. Point out that well over half of the territory of Peru lies within the Amazon Basin. Model the pronunciation of various features on the map and encourage students to tell what they know about Peru.

Assignment Ask students to read **Panorama** and answer the questions in **¿Qué aprendiste?** on page 229 as homework.

Present Ask volunteers to read sections of **El país en cifras**. After each section, ask other students questions about the content of what has been read. Point out that Iquitos, Peru's port city on the Amazon river, is an Atlantic port. Ocean-going ships travel over 2,300 miles up the Amazon river to reach Iquitos.

Increíble pero cierto
In recent years, the **El Niño** weather phenomenon has caused flooding in the deserts of southern Peru. The Peruvian government is currently taking steps to preserve the **Líneas de Nazca** from further deterioration due to floods in the hope that scientists will some day discover more about their origins and meaning.

Perú

NATIONAL STANDARDS connections cultures

El país en cifras

- **Área:** 1.285.220 km² (496.224 millas²), *un poco menos que el área de Alaska*
- **Población:** 26.523.000
- **Capital:** Lima—7.745.000
- **Ciudades principales:** Arequipa—764.000, Trujillo—643.000, Chiclayo—527.000, Callao—442.000, Iquitos—348.000

SOURCE: Population Division, UN Secretariat

Iquitos es un puerto muy importante en el río Amazonas. Desde Iquitos se envían a otros lugares muchos productos, incluyendo goma, nueces, madera, arroz, café y tabaco. Iquitos es también un destino popular para los ecoturistas que visitan la selva.

- **Moneda:** nuevo sol
- **Idiomas:** español (oficial), quechua (oficial), aymará

Bandera del Perú

Peruanos célebres

- Clorinda Matto de Turner, escritora (1854-1901)
- César Vallejo, poeta (1892-1938)
- Javier Pérez de Cuellar, diplomático (1920-)
- Mario Vargas Llosa, novelista (1936-)

Mario Vargas Llosa

Desde *From* se envían *are shipped* goma *rubber* nueces *nuts* madera *timber* arroz *rice* selva *jungle*

Bailando Marinera Norteña en Trujillo

Fuente de la Justicia en Lima

Calle en la ciudad de Iquitos

Mercado indígena en

recursos

R | WB pp. 83-84 | vistasonline.com

¡Increíble pero cierto!

Hace más de dos mil años la civilización Nazca de Perú grabó más de 2.000 km de líneas en el desierto. Los dibujos sólo son descifrables desde el aire. Uno de ellos es un condor del tamaño de un estadio. Las Líneas de Nazca son aún uno de los grandes misterios de la humanidad.

TEACHING OPTIONS

Heritage Speakers Ask Spanish speakers from Peru or who have visitied Peru to make a short presentation to the class about their impressions. Encourage them to speak of the region they are from or visited and how it differs from other regions in this vast country. If they have photographs, ask them to bring them to class to illustrate their talk.

TPR Invite students to take turns guiding the class on tours of Peru's waterways: one student gives directions, and the others follow by tracing the route on their map of Peru. For example: **Comenzamos en el Río Amazonas, pasando por Iquitos hasta llegar al Río Ucayali.**

Lugares • Lima

Lima es una ciudad moderna y antigua a la vez. La hermosa Iglesia de San Francisco es notable por la influencia de la arquitectura árabe. También son fascinantes las exhibiciones sobre los incas en el Museo del Oro del Perú y en el Museo Nacional de Antropología y Arqueología. Barranco, el barrio bohemio de la ciudad, es famoso por su gran ambiente cultural y sus bares y restaurantes.

Lugares • Machu Picchu

A 80 km (50 millas) al noroeste de Cuzco están las ruinas de Machu Picchu, una ciudad antigua del imperio inca. Esta ciudad está a una altitud de 2.350 metros (7.710 pies), entre dos cimas altísimas de los Andes. Cuando los conquistadores españoles llegaron a Perú nunca encontraron la ciudad de Machu Picchu. Sus ruinas quedaron escondidas hasta 1911, cuando el arqueólogo norteamericano Hiram Bingham las descubrió. Todavía no se sabe ni cómo se construyó una ciudad a tanta altura, ni por qué los incas abandonaron el lugar.

Economía • Llamas y alpacas

El Perú se conoce por sus llamas, alpacas, guanacos y vicuñas, todos animales mamíferos parientes del camello. Estos animales todavía son de enorme importancia para la economía del país. Dan lana para ropa, mantas, bolsas y artículos turísticos. La llama se usa también para la carga y el transporte.

Historia • Los incas

Antes del siglo XVI, los incas desarrollaron sistemas avanzados de comunicaciones y de contabilidad y construyeron acueductos, calles y templos. El 24 de junio, día del solsticio de invierno, los descendientes de los incas se reúnen en Cuzco para darle la bienvenida al sol en un festival espectacular, el Inti Raymi.

¿Qué aprendiste? Responde a las preguntas con una frase completa.

1. ¿Qué productos envía Iquitos a otros lugares? Iquitos envía goma, nueces, madera, arroz, café y tabaco.
2. ¿Cuáles son las lenguas oficiales del Perú? Las lenguas oficiales del Perú son el español y el quechua.
3. ¿Por qué es notable la Iglesia de San Francisco en Lima? Es notable por la influencia de la arquitectura árabe.
4. ¿Por qué los conquistadores españoles no encontraron la ciudad de Machu Picchu? No la encontraron porque está escondida entre dos cimas altísimas.
5. ¿Qué hacen los peruanos con la lana de sus llamas y alpacas? Hacen ropa, mantas, bolsas y artículos turísticos.
6. ¿Quiénes celebran el Inti Raymi? Los descendientes de los incas celebran el Inti Raymi.

Conexión Internet Investiga estos temas en el sitio **www.vistasonline.com.**

1. Investiga la cultura incaica. ¿Cuáles son algunos de los aspectos interesantes de su cultura?
2. Busca información sobre dos artistas, escritores o músicos peruanos, y presenta un breve informe a tu clase.

antigua *old* a la vez *at the same time* cimas *summits* escondidas *hidden* no se sabe *is not known* Oro *Gold* barrio *neighborhood* se conoce *is known* mamíferos *mammalian* mantas *blankets* desarrollaron *developed* contabilidad *accounting* construyeron *built* calles *roads* bienvenida *welcome* sol *sun*

TEACHING OPTIONS

Variación léxica Some of the most familiar words to have entered Spanish from the Quechua language are the names of animals native to the Andean region, such as **el cóndor, la llama, la puma,** and **la vicuña**. These words later passed from Spanish to a number of European languages, including English. **La alpaca** comes not from Quechua, the language of the Incas and their descendents, who inhabit most of the Andean region, but from Aymara, the language of native American people who live near Lake Titicaca on the Peruvian-Bolivian border. Most students are probably familiar with the traditional Quechua tune, **El cóndor pasa**, popularized in a version by Simon and Garfunkle.

Lima Lima is rich in colonial architecture. (*Américas*, October 2000, pages 16–23 has many photos of colonial Lima.) It is also the home of the University of San Marcos, established in 1551, the oldest university in South America.

Macchu Picchu The ruins cover an area of five square miles of terrace construction. Over 3,000 steps link its various levels. Some archeologists believe the city was the capital of the Incas before they moved to Cuzco. It was also their last fortress after the Spanish conquest.

Llamas y alpacas Of the camel-like animals of the Andes, only the sturdy llama has been domesticated as a pack animal. Its long, thick coat also provides fiber that is woven into a coarser grade of cloth. The more delicate alpaca and vicuña are raised only for their beautiful coats, used to create extremely high-quality cloth. The guanaco has never been domesticated.

Los incas Another invention of the Inca were the **quipus**, clusters of knotted strings that were a means of keeping records and sending messages. A **quipu** consisted of a series of small cords with knots in them attached to a larger cord. A cord's color, place, size, and the knots in it all had significance.

¿Qué aprendiste? Go over the questions and answers with the whole class.

Assignment Have students do activites in **Student Activities Manual: Workbook,** pages 83–84.

Conexión Internet Students will find information about Peru at **www.vistasonline.com**, as well as links to other sites that can help them in their research.

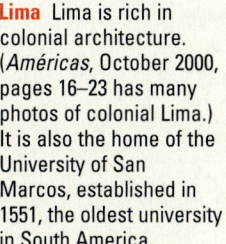

vocabulario

Los verbos reflexivos

acordarse (de) (o:ue)	*to remember*
acostarse (o:ue)	*to go to bed*
afeitarse	*to shave*
bañarse	*to bathe; take a bath*
cepillarse el pelo	*to brush one's hair*
cepillarse los dientes	*to brush one's teeth*
despedirse (de) (e:i)	*to say good-bye (to)*
despertarse (e:ie)	*to wake up*
dormirse (o:ue)	*to go to sleep; to fall asleep*
ducharse	*to shower; to take a shower*
enojarse (con)	*to get angry (with)*
irse	*to go away; to leave*
lavarse la cara	*to wash one's face*
lavarse las manos	*to wash one's hands*
levantarse	*to get up*
llamarse	*to be called; to be named*
maquillarse	*to put on one's makeup*
peinarse	*to comb one's hair*
ponerse	*to put on*
ponerse + *adj.*	*to become + adj.*
preocuparse	*to worry (about)*
probarse	*to try on*
quedarse	*to stay; to remain*
quitarse	*to take off*
sentarse (e:ie)	*to sit down*
sentirse (e:ie)	*to feel*
vestirse (e:i)	*to get dressed*

En el baño

el baño, el cuarto de baño	*bathroom*
el champú	*shampoo*
la crema de afeitar	*shaving cream*
el despertador	*alarm clock*
la ducha	*shower*
el espejo	*mirror*
el jabón	*soap*
el lavabo	*sink*
el maquillaje	*make-up*
la toalla	*towel*

Palabras de secuencia

antes (de)	*before*
después	*afterwards; then*
después de	*after*
durante	*during*
entonces	*then*
luego	*afterwards; then*
más tarde	*later*
por último	*finally*

Palabras afirmativas y negativas

algo	*something; anything*
alguien	*someone; somebody; anyone*
alguno/a, algún, algunos/as	*some; any*
jamás	*never; not ever*
nada	*nothing; not anything*
nadie	*no one; nobody; not anyone*
ni... ni	*neither... nor*
ninguno/a, ningún	*no; none; not any*
nunca	*never; not ever*
o... o	*either... or*
siempre	*always*
también	*also; too*
tampoco	*neither; not either*

Gustar y verbos similares

aburrir	*to bore*
encantar	*to like very much; to love (inanimate things)*
faltar	*to lack; to need*
fascinar	*to fascinate*
gustar	*to be pleasing to; to like*
importar	*to be important to; to matter*
interesar	*to be interesting to; to interest*
me gustaría(n) ...	*I would like...*
molestar	*to bother; to annoy*
quedar	*to be left over; to fit (clothing)*

Palabras adicionales

llamar (por teléfono)	*to call (on the phone)*
por la mañana	*in the morning*
por la noche	*at night*
por la tarde	*in the afternoon; in the evening*
la rutina diaria	*daily routine*

Expresiones útiles	*See page 205.*

La comida

8

Communicative Goals

You will learn how to:

- **Order food in a restaurant**
- **Talk about and describe food**

Lesson Goals

In **Lesson 8** students will be introduced to the following:
- food terms
- meal-related words
- preterite of stem-changing verbs
- double object pronouns
- converting **le** and **les** to **se** with double object pronouns
- uses of **saber** and **conocer**
- more uses of personal **a**
- comparitives and superlatives
- pronouns as objects of prepositions
- pronoun-preposition combinations **conmigo** and **contigo**
- reading for the main idea
- expressing and supporting opinions
- writing a restaurant review
- taking notes while listening
- planning a new restaurant and designing its menu
- cultural, geographic, and historical information about Guatemala

Lesson Preview

Have students look at the photo. Say: **Es una foto de una chica comprando fruta.** Then ask: **¿Qué es el hombre? ¿De qué colores son las frutas? ¿Conocen todas estas frutas? ¿Les gusta comer estas frutas?**

INSTRUCTIONAL RESOURCES

Student Activities Manual: Workbook, 85–96
Student Activities Manual: Lab Manual, 261–267
Student Activities Manual: Video Activities, 341–342
Instructor's Resource Manual: Hojas de actividades, 17–20
Instructor's Resource Manual: Answer Keys
Instructor's Resource Manual: Vocabulario adicional, 55
Tapescript/Videoscript
Overhead Transparencies, 33–35

Student Cassette/CD
Lab Cassette/CD
Video Program
CD-ROM
Website: **www.vistasonline.com**
Testing Program: Prueba A, Prueba B

Section Goals
In **Contextos** students will learn and practice:
- food names
- meal-related vocabulary

Instructional Resources
Student Activities Manual: Workbook, 85–86; Lab Manual, 261
Vocabulario adicional 55
Transparencies 33–34
Student Cassette/CD

Before Presenting Contextos Tell what you are going to have for lunch, writing food vocabulary on the board. Say: **Tengo hambre y voy a preparar una hamburguesa. ¿Qué ingredientes necesito? Pues, carne de res molida, queso, tomates, lechuga y mayonesa. También voy a preparar una ensalada. ¿Con qué ingredientes preparo la ensalada? A ver, lechuga, tomates, zanahorias,...** Tell students they are now going to learn the Spanish words for foods. **Assignment** Have students study **La comida,** pages 232–233, and prepare the activities on page 233 as homework.

Present Give students two minutes to review the market scene on pages 232–233. Then project **Transparency 33.** Ask: **¿Sí o no? ¿Hay bananas en el dibujo del mercado? (Sí.) ¿Qué otras frutas hay? Y ¿hay cerveza? (No.)** and so forth. Next mention typical dishes and ask students to tell what ingredients are used to make them. Suggestions: **una ensalada verde, una ensalada de fruta, un sándwich.**

Ask students what some of their favorite foods are. Ask: **Y tú, _____, ¿qué te gusta comer?** Offer help with unfamiliar vocabulary, drawing pictures on the board or using your picture file to illustrate these items.

La comida

Más vocabulario

el/la camarero/a	*waiter*
la comida	*food; meal*
el/la dueño/a	*owner; landlord*
los entremeses	*hors d'oeuvres*
el menú	*menu*
el plato (principal)	*(main) dish*
la sección de (no) fumar	*(non) smoking section*
el aceite	*oil*
el agua (mineral)	*(mineral) water*
el ajo	*garlic*
las arvejas	*peas*
el azúcar	*sugar*
la bebida	*drink*
los cereales	*cereal; grain*
la cerveza	*beer*
los frijoles	*beans*
la leche	*milk*
la margarina	*margarine*
la mayonesa	*mayonnaise*
el melocotón	*peach*
la papa	*potato*
el pollo (asado)	*(roast) chicken*
el queso	*cheese*
el refresco	*soft drink*
el sándwich	*sandwich*
el vinagre	*vinegar*
el yogur	*yogurt*
delicioso/a	*delicious*
rico/a	*tasty; delicious*
sabroso/a	*tasty; delicious*

Variación léxica

camarones ⟷ gambas
camarero ⟷ mesero (*Amér. L.*), mesonero (*Ven.*), mozo (*Arg., Chile, Urug., Perú*)
refresco ⟷ gaseosa (*Amér. C., Amér. S.*)
sándwich ⟷ bocadillo (*Esp.*)

recursos

R	SCASS./CD	WB	LM	LCASS./CD
	Lección 8	pp. 85-86	p. 261	Cass. 4B/CD4

TEACHING OPTIONS

Extra Practice To review vocabulary for colors, ask students what colors the following food items are: **las bananas (amarillas), las uvas (verdes o moradas), las zanahorias (anaranjadas), los tomates (rojos), los frijoles (blancos, marrones, rojos o negros).**

Variación léxica Point out that food vocabulary varies from region to region in the Spanish-speaking world. When the Spanish visited the New World, they introduced many foods unknown to the indigenous peoples, and likewise they took back many food items previously unknown in Europe. Also point out the different names for fruits and vegetables in **¡Lengua viva!** on page 233.

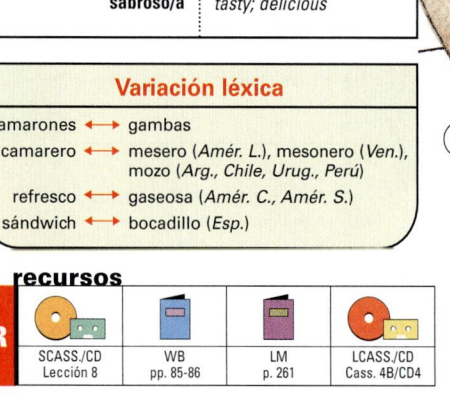

¡LENGUA VIVA!

Many fruits and vegetables have a variety of names:

arveja ↔ guisante, chícharo
banana ↔ banano, plátano, guineo
cacahuate ↔ maní
champiñón ↔ seta, hongo
frijol ↔ habichuela
maíz ↔ choclo, elote
papa ↔ patata
tomate ↔ jitomate

Práctica

1 Escuchar Indica si las frases que vas a escuchar son **ciertas** o **falsas**, según el dibujo. Después, corrige (*correct*) las frases falsas.

1. Cierta
2. Falsa El hombre compra una naranja.
3. Cierta
4. Falsa El pollo es una carne y la zanahoria es una verdura.
5. Cierta
6. Falsa El hombre y la mujer no compran vinagre.
7. Falsa La naranja es una fruta.
8. Falsa La chuleta de cerdo es una carne.
9. Falsa El limón es una fruta y el jamón es una carne.
10. Cierta

2 Identificar Identifica la palabra que no está relacionada con su grupo.

1. champiñón • cebolla • banana • zanahoria ___banana___
2. camarones • ajo • atún • salmón ___ajo___
3. aceite • leche • refresco • agua mineral ___aceite___
4. jamón • chuleta de cerdo • vinagre • carne de res ___vinagre___
5. cerveza • lechuga • arvejas • frijoles ___cerveza___
6. carne • pescado • mariscos • camarero ___camarero___
7. pollo • naranja • limón • melocotón ___pollo___
8. maíz • queso • tomate • champiñón ___queso___
9. rico • sabroso • menú • delicioso ___menú___
10. pescado • mariscos • salmón • bebida ___bebida___

3 Completar Completa las frases con las palabras más lógicas.

1. ¡Me gusta mucho este plato! Es ___b___.
   a. feo b. sabroso c. antipático
2. Camarero, ¿puedo ver el ___c___, por favor?
   a. aceite b. maíz c. menú
3. A Elena no le gusta la ___a___ pero le gusta mucho la fruta.
   a. carne b. uva c. naranja
4. Carlos y yo bebemos siempre agua ___b___.
   a. cómodo b. mineral c. principal
5. Antes de su plato principal, Maribel comió ___b___.
   a. azúcar b. entremeses c. cerveza
6. El plato del día es ___a___.
   a. el pollo asado b. la mayonesa c. el ajo
7. Margarita es vegetariana. Ella come ___a___.
   a. frijoles b. chuletas c. jamón
8. Mi hermana le sirve ___c___ a su niña.
   a. ajo b. vinagre c. yogur

1 Present Have students check their answers by going over the tapescript questions with the whole class.

1 Tapescript **1. La langosta está cerca de los camarones. 2. El hombre compra una pera. 3. La lechuga es una verdura. 4. El pollo y la zanahoria son carnes. 5. La cebolla está cerca del maíz. 6. El hombre y la mujer compran vinagre. 7. La naranja es una verdura. 8. La chuleta de cerdo es pescado. 9. El limón y el jamón son frutas. 10. El pavo está cerca del pollo.**
Student Cassette/CD

1 Expand Give students three minutes to write three additional true-false statements based on the drawing. Ask volunteers to read their statements aloud. The rest of the class indicates whether the statements are true or false, correcting the false statements.

2 Expand Go over answers quickly in class. After each answer, have students indicate why a particular item doesn't belong. Ex: **El champiñón, la cebolla y la zanahoria son verduras. La banana es una fruta.**

3 Present If the activity was done as homework, quickly go over answers in class. Ask students to give answers in the form of complete statements.

3 Expand Give additional statements, which students must complete. Ex: **Un vegetariano no come ____. (carne) El atún y el salmón son tipos de ____. (pescado)** and so forth.

Assignment Have students study the meal vocabulary on page 234 and prepare the activities on pages 235–236 as homework.

TEACHING OPTIONS

Game Play **Concentración**. On 8 cards, write names of food items. On another 8 cards, draw or paste a picture that matches each food item. Place the cards face-down in four rows of four. In pairs, students select two cards. If the two cards match, the pair keeps them. If the two cards don't match, students replace them in their original positions. The group with the most cards at the end wins.

Game Play a modified version of Twenty Questions. Ask a volunteer to think of a food item from the vocabulary drawing or list. Other students get one chance each to ask a yes-no question until someone guesses the item correctly. Limit attempts to 10 questions per item. You may want to write some phrases on the board to cue students' questions. Ex: **¿Es una fruta? ¿Es roja?** and so forth.

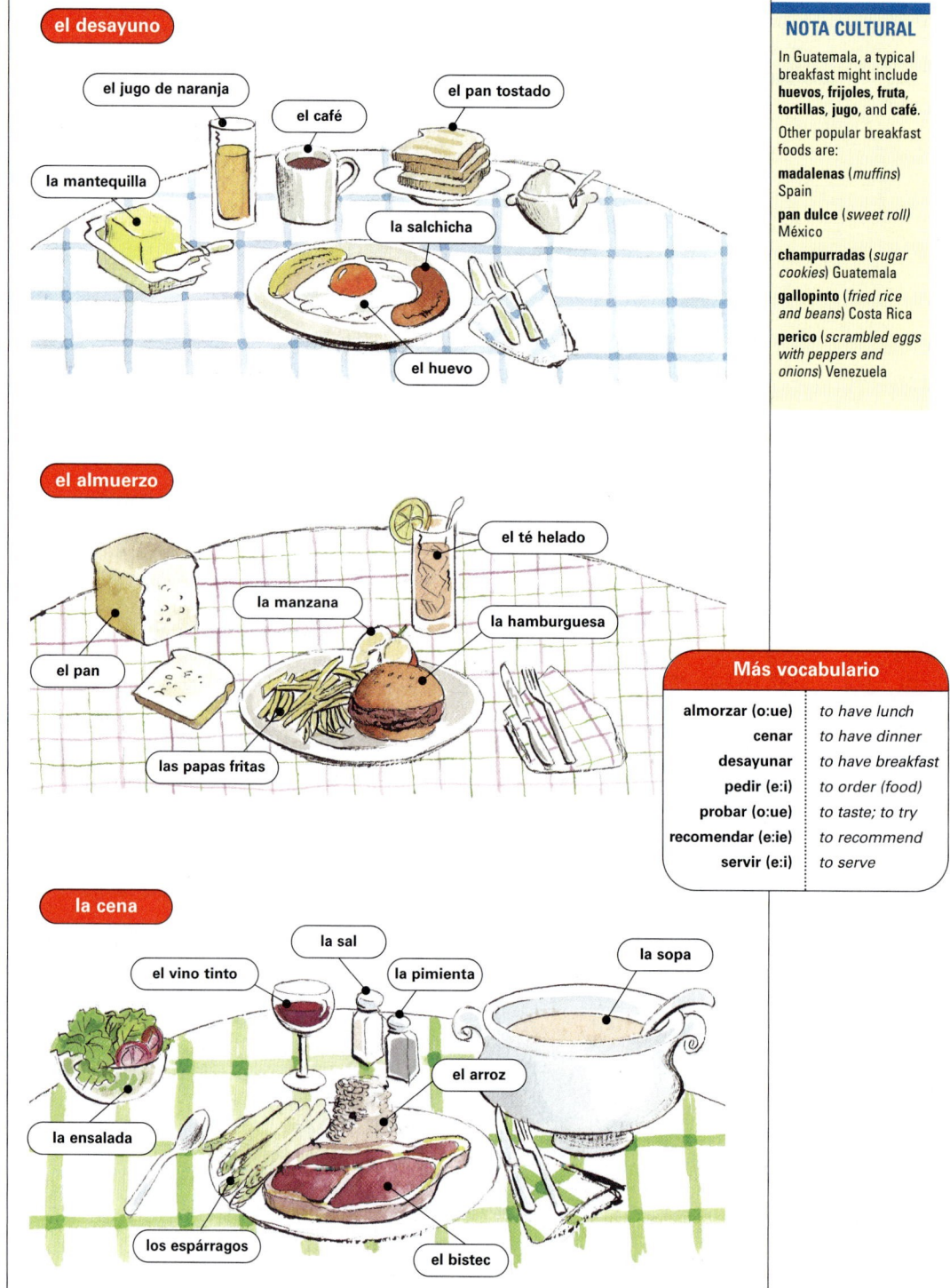

El desayuno, el almuerzo, la cena

Present

- Give students two minutes to review the three drawings on page 234.
- Involve the class in a conversation about meals. Say: **Por lo general, desayuno sólo café con leche y pan tostado, pero cuando tengo mucha hambre desayuno dos huevos y una salchicha también. ____, ¿qué desayunas tú?**
- Project **Transparency 34**. Say: **Mira el desayuno aquí. ¿Qué desayuna esta persona?** Go over the items pictured. Then continue to **el almuerzo** and **la cena.** Have students identify the food items and participate in a wide-ranging conversation about their eating habits. Get them to talk about what, when, and where they eat. Say: **Yo siempre desayuno en casa, pero casi nunca almuerzo en casa. ¿A qué hora almuerzan Uds. por lo general?**
- Ask students to tell you their favorite things to eat for each of the three meals. Ex: ____, **¿qué te gusta desayunar?** You may want to introduce additional items such as **los espaguetis, la pasta, la pizza.**

Nota cultural

Suggestion Have students read **Nota cultural.** Also point out that **el almuerzo** is usually the main meal of the day, consists of several courses, and is enjoyed at a leisurely pace. **La cena** in Hispanic countries is typically much lighter than **el almuerzo.**

Note: At this point you may want to present *Los alimentos y su preparación,* **Vocabulario adicional 55**, in the **Instructor's Resource Manual.**

el desayuno

el almuerzo

la cena

NOTA CULTURAL

In Guatemala, a typical breakfast might include **huevos, frijoles, fruta, tortillas, jugo,** and **café.**

Other popular breakfast foods are:

madalenas (*muffins*) Spain

pan dulce (*sweet roll*) México

champurradas (*sugar cookies*) Guatemala

gallopinto (*fried rice and beans*) Costa Rica

perico (*scrambled eggs with peppers and onions*) Venezuela

Más vocabulario

almorzar (o:ue)	*to have lunch*
cenar	*to have dinner*
desayunar	*to have breakfast*
pedir (e:i)	*to order (food)*
probar (o:ue)	*to taste; to try*
recomendar (e:ie)	*to recommend*
servir (e:i)	*to serve*

TEACHING OPTIONS

Small Groups In groups of three or four, students create a menu for a special occasion. Ask them what they are going to serve for **el primer plato**, **el plato principal**, and to drink. Write **el postre** on the board and explain that it means *dessert*. Explain that in Spanish-speaking countries fresh fruit and cheese are common as dessert, but you may also want to give **el pastel** (*pie, cake*) and **el helado** (*ice cream*). Students present their menu to the class.

Listening Comprehension Prepare descriptions of five to seven different meals, with a mix of breakfasts, lunches, and dinners. Have students write down what you say as a dictation. Based on the food items contained in the meal, students decide whether it is a **comida hispana** or a **comida norteamericana**.

4 **Completar** Trabaja con un(a) compañero/a de clase para relacionar cada producto con el grupo alimenticio (*food group*) correcto.

modelo

La carne es del grupo uno.

el aceite	la carne	las bananas	los espárragos
el azúcar	los cereales	la leche	el arroz
el café	los frijoles	el pescado	

1. La leche y el queso son del grupo cuatro.
2. Los frijoles son del grupo ocho.
3. El pescado y el pollo son del grupo tres.
4. El aceite es del grupo cinco.
5. El azúcar es del grupo dos.
6. Las manzanas y las bananas son del grupo siete.
7. El café es del grupo seis.
8. Los cereales son del grupo diez.
9. Los espárragos y los tomates son del grupo nueve.
10. El pan y el arroz son del grupo diez.

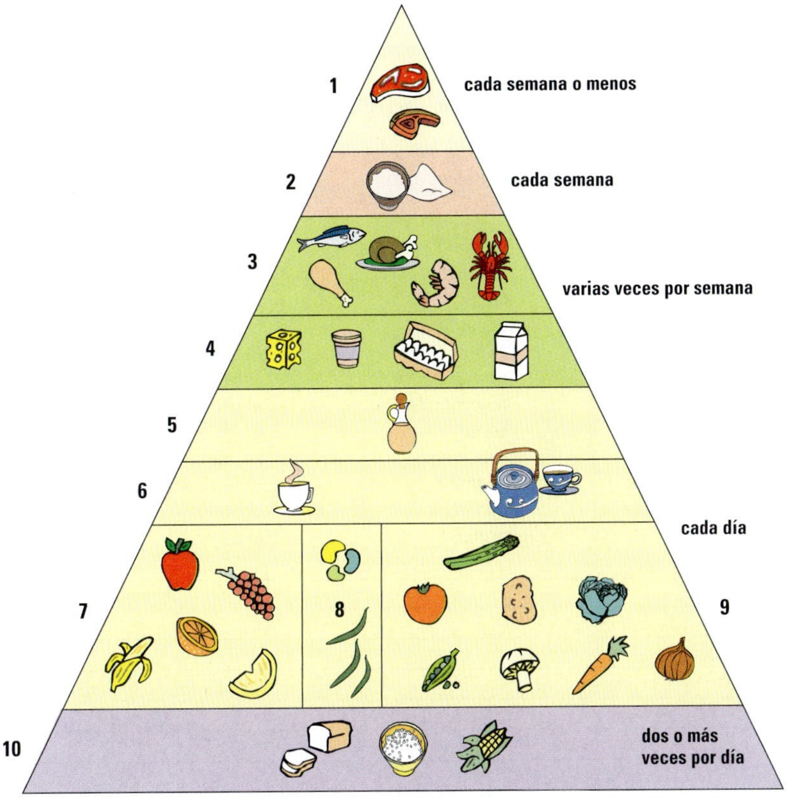

La Pirámide Alimenticia Latinoamericana

4 Present If this activity was done as homework, quickly go over answers in class. Then, ask students to explain the relevance of foods on the base of the pyramid when compared with foods on the top of it. (The foods on the bottom of the pyramid are essential dietary requirements. As one moves closer to the top of the pyramid, the food items become less essential to daily requirements but help to balance out a diet overall.)

4 Expand Ask additional questions about the **pirámide alimenticia.** Ask: **¿Qué comidas se deben comer varias veces por semana? ¿Qué se debe comer cada día? ¿Cuáles son los productos que aparecen en el grupo 4? ¿y en el grupo 7?** and so forth. Get students to talk about what they eat. **¿Comen Uds. carne sólo una vez a la semana o menos? ¿Qué comidas comen Uds. dos o más veces al día? ¿Toman café cada día?**

Expand Ask students if they know which food groups and food products comprise the food pyramid used in this country. If you can get a copy of one, bring it in to class and compare similarities and differences between the dietary requirements among cultures.

TEACHING OPTIONS

Heritage Speakers Ask heritage speakers talk about food items or dishes unique to their country of origin that are not typically found in this country. Have them describe what the item looks and tastes like. If the item is a dish, they should briefly describe how to prepare it if they know how to do so.

Extra Practice Have students draw food pyramids based not on what they should eat but on what they actually do eat as part of their diet. Students should be encouraged to include drawings or magazine cutouts in order to enhance the visual presentation. Then have students present their pyramids to the class.

5 Present If the activity was done as homework, quickly go over the answers in class. If not, you may want to have the students work in pairs with one student's book open to page 235 and the other's open to page 236.

5 Expand Give students two minutes to create three additional true-false statements that their partner must answer. Then ask volunteers to present their sentences for the rest of the class to answer.

6 Present If the activity was done as homework, ask volunteers to present their sentences to the class. You may wish for students to turn in their sentences for grading.

6 Expand Ask individual students what people in the activity logically do. Point out that there are many possible answers to your questions. Ex: **¿Qué hace la camarera en el restaurante? ¿Qué hace el dueño?** and so forth.

Nota cultural
Present Have students read the **Nota cultural** sidebar. Ask them if they know of any essential components of the diet of this country. Ask them if there are any essentials in their personal diets, ones they can't live without.

5 **¿Cierto o falso?** Consulta la Pirámide Alimenticia Latinoamericana e indica si las frases son ciertas o falsas. Corrige las frases falsas.

modelo
El queso está en el grupo diez.
Falso. En ese grupo están el maíz, el pan y el arroz.

1. La manzana, la banana, el limón y las arvejas están en el grupo siete.
Falso. En ese grupo están la manzana, las uvas, la banana, la naranja y el limón.
2. En el grupo cuatro están los huevos, la leche y el aceite.
Falso. En ese grupo están los huevos, la leche, el queso y el yogur.
3. El azúcar está en el grupo dos.
Cierto.
4. En el grupo diez están el pan, el arroz y el maíz.
Cierto.
5. El pollo está en el grupo uno.
Falso. En ese grupo están el bistec y la chuleta de cerdo.
6. En el grupo nueve están la lechuga, el tomate, las arvejas, la naranja, la papa, los espárragos y la cebolla. Falso. En ese grupo están la lechuga, el tomate, las arvejas, la zanahoria, la papa, los espárragos, la cebolla y el champiñón.
7. En el grupo seis están el café y el té.
Cierto.
8. En el grupo cinco está el arroz.
Falso. En ese grupo está el aceite.
9. En el grupo tres están el pescado, el yogur y el bistec.
Falso. En ese grupo están el pescado, el pollo, el pavo, los camarones y la langosta.
10. En el grupo ocho está la cerveza.
Falso. En ese grupo están los frijoles.

6 **Combinar** Combina palabras de cada columna, en cualquier orden (*any*) orden, para formar diez frases lógicas sobre las comidas. Añade otras palabras si es necesario.

Answers will vary.

modelo
La camarera nos sirve el almuerzo.

A	B	C
El/La camarero/a	almorzar	el almuerzo
El/La dueño/a	cenar	la sección de no fumar
Mi familia	desayunar	la cena
Mi novio/a	pedir	el desayuno
Mis amigos y yo	probar	la ensalada
Tía Ana	recomendar	el melocotón
Miguel	servir	el restaurante
Teresa y Pablo	sentarse	el jugo de naranja
Mi hermano/a	gustar	el refresco
El/La médico/a	necesitar	el plato
Yo	preferir	el arroz

1. ______________________
2. ______________________
3. ______________________
4. ______________________
5. ______________________
6. ______________________
7. ______________________
8. ______________________
9. ______________________
10. ______________________

NOTA CULTURAL

Rice is a staple of Caribbean, Central American, and Mexican cuisine. It often accompanies main dishes and is served with beans, as in Guatemala's **arroz con frijoles**. It's also frequently the main dish, as in **arroz con pollo** (*chicken and rice casserole*).

TEACHING OPTIONS

Extra Practice To review and practice the preterite along with food vocabulary, have students write a paragraph in which they describe what they ate up to this point today. Students should also indicate whether this meal or collection of meals represents a typical day for them. If not, they should explain why.

Small Groups In groups of two or three, students role-play a situation in a restaurant. One or two students play the customers and the other plays the **camarero/a**. Offer the following sentences on the board as suggested phrases: **¿Están listos para pedir?, ¿Qué nos recomienda Ud.?, ¿Me trae ____, por favor?, ¿Y para empezar?, A sus órdenes, la especialidad de la casa.**

NATIONAL communication STANDARDS

Comunicación

7

Un menú Con un(a) compañero/a de clase, usa la Pirámide Alimenticia Latinoamericana de la página 235 para crear un menú para una cena especial. Incluye alimentos de los diez grupos para los entremeses, los platos principales y las bebidas. Luego presenta el menú a la clase. Answers will vary.

8

Conversación En grupos, contesten las siguientes preguntas. Answers will vary.

1. ¿A qué hora, dónde y con quién cenas?
2. ¿Qué comidas te gustan más para la cena?
3. ¿A qué hora, dónde y con quién almuerzas?
4. ¿Cuáles son las comidas más (*most*) típicas de tu almuerzo?
5. ¿Desayunas? ¿Qué comes y bebes por la mañana?
6. ¿Qué comida deseas probar?
7. ¿Comes cada día comidas de los diferentes grupos de la pirámide alimenticia? ¿Cuáles son las comidas y bebidas más frecuentes en tu dieta?
8. ¿Qué comida recomiendas a tus amigos? ¿Por qué?
9. ¿Eres vegetariano/a? ¿Crees que ser vegetariano/a es una buena idea? ¿Por qué?
10. ¿Te gusta cocinar (*cook*)? ¿Qué comidas preparas para tus amigos? ¿Para tu familia?

¡LENGUA VIVA!
In addition to **beber**, the verb **tomar** is often used to express *to drink*.

9

Describir Con dos compañeros/as de clase, describe las dos fotos, contestando las siguientes preguntas. Answers will vary.

- ¿Quiénes están en las fotos?
- ¿Dónde están?
- ¿Qué hora es?
- ¿Qué comen y qué beben?

TEACHING OPTIONS

Small Groups In groups of two to four, students prepare brief skits that have something to do with food. The skits may involve being in a market, in a restaurant, in a café, inviting people over for dinner, and so forth. You may wish to have students form groups and settle on their situations and roles as homework before presenting the skits in class.

Game Play a game of continuous narration. One student begins with: **Voy a preparar** (*name of dish*) **y voy al mercado. Necesito comprar...** and names one food item. The next student then repeats the entire narration, adding another food item. Continue on through various students. When the possibilities for that particular dish are used up, have another student begin with another dish, repeating the process.

7 Present Have students work on their menu with one student's book open to page 235 and the other's open to page 237. Emphasize the fact that students must include at least one item from each group in the **pirámide alimenticia.**

7 Expand Ask students why they chose their food items—because they are personal preferences, for their health benefits, or because they went with other foods. Ex: **¿Por qué decidiste en espárragos? ¿Te gustan mucho? ¿Son saludables? Van bien con el pescado, ¿verdad?**

8 Present Have students work in groups of three to five, taking turns asking and answering questions.

¡Lengua viva! Explain that students already know several uses of **tomar. (tomar clases, tomar fotos, tomar el sol)** Explain that **tomar + *bebida*** is common in all Spanish-speaking countries. Ex: **¿Quieres tomar un café?**

8 Expand Ask the same questions of individual students. Ask other students to verify what their classmates answer.

9 Present Give students three or four minutes to describe the photos. You may also want them to write out their descriptions for handing in later.

9 Expand Using your picture file or magazine pictures that show people in eating situations, have students describe what's going on in them: who the people are, what they're eating and drinking, and so forth.

Assignment Have students do the activities in **Student Activities Manual: Workbook,** pages 85–86.

¿Qué tal la comida?

communication cultures — NATIONAL STANDARDS

Don Francisco y los estudiantes van al restaurante El Cráter.

PERSONAJES

MAITE

INÉS

DON FRANCISCO

ÁLEX

JAVIER

DOÑA RITA

CAMARERO

1

JAVIER ¿Sabes dónde estamos?

INÉS Mmm, no sé. Oiga, don Francisco, ¿sabe Ud. dónde estamos?

DON FRANCISCO Estamos cerca de Cotacachi.

2

ÁLEX ¿Dónde vamos a almorzar, don Francisco? ¿Conoce un buen restaurante en Cotacachi?

DON FRANCISCO Pues, conozco a doña Rita Perales, la dueña del mejor restaurante de la ciudad, el restaurante El Cráter.

3

DOÑA RITA Hombre, don Paco, ¿Ud. por aquí?

DON FRANCISCO Sí, doña Rita... y hoy le traigo clientes. Le presento a Maite, Inés, Álex y Javier. Los llevo a las montañas para ir de excursión.

6

MAITE Voy a tomar un caldo de patas y un lomo a la plancha.

JAVIER Para mí las tortillas de maíz y el ceviche de camarón.

ÁLEX Yo también quisiera las tortillas de maíz y el ceviche.

INÉS Voy a pedir caldo de patas y lomo a la plancha.

7

DON FRANCISCO Yo quiero tortillas de maíz y una fuente de fritada, por favor.

DOÑA RITA Y de tomar, les recomiendo el jugo de piña, frutilla y mora. ¿Se lo traigo a todos?

TODOS Sí, perfecto.

8

CAMARERO ¿Qué plato pidió Ud.?

MAITE Un caldo de patas y lomo a la plancha.

recursos

R — VIDEO Lección 8 | VM pp. 341-342

Section goals

In **Fotonovela** students will:

- receive comprehensible input from free-flowing discourse
- learn functional phrases that preview lesson grammatical structures

Instructional Resources
Student Activities Manual: Video Activities 341–342
Video Program (Start: 00:39:36)

Video Synopsis Don Francisco takes the travelers to the **Restaurante El Cráter** for lunch. The owner of the restaurant, doña Rita, welcomes the group and makes recommendations about what to order. After the food is served, don Francisco and doña Rita plan a surprise birthday party for Maite.

Before Presenting Fotonovela Have the class predict the content of the **Fotonovela** based on its title and the video stills. Record the predictions.

Assignment Have students study **Fotonovela** and **Expresiones útiles** for the next class.

Warm-up Quickly review the predictions made in the preceding class and ask your students a few questions to help them summarize this episode.

Present Ask students about their favorite restaurants, using the active vocabulary in **Expresiones útiles.** Ex: **¿Conoces un buen restaurante en esta ciudad? ¿Cómo se llama? Cuando vas a ____, ¿qué pides? ¿Qué tal la comida en ____?**

Continued on page 239.

TEACHING OPTIONS

Video Tips General suggestions for using video clips in the classroom can be found on page IAE-13 of the **Instructor's Annotated Edition**.

¿Qué tal la comida? Play the first half of the **¿Qué tal la comida?** segment of this video module and have the class give you a description of what they see. Write their observations on the board, pointing out any incorrect information. Repeat this process to allow the class to pick up more details of the plot. Then ask your students to use the information they have accumulated to guess what happens in the rest of the segment. Write their guesses on the board. Then play the entire segment and, through discussion, help the class summarize the plot.

DOÑA RITA ¡Bienvenidos al restaurante El Cráter! Están en muy buenas manos... don Francisco es el mejor conductor del país. Y no hay nada más bonito que nuestras montañas. Pero si van a ir de excursión deben comer bien. Vengan chicos, por aquí.

JAVIER ¿Qué nos recomienda Ud.?

DOÑA RITA Bueno, las tortillas de maíz son riquísimas. La especialidad de la casa es el caldo de patas... ¡tienen que probarlo! El lomo a la plancha es un poquito más caro que el caldo pero es sabrosísimo. También les recomiendo el ceviche y la fuente de fritada.

DOÑA RITA ¿Qué tal la comida? ¿Rica?

JAVIER Rica, no. ¡Riquísima!

ÁLEX Sí, y nos la sirvieron tan rápidamente.

MAITE Una comida deliciosa, gracias.

DON FRANCISCO Hoy es el cumpleaños de Maite...

DOÑA RITA ¡Ah! Tenemos unos pasteles que están como para chuparse los dedos...

Enfoque cultural La comida hispana

La cocina (*cuisine*) hispana es una combinación de comidas e ingredientes de varias regiones. La carne de res, la papa, el maíz y el chile, por ejemplo, son característicos de los países andinos. Los frijoles, el arroz, la caña de azúcar y la banana son productos típicos de los países del Caribe. La cocina española incorpora pescados y carnes cocinados (*cooked*) con condimentos como el ajo y la cebolla. La comida típica de Centroamérica es similar a la mexicana y consta de (*consists of*) carne, pescados, chile, tortillas y salsas.

Expresiones útiles

Finding out where you are

- **¿Sabe Ud./Sabes dónde estamos?**
  Do you know where we are?
- **Estamos cerca de Cotacachi.**
  We're near Cotacachi.

Talking about people and places you're familiar with

- **¿Conoce Ud./Conoces un buen restaurante en Cotacachi?**
  Do you know a good restaurant in Cotacachi?
- **Sí, conozco varios.**
  Yes, I know several.
- **¿Conoce/Conoces a doña Rita?**
  Do you know doña Rita?

Ordering food

- **¿Qué le puedo traer?**
  What can I bring you?
- **Voy a tomar/pedir un caldo de patas y un lomo a la plancha.**
  I am going to have/to order the beef soup and grilled flank steak.
- **Para mí las tortillas de maíz y el ceviche de camarón, por favor.**
  Corn tortillas and lemon-marinated shrimp for me, please.
- **Yo también quisiera...**
  I also would like...
- **Y de tomar, el jugo de piña, frutilla y mora.**
  And pineapple/strawberry/ blackberry juice to drink.
- **¿Qué plato pidió Ud.?**
  What did you order?
- **Yo pedí un caldo de patas.**
  I ordered the beef soup.

Talking about the food at a restaurant

- **¿Qué tal la comida?**
  How is the food?
- **Muy rica, gracias.**
  Very tasty, thanks.
- **¡Riquísima!**
  Extremely delicious!

Have the class read through the entire **Fotonovela**, with volunteers playing the parts of don Francisco, Javier, Inés, Álex, Maite, doña Rita and the **Camarero**. Model correct pronunciation as needed. You may want to have students take turns playing the roles so that more students have the opportunity to participate. See ideas for using the video in **Teaching Options**, page 238.

Comprehension Check Check comprehension of the **Fotonovela** episode by doing Activity 1, **Escoger**, page 240, orally with the whole class.

Suggestion Point out some of the unfamiliar structures in **Expresiones útiles**, which will be taught in detail in **Estructura**. Draw attention to the verb **pidió**. Explain that this is a form of the verb **pedir**, which has a stem change in the third person forms in the preterite. Point out the phrase **para mí** and tell the class that **mí** is a pronoun used as an object of a preposition. Now have the class read the caption for video still 5 of the **Fotonovela**. Explain that **más caro que** is an example of a comparison. Point out that in caption 9, **nos la** is an example of an indirect object pronoun and a direct object pronoun used together. Tell your students that they will learn more about these concepts in the upcoming **Estructura** section.

Assignment Have students do activities 2–4 in **Reacciona a la fotonovela**, page 240, as homework.

TEACHING OPTIONS

Enfoque cultural Point out that meal times in Spanish-speaking countries differ somewhat from country to country and differ significantly from the typical meal times in the United States. Breakfast (**el desayuno**) is often eaten between the hours of 7 and 9 in the morning, while lunch (**el almuerzo**) is usually eaten around 2 or 3 p.m. Late in the afternoon, some families have a snack (**merienda**) to tide them over until the last meal of the day (**la cena**), which is typically not very large and is served between 8 and 11 in the evening. Your students might also be interested to know that it is customary for family members to remain at the dinner table after the meal is over for an after-meal chat, **la sobremesa**. Tell students that in Spanish-speaking countries it is much less likely for family members to eat their meals on the run and separately from other members of the family than it is in the United States.

Reacciona a la fotonovela

1 **Escoger** Escoge la respuesta (*answer*) que completa mejor (*best*) cada oración.

1. Don Francisco lleva a los estudiantes a __c__ en el restaurante de una amiga.
   a. cenar b. desayunar c. almorzar
2. Doña Rita es __b__.
   a. la hermana de don Francisco b. la dueña del restaurante
   c. una camarera que trabaja en El Cráter
3. Doña Rita les recomienda a los viajeros __a__.
   a. el caldo de patas y el lomo a la plancha
   b. el bistec, las verduras frescas y el vino tinto c. unos pasteles
4. Inés va a pedir __c__.
   a. las tortillas de maíz y una fuente de fritada
   b. el ceviche de camarón y el caldo de patas
   c. el caldo de patas y el lomo a la plancha

2 **Identificar** Indica quién puede decir las siguientes frases.

1. No me gusta esperar en los restaurantes. ¡Qué bueno que nos sirvieron rápidamente! Álex
2. Les recomiendo la especialidad de la casa. doña Rita
3. ¡Maite y yo pedimos los mismos platos! Inés
4. Disculpe, señora... ¿qué platos recomienda Ud.? Javier
5. Yo conozco a una señora que tiene un restaurante excelente. Les va a gustar mucho. don Francisco
6. Hoy es mi cumpleaños (*birthday*). Maite

3 **Preguntas (*Questions*)** Contesta las siguientes preguntas sobre la **Fotonovela.**

1. ¿Dónde comieron don Francisco y los estudiantes?
   Comieron en el restaurante de doña Rita/El Cráter.
2. ¿Cuál es la especialidad de El Cráter?
   La especialidad de la casa es el caldo de patas.
3. ¿Qué pidió Inés? ¿Y Álex? ¿Qué tomaron todos? Inés pidió el caldo de patas y lomo a la plancha. Álex pidió las tortillas de maíz y el ceviche de camarón. Todos tomaron el jugo.
4. ¿Qué tal los pasteles en El Cráter?
   Los pasteles en El Cráter son sabrosísimos.

4 **En el restaurante**

1. Prepara con un(a) compañero/a una conversación en la que le preguntas si conoce algún buen restaurante en tu comunidad. Tu compañero/a responde que él/ella sí conoce un restaurante que sirve una comida deliciosa. Lo/La invitas a cenar y tu compañero/a acepta. Determinan la hora para verse en el restaurante y se despiden (*say goodbye*).
2. Trabaja con un(a) compañero/a para representar los papeles (*roles*) de un(a) cliente/a y un(a) camarero/a en un restaurante. El/La camarero/a te pregunta qué te puede servir y tú preguntas cuál es la especialidad de la casa. El/La camarero/a te dice cuál es la especialidad y te recomienda algunos platos del menú. Tú pides entremeses, un plato principal y una bebida. El/La camarero/a te da las gracias y luego te sirve la comida.

NOTA CULTURAL

Ceviche is a typical South American dish made with raw fish, shrimp or shellfish, onions, and hot peppers. The ingredients are marinated in lime juice and salt for several hours before serving.

CONSÚLTATO

Indefinite and negative words
To review indefinite words like **algún**, see Lesson 7, section 7.2, p. 212.

NATIONAL communication STANDARDS

Reacciona a la fotonovela

1 Warm-up Ask your students these questions before having them complete this activity: **¿Qué es El Cráter? ¿Quién es doña Rita? ¿Cuáles son algunas de las comidas en el menú?**

2 Present To make this activity more challenging, have your students close their books. Then read each item aloud and have the class guess who would have made each statement.

2 Expand Give the class these additional items: **7. Les van a gustar muchísimo nuestras montañas. (doña Rita) 8. ¿Les gustó la comida? (doña Rita) 9. Para mí las tortillas de maíz y la fuente de fritada. (don Francisco)**

3 Present Ask volunteers to share answers to the questions.

4 Possible responses
Conversation 1:
S1: Oye, María, ¿conoces un buen restaurante en esta ciudad?
S2: Sí... el restaurante El Pescador sirve comida sabrosísima.
S1: ¿Por qué no vamos a El Pescador esta noche?
S2: ¿A qué hora?
S1: ¿A las ocho?
S2: Perfecto.
S1: Está bien. Nos vemos a las ocho.
S2: Adiós.
Conversation 2:
S1: ¿Qué le puedo traer?
S2: Bueno, ¿cuáles son las especialidades de la casa?
S1: La especialidad de la casa es el lomo a la plancha. También recomiendo el caldo de patas.
S2: Mmm... voy a pedir los camarones y el lomo a la plancha. De tomar, voy a pedir el jugo de piña.
S1: Gracias, señor.

TEACHING OPTIONS

Extra practice Ask your students these questions about the **Fotonovela**. Ex: **¿En qué ciudad está el Restaurante El Cráter?** (Cotacachi) **¿Qué pidió Javier en el restaurante?** (tortillas de maíz, ceviche de camarón) **¿Qué pidió don Francisco?** (tortillas de maíz, fuente de fritada) **¿Cuándo es el cumpleaños de Maite?** (hoy)

Small groups Have your students work in groups to prepare a skit in which a family goes to a restaurant, is seated by a waitperson, examines the menu, and orders dinner. Each family member should ask a few questions about the menu and then order an entree and a drink. Have one or two groups perform the skit in front of the class.

comparisons NATIONAL STANDARDS

Pronunciación

ll, ñ, c, and z

pollo	**llave**	**ella**	**cebolla**

Most Spanish speakers pronounce the letter **ll** like the *y* in *yes.*

mañana	**señor**	**baño**	**niña**

The letter **ñ** is pronounced much like the *ny* in *canyon.*

café	**colombiano**	**cuando**	**rico**

Before **a**, **o**, or **u**, the Spanish **c** is pronounced like the *c* in *car.*

cereales	**delicioso**	**conducir**	**conocer**

Before **e** or **i**, the Spanish **c** is pronounced like the *s* in *sit*. (In parts of Spain, **c** before **e** or **i** is pronounced like the *th* in *think.*)

zeta	**zanahoria**	**almuerzo**	**cerveza**

The Spanish **z** is pronounced like the *s* in *sit.* (In parts of Spain, **z** before a vowel is pronounced like the *th* in *think.*)

Práctica Lee las palabras en voz alta.

1. mantequilla
2. cuñado
3. aceite
4. manzana
5. español
6. cepillo
7. zapato
8. azúcar
9. quince
10. compañera
11. almorzar
12. calle

Oraciones Lee las oraciones en voz alta.

1. Mi compañero de cuarto se llama Toño Núñez. Su familia es de la ciudad de Guatemala y de Quetzaltenango.
2. Dice que la comida de su mamá es deliciosa, especialmente su pollo al champiñón y sus tortillas de maíz.
3. Creo que Toño tiene razón porque hoy cené en su casa y quiero volver mañana para cenar allí otra vez.

Refranes Lee los refranes en voz alta.

Las apariencias engañan.[1]

Panza llena, corazón contento.[2]

1 Looks can be deceiving.
2 A full belly makes a happy heart.

recursos

R			
	SCASS./CD Lección 8	LM p. 262	LCASS./CD Cass. 4B/CD4

Section Goals

In **Pronunciación** students will be introduced to the pronunciation of the letters **ll**, **ñ**, **c**, and **z**

Instructional Resources
Student Activities Manual: Lab Manual, 262
Student Cassette/CD

Present

- Point out that the Spanish letter **ll** is usually pronounced like the English *y*. Write the example words on the board and ask for volunteers to pronounce them.
- Ask the class how the letter **ñ** is pronounced. (like the *ny* in *canyon*) Pronounce the example words and have the class repeat after you.
- Tell the class that **c** is pronounced like the English *c* in *car* before **a**, **o**, or **u**. Pronounce the example words and ask individual students to repeat.
- Ask the class how most Spanish speakers pronounce the letter **c** when it appears before **e** or **i**. (like the English *s*) Then point out that **c** before **e** or **i** is pronounced like the English *th* in some parts of Spain. Write the example words on the board and ask for volunteers to pronounce them.
- Explain that the Spanish **z** is usually pronounced like the English *s*. Mention that in parts of Spain, **z** is pronounced like the English *th*. Pronounce the example words and ask the class to repeat.

Práctica/Oraciones/Refranes Model the pronunciation of each word or sentence, having students repeat after you.

TEACHING OPTIONS

Extra Practice Write the names of a few distinguished Guatemalans on the board and ask for a volunteer to pronounce each one. Ex: Luis Cardoza y Aragón (writer), Carlos Mérida (painter), Enrique Gómez Carrillo (writer), José Milla (writer), Alonso de la Paz (sculptor). Repeat the process with a few city names: Villanueva, Zacapa, Escuintla, Cobán.

Pairs Have the class work in pairs to practice the pronunciation of the sentences given in Activity 2 (**Identificar**) on page 240. Encourage your students to help their partners if they have trouble pronouncing a particular word. Circulate around the class and model correct pronunciation as needed, focusing on the letters **ll**, **ñ**, **c**, and **z**.

8.1 Preterite of stem-changing verbs

NATIONAL comparisons STANDARDS

ANTE TODO As you learned in Lesson 6, **-ar** and **-er** stem-changing verbs have no stem change in the preterite. **-Ir** stem-changing verbs, however, do have a stem change. Study the following charts and observe where the stem changes occur.

Preterite of *-ir* stem-changing verbs

		servir *(to serve)*	**dormir** *(to sleep)*
SINGULAR FORMS	yo	serví	dormí
	tú	serviste	dormiste
	Ud./él/ella	s**i**rvió	d**u**rmió
PLURAL FORMS	nosotros/as	servimos	dormimos
	vosotros/as	servisteis	dormisteis
	Uds./ellos/ellas	s**i**rvieron	d**u**rmieron

- Stem-changing **-ir** verbs, in the preterite only, have a stem change in the third-person singular and plural forms. The stem change consists of either **e** to **i** or **o** to **u**.

  (e → i) pedir: p**i**dió, p**i**dieron (o → u) morir: m**u**rió, m**u**rieron (*to die*)

Perdón, ¿quiénes pidieron las tortillas de maíz?

¿Y qué plato pidió usted?

¡INTÉNTALO! Cambia los infinitivos al pretérito.

1. Yo ___serví___. (servir, dormir, pedir, preferir, repetir, seguir)
   dormí, pedí, preferí, repetí, seguí
2. Ud. _________. (morir, conseguir, pedir, sentirse, despedirse, vestirse)
   murió, consiguió, pidió, se sintió, se despidió, se vistió
3. Tú _________. (conseguir, servir, morir, pedir, dormir, repetir)
   conseguiste, serviste, moriste, pediste, dormiste, repetiste
4. Ellas _________. (repetir, dormir, seguir, preferir, morir, servir)
   repitieron, durmieron, siguieron, prefirieron, murieron, sirvieron
5. Nosotros _________. (seguir, preferir, servir, vestirse, despedirse, dormirse)
   seguimos, preferimos, servimos, nos vestimos, nos despedimos, nos dormimos
6. Uds. _________. (sentirse, vestirse, conseguir, pedir, despedirse, dormirse)
   se sintieron, se vistieron, consiguieron, pidieron, se despidieron, se durmieron
7. Él _________. (dormir, morir, preferir, repetir, seguir, pedir)
   durmió, murió, prefirió, repitió, siguió, pidió

Section Goals

In **Estructura 8.1**, students will be introduced to the preterite of stem-changing verbs.

Instructional Resources
Student Activities Manual: Workbook, 87–88; Lab Manual, 263

Before Presenting Estructura 8.1 Review present-tense forms of **-ir** stem-changing verbs **pedir** and **dormir**. Also review formation of the preterite of regular **-ir** verbs, using **escribir** and **recibir** as models. Tell students that they are now going to study **-ir** verbs that change their stem vowel in the preterite. **Assignment** Have students study **Estructura 8.1** and do the exercises on pages 242–243 for the next class.

Preterite of -ir stem-changing verbs
Present
- Work through the explanation and model pronunciation of the verb forms in the chart. Give model sentences that use these verbs in the preterite, emphasizing third-person forms.
- Emphasize that only the third-person singular and plural forms have a stem change in them.
- Point out that **morir** means *to die* and offer sample sentences using third-person preterite forms of the verb. Ex: **No tengo bisabuelos. Ya murieron.**
- Other **-ir** verbs that change their stem vowel in the preterite: **conseguir, despedirse, divertirse, pedir, preferir, repetir, seguir, sentir, sugerir, vestirse**

Close To consolidate entire section, do **¡Inténtalo!** with the whole class.

TEACHING OPTIONS

Extra Practice Do a pattern practice drill. Write a stem-changing **-ir** verb on the board and ask individual students to provide preterite forms for the different subject pronouns and/or names you call out. Ex: **seguir/Miguel (siguió)** Reverse activity by calling out a conjugated form and asking students to give the appropriate subject pronoun. Ex: **pidieron (ellos, ellas, Uds.)**

Pairs Ask students to work in pairs to come up with 10 original sentences in which they use third-person preterite forms of stem-changing **-ir** verbs. Point out that students should try to use many of the vocabulary items from **Contextos** in their sentences. Pairs then share their sentences with the rest of the class.

Práctica

1 **Completar** Completa las siguientes frases para describir lo que pasó anoche en el restaurante El Famoso.

1. Paula y Humberto Suárez llegaron al restaurante El Famoso a las ocho y ___siguieron___ (seguir) al camarero a una mesa en la sección de no fumar.
2. El Sr. Suárez ___pidió___ (pedir) una chuleta de cerdo. La Sra. Suárez decidió probar los camarones.
3. Para tomar, los dos ___pidieron___ (pedir) vino tinto.
4. El camarero ___repitió___ (repetir) el pedido (*the order*) para confirmarlo.
5. La comida tardó mucho (*took a long time*) en llegar y los Srs. Suárez ___se durmieron___ (dormirse) esperando la comida.
6. A las nueve el camarero les ___sirvió___ (servir) la comida.
7. Después de comer la chuleta de cerdo, el Sr. Suárez ___se sintió___ (sentirse) muy mal.
8. De repente, el Sr. Suárez se ___murió___ (morir).
9. Pobre Sr. Suárez... ¿por qué no ___pidió___ (pedir) los camarones?

2 **El camarero loco** En el restaurante La Hermosa trabaja un camarero muy loco que siempre comete muchos errores. Indica lo que los clientes pidieron y lo que el camarero les sirvió.

modelo

Armando / papas fritas

Armando pidió papas fritas pero el camarero le sirvió maíz.

1. Nosotros / jugo de naranja Nosotros pedimos jugo de naranja pero el camarero nos sirvió papas.
2. Beatriz / queso Beatriz pidió queso pero el camarero le sirvió uvas.
3. Tú / arroz Tú pediste arroz pero el camarero te sirvió arvejas.

4. Elena y Alejandro /atún Elena y Alejandro pidieron atún pero el camarero les sirvió camarones (mariscos).
5. Ud. / agua mineral Ud. pidió agua mineral pero el camarero le sirvió vino tinto.
6. Yo / hamburguesa Yo pedí una hamburguesa pero el camarero me sirvió zanahorias.

Práctica

1 Present If activity was done as homework, quickly go over answers in class. If not, you may want students to do the activity in pairs.

1 Expand Ask students to work in pairs to come up with an alternate ending to the narration, using stem-changing **-ir** verbs in the preterite. Pairs then share their endings with the class. The class can vote on the most original ending.

2 Present
- Explain that the drawings represent food items that the waiter brought but that the customers didn't order.
- Point out that students will need to use indirect object pronouns with the verb **servir** in their responses.
- Go through the **Modelo** with the whole class.

2 Expand In pairs, students redo the activity, this time role-playing the customer and the waiter. Model the possible interaction between the students. Ex: **E1: Perdón, pero pedí papas fritas y Ud. me sirvió maíz. E2: ¡Ay, perdón! (¡Lo siento!) Le traigo papas fritas enseguida** (right away). Students take turns playing the role of customer and waiter.

TEACHING OPTIONS

Video Show the video again to give students more input with stem-changing **-ir** verbs in the preterite. Have them write down all the stem-changing forms (third person singular and plural) they hear. Stop the video where appropriate to discuss how certain verbs were used and to ask comprehension questions. Ex: **¿Qué pidió Maite? ¿Cómo sirvieron la comida?** and so forth.

Listening Comprehension Prepare descriptions of five easily recognizable people in which you use the stem-changing forms of **-ir** verbs in the preterite. Write their names on the board in random order. Then read your descriptions, having students match the description to the appropriate name. Ex: **Murió en un accidente de avión en 1999. (John F. Kennedy, Jr.)**

3 Present
- Inform students that there are many possible ways to complete each sentence, provided that it makes sense, as in the model.
- You may wish for students to complete the activity in pairs.

3 Expand Have students share their sentences with the class. Ask comprehension questions of the other students based on what was said. Ex: ____ **jugó al baloncesto, pero ¿qué jugaron Tomás y Paco?**

4 Present Give students about 10 minutes to interview each other. Make sure students write down their partner's answers.

4 Expand Ask students to reveal their partner's answers to the questions in the interview. Remind students that they will be giving the answers using the third-person singular (and, possibly in a few cases, plural) form of the verbs.

4 Expand Ask volunteers to ask the same questions of you. Make sure that students address you as **Ud.**

5 Present Have students get into groups of three or four. Allow them five minutes to create their description.

Consúltalo Suggestion In addition to pointing out words and expressions that may signal the preterite, remind students about transition words that help to move the flow of a narration. Ex: **primero, después, luego, también,** and so forth.

5 Expand Have groups present their descriptions to the class in the form of a cohesive narration.

Assignment Have students do activities in **Student Activities Manual: Workbook,** pages 87–88.

Comunicación

NATIONAL communication STANDARDS

3 Oraciones Completa las oraciones de una manera lógica. Answers will vary.

modelo

Yo jugué al baloncesto pero Tomás y Paco...
Yo jugué al baloncesto pero Tomás y Paco jugaron al tenis.

1. Mi compañero/a de cuarto se despertó tarde pero yo...
2. Yo pedí ensalada de frutas pero mis amigos...
3. Lorena me recomendó el bistec pero Sofía y Carolina...
4. Esteban almorzó al mediodía pero yo...
5. Yo serví la carne pero Alonso...
6. Yo me dormí temprano pero ellos...
7. Nosotros preferimos los mariscos pero Sandra...
8. Celia se sintió enferma pero nosotros...
9. Nosotros repetimos el postre pero ustedes...
10. Yo seguí todas las instrucciones del profesor pero Manuela...

4 Entrevista Trabajen en parejas y túrnense para entrevistar a su compañero/a. Answers will vary.

1. ¿Te acostaste tarde o temprano anoche? ¿A qué hora te dormiste? ¿Dormiste bien?
2. ¿A qué hora te despertaste esta mañana? Y ¿a qué hora te levantaste?
3. ¿A qué hora vas a acostarte esta noche?
4. ¿Llegaste a tiempo (*on time*) a la clase de español?
5. ¿Cuándo empezaste a estudiar español?
6. ¿Quién preparó la cena en tu casa anoche? Y ¿quién la sirvió?
7. ¿Quién va a preparar y servir la cena en tu casa esta noche?
8. ¿Se durmió alguien en alguna de tus clases la semana pasada? ¿En qué clase?

Síntesis

5 Describir En grupos, estudien la foto y las preguntas que siguen. Luego, describan la cena romántica de Eduardo y Rosa.

- ¿Adónde salieron a cenar?
- ¿Qué pidieron?
- ¿Les sirvieron la comida rápidamente?
- ¿Les gustó la comida?
- ¿Cuánto costó?
- ¿Van a volver a este restaurante en el futuro?

CONSÚLTALO

Words commonly used with the preterite
To review time expressions such as **anoche**, see Lesson 6, Section 6.1, p. 177.

NATIONAL communication STANDARDS

TEACHING OPTIONS

Pairs In pairs, students take turns telling each other about a memorable experience in a restaurant, whether it was a date, whether they were with family or friends, and so forth. Students should be encouraged to take notes as their partner narrates. Then have students reveal what their partner told them.

Extra Practice Using your picture file or magazine pictures that show restaurant scenes, have students describe them in the past tense, using the preterite. Write on the board some stem-changing **-ir** verbs that might apply to what's going on in the pictures.

8.2 Double object pronouns

ANTE TODO In Lessons 5 and 6, you learned that direct and indirect object pronouns replace nouns and that they often refer to nouns that have already been referenced. You will now learn how to use direct and indirect object pronouns together. Observe the following diagram.

Indirect Object Pronouns			Direct Object Pronouns	
me	nos	+	lo	los
te	os		la	las
le (se)	les (se)			

▶ When direct and indirect object pronouns are used together, the indirect object pronoun always precedes the direct object pronoun.

		DOUBLE OBJECT PRONOUNS
El camarero **me** (I.O.) muestra **el menú** (D.O.).	→	El camarero **me lo** muestra.
The waiter shows me the menu.		*The waiter shows it to me.*
Nos (I.O.) sirven **los platos** (D.O.).	→	**Nos los** sirven.
They serve us the dishes.		*They serve them to us.*
Maribel **te** (I.O.) pidió **una hamburguesa** (D.O.).	→	Maribel **te la** pidió.
Maribel ordered a hamburger for you.		*Maribel ordered it for you.*

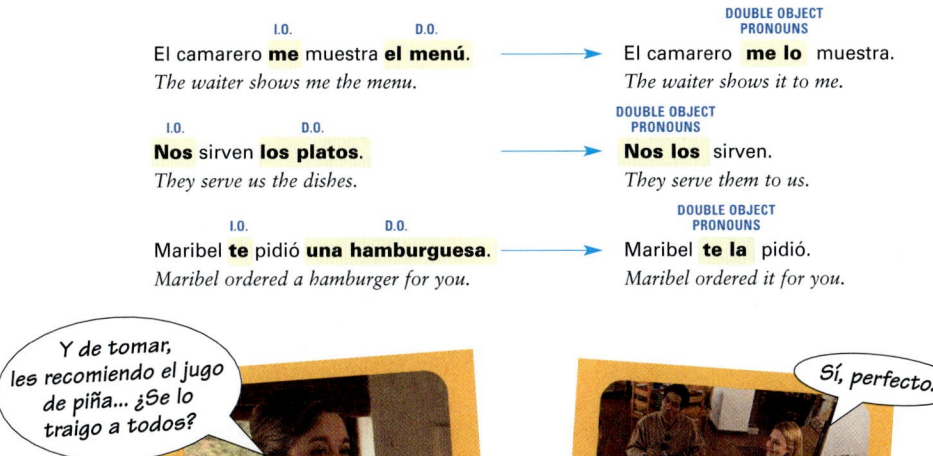

Y de tomar, les recomiendo el jugo de piña... ¿Se lo traigo a todos?

Sí, perfecto.

▶ In Spanish, two pronouns that begin with the letter **l** cannot be used together. Therefore, the indirect object pronouns **le** and **les** always change to **se** when they are used with **lo, los, la,** and **las.**

		DOUBLE OBJECT PRONOUNS
Le (I.O.) escribí **la carta** (D.O.).	→	**Se la** escribí.
I wrote him the letter.		*I wrote it to him.*
Les (I.O.) sirvió **los entremeses** (D.O.).	→	**Se los** sirvió.
He served them the hors d'oeuvres.		*He served them to them.*

TEACHING OPTIONS

Extra Practice Write six sentences on the board for students to express using double object pronouns. Ex: **Rita les sirvió la cena a los viajeros. (Rita se la sirvió.)**

Pairs In pairs, students write five sentences that contain both direct and indirect objects (not pronouns). Their partners must express the sentences using double object pronouns.

Video Show the video again to give students more input containing double object pronouns. Stop the video where appropriate to discuss how double object pronouns were used and to ask comprehension questions.

Section Goals

In **Estructura 8.2** students will be introduced to:
- the use of double object pronouns
- converting **le** and **les** into **se** when used with third person direct object pronouns

Instructional Resources
Student Activities Manual: Workbook, 89–90; Lab Manual, 264
Hoja de actividades 17

Before Presenting Estructura 8.2 Briefly review direct object pronouns (**Estructura 5.4**) and indirect object pronouns (**Estructura 6.2**). Give sentences and have students convert objects into object pronouns. Ex: **Sara escribió la carta. (Sara la escribió.) Mis padres escribieron una carta. (yo) Mis padres me escribieron una carta.**

Assignment Have students study **Estructura 8.2** and prepare the activities on pages 246–247 as homework.

Double object pronouns

Present Work through explanation and diagram and model sample sentences. Emphasize the fact that the indirect object pronoun always comes before the direct object pronoun in these constructions.

Go over explanation of converting **le** and **les** into **se** when used with a third-person direct object pronoun. Model additional examples for the students, asking them to make the conversion with **se**. Remind students that with double object pronouns in the third person they only need to concentrate on the gender and number of the direct object pronoun. The indirect object pronoun will always be **se**.

Ask students questions to which they respond with third-person double object pronouns. Ex: **¿Le recomiendas el ceviche a ____? (Sí, se lo recomiendo.) ¿Les preparas pizza para los amigos? (Sí, se la preparo los sábados.) ¿Les traes sándwiches para tus compañeros? (Sí, se los traigo.)**

Explain that in negative sentences with two object pronouns, the negaive comes before the object pronouns. Ex: **—¿Les compras helados a toda la clase? —¿No, no se los compro.**

Work through clarification of **se** in double object pronoun sentences. Model additional sentences that use this construction. Point out that names may also be used in this construction. Ex: **Se lo vendió a la Sra. Gutiérrez.**

Point out and model double pronoun placement with infinitives and present participles. Practice this by giving sentences that display one method of pronoun placement and ask students to restate the sentence in another way. Ex: **Se lo voy a mandar. = Voy a mandárselo.**

¡Atención! Point out and emphasize the need for a written accent to maintain the original stress of the infinitive or present participle. Give additional examples on the board.

Close Consolidate entire section by doing **¡Inténtalo!** with the whole class.

- Because **se** has multiple meanings, Spanish speakers often clarify to whom the pronoun refers by adding **a Ud., a él, a ella, a Uds., a ellos,** or **a ellas.**

¿El sombrero? Carlos **se** lo vendió **a ella.**	¿Las verduras? Ellos **se** las compran a **Ud.**
The hat? Carlos sold it to her.	*The vegetables? They buy them for you.*

- Double object pronouns follow the same rules for placement as single object pronouns. They are placed before a conjugated verb, and, with infinitives and present participles, they may be placed before the conjugated verb or attached to the end of the infinitive or present participle.

DOUBLE OBJECT PRONOUNS	DOUBLE OBJECT PRONOUNS
Te lo voy a mostrar.	Voy a mostrár**telo**.
DOUBLE OBJECT PRONOUNS	DOUBLE OBJECT PRONOUNS
Nos las están sirviendo.	Están sirviéndo**noslas**.

¡ATENCIÓN!

When pronouns are attached to an infinitive or a present participle, an accent mark is added to maintain the original stress. You will learn more about accents in **Ortografía**, p. 305.

mostrar → **mostrártelo**

sirviendo → **sirviéndonoslas**

Qué tal
la comida,
¿rica?

Sí, y nos
la sirvieron tan
rápidamente.

¡INTÉNTALO! Escribe el pronombre de objeto directo o indirecto que falta en cada frase.

Objeto directo

1. ¿La ensalada? El camarero nos __la__ sirvió.
2. ¿El salmón? La dueña me __lo__ recomienda.
3. ¿La comida? Voy a preparárte __la__.
4. ¿Las bebidas? Estamos pidiéndose __las__.
5. ¿Los refrescos? Te __los__ puedo traer ahora.
6. ¿Los platos de arroz? Van a servírnos __los__ después.

Objeto indirecto

1. ¿Puedes traerme tu plato? No, no __te__ lo puedo traer.
2. ¿Quieres mostrarle la carta? Sí, voy a mostrár __se__ la ahora.
3. ¿Les serviste la carne? No, no __se__ la serví.
4. ¿Vas a leerle el menú? No, no __se__ lo voy a leer.
5. ¿Me recomiendas la langosta? Sí, __te__ la recomiendo.
6. ¿Cuándo vas a prepararnos la cena? __Se__ la voy a preparar en una hora.

TEACHING OPTIONS

Pairs Have students create five dehydrated sentences for their partner to complete. They should include the following elements: subject / action / direct object / indirect object (name or pronoun). Ex: **Carlos / escribe / carta / Marta**. Their partner should "hydrate" this particular sentence as follows: **Carlos se la escribe (a Marta).**

Large Groups Split the class into two groups. Give cards that contain verbs that can take a direct object to one group. The other group gets cards containing nouns. Then select one member from each group to stand up and show his or her card. Another student converts the two elements into a sentence using double object pronouns: **mostrar / el libro** → [Name of student] **se lo va a mostrar**. Be sure each sentence makes sense.

Práctica

AYUDA

Here are some other useful expressions:

ahora mismo *right now*

inmediatamente *immediately*

¡A la orden! *At your service.*

¡Ya voy! *I'm on my way.*

1 **Responder** Imagínate que trabajas de camarero/a en un restaurante. Responde a las órdenes de estos clientes usando pronombres.

modelo

Sra. Gómez: Una ensalada, por favor.
Sí, señora. Enseguida (*Right away*) se la traigo.

1. Sr. López: La mantequilla, por favor. Sí, señor. Enseguida se la traigo.
2. Srta. Rivas: Los camarones, por favor. Sí, señorita. Enseguida se los traigo.
3. Sra. Lugones: El pollo asado, por favor. Sí, señora. Enseguida se lo traigo.
4. Tus compañeros/as de cuarto: Un café, por favor. Sí, chicos. Enseguida se lo traigo.
5. Tu profesor(a) de español: Papas fritas, por favor. Sí, profesor(a). Enseguida se las traigo.
6. Dra. González: La chuleta de cerdo, por favor. Sí, doctora. Enseguida se la traigo.
7. Tus padres: Los champiñones, por favor. Sí, señores. Enseguida se los traigo.
8. Dr. Torres: La cuenta (*check*), por favor. Sí, doctor. Enseguida se la traigo.

2 **¿Quién?** La Sra. Cevallos está hablando sola de los planes para una cena con su familia y sus amigos. Cambia los sustantivos (*nouns*) subrayados por pronombres de objeto directo y haz los otros cambios necesarios.

modelo

¡No tengo carne! ¿Quién va a traerme la carne del supermercado? (Mi esposo)
Mi esposo va a traérmela./Mi esposo me la va a traer.

1. ¡Las invitaciones! ¿Quién les mandó las invitaciones a los invitados (*guests*)? (Mi hija) Mi hija se las mandó.
2. No tengo tiempo de ir a la panadería (*bakery*). ¿Quién me puede comprar el pan? (Mi hijo) Mi hijo puede comprármelo./Mi hijo me lo puede comprar.
3. ¡Ay! No tengo suficientes platos. ¿Quién puede prestarme los platos que necesito? (Mi mamá) Mi mamá puede prestármelos./Mi mamá me los puede prestar.
4. Nos falta mantequilla. ¿Quién nos trae la mantequilla? (Mi cuñada) Mi cuñada nos la trae.
5. ¡Los postres! ¿Quién está preparándonos los postres? (Silvia y Renata) Silvia y Renata están preparándonoslos./Silvia y Renata nos los están preparando.
6. No hay suficientes sillas. ¿Quiénes nos traen las sillas que faltan? (Héctor y Lorena) Héctor y Lorena nos las traen.
7. No tengo tiempo de pedirle el azúcar a Mónica. ¿Quién puede pedirle el azúcar? (Mi hijo) Mi hijo puede pedírselo./Mi hijo se lo puede pedir.
8. ¿Quién va a servirles la cena a los invitados? (Mis hijos) Mis hijos van a servírsela./Mis hijos se la van a servir.

Ayuda

Present Model the helpful phrases in sentences. Point out that **ahora mismo, inmediatamente,** and **ya** can replace **enseguida** in the **Modelo** for Activity 1.

1 Present If activity was done as homework, quickly go over answers in class. If not, you may want to have students complete the activity in pairs, taking turns playing the role of customer and waiter.

1 Expand Do the activity with the whole class, selecting a student to play the role of customer and another to play the role of waiter for each item.

2 Present If activity was done as homework, quickly go over answers in class. If not, have students read directions. Read the **Modelo** aloud. If you choose to do this activity with the whole class, read aloud the sentences in the book and call on individual students to give the correct responses. In cases where there is more than one correct response, have student say both.

2 Expand Change the people in parentheses to different subjects in order for the students to use different persons and numbers of the verbs.

2 Expand Using your picture file or magazine pictures, ask students who is doing what to whom in the pictures. Ex: **La señora les muestra la casa a los jóvenes. Se la muestra a los jóvenes.**

TEACHING OPTIONS

Heritage Speakers Ask heritage speakers to talk about a favorite gift they received. Write **regalar** on the board and explain that it means *to give* (*a gift*). Students should talk about what they received, who gave it to them (**regalar**), why, and so forth. Ask comprehension questions of the rest of the class.

Game Play **Concentración**. Write sentences that use double object pronouns on each of 8 cards. On another 8 cards, draw or paste a picture that matches each description. Place the cards face-down in four rows of four. In pairs, students select two cards. If the two cards match, the pair keeps them. If the two cards don't match, students replace them in their original position. The group with the most cards at the end wins.

3 Present Have students read directions as you model sample sentences with a volunteer. Continue the model by asking: **—¿Cuándo nos lo enseña? —Nos lo enseña los lunes, miércoles, jueves y viernes.** Emphasize that students use **¿Quién?** and **¿Cuándo?** in their questions. Students should take turns asking and answering the questions.

3 Expand Ask questions of individual students. Then ask them why they answered as they did. Students answer using double object pronouns. Ex: **—¿Quién te enseña español? —Ud. me lo enseña. —¿Por qué? —Ud. me lo enseña porque es profesora de español.**

4 Present Emphasize that students are to answer the questions with complete sentences.

4 Expand Ask the questions of individual students. Then verify class comprehension by asking other students to repeat the information given.

5 Present This is another information-gap activity, in which each student possesses information that his or her partner needs. Students get the needed information by asking questions. Distribute the top half of **Hoja de actividades 17** to one of the partners and the bottom half to the other.

5 Expand Using your own copy of both parts of the **Hoja de actividades**, ask individual students questions about the information.

Assignment Have students do activities in **Student Activities Manual: Workbook,** pages 89–90.

Comunicación

NATIONAL communication STANDARDS

3

Contestar Trabajen en parejas y háganse preguntas usando las palabras interrogativas **¿Quién?** o **¿Cuándo?** Sigan el modelo. Answers will vary.

modelo

nos enseña español
Estudiante 1: ¿Quién nos enseña español?
Estudiante 2: La profesora Camacho nos lo enseña.

1. te puede explicar (*explain*) la tarea cuando no la entiendes
2. les vende los libros de texto a los estudiantes
3. te escribe mensajes electrónicos
4. te prepara la comida
5. te compró esa blusa
6. le enseñó español al/a la profesor(a)
7. vas a comprarme boletos (*tickets*) para un concierto
8. me vas a prestar tu computadora
9. nos va a recomendar el menú de la cafetería
10. me vas a mostrar tu casa o apartamento

4

Preguntas Hazle estas preguntas a un(a) compañero/a. Answers will vary.

1. ¿Me prestas tu coche (*car*)? ¿Ya le prestaste tu coche a otro/a amigo/a?
2. ¿Me puedes comprar un coche nuevo?
3. ¿Quién te presta dinero cuando lo necesitas?
4. ¿Les prestas dinero a tus amigos/as? ¿Por qué?
5. ¿Les prestas tu casa a tus amigos/as? ¿Por qué?
6. ¿Nos compras el almuerzo a mí y a los otros compañeros de clase?
7. ¿Me describes tu casa?
8. ¿Quién te va a preparar la cena esta noche?
9. ¿Quién te va a preparar el desayuno mañana?
10. ¿Vas a leerles la historia de Blanca Nieves (*Snow White*) a tus nietos/as? ¿Qué otras historias les vas a leer?

Síntesis

5

Regalos de Navidad Tu profesor(a) va a darte (*to give you*) una hoja de actividades. En parejas, cada un(a) de Uds. tiene parte de la lista de los regalos de Navidad (*Christmas gifts*) que Berta pidió y los regalos que sus parientes le compraron. Conversen entre Uds. para completar sus listas.

NATIONAL communication STANDARDS

modelo

Estudiante 1: ¿Qué le pidió Berta a su mamá?
Estudiante 2: Le pidió una computadora.
Estudiante 1: ¿Se la compró?
Estudiante 2: Sí, se la compró.

NOTA CULTURAL

Holiday celebrations last into January in Hispanic countries. In some places, although Christmas is celebrated, gifts are not given until **el Día de los Reyes Magos** (Three Kings' Day, or Epiphany) on January 6. Traditionally, children put straw in their shoes for the Three Kings' camels. In the morning, the straw is gone and in its place are presents.

TEACHING OPTIONS

Heritage Speakers Ask heritage speakers if they or their families celebrate el **Día de los Reyes Magos** (Epiphany, January 6). Ask them to expand on the information given in the **Nota cultural** sidebar and to tell whether **los Reyes** is more important for them than **la Navidad** or not.

Large Groups Divide the class in half. To each member of one half of the class give a strip of paper that contains a question on it. Ex: **¿Te compró ese suéter tu novia?** To each member of the other half of the class give the answer to that question. Ex: **Sí, ella me lo compró.** Students must find their partner. Take care not to create sentences that can have more than one match.

8.3 Saber and conocer

NATIONAL STANDARDS comparisons

ANTE TODO Spanish has two verbs that mean to know, **saber** and **conocer**, which cannot be used interchangeably. Note that all forms of **saber** and **conocer** are regular in the present tense except their **yo** forms.

Saber* and *conocer

		saber *(to know)*	conocer *(to know)*
SINGULAR FORMS	yo	**sé**	**conozco**
	tú	**sabes**	**conoces**
	Ud./él/ella	**sabe**	**conoce**
PLURAL FORMS	nosotros/as	**sabemos**	**conocemos**
	vosotros/as	**sabéis**	**conocéis**
	Uds./ellos/ellas	**saben**	**conocen**

¡ATENCIÓN!
The following verbs are also conjugated like **conocer**:
conducir *to drive*
ofrecer *to offer*
parecer *to seem*
traducir *to translate*

- **Saber** means *to know a fact or piece(s) of information* or *to know how to do something.*

No **sé** tu número de teléfono.
I don't know your telephone number.

Mi hermana **sabe** hablar francés.
My sister knows how to speak French.

- **Conocer** means *to know* or *be familiar/acquainted* with a person, place, or thing.

¿**Conoces** la ciudad de Nueva York?
Do you know New York City?

No **conozco** a tu amigo Esteban.
I don't know your friend Esteban.

- When the direct object of **conocer** is a person or pet, the personal **a** is used.

¿Conoces los restaurantes de Tegucigalpa? *but* ¿Conoces a Rigoberta Menchú?

¡INTÉNTALO! Escribe las formas apropiadas de los siguientes verbos.

saber

1. José no __sabe__ la hora.
2. Sara y yo __sabemos__ jugar al tenis.
3. ¿Por qué no __sabes__ tú estos verbos?
4. Mis padres __saben__ hablar japonés.
5. Yo __sé__ a qué hora es la clase.
6. Ud. no __sabe__ dónde vivo.
7. Mi hermano no __sabe__ nadar.
8. Nosotros __sabemos__ muchas cosas.
9. Carlos nunca __sabe__ qué hora es.
10. Yo __sé__ dónde comer bien.

verbos como **conocer**

1. Ud. y yo __conocemos__ (conocer) bien Miami.
2. Mi compañero __conduce__ (conducir) muy mal.
3. Esta clase __parece__ (parecer) muy buena.
4. Ellos siempre me __ofrecen__ (ofrecer) ayuda.
5. Yo __traduzco__ (traducir) del chino al inglés.
6. Ana, ¿__conoces__ (conocer) los poemas de Mistral?
7. Luis, ¡__pareces__ (parecer) triste!
8. Uds. __conducen__ (conducir) con cuidado.
9. Yo siempre __ofrezco__ (ofrecer) café a mis amigos.
10. Nadie me __conoce__ (conocer) bien.

TEACHING OPTIONS

Video Show the video again to give students more input with **saber** and **conocer**. Stop the video where appropriate to discuss how **saber** and **conocer** were used and to ask comprehension questions.

Extra Practice Call out several sentences in English which use *to know*. Have students say whether they would use **saber** or **conocer** to translate it. Ex: I know the answer to that question. (**saber**) He doesn't know the president. (**conocer**) and so forth. Also ask students to translate the sentences you give orally.

Section Goals

In **Estructura 8.3** students will learn:
- the uses of **saber** and **conocer**
- more uses of the personal **a**

Instructional Resources
Student Activities Manual: Workbook, 91; Lab Manual, 265
Hoja de actividades 18

Before Presenting Estructura 8.3 Write **saber** on the board and explain that it means to know. Model **saber** by asking several questions with it: Ex: _____, **¿sabes mi número de teléfono? ¿Sabes dónde está la biblioteca?** Next, write **conocer** on the board and explain that it also means to know, without explaining the difference between the two. Ask questions using conocer. Ex: _____, **¿conoces a esta persona aquí? ¿Me conoces también?** Ask further questions using both verbs. Then help students infer the difference in use between the two verbs. **Assignment** Have students study **Estructura 8.3** and prepare the activities on pages 249–250 as homework.

Saber* and *conocer
Present
- Model the paradigms for **saber** and **conocer**, emphasizing that only the first-person singular forms are irregular.
- Go through each point and example sentence, adding further illustrative examples.
- Point out that **saber** + *infinitive* means to know how to (do something)
- Review the use of the personal **a**, presented in **Estructura 5.4.**

¡Atención! Work through conjugations of the verbs in the **¡Atención!** sidebar.

Close Consolidate entire section by doing **¡Inténtalo!** with the whole class.

1 Present If activity was done as homework, quickly go over answers in class.

1 Expand Make statements that use **saber** and **conocer** to describe famous people. Students have to guess who you are. Ex: **Sé jugar al tenis muy bien. También conozco muy bien a Venus Williams porque ella es mi hermana. ¿Quién soy? (Serena Williams)**

2 Present If activity was done as homework, quickly go over answers in class. If not, you may wish for students to do activity in pairs.

2 Expand In pairs, students create three original questions using the verbs **conocer**, **conducir**, **ofrecer**, and **saber**, which their partner answers in complete sentences. Call on volunteers to present their questions to the entire class for other volunteers to answer.

3 Present If activity was done as homework, call on individual students to share their sentences with the class.

3 Expand Ask students personalized questions about what they know how to do or whom they know. Ask comprehension questions of other students in class to verify information. Ex: ____, **¿tienes un pasatiempo? ¿Qué hay que saber para practicar tu pasatiempo? ¿Conoces a otros aficionados de ese pasatiempo?**

Práctica

CONSÚLTALO

Panorama Locate the Guatemalan cities mentioned here, on p. 266.

1 **Completar** Completa las frases con la forma apropiada de **saber** o **conocer.**

1. Mi hermana mayor __sabe__ conducir, pero yo no __sé__.
2. —¿__Conoces__ a Carla, mi sobrina? —No, no la __conozco__.
3. —¿__Saben__ Uds. el número de Marta? —Nosotras no lo __sabemos__.
4. —Nosotros no __conocemos__ Guatemala. —Ah, ¿no? Yo __conozco__ bien las ciudades de Escuintla, Mazatenango, Quetzaltenango y Antigua.
5. —Todavía no __conozco__ a tu novio. —Sí, ya lo __sé__. Mañana te lo presento.
6. Yo __sé__ esquiar, pero Tino y Luis son pequeños y no __saben__.
7. Roberto __conoce__ bien el Popol Vuh, el libro sagrado de los mayas, y también __sabe__ leer los jeroglíficos de los templos mayas.

2 **Emparejar** Empareja (*match*) las oraciones de la columna A con las oraciones de la columna B y escribe la forma correcta de los verbos en la columna B.

A

1. María del Carmen tiene mucha sed. b
2. ¿Puedes traducir la carta del Sr. Jiménez? d
3. ¿Sabes cuándo es el concierto de Shakira? e/c
4. Gloria, tú no tienes automóvil, ¿verdad? f
5. Ése es el hijastro de mi cuñada María José. a
6. ¿A qué hora vuelve el ingeniero? c/e

B

a. ¿Ah, sí? Pues no lo __conozco__ (conocer). ¡Qué guapo!
b. Con gusto le __ofrezco__ (ofrecer) una bebida.
c. No __sé__ (saber). No me acuerdo.
d. En este instante no puedo, pero más tarde se la __traduzco__ (traducir).
e. No lo sé, pero si __consigo__ (conseguir) la información te llamo.
f. No, pero __conduzco__ (conducir) el de mis padres.

3 **Combinar** Combina las columnas A, B y C para hacer oraciones completas.

modelo

No conozco a Stephen King. / Stephen King conoce a Meg Ryan.

A	B	C
Connie Chung	(no) conocer	Meg Ryan
Bill Gates	(no) saber	cantar
Gloria Estefan y Ricky Martin		el lago de Atitlán en Guatemala
Billy Crystal		hablar dos lenguas extranjeras
Stephen King		hacer reír a la gente
Whoopie Goldberg		la fecha de hoy
yo		escribir novelas de horror
tú		programar computadoras
tu compañero/a		Steve Jobs
tu profesor(a)		muchas personas importantes

TEACHING OPTIONS

Extra Practice Have students write down three things they know how to do well (**saber** + *infinitive* + **bien**). Collect the papers and read the sentences. The rest of the class tries to guess who wrote the sentences. This same activity could also be done with **conocer**. Students guess who wrote the sentences based on people or places that student knows or is familiar with.

Extra Practice Students write down six things they know how to do. Then they circulate around the room, asking their classmates if they know how to do those things as well. Ex: **Sé tocar el piano. ¿Sabes tocar el piano también?** When they find someone that answers **sí**, they ask that person to sign next to the activity (**Firma aquí, por favor.**). Have students try to get signatures for all their activities.

Comunicación

4

Entrevista Pregúntale a un(a) compañero/a qué deportes practica y por qué.

modelo

Estudiante 1: ¿Sabes esquiar? (bucear, nadar, patinar, escalar montañas, jugar vóleibol, etc.)
Estudiante 2: Sí, sé esquiar porque aprendí de niño./ Sí, sé esquiar porque me gusta mucho la nieve./ No, no sé esquiar, pero me gustaría saber.

5

Encuesta Tu profesor(a) va a darte (*to give you*) una hoja de actividades. Camina por la clase y pregúntales por lo menos (*at least*) a dos compañeros qué ciudades de la lista conocen y por qué. Toma nota de sus respuestas y luego informa a la clase de los resultados.

Austin	Cincinnati	Los Angeles	New Orleans	St. Louis
Boston	Denver	Memphis	New York	San Francisco
Chicago	Kansas City	Miami	Phoenix	Seattle

6

Preguntas Con un(a) compañero/a, háganse las siguientes preguntas.

1. ¿Qué restaurantes buenos conoces? ¿Vas mucho a comer a los restaurantes?
2. En tu familia, ¿quién sabe cantar mejor (*best*)? ¿Tu opinión es objetiva?
3. ¿Conoces a algún artista hispano?
4. ¿Sabes usar bien el Internet? ¿Te parecen fáciles o difíciles las computadoras?
5. ¿Sabes escuchar cuando alguien te habla de sus problemas?
6. ¿Conoces a algún (alguna) chef famoso/a? ¿Qué tipo de comida prepara?
7. ¿Conoces a algún (alguna) escritor(a) famoso/a?
8. ¿Sabes si ofrecen cursos de administración de empresas en la universidad?

Síntesis

7

Conversar En parejas, túrnense para hacerse preguntas usando las frases de la lista. Luego informen a la clase de los resultados.

modelo

conocer el estado de Utah
Estudiante 1: ¿Conoces el estado de Utah?
Estudiante 2: Sí, conozco el estado de Utah./ Yo no, pero mi novio sí lo conoce.

traducir bien
conducir muy mal
estudiar mucho
preocupar(se) demasiado
creer que siempre tiene razón
peinar(se) de una manera elegante
saber afeitarse con sólo una mano
saber maquillarse muy bien
conocer a alguien famoso
saber quedarse en silencio
conocer el Gran Cañón
saber seleccionar platos del menú

AYUDA

Whereas in English we make contrasts by using *do/does*, in Spanish it is common to use **sí/no**.

Yo no lo conozco, pero mi novio **sí lo conoce**.

*I don't know it, but my boyfriend **does**.*

TEACHING OPTIONS

Pairs Ask students to individually write brief paragraphs in which they use the verbs presented in this section. Then they exchange their papers with a partner. Students should help each other to make the paragraphs as error-free as possible. Collect the papers for grading.

Extra Practice Ask individual students questions that are most likely not true for them. When students give a negative answer, they should indicate someone else for whom the question would be true. Ex: ____, **¿conoces a Martin Sheen? No, no lo conozco, pero Rob Lowe sí lo conoce.**

4 Present Point out that students should not simply answer with **sí** or **no** but should expand upon their answers.

4 Expand Ask individual students what their partner knows how to do. The partner verifies the information.

5 Present Explain that if the city in which the university is found is on the list, that city is not valid for the activity. Distribute **Hoja de actividades 18**.

5 Expand If you also know any of the cities mentioned in class, converse with students about your experiences.

6 Present Give pairs five minutes to complete the activity. Make sure students take turns asking and answering questions.

6 Expand Ask questions of the whole class to find someone for whom these questions are true. Ask for additional information. Ex: **¿Quién conoce un buen restaurante? ¿Ah, sí? ¿Cuál es? ¿Por qué es tan bueno?** and so forth.

7 Present Give students several minutes to form questions that they would like to ask their partner.

Ayuda
Present Explain that these uses of **sí** and **no** may help them in the activity and in conversations with others.

7 Expand Ask for whom in the class the items listed are true. Try to get as much information as possible. **¿Quién conoce el estado de Utah? ¿Ah, sí? ¿Por qué lo conoces?** and so forth.

Assignment Have students do activities in **Student Activities Manual: Workbook**, page 91.

Section Goals

In **Estructura 8.4** students will be introduced to:
- comparisons of inequality
- comparisons of equality
- superlatives
- irregular comparative and superlative words

Instructional Resources
Student Activities Manual: Workbook, *92–93; Lab Manual, 266*
Hoja de actividades 19

Before Presenting Estructura 8.4
Introduce the concept of comparisons. Write **más + *adjective* + que** and **menos + *adjective* + que** on the board, explaining their meaning. Illustrate with examples. Ex: **Esta clase es más grande que la clase de la tarde. La clase de la tarde es menos inteligente que ésta.** **Assignment** Have students study **Estructura 8.4** and prepare the activities on pages 255–256 as homework.

Present Model the pronunciation of each example in **Ante todo** and use it in a sentence.

Comparisons of inequality
Present Work through the explanations and model example sentences. Give additional examples using adjectives, adverbs, and nouns.

In examples where the second term of a comparison is a pronoun, emphasize that in Spanish subject pronouns are used. Ex: **Mi hermana es más alta que yo.** (It is a common error in English to use object pronouns here, and students may be inclined to carry that error into Spanish.)

¡Atención! Emphasize the use of **de** instead of **que** when the comparison comes before a number.

Continued on page 253.

8.4 Comparisons and superlatives

NATIONAL STANDARDS comparisons

ANTE TODO Spanish and English use comparisons to indicate which of two people or things has a lesser, equal, or greater degree of a quality. Both languages also use superlatives to express the highest or lowest degree of a quality.

Comparisons

menos interesante *less interesting*	más rápido *quicker*	tan sabroso como *as delicious as*

Superlatives

el mejor *the best*	el peor *the worst*	el más rápido *the fastest*

Comparisons of inequality

▶ Comparisons of inequality are formed by placing **más** (*more*) or **menos** (*less*) before adjectives, adverbs, and nouns and **que** (*than*) after them.

más/menos + [*adjective* / *adverb* / *noun*] + **que**

adjectives

Los bistecs son **más caros que** el pollo.
Steaks are more expensive than chicken.

Estas uvas son **menos sabrosas que** esa pera.
These grapes are less tasty than that pear.

adverbs

Me acuesto **más tarde que** tú.
I go to bed later than you (do).

Mi hermano corre **menos rápido que** Alfredo.
My brother runs less quickly than Alfredo.

nouns

Juan prepara **más platos que** José.
Juan prepares more dishes than José.

Susana come **menos carne que** Enrique.
Susana eats less meat than Enrique.

¡ATENCIÓN!

Note that while English has a comparative form for short adjectives (*faster*), such forms do not exist in Spanish (**más** rápido).

•••

When the comparison involves a numerical expression, **de** is used before the number instead of **que**.

Hay más **de** cincuenta naranjas.

Llego en menos **de** diez minutos.

Tengo más hambre que un elefante.

El lomo a la plancha es un poquito más caro pero es sabrosísimo.

▶ With verbs, the following construction is used to make comparisons of inequality:

[*verb*] + **más/menos que**

Mis hermanos **comen más que** yo.
My brothers eat more than I (do).

Arturo **duerme menos que** su padre.
Arturo sleeps less than his father (does).

TEACHING OPTIONS

Extra Practice Ask questions of students that make comparisons of inequality using adjectives, adverbs, and nouns. Ex: **¿Qué es más sabroso que una ensalada de frutas? ¿Quién se despierta más tarde que tú? ¿Quién tiene más libros que yo?** Then ask questions that use verbs in their construction. Ex: **¿Quién en la clase habla más que yo?**

Heritage Speakers Ask heritage speakers to give four to five sentences in which they compare themselves to members of their families. Make sure that the comparisons are ones of inequality. Ask other students in the class to report what the heritage speakers said as comprehension.

Comparisons of equality

The following construction is used to make comparisons of equality.

tan + [*adjective* / *adverb*] + **como**   **tanto/a(s)** + [*singular noun* / *plural noun*] + **como**

¡ATENCIÓN!

Note that **tanto** acts as an adjective and therefore agrees in number and gender with the noun it modifies: **tantas cosas**.

•••

Tan and **tanto** can also be used for emphasis, rather than to compare, with these meanings: **tan** *so*, **tanto** *so much*, **tantos/as** *so many*.

¡Tu almuerzo es **tan** grande!
*Your lunch is **so** big!*

¡Comes **tanto**!
*You eat **so much**!*

¡Comes **tantas** manzanas!
*You eat **so many** apples!*

¿Qué tal tu ceviche?

La comida es tan rica como en España.

Yo comí **tanta comida como** tú.
I ate as much food as you (did).

Uds. probaron **tantos platos como** él.
You tried as many dishes as they did.

▶ Comparisons of equality with verbs are formed by placing **tanto como** after the verb. Note that in this construction **tanto** does not change in number or gender.

[*verb*] + **tanto como**

No **duermo tanto como** mi tía.
I don't sleep as much as my aunt.

Estudiamos tanto como ustedes.
We study as much as you (do).

Superlatives

▶ The following construction is used to form superlatives. Note that the noun is always preceded by a definite article and that **de** is equivalent to the English *in* or *of*.

el/la/los/las + [*noun*] + **más/menos** + [*adjective*] + **de**

¡ATENCIÓN!

While **más** alone means *more*, after **el** or **la** (or **los** or **las**), it means *most*.

Es **el café más rico del** país.
It's the most delicious coffee in the country.

Es el menú **menos caro de** todos estos.
It is the least expensive menu of all of these.

▶ The noun in a superlative construction can be omitted if it is clear who is the person, place, or thing being referred to.

¿El restaurante El Cráter?
Es **el más elegante** de la ciudad.
¿The El Cráter restaurant?
It's the most elegant one in the city.

Recomiendo el pollo asado.
Es **el más sabroso** del menú.
I recommend the roast chicken.
It's the most delicious on the menu.

TEACHING OPTIONS

Extra Practice Have students write three original comparative or superlative sentences that describe themselves. Ex: **Soy el jugador más bajo del equipo de baloncesto.** Then collect the papers and read the sentences aloud. See if the rest of the class can guess who wrote each description.

Game Divide the class into two groups, A and B. Place the names of 20 famous people into a hat. Select a member from each group to draw a name. The student from group A then has 10 seconds to compare those two famous people. If the student has made a logical comparison, team A gets a point. Then it's team B's turn to make a different comparison, and so forth. The team with the most points at the end wins.

Comparisons of Equality

Present Work through explanation, diagram, and example sentences. Model additional sentences using this construction. Practice it by asking the class questions whose responses require the construction. Ex: **¿Quién es tan guapa como Jennifer López? ¿Quién tiene tanto dinero como Tiger Woods?** and so forth.

Contrast uses of **tan… como** and **tanto/a/os/as… como.** Point out that **tanto/a/os/as** in this construction is an adjective and must agree with the noun it modifies. Ask questions that involve comparisons with yourself. **¿Quién es tan alto como yo? Y ¿quién está tan cansado como yo? ¿Quién se acostó tan tarde como yo? ¿Quién habla tantas lenguas como yo? ¿Quién bebe tanto café como yo?**

Draw students' attention to the first **¡Atención!** sidebar on this page. Involve class in a conversation about themselves and classroom objects. Ex: ____, **¿por qué tienes tantas plumas? ¿Necesitas tantas? ____, cómo tu mochila es tan grande, puedes llevar muchos libros, ¿no? ¿Quién más tiene una mochila tan grande?**

Superlatives

Present Work through explanation, diagram, and model sentences. Model additional sentences that practice this construction and ask questions of students. Ex: **¿Cuál es la clase más difícil de esta universidad? Y ¿la más fácil?**

¡Atención!

Suggestion Point out that the superlative for less or fewer (**menos**) is least.

Irregular comparisons and superlatives

Irregular comparative and superlative forms

Adjective		Comparative form		Superlative form	
bueno/a	*good*	**mejor**	*better*	**el/la mejor**	*(the) best*
malo/a	*bad*	**peor**	*worse*	**el/la peor**	*(the) worst*
grande	*big*	**mayor**	*bigger*	**el/la mayor**	*(the) biggest*
pequeño	*small*	**menor**	*smaller*	**el/la menor**	*(the) smallest*
viejo/a	*old*	**menor**	*younger*	**el/la menor**	*(the) youngest*
joven	*young*	**mayor**	*older*	**el/la mayor**	*(the) oldest*

- When **grande** and **pequeño/a** refer to age, the irregular comparative and superlative forms, **mayor** and **menor**, are used. However, when these adjectives refer to size, the regular forms, **más grande** and **más pequeño/a**, are used.

Isabel es **la mayor** de su familia.
Isabel is the oldest in her family.

Tu ensalada es **más grande** que esa.
Your salad is bigger than that one.

Yo soy **menor** que tú.
I'm younger than you.

Pedí **el plato más pequeño** del menú.
I ordered the smallest dish on the menu.

- The adverbs **bien** and **mal** have the same irregular comparative forms as the adjectives **bueno/a** and **malo/a**.

Julio nada **mejor** que los otros chicos.
Julio swims better than the other boys.

Ellas cantan **peor** que las otras chicas.
They sing worse than the other girls.

CONSÚLTALO

Descriptive adjectives
To review how **bueno**, **malo**, and **grande** shorten before nouns, see Lesson 3, section 3.1, p.80.

Irregular comparisons and superlatives
Present/Expand
- Model irregular comparative and superlative forms in the chart. Ask questions and give examples to practice these forms. Ex: **¿Quién es el o la menor de su familia? ¿Ah, sí? ¿Cuántos hermanos mayores tienes?** and so forth.
- Point out that irregular superlatives for **bueno/a** and **malo/a** are also irregular in English: better and worse, respectively.
- Work through subsequent explanations and examples. Stress the differences between **grande—mayor** and **pequeño/a—menor** when referring to age.
- Emphasize that the same superlatives are used for adverbs **bien** and **mal** as for adjectives **bueno/a** and **malo/a.**

Consúltalo
Present Point out this sidebar to students. Review shortening of these adjectives as necessary for your class.

TEACHING OPTIONS

Large Groups Divide students into groups of six. Give cards with adjectives listed at the top of page 254 to one group. Give cards with the corresponding irregular comparative form to another group. Students must find their partner. To avoid confusion, make duplicate cards of **mayor** and **menor**.

Extra Practice Ask students questions with superlatives about things and places at your university, in your city/town, in the class, and so forth. Include a good mix of regular and irregular superlative forms. Ex: **¿Cuál es el edificio más grande del campus? ¿Cuál es la peor clase de la universidad?** and so forth.

Absolute Superlatives

- In Spanish the absolute superlative is equivalent to *extremely, exceptionally, super,* or *very* before an adjective or adverb. You encountered an absolute superlative when you learned how to say **Me gusta(n) muchísimo...**

- To form the absolute superlative of most adjectives and adverbs, drop the final vowel or consonant and add **-ísimo.**

malo → mal- → malísimo

¡El bistec está **malísimo**!
The steak is very bad!

mucho → much- → muchísimo

Comes **muchísimo**.
You eat a lot (very, very much).

difícil + -ísimo → dificilísimo

Esta prueba es **dificilísima**.
This quiz is exceptionally difficult.

fácil + ísimo → facilísimo

Los exámenes son **facilísimos**.
The tests are extremely easy.

- Adjectives and adverbs whose stem ends in **c, g,** or **z** change spelling to **qu**, **gu**, and **c** in the absolute superlative.

rico → riquísimo **largo → larguísimo** **feliz → felicísimo**

- Adjectives that end in **-n** or **-r** normally form the absolute superlative by adding **-císimo.**

joven + -císimo → jovencísimo **trabajador + -císimo → trabajadorcísimo**

¡INTÉNTALO! Escribe el equivalente de las palabras en inglés.

Comparativos

1. (*than*) Ernesto mira más televisión _que_ Alberto.
2. (*less*) Tú eres _menos_ simpático que Federico.
3. (*as much*) La camarera sirve _tanta_ carne como pescado.
4. (*more*) Conozco _más_ restaurantes que tú.
5. (*as much as*) No estudio _tanto como_ tú.
6. (*as*) ¿Sabes jugar al tenis tan bien _como_ tu hermana?
7. (*as many*) ¿Puedes beber _tantos_ refrescos como yo?
8. (*as*) Mis amigos parecen _tan_ simpáticos como Uds.

Superlativos

1. (*the most intelligent*) Marisa es _la más inteligente_ de todas.
2. (*the least boring*) Ricardo y Tomás son _los menos aburridos_ de la fiesta.
3. (*the worst*) Miguel y Antonio son _los peores_ estudiantes de la clase.
4. (*the oldest*) Mi profesor de biología es _el mayor_ de la universidad.
5. (*extremely delicious*) El pollo de esta tienda es _riquísimo_.
6. (*the youngest*) Carlos es _el menor_ de mis hermanos.
7. (*the best*) Este plato es _el mejor_ del restaurante.
8. (*extremely tall*) Sara es _altísima_.

Absolute Superlatives
Present Work through explanation of the absolute superlative, modeling their formation and pronunciation. Point out that the absolute superlative doesn't really imply a comparison. The **-ísimo/a** suffix is an intensifier. **Riquísimo**, for instance, does not mean *the richest*, but *extremely/exceptionally/very rich.*

Stress the dropping of the final vowel in adjectives and adverbs.

Point out that spelling changes that adjectives and adverbs whose stem ends in **c**, **g**, or **z** undergo are made in order to keep the consonant sound of that stem, and they mirror the spelling changes that verb stems ending in these consonants undergo when the personal ending **-é** is attached.

You may want to point out that absolute superlative forms using **–císimo** are rarely used.

Suggestion You may also want to point out that an irregular absolute superlative exists for **bueno/a**: **bonísimo/a**. However, over time this form has become archaic, and **buenísimo/a** is the favored form now in popular usage.

Close Consolidate entire section by doing **¡Inténtalo!** with the whole class.

TEACHING OPTIONS

Extra Practice Give 6–10 comparative and superlative sentences orally to practice listening comprehension. Dictate the sentences, then give students about 30 seconds per sentence to write the direct opposite. Ask volunteers to present their opposite sentences. Ex: **Ernesto mira más televisión que Alberto. (Alberto mira menos televisión que Ernesto.)**

Heritage Speakers Ask heritage speakers to discuss whether absolute superlatives are common in their culture or not (some regions and countries use them less frequently than others). Also have them discuss under what circumstances absolute superlatives are most frequently used, such as when talking about food, people, events, and so forth.

Práctica

1 **Escoger** Escoge (*Choose*) la palabra correcta del paréntesis para comparar a dos hermanas muy diferentes. Haz (*Make*) las adaptaciones necesarias.

1. Lucila es más alta y más bonita ___que___ Tita. (de, más, menos, que)
2. Tita es más delgada porque practica ___más___ deportes que su hermana. (de, más, menos, que)
3. Lucila es más ___simpática___ que Tita porque es alegre. (listo, simpático, bajo)
4. A Tita le gusta quedarse en casa. Va a ___menos___ fiestas que su hermana. (de, más, menos, que) Es tímida e inteligente. ___Estudia___ más que Lucila. (abrir, oír, estudiar) Ahora está tomando más ___de___ cinco clases. (de, más, menos, que)
5. Lucila se preocupa ___menos___ que Tita por estudiar. (de, más, menos, que) ¡Son ___tan___ diferentes!, pero se llevan muy bien. (como, tan, tanto)

2 **Emparejar** Completa las oraciones (*sentences*) de la columna A con palabras o frases de la columna B para comparar a Mario y a Luis, los novios de Lucila y Tita.

A

1. Mario es ___tan interesante___ como Luis.
2. Mario viaja tanto ___como___ Luis.
3. Luis habla ___tantas___ lenguas extranjeras como Mario.
4. Luis habla ___francés___ tan bien como Mario.
5. Mario tiene tantos ___amigos extranjeros___ como Luis.
6. ¡Qué casualidad (*coincidence*)! Mario y Luis también son hermanos, pero no hay tanta ___diferencia___ entre ellos como entre Lucila y Tita.

B

tantas
diferencia
tan interesante
amigos extranjeros
como
francés

3 **Completar** Tu profesor(a) va a darte (*to give you*) una hoja de actividades con descripciones de José Valenzuela Carranza y Ana Orozco Hoffman. Completa las oraciones acerca de (*about*) Ana, José, y sus familias con las palabras de la lista.

atlética	del	mejor	peor
altísima	la	menor	periodista
bajo	más	guapísimo	trabajadorcísimo
de	mayor	Orozco	Valenzuela

1. José es el ___menor___ y el más ___bajo___ de su familia. Es ___guapísimo___ y ___trabajadorcísimo___. Es el mejor ___periodista___ de 2000 y el ___peor___ jugador de baloncesto.
2. Ana es la más ___atlética___ y ___la___ mejor jugadora de baloncesto. Es la ___mayor___ de sus hermanos y es ___altísima___. Estudió la profesión ___más___ difícil ___de___ todas.
3. Jorge es el ___mejor___ jugador de juegos electrónicos.
4. Mauricio es el menor de la familia ___Orozco___.
5. El abuelo es el ___mayor___ de la familia Valenzuela.
6. Fifí es la perra más antipática ___del___ mundo.

1 Warm-up You may wish to quickly review the use of **de** before numerals in comparisons.

1 Present If activity was done as homework, quickly go over answers in class.

1 Expand Ask two students a question, then have another student compare them. Ex: ____, **¿cuántas horas de televisión miras cada día? ¿Y tú, ____? ____, haz una comparación.** Ask several pairs of students different types of questions. Possible questions: **¿Cuántas veces a la semana sales para comer en un restaurante? ¿Cuáles prefieres, las películas de aventuras o las dramas? ¿Estudias más para la clase de español o la clase de matemáticas?**

2 Present If activity was done as homework, quickly go over answers in class.

2 Expand Turn the activity's statements into questions and ask them of members of the class. Have students make up answers that involve comparisons.

3 Present Distribute the top part of **Hoja de actividades 19** to half the students and the bottom part to the rest. Explain to the class that information from both parts of the **Hoja** is necessary to complete the activity.

3 Expand Go over answers in class, asking individual students to complete the statements.

3 Expand In pairs, have students select a member of their family or a close friend and describe him or her using comparatives and superlatives. Ask volunteers to share their description with the class.

TEACHING OPTIONS

Extra Practice Using your picture file, magazine pictures, or your own drawings, show a family whose members vary widely in different aspects: age (write a number on each person that indicates how old he or she is), height, weight, and so forth. Ask students to make comparisons of that family. Give names to each family member so that they are easier to identify.

Large Groups Divide the class into two groups. Survey each group to get information about various topics. Ex: **¿Cuántos de Uds. hacen ejercicios cada día? ¿Cuántos salen al cine cada fin de semana? ¿Cuántos comen la comida rápida tres veces a la semana?** Ask for a show of hands and tally the number of hands. Then have students make comparisons between the two groups based on the information given.

NATIONAL communication STANDARDS

Comunicación

4

Intercambiar En parejas, hagan comparaciones sobre diferentes cosas. Pueden usar las sugerencias de la lista u otras ideas. Answers will vary.

AYUDA

You can use the following adjectives in your comparisons.

bonito/a
caro/a
elegante
interesante
inteligente

modelo

Estudiante 1: Los pollos de Pollitos del Corral son los mejores del mundo.
Estudiante 2: Pues yo creo que los pollos de Rostipollos son tan buenos como los pollos de Pollitos del Corral.
Estudiante 1: Mmm... no tienen tanta mantequilla como los pollos de Pollitos del Corral. Tienes razón. Son sabrosísimos.

restaurantes en tu ciudad/pueblo
cafés en tu ciudad/pueblo
tiendas en tu ciudad/pueblo

periódicos en tu ciudad/pueblo
revistas favoritas
libros favoritos

comidas favoritas
los profesores de las clases
los cursos que toman

5

Conversar En grupos, túrnense (*take turns*) para hacer comparaciones entre Uds. mismos (*yourselves*) y una persona de cada categoría de la lista. Answers will vary.

- una persona de tu familia
- un(a) amigo/a especial
- un(a) persona famosa

NATIONAL communication STANDARDS

Síntesis

6

Representar En grupos, preparen un diálogo sobre dos personas interesantes pero muy diferentes. Digan (*say*) por qué las conocen, qué saben hacer y cómo son.

Answers will vary.

modelo

Estudiante 1: ¿Conoces a Carolina y a Catalina?
Estudiante 2: Sí, las conozco de la escuela. ¿Por qué las conoces tú?
Estudiante 1: Porque vamos al mismo gimnasio. Son muy atléticas.
Estudiante 3: Sí, las dos hacen deporte, pero Catalina es la más atlética.

4 Present Ask a volunteer to model the sample conversation with you. Point out that this activity gives students a chance to express their personal opinions as well as to make comparisons. Give students 10 minutes to make comparisons and converse about their personal preferences.

4 Expand Ask pairs of volunteers to present one of their conversations to the class. Then survey the class to see which of the students the class agrees with more.

5 Present Model the activity by making a few comparisons between yourself and some celebrity. Then, give groups six minutes to make their comparisons.

5 Expand Ask a volunteer to share his or her comparisons. Then make comparisons between yourself and the student or yourself and the person the student mentioned. Continue to do this for three or four students.

6 Present Give groups three minutes to discuss the two people. You may want to do the activity with the whole class. You suggest names of two people to begin the first discussion. Continue discussing different people in order to give more students the opportunity to participate.

6 Expand Ask groups to share their discussion with the class. Students may even recreate their conversation in order to do this.

Assignment Have students do activities in **Student Activities Manual: Workbook,** pages 92–93.

TEACHING OPTIONS

Extra Practice As a listening comprehension activity, prepare short descriptions of five easily recognizable people in which you compare them to other recognizable people. Write their names on the board in random order. Then read your descriptions, having students match the description to the appropriate name. Ex: **Esta persona es más famoso que Enrique Iglesias pero es tan guapo como él. (Ricky Martin)**

TPR Give the same types of objects to different students but in different numbers. For example, hand out three books to one student, one book to another, and four to another. Then call on individuals to make comparisons between the students based on the number of objects they have.

Section Goals

In **Estructura 8.5** students will be introduced to:
- pronouns as objects of prepositions
- the pronoun-preposition combinations **conmigo** and **contigo**

Instructional Resources
Student Activities Manual: Workbook, 94; Lab Manual, 267
Hoja de actividades 20

Before Presenting Estructura 8.5 Review prepositions of location from **Estructura 2.3**. Use prepositional pronouns as you describe yourself and others in relation to people and things. Say: **¿Quién está delante de mí? Sí, ____ está delante de mí. ¿Y quién está detrás de ella? Sí, ____ está detrás de ella,** and so forth. Tell students that they are now going to learn the forms of the pronouns that follow prepositions.

Assignment Have students study **Estructura 8.5** and prepare **¡Inténtalo!** and Activity 1 on pages 258–259 as homework.

Pronouns after prepositions

Present Work through explanation of the object of a preposition and model prepositional pronouns in the chart. Students will recognize all of these except **mí** and **ti**. Emphasize that, except for **mí** and **ti**, the other prepositional pronouns are the same as subject pronouns.

Point out the written accent on **mí** in order to differentiate it from the possessive adjective **mi**. Also, draw students' attention to the fact that **ti** does not have a written accent. (The possessive adjective is **tu**.)

Close Consolidate entire section by doing **¡Inténtalo!** with the whole class.

8.5 Pronouns after prepositions

NATIONAL STANDARDS comparisons

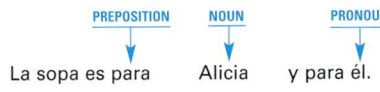

ANTE TODO In Spanish, as in English, the object of a preposition is the noun or pronoun that follows a preposition. Observe the following diagram.

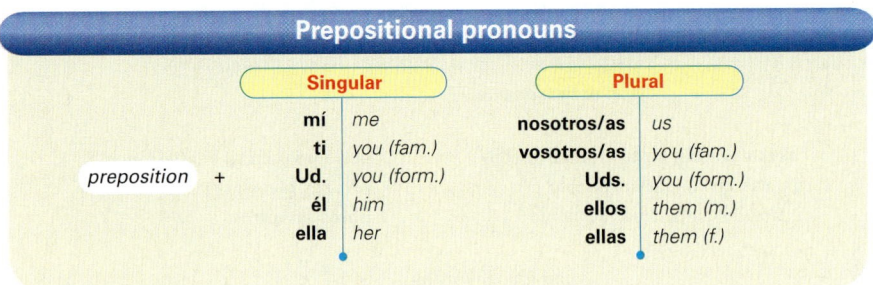

La sopa es para (PREPOSITION) Alicia (NOUN) y para él (PRONOUN).

Prepositional pronouns

		Singular		Plural	
preposition	+	**mí**	*me*	**nosotros/as**	*us*
		ti	*you (fam.)*	**vosotros/as**	*you (fam.)*
		Ud.	*you (form.)*	**Uds.**	*you (form.)*
		él	*him*	**ellos**	*them (m.)*
		ella	*her*	**ellas**	*them (f.)*

- Note that, except for **mí** and **ti,** these pronouns are the same as the subject pronouns.

- The preposition **con** combines with **mí** and **ti** to form **conmigo** and **contigo,** respectively.

  —¿Quieres venir **conmigo** a París?
  Do you want to come with me to Paris

  —Sí, gracias, me gustaría ir **contigo.**
  Yes, thanks, I would like to go with you.

- The preposition **entre** is followed by **tú** and **yo** instead of **ti** and **mí.**

  Papá va a sentarse **entre tú y yo**.
  Dad is going to sit between you and me.

¡ATENCIÓN!
Mí (*me*) has an accent mark to distinguish it from the possessive adjective **mi** (*my*).

¡INTÉNTALO! Completa las siguientes frases con las preposiciones y los pronombres apropiados.

1. *(with him)* No quiero ir con él.
2. *(for her)* Los libros son para ella.
3. *(for me)* Los mariscos son para mí.
4. *(with you,* pl. form.*)* Preferimos estar con Uds..
5. *(with you,* fam.*)* Me gusta salir contigo.
6. *(with me)* ¿Por qué no quieres venir conmigo?
7. *(for her)* El té es para ella.
8. *(for them,* m.*)* La habitación es muy pequeña para ellos.
9. *(with them,* f.*)* Anoche cené muy bien con ellas.
10. *(for you,* fam.*)* Este reloj es para ti.
11. *(with you,* fam.*)* Nunca me aburro contigo.
12. *(with you,* pl. form.*)* ¡Qué bien que vamos con Uds..
13. *(for you,* fam.*)* Para ti es todo muy fácil.
14. *(for them,* f.*)* Para ellas no hay fronteras.

TEACHING OPTIONS

Extra Practice Describe someone in the classroom using prepositions of location, but don't indicate who that person is. Ex: **Esta persona está sentada entre la ventana y ____. Y está enfrente de mí.** The rest of the class has to guess the person being described. Once students have this model, ask individuals to create similar descriptions so that their classmates may guess who is being described.

Game Divide the class into two groups. One student from the first group chooses an item that's in the classroom and writes it down. Call on five students from the other group one at a time to ask questions about where this item is. Ex: **¿Está cerca de mí?** The first student can respond with **sí, no, caliente,** or **frío**. If a team guesses the item within five tries, give them a point. If not, give the other team a point. The team with the most points wins.

Práctica

1 **Completar** David sale con sus amigos a comer. Para saber quién come qué, lee el mensaje electrónico que David le envió (*sent*) a Cecilia dos días después y completa el diálogo en el restaurante con los pronombres apropiados.

modelo

Camarero: Los camarones en salsa verde, ¿para quién son?
David: Son para ___ella___.

CAMARERO	El filete de pescado, ¿para quién es?
DAVID	Es para ___mí___.
CAMARERO	Aquí está. ¿Y el arroz con mariscos y las langostas?
DAVID	El arroz con mariscos es para ___ella___.
SILVIA Y DIANA	Las langostas son para ___nosotras___.
CAMARERO	Tengo un bistec grande...
DAVID	Cecilia, es para ___ti___, ¿no es cierto? (*Cecilia nods.*) Y el bistec más pequeño es para ___él___.
CAMARERO	¿Quién va a tomar vino tinto?
MIGUEL	Es para todos ___nosotros___, y el pollo es para ___mí___.
CAMARERO	(*a la profesora*) Entonces la ensalada verde es para ___usted___.

Para | Asunto

Hola,Cecilia:
¿Recuerdas la comida del viernes? Quiero repetir el menú en mi casa el miércoles. Ahora voy a escribir lo que comimos, luego me dices si falta algún plato. Yo pedí el filete de pescado y Maribel camarones en salsa verde. Tatiana pidió un plato grandísimo de arroz con mariscos. Diana y Silvia pidieron langostas, ¿te acuerdas? Y tú, ¿qué pediste? Ah, sí, un bistec grande con papas. Héctor también pidió un bistec, pero más pequeño. Miguel pidió pollo y vino tinto para todos. Y la profesora comió ensalada verde porque está a dieta. ¿Falta algo? Espero tu mensaje. Hasta pronto. David.

NATIONAL communication STANDARDS

Comunicación

2 **Compartir** Tu profesor(a) va a darte (*to give you*) una hoja de actividades en la que hay un dibujo. En parejas, hagan preguntas para saber dónde está cada una de las personas en el dibujo. Uds. tienen dos versiones diferentes de la ilustración. Al final (*end*) deben saber dónde está cada persona.

modelo

Estudiante 1: ¿Quién está al lado de Yolanda?
Estudiante 2: Alfredo está al lado de ella.

Alfredo	Dolores	Rubén	Raúl
Sra. Blanco	Enrique	Óscar	Sra. Gómez
Carlos	Graciela	Leonor	Yolanda

1 Present If activity was done as homework, quickly go over answers in class. If activity was not done as homework, read the **Modelo**, and give students five minutes to read the e-mail message and to complete the items in the activity. You may also wish for individual students to take turns reading the e-mail message aloud while the rest of the class follows along. Point out that students are to fill the blanks with prepositional pronouns, not names of the people in the dialogue.

1 Expand In small groups, have students play the roles of the people mentioned in the e-mail message. Individuals take turns asking who certain dishes are for. Students answer using prepositional pronouns. Ex: S1: **¿Para quién son los camarones?** S2: **Son para mí.**: S1: **¿Y el bistec? : S2: Son para él.**

2 Present Distribute copies of the top part of **Hoja de actividades 20** to one member of the pair and the bottom part to the other. Go over the directions with the class and give pairs five minutes to complete the activity. Tell pairs that when they decide where each person is, they should jot that information down.

2 Expand Using both versions of the illustration as a guide, ask questions of the whole class to find out where the people are. Ex: **¿Quién sabe dónde está la Sra. Blanco?**

Assignment Have students do activities in **Student Activities Manual: Workbook,** page 94.

TEACHING OPTIONS

Video Show the video module again to give students more input containing prepositional pronouns. Stop the video where appropriate to discuss how certain pronouns were used and to ask comprehension questions.

Large Groups Give half of the class cards that contain an activity (Ex: **jugar al baloncesto**) and give the other half cards that contain a place (Ex: **el gimnasio**). Activity card students circulate around the room to find places that match their activities. Ex: S1: **Voy a jugar al baloncesto. ¿Puedo ir contigo?** S2: **Pues, yo voy al museo. No puedes ir conmigo.** or **Voy al gimnasio. Sí, puedes ir conmigo.**

Section Goals

In **Lectura** students will:
- learn to identify the main idea in a text
- read a content-rich menu and restaurant review

Antes de leer

Tell students that recognizing the main idea of a text will help them unlock the meaning of unfamiliar words and phrases they come across while reading. Tell them to check the title first. The main idea is often expressed in the title. Tell them to read the topic sentence of each paragraph before they read the full text, so they will get a sense of the main idea.

Examinar el texto First, have students scan the menu. Ask how the title and subheadings help predict the content. Ask volunteers to state the meaning of each category of food served: **Entremeses** (Hors d'oeuvres), **Sopas** (Soups), **Entradas** (Entrees), **Postres** (Desserts), and **Bebidas** (Beverages). Then have students scan the newspaper article. Ask them how the title and the format (the box with ratings) of the text give clues to the content.

Identificar la idea principal Ask students to read the column heading and the title of the article and predict the subject of the article and the author's purpose. Then have students read the topic sentence of the first paragraph and state the main idea. Finally, have them read the entire paragraph.

Assignment Have students read **Menú** and **Cuatro estrellas para La feria del maíz** as well as the activities in **Después de leer** for the next class.

Lectura

NATIONAL STANDARDS communication cultures

Antes de leer

Estrategia
Reading for the main idea

As you know, you can learn a great deal about a reading selection by looking for cognates, titles and subtitles, and formatting. You can skim to get the gist of the reading selection and scan it for specific information. Reading for the main idea is another useful strategy; it involves locating the topic sentences of each paragraph in order to determine the author's purpose for writing a particular piece. Topic sentences can provide clues about the content of each paragraph, as well as the general organization of the reading. Your choice of which reading strategies to use will depend on the style and format of each reading selection.

Examinar el texto

En esta sección tenemos dos textos diferentes. ¿Qué estrategias puedes usar para leer la crítica culinaria? ¿Cuáles son las apropiadas para familiarizarte con el menú? Utiliza las estrategias más eficaces para cada texto. ¿Qué tienen en común? ¿Qué tipo de comida sirven en el restaurante?

Identificar la idea principal

Lee la primera frase de cada párrafo de la crítica culinaria del restaurante **La feria del maíz.** Apunta el tema prinicipal de cada párrafo. Luego lee todo el primer párrafo. ¿Crees que el restaurante le gustó al/a la autor(a) de la crítica culinaria? ¿Por qué? Ahora lee la crítica entera. En tu opinión, ¿cuál es la idea principal de la crítica? ¿Por qué la escribió el/la autor(a)? Compara tus opiniones con las de un(a) compañero/a.

MENÚ

Entremeses

Tortilla servida con
• Ajiaceite (chile, aceite) • Ajicomino (chile, comino)

Pan tostado servido con
• Queso frito a la pimienta • Salsa de ajo y mayonesa

Sopas

• Tomate • Cebolla • Verduras • Pollo y huevo
• Carne de res • Mariscos

Entradas

Tomaticán
(tomate, patatas, maíz, chile, guisantes, zanahorias y verduras)

Tamales
(maíz, azúcar, ajo, cebolla)

Frijoles enchilados
(frijoles negros, carne de cerdo o de res, arroz, chile)

Chilaquil
(tortilla de maíz, queso, hierbas y chile)

Tacos
(tortillas, pollo, verduras y mole)

Cóctel de mariscos
(camarones, langostas, vinagre, sal, pimienta, aceite)

Postres

• Plátanos caribeños • Cóctel de frutas al ron
• Uvate (uvas, azúcar de caña y ron) • Flan Napolitano
• Helado de piña y naranja • Pastel de yogur

Después de leer

Preguntas

En parejas, contesten las siguientes preguntas sobre la crítica culinaria de **La feria del maíz.** Answers will vary.

1. ¿Quién es el dueño y chef de **La feria del maíz**?
2. ¿Qué tipo de comida se sirve en el restaurante?
3. ¿Cuál es el problema con el servicio?
4. ¿Cómo es el ambiente del restaurante?
5. ¿Qué comidas probó el autor de la crítica culinaria?
6. ¿Quieren probar Uds. el restaurante **La feria del maíz**? ¿Por qué?

TEACHING OPTIONS

Heritage Speakers Ask Spanish speakers to create a dinner menu featuring their favorite dishes, including lists of ingredients similar to those in the menu above. Have Spanish speakers make copies of their menus, distribute them, and answer questions from classmates about how dishes are prepared or unfamiliar vocabulary.

Heritage Speakers If a Spanish speaker has visited Guatemala and dined in restaurants or cafés, ask him or her to prepare a short presentation about his or her experiences there. Of particular interest would be a comparison and contrast of city vs. small town restaurants. If possible, the presentation should be illustrated with menus from the restaurants, advertisements, or photos and articles of the country.

23F

Gastronomía

Cuatro estrellas para La feria del maíz

Sobresaliente. En el nuevo restaurante **La feria del maíz** Ud. va a encontrar la perfecta combinación entre la comida tradicional y el encanto de la vieja Antigua. Ernesto Sandoval, antiguo jefe de cocina del famoso restaurante **El fogón**, ha conseguido superarse en su nueva aventura culinaria.

El gerente, el experimentado José Sierra, controla a la perfección la calidad del servicio. El mesero que me atendió esa noche fue muy amable en todo momento. Sólo hay que comentar que, debido al éxito inmediato de **La feria del maíz**, se necesitan más meseros para atender a los clientes de una forma más eficaz. En esta ocasión, el mesero tardó unos veinte minutos en traerme la bebida.

Afortunadamente, no me importó mucho la espera entre plato y plato, pues el ambiente es tan agradable que me sentí como en casa. Por fuera, la fachada del restaurante mantiene el estilo colonial de Antigua. Por dentro, el estilo es elegante y rústico a la vez. Cuando el tiempo lo permite, se puede comer también en el patio, lleno de flores.

El servicio de meseros y el ambiente agradable del local pasan a un segundo plano cuando llega la comida, de una calidad y consistencia extraordinarias. Las tortillas están hechas en casa, y se sirven con un ajiaceite delicioso. La sopa de mariscos es excelente, y los tamales, pues, tengo que confesar que son mejores que los de mi abuelita. También recomiendo los tacos de pollo, servidos con un mole muy rico. De postre, don Ernesto me preparó su especialidad, un flan napolitano sabrosísimo.

Los precios pueden parecer altos para una comida tradicional, sin embargo, la calidad de los productos con que se cocinan los platos y el ambiente acogedor de **La feria del maíz** hacen que la experiencia valga la pena.

La feria del maíz
13 calle 4-41 Zona 1
La Antigua, Guatemala
2329912

lunes a sábado
10:30am-11:30pm
domingo 10:00am-10:00pm

Comida 🍴🍴🍴🍴🍴
Servicio 🍴🍴🍴
Ambiente 🍴🍴🍴🍴
Precio 🍴🍴🍴

Bebidas

- Cerveza negra • Chilate (bebida de maíz, chile y cacao)
- Jugos de fruta • Agua mineral • Té helado
- Vino tinto/blanco • Ron

Sobresaliente *Outstanding* ha conseguido superarse *has outdone himself* gerente *manager* altos *high* hacen...pena *make the experience well worthwhile*

Un(a) guía turístico/a

Tú eres un(a) guía turístico/a en Guatemala. Estás en el restaurante **La feria del maíz** con un grupo de turistas americanos. Ellos no hablan español y quieren comer, pero necesitan tu ayuda. ¿Cuál es el error de cada turista?

1. La Sra. Johnson es diabética y no puede comer azúcar. Pide sopa de verdura y tamales. No pide nada de postre.
   No debe pedir los tamales porque tienen azúcar.
2. Los señores Petit son vegeterianos y piden sopa de tomate, frijoles enchilados y plátanos caribeños.
   No deben pedir los frijoles enchilados porque tienen carne.
3. El Sr. Smith, que es alérgico al chocolate, pide tortilla servida con ajiaceite, chilaquil y chilate para beber.
   No debe pedir chilate porque tiene cacao.
4. La adorable hija del Sr. Smith tiene sólo cuatro años y le gustan mucho las verduras y las frutas naturales. Su papá le pide tomiticán y un cóctel de frutas.
   No debe pedir el cóctel de frutas porque tiene ron.
5. La Srta. Jackson está a dieta y pide uvate, flan napolitano y helado.
   No debe pedir postres porque está a dieta.

TEACHING OPTIONS

Extra Practice Ask students to review the exercises in **Un(a) guía turistico/a**, write dialogue, and act out the scene involving a tour guide eating lunch in a Guatemalan restaurant with several American tourists. Have them work in groups of 8 to assign the following roles: **mesero, guía turístico/a, Sra. Johnson, los señores Petit, Sr. Smith, la hija de Sr. Smith,** and **Srta. Jackson**. Each group can perform for the class.

Variación léxica Tell students that the adjective of place or nationality (**gentilicio**) for Guatemala is **guatemalteco/a**. Guatemalans often use a more colloquial term, **chapín**, as a synonym for **guatemalteco/a**.

Heritage Speakers Ask Spanish speakers to describe restaurant etiquette in Spanish-speaking countries. Have them discuss how to order, call a food server, ask for the check, tip, and so forth.

Después de leer

Preguntas

Suggestion Have students quickly review the article before answering the questions. Suggest that pairs take turns answering the questions. The student who does not answer a question should find the line of text that contains the answer. When pairs have finished, go over the answers orally with the whole class.

Suggestion If students have trouble inferring the meaning of any word or phrase, help them identify the corresponding context clues and explain any unfamiliar vocabulary.

Expand If you wish, expand the activity with these questions. **7. ¿Cómo fue el mesero que atendió al crítico? (Fue muy amable, pero muy ocupado con otros clientes del restaurante.) 8. ¿Cuál fue la opinión del crítico respecto a la comida? (Lo encontró todo de muy alta calidad.) 9. ¿Cómo son los precios de La feria del maíz? (Son altos, pero la calidad de la comida los justifica.)**

Un(a) guía turístico/a

Suggestion This activity is also appropriate for pairs to do in class if you have not assigned it as homework. Have partners read aloud one sentence at a time. Ask pairs to work together to check the menu and state why each customer should not order the item(s) he or she has selected.

The Affective Dimension A source of discomfort in travel can be unfamiliar foods. Tell students that by learning about the foods of a country they are going to visit they can make that part of their visit even more enjoyable.

Section Goals

In **Escritura** students will:
- learn to express and support opinions
- integrate in written form vocabulary and structures taught in **Lesson 8**
- write a restaurant review

Tema

Present Go over the directions with the class, explaining that each student will rate (**puntuar**) a local restaurant and write a review of a meal there, including a recommendation for future restaurant-goers.

Estrategia

Present Explain to students that when they write a restaurant review it is helpful to have some way of organizing the details required to support the rating. Have groups of three or four students write a list of questions in Spanish that readers of restaurant reviews might ask and use these to create a rating sheet. Tell them to refer to the list of questions on page 262 as a guide. Encourage students to leave space for comments in each category so they can record details that support their opinions. Suggest they fill out the rating sheet during the various stages of the meal.

Assignment Have students prepare **Ideas y organización** and **Primer borrador** for a class that takes place after they have visited a restaurant and filled out the rating sheet.

Escritura

NATIONAL communication STANDARDS

Estrategia

Expressing and supporting opinions

Written reviews are just one of many kinds of writing which require you to state your opinions. In order to convince your reader to take your opinions seriously, it is important to support them as thoroughly as possible. Details, facts, examples, and other forms of evidence are necessary. In a restaurant review, for example, it is not enough just to rate the food, service and atmosphere. Readers will want details about the dishes you ordered, the kind of service you received, and the type of atmosphere you encountered. If you were writing a concert or album review, what kinds of details might your readers expect to find?

It is easier to include details that support your opinions if you plan ahead. Before going to a place or event that you are planning to review, write a list of questions that your readers might ask. Decide which aspects of the experience you are going to rate and list the details that will help you decide upon a rating. You can then organize these lists into a questionnaire and a rating sheet. Bring these forms with you to help you make your opinions and to remind you of the kinds of information you need to gather in order to support those opinions. Later, these forms will help you organize your review into logical categories. They can also provide the details and other evidence you need to convince your readers of your opinions.

Tema

Una crítica culinaria

Escribe una crítica culinaria sobre un restaurante local para el periódico de la universidad. Puntúa el restaurante de una a cinco estrellas y anota tus recomendaciones para futuros clientes del restaurante. Incluye tus opiniones acerca de:

- La comida
  ¿Qué tipo de comida es? ¿Qué tipo de ingredientes se usan? ¿Es de buena calidad? ¿Cuál es el mejor plato? ¿Y el peor? ¿Quién es el chef?
- El servicio
  ¿Hay que esperar mucho para conseguir una mesa? ¿Tiene el camarero un buen conocimiento del menú? ¿Atienden a los clientes con rapidez y cortesía?
- El ambiente
  ¿Cómo es la decoración del restaurante? ¿Es el ambiente informal o elegante? ¿Hay música o algún tipo de entretenimiento? ¿Hay un bar? ¿Un patio?
- Información práctica
  ¿Cómo son los precios? ¿Se aceptan tarjetas de crédito? ¿Cuál es la dirección y el número de teléfono? ¿Quién es el dueño? ¿El gerente?

crítica culinaria *restaraunt review* acerca de *about* Puntúa *rate* estrellas *stars* se usan *are used* calidad *quality* amibiente *atmosphere* entretenimiento *entertainment* dirección *address*

TEACHING OPTIONS

Proofreading Activity Copy the following sentences containing mistakes onto the board or a transparency as a proofreading activity to do with the whole class.

1. **El Dr. Cavazos pedió un plato de tomaticán, pero el mesero lo servió a mí.**
2. **El tomaticán no es para mi. Puede Ud. servirlelo al Dr. Cavazos.**
3. **No conozco qué pedir de postre. Me recomienda Ud. un postre ricísimo?**
4. **¿Sabes un buen restaurante por aquí? Sí, el restaurante Eldorado es el más bueno de la ciudad.**
5. **¡Ay, entre ti y mí, el restaurante Eldorado es el peor de la ciudad!**
6. **Pedí una sopa de res bien caliente, ¡pero la me servieron fría!**

Plan de escritura

1 Ideas y organización

Usa un mapa de ideas para organizar tus comentarios sobre el **¿qué?, ¿quién?, ¿cuándo?, ¿dónde?, ¿cómo?** y **¿por qué?** de tu visita al restaurante y tu evaluación. Recuerda que tu artículo debe tener un título interesante para captar el interés del lector. Utiliza un esquema para organizar las diferentes partes de tu composición.

2 Primer borrador

Utilizando tus notas de **Ideas y organización,** escribe el primer borrador de tu artículo. Intenta usar el diccionario como último recurso.

3 Comentario

Intercambia tu composición con un(a) compañero/a. Lee su borrador y anota los aspectos mejor escritos de su crítica, por ejemplo cómo expresa su opinión acerca de la comida. Utiliza estas preguntas para evaluar el trabajo de tu compañero/a:

1. ¿Es interesante el título del artículo?
2. ¿Incluye toda la información pertinente?
3. ¿Está bien organizado el artículo?
4. ¿Está la opinión del/de la autor(a) apoyada con detalles específicos?
5. ¿Ves errores gramaticales u ortográficos?

4 Redacción

Revisa el primer borrador según las indicaciones de tu compañero/a. Incorpora nuevas ideas y/o más información para reforzar tu opinión. Utiliza esta guía para hacer la última revisión antes de escribir tu copia final.

1. Subraya cada verbo para comprobar la concordancia con el sujeto. ¡Cuidado con el pretérito!
2. Revisa la concordancia entre los sustantivos, los artículos y los adjetivos.
3. Comprueba el uso correcto de los pronombres.
4. Consulta tus **Anotaciones para mejorar la escritura** antes de revisar la ortografía y la puntuación.

5 Evaluación y progreso

Comprueba si hay un(a) compañero/a en la clase que conoce el restaurante evaluado en tu artículo y viceversa. Intercambien sus reportajes y después responde a estas preguntas.

- ¿Estás de acuerdo con la evaluación de tu compañero/a?
- ¿Qué impresiones del restaurante fueron similares o diferentes?

Lee los comentarios y las correcciones de tu profesor(a). Anota los errores más básicos en tu lista **Anotaciones para mejorar la escritura** en tu **Carpeta de trabajos.**

lector *reader* **esquema** *outline* **Intenta** *Try to* **Intercambia** *Exchange* **escritos** *written* **apoyada** *supported*

Comentario

Present Go over guide questions 1–5 with the class and allow five minutes for peer review.

Assignment Have students prepare **Redacción** as homework.

Evaluación y progreso Give the class five minutes to compare final drafts.

Writing Sample Here is an example restaurant review that would constitute superior writing achievement.

La Paz ya no es sobresaliente

La Paz
444 Avenida de los Ángeles

martes a domingo
11:00 am – 11:00 pm
cerrado los lunes

Desafortunadamente, ya no puedo dar cinco estrellas al restaurante que antes fue uno de los mejores de esta ciudad.

El antiguo dueño del restaurante La Paz lo vendió. Parece que el nuevo dueño cambió no sólo el ambiente pero también el menú. Por fuera, parece una casa ordinaria. Por dentro, tiene muchas mesas y es difícil caminar por entre ellas. Ya no hay mesas en el patio.

Hay pocos platos en el menú. Pedí sopa de verduras y pollo con salsa verde. Esperé mucho tiempo para la comida porque no hay suficientes meseros. Cuando llegó la sopa, me la sirvieron fría. No sé cuáles son los ingredientes de la salsa, pero ésta no me gustó nada. Sólo sirven flan de postre y no es muy sabroso.

No hay duda que hay mucho que hacer para mejorar este restaurante. Voy a esperar tres meses y probarlo de nuevo.

EVALUATION: Crítica culinaria

Criteria	Scale
Content	1 2 3 4 5
Organization	1 2 3 4 5
Use of details to support opinions	1 2 3 4 5
Accuracy	1 2 3 4 5

Scoring	
Excellent	18–20 points
Good	14–17 points
Satisfactory	10–13 points
Unsatisfactory	< 10 points

Section Goals

In **Escuchar** students will:

- use the strategy of jotting down notes
- listen to a short paragraph and note down its main points
- answer questions based on a recorded interview

Instructional Resource
Student Cassette/CD

Preparación Invite students to look at the photo and predict who they think Ramón Acevedo is and what he is going to talk about.

Estrategia
Script
Sandra está avergonzada. Ayer fue a sus clases sin peinarse ni maquillarse. ¡Y la ropa que llevaba! ¡Una camiseta vieja con unos pantalones morados y unas sandalias rosadas! Hablé con ella y me contó que tiene muchos problemas. Salió muy mal en el examen, su abuela está enferma y también su novio se enojó con ella anteayer.

Assignment Have students do the activities in **Ahora escucha** and **Comprensión** as homework. Verify the response to **Ahora escucha** and go over **Seleccionar** and **Preguntas** by reading each item and indicating individuals to answer.

Ahora escucha
Script
Bienvenidos a "La hora de la cocina". Hoy vamos a preparar un menú de Guatemala: pavo relleno, verduras en escabeche y un rico dulce de leche. Bueno, vamos a comenzar con el pavo relleno. Necesitan los siguientes ingredientes para servir de diez a doce personas; 1 pavo de 6 kilos, 500 gramos de carne de cerdo, 250 gramos de papas, 250 gramos de zanahorias, pimienta, sal, ajo, consomé, aceite y margarina.
Vamos a comenzar con el relleno. Hay que picar la carne de cerdo y las verduras en pedazos de un centímetro o menos. Ponemos a freír la carne con el ajo. Ponemos las papas a cocinar en un poco de agua. En otra sartén, vamos a freír las zanahorias en aceite, y añadimos las papas cocinadas, pimienta y consomé.
Bueno, ya están las verduras. Las revolvemos con la carne. Ahora, vamos a preparar el pavo. Tenemos que lavarlo bien. Le ponemos sal y pimienta por dentro y le ponemos el relleno. Hay que ponerle sal y pimienta por fuera, untarlo con margarina, y cubrirlo con papel de aluminio. Ya estamos listos para ponerlo en el horno a 325 grados por unas 4 horas, más o menos. Les recomiendo un vino blanco para acompañar este plato. ¡Delicioso!
Regresaremos en unos minutos después de los siguientes anuncios importantes. ¡No se vayan! Vamos a preparar unas sabrosas verduras en escabeche.

Escuchar

NATIONAL communication STANDARDS

Preparación

Según el dibujo, ¿quién es Ramón Acevedo? ¿Sobre qué crees que va a hablar?

Estrategia

Jotting down notes as you listen

Jotting down notes while you listen to a conversation in Spanish can help you keep track of the important points or details. It will help you to focus actively on comprehension rather than on remembering what you have heard. To practice this strategy, you will now listen to a paragraph. Jot down the main points you hear.

Ahora escucha

Ahora escucha a Ramón Acevedo. Toma apuntes de las instrucciones que él da en los espacios en blanco.

Ingredientes del relleno:	Poner dentro del pavo:
carne de cerdo	relleno
zanahorias	sal
papas	pimienta
ajo	
consomé	
pimienta	
aceite	

Instrucciones para cocinar:

untarlo con ___margarina___
cubrir con ___papel___ de aluminio
poner en el horno a ___325___ grados
por ___cuatro___ horas

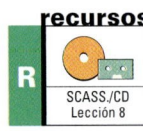

recursos
R — SCASS./CD Lección 8

Según *According to* **apuntes** *notes* **cocinar** *to cook* **untarlo** *spread* **horno** *oven*

En Guatemala, el pavo relleno es un plato popular para celebrar la Navidad y el Año Nuevo.

Comprensión

Seleccionar

Usa tus apuntes para seleccionar la respuesta correcta para cada oración.

1. Ramón Acevedo prepara un menú ideal para ___c___.
   a. una familia de tres personas b. una chica y su novio
   c. una familia de once
2. Este plato es perfecto para la persona a la que le gustan ___b___.
   a. los mariscos y la langosta
   b. la carne de cerdo y las papas
   c. los espárragos y los frijoles
3. Este plato es ideal para el/la cocinero/a que ___a___.
   a. tiene mucho tiempo b. tiene mucha prisa
   c. no tiene horno

Preguntas

Con dos o tres compañeros, respondan a las preguntas.

1. ¿Es similar el plato que prepara Ramón Acevedo a algún plato que Uds. comen? ¿En qué es similar? ¿En qué es distinto?
2. Escriban una variación de la receta de Ramón Acevedo. Usen ingredientes interesantes. ¿Es mejor su receta que la del Sr. Acevedo? ¿Por qué?

NATIONAL STANDARDS: communication, cultures, connections, communities

Proyecto

Crea un nuevo restaurante guatemalteco

Imagina que vas a abrir un restaurante en la capital de Guatemala. Necesitas decidir qué vas a servir y a qué precio, y dónde vas a abrir el restaurante.

1 Diseña el menú

El menú contiene toda la información importante para la creación de tu nuevo negocio. Usa los **Recursos para la investigación** para investigar cuáles son las comidas típicas y populares de Guatemala y saber cuál es la moneda de Guatemala para ponerles precio a las comidas del restaurante. El menú puede incluir esta información:

- el nombre del restaurante
- la dirección del restaurante, tomando en cuenta el diseño de la capital y la organización de sus calles y avenidas
- las comidas típicas de Guatemala que vas a servir, con una variedad de platos, incluyendo platos principales, ensaladas, postres y bebidas
- los precios de los platos en moneda guatemalteca

Palabras útiles

el postre	*dessert*
el flan	*baked custard*
el pastel	*cake; pie*
el helado	*ice cream*
el dulce	*sweet, candy*
la galleta	*cookie*

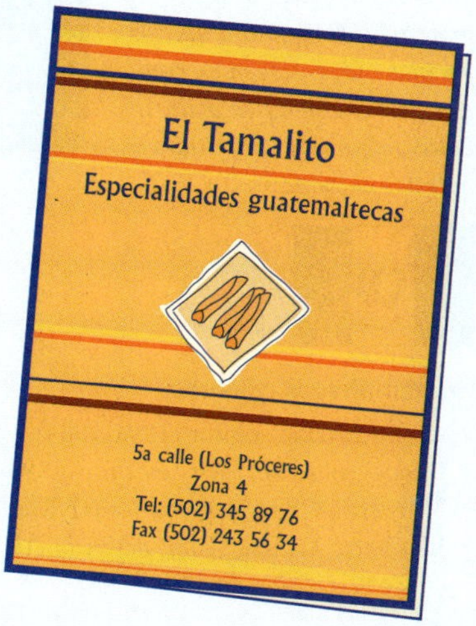

2 Presenta la información

Con tres o cuatro compañeros/as habla del plan que tienes para tu restaurante. Muéstrales el menú que diseñaste. Háblales de la comida que vas a servir. Pregúntales qué platos piensan que son los más sabrosos.

Diseña *Design* negocio *business* tomando en cuenta *taking into account* Háblales *Talk to them* recetas *recipes* cambio de moneda *currency exchange* libros de cocina *cookbooks*

recursos para la investigación

Internet Palabras clave: Guatemala, recetas, cambio de moneda, Ciudad de Guatemala	**Comunidad** Estudiantes o profesores que son de Guatemala o que viajaron a Guatemala, guatemaltecos que viven en la comunidad
Biblioteca Guías turísticas, periódicos con datos de cambio de moneda, almanaques	**Otros recursos** Libros de cocina de la América Central

EVALUATION: Plan/Menú

Criteria	Scale
Content	1 2 3 4
Organization	1 2 3 4
Accuracy	1 2 3 4
Oral Presentation	1 2 3 4
Creativity	1 2 3 4

Scoring	
Excellent	18–20 points
Good	14–17 points
Satisfactory	10–13 points
Unsatisfactory	< 10 points

Section Goals

In **Proyecto** students will:
- plan for a restaurant opening in Guatemala City
- design a menu
- integrate vocabulary and structures taught in **Lesson 8**

Before Assigning Proyecto Students will need approximately a week to complete the project, so at the beginning of that time period, have them open their books to page 265 and glance over **Proyecto**. Explain that they are going to plan to open a Guatemalan restaurant and design its menu.

Assignment Have students read page 265 and follow directions in **Diseña el menú** to complete their menu.

Diseña el menú

Suggestions
- Provide students with several menus written in Spanish and English. Ask them to discuss the good and bad points of the design features of each, integrating what works well into their menus.
- Students can seek recipes or information on Guatemalan dishes by using the key words and phrases **comidas típicas de Guatemala, recetas guatemaltecas** or **recetas chapinas.**

Presenta la información

Suggestion
- Students will present their menus and plans in small groups. Have the groups arrange their desks so they face each other for the presentations.
- You may wish to encourage students to bring in dishes they have prepared or to have the restaurant plans revealed in a restaurant after a meal.

Section Goals
In **Panorama**, students will read about the geography and culture of Guatemala.

Instructional Resources
Student Activities Manual: Workbook, 95–96
Transparency 35

Guatemala

Before Presenting Panorama Have students use the map in their books or project **Transparency 35**. Point out that Guatemala has three main climatic regions, the tropical Pacific and Caribbean coasts, the highlands (southwest) and jungle lowlands (north). Ask volunteers to read aloud the names of the cities, mountains, and rivers of Guatemala. Point out that indigenous languages are the source of many place names.

Assignment Have students read **Panorama** and write out the answers to the questions in **¿Qué aprendiste?** on page 267 as homework.

Present Ask volunteers to read each section of **El país en cifras**. As you read about the languages of Guatemala, you might point out that there are many Guatemalans who are monolingual in either Spanish or a Mayan language. Many are bilingual, speaking an indigenous language and Spanish. When students look at the Guatemalan flag, lead them to notice that the quetzal is featured prominently in the shield in the center.

Increíble pero cierto Guatemala is internationally renowned for the incredible wealth and diversity of its textile arts. Each village has a traditional "signature" weaving style that allows those in the know to quickly identify where each beautiful piece comes from.

Guatemala

NATIONAL STANDARDS connections cultures

El país en cifras

- **Área:** 108.890 km² (42.042 millas²), *un poco más pequeño que Tennessee*
- **Población:** 11.995.000
- **Capital:** la ciudad de Guatemala—3.491.000
- **Ciudades principales:** Quezaltenango—101.000, Escuintla—68.000, Mazatenango—42.000, Puerto Barrios—39.000

SOURCE: Population Division, UN Secretariat

- **Moneda:** quetzal
- **Idiomas:** español (oficial), lenguas mayas

El español es la lengua de un 60 por ciento de la población, mientras que el otro 40 por ciento tiene una de las lenguas mayas (cakchiquel, quiché, y kekchícomo entre otras) como materna. Una palabra que las lenguas mayas tienen en común es ixim, que significa maíz, un cultivo de mucha importancia en estas culturas.

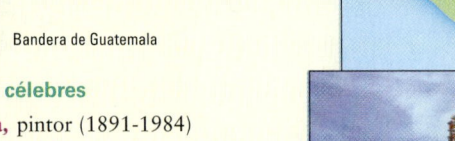

Bandera de Guatemala

Guatemaltecos célebres

- **Carlos Mérida,** pintor (1891-1984)
- **Miguel Ángel Asturias,** escritor (1899-1974)
- **Margarita Carrera,** poeta y ensayista (1929-)
- **Rigoberta Menchú Tum,** activista (1959-)

recursos
R | WB pp. 95-96 | vistasonline.com

por ciento *percent* cultivo *crop* tinte *dye* zancudos *mosquitos* aplastados *crushed* hace... destiñan *keeps the colors from running* hayan tejido *have woven*

¡Increíble pero cierto!

¿Qué ingrediente secreto se encuentra en las telas tradicionales de Guatemala? ¡El mosquito! El excepcional tinte es producto de una mezcla de flores y de zancudos aplastados. El insecto hace que los colores no se destiñan. Quizás ésta es la razón por la que los artesanos, agradecidos, hayan tejido la figura del zancudo en muchos huipiles.

TEACHING OPTIONS

Worth Noting Although the indigenous population of Guatemala is Mayan, many place names in southwestern Guatemala are in Náhuatl, the language of the Aztecs of Central Mexico. How did this happen? In the sixteenth century, Guatemala was conquered by Spaniards who came from the Valley of Mexico after having overthrown the Aztec rulers there. These conquistadors were accompanied by large numbers of Náhuatl-speaking allies, and it was these allies who renamed the captured Mayan strongholds with Náhuatl names. The suffix **-tenango** which appears in many of these names means "place with a wall," that is a fortified place. **Quetzaltenango**, then, means fortified place of the quetzal bird; **Mazatenango** means fortified place of the deer.

Ciudades • La Antigua Guatemala

La Antigua Guatemala fue fundada en 1543. Fue una capital de gran importancia hasta 1773, cuando un terremoto la destruyó. La Antigua Guatemala ha conservado el carácter original de su arquitectura y hoy día se ha convertido en uno de los centros turísticos del país. Su celebración de la Semana Santa es, para muchas personas, la más importante del hemisferio.

Naturaleza • El quetzal

El quetzal simbolizaba la libertad para los antiguos mayas porque creían que este pájaro no podía vivir en cautividad. En la actualidad el quetzal es el símbolo nacional. El pájaro da su nombre a la moneda nacional y aparece en los billetes del país. Desafortunadamente, está en peligro de extinción. Para protegerlo, el gobierno mantiene una reserva biológica especial.

Historia • Los mayas

Desde 1500 a.C. hasta 900 d.C. los mayas habitaron gran parte de lo que ahora es Guatemala. Su civilización era muy avanzada. Construyeron pirámides, templos y observatorios; descubrieron y usaron el cero antes que los europeos, y desarrollaron un calendario complejo y preciso.

Artesanía • La ropa tradicional

La ropa tradicional de los guatemaltecos refleja el sentido del orden y el amor a la naturaleza de la cultura maya. Es de colores vivos y tiene formas geométricas en los diseños. Además, el diseño y los colores de cada *huipil* indican el pueblo de origen y a veces el sexo y la edad de la persona que lo lleva.

¿Qué aprendiste? Responde a las preguntas con una frase completa.

1. ¿Qué significa la palabra *ixim?* La palabra ixim significa maíz.
2. ¿Quién es Rigoberta Menchú? Rigoberta Menchú es una activista de Guatemala.
3. ¿Qué pájaro representa a Guatemala? El quetzal representa a Guatemala.
4. ¿Qué simbolizaba el quetzal para los mayas? El quetzal simbolizaba la libertad para los mayas.
5. ¿Cuál es la moneda nacional de Guatemala? La moneda nacional de Guatemala es el quetzal.
6. ¿Qué celebración de La Antigua Guatemala es la más importante del hemisferio para muchas personas? La celebración de la Semana Santa de La Antigua Guatemala es la más importante del hemisferio para muchas personas.
7. ¿Qué construyeron los mayas? Los mayas construyeron pirámides, templos y observatorios.
8. ¿Qué descubrieron los mayas antes que los europeos? Los mayas descubrieron el cero antes que los europeos.
9. ¿Qué refleja la ropa tradicional de los guatemaltecos? La ropa refleja el sentido del orden y el amor a la naturaleza de la cultura maya.
10. ¿Qué indica un huipil con su diseño y sus colores? Con su diseño y colores, un huipil indica el pueblo de origen y a veces el sexo y la edad de la persona que lo lleva.

Conexión Internet Investiga estos temas en el sitio **www.vistasonline.com.**

1. Busca información sobre Rigoberta Menchú. ¿De dónde es? ¿Qué libros ha publicado (*has she published*)? ¿Por qué es famosa?
2. Estudia un sitio arqueológico en Guatemala para aprender más sobre los mayas, y prepara un breve informe para tu clase.

terremoto *earthquake* destruyó *destroyed* ha conservado *has preserved* se ha convertido *has turned into* Semana Santa *Holy Week* simbolizaba *symbolized* antiguos *ancient* cautividad *captivity* pájaro *bird* billetes *paper money* peligro *danger* protegerlo *protect it* Construyeron *They constructed* descubrieron *discovered* desarrollaron *developed* complejo *complex* sentido del orden *sense of order* vivos *bright* diseños *designs*

La Antigua Guatemala Students can use tour books and the Internet to learn more about **Semana Santa** celebrations in this Guatemalan city, usually referred to simply as Antigua. Encourage short presentations to the class.

El quetzal Recent conservation efforts in Guatemala, Costa Rica, and other Central American nations have focused on preserving the cloud forests (**bosque nuboso**) that are home to the quetzal.

Los mayas Today ethnobotanists are working with Mayan traditional healers to learn about medicinal uses of plants of the region.

La ropa tradicional Many indigenous Guatemalans still wear traditional garb richly decorated with embroidery. The **huipil** is a long, sleeveless tunic worn by women. A distinctively woven **faja**, or waist sash, identifies the town or village each woman comes from.

¿Qué aprendiste? Go over the questions and answers with students, making sure everyone understands unfamiliar words and what the correct answers are.

Assignment Have students do activites in **Student Activities Manual: Workbook,** pages 95–96.

Conexión Internet Students will find information about Guatemala at **www.vistasonline.com,** as well as links to other sites that can help them in their research.

TEACHING OPTIONS

Worth Noting Spanish is a second language for over 40% of Guatemalans. Students may be interested to learn that Guatemala has many bilingual education programs, where native languages are used in addition to Spanish for instructional purposes. There are also many government-sponsored Spanish as a Second Language (SSL) programs, offered through schools and radio or television. Speakers of Guatemala's indigenous languages often encounter problems similar to those found by other learners of Spanish: difficulty with concordance of number and gender.

vocabulario

Comidas

el/la camarero/a	*waiter*
la comida	*food; meal*
el/la dueño/a	*owner; landlord*
el menú	*menu*
la sección de (no) fumar	*(non) smoking section*
el almuerzo	*lunch*
la cena	*dinner*
el desayuno	*breakfast*
los entremeses	*hors d'oeuvres*
el plato (principal)	*(main) dish*
delicioso/a	*delicious*
rico/a	*tasty; delicious*
sabroso/a	*tasty; delicious*
almorzar (o:ue)	*to have lunch*
cenar	*to have dinner*
desayunar	*to have breakfast*
pedir (e:i)	*to order (food)*
probar (o:ue)	*to taste; to try*
recomendar (e:ie)	*to recommend*
servir (e:i)	*to serve*

Las frutas

la banana	*banana*
las frutas	*fruits*
el limón	*lemon*
la manzana	*apple*
el melocotón	*peach*
la naranja	*orange*
la pera	*pear*
la uva	*grape*

Las verduras

el arroz	*rice*
la cebolla	*onion*
el champiñón	*mushroom*
la ensalada	*salad*
los espárragos	*asparagus*
los frijoles	*beans*
las arvejas	*peas*
la lechuga	*lettuce*
el maíz	*corn*
las papas/patatas (fritas)	*(fried) potatoes; French fries*
el tomate	*tomato*
las verduras	*vegetables*
la zanahoria	*carrot*

La carne y el pescado

el atún	*tuna*
el bistec	*steak*
los camarones	*shrimp*
la carne	*meat*
la carne de res	*beef*
la chuleta (de cerdo)	*(pork) chop*
la hamburguesa	*hamburger*
el jamón	*ham*
la langosta	*lobster*
los mariscos	*shellfish*
el pescado	*fish*
el pollo (asado)	*(roast) chicken*
la salchicha	*sausage*
el salmón	*salmon*

Otras comidas

el aceite	*oil*
el azúcar	*sugar*
el ajo	*garlic*
los cereales	*cereal; grains*
el huevo	*egg*
la mantequilla	*butter*
la margarina	*margarine*
la mayonesa	*mayonnaise*
el pan (tostado)	*(toasted) bread*
la pimienta	*black pepper*
el queso	*cheese*
la sal	*salt*
el sándwich	*sandwich*
la sopa	*soup*
el vinagre	*vinegar*
el yogur	*yogurt*

Bebidas

el agua (mineral)	*(mineral) water*
la bebida	*drink*
el café	*coffee*
la cerveza	*beer*
el jugo (de fruta)	*(fruit) juice*
la leche	*milk*
el refresco	*soft drink*
el té (helado)	*(iced) tea*
el vino (blanco/tinto)	*(white/red) wine*

Verbos

conocer	*to know; to be acquainted with*
conducir	*to drive*
ofrecer	*to offer*
parecer	*to seem; to appear*
saber	*to know; to know how*
traducir	*to translate*
morir (o:ue)	*to die*

Las comparaciones

como	*like; as*
más de (*+ number*)	*more than*
más… que	*more … than*
menos de (*+ number*)	*less than*
menos… que	*less … than*
tan… como	*as … as*
tantos/as… como	*as many… as*
tanto… como	*as much… as*
el/la mayor	*the oldest*
el/la mejor	*the best*
el/la menor	*the youngest*
el/la peor	*the worst*
mejor	*better*
peor	*worse*

Palabras adicionales

conmigo	*with me*
contigo	*with you* (fam.)
despacio	*slowly*
rápido/a	*quickly; fast*

Pronouns after prepositions	*See page 258.*
Expresiones útiles	*See page 239.*

Las fiestas

9

Communicative Goals

You will learn how to:

- Express congratulations.
- Express gratitude.
- Ask for and pay the bill at a restaurant.

contextos

fotonovela

The students and don Francisco order desert while doña Rita surprises Maite by serving a bottle of wine for her birthday. Everyone congratulates Maite and expresses their gratitude to doña Rita.

estructura

adelante

Lectura: Read the society pages from a newspaper.
Escritura: Write an essay about celebrations.
Escuchar: Listen to a conversation about an anniversary party.
Proyecto: Write an article about a Chilean holiday.

panorama

Lesson Goals

In **Lesson 9** students will be introduced to the following:

- terms for parties and celebrations
- words for stages of life and interpersonal relations
- present tense of **dar** and **decir**
- irregular preterites
- verbs that change meaning in the preterite
- uses of **¿qué?** and **¿cuál?**
- recognizing word families
- using a Venn diagram to organize information
- writing a comparative analysis
- using context to infer the meaning of unfamiliar words
- writing an article about a Chilean festival
- cultural, geographic, and economical information about Chile

Lesson Preview

Have students look at the photo. Say: **Es una foto de una fiesta.** Then ask: **¿De qué colores son los globos? ¿Cuántas personas hay en la foto?¿Cómo están las personas? ¿Para quién es ése un día especial?**

INSTRUCTIONAL RESOURCES

Student Activities Manual: Workbook, 97–106
Student Activities Manual: Lab Manual, 269–274
Student Activities Manual: Video Activities, 343–344
Instructor's Resource Manual: Hojas de actividades, 21–24
Instructor's Resource Manual: Answer Keys
Tapescript/Videoscript
Overhead Transparencies, 36–37
Student Cassette/CD
Lab Cassette/CD
Video Program
CD-ROM
Website: **www.vistasonline.com**
Testing Program: Prueba A, Prueba B

Section Goals

In **Contextos**, students will learn and practice:
- vocabulary related to parties and celebrations
- vocabulary used to talk about stages of life and interpersonal relations

Instructional Resources
Student Activities Manual: Workbook, 97–98; Lab Manual, 269
Transparency 36
Hoja de actividades 21
Student Cassette/CD

Before Presenting Contextos Introduce active lesson vocabulary. Ask volunteers if they went to a party recently. Say: **¿Quiénes de Uds. fueron a una fiesta el fin de semana pasado? ¿Ah, sí? ¿Qué tomaste allí? ¿Comiste algo? ¿Bailaste? ¿Escuchaste música?** Write **divertirse** on the board and explain that it means *to have fun*. Ask: **¿Te divertiste allí?** Also write **pasarlo bien** on the board and explain that it means to have a good time. Say: **Ah, te divertiste mucho allí. Entonces, lo pasaste bien, ¿no? No lo pasaste mal.** Ask various students various questions.
Assignment Have students study **Contextos** and do the exercises in **Práctica** as homework.

Present Give students two minutes to review the party scene on pages 270–271. Then project **Transparency 36.** Have students respond to your true-false statements about the scene. Ex: **¿Cierto o falso? Es una fiesta de cumpleaños. (Cierto.) Muchas personas lo pasan mal en la fiesta. (Falso.)** Next, engage students in a conversation about what types of parties they like best and why. Say: **¿Qué tipo de fiesta te gusta más? ¿Te gusta recibir regalos? ¿Te gusta comer muchos dulces?** and so forth.

Las fiestas

Más vocabulario

la amistad	*friendship*
el amor	*love*
el aniversario de bodas	*wedding anniversary*
la boda	*wedding*
el cumpleaños	*birthday*
el día de fiesta	*holiday*
el divorcio	*divorce*
el matrimonio	*marriage*
la Navidad	*Christmas*
el/la recién casado/a	*newlywed*
la quinceañera	*young woman's fifteenth birthday celebration*
la sorpresa	*surprise*
cambiar (de)	*to change*
celebrar	*to celebrate*
cumplir años	*to have a birthday*
dejar una propina	*to leave a tip*
divertirse (e:ie, i)	*to have fun*
graduarse (en)	*to graduate (from)*
invitar	*to invite*
jubilarse	*to retire (from work)*
nacer	*to be born*
odiar	*to hate*
pagar la cuenta	*to pay the bill*
pasarlo bien/mal	*to have a good/bad time*
reírse (e:i, i)	*to laugh*
relajarse	*to relax*
sorprender	*to surprise*
sonreír (e:i, i)	*to smile*
juntos/as	*together*

Variación léxica

pastel ⟷ torta (*Arg., Venez.*)
comprometerse ⟷ prometerse (*Esp.*)

recursos

R			
SCASS./CD Lección 9	WB pp. 97-98	LM p. 269	LCASS./CD Cass. 5A/CD5

TEACHING OPTIONS

Extra Practice Ask students questions about birthdays and other celebrations and what days and months they fall on. Ask: ____, **¿cuándo es tu cumpleaños? (¿Qué día naciste?) ¿Estás casado/a? ¿Cuándo es tu aniversario de bodas?** Verify comprehension by asking other students to repeat. Then ask more general questions: **¿Cuándo es el Día de la Independencia de este país? ¿Cuándo es la Navidad?** and so forth.

Worth Noting Point out that in addition to or instead of celebrating their birthday, many Hispanics celebrate their **día del santo**, or Saint's Day. This is the day that celebrates the saint for whom a person was named. In many Hispanic countries, the **día del santo** is just as important and significant in an individual's life as his or her **cumpleaños**.

Relaciones personales

casarse (con)	*to get married (to)*
comprometerse (con)	*to get engaged (to)*
divorciarse (de)	*to get divorced (from)*
enamorarse (de)	*to fall in love with*
llevarse bien/mal (con)	*to get along well/badly (with)*
romper (con)	*to break up (with)*
salir (con)	*to go out (with); to date*
separarse (de)	*to separate (from)*
tener una cita	*to have a date; to have an appointment*

Práctica

1 Escuchar Escucha la conversación e indica si las oraciones son **ciertas** o **falsas**.

1. A Silvia no le gusta mucho el chocolate. Falsa.
2. Silvia sabe que sus amigos le van a hacer una fiesta. Falsa.
3. Los amigos de Silvia le compraron un pastel de chocolate. Cierta.
4. Los amigos brindan por Silvia con refrescos. Cierta.
5. Silvia y sus amigos van a comer helado. Cierta.
6. Los amigos de Silvia le van a servir flan y galletas. Falsa.

2 Emparejar Indica la letra de la frase que mejor completa cada oración.

a. se jubiló	d. nos divertimos	g. se llevan bien
b. dejó una propina	e. nació	h. lo pasaron mal
c. sonrío	f. se casaron	i. tenemos una cita

1. María y su esposo _g_. Son muy felices.
2. Pablo y yo _d_ en la fiesta. Bailamos y comimos mucho.
3. Manuel y Felipe _h_ en el cine. La película fue muy mala.
4. ¡Tengo una nueva sobrina! Ella _e_ ayer por la mañana.
5. Mi madre le _b_ muy grande al camarero.
6. Mi padre _a_ hace un año.
7. A Elena le gustan las galletas. Ella _c_ después de comérselas todas.
8. Jorge y yo _i_ esta noche. Vamos a ir a un restaurante muy elegante.
9. Jaime y Laura _f_ el septiembre pasado. La boda fue maravillosa.

3 Completar Completa las frases con palabras del nuevo vocabulario.

1. Susana _celebra_ su cumpleaños con su familia y sus amigos con una gran fiesta.
2. Su mamá invitó a mucha gente pero todos los _invitados_ llegaron tarde.
3. Su papá contó chistes (*jokes*) y todos _se rieron_.
4. A Susana le _regalaron_ muchos regalos.
5. El hermano de Susana comió muchos trozos (*pieces*) del _pastel de chocolate_ porque a él le gusta mucho el chocolate.
6. Susana está un poco triste porque ayer _rompió con_ su novio.
7. Su amiga, Anabela, va a _casarse_ con su novio en dos semanas.

TEACHING OPTIONS

Heritage Speakers Ask heritage speakers about some Hispanic holidays or other celebrations that they or their families typically celebrate, such as **el Día de los Reyes Magos, el día del santo, la quinceañera, el Cinco de Mayo, and el Día de los Muertos**. Ask speakers to elaborate on what the celebrations are like: who attends, what they eat and drink, why those days are celebrated, and so forth.

Game Play **Concentración**. Write vocabulary items that pertain to parties and celebrations on each of 8 cards. On another 8 cards, draw or paste a picture that matches each description. Place the cards face-down in four rows of four. In pairs, students select two cards. If the two cards match, the pair keeps them. If the two cards don't match, students replace them in their original position. The pair with the most cards at the end wins.

1 Present Have students check their answers by going over the tapescript questions with the whole class.

1 Tapescript E1: ¿Estamos listos, amigos? E2: Creo que sí. Aquí tenemos el pastel y el helado… E3: De chocolate, espero. Uds. saben cómo le encanta a Silvia el chocolate… E2: Por supuesto, el chocolate para Silvia. Bueno, un pastel de chocolate, el helado… E3: ¿El helado es de la cafetería o lo compraste cerca de la residencia estudiantil? E2: Lo compré en la tienda que está al lado de nuestra residencia. Es mejor que el helado de la cafetería. E1: Psstt… aquí viene Silvia… E1, E2, E3: ¡Sorpresa! ¡Sorpresa, Silvia! ¡Felicidades! E4: ¡Qué sorpresa! E3: ¿Y cuántos años cumples? E4: Dieciocho. ¡Gracias, amigos, muchas gracias! E1: Y ahora, ¡brindamos por nuestra amiga! E2: ¿Con qué brindamos? ¿Con el champán? E1: ¡Cómo no! ¡Por nuestra amiga Silvia, la más joven de todos nosotros!
Student Cassette/CD

2 Present If activity was done as homework, quickly go over answers in class.

2 Expand Have students write three sentences based on the drawing on pages 270–271, leaving out a word or phrase from the vocabulary. In pairs, students complete their partner's sentence. Ex: **Dos personas ____ con champán. (brindan)**

3 Present If activity was done as homework, quickly go over answers in class.

3 Expand Ask students personalized questions using verbs from the **Más vocabulario** box on page 271. Ex: **¿Con quién te llevas muy bien? ¿Con quién te llevas mal?**

Las etapas de la vida de Sergio
Present Engage students in a conversation about the stages in Sergio's life illustrated here. Say: **Mira el bebé Sergio en el primer dibujo. ¡Qué contento está! ¿Qué hace en el segundo dibujo? Está jugando con un triciclo, ¿no? ¿Quiénes se acuerdan de cómo jugaron en su niñez?** Continue in this manner until you have covered all the vocabulary in **Más vocabulario**.

4 Warm-up Before beginning the activity, make sure students have studied the new vocabulary items in this section. Ask several brief comprehension questions of a yes-no variety. Have students correct false statements. Ex: **Un soltero es un hombre que no está casado. (Sí.) La vejez ocurre antes de la niñez. (No, la vejez ocurre antes de la muerte.)** and so forth.

4 Present If activity was done as homework, quickly go over answers in class.

4 Expand Students create three original sentences that describe events mentioned in **Más vocabulario** on page 272. Then a partner has to name the event described. **Lourdes y Mario llevan diez años de casados. (el aniversario de bodas)**

5 Present Explain that students are to give the opposite of the underlined words in their answers.

5 Expand Have students write down five adjectives or characteristics that describe their ideal husband or wife. In pairs, students explain the characteristics that their ideal mate should have and why they chose those characteristics.

Las etapas de la vida de Sergio

Más vocabulario

las etapas de la vida	*the stages of life*
la muerte	*death*
estado civil	*marital status*
casado/a	*married*
divorciado/a	*divorced*
soltero/a	*single*
separado/a	*separated*
viudo/a	*widower/widow*

4 **Las etapas de la vida** Identifica las etapas de la vida que se describen (*are described*) en las siguientes (*following*) frases.

1. Mi abuela se jubiló y se mudó (*moved*) a Viña del Mar. la vejez
2. Mi padre trabaja para una compañía grande en Santiago. la madurez
3. ¿Viste a mi nuevo sobrino en el hospital? Es precioso y ¡tan pequeño! el nacimiento
4. Mi abuelo murió este año. la muerte
5. Mi hermana se enamoró de un chico nuevo en la escuela. la adolescencia
6. ¿Mi hermano? Tiene 22 años y le encantan los juegos de video. la juventud
7. Mi hermana pequeña juega con muñecas (*dolls*). la niñez

NOTA CULTURAL

Viña del Mar is a seaside town west of Santiago, Chile. In addition to its wonderful beaches, hotels, casinos, and restaurants, an international song festival takes place there every year.

5 **Opuestos** Túrnate (*Take turns*) con un(a) compañero/a para decir que sus afirmaciones son falsas y corrígelas usando los opuestos de las expresiones subrayadas.

modelo
Estudiante 1: Nuestros amigos lo pasaron mal en la playa.
Estudiante 2: No, te equivocas (*you're wrong*). Ellos lo pasaron bien.

1. Fernando odia a Merche. No, te equivocas. Fernando quiere a Merche.
2. Rafael se comprometió con Alicia. No, te equivocas. Rafael rompió con Alicia.
3. Nadia se separó de Eduardo, ¿no? No, te equivocas. Nadia y Eduardo están juntos.
4. La juventud es la etapa de la vida cuando nos jubilamos. No, te equivocas. La vejez es la etapa de la vida cuando nos jubilamos.
5. El nacimiento es el fin de la vida. No, te equivocas. La muerte es el fin de la vida.
6. A los sesenta y cinco años muchas personas comienzan a trabajar. No, te equivocas. A los sesenta y cinco años muchas personas se jubilan.
7. Julián y Pepi se divorcian mañana. No, te equivocas. Ellos se casan mañana.

AYUDA

Other ways to contradict someone:

No es verdad.
It's not true.

Creo que no.
I don't think so.

¡Claro que no!
Of course not!

¡Que va!
Go on!

TEACHING OPTIONS

Small Groups In groups of two to four, students perform a skit whose content describes and/or displays a particular stage of life (youth, old age, etc.) or marital status (married, single, divorced). The rest of the class has to try to figure out what the group is displaying.

Game Play a modified version of Twenty Questions. Ask a volunteer to think of a famous person. Other students get one chance each to ask a yes-no question until someone guesses the item correctly. Limit attempts to 10 questions per famous person. Point out that students can narrow down their selection by using vocabulary about the stages of life and marital status.

Comunicación

NATIONAL communication STANDARDS

6 **Una fiesta** Trabaja con dos compañeros/as para planear una fiesta. Recuerda incluir la siguiente información. Answers will vary.

1. ¿Qué tipo de fiesta es? ¿Dónde va a ser? ¿Cuándo va a ser?
2. ¿A quiénes van a invitar?
3. ¿Qué van a comer? ¿Quiénes van a llevar o a preparar la comida?
4. ¿Qué van a beber? ¿Quiénes van a llevar las bebidas?
5. ¿Qué van a hacer todos durante la fiesta?

7 **Encuesta** Tu profesor(a) va a darte (*to give you*) una hoja de actividades. Haz las preguntas de la hoja a dos o tres compañeros/as de clase para saber qué actitudes tienen en sus relaciones personales. Luego comparte los resultados de la encuesta (*survey*) con la clase y comenta tus conclusiones. Answers will vary.

Preguntas	Nombres	Actitudes
1. ¿Te importa la amistad? ¿Por qué?		
2. ¿Es mejor tener un buen amigo/a o muchos amigos/as?		
3. ¿Cuáles son las características que buscas en tus amigos/as?		
4. ¿Tienes novio/a? ¿A qué edad (age) es posible enamorarse?		
5. ¿Deben las parejas hacer todas las cosas juntos? ¿Deben tener las mismas opiniones? ¿Por qué?		

¡LENGUA VIVA!
While **a buen/a amigo/a** is a *good friend*, the term **amigo/a íntimo/a** refers to a *close friend*, or a very good friend, without any sexual overtones.

8 **Una fiesta memorable** Cuenta (*Tell*) la historia de una fiesta memorable. La historia debe incluir la siguiente información. Answers will vary.

- ¿Qué?
- ¿Cuándo?
- ¿Dónde?
- ¿Quién?
- ¿Cómo?
- ¿Cuántos?
- ¿Por qué?

9 **Minidrama** En parejas, consulten la ilustración de la página 272, y luego preparen un minidrama para representar (*to act out*) las etapas de la vida de una persona real o imaginaria. Answers will vary.

TEACHING OPTIONS

Extra Practice Using your picture file or magazine pictures, display images that pertain to parties or celebrations, stages of life, or interpersonal relations. Have students describe the pictures and make guesses about who the people are, how they are feeling, and so forth.

Extra Practice As a listening comprehension activity, prepare short descriptions of five easily recognizable people. Use as much active lesson vocabulary as possible. Write their names on the board in random order. Then read your descriptions, having students match the description to the appropriate name. Ex: **Esta mujer actúa en muchas películas. Tiene unas treinta años y está casada con Tom Cruise. (Nicole Kidman)**

6 Present Give students 10 minutes in their groups to plan the party.

6 Expand Ask volunteer groups to talk to the class about the party they have just planned.

6 Expand Have students make invitations for their party. You may also want to have a contest. Ask the class to judge which invitation is the cleverest, funniest, most elegant, and so forth.

7 Present Distribute **Hoja de actividades 21.** Give students 8 minutes to ask other group members the questions. Have students take turns asking and answering questions.

7 Expand Take a survey of the attitudes found in the entire class. Write down individual items on the board and ask for a show of hands. Ex: **¿Quiénes creen que es más importante tener un buen amigo que muchos amigos? ¿Quiénes creen que es más importante tener muchos amigos que un buen amigo?** and so forth. Tally the results of the survey.

8 Present You may also want to assign this as written homework to be handed in later.

8 Expand Ask volunteers to talk about their memorable party experience. Ask other students comprehension questions about what was said.

9 Present Have students select their partner and work on the skit as homework before performing it in class.

9 Expand After all skits have been presented, have the class vote on the most original, funniest, truest to life, and so forth.

Assignment Have students prepare the activities in **Student Activities Manual: Workbook,** pages 97–98.

Section goals

In **Fotonovela** students will:

- receive comprehensible input from free-flowing discourse
- learn functional phrases that preview lesson grammatical structures

Instructional Resources
Student Activities Manual: Video Activities 343–344
Video Program (Start: 00:47:00)

Video Synopsis While the travelers are looking at the dessert menu, Sra. Perales and the waiter bring in some flan, a cake, and some wine to celebrate Maite's birthday. The group leaves Sra. Perales a nice tip, thanks her, and says goodbye.

Before Presenting Fotonovela Have your students read the first line of dialogue in each **Fotonovela** segment and then make an educated guess about what happens in this **Fotonovela** episode. Record their guesses.

Assignment Have students study **Fotonovela** and **Expresiones útiles** as homework.

Warm-up Quickly review the guesses your students made about the **Fotonovela** in the previous class. Through discussion, guide the class to a correct summary of the plot.

Present Go through the **Expresiones útiles**, asking for a volunteer to pronounce each expression. Model correct pronunciation as needed. Check comprehension of this active vocabulary by asking **¿Cómo se dice...?** questions. Ex: **¿Cómo se dice *congratulations* en español?**

Continued on page 275.

¡Feliz cumpleaños, Maite!

NATIONAL STANDARDS communication cultures

Don Francisco y los estudiantes celebran el cumpleaños de Maite en el restaurante El Cráter.

PERSONAJES

MAITE

INÉS

DON FRANCISCO

ÁLEX

JAVIER

DOÑA RITA

CAMARERO

1

INÉS A mí me encantan los dulces. Maite, ¿tú qué vas a pedir?

MAITE Ay, no sé. Todo parece tan delicioso. Quizás el pastel de chocolate.

2

JAVIER Para mí el pastel de chocolate con helado. Me encanta el chocolate. Y tú Álex, ¿qué vas a pedir?

ÁLEX Generalmente prefiero la fruta, pero hoy creo que voy a probar el pastel de chocolate.

DON FRANCISCO Yo siempre tomo un flan y un café.

3

DOÑA RITA & CAMARERO ¡Feliz cumpleaños, Maite!

INÉS ¿Hoy es tu cumpleaños, Maite?

MAITE Sí, el 22 de junio. Y parece que vamos a celebrarlo.

TODOS MENOS MAITE ¡Felicidades!

6

ÁLEX Yo también acabo de cumplir los veintitrés años.

MAITE ¿Cuándo?

ÁLEX El cuatro de mayo.

7

DOÑA RITA Aquí tienen un flan, pastel de chocolate con helado... y una botella de vino para dar alegría.

MAITE ¡Qué sorpresa! ¡No sé qué decir! Muchísimas gracias.

8

DON FRANCISCO El conductor no puede tomar vino. Doña Rita, gracias por todo. ¿Puede traernos la cuenta?

DOÑA RITA Enseguida, Paco.

recursos

R	VIDEO Lección 9	VM pp. 343-344

TEACHING OPTIONS

Video Tips General suggestions for using video clips in the classroom can be found on page IAE-13 of the **Instructor's Annotated Edition**.

¡Feliz cumpleaños, Maite! As an advance organizer, ask your students to brainstorm a list of things that might happen in a surprise birthday party. Then play the **¡Feliz cumpleaños, Maite!** segment of this video module once, asking your students to take notes about what they see and hear. After viewing this video segment, have students use their notes to tell you what happened in this episode. Then play the segment again to allow your students to refine their notes. Repeat the discussion process and lead the class to an accurate summary of the plot.

4

MAITE ¡Gracias! Pero, ¿quién le dijo que es mi cumpleaños?

DOÑA RITA Lo supe por don Francisco.

5

ÁLEX Ayer te lo pregunté, ¡y no quisiste decírmelo! ¿Eh? ¡Qué mala eres!

JAVIER ¿Cuántos años cumples?

MAITE Veintitrés.

9

INÉS Creo que debemos dejar una buena propina. ¿Qué les parece?

MAITE Sí, vamos a darle una buena propina a la Sra. Perales. Es simpatiquísima.

10

DON FRANCISCO Gracias una vez más. Siempre lo paso muy bien aquí.

MAITE Muchísimas gracias, Sra. Perales. Por la comida, por la sorpresa y por ser tan amable con nosotros.

Enfoque cultural Las celebraciones hispanas

Las celebraciones de la independencia, los carnavales y la Semana Santa son fiestas importantísimas en los países hispanos. Las fechas de Navidad y Noche Vieja (*New Year's Eve*) son, quizás, las más festejadas (*celebrated*). Otra celebración importante es el santo. Cada día del año tiene un santo asignado, y algunas personas que se llaman igual que el santo del día (*who have the same name as the day's saint*) lo celebran. El 19 de marzo, por ejemplo, los que se llaman José o Josefa celebran el día de San José.

Expresiones útiles

Celebrating a birthday party

- **¡Feliz cumpleaños!**
  Happy birthday!
- **¡Felicidades!**
  Congratulations! (for an event such as a birthday or anniversary)
- **¡Felicitaciones!**
  Congratulations! (for an event such as an engagement or a good grade on a test)

- **¿Quién le dijo que es mi cumpleaños?**
  Who told you that it's my birthday?
- **Lo supe por don Francisco.**
  I found it out through don Francisco.

- **¿Cuántos años cumples/cumple Ud.?**
  How old are you now?
- **Veintitrés.**
  Twenty-three.

Asking for and getting the bill

- **¿Puede traernos la cuenta?**
  Can you bring us the bill?
- **La cuenta, por favor.**
  The bill, please.
- **Enseguida, señor/señora/señorita.**
  Right away, sir/ma'am/miss.

Expressing gratitude

- **¡(Muchas) gracias!**
  Thank you (very much)!
- **Muchísimas gracias.**
  Thank you very, very much.
- **Gracias por todo.**
  Thanks for everything.
- **Gracias una vez más.**
  Thanks again. (lit. Thanks one more time.)

Leaving a tip

- **Creo que debemos dejar una buena propina. ¿Qué les parece?**
  I think we should leave a good tip. What do you guys think?
- **Sí, vamos a darle una buena propina.**
  Yes, let's give her a good tip.

To practice pronunciation, read a few lines from the **Fotonovela** and have the class repeat. Then go through the **Fotonovela**, asking for volunteers to read the various parts. You may want to repeat this process with new volunteers so that more students will be able to participate. Correct any errors in pronunciation that interfere with comprehension. See ideas for using the video in **Teaching Options**, page 274.

Comprehension Check Check comprehension of the **Fotonovela** episode by doing Activity 1, **Completar**, page 276, orally with the whole class.

Suggestion Have the class look at the **Expresiones útiles**. Point out the word **darle**. Tell the class that **dar** means to give and that it is often used with indirect object pronouns. Draw attention to the forms **dijo** and **supe**. Explain that these are irregular preterite forms of the verbs **decir** (*to say, to tell*) and **saber**. Point out the phrase **no quisiste decírmelo** under video still five of the **Fotonovela**. Explain that **quisiste** is an irregular preterite form of the verb **querer**. You might want to tell the class that **no querer** in the preterite means *to refuse*. Tell your students that they will learn more about these concepts in the upcoming **Estructura** section.

Assignment Have students do activities 2–4 in **Reacciona a la fotonovela**, page 276, as homework.

TEACHING OPTIONS

Enfoque cultural Tell the class that many young girls eagerly anticipate their **quinceañera**, or fifteenth birthday party, which celebrates their transition into adulthood. The **quinceañera** is frequently a lavish event with live music, catered food, and a long list of guests, who include people of all ages, especially the girl's parents, grandparents, aunts, and uncles, not just friends of the girl's own age. You might want to mention that for young men, the coming-of-age party traditionally coincides with the eighteenth or twenty-first birthday. Tell the class that many other events are celebrated by families in the Spanish-speaking world, including weddings, anniversaries, and graduations. Ask heritage speakers if they are aware of any other specific celebrations or festivals in the Hispanic world.

Reaccciona a la fotonovela

1 Expand Have your students work in pairs or small groups to write a question that would have elicited each of these statements.

2 Warm-up Ask your students these questions before doing this activity: **¿A quién le gusta mucho la fruta?** (a Álex) **¿A quién le gusta muchísimo el chocolate?** (a Javier) **¿Quién no puede tomar vino?** (don Francisco)

2 Expand Give these additional items to your students: **7. ¡No me lo puedo creer! ¿Pastel de chocolate y flan para mí? (Maite) 8. ¿Mi cumpleaños? Es el cuatro de mayo. (Álex)**

3 Warm-up Have the class review the vocabulary items on pages 270-271 before doing this activity.

4 Possible response
E1: ¡Feliz cumpleaños! ¿Cuántos años cumples hoy?
E2: ¡Muchas gracias! Cumplo diecinueve.
E3: Buenas tardes. ¿En qué les puedo servir?
E1: Quisiera el pastel de chocolate y un café, por favor.
E2: Voy a pedir el pastel de chocolate con helado, y de tomar, un café. [LATER...]
E1: Señorita, ¿puede traernos la cuenta?
E3: Enseguida, señor.
E2: La camarera fue muy amable. Debemos dejarle una buena propina, ¿no crees?
E1: Sí. Y yo voy a pagar la cuenta, como es tu cumpleaños.
E2: Yo te ayudo. Gracias por todo...

Reacciona a la fotonovela

1 Completar Completa las frases con la información correcta, según la fotonovela.

1. De postre, don Francisco siempre pide ___un café y un flan___.
2. A Javier le encanta ___el chocolate___.
3. Álex cumplió los ___veintitrés___ años ___el cuatro de mayo___.
4. Hoy Álex quiere tomar algo diferente. De postre, quiere pedir ___un pastel de chocolate___.
5. Los estudiantes van a dejar ___una buena propina___ a doña Rita.

2 Identificar Identifica quién puede decir las siguientes frases.

1. Gracias, doña Rita, pero no puedo tomar vino. don Francisco
2. ¡Qué simpática es doña Rita! Fue tan amable conmigo. Maite
3. A mí me encantan los dulces y los pasteles, ¡especialmente si son de chocolate! Javier
4. Mi amigo acaba de informarme que hoy es el cumpleaños de Maite. doña Rita
5. ¿Tienen algún postre de fruta? Los postres de fruta son los mejores. Álex
6. Me parece una buena idea dejarle una buena propina a la dueña. ¿Qué piensan Uds.? Inés

NOTA CULTURAL

Tipping in Latin America and Spain is not as customary as it is in the United States. Since the waitstaff isn't as dependent on tips, only small tips are left. However, it's generally a good idea to tip well when large parties are served or the service is exceptional.

3 Completar Selecciona algunas de las opciones de la lista para completar las frases.

pedir	una botella de vino	la cuenta	el amor
la quinceañera	la galleta	una sorpresa	¡Qué sorpresa!
celebrar	un postre	el divorcio	día de fiesta

1. Maite no sabe que van a celebrar su cumpleaños porque es ___una sorpresa___.
2. Cuando una pareja celebra su aniversario y quiere tomar algo especial, compra ___una botella de vino___.
3. Después de una cena o un almuerzo, es normal pedir ___postre/la cuenta___.
4. De postre, Inés y Maite no saben exactamente lo que van a ___pedir___.
5. Después de comer en un restaurante, tienes que pagar ___la cuenta___.
6. Una pareja de enamorados nunca piensa en ___el divorcio___.
7. Hoy no trabajamos porque es un ___día de fiesta___.

CONSÚLTALO

Lectura The Latin American version of the debutante party is the **quinceañera**. A party for a girl turning fifteen, it is the moment when she is "presented" to society. To read more, see p. 287.

4 Fiesta sorpresa Trabajen en grupos para representar una conversación en la que uno/a de Uds. está celebrando su cumpleaños en un restaurante. Un(a) amigo/a le desea feliz cumpleaños a su compañero/a y le pregunta cuántos años cumple. Luego, cada uno/a le pide al/a la camarero/a un postre y algo para beber. Después de terminar los postres, un(a) amigo/a pide la cuenta y otro/a habla de dejar una propina. Los dos que no cumplen años dicen que quieren pagar la cuenta y el/la que cumple años les da las gracias por todo. Answers will vary.

NATIONAL communication STANDARDS

TEACHING OPTIONS

Extra practice Ask volunteers to ad-lib the **Fotonovela** episode for the class. Assure them that it is not necessary to memorize the **Fotonovela** or stick strictly to its content. They should try to get the general meaning across with the vocabulary and expressions they know, and they should also feel free to be creative. Give them time to prepare.

Pairs Have your students work in pairs to tell each other about celebrations in their families. Remind them to use as many expressions as possible from the **Expresiones útiles** on page 275, as well as the vocabulary on pages 270–271. Follow up by asking a few students to describe celebrations in their partners' families.

Pronunciación

The letters h, j, and g

helado **hombre** **hola** **hermosa**

The Spanish **h** is always silent.

José **jubilarse** **dejar** **pareja**

The letter **j** is pronounced much like the English *h* in *his.*

agencia **general** **Gil** **Gisela**

The letter **g** can be pronounced three different ways. Before **e** or **i**, the letter **g** is pronounced much like the English *h.*

Gustavo, gracias por llamar el domingo.

At the beginning of a phrase or after the letter **n**, the Spanish **g** is pronounced like the English *g* in *girl.*

Me gradué en agosto.

In any other position, the Spanish **g** has a somewhat softer sound.

Guerra **conseguir** **guantes** **agua**

In the combinations **gue** and **gui**, the **g** has a hard sound and the **u** is silent. In the combination **gua**, the **g** has a hard sound and the **u** is pronounced like the English *w.*

Práctica Lee las palabras en voz alta, prestando atención a la **h**, la **j** y la **g**.

1. hamburguesa	5. geografía	9. seguir	13. Jorge
2. jugar	6. magnífico	10. gracias	14. tengo
3. oreja	7. espejo	11. hijo	15. ahora
4. guapa	8. hago	12. galleta	16. guantes

Oraciones Lee las oraciones en voz alta, prestando atención a la **h**, la **j** y la **g**.

1. Hola. Me llamo Gustavo Hinojosa Lugones y vivo en Santiago de Chile.
2. Tengo una familia grande; somos tres hermanos y tres hermanas.
3. Voy a graduarme en mayo.
4. Para celebrar mi graduación mis padres van a regalarme un viaje a Egipto.
5. ¡Qué generosos son!

Refranes Lee los refranes en voz alta, prestando atención a la **h**, la **j** y la **g**.

A la larga, lo más dulce amarga.[1]

El hábito no hace al monje.[2]

1 Too much of a good thing.
2 The clothes don't make the man.

recursos

R	SCASS./CD Lección 9	LM p. 270	LCASS./CD Cass. 5A/CD5

TEACHING OPTIONS

Extra Practice Write the names of these Chilean cities on the board and ask for a volunteer to pronounce each one: Santiago, Antofagasta, Rancagua, Coihaique. Repeat the process with the names of these Chilean writers: Alberto Blest Gana, Vicente Huidobro, Gabriela Mistral, Juan Modesto Castro.

Pairs Have your students work in pairs to read aloud the sentences in Activity 2, **Identificar**, page 276. Encourage your students to help their partners if they have trouble pronouncing a particular word. Circulate around the class and model correct pronunciation as needed, focusing on the letters **h, j,** and **g**.

Section Goals

In **Pronunciación** students will be introduced to the pronunciation of **h, j,** and **g.**

Instructional Resources
Student Activities Manual: Lab Manual, 270
Student Cassette/CD

Present

- Ask the class how the Spanish **h** is pronounced. (It is silent.) Ask for volunteers to pronounce the example words.
- Explain that **j** is pronounced much like the English *h*. Pronounce the words **José, jubilarse, dejar,** and **pareja** and ask the class to repeat after you.
- Draw attention to the fact that the letter **g** is pronounced like the English *h* before **e** or **i**. Write the words **agencia, general, Gil,** and **Gisela** on the board and ask for volunteers to pronounce them.
- Point out that the letter **g** is pronounced like the English *g* at the beginning of a phrase or after the letter **n**. Pronounce the example sentence and have the class repeat after you.
- Explain that in any other position, particularly between vowels, **g** has a softer sound. Pronounce the example sentence and have the class repeat after you.
- Tell the class that in the combinations **gue** and **gui, g** has a hard sound and **u** is not pronounced. Explain that in the combination **gua**, the **u** sounds like the English *w*. Read the example words aloud and have the class repeat them.

Práctica/Oraciones/Refranes Model the pronunciation of each word or sentence, having students repeat after you.

Section Goals

In **Estructura 9.1** students will be introduced to the present tense of **dar** and **decir**.

Instructional Resources
Student Activities Manual: Workbook, 99; Lab Manual, 271

Before Presenting Estructura 9.1 Review forms of **e:i** stem-changing verbs **pedir, vestirse, servir,** as well as verbs with irregular **yo** forms like **hacer, poner, salir** (whose **yo** forms contain a **g** in the stem). Also review indirect object pronouns, as they are used frequently with the verbs **dar** and **decir**.
Assignment Have students study **Estructura 9.1** and prepare the activities (through Activity 2) on pages 278–279 as homework.

Dar and decir
Present
- Work through explanation and verb chart, modeling pronunciation of the verb forms.
- Emphasize that the **yo** forms of these verbs are irregular. The rest of the forms of **dar** are regular, while **decir** acts like an **e:i** stem-changing verb.
- Stress that indirect object pronouns are often used with these verbs and give additional examples.

¡Atención!
Present Have students look over the phrases with **dar** and **decir**. You may want to point out another common phrase in Spanish, **dar las gracias**. Contrast this with English *to say thanks* and emphasize that **decir** is not used in this phrase in Spanish.

Close Consolidate entire section by doing **¡Inténtalo!** with the whole class.

9.1 Dar and decir

NATIONAL STANDARDS comparisons

Dar** and **decir

		dar *(to give)*	**decir** *(to say; to tell)*
SINGULAR FORMS	yo	**doy**	**digo**
	tú	das	dices
	Ud./él/ella	da	dice
PLURAL FORMS	nosotros/as	damos	decimos
	vosotros/as	dais	decís
	Uds./ellos/ellas	dan	dicen
	present participle	**dando**	**diciendo**

- **Dar** and **decir** are both irregular in the first person singular of the present tense. The other forms of **dar** are regular, and those of **decir** follow the pattern of **-ir** stem-changing verbs **(e:i).**
- Both **dar** and **decir** are frequently used with indirect object pronouns, as well as with double object pronouns.

Mis padres **me dan** muchos regalos. → Mis padres **me los dan**.
My parents give me a lot of gifts. → *My parents give them to me.*

Te digo la respuesta. → **Te la digo.**
I am telling you the answer. → *I am telling it to you.*

¡ATENCIÓN!

Here are some common expressions with **dar** and **decir**:

dar consejos *to give advice*
dar un regalo *to give a present*
dar alegría *to give joy/happiness*
dar una fiesta *to throw a party*
decir la verdad *to tell the truth*
decir mentiras *to tell lies*
decir que *to say that*
dar un beso *to give a kiss*

¡INTÉNTALO! Completa las frases con las formas correctas de los verbos indicados.

dar

1. Mis amigos me __dan__ consejos.
2. Graciela y yo le __damos__ regalos a Miguel.
3. Yo te __doy__ este libro.
4. Tú les __das__ tu dirección electrónica a tus amigos.
5. Mi padre nos __da__ dulces.
6. Mis hijos me __dan__ mucha alegría.

decir

1. Yo siempre te __digo__ la verdad.
2. Elena y yo les __decimos__ nuestra dirección.
3. Isabel no nos __dice__ mentiras.
4. Mis hermanos me __dicen__ todo.
5. Tú les __dices__ tu número de teléfono.
6. Uds. me __dicen__ la fecha del examen.

TEACHING OPTIONS

Extra Practice As a rapid response drill, call out subject pronouns and have students respond with the correct form of **dar** or **decir**. Reverse the drill by starting with forms of **dar** and **decir** and asking students to give the corresponding subject pronouns.

Extra Practice Ask students questions using the phrases in **¡Atención!**. Ex: ____, **¿quién te da consejos? ¿A quién le das consejos?** and so forth. Verify student comprehension by asking other students questions that require them to confirm the answers given. Ex: ____, **¿a quién le da ____ consejos? ¿____ le da consejos a su hermano menor?**

Práctica

1 Completar Completa estas conversaciones con la forma correcta de **dar** o **decir.**

HIJO Papá, ¿me __das__ (dar) diez pesos para ir al cine?
PADRE ¿Qué __dices__ (decir)? Te __doy__ (dar) dinero todas las semanas. ¿Por qué no se lo pides a tu mamá?
HIJO Mamá __dice__ (decir) que no tiene dinero.

SUSANA Oye, Armando, ¿oíste que Adela __da__ (dar) una fiesta de fin de año?
ARMANDO No… ¿a qué hora empieza?
SUSANA A las ocho. Todos __dicen__ (decir) que va a ser estupenda.

2 Combinar Combina elementos de las tres columnas y agrega (*add*) todas las palabras necesarias para formar frases completas.

modelo
Mis amigos y yo siempre les damos regalos a nuestros profesores.

yo	siempre	dar consejos
tú	nunca	decir la verdad
mi compañero/a		dar fiestas
mi mejor amigo/a		dar alegría
Mis amigos y yo		decir mentiras
Mis padres		dar regalos

Comunicación

3 Preguntas En parejas, túrnense para hacerse estas preguntas. Answers will vary.

1. ¿Te dan tus profesores mucha tarea? ¿Qué dices cuando te la dan?
2. ¿Les dan los profesores muchos exámenes a los estudiantes?
3. ¿Das una fiesta este fin de semana? ¿Sabes quiénes dan una fiesta?
4. ¿Te gusta dar fiestas? ¿Por qué sí o no?
5. ¿Les das regalos a todos tus amigos? ¿Cuándo les das regalos y por qué?
6. ¿Qué dices cuando alguien te da un regalo?
7. ¿Tus padres te dan muchos consejos? ¿Qué te dicen? ¿Siempres sigues sus consejos?
8. ¿Qué otras personas te dan consejos? ¿Te dan consejos buenos o malos?
9. ¿A quiénes das consejos?
10. ¿Quiénes te dan dinero? ¿Por qué te lo dan?
11. ¿Les das dinero a tus amigos? ¿Por qué sí o por qué no?
12. ¿Siempre les dices la verdad a tus amigos? ¿Y a tus profesores?

4 Debate En grupos, comenten estos temas (*topics*). Hagan una lista de las razones (*reasons*) que tienen para defender sus opiniones en cada caso e informen a la clase. Answers will vary.

- ¿Es mejor decir siempre la verdad?
- ¿Es mejor dar regalos o recibirlos?

TEACHING OPTIONS

Heritage Speakers Ask heritage speakers to talk about a particular time in their lives when when one of the following situations went wrong: they gave poor advice to someone (**dar consejos**), they told a lie (**decir una mentira**), or they threw a huge party (**dar una fiesta**). (This will also preview irregular preterite forms of **dar** and **decir** that will be presented in **Estructura 9.2.**)

Small Groups In groups of three or four, students create three sentences each that use the verbs **dar** and **decir**. Two of the sentences must be true for them and the third must be false. Students read their sentences aloud to their group in random order. The other members of the group try to figure out which of the three sentences is false.

1 Present If activity was done as homework, quickly go over answers in class.

1 Expand Have individual students read the roles in the activity.

1 Present If activity was done as homework, ask volunteers to share some of their sentences with the class. If not, you may wish for students to do this activity in pairs. Have pairs create as many sentences as they can.

2 Expand Ask questions of students that expand on their answers in order to get more information. Ex: **—Yo siempre doy consejos. —¿A quién le das consejos? ¿Siempre son buenos?** and so forth.

3 Present Give students five minutes to complete activity. Make sure students take turns asking and answering the questions.

3 Expand Ask the questions of individual students. Ask related questions as necessary in order to get additional information. Verify student comprehension by asking other students questions that require them to confirm what was said.

4 Present Give groups four to five minutes to discuss each topic. Ask them to jot down their ideas as a group for presenting to the class afterward.

4 Expand As an alternate way of conducting the activity, split the class into four equal groups. Two groups will debate each topic, with one group taking the pro view and one taking the con view. Then the groups conduct the debates in front of the whole class.

Assignment Have students do activities in **Student Activities Manual: Workbook,** page 99.

Section Goals

In **Estructura 9.2** students will be introduced to the irregular preterites of several common verbs.

Instructional Resources
Student Activities Manual: Workbook, 100–101; Lab Manual, 272
Hoja de actividades 22

Before Presenting Estructura 9.2 Quickly review the present tense of a stem-changing verb such as **pedir**. Write the paradigm on the board and point out the stem-changing forms. Tell students that several important verbs, such as **tener, venir,** and **decir,** also have stem changes in the preterite and that they are now going to learn these. **Assignment** Have students study **Estructura 9.2** and do the exercises on pages 281–282 as homework.

Preterite of *tener, venir,* and *decir*

Present Work through the paradigms of **tener, venir,** and **decir,** modeling pronunciation. Point out the stem vowel and consonant changes and emphasize that in the first-person singular of these verbs the stress remains on the stem vowel, unlike regular preterites, where it moves to the ending **-é**. When you get to **dijeron,** explain that the expected **-i-** of the preterite ending (**-ieron**) does not appear after stems that end in **-j**. Except for the irregular stem, the first-person singular, and the lack of an **-i-** in the third-person plural, the preterites of these irregular verbs are the same as regular preterites. Tell students that when they learn the preterite of irregular verbs, they should memorize the first-person singular form because all the other forms of the preterite can be built on it according to rules they already know for regular preterites.

Continued on page 281.

9.2 Irregular preterites

NATIONAL comparisons STANDARDS

ANTE TODO You already know that the verbs **ir** and **ser** are irregular in the preterite. You will now learn other verbs whose preterite forms are also irregular.

Preterite of *tener, venir* and *decir*

		tener (e → u)	**venir** (e → i)	**decir** (e → i)
SINGULAR FORMS	yo	tuve	vine	dije
	tú	tuv**iste**	vin**iste**	dij**iste**
	Ud./él/ella	tuv**o**	vin**o**	dij**o**
PLURAL FORMS	nosotros/as	tuv**imos**	vin**imos**	dij**imos**
	vosotros/as	tuv**isteis**	vin**isteis**	dij**isteis**
	Uds./ellos/ellas	tuv**ieron**	vin**ieron**	dij**eron**

▶ In the chart above, observe how the conjugations of these verbs show a stem change. The **e** in **tener** changes to **u**, the **e** in **venir** and **decir** changes to **i**, and the **c** in **decir** changes to **j**.

▶ The following verbs observe similar stem-changes to **tener, venir** and **decir**.

INFINITIVE	U-STEM	PRETERITE FORMS
poder	pud-	pude, pudiste, pudo, pudimos, pudisteis, pudieron
poner	pus-	puse, pusiste, puso, pusimos, pusisteis, pusieron
saber	sup-	supe, supiste, supo, supimos, supisteis, supieron
estar	estuv-	estuve, estuviste, estuvo, estuvimos, estuvisteis, estuvieron

INFINITIVE	I-STEM	PRETERITE FORMS
querer	quis-	quise, quisiste, quiso, quisimos, quisisteis, quisieron
hacer	hic-	hice, hiciste, hizo, hicimos, hicisteis, hicieron

INFINITIVE	J-STEM	PRETERITE FORMS
traer	traj-	traje, trajiste, trajo, trajimos, trajisteis, trajeron
conducir	conduj-	conduje, condujiste, condujo, condujimos, condujisteis, condujeron
traducir	traduj-	traduje, tradujiste, tradujo, tradujimos, tradujisteis, tradujeron

¡ATENCIÓN!

The endings of these verbs are the regular preterite endings of **-er/-ir** verbs, except for the **yo** and **Ud.** forms. Note that these two endings are unaccented.

•••

The verbs with **j**-stems omit the letter **i** in the **Uds.** form. For example, **tener** → **tuvieron**, but **decir** → **dijeron**.
Most verbs that end in **-cir** are **j**-stem verbs in the preterite. For example, **producir** → **produje, produjiste,** etc.

ORBITEL
$5.000
$10.000
$20.000
¿Dijiste larga distancia?
En tarjetas prepagadas ninguna te da más minutos para hablar

TEACHING OPTIONS

Extra Practice Do a pattern practice drill. Give an infinitive and ask individual students to provide conjugations for the different subject pronouns and/or names you suggest. Reverse activity by saying a conjugated form and asking students to give the appropriate subject pronoun.

Game Divide the class into two teams. Indicate one team member at a time, alternating between teams. Give a verb in its infinitive form and a subject pronoun. The team member should give the correct preterite form. Give a point per correct answer. Deduct a point for each wrong answer. The team with the most points at the end of play wins.

The preterite of *dar*

yo	**di**	nosotros/as	**dimos**
tú	**diste**	vosotros/as	**disteis**
Ud./él/ella	**dio**	Uds./ellos/ellas	**dieron**

SINGULAR FORMS — PLURAL FORMS

- The endings for **dar** are the same as the regular preterite endings for **–er** and **–ir** verbs, except that there are no accent marks.

La camarera me **dio** el menú.
The waiter gave me the menu.

Le **di** a Juan algunos consejos.
I gave Juan some advice.

Los invitados le **dieron** un regalo.
The guests gave him/her a gift.

Nosotros **dimos** una gran fiesta.
We gave a great party.

- The preterite of **hay** (*inf.* **haber**) is **hubo** (*there was; there were*).

CONSÚLTALO

Note that there are other ways to say *there was* or *there were* in Spanish. See Lesson 10, section 10.1, p.306.

Doña Rita les dio una botella de vino a los viajeros.

Hubo una fiesta en el restaurante El Cráter.

¡INTÉNTALO! Escribe en cada espacio en blanco la forma correcta en pretérito del verbo que está entre paréntesis.

1. (querer) tú quisiste
2. (decir) Ud. dijo
3. (hacer) nosotras hicimos
4. (traer) yo traje
5. (conducir) ellas condujeron
6. (estar) ella estuvo
7. (tener) tú tuviste
8. (dar) ella y yo dimos
9. (traducir) yo traduje
10. (haber) ayer hubo
11. (saber) Ud. supo
12. (poner) ellos pusieron
13. (venir) yo vine
14. (poder) tú pudiste
15. (querer) Uds. quisieron
16. (estar) nosotras estuvimos
17. (decir) tú dijiste
18. (saber) ellos supieron
19. (hacer) él hizo
20. (poner) yo puse
21. (traer) nosotras trajimos
22. (tener) yo tuve
23. (dar) tú diste
24. (poder) Uds. pudieron

TEACHING OPTIONS

Video Show the video again to give students more input containing irregular preterite forms. Stop the video where appropriate to discuss how certain verbs were used and to ask comprehension questions.

Extra Practice Have students write down six things they brought to class today. Then they walk around the room asking other students if they also brought those items (**¿Trajiste llaves a clase hoy?**). When they find a student that answers **sí,** they ask that student to sign his or her name next to that item (**Firma aquí, por favor.**). Can students get signatures for all the items they brought to class?

Draw students' attention to the three patterns of stem changes in the listed verbs. Point out the spelling change in the third-person singular of **hacer** (**hizo**), noting that this change preserves the pronunciation of soft **c** before **o**, a spelling change that they have already observed in other verbs.

Test comprehension by randomly calling out an infinitive of one of these verbs and a subject pronoun. Signal a student to give you the corresponding preterite form. Continue until you have covered a majority of the forms and given most of the class an opportunity to respond.

The preterite of *dar*

Present Model pronunciation of preterite forms of **dar**. Emphasize that endings are the same as for **–er** and **–ir** verbs. Also emphasize that no accent marks accompany these forms.

Point out that **hubo** is used when talking about a specific occurrence, such as **Hubo un accidente**.

Use the preterite forms of all these verbs by talking about what you did in the recent past and then asking students questions that involve them in a conversation about what they did in the recent past. (Avoid the preterite of **poner, saber,** and **querer** for the moment.) Ex: **El sábado pasado tuve que ir a la fiesta de cumpleaños de mi nieta. Cumplió siete años. Hubo muchos chicos de su edad en la fiesta. Le di un bonito regalo. ____, ¿tuviste que ir a una fiesta sábado? ¿No? Pues, ¿qué hiciste sábado?** and so forth.

Close Consolidate entire section by doing **¡Inténtalo!** with the whole class.

1 Present If activity was done as homework, quickly go over answers in class.

1 Expand Ask individual students about the last time they threw a party. Ex: **La última vez que diste una fiesta, ¿quiénes estuvieron allí? ¿Vino alguien que no invitaste? ¿Qué trajeron los invitados?** and so forth.

Nota cultural
Suggestion You may want to point out the drawing of **flan de caramelo** on page 270. You may also want to bring some into class to have students sample it.

2 Present If activity was done as homework, quickly go over answers in class. If not, you may wish for students to do the activity in pairs.

2 Suggestion There are several possible answers other than those given in the annotations. Encourage the class to see how many sentences using the target verbs it can come up with to describe each drawing.

2 Expand Using your picture file or magazine pictures, show images similar to those in the activity. Students narrate what's happening in the images using irregular preterite verb forms.

Práctica

1 Completar Completa estas frases con el pretérito de los verbos entre paréntesis.

1. El sábado ___hubo___ (haber) una fiesta sorpresa para Elsa en mi casa.
2. Sofía ___hizo___ (hacer) un pastel para la fiesta y Miguel ___trajo___ (traer) un flan.
3. Los amigos y parientes de Elsa ___vinieron___ (venir) y ___trajeron___ (traer) regalos.
4. El hermano de Elsa no ___vino___ (venir) porque ___tuvo___ (tener) que trabajar.
5. Su tía María Dolores tampoco ___pudo___ (poder) venir.
6. Cuando Elsa abrió la puerta, todos gritaron: (*shouted*) "¡Feliz cumpleaños!" y su esposo le ___dio___ (dar) un beso.
7. Al final de la fiesta, todos ___dijeron___ (decir) que se divirtieron mucho.
8. La fiesta le ___dio___ (dar) a Elsa tanta alegría que no ___pudo___ (poder) dormir esa noche.

NOTA CULTURAL
A very popular dessert in Spanish-speaking countries, **flan** is a gelatinous custard made with eggs and topped with a caramel sauce. Delicious variations exist made with fruit or cheese.

2 Describir Usa los verbos apropiados para describir lo que estas personas hicieron.

dar	hacer	venir	traducir
estar	poner	tener	traer

1. El Sr. López
El Sr. López le dio dinero a su hijo.

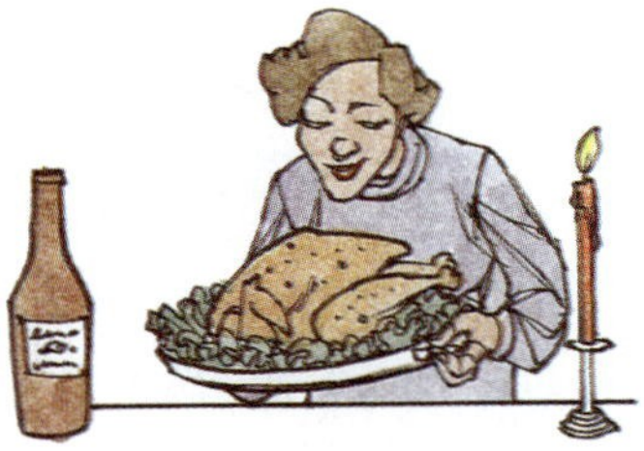

2. Norma
Norma puso el pavo en la mesa.

3. Anoche nosotros
Anoche nosotros tuvimos (hicimos/dimos) una fiesta de Navidad./Anoche nosotros estuvimos en una fiesta de Navidad.

4. Roberto y Elena
Roberto y Elena le trajeron/dieron un regalo a su amigo.

TEACHING OPTIONS

Heritage Speakers Ask heritage speakers to talk about a party they once attended. They should include information on what kind of party it was, who was there, what people brought, what the guests did, and so forth. Verify comprehension by asking other students in the class to relate what was said.

Small Groups In groups of three or four, each student writes three sentences using irregular preterites. Two of the sentences must be true for them and the third must be false. The other members of the group have to guess which of the sentences is the false one. This can also be done with the whole class.

Comunicación

3 Preguntas En parejas, túrnense para hacerse estas preguntas. Answers will vary.

1. ¿Qué hiciste anoche?
2. Y tu compañero/a, ¿qué hizo?
3. ¿Quiénes no estuvieron en clase la semana pasada?
4. ¿Qué trajiste a clase hoy?
5. ¿Hiciste la tarea para esta clase? ¿Cuándo la hiciste? ¿Se la diste al/a la profesor(a)?
6. ¿Hubo una fiesta en tu casa o residencia el sábado pasado?
7. ¿Alguien te dio una fiesta de cumpleaños el año pasado? ¿Quién?
8. ¿Cuándo fue la última (*last*) vez que tus parientes vinieron a visitarte? ¿Te trajeron algo? ¿Qué te trajeron?
9. ¿Les diste a tus padres un regalo para su aniversario? ¿Qué les regalaste?
10. ¿Le dijiste una mentira a tu novio/a o esposo/a la semana pasada?

4 Encuesta Tu profesor(a) va a darte una hoja de actividades. Circula por la clase y haz preguntas hasta que encuentres a alguien que corresponda a cada descripción de la lista. Luego informa a la clase de los resultados de tu encuesta.

Descripciones	Nombres
1. Tuvo un examen ayer.	
2. Trajo dulces a clase.	
3. Condujo su carro a clase.	
4. Estuvo en la biblioteca ayer.	
5. Dio consejos a alguien ayer.	
6. No pudo levantarse esta mañana.	
7. Hizo un viaje a un país hispano en el verano.	
8. Tuvo una cita anoche.	
9. Fue a una fiesta el fin de semana pasado.	
10. Tuvo que trabajar el sábado pasado.	

Síntesis

5 Conversación Trabaja con un(a) compañero/a para comparar cómo celebraron Uds. el Día de Acción de Gracias (*Thanksgiving Day*) en casa el año pasado. Incluyan la siguiente información en la conversación. Answers will vary.

- Cuál fue el menú
- Quiénes vinieron a la comida y quiénes no pudieron venir
- Quiénes prepararon la comida o trajeron algo
- Si Uds. tuvieron que preparar algo
- Lo que la gente hizo antes y después de comer

TEACHING OPTIONS

Extra Practice Ask students to write a brief composition on the **Fotonovela** from this lesson. Students should write about where the characters were, what they were doing, who ordered what, what they said to each other, and so forth. (Note: Students should stick to completed actions in the past [preterite]. The use of the imperfect for narrating a story will not be presented until **Lesson 10.**)

Large Groups Divide the class in half. To each member of one half of the class give a strip of paper that contains a question on it. Ex: **¿Quién me trajo el pastel de cumpleaños?** To each member of the other half of the class give the answer to that question. Ex: **Marta te lo trajo.** Students must find their partner.

3 Present Give students four to five minutes to complete the activity. Make sure students take turns asking and answering the questions.

3 Expand Ask the questions of individual students. Try to get additional information from the students when possible. Ex: **¿Hubo una fiesta en tu casa o residencia el sábado pasado? ¿Sí? ¿Quiénes estuvieron en la fiesta?** and so forth. Verify comprehension by asking other students questions that require them to respond to what was said. Ex: ____, **¿fuiste a la fiesta en la residencia de ____?**

4 Present Have students read directions. Point out that in order to get information they must form questions using the **tú** form of the verbs in the preterite. Ex: **¿Tuviste un examen ayer? ¿Trajiste dulces a clase?** and so forth. Give the class about 10 minutes to complete the activity. Distribute **Hoja de actividades 22**.

4 Expand Write items 1–10 on the board and ask for a show of hands for each item. Ex: **¿Quién tuvo un examen ayer?** Write tally marks next to each item to find out which activity was most popular.

5 Present
- Give students 10 minutes in pairs to complete the activity. You may wish for students to write down their information in the form of a composition to hand in later.
- If students don't or didn't celebrate Thanksgiving Day, ask them to talk about another holiday or special event that involved family or friends and a large meal.

Assignment Have students do activities in **Student Activities Manual: Workbook,** pages 100–101.

Section Goals

In **Estructura 9.3** students will be introduced to verbs that change meaning in the preterite tense.

Instructional Resources
Student Activities Manual: Workbook, 102; Lab Manual, 273

Before Presenting Estructura 9.3
Introduce the preterite of **conocer**. Say: **Conozco a Uds. muy bien ahora. Pero me acuerdo del día en que los conocí por primera vez. ¿Uds. se acuerdan del día en que nos conocimos por primera vez?** Explain that **conocer** changes meaning when used in the preterite. When used in the preterite, it means *met, got acquaited with, got to know.* Explain to students that several important verbs change meaning when used in the preterite.
Assignment Have students study **Estructura 9.3** and do the activities on pages 284-285 (Except activities 3–4) as homework.

Present
- Work through explanation and model sentences in the verb chart. Offer additional sample sentences as necessary.
- Stress that **poder** in the preterite means *to try and succeed.* **No poder** means *to try and not succeed.*
- Stress that **querer** in the preterite also means *to try.* **No querer** means *to refuse.*

Close Consolidate entire section by doing **¡Inténtalo!** with the whole class.

9.3 Verbs that change meaning in the preterite

NATIONAL STANDARDS comparisons

ANTE TODO The verbs **conocer, saber, poder,** and **querer** change meanings when used in the preterite. Because of this, each of them corresponds to more than one verb in English.

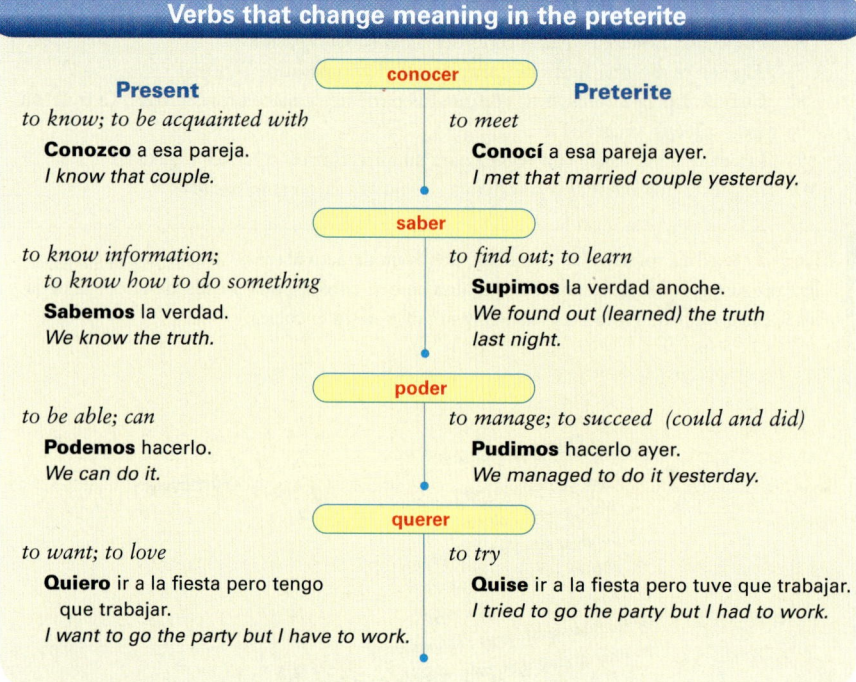

Verbs that change meaning in the preterite

	Present	Preterite
conocer	*to know; to be acquainted with* **Conozco** a esa pareja. *I know that couple.*	*to meet* **Conocí** a esa pareja ayer. *I met that married couple yesterday.*
saber	*to know information; to know how to do something* **Sabemos** la verdad. *We know the truth.*	*to find out; to learn* **Supimos** la verdad anoche. *We found out (learned) the truth last night.*
poder	*to be able; can* **Podemos** hacerlo. *We can do it.*	*to manage; to succeed (could and did)* **Pudimos** hacerlo ayer. *We managed to do it yesterday.*
querer	*to want; to love* **Quiero** ir a la fiesta pero tengo que trabajar. *I want to go the party but I have to work.*	*to try* **Quise** ir a la fiesta pero tuve que trabajar. *I tried to go the party but I had to work.*

¡ATENCIÓN!
In the preterite, the verbs **poder** and **querer** have different meanings, depending on whether they are used in affirmative or negative sentences.
pude *I was able (to)*
no pude *I failed (to)*
quise *I tried (to)*
no quise *I refused (to)*

¡INTÉNTALO! Cambia los verbos del presente al pretérito.

1. No quiero hacerlo.
   No ___quise___ hacerlo.
2. ¿Sabes la respuesta?
   ¿ ___Supiste___ la respuesta?
3. Las chicas pueden divertirse.
   Las chicas ___pudieron___ divertirse.
4. ¿Conoces a los recién casados?
   ¿ ___Conociste___ a los recién casados?
5. No puedo encontrar a Patricia.
   No ___pude___ encontrar a Patricia.
6. Josefina quiere relajarse.
   Josefina ___quiso___ relajarse.
7. Conocemos a Julio.
   ___Conocimos___ a Julio hoy.
8. Ella no puede venir a la fiesta.
   Ella no ___pudo___ venir a la fiesta.
9. Queremos pasarlo bien.
   ___Quisimos___ pasarlo bien.
10. Uds. saben del problema, ¿no?
    Uds. ___supieron___ del problema, ¿no?
11. No queremos ir a la fiesta.
    No ___quisimos___ ir a la fiesta.
12. Puedes venir conmigo
    ___Pudiste___ venir conmigo.

TEACHING OPTIONS

Extra Practice Give sentences using **conocer, saber, poder,** and **querer** in the present tense that will be logical when converted into the preterite. Have students convert them and explain (in English) how the meanings of the sentences change. Ex: **Sé la fecha de la fiesta. Gustavo puede comprar un regalo bonito. Queremos conocer a los invitados. Felipe y Paula no quieren ir a la fiesta. No puedo hacer un flan.**

Heritage Speakers Ask heritage speakers to talk about one of the following situations in the past: (1) when they found out there was no Santa Claus (**saber**), (2) when they met their best friend (**conocer**), or (3) something they tried to do but couldn't (**querer/no poder**). Verify student comprehension by asking other students to relate what was said.

Práctica

NOTA CULTURAL

Easter Island, or **Isla de Pascua,** is a remote Chilean territory located in the South Pacific. The immense statues found there are one of the world's greatest mysteries: no one knows how or why they were built. To learn more, see p. 294.

1 **Oraciones** Forma frases con los siguientes elementos. Usa el pretérito.

1. Anoche / nosotros / saber / que / Carlos y Eva / divorciarse
   Anoche nosotros supimos que Carlos y Eva se divorciaron.
2. Tú / conocer / Nora / clase / historia / ¿no?
   Conociste a Nora en la clase de historia, ¿no?
3. ¿Poder / Uds. / visitar / isla de Pascua?
   ¿Pudieron Uds. visitar la isla de Pascua?
4. Ayer / yo / saber / que / Paco / querer / romper / Olivia
   Ayer yo supe que Paco quiso romper con Olivia.
5. El señor Navarro / querer / jubilarse / pero / no poder
   El señor Navarro quiso jubilarse pero no pudo.
6. Gustavo y Elena / conocer / mi esposo / quinceañera
   Gustavo y Elena conocieron a mi esposo en la quinceañera.
7. Yolanda / no poder / dormir / anoche
   Yolanda no pudo dormir anoche.
8. Irma / saber / que / nosotros / comer / galletas
   Irma supo que nosotros comimos las galletas.

Comunicación

2 **Completar** Completa estas frases de una manera lógica. Answers will vary.

1. Ayer mi compañero/a de cuarto supo...
2. Esta mañana no pude...
3. Conocí a mi mejor amigo/a en...
4. Mis padres no quisieron...
5. Mi mejor amigo/a no pudo...
6. Mi novio/a y yo nos conocimos en...
7. La semana pasada supe...
8. Ayer mis amigos quisieron...

3 **Telenovela** (*Soap opera*) En parejas, escriban el diálogo para una escena de una telenovela. La escena trata de (*is about*) una situación amorosa entre tres personas: Mirta, Daniel y Raúl. Usen el pretérito de **conocer, poder, querer** y **saber** en su diálogo. Answers will vary.

Síntesis

4 **Conversación** En una hoja de papel, escribe dos listas: las cosas que hiciste durante el fin de semana y las cosas que quisiste hacer pero no pudiste. Luego, con un(a) compañero/a, comparen sus listas y expliquen por qué no pudieron hacer esas cosas. Answers will vary.

TEACHING OPTIONS

Video Show the video again to give students more input containing verbs that change meaning in the preterite. Stop the video where appropriate to discuss how certain verbs were used and to ask comprehension questions.

Pairs In pairs, students write three sentences using verbs that change meaning in the preterite. Two of the sentences must be true for them and the third must be false. Their partner has to guess which of the sentences is the false one. This can also be done with the whole class.

1 Present If activity was done as homework, go over answers quickly in class.

1 Expand In pairs, students create five similar dehydrated sentences for their partner to complete, using the verbs **conocer, saber, poder,** and **querer.** After pairs have completed this, ask for volunteers to share some of their dehydrated sentences. Write them on the board and have the rest of the class "hydrate" them.

2 Present If activity was done as homework, quickly go over answers in class.

2 Expand Ask for volunteers to share their sentence completions.

2 Expand Share with the class some recent things you found out, tried to do but couldn't, or the names of people you met, inviting students to respond.

3 Present Have groups write their dialogues as homework before presenting their skits in class. Students may also work with more than one person, if they wish.

3 Present Point out that, unlike soap operas in this country, Hispanic soap operas run for a limited period of time, like a mini-series, and then end.

3 Expand Have groups present their skits. The class may vote for the funniest, most original, and so forth.

Síntesis

4 Present Have students prepare their lists as homework before getting together with a partner to discuss them.

4 Expand Ask for volunteers to share some of the things they did and those they were unable to do. **Assignment** Have students do activities in **Student Activities Manual: Workbook,** page 102.

Section Goals
In **Estructura 9.4** students will review:
- the uses of **¿qué?** and **¿cuál?**
- interrogative words and phrases

Instructional Resources
Student Activities Manual: Workbook, 103–104; Lab Manual, 274
Hoja de actividades 23–24

Before Presenting Estructura 9.4 Review the question words **¿qué?** and **¿cuál?** Write incomplete questions on the board and ask students which interrogative word best completes each question. Ex: **¿____ es tu número de teléfono? (Cuál) ¿____ es esto? (Qué)** and so forth.
Assignment Have students study **Estructura 9.4** and do **¡Inténtalo!** and Activity 1 on pages 286–287 as homework.

Present
- Work through explanation, modeling sample sentences and offering additional ones.
- Point out that, while both question words mean what/which, **¿qué?** is typically used before a noun, while **¿cuál?** is used with a verb. Ex: **¿Qué clase te gusta más? ¿Cuál es tu clase favorita?**
- Review and work through chart of interrogative words and phrases. Ask students personalized questions using each of them and invite them to ask you questions.

Close Consolidate entire section by doing **¡Inténtalo!** with the whole class.

9.4 ¿Qué? and ¿cuál?

NATIONAL STANDARDS comparisons

ANTE TODO You've already learned how to use interrogative words and phrases. As you know, **¿qué?** and **¿cuál?** or **¿cuáles?** mean *what?* or *which?* However, they are not interchangeable.

▶ **¿Qué?** is used to ask for a definition or an explanation.

¿Qué es el flan?
What is flan?

¿Qué estudias?
What do you study?

▶ **¿Cuál(es)?** is used when there is a choice among several possibilities.

¿Cuál quieres, el más corto o el más largo?
Which (one) do you want, the shortest or the longest?

¿Cuáles son tus medias, las negras o las blancas?
Which ones are your socks, the black ones or the white ones?

▶ **¿Cuál?** can not be used before a noun; in this case, **¿qué?** is used.

¿Cuál es tu color favorito?
What is your favorite color?

¿Qué colores te gustan?
What colors do you like?

▶ **¿Qué?** used before a noun, has the same meaning as **¿cuál?**

¿Qué regalo te gusta?
What (Which) gift do you like?

¿Qué dulces quieren Uds.?
What (Which) sweets do you want?

Interrogative words and phrases

¿a qué hora?	*at what time?*	**¿cuánto/a?**	*how much?*
¿adónde?	*(to) where?*	**¿cuántos/as?**	*how many?*
¿cómo?	*how?*	**¿de dónde?**	*from where?*
¿cuál(es)?	*what?; which?*	**¿dónde?**	*where?*
¿cuándo?	*when?*	**¿qué?**	*what?; which?*
		¿quién(es)?	*who?*

¡INTÉNTALO! Completa las preguntas con **¿qué?** o **¿cuál(es)?**, según el contexto.

1. ¿ Cuál de los dos te gusta más?
2. ¿ Cuál es tu teléfono?
3. ¿ Qué tipo de pastel pediste?
4. ¿ Qué es una quinceañera?
5. ¿ Qué haces ahora?
6. ¿ Cuáles son tus platos favoritos?
7. ¿ Qué bebidas te gustan más?
8. ¿ Qué es esto?
9. ¿ Cuál es el mejor?
10. ¿ Cuál es tu opinión?
11. ¿ Qué fiestas celebras tú?
12. ¿ Qué vino prefieres?
13. ¿ Cuál es tu clase favorita?
14. ¿ Qué pones en la mesa?
15. ¿ Qué restaurante prefieres?
16. ¿ Qué estudiantes estudian más?
17. ¿ Qué quieres comer esta noche?
18. ¿ Cuál es la tarea para mañana?
19. ¿ Qué color prefieres?
20. ¿ Qué opinas?

TEACHING OPTIONS

Extra Practice Ask questions of individual students, using **¿qué?** and **¿cuál?** Make sure a portion of the questions are general and information-seeking in nature (**¿qué?**). Ex: **¿Qué es una guitarra? ¿Qué es un elefante?** This is also a good way for students to practice circumlocution (**Es una cosa que...**).

Extra Practice Students write one question using each of the interrogative words or phrases in the chart on page 286. Then they ask those questions of a partner, who must answer in complete sentences.

Práctica

1 **Completar** Completa estas frases con una palabra interrogativa. Luego, túrnate con un(a) compañero/a para hacer y contestar las preguntas. **¡Ojo!** A veces se puede usar más de una palabra interrogativa.

1. ¿En ___qué___ país nacieron tus padres?
2. ¿___Cuál___ es la fecha de tu cumpleaños?
3. ¿___Dónde___ naciste?
4. ¿___Cuál___ es tu estado civil?
5. ¿___Cómo/Cuándo/Dónde___ te relajas?
6. ¿___Cuáles___ son tus programas favoritos de la televisión?
7. ¿___Quién___ es tu mejor amigo?
8. ¿___Adónde___ van tus amigos para divertirse?
9. ¿___Qué___ postres te gustan? ¿___Cuál___ te gusta más?
10. ¿___Qué___ problemas tuviste el primer día de clase?

Comunicación

2 **Una invitación** En parejas, lean esta invitación. Luego, túrnense para hacerse preguntas basadas en la información de la invitación. Answers will vary.

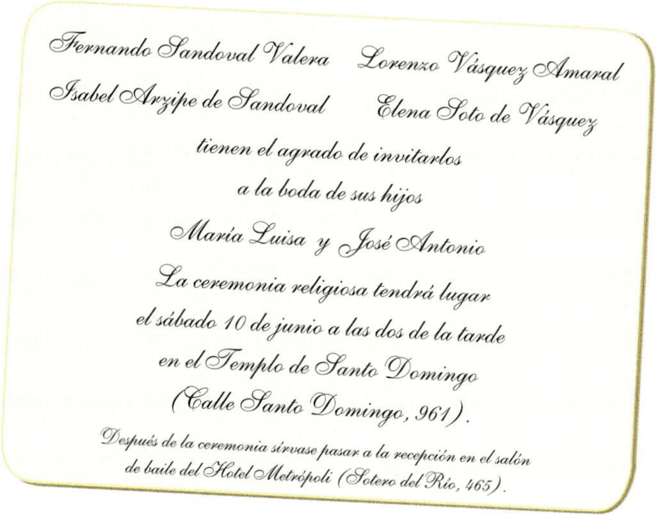
Fernando Sandoval Valera *Lorenzo Vásquez Amaral*
Isabel Arzipe de Sandoval *Elena Soto de Vásquez*
tienen el agrado de invitarlos
a la boda de sus hijos
María Luisa y José Antonio
La ceremonia religiosa tendrá lugar
el sábado 10 de junio a las dos de la tarde
en el Templo de Santo Domingo
(Calle Santo Domingo, 961).
Después de la ceremonia sírvase pasar a la recepción en el salón de baile del Hotel Metrópoli (Sotero del Río, 465).

¡LENGUA VIVA!
The word **invitar** is not used exactly like *invite*. If you say **Te invito (a) un café,** it means that you are offering to buy that person a coffee. **Te/le/les invito,** said alone, means *It's on me.*

3 **Situación** Trabaja con un(a) compañero/a. Una persona va a ser el/la director(a) de banquetes del Hotel Metrópoli. La otra persona es el padre o la madre de María Luisa, quien quiere hacer los arreglos (*plans*) para una recepción después de la boda de su hija. Su profesor(a) va a darles hojas de actividades para la situación. Answers will vary.

1 Present If filling in the blanks was done as homework, go over the questions quickly with the whole class. If not, give pairs three minutes to work together to fill in the blanks before you go over the questions.

1 Expand Give pairs five minutes to take turns asking and answering the questions. Then, with the whole class, conduct a conversation to find out what the class's consensus on some of the questions is.

2 Present Give students five minutes to complete the activity.

¡Lengua viva! Present Have students read **¡Lengua viva!** sidebar. Ask them to practice using **invitar** in this way with a classmate.

2 Expand Ask your own questions about the realia (**¿dónde? ¿qué? ¿cuándo?** and so forth). Alternatively, you may ask students to share some of the questions they asked their partner, which other students answer in complete sentences.

3 Present This activity is based on the wedding invitation in **Comunicación 2**. Distribute **Hoja de actividades 23** to one member of the pair and **Hoja de actividades 24** to the other. Give students about six minutes to complete activity.

3 Expand With their same partner and/or others, students prepare a **telenovela** skit with characters from the wedding invitation. Encourage students to use interrogative words as well as verbs that change meaning in the preterite.

Assignment Have students do activities in **Student Activities Manual: Workbook,** pages 103–104.

TEACHING OPTIONS

Pairs In pairs, students prepare a skit between two friends talking. One of the friends is planning a surprise party (**fiesta de sorpresa**) for a mutual friend. However, the other person reveals that he or she doesn't care all that much for the party honoree and tells why. The class can vote for the funniest or most original skit.

Game Play a game of *Jeopardy*®. Prepare five answers for each of six categories (30 questions in all), each in varying degrees of difficulty. Ask for three volunteers to play. Students must give their answers in the form of a question. You may also decrease the number of questions and have additional volunteers participate in the game.

Section Goals

In **Lectura** students will:
- learn to use word families to infer meaning in context
- read content-rich texts

Antes de leer

Introduce the strategy. Write **conocer** on the board, reminding students of the meaning *to know, be familiar with*. Next to it, write **conocimiento** and **conocido**. Tell students that recognizing the family relationship between a known word and unfamiliar words can help them infer the meaning of the words they don't yet know. Guide students to see that **conocimiento** is a noun meaning *knowledge, familiarity* and **conocido** is an adjective form of the verb meaning *known* or *well-known*.

Examinar el texto Have students scan the text for clues to its contents. Ask volunteers to tell what kind of text it is and how they know. Headlines (**titulares**), photos, and layout (**composición de la página**) reveal that it is the society news (**notas de sociedad**) in a newspaper.

Raíces Go over the instructions and the **Modelo** with the whole class. Have students fill in the rest of the chart after they have read **Vida social**.

Assignment Have students read **Vida social** and prepare the exercises in **Raíces** and **Después de leer** as homework.

Lectura

National Standards: communication, cultures

Antes de leer

Estrategia
Recognizing word families

Recognizing root words can help you guess the meaning of words in context, ensuring better comprehension of a reading selection. Using this strategy will enrich your Spanish vocabulary as well.

Examinar el texto

Familiarízate con el texto usando las estrategias de lectura más efectivas para ti. ¿Qué tipo de documento es? ¿De qué tratan las cuatro secciones del documento? Explica tus respuestas.

Raíces

Completa el siguiente cuadro para ampliar tu vocabulario. Usa palabras de la lectura de esta lección y el vocabulario de las lecciones anteriores. ¿Qué significan las palabras que escribiste en el cuadro?

modelo

Verbo	Sustantivos	Otras formas
agradecer	agradecimiento/ gracias	agradecido

1. estudiar	estudiante *student*	estudiado *studied*
2. celebrar *to celebrate*	celebración *celebration*	celebrado
3. bailar *to dance*	baile	bailable *danceable*
4. bautizar	bautismo *baptism*	bautizado *baptized*

¿De qué tratan...? *What are they about?* Raíces *Roots* cuadro *chart*

Vida social

Matrimonio Espinoza Álvarez-Reyes Salazar

El día sábado 30 de octubre de 2000 a las 19 horas, se celebró el matrimonio de Silvia Reyes y Carlos Espinoza en la Catedral de Santiago. La ceremonia fue oficiada por el pastor Federico Salas y participaron los padres de los novios, el señor Jorge Espinoza y señora, y el señor José Alfredo Reyes y señora.

Después de la ceremonia, los padres de los recién casados ofrecieron una fiesta con baile en el restaurante Doña Mercedes.

Bautismo

José María recibió el bautismo el 30 de septiembre de 2000.

Sus padres, don Roberto Lagos Moreno y doña María Angélica Sánchez, compartieron la alegría de la fiesta con todos sus parientes y amigos. La ceremonia religiosa se realizó en la Catedral de Aguas Blancas. Después de la ceremonia, padres, parientes y amigos celebraron una fiesta en la residencia de la familia Lagos.

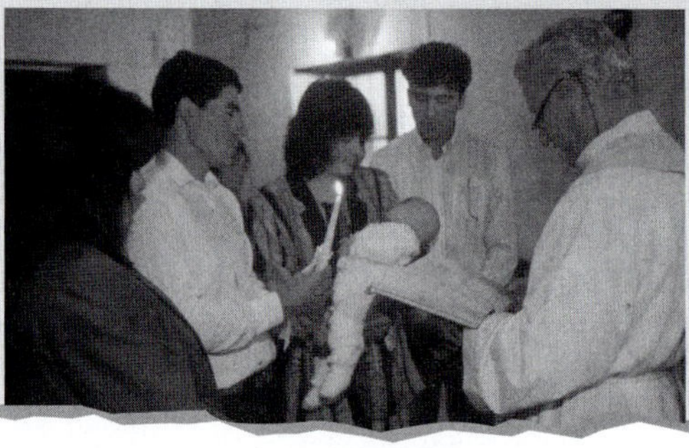

TEACHING OPTIONS

Heritage Speakers Ask Spanish speakers to analyze the word **quinceañera** and tell what two words and which suffix it is made of. (*quince* + *año* + *-era*) The suffix *-ero/a* indicates the word is an adjective. Basically **quinceañera** means *related to the fifteenth year*. It refers to both the party and the young woman. Then have them share what they know about the coming of age event for a 15-year-old girl celebrated throughout Latin America.

Extra Practice Here are some related words of which at least one form will be familiar to students. Guide them to recognize the relationship between words and meanings. **idea, ideal, idealismo, idealizar, idear, ideario, idealista • conservar, conservación, conserva, conservador • bueno, bondad, bondadoso, bonito • habla, hablador, hablar, hablante, hablado**

32B

Fiesta quinceañera

El médico don Amador Larenas Fernández y la señora Felisa Vera de Larenas celebraron los quince años de su hija Ana Ester junto a sus parientes y amigos. La quinceañera tiene su residencia en la ciudad de La Paz y es estudiante del Colegio Francés. La fiesta de presentación en sociedad de la señorita Ana Ester fue el día viernes 24 de mayo a las 19 horas en el Club Español. Entre los invitados especiales se encontraron el alcalde de la ciudad, don Pedro Castedo y su esposa. La música estuvo a cargo de la Orquesta Americana. ¡Feliz cumpleaños! le deseamos a la señorita Ana Ester en su fiesta bailable.

Expresión de Gracias

Carmen Godoy Tapia

Agradecemos sinceramente a todas las personas que nos acompañaron en el último adiós de nuestra apreciada esposa, madre, abuela y tía, la señora Carmen Godoy Tapia. El funeral tuvo lugar el día 28 de abril de 2000 en la ciudad de Capri. La vida de Carmen Godoy fue un ejemplo de trabajo, amistad, alegría y amor para todos nosotros. La familia agradece de todo corazón a todos los parientes y amigos su asistencia al funeral.

Su esposo, hijos y familia.

será *will be* **ofrecerán** *will throw* **alcalde** *mayor* **tuvo lugar** *took place* **agradecemos** *we thank* **de todo corazón** *sincerely* **asistencia** *attendance*

Después de leer

Corregir

Escribe estos comentarios otra vez para corregir la información errónea.

1. El alcalde y su esposa asistieron a la boda de Silvia y Carlos. El alcalde y su esposa asistieron a la fiesta de quinceañera de Ana Ester.
2. Todos los anuncios tratan de eventos felices. Tres de los anuncios tratan de eventos felices. Uno de los anuncios trata de una muerte.
3. Ana Ester Larenas cumple dieciséis años. Ana Ester Larenas cumple quince años.
4. Amador Larenas y Felisa Vera son hermanos. Amador Larenas y Felisa Vera están casados.
5. Carmen Godoy Tapia agradeció a las personas que asistieron al funeral. La familia de Carmen Godoy Tapia agradeció a las personas su asistencia al funeral.

Identificar

Escribe el nombre de la(s) persona(s) descrita(s).

1. Dejó viudo a su esposo en la primavera de 2000. Carmen Godoy Tapia
2. Sus padres y todos los invitados brindaron por él, pero él no entendió por qué. José María
3. El Club Español les presentó una cuenta considerable para pagar. don Amador Larenas Fernández y doña Felisa Vera de Larenas
4. Unió a los novios en santo matrimonio. el pastor Federico Salas
5. La celebración de su cumpleaños marcó el principio de su vida adulta. Ana Ester

Un anuncio

Trabaja con dos o tres compañeros/as de clase e inventen un anuncio breve sobre una celebración importante. Esta celebración puede ser una graduación, un matrimonio o una gran fiesta en la que Uds. participan. Incluyan la siguiente información.

1. Nombres de los participantes
2. La fecha, la hora y la dirección
3. Otros detalles de interés

anuncios *announcements* **tratan de** *have to do with* **agradeció** *thanked* **descritas** *described* **principio** *beginning* **Unió** *He united*

Después de leer

Corregir

Suggestion If you have assigned this as homework, go over the answers with the whole class, asking volunteers to correct each false statement and point out the location in the text where they found the correct answer. This activity is also suitable for pairs to do in class if you have not assigned it as homework. Have partners take turns reading the false statements aloud and looking in the text for the answers.

Identificar

Suggestion If students have trouble inferring the meaning of any word or phrase, help them identify the corresponding context clues and explain any unfamiliar vocabulary.

Expand Have pairs write one question for each of the five items and exchange them with another pair who answers the questions.

Un anuncio

Suggestion You may wish to provide students with examples of announcements from Spanish newspapers to analyze and use as models.

Suggestion Have Spanish speakers work with those who are being exposed to Spanish for the first time. When students are finished writing, ask them to read their announcements aloud. You may wish to have students combine the articles to create their own **Vida social** page for a class newspaper.

TEACHING OPTIONS

Variación léxica Ask Spanish speakers to tell the class other terms they use to refer to various types of celebrations. Possible responses: wedding: **matrimonio, boda, casamiento**; graduation: **graduación, promoción**; birthday: **cumpleaños, día del santo.**

Heritage Speaker If a Spanish speaker has attended a wedding, baptism, funeral, or other similar celebration in a Spanish-speaking country, ask him or her to prepare a short presentation about the event.

Game Have students describe the people mentioned in the announcements they wrote for the above activity **Un anuncio**; their classmates will guess which person in the announcement they are describing. They may extend the game by giving clues about the event and having classmates guess the event.

Section Goals

In **Escritura** students will:
- create a Venn diagram to organize information
- learn words and phrases that signal similarity and difference
- write a comparative analysis

Tema
Present Explain to students that to write a comparative analysis, they will need to use words or phrases that signal similarities (**similtudes**) and differences (**diferencias**). Model the pronunciation of the words and expressions under **Escribir una composición** with the whole class. Then have volunteers use them in sentences to express the similarities and differences listed in the Venn diagram.

Estrategia
Present Explain that a graphic organizer such as a Venn diagram is a great way to record information and visually organize details to be compared and contrasted in a comparative analysis. Draw a Venn diagram with the headings **Mi primer día de la escuela secundaria, Mi primer dia de la universidad,** and subheadings **Diferencias** and **Similtudes**. Tell students they are going to complete a Venn diagram to compare their first day of high school and their first day of college. Explaining any unfamiliar vocabulary, guide students in listing the similarities and differences of the two events. Then discuss with the whole class how these events are alike and how they are different using some of the terms to signal similarities and differences.
Assignment Have students prepare **Ideas y organización** and **Primer borrador** as homework. Tell students to keep the Venn diagram they use to organize their first draft.

Escritura

Estrategia

Planning and writing a comparative analysis

Writing any kind of comparative analysis requires careful planning. Venn diagrams are useful for organizing your ideas visually before comparing and contrasting people, places, objects, events, or issues. To create a Venn diagram, draw two circles that overlap and label the top of each circle. List the differences between the two elements in the outer rings of the two circles, then list their similarities where the two circles overlap. Review the following example.

Diferencias y similitudes

Boda de Silvia Reyes y Carlos Espinoza
Diferencias:
1. Primero hay una celebración religiosa.
2. Se celebra en un restaurante.
Similitudes:
1. Las dos fiestas se celebran por la noche.
2. Las dos fiestas son bailables.
Quinceañera de Ana Ester Larenas Vera
Diferencias:
1. Se celebra en un club.
2. Vienen invitados especiales.

La lista de palabras y expresiones de la derecha puede ayudarte a escribir este tipo de ensayo (*essay*).

Tema

Escribir una composición

Compara una celebración familiar (como una boda o una fiesta de cumpleaños o una graduación) a la que tú asististe recientemente con otro tipo de celebración. Utiliza palabras y expresiones de la siguiente lista.

Para expresar similitudes

además, también	*also*
al igual que	*the same as*
como	*as, like*
de la misma manera	*in the same manner (way)*
del mismo modo	*in the same manner (way)*
tan + adjetivo + como	*as + adjective + as*
tanto/a(s) + sustantivo + como	*as many (much) + noun + as*

Para expresar diferencias

a diferencia de	*unlike*
a pesar de	*in spite of*
aunque	*although*
en cambio	*on the other hand*
más/menos... que	*more/less . . . than*
no obstante	*nevertheless; however*
por otro lado	*on the other hand*
por el contrario	*on the other hand*
sin embargo	*nevertheless; however*

TEACHING OPTIONS

Proofreading Activity Copy on the board or onto a transparency the following items containing mistakes as a proofreading activity to do with the whole class.

1. **Concepción me deció que habió muchos invitados en su fiesta de cumpleaños.**
2. **¿Cuáles consejos siempre los dan a los recien casados?**
3. **Los invitados trajieron muchos regalos cuando venieron a la fiesta.**
4. **¿Cuál pensaste cuando sabiste las noticias de la boda?**
5. **Viné a la fiesta pero no pasé lo bien.**
6. **¿Qué me deces si te do un regalo bonito?**
7. **Me dijieron que Isabel rompió con Mario. ¿Cuál piensas tú?**

Plan de escritura

1 Ideas y organización

Tómate unos minutos para decidir qué celebraciones vas a comparar. Utiliza un diagrama de Venn para anotar las similitudes y las diferencias entre las dos celebraciones.

2 Primer borrador

Utiliza tus notas de **Ideas y organización** para escribir el primer borrador de tu composición. Escribe todo lo que puedas sin consultar en ningún sitio. Después consulta el texto y tus apuntes de clase. Usa el diccionario como último recurso.

3 Comentario

Intercambia tu composición con un(a) compañero/a. Lee su borrador y anota sus ideas en un diagrama de Venn. Comparte tu diagrama de Venn con el diagrama que él/ella preparó antes. Después:

1. Ofrécele algunas sugerencias para mejorar su composición.
2. Si ves algunos errores gramaticales u ortográficos, coméntaselos. Si él/ella tiene dificultad en realizar un diagrama de Venn basado en tu composición, debes cambiar la organización de la composición. Incorpora nuevas ideas y/o más información para ampliar la comparación entre las celebraciones.

4 Redacción

Utiliza esta guía para hacer la última revisión antes de escribir tu copia final.

1. Subraya cada verbo para comprobar la concordancia con el sujeto. ¡Cuidado con los verbos irregulares en el pretérito!
2. Revisa la concordancia entre los sustantivos y los adjetivos en cada oración.
3. Comprueba el uso correcto de los pronombres.
4. Revisa la ortografía y la puntuación otra vez con la ayuda de tus **Anotaciones para mejorar la escritura.**

5 Evaluación y progreso

Intercambia tu composición con otro/a compañero/a. Lee su composición y escribe una evaluación del contenido. Utiliza las palabras y expresiones que aprendiste en la Lección 8. Cuando tu profesor(a) devuelva tu trabajo, lee sus comentarios y correcciones con cuidado. Anota tus errores más importantes en tu lista de **Anotaciones para mejorar la escritura** en tu **Carpeta de trabajos.**

composición *essay* a la que tú asististe recientemente *that you recently attended* apuntes *notes* último *last* Intercambia *Exchange* Ofrécele *Offer him/her* sugerencias *suggestions* ortográficos *spelling* coméntaselos *comment on them* ampliar *expand* Subraya *Underline* Comprueba *Check* concordancia *agreement* contenido *contents*

EVALUATION: Composición

Criteria	Scale
Content	1 2 3 4
Organization	1 2 3 4
Use of comparisons/contrasts	1 2 3 4
Use of vocabulary	1 2 3 4
Accuracy	1 2 3 4

Scoring	
Excellent	18–20 points
Good	14–17 points
Satisfactory	10–13 points
Unsatisfactory	< 10 points

Comentario

Present Go over questions 1 and 2 with the whole class so peer readers understand their task. Then have pairs exchange compositions. Allow five minutes for reading and making a Venn diagram. Allow five minutes for comments.

Assignment Have students prepare **Redacción** as homework. Ask them to rewrite their drafts incorporating the peer comments and following the directions in **Redacción**. Tell them to prepare a clean copy of their final draft to hand in.

Evaluación y progreso

Give the class five minutes to exchange and comment on their final drafts. Then have them hand them in to you.

Writing Sample

Here is a sample composition that would constitute superior writing achievement.

Dos celebraciones bonitas

En mi familia se celebraron dos eventos bonitos este año. Primero, en abril se celebró la boda de mi prima Juana. Después en noviembre se celebró la quinceañera de mi hermana Elena.

Las dos celebraciones tuvieron mucho en común. En las dos ocasiones se celebró una ceremonia religiosa. Hubo muchos parientes y amigos que vinieron a la quinceañera al igual que a la boda. ¡Todos bailamos en las fiestas!

Sin embargo, también hubo diferencias. La boda se celebró en una iglesia durante el día. En cambio, la quinceañera se celebró en un club por la noche. En la quinceañera Elena pasó de niña a mujer. En la boda, Juana pasó de soltera a mujer casada.

Me divertí en las dos celebraciones pero creo que me divertí más en la quinceañera.

Section Goals

In **Escuchar** students will:

- use context to infer meaning of unfamiliar words
- answer questions based on a recorded conversation

Instructional Resource
Student Cassette/CD

Preparación Have students read the invitation and guess what Rosa and Josefina will be talking about in the recorded conversation.

Estrategia
Script Hoy mi sobrino Gabriel cumplió seis años. Antes de la fiesta, ayudé a mi hermana a decorar la sala con globos de todos los colores, pero ¡qué bulla después!, cuando los niños se pusieron a estallarlos todos. El pastel de cumpleaños estaba riquísimo y cuando Gabriel sopló las velas, apagó las seis. Los otros niños le regalaron un montón de juguetes, y nos divertimos mucho.

Assignment Have students do the activities in **Ahora escucha** and **Comprensión** as homework.

Ahora escucha
Script
Josefina: Rosa, ¿te divertiste anoche en la fiesta?
Rosa: Sí, me divertí más en el aniversario que en la boda. ¡La fiesta estuvo fenomenal! Fue buena idea festejar el aniversario en un restaurante. Así todos pudieron relajarse.
Josefina: En parte, yo lo disfruté porque son una pareja tan linda; qué dicha que estén tan enamorados después de dos años de matrimonio. Me gustaría tener una relación como la de ellos. Y también saberlo celebrar con tanta alegría. ¡Pero qué cantidad de comida y bebida! ¿Te imaginas cómo va a ser la fiesta de bautizo del primer hijo?
Rosa: Es verdad que Margarita y Roberto exageran un poco con sus fiestas, pero son de la clase de gente que le gusta celebrar los eventos de la vida. Y como tienen tantas amistades y dos familias tan grandes....
Josefina: Oye, Rosa, hablando de familia, ¿llegaste a conocer al cuñado de Magali? Es soltero, ¿no? Quise bailar con él pero no me sacó a bailar.
Rosa: Hablas de Rafael. Es muy bien parecido; ¡ese pelo...! Estuve hablando con él después del brindis. Me dijo que no le gustan ni el champán ni el vino; él finge tomar cuando brindan porque no lo soporta. No te sacó a bailar porque él y Susana estaban juntos en la fiesta.
Josefina: De todos modos, aun sin Rafael, bailé toda la noche. Lo pasé muy, pero muy bien.

Escuchar

NATIONAL communication STANDARDS

Preparación

Lee la invitación. ¿De qué crees que van a hablar Rosa y Josefina?

Margarita Robles de García
y Roberto García Olmos

Piden su presencia en la celebración
del segundo aniversario de bodas
el día 13 de marzo de 2001
con una misa en la Iglesia Virgen del Coromoto
a las 6:30

seguida por cena y baile
en el restaurante El Campanero,
Calle Principal, Las Mercedes
a las 8:30

Estrategia

Guessing the meaning of words through context

When you hear an unfamiliar word, you can often guess its meaning by listening to the words and phrases around it. To practice this strategy, you will now listen to a paragraph. Jot down the unfamiliar words that you hear. Then listen to the paragraph again and jot down the word or words that are the most useful clues to the meaning of each unfamiliar word.

Ahora escucha

Ahora escucha la conversación entre Josefina y Rosa. Cuando oigas una de las palabras de la primera columna A, usa el contexto para identificar el sinónimo o la definición en la columna B.

A

_d_ **festejar**
_c_ **dicha**
_h_ **bien parecido**
_g_ **finge (fingir)**
_b_ **soporta (soportar)**
_e_ **yo lo disfruté (disfrutar)**

B

a. conmemoración religiosa de una muerte
b. tolera
c. suerte
d. celebrar
e. me divertí
f. horror
g. crea una ficción
h. guapo

Comprensión

¿Cierto o falso?

Lee cada frase e indica si lo que dice es **cierto** o **falso**. Corrige las frases falsas.

1. A la fiesta de Margarita y Roberto no fueron tantos invitados porque Margarita y Roberto no conocen a mucha gente. Falso. Fueron muchos invitados porque Margarita y Roberto tienen muchas amistades y familias grandes.
2. Algunos fueron a la fiesta con una pareja y otros fueron sin compañero/a. Cierto.
3. Margarita y Roberto decidieron celebrar el segundo aniversario porque no celebraron el matrimonio con una fiesta. Falso. Celebraron el segundo aniversario porque les gustan las fiestas.
4. A Rosa y a Josefina les parece interesante Rafael. Cierto.
5. Josefina se divirtió mucho en la fiesta porque bailó toda la noche con Rafael. Falso. Josefina se divirtió mucho pero bailó con otros, no con Rafael.

Preguntas

1. ¿Son solteras Rosa y Josefina? ¿Cómo lo sabes? Parece que las dos chicas son solteras. Les interesa mucho un muchacho que fue a la fiesta y Josefina dice que quiere tener una relación como la relación de Margarita y Roberto.
2. ¿Tienen las chicas una amistad de mucho tiempo con la pareja que celebra su aniversario? ¿Cómo lo sabes? Sí, parece que las chicas son buenas amigas de Margarita y de Roberto. Hablan de la celebración de la boda y piensan estar en el bautizo del primer hijo también.

Proyecto

Prepara un reportaje

Imagina que eres periodista en un día de fiesta en Chile. Vas a escribir un artículo o reportaje para describir ese día y las cosas que hiciste.

1 Escribe un artículo

Escribe un artículo de un día de fiesta o de una celebración que viste en Chile. Usa los **Recursos para la investigación** para investigar las fiestas nacionales, las celebraciones y los festivales de Chile. Elige la celebración que más te interesa y busca información y fotos de la fiesta. El artículo puede incluir esta información:

- el nombre de la celebración
- cuándo fue
- cómo celebraron el día festivo, incluyendo la ropa especial que usaron, la comida, la música y el baile
- qué hiciste tú durante la celebración
- fotos de la celebración (en colores, si es posible)

2 Presenta la información

Presenta el artículo a la clase. Puedes fotocopiar el artículo para darles copias a tus compañeros/as. Habla del día festivo en que participaste. Informa a tus compañeros/as de lo que celebra la fiesta, de lo que hizo la gente y de lo que tú hiciste en particular. Quieres interesar a toda la clase en la celebración y por lo tanto es importante explicar los detalles y presentar fotos en colores.

Elige *Choose* por lo tanto *therefore* detalles *details*

recursos para la investigación

Internet Palabras clave: Chile, festividad(es), festival(es), fiestas religiosas	**Comunidad** Estudiantes o profesores que son de Chile o que viajaron a Chile, chilenos que viven en la comunidad
Biblioteca Libros de cultura o de folklore, guías turísticas, revistas	**Otros recursos** Videos turísticos de Chile

Section Goals

In **Proyecto** students will:
- pretend they are journalists in Chile
- investigate and write an article about a Chilean festival

Before Assigning Proyecto Students will need approximately a week to complete the project, so at the beginning of that time period, have them open their books to page 293 and glance over **Proyecto**. Tell them that they are going to use their Spanish skills as they carry out research on festivals in Chile. Tell them that when they finish their research, they will write an article on a Chilean festival; for example, Semana Santa (Holy Week), which takes place in March or April, or Día de la independencia (Independence Day), which is September 18.

Assignment Have students read page 293 and follow directions in **Prepara un reportaje** to complete their article.

Escribe un artículo

Suggestions
- Students may wish to interview someone who has recently visited Chile.
- If possible, provide students with examples of articles written in Spanish about festivals in Spanish-speaking countries
- Students can seek information on Chilean festivals by using the Spanish key words and phrases **fiestas típicas de Chile, fiestas chilenas or festivales chilenos.**

Presenta la información

Suggestion
- You may wish to have students present the articles as though they were giving the article at a live broadcast of the event.
- You may wish to do a few presentations at a time over several days.

EVALUATION: Artículo

Criteria	Scale
Content	1 2 3 4
Organization	1 2 3 4
Use of comparisons/contrasts	1 2 3 4
Visual Appeal	1 2 3 4
Oral Presentation	1 2 3 4

Scoring	
Excellent	18–20 points
Good	14–17 points
Satisfactory	10–13 points
Unsatisfactory	< 10 points

Section Goals

In **Panorama**, students will read about the geography, culture, and economy of Chile.

Instructional Resources
Student Activities Manual: Workbook, 105–106
Transparency 37

Chile

Before Presenting Panorama Ask students to look at the map of Chile or project **Transparency 37**, and to talk about the physical features of the country. Have a volunteer read about the Area of Chile. Point out that Chile is 2,880 miles from north to south, but no more than 264 miles from east to west. Look at the call-out photos and read the captions. Guide students to see that Chile has a variety of climates.

Assignment Have students read **Panorama** and write out the completed questions and anwers in **¿Qué aprendiste?** on page 295 as homework.

Present Ask volunteers to read each section of **El país en cifras**. After reading about the **Chilenos célebres,** you may want to give students more information about O'Higgins. They can probably guess correctly that his father was an Irish immigrant, but should also know that he is considered one of the founders of modern Latin America, along with Simón Bolívar and José de San Martín. These "founding fathers" are called **los próceres**.

Increíble pero cierto Chile lies in a seismically active zone and has developed state-of-the-art seismic engineering in order to address architectural vulnerability and other issues that impact this earthquake-prone region.

Chile

NATIONAL STANDARDS connections cultures

El país en cifras

- **Área:** 756.950 km^2 (292.259 millas^2), *dos veces el área de Montana*
- **Población:** 15.589.000 *Aproximadamente el 80 por ciento de la población es urbana, y la tercera parte de los chilenos vive en la capital.*
- **Capital:** Santiago de Chile—5.720.000
- **Ciudades principales:** Concepción—356.000, Viña del Mar—326.000, Valparaíso—283.000, Temuco—246.000

SOURCE: Population Division, UN Secretariat

- **Moneda:** peso chileno
- **Idiomas:** español (oficial), mapuche

Bandera de Chile

Chilenos célebres

- **Bernardo O'Higgins,** militar y héroe nacional (1778-1842)
- **Gabriela Mistral,** poeta y diplomática (1889-1957)
- **Pablo Neruda,** poeta (1904-1973)
- **Isabel Allende,** novelista (1942-)

Pablo Neruda

la tercera parte *a third* **militar** *soldier*

Pescadores de Valparaíso

Palacio de la Moneda en Santiago

Una calle de Santiago

Vista de la costa de Viña del Mar

Madre e hija en Temuco

recursos

R	WB pp. 105-106	WB, Repaso 7-9 pp. 107-108	vistasonline

¡Increíble pero cierto!

El terremoto más grande de la historia tuvo lugar en Chile el 22 de mayo de 1960. Registró la intensidad récord de 9.5 en la escala de Richter. 2.000 personas murieron, 3.000 resultaron heridas, 2.000.000 perdieron su hogar y la geografía del país se modificó notablemente.

TEACHING OPTIONS

Heritage Speaker Invite Spanish speakers to prepare a poem by **Pablo Neruda** to read aloud for the class. Many of the **Odas elementales,** such as **Oda a la alcachofa, Oda al tomate,** and **Oda a la cebolla** are written in simple language. Prepare copies of the poem beforehand and go over unfamiliar vocabulary with the class.

Worth Noting Chile's geography encompasses the greatest of extremes. Though it is the second smallest Spanish-speaking country in South America (only Ecuador is smaller), it has 2,800 miles of coastline. In the north is the Desert of Atacama, the driest region on earth. Some of the highest peaks in the Andes lie on Chile's border with Argentina. Chile's agricultural region is a valley the size of central California's. The southern archipelago is cool, foggy, and rainy, like the Alaska panhandle.

Lugares • La Isla de Pascua

La Isla de Pascua recibió ese nombre porque los exploradores holandeses llegaron a la isla por primera vez el día de Pascua de 1722. Ahora es parte del territorio de Chile. La Isla de Pascua es famosa por los *moai*, estatuas enormes que representan personas con rasgos muy exagerados. Estas estatuas las construyeron los *rapa nui*, los antiguos habitantes de la zona. En la actualidad no se sabe mucho sobre los *rapa nui* ni tampoco se sabe por qué decidieron abandonar la isla.

Deportes • Los deportes de invierno

Hay muchos lugares para practicar los deportes de invierno en Chile porque las montañas nevadas de los Andes ocupan gran parte del país. El Parque Nacional de Villarrica, por ejemplo, situado al pie de un volcán y junto a un lago, es un sitio popular para el esquí y el *snowboard*. Para los que prefieren deportes más extremos, el centro de esquí Valle Nevado ofrece el heli-esquí.

Ciencias • Astronomía

Los observatorios chilenos, situados en los Andes, son lugares excelentes para las observaciones astronómicas. Científicos de todo el mundo van a Chile para estudiar las estrellas y otros fenómenos de la galaxia. Hoy día Chile está construyendo observatorios y telescopios nuevos que darán imágenes aún más nítidas del universo.

Economía • El vino

La producción de vino comenzó en Chile en el siglo XVI. Ahora la industria del vino constituye una parte importante de la actividad agrícola del país y la exportación de sus productos ha subido mucho en los últimos años. Los vinos chilenos reciben el aprecio internacional por su gran variedad, sus ricos y complejos sabores y su precio moderado. Los más conocidos internacionalmente son los vinos de Aconcagua, de Santiago y de Huasco.

¿Qué aprendiste? Responde a las preguntas con una frase completa.

1. ¿Qué porcentaje (*percentage*) de la población chilena es urbana?
   El 80 por ciento de la población chilena es urbana.
2. ¿Qué son los *moai*? ¿Dónde están?
   Los *moai* son estatuas enormes en la Isla de Pascua.
3. ¿Qué deporte extremo se practica (*is practiced*) en el centro de esquí Valle Nevado?
   Se practica el *heli-esquí*.
4. ¿Por qué van a Chile científicos de todo el mundo? Van a Chile porque los observatorios chilenos son lugares excelentes para las observaciones astronómicas.
5. ¿Cuándo comenzó la producción de vino en Chile?
   Comenzó en el siglo XVI.
6. ¿Por qué reciben los vinos chilenos el aprecio internacional? Lo reciben por su variedad, sus ricos y complejos sabores y su precio moderado.

Conexión Internet Investiga estos temas en el sitio **www.vistasonline.com**.

1. Busca información sobre Pablo Neruda e Isabel Allende. ¿Dónde y cuándo nacieron? ¿Cuáles son algunas de sus obras (*works*)? ¿Cuáles son algunos de los temas de sus obras?
2. Busca información sobre sitios donde los chilenos y los turistas practican deportes de invierno en Chile. Selecciona un sitio y descríbelo a tu clase.

La Isla de Pascua *Easter Island* holandeses *Dutch* no se sabe mucho *not much is known* junto a *beside* lago *lake* los que *those who* Científicos *Scientists* estrellas *stars* Hoy día *Currently* darán imágenes aún más nítidas *will yield even clearer images* siglo *century* ha subido *has gone up* últimos años *recent years* complejos sabores *complex flavors*

TEACHING OPTIONS

Worth Noting The native Mapuche people of southern Chile are a small minority of the Chilean population today, but have maintained a strong cultural identity since the time of their first contact with Europeans. In fact, they resisted conquest so well that it was only in the late 19th century that the government of Chile could assert actual sovereignty over the region south of the river Bío-bío. The majority of Chileans are of European descent. Chilean Spanish is much less infused with indigenous lexical items than is the Spanish of countries such as Guatemala and Mexico, where the larger indigenous population has made a greater impact on the language.

La Isla de Pascua With its vibrant Polynesian culture, Easter Island is unlike anywhere else in Chile. Located 2,000 from the nearest island and 4,000 miles from the Chilean coast, it is one of the most isolated places on earth. Until the 1960s, it was visited once a year by a Chilean warship bringing supplies. Now there are regular air connections to Santiago.

Los deportes de invierno Remind students that some of the highest mountains in South America lie along the border Chile shares with Argentina. In the south is the **Parque Nacional Torres del Paine**, a national park featuring ice caverns, deep glacial trenches, and other spectacular features.

Astronomía In 1962, the Cerro Tololo Inter-American Observatory was founded as a joint project between Chilean and American astronomers. Since that time, so many other major telescopes have been installed for research purposes that Chile can now claim to have the highest concentration of telescopes in the world!

El vino Invite students to research the wine-growing regions of Chile and to compare them to wine-growing regions in California, France, or other wine-producing areas.

¿Qué aprendiste? Go over the questions and answers with students.

Assignment Have students do activites in **Student Activities Manual: Workbook,** pages 105–106.

Conexión Internet Students will find information about Chile at **www.vistasonline.com**, as well as links to other sites that can help them in their research.

9 vocabulario

Celebraciones

el aniversario (de bodas)	*(wedding) anniversary*
la boda	*wedding*
el día de fiesta	*holiday*
el cumpleaños	*birthday*
la fiesta	*party*
el/la invitado/a	*guest*
la Navidad	*Christmas*
la quinceañera	*young woman's fifteenth birthday celebration*
la sorpresa	*surprise*
brindar	*to toast* (drink)
celebrar	*to celebrate*
cumplir años	*to have a birthday*
dejar una propina	*to leave a tip*
divertirse (e:ie, i)	*to have fun*
invitar	*to invite*
pagar la cuenta	*to pay the bill*
pasarlo bien (mal)	*to have a good (bad) time*
regalar	*to give* (as a gift)
reírse (e:ie, i)	*to laugh*
relajarse	*to relax*
sonreír (e:ie, i)	*to smile*
sorprender	*to surprise*

Postres y otras comidas

el bizcocho	*biscuit*
la botella (de vino)	*bottle (of wine)*
el champán	*champagne*
el flan (de caramelo)	*baked (caramel) custard*
los dulces	*sweets; candy*
la galleta	*cookie*
el helado	*ice cream*
el pastel (de chocolate)	*(chocolate) cake; pie*
el pastel de cumpleaños	*birthday cake*
el postre	*dessert*

Relaciones personales

la amistad	*friendship*
el amor	*love*
el divorcio	*divorce*
el estado civil	*marital status*
el matrimonio	*marriage*
la pareja	(married) *couple; partner*
el/la recién casado/a	*newlywed*
casarse (con)	*to get married (to)*
comprometerse (con)	*to get engaged (to)*
divorciarse (de)	*to get divorced (from)*
enamorarse (de)	*to fall in love (with)*
llevarse bien/mal (con)	*to get along well/ badly (with)*
odiar	*to hate*
romper (con)	*to break up (with)*
salir (con)	*to go out (with); to date*
separarse (de)	*to separate (from)*
tener una cita	*to have a date; to have an appointment*
casado/a	*married*
divorciado/a	*divorced*
juntos/as	*together*
soltero/a	*single; unmarried*
separado/a	*separated*
viudo/a	*widower/widow*

Palabras adicionales

la alegría	*joy*
el apellido	*last name*
el beso	*kiss*
el consejo	*(a piece of) advice*
la mentira	*lie*
la respuesta	*answer*
la verdad	*truth*

Las etapas de la vida

la adolescencia	*adolescence*
la etapa	*stage; step*
la juventud	*youth*
la madurez	*maturity; middle age*
la muerte	*death*
el nacimiento	*birth*
la niñez	*childhood*
la vejez	*old age*
la vida	*life*
cambiar (de)	*to change*
graduarse (en)	*to graduate (from)*
jubilarse	*to retire (from work)*
nacer	*to be born*

Verbos

dar	*to give*
decir (que)	*to say (that); to tell (that)*

Expresiones útiles	*See page 275.*

En el consultorio

10

Communicative Goals

You will learn how to:

- Describe how you feel physically.
- Talk abouth health and medical conditions

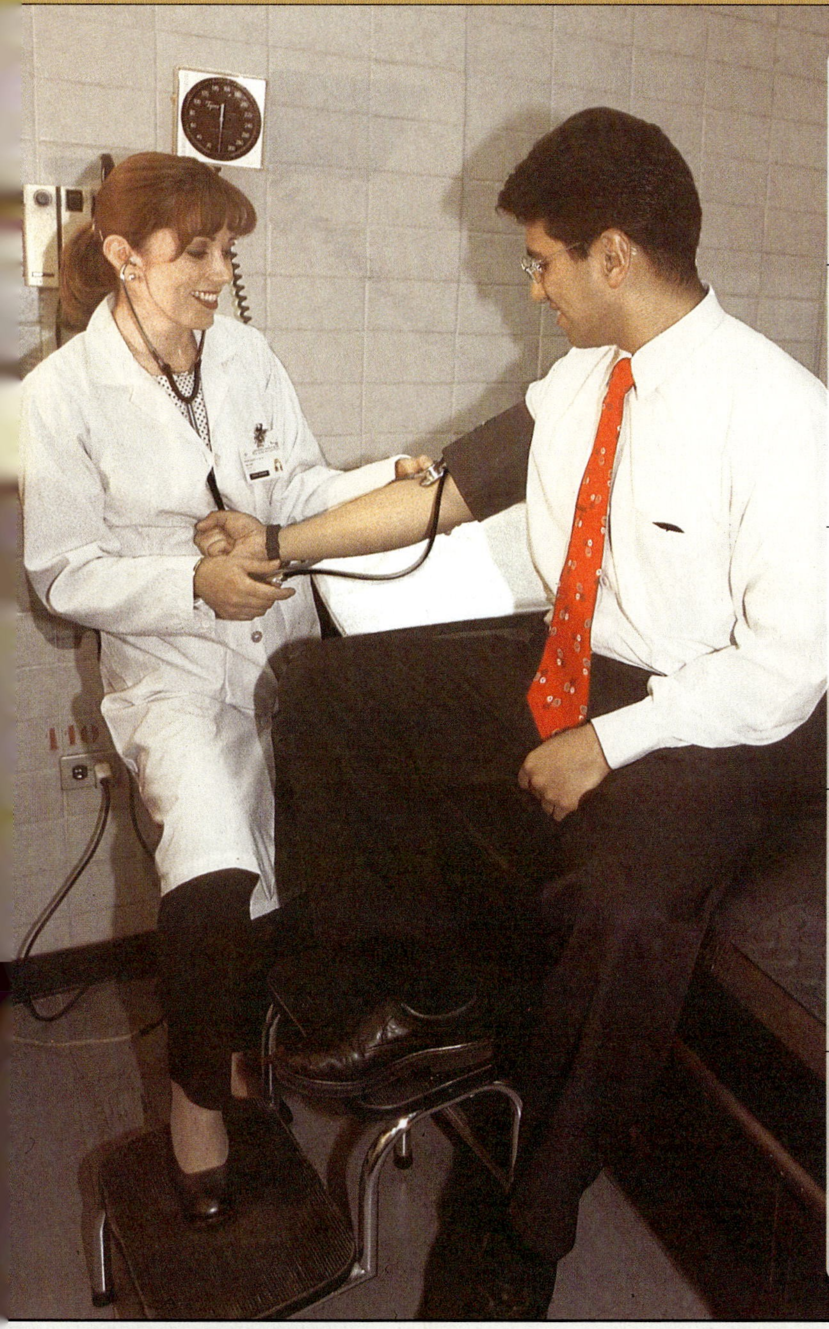

contextos

fotonovela

Javier hurts himself on the bus. Don Francisco takes him to see Dra. Márquez who, after examining him, concludes that he has only twisted his ankle.

estructura

adelante

panorama

Lesson Goals

In **Lesson 10** students will be introduced to the following:
- names of parts of the body
- health-related terms
- imperfect tense
- impersonal constructions with **se**
- using **se** for unplanned events
- forming adverbs using *adjective* + **-mente**
- common adverbs and adverbial expressions
- time expressions with **hacer**
- activating background knowledge
- avoiding redundancy
- writing a medical report
- listening for specific information
- writing and delivering a speech on the Costa Rican political or social system for a conference
- cultural, geographic, and economical information about Costa Rica

Lesson Preview

Have students look at the photo. Say: **Es una foto de una doctora y un paciente. Están en el consultorio.** Then ask: **¿Cuál es la doctora, el hombre o la mujer? ¿Quién es el paciente? ¿Está bien el paciente?**

INSTRUCTIONAL RESOURCES

Student Activities Manual: Workbook, 109–120
Student Activities Manual: Lab Manual, 275–280
Student Activities Manual: Video Activities, 345–346
Instructor's Resource Manual: Hojas de actividades, 25–26
Instructor's Resource Manual: Answer Keys
Instructor's Resource Manual: Vocabulario adicional, 56
Tapescript/Videoscript
Overhead Transparencies, 38–39

Student Cassette/CD
Lab Cassette/CD
Video Program
CD-ROM
Website: **www.vistasonline.com**
Testing Program: Prueba A, Prueba B

Section Goals

In **Contextos**, students will learn and practice:
- names of parts of the body
- vocabulary for talking about illnesses and accidents
- vocabulary associated with medical visits

Instructional Resources
Student Activities Manual: Workbook, 109–110; Lab Manual, 275
Vocabulario adicional 56
Transparency 38
Student Cassette/CD

Before Presenting Contextos Introduce active lesson vocabulary. Using cognate vocabulary, pointing to parts of your body, and pantomiming procedures, talk about a hospital visit, real or imaginary. Use the imperfect as input before it's presented to students in **Estructura 10.1.** Ex: **Recientemente fui al hospital. Me dolía la cabeza, la garganta, los ojos, la nariz... El médico me puso una inyección con antibióticos. Me recetó otra medicina y fui a la farmacia. Pero luego descubrí que tenía infección...** Ask comprehension questions and point to body parts. Ex: **¿Me dolía la nariz? ¿el brazo? ¿la cabeza?** and so forth.
Assignment Have students study **Contextos** and do the exercises in **Práctica** as homework.

Present Give students two minutes to review the doctor's office scene on pages 298–299. Then project **Transparency 38.** Have students refer to the scene and the vocabulary boxes as you give yes-no statements about the new vocabulary. Ex: **¿Sí o no? La enfermera le toma la temperatura a la paciente. (Sí.) La médica le pone una inyección al hombre. (No.)** Then ask volunteers to describe what's going on in the scene, using as much of the new vocabulary as possible.

En el consultorio

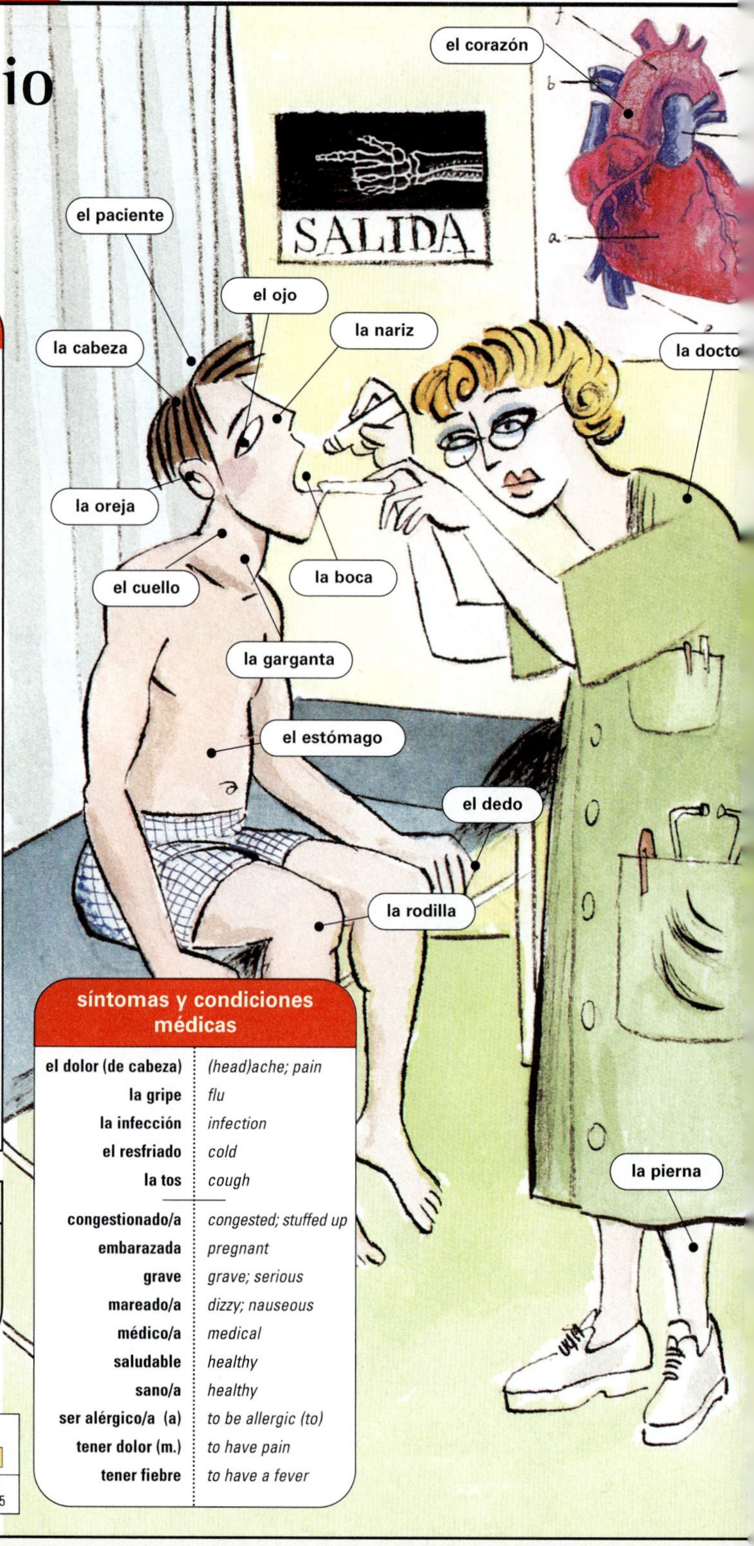

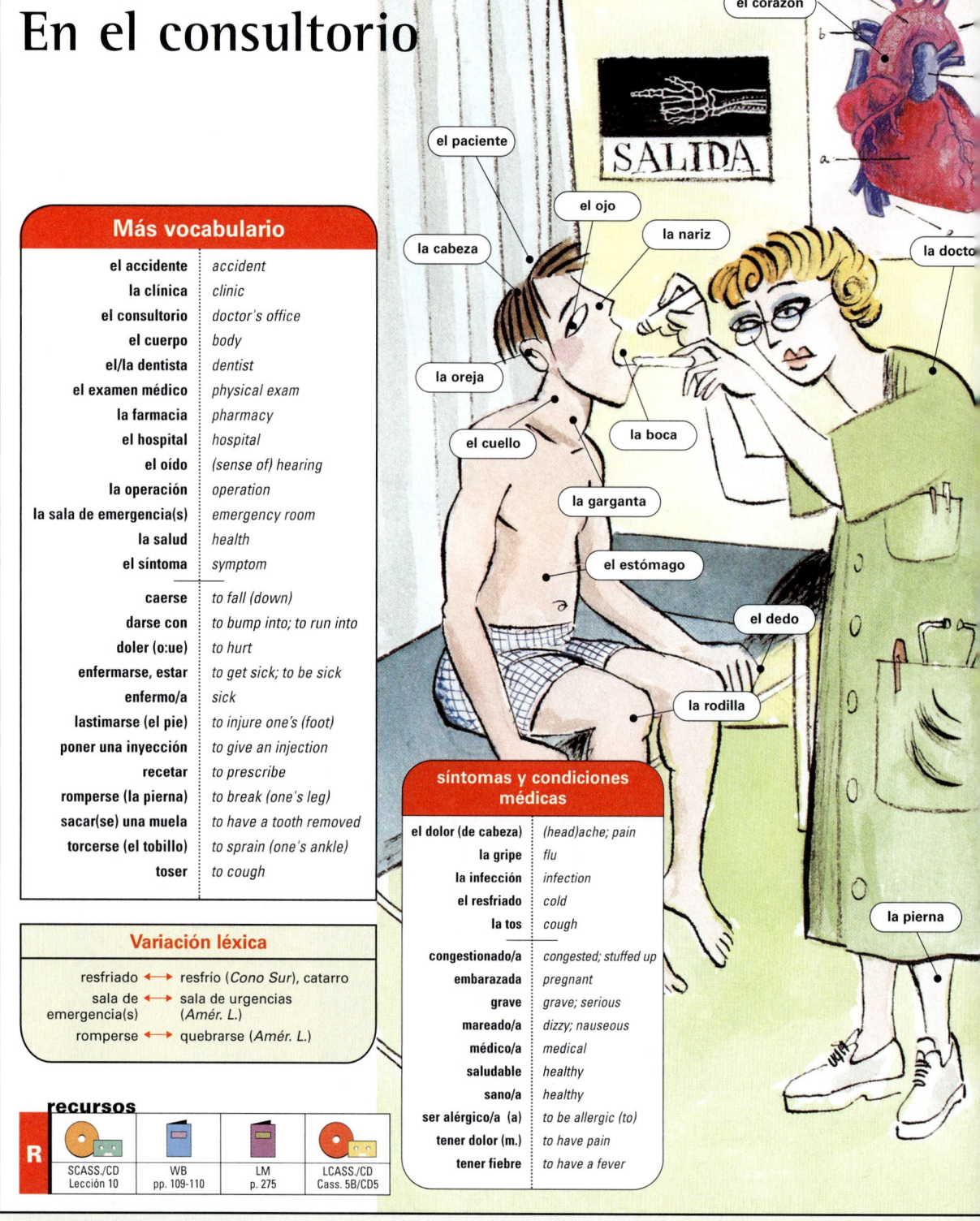

Más vocabulario

el accidente	*accident*
la clínica	*clinic*
el consultorio	*doctor's office*
el cuerpo	*body*
el/la dentista	*dentist*
el examen médico	*physical exam*
la farmacia	*pharmacy*
el hospital	*hospital*
el oído	*(sense of) hearing*
la operación	*operation*
la sala de emergencia(s)	*emergency room*
la salud	*health*
el síntoma	*symptom*
caerse	*to fall (down)*
darse con	*to bump into; to run into*
doler (o:ue)	*to hurt*
enfermarse, estar	*to get sick; to be sick*
enfermo/a	*sick*
lastimarse (el pie)	*to injure one's (foot)*
poner una inyección	*to give an injection*
recetar	*to prescribe*
romperse (la pierna)	*to break (one's leg)*
sacar(se) una muela	*to have a tooth removed*
torcerse (el tobillo)	*to sprain (one's ankle)*
toser	*to cough*

síntomas y condiciones médicas

el dolor (de cabeza)	*(head)ache; pain*
la gripe	*flu*
la infección	*infection*
el resfriado	*cold*
la tos	*cough*
congestionado/a	*congested; stuffed up*
embarazada	*pregnant*
grave	*grave; serious*
mareado/a	*dizzy; nauseous*
médico/a	*medical*
saludable	*healthy*
sano/a	*healthy*
ser alérgico/a (a)	*to be allergic (to)*
tener dolor (m.)	*to have pain*
tener fiebre	*to have a fever*

Variación léxica

resfriado ⟷ resfrío (*Cono Sur*), catarro
sala de emergencia(s) ⟷ sala de urgencias (*Amér. L.*)
romperse ⟷ quebrarse (*Amér. L.*)

recursos

R	SCASS./CD Lección 10	WB pp. 109-110	LM p. 275	LCASS./CD Cass. 5B/CD5

TEACHING OPTIONS

TPR Play a game of Simon Says (**Simón dice...**). Write **toquen** on the board and explain that it means *touch*. Start by saying: **Simón dice... toquen la nariz.** Students are to touch their nose and keep their hand there until instructed to do otherwise. Work through various parts of the body. Be sure to give instructions without saying **Simón dice...** once in awhile.

Variación léxica Point out differences in vocabulary related to health, as well as some false cognates students should be aware of. **Embarazada** means *pregnant*, not *embarrassed*. You may also want to present **constipado/a** and explain that it does not mean *constipated*, but rather *congested; stuffed up*.

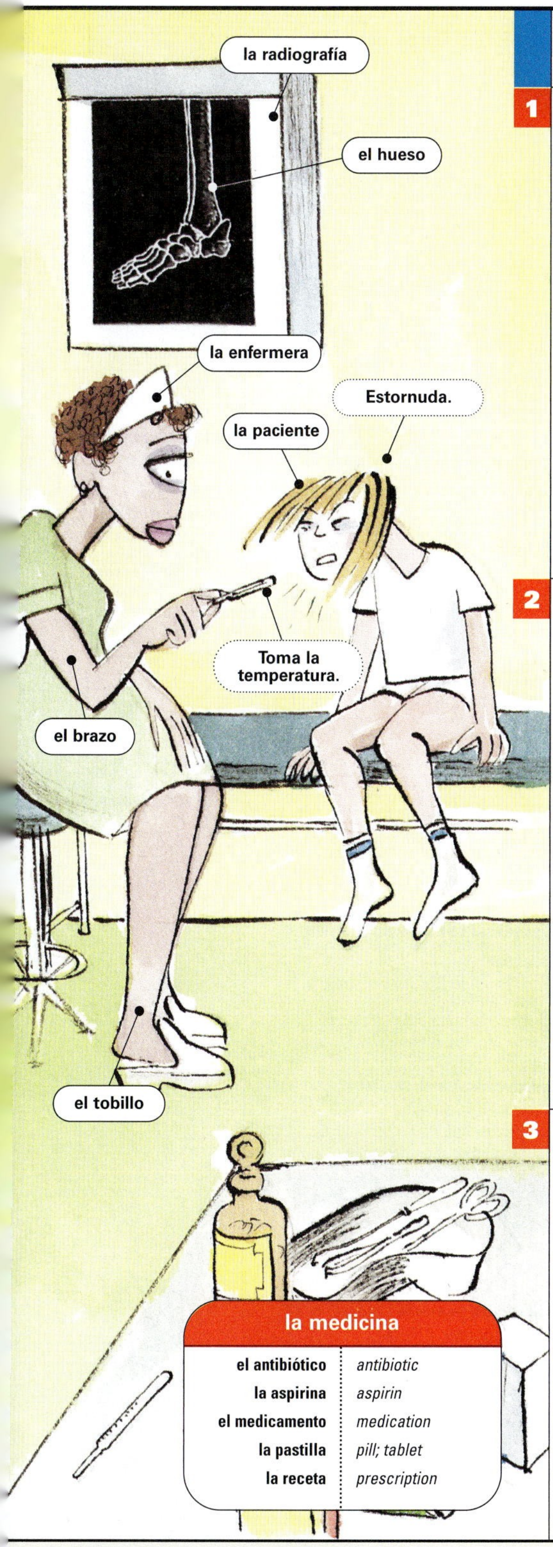

la medicina	
el antibiótico	*antibiotic*
la aspirina	*aspirin*
el medicamento	*medication*
la pastilla	*pill; tablet*
la receta	*prescription*

Práctica

1 Escuchar Escucha las frases y selecciona la respuesta más adecuada.

a. Tengo dolor de cabeza y fiebre.
b. No fui a la clase porque estaba enfermo.
c. Me caí ayer jugando al tenis.
d. Debes ir a la farmacia.
e. Porque tengo la gripe.
f. Sí, tengo mucha tos por las noches.
g. Lo llevaron directamente a la sala de emergencia.
h. No sé. Todavía tienen que tomarme la temperatura.

1. c
2. e
3. g
4. d
5. f
6. h
7. a
8. b

2 Completar Completa las siguientes frases con una palabra de la misma familia de la palabra subrayada. Usa la forma correcta de cada palabra.

1. Cuando oyes algo, usas el oído, que es uno de los cinco sentidos.
2. Cuando te enfermas, te sientes enfermo/a y necesitas ir al consultorio para ver a la enfermera.
3. El médico examina tu salud durante tu examen médico anual.
4. ¿Alguién estornudó? Creo que oí un estornudo (*sneeze*).
5. No puedo arrodillarme (*kneel down*) porque me lastimé la rodilla en un accidente de coche.
6. ¿Vas al consultorio para consultar al médico?
7. Si te rompes (*break*) un diente, vas al dentista.
8. Si tienes una infección de garganta, tu garganta está infectada.

3 Contestar Mira el dibujo de las páginas 298 y 299 y contesta las preguntas. Answers will vary.

1. ¿Qué hace la doctora?
2. ¿Qué hay en la pared?
3. ¿Qué hace la enfermera?
4. ¿Qué hace el paciente?
5. ¿A quién le duele la garganta?
6. ¿Qué hace la paciente?
7. ¿Qué tiene la paciente?

1 Present Have students check their answers as you go over the tapescript questions with the whole class.

1 Tapescript
1. ¿Cuándo te caíste? 2. ¿Por qué vas al médico? 3. ¿Adónde llevaron a Juan después del accidente? 4. ¿Adónde debo ir para conseguir estas pastillas? 5. ¿Tienes mucha tos? 6. ¿Tienes fiebre? 7. ¿Cuáles son sus síntomas, señor? 8. Ayer no te vi en la clase de biología. ¿Por qué?
Student Cassette/CD

2 Present
- If activity was done as homework, quickly go over in class.
- Have students say which part of speech the underlined word is and which part of speech the word they write on the blank is.

2 Expand Give students four minutes to write two additional sentences following the pattern of those in the activity. Their partner has to come up with the correct missing word.

2 Present If activity was done as homework, ask individual students to give the answers to the questions. If not, you may wish for students to complete the activity in pairs.

3 Expand Ask additional questions about the doctor's office scene for volunteers to answer. Ex: **¿Quiénes trabajan en el consultorio? (la médica/doctora, la enfermera), ¿Qué hace la chica? (Estornuda.)**, and so forth.

TEACHING OPTIONS

Game Play **Concentración**. On 8 cards, write names for parts of the body or items found in a doctor's office. On another 8 cards, draw or paste a picture that matches each description. Place the cards face-down in four rows of four. In pairs, students select two cards. If the two cards match, the pair keeps them. If the two cards don't match, students replace them in their original position. The group with the most cards at the end wins.

Heritage Speakers Ask heritage speakers to describe a visit they made to a doctor's office. Verify comprehension by having students relate what was said. On the board write any nonactive vocabulary that the native speakers may use, such as **auscultar los pulmones, sacar la lengua, tomar la presión arterial, la sangre,** and so forth.

4 Present Ask volunteers to read aloud the **Modelo**. Point out that there are often several parts of the body that may be associated with each activity. Encourage students to list as many as they can. This activity is also suitable for doing with the whole class.

4 Expand Say parts of the body and ask pairs of students to associate them with as many activities as they can.

5 Present Ask volunteers to read each sentence of the directions. Make sure everyone understands what the directions are. Give students five minutes to complete the survey and to tally their results.

5 Expand Write the three categories with their point totals on the board. Ask for a show of hands for those who fall into the different groups based on their point totals. Analyze the trends of the class—are your students healthy or unhealthy?

5 Expand Ask for volunteers from each of the three groups to explain whether they think the results of the survey are accurate or not. Ask them to give examples based on their own eating, exercise, and other health habits.

Note: At this point you may want to present *El cuerpo y la salud*, **Vocabulario adicional 56,** in the **Instructor's Resource Manual.**

4 **Asociaciones** Trabajen en parejas para identificar las partes del cuerpo que Uds. asocian con las siguientes actividades. Sigan el modelo. Answers will vary.

modelo

nadar
Estudiante 1: Usamos los brazos para nadar.
Estudiante 2: Usamos las piernas también.

1. hablar por teléfono
2. tocar el piano
3. correr en el parque
4. escuchar música
5. ver una película
6. toser
7. llevar zapatos
8. comprar perfume
9. estudiar biología
10. comer lomo a la plancha

5 **Cuestionario** Contesta el cuestionario seleccionando las respuestas que reflejen mejor tus experiencias. Suma (*Add*) los puntos de cada respuesta y anota el resultado. Después, con el resto de la clase, compara y analiza los resultados del cuestionario y comenta lo que dicen de la salud y de los hábitos de todo el grupo. Answers will vary.

AYUDA

Remember that in Spanish, body parts are usually referred to with an article and not a possessive: **Me duelen los pies.** The idea of "my" is expressed by the indirect object pronoun **me.**

¿Tienes buena salud?

27-30 puntos	Salud y hábitos excelentes
23-26 puntos	Salud y hábitos buenos
22 puntos o menos	Salud y hábitos problemáticos

1. ¿Con qué frecuencia te enfermas? (resfriados, gripe, etc.)
Cuatro veces por año o más. (1 punto)
Dos o tres veces por año. (2 puntos)
Casi nunca. (3 puntos)

2. ¿Con qué frecuencia tienes dolores de estómago o problemas digestivos?
Con mucha frecuencia. (1 punto)
A veces. (2 puntos)
Casi nunca. (3 puntos)

3. ¿Con qué frecuencia sufres de dolores de cabeza?
Frecuentemente. (1 punto)
A veces. (2 puntos)
Casi nunca. (3 puntos)

4. ¿Comes verduras y frutas?
No, casi nunca como verduras ni frutas. (1 punto)
Sí, a veces. (2 puntos)
Sí, todos los días. (3 puntos)

5. ¿Eres alérgico/a algo?
Sí, a muchas cosas. (1 punto)
Sí, a algunas cosas. (2 puntos)
No. (3 puntos)

6. ¿Haces ejercicios aeróbicos?
No, casi nunca hago ejercicios aeróbicos. (1 punto)
Sí, a veces. (2 puntos)
Sí, con frecuencia. (3 puntos)

7. ¿Con qué frecuencia te haces un examen médico?
Nunca o casi nunca. (1 punto)
Cada dos años. (2 puntos)
Cada año y/o antes de practicar un deporte. (3 puntos)

8. ¿Con qué frecuencia vas al dentista?
Nunca voy al dentista. (1 punto)
Sólo cuando me duele una muela. (2 puntos)
Por lo menos una vez por año. (3 puntos)

9. ¿Qué comes normalmente por la mañana?
No como nada por la mañana. (1 punto)
Tomo una bebida dietética. (2 puntos)
Como cereal y fruta. (3 puntos)

10. ¿Con qué frecuencia te sientes mareado/a?
Frecuentemente. (1 punto)
A veces. (2 puntos)
Casi nunca. (3 puntos)

TEACHING OPTIONS

Pairs In pairs, students interview each other using the questions from the realia piece in Activity 5. However, students are not limited to the choices given for answers if they can make other statements that are true for them. Then have students present the results of their interview in class. Does the interviewer think that his or her partner is in great health, relatively good health, or poor health?

Game Play a modified version of Twenty Questions. Ask a volunteer to think of a part of the body. Other students get one chance each to ask a yes-no question until someone guesses the item correctly. Limit attempts to 10 questions per item. You may want to write some phrases on the board to cue students' questions. Encourage students to guess by associating activities with various parts of the body.

Comunicación

6 **En el consultorio** Trabajen en parejas y túrnense para representar los papeles (*roles*) de un(a) médico/a y su paciente. Sigan el modelo. Answers will vary.

modelo

Estudiante 1: Me duele la garganta y toso.
Estudiante 2: Creo que Ud. tiene una infección de la garganta. Voy a recetarle un antibiótico.

7 **¿Qué le pasó?** Trabajen en un grupo de dos o tres personas. Hablen de lo que les pasó y de cómo se sienten las personas que aparecen en los dibujos. Answers will vary.

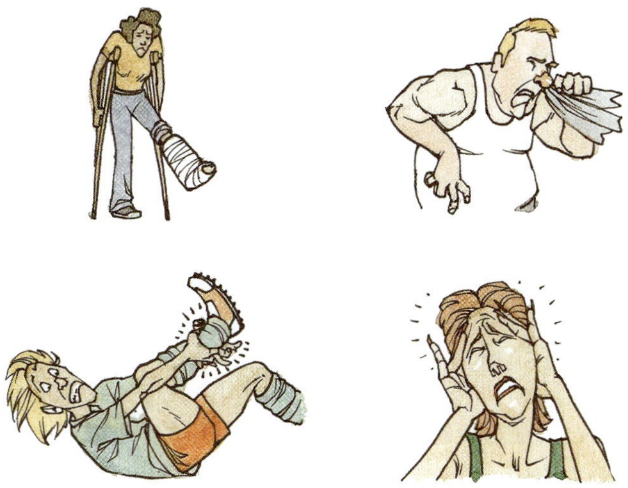

8 **Un accidente** Cuéntale (*Tell*) a la clase un accidente o una enfermedad que tuviste. Incluye información que conteste las siguientes preguntas. Answers will vary.

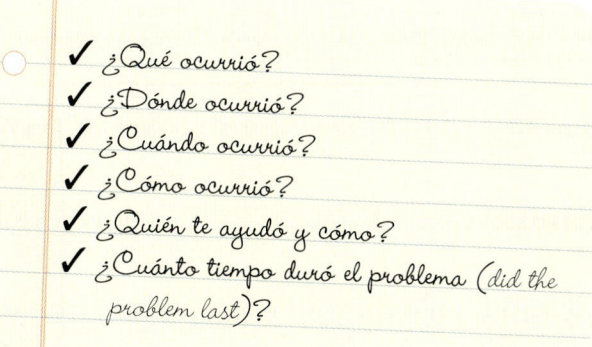

- ✓ ¿Qué ocurrió?
- ✓ ¿Dónde ocurrió?
- ✓ ¿Cuándo ocurrió?
- ✓ ¿Cómo ocurrió?
- ✓ ¿Quién te ayudó y cómo?
- ✓ ¿Cuánto tiempo duró el problema (*did the problem last*)?

TEACHING OPTIONS

Small Groups Prepare four different descriptions of a fantastical beast or alien. Ex: **Tiene dos narices y tres ojos. Los ojos están encima de la cabeza,** and so forth. Read each description line-by-line to groups of three or four. Members of the group take turns drawing the description on the board. Did they get the description right?

Extra Practice Have students write physical descriptions of themselves. Students should use as much vocabulary from this lesson as they can. Collect the papers and read the descriptions aloud. The rest of the class has to guess who is being described. Write **Mido ____ pies y ____ pulgadas** on the board and explain that it means *I am ____ feet, ____ inches tall* in order to help students with their descriptions.

Successful Language Learning Tell your students to imagine situations in which they commonly see a doctor and to think about what they would say in Spanish in each of these situations.

6 Present Ask volunteers to read aloud the **Modelo**. Give students three to four minutes to come up with various interactions. Make sure students take turns playing the patient and the doctor.

6 Expand You may wish students to role-play a skit about a visit to the doctor's office and then have them perform it for the class. Assign groups and roles as homework before having students perform the skits.

7 Present Give students several minutes in groups to come up with their possibilities.

7 Expand Ask students to list the various possibilities of what happened to these people and how they feel. How many different situations can your students come up with?

7 Expand Choose from your picture file images related to illness, medicine, and medical appointments. Have students describe what is going on in the images.

8 Present Give students five to six minutes to prepare their answers to these questions. Alternatively, you may have students do this activity for homework and then have them tell the class about the illness or accident. You may also wish for students to write it out for handing in later.

8 Expand Talk about an illness or accident you may have had.

Assignment Have students do the activities in **Student Activities Manual: Workbook,** pages 109–110.

Section goals

In **Fotonovela** students will:

- receive comprehensible input from free-flowing discourse
- learn functional phrases that preview lesson grammatical structures

Instructional Resources
Student Activities Manual: Video Activities 345–346
Video Program (Start: 00:52:19))

Video Synopsis While on the bus, Javier injures his foot. Don Francisco tells group they are close to the clinic of a friend of his, Dra. Márquez. Dra. Márquez determines that Javier simply twisted his ankle. She prescribes some pain medication and sends Javier and don Francisco on their way.

Before Presenting Fotonovela Have your students cover the **Expresiones útiles** with a sheet of paper and scan the **Fotonovela** for words and expressions related to health care. Then have them predict what will happen in this episode. **Assignment** Have students study **Fotonovela** and **Expresiones útiles** as homework.

Warm-up Quickly review the predictions made in the preceding class, asking a few questions that guide students in summarizing this episode.

Present Read the **Expresiones útiles** aloud and have the class repeat. Then ask individual students a few questions. Ex: **¿Te duele la cabeza? ¿Eres alérgico a algún medicamento?**

Continued on page 303.

¡Uf! ¡Qué dolor!

NATIONAL communication cultures STANDARDS

Don Francisco y Javier van a la clínica de la doctora Márquez.

PERSONAJES

INÉS

DON FRANCISCO

JAVIER

DRA. MÁRQUEZ

1

JAVIER Estoy aburrido... tengo ganas de dibujar. Con permiso.

2

INÉS ¡Javier! ¿Qué te pasó?

JAVIER ¡Ay! ¡Uf! ¡Qué dolor! ¡Creo que me rompí el tobillo!

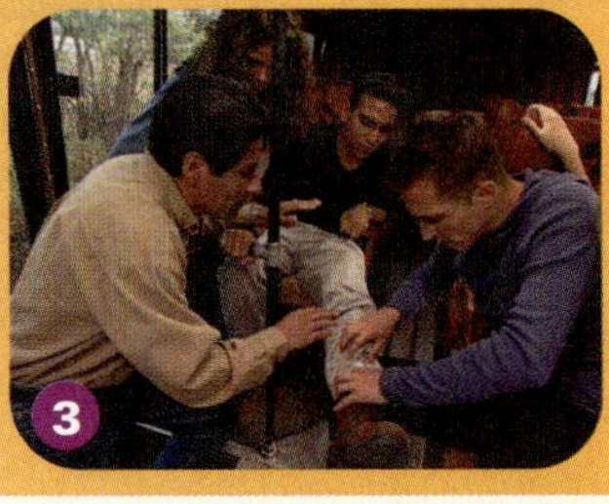
3

DON FRANCISCO No te preocupes, Javier. Estamos cerca de la clínica donde trabaja la doctora Márquez, mi amiga.

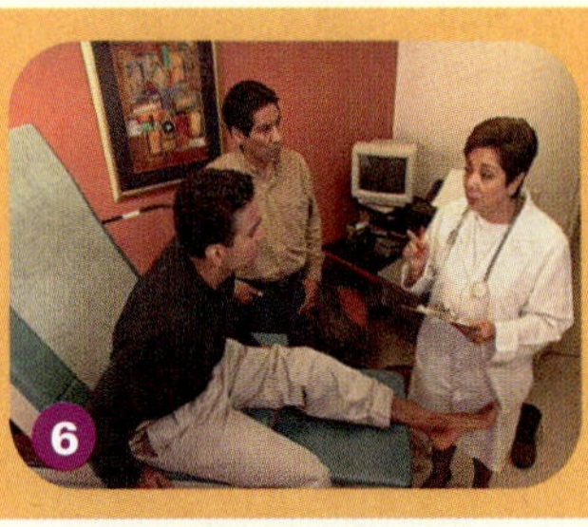
6

DRA. MÁRQUEZ ¿Cuánto tiempo hace que se cayó?

JAVIER Ya se me olvidó... déjeme ver... este... eran más o menos las dos o dos y media cuando me caí... o sea hace más de una hora. ¡Me duele mucho!

DRA. MÁRQUEZ Bueno, vamos a sacarle una radiografía. Queremos ver si se rompió uno de los huesos del pie.

7

DON FRANCISCO Sabes, Javier, cuando era chico yo les tenía mucho miedo a los médicos. Visitaba mucho al doctor porque me enfermaba con mucha frecuencia... tenía muchas infecciones de la garganta. No me gustaban las inyecciones ni las pastillas. Una vez me rompí la pierna jugando al fútbol...

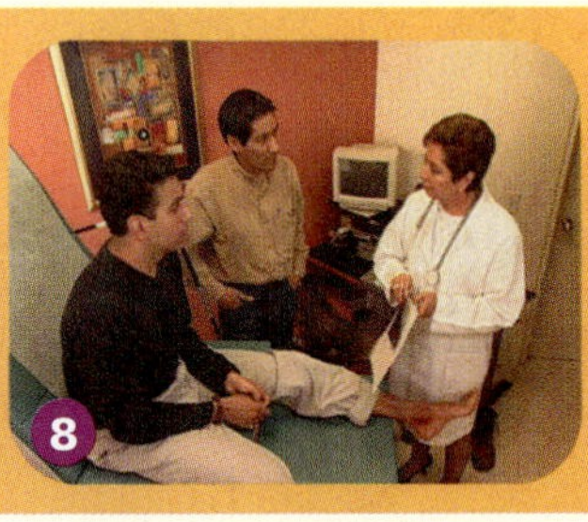
8

JAVIER ¡Doctora! ¿Qué dice? ¿Está roto el tobillo?

DRA. MÁRQUEZ Tranquilo, le tengo buenas noticias, Javier. No está roto el tobillo. Apenas está torcido.

recursos

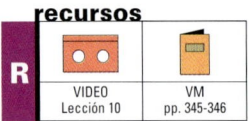

R	VIDEO Lección 10	VM pp. 345-346

TEACHING OPTIONS

Video Tips General suggestions for using video clips in the classroom can be found on page IAE-13 of the **Instructor's Annotated Edition.**

¡Uf! ¡Qué dolor! Play the **¡Uf! ¡Qué dolor!** segment of this video module and have your students jot down key words that they hear. Then have them work in small groups to prepare a brief plot summary based on their lists of key words. Play the segment again and have students return to their groups to refine their summaries. Finally, discuss the plot of this episode with the entire class and correct any errors of fact or sequencing that students may have.

JAVIER ¿Tengo dolor? Sí, mucho. ¿Dónde? En el tobillo. ¿Tengo fiebre? No lo creo. ¿Estoy mareado? Un poco. ¿Soy alérgico a algún medicamento? No. ¿Embarazada? Definitivamente NO.

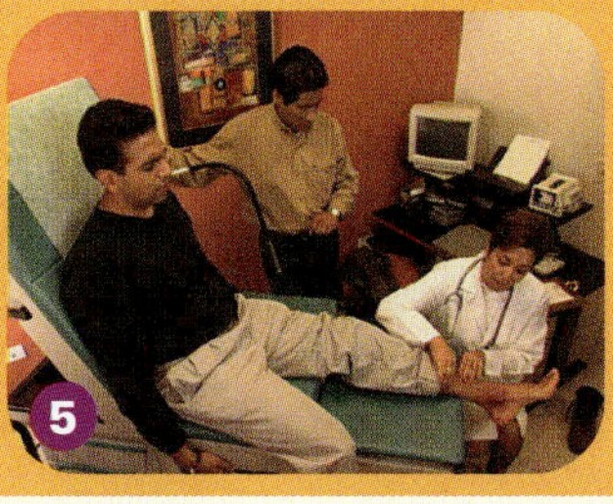

DRA. MÁRQUEZ ¿Cómo se lastimó el pie?

JAVIER Me caí cuando estaba en el autobús.

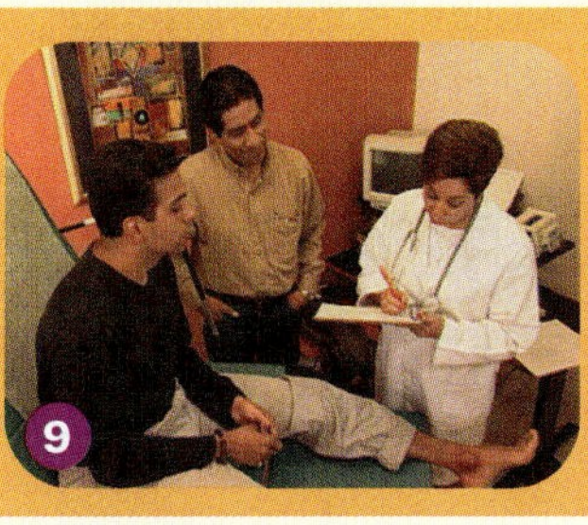

JAVIER Pero, ¿voy a poder ir de excursión con mis amigos?

DRA. MÁRQUEZ Creo que sí. Pero debe descansar y no caminar mucho durante un par de días. Le receto unas pastillas para el dolor.

DRA. MÁRQUEZ Adiós, Francisco. Adiós, Javier. ¡Cuidado! ¡Buena suerte en las montañas!

Enfoque cultural La medicina en los países hispanos

Varios factores económicos y culturales hacen que el sistema de sanidad de los países hispanos sea diferente del sistema estadounidense. En las farmacias, muchas veces las personas consultan sus síntomas con el farmacéutico y él mismo (*he himself*) les da el medicamento, sin necesidad de recetas médicas. La influencia de las culturas indígenas se refleja en la importancia que tienen los curanderos (*folk medicine practitioners*) en muchas regiones. Éstos combinan hierbas medicinales y elementos religiosos para curar las enfermedades.

Expresiones útiles

Discussing medical conditions

▶ **¡Ay, qué dolor!**
Oh, what pain!
▶ **Creo que me rompí el tobillo.**
I think I broke my ankle.

▶ **¿Cómo se lastimó el pie?**
How did you hurt your foot?
▷ **Me caí en el autobús.**
I fell when I was on the bus.

▶ **¿Te duele el tobillo?**
Does your ankle hurt? (fam.)
▶ **¿Le duele el tobillo?**
Does your ankle hurt? (form.)
▷ **Sí, (me duele) mucho.**
Yes, (it hurts) a lot.

▶ **¿Es Ud. alérgico/a a algún medicamento?**
Are you allergic to any medication?
▷ **Sí, soy alérgico/a a la penicilina.**
Yes, I'm allergic to penicillin.

▶ **¿Está roto el tobillo?**
Is the ankle broken?
▷ **No está roto. Apenas está torcido.**
It's not broken. It's just twisted.
▶ **Le receto unas pastillas para el dolor.**
I'll prescribe some pills for the pain.

Talking about childhood medical problems

▶ **¿Te enfermabas frecuentemente?**
Did you get sick frequently? (fam.)
▷ **Sí, me enfermaba frecuentemente.**
Yes, I used to get sick frequently.

▶ **Tenía muchas infecciones.**
I used to get a lot of infections.
▶ **No me gustaban las inyecciones ni las pastillas.**
I didn't like injections or pills.

After you have worked through **Expresiones útiles**, ask students to read the **Fotonovela** conversation in groups of four. Give groups time to assign roles and practice reading their parts. Ask one or two groups to present the episode to the rest of the class. See ideas for using the video in **Teaching Options**, page 302.

Comprehension Check Check comprehension of the **Fotonovela** episode by doing Activity 1, **¿Cierto o falso?**, page 304, orally with the whole class.

Suggestion Have the class look at the **Expresiones útiles**. Point out the verb forms **enfermaba, enfermabas, tenía,** and **gustaban**. Explain that these are imperfect tense forms, used here to talk about habitual events in the past. Point out the adverb **frecuentemente** and tell the class that that many adverbs end in **–mente**. In frame six of the **Fotonovela**, point out the phrase **se me olvidó** and inform the class that **se** constructions are often used to talk about unplanned events. Tell your students that they will learn more about these concepts in the upcoming **Estructura** section.

Successful Language Learning Tell your students that before traveling to a Spanish-speaking country, they should make a list of their allergies and medical needs and learn how to say them in Spanish.

Assignment Have students do Activities 2–4 in **Reacciona a la fotonovela**, page 304, as homework.

TEACHING OPTIONS

Enfoque cultural Explain to the class that most Spanish-speaking countries, including Spain, Mexico, and Costa Rica, offer free health care to all citizens through systems of state-run hospitals and clinics. Point out that residents of large, cosmopolitan areas generally have access to a wide variety of medical specialists and to the latest advances in health care. The same cannot usually be said about people who live in rural areas. Although many residents of rural areas have access to doctors, hospitals, and public health clinics, some, either by necessity or by choice, seek medical assistance from **curanderos** (*folk medicine practitioners*) and **parteras** (*midwives*).

Reacciona a la fotonovela

1 Expand Give these additional items to the class: **6. Javier tiene el tobillo roto. (Falso. No está roto el tobillo. Está torcido.) 7. La doctora Márquez le receta un poco de penicilina. (Falso. Le receta unas pastillas para el dolor).**

2 Expand Give these additional items to the class: **7. Le voy a recetar unas pastillas para el dolor. (Dra. Márquez) 8. Cuando era niño no me gustaba mucho ir al doctor. (don Francisco)**

3 Present Ask for a volunteer to write the sentences on the chalkboard in the correct order.

4 Possible response
S1: Buenos días. ¿Cómo se lastimó?
S2: Bueno, doctor, me caí en casa.
S1: ¿Y cuánto tiempo hace que se cayó?
S2: Hace más de dos horas. Creo que me rompí el dedo.
S1: ¿Ah, sí? ¿Le duele mucho?
S2: Me duele muchísimo, doctor. Y estoy mareada.
S1: Bueno, le voy a sacar una radiografía primero.
S2: ¿Está roto el dedo?
S1: No se preocupe, señorita. No está roto el dedo. Apenas le duele mucho. Le receto unas pastillas para el dolor.
S2: Sí, doctor. Gracias.

The Affective Dimension
Point out to your students that they are more likely to feel anxious about speaking Spanish during a medical emergency. Tell them to rehearse phrases that they might use in such a situation and to visualize themselves remaining calm.

Reacciona a la fotonovela

1 **¿Cierto o falso?** Decide si lo que dicen las siguientes frases sobre Javier es cierto o falso. Corrige las frases falsas.

	Cierto	Falso	
1. Está aburrido y tiene ganas de hacer algo creativo.	✓	❍	
2. Cree que se rompió la rodilla.	❍	✓	Cree que se rompió el tobillo.
3. Se lastimó cuando se cayó en el autobús.	✓	❍	
4. Es alérgico a dos medicamentos.	❍	✓	No es alérgico a ningún medicamento.
5. No está mareado pero sí tiene un poco de fiebre.	❍	✓	Está un poco mareado pero no tiene fiebre.

2 **Identificar** Identifica quién puede decir las siguientes frases.

1. Hace años me rompí la pierna cuando estaba jugando al fútbol. don Francisco
2. Hace más de una hora que me rompí la pierna. Me duele muchísimo. Javier
3. Tengo que sacarle una radiografía. No sé si se rompió uno de los huesos del pie. Dra. Márquez
4. No hay problema, vamos a ver a mi amiga la doctora. don Francisco
5. Bueno, parece que el tobillo no está roto. Qué bueno, ¿no? Dra. Márquez
6. No sé si voy a poder ir de excursión con el grupo. Javier

DRA. MÁRQUEZ

DON FRANCISCO

JAVIER

NOTA CULTURAL
Besides Costa Rica (see Panorama, p.324), Spain, Mexico, and Argentina are other countries where medical care is free. In Spain, for example, medical care is subsidized with public funds.

3 **Ordenar** Pon los siguientes eventos en el orden correcto.

a. La doctora le saca una radiografía. 4
b. La doctora le receta unas pastillas para el dolor. 6
c. Javier se lastima el tobillo en el autobús. 2
d. Don Francisco le habla a Javier de cuando era chico. 5
e. Javier quiere dibujar un rato (*a while*). 1
f. Don Francisco lo lleva a una clínica. 3

4 **En el consultorio** Trabajen en parejas para representar los papeles (*roles*) de un(a) médico/a y su paciente. El/La paciente se cayó en su casa y piensa que se rompió un dedo. Preparen una conversación en la que el/la médico/a le pregunta al/a la paciente si le duele y cuánto tiempo hace que se cayó. El/La paciente describe su dolor. Finalmente, el/la médico/a le recomienda un tratamiento (*treatment*). Usen las siguientes preguntas y frases en su conversación. Answers will vary.

NATIONAL communication STANDARDS

¿Cómo se lastimó...?	Estoy...
¿Le duele...?	¿Es usted alérgico/a a algún medicamento?
¿Cuánto tiempo hace que...?	Usted debe...
Tengo...	

TEACHING OPTIONS

Heritage Speakers Ask any heritage speakers in your class to prepare a poster that gives information about the health care system of their country of origin or other Spanish-speaking countries they have visited. You may want to display the posters in your classroom.

Extra Practice Ask your students a few questions about the **Fotonovela**. Ex: **1. ¿Quién se lastimó en al autobús? (Javier) 2. ¿Cómo se llama la amiga de don Francisco? (Dra. Márquez) 3. ¿Adónde lleva don Francisco a Javier? (a la clínica de la Dra. Márquez) 4. ¿Quién tenía muchas infecciones de la garganta? (don Francisco)**

Ortografía

El acento y las sílabas fuertes

In Spanish, written accent marks are used on many words. Here is a review of some of the principles governing word stress and the use of written accents.

as-pi-ri-na **gri-pe** **to-man** **an-tes**

In Spanish, when a word ends in a vowel, **-n**, or **-s**, the spoken stress usually falls on the next-to-last syllable. Words of this type are very common and do not need a written accent.

a-sí **in-glés** **in-fec-ción** **hé-ro-e**

When a word ends in a vowel, **-n**, or **-s**, and the spoken stress does *not* fall on the next-to-last syllable, then a written accent is needed.

hos-pi-tal **na-riz** **re-ce-tar** **to-ser**

When a word ends in any consonant *other* than **-n** or **-s**, the spoken stress usually falls on the last syllable. Words of this type are very common and do not need a written accent.

lá-piz **fút-bol** **hués-ped** **sué-ter**

When a word ends in any consonant *other* than **-n** or **-s** and the spoken stress does *not* fall on the last syllable, then a written accent is needed.

far-ma-cia **bio-lo-gí-a** **su-cio** **frí-o**

Diphthongs (two weak vowels or a strong and weak vowel together) are normally pronounced as a single syllable. A written accent is needed when a diphthong is broken into two syllables.

sol **pan** **mar** **tos**

Spanish words of only one syllable do not usually carry a written accent.

Práctica Busca las palabras que necesitan acento y escribe su forma correcta.

1. sal-mon salmón
2. ins-pec-tor
3. nu-me-ro número
4. fa-cil fácil
5. ju-go
6. a-bri-go
7. ra-pi-do rápido
8. sa-ba-do sábado
9. vez
10. me-nu menú
11. o-pe-ra-cion operación
12. im-per-mea-ble
13. a-de-mas además
14. re-ga-te-ar
15. an-ti-pa-ti-co antipático
16. far-ma-cia
17. es-qui esquí
18. pen-sion pensión
19. pa-is país
20. per-don perdón

El ahorcado (*Hangman*) Juega al ahorcado para adivinar las palabras.

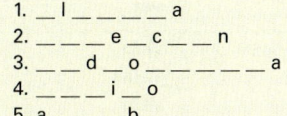

1. _ l _ _ _ _ a — Vas allí cuando estás enfermo. clínica
2. _ _ _ e _ c _ _ n — Se usa para poner una vacuna (*vaccination*). inyección
3. _ _ d _ o _ _ _ _ _ _ a — Ves los huesos. radiografía
4. _ _ _ i _ o — Trabaja en un hospital. médico
5. a _ _ _ b _ _ _ _ _ _ _ — Es una medicina. antibiótico

TEACHING OPTIONS

Extra Practice Have your students close their books. Then give them the sentences in Activity 1, **¿Cierto o falso?**, page 304 as a dictation. Say each sentence twice slowly and once at normal speed to give your students enough time to write. Then have your students open their books and check their work.

Pairs Ask your students to work in pairs to explain why each word in the **Práctica** activity does or does not have a written accent mark. The same process can be followed with the words in the **El ahorcado** activity.

Section Goals

In **Ortografía** students will review
- word stress
- the use of written accent marks

Present
- Words that end in a vowel, **-n**, or **-s** are usually stressed on the next-to-last syllable. Write the example words on the board and have the class repeat them.
- When a word ends in a vowel, **-n** or **-s** and the next-to-last syllable isn't stressed, a written accent is always used to show which syllable is stressed. Write the example words on the board without written accents. Pronounce each word and ask where its written accent should go.
- No written accent is needed in words that end in a consonant other than **-n** or **-s** and are stressed on the last syllable. Write **hospital** and **recetar** on the board and pronounce each word.
- A written accent is needed when a word that ends in any consonant other than **-n** or **-s** is not stressed on the last syllable. Pronounce the example words and have students write them.
- Normally when a weak vowel (**i, u**) is next to a strong vowel (**a, o, e**) they are pronounced as one syllable (**farmacia**). When they are not pronounced as one syllable a written accent is used to show that the vowels are in separate syllables (**biología**).
- Write **pan** and **sol** on the board and point out that one-syllable words usually don't have a written accent.

Práctica/El ahorcado
Work through these activities with the class to practice the use of written accents.

Section Goals

In **Estructura 10.1**, students will learn the imperfect tense.

Instructional Resources
Student Activities Manual: Workbook, 111–112; Lab Manual, 277
Hoja de actividades 25

Before Presenting Estructura 10.1 Ask volunteers to answer questions about childhood illnesses and injuries. Ex: **Cuando eras chico/a, ¿te enfermabas con frecuencia? ¿Te rompiste la pierna alguna vez? ¿Tuviste sarampión** (measles)? (Use mime to elicit understanding of unfamiliar vocabulary or simply say the English word, if necessary.) Then draw a horizontal line on the board and write under it: **cuando era chico/a.** Draw intersecting vertical lines on it at various points labeling them with the medical conditions described by volunteers. Ex: **Tuve sarampión. Me rompí el brazo. Estuve seis días en el hospital,** and so forth. Tell students they already know how to use the preterite tense to describe past actions; now they are going to learn another way to describe things that happened in the past. **Assignment** Have students study **Estructura 10.1** and prepare the exercises on pages 307–308 as homework.

Present Work through the discussion of the imperfect of regular verbs point by point, writing examples on the board. Test comprehension as you proceed by asking volunteers to supply the correct form of verbs for the subjects you suggest.
Go over the points outlined in **¡Atención!**

Continued on page 307.

10.1 The imperfect tense

NATIONAL STANDARDS comparisons

ANTE TODO In Lesson 8 you learned how to form and use the preterite tense. You will now learn the imperfect tense, which you can use to describe past activities in a different way.

The imperfect of regular verbs

		cantar	beber	escribir
SINGULAR FORMS	yo	cant**aba**	beb**ía**	escrib**ía**
	tú	cant**abas**	beb**ías**	escrib**ías**
	Ud./él/ella	cant**aba**	beb**ía**	escrib**ía**
PLURAL FORMS	nosotros/as	cant**ábamos**	beb**íamos**	escrib**íamos**
	vosotros/as	cant**abais**	beb**íais**	escrib**íais**
	Uds./ellos/ellas	cant**aban**	beb**ían**	escrib**ían**

¡ATENCIÓN!
Note that the imperfect endings of **–er** and **–ir** verbs are the same. Also note that the **nosotros** form of **–ar** verbs always carries an accent mark on the first **a** of the ending. All forms of **–er** and **–ir** verbs, carry an accent on the first **i** of the ending.

Sabes, Javier, cuando era chico yo les tenía mucho miedo a los médicos.

De niño tenía que ir mucho a una clínica en San Juan. ¡No me gustaban nada las inyecciones!

▶ Although many verbs have stem changes in the present and preterite tenses, these same verbs do not have stem changes in the imperfect.

entender (e: ie)
servir (e:i, i)
doler (o:ue)
jugar (u:ue)

Entendíamos japonés.
El camarero les **servía** el café.
A Javier le **dolía** el tobillo.
Yo **jugaba** al tenis con mi compañero de cuarto.

▶ The imperfect form of **hay** is **había** *(there was; there were; there used to be).*

Había un solo médico en la sala.
There was only one doctor in the room.

Había dos pacientes allí.
There were two patients there.

Irregular verbs in the imperfect

		ir	ser	ver
SINGULAR FORMS	yo	iba	era	veía
	tú	ib**as**	er**as**	veí**as**
	Ud./él/ella	iba	era	veía
PLURAL FORMS	nosotros/as	íb**amos**	ér**amos**	veí**amos**
	vosotros/as	ib**ais**	er**ais**	veí**ais**
	Uds./ellos/ellas	ib**an**	er**an**	veí**an**

¡ATENCIÓN!
Ir, **ser**, and **ver** are the only verbs in Spanish that are irregular in the imperfect.

TEACHING OPTIONS

Extra Practice To provide oral practice with the imperfect tense, change the pronouns in **¡Inténtalo!** on page 307. Have students give the appropriate forms for each infinitive listed.

Heritage Speakers Have Spanish speakers compare and contrast cultural concepts of medical treatment in their home communities and the United States. Ask them to use the imperfect tense to describe how medical problems and emergencies were handled in their family.

CONSÚLTALO

You will learn more about the contrast between the preterite and the imperfect in Lesson 11, page 236.

Uses of the imperfect

- The imperfect is used to describe past events in a different way than the preterite. As a general rule, the imperfect is used to describe actions which are seen by the speaker as incomplete or "continuing," while the preterite is used to describe actions which have been completed. The imperfect expresses what was happening at a certain time or how things used to be. The preterite, in contrast, expresses a completed action.

—¿Qué te **pasó**? *What happened to you?*	—Me **torcí** el tobillo. *I sprained my ankle.*
—¿Dónde **vivías** de niño? *Where did you live as a child?*	—**Vivía** en San José. *I lived in San José.*

- The following words and expressions are often used with the imperfect because they express habitual or repeated actions: **de niño** (*as a child*), **todos los días** (*every day*), **mientras** (*while*).

Uses of the imperfect

Habitual or repeated actions	**Íbamos** al parque los domingos. *We used to go to the park on Sundays.*
Events or actions that were in progress	Yo **leía** mientras él **estudiaba**. *I was reading while he was studying.*
Physical characteristics	**Era** alto y guapo. *He was tall and handsome.*
Mental or emotional states	**Quería** mucho a su familia. *He loved his family very much.*
Time-telling	**Eran** las tres y media. *It was 3:30.*
Age	Los niños **tenían** seis años. *The children were six years old.*

¡INTÉNTALO! Indica la forma correcta de cada verbo en el imperfecto.

1. Yo hablaba (hablar, bailar, descansar, correr, comer, decidir, vivir)
   bailaba, descansaba, corría, comía, decidía, vivía
2. Tú ______ (nadar, encontrar, comprender, venir, ir, ser, ver)
   nadabas, encontrabas, comprendías, venías, ibas, eras, veías
3. Ud. ______ (hacer, regatear, asistir, ser, pasear, poder, ir)
   hacía, regateaba, asistía, era, paseaba, podía, iba
4. Nosotras ______ (ser, tomar, ir, poner, seguir, ver, pensar)
   éramos, tomábamos, íbamos, poníamos, seguíamos, veíamos, pensábamos
5. Ellos ______ (salir, viajar, ir, querer, ser, pedir, empezar)
   salían, viajaban, iban, querían, eran, pedían, empezaban
6. Yo ______ (ver, estornudar, sufrir, ir, dar, ser, toser)
   veía, estornudaba, sufría, iba, daba, era, tosía

TEACHING OPTIONS

Video Show the video again to give students more input about the use of the imperfect. Stop the video at appropriate moments to contrast the use of preterite and imperfect tenses.

Game Divide the class into two teams. Indicate one team member at a time, alternating between teams. Give a certain infinitive and name a subject for which the team member should supply the correct form of the verb in the imperfect. Give a point per correct answer. Deduct a point for each wrong answer. The team with the most points at the end of play wins.

Irregular verbs in the imperfect

Present Work through the three irregular verbs: **ir, ser,** and **ver**. Point out the accentuation in the **nosotros** forms of **ir** and **ser**. Reassure students that **ir, ser,** and **ver** are the only irregular verbs in the imperfect tense.

Suggestion After you have presented the imperfect forms of regular and irregular verbs, consolidate by doing **¡Inténtalo!** below.

Uses of the imperfect

Warm-up Ask students to compare and contrast a home video with a snapshot in the family picture album. Then call their attention to the brief description of uses of the imperfect. Which actions would be best captured by a home video? (Continuing actions; incomplete actions; what was happening; how things used to be). Which actions are best captured in a snapshot? (a completed action)

Present Work through the uses of the imperfect, asking students to answer questions about themselves in the past using the examples as a model. Ex: **Y tú, ____, ¿ibas al parque los domingos cuando eras chico/a? ¿Qué hacías mientras tu madre preparaba la comida? ¿Cómo eras de niño?** and so forth.

Successful Language Learning Ask students to think about things they used to do when younger and imagine how to say them in Spanish. This is good practice for real-life conversations because people often talk about their childhoods when making new friends.

Close Have students open to **Fotonovela**, pages 302–303. Ask questions about the characters using the imperfect tense. Have students answer with complete sentences.

1 Warm-up Review the forms of the imperfect by calling out an infinitive and a series of subject pronouns. Ask volunteers to give the corresponding forms. Ex: **doler. Ud. (dolía) yo (dolía) nosotros (dolíamos).** Include irregular verbs.

1 Present As a model, write the following sentences on the board and have volunteers supply the verb forms and then reorder the sentences.
- **No ____ (dormir) bien. (dormía/1)**
- **____ (ser) la una de la mañana cuando llamé al doctor. (era/3)**
- **Me desperté a las once porque ____ (sentirse) mal. (me sentía/2)**

1 Expand Have students write a dialogue between Miguelito and his friends in which he relates what happened after the accident.

2 Present Model the activity for the students. Ex: **El doctor Sanz/trabajar/en la clínica Mayo. (El doctor Sanz trabajaba en la clínica Mayo.)**

2 Suggestion After going over the answers, ask students to identify the reason the imperfect was necessary in each sentence. Ex: Was a continuing action described? Were physical characteristics described? and so forth.

3 Present Model the activity by asking a volunteer to complete the first sentence.

3 Expand Write these sentences on the board, and have students complete them in pairs. **1. Fui al doctor porque ____. 2. Tuvo que ir al dentista porque ____. 3. El médico le dio unas pastillas porque ____. 4. La enfermera le tomó la temperatura porque ____.**

Práctica

1 Completar Primero, completa las frases con la forma correcta de los verbos. Luego, pon las oraciones en un orden lógico y compara tus respuestas con las de un(a) compañero/a.

1. El doctor dijo que no __era__ (ser) nada grave. 7
2. El doctor __quería__ (querer) ver la nariz del niño. 6
3. Su mamá __estaba__ (estar) dibujando cuando Miguelito entró llorando. 3
4. Miguelito __tenía__ (tener) miedo. Fueron a la sala de emergencias. 4
5. Miguelito no __iba__ (ir) a jugar más. Ahora quería ir a casa a descansar. 8
6. Los niños __jugaban__ (jugar) al béisbol en el patio. 2
7. __Eran__ (ser) las dos de la tarde. 1
8. El niño le dijo a la enfermera que __le dolía__ (dolerle) la nariz. 5

2 Transformar Forma oraciones completas. Usa las formas correctas del imperfecto y añade todas las palabras necesarias.

1. Julieta y César / ser / paramédicos
   Julieta y César eran paramédicos.
2. trabajar / juntos y / llevarse / bien
   Trabajaban juntos y se llevaban muy bien.
3. cuando / haber / accidente, / siempre / analizar / situación / con cuidado
   Cuando había un accidente, siempre analizaban la situación con cuidado.
4. preocuparse / mucho / por / pacientes
   Se preocupaban mucho por los pacientes.
5. si / paciente / tener / mucho / dolor, / ponerle / inyección
   Si el paciente tenía mucho dolor, le ponían una inyección.

3 En el hospital Completa las frases con las formas correctas del imperfecto de los verbos de la lista. Algunos verbos se usan más de una vez.

doler	mirar	querer	enfermarse
esperar	estar	poder	sentirse
estornudar	toser	tener	caerse

1. Después de correr 10 kilómetros, a Dora le __dolían__ muchísimo los pies.
2. Ema __miraba__ el termómetro; con tanta fiebre no __podía__ leerlo.
3. Arturo __esperaba__ porque la enfermera __estaba__ muy ocupada.
4. Carolina y Juan __tosían__ mucho y __se sentían__ muy congestionados porque __tenían__ la gripe.
5. Lorenzo __tenía__ dolor de muelas pero no __quería__ ir al dentista.
6. Paco y Luis __tenían__ dolor de estómago y __querían__ unas pastillas para el dolor.
7. A Juan le __dolía__ la cabeza y __se sentía__ mareado.
8. Luisa __estornudaba__ mucho porque es alérgica al polen.
9. Antes de la operación le __dolía__ todo el cuerpo.
10. De niño, nunca __quería__ ir al médico.
11. Mi hermana __se enfermaba__ con mucha frecuencia cuando era pequeña.
12. Juan Carlos siempre __se caía__ de la bicicleta.

TEACHING OPTIONS

TPR Model gestures for physical or emotional states using the imperfect. Ex: **Me dolía la cabeza.** (furrow your brow and rub your forehead); **Tenía fiebre** (fan yourself); and so forth. Have students stand. Say an expression at random (**Estornudabas**) and signal a student to perform the appropriate gesture. Keep the pace rapid. Vary by pointing to more than one student (**Uds. se enfermaban**).

Small groups Have students write about a favorite or not-fondly-remembered doctor or dentist from the past. Refer them to Activity 2 for ideas. When they are finished, have them read each others descriptions in groups of four.

Extra Practice Have students bring in video clips from popular movies. Choose three or four clips and have the students describe the events after viewing.

Comunicación

4 **Entrevista** Trabajen en parejas. Un(a) estudiante usa estas preguntas para entrevistar a su compañero/a. Luego compartan los resultados de la entrevista con la clase.

Answers will vary.

1. Cuando eras estudiante de primaria, ¿te gustaban tus profesores/as?
2. ¿Veías mucha televisión cuando eras niño?
3. Cuando tenías diez años, ¿cuál era tu programa de televisión favorito?
4. Cuando eras niño/a, ¿qué hacía tu familia durante las vacaciones?
5. ¿Cuántos años tenías en 1993?
6. Cuando eras estudiante de secundaria, ¿qué hacías con tus amigos/as?
7. Cuando tenías quince años, ¿cuál era tu grupo musical favorito?
8. Antes de tomar esta clase, ¿sabías hablar español?

5 **Describir** En parejas, túrnense para describir lo que hacían durante algunos momentos de su vida. Pueden usar las sugerencias de la lista u otras ideas. Luego informen a la clase sobre la vida del/de la compañero/a. Answers will vary.

modelo

De niña, mi familia y yo siempre íbamos a Puntarenas. Tomábamos el tren. Salíamos a las 6 de la mañana. Todos los días nadábamos. En Navidad mis papás siempre hacían una gran fiesta. Mi mamá y mis tías preparaban un montón de comida. Toda la familia venía.

- Las vacaciones cuando eras niño/a
- Ocasiones especiales
- Qué hacías durante el verano
- Celebraciones con tus amigos/as
- Celebraciones con tu familia
- Cómo era tu escuela
- Cómo eran tus amigos/as
- Los viajes que hacías
- A qué jugabas
- Cuándo te sentías enfermo/a

Síntesis

6 **En el consultorio** Tu profesor(a) va a darte una hoja de actividades. La hoja contiene una lista de las personas que fueron al consultorio del Dr. Donoso ayer. En parejas indiquen a qué hora llegaron las personas al consultorio y cuáles eran sus problemas. Answers will vary.

4 Present Give students five minutes to carry out the interview. You might want students to take turns answering and asking the questions.

4 Expand If both students answer the questions, have them record the results of their interviews in a Venn diagram, which they can use to present the information to the class.

5 Present Go over the instructions with the class. Then ask volunteers to read the **Modelo** aloud. Give students five minutes to prepare their descriptions. Alternatively, you might want to assign this activity as a short written composition.

5 Suggestion Before you have students report to the whole class, divide the class into groups of four. After each report, give the groups two minutes to compose a question for the presenter. Then have the groups take turns asking the student about his/her experiences.

6 Present Go over the directions before assigning the activity to pairs of students. Distribute a copy of the top part of **Hoja de actividades 25** to one of the pair and the bottom part to the other.

6 Expand Have pairs dramatize their dialogue for each other.

Assignment Have students do activities in **Student Activities Manual: Workbook,** pages 111–112.

TEACHING OPTIONS

Large group Label the four corners of the room as follows: **La Revolución Americana, Tiempos prehistóricos, El Imperio Romano, El Japón de los samurai.** Then have students go to the corner that best describes what historical period they would visit if they could. Each group should then talk among themselves about their reasons for choosing that period using the imperfect tense. A spokesperson will summarize the group response to the rest of the class.

Game Divide the class into groups of three. Each group should decide on a historical or fictional villain. When it is their turn, they will give the class one hint. The other groups are allowed three questions, which must be answered truthfully. At the end of the question/answer session, groups must guess the identity. Award one point for each correct guess and two to any group able to stump the class.

Lesson Goals

In **Estructura 10.2** students will be introduced to:

- impersonal constructions with **se**
- using **se** for unplanned events

Instructional Resources *Student Activities Manual: Workbook, 113–114; Lab Manual, 278*

Before Presenting Estructura 10.2 Have students look at the three signs in the grammatical explanation, and ask simple questions about the situations. Ex: **En esta playa, ¿podemos nadar? El Grupo Tecno, ¿qué buscan? ¿Encontramos estas instrucciones en una puerta o en una ventana?**

Assignment Have students study **Estructura 10.2** and prepare the exercises on pages 311–312 as homework.

Present Work through the discussion of impersonal constructions with **se** point by point, writing examples on the board. Test comprehension as you proceed by asking volunteers to answer questions based on similar constructions. Ex: **¿Se habla español en Inglaterra? (No, se habla inglés.) ¿Dónde se hacen las películas norteamericanas? (Se hacen en Hollywood)** and so forth.

Suggestion Review **¡Atención!** with the class and provide further examples. Ex: **En Suiza, se hablan alemán, francés e italiano.**

Close Do Part A of **¡Inténtalo!** on page 311 orally with the whole class.

10.2 Constructions with **se**

ANTE TODO In Lesson 7 you learned how to use **se** as the third person reflexive pronoun (**El se despierta. Ellos se visten. Ella se baña.**). **Se** can also be used to form constructions in which the person performing the action is not expressed or is de-emphasized.

Impersonal constructions with *se*

- In Spanish, verbs that are not reflexive can be used with **se** to form impersonal constructions. These are statements in which the person performing the action is not expressed or defined. In English, the passive voice or indefinite subjects *(you, they, one)* are used.

Se habla español en Costa Rica. *Spanish is spoken in Costa Rica.*	**Se puede leer** en la sala de espera. *You can read in the waiting room.*
Se hacen operaciones aquí. *They perform operations here.*	**Se necesitan** medicinas enseguida. *They need medicines right away.*

¡ATENCIÓN!
Note that the third person singular verb form is used with singular nouns and the third person plural form is used with plural nouns:
Se vende ropa.
Se venden camisas.

- You often see the impersonal **se** in signs, advertisements, and directions.

SE PROHIBE NADAR

Se necesitan programadores
GRUPO TECNO
Tel. 778-34-34

ENTRADA

Se entra por la izquierda

Se for unplanned events

¿Cuánto tiempo hace que se cayó?
Ya se me olvidó.

Bueno, vamos a sacarle una radiografía para ver si se le rompió el hueso.

- **Se** is also used to form statements that describe accidental or unplanned events. In this construction, the person who performs the action is de-emphasized, so as to imply that the accident or unplanned event is not his or her direct responsibility. These statements are constructed using the following pattern.

se	+	[INDIRECT OBJECT PRONOUN]	+	[VERB]	+	[SUBJECT]
Se		me		cayó		la pluma.

TEACHING OPTIONS

TPR Use impersonal constructions with **se** to have students draw what you say. Ex: You say: **Se prohíbe entrar** and students draw a door with a diagonal line through it. Other possible expressions could be: **Se sale por la derecha. Se permiten perros. Se prohíben botellas.**

Extra Practice Have students bring in common icons or international signs. They can find these on the Internet. Then pair students to write directions using **se** for each of the icons and signs. Ex: **No se entra. No se pasa. Se habla español.**

- In this type of construction, what would normally be the direct object of the sentence becomes the subject, and it agrees with the verb, not with the indirect object pronoun.

	I.O. PRONOUN	VERB	SUBJECT
Se	me te le nos os les	perdieron cayó dañó rompieron olvidaron	las llaves. la taza. el radio. las botellas. las pastillas.

CONSÚLTALO
See Lesson 8, page 258 for an explanation of prepositional pronouns.

- The following verbs are the ones most frequently used with **se** to describe unplanned events. Note also that while Spanish has a verb for *fall* (**caer**), there is no exact translation for *drop*; **dejar caer** (*let fall*) is often used, to mean *to drop*.

caer	*to fall; to drop*	**perder (e: i, i)**	*to lose*
dañar	*to damage; to break down*	**quedar**	*to be left behind*
olvidar	*to forget*	**romper**	*to break*

- To clarify or emphasize who is the person involved in the action, this construction commonly begins with the preposition **a** + [*noun*] or **a** + [*prepositional pronoun*].

Al estudiante se le perdió la tarea.
The student lost his homework.

A Diana se le olvidó ir a clase ayer.
Diana forgot to go to class yesterday.

A mí se me cayeron los cuadernos.
I dropped the notebooks.

A Uds. se les quedaron los libros en casa.
You left the books at home.

¡INTÉNTALO! Completa las frases de la columna A con **se** impersonal y los verbos correspondientes en presente. Completa las frases de la columna B con **se** para sucesos imprevistos y los verbos en pretérito.

A

1. Se enseñan (enseñar) cinco lenguas en esta universidad.
2. Se come (comer) muy bien en El Cráter.
3. Se venden (vender) muchas camisetas allí.
4. Se sirven (servir) platos exquisitos cada noche.
5. Se necesita (necesitar) mucho dinero.
6. Se busca (buscar) secretaria.

B

1. Se me rompieron (*I broke*) las gafas.
2. Se te cayeron (*You* (fam.) *dropped*) las pastillas.
3. Se les perdió (*They lost*) la receta.
4. Se le quedó (*You* (form.) *left*) aquí la radiografía.
5. Se nos olvidó (*We forgot*) pagar la medicina.
6. Se les quedaron (*They left*) los cuadernos en casa.

Successful Language Learning Tell your students that this construction has no exact equivalent in English. Tell them to examine the examples in the textbook and make up examples of their own in order to get a feel for how this construction works.

Present Work through the discussion of **se** for unplanned events point by point, writing examples on the board. Test comprehension as you proceed by asking volunteers to change sentences from plural to singular and vice versa. Ex: Se me perdieron las llaves. **(Se me perdió la llave.)**

Expand Have students finish sentences using a construction with **se** to express an unplanned event. Ex: **Al doctor (se le cayó el termómetro). A la profesora (se le quedaron los papeles en casa)** and so forth.

Involve students in a conversation about unplanned events that happened to them recently. Say: **Se me olvidaron los lentes oscuros esta mañana. ¡Qué lata! Y a ti, ____, ¿se te olvidó algo esta mañana? ¿Qué se te olvidó?** Continue the conversation with other verbs in statements and questions about unplanned events. **Ex: ¿A quién se le perdió algo importante esta semana? ... ¿Ah, sí? Y ¿qué se te perdió, ____? ... Y ¿no lo encontraste en ninguna parte? Lo siento, ____.** and so forth.

Close Do part **B** of **¡Inténtalo!** orally as a class.

TEACHING OPTIONS

Video Show the video again to give students more input containing constructions with **se**. Have students write down all the examples of the construction as they can. After viewing the video, have students edit their lists and cross out any reflexive verbs that they mistakenly understood to be constructions with **se.**

Heritage Speakers Ask Spanish speakers to write a fictional or true account of a day in which everything went wrong. Ask them to include as many constructions with **se** as possible. Have them read their accounts aloud to the class to give extra practice to the rest of the students.

Práctica

1 **¿Cierto o falso?** Lee estas oraciones sobre la vida en 1901. Indica si lo que dice cada oración es cierto o falso. Luego corrige las oraciones falsas.

1. Se veía mucha televisión. Falso. No se veía mucha televisión. Se leía mucho.
2. Se escribían muchos libros. Cierto.
3. Se viajaba mucho en tren. Cierto.
4. Se montaba a caballo. Cierto.
5. Se mandaba mucho correo electrónico. Falso. No se mandaba correo electrónico. Se mandaban muchas cartas y postales.
6. Se preparaban muchas comidas en casa. Cierto.
7. Se llevaban minifaldas. Falso. No se llevaban minifaldas. Se llevaban faldas largas.
8. Se pasaba mucho tiempo con la familia. Cierto.

2 **Traducir** Traduce estos letreros (*signs*) y anuncios (*ads*) al español.

1. Engineers needed Se necesitan ingenieros
2. Eating and drinking prohibited Se prohíbe comer y beber
3. Programmers sought Se buscan programadores
4. We speak English Se habla inglés
5. Computers sold Se venden computadoras
6. No talking Se prohíbe hablar
7. Teacher needed Se necesita profesor / profesora
8. Books sold Se venden libros
9. Do not enter Se prohíbe entrar
10. Spanish spoken Se habla español

3 **¿Qué pasó?** Mira los dibujos e indica lo que pasó en cada uno.

1. camarero / pastel

Al camarero se le cayó el pastel.

2. Sr. Álvarez / espejo

Al señor Álvarez se le rompió el espejo.

3. Arturo / tarea

A Arturo se le olvidó la tarea.

4. Sra. Domínguez / llaves

A la Sra. Domínguez se le perdieron las llaves.

5. Carlos y Lupe / botellas de vino

A Carlos y Lupe se les rompieron dos botellas de vino.

6. Juana / platos

A Juana se le rompieron los platos.

1 Present Go through the activity orally with the whole class.

1 Expand Change the date from 1901 to 1999 and go through the exercise again orally.

1 Expand Have students work in pairs and write a description, using constructions with **se**, of a certain historical period such as the French or American Revolution, the Sixties, Prohibition, and so forth. Then have pairs form groups of six to read their descriptions aloud.

2 Present Model the activity by asking volunteers to translate similar sentences. Ex: Nurse sought. **(Se busca enfermero/a.)** Used books bought. **(Se compran libros usados.)**

2 Suggestion Ask students to describe where these signs could be found locally.

3 Warm-up Have students work in pairs to brainstorm verbs that could be used to complete this activity.

3 Expand Use pictures from your picture file to have students continue describing past events using constructions with **se**.

TEACHING OPTIONS

Extra Practice Have students imagine that they have just just seen a movie about the future. Have them work in groups to prepare a description of the way of life portrayed in the movie using the imperfect tense and constructions with **se**. Ex: **No se necesitaba trabajar. Se usaban róbots para hacer todo. Se viajaba por telepatía. No se comía nada sino en los fines de semana.**

Game Divide the class into groups of four. Have each group think of a famous place or public building and compose four signs that could be found on the premises. Groups will take turns reading their signs aloud. Each group that correctly identifies the place or building receives a point. Award two points to the group that is able to stump the rest of the class.

NATIONAL communication STANDARDS

Comunicación

4 **Preguntas** Trabajen en parejas y usen estas preguntas para entrevistarse. Answers will vary.

1. ¿Qué comidas se sirven en tu restaurante favorito?
2. ¿Se te olvidó invitar a alguien a tu última fiesta o comida?
3. ¿A qué hora se abre la cafetería de tu universidad?
4. ¿Alguna vez se te quedó algo importante en la casa?
5. ¿Alguna vez se te perdió algo importante durante un viaje?
6. ¿Qué se vende en la librería de la universidad?
7. ¿Sabes si en la librería se aceptan cheques?
8. ¿Alguna vez se te rompió un plato o un vaso (*glass*)?
9. ¿Alguna vez se te cayó una botella de vino?

5 **Minidiálogos** En parejas, preparen los siguientes minidiálogos. Luego preséntenlos a la clase. Answers will vary.

1. A Spanish professor asks for a student's workbook. The student explains why he or she doesn't have it.
2. A tourist asks the bellhop where the best food in the city is served, and the bellhop gives several suggestions.
3. A patient tells the doctor that he or she can't walk. The doctor examines the patient and explains what's wrong.
4. A parent asks a child how the plates got broken. The child apologizes profusely and explains what happened.

NATIONAL communication STANDARDS

Síntesis

6 **Anuncios** En grupos, preparen dos anuncios de televisión para presentar a la clase. Usen el imperfecto y por lo menos dos construcciones con **se** en cada uno. Answers will vary.

modelo

Se me cayeron unos libros en el pie y me dolía mucho. Pero ahora no, gracias a SuperAspirina 500. ¡Dos pastillas y se me fue el dolor! Se puede comprar SuperAspirina 500 en todas las farmacias Recetamax.

TEACHING OPTIONS

Extra Practice Write the following sentence fragments on the board and ask students to supply several logical endings using a construction with **se: 1. Cuando subía al avión, ____. (se le cayó la maleta; se le torció el pie) 2. Una vez cuando comía en un restaurante elegante, ____. (se me rompió un vaso; me dio un dolor de estómago) 3. Ayer cuando venía a clase, ____. (se me rompió la bicicleta; me caí y se me rompió el brazo). 4. Cuando era niño/a, ____. (siempre se me olvidaban las cosas; se me dolía siempre la cabeza) 5. El otro día cuando lavaba los platos, ____. (se me rompieron tres vasos; se me olvidó el detergente)**

4 Present Model a detailed answer by choosing among questions 4, 5, 8, and 9, providing as many details as possible for the students. Ex: **Una vez cuando era adolescente se me cayó un plato de pavo que servía mi madre en una cena. Pero mi madre no se enfadó. Me dijo: —No te preocupes, hija. Recógelo** (mimic picking something up) **y puede traer el otro pavo que está en la cocina.**

4 Suggestion Point out in the directions that **entrevistarse** means *interview one another.* Pairs should take turns asking and answering questions. Also point out that while some of these questions can be answered with *yes* or *no,* it is preferable to answer with as much information as possible.

4 Expand Have each pair decide on the most unusual answer to the questions in the **entrevista**. Ask the student to describe the event to the class.

5 Warm-up Have students brainstorm ideas for their role-plays using idea maps.

5 Suggestion Encourage students to develop their own scenarios for role-play.

6 Present Model the activity with the whole class before having groups work together by reading the **Modelo**.

6 Expand After all the groups have presented their ads, have each group write a letter of complaint. Their letter should be directed to one of the other groups, claiming false advertising.

Assignment Have students do activities in **Student Activities Manual: Workbook,** pages 113–114.

Section Goals

In **Estructura 10.3** students will learn:
- the formation of adverbs using *adjective* + **-mente**
- common adverbs and adverbial expressions

Instructional Resources
Student Activities Manual: Workbook, 115–116; Lab Manual, 279
Hoja de actividades 26

Before Presenting Estructura 10.3 Use your picture file to review known adverbs. Ex: **Mira la foto que tengo *aquí*. *Hoy* esta chica se siente *bien*, pero *ayer* se sentía *mal*...** Write adverbs on the board as you proceed. Explain that adverbs tell how, when, and where actions take place. Tell students that they are going to learn to form the most common type of adverb.

Assignment Have students study **Estructura 10.3** and prepare **¡Inténtalo!** and Activity 1 on pages 314–315 as homework.

Present Work through the formation of adverbs that end in **-mente**. Then ask volunteers to convert known adjectives into adverbs and then use them in a sentence: **abierto, agradable, alegre, amable, avergonzado, cansado, cómodo, contento, desordenado, difícil, equivocado, fácil, feliz, nervioso, ordenado, preocupado, seguro, triste.** Ex: **cómodo/cómodamente: Alberto se sentó cómodamente en la silla.**

Point out that adjectives that have an accent keep it when adding **-mente**. Ex: **cómodamente, comúnmente.**

Common adverbs and adverbial expressions Model the pronunciation of the expressions and use them in sentences.

Close Consolidate by doing **¡Inténtalo!** on page 314.

10.3 Adverbs

NATIONAL STANDARDS comparisons

ANTE TODO Adverbs are words that describe how, when, and where actions take place. They can modify verbs, adjectives, and even other adverbs. In previous lessons, you have already learned many Spanish adverbs. Study the adverbs in the list below and see if you can determine what they mean.

bien	nunca	temprano
mal	hoy	ayer
muy	siempre	aquí

- The most common adverbs are those which end in **-mente.** These are equivalent to the English adverbs which end in *-ly.*

lentamente *slowly* — **generalmente** *generally*
verdaderamente *truly, really* — **simplemente** *simply*

- To form adverbs which end in **-mente,** add **-mente** to the feminine form of the adjective. If the adjective does not have a special feminine form, just add **-mente** to the standard form.

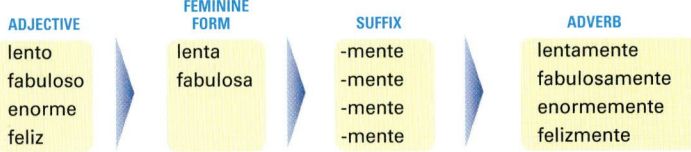

ADJECTIVE	FEMININE FORM	SUFFIX	ADVERB
lento	lenta	-mente	lentamente
fabuloso	fabulosa	-mente	fabulosamente
enorme		-mente	enormemente
feliz		-mente	felizmente

- Adverbs that end in **-mente** generally follow the verb, while adverbs that modify an adjective or another adverb precede the word they modify.

Javier dibuja **maravillosamente.**
Javier draws wonderfully.

Inés está **casi siempre** ocupada.
Inés is almost always busy.

Common adverbs and adverbial expressions

a menudo	*often*	**así**	*like this; so*	**menos**	*less*
a tiempo	*on time*	**bastante**	*enough; rather*	**muchas veces**	*a lot; many times*
a veces	*sometimes*	**casi**	*almost*	**poco**	*little*
además (de)	*furthermore; besides*	**con frecuencia**	*frequently*	**por lo menos**	*at least*
apenas	*hardly; scarcely*	**de vez en cuando**	*from time to time*	**pronto**	*soon*

¡INTÉNTALO! Transforma los siguientes adjetivos en adverbios.

1. alegre alegremente
2. constante constantemente
3. gradual gradualmente
4. perfecto perfectamente
5. real realmente
6. frecuente frecuentemente
7. tranquilo tranquilamente
8. regular regularmente
9. maravilloso maravillosamente
10. normal normalmente
11. básico básicamente
12. afortunado afortunadamente

TEACHING OPTIONS

Heritage Speakers Have Spanish speakers interview an older member of their home community about daily life when he or she was a young adult. Students should write a summary of the information, using at least eight of the common adverbs and adverbial expressions listed.

Extra Practice Have pairs of students write sentences using adverbs such as **nunca, hoy, lentamente,** and so forth. When they have finished, ask volunteers to dictate their sentences to you to write on the board. After you have written a sentence and corrected any errors, ask volunteers to suggest a sentence that uses the antonym of the adverb.

Práctica

1 **Escoger** Completa las oraciones con los adverbios adecuados.

1. La cita era para las dos pero llegamos ___tarde___. (aquí, nunca, tarde)
2. El problema fue que ___ayer___ se nos rompió el despertador. (aquí, ayer, así)
3. La recepcionista no se enojó porque sabe que normalmente llego ___a tiempo___. (a veces, a tiempo, poco)
4. ___Por lo menos___ el doctor estaba listo. (por lo menos, mal, casi)
5. ___Apenas___ tuvimos que esperar cinco minutos. (así, además, apenas)
6. El doctor dijo que nuestra hija Irene necesitaba una operación ___inmediatamente___. (temprano, menos, inmediatamente)
7. Cuando salió de la operación, le preguntamos ___nerviosamente___ al doctor cómo estaba Irene. (con frecuencia, nerviosamente, muchas veces)
8. ___Afortunadamente___ nos contestó que Irene estaba bien. (por lo menos, afortunadamente, a menudo)

Comunicación

NATIONAL communication STANDARDS

2 **¿Con qué frecuencia?** Tu profesor(a) va a darte una hoja de actividades. Circula por la clase y pregúntales a tus compañeros/as con qué frecuencia ellos/ellas y sus amigos/as hacen las cosas que se mencionan en la lista. Anota sus respuestas y luego compartan la información con la clase. Answers will vary.

Actividades	con mucha frecuencia	de vez en cuando	casi nunca	nunca
1. nadar				
2. jugar al tenis				
3. hacer la tarea				
4. salir a bailar				
5. mirar la televisión				
6. dormir en clase				
7. perder las gafas				
8. tomar medicina				
9. ir al dentista				

1 Warm-up Review common adverbs and adverbial expressions by drawing a three-column chart on the board. Title the columns: **¿Cómo?**, **¿Cuándo?**, and **¿Dónde?**. Ask volunteers to call out adverbs for each column. Write the correct answers on the board. Ex: **¿Cómo?—a tiempo, lentamente, temprano; ¿Cuándo?—nunca, siempre, a menudo; ¿Dónde?—aquí, allí**

1 Expand Ask students to rewrite each sentence so it makes sense with one of the other adverbs in parentheses.

2 Present Model one or two of the questions for the whole class. Ex: **¿Con qué frecuencia nadas? ¿Nadas con mucha frecuencia, de vez en cuando, casi nunca o nunca?** Then distribute **Hoja de actividades 26.** Point out that for Item 10 each student is to choose his or her own activity. Give class ten minutes to complete the activity.

2 Expand After collecting the papers, ask personalized questions about the activities. Ex: ____, **¿con qué frecuencia nadas en la piscina de la universidad?** ____, **¿nunca sales a bailar por la noche?**

TEACHING OPTIONS

Extra Practice Here are five sentences containing adverbs to use as a dictation. **1. A mi profesor de español siempre se le olvidan las cosas. 2. Con frecuencia se pone dos zapatos diferentes por la mañana. 3. De vez en cuando trae un calcetín negro y otro blanco. 4. De vez en cuando se les pierden los papeles. 5. Felizmente es un profesor excelente y siempre aprendemos mucho en su clase.**

Game Divide the class into groups of three. Each group should have a piece of paper or a transparency. Say the name of a historical figure and give groups three minutes to write down as many facts as they can about that person, using adverbs and adverbial expressions. At the end of each round, have groups project their answers or read them aloud. Award one point to the group with the most correct answers for each historical figure.

Section goals
In **Estructura 10.4** students will learn time expressions with **hacer.**

Instructional Resources
Student Activities Manual: Workbook, 117–118; Lab Manual, 280

Before Presenting Estructura 10.4 Draw a time line on the board going from the first day of class through today. Mark two or three significant events such as mid-term or holidays. Ex: **17 de enero: Día de los Derechos Civiles.** Then model time expressions using hacer to talk about the semester so far. **Ex: Hace tres meses que Uds. estudian español. Celebramos el Día de los Derechos Civiles hace tres semanas.**

Assignment Have students study **Estructura 10.4** and prepare **¡Inténtalo!** and Activity 1 on pages 316–317.

Present Work through the discussion of time expressions with **hacer**, point by point, writing examples on the board. Test comprehension as you proceed by asking volunteers to answer questions about their experience on campus. Ex: **Hace seis años que enseño aquí. ¿Cuánto tiempo hace que tú estudias aquí?**

Expand Formulate a list of five news events that have happened over the last few months and write them on the board. Ask questions about the time frame of these events using expressions with hacer. Ex: **¿Cuánto tiempo hace que elegimos el nuevo presidente de los Estados Unidos? ¿Cuánto tiempo hace que el huracán ____ pasó por la Florida?**

10.4 Time expressions with **hacer**

NATIONAL STANDARDS comparisons

▶ Spanish and English use different constructions to tell how long something has been going on.

Hace dos años que vivo aquí.
I've lived here for two years.

Hace un mes que esta aquí.
He's been here for a month.

English uses the present perfect (*I've lived*) or the present perfect progressive (*I've been living*) plus the preposition *since* or *for*. Spanish, in contrast, uses the present tense (**vivo**) plus the expression **hace... que...** (literally, *it makes... that...*).

Hace + [*period of time*] + **que** + [*present tense*]

Hace un mes que trabaja aquí.
He's worked (or been working) here for a month.

Hace tres años que estudian.
They've studied (or been studying) for three years.

▶ The question form **¿Cuánto tiempo hace que...?** is used with the present tense to ask how long something has been going on.

—**¿Cuánto tiempo hace que hablas** español?
(For) how long have you been speaking Spanish?

—**Hace tres años que hablo español.**
I've been speaking Spanish for three years.

—**¿Cuánto tiempo hace que tose** su hija?
How long has your daughter been coughing?

—**Hace dos días que tose.**
She's been coughing for two days.

▶ If the preterite is used instead of the present tense, it tells how long ago something happened. In this case, the **hacer** expression can either precede or follow the rest of the sentence. If it follows, the **que** is not needed.

Hace + [*period of time*] + **que** + [*preterite tense*]
or
[*Preterite tense*] + **hace** + [*period of time*]

—**¿Cuánto tiempo hace que** Ud. **se lastimó** el pie?
How long ago did you hurt your foot?

—**Hace** un mes **que me lastimé** el pie. *or*
—**Me lastimé** el pie **hace un mes.**
I hurt my foot a month ago.

¡INTÉNTALO! Completa las oraciones utilizando expresiones de tiempo con **hacer**. Usa el tiempo presente en las oraciones 1 a 3 y el pretérito en las oraciones 4 a 6.

1. Ana / estudiar / veinte minutos Hace veinte minutos que Ana estudia.
2. Nosotros / estar enfermos / una semana Hace una semana que (nosotros) estamos enfermos.
3. Tú / tener fiebre / tres días Hace tres días que (tú) tienes fiebre.
4. Alberto / llegar / dos horas Hace dos horas que Alberto llegó.
5. Yo / hacer la tarea / una hora Hace una hora que (yo) hice la tarea.
6. Ellas / jugar al fútbol / dos horas Hace dos horas que (ellas) jugaron al fútbol.

TEACHING OPTIONS

Pair Have students make a personal time line that includes a minimum of five events. Have them exchange their time lines with a partner and report the events recorded on the time line they receive to the class, using time expressions with **hacer**.

Heritage Speakers Ask Spanish speakers to use the Internet to research historical information about their cultural community. Have them prepare an informative presentation for the class that uses time expressions with **hacer**.

Práctica

1 **Minidiálogos** Completa los minidiálogos con las palabras adecuadas.

1. **JUAN** ¿ Cuánto tiempo hace que vives en esta ciudad?
   DORA Mmm... Hace dos años que vivo aquí.
2. **SARA** ¿Cuánto tiempo hace que ustedes llegaron?
   LUPE Llegamos hace una hora.
3. **SILVIA** ¿Cuánto tiempo hace que sales con Julia?
   CARLOS Hace un año.
4. **ROSA** ¿Cuánto tiempo hace que te lastimaste el pie?
   PACO Me lastimé el pie hace un mes.
5. **ALINA** ¿ Cuántos años hace que estudias alemán?
   MARTA Hace cinco años que lo estudio.
6. **ARMANDO** Tú y Laura se casaron hace dos años, ¿no?
   ALBERTO No, hace tres años que nos casamos.

Comunicación

2 **Conversación** En parejas, háganse preguntas personales utilizando expresiones con **hacer**. Luego, compartan con la clase lo que averiguaron (*found out*).

modelo

Estudiante 1: ¿Cuánto tiempo hace que vives en esta ciudad?
Estudiante 2: Dos meses. ¿Cuánto tiempo hace que hablaste con tu mejor amigo/a?

Síntesis

3 **Lectura** Trabajen en parejas. Lean la información sobre Costa Rica. Luego, háganse preguntas basadas en la información. Answers will vary.

modelo

¿Cuánto tiempo hace que Óscar Arias ganó el Premio Nobel de la Paz? Hace más de diez años.

¡En breve!

COSTA RICA

- En 1502 Cristóbal Colón llegó al área que ahora se conoce como Puerto Limón.
- La Universidad de Costa Rica se fundó en 1940.
- El periódico La Nación se fundó en 1946.
- Se abolió el ejército en 1948.
- La Guerra Civil tuvo lugar en 1948.
- En 1970 se estableció un extenso sistema de parques nacionales.
- Óscar Arias, presidente de 1986 a 1990, ganó el Premio Nobel de la Paz en 1987.

1 Present Model the activity by writing the following example on the board and having a volunteer fill in the blanks. **¿Cuánto ____ (tiempo) hace que conoces a Vilma? Sólo hace tres meses ____ (que) nos conocemos.**

1 Expand Ask questions about the information included in the **minidiálogos**. Ex: **¿Cuándo empezó Marta a estudiar el español?**

2 Present/Warm-up Model the activity by asking a volunteer to read the **Modelo** aloud with you. Then have students brainstorm suitable questions for the **Conversación**, and write them on the board.

2 Suggestion Instead of having pairs report to the whole class, group three pairs together and have them report to each other.

3 Present Model the activity by reading the **Modelo** aloud before assigning partners.

3 Expand Ask students to go to the home page of your college or university and write a short fact sheet about its history similar to the chart that appears in **Síntesis**. Have them include a time expression that uses **hacer** with every fact. Ex: **La universidad se fundó en 1893, hace 104 años.**

Assignment Have students do activities in **Student Activities Manual: Workbook**, pages 117–118.

TEACHING OPTIONS

Small Groups Have students get together in small groups to talk about their favorite classes and teachers. They should describe the classes and the teachers and indicate why they like them. They should also mention what days and times they attend each class. You may want to ask for a few volunteers to present a summary of their conversation.

Game Ask students to bring in one trivia question and answer using the past tense for each of the following categories: **Ciencias, Deportes, Historia, Cine y televisión.** Collect the papers, and divide the class into groups of three. Groups take turns picking a category and answering one question developed by a member of another group. The group with the most points wins.

Section Goals

In **Lectura** students will:
- learn to activate background knowledge to understand a reading selection
- read a content-rich text on health care while traveling

Antes de leer

Introduce the strategy. Tell students that they will find it easier to understand the content of a reading selection on a particular topic by reviewing what they know about the subject before reading. Then ask students to brainstorm things they know to do to stay healthy while traveling. Possible responses: don't drink the water, don't eat raw fruit or vegetables, pack personal medical supplies that may not be available at the destination, and so forth.

Examinar el texto
After pairs have shared their observations about the text and answered the questions, go over the bulleted points with the whole class. Students should mention that the text is an interview (**entrevista**) by a journalist (**periodista**) of an author (**autora**) whose book is about health care while traveling.

Conocimiento previo
After pairs have discussed these five points, go through them with the whole class.

Assignment Have students read **Entrevista a Carla Baron** and prepare the activities in **Después de leer** as homework.

The Affective Dimension
Remind your students that they will probably feel less anxious about reading in Spanish if they follow the suggestions in the **Estrategia** sections, which are designed to reinforce and increase reading comprehension skills.

Lectura

Antes de leer

Estrategia

Activating background knowledge

Using what you already know about a particular subject will often help you better understand a reading selection. For example, if you read an article about a recent medical discovery, you might think about what you already know about health in order to understand unfamiliar words or concepts.

Examinar el texto

Utiliza las estrategias de lectura que tú consideras las más efectivas para hacer unas observaciones preliminares acerca del texto. Después trabajen en parejas para comparar sus observaciones acerca del texto. Luego contesten las siguientes preguntas:
- Analiza el formato del texto. ¿Qué tipo de texto es? ¿Dónde crees que se publicó este artículo?
- ¿Quiénes son Carla Baron y Tomás Monterrey?
- Mira la foto del libro. ¿Qué sugiere el título del libro sobre su contenido?

Conocimiento previo

Ahora comparen su conocimiento previo sobre el cuidado de la salud en los viajes. Consideren las siguientes preguntas:
- ¿Viajaste alguna vez a otro estado o a otro país?
- ¿Tuviste algunos problemas durante tus viajes a causa del agua, de la comida o del clima del país?
- ¿Olvidaste poner en tu maleta algún medicamento u otro producto que después necesitaste para prevenir o curar un problema de salud?
- ¿Qué más información tienes sobre el tema a través de las historias de otras personas o de lo que has leído?
- Imagina que un(a) amigo/a tuyo/a se va de viaje. Dile por lo menos cinco cosas que debe hacer para prevenir cualquier problema de salud.

Conocimiento previo *Background knowledge* **a causa de** *due to* **prevenir** *prevent* **a través de** *through* **lo...leído** *what you have read* **tuyo** *of yours*

Libro de la semana

Después de leer

Correspondencias Busca las correspondencias entre los Problemas y las Recomendaciones.

Problemas

1. el agua __b__
2. el sol __d__
3. la comida __a__
4. la identificación __e__
5. el clima __c__

Recomendaciones

a. Hay que adaptarse a los ingredientes no familiares.
b. Toma sólo productos purificados (*purified*).
c. Es importante llevar ropa adecuada cuando viajas.
d. Lleva loción o crema con alta protección solar.
e. Lleva tu pasaporte.

TEACHING OPTIONS

Heritage Speakers Have pairs of Spanish speakers interview each other about health problems they have encountered while traveling. First, have them brainstorm a list of pertinent questions, then have them take turns asking and answering them. After the interview each student writes up a short paragraph about his or her own experience.

Small Groups Have groups of three select a country they would like to visit. Ask students to research what food and beverage precautions should be taken (**precauciones que se deben tomar**) by visitors to that country. Students should mention precautions such as not eating undercooked meat, uncooked seafood or vegetables, raw fruits, or unpasteurized dairy products, and not drinking tap water or drinks with ice or mixed with water.

Entrevista a Carla Baron

por Tomás Monterrey

Tomás: ¿Por qué escribió su libro *Cómo tener un viaje saludable y feliz?*

Carla: Me encanta viajar, conocer otras culturas y escribir. Mi primer viaje lo hice cuando era estudiante universitaria. Todavía recuerdo el día en que llegamos a San Juan, Puerto Rico. Era el panorama ideal para unas vacaciones maravillosas, pero al llegar a la habitación del hotel, bebí mucha agua de la llave y luego pedí un jugo de frutas con mucho hielo. El clima en San Juan es tropical y yo tenía mucha sed y calor. Las consecuencias llegaron en menos de media hora: pasé dos días con dolor abdominal y corriendo hacia el cuarto de baño cada 10 minutos. Desde entonces, siempre que viajo sólo bebo agua mineral y llevo un pequeño bolso con medicinas necesarias como pastillas para el dolor y también bloqueador solar, una crema repelente de mosquitos y un desinfectante.

Tomás: ¿Son reales las situaciones que se narran en su libro?

Carla: Sí, son reales y son mis propias historias. A menudo los autores crean caricaturas divertidas de un turista en dificultades. ¡En mi libro la turista en dificultades soy yo!

Tomás: ¿Qué recomendaciones puede hallar el lector en su libro?

Carla: Bueno, mi libro es anecdótico y humorístico, pero el tema de la salud se trata de manera seria. En general, se dan recomendaciones sobre ropa adecuada para cada sitio, consejos para protegerse del sol, y comidas y bebidas adecuadas para el turista que viaja a cualquier país del Caribe o de la América del Sur.

Tomás: ¿Tiene algún consejo para las personas que se enferman en sus viajes?

Carla: Muchos turistas toman el avión sin saber nada acerca del país que van a visitar. Ponen toda su ropa en la maleta, toman el pasaporte, la cámara fotográfica y ¡a volar! Es necesario tomar precauciones porque nuestro cuerpo necesita adaptarse al clima, al sol, a la humedad, al agua y a la comida. Se trata de viajar, disfrutar de las maravillas del mundo y regresar a casa con hermosos recuerdos. En resumen, la clave es "prevenir en vez de curar".

llave *faucet* hielo *ice* hacia *toward* reales *true* propias *own* historias *stories* hallar *to find* se trata *is treated* cualquier *any* sin *without* acerca del *about* volar *to fly* Se trata de *It's a question of* disfrutar de *to enjoy* clave *key* en vez de *instead of*

Seleccionar Selecciona la respuesta correcta.

1. El tema principal de este libro es __d__.
   a. Puerto Rico b. la salud y el agua c. otras culturas
   d. el cuidado de la salud en los viajes
2. Las situaciones narradas en el libro son __a__.
   a. autobiográficas b. inventadas c. ficticias
3. ¿Qué recomendaciones no vas a encontrar en este libro? __d__
   a. cómo vestirse adecuadamente
   b. cómo prevenir las quemaduras solares
   c. consejos sobre la comida y la bebida
   d. cómo dar propina en los países del Caribe o de América del Sur
4. En opinión de la Srta. Baron, __b__.
   a. es bueno tomar agua de la llave y beber jugo de frutas con mucho hielo
   b. es mejor tomar solamente agua embotellada (*bottled*)
   c. los minerales son buenos para el dolor abdominal
   d. es importante visitar el cuarto de baño cada 10 minutos
5. ¿Cuál de los siguientes productos no usa la autora cuando viaja a otros países? __c__
   a. desinfectante
   b. cremas preventivas
   c. un libro anecdótico y humorístico
   d. pastillas medicinales

Después de leer

Correspondencias

Suggestion Ask students to work together in pairs to use cognates and context clues to match **Problemas** with **Recomendaciones**. When pairs are finished, go over the answers to items 1–5 orally with the whole class.

Seleccionar

Suggestion This activity is also appropriate for groups of students to do in class if you have not assigned it as homework. Have volunteers read aloud one sentence at a time. Ask groups to work together to complete each sentence in the paragraph. Have students check their work by locating the sections in the text where the answers can be found.

Suggestion Ask the questions of the whole class. Ask volunteers to answer orally or to write their answers on the board.

TEACHING OPTIONS

Pairs Ask pairs to use the items in **Correspondencias** on page 318 as a model. Have them work together to write additional possibilities for **Problemas y Recomendaciones**. Ex.: **Problema: el dinero; Recomendación: lleva cheques de viajero o una tarjeta de crédito internacional**. When pairs have completed five more items, have them exchange their items with another pair who can match them.

Heritage Speakers Ask Spanish speakers to prepare a short presentation of health tips for traveling in their countries. Students should include information on any immunizations that may be required; appropriate clothing, particularly for countries in which the seasons are opposite ours; spicy regional foods or dishes that may cause digestive problems; and so forth.

Section Goals

In **Escritura** students will:
- learn to avoid redundancies
- integrate **Lesson 10** vocabulary and structures
- write a medical report in Spanish

Tema

Present Discuss what types of information may be included in a medical report completed by an emergency room nurse. Review orally with the whole class the suggested details to include on page 320, clarifying any unfamiliar vocabulary.

Estrategia

Successful Language Learning Tell your students that they should use the **Estrategia** information to avoid redundancies whenever they write in Spanish. Point out that they can also apply these strategies when they write in English.

Present Have a volunteer write the paragraph labeled *Redundant* on the board as you dictate it. Ask a volunteer to read the second sentence and identify the redundancy (**redundancia**). The student should say it is not necessary to mention the word **Susana** again and that the direct object pronoun la can be used (**se la lastimó**) because **se lastimó la rodilla** has already been stated. Ask another volunteer to record the sentences in the second paragraph as they are dictated.

Assignment Have students prepare **Ideas y organización** and **Primer borrador** as homework.

The Affective Dimension Students will feel less anxious about writing in Spanish if they follow the advice in the **Estrategia, Tema,** and **Plan de escritura** sections. These offer step-by-step support for the writing process.

Escritura

Estrategia

Avoiding redundancies

Redundancy is the needless repetition of words or ideas. To avoid redundancy with verbs and nouns, consult a Spanish language thesaurus (**Diccionario de sinónimos**). You can also avoid redundancy by using direct object pronouns, possessive adjectives, demonstrative adjectives and pronouns, and prepositional pronouns. Remember that in Spanish, subject pronouns are generally used only for clarification, emphasis, or contrast. Study the example below:

Redundant:

Susana se lastimó la rodilla ayer. Susana estaba corriendo por el parque cuando se cayó y se lastimó la rodilla. La madre de Susana llevó a Susana a la sala de emergencia.

Improved:

Susana se lastimó la rodilla ayer. Estaba corriendo por el parque cuando se cayó y se la lastimó. Su madre la llevó a la sala de emergencia.

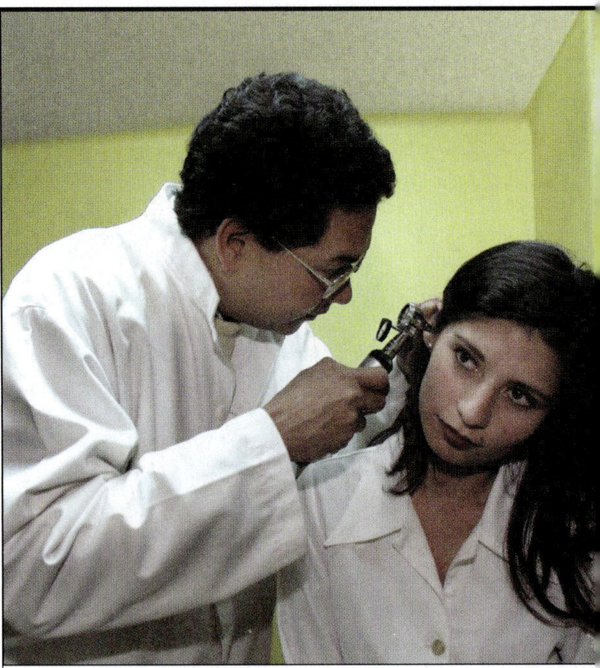

Tema

Escribir un parte médico

Imagina que eres un(a) enfermero/a en la sala de emergencia de un hospital. Acabas de tener un día sumamente ocupado, con todo tipo de pacientes y de problemas médicos. Antes de salir del trabajo, tienes que escribir el parte médico del día para tu supervisor(a). Incluye todos los detalles del día. Mira la siguiente lista para ver algunas sugerencias de los detalles que puedes incluir en tu parte médico.

- Descripciones de los pacientes
  - Nombre
  - Edad
  - Características físicas
  - Historial médico
- Descripciones de los síntomas
  - Enfermedades
  - Accidentes
  - Problemas médicos
  - Otros síntomas
- Descripciones del tratamiento
  - Diagnósticos del médico
  - Tratamientos
  - Recetas
  - Operaciones

TEACHING OPTIONS

Proofreading Activity Copy the following dialogue containing mistakes onto the board or a transparency as a proofreading activity to do with the whole class.

1. **¿Cuánto tiempo hace que te rompía la pierna? ¿Hace por menos un año?**
2. **Cuando fui niño, ía al médico con frecuencia.**
3. **Juan siempre tuvo un resfriado y le dolió la cabeza.**
4. **Lourdes caminó por el campus cuando se le caía las llaves.**
5. **Fue las diez de la mañana en punto cuando llegabamos a la clase.**
6. **¿Uds. se les olvidaba la tarea ayer?**
7. **De niño casi cantabamos el himno nacional en la clase.**

Plan de escritura

1 Ideas y organización

Después de pensar en el tema durante unos minutos, apunta tus ideas. Utiliza un mapa de ideas para organizar el borrador de tu parte médico.

2 Primer borrador

Utiliza tus notas de **Ideas y organización** para escribir el primer borrador de tu parte. Usa el diccionario solamente como último recurso y no te olvides de repasar tu lista de **Anotaciones para mejorar la escritura** en tu **Carpeta de trabajos.**

3 Comentario

Intercambia tu composición con un(a) compañero/a. Lee su borrador y anota los aspectos mejor escritos. Compartan sus impresiones utilizando esta guía:

1. ¿Incluye toda la información pertinente?
2. ¿Está bien organizado?
3. ¿Hay alguna redundancia?
4. ¿Qué sugerencias puedes darle al/a la escritor(a) para mejorar su composición?
5. ¿Ves errores gramaticales u ortográficos?

4 Redacción

Revisa el primer borrador según las indicaciones de tu compañero/a. Incorpora nuevas ideas y/o más información si es necesario. Utiliza esta guía para hacer la última revisión antes de escribir la versión final del parte médico:

1. Subraya el sujeto de cada oración. Si es necesario, usa pronombres u otro elemento gramatical para eliminar la redundancia.
2. Subraya dos veces cada verbo para comprobar la concordancia con el sujeto. ¡Cuidado con los verbos irregulares en el pretérito!
3. Revisa la concordancia entre los sustantivos y los adjetivos en cada oración.
4. Comprueba el uso correcto de los pronombres.
5. Consulta tus **Anotaciones para mejorar la escritura** antes de revisar la ortografía y la puntuación.

5 Evaluación y progreso

Trabaja con dos o tres compañeros/as. Utilicen una parte de cada composición para formular una nueva redacción y compártanla con la clase. Cuando tu profesor(a) te devuelva tu trabajo, lee sus comentarios y correcciones y anota los errores de conceptos fundamentales en tu lista de **Anotaciones para mejorar la escritura** en tu **Carpeta de trabajos.**

parte médico *medical report* historial médico *medical history* tratamiento *treatment* devuelva *returns* redacción *version*

EVALUATION: Parte médico

Criteria	Scale
Content	1 2 3 4 5
Organization	1 2 3 4 5
Use of Vocabulary	1 2 3 4 5
Grammatical Accuracy	1 2 3 4 5

Scoring	
Excellent	18–20 points
Good	14–17 points
Satisfactory	10–13 points
Unsatisfactory	< 10 points

Comentario

Present Go over guide questions 1–5 with the whole class so peer readers understand their task. Then have pairs of students exchange medical reports. Allow five minutes for reading and comments. Allow five minutes for discussing comments.

Assignment Have students prepare **Redacción** for the next class. Ask them to rewrite their drafts, incorporating the peer comments and following the directions in **Redacción**. Tell them to prepare a clean copy of their final draft to hand in.

Evaluación y progreso Give groups ten minutes to exchange their reports and create a new one to present to the class.

Writing Sample Here is a sample medical report that would constitute superior writing achievement.

Paciente: Salvador Méndez Arguello, 45 años, alto, gordo, costarriquense

Historia médica: El Sr. Méndez, turista en nuestro país, tiene historia de problemas con alergias y sinusitis.

Síntomas: Sr. Méndez fue en una excursión turística a las ruinas de Monte Albán, cerca de la ciudad de Oaxaca. Hacía mucho calor y pasaba todo el día caminando por las ruinas. Luego, caminó por la ciudad. Hubo mucha contaminación por los coches y autobuses y empezó a toser muchísimo. Por la noche, Sr. Méndez se quejaba de un dolor de cabeza, estaba mareado, y cuando empezó a vomitar, su esposa llamó una ambulancia.

Diagnóstico: sinusitis grave a causa de los contaminantes en el aire y el calor

Tratamiento: Debe tomar los antibióticos que se le recetó.

Escuchar

Preparación

Mira las foto. En tu opinión, ¿con quién está conversando Carlos Peña? ¿De qué están hablando?

Estrategia

Listening for specific information

You can listen for specific information effectively once you identify the subject of a conversation and use your background knowledge to predict what kinds of information you might hear. To practice this strategy, you will listen to a paragraph from a letter Marta wrote to a friend about her fifteenth birthday celebration. Before you listen to the paragraph, use what you know about this type of party to predict the content of the letter. What kinds of details might Marta include in her description of the celebration? Now listen to the paragraph and jot down the specific information Marta relates. Then compare these details to the predictions you made about the letter.

Ahora escucha

Ahora escucha la conversación de la señorita Méndez y Carlos Peña. Marca las frases donde se mencionan los síntomas de Carlos.

1. ___ **Tiene infección en los ojos.**
2. ___ **Se lastimó el dedo.**
3. _✔_ **No puede dormir.**
4. _✔_ **Siente dolor en los huesos.**
5. ___ **Está mareado.**
6. _✔_ **Está congestionado.**
7. ___ **Le duele el estómago.**
8. _✔_ **Le duele la cabeza.**
9. ___ **Es alérgico a la aspirina.**
10. _✔_ **Tiene tos.**
11. _✔_ **Le duele la garganta.**
12. ___ **Se rompió la pierna.**
13. ___ **Tiene dolor de oído.**
14. _✔_ **Tiene frío.**

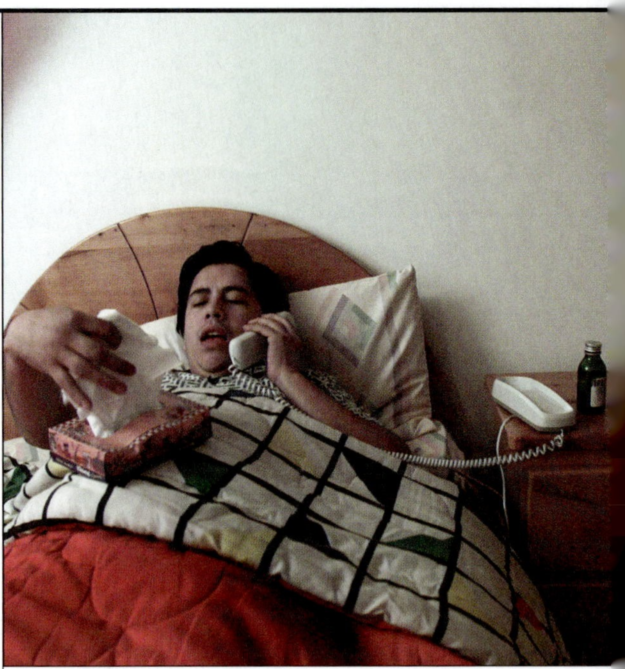

Comprensión

Preguntas

1. ¿Tiene fiebre Carlos? Carlos no sabe si tiene fiebre pero tiene mucho frío y le duelen los huesos.
2. ¿Cuánto tiempo hace que le duele la garganta a Carlos? Hace cinco días que le duele la garganta.
3. ¿Qué tiene que hacer el médico antes de recetarle algo a Carlos? Tiene que ver si tiene una infección.
4. ¿A qué hora es su cita con el médico? Es a las tres de la tarde.
5. Después de darle una cita con el médico, ¿qué otra información le pide a Carlos la señorita del consultorio? Le pide su nombre, su fecha de nacimiento y su número de teléfono.
6. En tu opinión, ¿qué tiene Carlos? ¿La gripe? ¿Un resfriado? ¿Alergias? Explica tu opinión. Answers will vary.

Diálogo

Con un(a) compañero/a, escribe el diálogo entre el Dr. Aguilar y Carlos Peña en el consultorio del médico. Usa la información del diálogo telefónico para pensar en lo que dice el médico mientras examina a Carlos. Imagina cómo responde Carlos y qué preguntas le hace al médico. ¿Cuál es el diagnóstico del médico?

Section Goals

In **Escuchar** students will:
- listen to a short paragraph and identify the topic
- answer questions based on the content of a recorded conversation

Preparación
Warm-up Have students look at the photo and guide them to see that Carlos Peña is talking to a health care provider about his illness.

Estrategia
Script Ya sé que no pudiste venir a mi quinceañera. ¡Cuánto lo siento, Juanita! Vinieron muchos invitados, ¡creo que eran más de cien! Todos se divirtieron y yo lo pasé fenomenal. Llevé un traje largo y rosado con mucho encaje, y guantes y zapatos del mismo color. Mi tía Rosa, la madrina de la fiesta, me preparó el pastel. Me imagino que sabes que el pastel era de chocolate porque me fascina el chocolate. Me dieron muchos regalos. ¡Imagínate!, mis abuelos me regalaron un viaje para ir a visitarte.

Ahora Escucha
Script
Srta. Méndez: Consultorio del Dr. Aguilar. Buenos días.
Carlos Peña: Buenos días, señorita. Habla Carlos Peña. Mire, no me siento nada bien.
Srta. Méndez: ¿Qué tiene?
Carlos Peña: Tengo mucha tos. Apenas me deja dormir. Estoy muy congestionado y tengo un tremendo dolor de cabeza.
Srta. Méndez: ¿Cuánto tiempo hace que se siente así?
Carlos Peña: Bueno, hace cinco días que me empezó a doler la garganta. Fue de mal en peor.
Srta. Méndez: ¿Tiene fiebre?
Carlos Peña: Pues, en realidad, no lo sé. No me tomé la temperatura, pero creo que sí tengo fiebre porque tengo mucho frío y me duelen los huesos.
Srta. Méndez: Pienso que Ud. tiene la gripe. Primero hay que verificar que no tiene una infección, pero creo que el doctor le va a recetar algo que va a ayudarle. Le puedo dar una cita con el médico hoy a las tres de la tarde.
Carlos Peña: Excelente.
Srta. Méndez: ¿Cómo me dijo que se llama?
Carlos Peña: Carlos Peña, señorita.
Srta. Méndez: ¿Y su fecha de nacimiento y su teléfono, por favor?
Carlos Peña: 4 de octubre de 1983, y mi teléfono... seis cuarenta y tres, veinticinco, cincuenta y dos.
Srta. Méndez: Muy bien. Hasta las tres.
Carlos Peña: Sí. Muchas gracias, señorita, y hasta luego.

communication
cultures
connections
communities

Proyecto

Participa en una conferencia

Imagina que eres un conferenciante que está preparando una conferencia en la que vas a hablar sobre el sistema político y social costarricense.

1 Prepara la presentación

Prepara una presentación sobre dos o tres de los sistemas políticos y sociales de Costa Rica que más te interesan. Aquí tienes una lista de los posibles temas que puedes cubrir en tu presentación.

- El sistema de sanidad: el seguro médico, la eficacia del sistema, la repercusión económica
- El sistema educativo: la enseñanza pública, las universidades
- Las ayudas sociales: las ayudas para las víctimas de los accidentes de trabajo, las ayudas a la maternidad
- El gobierno: la democracia, los partidos políticos
- El sistema jurídico
- La defensa nacional y la eliminación del ejército

Usa los **Recursos para la investigación** para buscar información sobre los temas sociales que elijas para la conferencia.

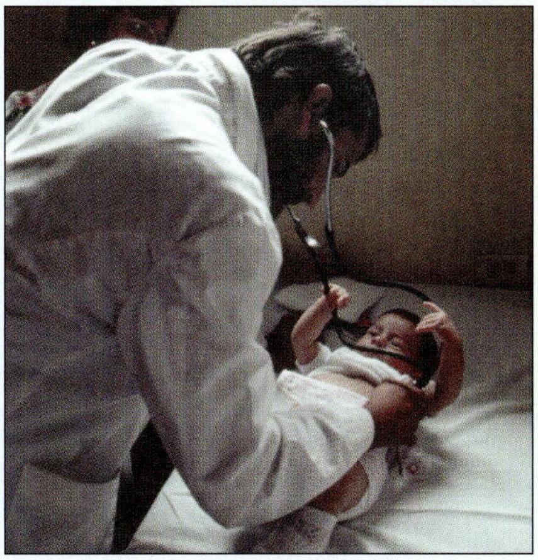

En los hospitales públicos de Costa Rica, como el Hospital de los Niños, los servicios médicos son gratuitos.

2 Presenta la información

Presenta tu información en la conferencia y pregúntales después a tus compañeros/as su opinión sobre el sistema político y social de Costa Rica. ¿Qué tiene en común este sistema con el de los Estados Unidos? ¿En qué se diferencian los dos sistemas?

conferenciante *lecturer* conferencia *lecture* cubrir *to cover* sistema sanitario *health care system* seguro *insurance* ayudas *assistance* jurídico *legal* elijas *you select*

recursos para la investigación

Internet Palabras clave: Costa Rica, San José, seguro médico, gobierno	**Comunidad** Estudiantes y profesores que son de Costa Rica o que han viajado allí
Biblioteca Enciclopedias, libros sobre Costa Rica, libros sobre sistemas políticos y sociales	**Otros recursos** Embajadas o consulados costarricenses

Section Goals

In **Proyecto** students will:
- use Spanish as they research and interact with the wider world
- write and deliver a speech on the Costa Rican political or social system as a speaker at a conference
- learn about Costa Rican political and social systems

Before Assigning Proyecto Students will need approximately a week to complete the project, so at the beginning of that time period, have them open their books to page 323 and glance over **Proyecto**.

Prepara la presentación Suggestions
- Review the suggested topics. Clarify any unfamiliar vocabulary. Explain to students that Costa Rica's political and social systems fall under **Ministerios** (Ministries), for example, **Ministerio de Salud** (Ministry of Health), **Ministerio de Educación** (Ministry of Education), and so forth.
- You may wish to have students work in groups of six to divide up the research. Then they can designate a group member or group members to give the speech.

Presenta la información Suggestions
- Have students organize a mock conference (**conferencia simulada**) in which every group's representative or student gives his or her speech in front of all the conference participants.
- In lieu of the standard presentation to a passive audience, invite students to guide an interactive question-and-answer session with their classmates.
- You may wish to set aside sufficient class time to do a few presentations at a time until all students have had a chance to present.

EVALUATION: Conferencia

Criteria	Scale
Content	1 2 3 4
Organization	1 2 3 4
Accuracy	1 2 3 4
Comprehensibility	1 2 3 4
Creativity	1 2 3 4

Scoring	
Excellent	18–20 points
Good	14–17 points
Satisfactory	10–13 points
Unsatisfactory	< 10 points

Section Goals

In **Panorama**, students will read about the geography and culture of Costa Rica.

Instructional Resources
Student Activities Manual: Workbook, 119–120
Transparency 39

Costa Rica

Before Presenting Panorama Have students look at the map of Costa Rica or project **Transparency 39.** Encourage students to mention the physical features that they notice. Ask volunteers to read the labeled features. Model pronunciation as necessary. Ask volunteers to read each of the call-out captions. Discuss the images in the call-out photos.

Assignment Have students read **Panorama** and write out the completed sentences in **¿Qué aprendiste?** on page 325 as homework.

Present Ask volunteers to read aloud each section of **El país en cifras**. After each section, ask other students questions about the content of what has been read. Ex: **¿Cuáles son las masas de agua en que tiene costas Costa Rica? ¿Las ciudades principales, en qué lado de la Cordillera Central se quedan?** When reading about Costa Rica's population, point out that the country has over a 90% literacy rate, the best in Latin America. Point out that Oscar Arias received the Nobel Peace Prize for his work in resolving civil wars in the other Central American countries during the 1970s.

Increíble pero cierto Costa Rica has one of the most long-standing democratic traditions in America. Although it has no army, it does have a national police force and a rural guard.

Costa Rica

NATIONAL STANDARDS connections cultures

El país en cifras

- **Área:** 51.100 km^2 (19.730 millas^2), *aproximadamente el área de Virginia Occidental*
- **Población:** 4.200.000

Costa Rica es el país de Centroamérica con la población más homogénea. El 98% de sus habitantes es blanco y mestizo. Más del 50% de la población es de descendencia española y un alto porcentaje tiene sus raíces en otros países europeos.

- **Capital:** San José —1.037.000
- **Ciudades principales:** Alajuela —173.000, Cartago —119.000, Puntarenas —102.000, Heredia —73.000

SOURCE: Population Division, UN Secretariat

- **Moneda:** colón costarricense
- **Idiomas:** español (oficial)

Bandera de Costa Rica

Celebración del Viernes Santo

Cráter del Volcán Poá

El Gran Hotel en San José

Iglesia en Cartago

Costarricenses célebres

- Carmen Lira, escritora (1888–1949)
- Chavela Vargas, cantante (1919-)
- Óscar Arias Sánchez, político (1949-)
- Claudia Poll, nadadora olímpica (1972-)

Óscar Arias recibió el Premio Nobel de la Paz en 1987.

recursos

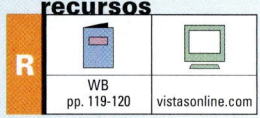

R | WB pp. 119-120 | vistasonline.com

homogénea *homogenous* mestizo *of indigenous and white parentage* descendencia *descent* raíces *roots* nadadora *swimmer*

¡Increíble pero cierto!

Costa Rica es el único país latinoamericano que no tiene ejército. Sin gastos militares, el gobierno ha podido invertir más en la educación y las artes. En la foto aparece el Museo Nacional de Costa Rica, antiguo cuartel del ejército.

TEACHING OPTIONS

Heritage Speaker Invite students of Costa Rican backgrounds or from other countries of Central America to share information about the national nicknames that Central Americans use for each other. Costa Ricans are called **ticos**, Nicaraguans are called **nicas**, and Guatemalans are called **chapines**.

Variación léxica If you visit Costa Rica, you may hear a few interesting colloquialisms such as these. **Pulpería** is the word for the *corner grocery store*. A gas station is called a **bomba**, literally a *pump*. A city block is called **cien metros**, literally *a hundred meters*.

Lugares • Los parques nacionales

Establecido para proteger los delicados ecosistemas de la región y su biodiversidad, el sistema de parques nacionales cubre el 12% del territorio de Costa Rica. En los parques, los ecoturistas pueden ver hermosas cataratas, montañas y cuevas, además de una multitud de plantas exóticas. Algunos parques ofrecen también la oportunidad de ver quetzales, monos, jaguares, armadillos, osos perezosos y elegantes mariposas en su hábitat natural.

Economía • Las plantaciones de café

Costa Rica fue el primer país centroamericano en desarrollar la industria cafetera. En el siglo XIX los costarricenses empezaron a exportar su café, de rico aroma y sabor, a Inglaterra, lo cual contribuyó mucho a la prosperidad de la nación. Hoy día más de 50.000 costarricenses trabajan cultivando el café, que representa alrededor del 15% de las exportaciones anuales del país.

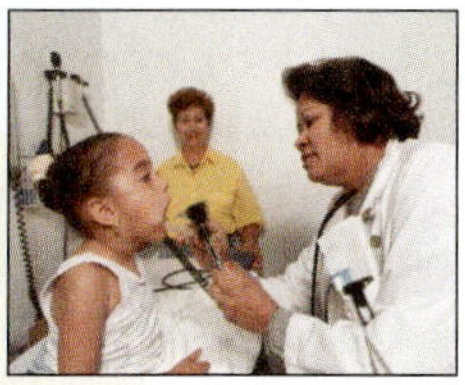

Sociedad • Una nación progresista

Un modelo de democracia y de estabilidad, Costa Rica es también uno de los países más progresistas del mundo. Provee servicios médicos gratuitos a todos sus ciudadanos y también a los turistas. En 1870 Costa Rica eliminó la pena de muerte y en 1949 eliminó el ejército e hizo obligatoria y gratuita la educación para todos los costarricenses.

Bañistas en Limón

¿Qué aprendiste? Responde a las preguntas con una frase completa.

1. ¿Cómo se llama la capital de Costa Rica? La capital de Costa Rica se llama San José.
2. ¿Quién es Claudia Poll? Claudia Poll es una nadadora olímpica.
3. ¿Qué porcentaje del territorio de Costa Rica cubren los parques nacionales? Los parques nacionales cubren el 12% del territorio de Costa Rica.
4. ¿Qué protegen los parques nacionales? Los parques nacionales protegen los delicados ecosistemas de la región y su biodiversidad.
5. ¿Qué pueden ver los turistas en los parques nacionales? En los parques nacionales, los turistas pueden ver cataratas, montañas, cuevas y muchas plantas exóticas.
6. ¿Cuántos costarricenses trabajan en las plantaciones de café hoy día? Más de 50.000 costarricenses trabajan en las plantaciones de café hoy día.
7. ¿Cuándo eliminó Costa Rica la pena de muerte? Costa Rica eliminó la pena de muerte en 1870.

Conexión Internet Investiga estos temas en el sitio **www.vistasonline.com.**

1. Busca información sobre Óscar Arias Sánchez. ¿Quién es? ¿Por qué se le considera (*is he considered*) un costarricense célebre?
2. Busca información sobre los artistas de Costa Rica. ¿Qué artista, escritor o cantante te interesa más? ¿Por qué?

Establecido *Established* proteger *protect* cubre *covers* cataratas *waterfalls* cuevas *caves* además de *in addition to* monos *monkeys* osos perezosos *sloths* mariposas *butterflies* desarrollar *develop* cafetera *coffee (adj.)* siglo *century* sabor *flavor* Inglaterra *England* Hoy día *Nowadays* alrededor del *around* mundo *world* Provee *It provides* gratuitos *free* ciudadanos *citizens* pena de muerte *death penalty* ejército *army*

Los parques nacionales Costa Rica's system of national parks was begun in the 1960s. With the addition of buffer zones in which some logging and farming are allowed, the percentage of Costa Rica's territory protected by environmental legislation rose to 27%.

Las plantaciones de café Invite students to prepare a coffee-tasting session, where they sample the coffees of Central America. You may wish to compare them to South American or African coffees as well. Teach vocabulary to describe the flavors: **rico, amargo, fuerte,** and so forth.

Una nación progresista Because of its mild climate (both physically and politically), Costa Rica has become a major destination for retired and expatriate Americans. Survey students to see how many have visited Costa Rica already, and how many know of friends or family who have visited or live there.

¿Qué aprendiste? Go over the questions and answers with students, making sure everyone understands unfamiliar words and what the correct answers are.

Assignment Have students do activites in **Student Activities Manual: Workbook,** pages 119–120.

Conexión Internet Students will find information about Costa Rica at **www.vistasonline.com,** as well as links to other sites that can help them in their research.

TEACHING OPTIONS

Worth Noting Costa Rica has three types of lands protected by ecological legislation, **parques nacionales, refugios silvestres,** and **reservas biológicas**. Costa Rica's most famous protected area is the **Reserva Biológica Bosque Nuboso Monteverde** (Monte Verde Cloud Forest Biological Reserve) where over 400 different species of birds have been recorded. The town of Monteverde was founded by Quakers from the United States in 1951 who began dairy farming and cheese-making there. In order to protect the watershed, the settlers decided to preserve about a third of their property as a biological reserve. In 1972 this area was more than doubled, and this became the **Reserva Biológica**. Today Monteverde still has a cheese factory (**La Fábrica**) and its cheeses are sold throughout the country.

10 vocabulario

El cuerpo

la boca	*mouth*
el brazo	*arm*
la cabeza	*head*
el corazón	*heart*
el cuello	*neck*
el cuerpo	*body*
el dedo	*finger*
el estómago	*stomach*
la garganta	*throat*
el hueso	*bone*
la nariz	*nose*
el oído	*(sense of) hearing*
el ojo	*eye*
la oreja	*(outer) ear*
el pie	*foot*
la pierna	*leg*
la rodilla	*knee*
el tobillo	*ankle*

La salud

el accidente	*accident*
el antibiótico	*antibiotic*
la aspirina	*aspirin*
la clínica	*clinic*
el consultorio	*doctor's office*
el/la dentista	*dentist*
el dolor (de cabeza)	*(head)ache; pain*
el/la enfermero/a	*nurse*
el examen médico	*physical exam*
la farmacia	*pharmacy*
la gripe	*flu*
el hospital	*hospital*
la infección	*infection*
el medicamento	*medication*
la medicina	*medicine*
la operación	*operation*
el/la paciente	*patient*
la pastilla	*pill; tablet*
la radiografía	*X-ray*
la receta	*prescription*
el resfriado	*cold (illness)*
la sala de emergencia(s)	*emergency room*
la salud	*health*
el síntoma	*symptom*
la tos	*cough*

Verbos

caerse	*to fall (down)*
dañar	*to damage; to break down*
darse con	*to bump into; to run into*
doler (o:ue)	*to hurt*
enfermarse	*to get sick*
estar enfermo/a	*to be sick*
estornudar	*to sneeze*
lastimarse (el pie)	*to hurt one's (foot); to injure one's (foot)*
olvidar	*to forget*
poner una inyección	*to give an injection*
prohibir	*to prohibit*
quedar	*to be left behind*
recetar	*to prescribe*
romper	*to break*
romperse (la pierna)	*to break (one's leg)*
sacar(se) una muela	*to have a tooth removed*
ser alérgico/a (a)	*to be allergic (to)*
tener dolor (*m.*) de (rodilla)	*to have a pain in one's (knee)*
tener fiebre (*f.*)	*to have a fever*
tomar la temperatura	*to take someone's temperature*
torcerse (el tobillo)	*to sprain (one's ankle)*
toser	*to cough*

Adjetivos

congestionado/a	*congested; stuffed-up*
embarazada	*pregnant*
grave	*grave; serious*
mareado/a	*dizzy; nauseous*
médico/a	*medical*
saludable	*healthy*
sano/a	*healthy*

Adverbios

a menudo	*often*
a tiempo	*on time*
a veces	*sometimes*
además (de)	*furthermore; besides*
apenas	*hardly; scarcely*
así	*like this; so*
bastante	*enough; rather*
casi	*almost*
con frecuencia	*frequently*
de niño	*as a child*
de vez en cuando	*from time to time*
mientras	*while*
menos	*less*
muchas veces	*a lot; many times*
poco	*little*
por lo menos	*at least*
pronto	*soon*
todos los días	*every day*

Otras palabras y expresiones

Hace + *time* + **que** + *verb in the preterite*	*to have done something in the past (ago)*
Hace + *time* + **que** + *verb in the present*	*to have been doing something for a period of time*

Expresiones útiles	*See page 303.*

La tecnología

11

Communicative Goals

You will learn how to:

- **Talk about using technology and electronic products.**
- **Use common expressions on the telephone.**
- **Talk about car trouble.**

contextos

pages 328-331
- The car and its accessories
- Electronic products
- Computers and peripherals

fotonovela

pages 332-335
Inés and Javier tease Álex for his obsession with computers. Don Francisco asks everyone to get off because of mechanical problems with the bus. Inés and Alex come to the rescue.

estructura

pages 336-349
- The preterite and the imperfect
- **Por** and **para**
- Reciprocal reflexives
- Stressed possessive adjectives and pronouns

adelante

pages 350-355
Lectura: Read an article about the Internet.
Escritura: Write about an experience with technology.
Escuchar: Listen to a commercial about computers.
Proyecto: Create an advertisement for an Internet café.

panorama

pages 356-357
Featured Country: Argentina
- European immigration
- The spell of the Tango
- Iguazú Falls
- Buenos Aires: the "Paris" of South America

Lesson Goals

In **Lesson 11** students will be introduced to the following:
- terms related to cars and driving
- names of electronic products
- computer and technology-related words
- uses of the preterite and imperfect tenses
- uses of **por** and **para**
- reciprocal reflexive verbs
- stressed possessive adjectives and pronouns
- recognizing borrowed words
- writing a narrative using preterite and imperfect tenses
- recognizing the genre of spoken discourse
- creating an advertisement for a cybercafé
- cultural, geographic, and historical information about Argentina

Lesson Preview

Have students look at the photo. Say: **El hombre en esta foto usa una computadora y un teléfono celular**. Then ask: **¿Dónde está la computadora? ¿Al hombre le gusta la tecnología? ¿Dónde usan Uds. las computadoras? ¿Usan Uds. los teléfonos celulares?**

INSTRUCTIONAL RESOURCES

Student Activities Manual: Workbook, 121–134
Student Activities Manual: Lab Manual, 281–286
Student Activities Manual: Video Activities, 347–348
Instructor's Resource Manual: Hojas de actividades, 27–28
Instructor's Resource Manual: Answer Keys
Tapescript/Videoscript
Overhead Transparencies, 40–42
Student Cassette/CD
Lab Cassette/CD
Video Program
CD-ROM
Website: **www.vistasonline.com**
Testing Program: Prueba A, Prueba B

Section Goals

In **Contextos**, students will learn and practice:
- vocabulary related to cars and driving
- names of electronic items
- computer and technology-related vocabulary

Instructional Resources
Student Activities Manual: Workbook, 121–122; Lab Manual, 281
Transparencies 40–41
Student Cassette/CD

Before Presenting Contextos Introduce active lesson vocabulary. Using cognate vocabulary, ask students about cars. Ask: **¿Cuántos de Uds. tienen carro? ¿Qué tipo de carro es? ¿Cuántas veces a la semana tienes que llenar el tanque? ¿Cuánto cuesta la gasolina ahora?** and so forth. Also ask students about electronic items they may have. Ask: **¿Cuántos de Uds. tienen cámara de video? ¿Cuántos tienen fax en su casa? ¿Para qué usas el fax? ¿Cuántos tienen teléfono celular? ¿Cuántas veces al día lo usas?** and so forth.

Assignment Have students study **Contextos** and do the exercises in **Práctica** as homework.

Present
- Give students two minutes to review the gas station scene. Then project **Transparency 40**. Have students refer to the scene as you give true-false statements about it. Ex: **¿Cierto o falso? Hay un hombre que habla por teléfono celular. (Cierto.) Un mecánico limpia el parabrisas. (Falso.)**
- Ask students about electronic items by giving true-false statements about associations. Ex: **El control remoto se usa con el televisor. (Cierto.)**

La tecnología

Más vocabulario

la autopista, la carretera	*highway*
la avenida	*avenue*
el bulevar	*boulevard*
la calle	*street*
el camino	*road*
la circulación, el tráfico	*traffic*
los frenos	*brakes*
el garaje, el taller (mecánico)	*(mechanic's) garage; repair shop*
el kilómetro	*kilometer*
la licencia de conducir	*driver's license*
el/la mecánico/a	*mechanic*
la milla	*mile*
el motor	*motor*
la mujer policía	*police officer (f.)*
la multa	*fine*
la policía	*police (force)*
la velocidad máxima	*speed limit*
arrancar	*to start*
arreglar	*to fix; to arrange*
bajar	*to go down*
bajar(se) de	*to get off of/out of (a vehicle)*
chocar (con)	*to run into; to crash*
conducir, manejar	*to drive*
estacionar	*to park*
parar	*to stop*
subir	*to go up*
subir(se) a	*to get on/into (a vehicle)*
lento/a	*slow*
lleno/a	*full*

Variación léxica

baúl ⟷ cajuela (*Méx.*); maletera (*Perú*)
gasolinera ⟷ bencinera (*Chile*)

recursos

R	SCASS./CD Lección 11	WB pp. 121-122	LM p. 281	LCASS./CD Cass. 6A/CD6

TEACHING OPTIONS

Small Groups Draw a picture of a car on the board. Be sure to include identifiable parts of the car (windshield, steering wheel, tires, gas tank, trunk, hood). Make cards that contain the Spanish names for these items and place tape on the back of the cards. In groups of three or four, students try to place the cards on the corresponding part of the drawing. You can do the same with a street scene or a living room scene to practice other vocabulary.

Variación léxica Talk about word relationships for the items in this box. Ask students if they can explain why a trunk is named **maletera** in Peru (it's a place where one puts the **maletas**). Also explain that **cajuela** is a word that is related to others that mean similar things: **caja** (*box*), **cajón** (*drawer*). Also point out that a **bencinera** refers to **la bencina** (*benzene*), a chemical compound used to fuel motor vehicles.

La tecnología

la calculadora	*calculator*
la cámara (de video)	*video camera*
el canal	*(TV) channel*
la cinta	*(audio) tape*
la contestadora	*answering machine*
el control remoto	*remote control*
el disco compacto	*compact disk*
el estéreo	*stereo*
el *fax*	*fax (machine)*
la televisión por cable	*cable television*
el televisor	*television set*
el tocadiscos compacto	*compact disk player*
el video(casete)	*video(cassette)*
la videocasetera	*VCR*
apagar	*to turn off*
funcionar	*to work*
llamar	*to call*
poner, prender	*to turn on*
sonar (o:ue)	*to ring*
descompuesto/a	*not working; out of order*

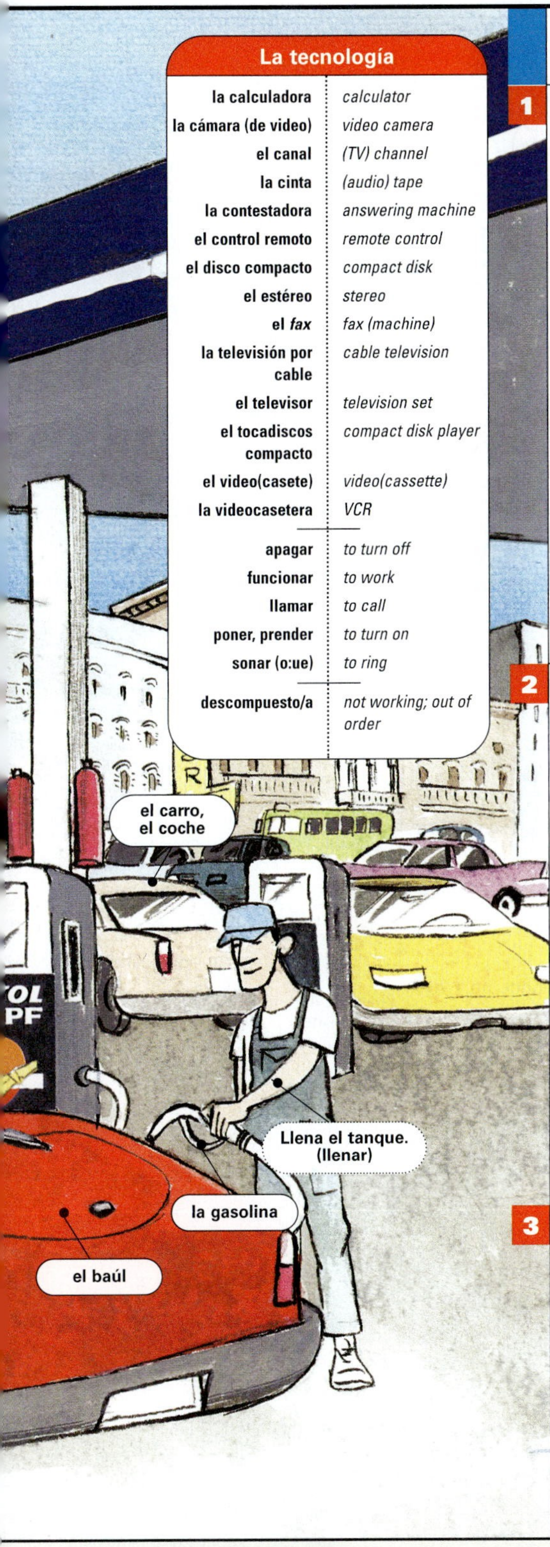

Práctica

1 Escuchar Escucha la conversación entre un joven y el empleado de una gasolinera. Después completa las oraciones.

1. El empleado de la gasolinera llena el tanque, revisa el aceite y __b__.
   a. estaciona b. limpia el parabrisas c. maneja
2. La próxima semana el joven tiene que __a__.
   a. manejar hasta Córdoba b. manejar hasta la gasolinera c. revisar las llantas
3. El joven va a volver mañana porque el empleado __b__.
   a. va a llenar el tanque b. va a revisar los frenos c. va a darle una multa
4. Para revisar los frenos, el empleado necesita __c__.
   a. un par de minutos b. un par de días c. un par de horas
5. Hoy el joven va __c__.
   a. a Córdoba b. a las montañas c. a la playa
6. La gasolina cuesta __a__.
   a. 22 pesos b. 32 pesos c. 24 pesos

2 Oraciones Escribe oraciones usando los elementos siguientes. Usa el pretérito y agrega (*add*) las palabras necesarias.

1. Marisa / poner / su / maletas / baúl
   Marisa puso sus maletas en el baúl.
2. Yo / apagar / radio / diez / noche
   Yo apagué el radio a las diez de la noche.
3. ¿Quién / poner / videocasetera?
   ¿Quién puso la videocasetera?
4. Daniel y su esposa / comprar / coche / nuevo / ayer
   Daniel y su esposa compraron un coche nuevo ayer.
5. Sara y yo / ir / gasolinera / para / llenar / tanque
   Sara y yo fuimos a la gasolinera para llenar el tanque.
6. Jaime / decidir / comprar / calculadora / nuevo
   Jaime decidió comprar una calculadora nueva.
7. Sandra / perder / control remoto
   Sandra perdió el control remoto.
8. David / poner / contestadora / y / acostarse
   David puso la contestadora y se acostó.
9. teléfono / sonar / pero / yo / no contestar
   El teléfono sonó pero yo no contesté.
10. Yo / comprar / llanta / nuevo / para / coche
    Yo compré una llanta nueva para el coche.

3 Completar Completa las siguientes frases con las palabras correctas.

1. Para poder conducir legalmente necesitas... una licencia de conducir.
2. Para parar tu coche necesitas usar... los frenos.
3. Si tu carro no funciona debes llevarlo a... un mecánico / un taller.
4. Para llenar el tanque de tu coche necesitas ir a... la gasolinera.
5. Para que (*In order that*) funcione bien el motor, es importante revisar... el aceite.
6. Otra palabra para autopista es... carretera.
7. Si manejas demasiado rápido, la policía te puede dar... una multa.
8. Otra palabra para coche es... carro.

TEACHING OPTIONS

Pairs Have pairs of students role-play one of the following situations: (1) a visit to a service station, where one student plays the driver while the other plays the mechanic, (2) a police officer gives a driver a ticket, (3) one driver crashes his or her car into the car of another driver. Write helpful vocabulary on the board for students who choose to act out the second situation: **ponerle una multa, exceder la velocidad máxima.**

Heritage Speakers Ask heritage speakers to tell about receiving their driver's license: how old they were, what they did right away and with whom, and so forth. Verify comprehension by asking other members of the class to relate what was said.

1 Present Have students check their answers by going over the tapescript questions with the whole class.

1 Tapescript
EMPLEADO: Buenos días. ¿En qué le puedo servir hoy?
JÓVEN: Buenos días. Quiero llenar el tanque y revisar el aceite, por favor.
E: Con mucho gusto. Si quiere, también le limpio el parabrisas.
J: Sí, gracias. Ah, y la próxima semana tengo que manejar hasta Córdoba. ¿Puede revisar los frenos también?
E: Claro que sí, pero voy a tardar un par de horas.
J: Entonces, mejor regreso mañana para que revise los frenos. Ahora voy a la playa, y no quiero esperar. ¿Cuánto le debo por la gasolina?
E: Veintidós pesos, por favor.
J: Aquí tiene. Hasta mañana.
E: Gracias y hasta mañana.
Student Cassette/CD

2 Present If activity was done as homework, quickly go over answers.

2 Expand In pairs, students create three similar dehydrated sentences for their partner to complete. Then ask volunteers to share some of their dehydrated sentences. Write them on the board and have the rest of the class "hydrate" them.

3 Present If activity was done as homework, quickly go over answers in class. If not, give students three minutes to complete activity.

3 Expand In pairs, students create three similar sentences for their partner to complete. Then ask volunteers to share some of their incomplete sentences. Write them on the board and have the rest of the class complete them.

La computadora
Present Have students open their books to the drawing on page 330 or project **Transparency 41**. Ask students questions to elicit computer vocabulary and involve students in a conversation about their computer use. Ex: **¿La computadora, es portatil o no? (Es portátil.) ¿Qué se usa para mover el cursor? (un ratón) ¿Qué se necesita para hacer una conexión Internet? (un módem) ¿Quiénes navegan en la red? ¿Cuál es tu sitio web favorito?**

4 Warm-up Before beginning the activity, make sure students have studied the items in the drawing and in the **La computadora** box. Ask several brief comprehension questions of a yes-no variety. Ex: **¿Sí o no? Se usa la impresora para imprimir documentos. (Sí.) Se usa el ratón para escribir con el teclado. (No.)**

4 Present If activity was done as homework, quickly go over answers in class. You may wish to have individual students read through the items aloud. If not, you can assign the dialogue to pairs, with each student completing the sentences of one of the two speakers.

4 Expand Ask volunteers to talk about problems they have had with computers and technology. Possible subjects are: the crashing of a computer (**fallar**), a malfunctioning printer, slow Internet access, and so forth.

La computadora

el archivo	*file*
el Internet	*Internet*
el módem	*modem*
la página principal	*home page*
el programa de computación	*software*
la red	*network; Internet*
el sitio Web	*website*
guardar	*to save*
imprimir	*to print*
navegar (en)	*to surf (the Internet)*

4 Diálogo Completa el diálogo con las formas correctas de las siguientes palabras.

arreglar	funcionar	llamar	prender
descompuesto	la impresora	navegar	la red
el disco	imprimir	la pantalla	el teléfono celular

JUAN CARLOS Mariana, la computadora portátil no ___funciona___. Ven a ver, no veo nada en ___la pantalla___.

MARIANA Pues, ¿la ___prendiste___?

JUAN CARLOS Claro que sí, ¡no soy tonto! ¿Piensas que tiene un virus?

MARIANA Espero que no. Vamos a ver... Ay, Juan Carlos, te olvidaste de poner la batería.

JUAN CARLOS Ah sí, tienes razón... Mariana, ahora no puedo conectarme a ___la red___. Parece que el módem está ___descompuesto___. ¿Sabes cómo lo puedo ___arreglar___?

MARIANA ¡Ay, mi amor! No es eso. Es que estoy hablando por teléfono con Sara. Si quieres, la puedo ___llamar___ por ___el teléfono celular___.

JUAN CARLOS Sí, gracias... bueno, ahora sí estoy conectado. Voy a ___navegar___ un rato, y después voy a ___imprimir___ el trabajo para mi clase de historia... pero, Mariana, ¿dónde está ___la impresora___?

MARIANA Lo siento, ésa sí está descompuesta. Pablo la está arreglando. No sé cómo vas a imprimir tu trabajo ahora.

JUAN CARLOS No te preocupes. Puedo llevar ___el disco___ a la universidad.

MARIANA ¡Qué buena idea! ¡Eres tan inteligente, mi amor!

NOTA CULTURAL

Cellular phones have become very popular in Latin America. In Chile, for example, where their use in automobiles is restricted by law, they have become such a status symbol that police have stopped motorists for using cell phones only to find that the phones were fake!

TEACHING OPTIONS

Extra Practice Students write down a list of six electronic or other technology items they have or use frequently. Then they circulate around the room asking other students if they have those items too. When someone answers affirmatively, the student asks for his or her signature (**Firma aquí, por favor**). Students should try to get a different signature for each item.

Game Play **Concentración**. On 8 cards, write names of electronic items or parts of cars. On another 8 cards, draw or paste a picture that matches each of the first 8 cards. Place the cards face-down in four rows of four. In pairs, students select two cards. If the two cards match, the pair keeps them. If the two cards don't match, students replace them in their original position. The group with the most cards at the end wins.

NATIONAL communication STANDARDS

Comunicación

CONSÚLTALO

Time expressions with hacer To review expressions like **hace...que**, see Lesson 10, section 10.4, p. 316.

5 **Preguntas** Trabajen en grupos para contestar las siguientes preguntas. Después compartan sus respuestas con la clase. Answers will vary.

1. a. ¿Tienes licencia de conducir?
   b. ¿Cuánto tiempo hace que la recibiste?
   c. ¿Tienes carro?
2. a. ¿Siempre paras cuando ves la luz amarilla del semáforo?
   b. ¿Manejas muy rápido? ¿Sobrepasas (*Do you exceed*) la velocidad máxima?
   c. ¿Recibes muchas multas de la policía de tráfico?
   d. ¿Chocaste con otro coche el año pasado?
3. ¿Cuáles de las siguientes actividades haces tú normalmente: llenar el tanque, limpiar el parabrisas, lavar (*wash*) el coche, revisar el aceite, cambiar el aceite, revisar las llantas, llenar las llantas de aire, arreglar el carro?
4. ¿Qué se puede hacer para hacer más seguras las calles, las avenidas y los bulevares de tu ciudad?
5. a. ¿Miras la televisión con frecuencia?
   b. ¿Qué programas ves?
   c. ¿Tienes televisión por cable?
   d. ¿Tienes una videocasetera? ¿Un DVD? ¿Un DVD en la computadora?
   e. ¿Cómo escuchas música: por radio, estéreo, *walkman*, tocadiscos compacto o computadora?
6. a. ¿Tienes un teléfono celular? ¿Un buscapersonas (*pager*)?
   b. Para comunicarte con tus amigos/as, ¿qué utilizas más: el teléfono, el teléfono por Internet o el correo electrónico?
   c. En tu opinión, ¿cuáles son las ventajas (*advantages*) y desventajas de los diferentes modos de comunicación?
7. a. ¿Con qué frecuencia usas la computadora?
   b. ¿Tienes una computadora personal?
   c. ¿Qué programas de computación tienes?
   d. ¿Tienes tu propia página principal? ¿Cómo es?
8. ¿Cómo usas la tecnología para divertirte? ¿y para comunicarte? ¿y para trabajar?

6 **Situación** Con un(a) compañero/a de clase, prepara una conversación entre el/la director(a) de ventas (*sales*) de una tienda de computadoras y uno de los clientes siguientes. El/La director(a) de ventas debe hacer preguntas para saber lo que el cliente desea hacer con la computadora y mostrarle la computadora que debe comprar. Answers will vary.

1. el padre o la madre de un niño de seis años
2. una jubilada (*female retiree*) que quiere aprender cosas nuevas
3. una mujer que va a crear una empresa (*business*) nueva en su casa
4. un estudiante que va a ir a la universidad y no sabe nada de computadoras
5. un hombre de negocios (*businessman*) que viaja mucho

7 **El taller** En parejas, escriban un diálogo entre un(a) mecánico/a y un(a) cliente/a cuyo (*whose*) coche se dañó (*was damaged*) en un accidente. El/La cliente/a le dice al/a la mecánico/a qué ocurrió en el accidente y los dos hablan de las partes dañadas (*damaged*). Answers will vary.

TEACHING OPTIONS

Extra Practice Have students do an Internet research project on technology and technology terminology in the Spanish-speaking world. Suggest possible topics and sites where students may begin in order to look for information. Have students write out their reports and present them to the class. You may also wish for students to hand in their reports to be graded.

Small/Large Groups Stage a debate about the role of technology in today's world. Propose this debate topic: **La tecnología: ¿beneficio o no?** Divide each group in half, assigning each a position. Allow groups time to plan their arguments before staging the debate. Alternately, you may divide the class into two large groups to have the debate with the entire class.

5 Present Give students about 10 minutes to complete the activity. Go over answers in class by asking the questions of individual students.

5 Expand Write names of electronic communication devices on the board (**teléfono celular, fax, buscapersonas, computadora,** and so forth). Then survey the class, asking for a show of hands, to find out how many people own or use these items. Analyze the trends of the class and whether the students are highly "connected" or not.

6 Present Have students read directions. Ask volunteers to read aloud the list of clients. Give them five to six minutes to complete their conversations. You may also assign conversations as homework before students present them in class.

6 Expand Have students present their conversations to the class.

Successful Language Learning Point out to your students that they will be likely to shop in a store if they travel to a Spanish-speaking country. Tell them to use Activity 6 to rehearse things they might say in shopping situations.

7 Present Give students a few minutes in class to discuss their roles and conversations, then assign the actual writing of the conversations as homework.

7 Expand Have students present their conversations to the class. You can hold a vote for the funniest, most original, and so forth.

Assignment Have students do the activities in **Student Activities Manual: Workbook,** pages 121–122.

Section goals

In **Fotonovela** students will:

- receive comprehensible input from free-flowing discourse
- learn functional phrases that preview lesson grammatical structures

Instructional Resources
Student Activities Manual: Video Activities 347–348
Video Program (Start: 00:58:05)

Video Synopsis On the way to Ibarra, the bus breaks down. Don Francisco can't locate the problem, but Inés, an experienced mechanic, diagnoses it as a burned out alternator. Álex uses his cell phone to call don Francisco's friend, Sr. Fonseca, who is a mechanic. Maite and don Francisco praise Inés and Álex for saving the day.

Before Presenting Fotonovela Have your students cover the **Fotonovela** dialogue and guess what happens in this episode based on the video stills only. Record their guesses.

Assignment Have students study **Fotonovela** and **Expresiones útiles** as homework.

Warm-up Quickly review the guesses your students made about the plot in the preceding class. Confirm the correct guesses and ask your students a few questions to guide them in summarizing this episode.

Present Read the **Expresiones útiles** aloud and have the class repeat. Check comprehension of this active vocabulary by asking **¿Cómo se dice...?** questions. Ex: **¿Cómo se dice en español** *We're twenty kilometers from the city?*

Continued on page 333.

Tecnohombre, ¡mi héroe!

El autobús se daña.

PERSONAJES

MAITE

INÉS

DON FRANCISCO

ÁLEX

JAVIER

SR. FONSECA

1

ÁLEX ¿Bueno? ... Con él habla... Ah, ¿cómo estás? ... Aquí, yo muy bien. Vamos para Ibarra. ¿Sabes lo que pasó? Esta tarde íbamos para Ibarra cuando Javier tuvo un accidente en el autobús. Se cayó y tuvimos que llevarlo a una clínica.

2

JAVIER Episodio veintiuno: Tecnohombre y los superamigos suyos salvan el mundo una vez más.

INÉS Oh, Tecnohombre, ¡mi héroe!

MAITE ¡Qué cómicos! Un día de éstos, ya van a ver...

3

ÁLEX Van a ver quién es realmente Tecnohombre. Mis superamigos y yo nos hablamos todos los días por el teléfono Internet, trabajando para salvar el mundo. Pero ahora, con su permiso, quiero escribirle un mensaje electrónico a mi mamá y navegar en la red un ratito.

6

INÉS Pues... no sé... creo que es el alternador. A ver... sí... Mire, don Francisco... está quemado el alternador.

DON FRANCISCO Ah, sí. Pero aquí no podemos arreglarlo. Conozco a un mecánico pero está en Ibarra, a veinte kilómetros de aquí.

7

ÁLEX ¡Tecnohombre, a sus órdenes!

DON FRANCISCO ¡Eres la salvación, Álex! Llama al Sr. Fonseca al cinco, treinta y dos, cuarenta y siete, noventa y uno. Nos conocemos muy bien. Seguro que nos ayuda.

8

ÁLEX Buenas tardes. ¿Con el Sr. Fonseca por favor? ... Soy Álex Morales, cliente de Ecuatur. Le hablo de parte del señor Francisco Castillo... Es que íbamos para Ibarra y se nos dañó el autobús. ... Pensamos que es el... el alternador... Estamos a veinte kilómetros de la ciudad...

recursos

R	VIDEO Lección 11	VM pp. 347-348

TEACHING OPTIONS

Video Tips General suggestions for using video clips in the classroom can be found on page IAE-13 of the **Instructor's Annotated Edition**.

Tecnohombre, ¡mi héroe! Make a photocopy of the videoscript and white out 7–10 words in order to create a master for a cloze activity. Hand out photocopies of the master to your students and have them fill in the missing words as they watch the **Tecnohombre, ¡mi héroe!** video module.

You may want to show the segment twice or more if your students experience difficulties with this activity. You may also want your students to share their pages in small groups and help each other fill in any gaps.

DON FRANCISCO Chicos, creo que tenemos un problema con el autobús. ¿Por qué no se bajan?

DON FRANCISCO Mmm, no veo el problema.

INÉS Cuando estaba en la escuela secundaria, trabajé en el taller de mi tío. Me enseñó mucho sobre mecánica. Por suerte, arreglé unos autobuses como éste.

DON FRANCISCO ¡No me digas! Bueno, ¿qué piensas?

SR. FONSECA Creo que va a ser mejor arreglar el autobús allí mismo. Tranquilo, enseguida salgo.

ÁLEX Buenas noticias. El Sr. Fonseca viene enseguida. Piensa que puede arreglar el autobús aquí mismo.

MAITE ¡La Mujer Mecánica y Tecnohombre, mis héroes!

DON FRANCISCO ¡Y los míos también!

Enfoque cultural El transporte en la ciudad

En las ciudades hispanas suele haber (*there is usually*) más transporte público que en las estadounidenses y sus habitantes dependen menos de los carros. En los países hispanos también es más frecuente el uso de carros pequeños y de motocicletas que gastan poca gasolina. En las ciudades españolas, por ejemplo, la gasolina es muy cara y también hay poco espacio para el estacionamiento (*parking*); por eso es tan frecuente el uso de vehículos pequeños y económicos.

Expresiones útiles

Talking on the telephone

- **Aló./¿Bueno?/Diga.**
  Hello.
- **¿Quién habla?**
  Who is speaking?
- **¿De parte de quién?**
  Who is calling?
- **Con él/ella habla.**
  This is he/she.
- **Le hablo de parte de Francisco Castillo.**
  I'm speaking to you on behalf of Francisco Castillo.
- **¿Puedo dejar un recado?**
  May I leave a message?
- **Está bien. Llamo más tarde.**
  That's fine. I'll call later.

Talking about bus or car problems

- **¿Qué pasó?**
  What happened?
- **Se nos dañó el autobús.**
  The bus broke down.
- **Se nos pinchó una llanta.**
  We had a flat tire.
- **Está quemado el alternador.**
  The alternator is burned out.

Saying how far away things are

- **Está a veinte kilómetros de aquí.**
  It's twenty kilometers from here.
- **Estamos a veinte kilómetros de la ciudad.**
  We're twenty kilometers from the city.

Expressing surprise

- **¡No me digas!**
  You don't say! (fam.)
- **¡No me diga!**
  You don't say! (form.)

Offering assistance

- **A sus órdenes.**
  At your service.

Additional vocabulary

- **aquí mismo**
  right here

Have the class read through the entire **Fotonovela**, with volunteers playing the various roles. Correct pronunciation errors that affect comprehension. You may want to have students take turns playing the roles so that more students have the opportunity to participate. See ideas for using the video in **Teaching Options**, page 332.

Comprehension Check Check comprehension of the **Fotonovela** episode by doing Activity 1, **Seleccionar**, page 334, orally with the whole class.

Suggestion Have students read the caption of the first video still. Point out the sentence **Esta tarde íbamos para Ibarra cuando Javier tuvo un accidente en el autobús.** Note that the imperfect tense is used in this sentence to describe an ongoing action in the past, while the preterite is used to talk about a completed action. Now draw the attention of the class to the phrase **nos hablamos** in the caption of the third video still. Explain that this is a reciprocal reflexive construction that expresses a shared action between Álex and his friends. Finally, point out the words **los míos** in the caption of the tenth video still and tell the class that this is an example of a possessive pronoun. Tell your students that they will learn more about these concepts in the upcoming **Estructura** section.

Assignment Have students do Activities 2–4 in **Reacciona a la fotonovela**, page 334, as homework.

TEACHING OPTIONS

Enfoque cultural Like most large cities in the United States, large cities in the Spanish-speaking world often experience traffic gridlock. To address this problem, large cities in Spanish-speaking countries have emphasized public transportation. Almost all of them have extensive public bus systems. Mexico City, with a population estimated at over 20 million, has been singled out for particular praise because of its **metro** (*subway*) system. The Mexico City metro, which is efficient and well maintained, costs very little to ride and provides transportation to approximately 4.4 million riders on its ten lines each day. Though its 154 stations are notably attractive, two downtown stations are of more than transportation interest. The Insurgentes station is packed with market stalls of every type, and the Pino Suárez station, near the national palace, houses an Aztec pyramid, unearthed during the excavations when the metro was built.

Reacciona a la fotonovela

2 Expand Give these additional items to the class: **6. El problema es el alternador, creo.** (Inés) **7. Hola. ¿Está el Sr. Fonseca?** (Álex) **8. Tengo ganas de navegar en la red.** (Álex)

3 Expand Have your students write a sentence that includes the word **volante** and another sentence that includes **lleno**.

4 Possible response
S1: ¿Bueno?
S2: Aló, ¿está el señor Martínez?
S1: Con él habla.
S2: Tengo un problema con mi coche. Se me dañó en la carretera.
S1: ¿Qué pasó?
S2: No sé exactamente. Paró y ahora no arranca. No sé si es el alternador.
S1: Tengo que revisarlo. ¿Dónde está usted ahora?
S2: Estoy a dos kilómetros de su taller. ¿Puede arreglar el coche aquí mismo?
S1: No sé, señora, pero voy a ver. Vengo enseguida, ¿está bien?
S2: ¡Muchísimas gracias!

Successful Language Learning Ask your students how they are progressing in understanding spoken Spanish in class, on the video, and on audiotape. Ask them what strategies they have been using to increase their comprehension.

The Affective Dimension Point out to your students that talking on the phone can be more stressful than talking with someone in person because they can't see the other person's facial expressions or gestures. Remind your students that they don't need to be able to understand every word, and that they should ask the other person to repeat if necessary.

Reacciona a la fotonovela

1 Seleccionar Selecciona las respuestas que completan correctamente las siguientes frases.

1. Álex quiere __b__.
   a. llamar a su mamá por teléfono celular b. escribirle a su mamá y navegar en la red c. hablar por teléfono Internet y navegar en la red
2. Se les dañó el autobús. Inés dice que __a__.
   a. el alternador está quemado b. se les pinchó una llanta c. el taller está quemado
3. Álex llama al mecánico, el señor __c__.
   a. Castillo b. Ibarra c. Fonseca
4. Maite llama a Inés la "Mujer Mecánica" porque antes __a__.
   a. trabajaba en el taller de su tío b. arreglaba computadoras c. conocía a muchos mecánicos
5. El grupo está a __c__ de la ciudad.
   a. veinte millas b. veinte grados centígrados c. veinte kilómetros

NOTA CULTURAL

In the U.S., Internet addresses typically end with *.com*, *.net*, or *.edu*. Other countries each have their own unique domain code. Here are the codes for some Spanish-speaking countries:

Argentina	**ar**
Colombia	**co**
Mexico	**mx**
Spain	**es**
Venezuela	**ve**

2 Identificar Identifica quién puede decir las siguientes frases.

1. Gracias a mi tío tengo un poco de experiencia arreglando autobuses. Inés
2. Sé manejar un autobús pero no sé arreglarlo. ¿Por qué no llamamos a mi amigo? don Francisco
3. Sabes, admiro mucho a la Mujer Mecánica y a Tecnohombre. Maite
4. Aló... Sí, ¿de parte de quién? Álex
5. El nombre de Tecnohombre fue idea mía. ¡Qué cómico!, ¿no? Javier

3 Completar Completa las siguientes frases con palabras de la lista.

computadora portátil	lleno	descompuesto
un parabrisas	"Diga"	"No me diga"
un teclado	el volante	el capó

1. La computadora de Álex tiene una pantalla, un monitor y __un teclado__.
2. Si tu coche no arranca, debes levantar __el capó__ y ver cuál es el problema.
3. Se les dañó el autobús en la carretera. Ahora está __descompuesto__.
4. Cuando Álex le escribe una carta a su mamá lo hace en su __computadora portátil__.
5. Cuando contestas el teléfono, debes decir: __"Diga"__.

¡LENGUA VIVA!

There are various ways to say that a car is broken down. Synonyms for **descompuesto** include **averiado, roto, varado**, and **en pana**. You can also say **se rompió** or simply **no funciona**.

• • •

While **rueda** means *wheel everywhere*, *tires* are variously called **llantas, neumáticos, gomas**, and **cauchos**.

4 Situaciones Trabaja con un(a) compañero/a para representar los papeles de un(a) mecánico/a y un(a) conductor(a). El/La conductor(a) llama al/a la mecánico/a por teléfono y explica cuál es el problema del coche. Después indica dónde está en relación con el taller. El/La mecánico/a dice que puede ir enseguida. Usen estas preguntas y frases en su conversación:

- Aló/¿Bueno?/Diga
- ¿Quién habla?
- Con él/ella habla.
- ¿Qué pasó?
- Se me dañó el coche.
- Estoy a... kilómetros de...

NATIONAL communication STANDARDS

TEACHING OPTIONS

Extra Practice Have each student choose one of the video characters and then prepare a five to six sentence summary of the day's events from that person's point of view. Have a few volunteers read their summaries to the class; the class will guess which video character would have given each summary.

Small Groups Have the class work in small groups to write questions about the **Fotonovela**. Have each group hand its questions to another group, which will write the answers. For example, G1: **¿A quién llamó Álex?** G2: **Álex llamó al Sr. Fonseca, el mecánico**.

Ortografía

La acentuación de palabras similares

Although accent marks usually indicate which syllable in a word is stressed, they are also used to distinguish between words that have the same or similar spellings.

Él maneja el coche. **Sí, voy si quieres.**

Although one-syllable words do not usually carry written accents, some *do* have accent marks to distinguish them from words that have the same spelling but different meanings.

Sé cocinar. **Se baña.** **¿Tomas té?** **Te duermes.**

Sé (*I know*) and **té** (*tea*) have accent marks to distinguish them from the pronouns **se** and **te**.

para mí **mi cámara** **Tú lees.** **tu estéreo**

Mí (*me*) and **tú** (*you*) have accent marks to distinguish them from the possessive pronouns **mi** and **tu**.

¿Por qué vas? **Voy porque quiero.**

Several words of more than one syllable also have accent marks to distinguish them from words that have the same or similar spellings.

Éste es rápido. **Este módem es rápido.**

Demonstrative pronouns have accent marks to distinguish them from demonstrative adjectives.

¿Cuándo fuiste? **Fui cuando me llamó.**
¿Dónde trabajas? **Voy al taller donde trabajo.**

Adverbs have accent marks when they are used to convey a question.

Práctica Marca los acentos en las palabras que los necesitan.

ANA Alo, soy Ana. ¿Que tal? Aló/¿Qué?
JUAN Hola, pero...¿por que me llamas tan tarde? ¿por qué?
ANA Porque mañana tienes que llevarme a la universidad. Mi auto esta dañado. está
JUAN ¿Como se daño? ¿Cómo?/dañó
ANA Se daño el sabado. Un vecino (*neighbor*) choco con el. dañó/sábado/chocó/él

Crucigrama Utiliza las siguientes pistas (*clues*) para completar el crucigrama. ¡Ojo con los acentos!

Horizontales

1. Él ________ levanta.
4. No voy ________ no puedo.
7. Tú ________ acuestas.
9. ¿ ________ es el examen?
10. Quiero este video y ________.

Verticales

2. ¿Cómo ________ Ud.?
3. Eres ________ mi hermano.
5. ¿ ________ tal?
6. Me gusta ________ suéter.
8. Navego ________ la red.

	1 S	2 E			3 C				
		S		4 P	O	R	5 Q	U	6 E
		7 T	8 E		M		U		S
9 C	U	Á	N	D	O		10 É	S	E

Section Goals

In **Ortografía** students will learn about the use of accent marks to distinguish between words words that have the same or similar spellings.

Present

- The word **él** (*he*) has a written accent, but **el** (*the*) does not. Write the example sentences on the board without accent marks. Ask where the written accents should go.
- Accent marks distinguish **sé** (*I know*) from **se** (*pronoun*), and **té** (*tea*) from **te** (*pronoun*). Pronounce the samples and have students write them on the board.
- Written accents distinguish **mí** (*me*) from **mi** (*my*) and **tú** (*you*) from **tu** (*your*). Write the examples on the board without written accents. Ask where the written accents should go.
- **¿Por qué?** (*Why?*) has a written accent, unlike **porque** (*because*). Say the example sentences aloud and have volunteers write them on the board.
- Demonstrative pronouns have accents but demonstrative adjectives don't. Pronounce the example sentences, emphasizing the difference in stress between **por qué** and **porque**. Have students write them on the board.
- The interrogative words **¿cuándo?** and **¿dónde?** have written accents, but the adverbs **cuando** and **donde** don't. Pronounce the examples aloud and have students write them on the board.

Práctica/Crucigrama
Work through these activities with the class to practice the use of written accents.

TEACHING OPTIONS

Small Groups Have your students work in groups to explain which words in the **Práctica** activity need written accents and why. If necessary, have your students quickly review the information about accents in the **Ortografía** section of **Lesson 10**, page 305.

Extra Practice Write these sentences on the board or on a transparency without accent marks. **Esta es mi camara. • Papa la trajo del Japon para mi. • ¿Donde encontraste mi mochila? ¡Pues, donde lo dejaste, claro! • ¿Cuando visito Buenos Aires Mario? Se que Lourdes fue alli el año pasado, pero ¿cuando fue el? • ¿Me explicas por que llegas tarde? Porque mi coche está descompuesto.**

Section Goals

In **Estructura 11.1** students will compare and contrast the uses and meanings of the preterite and imperfect tenses.

Instructional Resources
Student Activities Manual: Workbook, 123–126; Lab Manual, 283
Hoja de actividades 27

Before Presenting Estructura 11.1 Have a volunteer read Inés's words in the caption of the fifth video still on page 333. Ask which verbs are preterite (**estaba**) and which are imperfect (**trabajé, enseñó, arreglé**). Explain to students that they are now going to learn how Spanish uses these two past tenses to express differences in meaning.

Assignment Have students study **Estructura 11.1** and prepare the activities on pages 337–338 as homework.

Present Go through these items by contrasting the preterite and imperfect point by point. As you do so, give other, personalized examples for each point. Ex: **El año pasado compré un nuevo coche. Esperaba comprar uno más barato pero no pude. • Vivía en Santa Bárbara de niño. Íbamos a la playa todos los domingos durante el verano. Un verano se me rompió un brazo.** and so forth.

Emphasize that the speaker's perspective on the past events is important to whether the preterite or the imperfect is appropriate. When a speaker focuses on the beginning or end of an action, the preterite is appropriate. When a speaker is not focusing on the beginning or end, the imperfect is appropriate.

Continued on page 337.

11.1 The preterite and the imperfect

NATIONAL comparisons STANDARDS

ANTE TODO Now that you have learned the forms of the preterite and imperfect, you will learn more about how they are used. The preterite and the imperfect are not interchangeable. In Spanish, the choice between these two tenses depends on the context and on the point of view of the speaker.

Por suerte, arreglé unos autobuses como éste.

Íbamos para Ibarra y se nos dañó el autobús.

COMPARE & CONTRAST

Uses of the preterite

- To express actions that are viewed by the speaker as completed

Don Francisco **estacionó** el autobús.
Don Francisco parked the bus.

Fueron a Buenos Aires ayer.
They went to Buenos Aires yesterday.

- To express the beginning or end of a past action

La película **empezó** a las nueve.
The movie began at nine o'clock.

Ayer **terminé** el proyecto para la clase de química.
Yesterday I finished the project for chemistry class.

- To narrate a series of past actions or events

Prendí la computadora, **leí** mi correo electrónico y luego le **escribí** un mensaje a Inés.
I turned on the computer, read my e-mail, and then wrote Inés a message.

Don Francisco **paró** el autobús, **abrió** la ventanilla y **saludó** a doña Rita.
Don Francisco stopped the bus, opened the window, and greeted doña Rita.

Uses of the imperfect

- To describe an ongoing past action with no reference to its beginning or end

Maite **conducía** muy rápido en Madrid.
Maite was driving very fast in Madrid.

Javier **esperaba** en el garaje.
Javier was waiting in the garage.

- To express habitual past actions and events

Cuando **era** joven, jugaba al tenis.
When I was young, I used to play tennis.

Álex siempre **revisaba** su correo electrónico a las tres.
Álex always checked his e-mail messages at three o'clock.

- To describe mental, physical, and emotional states or conditions

La chica **quería** descansar. **Se sentía** mal y **tenía** dolor de cabeza.
The girl wanted to rest. She felt ill and had a headache.

Ellos **eran** altos y **tenían** ojos verdes.
They were tall and had green eyes.

Estábamos felices de ver a la familia.
We were happy to see the family.

TEACHING OPTIONS

Extra Practice Write in English a simple, humorous retelling of a well-known fairy tale. Read it to the class, pausing after each verb in the past to ask the class whether the imperfect or preterite would be used in Spanish. Ex: Once upon a time there was a girl named Red Riding Hood. She wanted to take lunch to her ailing grandmother. She put a loaf of bread, a wedge of cheese, and a bottle of beaujoulais in a basket and set off through the woods. Meanwhile, farther down the path, a big, ugly, snaggle-toothed wolf was leaning against a tree, filing his nails . . .

Pairs On separate slips of paper, have students write six true statements, one for each of the uses of the preterite and imperfect in **Compare & Contrast**. Have them mix up the slips and exchange them with a partner, who will identify the preterite or imperfect use the sentence illustrates.

- The preterite and the imperfect often appear in the same sentence. In such cases the imperfect describes what *was happening*, while the preterite describes the action that "interrupted" the ongoing activity.

Navegaba en la red cuando **sonó** el teléfono.
I was surfing the web when the phone rang.

Maite **leía** el periódico cuando llegó Álex.
Maite was reading the newspaper when Álex arrived.

- You will also see the preterite and the imperfect used together in lengthy narratives such as fiction stories, news stories, and retelling of events. In these cases the imperfect provides all of the background information, such as the time, the weather, and the location, while the preterite indicates the specific events that occurred.

Eran las dos de la mañana y el detective ya no **podía** mantenerse despierto. **Se bajó** lentamente del coche, **estiró** las piernas y **levantó** los brazos hacia el cielo oscuro.
It was two in the morning, and the detective could no longer stay awake. He slowly stepped out of the car, stretched his legs, and raised his arms towards the darkened skies.

La luna **estaba** llena y no **había** en el cielo ni una sola nube. De repente, el detective **escuchó** un grito espeluznante proveniente del parque.
The moon was full and there wasn't a single cloud in the sky. Suddenly, the detective heard a piercing scream coming from the park.

NASA • La sonda se estrelló antes de orbitar

Mars cayó en Marte

La agencia espacial estadounidense perdió la comunicación con la sonda Mars Climate Orbiter, justo en el momento en que se ponía en órbita alrededor de Marte. La nave se estrelló por un error de navegación importante. Se habían invertido USD 25 millones y sería la primera estación meteorológica interplanetaria. PASE A LA A6

NOTA CULTURAL

The **pampa** or **pampas** is a vast region of flat grasslands which covers the majority of Argentina's interior, ranging from prairies to desert. The **pampas** were the home of the **gauchos**, nomadic cowboys known for their skill at riding horses and using a lasso and bolas

¡INTÉNTALO!

Completa estas historias (*stories*) con el pretérito o el imperfecto y explica por qué se usa ese tiempo verbal en cada ocasión.

El pretérito

1. (ir) Tomás y yo ___fuimos___ al parque ayer.
2. (nadar) ___Nadamos___ por la tarde.
3. (tomar) Después ___tomamos___ el sol.
4. (regresar) ___Regresamos___ a casa a las cinco.
5. (leer) Tomás preparó la cena. Yo ___leí___ el periódico.
6. (dormirse) Mientras Tomás veía una película, yo ___me dormí___.

El imperfecto

1. (ser) ___Eran___ las doce.
2. (haber) ___Había___ mucha gente en la calle.
3. (estar) Los novios ___estaban___ en el café.
4. (almorzar) Todos los días ___almorzaban___ juntos.
5. (servir) El camarero les ___servía___ ensaladas.
6. (llover) Cuando los novios salieron del café, ___llovía___.

Explain that when talking about or narrating events in the past, both the imperfect and the preterite are necessary, and that they frequently appear in the same sentence. Read the examples that show the imperfect as describing "background" conditions and the preterite describing "interrupting" actions. Then give more examples from your own experience. Ex: **Quería ver la nueva película ____, pero anoche sólo pude ir a la última función. La película era buena, pero terminó muy tarde. Era la una cuando llegué a casa. Como resultado me acosté muy tarde y esta mañana cuando me levanté estaba cansadísimo.**

Suggestion Have students find the example of an interrupted action in the realia.

Expand Involve the class in a conversation about things they have done in the past. Ask: ____, **¿viste la película ____? ¿La gustó? ¿La querías ver por mucho tiempo? ____, ¿qué hiciste recientemente que querías hacer por mucho tiempo? ____, ¿cuántos años tenía cuando aprendiste a conducir un coche? ¿Quién te enseñó conducir? ¿Estaba muy tranquila cuando estabas al volante?**

Close Call on volunteers to read their answers to **¡Inténtalo!** Have them explain why the preterite or imperfect was used in each case. Then call on different students to create other sentences illustrating the same uses.

TEACHING OPTIONS

Pairs Ask students to narrate the most interesting, embarassing, exciting, annoying thing that has happened to them recently. Tell them to describe what happened and how they felt, using preterite and imperfect verbs.

Heritage Speakers Ask Spanish speakers to write a summary of what happened in the **Fotonovela**. Tell them that their summaries should first set the scene and establish background information about the characters, where they are, and what they were doing, then explain what happened.

1 Present Ask volunteers to read the completed sentences. Have them explain the reason they chose the preterite or imperfect in each case. If there was a word or expression that triggered one tense or the other, have them point it out.

2 Expand After students have successfully completed the exercise, ask them the following comprehension questions about the article. **¿Qué pasó ayer? ¿Dónde hubo el accidente? ¿Cómo estaba el tiempo? ¿Qué le pasó a la mujer que manejaba? ¿Y a su pasajero? ¿Qué hizo el conductor del autobús? ¿Qué les pasó a los pasajeros del autobús?**

2 Expand Have students write a short news article about a current event that has happened in their community, following the model of the article in the activity.

3 Present Model the activity by completing the first item in several different ways.

3 Expand After students have compared their sentences, ask them to report to the class the most interesting things their partner said.

3 Expand Ask students to expand on one of their sentences, creating a paragraph about an imaginary or actual past experience.

Práctica

1 Seleccionar Utiliza el tiempo verbal adecuado, según (*according to*) el contexto.

1. Arturo ___manejaba___ (manejar) por la autopista cuando de repente ___vio___ (ver) que le ___seguían___ (seguir) dos policías. Él ___paró___ (parar) el coche, y los policías ___se aproximaron___ (*approached*) (aproximarse) al coche y le ___pidieron___ (pedir) la licencia de conducir.
2. Tú ___aprendiste___ (aprender) a manejar cuando ___tenías___ (tener) quince años, ¿no?
3. Esta mañana se me ___pinchó___ (pinchar) una llanta. ___Fui___ (Ir) a buscar la llanta de repuesto (*spare*) en el baúl, pero cuando la ___encontré___ (encontrar), también ___estaba___ (estar) desinflada (*flat*).
4. El lunes mi papá ___llevó___ (llevar) el carro al taller mecánico porque los frenos ___hacían___ (hacer) un ruido extraño (*strange noise*). El mecánico los ___revisó___ (revisar) pero no ___pudo___ (poder) encontrar ningún problema.
5. De niño, mi hijo siempre ___decía___ (decir) que ___quería___ (querer) ser mecánico porque le ___fascinaban___ (fascinar) los motores de los carros.
6. Nosotros ___estacionamos___ (estacionar) el carro y después ___fuimos___ (ir) a ver las cataratas (*waterfalls*) de Iguazú. ___Fue___ (Ser) un viaje magnífico.

CONSÚLTALO

The **Cataratas de Iguazú** are a chain of nearly 300 waterfalls that make up one of the most magnificent sights in South America. To learn more, see **Panorama** p.357.

2 Completar Completa esta noticia con la forma correcta del pretérito o el imperfecto.

Un accidente trágico

Ayer temprano por la mañana ___hubo___ (haber) un trágico accidente en la calle Ayacucho en el centro de Buenos Aires cuando un autobús ___chocó___ (chocar) con un carro. La mujer que ___manejaba___ (manejar) el carro ___murió___ (morir) al instante y los paramédicos ___tuvieron___ (tener) que llevar a su pasajero al hospital porque ___sufrió___ (sufrir) varias fracturas y una conmoción (*concussion*) cerebral. Su estado de salud es todavía muy grave. El conductor del autobús ___dijo___ (decir) que no ___vio___ (ver) el carro hasta el último (*last*) momento porque ___había___ (haber) mucha niebla y ___estaba___ (estar) lloviendo. Él ___intentó___ (intentar) (*to attempt*) dar un viraje brusco (*to swerve*), pero ___perdió___ (perder) el control del autobús y no ___pudo___ (poder) evitar (*to avoid*) el choque. Según nos informaron, ___no se lastimó___ (lastimarse) ningún pasajero.

CONSEJOS

Reading Spanish-language newspapers is a good way to practice verb tenses. You will find that both the imperfect and the preterite occur with great regularity. Many newsstands carry international papers, and many Spanish-language newspapers (such as Spain's *El País*, Mexico's *Reforma*, and Argentina's *Clarín*) are now on the Web.

3 Completar Completa las frases de una manera lógica. Usa el pretérito o el imperfecto. En parejas, comparen sus respuestas. Answers will vary.

1. De niño/a, yo...
2. Yo manejaba el coche mientras...
3. Anoche mi novio/a...
4. Ayer el/la profesor(a)...
5. La semana pasada un(a) amigo/a...
6. A menudo mi madre...
7. Esta mañana en la cafetería...
8. Navegábamos en la red cuando...

TEACHING OPTIONS

Small Groups Have students work in groups of four to write a short article about an imaginary road trip they took last summer. Students should use the imperfect to set the scene and the preterite to narrate the events. Each student should contribute three sentences to the article. When finished, have students read their articles to the class.

Heritage Speakers Ask Spanish speakers to write a brief narration of a well-known fairy tale such as Little Red Riding Hood (**Caperucita roja**), Goldilocks and the Three Bears (**Ricitos de Oro y los tres osos**), or Tom Thumb (**Pulgarcito**). Allow them to change details as they see fit, modernizing the story or setting it in another country, for example, but tell them to pay special attention to the use of preterite and imperfect verbs. Have them share their retellings with the class.

Comunicación

4 **Entrevista** Usa estas preguntas para entrevistar a un(a) compañero/a acerca de su primer(a) novio/a. Si quieres, puedes añadir (*to add*) otras preguntas. Answers will vary.

1. ¿Quién fue tu primer(a) novio/a?
2. ¿Cuántos años tenían Uds. cuando se conocieron?
3. ¿Cómo era él/ella?
4. ¿Qué le gustaba hacer? ¿Le interesaban los deportes?
5. ¿Por cuánto tiempo salieron Uds.?
6. ¿Qué hacían Uds. cuando salían?
7. ¿Pensaban casarse?
8. ¿Cuándo y por qué rompieron Uds.?

5 **Encuesta** Tu profesor(a) va a darte una hoja de actividades. Circula por la clase y pregúntales a tus compañeros/as con qué frecuencia hicieron las actividades de la lista en el pasado. Informa a la clase de los resultados de tu encuesta. Answers will vary.

Actividades	Nombres	Frecuencia
1. Cambiar una llanta pinchada		
2. Ir al taller mecánico		
3. Revisar el aceite del carro		
4. Chocar con otro carro		
5. Comprar discos compactos		
6. Usar una cámara de video		
7. Crear un sitio Web		
8. Usar un teléfono celular		

6 **Situación** Anoche alguien robó (*stole*) el examen de la Lección 11 de la oficina de tu profesor(a) y tú tienes que averiguar (*to find out*) quién lo hizo. Pregúntales a tres compañeros dónde estaban, con quién estaban y qué hicieron entre las ocho y las doce de la noche. Answers will vary.

Síntesis

7 **Escribir** Escribe una composición breve sobre la primera vez que manejaste un carro o el día en que fuiste al Departamento de Tráfico para conseguir tu licencia de conducir. Incluye los siguientes puntos en tu composición: una descripción del día, la hora y el tiempo, tu edad (*age*), qué pasó y cómo te sentías. Answers will vary.

TEACHING OPTIONS

Small Groups Have students write and perform a dialogue for the class. Three customers are trying to explain to a gas station attendant what happened to them and why their vehicles need repair. Students should use the preterite and imperfect as appropriate.

Game On your computer, create a short narrative in past time based on a well-known story. Double space between each sentence so the sentences may be easily cut apart into strips. Print two copies of the sentences and cut them apart. Then make a copy of the file and edit it, changing all preterites to imperfects and vice versa. Print out two copies of this version and cut the sentences apart. Into each of two bags put a complete set of each version of the story, mix the strips up, and challenge two groups to reconstruct the correct version of the story. The group that does so first wins.

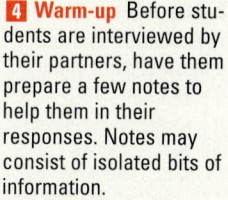

4 Warm-up Before students are interviewed by their partners, have them prepare a few notes to help them in their responses. Notes may consist of isolated bits of information.

4 Expand Have students write a summary of their partner's responses, omitting all names. Collect the summaries, then read them to the class. Have students guess who had the relationship described in the summary.

5 Warm-up Call on students to model each question in the survey before students do the survey on their own.

5 Present Distribute **Hoja de Actividades 27** and give students ten minutes to circulate around the classroom collecting responses.

6 Expand Have students decide who in their group would be the most likely thief based on his/her responses. Ask the group to prepare a police report explaining why they believe their suspect is the culprit.

7 Warm-up Before students begin to write, have them list information they plan to include in their composition, such as their age, the time, the date, what the weather was like, and so forth. Next, have them list the events of the day in the order they happened. Finally, have students prepare an outline for their essays.

7 Present After students write a draft of their composition, have them check the use of each verb to be sure it matches the tense they chose. Students should make necessary corrections before turning in their essays.

Assignment Have students do activities in **Student Activities Manual: Workbook,** pages 123–126.

Section Goals

In **Estructura 11.2** students will learn when to use **por** and **para.**

Instructional Resources
Student Activities Manual: Workbook, 127–128; Lab Manual, 284
Hoja de actividades 28

Before Presenting Estructura 11.2 Have a volunteer read the caption of the third video still on page 332. Focus on **...nos hablamos todos los días por el teléfono Internet, trabajando para salvar el mundo.** Tell students that they have already leaned most of the uses of the prepositions **por** and **para**, but that they are now going to compare and contrast their uses in detail and learn a few new uses.
Assignment Have students study **Estructura 11.2** and prepare the activities on pages 341–342 as homework.

Present Discuss each of the uses of **por** listed, adding other examples as you do so. Then ask students to translate phrases requiring **por**. Say: **¿Cómo se dice?:** *talk by phone; send information by e-mail; walk across campus; walk along Béquer Street; arrive in the afternoon/in the morning; be worried about the accident/about your friend; go 30 miles per hour; study for four hours; work for your uncle; buy groceries for your grandmother;* and so forth.

11.2 Por and para

NATIONAL STANDARDS comparisons

ANTE TODO Unlike English, Spanish has two words that mean *for*: **por** and **para.** These two prepositions are not interchangeable. Study the following charts to see how they are used.

Es para usted.
Es un cliente de
don Paco.

Álex habla por
teléfono.

Por **is used to indicate...**

▶ **Motion or a general location** *(around, through, along, by)*	La excursión nos llevó **por** el centro. *The tour took us through downtown.* Pasamos **por** el parque y **por** el río. *We passed by the park and along the river.*
▶ **Duration of an action** *(for, during, in)*	Estuve en la Patagonia **por** un mes. *I was in Patagonia for a month.* Miguel estudió **por** la noche. *Miguel studied during the night.*
▶ **Reason or motive for an action** *(because of, on account of, on behalf of)*	Lo hizo **por** su familia. *She did it on behalf of her family.* Papá llegó a casa tarde **por** el tráfico. *Dad arrived home late because of the traffic.*
▶ **Object of a search** *(for, in search of)*	Vengo **por** ti a las ocho. *I'm coming for you at eight.* Maite fue **por** su cámara. *Maite went in search of her camera.*
▶ **Means by which something is done** *(by, by way of, by means of)*	Ellos viajan **por** la autopista. *They travel by (by way of) the highway.* ¿Hablaste con la policía **por** teléfono? *Did you talk to the police by (on the) phone?*
▶ **Exchange or substitution** *(for, in exchange for)*	Le di dinero **por** la videocasetera. *I gave him money for the VCR.* Muchas gracias **por** el video. *Thank you very much for the video.*
▶ **Unit of measure** *(per, by)*	José manejaba a 120 kilómetros **por** hora. *José was driving 120 kilometers per hour.*

¡ATENCIÓN!

Por is also used in several idiomatic expressions, including:
por aquí *around here*
por ejemplo *for example*
por eso *that's why; therefore*
por fin *finally*

¡ATENCIÓN!

Remember that when giving an exact time, **de** is used instead of **por** before **la mañana, la tarde**, etc.

La clase empieza a las nueve **de** la mañana.

• • •

In addition to **por**, **durante** is also commonly used to mean *for* when referring to time.

Esperé al médico **durante** cincuenta minutos.

TEACHING OPTIONS

TPR Call out a sentence, omitting either **por** or **para**. If students think **por** should be used in the sentence, they raise one hand. If they think **para** should be used, they raise two hands. Avoid cases where either **por** or **para** could be used. Ex: **Tengo que leer el capítulo 9 ____ mañana.** (two hands) **Jimena trabaja ____ la noche.** (one hand) **Estaba en Buenos Aires ____ el mes de marzo.** (one hand)

Game Divide the class into four or five teams, giving each team a large piece of paper. Call out a use of either **por** or **para**. Teams have one minute to write as many sentences as they can, employing that use. Check answers by having a volunteer read his or her team's sentences. Give a point for each correct sentence. Keep score on the board. The team with the most sentences wins.

***Para* is used to indicate...**

▶ **Destination** (*toward, in the direction of*)	Salimos **para** Córdoba el sábado. *We are leaving for Córdoba on Saturday.*
▶ **Deadline or a specific time in the future** (*by, for*)	Él va a arreglar el carro **para** el viernes. *He will fix the car by Friday.*
▶ **Purpose or goal +** ***infinitive*** (*in order to*)	Juan estudia **para** (ser) mecánico. *Juan is studying to be a mechanic.*
▶ **Purpose +** ***noun*** (*for, used for*)	Es una llanta **para** el carro. *It's a tire for the car.*
▶ **The recipient of something** (*for*)	Compré una calculadora **para** mi hijo. *I bought a calculator for my son.*
▶ **Comparison with others or an opinion** (*for, considering*)	**Para** un joven, es demasiado serio. *For a young person, he is too serious.* **Para** mí, esta lección no es difícil. *For me, this lesson isn't difficult.*
▶ **In the employ of** (*for*)	Sara trabaja **para** Telecom Argentina. *Sara works for Telecom Argentina.*

▶ In many cases it is grammatically correct to use either **por** or **para** in a sentence. The meaning of the sentence is different, however, depending on which preposition is used.

Caminé **por** el parque.
I walked through the park.

Caminé **para** el parque.
I walked to (toward) the park.

Trabajó **por** su padre.
He worked for (in place of) his father.

Trabajó **para** su padre.
He worked for his father('s company).

¡INTÉNTALO! Completa estas frases con las preposiciones **por** o **para.**

1. Jugamos al fútbol __por__ la mañana.
2. Necesitas un módem __para__ navegar en la red.
3. Entraron __por__ la puerta.
4. Quiero un pasaje __para__ Buenos Aires.
5. __Para__ arrancar el carro, necesito la llave.
6. Arreglé el televisor __para__ mi amigo.
7. Estuvieron nerviosos __por__ el examen.
8. ¿No hay una gasolinera __por__ aquí?
9. Esta computadora es __para__ Ud.
10. Juan está enfermo. Tengo que trabajar __por__ él.
11. Estuvimos en Cancún __por__ dos meses.
12. __Para__ mí, el español es difícil.
13. Tengo que estudiar la lección __para__ el lunes.
14. Voy a ir __por__ el camino más corto.
15. Compré dulces __para__ mi novia.
16. Compramos el auto __por__ un buen precio.

TEACHING OPTIONS

Extra Practice Give each student in the class a strip of paper on which you have written one of the uses of **por** or **para**, or a sentence that is an example of one of the uses. Have students circulate around the room until they find the person who has the match for their use or sentence. After everyone has found a partner, the pairs read their sentences and uses to the class.

Pairs/Game Have students create cards for a memory game. There should be one card for each use of **por** and **para**, and one card with a sentence illustrating each use, for a total of 28 cards. When finished, students lay all the cards face down. Then, taking turns, students uncover two cards at a time, trying to match a use to a sentence. The student with the most matches wins.

Create a matching activity for the uses of **para**. Write on the board sentences exemplifying each use of **para** listed, but not in the order they are given in the text. Say each sentence aloud as you write it. Ex:

1. **El Sr. López compró el Ferrari para Mariana.**
2. **Este autobús va para Corrientes.**
3. **Para don Francisco, conducir un autobús no es nada difícil.**
4. **Don Francisco trabaja para Ecuatur.**
5. **Estudia para llegar a ser ingeniero.**
6. **El baúl es para las maletas.**
7. **Tengo que pagar la multa para lunes.**

To the right of the sentences, list the uses of **para**:

a. **Destination**
b. **Deadline**
c. **Purpose +** *infinitive*
d. **Purpose +** *noun*
e. **Recipient**
f. **Comparison or opinion**
g. **Employment**

Call on individuals to match each sentence with its usage. As you go through the matching, discuss each choice and provide further examples.

Next, have students make two flashcards. On one they write **por** and on the other **para**. Call out one of the uses for either word. Students show the appropriate card. Then, call on a volunteer to write a sentence illustrating that use on the board. The class determines whether the sentence is correct or not.

Finally, point to the example sentences in which either **por** or **para** is correct. Explain that it is important to use these prepositions correctly, since not doing so could result in misunderstanding.

Suggestion Do **¡Inténtalo!** as a whole class activity to check comprehension after your presentation.

1 Present Go over the activity orally with the class. Ask volunteers to read each complete sentence and explain their choice of **por** or **para**.

1 Expand After students have completed the activity, have them list the uses of **por** and **para** in the paragraph. Then ask them to work in pairs to add sentences to the paragraph, employing the remaining uses of **por** and **para**. (Remaining uses of **por**: reason or motive, object of search, means, unit of measure; remaining uses of **para**: destination, deadline, purpose + *noun*, comparison, employment) Go over the additional sentences orally with the class.

2 Warm-up Model the activity by creating a sentence with an element from each column. Ask a volunteer to explain your choice of **por** or **para**.

2 Present Divide the class into groups of three. Give groups five minutes to write as many sentences as they can combining elements from each column. Have groups compare their sentences.

3 Present Have students take turns describing in detail to a partner what they see in each drawing. They should talk about who or what is in the drawing, and what is happening. Explain that there may be several possible responses to each drawing.

3 Expand Have students take turns with a partner to expand their descriptions to a short oral narrative. After each drawing has been described, ask students to pick two or three of their narratives and link them into a story.

Práctica

1 Completar Completa este párrafo con las preposiciones **por** o **para.**

El mes pasado mi esposo y yo hicimos un viaje a Buenos Aires y sólo pagamos dos mil dólares ___por___ los pasajes. Estuvimos en Buenos Aires ___por___ una semana y recorrimos toda la ciudad. Durante el día caminamos ___por___ la plaza San Martín, el microcentro y el barrio de La Boca, donde viven muchos artistas. ___Por___ la noche fuimos a una tanguería, que es una especie de teatro ___para___ mirar a la gente bailar tango. Dos días después decidimos hacer una excursión ___por___ las pampas ___para___ ver el paisaje y un rodeo con gauchos. ___Por___ eso, alquilamos (*we rented*) un carro y pasamos unos días muy agradables. El último *(last)* día que estuvimos en Buenos Aires fuimos a Galerías Pacíficas ___para___ comprar recuerdos (*souvenirs*) ___para___ nuestros hijos y nietos. Compramos tantos regalos que tuvimos que pagar impuestos (*duties*) cuando pasamos ___por___ la aduana al regresar.

2 Oraciones Añade (*Add*) **por** o **para** y forma frases con los siguientes elementos. Answers will vary.

A	B	C	D
(no) fui	al mercado	comprar frutas	coche
(no) fuimos	a las montañas	tres días	esquiar
	a Mar del Plata	razones económicas	mi madre
		tomar el sol	nadar

3 Describir Usa **por** o **para** y el tiempo presente para describir estos dibujos. Answers will vary.

1. ______________

2. ______________

3. ______________

4. ______________

5. ______________

6. ______________

CONSÚLTALO

To learn more about Buenos Aires, Argentina's capital, see **Panorama** p. 356.

NOTA CULTURAL

Mar del Plata is a resort city on the coast of Argentina. Known as "the Pearl of the Atlantic," the city is visited by large numbers of vacationers for its beaches and casinos.

TEACHING OPTIONS

Large Group Have students create ten questions for a survey about the use of modern technology. Questions should include as many uses of **por** and **para** as possible. When finished, have students administer their survey to five different people in the room, then compile their results.
Ex: **¿Por cuántas minutos al día hablas por teléfono celular?**

Heritage Speakers Ask native Spanish speakers to imagine they are explaining to a younger sibling how to maintain the family car and why certain types of maintenance are necessary. Students should employ as many different uses of **por** and **para** in their explanations as possible.

Comunicación

4 **Descripciones** Usa **por** o **para** y completa estas frases de una manera (*manner*) lógica. Luego, compara tus respuestas con las de un(a) compañero/a. Answers will vary.

1. En casa, hablo con mis amigos...
2. Mi padre/madre trabaja...
3. Ayer fui al taller...
4. Los miércoles tengo clases...
5. A veces voy a la biblioteca...
6. Esta noche tengo que estudiar...
7. Necesito... dólares...
8. Compré un regalo...
9. Mi mejor amigo/a estudia...
10. Necesito hacer la tarea...

5 **Encuesta** Tu profesor(a) va a darte una hoja de actividades. Camina por la clase y haz preguntas hasta que encuentres a alguien que responda a cada descripción que se menciona en la lista. Luego presenta los resultados a la clase. Answers will vary.

Descripciones	Nombres
1. En casa tiene televisión por cable.	
2. Anoche durmió por ocho horas.	
3. No le gusta hablar cuando se levanta por las mañanas.	
4. Hoy pasó por una gasolinera.	

6 **Situación** Dramatiza esta situación con un(a) compañero/a. Uno de Uds. quiere comprar un carro y necesita que su padre/madre le preste dinero. Para convencerlo/la, el/la hijo/a menciona varias razones por las cuales (*which*) necesita el carro. Answers will vary.

Síntesis

7 **Una subasta (*auction*)** Trabajen en grupos. Cada estudiante debe traer un objeto o una foto del objeto para vender a la clase. Luego, un(a) estudiante es el/la vendedor(a) y los otros son los postores (*bidders*). Para empezar la subasta, el/la vendedor(a) tiene que describir el objeto y explicar para qué se usa y por qué alguien debe comprarlo. Answers will vary.

modelo

Vendedor(a) Aquí tengo una videocasetera Sony. Pueden usar esta videocasetera para ver películas en su casa o para grabar (*to record*) sus programas favoritos. Sólo hace un año que la compré y todavía funciona perfectamente. ¿Quién ofrece $150.00 para empezar?
Postor(a) 1 Te doy $50.00.
Vendedor(a) ¿Quién me ofrece $60.00 por la videocasetera? Es una ganga a este precio. Yo pagué $200.00 por ella.
Postor(a) 2 Te doy $60.00 por la videocasetera.

TEACHING OPTIONS

Small Groups Have students create a television advertisement for a car or piece of technological equipment. Students should describe the item, why the customer should buy it, how much it costs, explain that the item is on sale only until a certain date, and detail any possible trade-ins. Students should use **por** and **para** when possible in their ad.

Extra Practice For students still having trouble with distinguishing between **por** and **para**, have them create a mnemonic device, like a story or chant, for remembering the different uses. Ex: **Busqué POR por el parque, por el río y por el centro. Busqué por horas, por todos los estudiantes confundidos. Viajé por carro, por tren y por avión.** Do the same for **para**.

4 Present Model the activity by completing one of the sentence starters in two different ways.

4 Expand Have students discuss the uses of **por** and **para** they employed, and say whether they used **por** or **para** more. If one use predominated, have students create new sentences, employing other uses of **por** or **para**.

5 Present Distribute **Hoja de actividades 28** to each student and allow five minutes to complete the activity.

5 Expand Go over the survey results with the whole class to determine class trends. Ask: **¿Cuántos tienen televisión por cable en casa?** Record number on the board. Ask volunteers questions about the results. Ex: **¿Qué porcentaje de la clase durmió ocho horas anoche? ¿Qué porcentaje no?**

6 Warm-up Allow five minutes for pairs to prepare their dialogues. You may wish for students to jot down some notes before presenting their dialogues to the class.

7 Warm-up Before the bidding begins, display the items to be auctioned off and name them. Invite students to walk around with their group members and discuss what the items are, their purposes, and how much they will pay for them.

7 Present Have groups prepare the opening statements for the items their members brought. Students then take turns opening up the bidding for the entire class. Nongroup members may bid on each item. Group members bid to keep the bidding alive.

Assignment Have students do activities in **Student Activities Manual: Workbook**, pages 127–128.

Section Goals

In **Estructura 11.3** students will learn the use of reciprocal reflexives.

Instructional Resources *Student Activities Manual: Workbook, 129–130; Lab Manual, 285*

Before Presenting Estructura 11.3 Ask an individual to explain what reflexive verbs are. Ask volunteers to provide examples. Review reflexive verbs and pronouns by asking students questions about their personal routine. Ex: **Yo me desperté a las seis de la mañana. Y tú, ____, ¿a qué hora te despertaste?** Have students read the caption to the third video still, drawing attention to **...nos hablamos todos los días por teléfono Internet...** Ask students if they think **nos hablamos** is reflexive (*we speak to ourselves*), leading them to see that it is reciprocal (*we speak to one another*).

Assignment Have students study **Estructura 11.3** and prepare **¡Inténtalo!** on page 344 and Activities 1 and 2 on page 345 as homework.

Present Explain that reciprocal reflexives are logically used only in the plural since they express a reciprocal action between more than one person or thing. After going over the example sentences, ask students questions that contain or require reciprocal constructions. Ex: **¿Los estudiantes y los profesores siempre se saludan? ¿Se ven ustedes con frecuencia durante la semana? ¿Los candidatos siempre se respetan?**

Close Review the answers to **¡Inténtalo!** orally with the class, having students give the English translation for each item.

11.3 Reciprocal reflexives

NATIONAL STANDARDS comparisons

ANTE TODO In Lesson 7, you learned that reflexive pronouns indicate that the subject of a sentence does the action to itself. Reciprocal pronouns, on the other hand, express a shared or reciprocal action between two or more people or things. In this context, the reflexive pronoun means *(to) each other* or *(to) one another*.

Luis y Marta **se** miran en el espejo.
Luis and Marta look at themselves in the mirror.

Luis y Marta **se** miran.
Luis and Marta look at each other.

▶ Only the plural forms of the reflexive pronouns **(nos, os, se)** are used to express reciprocal actions because the action must involve more than one person or thing.

Cuando **nos vimos** en la calle, **nos abrazamos**.
When we saw each other on the street, we hugged one another.

Uds. **se** van a **encontrar** en el Café Tortoni, ¿no?
You are meeting each other at the Café Tortoni, right?

Nos ayudamos cuando usamos la computadora.
We help each other when we use the computer.

Las amigas **se saludaron** y **se besaron**.
The friends greeted each other and kissed one another.

¡INTÉNTALO! Indica el reflexivo recíproco adecuado y el presente o el pretérito de estos verbos.

El presente

1. (escribir) Los novios _se escriben_.
   Nosotros _nos escribimos_.
   Ana y Ernesto _se escriben_.
2. (escuchar) Mis tíos _se escuchan_.
   Nosotros _nos escuchamos_.
   Ellos _se escuchan_.
3. (ver) Nosotros _nos vemos_.
   Fernando y Tomás _se ven_.
   Uds. _se ven_.
4. (llamar) Ellas _se llaman_.
   Mis hermanos _se llaman_.
   Pepa y yo _nos llamamos_.

El pretérito

1. (saludar) Nicolás y tú _se saludaron_.
   Nuestros vecinos _se saludaron_.
   Nosotros _nos saludamos_.
2. (hablar) Los amigos _se hablaron_.
   Elena y yo _nos hablamos_.
   Nosotras _nos hablamos_.
3. (conocer) Alberto y yo _nos conocimos_.
   Uds. _se conocieron_.
   Ellos _se conocieron_.
4. (odiar) Ana y Javier _se odiaron_.
   Los primos _se odiaron_.
   Mi hermana y yo _nos odiamos_.

TEACHING OPTIONS

Extra Practice Have students write sentences using the following verbs to describe what they and their significant other or best friend do together, or what their friends do together: **llamarse por teléfono..., verse..., decirse..., ayudarse..., encontrarse..., reunirse...** Ex: **Mi amigo y yo siempre nos hablamos de todo.**

Pairs Have students write and perform a dialogue in which they discuss two friends who are romantically involved, but have had a misunderstanding. Ask students to try and incorporate the following verbs: **conocerse, encontrarse, quererse, hablarse, enojarse, besarse, mirarse,** and **entenderse.**

Práctica

1 **Un amor recíproco** Describe a Laura y a Elián usando los verbos recíprocos.

modelo

Laura veía a Elián todos los días. Elián veía a Laura todos los días.
Laura y Elián se veían todos los días.

1. Laura conocía bien a Elián. Elián conocía bien a Laura.
   Laura y Elián se conocían bien.
2. Laura miraba a Elián con amor. Elián la miraba con amor también.
   Laura y Elián se miraban con amor.
3. Laura entendía bien a Elián. Elián entendía bien a Laura.
   Laura y Elián se entendían bien.
4. Laura hablaba con Elián todas las noches por teléfono. Elián hablaba con Laura todas las noches por teléfono.
   Laura y Elián se hablaban todas las noches por teléfono.
5. Laura ayudaba a Elián con los problemas. Elián la ayudaba también con los problemas.
   Laura y Elián se ayudaban con los problemas.

2 **Describir** Mira los dibujos y describe lo que estas personas hicieron.

¡LENGUA VIVA!
In Argentina and other parts of Latin America, the pronoun **vos** is often used in place of **tú** when speaking to friends. In this case, the **tú** verb forms are used, but they are accented on the final syllable (and there are no stem changes).
Vos, ¿qué pensás? ¿Qué querés comer?

1. Las hermanas se abrazaron.

2. Ellos se besaron.

3. Gilberto y Mercedes no se miraron / no se hablaron / se enojaron.

4. Tú y yo nos saludamos / nos encontramos en la calle.

Comunicación

NATIONAL communication STANDARDS

3 **Preguntas** En parejas, túrnense para hacerse estas preguntas. Answers will vary.

1. ¿Se vieron tú y tu mejor amigo/a ayer? ¿Cuándo se ven Uds. normalmente?
2. ¿Dónde se encuentran tú y tus amigos?
3. ¿Se ayudan tú y tu mejor amigo/a con sus problemas?
4. ¿Se entienden bien tú y tu novio/a?
5. ¿Dónde se conocieron tú y tu novio/a? ¿Cuánto tiempo hace que se conocen Uds.?
6. ¿Cuándo se dan regalos tú y tu novio/a?
7. ¿Se escriben tú y tus amigos por correo electrónico o prefieren llamarse por teléfono?
8. ¿Siempre se llevan bien tú y tu compañero/a de cuarto? Explica.

1 Warm-up Review conjugations of the imperfect tense before beginning the activity. Model the activity by reading through the **Modelo**.

1 Expand Have students expand upon the sentences to create a story about Laura and Elián falling in love.

1 Expand Have students rewrite the sentences, imagining that they are talking about themselves and their significant other.

2 Warm-up Ask a volunteer to read the directions. Point out that responses should use the preterite tense. Ask the class to describe what is going on in each illustration, suggesting appropriate verbs.

3 Warm-up Ask students to read through the questions and prepare short answers (not complete sentences) for each before talking to their partner.

3 Present Have students interview their partners, asking all the questions before switching roles. As students listen to their partners' answers, they should verify what they hear by paraphrasing or summarizing their partners' responses.

3 Expand Have students ask follow-up questions after their partners have asked the original ones. Ex: **¿A qué hora se vieron ayer? ¿Dónde se vieron? ¿Por qué se vieron ayer? ¿Para qué se ven Uds. normalmente?**

Assignment Have students do the activities in the **Student Activities Manual: Workbook**, pages 129–130.

TEACHING OPTIONS

Game Divide the class into groups of four to play a guessing game. Write a verb on the board. Groups have 20 seconds to come up with a famous couple or two famous people or entities that behave or feel that way toward each other. The verb may be in the present, imperfect, or preterite tense. Ex: **quererse—Romeo y Julieta se querían.** All groups with a correct answer earn a point.

TPR Call on a pair of volunteers to act out a reciprocal action. The class will guess the action, using the verb in a sentence.

Heritage Speakers Ask Spanish speakers to summarize the action of their favorite love story, soap opera, or television drama. They should try to use as many reciprocal reflexives as possible in their summary.

Section Goals

In **Estructura 11.4** students will learn:
- the stressed possessive adjectives and pronouns
- placement of stressed possessive adjectives

Instructional Resources *Student Activities Manual: Workbook, 131–132; Lab Manual, 286*

Before Presenting Estructura 11.4 Ask a few questions that involve possessive adjectives and respond to student answers with statements that involve the stressed possessive pronouns. Write each stressed pronoun you introduce on the board as you say it. Ex: ____, **¿es éste tu lápiz? (Sí.) Pues, este lápiz es tuyo,** ____. Show your own pencil. **Éste es mi lápiz. Este lápiz es mío.** Say: **Clase,** (pointing to first pencil) **este lápiz es suyo y** (holding up your pencil) **este es mío.** Tell students they are now going to learn the stressed forms of possessive pronouns and adjectives.

Assignment Have students study **Estructura 11.4** and do the exercises on pages 347–348 as homework.

Present Write the masculine forms of the stressed possessive adjectives/pronouns on the board, modeling their pronunciation as you do so. Ask volunteers to give the feminine and plural forms. Work through each point about the agreement and position of stressed possessive adjectives. Emphasize that when a stressed possessive adjective is used, the word it modifies is preceded by an article.

Continued on page 347.

11.4 Stressed possessive adjectives and pronouns

NATIONAL STANDARDS comparisons

ANTE TODO In contrast to English, Spanish has two types of possessive adjectives: the unstressed (or short) forms you learned in Lesson 3 and the stressed (or long) forms. The stressed possessive adjectives are used for emphasis or to express the English phrases *of mine, of yours, of his,* and so on.

Stressed possessive adjectives and pronouns

Masculine	Feminine	Masculine	Feminine	
mío	**mía**	**míos**	**mías**	*my; (of) mine*
tuyo	**tuya**	**tuyos**	**tuyas**	*your; (of) yours* (fam.)
suyo	**suya**	**suyos**	**suyas**	*your; (of) yours* (form.)*; his; (of) his; her; (of) hers; its*
nuestro	**nuestra**	**nuestros**	**nuestras**	*our; (of) ours*
vuestro	**vuestra**	**vuestros**	**vuestras**	*your; (of) yours* (fam.)
suyo	**suya**	**suyos**	**suyas**	*your; (of) yours* (form.)*; their; (of) theirs*

¡ATENCIÓN!

Used with **un/una**, these possessives are similar in meaning to the English expression *of mine/yours/etc.*

Juancho es un amigo mío.
Juancho is a friend of mine.

▶ Stressed possessive adjectives must agree in gender and number with the nouns they modify.

su impresora → la impresora **suya**
her printer → *her printer*

nuestros televisores → los televisores **nuestros**
our television sets → *our television sets*

▶ Stressed possessive adjectives are placed after the noun they modify, while unstressed possessive adjectives are placed before the noun.

Son **mis** llaves. — Son las llaves **mías**.
They are my keys. — *They are my keys.*

▶ A definite article, an indefinite article, or a demonstrative adjective usually precedes a noun modified by a stressed possessive adjective.

Me encantan {
unos discos compactos **tuyos**. *I love some compact discs of yours.*
los discos compactos **tuyos**. *I love your compact discs.*
estos discos compactos **tuyos**. *I love these compact discs of yours.*

▶ Since **suyo, suya, suyos,** and **suyas** have more than one meaning, you can avoid confusion by using the construction: [*article*] + [*noun*] + **de** + [*subject pronoun*].

el teclado **suyo** ←
el teclado **de él/ella** — *his/her keyboard*
el teclado **de Ud.** — *your keyboard*
el teclado **de ellos/ellas** — *their keyboard*
el teclado **de Uds.** — *your keyboard*

TEACHING OPTIONS

TPR Place different objects and/or photos of objects in a large bag. Ask students to retrieve one item from the bag as you whisper a name or names of people in the classroom into the students' ear. The students then mime how to use the item and to whom the item belongs. The class makes guesses like the following: **Es el carro de Roberto y de Chela. Es el carro suyo.**

Extra Practice Refer students to the chart of possessive adjectives on this page. Call out a noun and subject, then ask students to tell you which adjective they would use. Ex: **discos compactos, ustedes (suyos)**

Possessive pronouns

> **CONSÚLTALO**
>
> **Possessive adjectives** Note that this is the same construction you learned in Lesson 3 for clarifying **su** and **sus**. To review unstressed possessive adjectives, see Lesson 3, section 3.2, p. 83.

- Possessive pronouns are used to replace a noun + [*possessive adjective*]. In Spanish, the possessive pronouns have the same forms as the stressed possessive adjectives, and they are preceded by a definite article.

la calculadora **nuestra**	**la nuestra**
el *fax* **tuyo**	**el tuyo**
los archivos **suyos**	**los suyos**

- A possessive pronoun agrees in number and gender with the noun it replaces.

—Aquí está **mi coche.** ¿Dónde está **el tuyo**?
Here's my car. Where is yours?

—**El mío** está en el taller de mi hermano.
Mine is at my brother's garage.

—¿Tienes **las cintas** de Carlos?
Do you have Carlos' tapes?

—No, pero tengo **las nuestras.**
No, but I have ours.

> **¡LENGUA VIVA!**
>
> The definite article (**el/la**) is usually omitted when a stressed possessive follows the verb **ser**.
>
> Perdone, ¿pero **es** esta cámara **suya**?
>
> No, no **es mía**.

Episodio veintiuno: Tecnohombre y los superamigos suyos salvan el mundo una vez más.

La mujer mecánica y el tecnohombre, ¡mis héroes!
¡Y los míos también!

¡INTÉNTALO! Indica las formas tónicas (*stressed*) de estos adjetivos posesivos y los pronombres posesivos correspondientes.

	adjetivos	pronombres
1. su videocasetera	la videocasetera suya	la suya
2. mi televisor	el televisor mío	el mío
3. nuestros discos	los discos nuestros	los nuestros
4. tus cintas	las cintas tuyas	las tuyas
5. su módem	el módem suyo	el suyo
6. mis videos	los videos míos	los míos
7. nuestra impresora	la impresora nuestra	la nuestra
8. tu estéreo	el estéreo tuyo	el tuyo
9. nuestro carro	el carro nuestro	el nuestro
10. mi computadora	la computadora mía	la mía

TEACHING OPTIONS

Video Replay the **Fotonovela**, having students listen for each use of an unstressed possessive adjective and write down the sentence in which it occurs. Next, have students rewrite those sentences using a stressed possessive adjective. Then, discuss how the use of stressed possessive adjectives affected the meaning or fluidity of the sentences.

Pairs Tell students that their laundry has gotten mixed up with their roommate's and since they are the same size and have the same tastes in clothing, they can't tell what belongs to whom. Have them ask each other questions about different articles of clothing. Ex: **—¿Son tuyos estos pantalones de rayas? —Sí, son míos. —Y ¿estos calcetines rojos son tuyos? —Sí, son míos, pero esta camisa grandísima no es mía.**

Explain that the possessive pronouns have the same forms as the stressed possessive adjectives, that they are always preceeded by an article, and that they agree in gender and number with the noun they replace.

Point out that the function of the stressed possessives is to give emphasis. They are often used to point up contrasts. Ex: **¿Tú carro es azul? Pues el carro mío es rojo cereza. Y ¿tu computadora es de 1998? Pues, la mía es totalmente nueva. Y ¿tu cámara todavía utiliza película? Pues, la mía es digitalizada.**

Next, use a balled-up piece of paper to practice. Call out a sentence using an unstressed possessive adjective. Toss the balled-up piece of paper to a student who restates the sentence, using a stressed possessive adjective. That student, in turn, tosses the ball to another student, who states the sentence using a possessive pronoun and tosses the ball back to you. Ex: **Nuestro módem es nuevo. El módem nuestro es nuevo. El nuestro es nuevo.**

Suggestion After students have completed the above mentioned ball-toss activity, have volunteers write the answers to **¡Inténtalo!** on the board.

Close Ask students questions using unstressed possessive adjectives or the article + *noun* + **de** + *name* construction, having them answer with a possessive pronoun. Ex: **Es tu cuaderno, ¿verdad? (Sí, es el mío.) Clase, ¿son éstos sus exámenes? (Sí, son los nuestros.) Este mochila negra es de Mónica, ¿no? (No, no es la suya. La mochila roja es la suya.)**

1 Present Go over the sentences orally with the whole class. Ask volunteers to read each sentence aloud.

1 Expand Have students work in pairs to write four sentences that use stressed possessive adjectives or possessive pronouns. Have them "dehydrate" their sentences following the model of this activity and then exchange them with another pair that "rehydrates" them.

2 Warm-up Review the technological vocabulary on pages 329–330. Then, call on two volunteers to read the **Modelo**.

2 Expand Have students continue the activity, using the following six items: **las cintas, la impresora, el walkman, los videos, el teléfono celular,** and **las videocaseteras.**

3 Present Call on pairs of volunteers to read each item. Then, have them explain why they chose the possessive pronoun they did.

3 Expand Have students create dialogues, modeled after the ones in the activity, and perform them for the class. Each dialogue should consist of at least six lines and use as many stressed possessive adjectives and pronouns as possible.

Práctica

1 Frases Forma frases con las siguientes palabras. Usa el presente.

1. Un / amiga / suyo / vivir / Córdoba Una amiga suya vive en Córdoba.
2. ¿Me / prestar / calculadora / tuyo? ¿Me prestas la calculadora tuya?
3. El / coche / suyo / nunca / funcionar / bien El coche suyo nunca funciona bien.
4. No / nos / interesar / problemas / suyo No nos interesan los problemas suyos.
5. Yo / querer / cámara / mío / ahora mismo Yo quiero la cámara mía ahora mismo.
6. Un / amigos / nuestro / manejar / como / loco Unos amigos nuestros manejan como locos.

2 ¿Es suyo? Un policía ha capturado al hombre que robó (*robbed*) en tu casa. Ahora quieren saber qué cosas son tuyas. Túrnate con un(a) compañero/a para hacer el papel del policía y usa las pistas (*clues*) para contestar las preguntas.

modelo

No/viejo

Policía: Esta calculadora, ¿es suya?

Estudiante: No, no es mía. La mía era más vieja.

1. Sí Este estéreo, ¿es suyo?/Sí, es mío.

2. Sí Esta computadora portátil, ¿es suya?/Sí, es mía.

4. Sí Este radio, ¿es suyo?/ Sí, es mío.

4. No/grande Este televisor, ¿es suyo?/ No, no es mío. El mío era más grande.

5. No/pequeño Esta cámara de video, ¿es suya?/ No, no es mía. La mía era más pequeña.

6. No/de Shakira Estos discos compactos, ¿son suyos?/ No, no son míos. Los míos eran de Shakira.

NOTA CULTURAL

Shakira, a singer/songwriter from Colombia with an unusual and intriguing brand of Latin pop music, skyrocketed at age 18 to the top of the Latin music scene.

3 Conversaciones Completa estas conversaciones con las formas adecuadas de los pronombres posesivos.

1. —La casa de los Ortiz estaba en la avenida 9 de Julio. ¿Dónde estaba la casa de Uds.?
   —__La nuestra__ estaba en la calle Bolívar.
2. —A Carmen le encanta su monitor nuevo.
   —¿Sí? A José no le gusta __el suyo__.
3. —Puse mis discos aquí. ¿Dónde pusiste __los tuyos__, Alfonso?
   —Puse __los míos__ en el escritorio.
4. —Se me olvidó traer mis cintas. ¿Trajeron Uds. __las suyas__?
   —No, dejamos __las nuestras__ en casa.
5. —Yo compré una computadora de Gateway y Marta compró __la suya__ de Dell. ¿De qué marca (*brand*) es __la tuya__?
   —__La mía__ es de IBM.

TEACHING OPTIONS

Large Groups Have students bring in a photo of their favorite car and tell them to imagine that everyone in town is picking up his or her car at the mechanic's shop at the same time. Have students role-play a scene among the mechanic and several customers in which the mechanic tries to determine which car belongs to whom.

Pairs Have students make a wish list consisting of 10 items, then give it to another pair. Students should decide who gets what on the list, justifying their claim. Ex: **La bicicleta nueva es mía. La necesito para ir a la universidad.** Students should try to use at least one possessive adjective or pronoun in their claims.

Comunicación

4 Identificar Trabajen en grupos. Cada persona da tres objetos. Pongan (*Put*) todos los objetos juntos. Luego, una persona escoge uno o dos objetos y le pregunta a otro estudiante si esos objetos son suyos. Usen los pronombres posesivos en sus preguntas. Answers will vary.

modelo

Estudiante 1: *Felipe, ¿son tuyas estas cintas?*
Estudiante 2: *Sí, son mías.*
No, no son mías. Son las cintas de Bárbara.

5 Comparar Trabajen en parejas. Intenta (*Try to*) convencer a tu compañero/a de que algo que tú tienes es mejor que el que él/ella tiene. Pueden hablar de sus carros, estéreos, discos compactos, clases, horarios o trabajos. Answers will vary.

modelo

Estudiante 1: *Mi computadora tiene una pantalla de quince pulgadas (inches). ¿Y la tuya?*
Estudiante 2: *La mía es mejor porque tiene una pantalla de diecisiete pulgadas.*
Estudiante 1: *Pues la mía...*

Síntesis

6 Anuncios Lee este anuncio (*ad*) con un(a) compañero/a. Luego, preparen su propio (*own*) anuncio usando los adjetivos o los pronombres posesivos. Presenten el anuncio a la clase. Answers will vary.

Esta computadora y esta impresora pueden ser suyas por sólo
$899
Características de la computadora
• Procesador: Intel Pentium III a 1000 Mhz
• 256Mb de memoria
• Disco duro de 24 Gb
• Módem: 56 Kbps
• Sistema operativo: Windows 2000
Características de la impresora
• Velocidad 5 páginas por minuto en blanco y negro
• Resolución de 600 x 600
El precio incluye un año de servicio de Internet gratis.
Para más información, llame al 362-1990 o visite nuestro sitio Web www.fiera.com.

TEACHING OPTIONS

Large Group Ask each student to bring in a photo of an object. Tell students not to tell anyone what their object is and place it in a large sack. Call students up one at a time to choose a photo from the sack. Students then circulate around the classroom, trying to find the owner of their photo. Ex: **¿Es tuyo este disco compacto? (No, no es mío.** or **Sí, es mío.)**

Heritage Speakers Have native Spanish speakers imagine that they are salespersons at a car dealership and they are writing a letter to a customer explaining why their cars are better than those of the other two dealerships in town. Students should compare several attributes of the cars and use stressed possessive adjectives and pronouns when appropriate.

4 Suggestion If students can't bring in three objects, have them either find photos of objects or draw them. Students should try to find one feminine, one masculine, and one plural object to do the activity.

5 Warm-up Before beginning the activity, have students make a list of objects to compare. Next, have them brainstorm as many different qualities, or features, of those objects they can think of. Finally, have them list adjectives or other descriptors that they might use to compare the objects they've chosen.

5 Present Ask two volunteers to read the **Modelo**. Encourage students to discuss three different objects and make at least two comparisons for each object. After they have finished practicing with their partners, have students pick their best mini-discussion and present it to the class.

6 Warm-up After students have decided on the product they would like to advertise, have them decide who their target market is and what type of advertising would appeal to that market.

6 Present Have students find a photo or create a drawing of the product in their ad. Next, have them make a list of the product's features, noting what about those features makes their product stand out from the competition. Finally, have them brainstorm sentences that "sell" their product to a target audience. Have students put all these elements together to write their advertisement.

6 Expand Have students decide how they would change their ad if they were to market their product for television or radio.

Section Goals

In **Lectura** students will:
- learn to recognize borrowed words
- increase their reading comprehension in Spanish by using borrowed words to predict content
- read a content-rich text with borrowed words about Internet use in Argentina

Antes de leer

Introduce the strategy. Tell students that recognizing words borrowed from English will help them understand unfamiliar texts.

Examinar el texto Ask students to scan the text for borrowed words. When they are finished, ask volunteers to tell what the text is about. (Internet use in Argentina)

Buscar Ask volunteers to read aloud paragraphs of the text. After each paragraph is read aloud, have a volunteer tell whether the paragraph contains any borrowed words and write them on the board. When students finish the article, model for the whole class the pronunciation of the borrowed words.

Predecir After pairs have answered the questions, go over items 1–3 orally with the whole class. Discuss how borrowed words coupled with other context clues helped them predict content.

Assignment Have students read **Los argentinos atrapados en la Red** and prepare the first two activities in **Después de leer** as homework

Lectura

NATIONAL communication cultures STANDARDS

Antes de leer

Estrategia
Recognizing borrowed words

One way languages grow is by borrowing words from each other. English words that relate to technology are often borrowed by Spanish and other languages throughout the world. Sometimes the words are modified slightly to fit the sounds of the languages that borrow them. When reading in Spanish, you can often increase your understanding by looking for words borrowed from English or other languages you know.

Examinar el texto

Mira brevemente la selección. ¿De qué trata? ¿Cómo lo sabes?

Buscar

Esta lectura contiene varias palabras tomadas del inglés. Trabaja con un(a) compañero/a para encontrarlas. Internet, fax, computadora, clic

Predecir

Trabaja con un(a) compañero/a para contestar las siguientes preguntas.

1. Examina el título, las tablas y el vocabulario. ¿Qué te dicen sobre el contenido del texto?
2. Usa tu experiencia personal para predecir los tipos de tecnologías incluidas en el artículo:
   - ¿Qué tipos de tecnologías se han desarrollado desde que tú naciste?
   - ¿Y en la década pasada?
   - ¿Y en el pasado año?
3. ¿Cómo han afectado las nuevas tecnologías
   - a los empresarios?
   - a los estudiantes?
   - a las familias?

brevemente *briefly* ¿De qué trata? *What is it about?* tomadas *taken* empresarios *business owners*

La tecnología

Los argentinos atrapados en la Red

En el primer año del nuevo milenio, el número de usuarios de Internet superó el millón en la Argentina. Así lo indica un informe con datos recopilados por el gerente de Marketing de Telecom, José Pagés. Asimismo, la conexión al Internet desde los hogares creció un 60 por ciento en el último año.

Como demuestran estas cifras, es sin duda el Internet la novedad tecnológica que está teniendo un mayor impacto social, especialmente entre los jóvenes. En el año 2000 ya existían en el país más de dos millones de computadoras personales—una computadora por cada 15 habitantes. Unas 900.000 máquinas, el 40% del total, están en las viviendas particulares. Los argentinos que instalan una PC en su hogar la utilizan principalmente, al igual que ocurre en los Estados Unidos y en otros países, para recibir y enviar correo electrónico, navegar en la Red en busca de noticias e información, como procesadores de textos y para jugar.

Este apabullante auge en el uso de la Red refleja la aceptación de las novedades tecnológicas en todos los sectores de la sociedad. Las escuelas incorporan la computación como curso oficial desde el año 1990 y las empresas ya trabajan con sofisticadas redes de comunicaciones. Las computadoras y el *fax* no faltan en casi ningún negocio y los niños

La tecnología en la Argentina

1990 Argentina se conectó a la Red junto con Austria, Bélgica, Brasil, Chile, Grecia, India, Irlanda, Corea, España y Suiza.

1995 965 personas de cada 100.000 tenían un teléfono celular.

TEACHING OPTIONS

Extra Practice Provide students with brief texts in Spanish on inflation, unemployment, or a topic that lends itself to numerical expressions, particularly percentages. Ask them to scan the text and write two or three corresponding questions, such as: **¿Cuánto subió la inflación este mes?** Have students exchange articles and questions with a partner and answer one another's questions.

Game Have students describe an type of new technology that has changed their lives; their classmates will guess what they are describing. Tell students to present the most general clues first, moving toward more specific clues: Ex. **Con esto puedo enviar mensajes a mis amigos. Y los amigos míos pueden leerlos y responderme casi inmediatamente. (correo electrónico)**

24D

aprenden con programas de computación educativos. Los gauchos usan teléfono celular y los aficionados al fútbol siguen los partidos internacionales en la televisión por cable.

En este ambiente tecnológico favorable, los servicios de la Red se multiplican. En marzo del año 2000, 52.400 argentinos compraron por Internet y gastaron cerca de 3 millones de pesos. El 98% de los que compraron productos por la Red volvería a hacerlo y el 61% de los que jamás compraron vía Internet está dispuesto a hacerlo este año.

En medio de este gran abanico de posibilidades tecnológicas no hay que olvidar a los jóvenes fanáticos del mundo digital que ya están armando su propia empresa de Internet. Es pues el futuro ya una realidad en la vida de los argentinos, que han descubierto que el mundo tan sólo está a un clic de distancia.

Proyección de usuarios del Internet en la Argentina

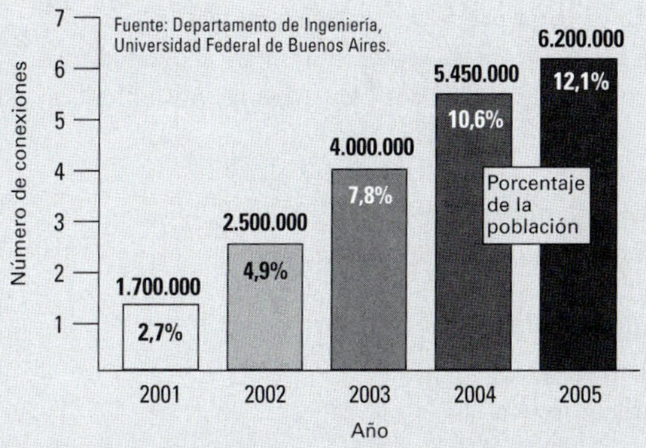

1998 Argentina tenía casi 3.500.000 de abonados a la televisión por cable.

2000 El número de usuarios del Internet superó el millón.

1999 La página web de la Universidad de Buenos Aires (UBA) recibió cerca de 25.000 mensajes de correo electrónico.

superó *exceeded* recopilados *compiled* Asimismo *Likewise*
hogares *homes* mayor *greater* apabullante auge *overwhelming increase*
gauchos *Argentine cowboys* abanico *range*
están armando *are putting together* abonados *subscribers*

Después de leer

Completar

Completa las siguientes frases según el texto.

1. En el año 2000 el número de usuarios superó el millón.
2. Según el artículo, el sector de la población argentina más afectado por los avances tecnológicos es la juventud.
3. Los argentinos utilizan las PC en casa para recibir y enviar correo electrónico, navegar en la Red, como procesadores de textos y para jugar.
4. La computación como curso oficial se estableció en el año mil novecientos noventa.
5. Los aficionados argentinos al fútbol ven partidos internacionales en la televisión por cable.

Interpretar las estadísticas

Responde a las siguientes preguntas utilizando la "Proyección de usuarios del Internet en la Argentina".

1. ¿Entre qué años se proyecta el mayor aumento en el número de usuarios? entre los años 2002 y 2003
2. ¿Para qué año se piensa que casi cinco millones y medio de argentinos van a estar conectados al Internet? para el año 2004
3. Según la proyección, ¿qué porcentaje de la población argentina va a usar el Internet en el año 2002? 4,9%.
4. Según la proyección, ¿qué porcentaje de la población argentina va a tener acceso al Internet en el año 2005? 12,1%

Conversar

Con dos o tres compañeros/as, hablen de los siguientes temas.

1. De todas las nuevas tecnologías que se describen en el artículo, ¿cuáles usan ustedes?
2. ¿Cómo afectan la vida de las personas las tecnologías descritas? ¿Qué aspectos de la vida se simplifican? ¿Qué problemas plantea el desarrollo de nuevas tecnologías?
3. ¿Qué cambios se predicen tanto en los Estados Unidos como en la Argentina debido al creciente (*due to the growing*) número de usuarios del Internet?

Después de leer

Completar

Suggestion If you have assigned this activity as homework, go over the responses with the whole class. If students have difficulty with any item, have them work in pairs to locate the source of that information in the text.

Interpretar las estadísticas

Suggestion You may wish to remind students of the terms **punto** (point, period) and **coma** (comma), as they are used in numerical expressions.

Suggestion Ask students to look at the bar graph on page 351 and remind them that when representing numbers, Spanish generally uses a comma where English speakers would expect a decimal point (in fractions), and a point where English speakers would expect a comma (to separate hundreds).

Suggestion This activity is also appropriate for groups of students to do in class if you have not assigned it as homework. Have volunteers read aloud one question at a time. Ask groups to work together and use the bar graph to answer each question.

Conversar

Suggestion Give small groups ten minutes to complete the activity.

TEACHING OPTIONS

Small Groups Ask students to work in groups of six. Tell them to improvise and create a humorous story as a group. Ask one person in the group to start it off by giving an introductory sentence, such as: **Ayer estuvimos en el coche y ocurrió algo muy raro.** Others add sentences with additional details to complete the story. Encourage students to be creative and make the story as long as they wish.

Pairs Ask students to work together to create answers and corresponding questions. Have one partner create the answers to questions about the Internet. The other partner develops the questions that relate to the answers. Then partners switch roles.

Section Goals

In **Escritura** students will:
- write a narrative using preterite and imperfect
- integrate lesson vocabulary structures in their narrative

Tema

Present Go over the directions with the whole class. Explain that the story or composition students are to write will be about something that occurred in the past. Encourage them to brainstorm as many details as possible about the event before they begin writing. Tell them that one way of organizing a narrative is by chronological order.

Estrategia

Present Write the following sentences on the board: **1. Gloria paró para contestar su teléfono celular. 2. Cuando mi papá era joven, no tenían computadoras. 3. Fue a comprar una computadora la semana pasada. 4. Mis abuelos estaban felices de ver la foto de su nieto en su correo electrónico.** Ask volunteers to explain why the preterite or imperfect tense was used in each case.

Then give the class ten minutes write down actions for their composition in preterite or imperfect and compare their lists with those of a few classmates.

Assignment Have students prepare **Ideas y organización** and **Primer borrador** as homework.

Successful Language Learning Remind your students to check for the correct use of the preterite and the imperfect whenever they write about the past in Spanish. Tell them they may find it helpful to memorize the summary of preterite versus imperfect in the **Estrategia**.

Escritura

NATIONAL communication STANDARDS

Estrategia

Mastering the simple past tenses

In Spanish, when you write about events that occurred in the past you will need to know when to use the preterite and when to use the imperfect tense. A good understanding of the uses of each tense will make it much easier to determine which one to use as you write.

Look at the following summary of the uses of the preterite and the imperfect and write your own example sentence for each of the rules described.

Preterite vs. imperfect

Preterite

1. Actions viewed as completed
____
____
2. Beginning or end of past actions
____
____
3. Series of past actions
____
____

Imperfect

1. Ongoing past actions
____
____
2. Habitual past actions
____
____
3. Mental, physical, and emotional states in the past
____
____

Get together with a few classmates to compare your example sentences. Then use the chart and your example sentences as a guide to help you decide which tense to use as you are writing the sentences of a story or other narration about the past.

Tema

Escribir una historia

Escribe una historia acerca de una experiencia tuya (o de otra persona) con máquinas (*machines*) electrónicas o con carros. Tu historia puede ser real o imaginaria y puede tratar de un incidente divertido, humorístico o desastroso. Incluye todos los detalles posibles. Algunas posibilidades son:

Máquinas electrónicas
- una computadora
- un *fax*
- una impresora
- un teléfono celular
- una videocasetera

Carros
- un carro nuevo
- un accidente
- un problema mecánico
- una llanta pinchada
- un viaje en carro

tratar de *deal with* desastroso *disastrous* pinchada *flat*

TEACHING OPTIONS

Proofreading Activity Copy the following sentences containing mistakes onto the board or a transparency as a proofreading activity to do with the whole class.
1. **David comía un sándwich, mientras buscó información en el Internet por un informe sobre la Argentina.**
2. **Siempre revisé mío correo electrónico por la mañana.**
3. **Pasa para mi apartamento y mira la mía computadora nueva.**
4. **De repente el carro suo se arrancaba.**
5. **Rita y Eugenia se habla para teléfono celular cada día.**
6. **¡Y al clímax del concierto sonaba un teléfono celular! ¡Qué disastre! Siempre apago mío.**

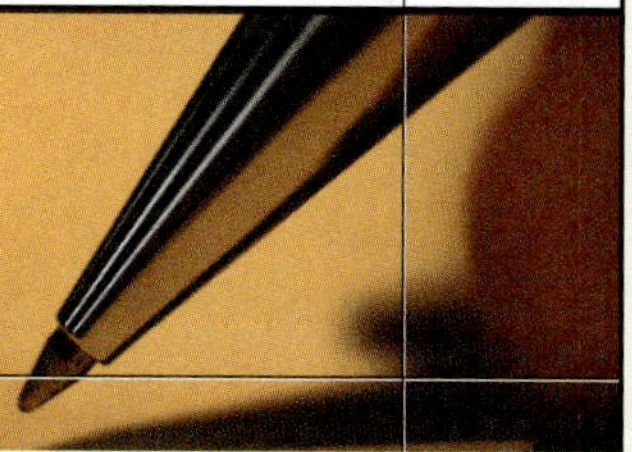

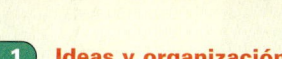

Plan de escritura

1 Ideas y organización

Haz una lista de todos los detalles que quieres narrar. Escoge los detalles más interesantes para tu narración.

2 Primer borrador

Utilizando tus apuntes de **Ideas y organización** y tu lista de los usos del pretérito y el imperfecto, escribe el primer borrador de tu historia.

3 Comentario

Intercambia tu historia con un(a) compañero/a. Lee su borrador y reflexiona sobre las partes mejor escritas de su historia. Comparte tus impresiones. Utiliza esta guía para evaluar el trabajo de tu compañero/a:

1. ¿Son interesantes los detalles de la narración? ¿Necesita más detalles o menos detalles?
2. ¿Contiene redundancias la narración? ¿Cómo pueden eliminarse?
3. ¿Es lógica la secuencia de los eventos?
4. ¿Se usan correctamente el pretérito y el imperfecto?
5. ¿Notas errores de gramática o de ortografía?

4 Redacción

Revisa el primer borrador según las indicaciones de tu compañero/a. Si es necesario, incorpora nuevas ideas para enriquecer la narración de los eventos. Utiliza esta guía para hacer la última revisión antes de escribir tu copia final:

1. Subraya cada verbo para comprobar el uso del pretérito y del imperfecto.
2. Revisa la concordancia entre el sujeto y el verbo de cada frase.
3. Revisa la concordancia entre los sustantivos y los adjetivos.
4. Revisa los pronombres para comprobar el uso correcto de cada uno.
5. Revisa la ortografía y la puntuación otra vez con la ayuda de tus **Anotaciones para mejorar la escritura.**

5 Evaluación y progreso

Reúnete con tres compañeros/as. Doblen la parte superior de cada composición para esconder el nombre del/de la autor(a). Intercambien sus composiciones con otro grupo. Lean los trabajos del otro grupo e intenten determinar de quién es cada composición. Como último paso, lee con interés los comentarios y las correcciones de tu profesor(a), anotando los errores en las **Anotaciones para mejorar la escritura** en tu **Carpeta de trabajos.**

Reúnete *Get together* Doblen *Fold back* esconder *to hide*

EVALUATION: Historia

Criteria	Scale
Content	1 2 3 4
Organization	1 2 3 4
Use of preterite and imperfect	1 2 3 4
Use of vocabulary	1 2 3 4
Accuracy and Mechanics	1 2 3 4

Scoring	
Excellent	18–20 points
Good	14–17 points
Satisfactory	10–13 points
Unsatisfactory	< 10 points

Comentario

Present Go over guide questions 1–5 with the whole class so peer readers understand their task. Then have pairs of students exchange compositions. Allow five minutes for reading and comments. Allow five minutes for discussing comments.

Assignment Have students prepare **Redacción** as homework. Ask them to rewrite their drafts, incorporating the peer comments and following the directions in **Redacción.**

Evaluación y progreso Give the class five minutes to exchange and comment on the final drafts of their compositions. Then have them hand them in to you.

Writing Sample Here is a sample of a composition that would contitute a superior writing achievement.

La tecnología y el abuelo mío

A mi abuelo no le gustaban las cosas nuevas ni los cambios. Era un hombre muy conservador. Pero cuando mi abuela le compró una computadora portátil para su cumpleaños, hubo un gran cambio en casa de mis abuelos.

No sé cómo ocurrió, pero de repente mi abuelo empezó a aprender todo lo que podía acerca de cómo funcionaba la computadora y todos los programas que le interesaban.

Antes escribía todo a mano. Empezó a escribir todo con la computadora: cartas, listas, recetas, y mucho más. Conseguí una conexión Internet y comenzó a enviar mensajes electrónicos a todo el mundo. Aprendió mucho en muy poco tiempo.

Y si eso no fue suficiente, ¡ayer se le compró un teléfono celular a mi abuela!

Section Goals

In **Escuchar** students will:
- practice recognizing the genre of two short examples of spoken discourse
- answer questions based on a broadcast advertisement for a computer center

Instructional Resource
Student Cassette/CD

Preparación
Warm-up Have students look at the photo and describe what they see. Guide them to see that Ricardo Moreno is broadcasting from a radio studio.

Estrategia
Script **(1) Buenos días. Hoy tenemos la gran oportunidad de conversar con el futbolista Carlos Roa del equipo argentino. Carlos, ¿qué opinas del partido que ganaron contra Chile? (2) Buenos días. Ésta es la residencia del arquitecto Rivera. No hay nadie en casa en estos momentos. Por favor, deje un mensaje y lo llamaré lo más pronto posible.**

Assignment Have students do the activities in **Ahora escucha** and **Comprensión** as homework. At that time, verify the responses to **Ahora escucha** with the whole class and go over **Identificar** and **¿Cierto o falso?** by reading each question aloud and calling on different students to answer.

Ahora escucha
Script **¡Por fin! Una computadora que sirve para todas sus necesidades. Con sólo esta modernísima computadora y una línea telefónica de alta velocidad usted tiene a su alcance el infinito mundo del Internet. Le da la conveniencia de mandar un fax por medio del módem interior y de divertirse con su música favorita gracias al CD-ROM. Por el mismo precio, usted también recibe un monitor a colores y una impresora láser. El teclado ha sido diseñado especialmente para no causar dolor en las manos o los brazos. Esta oportunidad sólo se ofrece este mes. Venga inmediatamente a Mundo de Computación en Paseo Las Américas para aprovecharse de esta ganga. O mire el sitio Web en la dirección www.mundodecom.ar.**

Escuchar

Preparación

Mira la foto de Ricardo Moreno. ¿Qué ideas te da sobre el género del discurso que vas a oír?

Estrategia

Recognizing the genre of spoken discourse

You will encounter many different genres of spoken discourse in Spanish. For example, you may hear a political speech, a radio interview, a message on an answering machine, or a news broadcast. Try to identify the genre of what you hear so that you can activate your background knowledge about that type of discourse and identify the speakers' motives and intentions. To practice this strategy, you will now listen to two short selections. Identify the genre of each one. entrevista, mensaje de contestadora

Ahora escucha

Mientras escuchas a Ricardo Moreno, selecciona el género al que corresponde su discurso. Luego, identifica de qué habla y su propósito.

1. ¿Qué tipo de discurso es? c
   a. las noticias por radio o televisión
   b. una conversación entre amigos
   c. un anuncio comercial
   d. una reseña de una película
2. ¿De qué habla? c
   a. del tiempo
   b. de su vida
   c. de un producto o servicio
   d. de algo que oyó o vio
3. ¿Cuál es el propósito? b
   a. relacionarse con alguien
   b. vender
   c. informar
   d. dar opiniones

recursos
R — SCASS./CD Lección 11

Comprensión

Identificar

Indica si la siguiente información está incluida en el discurso; si está incluida, escribe los detalles que escuchaste.

	Sí	No
1. Describe el producto o servicio. *tiene impresora, monitor a colores, fax*	✓	
2. Explica cómo está de salud.		✓
3. Informa sobre cuánto cuesta el producto. *es una ganga*	✓	
4. Pide tu opinión.		✓
5. Explica por qué es mejor que otros productos. *tiene teclado especial*	✓	
6. Informa sobre el tiempo para mañana.		✓
7. Informa dónde se puede conseguir el producto. *en Mundo de Computación*	✓	
8. Informa sobre las noticias del mundo.		✓

Haz un anuncio

Con tres o cuatro compañeros, hagan un anuncio comercial de algún producto. Acuérdense de dar toda la información necesaria. Después presenten su anuncio a la clase.

género *genre* propósito *purpose* noticias *news* anuncio *advertisement* reseña *review*

communication
cultures
connections
communities

Proyecto

Promociona un nuevo cibercafé

Imagina que trabajas para una agencia de publicidad en Argentina. Tienes que crear un anuncio para promocionar un nuevo cibercafé en Buenos Aires.

1 Diseña el anuncio

Crea un anuncio para una revista, teniendo en cuenta el mercado argentino. Usa los **recursos para la investigación** para encontrar información sobre cibercafés en países hispanos. Investiga también el mercado argentino para poder explicar por qué es necesario un nuevo cibercafé en la capital. El anuncio debe:

- describir toda la tecnología que se ofrece a los clientes, incluyendo fotos o dibujos si es posible.
- explicar por qué este cibercafé es mejor que los que ya existen en Buenos Aires.
- hablar de los precios, de la zona donde está ubicado y de otros servicios importantes que se ofrecen en el cibercafé.

2 Presenta la información

Usa el anuncio de revista como base para hacer un anuncio publicitario de radio. Puedes presentar el anuncio a tus compañeros/as en persona o lo puedes grabar para la clase. El anuncio debe animar a tus compañeros/as a visitar el cibercafé.

teniendo en cuenta *keeping in mind* está ubicado *is located* anuncio publicitario *advertisement; commercial* mostrar *to show*

recursos para la investigación

Internet Palabras clave: cibercafé, Buenos Aires, Internet, tecnología	**Comunidad** Personas que conocen los nuevos adelantos en el Internet, o que han estado en un cibercafé, estudiantes o profesores argentinos
Biblioteca Revistas de Internet, periódicos	**Otros recursos** Anuncios de cibercafés en el Internet

Section Goals

In **Proyecto** students will:
- use Spanish as they research and interact with the wider world
- create a magazine advertisement for a cybercafé en Buenos Aires
- create a radio advertisement for the cybercafé

Before Assigning Proyecto

Students will need approximately a week to complete the project, so at the beginning of that time period, have them open their books to page 355 and glance over **Proyecto**. Tell them they are going to create an advertisement for a cybercafé that they will use to make a radio commercial.

Diseña el anuncio Suggestions

- Bring in examples of advertisements for technology products in Spanish-language magazines for students to examine.
- Students may never have heard a Spanish-language radio advertisement. Record some from your local Spanish-language radio station and play them for the class.
- Students may have the capability of creating a banner ad or a Web page to advertise their cybercafé.

Presenta la información Suggestions

- Students may have the capability of videotaping a commercial for their cybercafé.
- You may wish to set aside sufficient class time to do a few presentations at a time until all students have had a chance to present.

EVALUATION: Anuncio

Criteria	Scale
Content	1 2 3 4
Organization	1 2 3 4
Accuracy	1 2 3 4
Creativity	1 2 3 4
Oral Presentation	1 2 3 4

Scoring	
Excellent	18–20 points
Good	14–17 points
Satisfactory	10–13 points
Unsatisfactory	< 10 points

Section Goals

In **Panorama**, students will read about the geography, history, and culture of Argentina.

Instructional Resources
Student Activities Manual: Workbook, 133–134
Transparency 42

Argentina
Before Presenting Panorama Have students look at the map of Argentina or project **Transparency 42**. Ask volunteers to read the labels and discuss the topography of Argentina. Guide students to recognize Argentina's great size and the variety of topographical features, such as mountains (**los Andes**), vast plains (**las pampas**), large rivers.
Assignment Have students read **Panorama** and write out the anwers to the questions in **¿Qué aprendiste?**, page 357, for the next class.

Present Look at the call-out photos and read the labels. Point out that Argentina is one of the largest beef producers in the world and that **gauchos** have played an important role in the culture of the country. **Bariloche** is an important winter recreation area. Remind students that June–August is winter in the southern hemisphere. **Patagonia** is very sparcely populated, but **Buenos Aires** is a metropolis about the size of New York City. Invite students to mention anything they know about Argentina. Then, ask volunteers to read each section of **El país en cifras**.

Increíble pero cierto Under the leadership of General José de San Martín, Argentina won its independence from Spain on July 9, 1816. Like Simón Bolívar, San Martín is venerated as one of the great heroes of Latin America.

Argentina

NATIONAL STANDARDS connections cultures

El país en cifras

- **Área:** 2.780.400 km² (1.074.000 millas²)
Argentina es el país de habla española más grande del mundo. Su territorio es dos veces el tamaño de Alaska.
- **Población:** 37.944.000
- **Capital:** Buenos Aires —12.830.000
En Buenos Aires vive cerca del cuarenta por ciento de la población total del país. La ciudad es conocida como el "París de Sudamérica" por el estilo parisino de muchas de sus calles y edificios.

Buenos Aires

- **Ciudades principales:** Córdoba —1.482.000, Rosario —1.314.000, Mendoza —982.000

SOURCE: Population Division, UN Secretariat

- **Moneda:** peso argentino
- **Idiomas:** español (oficial), guaraní

Bandera de Argentina

Argentinos célebres

- Jorge Luis Borges, escritor (1899–1986)
- María Eva Duarte de Perón ("Evita"), primera dama (1919–1952)
- Mercedes Sosa, cantante (1935–)
- Gato Barbieri, saxofonista (1935–)

conocida *known* parisino *Parisian* primera dama *First Lady* ancha *wide* lado *side* mide *it measures* campo *field*

recursos
R
WB pp. 133-134
vistasonline.com

¡Increíble pero cierto!

La Avenida 9 de Julio en Buenos Aires es la calle más ancha del mundo. De lado a lado mide cerca de 140 metros, lo que es equivalente a un campo y medio de fútbol. Su nombre conmemora el día de la independencia de Argentina.

TEACHING OPTIONS

Worth Noting The Argentinian cowboy, the **gaucho**, has played as significant a role in the folklore of Argentinian as the cowboy of the Old West has played in that of the United States. Two classic works of Argentinan literature focus on the gaucho. **El gaucho Martín Fierro**, an epic poem by José Hernández (1834–1886) celebrates the gaucho's fiercely independent way of life. Diego Sarmiento (1811–1888) subtitled his great work **Facundo: Civilización y barbarie**, and saw the nomadic, uneducated gauchos as hinderances in Argentina's pursuit of economic, social, and political progress.

Extra Practice Have partners listen to a song on one of the many recordings by singer Mercedes Sosa. Then, they can work together to transcribe the lyrics. Invite volunteers to share their work with the class.

BRASIL

Historia • Inmigración europea

Se dice que la Argentina es el país más "europeo" de toda la América Latina. Esto se debe a que, después del año 1880, una gran cantidad de inmigrantes dejó Europa para establecerse en este país. Las diferentes culturas de estos inmigrantes, que venían principalmente de Italia, Alemania, España e Inglaterra, han dejado una profunda huella en la música, el cine, el arte y la arquitectura de la Argentina.

Artes • El tango

El tango, un baile cuyos sonidos y ritmos tienen raíces africanas, italianas y españolas, es uno de los símbolos culturales más importantes de la Argentina. Se originó entre los bonaerenses, muchos de ellos inmigrantes, en la década de 1880. Se hizo popular en París y luego entre la clase alta de Argentina. En un principio, el tango era un baile provocativo y violento, pero se hizo más romántico durante los años 30. Hoy día es popular en todo el mundo.

Lugares • Las cataratas de Iguazú

Entre las fronteras de la Argentina, el Paraguay y el Brasil, al norte de Buenos Aires y cerca de la confluencia de los ríos Iguazú y Paraná, están las famosas cataratas de Iguazú. Estas extensas e imponentes cataratas tienen unos 70 m (230 pies) de altura y, en época de lluvias, llegan a medir 4 km (2.5 mi) de ancho. Situadas en el Parque Nacional de Iguazú, las cataratas son uno de los sitios turísticos más visitados de la América del Sur.

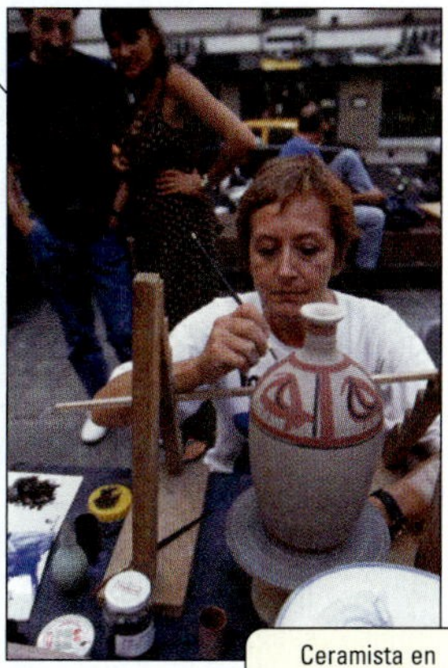
Ceramista en Buenos Aires

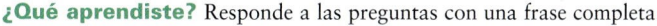

¿Qué aprendiste? Responde a las preguntas con una frase completa.

1. ¿Qué porcentaje de la población de la Argentina vive en la capital?
   Cerca del cuarenta por ciento de la población de la Argentina vive en la capital.
2. ¿Quién es Mercedes Sosa?
   Mercedes Sosa es una cantante argentina.
3. Se dice que la Argentina es el país más europeo de América Latina. ¿Por qué? Se dice que la Argentina es el país más europeo de la América Latina porque muchos inmigrantes europeos se establecieron allí.
4. ¿Qué tipo de baile es uno de los símbolos culturales más importantes de la Argentina?
   El tango es uno de los símbolos culturales más importantes de la Argentina.
5. ¿Dónde y cuándo se originó el tango?
   El tango se originó entre los bonaerenses en la década de 1880.
6. ¿Cómo era el tango en un principio?
   En un principio, el tango era un baile provocativo y violento.
7. ¿En qué parque nacional están las cataratas de Iguazú?
   Las cataratas de Iguazú están en el Parque Nacional de Iguazú.

Conexión Internet Investiga estos temas en el sitio **www.vistasonline.com.**

1. Busca información sobre el tango. ¿Te gustan los ritmos y sonidos del tango? ¿Por qué? ¿Se baila el tango en tu comunidad?
2. ¿Quiénes fueron Juan y Eva Perón y qué importancia tienen en la historia de la Argentina?

Esto se debe a que *This is due to the fact that* principalmente *mainly* han dejado una profunda huella *have left a deep mark* cuyos *whose* raíces *roots* bonaerenses *people of Buenos Aires* En un principio *At first* Hoy día *Nowadays* mundo *world* cataratas *waterfalls* confluencia *junction* imponentes *imposing* altura *height*

TEACHING OPTIONS

Variación léxica Argentinians frequently use the word **¡che!** to get the attention of someone they are talking to. **Che** also serves as a kind of spoken exclamation point with which Argentinians pepper their speech. This is so noticable to outsiders that Argentinians are often given the nickname **Che** in other parts of the Spanish-speaking world. Another notable feature of Argentinian Spanish is the existence, alongside **tú**, of **vos** as the second-person singular familiar pronoun. While **vos** is also heard in other parts of Latin America, in Argentina is it accompanied by corresponding verb forms in the present tense. Here are some equivalents: **vos contás/tú cuentas, vos pensás/tú piensas, vos sos/tú eres, vos ponés/ tú pones, vos venís/tú vienes.**

Inmigración europea Among the European immigrants who arrived in waves on Argentina's shores were thousands of Jews. An interesting chapter in the history of the **pampas** features Jewish **gauchos**. A generous pre-Zionist philanthropist purchased land for Jews who settled on the Argentine grasslands. At one time, the number of Yiddish-language newspapers in Argentina was second only to that of New York City.

El tango The great classic interpreter of tango was Carlos Gardel (1890–1935). If possible, bring in a recording of his version of a tango such as **"Cuesta abajo"** or **"Volver."** A modern exponent of tango was Astor Piazzola (1921–1992). His **tango nuevo** has found interpreters such as chellist Yo-Yo Ma and the Kronos Quartet.

Las cataratas de Iguazú In the **Guaraní** language, Iguazú means "big water." The falls are three times wider than Niagara and have been declared a World Heritage Site by UNESCO. Iguazú National Park was established in 1934 to protect and preserve this natural treasure.

¿Qué aprendiste? Go over the questions and answers with students, making sure everyone understands unfamiliar words and what the correct answers are.

Assignment Have students do activities in **Student Activities Manual: Workbook,** pages 133–134.

Conexión Internet Students will find information about Argentina at **www.vistasonline.com,** as well as links to other sites that can help them in their research.

11 vocabulario

La tecnología

la calculadora	*calculator*
la cámara (de video)	*(video) camera*
el canal	*(TV) channel*
la cinta	*(audio)tape*
la contestadora	*answering machine*
el control remoto	*remote control*
el disco compacto	*compact disk*
el estéreo	*stereo*
el *fax*	*fax (machine)*
el radio	*radio (set)*
el teléfono (celular)	*(cell) telephone*
la televisión por cable	*cable television*
el televisor	*televison set*
el tocadiscos compacto	*compact disk player*
el video(casete)	*video(cassette)*
la videocasetera	*VCR*
el *walkman*	*walkman*
apagar	*to turn off*
funcionar	*to work*
llamar	*to call*
poner, prender	*to turn on*
sonar (o:ue)	*to ring*
descompuesto/a	*not working; out of order*

La computadora

el archivo	*file*
la computadora portátil	*portable computer; laptop*
el disco	*(computer) disk*
la impresora	*printer*
el Internet	*Internet*
el módem	*modem*
el monitor	*(computer) monitor*
la página principal	*home page*
la pantalla	*screen*
el programa de computación	*software*
el ratón	*mouse*
la red	*network; Internet*
el sitio Web	*Web site*
el teclado	*keyboard*
guardar	*to save*
imprimir	*to print*
navegar (en)	*to surf (the Internet)*

El carro

la autopista, la carretera	*highway*
la avenida	*avenue*
el baúl	*trunk*
el bulevar	*boulevard*
la calle	*street*
el camino	*road*
el capó	*hood*
el carro, el coche	*car*
la circulación, el tráfico	*traffic*
los frenos	*brakes*
el garaje, el taller (mecánico)	*garage; (mechanic's) repair shop*
la gasolina	*gasoline*
la gasolinera	*gas station*
el kilómetro	*kilometer*
la licencia de conducir	*driver's license*
la llanta	*tire*
el/la mecánico/a	*mechanic*
la milla	*mile*
el motor	*motor*
la multa	*fine*
el parabrisas	*windshield*
el policía/la mujer policía	*police officer*
la policía	*police (force)*
el semáforo	*traffic light*
la velocidad máxima	*speed limit*
el volante	*steering wheel*
arrancar	*to start*
arreglar	*to fix; to arrange*
bajar	*to go down*
bajar(se) de	*to get off of/out of (a vehicle)*
chocar (con)	*to run into*
conducir, manejar	*to drive*
estacionar	*estacionar to park*
llenar (el tanque)	*to fill (the tank)*
parar	*to stop*
revisar (el aceite)	*to check (the oil)*
subir	*to go up*
subir(se) a	*to get on/into (a vehicle)*
lento/a	*slow*
lleno/a	*full*

Verbos

abrazar(se)	*to hug; to embrace (each other)*
ayudar(se)	*to help (each other)*
besar(se)	*to kiss (each other)*
encontrar(se)	*to meet (each other); to find (each other)*
saludar(se)	*to greet (each other)*

Otras palabras y expresiones

para	*for; in order to*
por	*for; by; by means of; through; along; during; in; because of; due to; in exchange for; for the sake of; on behalf of*
por aquí	*around here*
por ejemplo	*for example*
por eso	*that's why; therefore*
por fin	*finally*

Stressed possessive adjectives and pronouns	*See page 346.*
Expresiones útiles	*See page 333.*

La vivienda

12

Communicative Goals

You will learn how to:

- Welcome people to your home.
- Describe your house or apartment.
- Talk about household chores.
- Give instructions.

contextos

fotonovela

The students arrive at the home of Sra. Vives in Ibarra. After welcoming them, Sra Vives shows them the house and assigns the bedrooms. Don Francisco reminds the students of their early start in the morning.

estructura

adelante

Lectura: Read about **Palacio de las Garzas.**
Escritura: Write a rental agreement.
Escuchar: Listen to a conversation about finding a home.
Proyecto: Plan your dream vacation home.

panorama

Featured Country: Panamá
- The Panamá Canal
- Mola textiles
- Scuba diving in the Caribbean

Lesson Goals

In **Lesson 12** students will be introduced to the following:
- terms for parts of a house
- names of common household objects
- terms for household chores
- rules for capitalization in Spanish
- relative pronouns
- formal commands
- object pronouns with formal commands
- present subjunctive
- subjunctive with verbs and expressions of will and influence
- locating the main parts of a sentence
- using linking words
- writing a lease agreement
- using visual cues while listening
- writing a letter to a contractor describing a house to be built
- cultural and geographic information about Panama

Lesson Preview
Have students look at the photo. Ask: **¿Qué ven en la foto? ¿De dónde salen las chicas? ¿Cómo es la puerta?**

INSTRUCTIONAL RESOURCES

Student Activities Manual: Workbook, 135–146
Student Activities Manual: Lab Manual, 287–292
Student Activities Manual: Video Activities, 349–350
Instructor's Resource Manual: Answer Keys
Tapescript/Videoscript
Overhead Transparencies, 43–46
Student Cassette/CD
Lab Cassette/CD
Video Program
CD-ROM
Website: **www.vistasonline.com**
Testing Program: Prueba A, Prueba B

Section Goals

In **Contextos**, students will learn and practice:
- names of rooms in a home
- names of common household objects
- terms for household chores

Instructional Resources
Student Activities Manual: Workbook, 135–136; Lab Manual, 287
Transparencies 43–44
Student Cassette/CD

Before Presenting Contextos Project **Transparency 43** and describe the house, naming the kinds of rooms and introducing those that aren't shown. Ex: **Ésta es la casa de los Hernández. Hay una sala grande, un dormitorio, una oficina, una cocina y un altillo. También hay un cuarto de baño, un sótano, un patio y un garaje, pero no vemos estos cuartos en la ilustración.** Tell students they are now going to learn vocabulary related to houses.

Assignment Have students study **Contextos** and prepare the exercises on pages 361–362 as homework.

Present Give students two minutes to review the parts of the house on pages 360–361. Then project **Transparency 43**. Ask open-ended questions about the house and housework. Ex: **¿Dónde se pone la comida después de regresar del supermercado? ¿Qué se hace en la oficina?** and so forth. After you have gone over most of the vocabulary, personalize questions, getting students to talk to you and one another about themselves and their living arrangements. ____, **¿vives en una residencia o en un apartamento? ¿Cuántos cuartos hay? Y tú, ____, vives en un apartamento con cinco cuartos?** and so forth.

La vivienda

Más vocabulario

las afueras	*suburbs; outskirts*
el alquiler	*rent (payment)*
el ama (*m., f.*) de casa	*housekeeper; caretaker*
el balcón	*balcony*
el barrio	*neighborhood*
la cafetera	*coffee maker*
el cartel	*poster*
el edificio de apartamentos	*apartment building*
el electrodoméstico	*electrical appliance*
la entrada	*entrance*
la escalera	*stairs; stairway*
el garaje	*garage*
el (horno de) microondas	*microwave (oven)*
el jardín	*garden; yard*
la lavadora	*washing machine*
la luz	*light, electricity*
la mesita de noche	*night stand*
los muebles	*furniture*
el pasillo	*hallway*
el patio	*patio; yard*
la pintura	*painting; picture*
la secadora	*clothes dryer*
el sótano	*basement; cellar*
la tostadora	*toaster*
el/la vecino/a	*neighbor*
la vivienda	*housing*
alquilar	*to rent*
mudarse	*to move (from one house to another)*

Variación léxica

alcoba, dormitorio ⟷ aposento (*Rep. Dom.*); recámara (*Méx.*)
apartamento ⟷ departamento (*Amér. L.*); piso (*Esp.*)
lavar los platos ⟷ lavar/fregar los trastes (*Amér. C., Rep. Dom.*)

recursos

R	SCASS./CD Lección 12	WB pp. 135-136	LM p. 287	LCASS./CD Cass. 6B/CD6

Los quehaceres domésticos

arreglar	*to neaten; to straighten up*
barrer el suelo	*to sweep the floor*
cocinar	*to cook*
ensuciar	*to get (something) dirty*
hacer quehaceres domésticos	*to do household chores*
lavar (el suelo, los platos)	*to wash (the floor, the dishes)*
limpiar la casa	*to clean the house*
planchar la ropa	*to iron the clothes*
quitar la mesa	*to clear the table*

TEACHING OPTIONS

Extra Practice Ask students to complete these analogies.
1. **aspiradora : ____ (alfombra) :: lavadora : ropa** (***aspiradora* es a ____ como *lavadora* es a *ropa***)
2. **frío : calor :: congelador : ____ (horno)**
3. **cama : alcoba :: ____ (escritorio) : oficina**
4. **platos : cocina :: carro : ____ (garaje)**

Variación léxica Ask Spanish speakers to tell the class any other terms they use to refer to rooms in a home. Ex: **alcoba, dormitorio = aposento (*D.R.*), recámara (*Mex.*); lavar los platos = fregar los trastes (*D.R.*); despensa = gabinete (*P.R.*), alacena (*Mex.*)** Also ask Spanish speakers to describe typical homes in their home community.

Práctica

1 Escuchar Escucha la conversación y completa las frases.

1. Pedro va a limpiar primero la sala.
2. Paula va a comenzar en la cocina.
3. Pedro le recuerda (*reminds*) a Paula que debe hacer la cama en la alcoba de huéspedes.
4. Pedro va a planchar la ropa en el sótano.
5. Pedro también va a limpiar la oficina.
6. Ellos están limpiando la casa porque la madre de Pedro va a visitarlos.

2 Escoger Escoge la letra de la respuesta correcta.

1. Cuando quieres salir al aire libre y estás en el tercer piso, vas b.
   a. al pasillo b. al balcón c. al sótano
2. Cuando quieres tener una lámpara y un despertador cerca de tu cama, puedes ponerlos en c.
   a. el barrio b. el cuadro c. la mesita de noche
3. Si no quieres vivir en el centro de la ciudad, puedes mudarte b.
   a. al alquiler b. a las afueras c. a la vivienda
4. Guardamos (*We keep*) los pantalones, las camisas y los zapatos en b.
   a. la secadora b. el armario c. el patio
5. Para subir de la planta baja al primer piso, usamos c.
   a. las entradas b. los carteles c. las escaleras
6. Ponemos cuadros y pinturas en a.
   a. las paredes b. los quehaceres c. los jardines

3 Definiciones En parejas, identifiquen cada cosa que se describe. Luego inventen sus propias descripciones de algunas palabras y expresiones de las páginas 360 y 361.

modelo

Estudiante 1: Si vives en un apartamento, lo tienes que pagar cada mes.

Estudiante 2: el alquiler

1. Es donde pones la cabeza cuando duermes. una almohada
2. Es el quehacer doméstico que haces después de comer. lavar los platos/quitar la mesa
3. Cubren (*They cover*) las ventanas y decoran la sala a la vez (*at the same time*). las cortinas
4. Algunos ejemplos son las cómodas, las mesitas y los sillones. los muebles
5. Son las personas que viven en tu barrio. los vecinos

TEACHING OPTIONS

Small Groups Have groups of three interview each other about their dream house, one conducting the interview, one answering, and one taking notes. At three-minute intervals have students switch roles until each has been interviewer, interviewee, and note-taker. Then pair up the groups and have them report to one another using their notes.

Game Ask students to bring in pictures of mansions, castles or palaces. Divide the class into groups of three, and have each group write a description of the rest of the residence that isn't visible. Have each group read its description aloud. To determine the winner, ask the students to vote for the best description.

Práctica

1 Present Help students check their answers by converting each sentence into a question and asking volunteers to give the correct response. Ex: **¿Qué es lo que va a limpiar Pedro primero? ¿Dónde va a comenzar Paula?**

Tapescript
PEDRO: Paula, tenemos que limpiar toda la casa esta mañana. ¿Por dónde podemos empezar?
PAULA: Pienso empezar por la cocina. Voy a lavar los platos, sacar la basura y barrer el suelo.
PE: Pues, primero voy a limpiar la sala. Necesito pasar la aspiradora y sacudir los muebles.
PA: Despúes de la sala, ¿qué cuarto quieres limpiar?
PE: Después quiero limpiar la oficina.
PA: Entonces yo voy a limpiar la alcoba de huéspedes.
PE: Bueno. Debes hacer la cama en esa alcoba también.
PA: Ya lo sé. Ah, ¿puedes planchar la ropa en el sótano, Pedro?
PE: Sí… Espero que todo vaya bien durante la visita de mi madre.
PA: Sí. Pues yo espero que ella no venga hasta que todo esté limpio. ¡No nos queda mucho tiempo para terminar!
Student Cassette/CD

2 Present Go over the answers by turning the statements into questions. Ex: **Cuando quieres salir al aire libre y estás el tercer piso, ¿adónde vas?**

3 Present Model the activity by reading **Modelo** and providing a second example such as **Sirve para pasar de un cuarto al otro. (el pasillo)**

Successful Language Learning Have students list in English the rooms in their homes and the things in each room, then write the Spanish equivalent of each term.

El comedor
Present Project **Transparency 44** and ask volunteers to name the items on the table. Guide them to mention any item they fail to mention. Then talk about the uses of the silverware (**cubiertos**) and glassware (**cristalería**) and china (**vajilla**) pictured. Ex: **La copa sirve para tomar vino, pero la taza es para el café o el té. • La cuchara sirve para tomar sopa. • El tenedor sirve para llevar a la boca la carne y el pescado.** and so forth.

4 Expand Ask volunteers to answer questions modeled on the partial sentences in Activity 4. Ex: **¿Qué se necesita para comer la carne? Para comer un helado, ¿qué se necesita?**

4 Expand Using pictures from your picture file, ask students what utensils are needed. Ex: **¿Con qué se come este taco? (Con las manos) ¿Qué se necesita para comer este plato de espaguetis? (Un tenedor y una cuchara)** and so forth.

5 Present Before breaking the class into groups, model the activity using your own situation. Ex: **En casa, mi marido siempre pasa la aspiradora, pero yo sacudo los muebles. Mi hijo saca la basura cada noche. Cada uno hace su cama antes de salir de la casa por la mañana.**

5 Expand Ask students to name the worst possible place to have to do each of the chores listed. Ex: **¿Cuál es el lugar donde menos te gustaría sacar la basura? (Yankee Stadium después del *World Series*.) ¿Donde menos te gustaría pasar la aspiradora? (En la Casa Blanca.)**

el comedor

4 Completar Completa las siguientes frases con la palabra más adecuada.

1. Para tomar vino necesitas... una copa
2. Para comer una ensalada necesitas... un tenedor/un plato
3. Para tomar café necesitas... una taza
4. Para poner la comida en la mesa necesitas... un plato/poner la mesa
5. Para limpiarte la boca después de comer necesitas... una servilleta
6. Para cortar (*to cut*) un bistec necesitas... un cuchillo
7. Para tomar agua necesitas... un vaso
8. Para tomar sopa necesitas... una cuchara/un plato

5 Los quehaceres Trabajen en grupos para indicar quién hace estos quehaceres domésticos en su casa. Luego contesten las preguntas. Answers will vary.

pasar la aspiradora	sacar la basura	cocinar
sacudir los muebles	hacer las camas	lavar la ropa
barrer el suelo	lavar los platos	planchar la ropa

- ¿Quién hace más quehaceres, tú o tus compañeros/as?
- ¿Son hombres o mujeres las personas que hacen la mayoría de los quehaceres?
- ¿Piensas que debes hacer más quehaceres? ¿Por qué?

TEACHING OPTIONS

Heritage Speakers Have Spanish-speakers write a comparison and contrast of roles men and women play with regard to domestic chores in their home communities and mainstream United States. Encourage them to include their personal opinions about either or both situations.

Extra Practice Write the following partial sentences on the board, and have the students complete them. **1. Antes de pasar la aspiradora, tienes que... (sacudir los muebles). 2. Después de lavar y secar la ropa, normalmente... (tienes que plancharla). 3. Después de comer, tienes que... (lavar los platos). 4. Tienes que levantarte antes de... (hacer la cama). 5. Antes de sentarse a comer, tienes que... (poner la mesa).**

NATIONAL communication STANDARDS

Comunicación

6 **La vida doméstica** En parejas, describan las habitaciones que ven en estas fotos. Identifiquen y describan seis muebles o adornos (*accessories*) de cada foto y digan tres quehaceres que se pueden hacer en cada habitación. Answers will vary.

7 **Mi apartamento** Dibuja el plano de un apartamento amueblado (*furnished*) imaginario y escribe los nombres de las habitaciones y de los muebles. En parejas, pónganse espalda contra espalda (*sit back to back*). Uno de los dos describe su apartamento mientras su compañero/a lo dibuja según (*according to*) la descripción. Cuando terminen, miren el dibujo que hicieron. ¿Es similar al dibujo original? Hablen de los cambios que se necesitan hacer para mejorar el dibujo. Repitan la actividad intercambiando los papeles (*roles*). Answers will vary.

8 **Un(a) agente inmobiliario/a (*real estate*)** Trabajen en grupos para representar a un(a) agente inmobiliario/a y a sus clientes. El/La agente tiene varias casas para la venta (*for sale*) y debe mostrarlas (*show them*) y hablar de los muebles y del barrio que más le convienen (*suit*) a cada cliente. Los clientes son: Answers will vary.

- Una pareja que está esperando su segundo hijo
- Una pareja de jubilados que quieren tranquilidad
- Un grupo de estudiantes universitarios que quiere vivir fuera del campus (*off campus*) los últimos años de universidad
- Una familia con cinco niños

6 Present Model the activity using a picture from your picture file. Ex: (displaying a picture of a messy dining room) **¡Qué comedor más desordenado! ¡Es un desastre! Alguien debe quitar los platos sucios de la mesa. También es necesario sacudir los muebles y pasar la aspiradora. La mesa y las sillas son muy bonitas, pero el comedor está muy sucio ahora.**

6 Present Give students three minutes to look at the pictures and brainstorm possible answers before assigning pairs.

7 Warm-up Draw a map of a three-room apartment on the board. Ask volunteers to describe it.

7 Present Have students draw their maps before you assign pairs. Make sure they understand the activity so that their maps do not become too complicated.

7 Expand Have students make the suggested changes on their maps and repeat the activity again with a different partner.

8 Warm-up Before forming groups, have students work in pairs to brainstorm the topic. Suggest they use an idea map to jot down their ideas about **muebles** and **barrio** for each client.

8 Expand Ask different groups to describe one of the houses and neighborhoods they invented. Have the rest of the class guess for which client it was designed.

Assignment Have students do the activities in **Student Activities Manual: Workbook**, pages 135–136.

TEACHING OPTIONS

Extra Practice Have students complete the following cloze activity: **La vida doméstica de un estudiante universitario puede ser un desastre, ¿no? Nunca hay tiempo para hacer los ____ (quehaceres) domésticos. Sólo ____ (pasa) la aspiradora una vez al semestre y nunca ____ (sacude) los muebles. Los ____ (platos) sucios se acumulan en la ____ (cocina). Saca la ropa de la ____ (secadora) y la pone sin ____ (planchar). Y, ¿por qué hacer la ____ (cama)? ¡Se va a acostar en ella de nuevo este mismo día, ¿no?**

Game Have students bring in real-estate ads. Ask groups of three to write a description of a property. Groups then take turns reading their descriptions aloud. Other groups guess the price. The group that guesses the amount closest to the real price without going over scores a point.

Section goals

In **Fotonovela** students will:
- receive comprehensible input from free-flowing discourse
- learn functional phrases that preview lesson grammatical structures

Instructional Resources
Student Activities Manual: Video Activities 349–350
Video Program (Start: 01:04:59)

Video Synopsis Don Francisco and the students go to the house where they will stay before their hike. The housekeeper shows the students around the house. Don Francisco tells the students to help with the chores, and he advises them that their guide for the hike will arrive at seven the next morning.

Before Presenting Fotonovela Have your students guess what happens in this **Fotonovela** episode, based on its title and the video stills.

Assignment Have students study **Fotonovela** and **Expresiones útiles** as homework.

Warm-up Ask the class if this **Fotonovela** episode was what they expected, based on the predictions they made in the previous class. Through discussion, guide the class to a correct summary of the plot.

Present Read the **Expresiones útiles** aloud and have the class repeat. Check comprehension of this active vocabulary by asking **¿Cómo se dice...?** questions. Ex: **¿Cómo se dice en español *This is the living room?***

Continued on page 365.

¡Les va a encantar la casa!

Don Francisco y los estudiantes llegan a Ibarra.

PERSONAJES

INÉS

DON FRANCISCO

ÁLEX

JAVIER

SRA. VIVES

SRA. VIVES ¡Hola, bienvenidos!

DON FRANCISCO Sra. Vives, le presento a los chicos. Chicos, ésta es la Sra. Vives, el ama de casa.

SRA. VIVES Encantada. Síganme que quiero mostrarles la casa. ¡Les va a encantar!

SRA. VIVES Esta alcoba es para los chicos. Tienen dos camas, una mesita de noche, una cómoda... En el armario hay más mantas y almohadas por si las necesitan.

SRA. VIVES Ésta es la sala. El sofá y los sillones son muy cómodos. Pero, por favor, ¡no los ensucien!

SRA. VIVES Allí están la cocina y el comedor. Al fondo del pasillo hay un baño.

DON FRANCISCO Chicos, a ver... ¡atención! La Sra. Vives les va a preparar las comidas. Pero quiero que Uds. la ayuden con los quehaceres domésticos. Quiero que arreglen sus alcobas, que hagan las camas, que pongan la mesa... ¿entendido?

JAVIER No se preocupe... la vamos a ayudar en todo lo posible.

ÁLEX Sí, cuente con nosotros.

recursos

R	VIDEO Lección 12	VM pp. 349-350

TEACHING OPTIONS

Video Tips General suggestions for using video clips in the classroom can be found on page IAE-13 of the **Instructor's Annotated Edition**.

¡Les va a encantar la casa! Play the last half of the **Lesson 12** video episode, except the **Resumen** segment. Have your students summarize what they see and hear. Then have the class predict what will happen in the first half of the video episode, based on their observations. Write their predictions on the board. Then play the entire episode, including the **Resumen**, and, through discussion, guide the class to a correct summary of the plot.

SRA. VIVES Javier, no ponga las maletas en la cama. Póngalas en el piso, por favor.

SRA. VIVES Tomen Uds. esta alcoba, chicas.

INÉS Insistimos en que nos deje ayudarla a preparar la comida.

SRA. VIVES No, chicos, no es para tanto, pero gracias por la oferta. Descansen un rato que seguramente están cansados.

ÁLEX Gracias. A mí me gustaría pasear por la ciudad.

INÉS Perdone, don Francisco, ¿a qué hora viene el guía mañana?

DON FRANCISCO ¿Martín? Viene temprano, a las siete de la mañana. Les aconsejo que se acuesten temprano esta noche. ¡Nada de televisión ni de conversaciones largas!

ESTUDIANTES ¡Ay, don Francisco!

Enfoque cultural Las viviendas

Del mismo modo que en los países hispanos era típico construir las ciudades en torno a una plaza central, también era común construir las casas alrededor de un patio abierto central. Aunque esta arquitectura tradicional ya no es muy común, la importancia del patio sigue intacta en la cultura hispana. No es extraño ver crecer árboles de mangos y de aguacates en los patios de las casas de los países tropicales de América Latina. En el sur de España, los geranios y otras flores alegran los balcones y terrazas de las viviendas.

Expresiones útiles

Welcoming people

- **¡Bienvenido(s)/a(s)!**
  Welcome!

Showing people around the house

- **Síganme que quiero mostrarles la casa.**
  Follow me... I want to show you the house.
- **Esta alcoba es para los chicos.**
  This bedroom is for the guys.
- **Ésta es la sala.**
  This is the living room.
- **Allí están la cocina y el comedor.**
  The kitchen and dining room are over there.
- **Al fondo del pasillo hay un baño.**
  At the end of the hall there is a bathroom.

Telling people what to do

- **Quiero que la ayude(n) con los quehaceres domésticos.**
  I want you to help her with the household chores.
- **Quiero que arregle(n) su(s) alcoba(s).**
  I want you to straighten your room(s).
- **Quiero que haga(n) las camas.**
  I want you to make the beds.
- **Quiero que ponga(n) la mesa.**
  I want you to set the table.
- **Cuente con nosotros.**
  You can count on us.
- **Insistimos en que nos deje ayudarla a preparar la comida.**
  We insist that you let us help you make the food.
- **Le (Les) aconsejo que se acueste(n) temprano.**
  I recommend that you go to bed early.

Other expressions

- **No es para tanto.**
  It's not a big deal.
- **Gracias por la oferta.**
  Thanks for the offer.

To practice pronunciation, read a few lines from the **Fotonovela** aloud, having students repeat after you. Then have the class read through the entire **Fotonovela**, with volunteers playing the various parts. Model correct pronunciation as needed. See ideas for using the video in **Teaching Options**, page 364.

Comprehension Check Check comprehension of the **Fotonovela** episode by doing Activity 1, **¿Cierto o falso?**, page 366, orally with the whole class.

Suggestion Have the class look at the **Expresiones útiles**. Point out that the verbs **Síganme** and **Cuente** are command forms. Have the class guess which is an **usted** command and which is an **ustedes** command. Then point out the sentences that begin with **Quiero que…**, **Insistimos en que…**, and **Le (les) aconsejo que.** Explain that these sentences are examples of the present subjunctive with verbs of will or influence. Write two or three of these sentences on the board. Point out that the main clause in each sentence contains a verb of will or influence, while the subordinate clause contains a verb in the present subjunctive. Tell your students that they will learn more about these concepts in the upcoming **Estructura** section.

The Affective Dimension Tell students that travelers in a foreign country may feel culture shock for a while. These feelings are normal and tend to diminish with time.

Assignment Have students do Activities 2–4 in **Reacciona a la fotonovela**, page 366, as homework.

TEACHING OPTIONS

Enfoque cultural The "traditional" houses built around patios described here have very ancient roots, going back to the style of houses built by the Romans. The traditional Spanish house made a very clear separation between the interior of the house, which was a private and protected space, and the street, which was public and exposed. Modern residents of large cities in Spanish-speaking countries generally live in apartments, which are usually rented but are sometimes owned by the occupants. Explain that the first floor (**planta baja**) of many multistory buildings is occupied by places of business, while the upper floors consist of apartments. Point out that is not unusual for an apartment dweller in the United States to refer to his or her home as a house; explain that in Spanish-speaking countries, the word **casa** is often used in the same way.

Reacciona a la fotonovela

1 Expand Give these additional items to the class: **6. Álex quiere descansar. (Falso. Álex quiere pasear por la ciudad.) 7. Martín va a llegar mañana a las cuatro de la tarde. (Falso. Martín va a llegar a las siete de la mañana.**

2 Warm-up Have the class skim the **Fotonovela** on pages 364–365 before they begin this activity.

2 Expand Write these additional items on the board: **6. Ésta es la alcoba de las chicas. (Sra. Vives) 7. El guía va a llegar a las siete de la mañana. (don Francisco) 8. ¿Quieren descansar un rato? (Sra. Vives) 9. Chicos, les presento a la Sra. Vives. (don Francisco)**

3 Present This activity can be done either orally or in writing. It is suitable for whole-class work, group work, or pair work.

3 Expand Have your students work in pairs to write a new sentence in Spanish for each of the words in the word bank.

4 Possible response
S1: Quiero mostrarte mi casa. Ésta es la sala. Me gusta mirar la televisión allí. Aquí está la oficina. Allí hablo por teléfono y trabajo en la computadora. Éste es el garaje. Es donde tengo mis dos coches. Y aquí está la cocina, donde preparo las comidas. Quiero que me ayudes a sacudir los muebles y pasar la aspiradora.
S2: Está bien. Ahora quiero mostrarte mi apartamento....

Reacciona a la fotonovela

1 **¿Cierto o falso?** Indica si lo que dicen las siguientes frases es **cierto** o **falso**. Corrige las frases falsas.

	Cierto	Falso
1. Las alcobas de los estudiantes tienen dos camas, dos mesitas de noche y una cómoda. Tienen sólo una mesita de noche.	❍	✓
2. La señora Vives no quiere que Javier ponga las maletas en la cama.	✓	❍
3. El sofá y los sillones están en la sala.	✓	❍
4. Los estudiantes tienen que sacudir los muebles y sacar la basura. Tienen que arreglar las alcobas, hacer las camas y poner la mesa.	❍	✓
5. Los estudiantes van a preparar las comidas. La señora Vives va a preparar las comidas.	❍	✓

2 **Identificar** Identifica quién puede decir las siguientes frases.

1. Nos gustaría preparar la comida esta noche. ¿Le parece bien a Ud.? Inés
2. Miren, si quieren otra almohada o manta, hay más en el armario. Sra. Vives
3. Tranquilo, tranquilo, que nosotros vamos a ayudarla muchísimo. Javier
4. Tengo ganas de caminar un poco por la ciudad. Álex
5. No quiero que nadie mire la televisión esta noche. ¡Tenemos que levantarnos temprano mañana! don Francisco

3 **Completar** Completa las frases con la palabra correcta de la siguiente lista.

el garaje	la cocina	la sala
la alcoba	la oficina	el sótano

1. ¿Tienes hambre? Ahora mismo voy a preparar la cena en la cocina.
2. ¡Qué cansada estoy! Creo que voy a dormir un rato en la alcoba.
3. ¿Quieres conversar un rato o mirar la televisión? ¿Por qué no vamos a la sala?
4. Oye, quiero mirar la televisión contigo pero primero tengo que escribir un mensaje electrónico en la oficina.
5. El coche está descompuesto y no lo podemos usar. Ahora está en el garaje.

4 **Mi casa** Dibuja el plano (*floor plan*) de una casa o de un apartamento. Puede ser el plano de la casa o del apartamento donde vives o de donde te gustaría vivir. Después, trabajen en parejas y describan lo que se hace en cuatro de las habitaciones. Para terminar, pídanse (*ask for*) ayuda para hacer dos quehaceres domésticos. Pueden usar estas frases en su conversación. Answers will vary.

Quiero mostrarte...
Ésta es (la cocina).
Allí yo (preparo la comida).
Al fondo hay...
Quiero que me ayudes a (sacar la basura).

NATIONAL communication STANDARDS

TEACHING OPTIONS

TPR Have the class label various parts of the classroom with the names of rooms one would typically find in a house. Then have groups of three perform a skit in which the owner of the house is showing it to two inquisitive exchange students who are going to be spending the semester there. Give the groups time to prepare.

Game Have each of your students write a few sentences that one of the characters in this **Fotonovela** episode would say. They can look at the **Fotonovela** for ideas, but they shouldn't copy sentences from it word for word. Then have each student read his or her sentences to the class. The class will guess which character would say those things.

Ortografía

Las mayúsculas y las minúsculas

Here are some of the rules that govern the use of capital letters (**mayúsculas**) and lowercase letters (**minúsculas**) in Spanish.

Los estudiantes llegaron al aeropuerto a las dos.
Luego fueron al hotel.

In both Spanish and English, the first letter of every sentence is capitalized.

Rubén Blades **Panamá** **Colón** **los Andes**

The first letter of all proper nouns (names of people, countries, cities, geographical features, etc.) is capitalized.

Cien años de soledad ***Don Quijote de la Mancha***
El País ***Muy Interesante***

The first letter of the first word in titles of books, films, and works of art is generally capitalized, as well as the first letter of any proper names. In newspaper and magazine titles, as well as other short titles, the initial letter of each word is often capitalized.

la señora Ramos **don Francisco**
el presidente **Sra. Vives**

Titles associated with people are not capitalized unless they appear as the first word in a sentence. Note, however, that abbreviated titles are capitalized.

Último **Álex** **MENÚ** **PERDÓN**

Accent marks should be retained on capital letters. In practice, however, this rule is often ignored.

lunes **viernes** **marzo** **primavera**

The first letter of days, months, and seasons are not capitalized.

español **estadounidense** **japonés** **panameños**

The first letter of nationalities and languages are not capitalized.

Práctica Corrige las mayúsculas y minúsculas incorrectas.

1. soy lourdes romero. Soy Colombiana. Soy Lourdes Romero. Soy colombiana.
2. éste Es mi Hermano álex. Éste es mi hermano Álex.
3. somos De panamá. Somos de Panamá.
4. ¿es ud. La sra. benavides? ¿Es Ud. la Sra. Benavides?
5. ud. Llegó el Lunes, ¿no? Ud. llegó el lunes, ¿no?

Palabras desordenadas Lee el diálogo de las serpientes. Ordena las letras para saber de qué palabras se trata. Después escribe las letras indicadas para descubrir por qué llora Pepito.

Profesor Herrera, ¿es cierto que somos venenosas?
Sí, Pepito. ¿Por qué lloras?

m n a a P á ◯_ _ _ _ _ _
s t e m r a ◯_ _ _ _ _ _
i g s l é n _ _ _ ◯ _ _
y a U r u g u _ _ _ ◯ _ _ _
r o ñ e s a _ _ _ _ _ ◯

¡ _orque ___e acabo de morder la _en_u_!

1 Respuestas: Panamá, martes, inglés, Uruguay, señora. ¡Porque me acabo de morder la lengua!

venenosas *venomous*
morder *to bite*

Section Goals

In **Ortografía** students will learn about the rules for capitalization in Spanish.

Present

- Explain that both Spanish and English follow the same rules for capitalizing the first word of a sentence and proper names. Explain that in a few Spanish city and country names the definite article is considered part of the name, and is thus capitalized. Ex: **La Habana, La Coruña, La Haya, El Salvador**
- Spanish treatment of titles of books, film, and works of art differs from English. In Spanish, only the first word and any proper noun gets an initial capital. Spanish treatment of the names of newspapers and magazines is the same as in English. Tell students that **El País** is a newspaper and **Muy Interesante** is a magazine. All the items mention are italicized in print.
- Say that common titles of respect (**señor, señora, señorita, don,** and **doña**) are capitalized only when they are abbreviated or are the first word in a sentence.
- Mention that accent marks should be maintained on capital letters. Write the examples on the board; ask which letters should be capitalized.
- Say that the first letters of days, months, seasons, nationalities, and languages aren't capitalized except at the beginning of a sentence. Ask the class for some examples.

Práctica/Palabras desordenadas Work through these activities with the class to practice the use of capital letters and lowercase letters.

TEACHING OPTIONS

Pair Work Have your students work in pairs to circle all the capital letters in the **Enfoque cultural** on page 365. Then have them explain why each of these letters is capitalized. Afterward have them look through the **Enfoque cultural** for examples of uncapitalized words discussed in **Ortografía**.

Extra Practice Give this sentence to the class as a dictation: **El Dr. Guzmán, el amigo panameño de la Srta. Rivera, llegó a Quito el lunes doce de mayo.** Tell the class to abbreviate all titles. To allow your students time to write, read the sentence twice slowly and once at full speed. Then write the sentence on the board so that they can check their work.

Section Goal

In **Estructura 12.1** students will learn the relative pronouns and their use.

Instructional Resources *Student Activities Manual: Workbook, 137–138; Lab Manual, 289.*

Before Presenting Estructura 12.1 Have students open to the **Fotonovela**, 364–365. Ask open-ended questions about the situation and then rephrase the students' short answers into sentences using relative pronouns. Write your sentences on the board and underline the relative pronoun. Ex: **¿Quién va a preparar la comida? (la Sra. Vives) Sí, ella es la persona que va a preparar la comida. ¿Qué cuarto tiene un sofá y sillones cómodos? (la sala) Sí, la sala es el cuarto que tiene un sofá y sillones cómodos.** Tell students that they will now learn more about the use of relative pronouns.

Assignment Have students study **Estructura 12.1** and prepare the exercises on pages 369–370 as homework.

Present Work through the discussion of relative pronouns point by point, writing examples on the board.

Suggestion Discuss the term *relative pronoun* with students. Review the function of a pronoun and explain that a *relative* pronoun is one that *relates* a subordinate clause back to a noun or pronoun in the main clause.
Point out that *that, which, who,* and *whom* are all usually translated as **que**, but that when a relative pronoun referring to a person is the object of a preposition, **quien** is used. Emphasize the lack of accents on relative pronouns.

Continued on page 369.

12.1 Relative pronouns

NATIONAL STANDARDS comparisons

ANTE TODO In both English and Spanish, relative pronouns are used to combine two sentences or clauses that share a common element, such as a noun or pronoun. Study the following diagram.

Éste es **el cuarto** de Manuela.
This is Manuela's room.

Ella usa **el cuarto** para estudiar.
She uses the room to study.

Éste es el cuarto **que** Manuela usa para estudiar.
This is the bedroom that Manuela uses to study.

Lourdes es muy inteligente.
Lourdes is very intelligent.

Lourdes estudia español.
Lourdes is studying Spanish.

Lourdes, **quien** estudia español, es muy inteligente.
Lourdes, who studies Spanish, is very intelligent.

Pueden usar las almohadas que están en el armario.

Chicos, ésta es la Sra. Vives, quien les va a mostrar la casa.

- Spanish has three frequently-used relative pronouns, as shown in the following list.

que	*that; which; who*
quien(es)	*who; whom; that*
lo que	*that which; what*

¡ATENCIÓN!
Interrogative words (**qué**, **quién**, etc.) always carry an accent. Relative pronouns, however never carry a written accent.

- **Que** is the most frequently used relative pronoun. It can refer to things or to people. Unlike its English counterpart, *that*, **que** is never omitted.

¿Dónde está la cafetera **que** compré?
Where is the coffee maker (that) I bought?

El hombre **que** limpia es Pedro.
The man who is cleaning is Pedro.

- The relative pronoun **quien** refers only to people and is often used after a preposition or the personal **a.** Note that **quien** has only two forms: **quien** (singular) and **quienes** (plural).

¿Son las chicas **de quienes** me hablaste la semana pasada?
Are they the girls you told me about last week?

Eva, **a quien** conocí anoche, es mi nueva vecina.
Eva, whom I met last night, is my new neighbor.

TEACHING OPTIONS

Extra Practice Write the following sentences on the board, and have the student supply the correct relative pronoun: **1. Hay una escalera ____ (que) sube a la primera planta. 2. Elena es la muchacha a ____ (quien) presté la aspiradora. 3. ¿Dónde pusiste la ropa ____ (que) acabas de quitarte? 4. ¿Cuál es el señor de____ (quien) alquilas tu casa? 5. La cómoda ____ (que) compramos la semana pasada está en el dormitorio de mi hermana.**

Heritage Speakers Have Spanish speakers create descriptions of favorite gathering places in their home communities using complex sentences with relative pronouns. Possible sites might be the local parish, the town square, or a favorite park.

¡LENGUA VIVA!
In English, it is generally recommended to use *who(m)* to refer to people, and to use *that* and *which* to refer to things. In Spanish, however, it is perfectly acceptable to use **que** when referring to people.

▶ **Quien(es)** is occasionally used instead of **que** in clauses set off by commas.

Lola, **quien** es cubana, es médica.
Lola, who is Cuban, is a doctor.

Su tía, **que** es alemana, ya llegó.
His aunt, who is German, already arrived.

▶ Unlike **que** and **quien(es), lo que** doesn't refer to a specific noun. It refers to an idea, a situation, or a past event and means *what, that which,* or *the thing that.*

Este mercado tiene todo lo que Inés necesita.

A la Sra. Vives no le gustó lo que hizo Javier.

Este mercado tiene todo **lo que** Inés necesita.
This market has everything that Inés needs.

A la Sra. Vives no le gustó **lo que** hizo Javier con sus maletas.
Mrs. Vives didn't like what Javier did with his suitcases.

Lo que me molesta es el calor.
What bothers me is the heat.

Lo que quiero es una casa.
What I want is a house.

¡INTÉNTALO! Completa las siguientes oraciones con pronombres relativos.

1. Voy a utilizar los platos ___que___ me regaló mi abuela.
2. Ana comparte una casa con la chica a ___quien___ conocimos en la fiesta de Jorge.
3. Este apartamento tiene todo ___lo que___ necesitamos.
4. Puedes estudiar en la alcoba ___que___ está a la derecha de la cocina.
5. Los señores ___que___ viven en esa casa acaban de llegar de Centroamérica.
6. Los niños a ___quienes___ viste en nuestro jardín son mis sobrinos.
7. La piscina ___que___ ves desde la ventana es la piscina de mis vecinos.
8. Fue Úrsula ___quien___ ayudó a mamá con los quehaceres.
9. Ya te dije que es mi padre ___quien___ alquiló el apartamento.
10. ___Lo que___ te dijo Pablo no es cierto.
11. Tengo que sacudir los muebles ___que___ están en el altillo una vez al mes.
12. No entiendo por qué no lavaste los platos ___que___ te dije.
13. La mujer a ___quien___ saludaste vive en las afueras.
14. ¿Sabes ___lo que___ necesita esta alcoba?
15. ¡No quiero volver a hacer ___lo que___ hice ayer.
16. No me gusta vivir con personas a ___quien___ no conozco.

Test comprehension as you proceed by asking volunteers to answer questions about students and objects in the classroom. Ex: **¿Cómo se llama la estudiante que se sienta detrás de ____? ¿Cómo se llama el estudiante que entró en la clase tarde? ¿Cómo se llaman los estudiantes a los quienes acabo de hacer una pregunta? ¿Dónde está la tarea que Uds. hicieron para hoy?** and so forth.

Point out that **lo que** refers back, not to a specific noun, but to the content of the whole clause that preceeds it. Ex: **¿Tiene este apartamento lo que necesita Ud.? ¿Pudo Ud. comprar lo que quería en el mercado? Mario, este cuarto es un desastre, lo que me molesta mucho.**

Expand In the chalk tray, line up four to five pictures from your picture file. Ask questions that use relative pronouns or elicit them in student answers. Ex: **—¿Quién está comiendo una hamburguesa? —El muchacho que está sentado en la playa come una hamburguesa. • —¿Quién sabe lo que hace esta muchacha? • —A quién le da dinero este joven?**

Expand Ask students to make two short lists: **Lo que tengo en mi casa/Lo que quiero tener en mi casa.** Ask volunteers to read part of their lists to the class. Encourage a conversation by asking questions such as: **¿Es esto lo que tienes en casa tuya? ¿Es un ____ lo que quieres tú?**

Close Do **¡Inténtalo!** orally with the whole class.

TEACHING OPTIONS

Video Show the video again to give students more input containing relative pronouns. Stop the video where appropriate to discuss how relative pronouns were used.
Game Ask students to bring in some interesting pictures from magazines or the Internet, but tell them not to show these photos to one another. Divide the class into groups of three. Each group should pick a picture. One student will write an accurate description of it, and the others will write imaginary descriptions. Tell them to use relative pronouns in the descriptions. Each group will read its three descriptions aloud without showing the picture. Give the rest of the class two minutes to ask questions about the descriptions before guessing which is the accurate description. Award one point for a correct guess and two points to the team able to fool the class.

1 Warm-up Quickly review the relative pronouns **que, quien, quienes,** and **lo que,** asking volunteers to give an example of each.

1 Present Go over the activity with the whole class, asking different individuals to read each completed sentence and explain why they chose the completion they did.

1 Expand Ask students to write their own completions to each of the partial sentences. Then go over each item orally with the class, asking several volunteers to read their completions of the sentences.

2 Expand Ask questions about the content of the activity. **¿Quiénes quieren comprar una casa? (Jaime y Tina) ¿Qué casa quieren comprar? (Una casa que está en las afueras de la ciudad.) ¿De quién era la casa? (de una artista famosa) ¿Cómo venden la casa? (con todos los muebles que tenía) ¿Qué tipo de alfombra tiene la sala? (una alfombra persa que la artista trajo de Kuwait)**

3 Present Read aloud the **Modelo**, pointing out that the article **los** is replaced by the relative pronoun **que**.

3 Expand Have students pair up to write two more sentences about Javier and Ana's new home that contain relative pronouns.

Práctica

1 Combinar Combina elementos de la columna A y la columna B para formar oraciones lógicas.

A

1. Ése es el hombre __d__.
2. La mujer __a__.
3. No traje __e__.
4. ¿Te gusta el regalo __b__?
5. ¿Cómo se llama el programa __g__?
6. El profesor Montero, __c__.

B

a. con quien bailaba Fernando se llama Isabel
b. que te compró Cecilia
c. quien enseña biología en la universidad, es de Panamá
d. que arregló mi auto
e. lo que necesito para la clase de matemáticas
f. que comiste en el restaurante
g. que viste en la televisión anoche

2 Completar Completa la historia sobre la casa que Jaime y Tina quieren comprar, usando los pronombres relativos **que, quien, quienes** o **lo que.**

1. Jaime y Tina son los chicos a __quienes__ conocí la semana pasada.
2. Quieren comprar una casa __que__ está en las afueras de la ciudad.
3. Es una casa __que__ era de una artista famosa.
4. La artista, a __quien__ yo conocía, murió el año pasado y no tenía hijos.
5. Ahora se vende la casa con todos los muebles __que__ ella tenía.
6. La sala tiene una alfombra persa __que__ trajo de Kuwait.
7. Los armarios de toda la casa tienen mucho espacio, __lo que__ a Tina le encanta.

3 Combinar Javier y Ana acaban de casarse y han comprado una casa y muchas otras cosas. Combina sus declaraciones para formar una sola oración con los pronombres relativos **que, quien(es)** y **lo que.**

modelo

Vamos a usar los cubiertos nuevos mañana. Los pusimos en el comedor.
Mañana vamos a usar los cubiertos nuevos que pusimos en el comedor.

1. Tenemos una cafetera nueva. Mi prima nos la regaló.
   Tenemos una cafetera nueva que mi prima nos regaló.
2. Tenemos una cómoda nueva. Es bueno porque no hay espacio en el armario.
   Tenemos una cómoda nueva, lo que es bueno porque no hay espacio en el armario.
3. Esos platos no nos costaron mucho. Están encima del horno.
   Esos platos que están encima del horno no nos costaron mucho.
4. Esas copas me las regaló mi amiga Amalia. Ella viene a visitarme mañana.
   Esas copas me las regaló mi amiga Amalia, quien viene a visitarme mañana.
5. La lavadora está casi nueva. Nos la regalaron mis suegros.
   La lavadora que nos regalaron mis suegros está casi nueva.
6. La vecina nos dio una manta de lana. Ella la compró en México.
   La vecina nos dio una manta de lana que compró en México.

TEACHING OPTIONS

Extra Practice Have students use relative pronouns to complete this paragraph. ____ **(Lo que) tenemos que hacer es buscar otro apartamento ____ (que) se alquila. El apartamento ____ (que) tenemos sólo tiene dos alcobas. Necesitamos un apartamento ____ (que) tiene tres. Ayer hablamos con un compañero ____ (que) alquila una casa cerca de aquí. Buscamos algo similar a ____ (lo que) él tiene: tres alcobas, una cocina, una sala y dos cuartos de baño... ¡y un alquiler bajo! Nos dio el nombre de varios agentes a ____ (quienes) podemos contactar para más información.**

Pairs Ask students to write a description of a new household gadget, using relative pronouns. Their descriptions should include the purpose of the gadget and how it is used.

NATIONAL communication STANDARDS

Comunicación

4 **Entrevista** En parejas, túrnense para hacerse las siguientes preguntas. Answers will vary.

1. ¿Quién era la persona que más quehaceres domésticos hacía en tu casa cuando eras niño/a? ¿Quién era la persona que trabajaba más tiempo fuera de la casa?
2. ¿Cómo se llama el producto que usas para limpiar el piso?
3. ¿Dónde compras los productos que usas para limpiar la casa?
4. Cuando eras niño/a, ¿siempre hacías todo lo que te decían tus padres?
5. ¿Quiénes son las personas con quienes más sales los fines de semana? ¿Quién es la persona a quien más llamas por teléfono?
6. ¿Cuál es el deporte que más te gusta? ¿Cuál es el que menos te gusta?
7. ¿Cuál es el barrio de tu ciudad que más te gusta y por qué?
8. ¿Quién es la persona a quien más llamas cuando tienes problemas?
9. ¿Quién es la persona a quien más admiras? ¿Por qué?
10. ¿Qué es lo que más te gusta de tu casa?
11. ¿Qué es lo que más te molesta de tus amigos?
12. ¿Qué es lo que menos te gusta de tu barrio?

5 **Diálogo** En grupos, preparen un diálogo para presentar a la clase. Una persona hace el papel del/de la cliente/a que quiere comprar una casa; la otra es el/la agente. Utilicen pronombres relativos. Answers will vary.

modelo

Cliente: Me interesa comprar la casa que está enfrente del mar. ¿Cuántas alcobas tiene?
Agente: Tiene dos, pero la alcoba que tiene balcón es muy grande.
Cliente: Bueno, lo que quiero es una casa con tres alcobas. La persona con quien hablé ayer me dijo que la casa tenía tres alcobas.

NATIONAL communication STANDARDS

Síntesis

6 **Definir** En parejas, definan las palabras. Usen los pronombres **que, quien(es)** y **lo que.** Luego compartan sus definiciones con la clase. Answers will vary.

modelo

lavadora Es lo que se usa para lavar la ropa.
pastel Es un postre que comes en tu cumpleaños.

las afueras	enfermera	manta	tenedor
alquiler	flan	patio	termómetro
amigos	guantes	postre	vaso
aspiradora	jabón	sillón	vecino

AYUDA

Remember that **de**, followed by the name of a material, means *made of*.

Es de algodón. *It's made of cotton.*

Es un tipo de means *It's a kind/sort of...*

Es un tipo de flor. *It's a kind of flower.*

TEACHING OPTIONS

Small Groups Have students bring in pictures of houses (exterior only). Have students work in groups of three to write a description of what they imagine the interiors to be like. Remind them to use relative pronouns in their descriptions.

Extra Practice For practice in listening comprehension, prepare short descriptions of five easily recognizable residences. Write their names on the board in random order. Then read your descriptions as a dictation, having students copy your description and match the description to the appropriate name. Ex: **Es un castillo que está situado en una pequeña montaña cerca del océano Pacífico de California. Lo construyó un norteamericano que se consideraba bastante excéntrico. Es un sitio que visitan muchos turistas cada año.** (Hearst Castle).

4 Present Remind the questioners to take note of the answers that the student they question gives. Remind students that they should take turns asking and answering the questions. Allow pairs about ten minutes to complete the interview.

4 Expand Have pairs team up to form groups of four. Each student will report on his/her partner using the information obtained in the interview. Have all four students respond to each item before moving on to the next one.

4 Expand Give pairs of students three minutes to write four more questions modeled on the activity sentences. Ask each pair to exchange its questions with another.

5 Warm-up Have the whole class brainstorm real estate amenities before dividing into groups. Ask them the things they as potential buyers want in a house. Write the list on the board.

5 Present Ask volunteers to read the **Modelo**, then divide the class into small groups. Give groups ten minutes to prepare and practice their presentation.

6 Warm-up Ask a volunteer: **¿Qué es una lavadora? (Es el aparato en que se lava la ropa.)** Ask another: **Y un pastel, ¿qué es? (Es un dulce que se come de postre.)** The have volunteers read the **Modelo**. Point out that there are various acceptable definitions for each of the terms.

6 Suggestion Go over **Ayuda** before assigning the exercise to students.

Assignment Have students do activities in **Student Activities Manual: Workbook,** pages 137–138.

Section Goals

In **Estructura 12.2** students will learn:
- formal commands
- use of object pronouns with formal commands

Instructional Resources
Student Activities Manual: Workbook, 139–140; Lab Manual 290

Before Presenting Formal commands
Model the use of formal commands with simple examples using TPR and gestures. Ex: **Levántese**. (Make a rising motion with hands.) **Siéntense**. (Signal the class to sit down). Then point to individual students. Ex: ____, **levántese**. and so forth. Give other commands using **salga/salgan, vuelva/vuelvan,** and **venga/vengan.**
Assignment Have students study **Estructura 12.2** and prepare the exercises on pages 373–374 as homework.

Present Begin by explaining the concept of formal commands and reviewing the situations in which students would use **Ud./Uds**. Then write the following sentences on the board, contrasting their meaning with the examples in the text: **Habla con ellos. Come fruta y verduras. Lavan los platos ahora mismo. Beben menos té y café.**

Go through the forms listed, pronouncing them and giving other examples of their use. Emphasize that formal commands are based on the **yo** form of verbs, so, if students know that, they will have no trouble making most of the formal commands. Stress this as you give examples of verbs with irregular **yo** forms and stem-changing forms.

Consolidate by having volunteers give the command forms for other verbs, such as **alquilar, correr,** or **prohibir.**

12.2 Formal (Ud. and Uds.) commands

NATIONAL STANDARDS comparisons

ANTE TODO In Spanish, the command forms are used to give orders or advice. Formal commands are used with people you address as **Ud.** or **Uds.** Observe the following examples, then study the chart.

Hable con ellos, don Francisco.
Talk with them, don Francisco.

Coma frutas y verduras.
Eat fruits and vegetables.

Laven los platos ahora mismo.
Wash the dishes right now.

Beban menos té y café.
Drink less tea and coffee.

CONSEJOS

Learning these command forms will be very helpful since the same forms are used for the subjunctive, which you will begin learning in the next section.

Formal commands (*Ud.* and *Uds.*)

Infinitive	Present tense *yo* form	*Ud.* command	*Uds.* command
limpiar	limpi**o**	limpi**e**	limpi**en**
barrer	barr**o**	barr**a**	barr**an**
sacudir	sacud**o**	sacud**a**	sacud**an**
decir	dig**o**	dig**a**	dig**an**
salir	salg**o**	salg**a**	salg**an**
venir	veng**o**	veng**a**	veng**an**
volver (o:ue)	vuelv**o**	vuelv**a**	vuelv**an**
servir (e:i)	sirv**o**	sirv**a**	sirv**an**

- The **Ud.** and **Uds.** commands are formed by dropping the final **-o** of the **yo** form of the present tense. For **-ar** verbs, add **-e** or **-en**. For **-er** and **-ir** verbs, add **-a** or **-an**.

No se preocupe...
La vamos a ayudar en
todo lo posible.

- Verbs with irregular **yo** forms maintain the same irregularity in their formal commands. These verbs include **conducir, conocer, decir, hacer, ofrecer, oír, poner, salir, tener, traducir, traer, venir,** and **ver.**

Oiga, don Francisco...
Listen, don Francisco...

¡Salga inmediatamente!
Leave immediately!

Ponga la mesa, por favor.
Set the table, please.

Hagan la cama antes de salir.
Make the bed before leaving.

- Note also that stem-changing verbs maintain their stem-changes in **Ud.** and **Uds.** commands.

e:ie	o:ue	e:i
No **pierda** la llave.	**Vuelva** temprano, joven.	**Sirva** la sopa, por favor.
Cierren la puerta.	**Duerman** bien, chicos.	**Repitan** las frases.

TEACHING OPTIONS

Video Replay the video segment, having students focus on formal commands. Ask them to write down each formal command that they hear. Then form groups of three and have students compare their lists.

TPR Have students stand. Using the verbs presented in the discussion of formal commands, give random commands (Ex: **Barra el suelo. Lava los platos. Sacuda los muebles.**) and point to a student who should perform the appropriate gesture. Keep the pace rapid. Vary by calling out names of more than one student. (Ex: **Pongan la mesa. Hagan la cama.**)

CONSEJOS

These spelling changes are necessary to ensure that the words are pronounced correctly. See Lesson 8, p. 239, and Lesson 9, p. 271.

• • •

It may help you to study the following five series of syllables. Note that within each series, the consonant sound doesn't change.

sa se si so su
ca que qui co cu
za ce ci zo zu
ga gue gui go gu
ja ge gi jo ju

▶ Verbs ending in **-car, -gar,** and **-zar** have a spelling change in the command forms.

sa**car**	**c → qu**	sa**qu**e, sa**qu**en
ju**gar**	**g → gu**	jue**gu**e, jue**gu**en
almor**zar**	**z → c**	almuer**c**e, almuer**c**en

The following verbs have irregular formal commands.

Infinitive	*Ud.* command	*Uds.* command
dar	**dé**	**den**
estar	**esté**	**estén**
ir	**vaya**	**vayan**
saber	**sepa**	**sepan**
ser	**sea**	**sean**

▶ To make a formal command negative, simply place **no** before the verb.

No ponga las maletas en la cama.
Don't put the suitcases on the bed.

No ensucien los sillones.
Don't dirty the armchairs.

¡ATENCIÓN!

When a pronoun is attached to an affirmative command that has two or more syllables, an accent mark is added to maintain the original stress:

limpie → límpielo
lean → léanlo
diga → dígamela

▶ In affirmative commands, reflexive, indirect and direct object pronouns are always attached to the end of the verb.

Siénten**se**, por favor
Síga**me,** Laura.

Acuésten**se** ahora.
Póngan**las** en el suelo, por favor.

In negative commands, these pronouns always precede the verb.

No **se** preocupe.
No **me** lo dé.

No **los** ensucien.
No **nos las** traigan.

▶ **Ud.** and **Uds.** can be used with the command forms to strike a more formal tone. In such instances they follow the command form.

Muéstrele Ud. la foto a su amigo.
Show the photo to your friend.

Tomen Uds. esta alcoba.
Take this bedroom.

¡INTÉNTALO! Indica cuáles son los mandatos (*commands*) afirmativos y negativos correspondientes para cada ocasión.

1. escucharlo (Ud.) Escúchelo. No lo escuche.
2. decírmelo (Uds.) Díganmelo. No me lo digan.
3. salir (Ud.) Salga. No salga.
4. servírnoslo (Uds.) Sírvannoslo. No nos lo sirvan.
5. barrerla (Ud.) Bárrala. No la barra.
6. hacerlo (Ud.) Hágalo. No lo haga.
7. ir (Uds.) Vayan. No vayan.
8. sentarse (Uds.) Siéntense. No se sienten.

Explain that some formal command forms undergo spelling changes in order to preserve the pronunciation of hard **c,** hard **g,** and **z.** Call students' attention to **Consejos,** emphasizing that they have already encountered these spelling changes. Other familiar verbs that undergo these spelling changes are: **empezar, comenzar, buscar, pagar, llegar.**

Model the pronunciation of the verbs with irregular formal command forms and use each in an example sentence. Some of these forms are of most often used in set expression Ex: **Déme su nombre y edad, Sr. Álvarez. • Esté tranquila, Sra. López. Vamos a hacer lo posible para encontrar a Fluffy. • ¡Vaya con Dios! • Sepa Ud. bien, Sr. Gallardo, yo no estoy para bromas.**

Work through the discussion of negative commands, negative and affirmative comands with object pronouns, and the use of **Ud.** and **Uds.**, writing examples on the board. Test comprehension as you proceed by asking volunteers to supply the correct form of other verbs you suggest. Call students' attention to the explanation of accents outlined in **¡Atención!**

Close Do **¡Inténtalo!** orally with the whole class.

TEACHING OPTIONS

Extra Practice Write a list of situations on the board using singular and plural forms. Ex: **La cocina está sucia. Mis amigos y yo tenemos hambre. Tenemos miedo.** Then have students write responses in the form of commands. (**Límpiela. Hagan la cena. No tengan miedo.**)

Heritage Speakers Ask Spanish speakers to make a list of ten commands they would hear in their home communities that would probably not be heard elsewhere in the U.S.A. Ex: **Sírvale el café al niño. Acúestese después de almorzar.**

Práctica

1 **Completar** La Sra. González quiere mudarse de casa. Ayúdala a organizarse. Indica el mandato (*command*) formal de cada verbo.

1. Lea los anuncios (*ads*) del periódico y guárdelos. (leer, guardar)
2. Vaya personalmente y vea las casas Ud. misma. (ir, ver)
3. El día de la mudanza (*On moving day*) esté tranquila. Almuercen y hagan las camas temprano para poder descansar bien en la noche. (estar, almorzar)
4. Saque tiempo para hacer las maletas tranquilamente. No les haga las maletas a los niños más grandes. (sacar, hacerles)
5. Primero, dígales a todos en casa que Ud. va a estar ocupada. No les diga que Ud. va a hacerlo todo. (decirles, decirles)
6. Decida qué casa quiere y llame al agente. Pídale un contrato de alquiler. (llamar, pedirle)
7. No se preocupe. Sepa que todo va a salir bien. (preocuparse, saber)
8. Contrate un camión (*truck*) para ese día y pregúnteles la hora exacta de llegada. (contratar, preguntarles)

2 **¿Qué dicen?** Mira los dibujos y escribe un mandato lógico para cada uno. Usa palabras que aprendiste en las páginas 360 y 361.

1. Abran sus libros, por favor.

2. Cierre la puerta. ¡Hace frío!

3. Traiga Ud. la cuenta, por favor.

4. La cocina está sucia. Bárranla, por favor.

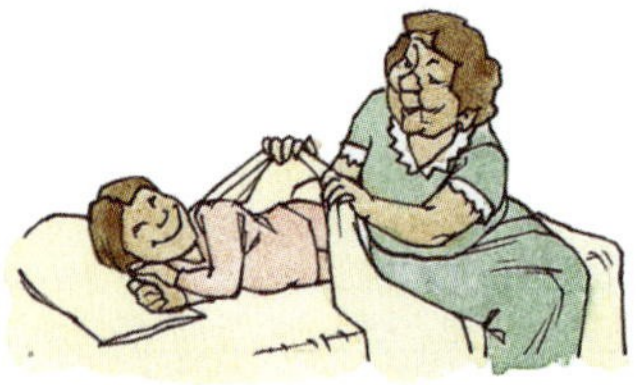

5. Duerma bien, niña.

6. Arreglen el cuarto, por favor. Está desordenado.

1 Present If you have assigned this activity as homework, go over the answers with the whole class, asking volunteers to read each completed item. Draw attention to the placement of object pronouns and the use of accent marks when the object pronouns are attached to the verbs. Then ask pairs to work together to put the items in order. If students haven't done the activity as homework, assign both completing the sentences and putting the items in order to pairs.

1 Expand Ask volunteers to give more organization tips not included in the activity for Sra. González.

1 Expand Have students work in pairs to formulate a list of instructions for the movers. Ex: **Tengan cuidado con los platos. No pongan los cuadros en una caja.** Working with the whole class, compare and contrast the commands the pairs have formulated.

2 Warm-up With the whole class, have volunteers describe the situation in each of the pictures. Be sure to have them identify who is speaking to whom.

2 Expand Continue the exercise orally by using pictures from your picture file.

TEACHING OPTIONS

Small groups Form small groups of students who have similar living arrangements, such as dormitories, at home, or in an apartment. Then have the groups make a list of suggestions for a newly arrived older resident. Ex: **No ponga Ud. la tele después de las diez. Saque Ud. la basura temprano. No estacione Ud. el carro en la calle. No invite a los amigos suyos a visitar después de las once.**

Extra Practice Here are five sentences to use as a dictation. Read each twice, pausing after the second time for students to write. **1. Saquen la basura a la calle. 2. Almuerce Ud. conmigo hoy. 3. Niños, jueguen en la calle. 4. Váyase inmediatemente. 5. Esté Ud. aquí a las diez.**

NATIONAL communication STANDARDS

Comunicación

3

Solucionar Trabajen en parejas para presentar los siguientes problemas. Un(a) estudiante presenta los problemas de la columna A y el/la otro/a los de la columna B. Usen mandatos y túrnense para ofrecer soluciones. Answers will vary.

modelo

Estudiante 1: Vilma se torció un tobillo jugando al tenis. Es la tercera vez.
Estudiante 2: No juegue más al tenis. / Vaya a ver a un especialista.

A

1. Se me perdió el libro de español con todas mis notas.
2. A Vicente se le cayó la botella de vino para la cena.
3. ¿Cómo? ¿Se te olvidó traer el traje de baño a la playa?
4. Se nos quedaron los boletos en la casa. El avión sale en una hora.

B

1. Mis hijas no se levantan temprano. Siempre llegan tarde a la escuela.
2. A mi hermana le robaron las maletas. Era su primer día de vacaciones.
3. Nuestra casa es demasiado pequeña para nuestra familia.
4. Me preocupo constantemente por Roberto. Trabaja demasiado.

4

Diálogos En parejas, escojan dos situaciones y preparen diálogos para presentar a la clase. Usen mandatos formales. Answers will vary.

modelo

Lupita: Sr. Ramírez, siento mucho llegar tan tarde. Mi niño se enfermó. ¿Qué debo hacer?
Sr. Ramírez: No se preocupe. Siéntese y descanse un poco.

SITUACIÓN 1 Profesor Rosado, no vine la semana pasada porque el equipo jugaba en Boquete. ¿Qué debo hacer para ponerme al día *(catch up)*?

SITUACIÓN 2 Los invitados de la boda llegan a las cuatro de la tarde, la mesa está sin poner y el champán sin servir. Los camareros apenas están llegando. ¿Qué deben hacer los camareros?

SITUACIÓN 3 Mi novio es un poco aburrido. No le gustan el cine, ni los deportes, ni salir a comer. Tampoco habla mucho. ¿Qué puedo hacer o qué le puedo decir?

SITUACIÓN 4 Tengo que preparar una presentación para mañana sobre el Canal de Panamá. ¿Por dónde comienzo?

CONSÚLTALO

Did you know that on December 31, 1999, The United States ceded control of the Panama Canal to the government of Panama, ending nearly 100 years of administration by the U.S.? To learn more, see **Panorama** p. 391.

NATIONAL communication STANDARDS

Síntesis

5

Presentar En grupos, preparen un anuncio *(ad)* de televisión para presentar a la clase. El anuncio debe tratar de *(be about)* un detergente, un electrodoméstico, una agencia inmobiliaria o un gimnasio. Usen mandatos, los pronombres relativos **(que, quien(es)** o **lo que)** y el impersonal **se.** Answers will vary.

modelo

Compre el lavaplatos Siglo XXI. Tiene todo lo que Ud. desea. Es el lavaplatos que mejor funciona. Venga a verlo ahora mismo... No pierda ni un minuto más. Se aceptan tarjetas de crédito.

TEACHING OPTIONS

Heritage Speakers Have Spanish speakers write a description of a household item commonly found in their homes, but not in mainstream U.S. homes. Ex: **comal, molcajete, cafetera exprés, paellera,** and so forth. Have them read their descriptions to the class.

Pairs Have pairs of students write a series of commands for a famous sports figure. Ex: (*John McEnroe*) **No se enoje. Tenga paciencia. Escuche a los árbitros** (*referees*). **No tire la raqueta.**

3 Present Model the activity by having two volunteers read the **Modelo**. Ask other volunteers to offer other suggestions. Ex: **Tenga Ud. más cuidado. Compre nuevos zapatos de tenis.**

3 Expand Ask pairs to pick their most humorous or unusual response to present to the class.

4 Present Make sure students know that each pair has to prepare two dialogues. Then ask volunteers to read the **Modelo**. Encourage students to expand their dialogues with questions and suggestions.

4 Expand Have each pair write another scenario on a sheet of paper. Then ask the pairs to exchange papers and give them two minutes to prepare another dialogue. Have them read their dialogues to the authors.

5 Present Read the **Modelo** aloud to the whole class, using your best "radio announcer" voice. Ask volunteers to point out the **mandatos, pronombres relativos** and the impersonal **se** in the **Modelo**. Divide the class into small groups. Have the groups choose a product or business and brainstorm positive attributes that they want to publicize. Make clear that an ad in which there is more than one speaker is perfectly acceptable. Give them sufficient time to prepare and practice.

5 Expand Ask different groups to read their commercials out loud to the class.

The Affective Dimension Students may feel more comfortable speaking if they assume the personae of celebrity endorsers when presenting the television commercial.

Assignment Have students do activities in **Student Activities Manual: Workbook,** pages 139–140.

Section Goals

In **Estructura 12.3** students will learn:
- present subjunctive of regular verbs
- present subjunctive of stem-changing verbs
- irregular verbs in the present subjunctive

Instructional Resources
Student Activities Manual: Workbook, 141–142; Lab Manual, 291

Before Presenting Estructura 12.3 Write sentences such as the following on the board in two columns labeled *Indicative* and *Subjunctive*: Col. 1: **Mi esposa lava los platos. Mi esposa barre el suelo. Mi esposa cocina.** Col 2: **Mi esposa quiere que yo lave los platos. Mi esposa quiere que yo barra el suelo. Mi esposa quiere que yo cocine.** Underline **yo lave**, asking students what the indicative form would be (**yo lavo**). Then underline **quiere que,** pointing out that this indicates an attitude toward the content of the subordinate clause (i.e. the wife's attitude toward the husband's washing dishes). Do the same for the other sentences. Tell students they are going to study the subjunctive mood, which expresses a speaker's attitude toward events, actions, or states he or she views as uncertain or hypothetical.

Assignment Have students study **Estructura 12.3** and prepare **¡Inténtalo!** on pages 378 and **Práctica** on page 379 as homework.

Continued on page 377.

12.3 The present subjunctive

NATIONAL comparisons STANDARDS

ANTE TODO With the exception of formal commands, all of the verb forms you have been using have been in the indicative mood. The indicative is used to state facts and to express actions or states that the speaker considers to be real and definite. In contrast, the subjunctive mood expresses the speaker's attitudes toward events, as well as actions or states the speaker views as uncertain or hypothetical.

Quiero que ustedes ayuden con los quehaceres domésticos.

Insistimos en que nos deje ayudarla a preparar la comida.

Present subjunctive of regular verbs

		hablar	comer	escribir
SINGULAR FORMS	yo	hable	coma	escriba
	tú	hables	comas	escribas
	Ud./él/ella	hable	coma	escriba
PLURAL FORMS	nosotros/as	hablemos	comamos	escribamos
	vosotros/as	habléis	comáis	escribáis
	Uds./ellos/ellas	hablen	coman	escriban

¡LENGUA VIVA!
You may think that English has no subjunctive, but it does! It used to be very common but now survives mostly in set expressions such as *if I were you* and *be that as it may*.

- The present subjunctive is formed very much like **Ud.** and **Uds.** commands. From the **yo** form of the present indicative, drop the **-o** ending, and replace it with the subjunctive endings.

INFINITIVE	PRESENT INDICATIVE	VERB STEM	PRESENT SUBJUNCTIVE
hablar	**hablo**	**habl-**	**hable**
comer	**como**	**com-**	**coma**
escribir	**escribo**	**escrib-**	**escriba**

- The present subjunctive endings are:

-ar verbs		*-er* and *-ir* verbs	
-e	**-emos**	**-a**	**-amos**
-es	**-éis**	**-as**	**-áis**
-e	**-en**	**-a**	**-an**

CONSEJOS
Note that, in the present subjunctive, **–ar** verbs use endings normally associated with present tense **–er** and **–ir** verbs. Likewise, **–er** and **–ir** verbs in the present subjunctive use endings normally associated with **–ar** verbs in the present tense. Note also that, in the present subjunctive, the **yo** form is the same as the **Ud./él/ella** form.

TEACHING OPTIONS

Large group You will need a wadded piece of paper or a beanbag for this activity. Have students arrange their chairs in a circle. Then say an infinitive of a regular verb and a subject pronoun. Ex: **alquilar/nosotros**. Throw the paper to a student. S/he must provide the correct subjunctive form (**alquilemos**).

Extra Practice Create sentences that use the subjunctive. Say the sentence, have students repeat. Then call out a different subject for the subordinate clause. Have students then say the sentence with the new subject, making all other necessary changes. Ex: **Quiero que Uds. trabajen mucho. Javier. (Quiero que Javier trabaje mucho.) Quiero que lleguen temprano. Nosotras. (Quiero que lleguemos temprano.)**

- Verbs with irregular **yo** forms show the same irregularity in the present subjunctive.

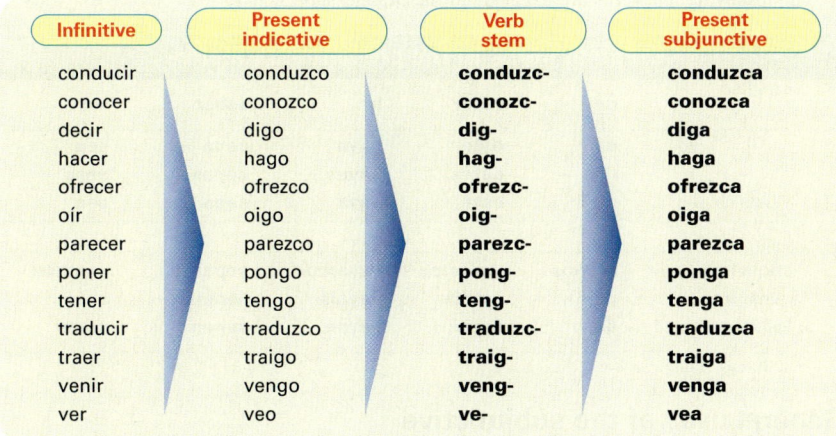

Infinitive	Present indicative	Verb stem	Present subjunctive
conducir	conduzco	**conduzc-**	**conduzca**
conocer	conozco	**conozc-**	**conozca**
decir	digo	**dig-**	**diga**
hacer	hago	**hag-**	**haga**
ofrecer	ofrezco	**ofrezc-**	**ofrezca**
oír	oigo	**oig-**	**oiga**
parecer	parezco	**parezc-**	**parezca**
poner	pongo	**pong-**	**ponga**
tener	tengo	**teng-**	**tenga**
traducir	traduzco	**traduzc-**	**traduzca**
traer	traigo	**traig-**	**traiga**
venir	vengo	**veng-**	**venga**
ver	veo	**ve-**	**vea**

- To maintain the **-c, -g,** and **-z** sounds, verbs ending in **-car, -gar,** and **-zar** have a spelling change in all forms of the present subjunctive.

sacar: sa**que**, sa**qu**es, sa**que**, sa**qu**emos, sa**qu**éis, sa**qu**en
jugar: jue**gu**e, jue**gu**es, jue**gu**e, ju**gu**emos, ju**gu**éis, jue**gu**en
almorzar: almuer**c**e, almuer**c**es, almuer**c**e, almor**c**emos, almor**c**éis, almuer**c**en

Present subjunctive of stem-changing verbs

¡ATENCIÓN!
Note that, in the present subjunctive, regular verbs have the same endings as irregular verbs, stem-changing verbs, and verbs that have a spelling change.

- **-Ar** and **-er** stem-changing verbs have the same stem changes in the subjunctive as they do in the present indicative.

pensar (e:ie): p**ie**nse, p**ie**nses, p**ie**nse, pensemos, penséis, p**ie**nsen
mostrar (o:ue): m**ue**stre, m**ue**stres, m**ue**stre, mostremos, mostréis, m**ue**stren
entender (e:ie): ent**ie**nda, ent**ie**ndas, ent**ie**nda, entendamos, entendáis, ent**ie**ndan
volver (o:ue): v**ue**lva, v**ue**lvas, v**ue**lva, volvamos, volváis, v**ue**lvan

- **-Ir** stem-changing verbs have the same stem changes in the subjunctive as they do in the present indicative, but in addition, the **nosotros/as** and **vosotros/as** forms undergo a stem change. The unstressed **e** changes to **i,** while the unstressed **o** changes to **u.**

pedir (e:i): p**i**da, p**i**das, p**i**da, p**i**damos, p**i**dáis, p**i**dan
sentir (e:ie): s**ie**nta, s**ie**ntas, s**ie**nta, s**i**ntamos, s**i**ntáis, s**ie**ntan
dormir (o:ue): d**ue**rma, d**ue**rmas, d**ue**rma, d**u**rmamos, d**u**rmáis, d**ue**rman

Present Review the meaning of mood as explained in **Ante todo**. It may help students to be aware that American English uses the subjunctive mood in certain cases. Ex: *I wish she were here. I insisted that he take notes. I suggest you be there tomorrow. If it were me, I would be happy. Be that as it may.*

Then work through the conjugation of regular verbs in the present subjunctive, emphasizing that the subjunctive is formed by adding subjunctive endings to the stem of the indicative **yo** form of a verb. Point out the relationship with formal (**Ud./Uds.**) commands. Draw students' attention to the contents of **Consejos**.

Check for understanding by asking volunteers to give subjunctive forms of other regular verbs from this lesson such as **planchar, barrer,** and **sacudir.**

Briefly work through the explanation of verbs with irregular **yo** forms, spelling changes, and changes to the stem vowel. Remind students that they have already studied each of these points when they learned the **Ud./Uds.** command forms. Pay special attention to the stem changes that take place in the **nosotros/as** and **vosotros/as** forms of **-ir** stem-changing verbs.

TEACHING OPTIONS

Pairs Have pairs of students role-play landlord/landlady and new resident. Students should refer to the **Fotonovela** as a model. Give pairs sufficient time to plan and practice. When all pairs have completed the activity, ask a few of them to introduce their characters and perform the dialogue for the whole class.

Heritage Speakers Ask Spanish speakers to compare male and female attitudes towards domestic life using the subjunctive. Ex: **Las mujeres quieren que los hombres...** **Los hombres insisten que...** Their comparative study should reflect values in their cultural communities.

Irregular verbs in the present subjunctive

Warm-up Before going over the chart of irregular verbs in the present subjunctive, ask the class if they recognize any of these forms. (The **Ud./Uds.** forms are the same as the formal commands.)

Present Model the pronunciation of these forms, having students repeat after you. Then give examples of sentences for one or two forms of each verb, using **Quiero que...** as the trigger. Ex: ____, **quiero que des tu lápiz a ____. Quiero que Uds. estén en la clase a las ____ en punto. Quiero que mi hija vaya de compras conmigo esta tarde. Quiero que Uds. sepan todas las formas del subjuntivo. Quiero que todos seamos felices.**

Draw attention to **¡Atención!** Use **haya** in an example sentence such as the following. Ex: **No quiero que haya discusiones.**

General uses of the subjunctive
Briefly go over the four principal uses of the subjunctive, explaining that in this lesson the emphasis will be on sentences that involve will and influence.

Explain that while the word *that* is usually optional in English, **que** is required in Spanish.

Check understanding by writing on the board *main clauses* + **que** that require a subjunctive in the subordinate clause. Invite volunteers to suggest several endings for each, using verbs they have just gone over. Ex: **Es importante que... (aprendamos español, yo entienda la lección, los estudiantes traigan sus libros.)**

Close Do **¡Inténtalo!** orally as a class.

Irregular verbs in the present subjunctive

- The following five verbs are irregular in the present subjunctive.

Irregular verbs in the present subjunctive

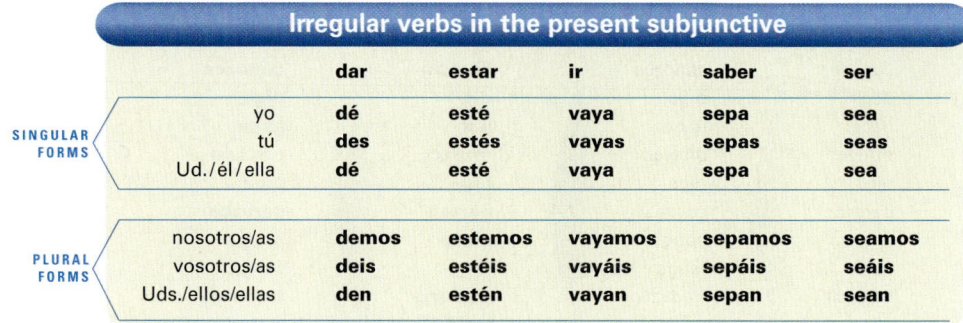

		dar	estar	ir	saber	ser
SINGULAR FORMS	yo	**dé**	**esté**	**vaya**	**sepa**	**sea**
	tú	**des**	**estés**	**vayas**	**sepas**	**seas**
	Ud./él/ella	**dé**	**esté**	**vaya**	**sepa**	**sea**
PLURAL FORMS	nosotros/as	**demos**	**estemos**	**vayamos**	**sepamos**	**seamos**
	vosotros/as	**deis**	**estéis**	**vayáis**	**sepáis**	**seáis**
	Uds./ellos/ellas	**den**	**estén**	**vayan**	**sepan**	**sean**

General uses of the subjunctive

- The subjunctive is mainly used to express: 1) will and influence, 2) emotion, 3) doubt, disbelief, and denial, and 4) indefiniteness and nonexistence.

- The subjunctive is most often used in complex sentences that consist of a main clause and a subordinate clause. The main clause contains a verb or expression that triggers the use of the subjunctive. The conjunction **que** connects the subordinate clause to the main clause.

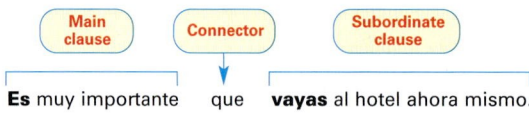

Main clause	Connector	Subordinate clause
Es muy importante	que	**vayas** al hotel ahora mismo.

- Some expressions are always followed by clauses in the subjunctive. These include:

Es bueno que... *It's good that...*	**Es mejor que...** *It's better that...*	**Es malo que...** *It's bad that...*
Es importante que... *It's important that...*	**Es necesario que...** *It's necessary that...*	**Es urgente que...** *It's urgent that...*

¡ATENCIÓN!
The subjunctive form of **hay** (*there is, there are*) is also irregular: **haya**.

¡INTÉNTALO! Indica el presente de subjuntivo de los siguientes verbos.

1. (alquilar, beber, vivir) yo alquile, beba, viva
2. (estudiar, aprender, asistir) tú estudies, aprendas, asistas
3. (encontrar, poder, dormir) él encuentre, pueda, duerma
4. (hacer, tener, venir) nosotras hagamos, tengamos, vengamos
5. (dar, hablar, escribir) ellos den, hablen, escriban
6. (pagar, empezar, buscar) Uds. paguen, empiecen, busquen
7. (ser, ir, saber) yo sea, vaya, sepa
8. (estar, dar, oír) tú estés, des, oigas
9. (arreglar, leer, abrir) nosotros arreglemos, leamos, abramos
10. (cantar, leer, vivir) ellas canten, lean, vivan

TEACHING OPTIONS

Video Show the video module again to give students more comprehensible input that uses the present subjunctive. Stop the video where appropriate and ask students to say which of the four principal uses of the subjunctive (will and influence; emotion; doubt, disbelief, and denial; indefiniteness and non existence) is expressed in the sentence.
Extra Practice Here are five sentences containing verbs in the present subjunctive to use as a dictation. Read each twice, pausing after the second time for students to write. **1. Es urgente que encontremos una casa nueva. 2. Es mejor que cada uno tenga su propia alcoba. 3. Necesitamos una casa que esté cerca de la universidad. 4. No es urgente que nos mudemos inmediatemente. 5. Pero sí es importante que empecemos a buscar la casa ya.**

Práctica

1 Completar Completa las oraciones conjugando los verbos entre paréntesis. Luego empareja las oraciones del primer grupo con las del segundo grupo.

1. Es mejor que __cenemos__ en casa. (nosotros, cenar) b
2. Es importante que __tome__ algo para calmar el dolor. (yo, tomar) c
3. Señora, es urgente que le __saque__ la muela. Parece que tiene una infección. (yo, sacar) e
4. Es malo que Ana les __dé__ tantos dulces a los niños. (dar) a
5. Es necesario que __lleguen__ a la una de la tarde. (Uds., llegar) f
6. Es importante que __nos acostemos__ temprano. (nosotros, acostarse) d

a. Es importante que __coman__ más verduras. (ellos, comer)
b. No, es mejor que __salgamos__ a comer. (nosotros, salir)
c. Y yo creo que es urgente que __llames__ al doctor. (tú, llamar)
d. En mi opinión, no es necesario que __durmamos__ tanto. (nosotros, dormir)
e. ¿Ah, sí? ¿Es necesario que me __tome__ un antibiótico también? (yo, tomar)
f. Para llegar a tiempo, es necesario que __almorcemos__ temprano. (nosotros, almorzar)

Comunicación

NATIONAL communication STANDARDS

2 Minidiálogos En parejas, completen los minidiálogos de una manera lógica.
Answers will vary.

modelo
Miguelito: Mamá, no quiero arreglar mi cuarto.
Sra. Casas: *Es necesario que lo arregles. Y es importante que sacudas los muebles también.*

MIGUELITO Mamá, no quiero estudiar. Quiero salir a jugar con mis amigos.
SRA. CASAS ____________________

MIGUELITO Mamá, es que no me gustan las verduras. Prefiero comer pasteles.
SRA. CASAS ____________________

MIGUELITO ¿Tengo que poner la mesa, mamá?
SRA. CASAS ____________________

MIGUELITO No me siento bien, mamá. Me duele todo el cuerpo y tengo fiebre.
SRA. CASAS ____________________

3 Entrevista Trabajen en parejas. Entrevístense usando estas preguntas. Expliquen sus respuestas. Answers will vary.

1. ¿Es importante que los niños ayuden con los quehaceres domésticos?
2. ¿Es urgente que los norteamericanos aprendan otras lenguas?
3. Si un(a) norteamericano/a quiere aprender francés, ¿es mejor que lo aprenda en Francia?
4. En su universidad, ¿es necesario que los estudiantes vivan en residencias estudiantiles?
5. ¿Es bueno que todos los estudiantes participen en algún deporte?
6. ¿Es importante que todos los estudiantes asistan a la universidad?

1 Present If you have assigned this activity as homework, go over the answers with the whole class. If you haven't assigned it, the activity can also be done by pairs of students. One student completes the first group of sentences and the other completes the second. Have partners check each other's work before they match the sentence pairs.

1 Expand After students have paired the sentences from each group, have them continue a couple of the short dialogues with two more sentences using the subjunctive. Ex: **No es posible que encontremos un restaurante con mesas libres a las siete. Es mejor que salgamos ahora mismo para no tener ese problema.**

2 Present Ask two volunteers to read the **Modelo**. Then ask other volunteers to suggest two more responses for **Sra. Casas.**

2 Expand Ask volunteers to share their mini-dialogues with the rest of the class.

2 Expand Ask questions about **Miguelito** and **Sra. Casas** using the subjunctive. Ex: **¿En qué insiste la Sra. Casas? (Insiste en que Miguelito arregle su cuarto; coma verduras; ponga la mesa) ¿Qué quiere Miguel? (Quiere salir a jugar; comer pasteles)** and so forth.

3 Expand Ask students to report on their partners' answers using complete sentences and explanations. Ex: **¿Qué opina Moesha sobre los quehaceres de los niños? ¿Cree que es importante que ayuden?**

Assignment Have students do activities in **Student Activities Manual: Workbook,** pages 141–142.

TEACHING OPTIONS

Heritage Speakers Have Spanish speakers write ten sentences comparing mainstream social practices in the U.S. with those of their cultural communities. Ex: **En los Estados Unidos, es correcto que una señora le extienda la mano a un caballero. En nuestra cultura se considera mala educación que un caballero no le extienda la mano a una señora primero.**

Small groups Divide the class into groups of four. Assign each group one of the following personal characteristics: **apariencia física; dinero; inteligencia; personalidad.** Have groups use the subjunctive to write sentences about the importance or unimportance of this trait for certain individuals. Ex: **Para ser "Miss Universo" es importante que una chica sea guapa.**

Section Goals

In **Estructura 12.4** students will learn:
- the subjunctive with verbs and expressions of will and influence
- common verbs of will and influence

Instructional Resources
Student Activities Manual: Workbook, 143–144; Lab Manual, 292
Transparency 45

Before Presenting Estructura 12.4
Write the word **Recomendaciones** on the board. Ask volunteers for household tips and write them on the board in infinitive form with the student's name in parenthesis. Ex: **Hacer todos los quehaceres los sábados.** (Paul) **Lavar los platos en el lavaplatos.** (Sarah). When you have approximately ten suggestions, begin rephrasing them using verbs of will and influence with subordinate clauses. Ex: **Paul nos aconseja que hagamos todos los quehaceres los sábados. Sarah recomienda que lavemos los platos en el lavaplatos.** After you have modeled several responses, ask volunteers to continue. Give them cues such as **¿Qué sugiere ____?**
Assignment Have students study **Estructura 12.4** and prepare **¡Inténtalo!** on page 381 and Activity 1 on page 382 as homework.

Present Go over the points in **Ante todo**. Read aloud the examples in the captions to the video stills and following the first bullet. Point out that in each example the subject of the verb of influence in the main clause is different from the subject of the verb in the subordinate clause (i.e. someone wants to influence someone else.) Go through the list of verbs and impersonal expressions that generally take the subjunctive, giving examples of their usage and asking volunteers to give others.

12.4 Subjunctive with verbs of will and influence

NATIONAL STANDARDS comparisons

ANTE TODO You will now learn how to use the subjunctive with verbs and expressions of will and influence.

▶ Verbs of will and influence are often used when someone wants to affect the actions or behavior of other people.

Enrique **quiere** que salgamos a cenar.
Enrique wants us to go out for dinner.

Paola **prefiere** que cenemos en casa.
Paola prefers that we have dinner at home.

¡ATENCIÓN!
In English, constructions using the infinitive, such as *I want you to go*, are often used with verbs or expressions of will or influence.

▶ Here is a list of widely used verbs of will and influence.

Verbs of will and influence

aconsejar	*to advise*	**pedir** (e:i, i)	*to ask (for)*
desear	*to wish; to desire*	**preferir** (e:ie, i)	*to prefer*
importar	*to be important; to matter*	**prohibir**	*to prohibit*
insistir (en)	*to insist (on)*	**querer** (e:ie)	*to want*
mandar	*to order*	**recomendar** (e:ie)	*to recommend*
necesitar	*to need*	**rogar** (o:ue)	*to beg; to plead*
		sugerir (e:ie, i)	*to suggest*

▶ Some impersonal expressions, such as **es necesario que, es importante que, es mejor que** and **es urgente que,** are considered expressions of will or influence.

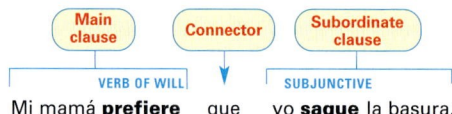

▶ When the main clause contains an expression of will or influence, the subjunctive is required in the subordinate clause, provided that the two clauses have different

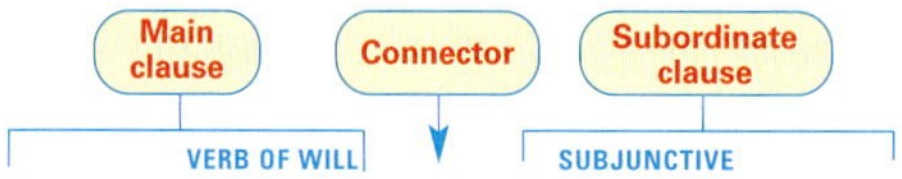

Mi mamá **prefiere** que yo **saque** la basura.

TEACHING OPTIONS

Small Groups Give groups of three five minutes to write nine sentences, each of which uses a different verb of will and influence with the subjunctive. Ask volunteers to write some of their group's best sentences on the board. Work with the whole class to read the sentences and correct any errors.

Extra Practice Have students finish the following incomplete sentences. **1. Yo insisto en que mis amigos… 2. No quiero que mi familia… 3. Para mí es importante que el amor… 4. Prefiero que mi residencia… 5. Mi novio/a no quiere que yo… 6. Los profesores siempre recomiendan a los estudiantes que… 7. El doctor sugiere que nosotros… 8. Mi madre me ruega que… 9. El policía manda que los estudiantes… 10. El fotógrafo prefiere que nosotras…**

Quiero que arreglen sus alcobas, que hagan las camas, que pongan la mesa...

...y les aconsejo que se acuesten temprano esta noche.

▶ Indirect object pronouns are often used with the verbs **aconsejar, importar, mandar, pedir, prohibir, recomendar, rogar,** and **sugerir.**

Te aconsejo que estudies.
I advise you to study.

Le sugiero que vaya a casa.
I suggest that he go home.

Les recomiendo que barran el suelo.
I recommend that you sweep the floor.

Le ruego que no venga.
I beg him not to come.

▶ Note that all the forms of **prohibir** in the present tense carry a written accent, except for the **nosotros** form: **prohíbo, prohíbes, prohíbe, prohibimos, prohibís, prohíben.**

Ella les **prohíbe** que miren la televisión.
She prohibits them from watching television.

Nos **prohíben** que nademos en la piscina.
They prohibit that we swim in the swimming pool.

▶ The infinitive is used with words or expressions of will and influence if there is no change of subject in the sentence.

No quiero **sacudir** los muebles.
I don't want to dust the furniture.

Paco prefiere **descansar.**
Paco prefers to rest.

Es importante **sacar** la basura.
It's important to take out the trash.

No es necesario **quitar** la mesa.
It's not necessary to clear the table.

¡INTÉNTALO! Completa cada oración con la forma correcta del verbo entre paréntesis.

1. Te sugiero que vayas (ir) con ella al supermercado.
2. Él necesita que yo le preste (prestar) dinero.
3. No queremos que tú hagas (hacer) nada especial para nosotros.
4. Mis papás quieren que yo limpie (limpiar) mi cuarto.
5. Nos piden que la ayudemos (ayudar) a preparar la comida.
6. Quieren que tú saques (sacar) la basura todos los días.
7. Quiero descansar (descansar) esta noche.
8. Es importante que Uds. limpien (limpiar) la casa.
9. Su tía les manda que pongan (poner) la mesa.
10. Te aconsejo que no salgas (salir) con él.
11. Mi tío insiste en que mi prima haga (hacer) la cama.
12. Prefiero ir (ir) al cine.
13. Es necesario estudiar (estudiar).
14. Recomiendo que ustedes pasen (pasar) la aspiradora.

TEACHING OPTIONS

Extra Practice Create sentences that follow the pattern of the sentences in **¡Inténtalo!**. Say the sentence, have students repeat it, then give a different subject pronoun for the subordinate clause, varying the person and number. Have students then say the sentence with the new subject, changing pronouns and verbs as necessary.

TPR Have students stand. At random call out implied commands using statements with verbs of will or influence and actions that can be pantomimed. Ex: **Quiero que laves los platos. • Insisto en que hagas la cama. • Te ruego que saques la basura. • Recomiendo que pases la aspiradora.** When you make a statement, point to a student to pantomime the action. Also use plural statements and point to more that one student. When you use negative statements, indicated students should do nothing. Keep the pace rapid.

Have a volunteer read the advertisement for Dentabrit and explain what the subject of each clause is.

Elicit indirect object pronouns with verbs of influence by making statements that give advice and asking students for advice. Personalize the statements and questions as much as is possible. Ex: **Yo siempre aconsejo a mis estudiantes que estudien mucho. Y, ¿qué me recomiendan Uds. a mí? • Mi coche no arranca cuando hace mucho frío. ¿Qué recomiendas, ____? • Tengo demasiados tareas para corregir. ____, ¿que sugieras? • Mi apartamento está siempre desordenado. ¿Que me aconseja? • Voy a tener huéspedes el fin de semana, ¿Qué recomiendan Uds. que veamos? ¿Qué sugieran que hagamos?** and so forth.

Then explain the accentuation of the verb **prohibir**. Remind students that **h** is always silent. Explain that the accent mark indicates that the vowels **o** and **i** are pronounced in separate syllables rather than as a diphthong. Have students listen for the difference as you pronounce **prohibe** and **prohíbe**.

Write the following sentences on the board: **Quiero que almuerces en la cafeteria. Quiero almorzar en la cafeteria.** Point out that, in the first example, the subject of **quiero** is different from **almuerces**. In the second example, there is no change of subject, so the infinitive is used rather than a subordinate clause with the subjunctive. Go over the examples in the text with the class.

Close To consolidate, do **¡Inténtalo!** orally as a class.

1 Present If you assigned this activity as homework, go over the answers with the whole class. You may ask two volunteers to take the parts of Irene and Julia. If you did not assign it, this activity is suitable to be completed by pairs. Each partner takes the role of either Irene or Julia.

1 Expand Have students write write a summary of the dialogue in the third person. Ask one or two volunteers to read their summaries. When there is an error in the use of the subjunctive, ask volunteers to help correct it.

2 Present Model the activity by asking two volunteers to read the **Modelo**. Then ask volunteers to offer other possible suggestions for **Isabel**.

2 Expand Have students create two suggestions for each person. In the second they should use an impersonal expression such as **Es importante... , Es mejor... ,** and so forth.

3 Present Model the activity by answering the first question orally yourself. Then remind students that they should take turns asking and answering questions.

3 Expand Have a conversation with class members about the information they learned in their interviews. Ask: **¿A quiénes siempre les dan consejos sus amigos? Y ¿quiénes siempre les dan consejos a los amigos suyos? ¿Qué tipo de cosas aconsejan?** and so forth.

Práctica

1 Completar Completa el diálogo con palabras de la lista.

ponga	sea	saber	haga
prohíbe	quiere	comas	diga
cocina	sé	ser	vaya

IRENE Tengo problemas con Vilma. Sé que debo hablar con ella. ¿Qué me recomiendas que le ___diga___?

JULIA Pues, necesito ___saber___ más antes de darte consejos.

IRENE Bueno, para empezar me ___prohíbe___ que traiga dulces a la casa.

JULIA Pero chica, tiene razón. Es mejor que tú no ___comas___ cosas dulces.

IRENE Sí, ya lo sé. Pero quiero que ___sea___ más flexible. Además, insiste en que yo ___haga___ todo en la casa.

JULIA Yo ___sé___ que Vilma ___cocina___ y hace los quehaceres todos los días.

IRENE Sí, pero siempre que hay fiesta me pide que ___ponga___ los cubiertos y las copas en la mesa y que ___vaya___ al sótano por las servilletas y los platos. ¡Es lo que más odio, ir al sótano!

JULIA Mujer, ¡Vilma sólo ___quiere___ que ayudes en la casa!

2 Aconsejar En parejas, lean lo que dice cada persona. Luego den consejos lógicos usando verbos como **aconsejar, recomendar** y **prohibir.** Sus consejos deben ser diferentes de lo que la persona quiere hacer. Answers will vary.

modelo

Isabel: Quiero conseguir un comedor con los muebles más caros del mundo.
Consejo: *Te aconsejamos que consigas unos muebles menos caros.*

1. **DAVID:** Pienso poner el congelador en el sótano.
2. **SARA:** Voy a ir a la gasolinera para comprar unas copas de cristal elegantes.
3. **SR. ALARCÓN:** Insisto en comenzar a arreglar el jardín en marzo.
4. **SRA. VILLA:** Quiero ver las tazas y los platos de la tienda El Ama de Casa Feliz.
5. **DOLORES:** Voy a poner servilletas de tela (*cloth*) para los cuarenta invitados.
6. **SR. PARDO:** Pienso poner todos mis muebles nuevos en el altillo.
7. **SRA. GONZÁLEZ:** Hay una fiesta en mi casa esta noche pero no quiero arreglar la casa.
8. **CARLITOS:** Hoy no tengo ganas de hacer las camas ni de quitar la mesa.

3 Preguntas En parejas, túrnense para contestar las preguntas. Usen el subjuntivo. Answers will vary.

1. ¿Te dan consejos tus amigos? ¿Qué te aconsejan? ¿Aceptas sus consejos? ¿Por qué?
2. ¿Qué te sugieren tus profesores que hagas antes de terminar los cursos que llevas?
3. ¿Insisten tus amigos en que salgas mucho con ellos?
4. ¿Qué quieres que te regalen tu familia y tus amigos/as en tu cumpleaños?
5. ¿Qué le recomiendas tú a un(a) amigo/a que no quiere salir los sábados con su novio/a?
6. ¿Qué les aconsejas a los nuevos estudiantes de tu universidad?

TEACHING OPTIONS

Small Groups Have small groups prepare skits in which a group of roommates are discussing how to equitably divide the household chores. Give groups time to prepare and practice their skits before presenting them to the class.

Game Give pairs of students five minutes to write a dialogue in which they use logically as many of the verbs of will and influence with the subjunctive as they can. After the time is up ask pairs the number of subjunctive constructions using verbs of will and influence they used in their dialogues. Have the top three or four perform their dialogues before the whole class.

NATIONAL communication STANDARDS

Comunicación

4 **Inventar** En parejas, preparen una lista de seis personas famosas. Un(a) estudiante da el nombre de una persona famosa y el/la otro/a le da un consejo. Answers will vary.

modelo

Estudiante 1: Judge Judy.
Estudiante 2: Le recomiendo que sea más simpática con la gente.
Estudiante 2: Leonardo DiCaprio.
Estudiante 1: Le aconsejo que haga más películas.

5 **Hablar** En parejas, miren la ilustración y denle consejos a Gerardo sobre cómo arreglar su casa. Usen expresiones impersonales y verbos como **aconsejar, sugerir** y **recomendar.** Answers will vary.

modelo

Es mejor que arregles el apartamento más a menudo.
Te aconsejo que no dejes para mañana lo que puedes hacer hoy.

NATIONAL communication STANDARDS

Síntesis

6 **El Dr. Freud** En grupos pequeños, preparen un párrafo corto sobre un problema que un paciente le presenta al Dr. Freud. Al terminar, cambien su párrafo con otro grupo. Luego, cada grupo prepara los consejos que el Dr. Freud le da al paciente. Preséntenle a la clase el intercambio (*exchange*) entre el Dr. Freud y el paciente. Answers will vary.

modelo

Grupo 1: Dr. Freud, me llamo Alicia y tengo diecisiete años. Mi mamá no quiere que yo vaya a ninguna parte (*anywhere*). No le importa que me aburra como una ostra (*oyster*). Me prohíbe conducir de noche y me siento muy sola.
Grupo 2: Alicia, le aconsejo que hable con su mamá. Tenga paciencia. Su mamá quiere protegerla, pero le recomiendo que le explique lo que siente.

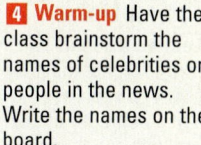

4 Warm-up Have the class brainstorm the names of celebrities or people in the news. Write the names on the board.

4 Present Ask a volunteer to read throught the **Modelo** with you. Ask volunteers for other suggestions they would make to Judge Judy and Leonardo DiCaprio.

4 Expand Ask each pair to pick out their favorite response and read it aloud to the class.

5 Warm-up With the whole class, ask volunteers to describe the illustration, naming everything they see and all the chores that need to be done. You may project **Transparency 45,** if you wish, instead of using the text illustration.

5 Present Ask: **¿Qué le aconsejan a Gerardo que haga para arreglar su casa?** Then read the **Modelo**.

5 Expand Have students change partners. They take turns playing the role of Gerardo and giving him advice. Ex: **—Sugiero que pongas la pizza en la basura. —Pero es la pizza de mi compañero de casa. Prefiero que él lo haga.**

6 Present Before assigning groups, model the activity by having two volunteers read the **Modelo**.

Assignment Have students do activities in **Student Activities Manual: Workbook,** pages 143–144.

TEACHING OPTIONS

Heritage Speakers Have Spanish speakers write a list of ten suggestions for non-Spanish speaking students participating in an exchange program in their cultural communities. Their suggestions should focus on participating in daily life in their host family's home.

Large Group Write the names of famous historical figures on individual sticky notes and place them on the students' backs. The students should circulate around the room giving each other advice that will help them guess their "identity."

Section Goals

In **Lectura** students will:
- learn to locate the main parts of a sentence
- read a content-rich text with long sentences

Antes de leer

Introduce the strategy. Tell students that if they have trouble reading long sentences in Spanish, they should pause to identify the main verb of the sentence and its subject. They should then reread the sentence in its entirety.

Examinar el texto Students should see from the layout (cover page with title, photo, and phone numbers; interior pages with an introduction and several headings followed by short paragraphs) that this is a brochure. Revealing cognates are: **información** (cover) and **residencia oficial del Presidente de Panamá** (introduction).

¿Probable o improbable? Ask volunteers to read aloud each question and answer it. Have a volunteer rephrase the improbable statement so that it is probable.

Frases largas Ask pairs to suggest a couple long sentences. Have them point out the main verb and subject. Then have a volunteer read the whole sentence.

Assignment Have students read **Bienvenidos al Palacio de Las Garzas** and prepare the activities in **Después de leer** as homework.

Lectura

NATIONAL STANDARDS communication cultures

Antes de leer

Estrategia

Locating the main parts of a sentence

Did you know that a text written in Spanish is an average of 15% longer than the same text written in English? Because the Spanish language tends to use more words to express ideas, you will often encounter long sentences when reading in Spanish. Of course, the length of sentences varies with genre and with authors' individual styles. To help you understand long sentences, identify the main parts of the sentence before trying to read it in its entirety. First locate the main verb of the sentence, along with its subject, ignoring any words or phrases set off by commas. Then reread the sentence, adding details like direct and indirect objects, transitional words, and prepositional phrases.

Examinar el texto

Mira el formato de la lectura. ¿Qué tipo de documento es? ¿Qué cognados encuentras en la lectura? ¿Qué te dicen sobre el tema de la selección?

¿Probable o improbable?

Mira brevemente el texto e indica si las siguientes frases son probables o improbables.

1. Este folleto es de interés turístico. probable
2. El folleto describe un lugar histórico cubano. improbable
3. El folleto incluye algunas explicaciones de arquitectura. probable
4. Esperan atraer visitantes al lugar. probable

Frases largas

Mira el texto y busca algunas frases largas. Con un(a) compañero/a, identifiquen las partes principales de la frase y después examinen las descripciones adicionales. ¿Qué significan las frases?

folleto *brochure* atraer *to attract* épocas *time periods* herencia *heritage*

Bienvenidos al Palacio de Las Garzas

El palacio está abierto de martes a domingo.
Para más información,
llame al teléfono 507-226-7000.
También puede solicitar un folleto
a la casilla 3467,
Ciudad de Panamá, Panamá.

Después de leer

Ordenar

Pon los siguientes eventos en el orden cronológico adecuado.

__3__ El palacio se convirtió en residencia presidencial.
__2__ Durante diferentes épocas, maestros, médicos y banqueros practicaron su profesión en el palacio.
__4__ El Dr. Belisario Porras ocupó el palacio por primera vez.
__1__ Los colonizadores construyeron el palacio.
__5__ Se renovó el palacio.
__6__ Los turistas pueden visitar el palacio de martes a domingo.

TEACHING OPTIONS

Heritage Speakers Ask Spanish speakers to give a brief presentation about the official residence of their home country. Tell them to include in their description recommendations to visitors about what rooms and objects are particularly noteworthy and should not be missed. If it is possible, they should illustrate their presentation with photographs or brochures.

Extra Practice Have students work in pairs to write ten suggestions, recommendations, or statements using the subjunctive for what their idea of a dream house **(la casa de mis sueños)** would be like. Ex: **Para mí es importante que haya una piscina de tamaño olímpico en la casa de mis sueños. Recomiendo que la cocina sea grande porque me gusta cocinar. Es necesario que tenga varios recámaras porque siempre tengo huéspedes.**

El Palacio de Las Garzas es la residencia oficial del Presidente de Panamá desde 1903. Fue construido en 1673 para ser la casa de un gobernador español. Con el paso de los años fue almacén, escuela, hospital, aduana, banco y por último, palacio presidencial.

En la actualidad el edificio tiene tres pisos, pero los planos originales muestran una construcción de un piso con un gran patio en el centro. La restauración del palacio comenzó en el año 1922 y los trabajos fueron realizados por el arquitecto Villanueva-Myers y el pintor Roberto Lewis. El palacio, un monumento al estilo colonial, todavía conserva su elegancia y buen gusto, y es una de las principales atracciones turísticas del barrio Casco Viejo.

Planta baja

El patio de las Garzas

Una antigua puerta de hierro recibe a los visitantes. El patio interior todavía conserva los elementos originales de la construcción: piso de mármol, columnas de perla gris y una magnífica fuente de agua en el centro. Aquí están las nueve garzas que dan el nombre al palacio y que representan las nueve provincias de Panamá.

Primer piso

El salón Amarillo

Aquí el turista puede visitar una galería de cuarenta y un retratos de gobernadores y personajes ilustres de Panamá. La principal atracción de este salón es el sillón presidencial, que se usa especialmente cuando hay cambio de presidente. Otros atractivos de esta área son el comedor de Los Tamarindos, que se destaca por la elegancia de sus muebles y sus lámparas de cristal, y el patio andaluz, con sus coloridos mosaicos que representan la unión de la cultura indígena y la española.

El salón Dr. Belisario Porras

Este elegante y majestuoso salón es uno de los lugares más importantes del Palacio de Las Garzas. Lleva su nombre en honor al Dr. Belisario Porras, quien fue tres veces presidente de Panamá (1912-1916, 1918-1920 y 1920-1924).

Segundo piso

Es el área residencial del palacio y el visitante no tiene acceso a ella. Los armarios, cómodas y espejos de la alcoba fueron comprados en Italia y Francia por el presidente Porras, mientras que las alfombras, cortinas y frazadas son originarias de España.

Garzas *Herons* solicitar *request* casilla *post office box*
Casco Viejo *Old Quarter* hierro *iron* mármol *marble* retratos *portraits*
destaca *stands out* frazadas *blankets*

Preguntas

Contesta las preguntas.

1. ¿Qué sala es notable por sus muebles elegantes y sus lámparas de cristal? el comedor de los Tamarindos
2. ¿En qué parte del palacio se encuentra la residencia del presidente? en el segundo piso
3. ¿Dónde empiezan los turistas su visita al palacio? en el patio de las Garzas
4. ¿En qué lugar se representa artísticamente la rica herencia cultural de Panamá? en el patio andaluz
5. ¿Qué salón honra la memoria de un gran panameño? el salón Dr. Belisario Porras
6. ¿Qué partes del palacio te gustaría más visitar? ¿Por qué? Explica tu respuesta. Answers will vary.

Conversación

En grupos de tres o cuatro estudiantes, hablen sobre lo siguiente:

1. ¿Qué tiene en común el Palacio de las Garzas con otras residencias presidenciales u otras casas muy grandes?
2. ¿Te gustaría vivir en el Palacio de las Garzas? ¿Por qué?
3. Imagina que puedes diseñar tu palacio ideal. Describe los planos para cada piso del palacio.

TEACHING OPTIONS

Variación léxica Point out that **piso** is a multiple-meaning word that may mean *floor, flooring; apartment, flat; story* (of a building). In Spanish, the **planta baja** of a building is its ground floor. The second story is called the **primer piso**; the third story is called the **segundo piso,** and so forth. The top floor in a building is called the **planta alta**. In the **Palacio de Las Garzas,** the **segundo piso** is also the **planta alta**.

Groups Ask students to work in groups of four or five to role-play a guided tour of the **Palacio de Las Garzas.** One group member plays the guide and the others play tourists. Encourage the guide to develop a script and the tourists to ask questions about the residence and its occupants. Give each group time to prepare and practice before performing their skit before the class.

Después de leer

Ordenar

Suggestion Quickly go over the correct order by asking a volunteer to read the sentence he or she believes should be first, another volunteer to read the sentence that should be second, and so forth. If there is any confusion, have students to refer back to the text for clarification.

Preguntas

Suggestion This activity is also appropriate for groups of students to do in class if you have not assigned it as homework. Have volunteers read aloud one question at a time. Ask groups to work together to answer each question.

Suggestion Have students rewrite the questions as statements, incorporating the answers in them. Ex: **El comedor de los Tamarindos es notable por sus muebles elegantes y sus lámparas de cristal.**

Conversación

Present Give groups five to ten minutes to have their conversation.

Expand After groups have finished their conversations, encourage the whole class to talk about the three questions. Besides asking the questions in the text, ask: **¿En qué se difiere el Palacio de Las Garzas de otras casas? ¿A quién no le gustaría vivir en el Palacio de Las Garzas? ¿Por qué? ¿Quién está de acuerdo?**

Section Goals

In **Escritura** students will:
- learn to use linking words
- integrate **Lesson 12** vocabulary and structures
- write a lease agreement

Tema
Present Review with students the details suggested for inclusion in the lease agreement. You may wish to present the following terms students can use in their agreements: **arrendatario** (tenant); **arrendador** (landlord); **propietario** (owner); **estipulaciones** (stipulations); **parte** (party); **de anticipación, de antelación** (in advance).

Suggestion Provide students with samples of legal documents in Spanish. (Many legal forms are downloadable from the Internet.) Go over the format of these documents with students, clarifying legal terminology as necessary.

Estrategia
Present Review the linking words in **Estrategia**. Point out that they are all words that students are familiar with. Ask volunteers to use a few of them in sentences.

Assignment Have students prepare **Ideas y organización** and **Primer borrador** as homework.

Escritura

NATIONAL communication STANDARDS

Estrategia

Using linking words

You can make your writing sound more sophisticated by using linking words to connect simple sentences or ideas and create more complex sentences. Consider the following passages, which illustrate this effect:

Without linking words

En la actualidad el edificio tiene tres pisos. Los planos originales muestran una construcción de un piso con un gran patio en el centro. La restauración del palacio comenzó en el año 1922. Los trabajos fueron realizados por el arquitecto Villanueva-Myers y el pintor Roberto Lewis.

With linking words

En la actualidad el edificio tiene tres pisos, pero los planos originales muestran una construcción de un piso con un gran patio en el centro. La restauración del palacio comenzó en el año 1922 y los trabajos fueron realizados por el arquitecto Villanueva-Myers y el pintor Roberto Lewis.

Linking words

cuando	*when*
mientras	*while*
pero	*but*
porque	*because*
pues	*since*
que	*that; who; which*
quien	*who*
sino	*but (rather)*
y	*and*
o	*or*

Tema

Escribir un contrato de arrendamiento

Eres el/la administrador(a) de un edificio de apartamentos. Prepara un contrato de arrendamiento para los nuevos inquilinos. El contrato debe incluir los siguientes detalles:

- La dirección del apartamento y del/de la administrador(a)
- Las fechas del contrato
- El precio del alquiler y el día que se debe pagar
- El precio del depósito
- Información y reglas acerca de:
  - la basura
  - el correo
  - los animales domésticos
  - el ruido
  - los servicios de electricidad y agua
  - el uso de electrodomésticos
- Otros aspectos importantes de la vida comunitaria

contrato de arrendamiento *lease* administrador(a) *manager* inquilinos *tenants* dirección *address* reglas *rules* ruido *noise* servicios *utilities*

TEACHING OPTIONS

Proofreading Activity Copy the following sentences containing mistakes onto the board or a transparency as a proofreading activity to do with the whole class.

1. **El agente nos recomienda que buscamos una casa de las afueras, la que no me gusta nada.**
2. **Nuestros amigos Panameños acaban de encontrar en el centro lo qué buscaban.**
3. **¿Es ésta la casa de quien me hablaste el Lunes?**
4. **Es necesario que Uds. pasan al balcón para ver el océano pacífico.**
5. **Por favor, entran Uds. en la sala y observan que es muy grande.**
6. **Los martínez, quiénes conocieron la semana pasada, son sus vecinos.**
7. **¿Sepan Uds. que el vecino del otro lado sea muy famoso?**

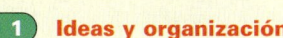

Plan de escritura

1 Ideas y organización

Después de pensar en el tema durante unos minutos, apunta tus ideas usando un mapa de ideas. Convierte el mapa en bosquejo para asegurar la organización lógica de tu escrito.

2 Primer borrador

Utiliza tu bosquejo de **Ideas y organización** para escribir el primer borrador del contrato. Consulta tus apuntes de clase y las **Anotaciones para mejorar la escritura** en tu **Carpeta de trabajos** para no repetir errores previos.

3 Comentario

Intercambia el contrato con un(a) compañero/a. Lee su borrador y anota las partes mejor escritas de su composición, especialmente el uso de las palabras de enlace. Compartan sus impresiones utilizando esta guía:

1. ¿Incluye toda la información pertinente?
2. ¿Hay una buena organización de los detalles específicos dentro del contrato?
3. ¿Emplea palabras de enlace para unir ideas y frases cortas?
4. ¿Qué sugerencias puedes dar al/a la escritor(a) para mejorar su documento?
5. ¿Ves errores gramaticales u ortográficos?

4 Redacción

Revisa el primer borrador según las indicaciones de tu compañero/a. Utiliza esta guía para hacer la última revisión antes de escribir tu versión final:

1. Utiliza palabras de enlace para unir las oraciones cortas.
2. Revisa la concordancia entre el sujeto y el verbo de cada oración.
3. Revisa la concordancia entre los sustantivos y los adjetivos.
4. Cuando es necesario, sustituye los sustantivos por pronombres u otro elemento gramatical para evitar la redundancia.
5. Consulta tus **Anotaciones para mejorar la escritura** antes de revisar la ortografía y la puntuación.

5 Evaluación y progreso

Trabaja con tres compañeros/as y lee sus trabajos. Después de escuchar atentamente las reglas de los "administradores", escoge las que, en tu opinión, garantizan una vida comunitaria tranquila. Explica tu elección. No olvides leer atentamente los comentarios y las correcciones de tu profesor(a). Finalmente, anota los errores fundamentales en las **Anotaciones para mejorar la escritura** en tu **Carpeta de trabajos.**

bosquejo *outline* palabras de enlace *linking words* tranquila *calm; quiet*

Comentario

Present Allow pairs five minutes for reading and commenting on their leases. Allow five minutes for discussing comments.

Assignment Have students prepare **Redacción** for the next class.

Evaluación y progreso Give the class five minutes to exchange and comment on the final drafts of their leases. Then have them hand them in to you.

Writing Sample Here is an example of a lease that would constitute a superior writing achievement.

Contrato de arrendamiento de vivienda

Arrendador: Don Fernando Cuevas

Arrendatarios: Don Rafael Calderón y Doña Ana Ugarte de Calderón

OBJETO DEL CONTRATO: Don Fernando Cuevas, propietaro de los Apartamentos Las Brisas, Avenida Arenales 445, Colón, Panamá, alquila el apartamento 10 a los arrendatarios.

ESTIPULACIONES: La duración del contrato es de un año, comenzando el 15 de septiembre de 2000. El alquiler mensual es de $750.00, pagable el 15 de cada mes. Hay un depósito de $750. Los arrendatarios pagan por separado los gastos de electricidad y agua. Los lunes pasan para recoger la basura. No se permite ningún animal. Se prohíben ruidos después de las 10 de la tarde.

En prueba de conformidad, ambas partes firman este contrato el 1 de septiembre de 2000.

EVALUATION: Contrato

Criteria	Scale
Content	1 2 3 4
Organization	1 2 3 4
Use of vocabulary	1 2 3 4
Use of linking words	1 2 3 4
Grammatical accuracy	1 2 3 4

Scoring	
Excellent	18–20 points
Good	14–17 points
Satisfactory	10–13 points
Unsatisfactory	< 10 points

Section Goals

In **Escuchar** students will:
- use visual clues to help them undersand an oral passage
- answer questions based on the content of a recorded conversation

Instructional Resource
Student Cassette/CD

Preparación
Warm-up Have students look at the drawing of a newspaper clipping. Ask them to describe what they see and read. Then have them guess the meaning of **Bienes raíces** (real estate).

Estrategia
Script En mi niñez lo pasé muy bien. Vivíamos en una pequeña casa en la isla Colón con vistas al mar. Pasaba las horas buceando alrededor de los arrecifes de coral. A veces me iba a pasear por las plantaciones de bananos o a visitar el pueblo de los indios guayamí. Otros días iba con mi hermano al mar en una pequeña lancha para pescar. Era una vida feliz y tranquila. Ahora vivo en la ciudad de Panamá. ¡Qué diferencia!

Ahora escucha
Script
Adriana: Mira, papá, tienen una sección especial de bienes raíces en el periódico. Felipe, mira esta casa... tiene un jardín enorme.
Felipe: ¡Qué linda! ¡Uy, qué cara! ¿Qué piensa Ud.? ¿Debemos buscar una casa o un apartamento?
Sr. Núñez: Bueno, hijos, hay muchas cosas que deben considerar. Primero, ¿les gustaría vivir en las afueras o en el centro de la ciudad?
Felipe: Pues, Sr. Núñez, yo prefiero vivir en la ciudad. Así tenemos el teatro, los parques, los centros comerciales... todo cerca de casa. Sé que Adriana quiere vivir en las afueras porque es más tranquilo.

Escuchar

Preparación

Mira el dibujo. ¿Qué pistas te da para comprender la conversación que vas a escuchar? ¿Qué significa *bienes raíces*?

Estrategia

Using visual cues

Visual cues like illustrations and headings provide useful clues about what you will hear. To practice this strategy, you will listen to a passage related to the following photo. Jot down the clues the photo gives you as you listen to a brief passage.

Ahora escucha

Mira los anuncios de esta página y escucha la conversación entre el Sr. Núñez, Adriana y Felipe. Luego indica si cada descripción se refiere a la casa ideal de Adriana y Felipe, a la casa del anuncio o al apartamento del anuncio.

Frases	La casa ideal	La casa del anuncio	El apartamento del anuncio
Es barato.	___	___	✔
Tiene cuatro alcobas.	___	✔	___
Tiene una oficina.	✔	___	___
Tiene un balcón.	___	___	✔
Tiene una cocina moderna.	___	✔	___
Tiene un jardín muy grande.	___	✔	___
Tiene un patio.	✔	___	___

18G

Bienes raíces

Se vende.
4 alcobas, 3 baños, cocina moderna, jardín con árboles frutales.
B/. 225.000

Se alquila.
2 alcobas, 1 baño.
Balcón. Urbanización Las Brisas. 525

Comprensión

Preguntas Answers will vary.

1. ¿Cuál es la relación entre el Sr. Núñez, Adriana y Felipe? ¿Cómo lo sabes?
2. ¿Qué diferencia de opinión hay entre Adriana y Felipe sobre dónde quieren vivir?
3. Usa la información de los dibujos y la conversación para entender lo que dice Adriana al final. ¿Qué significa "todo a su debido tiempo"?

Conversación Answers will vary.

1. ¿Qué tienen en común el apartamento y la casa del anuncio con el lugar donde tú vives?
2. ¿Qué piensas de la recomendación del Sr. Núñez?
3. ¿Qué tipo de sugerencias te da tu familia sobre dónde vivir?
4. ¿Dónde prefieres tú vivir? ¿en un apartamento o en una casa? Explica por qué.

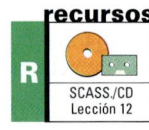

recursos
R
SCASS./CD Lección 12

pistas *clues* anuncio *advertisement*

Sr. Núñez: De todos modos van a necesitar un mínimo de dos alcobas, un baño, una sala grande... ¿Qué más?
Adriana: Es importante que tengamos una oficina para mí y un patio para las plantas.
Sr. Núñez: Como no tienen mucho dinero ahorrado, es mejor que alquilen un apartamento pequeño por un tiempo. Así pueden ahorrar su dinero para comprar la casa ideal. Miren este apartamento. Tiene un balcón precioso y está en un barrio muy seguro y bonito. Y el alquiler es muy razonable.
Felipe: Adriana, me parece que tu padre tiene razón. Con un alquiler tan barato, podemos comprar muebles y también ahorrar dinero cada mes.
Adriana: ¡Ay!, quiero mi casa. Pero, bueno, ¡todo a su debido tiempo!

NATIONAL STANDARDS communication cultures connections communities

Proyecto

Diseña una casa de vacaciones

Imagina que quieres construir una casa de vacaciones en Panamá. Vas a decidir dónde quieres construir la casa y cómo va a ser.

1 Escribe una carta al contratista

Escribe una carta detallada al contratista de obras, explicando dónde vas a construir la casa, cómo va a ser y los muebles que quieres para la casa. Primero usa los **Recursos para la investigación** para decidir en qué ciudad o región de Panamá quieres construir la casa. Busca fotos del lugar que escojas. Comienza la carta con el encabezamiento "Estimado/a Sr./Sra...." y concluye con "Atentamente" antes de tu firma. Tu carta al contratista de obras puede incluir la siguiente información:

- una descripción de la ubicación de la casa (selva, isla, valle, con vistas al mar, etc.)
- una explicación del tipo de casa que quieres (cuántos pisos, de madera, de cemento, etc.)
- un plano que tú dibujaste, incluyendo el nombre de cada cuarto de la casa
- una descripción de los muebles que debe llevar cada cuarto

2 Presenta la información a tus compañeros

Reúnete con 3 ó 4 compañeros/as. Muestra fotos y/o un mapa para mostrar dónde vas a construir la casa. Usa el plano para describirles la casa y todos los detalles especiales, incluyendo los muebles.

construir *to build* detallada *detailed* contratista de obras *building contractor* encabezamiento *salutation* firma *signature* ubicación *location* selva *forest; jungle* valle *valley* madera *wood* plano *floor plan*

recursos para la investigación

Internet Palabras clave: Panamá, fotos, turismo, casas, bienes raíces	**Comunidad** Personas de Panamá, personas que saben de los estilos y materiales de construcción en Centroamérica
Biblioteca Mapas, enciclopedias, guías turísticas, revistas	**Otros recursos** revistas y folletos turísticos que se pueden recortar (*cut up*), anuncios de casas

Section Goals

In **Proyecto** students will:
- use Spanish as they research and interact with the wider world
- write a letter to a contractor describing a house to be built

Before Assigning Proyecto

Students will need approximately a week to complete the project, so at the beginning of that time period, have them open their books to page 389 and glance over **Proyecto**. Tell them they are first going to write a letter to a contractor (**un contratista**) in Panamá describing the type of vacation home they want to have built and its specifications.

Escribe una carta al contratista Suggestions

- Provide samples of business letters in Spanish for students to use as models. Review the **saludo** (salutation), **cuerpo o texto de la carta** (body of the letter), and **despedida** (closing).
- Students may have the capability of using freeware or shareware programs available on the Internet to design floor plans (**planos**).

Presenta la información a tus compañeros Suggestions

- Students may have the capability of scanning a map of the area where they plan to build and creating a transparency to be shown on an overhead projector, or integrating the map into a multimedia presentation.
- You may wish to set aside sufficient class time to do a few presentations at a time until all students have had a chance to present.

EVALUATION: Casa de vacaciones

Criteria	Scale
Content	1 2 3 4
Organization	1 2 3 4
Use of vocabulary	1 2 3 4
Use of linking words	1 2 3 4
Grammatical accuracy	1 2 3 4

Scoring	
Excellent	18–20 points
Good	14–17 points
Satisfactory	10–13 points
Unsatisfactory	< 10 points

Section Goals

In **Panorama**, students will read about the geography and culture of Panama.

Instructional Resources
Student Activities Manual: Workbook, 145–146
Transparency 46

Panamá

Before Presenting Panorama Have students look at the map of Panama or project **Transparency 46** and discuss the physical features of the country. Point out the bodies of water that run along the coasts of Panama, and the canal that cuts through the isthmus (istmo). Then, have students look at the call-out photos and read the captions. point out that the Cuna people live on the San Blas islands in the Caribbean Sea.

Assignment Have students read **Panorama** and write out the anwers to the questions in **¿Qué aprendiste?**, page 391, as homework.

Present Ask volunteers to read each section of **El país en cifras**. Mention that the national currency, the balboa, is named for **Vasco Núñez de Balboa**, who explored the Isthmus of Panama in 1501. Tell students that **Chibcha** is a major indigenous language group, with dialects spoken by native people from central Colombia through eastern Nicaragua. After reading about the **Panameños célebres**, ask students to share what they know about the individuals listed and how they learned about them.

Increíble pero cierto The opening of the Panama Canal not only dramatically reduced the distance ships had to travel to get from the Atlantic Ocean to the Pacific, it also provided a much safer route than the stormy, perilous route around Cape Horn and through the Straits of Magellan.

Panamá

NATIONAL STANDARDS connections cultures

El país en cifras

Mujer cuna lavando una mola.

- **Área:** 78.200 km^2 (30.193 millas^2), *aproximadamente el área de Carolina del Sur*
- **Población:** 2.942.000
- **Capital:** La ciudad de Panamá — 1.228.000
- **Ciudades principales:** Colón — 138.000, David — 125.000

SOURCE: Population Division, UN Secretariat

- **Moneda:** balboa; Es equivalente al dólar estadounidense.

En Panamá circulan los billetes de dólar estadounidense. El país centroamericano, sin embargo, acuña sus propias monedas. "El peso" es una moneda grande equivalente a cincuenta centavos. La moneda de cinco centavos es llamada frecuentemente "real".

- **Idiomas:** español (oficial), chibcha, inglés

La mayoría de los panameños son bilingües. La lengua materna del 14% de los panameños es el inglés.

Bandera de Panamá

Panameños célebres

- **Manuel Antonio Noriega,** militar y dictador (1934-)
- **Rod Carew,** beisbolista (1945-)
- **Mireya Moscoso,** política (1947-)
- **Rubén Blades,** músico y político (1948-)

Un turista disfruta del bosque tropical colgado de un cable.

Ruinas de un fuerte panameño.

recursos

R | WB pp. 147-148 | vistasonline.com

acuñar *to mint* moneda *coin* centavos *cents* actualmente *currently* peaje *toll* promedio *average*

¡Increíble pero cierto!

¿Conocías estos datos sobre el Canal de Panamá?

- El viaje en barco de Nueva York a Tokio a través del Canal de Panamá es 3.000 millas más corto
- Su construcción costó 639 millones de dólares
- 38 barcos al día lo usan actualmente
- El peaje promedio cuesta 40.000 dólares

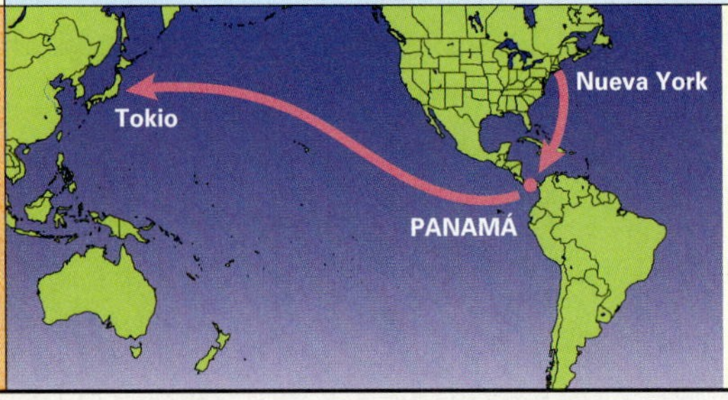

TEACHING OPTIONS

Heritage Speaker Invite Panamanian students or Spanish speakers who have visited Panama to share information about language patterns in Panama. Have them talk about what languages are spoken at home, what language is usually learned first, how English speakers acquire English, and so forth.

Extra Practice Rubén Blades changed the world of salsa music by introducing lyrics with social import into what had previously been simply dance music. If possible, bring in his recording **Buscando América**, and have students listen to "Padre Antonio y el monaguillo Andrés," based on the story of Archbishop Romero of El Salvador. Or, listen to the story of "Pedro Navaja" on **Siembra**, Blade's classic collaboration with Willie Colón. Have students write a summary of the song in English, or describe how Blades' salsa differs from traditional "romantic" salsa.

Lugares • El Canal de Panamá

El Canal de Panamá une los océanos Pacífico y Atlántico. Se empezó a construir en 1903 y se terminó diez años después. Es la fuente principal de ingresos del país, gracias al dinero que se recauda de los más de 12.000 buques que pasan anualmente por el canal.

Artes • La mola

La mola es una forma de arte textil de los cunas, una tribu indígena que vive en las islas San Blas en Panamá. Las molas se hacen con capas y fragmentos de tela de colores vivos. Sus diseños son muchas veces abstractos, inspirados en las formas del coral. Las molas tradicionales son las más apreciadas y sus diseños son completamente geométricos. Antes sólo se usaban como ropa, pero hoy día también se usan para decorar las casas.

Deportes • El buceo

Panamá, cuyo nombre significa "lugar de muchos peces", es un sitio excelente para los amantes del buceo, el buceo con esnórkel y la pesca. Las playas en los dos lados del istmo, el mar Caribe a un lado y el océano Pacífico al otro, son muy variadas. Unas están destinadas al turismo y otras poseen un gran valor ecológico por la riqueza y diversidad de su vida marina, abundante en arrecifes de coral. En la playa Bluff, por ejemplo, se pueden observar cuatro especies de tortugas en peligro de extinción.

Vista de la Ciudad de Panamá.

¿Qué aprendiste? Responde a las preguntas con una frase completa.

1. ¿Cuál es la lengua materna del catorce por ciento de los panameños?
   El inglés es la lengua materna del catorce por ciento de los panameños.
2. ¿A qué unidad monetaria (*monetary unit*) es equivalente el balboa?
   El balboa es equivalente al dólar estadounidense.
3. ¿Qué océanos une el Canal de Panamá?
   El Canal de Panamá une los océanos Atlántico y Pacífico.
4. ¿Quién es Rubén Blades?
   Rubén Blades es un músico y político panameño.
5. ¿Qué son las molas?
   Las molas son una forma de arte textil común entre los cunas.
6. ¿Cómo son los diseños de las molas?
   Sus diseños son abstractos.
7. ¿Para qué se usaban las molas antes?
   Las molas se usaban como ropa.
8. ¿Cómo son las playas de Panamá?
   Son muy variadas; unas están destinadas al turismo, otras tienen valor ecológico.
9. ¿Qué significa "Panamá"?
   "Panamá" significa "lugar de muchos peces".

Conexión Internet Investiga estos temas en el sitio **www.vistasonline.com.**

1. Investiga la historia de las relaciones entre Panamá y los Estados Unidos y la decisión de devolver (*give back*) el Canal a Panamá. ¿Estás de acuerdo con la decisión? Explica tu opinión.
2. Investiga los cunas u otro grupo indígena de Panamá. ¿En qué partes del país viven? ¿Qué lenguas hablan? ¿Cómo es su cultura?

une *connects* fuente *source* ingresos *income* se recauda *is collected* buques *ships* capas *layers* tela *fabric* vivos *bright* apreciadas *valued* hoy día *nowadays* cuyo *whose* peces *fish* amantes *lovers* buceo *diving* istmo *isthmus* poseen *possess* valor *value* riqueza *riches* arrecifes *reefs* tortugas *tortoises* peligro *danger*

El Canal de Panamá The Panama Canal is a lake-and-lock type of canal, connecting the Atlantic and Pacific oceans at one of the lowest points on the Continental Divide. It is about 40 miles long and is one of the two most strategic waterways on earth (the Suez Canal is the other).

La mola The Cuna people originally lived on mainland Panama, but preferred to move to the San Blas islands, where they could maintain their way of life. Elaborate traditions accompany every life-cycle event in Cuna culture, and many of these ceremonies are depicted on the elaborate appliqué **molas**, which are the pride of the Cuna women.

El buceo An excellent place for diving in Panama is the Parque Nacional Bastimentos, in the Archipiélago de Bocas del Toro. In this nature reserve, turtles nest on some of the beaches. Its coral reefs are home to over 200 species of tropical fish, in addition to lobsters and other sea life; manatees also inhabit these waters. The park is also known for its mangroves, which offer snorkelers another experience.

¿Qué aprendiste? Go over the questions and answers with students, making sure everyone understands unfamiliar words and what the correct answers are.

Assignment Have students do activites in **Student Activities Manual: Workbook,** pages 145–146.

Conexión Internet Students will find information about Panama at **www.vistasonline.com,** as well as links to other sites that can help them in their research.

TEACHING OPTIONS

Worth Noting The Cuna people have a strong, rich oral tradition. During regular community "meetings," ritual forms of speaking, including storytelling and speeches, are presented by community elders. It is only over the past decade that a written form of the Cuna language has been developed by "outsiders." However, as Spanish—and even English—begin to encroach more and more into Kuna Yala (the Cuna name for their homeland), linguistic anthropologists have highlighted the urgency of recording and preserving the rich Cuna oral tradition, fearing that the traditional Cuna language and culture will begin to be diluted by outside influences.

12 vocabulario

Viviendas

las afueras	*suburbs; outskirts*
el alquiler	*rent*
el ama (*m., f.*) de casa	*housekeeper; caretaker*
el barrio	*neighborhood*
el edificio de apartamentos	*apartment building*
el/la vecino/a	*neighbor*
la vivienda	*housing*
alquilar	*to rent*
mudarse	*to move (from one house to another)*

Cuartos y otros lugares

la alcoba, el dormitorio	*bedroom*
el altillo	*attic*
el balcón	*balcony*
la cocina	*kitchen*
el comedor	*dining room*
la entrada	*entrance*
la escalera	*stairs; stairway*
el garaje	*garage*
el jardín	*garden; yard*
la oficina	*office*
el pasillo	*hallway*
el patio	*patio; yard*
la sala	*living room*
el sótano	*basement; cellar*

Muebles y otras cosas

la alfombra	*carpet; rug*
la almohada	*pillow*
el armario	*closet*
el cartel	*poster*
la cómoda	*chest of drawers*
las cortinas	*curtains*
el cuadro	*picture*
el estante	*bookcase; bookshelves*
la lámpara	*lamp*
la luz	*light; electricity*
la manta	*blanket*
la mesita	*end table*
la mesita de noche	*night stand*
los muebles	*furniture*
la pared	*wall*
la pintura	*painting; picture*
el sillón	*armchair*
el sofá	*couch; sofa*

Electrodomésticos

la cafetera	*coffee maker*
la cocina, la estufa	*stove*
el congelador	*freezer*
el electrodoméstico	*electric appliance*
el horno (de microondas)	*(microwave) oven*
la lavadora	*washing machine*
el lavaplatos	*dishwasher*
el refrigerador	*refrigerator*
la secadora	*clothes dryer*
la tostadora	*toaster*

Para poner la mesa

la copa	*wineglass; goblet*
la cuchara	*(table or large) spoon*
el cuchillo	*knife*
el plato	*plate*
la servilleta	*napkin*
la taza	*cup*
el tenedor	*fork*
el vaso	*glass*
poner la mesa	*to set the table*
quitar la mesa	*to clear the table*

Quehaceres domésticos

arreglar	*to neaten; to straighten up*
barrer el suelo	*to sweep the floor*
cocinar	*to cook*
ensuciar	*to get (something) dirty*
hacer la cama	*make the bed*
hacer quehaceres domésticos	*to do household chores*
lavar	*to wash*
limpiar la casa	*to clean the house*
pasar la aspiradora	*to vacuum*
planchar la ropa	*to iron the clothes*
sacar la basura	*to take out the trash*
sacudir los muebles	*to dust the furniture*

Verbos y expresiones verbales

aconsejar	*to advise*
insistir (en)	*to insist (on)*
mandar	*to order*
recomendar (e:ie)	*to recommend*
rogar (o:ue)	*to beg; to plead*
sugerir (e:ie)	*to suggest*
Es bueno que…	*It's good that…*
Es importante que…	*It's important that…*
Es malo que…	*It's bad that…*
Es mejor que…	*It's better that…*
Es necesario que…	*It's necessary that…*
Es urgente que…	*It's urgent that…*

Relative pronouns	*See page 368.*
Expresiones útiles	*See page 365.*

La naturaleza

13

Communicative Goals

You will learn how to:

- Talk about and discuss the environment.
- Express your beliefs and opinions about issues.

Lesson Goals

In **Lesson 13** students will be introduced to the following:

- terms to describe nature and the environment
- conservation and recycling terms
- punctuation in Spanish
- subjunctive with verbs and expressions of emotion
- subjunctive with verbs and expressions of doubt, disbelief, and denial
- expressions of certainty
- conjunctions that require the subjunctive
- when the infinitive follows a conjunction
- negative and affirmative familiar **(tú)** commands
- recognizing the purpose of a text
- considering audience and purpose when writing
- writing a persuasive letter or article
- using background knowledge and context to guess meaning
- writing a letter in the role of an environmental activist
- cultural, geographic, and historical information about Colombia

Lesson Preview

Have students look at the photo. Say: **En esta foto, los jóvenes están en un sitio natural.** Then ask: **¿Cómo es la ropa del chico? ¿De la chica? ¿Qué hacen los jóvenes? ¿A Uds. les gusta estar en la naturaleza?**

INSTRUCTIONAL RESOURCES

Student Activities Manual: Workbook, 149–160
Student Activities Manual: Lab Manual, 293–298
Student Activities Manual: Video Activities, 351–352
Instructor's Resource Manual: Hojas de actividades, 29–30
Instructor's Resource Manual: Answer Keys
Instructor's Resource Manual: Vocabulario adicional, 57
Tapescript/Videoscript
Overhead Transparencies, 47–49
Student Cassette/CD
Lab Cassette/CD
Video Program
CD-ROM
Website: **www.vistasonline.com**
Testing Program: Prueba A, Prueba B

Section Goals

In **Contextos** students will learn and practice:
- terms to describe nature
- conservation terms

Instructional Resources
Student Activities Manual: Workbook, 149–150; Lab Manual, 293
Vocabulario adicional 57
Hoja de actividades 29
Transparencies 47–48
Student Cassette/CD

Before Presenting Contextos Write the headings **la naturaleza** and **la conservación** on the board, asking students to guess what the terms mean. Then, have two volunteers come to the board and write down all the English words the class can brainstorm pertaining to nature and conservation. After the class has produced at least 15 words under each heading, have students look in their texts to see how many of their Spanish equivalents they can find.
Assignment Have students study **Contextos** and do Activities 1, 2, and 5, pages 395–396, as homework.

Present Project **Transparency 47.** Point to vocabulary items illustrated and either say their Spanish names, having students repeat after you, or ask volunteers to say what each illustration is of. Then begin a conversation by asking personalized questions that recycle the items already covered and introduce those in **Más vocabulario.** Ex: **¿Cuáles son los recursos naturales de nuestra región? ¿Adónde van Uds. para hacer un picnic? ¿Cuáles son los problemas de contaminación del medio ambiente de nuestra región?** and so forth.

Note: At this point you may want to present *Los animales y las plantas,* **Vocabulario adicional 57,** in the **Instructor's Resource Book**.

La naturaleza

Más vocabulario

el animal	*animal*
el bosque (tropical)	*(tropical; rain) forest*
el cielo	*sky*
el desierto	*desert*
la estrella	*star*
la luna	*moon*
el mundo	*world*
la naturaleza	*nature*
la planta	*plant*
la región	*region; area*
la selva, la jungla	*jungle*
la tierra	*land; soil*
la conservación	*conservation*
la contaminación (del aire; del agua)	*(air; water) pollution*
la deforestación	*deforestation*
la ecología	*ecology*
el ecoturismo	*ecotourism*
la energía (nuclear; solar)	*(nuclear; solar) energy*
la extinción	*extinction*
el gobierno	*government*
la ley	*law*
la lluvia (ácida)	*(acid) rain*
el medio ambiente	*environment*
el peligro	*danger*
la población	*population*
el recurso natural	*natural resource*
la solución	*solution*
puro/a	*pure*

Variación léxica

césped ⟷ pasto (*Perú*); grama (*Venez.*); zacate (*Méx.*)

recursos

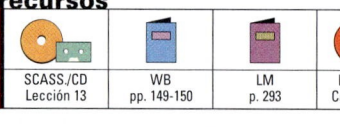

R			
SCASS./CD Lección 13	WB pp. 149-150	LM p. 293	LCASS./CD Cass. 7A/CD7

TEACHING OPTIONS

Variación léxica Tell students that they might see **hierba** spelled **yerba**. In either case, the pronunciation is the same. Ask Spanish speakers what the word for *grass* or *lawn* in their region is. Invite them also to think of other things found in nature that have more than one name. Ex: **culebra/serpiente/víbora** (*snake*); **piedra/roca** (*rock*); **bosque tropical/selva tropical** (*rain forest*)

Extra Practice Whisper a vocabulary word into a student's ear. That student should draw on the board a picture or pictures that explain the word. The class must guess the word, call it out, then spell it in Spanish as the volunteer writes it on the board. Repeat.

Práctica

1 Escuchar Mientras escuchas las frases, anota los sustantivos (*nouns*) que se refieren a las plantas, los animales, la tierra y el cielo.

Plantas	Animales	Tierra	Cielo
flores	perro	valle	sol
hierba	gatos	volcán	nubes
árboles	vacas	bosque tropical	estrellas

2 Seleccionar Selecciona la palabra que no está relacionada con cada grupo.

1. estrella • gobierno • luna • sol gobierno
2. gatos • peces • perros • hierba hierba
3. contaminación • extinción • ecoturismo • deforestación ecoturismo
4. lago • río • mar • peligro • peligro
5. vaca • gato • pájaro • población población
6. conservación • lluvia ácida • ecología • recurso natural lluvia ácida
7. cielo • cráter • aire • nube cráter
8. desierto • solución • selva • bosque solución
9. nube • cielo • lluvia • piedra piedra
10. flor • hierba • sendero • árbol sendero

3 Definir Trabaja con un(a) compañero/a para definir o describir cada palabra. Sigue el modelo. Answers will vary.

modelo

Estudiante 1: *¿Qué es el cielo?*
Estudiante 2: *El cielo está sobre la tierra y tiene nubes.*

1. la población
2. un valle
3. la lluvia
4. la naturaleza
5. un desierto
6. la extinción
7. la ecología
8. un sendero

4 Describir Trabajen en parejas para describir las siguientes fotos. Answers will vary.

1 Present Check the answers orally with the whole class.

Tapescript **1. Mi novio siempre me compra flores para nuestro aniversario. 2. Cuando era pequeño jugaba con mi perro todo el tiempo. 3. Javier prefiere jugar al fútbol norteamericano sobre hierba natural. 4. Antes de las vacaciones, los estudiantes tomaban el sol en el parque. 5. No puedo visitarte porque soy alérgico a los gatos. 6. Durante la tormenta, las nubes grises cubrían toda la ciudad. 7. Cerca de la casa de mi hermana hay un valle donde siempre hay muchas vacas. 8. Algunas noches vamos al campo para ver las estrellas. 9. El Puracé es un volcán activo en los Andes colombianos.10. Los árboles de los bosques tropicales contienen las curas para muchas enfermedades.**
Student Cassette/CD

2 Present Have students give answers and state a category for each group. Ex: **1. Cosas que están en el cielo.**

3 Present Give pairs about ten minutes to finish the activity. Then go through the terms, calling on several volunteers to read their definitions.

4 Present Have pairs include the following in the descriptions: objects in the photos, the colors, what the weather is like, the time of day, the country where the photo was taken. Ask students to pick a description to present to the class.

4 Expand Ask students to imagine the photos were taken on a recent vacation. Have students write a brief essay about their vacation, incorporating their descriptions.

TEACHING OPTIONS

TPR Make a series of true-false statements related to the lesson theme using the vocabulary. Tell students to remain seated if a statement is true and to stand if it is false. Ex: **A los gatos les gustan nadar en los lagos.** (Students stand.) **Los carros son responsables en parte de la contaminación del aire.** (Students remain seated.)

Game Have students fold a sheet of paper into 16 squares (four folds in half) and choose one vocabulary word to write in each square. Call out definitions for the vocabulary words. If students have the defined word, they mark their paper. The first student to mark four words in a row (across, down, or diagonally) calls out **"Loto"**. The student then reads his or her words to check if the definitions have been given.

El reciclaje

Recicla la lata de aluminio. (reciclar)
el envase de plástico
Recoge la botella de vidrio. (recoger)

La conservación

conservar	*to conserve*
contaminar	*to pollute*
controlar	*to control*
cuidar	*to take care of*
dejar de (+ *inf.*)	*to stop (doing something)*
desarrollar	*to develop*
descubrir	*to discover*
destruir	*to destroy*
estar afectado/a (por)	*to be affected (by)*
estar contaminado/a	*to be polluted*
evitar	*to avoid*
mejorar	*to improve*
proteger	*to protect*
reducir	*to reduce*
resolver (o:ue)	*to resolve; to solve*
respirar	*to breathe*

5 **Completar** Selecciona la palabra o la expresión adecuada para completar cada frase.

contaminar	se desarrollaron	resolver
controlan	descubrir	recoger
destruyen	están afectadas	cuidan
reciclamos	proteger	mejoramos

1. Si vemos basura en las calles, la debemos __recoger__.
2. Los científicos trabajan para __descubrir__ nuevas soluciones.
3. Es necesario que todos trabajemos juntos para __resolver__ los problemas del medio ambiente.
4. Debemos __proteger__ el medio ambiente porque hoy día está en peligro.
5. Muchas leyes nuevas __controlan__ el número de árboles que se puede cortar (*cut down*).
6. Las primeras civilizaciones __se desarrollaron__ cerca de los ríos y los mares.
7. Todas las personas del mundo __están afectadas__ por la contaminación.
8. Los turistas deben tener cuidado de no __contaminar__ las regiones que visitan.
9. Podemos conservar los recursos si __reciclamos__ el aluminio, el vidrio y el plástico.
10. La lluvia ácida, la contaminación y la deforestación __destruyen__ el medio ambiente.

El reciclaje* and *La conservación
Present Involve students in a discussion of recycling and conservation. Project **Transparency 48** and ask volunteers to describe what is happening in the drawing. Ask: **¿Quién me quiere describir lo que se ve en la ilustración? ¿Qué hace la señora de la izquierda? (Recicla una lata de aluminio.)** Cover the active vocabulary, then guide the coversation toward students' own experience and opinions. Ask questions like the following: **¿Tiene un buen programa de reciclaje nuestra ciudad? ¿Qué hacen Uds. para reducir la contaminación del medio ambiente? ¿Qué hace la universidad? ¿Cómo estamos afectados por la contaminación en nuestra ciudad/región? ¿Cuál es el mayor problema ecológico de nuestra region? ¿Hay cierto producto que evitan Uds. por razones ecológicos?**

Successful Language Learning Tell your students to look at the new verbs and expressions and imagine what kinds of things they might be able to say with them.

5 Present Check correct answers by going over the activity with the whole class. Ask individuals to read the completed sentences.

5 Expand After students have read their sentences, ask questions that require students to recycle the activity vocabulary. Ex: **¿Qué debemos hacer para mantener limpias de basura las calles? ¿Para qué trabajan los científicos? ¿Por qué es necesario que trabajemos para proteger el medio ambiente?**

5 Expand Have students write five more original sentences, using different forms of the verbs. Ask volunteers to share their sentences with the rest of the class.

TEACHING OPTIONS

Pairs Have pairs of students write each vocabulary word in **El reciclaje** and **La contaminación** on index cards. Pairs then shuffle the cards and take turns drawing from the stack. The student who draws a card then must make a comment about conservation or the environment, using the word he or she has drawn. One partner writes down the other partner's comment. After students finish the stack, call on volunteers to share their comments.

Small Groups Divide the class into groups of 3 or 4. Have each group make a list of 8 environmental problems in the region. Ask groups to trade lists. Have groups write solutions to the problems on the list they receive, and then give the lists back to the original group. After reading the solutions, the original groups should give reasons why the solutions are good or not.

Comunicación

6 **Encuesta** Tu profesor(a) te va a dar una hoja de actividades. Haz una encuesta a tus compañeros/as para saber el grado de importancia que les dan a los problemas que se mencionan en la lista y anota sus respuestas. Después dibuja una gráfica de barras (*bar graph*) para mostrar los resultados. Answers will vary.

modelo

Estudiante 1: ¿Qué importancia tiene la deforestación?
Estudiante 2: Pienso que el problema de la deforestación es importantísimo.

Escala (el grado de importancia)	Problemas	Nombres
importantísimo	1. la deforestación	
muy importante	2. la población	
importante	3. la contaminación del aire	
poco importante	4. la contaminación del agua	
no es importante	5. la reducción de los recursos naturales	

Ahora contesta estas preguntas.

1. ¿Qué problema consideras tú el más grave? ¿Por qué?
2. ¿Qué problema escogieron tus compañeros/as de clase como el más grave? ¿Estás de acuerdo (*Do you agree*) con ellos? ¿Por qué?
3. ¿Cómo se puede evitar o resolver el problema más importante?
4. ¿Es necesario resolver el problema menos importante? ¿Por qué?

7 **Situaciones** Trabajen en grupos pequeños para representar las siguientes situaciones. Answers will vary.

1. Un(a) representante de una agencia ambiental (*environmental*) habla con el/la presidente/a de una compañía industrial que está contaminando un río o el aire.
2. Un(a) guía de ecoturismo habla con un grupo sobre cómo disfrutar (*enjoy*) y conservar el medio ambiente.
3. Un(a) representante de la universidad habla con un grupo de nuevos estudiantes sobre la campaña (*campaign*) ambiental de la universidad y trata de reclutar (*tries to recruit*) miembros para un club que trabaja para la protección del medio ambiente.

8 **Escribir una carta** Trabajen en parejas para escribir una carta a una empresa real o imaginaria que esté contaminando el medio ambiente. Expliquen las consecuencias que sus acciones van a tener para el medio ambiente. Sugiéranle algunas ideas para que solucionen el problema. Utilicen por lo menos diez palabras de las páginas 394–396. Answers will vary.

TEACHING OPTIONS

Heritage Speakers Ask Spanish speakers to interview family members or people in the community about the environmental challenges in the region they come from. Encourage them to find out how the problems impact the land and the people. Have students report their findings to the class.

Large Groups Write environmental problems and possible solutions on separate index cards. Ex: **la destrucción de los bosques tropicales—limitar el número de árboles que se cortan; la contaminación de los ríos—reducir la cantidad de sustancias químicas vertidas en el agua**. Hand the cards out to students. Students with problem cards ask their classmates questions until they find a viable solution.

6 Warm-up Go over the instructions with the whole class. Ask volunteers to read the **Modelo**.

6 Present Distribute **Hoja de actividades 29** and allow 10–12 minutes for students to conduct the survey. Encourage students to circulate rapidly in order to speak with everyone in the class. Assign the bar graph as homework. Tell students that using graph paper will make the graph easier to draw. Divide the class into groups of five to discuss the follow-up questions. Groups should reach a consensus for each question, then report to the class.

7 Present Divide the class into groups of three. Have each group choose a situation, but make sure that all situations are covered. Have students take turns playing each role. After groups have had time to prepare their situations, invite some of them to present them before the rest of the class.

8 Warm-up Remind students that a business letter in Spanish begins with a salutation such as **Estimado(s) señor(es)** and ends with a closing such as **Atentamente**.

8 Present With the whole class, brainstorm a list of companies that are known to have had environmental problems. Ask the class to categorize the companies by what they produce and the problems they cause. Then divide the class into pairs and have them choose a company. Give them ten minutes to complete their letter.

Assignment Have students prepare the activities in **Student Activities Manual: Workbook**, pages 149–150.

Section goals

In **Fotonovela** students will:

- receive comprehensible input from free-flowing discourse
- learn functional phrases that preview lesson grammatical structures

Instructional Resources
Student Activities Manual: Video Activities 351–352
Video Program (Start: 01:10:38)

Video Synopsis Don Francisco introduces the students to Martín, who will be their guide on the hike. Martín takes the students to the site of the hike, where they discuss the need for environmental protection.

Before Presenting Fotonovela Have your students scan this **Fotonovela** episode and list words related to nature and the environment. Then have them predict what will happen in this episode, based on the words they listed and the video stills. Write down their predictions.
Assignment Have students study **Fotonovela** and **Expresiones útiles** as homework.

Warm-up Quickly review the guesses your students made about the **Fotonovela**. Through discussion, guide the class to a correct summary of the plot.

Present Read the **Expresiones útiles** aloud and have the class repeat. Then continue the conversation that you began in **Contextos** about the state of the environment in your area. Integrate **Expresiones útiles** into the conversation. Ex: **¿Cuál es el mayor problema de contaminación en esta región? ¿Qué creen Uds. que debemos hacer para proteger el medio ambiente?**

Continued on page 399.

¡Qué paisaje más hermoso!

NATIONAL STANDARDS communication cultures

Martín y los estudiantes visitan el sendero en las montañas.

PERSONAJES

MAITE

INÉS

DON FRANCISCO

ÁLEX

JAVIER

MARTÍN

1

DON FRANCISCO Chicos, les presento a Martín Dávalos, el guía de la excursión. Martín, nuestros pasajeros—Maite, Javier, Inés y Álex.

2

MARTÍN Mucho gusto. Voy a llevarlos al área donde vamos a ir de excursión mañana. ¿Qué les parece?

ESTUDIANTES ¡Sí! ¡Vamos!

3

MAITE ¡Qué paisaje más hermoso!

INÉS No creo que haya lugares más bonitos en el mundo.

6

JAVIER Entiendo que mañana vamos a cruzar un río. ¿Está contaminado?

MARTÍN En las montañas el río no parece estar afectado por la contaminación. Cerca de las ciudades, sin embargo, el río tiene bastante contaminación.

7

ÁLEX ¡Qué aire tan puro se respira aquí! No es como en la Ciudad de México... Tenemos un problema gravísimo de contaminación.

MARTÍN A menos que resuelvan ese problema, los habitantes van a sufrir muchas enfermedades en el futuro.

8

INÉS Creo que todos debemos hacer algo para proteger el medio ambiente.

MAITE Yo creo que todos los países deben establecer leyes que controlen el uso de automóviles.

recursos

R	VIDEO Lección 13	VM pp. 351-352

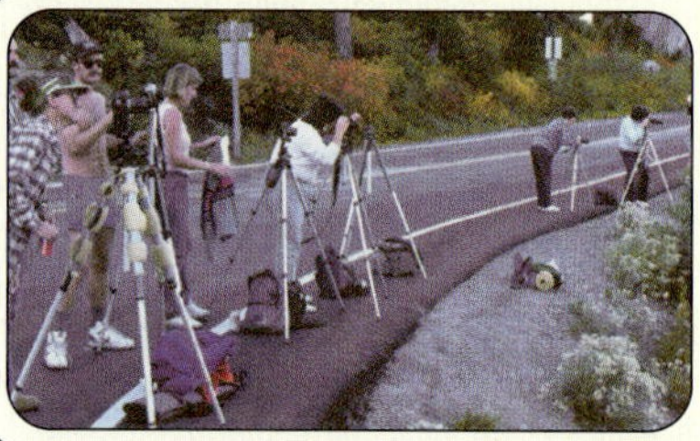

TEACHING OPTIONS

Video Tips General suggestions for using video clips in the classroom can be found on page IAE-13 of the **Instructor's Annotated Edition**.
¡Qué paisaje más hermoso! Play the video episode, not including the **Resumen** segment, and have your students give you a "play-by-play" description of the action. Write their descriptions on the board. Then replay it, asking the class to list any key words they hear. Write some of their key words on the board. Finally, discuss the material on the board with the class and guide the class toward a correct summary of the plot.

MARTÍN Esperamos que Uds. se diviertan mucho, pero es necesario que cuiden la naturaleza.

JAVIER Se pueden tomar fotos, ¿verdad?

MARTÍN Sí, con tal de que no toques las flores o las plantas.

ÁLEX ¿Hay problemas de contaminación en esta región?

MARTÍN La contaminación es un problema en todo el mundo. Pero aquí tenemos un programa de reciclaje. Si ves por el sendero botellas, papeles o latas, recógelos.

JAVIER Pero Maite, ¿tú vas a dejar de usar tu carro en Madrid?

MAITE Pues voy a tener que usar el metro... Pero tú sabes que mi coche es tan pequeñito... casi no contamina nada.

INÉS ¡Ven, Javier!

JAVIER ¡¡Ya voy!!

Expresiones útiles

Talking about the environment

- **¿Hay problemas de contaminación en esta región?**
  Are there problems with pollution in this region/area?
- **La contaminación es un problema en todo el mundo.**
  Pollution is a problem throughout the world.

- **¿Está contaminado el río?**
  Is the river polluted?
- **En las montañas el río no parece estar afectado por la contaminación.**
  In the mountains the river does not seem to be affected by pollution.
- **Cerca de las ciudades el río tiene bastante contaminación.**
  Near the cities, the river is pretty polluted.

- **¡Qué aire tan puro se respira aquí!**
  The air you breathe here is so pure!
- **Es necesario que cuiden la naturaleza.**
  It's necessary that you take care of nature.
- **Tenemos un problema gravísimo de contaminación.**
  We have an extremely serious problem with pollution.
- **Creo que todos debemos hacer algo para proteger el medio ambiente.**
  I think we should all do something to protect the environment.
- **No toques las flores o las plantas.**
  Don't touch the flowers or the plants.
- **Tenemos un programa de reciclaje.**
  We have a recycling program.
- **Si ves por el sendero botellas, papeles o latas, recógelos.**
  If you see bottles, papers, or cans along the trail, pick them up.

Enfoque cultural El ecoturismo

La contaminación es un problema en todo el mundo, incluyendo los países hispanohablantes. Sin embargo (*However*), el ecoturismo enseña a los turistas y a los habitantes de las regiones turísticas la importancia de cuidar el medio ambiente. El ecoturismo es muy popular en los bosques tropicales de países como Costa Rica y Perú, donde hay animales y plantas que están en peligro de extinción. Gracias al ecoturismo, los turistas visitan las tiendas propias de los habitantes de la zona y así se evita que el turismo altere estas regiones.

Have the class work in groups to read through the entire **Fotonovela** aloud, with volunteers playing the various parts. Circulate among the groups and model correct pronunciation as needed. See ideas for using the video in **Teaching Options**, page 398.

Comprehension Check Check comprehension of the **Fotonovela** episode by doing Activity 1, **Seleccionar**, page 400, orally with the whole class.

Suggestion Have the class look at video still 3 of the **Fotonovela**. Explain that **No creo que haya lugares más bonitos en el mundo** is an example of the present subjunctive used with an expression of doubt. In video still 4, point out that **Esperamos que Uds. se diviertan mucho** is an example of the present subjunctive with a verb of emotion. Draw attention to **con tal de que no toques las flores** in video still 4 and **a menos que resuelvan ese problema** in video still 7; explain that **con tal de que and a menos que** are conjunctions that are always followed by the subunctive. Then point out the word **recógelos** in video still 5; tell the class that this is an example of an affirmative **tú** command. Tell your students that they will learn more about these concepts in the upcoming **Estructura** section.

Assignment Have students do activities 2–4 in **Reacciona a la fotonovela**, page 400, as homework.

TEACHING OPTIONS

Enfoque cultural Many governments in the Spanish-speaking world have established national parks and biological reserves to preserve their natural treasures. Costa Rica and Ecuador, of course, are famous for their protection of ecological treasures. Some of the most famous are the following. **El Yunque**, located near San Juan, Puerto Rico, also known as the **Bosque Nacional del Caribe**, preserves a tract of the Caribbean rain forest. **Parque Nacional Manu**, in Peru's Amazon basin, is famous for its brilliantly colored macaws, its jaguars, ocelots, otters, and alligators. **Parque Nacional Canaima**, in the Guayana highlands of Venezuela, is home of the micro-ecologies of the **tepúyes** and **Salto Ángel**, the highest waterfall in the world. **Parque Nacional Torres del Paine** in Chilean Patagonia contains some of the most spectacularly rugged crags in the southern Andes.

Reacciona a la fotonovela

1 Present You may want to ask for volunteers to read each sentence aloud.

2 Warm-up Have the class skim the **Fotonovela** on pages 398–399 before they begin this activity.

3 Present You may want your students to work through these questions in pairs.

4 Possible response
S1: ¿Hay problemas de contaminación donde vives?
S2: Sí, tenemos un problema muy grave de contaminación de los ríos. Hay muchos papeles, botellas y latas en los ríos. En las montañas, los ríos no están afectados por la contaminación pero en las ciudades, sí. ¿En tu región hay problemas de contaminación?
S1: Sí, tenemos un problema gravísimo de contaminación del aire. ¡No se puede respirar aire puro! Esto causa enfermedades para los habitantes.
S2: Qué terrible. ¿Cómo podemos resolver los problemas de la contaminación?
S1: Bueno, nosotros tenemos un programa de reciclaje ahora. Reciclamos papeles, latas y botellas de vidrio y plástico . También algunas personas tratan de no usar el auto. Usan el metro o caminan al trabajo o a la universidad.

The Affective Dimension Many students feel nervous when called on to give an answer or to read aloud. You can minimize this source of anxiety by asking for volunteers and by having students work in pairs or groups.

Reacciona a la fotonovela

1 Seleccionar Selecciona la respuesta más lógica para cada frase.

1. Martín va a llevar a los estudiantes al lugar donde van a ___c___.
   a. contaminar el río b. bailar c. ir de excursión
2. El río está más afectado por la contaminación ___b___.
   a. cerca de los bosques b. en las ciudades c. en las montañas
3. Martín quiere que los estudiantes ___a___.
   a. limpien los senderos b. descubran nuevos senderos c. no usen sus autos
4. La naturaleza está formada por ___c___.
   a. los ríos, las montañas y las leyes b. los animales, las latas y los ríos
   c. los lagos, los animales y las plantas
5. La contaminación del aire puede producir ___b___.
   a. problemas del estómago b. enfermedades respiratorias c. enfermedades mentales

2 Identificar Identifica quién puede decir las siguientes frases. Puedes usar cada nombre más de una vez.

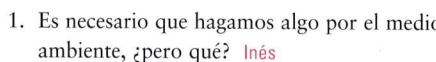

1. Es necesario que hagamos algo por el medio ambiente, ¿pero qué? Inés
2. En mi ciudad es imposible respirar aire limpio. ¡Está muy contaminado! Álex
3. En el futuro, a causa del problema de la contaminación, las personas van a tener problemas de salud. Martín
4. El metro es una excelente alternativa al coche. Maite
5. ¿Está limpio o contaminado el río? Javier
6. Puedes usar tu cámara pero sin tocar las plantas, por favor. Martín
7. De todos los lugares del mundo, me parece que éste es el mejor. Inés
8. Como todo el mundo usa automóviles, debemos hacer leyes para controlar cómo y cuándo usarlos. Maite

3 Preguntas Responde a las siguientes preguntas usando la información de **Fotonovela**.

1. Según Martín, ¿qué es necesario que hagan los estudiantes? ¿Qué no pueden hacer?
   Es necesario que cuiden la naturaleza. No pueden tocar las plantas ni las flores.
2. ¿Qué problemas del medio ambiente mencionan Martín y los estudiantes?
   Hay problemas de contaminación del aire y de los ríos.
3. ¿Qué cree Maite que deben hacer los países?
   Los países deben establecer leyes que controlen el uso de los automóviles.
4. ¿Qué cosas se pueden reciclar? Menciona tres.
   Se pueden reciclar las botellas, los papeles y las latas.
5. ¿Qué otro medio de transporte importante dice Maite que hay en Madrid?
   El metro es importante.

4 El medio ambiente En parejas, discutan algunos problemas ambientales y sus posibles soluciones. Usen las siguientes preguntas y frases en su conversación.
Answers will vary.

- ¿Hay problemas de contaminación donde vives?
- Tenemos un problema muy grave de contaminación de...
- ¿Cómo podemos resolver los problemas de la contaminación?

NATIONAL communication STANDARDS

TEACHING OPTIONS

Extra Practice You may want to use the sentences in Activity 1 or Activity 2 on page 400 for a dictation activity. Have your students close their books, then read each sentence twice slowly and once at regular speed. Then have your students open their books and correct any errors in their work.

Small Groups Have your students work in groups of three to write a short article about their environmental concerns for a local news letter (**boletín informativo**). Their articles should include a description of a few environmental problems and some suggestions for solving them. When groups have finished, have them share their articles with the rest of the class.

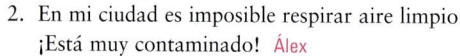

NATIONAL STANDARDS comparisons

Ortografía

Los signos de puntuación

In Spanish, as in English, punctuation marks are important because they help you express your ideas in a clear, organized way.

No podía ver las llaves. Las buscó por los estantes, las mesas, las sillas, el suelo; minutos después, decidió mirar por la ventana. Allí estaban...

The **punto y coma** (;), the **tres puntos** (...), and the **punto** (.) are used in very similar ways in Spanish and English.

Argentina, Brasil, Paraguay y Uruguay son miembros de Mercosur.

In Spanish, the **coma** (,) is not used before **y** or **o** in a series.

13,5% **29,2°** **3.000.000** **$2.999,99**

In numbers, Spanish uses a **coma** where English uses a decimal point and a **punto** where English uses a comma.

¿Dónde está? **¡Ven aquí!**

Questions in Spanish are preceded and followed by **signos de interrogación** (¿ ?), and exclamations are preceded and followed by **signos de exclamación** (¡ !).

Práctica Lee el párrafo e indica los signos de puntuación necesarios. Answers will vary.

Ayer recibí la invitación de boda de Marta mi amiga colombiana inmediatamente empecé a pensar en un posible regalo fui al almacén donde Marta y su novio tenían una lista de regalos había de todo copas cafeteras tostadoras finalmente decidí regalarles un perro ya sé que es un regalo extraño pero espero que les guste a los dos

¿Palabras de amor? El siguiente diálogo tiene diferentes significados (*meanings*) dependiendo de los signos de puntuación que utilizas y el lugar donde los pones. Intenta encontrar los diferentes significados. Answers will vary.

JULIÁN me quieres
MARISOL no puedo vivir sin ti
JULIÁN me quieres dejar
MARISOL no me parece mala idea
JULIÁN no eres feliz conmigo
MARISOL no soy feliz

TEACHING OPTIONS

Group Work Have your students work in pairs to write example sentences for each of the four punctuation rules explained in **Ortografía**. Then ask volunteers to write their sentences on the board. Work with the class as a whole to correct any errors of punctuation, grammar, or spelling.

Extra Practice With the entire class, go over the **¿Palabras de amor?** dialogue and point out how it can be punctuated in different ways to express opposite meanings. Reinforce this by having your students work in pairs to dramatize the dialogue in both ways. After the class has had time to prepare, ask a few pairs to present the contrasting dialogues to the class.

Section Goals

In **Ortografía** students will learn the use of punctuation marks in Spanish.

Present

- Explain that ellipsis marks are used in Spanish to indicate omissions and hesitations, but that there is no space before or between the marks in Spanish. There is, however, a space after them.
- Point out the lack of a comma before **y** or **o** in a series in Spanish.
- Model reading the numerical examples. Ex: **13,5% = trece coma cinco por ciento, 29,2° = veintinueve coma dos grados** Write English numbers on the board for translations into Spanish. Ex: 89.3%; 5,020,307 students; $13.50; 0.49%.
- Explain that the inverted question mark or exclamation point does not always come at the beginning of a sentence, but at the beginning of the part of the sentence where the question or exclamation begins. Ex: **—¿Cómo estás, Mirta? —¡Super bien, Andrés! Y tú, ¿cómo estás? —No me siento bien y me duele la cabeza, ¡caramba!**

Práctica/Palabras de amor Two possibilities for punctuation:

J: ¿Me quieres?
M: ¡No puedo vivir sin ti!
J: ¿Me quieres dejar?
M: No. Me parece mala idea.
J: ¿No eres feliz conmigo?
M: No. Soy feliz.

J: ¿Me quieres?
M: No. Puedo vivir sin ti.
J: ¡Me quieres dejar!
M: No me parece mala idea.
J: ¿No eres feliz conmigo?
M: No soy feliz.

Section Goals

In **Estructura 13.1** students will learn:
- to use the subjunctive with verbs and expressions of emotion
- common verbs and expressions of emotion

Instructional Resources
Student Activities Manual: Workbook, 151–152; Lab Manual, 295
Hoja de actividades 30

Before Presenting Estructura 13.1 Ask students to call out some of the verbs that trigger the subjunctive in subordinate clauses that follow them (**Verbs of will and influence,** page 380). Write them on the board and ask students use some of them in sentences. Then, quickly review the conjugation of a regular verb from the **-ar, -er,** and **-ir** conjugations. Tell students that they are now going to learn more verbs, verbs of emotion, that trigger the subjunctive in subordinate clauses that follow them. **Assignment** Have students study **Estructura 13.1** and do the exercises on pages 403–404 as homework.

Present Go through the grammar explanation and examples, pointing out the similarity between the subjunctive with verbs of emotion and the subjunctive with verbs of will and influence. Model the use of some of the common verbs and expressions of emotion in sentences. Ex: **Me molesta mucho que recojan la basura sólo una vez a la semana. Me sorprende que más gente no se interese por cuestiones del medio ambiente. Es ridículo que echemos tanto en la basura.** Then ask volunteers to use other verbs and expressions in sentences.

Continued on page 403.

13.1 The subjunctive with verbs of emotion

NATIONAL STANDARDS comparisons

ANTE TODO In the previous lesson, you learned how to use the subjunctive with expressions of will and influence. You will now learn how to use the subjunctive with verbs and expressions of emotion.

Main clause		Subordinate clause
Marta **espera**	que	yo **vaya** al lago este fin de semana.

▶ When the verb in the main clause of a sentence expresses an emotion or feeling such as hope, fear, joy, pity, surprise, etc., the subjunctive is required in the subordinate clause.

Nos alegramos de que te **gusten** las flores.
We are happy that you like the flowers.

Siento que tú no **puedas** venir mañana.
I'm sorry that you can't come tomorrow.

Temo que Ana no **pueda** ir mañana con nosotros.
I'm afraid that Ana won't be able to go with us tomorrow.

Le **sorprende** que Juan **sea** tan joven.
It surprises him that Juan is so young.

Esperamos que Uds. se diviertan mucho en la excursión.

Es triste que tengamos un problema grave de contaminación en la ciudad de México.

Common verbs and expressions of emotion

alegrarse (de)	*to be happy*	**tener miedo (de)**	*to be afraid (of)*
esperar	*to hope; to wish*	**es extraño**	*it's strange*
gustar	*to be pleasing; to like*	**es una lástima**	*it's a shame*
molestar	*to bother*	**es ridículo**	*it's ridiculous*
sentir (e:ie, i)	*to be sorry; to regret*	**es terrible**	*it's terrible*
sorprender	*to surprise*	**es triste**	*it's sad*
temer	*to be afraid; to fear*	**ojalá (que)**	*I hope (that); I wish (that)*

Me molesta que la gente no **recicle** el plástico.
It bothers me that people don't recycle plastic.

Es triste que tengamos problemas con la deforestación.
It's sad that we have problems with deforestation.

TEACHING OPTIONS

Large Group Have students circulate around the room, interviewing their classmates about their hopes and fears for the future. Ex: **¿Qué es lo que más esperas para el futuro? (Espero que encontremos una solución al problema de la contaminación.) ¿Qué es lo que más temes? (Temo que destruyamos nuestro medio ambiente.)** Encourage students to use the common verbs and expressions of emotion in their responses.

Extra Practice Ask students to imagine that they have just finished watching a documentary about pollution's affects. Have them write five responses to what they saw and heard, using different verbs or expressions of emotion in each sentence. Ex: **Me sorprende que el río esté contaminado.**

- As with expressions of will and influence, the infinitive, not the subjunctive, is used after an expression of emotion when there is no change of subject from the main clause to the subordinate clause. Compare these sentences.

Temo **llegar** tarde.	Temo que mi novio **llegue** tarde.
I'm afraid I'll arrive late.	*I'm afraid my boyfriend will arrive late.*

¡LENGUA VIVA!
Whether **Ojalá** is translated as *I hope* or *I wish* depends on whether it is followed by a verb in the present subjunctive or the past subjunctive, which you will learn in Lesson 16.

- The expression **ojalá (que)** means *I hope* or *I wish*, and it is always followed by the subjunctive. Note that the use of **que** with this expression is optional.

Ojalá (que) se conserven nuestros recursos naturales.	**Ojalá (que) recojan** la basura hoy.
I hope (that) our natural resources will be conserved.	*I hope (that) they collect the garbage today.*

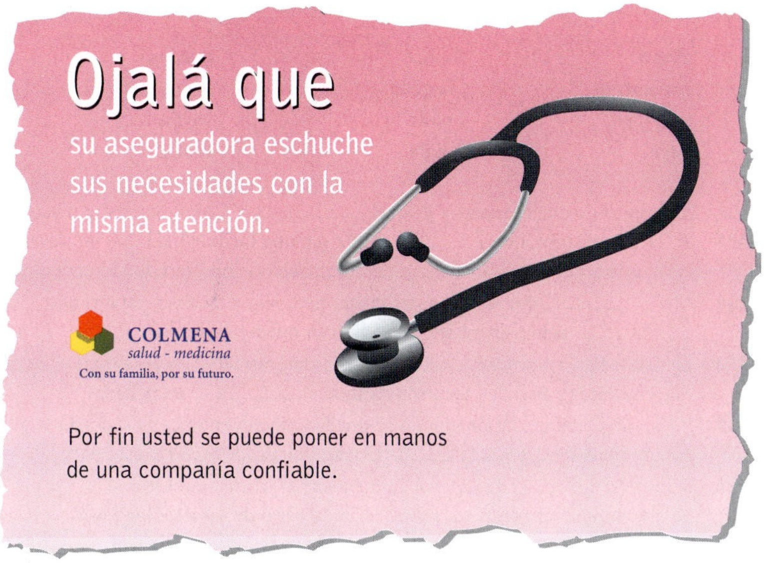

Ojalá que
su aseguradora eschuche sus necesidades con la misma atención.
COLMENA
salud - medicina
Con su familia, por su futuro.
Por fin usted se puede poner en manos de una companía confiable.

¡INTÉNTALO! Completa las oraciones con las formas correctas de los verbos.

1. Ojalá que ellos <u>descubran</u> (descubrir) nuevas formas de energía.
2. Espero que Ana nos <u>ayude</u> (ayudar) a recoger la basura en la carretera.
3. Es una lástima que la gente no <u>recicle</u> (reciclar) más.
4. Esperamos <u>proteger</u> (proteger) el aire de nuestra comunidad.
5. Me alegro de que mis amigos <u>quieran</u> (querer) conservar la naturaleza.
6. A mis padres les gusta que nosotros <u>participemos</u> (participar) en programas de conservación.
7. Es ridículo <u>contaminar</u> (contaminar) el medio ambiente.
8. Espero que tú <u>vengas</u> (venir) a la reunión (*meeting*) del Club de Ecología.
9. Siento que nuestras ciudades <u>estén</u> (estar) afectadas por la contaminación.
10. Ojalá que yo <u>pueda</u> (poder) hacer algo para reducir la contaminación.

TEACHING OPTIONS

Extra Practice Have students look at the drawing for **Contextos** on pages 394–395. Ask them to imagine they are one of the people pictured. Then have them write five sentences about how they feel from the point of view of that person. Ex: **Espero que a Alicia le guste la comida. Ojalá Gustavo no pierda las llaves del carro esta vez. Es ridículo que llevemos el perro y el gato en un picnic.**

Pairs Have students write five sentences describing nature or the environment. Students then read their sentences to a partner who will respond to each one, expressing a feeling or hope. Ex: **Hay muchos animales que están en peligro de extinción. (Es terrible que haya muchos animales en peligro de extinción.)**

Remind students that for a verb or expression to trigger the subjunctive in a following clause, the subject of the following clause must be different from that of the "triggering" verb. If the subject is the same, an infinitive phrase is used instead of a clause. Illustrate this point with examples like the following. Ex: **Juan espera hacer algo para aliviar el problema de la contaminación ambiental. Juan espera que el gobierno haga algo para aliviar el problema de la contaminación ambiental. • ¿Creen que es terrible no reciclar? ¿Creen que es terrible que yo no recicle? • ¿Les molesta sentarse aquí? ¿Les molesta que nos sentemos aquí?**

Go over the discussion of **ojalá**. Point out that the interjection **¡Ojalá!** comes from Arabic and means *Allah willing or God willing.* Thus, while it means *I hope . . .*, it's meaning can sometimes be more impersonal, such as *Let's hope that . . .* or *One would hope that . . .* Then ask a volunteer to read the advertisement for Colmena health insurance company. Ask the volunteer which verb is in the subjunctive and why.

Close Go over **¡Inténtalo!** orally with the whole class. Use a ball or balled-up piece of paper for an expansion activity. Read the beginning of one of the sentences (the words before the blank) and toss the ball to one of your students, who should then complete the sentence in an original manner using a the correct subjunctive form of a verb or infinitive. Continue until everyone has had a chance to finish a sentence.

The Affective Dimension Reassure students they will feel more comfortable with the subjunctive as they continue studying Spanish.

1 Warm-up Have students read the verbs and verb phrase listed before the activity. Have them point out which verbs are in the subjunctive and which ones trigger the subjunctive.

1 Present Ask individuals to read each completed sentence and explain why they chose the verb or expression they did.

1 Expansion Ask pairs of students to create an original dialogue based on the one in the activity. Students should use the subjunctive at least six times. Call on pairs to perform their dialogues for the class. Give awards for the following: best use of the subjunctive, best accents, and best performance.

2 Warm-up Have volunteers look at the dehydrated sentences and name elements that could trigger the subjunctive in a following clause. Ex: **1. esperar, ojalá 2. molestarme 3. alegrarme 4. ser terrible 5. tener miedo, ser triste 6. sorprenderme**

2 Present Go over the activity with the whole class. Ask volunteers to write their completed sentences on the board and then read them aloud. Correct spelling and grammar as necessary. After you have gone over the activity, invite volunteers to present it as a dialogue for the whole class.

Práctica

1 Completar Completa el diálogo con palabras de la lista. Compara tus respuestas con las de un(a) compañero/a.

Bogotá, Colombia

alegro	salga	puedan
encuentren	lleguen	tengo miedo de
reduzcan	molesta	vayan
estén	ojalá	visitar

OLGA Me alegro de que Adriana y Raquel ___vayan___ a Colombia. ¿Van a estudiar?

SARA Sí. Es una lástima que ___lleguen___ una semana tarde. Ojalá que la universidad las ayude a buscar casa. ___Tengo miedo de___ que no consigan dónde vivir.

OLGA Me ___molesta___ que seas tan pesimista, pero sí, yo también espero que ___encuentren___ gente simpática y que hablen mucho español.

SARA Sí, ojalá. Van a hacer un estudio sobre la deforestación en las costas. Es triste que en tantos países los recursos naturales ___estén___ en peligro.

OLGA Pues, me ___alegro___ de que no se queden mucho en la capital por la contaminación, pero ___ojalá___ tengan tiempo de viajar por el país.

SARA Sí, espero que ___puedan___ por lo menos ir al Museo del Oro. Sé que también esperan ___visitar___ la catedral de sal de Zipaquirá.

2 Transformar Transforma los siguientes elementos en frases completas para formar un diálogo entre Juan y la madre de Raquel. Añade palabras si es necesario. Luego, con un(a) compañero/a, presenta el diálogo a la clase. Answers will vary.

1. Juan, / esperar / (tú) escribirle / Raquel. / Ser / tu / novia. / Ojalá / no / sentirse / sola
   Juan, espero que (tú) le escribas a Raquel. Es tu novia. Ojalá (que) no se sienta sola.
2. molestarme / (Ud.) decirme / lo que / tener / hacer. / Ahora / mismo / estarle / escribiendo Me molesta que (Ud.) me diga lo que tengo que hacer. Ahora mismo le estoy escribiendo.
3. alegrarme / oírte / decir / eso. / Ser / terrible / estar / lejos / cuando / nadie / recordarte Me alegra oírte decir eso. Es terrible estar lejos cuando nadie te recuerda.
4. señora, / ¡yo / tener / miedo / (ella) no recordarme / mí! / Ser / triste / estar / sin / novia Señora, ¡yo tengo miedo que (ella) no me recuerde a mí! Es triste estar sin novia.
5. ser / ridículo / (tú) sentirte / así. / Tú / saber / ella / querer / casarse / contigo
   Es ridículo que te sientas así. Tú sabes que ella quiere casarse contigo.
6. ridículo / o / no, / sorprenderme / (todos) preocuparse / ella / y / (nadie) acordarse / mí Ridículo o no, me sorprende que todos se preocupen de ella y nadie se acuerde de mí.

NOTA CULTURAL

Although Colombia is very close to the equator, many of its cities are in the mountains, where the weather is permanently spring-like. Bogotá, the capital, is located at over 8,000 feet above sea level!

TEACHING OPTIONS

Game Write each of the common verbs and expressions of emotion (page 402) on slips of paper and put them in a box or bag. On separate strips write an equal number of infinitives and subject pronouns. Place these in a separate box or bag. Divide the class into two teams. One member of each team draws a slip of paper from each box and writes a sentence on the board using the sentence elements on both slips. If the sentence makes sense and the grammar is correct, that team gets a point. Play until every team member has had a chance to go to the board. The team with the most points at the end of play wins.

Pairs Have students tell a partner three things that bother him or her and three things he or she is happy about.

NATIONAL communication STANDARDS

Comunicación

3

Comentar En parejas, túrnense para formar oraciones sobre su ciudad, sus clases, su gobierno o algún otro tema, usando expresiones como **me alegro de que, temo que** y **es extraño que.** Luego reaccionen a los comentarios de su compañero/a. Answers will vary.

modelo

Estudiante 1: Me alegro de que vayan a limpiar el río.
Estudiante 2: Yo también. Me preocupa que el agua del río esté tan sucia.

4

Contestar Lee el mensaje electrónico que Raquel le escribió a su novio Juan. Luego, en parejas, contesten el mensaje usando expresiones como **me sorprende que, me molesta que** y **es una lástima que.** Answers will vary.

AYUDA

Echar de menos (a alguien) and **extrañar (a alguien)**, are two ways of saying *to miss (someone).*

Para	Asunto

Hola, Juan:

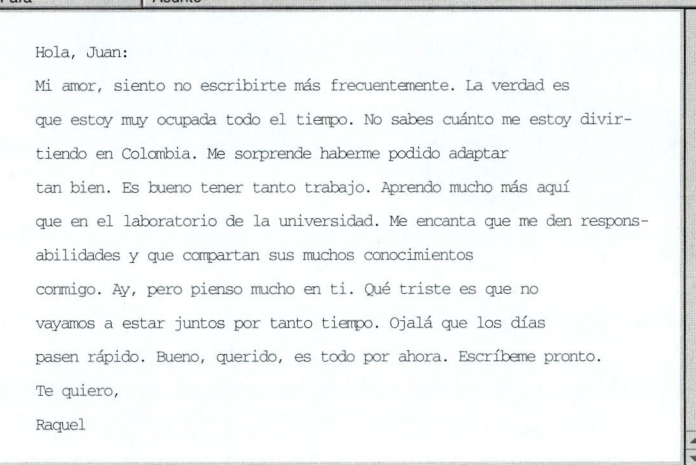

Mi amor, siento no escribirte más frecuentemente. La verdad es que estoy muy ocupada todo el tiempo. No sabes cuánto me estoy divirtiendo en Colombia. Me sorprende haberme podido adaptar tan bien. Es bueno tener tanto trabajo. Aprendo mucho más aquí que en el laboratorio de la universidad. Me encanta que me den responsabilidades y que compartan sus muchos conocimientos conmigo. Ay, pero pienso mucho en ti. Qué triste es que no vayamos a estar juntos por tanto tiempo. Ojalá que los días pasen rápido. Bueno, querido, es todo por ahora. Escríbeme pronto.

Te quiero,

Raquel

NATIONAL communication STANDARDS

Síntesis

5

Problemas Tu profesor(a) te va a dar una hoja de actividades. Escribe tres problemas ecológicos que te preocupen. Luego, circula por la clase y describe cada problema a un(a) compañero/a. Escribe las soluciones que te ofrece. Después, comparte la información con la clase. Answers will vary.

modelo

Estudiante 1: Me molesta que mi país no evite la deforestación.
Estudiante 2: Ojalá que el gobierno haga más para proteger los bosques.

TEACHING OPTIONS

Small Groups Divide students into groups of three. Have students write three predictions about the future on separate pieces of paper and put them in a sack. Students take turns drawing predictions and reading them to the group. Group members respond with an appropriate expression of emotion. Ex: **Voy a ganar millones de dólares algún día. (Me alegro que ganes millones de dólares.)**

Heritage Speakers Ask students to imagine that they are world leaders speaking at an environmental summit. Have students deliver a short speech to the class about some of the world's environmental problems and how they hope to solve them. Students should use as many verbs and expressions of emotion as possible.

3 Warm-up Have students divide a sheet of paper into four columns, with the following headings: **nuestra ciudad, las clases, el gobierno,** and another subject of their choosing. Then, have them brainstorm topics or issues for each column in preparation for the activity.

3 Present Ask two volunteers to read the **Modelo**. Then ask another volunteer to provide another sentence using **Me alegro que...** and another volunteer to react to that statement. Note: This activity is also suitable for groups of three. Have each student takes turns making comments, reacting, and writing the comments and reactions of their classmates to share with the class later.

4 Warm-up Introduce the two ways of saying *to miss (someone)* found in **Ayuda** by using them in sentences. Ex: **Te extraño, Luisa. Te echo de menos, Mario.**

4 Present Give pairs aproximately five minutes to read the e-mail and write their reponse. Give the class approximately ten minutes to complete the activity.

5 Present Ask a volunteer to read the **Modelo** with you. Distribute a copy of **Hoja de actividades 30** to each student.

5 Expand Have students work in groups of three to create a public service announcement. Groups should choose one of the ecological problems they mentioned in the activity, and include the proposed solutions for that problem in their announcement.

Assignment Have students do activities in **Student Activities Manual: Workbook, 151–152**

13.2 The subjunctive with doubt, disbelief, and denial

NATIONAL STANDARDS comparisons

ANTE TODO Just as the subjunctive is required with expressions of emotion, influence, and will, it is also used with expressions of doubt, disbelief, and denial.

Main clause — Subordinate clause

Dudan que su hijo les **diga** la verdad.

▶ The subjunctive is always used in a subordinate clause when there is a change of subject and the expression in the main clause implies negation or uncertainty.

¡No creo que haya lugares más bonitos en el mundo!

Dudo que el río esté contaminado aquí en las montañas.

▶ Here is a list of some common expressions of doubt, disbelief, or denial.

Expressions of doubt, disbelief, or denial

dudar	*to doubt*	**no es seguro**	*it's not certain*
negar (e:ie)	*to deny*	**no es verdad**	*it's not true*
no creer	*not to believe*	**es imposible**	*it's impossible*
no estar seguro/a (de)	*not to be sure*	**es improbable**	*it's improbable*
no es cierto	*it's not true; it's not certain*	**(no) es posible**	*it's (not) possible*
		(no) es probable	*it's (not) probable*

El gobierno **niega** que el agua **esté** contaminada.
The government denies that the water is contaminated.

Dudo que el gobierno **resuelva** el problema.
I doubt that the government will solve the problem.

Es probable que **haya** menos bosques y selvas en el futuro.
It's probable that there will be less forests and jungles in the future.

No es verdad que mi hermano **estudie** ecología.
It's not true that my brother studies ecology.

¡LENGUA VIVA!
In English, the expression *it is probable* indicates a fairly high degree of certainty. In Spanish, however, **es probable** implies uncertainty and therefore triggers the subjunctive in the subordinate clause: **Es muy probable que venga Elena.**

Section Goals

In **Estructura 13.2** students will learn:
- to use the subjunctive with verbs and expressions of doubt, disbelief, and denial
- common verbs and expressions of doubt, disbelief, and denial
- expressions of certainty

Instructional Resources
Student Activities Manual: Workbook, 153–154; Lab Manual, 296

Before Presenting Esctructura 13.2
Introduce a few of the expressions of doubt, disbelief, or denial by talking about a topic familiar to the whole class. Ex: **Dudo que el equipo de baloncesto vaya a ganar el partido este fin de semana. Es probable que el equipo contrario gane. No es cierto que el entrenador del nuestro equipo sea tan bueno como se dice.** and so forth. As you introduce each expression of doubt, disbelief, or denial, write it on the board, making sure that everyone understands its meaning and recognizes the subjunctive verb in the subordinate clause. Tell students that they are now going to learn another group of verbs and expressions that can trigger the subjunctive.

Assignment Have students prepare the activities on pages 407–408 as homework.

Present Go over **Ante Todo** and the example sentence, then ask volunteers to read the captions to the video stills, having them identify the phrase that triggers the subjunctive and the verb in the subjunctive. Model the pronunciation of each of the expressions of doubt, disbelief, or denial, having students repeat after you. Work through the model sentences and draw attention to **¡Lengua viva!** Point out that **es probable** and **es posible** are considered to express doubt.

TEACHING OPTIONS

Extra Practice Write these statements on the board, then ask students to write their reactions using a different expression of doubt, disbelief, or denial for each. **Muchos tipos de peces viven en el desierto. El cielo se está cayendo. Plantas enormes crecen en la luna. Los carros pequeños no contaminan. No hay ningún animal en peligro de extinción.**

Pairs Ask students to write five absurd statements. Students react to their partners' statements with an expression of doubt, disbelief, or denial as their partner reads them aloud. Ex: **Unos hombres verdes vienen a visitarme todos los días. (No creo que unos hombres verdes vengan a visitarte todos los días.)**

▶ The indicative is used in a subordinate clause when there is no doubt or uncertainty in the main clause. Here is a list of some expressions of certainty.

Expressions of certainty

no dudar	*not to doubt*	**estar seguro/a (de)**	*to be sure*
no cabe duda de	*there is no doubt*	**es cierto**	*it's true; it's certain*
no hay duda de	*there is no doubt*	**es seguro**	*it's certain*
no negar (e:ie)	*not to deny*	**es verdad**	*it's true*
		es obvio	*it's obvious*

No negamos que **hay** demasiados carros en las carreteras.
We don't deny that there are too many cars on the highways.

Es verdad que Colombia **es** un país bonito.
It's true that Colombia is a beautiful country.

No hay duda de que el Amazonas **es** uno de los ríos más largos.
There is no doubt that the Amazon is one of the longest rivers.

Es obvio que los tigres **están** en peligro de extinción.
It's obvious that tigers are in danger of extinction.

▶ In affirmative sentences, the verb **creer** expresses belief or certainty, so it is followed by the indicative. In negative sentences, however, when doubt is implied, **creer** is followed by the subjunctive.

No creo que **haya** vida en el planeta Marte.
I don't believe that there is life on the planet Mars.

Creo que **debemos** usar exclusivamente la energía solar.
I believe we should exclusively use solar energy.

▶ The expressions **quizás** and **tal vez** are usually followed by the subjunctive because they imply doubt about something.

Quizás haga sol mañana.
Perhaps it will be sunny tomorrow.

Tal vez veamos la luna esta noche.
Perhaps we will see the moon tonight.

¡INTÉNTALO! Completa estas frases con la forma correcta del verbo.

1. Dudo que ellos trabajen (trabajar).
2. Es cierto que él come (comer) mucho.
3. Es imposible que ellos salgan (salir).
4. Es probable que Uds. ganen (ganar).
5. No creo que ella vuelva (volver).
6. Es posible que nosotros vayamos (ir).
7. Dudamos que tú recicles (reciclar).
8. Creo que ellos juegan (jugar) al fútbol.
9. No niego que Uds. estudian (estudiar).
10. Es posible que ella no venga (venir) a casa.
11. Es probable que ellos duerman (dormir).
12. Es posible que Marta llame (llamar).
13. Tal vez Juan no nos oiga (oír).
14. No es cierto que ellos nos ayuden (ayudar).
15. Es obvio que Luis se aburre (aburrirse).
16. Creo que Juana va (ir) a casarse.

TEACHING OPTIONS

TPR Call out a series of sentences, using either an expression of certainty or an expression of doubt, disbelief, or denial. Have students stand if they hear an expression of certainty or remain seated if they hear an expression of doubt. Ex: **Es cierto que algunos pájaros hablan.** (students stand)

Extra Practice Have students write sentences about three things of which they are certain and three things they doubt or can't believe. Students should use a different expression for each of their sentences. Have students share some of their sentences with the class.

Present the expressions of certainty and work through the example sentences. Point out that adding **no** to an expression of doubt, disbelief, or denial, like **negar** or **dudar,** makes it an expression of certainty. Show how the inverse is the case with **creer**. Finally, point out that **tal vez** and **quizás** sometimes are followed by verbs in the indicative but that generally they are followed by verbs in the subjunctive.

Then engage students in a conversation about a topic familiar to the whole class as you did in **Before Presenting Estructura 13.2**, but this time invite students to respond by asking them questions that elicit their expressions of doubt, disbelief, or denial and expressions of certainty.

Ex: **En mi opinión, es cierto que el nuevo estadio daña el medio ambiente. ¿Qué creen Uds.? • No creo que terminen la nueva residencia antes de la próxima trimestre. ¿Creen Uds. que la terminen a tiempo? • Es improbable que se baje la matrícula el próximo año. ¿Qué creen Uds.? • No es cierto que la universidad tenga nuevo presidente antes del próximo año.**

Sugerencia Before checking **¡Inténtalo!**, have students read each item and mark whether the expression in the main clause is one of certainty or doubt. Then call on students to give their answers orally. Next, have students change the items in **¡Inténtalo!**, making the positive expressions negative, and the negative expressions positive. Students make the corresponding changes to their new sentences. For example, Item 1 becomes: **No dudo que ellos trabajan**.

1 Warm-up Before doing the first activity, model using the expressions in **Ayuda** by making a doubtful statement, then responding with one of the expressions. Use appropriate gestures as you do so. Ex: **¿Me dices que vas a viajar a Colombia para el fin de semana? ¡Qué va! ¡No vas a hacer eso!**

1 Present With a volunteer, read the **Modelo**, then add an additional response with another expression of doubt or disbelief from **Ayuda**. Go over the activity with the whole class. You play the role of Carolina, reading the printed sentences. Point to individuals to respond with disbelieve to your statements. If you wish, you may ask more than one student to respond to a given statement, using expressions of disbelief other than the one suggested.

1 Expand After you have gone through the statements in the exercise, you may continue by making other false statements such as the following: **Voy a hacer una excursión en el monte Rainier mañana. Mi abuela sólo come pasteles y cebollas.**

2 Present Go over the anwers with the whole class. Ask volunteers to read the completed sentences. Ask students to explain why they chose one verb form over another. After you finish, have pairs dramatize the dialogue together.

2 Sugerencia Introduce the vocabulary in **¡Lengua viva!** after completing Activity 2. Engage students in a short conversation about the Internet using the terms. Ex: **¿Es fácil conectarse con Internet usando las computadoras de la universidad? ¿Cuáles son sus sitios favoritos? ¿Quién conoce algunos sitios que tratan de la lengua española?**

Práctica

1 Dudas Carolina es una chica que siempre miente. Expresa tus dudas sobre lo que Carolina está diciendo ahora. Usa las expresiones entre paréntesis para tus respuestas.

modelo

El próximo año mi familia y yo vamos de vacaciones por diez meses. (dudar)

¡Ja! Dudo que vayan de vacaciones por ese tiempo. ¡Uds. no son ricos!

1. Estoy escribiendo una novela en español. (no creer)
   No creo que estés escribiendo una novela en español.
2. Mi tía es la directora del *Sierra Club*. (no ser verdad)
   No es verdad que tu tía sea la directora del Sierra Club.
3. Dos profesores míos juegan para los Osos *(Bears)* de Chicago. (ser imposible)
   Es imposible que dos profesores tuyos jueguen para los Osos.
4. Mi mejor amiga conoce al chef Emeril. (no ser cierto)
   No es cierto que tu mejor amiga conozca al chef Emeril.
5. Mi padre es dueño del Centro Rockefeller. (no ser posible)
   No es posible que tu padre sea dueño del Centro Rockefeller.
6. Yo ya tengo un doctorado *(doctorate)* en lenguas. (ser improbable)
   Es improbable que tengas un doctorado en lenguas.

AYUDA

Some useful expressions to express that you don't believe someone:

¡Qué va!
¡Imposible!
¡No te lo creo!
¡Es mentira!

2 Escoger Escoge las respuestas correctas para completar el diálogo. Luego dramatiza el diálogo con un(a) compañero/a.

RAÚL Uds. dudan que yo realmente ___estudie___ (estudio/estudie). No niego que a veces me ___divierto___ (divierto/divierta) demasiado, pero no cabe duda de que ___tomo___ (tomo/tome) mis estudios en serio. Estoy seguro de que cuando me vean graduarme van a pensar de manera diferente. Creo que no ___tienen___ (tienen/tengan) razón con sus críticas.

PAPÁ Es posible que tu mamá y yo no ___tengamos___ (tenemos/tengamos) razón. Es cierto que a veces ___dudamos___ (dudamos/dudemos) de ti. Pero no hay duda de que te ___pasas___ (pasas/pases) toda la noche en el Internet y oyendo música. No es nada seguro que ___estés___ (estás/estés) estudiando.

RAÚL Es verdad que ___uso___ (uso/use) mucho el Internet pero, ¡piensen! ¿No es posible que ___sea___ (es/sea) para buscar información para mis clases? ¡No hay duda de que el Internet ___es___ (es/sea) el mejor recurso del mundo! Es obvio que Uds. ___piensan___ (piensan/piensen) que no hago nada, pero no es cierto.

PAPÁ No dudo que esta conversación nos ___va___ (va/vaya) a ayudar. Pero tal vez esta noche ___puedas___ (puedes/puedas) trabajar sin música. ¿Está bien?

¡LENGUA VIVA!

Some useful Internet terms in Spanish:

dirección de Internet → *web address*
el sitio → *website*
la página → *page*
el enlace → *link*
navegar → *surf, browse*
hacer clic en → *click on*
bajar → *download*
conectarse → *log on*
desconectarse → *log off*

TEACHING OPTIONS

Large Groups Divide the class into groups of 5–7 students to stage an environmental debate. Some groups should play the role of environmental advocates while others represent industrialists and big business. Have students take turns presenting a policy platform for the group they represent. When they are finished, opposing groups express their doubts, disbeliefs, and denials.

Heritage Speakers Ask native speakers of Spanish to write an editorial about a current event or political issue in their community. In the body of their essay, students should include expressions of certainty as well as expressions of doubt, disbelief, or denial.

NATIONAL communication STANDARDS

Comunicación

3 **Diálogo** En parejas, miren la ilustración y desarrollen un diálogo interesante entre un(a) conservacionista y un(a) burócrata (*bureaucrat*) del gobierno. Answers will vary.

modelo

Conservacionista: Queremos reducir la contaminación del aire. Pero dudo que el gobierno nos vaya a ayudar.
Burócrata: Es obvio que el gobierno está haciendo muchas cosas para reducir la contaminación del aire.

4 **Adivinar** Escribe cinco oraciones sobre tu vida presente y futura. Cuatro deben ser falsas y sólo una debe ser cierta. Presenta tus oraciones al grupo. El grupo adivina (*guesses*) cuál es la oración cierta y expresa sus dudas sobre las falsas. Answers will vary.

modelo

Estudiante 1: Quiero irme un año a la selva a trabajar.
Estudiante 2: Dudo que te guste vivir en la selva.
Estudiante 3: En cinco años voy a ser presidente de los Estados Unidos.
Estudiante 2: No creo que seas presidente de los Estados Unidos en cinco años. ¡Tal vez en treinta!

AYUDA

Some verbs for talking about plans:
esperar → *to hope to*
querer → *to want to*
pretender → *to intend*
pensar → *to plan to*
pensar → *to be going*

NATIONAL communication STANDARDS

Síntesis

5 **Intercambiar** En grupos, escriban un párrafo sobre los problemas del medio ambiente en su estado o en su comunidad. Compartan su párrafo con otro grupo, que va a ofrecer opiniones y soluciones. Luego presenten su párrafo, con las opiniones y soluciones del otro grupo, a la clase. Answers will vary.

3 Warm-up Have the class as a whole brainstorm different topics that might be discussed.

3 Present Ask a volunteer to read the **Modelo** with you. Take the role of the **conservacionista**. After the volunteer has read the part of the **burócrata**, model adding an additional response, such as, **No creo que el gobierno esté haciendo tanto para reducir la contaminación del aire**. Then divide the class into teams; one representing the **conservacionista**, the other representing the **burócrata**. Individual students take turns making statements from the viewpoint of their party. The team for the opposing party responds to the statements, using an expression of certainty or doubt, disbelief, or denial.

4 Warm-up Review the vocabulary from **Ayuda** before students begin the activity.

4 Present Ask students to choose a secretary for their group to write down the group members' true statements to present to the class.

5 Expand Divide the class into groups of four. Ask group members to appoint a mediator to lead the discussion, a secretary to write the paragraph, a checker to proofread what was written, and a stenographer to take notes on the opinions and solutions of the other group.

5 Expand Have students create a poster illustrating the environmental problems in their community and proposing possible solutions.

Assignment Have students do the activities in the **Student Activities Manual: Workbook**, 153–154

TEACHING OPTIONS

Small Groups Give groups of three scenarios. Have students take turns playing a reporter interviewing the other two students about what is happening in each situation. The students being interviewed should use expressions of certainty or doubt, disbelief, and denial when responding to the reporter's questions. Possible scenarios: protest in favor of animal rights, a volcano about to erupt, a local ecological problem, a vacation in the mountains.

Game Divide the class into two teams. One team writes sentences with expressions of certainty while the other writes sentences with expressions of doubt, disbelief or denial. Put all the sentences in a hat. Students take turns drawing sentences for their team and stating the opposite of what the sentence says. The team with the most sentences using the correct mood wins.

Section Goals

In **Estructura 13.3**, students will learn:
- conjunctions that require the subjunctive
- when the infinitive follows a conjunction

Instructional Resources *Student Activities Manual: Workbook, 155; Lab Manual, 297*

Before Presenting Estructura 13.3 To introduce conjunctions that require the subjunctive, make a few statements about yourself. Ex: **Nunca llego a la clase tarde a menos que haya un problema con mi carro. Siempre leo mis mensajes electrónicos antes de que vaya a la clase. Camino a la clase con tal de que no llueve.** and so forth. After making each statement, write the conjunction on the board, explain its meaning, and repeat the statement so students hear the subjunctive in the subordinate clause. Tell students that in this lesson they will learn several conjunctions that are regularly followed by the subjunctive.

Assignment Have students study **Estructura 13.3** and prepare **¡Inténtalo!** and Activities 1 and 2 on pages 411–412 as homework.

Present Go over **Ante Todo** and the example sentence with the class. Then have volunteers read the captions to the video stills. Help them identify the conjunctions in the sentences and the subjunctive verbs in the subordinate clauses. Next, go over the discussion of adverbial clauses that express hypothetical situations and the example sentences that follow it.

Continued on page 411.

13.3 Conjunctions that require the subjunctive

NATIONAL STANDARDS comparisons

ANTE TODO In both Spanish and English, conjunctions are words or phrases that connect other words and clauses in sentences. Certain conjunctions commonly introduce adverbial clauses, which describe *how, why, when,* and *where* an action takes place.

Main clause	Conjunction	Adverbial clause
Vamos a visitar a Carlos	**antes de que**	**regrese** a California.

Se puede tomar fotos, ¿verdad?
Sí, con tal de que no toques las flores ni las plantas.

A menos que resuelvan el problema de la contaminación, los habitantes van a sufrir muchas enfermedades en el futuro.

- In Spanish, the subjunctive is used in an adverbial clause when it expresses a hypothetical situation, uncertainty as to whether an action or event will take place, or a condition that may or may not be fulfilled.

Voy a dejar un recado **en caso de que** Gustavo me llame.
I'm going to leave a message in case Gustavo calls me.

Voy al supermercado **para que** tengas algo de comer.
I'm going to the store so that you'll have something to eat.

CONSÚLTALO

Since much of the future (if not all!) is uncertain, the subjunctive is very commonly used when a subordinate clause expresses a future action. You will learn more about this in Lesson 14, section 14.2, p.440.

- Here is a list of the conjunctions that always require the subjunctive.

Conjunctions that require the subjunctive

a menos que	*unless*	**en caso (de) que**	*in case (that)*
antes (de) que	*before*	**para que**	*so that*
con tal (de) que	*provided that*	**sin que**	*without*

Algunos animales van a morir **a menos que** haya leyes para protegerlos.
Some animals are going to die unless there are laws to protect them.

Ellos nos llevan a la selva **para que** veamos las plantas tropicales.
They are taking us to the jungle so that we may see the tropical plants.

Voy a salir **sin que** mis hermanos me vean.
I'm going to leave without my brothers seeing me.

Voy a tomar esa clase **con tal de que** tú la tomes también.
I'm going to take that class provided that you take it too.

¡ATENCIÓN!

The expression **sin que** works differently than *without*. Whereas in English we say: *We do it without them (their) asking us*, in Spanish the second verb is conjugated, not a gerund: **Lo hacemos sin que nos lo pidan.**

TEACHING OPTIONS

Extra Practice Write the following partial sentences on the board. Have students complete them with true or invented information about their own lives. **Voy a terminar los estudios con tal de que..., Necesito $500 en caso de que..., Puedo salir este sábado a menos que..., El mundo cambia sin que..., Debo... antes de que..., Mis padres... para que yo...**

Video Have students divide a sheet of paper into four sections, labeling them **voluntad, emoción, duda,** and **conjunción**. Replay the video. Have them listen for each use of the subjunctive, marking the example they hear in the appropriate section. Play the video again, then have students write a short summary that includes each use of the subjunctive.

COMPARE & CONTRAST

You have learned that expressions of emotion, doubt, and will are followed by an infinitive when there is no change of subject from the main clause to the subordinate clause. An infinitive is also used after the prepositions **antes de, para,** and **sin** when there is no change of subject. Compare these sentences.

Te llamamos mañana **antes de que salgas** para Cartagena.
We will call you tomorrow before you leave for Cartagena.

Te llamamos mañana **antes de salir** para Cartagena.
We will call you tomorrow before leaving for Cartagena.

Tus padres trabajan mucho **para que tú puedas** vivir bien.
Your parents work a lot so that you are able to live well.

Tus padres trabajan muchísimo **para vivir** bien.
Your parents work very hard in order to live well.

In contrast, the subjunctive is always used after **a menos que, con tal (de) que,** and **sin que** even when there is no change of subject from the main clause to the subordinate clause.

Voy a llevarlos al río esta tarde **con tal (de) que** tenga tiempo.
I'm going to take them to the river provided that I have time.

Vamos de excursión mañana **a menos que estemos** enfermos.
We'll go hiking tomorrow unless we're feeling sick.

¡INTÉNTALO! Completa las oraciones con la forma correcta de los verbos entre paréntesis.

1. Voy a establecer un club de ecología para que mis amigos y yo podamos (poder) aprender más sobre el medio ambiente.
2. Siempre reciclo los envases de plástico para reducir (reducir) la contaminación del medio ambiente.
3. No podemos evitar la lluvia ácida a menos que el gobierno y la gente trabajen (trabajar) juntos para controlar la contaminación del aire.
4. El gobierno va a establecer parques nacionales para proteger (proteger) las selvas y los bosques.
5. Elisa quiere hablar con el presidente del club de ecología antes de que comience (comenzar) la reunión *(meeting)*.
6. No podemos conducir nuestros carros sin contaminar (contaminar) el aire.
7. Debemos recoger la basura en las calles y en las carreteras sin que nadie nos lo pida (pedir).
8. Debemos crear parques para proteger las aves y los otros animales en caso de que la gente destruya sus hábitats naturales.
9. No voy de excursión a menos que vaya (ir) también un guía.
10. Antes de nadar (nadar) en algún río pregunto si el agua está contaminada.

Help students see that in each case the conjunction introduces a situation that has not yet happened (will happen in the future) and which could turn out differently than expected (or hoped). Illustrate this by going over the list of conjunctions and their meanings with the example sentences that follow.

Discuss the contents of **¡Atención!** Illustrate the point by asking questions such as: **¿Hagan Uds. los ejercicios sin que yo les pida? ¿Saquen la basura sin que alguien les ayude?** and so forth.

Compare and Contrast Present As you work through the example sentences, point out that **antes de** and **para** (which are employed when there is no change in subject and which lack **que**) are prepositions, while **antes de que** and **para que** (which are employed to introduce a subordinate clause with a different subject) are conjunctions. Then write sentences that use **antes de, para,** and ask volunteers to rewrite them so that, instead of a preposition and an infinitive, they end with subordinate clauses. Ex: **Voy a hablar con Paula antes de partir para la clase. (...antes de que ella parta para la clase. ...antes de que Sergio le hable. ...antes de que ella compre esas botas.)**

Close Go over **¡Inténtalo!** orally with the whole class. Ask volunteers to read the sentences with the correct verb form and explain the reason they chose it.

TEACHING OPTIONS

TPR Make several statements, some with conjunctions followed by the infinitive and some with conjunctions followed by the subjunctive. After each statement, hold up two flashcards, one with *I* for infinitive and one with *S* for subjunctive. Students point to the card that represents what they heard. Ex: **Juan necesita un reloj para que llegue a tiempo. (S) No laven el carro para conservar el agua. (I)**

Extra Practice Have students use the following conjunctions to make statements about the environment: **para, para que, sin, sin que, antes de,** and **antes de que.** Ex: **Es importante empezar un programa de reciclaje antes de que tengamos demasiado basura. No es posible conservar los bosques sin que se deje de cortar tantos árboles.**

1 Present Go over the activity with the whole class, having volunteers read each complete sentence. After each item, ask another student to explain the reason the sentence requires a subjunctive form or an infinitive.

1 Expand Ask students to write new endings for each sentence. Ex: **Voy a llevar a mis hijos al parque pare que... hagan más ejercicio/jueguen con sus amigos/pasen más tiempo fuera de la casa.**

1 Expand Ask students to work in pairs to write six original complex sentences like the ones in the activity about a trip they plan to take. Have them use one conjunction that requires the subjunctive in each sentence.

2 Present Have four or five volunteers write their sentences on the board. Go over them with the whole class, correcting any errors. As you go through the items, ask volunteers who didn't write on the board to present their sentences orally.

2 Expand Have students write more than one way to finish each sentence in the activity.

3 Warm-up Write the expressions from **Ayuda** on the board. Model a statement about one of the organizations featured in the activity using an expression from **Ayuda**.

3 Expand Have students create a fund-raising advertisement for one of these organizations for their local newspaper. Students should state the goals of the organization, how these goals are in the public interest, and where and how a donation can be made.

Práctica

1 Completar La Sra. Montero habla de una excursión que quiere hacer con su familia. Completa las oraciones con la forma correcta de cada verbo.

1. Voy a llevar a mis hijos al parque para que aprendan (aprender) sobre la naturaleza.
2. Vamos a pasar todo el día allí con tal de que nosotros tengamos (tener) tiempo.
3. En bicicleta podemos explorar el parque sin caminar (caminar) demasiado.
4. Vamos a bajar al cráter a menos que se prohíba (prohibir).
5. Vamos a llevar al perro para que nos proteja (protegernos).
6. No pensamos ir muy lejos en caso de que llueva (llover).
7. Queremos cenar a la orilla (*shore*) del río a menos que no haya (haber) suficiente luz.
8. Mis hijos van a ver muchas cosas interesantes antes de salir (salir) del parque.

2 Oraciones Completa las siguientes oraciones de una manera lógica. Answers will vary.

1. No podemos controlar la contaminación del aire a menos que...
2. Voy a reciclar los productos de papel y de vidrio para que...
3. Con tal de que se ponga fin a (*put to an end*) la deforestación...
4. Debemos proteger los animales en peligro de extinción para que...
5. Mis amigos y yo vamos a recoger la basura de la universidad para...
6. No podemos desarrollar nuevas fuentes (*sources*) de energía sin...
7. Tenemos que eliminar la contaminación del agua para...
8. No podemos proteger a la naturaleza sin que...

3 Organizaciones En parejas, lean las descripciones de las organizaciones de conservación. Luego expresa en tus propias (*own*) palabras las opiniones de cada organización. Answers will vary.

Organización: Fundación Río Orinoco
Problema: La destrucción de los ríos
Solución: Programa para limpiar las orillas de los ríos y reducir la erosión y así proteger los ríos

Organización: Oficina de Turismo Internacional
Problema: Necesidad de mejorar la imagen del país en el mercado turístico internacional
Solución: Plan para promover el ecoturismo en los 33 parques nacionales usando agencias de publicidad e implementando un plan agresivo de conservación

Organización: Asociación Nabusimake-Pico Colón
Problema: Un lugar turístico popular en Sierra Nevada, Santa Marta, que necesita mejor mantenimiento
Solución: Programa de voluntarios para limpiar y mejorar los senderos

AYUDA

Here are some expressions you can use as you do **Práctica 3.**

Se puede evitar... con tal de que...
Es necesario... para que...
Debemos prohibir... antes de que...
No es posible... sin que...
Vamos a... en caso de que...
A menos que... no vamos a...

TEACHING OPTIONS

Pairs Ask students to imagine that unless some dramatic actions are taken, the world as we know it will end in five days. It is their responsibility as community leaders to give a speech warning people what will happen unless everyone takes action. Have students work with a partner to prepare a three minute presentation for the class, using as many different conjunctions that require the subjunctive as possible.

Small Group Divide the class into groups of four. The first student begins a sentence, the second picks a conjunction, and the third student finishes the sentence. The fourth student writes the sentence down. Students should take turns playing the different roles until they have created eight sentences.

Comunicación

4 **Preguntas** En parejas, túrnense para hacerse las siguientes preguntas. Answers will vary.

1. ¿Qué haces cada noche antes de acostarte?
2. ¿Qué haces en la clase cada día antes de que llegue el/la profesor(a)?
3. ¿Qué hacen tus padres para que puedas asistir a la universidad?
4. ¿Qué puedes hacer para mejorar tu español?
5. ¿Qué quieres hacer mañana a menos que haga mal tiempo?
6. ¿Qué haces en tus clases sin que los profesores lo sepan?

5 **Comparar** En parejas, comparen su rutina diaria con algo que van a hacer en el futuro. Usen conjunciones de la lista. Answers will vary.

antes de	con tal de que	para	sin
antes de que	en caso de que	para que	sin que

modelo

Estudiante 1: Siempre leo antes de acostarme pero hoy quiero estudiar para mi examen.

Estudiante 2: Todos los sábados llevo a mi primo al parque para que juegue. Pero el sábado que viene, con tal de que no llueva, lo voy a llevar a las montañas.

Síntesis

6 **Tic-Tac-Toe** En grupos de cuatro, formen dos equipos. Una persona comienza una frase y otra persona de su equipo la termina usando una conjunción de la gráfica (*chart*). El primer equipo que usa tres conjunciones seguidas (*in a row*) gana el *tic-tac-toe*. ¡Ojo! Hay que usar la conjunción y el verbo correctamente. Si no, ¡no cuenta! Answers will vary.

modelo

Equipo 1

Estudiante 1: Dudo que podamos eliminar la deforestación...

Estudiante 2: sin que nos ayude el gobierno.

Equipo 2

Estudiante 1: Creo que podemos conservar nuestros recursos naturales...

Estudiante 2: con tal de que todos hagamos algo para ayudar.

a menos que	con tal de que	para que
antes de que	para	sin que
sin	en caso de que	antes de

NOTA CULTURAL

Tic-tac-toe has various names in the Spanish-speaking world, including **tres en raya, tres en línea, ta-te-ti, gato, la vieja,** and **triqui-triqui.**

TEACHING OPTIONS

Heritage Speakers Ask native speakers if they ever played tic-tac-toe when growing up. What did they call it? Was it one of the names listed in the **Nota cultural**? Ask students the names of other childhood games they played and to describe them. Are the games similar to those played by the native English speakers in the class?

Pairs Ask pairs of students to interview each other about what they must do today in order for their future goals to become a reality. Students should state what their goals are, the necessary conditions to achieve them, and talk about obstacles they may encounter. Students should use as many conjunctions as possible in their interviews. Have students present their dialogues to the class.

4 Warm-up Give students a few minutes to read the questions and prepare their responses before working with a partner.

4 Expand When pairs have finished asking and answering the questions, work with the whole class, asking each of the questions to several individuals and asking other students to react to their classmates' responses. Ex: ____ **hace aeróbicos antes de acostarse. ¿Quién más hace ejercicios? ¡Uf! Hacer ejercicio me parece excesivo. ¿Quiénes ven la tele? ¿Nadie lee un libro antes de acostarse?** and so forth.

4 Expand You might have students ask Question 4 of five different classmates. Ask students to jot down the responses they get. Then, ask them questions such as these: **En su opinión, ¿cuál fue la respuesta mejor? ¿Y la respuesta más común?**

5 Present Ask a volunteer to read the **Modelo** with you. You take the part of **Estudiante 1**. After the volunteer has read the part of **Estudiante 2**, model another exchange using a preposition or conjunction from the word bank. Then allow pairs about ten minutes to prepare their exchanges. After they have finished, ask volunteers to share their best with the class.

6 Warm-up Have groups prepare a tic-tac-toe card like the one shown in **Síntesis**. Go over the instructions so there will be no confusion about the rules of the game. Then, ask four volunteers to read the **Modelo** for the class.

Assignment Have students do the activities in the **Student Activities Manual: Workbook,** page 155

Section Goals

In **Estructura 13.4**, students will learn:
- negative **tú** commands
- affirmative **tú** commands

Instructional Resources
Student Activities Manual: Workbook, 157–158; Lab Manual, 298

Before Presenting Estructura 13.4 Explain that students are about to learn the **tú** command forms, the forms they would use to tell someone whom they normally address as **tú** to do something. Reassure students that, with the exception of eight irregular forms, they have already encountered the **tú** command forms. Have them open to pages 404 and 408 and read the direction lines to the activities there. Help them recognize the **tú** command forms in the directions. Write the commands on the board as you identify them. Page 404—Activity 1: **completa, compara;** Activity 2: **transforma, añade.** Page 408—Activity 1: **expresa, usa;** Activity 2: **escoge, dramatiza.** Help students recognize that the affirmative **tú** command forms of regular verbs are the same as the third-person singular forms. Tell them they will also learn the negative **tú** command forms.

Assignment Have students study **Estructura 13.4** and do the exercises on pages 415–416 as homework.

Present Make clear that **tú** commands are spoken to people one addresses as **tú**. Then explain that the negative **tú** command of a verb is formed by **no** + **tú** form of the present subjunctive of that verb. Work through the chart of negative **tú** commands and the examples that follow, including the captions to the video stills.

Continued on page 415.

13.4 Familiar (tú) commands

ANTE TODO In Lesson 12, you learned how to use formal commands. You will now learn familiar (**tú**) commands. **Tú** commands are used when you want to give advice to or instruct someone you normally address with the familiar **tú.**

Negative *tú* commands

Infinitive	Present subjunctive	Negative *tú* command
cuidar	tú cuides	**no cuides** (tú)
tocar	tú toques	**no toques** (tú)
temer	tú temas	**no temas** (tú)
volver	tú vuelvas	**no vuelvas** (tú)
insistir	tú insistas	**no insistas** (tú)
pedir	tú pidas	**no pidas** (tú)

No toques las plantas, no salgas del sendero...

...pero si ves por el sendero botellas, papeles o latas, recógelos.

▶ Like **Ud.** and **Uds.** commands, negative **tú** commands have the same form as the **tú** form of the present subjunctive. Note that the pronoun **tú** is not used with familiar commands, except for emphasis.

Julia, no **molestes** a los animales.
Julia, don't annoy the animals.

Carlos, no **comas** esa planta.
Carlos, don't eat that plant.

Affirmative *tú* commands

Infinitive	Present indicative	Affirmative *tú* command
cuidar	cuida	**cuida** (tú)
tocar	toca	**toca** (tú)
temer	teme	**teme** (tú)
volver	vuelve	**vuelve** (tú)
insistir	insiste	**insiste** (tú)
pedir	pide	**pide** (tú)

▶ Unlike other command forms, affirmative **tú** commands do not resemble the forms of the present subjunctive. Instead, they usually have the same form as the third person singular of the present indicative.

Recicla el papel.
Recycle paper.

Protege nuestro medio ambiente.
Protect our environment.

¡ATENCIÓN!

As in other forms of the subjunctive, the negative familiar commands keep the same stem changes as the indicative. See Lesson 12, section 12.3, p.377.

LENGUA VIVA

To form affirmative **vosotros** commands, drop the **–r** from the infinitive and add **–d**:
evitar → evitad
pone → poned
salir → salid

Negative **vosotros** commands have the same form as the **vosotros** forms of the present subjunctive:
no evitéis
no pongáis
no salgáis

TEACHING OPTIONS

TPR Ask individual students to comply with a series of commands requiring them to perform actions or move around the room. While the student follows the command, the class writes it down as a volunteer writes it on the board. Be sure to use both positive and negative commands. Ex: **Recoge ese papel. Ponlo en la basura. Regresa a tu escritorio. No te sientes. Siéntate ahora.** and so forth.

Pairs Ask students to imagine they are starting an ecology club. Have them make a list of five things to do in order to get ready for the first meeting and five things not to do to make sure everything runs smoothly, using infinitives. Then have students take turns telling partners what to do or not do. Ex: **Usa papel reciclado para tomar las notas. Camina a la reunión; no vayas en carro.**

▶ There are eight irregular affirmative **tú** commands.

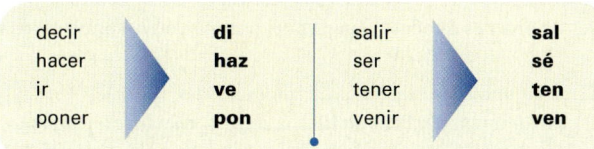

decir	**di**	salir	**sal**
hacer	**haz**	ser	**sé**
ir	**ve**	tener	**ten**
poner	**pon**	venir	**ven**

¡**Ten** cuidado con el perro!
Be careful with the dog!

¡**Sal** de aquí ahora mismo!
Leave here at once!

Pon las latas en la basura.
Put the cans in the trash.

Haz los ejercicios.
Do the exercises.

▶ Since **ir** and **ver** have the same **tú** command (**ve**), context will determine the meaning.

Ve al supermercado con José.
Go to the supermarket with José.

Ve ese programa... es muy interesante.
See that program... it's very interesting.

COMPARE & CONTRAST

The placement of reflexive and object pronouns in **tú** commands follows the same rules as in formal commands. Note that when a pronoun is attached to a command of more than two syllables, a written accent is used to maintain the original stress pattern. Compare the following examples.

¡Alégra**te**!
Be happy!

No **te** sientas triste.
Don't feel sad.

Di**me**.
Tell me.

No **me lo** digas.
Don't tell me (it).

¡Alégren**se**!
Be happy!

No **se** sientan tristes.
Don't feel sad.

Díga**me**.
Tell me.

No **me lo** diga.
Don't tell me (it).

LENGUA VIVA

Reflexive **vosotros** commands drop the **–d** and attach **os**:
sentaos
levantaos
The negative forms follow the normal pattern:
no os sentéis
no os levantéis

¡INTÉNTALO! Indica los mandatos (*commands*) familiares de estos verbos.

	Mandato afirmativo	Mandato negativo
1. cambiar	Cambia el aceite.	No cambies el aceite.
2. correr	Corre más rápido.	No corras más rápido.
3. salir	Sal ahora.	No salgas ahora.
4. tocar	Toca las flores.	No toques las flores.
5. venir	Ven aquí.	No vengas aquí.
6. levantarse	Levántate temprano.	No te levantes temprano.
7. volver	Vuelve pronto.	No vuelvas pronto.
8. hacerlo	Hazlo ya.	No lo hagas ahora.

TEACHING OPTIONS

Heritage Speakers Ask Spanish speakers to look for a how-to advertisement in a Spanish-language magazine or newspaper in which they find informal commands used. Have students bring a copy of the ad to class. Ask them to share the ad with the class and explain why they think informal commands were used instead of formal ones.

Extra Practice Have students imagine that they are a tour guide taking a group of college students on a trip to a national or state park. Have the guides make a handout of four things students must do and four things they must not do while visiting the park. Instruct them to use **tú** commands throughout. Then, write **Mandatos afirmativos** and **Mandatos negativos** on the board and ask individuals to write one of their commands in the appropriate column. Make corrections as necessary.

Test comprehension and practice negative **tú** commands by calling out the infinitives of a variety of regular verbs the students already know and signal individuals to convert them into negative commands. Ex: **conservar: no conserves, barrer: no barras, pedir: no pidas, insistir: no insistas** and so forth.

Affirmative tú commands Present Follow the same procedure to introduce the affirmative **tú** commands.

Model the pronunciation of the eight irregular affirmative **tú** commands. Point out that the negative **tú** commands of these verbs are formed in the regular way, i.e. **no** + **tú** form of the present subjunctive.

Note: If you are not teaching the **vosotros** forms, remind students now that the plural of tú commands is the **Uds.** command form. Ex: **decir: di, no digas, digan, no digan.** If you are teaching the **vosotros** forms, draw students' attention to the **Lengua viva** box on page 414 and use the procedure outlined above to introduce the forms.

Compare and contrast Present Ask students to explain what they remember about the placement of object and reflexive pronouns when they are used with formal (**Ud.**) commands. Point out that the same rules apply to **tú** commands. Go over **Compare and Contrast** and the example sentences. Then write several infinitive phrases such as the following on the board: **levantarse, decirme la verdad, leer el cuento a nosotros.** Have students write a positive and negative **tú** command for each phrase, replacing nouns with the appropriate object pronouns.

Close Go over the answers to **¡Inténtalo!** orally with the class.

1 Warm-up Before students complete the activity, ask them to say the eight verbs that have irregular affirmative **tú** commands.

1 Present Call on volunteers to write their answers on the board. Ask the class to make corrections to grammar or spelling as necessary.

1 Expand Continue this activity orally with the class, using regular verbs. Call out a negative command and designate individuals to make the corresponding positive command. Ex: **No sirvas la comida ahora. (Sirve la comida ahora.** or **Sírvela ahora.)**

2 Present Ask a volunteer to read the **Modelo** with you, then go over the activity with the whole class. You read Pedro's command and indicate an individual to give Marina's response. **Note:** This activity is also suitable to being done by pairs, who take turns playing the parts of Pedro and Marina.

3 Warm-up Go over **Lengua viva** with the class. Illustrate this usage with example sentences such as: **Rigo, ¡baja esa música, por favor! Es tan alta que Lourdes y yo no podemos conversar.**

3 Present Ask a volunteer to read the **Modelo**. Go over the answers to the activity orally with the class by reading each statement and cue and indicating an individual to give the command.

3 Expand Ask students to write sentences describing five additional situations in the Valenzuela household. Have students give their situations to a partner, who will write the corresponding command.

Práctica

1

Completar Unos amigos van a tener una cena en casa de Olga. Ella es la coordinadora y les da órdenes a todos. Completa el párrafo con la forma correcta de cada verbo.

1. No __vengas__ en una hora. __Ven__ ahora mismo. (venir)
2. __Haz__ el arroz a tiempo. Pero no lo __hagas__ demasiado temprano. (hacer)
3. No __vayas__ a la tienda a comprar los refrescos. __Ve__ al sótano. (ir)
4. __Dime__ que no quieres preparar la cebolla, pero no __me digas__ que no quieres ayudar. (decirme)
5. No __seas__ tan antipático con Katia. __Sé__ amable que es muy niña. (ser)
6. __Ten__ cuidado con el cuchillo, pero no __tengas__ miedo de usarlo. (tener)
7. __Sal__ al balcón, pero no __salgas__ al patio. Ayer llovió mucho. (salir)

2

Cambiar Pedro y Marina no pueden ponerse de acuerdo (*agree*) cuando le dan órdenes a su hijo Miguel. Lee las órdenes que Pedro le da a Miguel. Después, usa la información entre paréntesis para formar las órdenes que le da Marina. Sigue el modelo.

modelo

Recoge la basura. (poner la mesa)
No recojas la basura, Miguel. Pon la mesa.

1. Barre el suelo. (pasar la aspiradora) No barras el suelo, Miguel. Pasa la aspiradora.
2. Plancha la ropa. (hacer las camas) No planches la ropa, Miguel. Haz las camas.
3. Saca la basura. (quitar la mesa) No saques la basura, Miguel. Quita la mesa.
4. Ve al supermercado. (quedarte aquí) No vayas al supermercado, Miguel. Quédate aquí.
5. Pon el radio. (poner la televisión) No pongas el radio, Miguel. Pon la televisión.
6. Dale los libros a Katia. (dárselos a Juan) No le des los libros a Katia. Dáselos a Juan.
7. Prepara la cena. (limpiar el carro) No prepares la cena, Miguel. Limpia el carro.
8. Corta el césped. (bañar al gato) No cortes el césped, Miguel. Baña al gato.

3

Desastres La Sra. Valenzuela está pasando un mal día. Su casa está muy desordenada y le da órdenes a su esposo y a sus hijos/as para que ordenen todo. Forma los mandatos que ella le da a su familia. Answers will vary.

modelo

Hay mucha basura en la cocina. (Pilar)
Pilar, saca la basura de la cocina.

1. Las ventanas están abiertas. (Martín)
2. El perro ladra (*barks*) porque tiene hambre. (Lola)
3. La alfombra está sucia. (Pedro)
4. El gato se ha montado en la televisión. (Pilar)
5. Juanito está tirando los papeles del escritorio del Sr. Valenzuela. (Lola)
6. Pilar está escuchando música a todo volumen. (Martín)
7. Los muebles de la sala están llenos de polvo. (Pedro)
8. Las flores del jardín necesitan agua. (Lola)

LENGUA VIVA

While in English one says that the music is *loud* or *soft*, in Spanish one says **está alta** or **está baja**. The corresponding verbs are **subir** (*turn up*) and **bajar** (*turn down*)

TEACHING OPTIONS

TPR Have pairs of students brainstorm a list of actions that can be mimed. Then have them give each other **tú** commands based on the actions. Call on several pairs to demonstrate their actions for the class. When a repetoire of mimable actions is established, do rapid-fire TPR with the whole class using these commands/actions.

Pairs Have students create six questions about conservation, then work with a partner to ask and respond to the questions with positive and negative commands. If a student responds with a negative command, he or she must follow it with a positive command. Ex: **¿Debo reciclar las latas de aluminio? (Sí, recíclalas.) ¿Pongo los periódicos en la basura? (No, no los pongas en la basura. Recíclalos.)**

Comunicación

4 **Diálogo** En parejas, preparen un diálogo entre Ramón y Luisa Aguilera. Ellos se dan órdenes negativas y positivas sobre lo que tienen que hacer para llegar a tiempo a una fiesta. Usen mandatos afirmativos y negativos. Luego presenten el diálogo a la clase. Answers will vary.

modelo

Luisa: ¡Sal del cuarto de baño ya!
Ramón: ¡No me des órdenes!
Luisa: Pero tengo que maquillarme.
Ramón: Y yo tengo que ducharme. Oye, ¿qué hora es?
Luisa: Son las siete menos veinte.
Ramón: ¡Ay! ¡Tráeme una toalla!

5 **Órdenes** Circula por la clase e intercambia órdenes con tus compañeros/as. Debes seguir las órdenes que ellos te dan o reaccionar apropiadamente. Answers will vary.

modelo

Estudiante 1: Dame todo tu dinero.
Estudiante 2: No, no quiero dártelo. Muéstrame tu cuaderno.
Estudiante 1: Aquí está.
Estudiante 3: Ve a la pizarra y escribe tu nombre.
Estudiante 4: No quiero. Hazlo tú.

Síntesis

6 **Anuncios** Miren estos anuncios (*ads*). Luego, en grupos pequeños, preparen tres anuncios para asociaciones conservacionistas. Los anuncios pueden ser para un periódico, una revista, etc. Answers will vary.

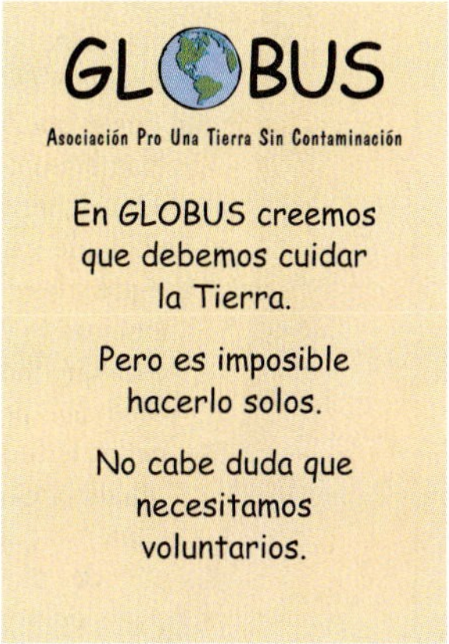

GLOBUS
Asociación Pro Una Tierra Sin Contaminación
En GLOBUS creemos que debemos cuidar la Tierra.
Pero es imposible hacerlo solos.
No cabe duda que necesitamos voluntarios.

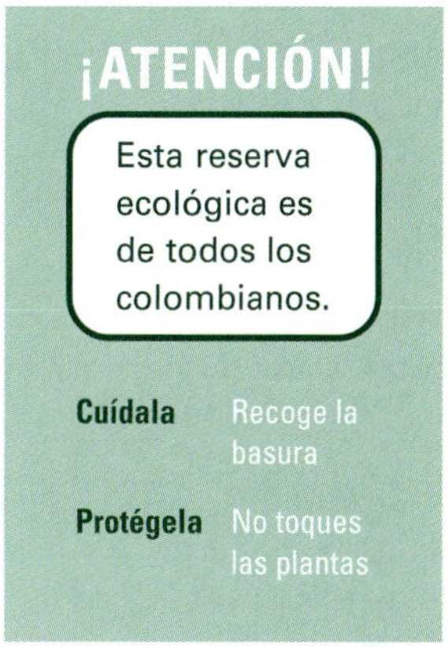

¡ATENCIÓN!
Esta reserva ecológica es de todos los colombianos.
Cuídala
Recoge la basura
Protégela
No toques las plantas

4 Warm-up With the whole class, brainstorm the things one has to do to get ready to go to a party. Write these ideas on the board.

4 Present Ask two volunteers to read the **Modelo** aloud. Give pairs five to seven minutes to prepare and practice their dialogues. Then have pairs present their dialogues to the class.

5 Warm-up Ask four volunteers to read the **Modelo**, then brainstorm some a list of things students might ask their classmates to do.

5 Expand Have volunteers report to the class what they were asked to do, what they did, and what they did not do.

6 Warm-up With the whole class, ask volunteers to read the ads. Ask comprehension questions about them. Ex: **¿Qué tipo de organización es Globus? ¿Qué hace? ¿Cuál es el objeto de la segunda anuncio?**

6 Present Divide the class into groups of three. Give groups these guidelines:

1. Use at least one affirmative and one negative informal command
2. Use the subjunctive with: one expression of emotion, one expression of doubt, and one conjunction;
3. Use one expression of certainty.

Assignment Have students do activities in the **Student Activities Manual: Workbook,** page 157–158.

TEACHING OPTIONS

Small Groups Divide the class into groups of four to practice all the **Estructuras** of the lesson. Student 1 makes a statement about the environment using an expression of emotion followed by the subjunctive. Student 2 responds with a statement of doubt or certainty. Student 3 adds an opinion, using a conjunction followed by the subjunctive, and Student 4 gives Student 1 an affirmative or negative command based on the previous comments made. Students should complete four rounds, alternating who starts the round.

Extra Practice Review the verbs on page 396 and informal commands by stating a verb, then calling on a volunteer to make an affirmative command using that verb. Call on a second volunteer to counter with a negative command.

Section Goals

In **Lectura** students will:
- learn that recognizing the purpose of a text can help them to understand it
- read a fable from ***El conde Lucanor***

Antes de leer
Introduce the strategy. Tell students that recognizing the writer's purpose will help them comprehend an unfamiliar text.

Examinar el texto Have students scan the text, using the reading strategies they have learned in order to determine the author's purpose. Then have them work with a partner to answer the questions. Students should recognize that the story is a fable because its characters are animals; it begins with the formulaic opening **Hubo una vez**; and it ends with an explanation of the story's meaning, a moral.

Predicciones After students have written their predictions, have them compare their answers with those of a classmate. Tell them that where their predictions differ they should refer back to the story for resolution.

Determinar el propósito Guide students to recognize that one of the traditional purposes of a fable is to teach a lesson about life. Tell them that as they read the fable they should try to express the lesson in their own words.

Assignment Have students read the selection from ***El conde Lucanor*** and prepare **Corregir** and **Contestar** on page 419 as homework.

Lectura

Antes de leer

Estrategia

Recognizing the purpose of a text

When you are faced with an unfamiliar text, it is important to determine the writer's purpose. If you are reading an editorial in a newspaper, for example, you know that the journalist's objective is to persuade you of his or her point of view. Identifying the purpose of a text will help you better comprehend its meaning.

Examinar el texto

Utiliza las estrategias de lectura para familiarizarte con el texto. Después contesta las siguientes preguntas y compara tus respuestas con las de un(a) compañero/a.

- ¿De qué trata la lectura?
- ¿Es una fábula, un poema, un artículo de periódico...?
- ¿Cómo lo sabes?

Predicciones

Lee estas predicciones sobre la lectura e indica si estás de acuerdo con ellas. Después compara tus opiniones con las de un(a) compañero/a.

1. La lectura es un género de ficción.
2. Los personajes son animales.
3. La acción tiene lugar en un zoológico.
4. Hay una moraleja.

Determinar el propósito

Con un(a) compañero/a, hablen de los posibles propósitos del texto. Consideren las siguientes preguntas.

- ¿Qué te dice el género del texto sobre los posibles propósitos del texto?
- ¿Piensas que el texto puede tener más de un propósito? ¿Por qué?

¿De qué trata la lectura? *What is the reading about?* fábula *fable* estás de acuerdo *you agree* género *type* personajes *characters* moraleja *moral* propósito *purpose*

De lo que le ocurrió a un zorro con un cuervo que tenía un pedazo de queso en el pico

(un fragmento de El conde Lucanor)

Don Juan Manuel

El noble español don Juan Manuel (1282–1348) es uno de los escritores más importantes de la literatura medieval. Sus historias inspiraron a autores tan célebres como Shakespeare y Cervantes. Su obra más conocida, El conde Lucanor, *es una colección de fábulas y cuentos didácticos populares cuyo objetivo era enseñar a través de la diversión. En esta ocasión presentamos la famosa fábula del zorro y el cuervo que siglos más tarde adaptó* La Fontaine.

Hubo una vez un cuervo que encontró un gran pedazo de queso. Lo tomó con el pico y se subió a un árbol para poder comérselo más tranquilamente, sin que nadie le molestara. Pasó en ese momento un zorro por el pie del árbol y al ver el queso que tenía el cuervo, comenzó a pensar en la manera de quitárselo. Y entonces le dijo:
—Don Cuervo, hace mucho tiempo que oí hablar de Ud., de su prudencia y de su nobleza. Lo busqué y hoy la fortuna hace que lo encuentre y, ahora que lo veo, entiendo que tiene más virtudes de las que todos me decían. Y para que vea que no lo digo por adular, ahora mismo voy a hablar de las virtudes que yo encuentro en Ud. y de las cualidades que la gente le critica. Toda la gente piensa que el color de sus plumas, de sus ojos, del pico, de las patas y de las uñas es de un color demasiado oscuro y por esa causa

TEACHING OPTIONS

Heritage Speakers Ask Spanish speakers to retell in their own words or perform a dramatic reading of this fable or any other fable with which they are familiar. If possible, have them make copies of the text for the class.

Pairs Write slogans like the following on the board: **Conserve el medio ambiente, Prohibido contaminar, Este planeta es para generaciones futuras.** Have pairs of students brainstorm other slogans for bumper stickers to promote environmental causes. Ask pairs to share their work with the whole class.

piensan que es menos bello. La gente no se da cuenta de su error, pues tan negras y tan brillantes son sus alas que parecen de color añil, al igual que las plumas del pavo real, que es el ave más hermosa del mundo. De la misma forma, sus ojos son negros, que es el color de ojos más bello, pues los ojos son para ver y todas las cosas negras las que más confortan la visión. Los ojos negros son, pues, los mejores y por eso los ojos más alabados son los de la gacela, que tiene los ojos más oscuros de entre todos los animales. También hay que decir que sus patas y uñas son más fuertes que las de ninguna ave del mismo tamaño, y que su vuelo es el de mayor ligereza, que no le preocupa volar en contra del viento por fuerte que sea, cosa que ninguna otra ave puede hacer con tanta agilidad como Ud. Y pienso yo, que como Dios hace todas las cosas con razón, estoy seguro de que no le negó otra virtud, pues no va a permitir que otra ave cante mejor que Ud. Y como Dios le ha hecho tan perfecto y sé que tiene más virtudes de las que yo oí antes de conocerle, le pido oir su canto que siempre estaré muy agradecido.

La intención del zorro era engañar al cuervo, pues todos sus razonamientos eran ciertos menos este último. Y cuando el cuervo vio cómo el zorro le alababa, y cómo le decía la verdad en todas las ocasiones, creyó que le decía la verdad en todo y que era su amigo. No sospechó que lo hacía para quitarle el queso que tenía en el pico, y entonces, abrió el pico para cantar. Al abrirlo cayó el queso a la tierra y el zorro lo tomó y se fue. Así engañó el zorro al cuervo, haciéndole creer que tenía más virtudes de las que tenía en realidad.

pedazo *piece* **pico** *beak*
didácticos *intended to instruct*
cuyo *whose* **a través de** *through* **zorro** *fox*
cuervo *crow* **siglos** *centuries* **adular** *to flatter*
patas *feet* **uñas** *claws* **se da cuenta de** *realizes*
añil *indigo* **pavo real** *peacock* **alabados** *praised*
gacela *gazelle* **tamaño** *size* **vuelo** *flight*
ligereza *agility* **volar** *to fly*
en contra de *against* **Dios** *God*
agradecido *grateful* **engañar** *to deceive*
alababa *praised*

Después de leer

Corregir

Escribe los siguientes comentarios otra vez, corrigiendo la información errónea.

1. Los personajes son un pavo real y una gacela.
   Los personajes son un zorro y un cuervo.
2. La narración tiene lugar en un zoológico.
   La narración tiene lugar en el campo.
3. El zorro adula al cuervo porque quiere ser su amigo.
   El zorro adula al cuervo porque quiere el pedazo de queso.
4. El cuervo engañó al zorro.
   El zorro engañó al cuervo.
5. La modestia no era una virtud del zorro.
   La modestia no era una virtud del cuervo.

Contestar

Contesta estas preguntas.

1. ¿Cuál es la moraleja de la fábula?
2. En tu opinión, ¿qué adjetivos describen mejor al zorro y al cuervo? Explica tu respuesta.
3. ¿Te gustaría ser amigo/a del zorro? ¿Y del cuervo? ¿Por qué?
4. ¿Qué otras fábulas o leyendas conoces? ¿Qué características tienen en común con esta fábula? ¿En qué son diferentes?
5. ¿Cuál fue el propósito de don Juan Manuel cuando escribió esta fábula?

Diálogos

En pequeños grupos, escojan una fábula que todos conozcan. Escriban un pequeño diálogo en el que cada uno interprete el papel de un personaje principal. No olviden incluir el papel del narrador, que será el que comparta la moraleja con el público al final de la representación. Consideren las siguientes ideas como punto de partida.

- La zorra y las uvas (*the fox and the grapes*)
- El lobo disfrazado de cordero (*the wolf in sheep's clothing*)
- La gallina de los huevos de oro (*the goose who laid the golden eggs*)
- La liebre y la tortuga (*the hare and the tortoise*)

escojan *choose* **papel** *role* **punto de partida** *point of departure*

Después de leer

Corregir
Suggestion Ask volunteers to write their corrected versions of the statements on the board. Responses will vary. Accept all reasonable responses.

Contestar
Suggestion For each question, ask several volunteers for their responses.

Diálogos
If necessary, ask volunteers to review the story line of each of these fables for the rest of the class. Then divide the class into groups of three or four students and assign a fable to each. Students will need to prepare and practice their presentations outside class time. Assign a specific date when you expect each group to perform its fable for the class. After each presentation, ask the narrator to write the moral (**moraleja**) of the fable on the board.

TEACHING OPTIONS

Extra Practice Ask students to look for other fables in Spanish. Have them check for fables written originally in Spanish as well as those that have been translated. Tell them they may find collections or individual books in the juvenile section of a library. Have students read the fable to the class.

Heritage Speakers As in other European languages, some expressions derived from Aesop's fables have become proverbial in Spanish. For example, in Spanish you can describe someone as a wolf in sheep's clothing (**lobo en piel de cordero**) and talk about killing the goose that laid the golden eggs (**matar la gallina de los huevos de oro**). Likewise, the English expression *Sour grapes!* has a Spanish equivalent, ***¡Están verdes!*** Ask Spanish speakers if they know of any other proverbial expressions in Spanish that have come from Aesop's fables.

Section Goals

In **Escritura** students will:
- learn about writer's audience and purpose
- integrate related vocabulary structures taught in **Lesson 13**
- write a persuasive letter or article in Spanish

Tema
Present If possible, provide students with samples of persuasive letters, such as letters to the editor, in Spanish. Go over any unfamiliar vocabulary. Ask students to identify the audience and the author's purpose for each letter.

Estrategia
Present Review the purpose and audience suggested, as well as questions 1–5, with the whole class. Then ask students to apply the answers to the questions to each of the scenarios listed in **Tema**. Students should discuss the purpose of their writing and how to determine their audience.

Assignment Have students prepare **Ideas y organización** and **Primer borrador** as homework.

The Affective Dimension After students have handed in their letters, ask them if the topics they chose interested them. Then discuss with them how their writing was influenced by their level of interest in the topic.

Escritura

NATIONAL STANDARDS communication cultures

Estrategia

Considering audience and purpose

All writing always has a specific purpose. During the planning stages, a writer must determine to whom he or she is addressing the piece and what he or she wants to express to the reader. Once you have defined both your audience and your purpose, you will be able to decide which genre, vocabulary, and grammatical structures will best serve your literary composition.

Let's say you want to share your thoughts on local traffic problems. Your audience can be either the local government or the community. You could choose to write a newspaper article, a letter to the editor, or a letter to the city's governing board. But first you should ask yourself these questions:

1. Are you going to comment on traffic problems in general, or are you going to point out several specific problems?
2. Are you simply intending to register a complaint?
3. Are you simply intending to inform others and increase public awareness of the problems?
4. Are you hoping to persuade others to adopt your point of view?
5. Are you hoping to inspire others to take concrete actions?

The answers to these questions will help you establish the purpose of your writing and determine your audience. Of course, your writing can have more than one purpose. For example, you may intend for your writing to both inform others of a problem and inspire them to take action.

Tema

Escribir una carta o un artículo

Escoge uno de los siguientes temas. Luego decide si vas a escribir una carta a un(a) amigo/a, una carta a un periódico, un artículo de periódico o de revista, etc.

1. Escribe sobre los programas que existen para proteger la naturaleza en tu comunidad. ¿Funcionan bien? ¿Participan todos los vecinos de tu comunidad en los programas? ¿Tienes dudas sobre el futuro del medio ambiente en tu comunidad?
2. Describe uno de los atractivos naturales de tu región. ¿Te sientes optimista sobre el futuro de tu región? ¿Qué están haciendo el gobierno y los ciudadanos de tu región para protegerla? ¿Es necesario hacer más?
3. Escribe sobre algún programa para proteger el medio ambiente a nivel nacional. ¿Es un programa del gobierno o de una empresa privada? ¿Cómo funciona? ¿Quiénes participan? ¿Tienes dudas sobre el programa? ¿Crees que debe cambiarse o mejorarse? ¿Cómo?

Escoge *Choose* ciudadanos *citizens* nivel *level* empresa *company* privada *private*

TEACHING OPTIONS

Proofreading Activity Copy the following sentences containing mistakes onto the board or a transparency as a proofreading activity to do with the whole class.

1. **Por qué no crees que la situación es seria?**
2. **Es terrible que esa compañía sigue contaminando las lagunas, los ríos, y los océanos.**
3. **No debemos esperar hasta que nuestros hijos se enferman para que preocuparnos con la contaminación ambiental.**
4. **¡No deja esa basura en el suelo, recojela!**
5. **Ojalá podemos encontrar soluciones a este problema, no tenemos mucho tiempo.**
6. **Dudo que el gobierno deja que pasan estas cosas.**

Plan de escritura

1 Ideas y organización

Toma unos minutos para contestar estas preguntas:

- ¿Cuál es el propósito de tu composición?
- ¿Quién va a leer tu composición?
- Utiliza las estrategias de organización, como un mapa de ideas o un esquema, para planear tu composición.

2 Primer borrador

Utilizando tus apuntes de **Ideas y organización,** escribe el primer borrador. No debes consultar el texto, los apuntes de clase ni el diccionario.

3 Comentario

Intercambia el primer borrador con un(a) compañero/a. Lee su borrador y comparte tu análisis utilizando esta guía:

a. ¿Está claro el borrador? ¿Cuál es el propósito de la composición de tu compañero/a?
b. ¿Incluye toda la información pertinente?
c. ¿Está bien organizado el borrador?
d. ¿Es interesante?
e. ¿Hay errores gramaticales u ortográficos?

4 Redacción

Revisa el primer borrador según las indicaciones de tu compañero/a. Si tu compañero/a tuvo dificultad en determinar el propósito de tu composición, repasa la sección de **Ideas y organización** antes de revisar tu borrador. Usa esta guía para hacer una última revisión antes de escribir la versión final:

a. Subraya cada verbo para comprobar la concordancia de los verbos y los sujetos.
b. Revisa la concordancia de los sustantivos y los adjetivos en cada oración.
c. Revisa los pronombres para comprobar el uso correcto de cada uno.
d. Revisa la ortografía y la puntuación otra vez con la ayuda de tus **Anotaciones para mejorar la escritura.**

5 Evaluación y progreso

Comparte tu versión final con dos compañeros/as de clase. Cada estudiante debe leer su versión en voz alta. Después los otros miembros del grupo deben hacerle preguntas o comentarios. El/La escritor(a) debe responder oralmente a cada pregunta o comentario. Lee con cuidado los comentarios que hace tu profesor(a) en tu trabajo y anota los errores más importantes en las **Anotaciones para mejorar la escritura** en tu **Carpeta de trabajos.**

propósito *purpose* **esquema** *outline* **apuntes** *notes* **Subraya** *Underline*

EVALUATION: Una carta o un artículo

Criteria	Scale
Content	1 2 3 4
Organization	1 2 3 4
Use of Vocabulary	1 2 3 4
Accuracy and Mechanics	1 2 3 4
Creativity	1 2 3 4

Scoring	
Excellent	18–20 points
Good	14–17 points
Satisfactory	10–13 points
Unsatisfactory	< 10 points

Comentario

Present Go over guide questions **a–e** with the whole class so peer readers understand their task. Then have pairs of students exchange drafts. Allow five minutes for reading and comments. Allow five minutes for discussing comments.

Assignment Have students prepare **Redacción** as homework. Ask them to rewrite their drafts, incorporating the peer comments and following the directions in **Redacción**. Tell them to prepare a clean copy of their final draft to hand in.

Evaluación y progreso

Give groups of three fifteen minutes to read aloud and comment on their letters or articles.

Writing Sample

Carta al director

Señor Director:

Hace cuarenta años que vivo en esta comunidad. Es una comunidad muy bonita y agradable porque hay muchos parques y otros lugares donde la gente puede ir para ver la naturaleza. Espero que toda la comunidad esté de acuerdo cuando digo que es importante que cuidemos de nuestros parques.

Ahora me preocupo por el Parque Robles. Ayer hice una excursión allí, y lo encontré en condiciones desastrosas. ¡Por todo el sendero que sigue el río encontré basura! Por supuesto, la recogí. Pero me siento mucho que los otros excursionistas no cuiden del parque.

Pronto ya no vamos a tener este bonito parque, a menos que hagamos algo. ¡Ya no podemos esperar más! Necesitamos que todos participen como voluntarios en un programa para mantener limpio el parque y proteger este tesoro.

Atentamente,
Linda Esquivel

Section Goals
In **Escuchar** students will:
- use background knowledge and context to guess the meaning of unknown words
- listen to a short speech

Instructional Resource
Student Cassette/CD

Preparación
Warm-up Have students look at the drawing and guess what it depicts.

Estrategia
Script **Es necesario que las casas del futuro sean construidas en barrios que tengan todos los recursos esenciales para la vida cotidiana: tiendas, centros comerciales, cines, restaurantes y parques, por ejemplo. El medio ambiente ya no soporta tantas autopistas llenas de coches y, por lo tanto, es importante que la gente pueda caminar para ir de compras o para ir a divertirse. Recomiendo que vivamos en casas con jardines compartidos para usar menos espacio y, más importante, para que los vecinos se conozcan.**

Have students do the activities in **Ahora escucha** and **Escoger** as homework. Verify the responses to **Ahora escucha** and **Escoger** with the whole class. Then ask pairs to complete **Ahora Uds.**

Ahora escucha
Script **Les vengo a hablar hoy porque aunque espero que el futuro sea color de rosa, temo que no sea así. Vivimos en esta tierra de preciosos recursos naturales— nuestros ríos de los cuales dependemos para el agua que nos da vida, el aire que respiramos, los árboles que nos protegen, los animales cuyas vidas están entrelazadas con nuestras vidas. Es una lástima que no apreciemos lo mucho que tenemos.**

Es terrible que haya días con tanta contaminación del aire que nuestros ancianos se enferman y nuestros hijos no pueden respirar. La tala de árboles es un problema grave... hoy día cuando llueve, el río Cauca se llena de tierra porque no hay árboles que aguanten la tierra. La contaminación del río está afectando gravemente la ecología de las playas de Barranquilla, una de nuestras joyas.

Ojalá que me oigan y piensen bien en el futuro de nuestra comunidad. Espero que aprendamos a conservar la naturaleza y que podamos cuidar el patrimonio de nuestros hijos.

Escuchar

NATIONAL communication STANDARDS

Preparación

Mira el dibujo. ¿Qué pistas te da sobre el tema del discurso de Soledad Morales?

Estrategia
Using background knowledge/ Guessing meaning from context

By using your background knowledge, you can anticipate the content of discourse that you hear in Spanish. If you hear words or expressions you do not understand, you can often guess their meanings based on the surrounding words. To practice these strategies, you will listen to a paragraph written by Jaime Urbinas, an urban planner. Before listening to the paragraph, write down what you think it will be about, based on Jaime Urbinas' profession. As you listen to the paragraph, jot down any words or expressions you don't know and use context clues to guess their meanings.

Ahora escucha

Vas a escuchar un discurso de Soledad Morales, una activista preocupada por el medio ambiente. Antes de escuchar, marca las palabras y frases que tú crees que ella va a usar en su discurso. Después marca las palabras y frases que escuchaste.

Palabras	Antes de escuchar	Después de escuchar
el futuro	______	✔
el cine	______	______
los recursos naturales	______	✔
el aire	______	✔
los ríos	______	✔
la contaminación	______	✔
las diversiones	______	______
la conservación	______	______

pistas *clues* discurso *speech*

Comprensión

Escoger

Subraya la definición correcta de cada palabra.
1. patrimonio (fatherland, heritage, acrimony) heritage
2. ancianos (elderly, ancient, antiques) elderly
3. entrelazadas (destined, interrupted, intertwined) intertwined
4. aguantar (to hold back, to destroy, to pollute) to hold back
5. apreciar (to value, to imitate, to consider) to value
6. tala (planting, cutting, watering) cutting

Ahora Uds.

Trabaja con un(a) compañero/a. Escriban seis recomendaciones que creen que la señora Morales va a dar en la siguiente parte de su discurso.
Answers will vary.

1. ______
2. ______
3. ______
4. ______
5. ______
6. ______

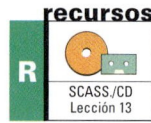

recursos
R SCASS./CD Lección 13

communication
cultures
connections
communities

Proyecto

Protege el medio ambiente

Imagina que eres un(a) activista ambiental en Colombia. Crees que es muy importante que se proteja la bella naturaleza del país.

1 Escribe una carta

Escribe una carta a un representante del gobierno colombiano para hablarle de tus preocupaciones, deseos y dudas sobre el futuro del medio ambiente en Colombia. Primero usa los **Recursos para la investigación** para informarte del paisaje y del medio ambiente de Colombia, incluyendo los problemas ambientales. Busca fotos que representen la información que encontraste. También investiga el nombre del representante del gobierno que está encargado del medio ambiente. Sigue este orden en tu carta:

- Encabeza la carta con "Estimado/a Sr./Sra. ..." y concluye con "Atentamente" antes de tu firma
- Explica lo que temes de los problemas ambientales, lo que esperas y tus dudas sobre el futuro
- Explica lo que recomiendas para resolver algunos de los problemas

2 Presenta la información

Lee la carta a tus compañeros/as. Muéstrales fotos del paisaje colombiano y fotos que muestren problemas ambientales para ayudarlos a entender por qué tus preocupaciones y recomendaciones son urgentes e importantes.

Las tortugas marinas están en grave peligro de extinción.

ambiental *environmental* encargado *in charge of* encabeza *write a salutation* firma *signature*

recursos para la investigación

Internet Palabras clave: Colombia, ecología, medio ambiente, contaminación, gobierno, Ministerio del Medio Ambiente, fotos	**Comunidad** Estudiantes o profesores que son de Colombia, personas de la comunidad que han viajado a Colombia
Biblioteca Revistas de organizaciones ambientales internacionales, periódicos	**Otros recursos** Comunicación con organizaciones ambientales internacionales por teléfono o correo electrónico

Section Goals

In **Proyecto** students will:
- use Spanish while researching and interacting with the wider world
- write a letter in the role of an environmental activist in Colombia

Before Assigning Proyecto Students will need approximately a week to complete the project, so at the beginning of that time period, have them open their books to page 423 and glance over **Proyecto**. Tell them they are going to write a letter about protecting the environment to the official of the Colombian government in charge of environmental affairs.

Escribe una carta
Suggestions
While the Internet can be a source of information on a wide range of topics, the reliability of such information is generally much more dubious than information gathered from printed sources. Tell students not to base all their research on Internet sources.

Presenta la información
Suggestions
- Students' presentations will be more interesting if they integrate visual aids such as posters, brochures, or music or audio recordings.
- You may wish to set aside sufficient class time to do a few presentations at a time until all students have had a chance to present.

EVALUATION: Una carta

Criteria	Scale
Content	1 2 3 4
Organization	1 2 3 4
Accuracy	1 2 3 4
Creativity	1 2 3 4
Oral Presentation	1 2 3 4

Scoring	
Excellent	18–20 points
Good	14–17 points
Satisfactory	10–13 points
Unsatisfactory	< 10 points

Section Goals

In **Panorama**, students will read about the geography, history, and culture of Colombia.

Instructional Resources
Student Activities Manual: Workbook, 159–160
Transparency 49

Colombia
Before Presenting Panorama Have students look at the map of Colombia or project **Transparency 49** and talk about the physical features of the country. Point out the three parallel ranges of the Andes in the west, and the Amazon Basin in the east and south. After students look at the call-out photos and read the captions, point out that there are no major cities in the eastern half of the country. Ask students to suggest reasons for the lack of population there.
Assignment Have students read **Panorama** and write out answers to the questions in **¿Qué aprendiste?** on page 425 as homework.

Present Ask volunteers to read aloud each section of **El país en cifras**. After reading the **Población** section, ask students what the impact might be of having 55% of the nation's territory unpopulated, and the sort of problems this might create for a national government. Remind students that **chibcha** is spoken as far north as Nicaragua. **Araucano** is a language spoken by indigenous people of the Andes.

Increíble pero cierto In their desperation to uncover the gold from Lake Guatavita, Spaniards made several attempts to drain the lake. Around 1545, Hernán Pérez de Quesada set up a bucket brigade that lowered the water level by several meters, allowing gold to be gathered.

Colombia

NATIONAL STANDARDS connections cultures

El país en cifras

- **Área:** 1,138.910 km² (439.734 millas²), *tres veces el área de Montana*
- **Población:** 43.821.000

De todos los países de habla hispana, sólo México tiene más habitantes que Colombia. Casi toda la población colombiana vive en las áreas montañosas y la costa occidental del país. Aproximadamente el 55% de la superficie del país está sin poblar.

- **Capital:** Santa Fé de Bogotá—6.547.000
- **Ciudades principales:** Cali—2.893.000, Medellín—3.070.000, Barranquilla—1.853.000, Cartagena—768.000

SOURCE: Population Division, UN Secretariat

Medellín

- **Moneda:** peso colombiano
- **Idiomas:** español (oficial), chibcha, araucano

Bandera de Colombia

Colombianos célebres

- **Edgar Negret,** escultor, pintor (1920-)
- **Gabriel García Márquez,** escritor (1928-)
- **Juan Pablo Montoya,** automovilista (1975-)
- **Shakira,** cantante (1977-)

habitantes *inhabitants* occidental *western* superficie *surface* sin poblar *unpopulated* escultor *sculptor* arrojaban *threw* macizo *solid* cacique *chief* dioses *gods* llevó *led* de oro *golden* ha encontrado *has found*

Baile típico de Barranquilla

Plaza Bolívar, Bogotá

Cultivo de caña de azúcar cerca de Cali

recursos
R | WB pp. 159-160 | vistasonline.com

¡Increíble pero cierto!

En el siglo XVI los exploradores españoles oyeron la leyenda de El Dorado. Esta leyenda cuenta que los indios, como parte de un ritual, arrojaban oro al lago Guatavita y el cacique se sumergía cubierto de oro en honor a los dioses. Aunque esto era cierto, muy pronto la exageración llevó al mito de una ciudad de oro.

Laguna de Guatavita

TEACHING OPTIONS

Heritage Speakers One of Colombia's contributions to Latin popular music is the dance form called the **cumbia**. The cumbia was born out of the fusion of musical elements contributed by each of Colombia's three main ethnic groups: Andean Indians, Africans, and Europeans. According to ethnomusicologists, the flutes and wind instruments characteristically used in the cumbia derive from Andean Indian music, the rhythms have their origin in African music, and the melodies are shaped by Spanish popular melodies. Cumbias are popular outside of Colombia, particularly in Mexico. Another Colombian dance form, this one native to the Caribbean coast, is the **vallenato**. In the vallenato, which is a fusion of African and European elements, the Andean element is missing. Encourage Spanish speakers to bring examples of cumbias and vallenatos for the class to listen to and compare and contrast.

Lugares • El Museo del Oro

El famoso Museo del Oro del Banco de la República fue fundado en Bogotá en 1939 para preservar las piezas de orfebrería de la época precolombina. En el museo, que tiene más de 30.000 piezas de oro, se pueden ver joyas, ornamentos sagrados y figuras que sirvieron de ídolos. El cuidado con el que están hechos los objetos de oro refleja la creencia de las tribus indígenas de que el oro era la expresión física de la energía creadora de los dioses.

Literatura • Gabriel García Márquez (1928-)

Gabriel García Márquez, ganador del Premio Nobel de Literatura en 1982, es uno de los escritores contemporáneos más importantes del mundo. García Márquez publicó su primer cuento en 1947, cuando era estudiante universitario. Su obra más conocida, *Cien años de soledad,* está escrita en el estilo literario llamado "realismo mágico", un estilo que mezcla la realidad con lo irreal y lo mítico.

Historia • Cartagena de Indias

Los españoles fundaron la ciudad de Cartagena de Indias en 1533 y construyeron a su lado la fortaleza más grande de las Américas, el Castillo de San Felipe de Barajas. En la ciudad de Cartagena se conservan muchos edificios de la época colonial, como iglesias, monasterios, palacios y mansiones. Cartagena es conocida también por el Festival de Música del Caribe y su prestigioso Festival Internacional de Cine.

BRASIL

¿Qué aprendiste? Responde a las preguntas con una frase completa.

1. ¿Qué idiomas se hablan en Colombia? En Colombia se hablan el español, el chibcha y el araucano.
2. ¿Qué país de habla hispana tiene más habitantes que Colombia? México tiene más habitantes que Colombia.
3. ¿Quién es Edgar Negret? Edgar Negret es un escultor y pintor colombiano.
4. ¿Por qué fue fundado el Museo del Oro? El Museo del Oro fue fundado para preservar las piezas de orfebrería de la época precolombina.
5. ¿Qué tipos de objetos hay en el Museo del Oro? En el Museo del Oro hay joyas, ornamentos religiosos y figuras que sirvieron de ídolos.
6. ¿Quién ganó el Premio Nobel de Literatura en 1982? Gabriel García Márquez ganó el Premio Nobel de Literatura en 1982.
7. ¿Cuál es la obra más famosa de García Márquez? *Cien años de soledad* es la obra más famosa de García Márquez.
8. ¿Qué es el "realismo mágico"? El "realismo mágico" es un estilo literario que mezcla la realidad con lo irreal y lo mítico.
9. ¿Qué construyeron los españoles al lado de la ciudad de Cartagena de Indias? Los españoles construyeron el Castillo de San Felipe de Barajas al lado de Cartagena de Indias.
10. ¿Qué festivales internacionales se celebran en Cartagena? Se celebran el Festival Internacional de Cine y el Festival de Música del Caribe.

Conexión Internet Investiga estos temas en el sitio **www.vistasonline.com.**

1. Busca información sobre las ciudades más grandes de Colombia. ¿Qué lugares de interés hay en estas ciudades? ¿Qué puede hacer el turista en estas ciudades?
2. Busca información sobre pintores y escultores colombianos como Edgar Negret, Débora Arango o Fernando Botero. ¿Cuáles son algunas de sus obras más conocidas? ¿Cuáles son sus temas?

Oro *Gold* fundado *founded* orfebrería *goldsmithing* joyas *jewels* sagrados *sacred* están hechos *are made* creencia *belief* creadora *creative* dioses *gods* ganador *winner* cuento *story* obra *work* más conocida *best- known* estilo *style* mezcla *mixes* mítico *mythical* fortaleza *fortress* se conservan *are preserved* iglesias *churches*

El Museo del Oro The native peoples from different regions of pre-Columbian Colombia developed distinct styles of working with gold. Some preferred to melt copper into the ore before working it, some pounded the gold, while others poured it into molds. If possible, bring photos of pre-Columbian gold work for the class to look at.

Gabriel García Márquez García Márquez was raised primarily by his maternal grandparents, who made a profound impression upon his life and his literature. His grandfather was a man of strong ideals and a military hero. His grand-mother held fast to many superstitious folk beliefs, which she espoused as gospel. Both of these elements surface in García Márquez's magical realism.

Cartagena de Indias Because Cartagena de Indias was the point of departure for shipments of Andean gold to Spain, it was the frequent target of pirate attacks from the 16th through the 18th centuries. It was beseiged on five occasions. The most famous seige was led by the English pirate Sir Francis Drake, in 1586. He held the city for 100 days, until the residents surrendered to him some 100,000 pieces of gold!

¿Qué aprendiste? Ask volunteers to give their answers to the questions.

Assignment Have students do activites in **Student Activities Manual: Workbook, pages 159–160.**

Conexión Internet Students will find information about Colombia at **www.vistasonline.com,** as well as links to other sites that can help them in their research.

TEACHING OPTIONS

Worth Noting Colombia, like other mountainous countries near the equator, does not experience the four seasons that are known in most of the United States. The average temperature of a given location does not vary much during the course of a year. Climate, however, changes dramatically with elevation, the higher altitudes being cooler than the low-lying ones. While the average temperature at sea level is 86°, 57° is the average temperature in Bogotá, the third highest capital in the world, behind La Paz, Bolivia, and Quito, Ecuador. When Colombians speak of **verano** or **invierno**, they are referring the the dry season **(verano)** and the rainy season **(invierno)**. When these seasons occur varies from one part of the country to another. In the Andean region, the **verano**, or dry season, generally falls between December and March.

13 vocabulario

La naturaleza

el árbol	*tree*
el bosque (tropical)	*(tropical; rain) forest*
el césped, la hierba	*grass*
el cielo	*sky*
el cráter	*crater*
el desierto	*desert*
la estrella	*star*
la flor	*flower*
el lago	*lake*
la luna	*moon*
el mundo	*world*
la naturaleza	*nature*
la nube	*cloud*
la piedra	*stone*
la planta	*plant*
la región	*region; area*
el río	*river*
la selva, la jungla	*jungle*
el sendero	*trail; trailhead*
el sol	*sun*
la tierra	*land; soil*
el valle	*valley*
el volcán	*volcano*

Animales

el animal	*animal*
el ave, el pájaro	*bird*
el gato	*cat*
el perro	*dog*
el pez	*fish*
la vaca	*cow*

El medio ambiente

la conservación	*conservation*
la contaminación (del aire; del agua)	*(air; water) pollution*
la deforestación	*deforestation*
la ecología	*ecology*
el ecoturismo	*ecotourism*
la energía (nuclear; solar)	*(nuclear; solar) energy*
el envase	*container*
la extinción	*extinction*
el gobierno	*government*
la lata	*(tin) can*
la ley	*law*
la lluvia (ácida)	*(acid) rain*
el medio ambiente	*environment*
el peligro	*danger*
la población	*population*
el reciclaje	*recycling*
el recurso natural	*natural resource*
la solución	*solution*
conservar	*to conserve*
contaminar	*to pollute*
controlar	*to control*
cuidar	*to take care of*
dejar de (+ *inf.*)	*to stop (doing something)*
desarrollar	*to develop*
descubrir	*to discover*
destruir	*to destroy*
estar afectado/a (por)	*to be affected (by)*
estar contaminado/a	*to be polluted*
evitar	*to avoid*
mejorar	*to improve*
proteger	*to protect*
reciclar	*to recycle*
recoger	*to pick up*
reducir	*to reduce*
resolver (o:ue)	*to resolve; to solve*
respirar	*to breathe*
de aluminio	*(made) of aluminum*
de plástico	*(made) of plastic*
de vidrio	*(made) of glass*
puro/a	*pure*

Emociones

alegrarse (de)	*to be happy*
esperar	*to hope; to wish*
sentir (e:ie, i)	*to be sorry; to regret*
temer	*to fear*
es extraño	*it's strange*
es una lástima	*it's a shame*
es ridículo	*it's ridiculous*
es terrible	*it's terrible*
es triste	*it's sad*
ojalá (que)	*I hope (that); I wish (that)*

Dudas y certezas

(no) dudar	*(not) to doubt*
(no) negar (e:ie)	*(not) to deny*
(no) creer	*(not) to believe*
es imposible	*it's impossible*
es improbable	*it's improbable*
es obvio	*it's obvious*
No cabe duda (de) que...	*There is no doubt that...*
No hay duda (de) que...	*There is no doubt that...*
(no) es posible	*it's (not) possible*
(no) es probable	*it's (not) probable*
(no) es cierto	*it's (not) certain*
(no) es verdad	*it's (not) true*
(no) es seguro	*it's (not) certain*

Conjunciones

a menos que	*unless*
antes (de) que	*before*
con tal (de) que	*provided (that)*
en caso (de) que	*in case (that)*
para que	*so that*
sin que	*without*

Expresiones útiles	*See page 399.*

En la ciudad

14

Communicative Goals

You will learn how to:

- Give advice to others.
- Give and receive directions.
- Discuss daily chores.

contextos

pages 428-431

- City life
- Daily chores
- Money and banking
- At a post office

fotonovela

pages 432-435

In preparation for the hike, Álex and Maite decide to go food shopping. On their way downtown, they ask a young man for directions.

estructura

pages 436-449

- The subjunctive in adjective clauses
- Conjunctions followed by the subjunctive or the indicative
- **Nosotros/as** commands
- Past participles used as adjectives

adelante

pages 450-455

Lectura: A short story by Marco Denevi
Escritura: Write directions for how to get to your home.
Escuchar: Listen to a conversation about a department store.
Proyecto: Create a brochure for a model community.

panorama

pages 456-457

Featured Country: Venezuela

- Oil: Economic engine of Venezuela
- Caracas: A modern metropolis
- Simón Bolívar: Liberator of South America

Lesson Goals

In **Lesson 14** students will be introduced to the following:

- names of commercial establishments
- banking terminology
- citing locations
- common Spanish abbreviations
- subjunctive in adjective clauses
- conjunctions followed by the subjunctive or indicative
- **nosotros/as** commands
- forming regular past participles
- irregular past participles
- past participles as adjectives
- identifying a narrator's point of view
- listing key words before writing
- giving directions in a letter
- listening for specific information and linguistic clues
- writing and presenting a brochure for a model community in Venezuela
- cultural, geographic, economic, and historical information about Venezuela

Lesson Preview

Have students look at the photo. Ask: **¿Qué ven en la foto? ¿Dónde están las personas? ¿Creen que los chicos viven en esta ciudad? ¿Creen que la mujer vive en esta ciudad?**

INSTRUCTIONAL RESOURCES

Student Activities Manual: Workbook, 161–172
Student Activities Manual: Lab Manual, 299–304
Student Activities Manual: Video Activities, 353–354
Instructor's Resource Manual: Hojas de actividades, 31–35
Instructor's Resource Manual: Answer Keys
Tapescript/Videoscript
Overhead Transparencies, 50–53
Student Cassette/CD
Lab Cassette/CD
Video Program
CD-ROM
Website: **www.vistasonline.com**
Testing Program: Prueba A, Prueba B

Section Goals

In **Contextos**, students will learn and practice:
- names of commercial establishments
- banking terminology
- citing locations

Instructional Resources
Student Activities Manual: Workbook, 161; Lab Manual, 299
Transparencies 50–51
Student Cassette/CD

Before Presenting Contextos Introduce active lesson vocabulary. Using realia or pictures from your picture file, ask volunteers to identify the items. Ex: **carne, zapato, pan,** and so forth. As students give their answers, write the names of corresponding establishments on the board (**carnicería, zapatería, panadería**). Then present banking vocabulary by miming common transactions. Ex: **Cuando necesito dinero, voy al banco. Escribo un cheque y lo cobro.**

Assignment Have students study **En la ciudad** and **En el correo** and prepare the activities on page 429 and Activity 4 on page 431 as homework.

Present Give students two minutes to review the drawing on pages 428–429. Then project **Transparency 50**. Have students refer to the picture to answer your questions about it. Ex: **¿Dónde queda el cajero automático? ¿Qué tienda queda entre la lavandería y la carnicería? ¿Qué establecimiento se encuentra encima del supermercado? Las dos señoras frente a la estatua, ¿de qué hablan? ¿Qué tipo de transacciones pueden hacerse en un banco?** and so forth until you have covered the active vocabulary.

Successful Language Learning Ask students to imagine how they would use this vocabulary when traveling.

En la ciudad

Más vocabulario

la frutería	*fruit store*
la heladería	*ice cream shop*
la pastelería	*pastry shop*
la pescadería	*fish market*
la cuadra	*(city) block*
la dirección	*address*
la esquina	*corner*
derecho	*straight (ahead)*
enfrente de	*opposite; facing*
hacia	*toward*
cruzar	*to cross*
doblar	*to turn*
hacer diligencias	*to run errands*
quedar	*to be located*
el cheque (de viajero)	*(traveler's) check*
la cuenta corriente	*checking account*
la cuenta de ahorros	*savings account*
ahorrar	*to save (money)*
cobrar	*to cash (a check)*
depositar	*to deposit*
firmar	*to sign*
llenar (un formulario)	*to fill out (a form)*
pagar a plazos	*to pay in installments*
pagar al contado, en efectivo	*to pay in cash*
pedir prestado	*to borrow*
pedir un préstamo	*to apply for a loan*
ser gratis	*to be free of charge*

Variación léxica

cheque de viajero ⟷ cheque de viaje (*Esp.*)
cuadra ⟷ manzana (*Esp.*)
direcciones ⟷ indicaciones (*Esp.*)
doblar ⟷ girar; virar; voltear
hacer diligencias ⟷ hacer mandados (*Amér. L.*)

recursos

R	SCASS./CD Lección 14	WB pp. 161-162	LM p. 229	LCASS./CD Cass. 7B/CD7

TEACHING OPTIONS

Heritage Speakers Have Spanish speakers write about shopping and banking customs in their home communities. Have them mention such things as business hours and the prevalance of specialty shops compared to supermarkets or department stories. Encourage them to compare and contrast customs cross-generationally as well as cross-culturally.

Pairs Have students individually draw schematic maps of a couple of blocks around a city square, labeling every establishment and naming the streets. Then have them write a description of the location of each establishment. When they have finished their descriptions, ask them to exchange them with a partner. They then use the written description to recreate the city map on which the description is based. Afterward, partners compare the original maps to the ones they created based on the descriptions.

Práctica

1 Escuchar Mira el mapa de las páginas 428 y 429. Luego escucha las frases e indica si lo que dice cada una es **cierto** o **falso**.

	Cierto	Falso		Cierto	Falso
1.	❍	✓	6.	✓	❍
2.	✓	❍	7.	✓	❍
3.	❍	✓	8.	❍	✓
4.	✓	❍	9.	❍	✓
5.	❍	✓	10.	✓	❍

2 Seleccionar Selecciona los lugares de la lista en los que haces las siguientes diligencias.

banco	frutería	pescadería
carnicería	joyería	salón de belleza
pastelería	lavandería	zapatería

1. comprar galletas pastelería
2. comprar manzanas frutería
3. comprar un collar (*necklace*) joyería
4. cortarte (*to cut*) el pelo salón de belleza
5. lavar la ropa lavandería
6. comprar pescado pescadería
7. comprar pollo carnicería
8. comprar sandalias zapatería

3 Completar Llena los espacios en blanco con las palabras más adecuadas.

1. El banco me regaló un reloj. Fue gratis.
2. Me gusta ahorrar dinero, pero no me molesta gastarlo.
3. La cajera me dijo que tenía que firmar el cheque en el dorso (*on the back*) para cobrarlo.
4. Para pagar con un cheque, necesito tener dinero en mi cuenta corriente.
5. Mi madre va a un cajero automático para obtener dinero en efectivo cuando el banco está cerrado.
6. Cada viernes, Julio lleva su cheque al banco y lo cobra para tener dinero en efectivo.
7. Cada viernes Ana lleva su cheque al banco y lo deposita en su cuenta de ahorros.
8. Anoche en el restaurante, Marco pagó en efectivo/al contado en vez de usar una tarjeta de crédito.
9. Cuando viajas, es buena idea llevar cheques de viajero.
10. Para pedir un préstamo, Miguel y Susana tuvieron que llenar cuatro formularios.

TEACHING OPTIONS

Game Play **Concentración.** On eight cards, write names of types of commercial establishments. On another 8 cards, draw or paste a picture that matches each commercial establishment. Place the cards face-down in four rows of four. In pairs, students select two cards. If the two cards match, the pair keeps them. If the two cards don't match, students replace them in their original position. The group with the most cards at the end wins.

Pairs Have each student write a shopping list (**lista de la compra/lista del mandado**) with ten items. Have students include items found in different stores. Then have them exchange their shopping list with a partner. Using the shopping list received, each student tells his or her partner where to go to get each item. Ex: **unas nuevas botas → Para comprar unas nuevas botas, tienes que ir a la zapatería que queda en la calle ____.**

1 Present Help students check their answers by reading each statement in the tapescript to the whole class and asking volunteers to say whether the statement is true or false. Have students correct the false statements by referring to the drawing on pages 428–429.

Tapescript **1. El supermercado queda al norte de la plaza, al lado de la lavandería. 2. La zapatería está al lado de la carnicería. 3. El banco queda al sur de la plaza. 4. Cuando sales de la zapatería, la lavandería está a su lado. 5. La carnicería está al lado del banco. 6. Cuando sales de la joyería, el cajero automático está a su lado. 7. No hay ninguna heladería cerca de la plaza. 8. La joyería está al oeste de la peluquería. 9. Hay una frutería al este de la plaza. 10. No hay ninguna pastelería cerca de la plaza.**
Student Cassette/CD

2 Present Model the activity by reading Item 1 to the class and asking **¿Dónde se compran galletas?** Guide them to see the correct response is **pastelería**.

2 Expand After students finish, ask them what other things could be bought in the establishments listed. Ex: **¿Qué más podemos comprar en la pastelería?**

3 Present Go over the answers with the whole class, asking volunteers to read each item.

3 Expand Ask students to compare and contrast two different facets of banking. Ex: ATM vs. traditional tellers; credit card vs. check; savings account vs. checking account. Have them work in groups of three to make a list of **Ventajas** (+) and **Desventajas** (-).

En el correo
Present Project **Transparency 51** and ask students questions about the picture to elicit active vocabulary. **¿Qué hace la señora en la ventanilla? Y la gente que espera detrás de ella, ¿qué hace?** and so forth. When you have covered the vocabulary, involve students in a conversation about mail and the post office. Ex: **Necesito estampillas. ¿Dónde está la oficina de correos más cerca de aquí? A mí me parece que la carta es una forma de escritura en vías de extinción. Desde que uso el correo electrónico, casi nunca escribo cartas. ¿Quiénes todavía escriben cartas?**

4 Present Go over the activity with the whole class. Ask volunteers to read each completed sentence.

4 Expand After you have gone over the activity, have students practice the dialogue with a partner.

4 Expand Have pairs create short dialogues similar to the one presented in the exercises, but set in a different place of business. Ex: **el salón de belleza, la pescadería.**

5 Warm-up Create a word bank of useful phrases on the board. Ask volunteers to suggest expressions and grammatical constructions that will help students develop their role plays.

5 Present Make sure students understand the activity before assigning small groups. Go over the new vocabulary once again by asking questions. Ex: **¿Cuándo pedimos un préstamo? ¿Los cheques son para una cuenta corriente o una cuenta de ahorros?** and so forth.

En el correo

4 **Diálogo** Completa el diálogo entre Juanita y el cartero con las palabras más adecuadas.

CARTERO Buenas tardes, ¿es Ud. la señorita Ramírez? Le traigo un ___paquete___.
JUANITA Sí, soy yo. ¿Quién lo envía?
CARTERO La Sra. Ramírez. Y también tiene Ud. dos ___cartas___.
JUANITA Ay, pero ¡ninguna es de mi novio! ¿No llegó nada de Manuel Fuentes?
CARTERO Sí, pero él echó la carta al ___buzón___ sin poner un ___sello___ en el sobre.
JUANITA Entonces, ¿qué recomienda Ud. que haga?
CARTERO Sugiero que vaya al ___correo___. Con tal de que pague el costo del sello, se le puede dar la carta sin ningún problema.
JUANITA Uy, otra diligencia, y no tengo mucho tiempo esta tarde para ___hacer___ cola en el correo, pero voy enseguida (*right away*). ¡Ojalá que sea una carta de amor!

¡LENGUA VIVA!
In Spanish, **Soy yo** means *That's me* or *It's me*. **¿Eres tú?/ ¿Es Ud.?** means *Is that you?*

5 **En el banco** Trabajen en grupos para representar estas situaciones. Answers will vary.

Un(a) empleado/a de un banco ayuda a...

1. un(a) estudiante universitario/a que quiere abrir una cuenta corriente.
2. una pareja de recién casados que quiere pedir un préstamo al banco para comprar una casa.
3. una persona que quiere información de los servicios que ofrece el banco.
4. un(a) estudiante que va a ir a estudiar al extranjero (*abroad*) y quiere saber qué tiene que hacer para llevar su dinero de una forma segura.

TEACHING OPTIONS

Extra Practice Ask students to surf the Internet for banks in Spanish-speaking countries. Have them write a summary of services, rates, hours, and so forth, offered by the bank.

Game Divide the class into two teams. They should sit in a row facing one another so that a person from team A is directly across from a person from team B. Begin with the first person and work your way down the row. Say a word, and the first person to make an association with a different word wins a point for his/her team. Ex: You say: **correos**. The person answers: **sello; cartero; carta.**

¡ATENCIÓN!

Note these different meanings:

quedar *to be located; to be left over; to fit*

quedarse *to stay, to remain*

6 **Diligencias** Trabajen en parejas para repartirse (*divide up*) las siguientes diligencias. Primero decidan quién va a hacer cada diligencia y después cuál es la manera más rápida de llegar a los diferentes sitios (*places*) desde el campus. Answers will vary.

modelo

Cobrar unos cheques

Estudiante 1: Yo voy a cobrar unos cheques. ¿Cómo llego al banco?

Estudiante 2: Conduce hacia el norte hasta cruzar la calle Oak. El banco queda en la esquina a la izquierda.

1. Enviar un paquete
2. Comprar botas nuevas
3. Comprar una torta de cumpleaños
4. Lavar unas camisas
5. Pedir un préstamo
6. Comprar helado
7. Cortarte el pelo
8. Comprar langosta

NOTA CULTURAL

El Hatillo is a small town near Caracas that is a popular for its quaint architecture, restaurants, and handicrafts shops.

CONSÚLTALO

Simón Bolívar (1783-1830) is considered the liberator of much of South America. In his honor, the Venezuelan unit of currency is called the *bolívar*. To learn more, see **Panorama** p. 457.

7 **El Hatillo** Trabajen en parejas para representar los papeles (*roles*) de un(a) turista que está perdido/a en El Hatillo y de un(a) residente de la ciudad que quiere ayudarle. Answers will vary.

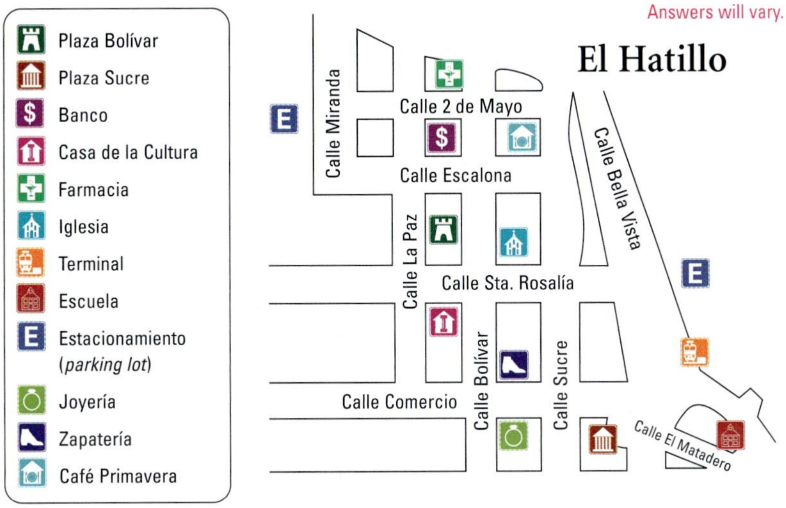

modelo

Plaza Sucre, Café Primavera

Estudiante 1: Perdón, ¿por dónde queda la Plaza Sucre?

Estudiante 2: Del Café Primavera, camine derecho por la calle Sucre hasta cruzar la calle Comercio. Doble a la izquierda y camine una cuadra. La Plaza Sucre queda a la derecha.

1. Plaza Bolívar, farmacia
2. Casa de la Cultura, Plaza Sucre
3. banco, terminal
4. estacionamiento (este), escuela
5. Plaza Sucre, estacionamiento (oeste)
6. joyería, banco
7. farmacia, joyería
8. zapatería, iglesia

8 **Direcciones** En grupos, escriban un minidrama en el que unos/as turistas están preguntando cómo llegar a diferentes sitios de la comunidad en la que viven Uds. Luego preséntenlo a la clase. Answers will vary.

6 Warm-up Draw a map of your campus and nearby streets with local commerce, asking students to direct you. Ex: **¿En qué calle queda el banco más cercano? ¿Qué tienda se encuentra en la esquina de ____ y ____?** and so forth.

6 Present Go over the directions and ask volunteers to read the **Modelo** before assigning the activity to pairs.

7 Warm-up Go over the icons in the legend to the map, pronouncing the places each represents and finding them on the map of El Hatillo. Model the pronunciation of the street names.

7 Present Read **Plaza Sucre** and **Café Primavera**, explaining that the task is to give directions to the first place from the second place. Ask students to find **Café Primavera** and **Plaza Sucre** on the map. Then read **Estudiante 1** in the **Modelo**. Give students a minute to find the route from the first place to the second. Then read **Estudiante 2**.

7 Expand Ask students to research El Hatillo on the Internet.

8 Warm-up As a class, brainstorm different tourist sites in and around your area. Write them on the board.

8 Present Using one of the sites listed on the board, model the activity by asking volunteers to give driving directions from campus.

TEACHING OPTIONS

Extra Practice Have pairs list the five best places for local college students. Ex: **la mejor pizza, el mejor corte de pelo,** and so forth. Then have them write directions to each place from campus. Expand to have students debate their choices.

Game Divide the class into groups of three. Each must write directions to a particular commercial establishment close to campus. The groups read their directions, and the other groups try to guess what errand they are running. Each group that guesses correctly wins a point.

Section Goals

In **Fotonovela** students will:

- receive comprehensible input from free-flowing discourse
- learn functional phrases that preview lesson grammatical structures

Instructional Resources *Student Activities Manual:Video Activities 353–354*
Video Program (Start 01:16:02)

Video Synopsis Don Francisco and Martín advise the students about things they need for the hike. Álex and Maite decide to go to the supermarket, the bank, and the post office. Álex and Maite get lost downtown, but a young man gives them directions. After finishing their errands, Álex and Maite return to the house.

Before Presenting Fotonovela Ask your students to predict what they would expect to see and hear in an episode in which the main characters get lost while running errands. Write down their predictions.

Assignment Have students study **Fotonovela** and **Expresiones útiles** as homework.

Warm-up Quickly review the predictions made in the preceding class and ask your students a few questions to help them summarize this episode.

Present Ask for volunteers to list a few expressions that would be used to get directions. Then ask for volunteers to give you directions to a nearby location. Ex: **Estoy perdido. ¿Hay un banco por aquí?**

Continued on page 433.

Estamos perdidos.

NATIONAL communication cultures STANDARDS

Maite y Álex hacen diligencias en el centro.

PERSONAJES

MAITE

INÉS

DON FRANCISCO

ÁLEX

JAVIER

MARTÍN

JOVEN

MARTÍN & DON FRANCISCO Buenas tardes.

JAVIER Hola. ¿Qué tal? Estamos conversando sobre la excursión de mañana.

DON FRANCISCO ¿Ya tienen todo lo que necesitan? A todos los excursionistas yo siempre les recomiendo llevar zapatos cómodos, una mochila, gafas oscuras y un suéter por si hace frío.

JAVIER Todo listo, don Francisco.

MARTÍN Les aconsejo que traigan algo de comer.

ÁLEX Mmm... no pensamos en eso.

MAITE ¡Deja de preocuparte tanto, Álex! Podemos comprar algo en el supermercado ahora mismo. ¿Vamos?

JOVEN ¡Hola! ¿Puedo ayudarte en algo?

MAITE Sí, estamos perdidos. ¿Hay un banco por aquí con cajero automático?

JOVEN Mmm... no hay ningún banco en esta calle que tenga cajero automático.

JOVEN Pero conozco uno en la calle Pedro Moncayo que sí tiene cajero automático. Cruzas esta calle y luego doblas a la izquierda. Sigues todo derecho y antes de que lleguen a la Joyería Crespo van a ver un letrero grande del Banco del Pacífico.

MAITE También buscamos un supermercado.

JOVEN Pues, allí mismo enfrente del banco hay un supermercado pequeño. Fácil, ¿no?

MAITE Creo que sí. Muchas gracias por su ayuda.

recursos

R	VIDEO Lección 14	VM pp. 353-354

TEACHING OPTIONS

Video Tips General suggestions for using video clips in the classroom can be found on page IAE-13 of the **Instructor's Annotated Edition**.

Estamos perdidos Play the **Resumen** segment of this video module without sound and ask the class to summarize what they see. Ask them to predict the content of the main video episode based on what they see in the **Resumen**. Write their predictions on the board. Then play the main video episode and the **Resumen** with sound. Finally, through questions and discussion, lead the class to a correct summary of the plot.

ÁLEX ¡Excelente idea! En cuanto termine mi café te acompaño.

MAITE Necesito pasar por el banco y por el correo para mandar unas cartas.

ÁLEX Está bien.

ÁLEX ¿Necesitan algo del centro?

INÉS ¡Sí! Cuando vayan al correo, ¿pueden echar estas postales al buzón? Además necesito unas estampillas.

ÁLEX Por supuesto.

MAITE Ten, guapa, tus sellos.

INÉS Gracias, Maite. ¿Qué tal les fue en el centro?

MAITE ¡Superbien! Fuimos al banco y al correo. Luego en el supermercado compramos comida para la excursión. Y antes de regresar, paramos en una heladería.

MAITE ¡Ah! Y otra cosa. Cuando llegamos al centro conocimos a un joven muy simpático que nos dio direcciones. Era muy amable... ¡y muy guapo!

Enfoque cultural Las tiendas especializadas

La popularidad de los supermercados está aumentando (*growing*) en los países hispanos, pero todavía muchas personas van a tiendas especializadas para comprar comidas como la carne, el pescado, el pan y los dulces. La pulpería, por ejemplo, es una tienda típica de las zonas rurales de algunos países de América Latina. La gente va a una pulpería para tomar una bebida o comprar productos esenciales. Otra tienda típica de algunos países hispanos es la rosticería, donde se asan (*roast*) y venden carnes para llevar (*takeout*).

Expresiones útiles

Giving advice

- **Les recomiendo/Hay que llevar zapatos cómodos.**
  I recommend that you/It's necessary to wear comfortable shoes.
- **Les aconsejo que traigan algo de comer.**
  I advise you to bring something to eat.

Talking about errands

- **Necesito pasar por el banco.**
  I need to go by the bank.
- **En cuanto termine mi café te acompaño.**
  As soon as I finish my coffee I'll go with you.

Getting directions

- **Estamos perdidos.**
  We're lost.

- **¿Hay un banco por aquí con cajero automático?**
  Is there a bank around here with an ATM?
- **Crucen esta calle y luego doblen a la izquierda/derecha.**
  Cross this street and then turn to the left/right.
- **Sigan todo derecho.**
  Go straight ahead.
- **Antes de que lleguen a la joyería van a ver un letrero grande.**
  Before you get to the jewelry store, you're going to see a big sign.

- **¿Por dónde queda el supermercado?**
  Where is the supermarket?
- **Está a dos cuadras de aquí.**
  It's two blocks from here.
- **Queda en la calle Flores.**
  It's on Flores street.
- **Pues, allí mismo enfrente del banco hay un supermercado.**
  Well, right in front of the bank there is a supermarket.

Ask for volunteers to read the various parts in the captions for video stills 1–5 of the **Fotonovela**. Correct any errors of pronunciation that would interfere with comprehension. Then have the class work in groups of four to read aloud the captions for video stills 6–10. See ideas for using the video in **Teaching Options**, page 432.

Comprehension Check Check comprehension of the **Fotonovela** episode by doing Activity 1, **¿Cierto o falso?**, page 434, orally with the whole class.

Suggestion Have the class look at the **Expresiones útiles**. Draw attention to the sentence **Estamos perdidos**. Tell the class that **perdidos** is a past participle of the verb **perder** and that it is used here as an adjective. Then point out the sentence **En cuanto termine mi café te acompaño.** Explain that the conjunction **en cuanto** must be followed by a verb in the present subjunctive if a future action is being expressed. Have the class look at the sentence **Cuando vayan al correo...** in the caption for frame 5 of the **Fotonovela** and guess why **Cuando** is followed by the present subjunctive. Tell your students that they will learn more about these concepts in the upcoming **Estructura** section.

Assignment Have students do activities 2–4 in **Reacciona a la fotonovela**, page 434, as homework.

TEACHING OPTIONS

Enfoque cultural You might want to introduce the names of these additional specialty shops: **el estanco** (a place where tobacco products, postcards, and stamps are sold) **la perfumería** (perfume shop), **el quiosco** (a newsstand where newspapers and magazines are sold), and **la relojería** (a shop that specializes in clocks and watches). Then write a list of items on the board and ask your students where they would go to obtain each one. Ex: **carne, pescado, libros, helado, fruta, comida, tarjetas postales, relojes, revistas, periódicos, cigarros, un pastel, un préstamo.**

Reacciona a la fotonovela

Reacciona a la fotonovela

1 Expand Give the class these additional items: **5. El joven llevó a Álex y a Maite al banco. (Falso. El joven les dio direcciones.) 6. Después de hacer sus diligencias, Maite y Álex fueron a una heladería. (Cierto.)**

2 Warm-up Ask the class a few questions about the **Fotonovela** before doing this activity. Ex: **¿Quién quería unas estampillas? (Inés) ¿Quién les dio direcciones a Álex y a Maite en el centro? (el joven)**

3 Present Have your students write these sentences on separate slips of paper so that they can rearrange them until they determine the correct order.

4 Possible response

S1: Voy al supermercado y a la heladería. ¿Quieres ir conmigo?

S2: Sí, en cuanto termine mi almuerzo te acompaño.

S1: Necesito pasar por el banco porque necesito dinero.

S2: Yo también necesito ir al banco. ¿Hay un banco por aquí con cajero automático?

S1: Hay un cajero automático a tres cuadras de aquí. Queda en la calle Libertad.

S2: También necesito ir a la lavandería y al correo para mandar unas cartas.

S1: Ningún problema... el correo y la lavandería están cerca del banco.

S2: Oye, ¿qué vas a hacer esta noche?

S1: Voy a ir a la fiesta que celebran para un amigo. ¿Quieres venir?

S2: ¡Sí, gracias!

1 **¿Cierto o falso?** Decide si lo que dicen las siguientes frases es **cierto** o **falso.** Corrige las frases falsas.

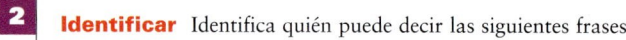

	Cierto	Falso	
1. Don Francisco insiste en que los excursionistas lleven una cámara.	○	✓	Don Francisco recomienda que los excursionistas lleven zapatos cómodos, una mochila, gafas oscuras y un suéter.
2. Inés escribió unas postales y ahora necesita mandarlas por correo.	✓	○	
3. El joven dice que el Banco del Atlántico tiene un cajero automático.	○	✓	El Banco del Pacífico tiene un cajero automático.
4. Enfrente del banco hay una heladería.	○	✓	Enfrente del banco hay un supermercado pequeño.

CONSÚLTALO

The subjunctive with verbs of will and influence To review the use of verbs like **insistir**, see Lesson 12, section 12.4, p. 380.

2 **Identificar** Identifica quién puede decir las siguientes frases.

1. Quiero ir contigo pero primero quiero terminar mi desayuno, ¿está bien? Álex
2. Insisto en que lleven ropa apropiada para una excursión como, por ejemplo, zapatos para caminar. don Francisco
3. Van a tener hambre en la excursión. ¿Por qué no traen un poco de fruta? Martín
4. Yo también necesito algo del correo. ¿Me puedes comprar unas estampillas? Inés
5. A ver... tengo que ir al banco, al supermercado y ¿qué más? Ah, necesito mandar unas cartas. Maite
6. Miren, después de doblar a la izquierda, van a ver el letrero del banco. Joven

3 **Ordenar** Pon los eventos de la **Fotonovela** en el orden correcto.

a. Un joven ayuda a Álex y a Maite a encontrar el banco porque están perdidos. 3
b. Álex y Maite comen un helado. 6
c. Inés les da unas postales a Maite y a Álex para echar al buzón. 2
d. Maite y Álex van al banco y al correo. 4
e. Álex termina su café. 1
f. Maite y Álex van al supermercado y compran comida. 5

4 **Conversación** Un(a) compañero/a y tú son vecinos/as. Uno/a de Uds. acaba de mudarse y necesita ayuda porque no conoce la ciudad. Los dos tienen que hacer algunas diligencias y deciden hacerlas juntos/as. Preparen una conversación breve en que hagan planes para ir a los siguientes lugares. Answers will vary.

- un banco
- una lavandería
- un supermercado
- una heladería
- una panadería

NATIONAL communication STANDARDS

AYUDA

primero *first*
luego *then*
¿Sabes dónde queda...? *Do you know where...is?*
¿Qué te parece? *What do you think?*
¡Cómo no! *Why not?*

TEACHING OPTIONS

Game Prepare several sets of directions that explain how to get to well-known places on campus or in your community, without mentioning the destinations by name. Read each set of directions out loud and ask the class to tell you where they would end up if they followed your directions.

Pairs Ask your students to work in pairs to create a skit in which a tourist asks for directions in a Spanish-speaking country. Give the class sufficient time to prepare and rehearse the skits, then ask for a few volunteers to present their skits to the class.

NATIONAL STANDARDS comparisons

Ortografía

Las abreviaturas

In Spanish, as in English, abbreviations are often used in order to save space and time while writing. Here are some of the most commonly used abbreviations in Spanish.

usted → **Ud.** **ustedes** → **Uds.**

As you have already learned, the subject pronouns **usted** and **ustedes** are often abbreviated.

don → **D.** **doña** → **Dña.** **doctor(a)** → **Dr(a).**
señor → **Sr.** **señora** → **Sra.** **señorita** → **Srta.**

These titles are frequently abbreviated.

centímetro → **cm** **metro** → **m** **kilómetro** → **km**
litro → **l** **gramo** → **gr** **kilogramo** → **kg**

The abbreviations for these units of measurement are often used, but without periods.

por ejemplo → **p. ej.** **página(s)** → **pág(s).**

These abbreviations are often seen in books.

derecha → **dcha.** **izquierda** → **izq. (izqda.)**
código postal → **C.P.** **número** → **n.º**

These abbreviations are often used in mailing addresses.

Banco → **Bco.** **Compañía** → **Cía.**
cuenta corriente → **c/c.** **Sociedad Anónima (*Inc.*)** → **S.A.**

These abbreviations are frequently used in the business world.

Práctica Escribe otra vez la siguiente información usando las abreviaturas adecuadas.

1. doña María Dña.
2. señora Pérez Sra.
3. Compañía Mexicana de Inversiones Cía.
4. usted Ud.
5. Banco de Santander Bco.
6. doctor Medina Dr.
7. Código Postal 03697 C.P.
8. cuenta corriente número 20-453 c/c., n.º

Emparejar En la tabla hay 9 abreviaturas. Empareja los cuadros necesarios para formarlas. S.A., Bco., cm, Dña., c/c., dcha., Srta., C.P., Ud.

S.	c.	C.	c	co.	U
B	c/	Sr	A.	D	dc
ta.	P.	ña.	ha.	m	d.

Section Goals

In **Ortografía** students will learn some common Spanish abbreviations

Present

- Remind the class that **usted** and **ustedes** are often abbreviated. Point out that the abbreviations begin with a capital letter, though the spelled-out forms do not.
- Write **D., Dña., Dr., Dra., Sr., Sra.,** and **Srta.** on the board. Ask the class what each abbreviation stands for. Again, point out that the abbreviations begin with a capital letter, though the spelled-out forms do not.
- Explain that the abbreviations for **centímetro, metro, kilómetro, litro, gramo,** and **kilogramo** don't use periods. Ask for volunteers to write the abbreviations on the board.
- Write **p. ej.** and **pág(s).** on the board and ask the class what each abbreviation stands for.
- Write **derecha, izquierda, código postal,** and **número** on the board. Ask for volunteers to write the abbreviations on the board. Point out that the period in n.º does not appear at the end of the abbreviation. Explain that the abbreviations for **primero** (**1.º**), **segunda** (**2.ª**), and so forth, also follow this pattern.
- Write **Bco., Cía., c/c.,** and **S.A.** on the board. Ask for volunteers to say what each abbreviation stands for.

Práctica/Emparejar Work through these activities with the class to practice the use of abbreviations in Spanish.

Successful Language Learning Tell students that the ability to recognize common abbreviations will make it easier for them to get along in a Spanish-speaking country.

TEACHING OPTIONS

Pairs Have the class work in pairs to write an imaginary mailing address that uses as many abbreviations as possible. Then have a few pairs write their work on the board and ask for volunteers to read the addresses aloud.

Extra Practice Write a list of abbreviations on the board; each abbreviation should have one letter missing. Have the class fill in the missing letters and tell you what each abbreviation stands for. Ex: **U__., D__a., g__, Bc__., d__ha., p__gs., __zq., S.__.**

14.1 The subjunctive in adjective clauses

NATIONAL STANDARDS comparisons

ANTE TODO In Lesson 13, you learned that the subjunctive is used in adverbial clauses after certain conjunctions. You will now learn how the subjunctive can be used in adjective clauses to express that the existence of someone or something is uncertain or indefinite.

¿Hay un banco por aquí que tenga cajero automático?

No hay ningún banco en esta calle que tenga cajero automático.

▶ The subjunctive is used in an adjective (or subordinate) clause that refers to a person, place, thing, or idea that either does not exist or whose existence is uncertain or indefinite. In the examples below, compare the differences in meaning between the statements using the indicative and those using the subjunctive.

Indicative	Subjunctive
Necesito **el libro** que **tiene** información sobre Venezuela. *I need the book that has information about Venezuela.*	Necesito **un libro** que **tenga** información sobre Venezuela. *I need a book that has information about Venezuela.*
Quiero vivir en **esta casa** que **tiene** jardín. *I want to live in this house that has a garden.*	Quiero vivir en **una casa** que **tenga** jardín. *I want to live in a house that has a garden.*
En mi barrio, hay **una heladería** que **vende** helado de mango. *In my neighborhood, there's an ice cream store that sells mango ice cream.*	En mi barrio no hay **ninguna heladería** que **venda** helado de mango. *In my neighborhood, there are no ice cream stores that sell mango ice cream.*

▶ When the adjective clause refers to a person, place, thing, or idea that is clearly known, certain, or definite, the indicative is used.

Quiero vivir en **la casa** que **tiene** jardín.
I want to live in the house that has a garden.

Busco **al profesor** que **enseña** japonés.
I'm looking for the professor who teaches Japanese.

Conozco **a alguien** que **va** a esa peluquería.
I know someone who goes to that beauty salon.

Tengo **un amigo** que **vive** cerca de mi casa.
I have a friend who lives near my house.

¡ATENCIÓN!

Adjective clauses are subordinate clauses that modify a noun or pronoun in the main clause of a sentence. That noun or pronoun is called the *antecedent*.

CONSÚLTALO

The future tense The verb in the main clause can also be in the future tense, which you will learn in Lesson 16. See Lesson 16, section 16.1, p.496.

Section Goals

In **Estructura 14.1** students will learn the use of the subjunctive in adjective clauses.

Instructional Resources *Student Activities Manual: Workbook, 163–164; Lab Manual, 301; Hojas de actividades 31–32*

Before Presenting Estructura 14.1 Use pictures from your picture file to compare and contrast the uses of the indicative and the subjunctive in adjective clauses. Ex: **Esta casa tiene una fuente en el jardín./Yo busco una casa que tenga piscina.; Este señor come insectos vivos./¿Conocen a alguien que coma insectos vivos?** Ask volunteers to answer questions that describe their wishes. Ex: **¿Qué buscas en una casa?** Tell students they are now going to learn how the subjunctive is used to express that the existence of someone or something is uncertain or indefinite. **Assignment** Have students study **Estructura 14.1** and prepare **¡Inténtalo!** on page 437 and Activities 1 and 2 on page 438 as homework.

Present Review the function of adjectives and adjective phrases before discussing the subjunctive in adjective clauses point by point. Call students' attention to the information in **¡Atención!** Ask volunteers to read the captions to the video stills and point out the subordinate adjective clause and its antecedent, then indicate the verb in present subjunctive. Then explain that in the first caption Maite is asking about a bank with an ATM, but she *doesn't know whether it exists or not.* In the second caption, the young man is certain about the *non-existence of the bank he is talking about.*

Continued on page 437.

TEACHING OPTIONS

Extra Practice To provide oral practice with adjective clauses in the subjunctive and indicative, create sentences that follow the pattern of the sentences in the examples. Say a sentence, have students repeat it, then change the main clause. Have students then say the sentence with the new clause, changing the subordinate clause as necessary. **Conozco una tienda donde se venden helados riquísimos. → Busco una tienda donde...**

Heritage Speakers Have Spanish speakers compare and contrast business establishments in their cultural communities and mainstream U.S.A. They should use both the indicative and the subjunctive, varying the verbs in the main clause as much as possible.

- The personal **a** is not used with direct objects that are hypothetical people. However, as you learned in Lesson 7, **alguien** and **nadie** are always preceded by the personal **a** when they function as direct objects.

Necesitamos **un empleado** que **sepa** usar computadoras. *We need an employee who knows how to use computers.*	Necesitamos **al empleado** que **sabe** usar computadoras. *We need the employee who knows how to use computers.*
Buscamos **a alguien** que **pueda** cocinar. *We're looking for someone who can cook.*	No conocemos **a nadie** que **pueda** cocinar. *We don't know anyone who can cook.*

¡ATENCIÓN!

Here are some verbs which are commonly followed by adjective clauses in the subjunctive:

necesitar	**encontrar**
querer	**conocer**
buscar	**haber**

- The subjunctive is commonly used in questions with adjective clauses when the speaker is trying to find out information about which he or she is uncertain. However, if the person who responds to the question knows the information, the indicative is used.

—¿Hay un parque que **esté** cerca de nuestro hotel? *Is there a park that's near our hotel?*	—Sí, hay un parque que **está** muy cerca del hotel. *Yes, there's a park that's very near the hotel.*

SECCION AMARILLA
Busque cualquier información que necesite.

¡INTÉNTALO! Escoge entre el subjuntivo o el indicativo para completar cada oración.

1. Necesito una persona que ___pueda___ (puede/pueda) cantar bien.
2. Buscamos a alguien que ___tenga___ (tiene/tenga) paciencia.
3. ¿Hay restaurantes aquí que ___sirvan___ (sirven/sirvan) comida japonesa?
4. Tengo una amiga que ___saca___ (saca/saque) fotografías muy bonitas.
5. Hay una carnicería que ___está___ (está/esté) cerca de aquí.
6. No vemos ningún apartamento que nos ___interese___ (interesa/interese).
7. Conozco a un estudiante que ___come___ (come/coma) hamburguesas todos los días.
8. ¿Hay alguien que ___diga___ (dice/diga) la verdad?

TEACHING OPTIONS

Pairs Ask pairs to use the sentences from **¡Inténtalo!** and the unused verbs **(puede, tiene, sirven, saque, esté, interesa, coma, dice)** and rewrite the sentence, changing the main clause accordingly.

Extra Practice Ask students to describe the ideal community. Their descriptions should include only sentences in the subjunctive. Refer them to the verbs included in **¡Atención!** to help them develop their descriptions.

As you discuss each section, be sure that students understand that, in each example that calls for the indicative in the subordinate clause, the subject of the main clause definitely knows that the direct object exists. On the other hand, in the examples that call for the subjunctive in the subordinate clause, the subject of the main clause either does not know whether the direct object exists or knows definitely that no such thing exists. Test comprehension as you proceed by asking volunteers to supply the correct form of verbs for adjective clauses you suggest. Ex: **Prefiero la playa donde ____ menos gente. (hay) Prefiero una playa donde ____ menos gente. (haya)** and so forth.

Work through the final two points concerning the use of the subjunctive in adjective clauses. Check for understanding by asking closed–ended questions and repeating the answer using complete sentence and the subjunctive. Ex: ____, **¿conoces a alguien que sepa hablar japonés? (no) ____ no conoce a nadie que sepa japonés, pero ____ conoce a una joven japonesa que estudia inglés.** Write the sentences on the board.

Suggestion Go over the information in **¡Atención!** Suggest main clauses with these verbs, and ask students to write the adjective clause. Ex: **Necesito un coche que... ; Busco al señor que... ; No hay nadie que...** and so forth. Then ask a volunteer to read the realia and explain why the verb **necesite** is in the subjunctive.

Close Do **¡Inténtalo!** orally as a whole class.

Práctica

1 Completar Completa estas frases con la forma correcta del indicativo o del subjuntivo de los verbos entre paréntesis.

1. Buscamos un hotel que ___tenga___ (tener) piscina.
2. ¿Sabe Ud. dónde ___queda___ (quedar) el Correo Central?
3. ¿Hay algún buzón por aquí donde yo ___pueda___ (poder) echar una carta?
4. Ana quiere ir a la carnicería que ___está___ (estar) en la avenida Lecuna.
5. Encontramos un restaurante que ___sirve___ (servir) comida venezolana típica.
6. ¿Conoces a alguien que ___sepa___ (saber) mandar un fax por computadora?
7. Necesitas al empleado que ___entiende___ (entender) este nuevo programa de computación.
8. No hay nada en este mundo que ___sea___ (ser) gratis.

2 Oraciones Forma frases con los siguientes elementos. Usa el presente del indicativo o del subjuntivo y luego, haz los cambios que sean necesarios.

1. mi / amigos / conocer / un / heladería / que / vender / helados / de / 51 / sabores (*flavors*)
   Mis amigos conocen una heladería que vende helados de cincuenta y un sabores.
2. ¿hay / alguien / que / saber / dirección / de / ese / heladería?
   ¿Hay alguien que sepa la dirección de esa heladería?
3. Marta / querer / comprarle / su / hija / un / zapatos / que / gustar
   Marta quiere comprarle a su hija unos zapatos que le gusten.
4. Ella / no / encontrar / nada / que / gustar / en / ese / zapatería
   Ella no encuentra nada que le guste en esa zapatería.
5. ¿tener / Ud. / algo / que / ser / más / barato?
   ¿Tiene Ud. algo que sea más barato?
6. ¿conocer / tú / alguno / banco / que / ofrecer / cuentas / corriente / gratis?
   ¿Conoces tú algún banco que ofrezca cuentas corrientes gratis?
7. nosotros / no / conocer / nadie / que / firmar / un / documento / sin / leerlo / primero
   Nosotros no conocemos a nadie que firme un documento sin leerlo primero.
8. no / hay / ninguno / cosa / que / a mí / interesar / en ese / joyería
   No hay ninguna cosa que a mí me interese en esa joyería.

3 Anuncios clasificados En parejas, lean estos anuncios y luego describan el tipo de persona u objeto que se busca. Answers will vary.

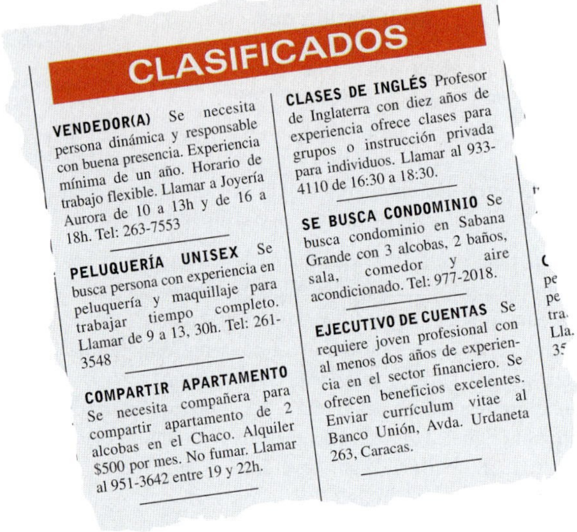

CLASIFICADOS

VENDEDOR(A) Se necesita persona dinámica y responsable con buena presencia. Experiencia mínima de un año. Horario de trabajo flexible. Llamar a Joyería Aurora de 10 a 13h y de 16 a 18h. Tel: 263-7553

PELUQUERÍA UNISEX Se busca persona con experiencia en peluquería y maquillaje para trabajar tiempo completo. Llamar de 9 a 13, 30h. Tel: 261-3548

COMPARTIR APARTAMENTO Se necesita compañera para compartir apartamento de 2 alcobas en el Chaco. Alquiler $500 por mes. No fumar. Llamar al 951-3642 entre 19 y 22h.

CLASES DE INGLÉS Profesor de Inglaterra con diez años de experiencia ofrece clases para grupos o instrucción privada para individuos. Llamar al 933-4110 de 16:30 a 18:30.

SE BUSCA CONDOMINIO Se busca condominio en Sabana Grande con 3 alcobas, 2 baños, sala, comedor y aire acondicionado. Tel: 977-2018.

EJECUTIVO DE CUENTAS Se requiere joven profesional con al menos dos años de experiencia en el sector financiero. Se ofrecen beneficios excelentes. Enviar currículum vitae al Banco Unión, Avda. Urdaneta 263, Caracas.

1 Warm-up Briefly review the use of the indicative and subjunctive in adjective clauses. Write two contrasting sentences on the board. Ex: **Conozco una pastelería donde sirven café. No hay ninguna pastelería en este barrio dónde sirvan café.** Then ask for volunteers to explain why the indicative/subjunctive was used in each sentence.

1 Present If you have assigned this activity as homework, you may ask pairs to exchange their sentences and check each other's work. After pairs have finished checking, go over the activity with the whole class.

1 Suggestion If you haven't assigned this activity as homework, it can be done in pairs. Have one student complete 1, 3, 5, and 7 while the other completes 2, 4, 6, and 8. Then ask them to check each other's work. Go over the activity with the entire class.

2 Warm-up Review the concept of main and subordinate clauses, reminding students that the subjunctive does not appear in the main clause. Then ask volunteers to write each "rehydrated" sentence on the board. Discuss and correct as necessary.

3 Warm-up Ask volunteers to discuss the types of information that can be found in classified ads. Write them on the board.

4 Present Give pairs ten minutes to read the ads and describe the kinds of people sought in each. Each student should describe three ads.

3 Expand Have pairs compose their own classified ad for one of the topics listed on the board but not covered in the activity.

TEACHING OPTIONS

Pairs Have students write a description of the kind of place where they would like to vacation, using the subjunctive. Then have them exchange papers and make suggestions as to places that satisfy the desired characteristics. Ex: **Quiero ir de vacaciones en un lugar donde pueda esquiar en julio. → Bariloche, Argentina, es un lugar donde puedes esquiar en julio.**

Extra Practice Here are five sentences to use as a dictation. Read each twice, pausing at natural breaks during the second reading to allow students time to write. **1. ¿Conoces una peluquería donde un corte de pelo no sea muy caro? 2. Sí, el salón de belleza que está al lado del banco tiene precios bajos. 3. No hay otra peluquería que tenga tan buen servicio. 4. Gracias, tú siempre me das consejos que me ayudan. 5. Espero que te guste la peluquería.**

NATIONAL communication STANDARDS

Comunicación

4

Completar Completa estas frases de una manera lógica. Luego, compara tus respuestas con las de un(a) compañero/a. Answers will vary.

1. Deseo un trabajo (*job*) que...
2. Algún día espero tener un apartamento (una casa) que...
3. Mis padres buscan un carro que..., pero yo quiero un carro que...
4. Tengo un(a) novio/a que...
5. Un consejero/a (*advisor*), debe ser una persona que...
6. Mi compañero/a de cuarto conoce a alguien que...
7. No conozco a nadie que...
8. Me gustaría conocer a alguien que...
9. En esta clase no hay nadie que...
10. No tengo ningún profesor que...

5

Encuesta Tu profesor(a) va a darte una hoja de actividades. Circula por la clase y pregúntales a tus compañeros/as si conocen a alguien que haga cada actividad que se menciona en la lista. Si dicen que conocen a una persona así, pregúntales quién es y anota sus respuestas. Luego informa a la clase de los resultados de tu encuesta. Answers will vary.

Actividades	Nombres	Respuestas
1. Trabajar en un supermercado		
2. Querer ser cartero/a		
3. No tener tarjeta de crédito		
4. Necesitar un préstamo		
5. Saber ahorrar dinero		
6. Hablar japonés		
7. Ser venezolano/a		
8. Graduarse este año		
9. Casarse en el verano		
10. Preocuparse por su situación económica		
11. Comprender el subjuntivo		
12. Pedir prestado el carro de sus padres		

NATIONAL communication STANDARDS

Síntesis

6

Agencia de viajes Tu profesor(a) va a darte una hoja de actividades con instrucciones. Trabaja con un(a) compañero/a para realizar esta actividad. Una persona va a ser un(a) agente de viajes, la otra va a ser el/la cliente. Answers will vary.

4 Present Model the activity by giving a personal example. Write, for example, **No conozco a ningún restaurante cercano que...** on the board, then complete the sentence. Ex: **No conozco ningún restaurante cercano que sirva comida venezolana. No conozco ningún restaurante cercano que tenga un patio grande.**

4 Expand Assign students to groups of six. Have each student compare his or her answers with those of the rest of the group. Then ask the group to make a visual representation of the group's responses to question 1, 2, 3, or 5. Designate a spokesperson from each group to explain the visual to the class.

5 Present Model one or two of the questions for the whole class. Then distribute copies of **Hoja de actividades 31** for students to fill in with their classmates' responses. Give the class ten minutes to complete the activity.

6 Present Before class, make half as many copies of **Hoja de actividades 32** as you have students and cut each **Hoja** in half. Divide the class into pairs, distributing the top half of the **Hoja** to one member of each pair and the bottom half of the **Hoja** to the other partner. Go over the instructions with the whole class.

Assignment Have students do activities in **Student Activities Manual: Workbook,** pages 163–164.

TEACHING OPTIONS

Video Show the video module again to give students more input on the use of the subjunctive in adjective clauses. Stop the video where appropriate to discuss why the subjunctive or indicative was/was not used.

Small Groups Ask students to bring in travel brochures or tourist information from the Internet. Divide the class into groups of four and have them write a short radio spot for one of the tourist locations using only the subjunctive and formal commands.

Section Goals
In **Estructura 14.2** students will learn:
- conjunctions followed by the subjunctive
- conjunctions followed by the indicative

Instructional Resources
Student Activities Manual: Workbook, 165–166; Lab Manual, 302
Hoja de actividades 33
Transparency 52

Before presenting Estructura 14.2
Describe what you are going to do in the near future by way of introducing conjunctions that may be followed by either the subjunctive or the indicative. Ex: **Voy a regresar a mi oficina en cuanto termine la clase. Tan pronto como llegue, voy a leer sus trabajos. Voy a seguir corrigiéndolos hasta que termine con todos.** As you say a sentence, write it on the board, underlining the conjunction and drawing attention to the subjunctive verb in the subordinate clause. Then tell students that they are going to learn a class of conjunctions that is sometimes followed by the subjunctive and sometimes by the indicative. **Assignment** Have students study **Estructura 14.2** and prepare the exercises on pages 441–442 as homework.

Warm-up Remind students of the grammatical function of conjunctions—to connect words, phrases, or clauses. Have volunteers read the captions to the video stills and locate the conjunctions, indicate the clauses the conjunctions connect, and tell which verb is in the subjunctive.

Present Model the pronunciation of the conjunctions, having students repeat after you. Then work through the explanation of conjunctions followed by the subjunctive and the examples.

Continued on page 441.

14.2 Conjunctions followed by the subjunctive or the indicative

ANTE TODO In Lesson 13, you learned that certain conjunctions are always followed by the subjunctive. There is another set of conjunctions that can be followed by either the subjunctive or the indicative, depending on the context in which they are used.

Cuando vayan al correo, ¿pueden echar estas postales al buzón?

- All of the conjunctions in the following list refer to time and are used to connect a main clause and a subordinate clause.

cuando	*when*
después (de) que	*after*
en cuanto	*as soon as*
hasta que	*until*
tan pronto como	*as soon as*

- The present subjunctive is required in the subordinate clause when the main clause expresses a future action or a condition that has not yet occurred.

Voy a firmar el cheque **tan pronto como** ellos me lo **den.**
I'm going to sign the check as soon as they give it to me.

Voy a llamarte **después de que** Miguel **se vaya.**
I'm going to call you after Miguel leaves.

- With this use of the present subjunctive, the verb in the main clause either is a command or refers to the future. Also, note that the main clause can come either before or after the subordinate clause.

Cuando tenga tiempo, **voy a enviar** esta carta a mi hija.
When I have time, I'm going to mail this letter to my daughter.

No salgas **hasta que** tú y tu hermano **limpien** su cuarto.
Don't go out until you and your brother clean your room.

TEACHING OPTIONS

Extra Practice Write the following sentences on the board and have students complete them with an appropriate verb in the subjunctive. **1. Cuando ____ (ir) a la pescadería, compra el pescado para la cena. (vayas) 2. En cuanto ____ (hacer) los mandados, voy a limpiar la casa. (haga) 3. Después de que nos ____ (llamar) Moisés por teléfono, podemos irnos. (llame) 4. Díselo a Isabel tan pronto como tú ____ (llegar) del trabajo.(llegues) 5. En cuanto ____ (encontrar) un cajero automático, vamos a depositar este cheque. (encontremos)**

Heritage Speakers Have Spanish speakers write ten sentences about things they are going to do after class, using **cuando, después de que, en cuanto, hasta que,** and **tan pronto como.** Then have them read their lists to one another.

CONSEJOS

Note that adverbs of time can help you determine whether an action is habitual or occurred in the past.

siempre, nunca, todos los días, etc. → indicative

ayer, el mes pasado, etc. → indicative

- If the verb in the main clause expresses a real-life action that habitually happens or that has happened in the past, the indicative, *not* the subjunctive, is used in the subordinate clause.

Habitual Actions → Indicative

Siempre pago al contado **cuando tengo** dinero.
I always pay in cash when I have money.

Por las mañanas, me ducho **en cuanto me despierto.**
In the morning, I take a shower as soon as I awake.

Nunca miro la televisión **hasta que termino** de comer.
I never watch television until I finish eating.

Siempre me afeito **después de que me ducho.**
I always shave after I take a shower.

Past Actions → Indicative

El sábado salí **tan pronto como pude.**
On Saturday I went out as soon as I could.

Envié el mensaje electrónico **en cuanto** lo **terminé.**
I sent the e-mail message as soon as I finished it.

Julia no me pudo mandar el paquete **hasta que supo** mi dirección.
Julia couldn't send me the package until she found out my address.

Fuimos de compras **después de que salimos** de la conferencia.
We went shopping after we left the conference.

Siempre garantizamos la energía
hasta que alguién los separa.
ISAGEN

¡INTÉNTALO! Completa las oraciones con el subjuntivo o el indicativo de los verbos.

1. Le voy a escribir tan pronto como ___tenga___ (tengo/tenga) tiempo.
2. Apaga la televisión en cuanto te lo ___pida___ (pido/pida).
3. Mi hermana me llamó ayer en cuanto ___volví___ (volví/vuelva) a la residencia.
4. Siempre ahorro dinero cuando ___como___ (como/coma) en casa.
5. Vamos a leer los documentos cuando los ___recibamos___ (recibimos/recibamos).
6. De niño, siempre iba a la heladería tan pronto como ___tenía___ (tenía/tenga) dinero.
7. Vamos a salir después de que el mesero nos ___dé___ (da/dé) la cuenta.
8. Espera aquí hasta que nosotros ___volvamos___ (volvemos/volvamos).
9. Siempre llamo a mis amigos en cuanto ___llego___ (llego/llegue) a casa.
10. Vamos a pedir la comida cuando tú ___tengas___ (tienes/tengas) hambre.

TEACHING OPTIONS

Video Show the video module again to give students more input containing the use of the subjunctive and indicative after **cuando, después de que, en cuanto, hasta que,** and **tan pronto como**. Stop the video at points where these conjunctions are used and discuss with your class why the subjunctive or the indicative was appropriate in each case.

Heritage Speakers Ask Spanish speakers to write an account of a planned future trip to their hometown. Tell them to use the subjunctive to describe what they will do when they arrive, contrasting these activities to what they habitually do here.

Write examples that illustrate **cuando, en cuanto,** and **hasta que** on the board. Point out that when the subjunctive is used in subordinate clauses like those in the examples, it refers to a future event, one that has not yet happened and could possibly not happen and, therefore, is not definite.

Check for understanding by supplying a main clause and asking volunteers to provide the subordinate clause. Ex: **Vamos a cenar tan pronto como... (Mamá vuelva de los mandados). No firmes el cheque hasta que... (llegues al banco)** and so forth.

Suggestion Write all the example sentences on page 440 on the board and have volunteers rewrite the sentences by inverting the clauses.

Explain that, while **cuando, después de que, en cuanto, hasta que, and tan pronto como** require the subjunctive when they refer to a future action, when they refer to a habitual action or an action in the past they take the indicative. Go through the examples with the class, then compare and contrast sentences such as the following:

Voy a mi oficina en cuanto termine la clase. • Siempre voy a mi oficina en cuanto termina la clase. • Ayer fui a mi oficina en cuanto terminó la clase. • Siempre iba a mi oficina en cuanto terminaba la clase.

Ask a volunteer to read the **ISAGEN** ad, pointing out the conjunction and subjunctive in the subordinate clause.

Close Do **¡Inténtalo!** orally with the whole class.

1 Warm-up Review the use of the subjunctive and indicative after conjunctions by comparing and contrasting sentences. Ex: **En cuanto los Gallardo llegaron a Caracas, nos llamaron. En cuanto Uds. lleguen a Caracas, llámenos.** Ask volunteers to identify past, habitual, or future actions.

1 Present Ask volunteers to read each completed item, explaining the choice of a subjunctive or indicative verb.

2 Suggestion If you have not assigned this activity as homework, you might have students complete it individually and then compare their answers in groups of three.

2 Present Go over the activity by asking volunteers to read each sentence aloud.

2 Expand Use a picture from your picture file and ask students to write a story about what will happen next. They can use the story in the activity as a guide.

Práctica

1 **Completar** Completa las oraciones con las formas adecuadas de los verbos en el indicativo o el subjuntivo. Piensa si cada verbo trata de una acción pasada o habitual (indicativo) o de una acción futura (subjuntivo).

1. Desde que (*since*) __empecé__ (empezar) a trabajar, siempre pago todo al contado. Pero algún día, cuando yo __compre__ (comprar) una casa, voy a tener que aprender a pagar a plazos.
2. Tan pronto como __fuimos__ (ir) todos a la panadería a comer pan dulce, empezó a llover. Yo le dije a Sandra: «No me muevo de aquí hasta que __salga__ (salir) el sol».
3. Hasta que tú __eches__ (echar) al buzón el cheque para la cuenta de la electricidad, no voy a estar tranquilo. Después de que tú __perdiste__ (perder) el trabajo el mes pasado, no pagamos muchas cosas a tiempo.
4. Te voy a llevar a la heladería de Macuto cuando yo __tenga__ (tener) tiempo. Después de que yo __termine__ (terminar) de estudiar en la universidad, voy a tener más tiempo libre.
5. Tan pronto como Uds. __se perdieron__ (perderse), ¿no pensaron en pedir direcciones? Normalmente, cuando Felipe y yo no __estamos__ (estar) seguros, buscamos una gasolinera para preguntar.

2 **Un cuento** Completa el cuento (*story*) con la forma adecuada de los siguientes verbos.

comer	despertar	ir	preparar
poder	terminar	dar	acompañar

Lupe se levantó por la mañana tan pronto como su marido se __fue__ de la casa. Ella le quería __dar__ una sorpresa de aniversario. Salió a la calle, hablando consigo misma (*talking to herself*): «Mañana sábado, cuando Félix se __despierte__, le voy a llevar el café a la cama, y en cuanto __coma__ su desayuno, le voy a pedir que me __acompañe__ a casa de mi prima para recoger unas cosas. Perfecto. Mientras todos preparan la fiesta sorpresa, nosotros vamos a ir a hacer diligencias. En cuanto __terminen__ de preparar todo, Rosa me va a llamar al teléfono celular». Esa mañana, Lupe fue al banco, al supermercado, a la peluquería... todo tenía que estar perfecto. Volvió a su casa tan pronto como __pudo__. Durante toda la tarde siguió pensando en todos los detalles, las invitaciones, la comida... Llegó su marido por la noche, se acostaron y a la mañana siguiente Félix no se despertó hasta que Lupe le __preparó__ su café.

TEACHING OPTIONS

Small groups Divide the class into groups of four. Put a writing prompt on the board. Ex: **Hacía frío y la noche estaba oscura. Mari Paz...** Ask students to finish the story in parts. The first student will complete the first sentence and pass the paper on to the next student. He or she will write a second sentence and pass it on. This should continue until the story has been completed or there are at least eight sentences.

Extra Practice Create prompts modeled on the sentences in Activity 1. Say the sentence or write it on the board, then provide different adverbs or tenses and ask the students to form the new sentence. Ex: **Tan pronto como llegaron esta tarde, salimos a dar un paseo. (mañana; la semana próxima; el sábado pasado)** and so forth.

Comunicación

3 **Encuesta** Tu profesor(a) va a darte una hoja de actividades. Hazles las preguntas de la tabla (*chart*) a tres compañeros/as de clase. Después, anota sus respuestas en la hoja de actividades. Answers will vary.

4 **Oraciones** Con un(a) compañero/a, completa las oraciones que siguen, basándote en tus propias experiencias. Puedes usar el verbo en el indicativo o en el subjuntivo. Answers will vary.

modelo

Hasta que sepa / supe...
No quiero ir a Venezuela hasta que sepa hablar el español.
No quise invitar a mi novia a comer hasta que supe cocinar.

1. Cuando compre / compré una casa...
2. En cuanto tenga / tuve que pedir prestado...
3. Tan pronto como abra / abrí una cuenta...
4. Hasta que estudie / estudié...
5. Después de que vaya / fui...
6. Cuando tenga / tuve suficiente dinero...
7. En cuanto cumpla / cumplí...
8. Cuando sea / era...

Síntesis

5 **¿Dónde queda?** En parejas, miren el mapa. Después, uno/a de los compañeros/as dice dónde está y adónde quiere llegar y el/la otro/a le da direcciones. Túrnense para pedir direcciones. Answers will vary.

modelo

Estudiante 1: *Estoy en el estacionamiento y quiero ir a la pescadería.*
Estudiante 2: *Cuando salgas del estacionamiento, dobla a la derecha y camina hasta que...*

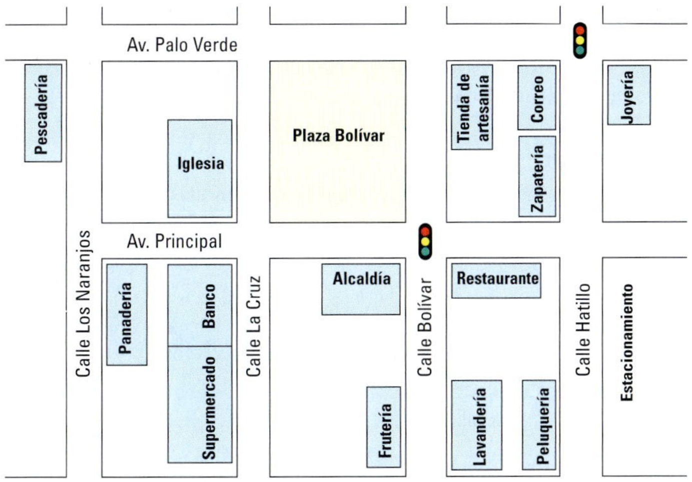

NOTA CULTURAL

Venezuela has the highest concentration in South America of people living in cities. 84% of the country's population lives in urban areas.

3 Present Model one or two of the questions for the whole class. Then distribute copies of **Hoja de actividades 33** for students to fill in with their classmates' responses.

3 Expand Call on different students to report on their group's results.

4 Present Read the **Modelo** and ask volunteers to explain why the subjunctive was used in the first sentence and the indicative in the second. Then model two more examples of **Hasta que sepa/supe...** that are true for you.

4 Expand Ask each pair to write the most original, most humorous, or most extraordinary response on a separate piece of paper. Read them aloud to the class and have the students guess to whom each statement refers.

5 Present Before assigning pairs, model the activity by having two volunteers read the **Modelo**. You may have pairs use the map in their texts or you may project **Transparency 52**, which contains the map.

5 Expand Reconstruct the activity on the basis of directions, and ask students to find your destination. Ex: **Salí de la iglesia a la Avenida Principal. Doblé a la izquierda y pasé dos esquinas. ¿Adónde fui? (Al restaurante.)**

Assignment Have students do activities in **Student Activities Manual: Workbook,** pages 165–166.

TEACHING OPTIONS

Small groups Ask students to bring in tourist information about Caracas or Maracaibo from a travel agency or from the Web. Have them create a day's itinerary for a tourist visiting the city for a day.

Game Divide the class into small groups. Begin a sentence and ask Group 1 to finish it. Ex: **En cuanto llegue a mi casa esta noche, (voy a acostarme).** If Group 1 does not answer correctly, it passes to Group 2 . Each grammatically correct answer scores a point.

Section goals

In **Estructura 14.3** students will learn **nosotros/as** commands.

Instructional Resources *Student Activities Manual: Workbook, 167–168; Lab Manual, 303*

Before Presenting Estructura 14.3 Model the **nosotros/as** commands by making suggestions to the whole group. Begin by having students respond to **tú** and **Uds.** commands, and then add commands for the class as a whole. Ex: ____, **abre el libro.** ____ **y** ____, **abran el libro. Ahora todos, abramos el libro. Abrámoslo.**

Assignment Have students study **Estructura 14.3** and prepare the exercises on pages 444–445.

Present Work through the explanation of **nosotros** commands point by point. Check cpmprehension by 1) asking volunteers to convert **Vamos a** + *infinitive* suggestions into **nosotros/as** commands, 2) calling out affirmative commands and pointing to individuals to convert them them into a negative commands (and vice versa), and 3) calling out commands with object nouns and asking volunteers to repeat the commands with the appropriate pronouns.

Make sure to discuss the information in **¡Atención!** when discussing object pronouns and **nosotros** commands.

Successful Language Learning Ask your students how they might use the **nosotros/as** commands when they are out with a group of Spanish speakers.

Close Do **¡Inténtalo!** orally as a class.

14.3 Nosotros/as commands

NATIONAL comparisons STANDARDS

ANTE TODO You have already learned familiar (**tú**) commands and formal (**Ud./Uds.**) commands. You will now learn **nosotros/as** commands, which are used to give orders or suggestions that include yourself and other people.

Nosotros/as commands correspond to the English *Let's*.

Crucemos la calle.	**No crucemos** la calle.
Let's cross the street.	*Let's not cross the street.*

▶ Both affirmative and negative **nosotros/as** commands are generally formed by using the first-person plural form of the present subjunctive.

¿Quieres ir al supermercado?

¡Excelente idea! ¡Vamos!

▶ The affirmative *Let's* + [*verb*] command may also be expressed with **vamos a** + [*infinitive*]. Remember, however, that **vamos a** + [*infinitive*] can also mean *we are going to (do something)*. Context and tone of voice determine which meaning is being expressed.

Vamos a cruzar la calle.	**Vamos a trabajar** mucho.
Let's cross the street.	*We're going to work a lot.*

▶ To express the command *Let's go*, the present indicative form of **ir** (**vamos**) is used, not the present subjunctive. For the negative command, however, the present subjunctive is used.

Vamos a la pescadería.	No **vayamos** a la pescadería.
Let's go to the fish market.	*Let's not go to the fish market.*

▶ Object pronouns are always attached to affirmative **nosotros/as** commands. A written accent is added to maintain the original stress.

Firmemos el cheque. → **Firmémoslo.** **Escribamos** a Ana y Raúl. → **Escribámosles.**

▶ Object pronouns are placed in front of negative **nosotros/as** commands.

No **les paguemos** el préstamo.	No **se lo digamos** a ellos.

¡ATENCIÓN!

When **nos** or **se** are attached to an affirmative **nosotros/as** command, the final **-s** is dropped.

Sentémonos allí.
Démoselo a ella.
Mandémoselo a ellos.

• • •

The **nosotros/as** command form of **irse** (*to go away*) is **vámonos** (negative **no nos vayamos**).

¡INTÉNTALO! Indica los mandatos afirmativos y negativos de la primera persona del plural (**nosotros/as**) de los siguientes verbos.

1. estudiar *estudiemos, no estudiemos*
2. cenar cenemos, no cenemos
3. leer leamos, no leamos
4. decidir decidamos, no decidamos
5. decir digamos, no digamos
6. cerrar cerremos, no cerremos
7. levantarse levantémonos, no nos levantemos
8. irse vámonos, no nos vayamos

TEACHING OPTIONS

TPR Brainstorm gestures related to the active vocabulary in **Lesson 14**. Have students stand. At random call out **nosotros/as** commands. All students should perform the appropriate gesture. Keep the pace rapid. Ex: **Crucemos la calle. Doblemos a la izquierda. Firmemos un cheque. Hagamos diligencias. Pidamos un préstamo. Llenemos un formulario.**

Extra Practice To provide oral practice with **nosotros/as** commands, create sentences with **vamos a** + *place of business*. Ex: **Vamos al banco. Vamos a la peluquería.** Say the sentence, have students repeat it, then call on individual students to add an appropriate **nosotros** command form. Ex: **Saquemos dinero. Cortémonos el pelo.**

Práctica

1 **Completar** Completa esta conversación con los mandatos de **nosotros/as.** Luego, representa la conversación con un(a) compañero/a.

MARÍA Sergio, ¿quieres hacer diligencias ahora o por la tarde?
SERGIO No ___las dejemos___ (dejarlas) para más tarde. ___Hagámoslas___ (Hacerlas) ahora. ¿Qué tenemos que hacer?
MARÍA Necesito comprar sellos.
SERGIO Yo también. ___Vamos___ (Ir) al correo.
MARÍA Pues, antes de ir al correo, necesito sacar dinero de mi cuenta corriente.
SERGIO Bueno, ___busquemos___ un cajero automático.
MARÍA ¿Tienes hambre?
SERGIO Sí. ___Crucemos___ (Cruzar) la calle y ___entremos___ (entrar) en ese café.
MARÍA Buena idea.
SERGIO ¿Nos sentamos aquí?
MARÍA No, no ___nos sentemos___ (sentarse) aquí; ___sentémonos___ (sentarse) enfrente de la ventana.
SERGIO ¿Qué pedimos?
MARÍA ___Pidamos___ (Pedir) café y pan dulce.

2 **Responder** Responde a cada mandato según las indicaciones. Usa los mandatos de **nosotros/as** y sustituye los pronombres por los objetos directos e indirectos.

modelo
Vamos a vender el carro. (Sí)
Sí, vendámoslo.

1. Vamos a levantarnos a las seis. (Sí) Sí, levantémonos a las seis.
2. Vamos a enviar los paquetes. (No) No, no los enviemos.
3. Vamos a depositar el cheque. (Sí) Sí, depositémoslo.
4. Vamos al supermercado. (No) No, no vayamos al supermercado.
5. Vamos a mandar esta tarjeta postal a nuestros amigos. (No) No, no se la mandemos.
6. Vamos a limpiar la habitación. (Sí) Sí, limpiémosla.
7. Vamos a mirar la televisión. (No) No, no la miremos.
8. Vamos a bailar. (Sí) Sí, bailemos.
9. Vamos a pintar la sala. (No) No, no la pintemos.
10. Vamos a comprar estampillas. (Sí) Sí, comprémoslas.

1 Warm-up Ask Spanish-speakers to talk about foods typically eaten at breakfast in their home communities and at what time breakfast is eaten.

1 Present Go over the activity with the whole class by having volunteers read each exchange in the conversation. After the class has checked the answers, divide it into pairs and give them sufficient time to practice and perform the conversation.

1 Expand Invite volunteers to perform the conversation for the class, ad-libbing additional material as they see fit.

2 Warm-up Quickly review the placement of direct and indirect object pronouns with affirmative and negative **nosotros/as** commands.

2 Present Model the activity by having two students read the **Modelo**. Go through the activity with the whole class. Read each item and cue and indicate an individual to respond. Vary the activity by changing the cues.

2 Suggestion This activity is also suitable to being done in pairs. Students take turns reading the statement and responding with a **nosotros/as** command.

TEACHING OPTIONS

Heritage Speakers Ask Spanish-speakers to write a dialogue using **nosotros/as** commands. The topic of the dialogue should be typical errands run in their home communities, such as **la tortillería, la droguería** and so forth. Have them read their dialogues to the class, making sure to note any new vocabulary on the board.

Game Divide the class into groups of three. Groups will take turns responding to your cues with a **nosotros/as** command. Ex: **Necesitamos pan. (Vayamos a la panadería.)** Give the cue. Allow the groups to confer and come up with a group answer, and then call on a specific group. Each correct answer earns a point.

3 Present Model the activity by writing a sentence such as the following on the board. Ex: **¿Completamos la actividad en clase o la hacemos de tarea? Completémosla en clase.**

3 Suggestion Ask students to expand their answers with a reason for their choice. Ex: **No nos quedemos en un hotel. Las pensiones son menos caras.**

4 Warm-up With the whole class, take a quick look at the types of information found in **Guía de Caracas.** Then ask a volunteer to read the **Modelo**. Discuss the information in **Nota cultural.**

4 Present Divide the class into groups of three or four students. Give groups ten minutes to complete the activity.

4 Suggestion Students who are interested may want to research on the Internet some of the places mentioned in the **Guía** and report back to the class.

5 Warm-up Before beginning the activity, have students brainstorm in Spanish different financial problems and solutions encountered by roommates sharing an apartment. Write them on the board.

5 Present Ask a volunteer to read the **Modelo**. Then allow pairs ten minutes to complete the activity.

5 Expand Call on different pairs to perform their **Situación** for the whole class.

Assignment Have students do activities in **Student Activities Manual: Workbook,** pages 167–168.

Comunicación

NATIONAL communication STANDARDS

3 **Preguntar** Tú y un(a) compañero/a están en Caracas. Túrnense para hacerse estas preguntas. Contesten las preguntas con un mandato afirmativo o negativo de **nosotros/as.** Answers will vary.

1. ¿Nos quedamos en un hotel o en una pensión?
2. ¿Cruzamos la calle aquí o caminamos una cuadra más?
3. ¿Vamos al supermercado o comemos en un restaurante?
4. ¿Vamos al cine en taxi o en autobús?
5. ¿Salimos para el cine a las seis o las seis y media?
6. ¿Hacemos cola o buscamos otra película?
7. ¿Volvemos al hotel después de la película o tomamos algo en un café?
8. ¿Pagamos la cuenta en efectivo o con tarjeta de crédito?

4 **Decisiones** Trabajen en grupos pequeños. Uds. están en Caracas por dos días. Lean esta página de una guía turística sobre la ciudad y decidan qué van a hacer hoy por la mañana, por la tarde y por la noche. Usen los mandatos afirmativos o negativos de **nosotros/as.** Answers will vary.

modelo

Visitemos el Museo de Arte Contémporaneo Sofía Imber esta tarde. Quiero ver las esculturas de Jesús Rafael Soto.

Guía de Caracas

MUSEOS
- **Museo de Arte Colonial** Avenida Panteón
- **Museo de Arte Contemporáneo Sofía Imber** Parque Central Esculturas de Jesús Rafael Soto y pinturas de Miró, Chagall y Picasso.
- **Galería de Arte Nacional** Parque Central. Colección de más de 4000 obras de arte venezolano.

SITIOS DE INTERÉS
- **Plaza Bolívar**
- **Jardín Botánico** Avenida Interna UCV. De 8:00 a 5:00.
- **Parque del Este** Avenida Francisco de Miranda Parque más grande de la ciudad con serpentarium.
- **Casa Natal de Simón Bolívar** Esquina de Sociedad de la avenida Universitaria. Casa colonial donde nació El Libertador.

RESTAURANTES
- **El Barquero** Avenida Luis Roche
- **Restaurante El Coyuco** Avenida Urdaneta
- **Restaurante Sorrento** Avenida Francisco Solano
- **Café Tonino** Avenida Andrés Bello

NOTA CULTURAL

Jesús Rafael Soto (1932–) is a modern Venezuelan sculptor/painter whose "kinetic" works often involve parts that shimmer and vibrate, bringing the viewer into closer contact with the work.

Síntesis

NATIONAL communication STANDARDS

5 **Situación** Tú y un(a) compañero/a viven juntos en un apartamento y tienen problemas económicos. Describan los problemas y sugieran algunas soluciones. Usen los mandatos afirmativos o negativos de **nosotros/as.** Answers will vary.

modelo

Es importante que reduzcamos nuestros gastos (expenses). Hagamos un presupuesto (budget).

TEACHING OPTIONS

Video Show the video again to give students more input containing **nosotros/as** commands. Ask students to write down all the examples they hear in the dialogue. When the video has finished, review the lists as a class.

Pairs Have students develop a role play in which two friends or a couple are deciding in which local restaurant to have dinner. Students should use **nosotros/as** commands as much as possible. Call on different pairs to perform their role plays for the class.

14.4 Past participles used as adjectives

NATIONAL comparisons STANDARDS

¡ATENCIÓN!

The past participles of **–er** and **–ir** verbs whose stems end in **–a, –e,** or **–o** carry a written accent mark on the **i** of the **–ido** ending.

caer	**caído**
creer	**creído**
leer	**leído**
oír	**oído**
reír	**reído**
sonreír	**sonreído**
traer	**traído**

ANTE TODO In Lesson 5, you learned about present participles (**estudiando**). Both Spanish and English have past participles. The past participles of English verbs often end in **–ed** (*to turn* → *turned*), but many are also irregular (*to buy* → *bought; to drive* → *driven*).

▶ In Spanish, regular **–ar** verbs form the past participle with **–ado.** Regular **–er** and **–ir** verbs form the past participle with **–ido.**

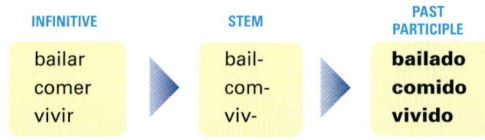

INFINITIVE	STEM	PAST PARTICIPLE
bailar	bail-	**bailado**
comer	com-	**comido**
vivir	viv-	**vivido**

Irregular past participles

abrir	**abierto**	morir	**muerto**
decir	**dicho**	poner	**puesto**
describir	**descrito**	resolver	**resuelto**
descubrir	**descubierto**	romper	**roto**
escribir	**escrito**	ver	**visto**
hacer	**hecho**	volver	**vuelto**

CONSEJOS

You already know several participles used as adjectives: **aburrido, interesado, nublado, perdido, etc.**

•••

Note that all irregular past participles except **dicho** and **hecho** end in **–to.**

▶ In Spanish, as in English, past participles can be used as adjectives. They are often used with the verb **estar** to describe a condition or state that results from an action. Like other Spanish adjectives, they must agree in gender and number with the nouns they modify.

En la entrada hay algunos letreros **escritos** en español.
In the entrance, there are some signs written in Spanish.

Tenemos la mesa **puesta** y la cena **hecha.**
We have the table set and dinner made.

La joyería **está cerrada.**
The jewelry store is closed.

El cheque ya **está firmado.**
The check is already signed.

¡INTÉNTALO! Indica la forma correcta del participio pasado de estos verbos.

1. hablar hablado
2. beber bebido
3. decidir decidido
4. romper roto
5. escribir escrito
6. cantar cantado
7. oír oído
8. traer traído
9. correr corrido
10. leer leído
11. ver visto
12. hacer hecho
13. morir muerto
14. reír reído
15. mirar mirado

TEACHING OPTIONS

Extra Practice To provide oral practice with past-participle agreement with the nouns they modify, create substitution drills. Ex: ***Felipe* está enojado. (Lupe/Los estudiantes/Mis hermanas/El profesor) • *El cheque* ya está firmado. (La carta/Las tarjetas/El artículo)** Say a sentence and have students repeat. Say a cue. Have students replace the subject of the original sentence with the cued subject and make any other necessary changes.

Game Divide the class into groups of five and have each team sit in a row. The first person in the row has a blank piece of paper. Have five infinitives in mind. Call out one of them. Allow the student with the paper 30 seconds to write down the past participle of the infinitive and pass the paper to the next in row in his team. The group with the most correct responses wins.

Section Goals

In **Estructura 14.4** students will learn:
- to form regular past participles
- irregular past participles
- to use past participles as adjectives

Instructional Resources
Student Activities Manual: Workbook, 169–170; Lab Manual, 308
Hojas de actividades 34–35

Before Presenting Estructura 14.4 Use your picture file to review some of the following regular past participles students have learned as adjectives: **aburrido, afectado, avergonzado, cansado, casado, cerrado, desordenado, enamorado, enojado, equivocado, mareado, ocupado, ordenado, preocupado.** As you review these forms, indicate the corresponding infinitives.

Assignment Have students study **Estructura 14.1** and prepare **¡Inténtalo!** on page 447 and Activity 1 on page 448 as homework.

Warm-up Work through the explanation of past participles as a grammatical concept as explained in **Ante todo.**

Present Discuss the formation of regular past participles. Check for understanding by calling out known infinitives and asking volunteers to give their past participles. Ex: **mirar, comprender, cumplir.** Make sure students note the accentuation rule outlined in **¡Atención!**

Then go over the irregular past participles one by one. Tell students that they will need to memorize these forms.

Finally, discuss the use of past participles as adjectives.

Close Consolidate by doing **¡Inténtalo!** as a class.

1 Suggestion Working with the whole class, ask volunteers to read each completed item.

1 Expand Have volunteers go to the board and rewrite each sentence in the activity, replacing the subject (or direct object in Item 6) with a subject (or object) of a different gender or number. Have them make all other necessary changes. Ask volunteers from the class to correct grammar and spelling as necessary.

2 Present Go over the directions with the whole class and ask two volunteers to read the **Modelo**. Divide the class into pairs, allowing about eight minutes to complete the activity. Remind pairs to take turns asking the questions and responding.

2 Expand Have students redo the activity using a negative response and a different past participle used as an adjective to provide a reason. Ex: **No, no están comprados porque el banco está cerrado hoy. No, nos están confirmadas porque el teléfono del hotel está ocupado.** and so forth.

3 Warm-up Allow a couple of minutes for students to make notes about the crime scene before assigning the activity to pairs.

3 Present Call the students' attention to the **Ayuda** section before having them begin the activity. Read the **Modelo** aloud.

3 Expand Have students give their answers in round robin format. Remind them that each contribution has to contain new information not already supplied by another pair.

Práctica

1 Completar Completa estas frases con la forma adecuada del participio pasado del verbo que está entre paréntesis.

1. El hombre descrito (describir) en ese documento es un criminal.
2. María Conchita Alonso es una actriz y cantante muy conocida (conocer).
3. ¿Está descubierto (descubrir) ya todo el petróleo de Venezuela?
4. Los libros usados (usar) son muy baratos.
5. Los documentos están firmados (firmar).
6. Tenemos el documento firmado (firmar) desde hace una semana.

2 Preparaciones Tú y tu compañero/a van a hacer un viaje. Túrnense para hacerse las siguientes preguntas sobre los preparativos (*preparations*). Usen el participio pasado en sus respuestas.

modelo

Estudiante 1: ¿Firmaste el cheque de viajero?
Estudiante 2: Sí, el cheque de viajero ya está firmado.

1. ¿Compraste los boletos para el avión? Sí, los boletos ya están comprados.
2. ¿Confirmaste las reservaciones para el hotel? Sí, las reservaciones ya están confirmadas.
3. ¿Firmaste tu pasaporte? Sí, mi pasaporte ya está firmado.
4. ¿Lavaste la ropa? Sí, la ropa ya está lavada.
5. ¿Resolviste el problema con el banco? Sí, el problema con el banco ya está resuelto.
6. ¿Pagaste todas las cuentas? Sí, las cuentas ya están pagadas.
7. ¿Hiciste todas las diligencias? Sí, todas las diligencias ya están hechas.
8. ¿Hiciste las maletas? Sí, las maletas ya están hechas.

3 Describir Tú y un(a) compañero/a son agentes de policía y tienen que investigar un crimen que ocurrió en el hotel Coliseo. Miren el dibujo y describan lo que encontraron al entrar en la suite del Sr. Villalonga. Usen el participio pasado en la descripción. Answers will vary.

modelo

La puerta del baño no estaba cerrada.

AYUDA

You may want to use the past participle of these verbs to describe the illustration.

abrir *to open*
desordenar *to make untidy*
hacer *to do, to make*
poner *to turn on (a machine)*
tirar *to throw*

TEACHING OPTIONS

Heritage Speakers Have Spanish speakers write a short description of their own home town. Encourage them to use active vocabulary from **Contextos** and at least twelve past participles used as adjectives in their descriptions.

Extra Practice Write these sentences on the board. Have students copy them and draw a happy/sad face next to each to show the situations and/or feelings expressed. Ex: **Ni está la comida hecha ni está la mesa puesta.** ☹

1. Tenemos ganado un viaje gratis a Venezuela. 2. Con el dinero ahorrado en las compras, podemos ir al cine. 3. Tuve que cerrar mi cuenta corriente por falta de dinero. 4. Con el préstamo del banco tenemos resuelto nuestro problema. 5. Vayamos a la pastelería de la esquina recientemente abierta.

Comunicación

4 **Preguntas** En parejas, túrnense para hacerse estas preguntas. Answers will vary.

1. ¿Quiénes están aburridos en la clase?
2. ¿Hay alguien que esté dormido en la clase?
3. ¿Dejas la luz prendida en tu cuarto?
4. ¿Está ordenado tu cuarto?
5. ¿Prefieres comprar libros usados o nuevos? ¿Por qué?
6. ¿Tienes mucho dinero ahorrado?
7. ¿Necesitas pedirles dinero prestado a tus padres?
8. ¿Estás preocupado/a por el medio ambiente?
9. ¿Qué haces cuando no estás preparado/a para una clase?
10. ¿Qué haces cuando estás perdido/a en una ciudad?

5 **Encuesta** Tu profesor(a) va a darte una hoja de actividades. Circula por la clase y haz preguntas hasta que encuentres a las personas que responden a cada descripción y anota sus respuestas. Luego informa a la clase de los resultados de tu encuesta. Answers will vary.

AYUDA

Remember that **llevar** means *to wear* in addition to *to take* or *to bring*.

Descripciones	Nombres	Otra información
1. Tiene algo roto. ¿Qué es?		
2. Lleva algo hecho en un país hispano. ¿Qué es?		
3. Tiene algo traído de otro país. ¿Qué es?		
4. Tiene las respuestas escritas en su libro.		
5. Tiene la cama hecha.		
6. Su cuarto está desordenado. ¿Por qué?		
7. Sabe los nombres de dos venezolanos muy conocidos. ¿Quiénes son?		
8. Está interesado/a en trabajar en un banco. ¿Por qué?		

Síntesis

6 **Situación** Tu profesor(a) va a darte una hoja de actividades. Trabaja con un(a) compañero/a. Una persona va a ser el/la recepcionista (*desk clerk*) en un hotel. La otra persona es un(a) huésped en el hotel. Answers will vary.

4 Suggestion Tell students they should try to use complex sentences whenever possible. Ex: **No hay nadie en la clase que esté aburrido porque todo es tan interesante.**

4 Expand Call on different students to tell their partner's response to the class.

5 Present Model one or two of the questions for the whole class. Ex: **¿Tienes algo que está roto? ¿Llevas algo hecho en un país hispano?** (Remind students that **llevar** can mean *wear* as well as *carry*.) Then distribute copies of **Hoja de actividades 34**. Allow ten minutes for completion of the activity.

5 Expand Have students work together in groups of four to compare their answers. Have them determine how many students have something broken, etc.

6 Warm-up Have students work with a classmate to brainstorm different types of interactions that take place between a hotel guest and the receptionist.

6 Present Divide the class into pairs, then distribute the top half of **Hoja de actividades 35** to one member of the pair, and the bottom half to another.

6 Expand Invite volunteers to present their conversations before the class.

Assignment Have students do activities in **Student Activities Manual: Workbook,** pages 169–170.

TEACHING OPTIONS

Pairs Have pairs make a promotional flyer for a new business in town. Their flyers should include at least three past participles used as adjectives. When they have finished, circulate the flyers in the class.

Game Divide the class into groups of three. Each group should think of a famous place or an historical monument. The other groups will take turns asking questions about the monument. Questions can only be answered with yes/no and each one should have a past participle used as an adjective. Ex: **¿Está abierto al público? ¿Es conocido solamente en este país?** The first group to guess the identity of the site wins a point.

Section Goals

In **Lectura** students will:
- learn the strategy of identifying a narrator's point of view
- read an authentic narrative in Spanish

Antes de leer

Introduce the strategy. Tell students that recognizing the point of view from which a narrative is told will help them comprehend the narrative.

Write the following first sentences of two narratives on the board and ask students to identify the point of view.

Cristóbal Colón vio por primera vez el territorio de Venezuela el 1.º de agosto de 1498 en su tercer viaje al Nuevo Mundo.

Muy pronto tuvimos que reconocer que no íbamos a solucionar el caso sin mucho trabajo.

Examinar el texto Ask students to read the first paragraph of **Grandezas de la burocracia** and determine whether the narrative is written in the first- or third-person point of view.

Seleccionar Have pairs of students work through this activity together before you go over the answers orally with the whole class. If pairs have difficulty answering any question, suggest one of the partners read aloud corresponding portions of the text.

Assignment Have students read **Grandezas de la burocracia** and prepare the activities in **Después de leer** as homework.

Lectura

Antes de leer

Estrategia

Identifying point of view

You can understand a narrative more completely if you identify the point of view of the narrator. You can do this by simply asking yourself from whose perspective the story is being told. Some stories are narrated in the first person. That is, the narrator is a character in the story, and everything you read is filtered through that person's thoughts, emotions, and opinions. Other stories have an omniscient narrator who is not one of the story's characters and who reports the thoughts and actions of all the characters.

Examinar el texto

Lee brevemente el cuento. ¿De qué trata? ¿Cómo lo sabes? ¿Se narra en primera persona o tiene un narrador omnisciente? ¿Cómo lo sabes?

Seleccionar

Completa cada frase con la información adecuada.

1. Los personajes son __a__.
   a. árabes b. franceses c. argentinos
2. Abderrahmán era __b__.
   a. el ingeniero más sabio de los árabes
   b. un califa importante
   c. supervisor de la construcción de la ciudad
3. El cuento tiene que ver con __a__.
   a. la construcción de una ciudad
   b. los problemas del califa con su esposa
   c. la burocracia en Bagdad
4. El supervisor de la construcción prometió terminar el proyecto dentro de __c__.
   a. diez años b. cuatro años c. un año

personajes *characters* cuento *story* tiene que ver con *has to do with* dentro de *within*

Grandezas de la burocracia

Marco Denevi

Marco Denevi nació en Buenos Aires, Argentina en 1922 y murió en la misma ciudad en 1998. Su novela Rosaura a las diez *le llevó a la fama en 1955. Escribió cuentos, novelas, obras teatrales y, a partir de 1980, se dedicó a escribir periodismo político. La obra de Denevi, candidato al Premio Nobel de Literatura, se caracteriza por su ingenio y sentido del humor.*

Después de leer

Completar

Completa cada frase con la información adecuada. Answers will v

1. Abderrahmán quería fundar ________.
2. Kamaru-l-Akmar prometió ________.
3. Después del primer año, Kamaru-l-Akmar pidió ________.
4. Abderrahmán se enojó porque ________.
5. Cuando Abderrahmán vio la ciudad, dijo que ________.
6. Mientras planeaban la futura ciudad, los ingenieros y arquitectos construyeron ________.

TEACHING OPTIONS

Heritage Speakers Ask Spanish speakers if they have visited an **alcázar** (fortress) or a **mesquita** (mosque) in Spain or another Spanish-speaking country. Ask them to give a brief presentation on the features of either of these structures, what they saw, and where. Ask them to display postcards, photos, or brochures as visual aids, if possible.

Pairs Have pairs of students work together to read **Grandezas de la burocracia** and write two questions about the selection. When they have finished, have them exchange their questions with another pair who can work together to answer them.

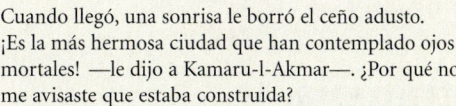

Cuentan que Abderrahmán decidió fundar la ciudad más hermosa del mundo, para lo cual mandó llamar a una multitud de ingenieros, de arquitectos y de artistas a cuya cabeza estaba Kamaru-l-Akmar, el primero y el más sabio de los ingenieros árabes.

Kamaru-l-Akmar prometió que en un año la ciudad estaría edificada, con sus alcázares, sus mezquitas y jardines más bellos que los de Susa y Ecbatana y aún que los de Bagdad. Pero solicitó al califa que le permitiera construirla con entera libertad y fantasía y según sus propias ideas, y que no se dignase verla sino una vez que estuviese concluida. Abderrahmán, sonriendo, accedió.

Al cabo del primero año Kamaru-l-Akmar pidió otro año de prórroga, que el califa gustosamente le concedió. Esto se repitió varias veces. Así transcurrieron no menos de diez años. Hasta que Abderrahmán, encolerizado, decidió ir a investigar.

Cuando llegó, una sonrisa le borró el ceño adusto. ¡Es la más hermosa ciudad que han contemplado ojos mortales! —le dijo a Kamaru-l-Akmar—. ¿Por qué no me avisaste que estaba construida?

Kamaru-l-Akmar inclinó la frente y no se atrevió a confesar al califa que lo que estaba viendo eran los palacios y jardines que los ingenieros, arquitectos y demás artistas habían levantado para sí mismos mientras estudiaban los planes de la futura ciudad.

Así fue construida Zahara, a orillas del Guadalquivir.

grandezas *grandeurs* a partir de 1980 *from 1980 on*
ingenio *creative mind* fundar *to found* sabio *wise*
estaría edificada *would be built* alcázares *fortresses*
mezquitas *mosques* aún *even*
sino una vez que estuviese concluida *until it was finished*
Al cabo de *At the end of* prórroga *extension*
transcurrieron *passed* encolerizado *angry*
le borró el ceño adusto *wiped the stern frown off his face*
frente *forehead* no se atrevió *didn't dare* a orillas de *on the shores of*

Contestar

Contesta estas preguntas.

1. Describe al califa y a Kamaru-l-Akmar. ¿Qué tipo de personas crees que son? Explica tu respuesta.
2. ¿Por qué el ingeniero no quiere que Abderrahmán vea la ciudad antes de que termine la construcción? Explica tu respuesta.
3. ¿Qué significa la palabra **burocracia?**
4. ¿Por qué este cuento se llama *Grandezas de la burocracia*?
5. ¿Crees que el narrador de este cuento está a favor de o en contra de la burocracia? Explica tu opinión.
6. ¿Cuáles son algunos ejemplos de la burocracia en tu vida?

Diálogo

Trabaja con un(a) compañero/a para preparar un diálogo en tres partes, basándose en la lectura. Después presenten el diálogo a la clase.

- Primera parte: El califa habla con el más sabio de los ingenieros sobre la ciudad que quiere fundar.
- Segunda parte: Kamaru-l-Akmar pide la séptima prórroga y explica por qué es necesaria. El califa se la concede pero no está muy contento.
- Tercera parte: Abderrahmán y Kamaru-l-Akmar visitan el lugar de construcción en el décimo año.

a favor de *in favor of* en contra de *against*

Después de leer

Completar

Suggestion You may have pairs of students work through this activity together before you go over the answers orally with the whole class. Ask pairs to find the correct answers to each item in the text. If pairs have difficulty answering any question, suggest one of the partners read aloud corresponding portions of the text.

Contestar

Suggestion Ask volunteers to answer questions orally in class. Involve the whole class in discussing opinions of **el califa** and **Kamaru-l-Akmar** as well as the meaning of the word **burocracia**.

Diálogo

Suggestion Give students sufficient time to prepare and practice their dialogues. Ask volunteers to perform their dialogues for the whole class.

Students may wish to make audio recordings of their presentations.

TEACHING OPTIONS

Heritage Speakers Have Spanish speakers bring a map (in Spanish) of a city where they have lived or visited. Have them describe important landmarks or points of interest. Spanish speakers should indicate the major highways, bridges (**puentes**), squares, and so forth, on the map as they describe the location of the points of interest and transportation routes.

TPR Have students work in pairs. One partner is blindfolded and the other gives directions to get from one place in the classroom to another. For example: **Te voy a decir cómo llegar de tu escritorio a la puerta del salón. Camina derecho cinco pasos. Toma tres pasos a la izquierda y luego dobla a la derecha y camina cuatro pasos para que no choques con el escritorio. Estás cerca a la puerta. Siga derecho dos pasos más. Allí está la puerta.**

Section Goals

In **Escritura** students will:
- learn to prepare for writing by making a list of key words they plan to use as they write
- write a letter to a friend or relative giving directions from the airport to the writer's house

Tema
Present Have students brainstorm and categorize a list of verbs, directions, and locations that they may use in their letters. Ask a volunteer to record students' suggestions in a word map on the board. Tell students they will be composing their directions using present tense imperatives or commands, for example, **conducir (conduzca, conduzcan), doblar (doble, doblen), seguir (siga, sigan)**; as well as directions **(este, oeste, sur, norte)**; and locations **(en frente de, al lado de, detrás de)**.

Estrategia
Present Discuss the importance of writing clear directions and the need to be precise, particularly if someone gets lost easily. In addition to the vocabulary reviewed above, you may wish to introduce some additional terms: **cerca** (near), **lejos** (far), **salida** (exit), **cruzarse, cruce** (intersect, intersection), **semáforo** (stoplight).

Suggestion Ask volunteers to work in pairs and to practice giving directions to one another from their house to the college or university. Remind them to ask questions for clarification.

Assignment Have students prepare **Ideas y organización** and **Primer borrador** as homework.

Escritura

NATIONAL communication STANDARDS

Estrategia

Listing key words

Once you have determined the purpose for a piece of writing and identified your audience, it is helpful to make a list of key words you can use while writing. If you were to write a description of your campus, for example, you would probably need a list of prepositions that describe location, such as **en frente de, al lado de,** and **detrás de.** Likewise, a list of descriptive adjectives would be useful to you if you were writing about the people and places of your childhood.

By preparing a list of potential words ahead of time, you will find it easier to avoid using the dictionary while writing your first draft. You will probably also learn a few new words in Spanish while preparing your list of key words.

Listing useful vocabulary is also a valuable organizational strategy, since the act of brainstorming key words will help you to form ideas about your topic. In addition, a list of key words can help you avoid redundancy when you write.

If you were going to draw a map of the community where you currently live, what words would be most helpful to you? Jot a few of them down and compare your list with a partner's. Did you choose the same words? Would you choose any different or additional words, based on what your partner wrote?

1. ______________________
2. ______________________
3. ______________________
4. ______________________
5. ______________________
6. ______________________

Tema

Escribir direcciones

Un(a) amigo/a o un(a) pariente que vive en otra ciudad te mandó una carta diciéndote que viene a visitarte el próximo mes. Tiene planes de alquilar un coche pero no sabe cómo llegar desde el aeropuerto a tu casa. Tú sabes que esta persona siempre anda perdida porque no le gusta pedir direcciones a los desconocidos.

Escríbele una carta en la cual le explicas claramente cómo llegar a tu casa. Incluye también un mapa detallado para que no se confunda.

Considera la siguiente lista de datos que puedes incluir en tu carta.

- Mandatos que describen en detalle cada cosa que la persona debe hacer para llegar a tu casa
- El nombre del aeropuerto
- Los nombres de las calles principales entre el aeropuerto y tu casa
- Los nombres de lugares importantes que la persona va a ver entre el aeropuerto y tu casa
- Un mapa que contenga dibujos o símbolos que representen los lugares importantes, y flechas que indiquen la ruta que la persona debe seguir

siempre anda perdida *is always getting lost* desconocidos *strangers*
claramente *clearly* flechas *arrows* mandatos *commands*

TEACHING OPTIONS

Proofreading Activity Copy the following items containing mistakes onto the board or a transparency as a proofreading activity to do with the whole class.

1. **Queremos vivir en una parte de la ciudad que tiene muchos árboles y que queda cerca al centro.**
2. **¿Hay un restaurante en el centro que tiene comida vegetariana y que está abierta los lunes?**
3. **Cuando llegamos al centro esta tarde, buscamos un buen restaurante.**
4. **A ver si la tienda esta cerrado cuando llegamos.**
5. **En cuanto encontremos una tienda donde se venden gafas de sol, compremosnoslas.**

Plan de escritura

1 Ideas y organización

Apunta las palabras y expresiones que más utilizas para dar direcciones, incluyendo los nombres de calles y lugares importantes en tu comunidad. Si quieres, puedes basar tus direcciones en una comunidad inventada por ti. Después planea la mejor ruta para llegar desde el aeropuerto hasta tu casa.

2 Primer borrador

Utilizando tu dibujo y la lista de palabras clave de **Ideas y organización,** escribe el primer borrador de las direcciones. Dibuja también un mapa que indique claramente la ruta. Utiliza el texto, los apuntes de clase y el diccionario solamente como último recurso.

3 Comentario

Intercambia tus direcciones con un(a) compañero/a. Comparte tus opiniones sobre el primer borrador utilizando estas preguntas como guía:

a. ¿Están claras las direcciones o necesitan alguna clarificación?
b. ¿Hay suficientes detalles? ¿Hay demasiados?
c. ¿Está claro el mapa? ¿Qué puede hacer tu compañero/a para hacerlo más claro?
d. ¿Hay errores de gramática, vocabulario o puntuación?
e. ¿Tienes otras sugerencias para mejorar las direcciones o el mapa?

4 Redacción

Revisa el primer borrador según las indicaciones de tu compañero/a. Utiliza la siguiente guía para hacer una última revisión antes de escribir tu versión final.

a. Mira las direcciones. ¿Omitiste detalles importantes? ¿Incluiste demasiados detalles?
b. Subraya todos los verbos. ¿Utilizaste la forma correcta de cada uno?
c. Revisa la ortografía y la puntuación una vez más con la ayuda de tus **Anotaciones para mejorar la escritura.**
d. Mira el mapa. ¿Está claro? ¿Necesitas hacer algo para clarificarlo?

5 Evaluación y progreso

Trabaja con un(a) compañero/a. Lee las instrucciones que escribió y mira el mapa que dibujó. Después, mirando solamente el mapa, dale las instrucciones al revés... es decir, cómo llegar de su casa al aeropuerto. Cuando recibas las correcciones y los comentarios de tu profesor(a), anota tus errores en las **Anotaciones para mejorar la escritura** en tu **Carpeta de trabajos.**

Comentario
Present Go over guide questions **a-e** with the class so peer readers understand their task. Then have pairs of students exchange letters. Allow five minutes for reading and comments.
Assignment Have students follow the directions in **Redacción** as homework.

Evaluación y progreso
Give the class ten minutes to carry out the activity. Then have students hand in their letters to you.

Writing Sample Here is a sample letter with directions that would constitute superior writing achievement.

Querida tía Carolina,

Ésta es la manera más fácil de ir del aeropuerto a mi casa. Mi dirección es calle Palmetto 329. Mi casa queda a unos 15 minutos del aeropuerto.

Hay sólo una salida del areopuerto. Busca un letrero que diga Carretera 26—Oeste. En cuanto ves el letrero, marca el número de millas. De allí, vas a viajar 12 millas hacia el norte.

Después de viajar 3 millas, verás un estadio a la izquierda. Sigue derecho hasta que la Carretera 26 cruce la Carreterra 60. Luego, busca la salida 102A y sal de la carreter. Ahora vas a estar en el camino San Andrés. Sigue derecho otra milla y media, y dobla a la izquierda en la calle Ventura. Sigue media cuadra y dobla a la derecha en la calle Palmetto.

Nuestra casa queda al lado izquierdo. Es casa amarilla. No te olvides el número de teléfono—777–7654—en caso de que te pierdas.

¡Nos vemos pronto! Recibe un abrazo de tu sobrina,

Gloria

EVALUATION: Direcciones

Criteria	Scale
Content	1 2 3 4
Organization	1 2 3 4
Use of vocabulary	1 2 3 4
Grammatical accuracy	1 2 3 4
Accuracy of map	1 2 3 4

Scoring	
Excellent	18–20 points
Good	14–17 points
Satisfactory	10–13 points
Unsatisfactory	< 10 points

Escuchar

NATIONAL communication STANDARDS

Preparación

Describe la foto. Según la foto, ¿qué información específica piensas que vas a oír en el diálogo?

Estrategia

Listening for specific information/ Listening for linguistic cues

As you already know, you don't have to hear or understand every word when listening to Spanish. You can often get the facts you need by listening for specific pieces of information. You should also be aware of the linguistic structures you hear. For example, by listening for verb endings, you can ascertain whether the verbs describe past, present, or future actions, and they can also indicate who is performing the action. To practice these strategies, you will listen to a short paragraph about an environmental issue. What environmental problem is being discussed? What is the cause of the problem? Has the problem been solved, or is the solution under development?

Ahora escucha

Lee estas frases y luego escucha la conversación entre Alberto y Eduardo. Indica si cada verbo se refiere a algo en el pasado, en el presente o en el futuro.

Acciones

1. Demetrio / comprar en Macro pasado
2. Alberto / comprar en Macro futuro
3. Alberto / estudiar psicología pasado
4. coche / tener frenos malos presente
5. Eduardo / comprar un anillo para Rebeca pasado
6. Eduardo / estudiar futuro

Comprensión

Descripciones

Marca las frases que describen correctamente a Alberto.

1. ✔ Es organizado en sus estudios.
2. ______ Compró un anillo para su novia.
3. ______ No le gusta tomar el metro.
4. ✔ No conoce bien la zona de Sabana Grande y Chacaíto.
5. ✔ No tiene buen sentido de la orientación.
6. ✔ Le gusta ir a los lugares que están de moda.

Preguntas

1. ¿Por qué Alberto prefiere ir en metro a Macro? porque es muy difícil estacionar el coche en Sabana Grande.
2. ¿Crees que Alberto y Eduardo viven en una ciudad grande o en un pueblo? ¿Cómo lo sabes? en una ciudad grande por que tiene metro.
3. ¿Por qué tiene tanto interés Alberto en ir a Macro? porque es el único que no ha ido.

Conversación

En grupos pequeños, hablen de sus tiendas favoritas y de cómo llegar a ellas desde la universidad. ¿En qué lugares tienen la última moda? ¿Los mejores precios? ¿Hay buenas tiendas cerca de la universidad? Answers will vary.

anillo *ring* sentido de la orientación *sense of direction*

Section Goals

In **Escuchar** students will:
- listen for specific information and linguistic clues
- answer questions based on a recorded conversation

Instructional Resource
Student Cassette/CD

Preparación
Warm-up Have students describe the photo. Guide them to guess who Demetrio and Alberto are and what they are doing.

Estrategia
Script Hace muchos años que los residentes de nuestra ciudad están preocupados por la contaminación del aire. El año pasado se mudaron más de cinco mil personas a nuestra ciudad. Hay cada año más carros en las calles y el problema de la contaminación va de mal en peor. Los estudiantes de la universidad de Puerto Ordaz piensan que este problema es importante; quieren diseñar carros que usen menos gasolina para evitar más contaminación ambiental.
Assignment Have students do **Ahora escucha** and **Comprensión** as homework. Verify the responses to **Ahora escucha** with the whole class and go over **Descripciones** and **Preguntas**. Then have groups of three do **Conversación**.

Ahora escucha
Script
Alberto: Demetrio me dijo que fue de compras con Carlos y Roberto a Macro.Y tú, Eduardo, ¿has ido? **Eduardo:** ¡Claro que sí, Alberto! Tienen las últimas modas. Me compré estos zapatos allí. ¡Carísimos!, pero me fascinan y, de ñapa, son cómodos. • **A:** Pues, ya terminé de estudiar para el examen de psicología. Creo que voy a ir esta tarde porque me siento muy fuera de la onda. ¡Soy el único que no ha ido a Macro! ¿Dónde queda? • **E:** Es por Sabana Grande. ¿Vas a ir en metro o en carro? • **A:** Es mejor ir en metro. Es muy difícil estacionar el carro en Sabana Grande. Tampoco me gusta manejarlo porque los frenos están malos. • **E:** Bueno, súbete al metro en la línea amarilla hasta Plaza Venezuela. Cuando salgas de la estación de metro dobla a la izquierda hacia Chacaíto. Sigue derecho por dos cuadras. • **A:** Ah, sí, enfrente de la joyería donde le compraste el anillo a Rebeca. • **E:** No, la joyería queda una cuadra hacia el sur. Pasa el Banco Mercantil y dobla a la derecha. Tan pronto como pases la pizzería Papagallo, vas a ver un letrero rojo grandísimo a mano izquierda que dice Macro. • **A:** Gracias, Eduardo. ¿No quieres ir? Así no me pierdo. • **E:** No, hoy no puedo. Tengo que estudiar y a las cuatro tengo una cita con Rebeca. Pero estoy seguro que vas a llegar sin ningún problema.

NATIONAL STANDARDS
communication
cultures

NATIONAL STANDARDS
connections
communities

Proyecto

Promociona una comunidad

Imagina que eres miembro de un grupo que está diseñando y promocionando una comunidad modelo en Venezuela.

1 Prepara un folleto

Crea un folleto para hacer publicidad de una comunidad modelo que van a construir en Venezuela. Usa los **Recursos para la investigación** para escoger el lugar ideal para el proyecto, considerando la geografía, el terreno, el clima, el acceso a ciudades grandes, los eventos culturales y los atractivos naturales. El folleto puede incluir la siguiente información:

- Un pequeño mapa de Venezuela que indica dónde está localizada la comunidad modelo
- Fotos de la zona
- Un mapa de la zona que muestra las tiendas y las atracciones principales del centro de la comunidad
- Una explicación de la ubicación ideal de la comunidad, incluyendo clima, atractivos naturales y acceso a ciudades importantes
- Varios párrafos que expliquen las características de la comunidad, sus atracciones y las razones por las cuales va a ser una comunidad mejor que las otras

2 Presenta la información

Reúnete con tres o cuatro compañeros/as. Usa el folleto como guía para promocionar la comunidad con tus compañeros. La meta de la presentación es mostrar que esta comunidad es única por su ubicación, atracciones y recursos.

Luego comparen las comunidades que han planeado. ¿Están en las mismas regiones geográficas o en lugares muy distintos? ¿Tienen las mismas atracciones culturales y naturales? ¿Qué ventajas especiales tiene cada una de sus comunidades?

folleto *brochure* promociona *promote* construir *to build* ubicación *location* meta *goal*

recursos para la investigación

Internet Palabras clave: Venezuela, ciudad, ciudades, fotos, geografía, atractivos, arte, cultura, mapa	**Comunidad** Profesores, estudiantes o personas en la comunidad que son venezolanas o que han viajado por Venezuela
Biblioteca Mapas, enciclopedias, revistas, guías turísticas	**Otros recursos** Hacer investigación de los recursos especiales que tienen las mejores comunidades

Section Goals

In **Proyecto** students will:
- learn about Venezuela, its geography, culture, and people
- use Spanish as they do research and interact with the wider world
- write and present a brochure for a model community in Venezuela

Before Assigning Proyecto Students will need approximately a week to complete the project, so at the beginning of that time period, have them open their books to page 455 and glance over **Proyecto**. Explain that they are going to use their research skills to prepare a brochure to promote a model community in Venezuela. Ask them to review the list of information to include and have them brainstorm what types of information they want to feature in their brochures.

Assignment Have students read page 455 and follow directions in **Prepara un folleto** to plan their presentation.

Prepara un folleto Suggestions
- Students may wish to interview local community designers or community developers to get first-hand information on what goes into developing a model community.
- You may wish to have students work in pairs, with one partner focusing on the residential areas and the other on the commercial areas of the community.
- Students may have the capability of creating an electronic brochure with multimedia or Web authoring software.

Presenta la información Suggestion If you assigned partners, you may wish to give pairs time to coordinate and practice their individual portions of the presentation.

EVALUATION: Folleto

Criteria	Scale
Content	1 2 3 4 5
Organization	1 2 3 4 5
Grammatical Accuracy	1 2 3 4 5
Creativity	1 2 3 4 5

Scoring	
Excellent	18–20 points
Good	14–17 points
Satisfactory	10–13 points
Unsatisfactory	< 10 points

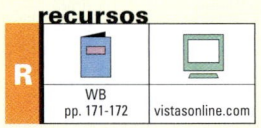

Section Goals

In **Panorama**, students will read about the history, geography, and economy of Venezuela.

Instructional Resources
Student Activities Manual: Workbook, 171–172 Transparency 53

Venezuela
Before Presenting Panorama Have students look at the map of Venezuela or project **Transparency 53** and talk about the physical features of the country. Have students trace the **Río Orinoco** and notice the types of terrain it runs through (such as **Los Llanos** and the Amazon basin). Note that the principal cities are all located along the Caribbean coast.
Assignment Have students read **Panorama** and write out the completed questions and anwers in **¿Qué aprendiste?** on page 457.

Present Ask volunteers to read each section of **El país en cifras**. Point out that the national currency is named for Simón Bolívar, the Latin American hero who played a central role in the struggle for independence from Spain. Point out that Bolívar's birthplace was Caracas. After reading about the **yanomami**, point out to students the vastness of Venezuela's jungle area, and remind them that various groups of indigenous people inhabit this largely undeveloped area.

Increíble pero cierto
Angel Falls is located in a rugged, inaccessible area of Venezuela, the Guyana Highlands, and is most easily viewed from the air. In fact, that is how the falls were first identified by Venezuelans in 1935. Subsequently, James C. Angel crash-landed a plane in the area, and made the first non-native exploration of this natural wonder.

Venezuela

NATIONAL STANDARDS connections cultures

El país en cifras

- **Área:** 912.050 km² (352.144 millas²), *aproximadamente dos veces el área de California*
- **Población:** 24.170.000
- **Capital:** Caracas—3.198.000
- **Ciudades principales:** Maracaibo—2.014.000, Valencia—2.068.000, Maracay—1.162.000, Barquisimeto—957.000

SOURCE: Population Division, UN Secretariat

- **Moneda:** bolívar
- **Idiomas:** español (oficial), arahuaco, caribe

El yanomami es uno de los idiomas indígenas que se habla en Venezuela. La cultura de los yanomami tiene su centro en el sur de Venezuela, en el bosque tropical. Muchos antropólogos han estudiado esta tribu por la agresividad que utiliza para defender sus tradiciones y costumbres.

Bandera de Venezuela

Venezolanos célebres

- **Teresa Carreño,** compositora y pianista (1853-1917)
- **Rómulo Gallegos,** escritor y político (1884-1979)
- **Andrés Eloy Blanco,** poeta (1897-1955)
- **Baruj Benacerraf,** científico (1920-)

Baruj Benacerraf, junto con dos de sus colegas, recibió el Premio Nobel por sus investigaciones en el campo de la inmunología y las enfermedades autoinmunes. Nacido en Caracas, Benacerraf también vivió en París y reside ahora en los Estados Unidos.

caída *drop*

Vista central de Caracas

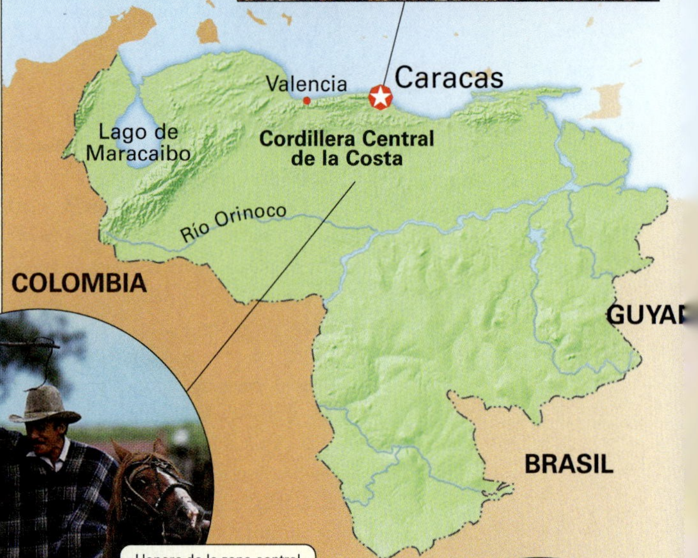

Llanero de la zona central de Venezuela.

Tres niños en una piragua

¡Increíble pero cierto!

Con una caída de 979 m. (3,212 pies) desde la meseta de Auyan Tepuy, Salto Ángel (*Angel Falls*), en Venezuela, es la catarata más alta del mundo, ¡diecisiete veces más alta que las cataratas del Niágara! James C. Angel la descubrió en 1937. Los indígenas de la zona la denominan Churún Merú.

recursos

R | WB pp. 171-172 | vistasonline.com

TEACHING OPTIONS

Variación léxica Venezuelan Spanish has a rich repertoire of regionalisms and colloquialisms. If your students go to Caracas, they are certainly going to hear the word **pana**, which means both **amigo** and **amiga**. Ex: **¡Eso es chévere, pana!** The Venezuelan equivalent of *guy* or *girl* is **chamo/a**. An inhabitant of the city of Caracas is a **caraqueño/a.** Some other words that are specific to Venezuela are **cambur** for **plátano** and **caraota** for **frijol**.

Worth Noting Rómulo Gallegos's great novel, *Doña Bárbara*, is set in the Llanos of Venezuela, a region known for its culture of cattle raising. The theme of the novel is one that has been dealt with by many Latin American writers, the struggle between **civilización y barbarie**.

Economía • El petróleo

La industria petrolera es muy importante para la economía venezolana. La mayor concentración de petróleo se encuentra debajo del lago Maracaibo, el lago más grande de América del Sur. En 1976 se nacionalizaron las empresas petroleras y pasaron a ser propiedad del estado con el nombre de Petróleos de Venezuela. Este producto representa más del 70% de las exportaciones del país, siendo Estados Unidos su principal comprador.

Actualidades • Caracas

Debido al boom petrolero de los años cincuenta, Caracas se ha convertido en una ciudad cosmopolita. Sus rascacielos y excelentes sistemas de transporte hacen que se cuente entre las ciudades más modernas de Latinoamérica. El metro, construido en 1983, es de los más recientes y sus extensas carreteras y autopistas conectan la ciudad con el interior del país. El corazón de la ciudad es el Parque Central, una zona de centros comerciales, tiendas, restaurantes y clubes.

Historia • Simón Bolívar (1783-1830)

A finales del siglo XVIII, Venezuela, al igual que otros países sudamericanos, todavía estaba bajo el dominio de la corona española. El general Simón Bolívar, nacido en Caracas, fue llamado "El Libertador" porque fue el líder del movimiento independentista sudamericano que liberó el área que hoy es Venezuela, Colombia, Ecuador, Perú y Bolivia. Con la ayuda de su lugarteniente, José Antonio Sucre, Bolívar contribuyó a formar el destino de América.

¿Qué aprendiste? Responde a las preguntas con una frase completa.

1. ¿Cuál es la moneda de Venezuela?
   La moneda de Venezuela es el bolívar.
2. ¿Quién fue Rómulo Gallegos?
   Rómulo Gallegos fue un escritor y político venezolano.
3. ¿Cuál es el lago más grande de América del Sur?
   El lago Maracaibo es el lago más grande de América del Sur.
4. ¿Cuál es el producto más exportado de Venezuela?
   El producto más exportado de Venezuela es el petróleo.
5. ¿Qué ocurrió en 1976 con las empresas petroleras?
   En 1976 las empresas petroleras se nacionalizaron.
6. ¿Cómo se llama la capital de Venezuela?
   La capital de Venezuela se llama Caracas.
7. ¿Qué hay en el Parque Central de Caracas?
   Hay centros comerciales, tiendas, restaurantes y clubes.
8. ¿Por qué es conocido Simón Bolívar como "El Libertador"? Simón Bolívar es conocido como "El Libertador" porque liberó de España el área que hoy es Venezuela, Colombia, Ecuador, Perú y Bolivia.
9. ¿Quién era el lugarteniente de Simón Bolívar? José Antonio Sucre era el lugarteniente de Simón Bolívar.

Tejedor en Los Aleros, aldea en los Andes de Venezuela

Conexión Internet Investiga estos temas en el sitio **www.vistasonline.com.**

1. Busca información sobre Simón Bolívar. ¿Cuáles son algunos de los episodios más importantes de su vida? ¿Crees que Bolívar fue un estadista (*statesman*) de primera categoría? ¿Por qué?
2. Prepara un plan para un viaje de ecoturismo por el Orinoco. ¿Qué quieres ver y hacer durante la excursión? ¿Por qué?

empresas petroleras *oil companies* se nacionalizaron *were nationalized* propiedad *property* comprador *buyer* Debido al *Due to* se ha convertido *has turned into* rascacielos *skyscrapers* hacen que se cuente *make it rank* más recientes *newest* siglo *century* corona *crown* nacido *born* lugarteniente *chief lieutenant*

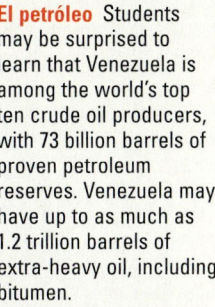

El petróleo Students may be surprised to learn that Venezuela is among the world's top ten crude oil producers, with 73 billion barrels of proven petroleum reserves. Venezuela may have up to as much as 1.2 trillion barrels of extra-heavy oil, including bitumen.

Caracas Both Caracas and Houston are major urban areas fueled by oil booms. Students may find it interesting to compare how these cities have developed: Houston's urban development is limited only by the coastline, allowing it to sprawl in all other directions; Caracas is hemmed into a narrow valley by two ranges of mountains, leading to its dense development and its many highrises.

Simón Bolívar The life of Simón Bolívar has inspired artists of every sort: from painters and sculptors to musician and writers. In 1989, Colombian Nobel winner Gabriel García Márquez published **El general en su laberinto**, his vision of Bolívar towards the end of his life, as he muses about the accomplishments and disappointments of his life.

¿Qué aprendiste? Go over the answers to the questions with students, making sure everyone understands unfamiliar words and what the correct answers are.

Assignment Have students do activites in **Student Activities Manual: Workbook,** pages 171–172.

Conexión Internet Students will find information about Venezuela at **www.vistasonline.com,** as well as links to other sites that can help them in their research.

TEACHING OPTIONS

Worth Noting Tell students that the **Salto Ángel**, besides being the highest uninterrupted waterfall in the world, falls from the top of a **tepuy** (pl. **tepúyes**), a flat-topped, sandstone mountain with vertical sides. Because of the isolation that results from their great elevation and their vertical sides, the top of each tepuy has its own closed ecology, featuring plants and animals of different species that grow nowhere else on earth, including the tops of neighboring tepúyes. The chilly, damp climate atop a tepuy differs so markedly from the tropical climate at its foot/base that species aclimatized to it cannot survive on the **sabana** below and vice versa. This ensures the isolation of the ecological system atop each tepuy.

Heritage Speakers Ask Spanish speakers who come from Venezuela or have visited there to tell the class about their experience of the country.

14 vocabulario

En la ciudad

el banco	*bank*
la carnicería	*butcher shop*
el correo	*post office*
la frutería	*fruit store*
la heladería	*ice cream shop*
la joyería	*jewelry store*
la lavandería	*laundromat*
la panadería	*bakery*
la pastelería	*pastry shop*
la peluquería, el salón de belleza	*beauty salon*
la pescadería	*fish market*
el supermercado	*supermarket*
la zapatería	*shoe store*
hacer cola	*to stand in line*
hacer diligencias	*to run errands*

En el correo

el cartero	*mail carrier*
el correo	*mail*
el paquete	*package*
la estampilla, el sello	*stamp*
el sobre	*envelope*
echar (una carta) al buzón	*to put (a letter) in the mailbox; to mail*
enviar, mandar	*to send; to mail*

En el banco

el cajero automático	*ATM*
la cuenta corriente	*checking account*
la cuenta de ahorros	*savings account*
el cheque (de viajero)	*(traveler's) check*
ahorrar	*to save (money)*
cobrar	*to cash (a check)*
depositar	*to deposit*
firmar	*to sign*
llenar (un formulario)	*to fill out (a form)*
pagar a plazos	*to pay in installments*
pagar al contado, en efectivo	*to pay in cash*
pedir prestado	*to borrow*
pedir un préstamo	*to apply for a loan*
ser gratis	*to be free of charge*

Conjunciones

después (de) que	*after*
en cuanto	*as soon as*
hasta que	*until*
tan pronto como	*as soon as*

Direcciones

la cuadra	*(city) block*
la dirección	*address*
la esquina	*corner*
el letrero	*sign*
cruzar	*to cross*
dar direcciones	*to give directions*
doblar	*to turn*
estar perdido/a	*to be lost*
quedar	*to be located*
(al) este	*(to the) east*
(al) norte	*(to the) north*
(al) oeste	*(to the) west*
(al) sur	*(to the) south*
derecho	*straight (ahead)*
enfrente de	*opposite; facing*
hacia	*toward*

Past participles used as adjectives	*See page 447.*
Expresiones útiles	*See page 433.*

El bienestar

15

Communicative Goals

You will learn how to:

- Talk about health, well being, and physical activities.
- Describe an action or event in the immediate past.
- Describe an action or event that ocurred before another past event.

contextos

pages 460-463

- Health and well being
- Exercise and physical activity
- Nutrition

fotonovela

pages 464-467

The students and Martín go on their long-awaited hike. Don Francisco greets them when they return at the end of the day, and listens to their reactions to what they saw and experienced.

estructura

pages 468-477

- The present perfect
- The past perfect
- The present perfect subjunctive

adelante

pages 478-483

Lectura: Read a short story with an unexpected ending.
Escritura: Write a personal health plan.
Escuchar: Listen to a radio program about exercise.
Proyecto: Create a brochure for a trip to Bolivia.

panorama

pages 484-485

Featured Country: Bolivia

- **Titicaca:** The highest lake in the world
- Andean music
- **Tiahuanaco:** City of the gods

Lesson Goals

In **Lesson 15** students will be introduced to the following:

- terms for health and exercise
- nutrition terms
- present perfect
- past perfect
- present perfect subjunctive
- making inferences
- organizing information logically when writing
- writing a personal fitness plan
- listening for the gist and for cognates
- writing a brochure for adventure travel in Bolivia
- cultural, geographic, and historical information about Bolivia

Lesson Preview

Have students look at the photo. Ask: **¿Qué ven en la foto? ¿Cómo es la chica? ¿Creen que la chica tiene mucha energía? ¿Creen que la chica está de buena salud?**

INSTRUCTIONAL RESOURCES

Student Activities Manual: Workbook, 173–182
Student Activities Manual: Lab Manual, 305–309
Student Activities Manual: Video Activities, 355–356
Instructor's Resource Manual: Hojas de actividades, 36–37
Instructor's Resource Manual: Answer Keys
Tapescript/Videoscript
Overhead Transparencies, 54–56
Student Cassette/CD
Lab Cassette/CD
Video Program
CD-ROM
Website: **www.vistasonline.com**
Testing Program: Prueba A, Prueba B

Section Goals

In **Contextos**, students will learn and practice:

- vocabulary used to talk about health and exercise
- vocabulary used to discuss nutrition and a healthy diet

Instructional Resources
Student Activities Manual: Workbook, 173–174; Lab Manual, 305
Hoja de actividades 36
Transparencies 54–55
Student Cassette/CD

Before Presenting Contextos Write **hacer ejercicios** on the board, then ask personalized questions such as the following, writing new vocabulary on the board: **¿Quiénes hacen ejercicios regularmente? ¿Hacen ejercicios aeróbicos? ¿Quiénes levantan pesas? ¿Quiénes no hacen ejercicios para nada?** Tell students that they are going to learn vocabulary related to exercise and nutrition. **Assignment** Have students study **Contextos** and do the activities on page 461 and Activity 4 on page 462 as homework.

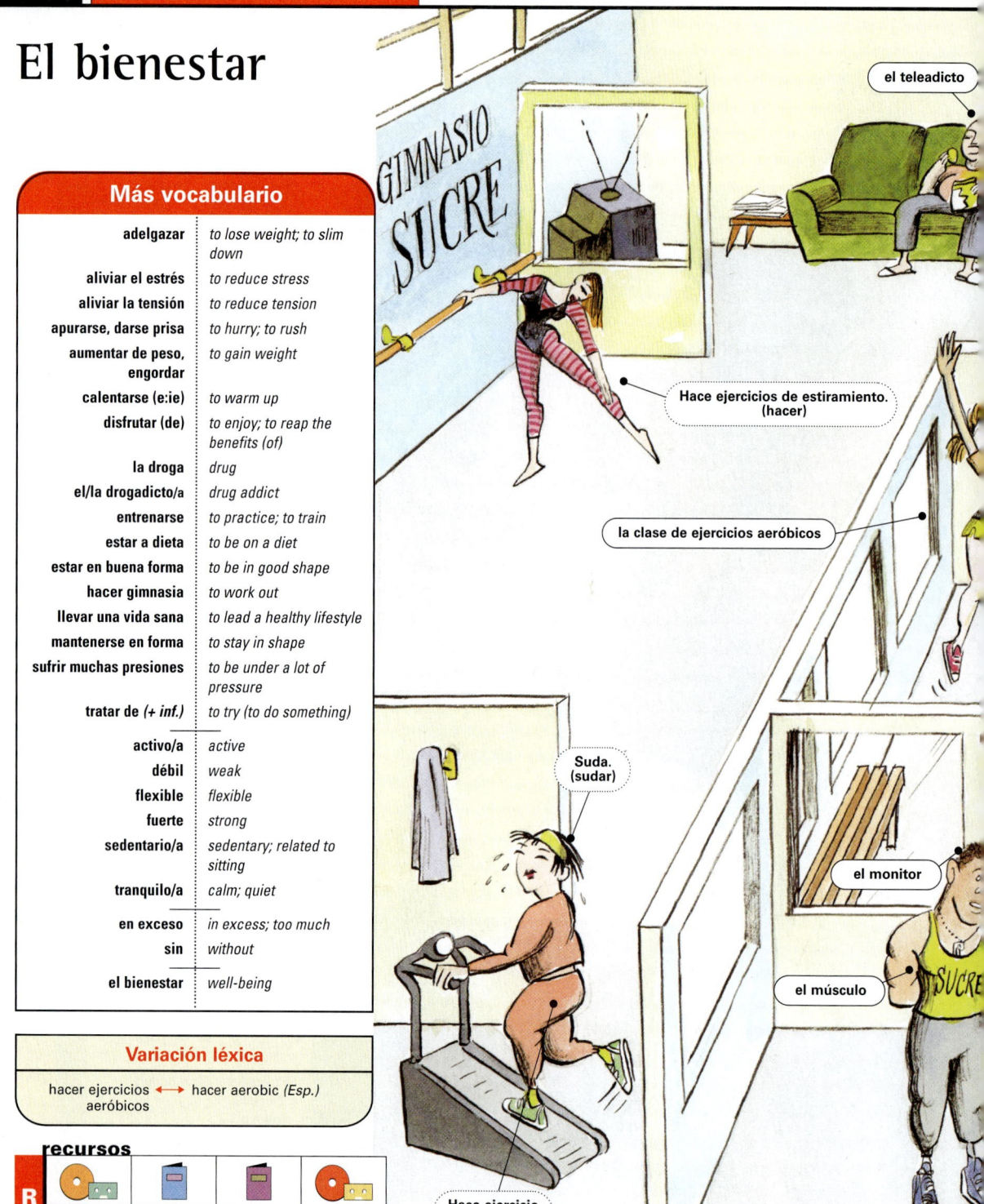

Present Project **Transparency 54.** Give the people in the transparency names and make statements and ask questions about their activities. Ex: **El Sr. Garza es teleadicto. Miren como hace ejercicios. Ve televisión y come papitas fritas. ¿Es activo o sedentario? ¿Lleva una vida sana?** After you have gone over the active vocabulary, ask students personalized questions about their exercise habits. Ex: **¿Qué hacen para aliviar el estrés? María, ¿qué haces para aliviar el estrés? ¿Creen que se puede hacer ejercicios en exceso? ¿Creen que es más importante ser flexible o ser fuerte?**

El bienestar

Más vocabulario

adelgazar	*to lose weight; to slim down*
aliviar el estrés	*to reduce stress*
aliviar la tensión	*to reduce tension*
apurarse, darse prisa	*to hurry; to rush*
aumentar de peso, engordar	*to gain weight*
calentarse (e:ie)	*to warm up*
disfrutar (de)	*to enjoy; to reap the benefits (of)*
la droga	*drug*
el/la drogadicto/a	*drug addict*
entrenarse	*to practice; to train*
estar a dieta	*to be on a diet*
estar en buena forma	*to be in good shape*
hacer gimnasia	*to work out*
llevar una vida sana	*to lead a healthy lifestyle*
mantenerse en forma	*to stay in shape*
sufrir muchas presiones	*to be under a lot of pressure*
tratar de (+ *inf.*)	*to try (to do something)*
activo/a	*active*
débil	*weak*
flexible	*flexible*
fuerte	*strong*
sedentario/a	*sedentary; related to sitting*
tranquilo/a	*calm; quiet*
en exceso	*in excess; too much*
sin	*without*
el bienestar	*well-being*

Variación léxica

hacer ejercicios aeróbicos ⟷ hacer aerobic *(Esp.)*

recursos

R				
	SCASS./CD Lección 15	WB pp. 173-174	LM p. 305	LCASS./CD Cass. 8A/CD8

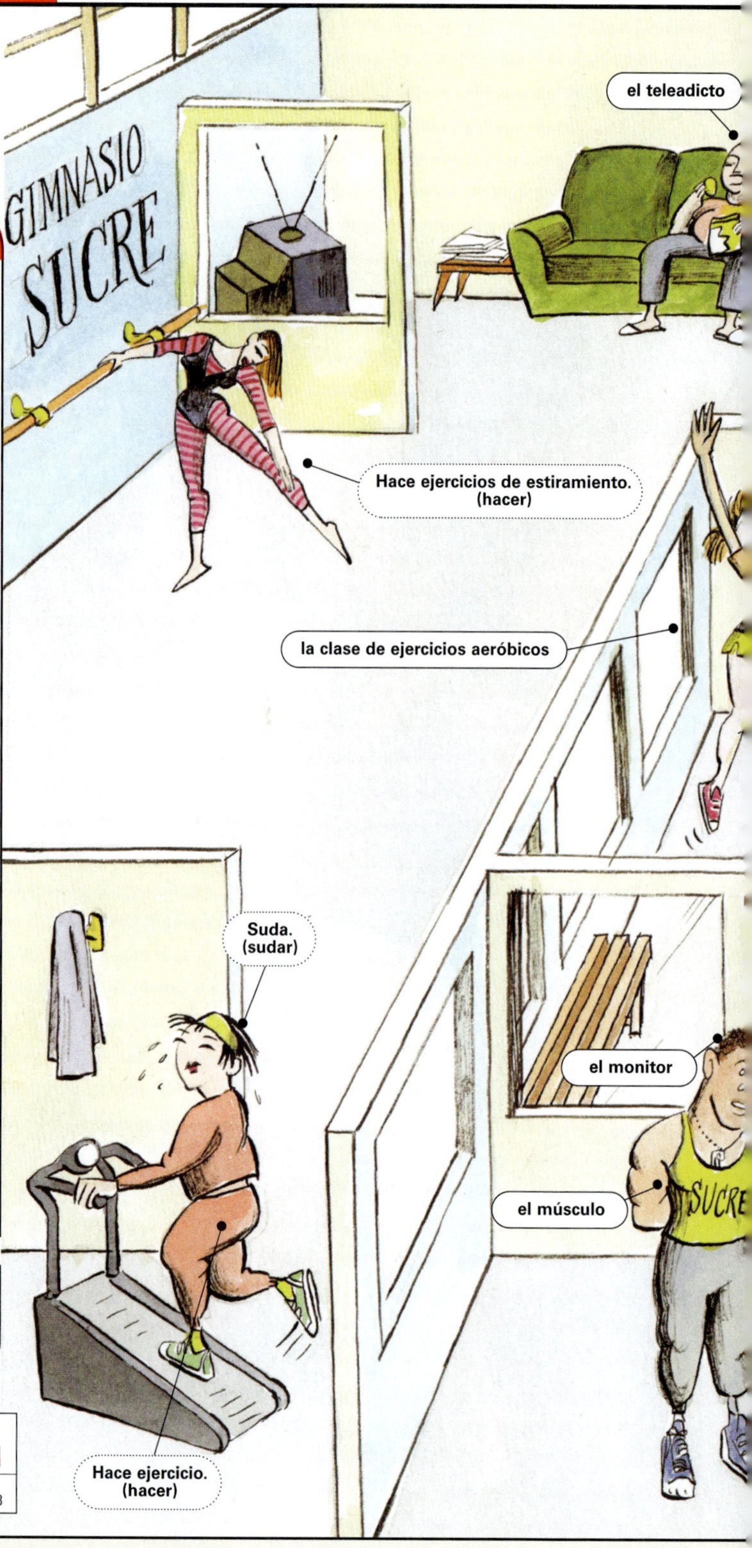

TEACHING OPTIONS

TPR Ask students to stand. Call out commands based on the lesson vocabulary. Ex: **¡Levanten pesas! ¡Hagan ejercicios aeróbicos! ¡Apúrense! ¡Descánsense!** and so forth. Working with students, invent a gesture to mime each activity. When you have invented gestures to cover all the vocabulary, carry out a TPR activity with the class. Keep the pace rapid. Vary singular and plural commands.

Variación léxica Point out that the fitness movement began in the United States and spread to other parts of the world; hence, many of the terms related to fitness are borrowed from English. Ask Spanish speakers if they can think of other fitness terms that may have been influenced by English.

No fumar.
el masaje
Hace ejercicios aeróbicos. (hacer)
Levanta pesas. (levantar)

Práctica

1 Escuchar Mira el dibujo en las páginas 460-461. Luego escucha las frases e indica si lo que se dice en cada frase es **cierto** o **falso.**

	Cierto	Falso
1.	○	✓
2.	○	✓
3.	✓	○
4.	✓	○
5.	✓	○
6.	○	✓
7.	○	✓
8.	✓	○
9.	○	✓
10.	○	✓

2 Identificar Identifica el opuesto (*opposite*) de cada palabra.

sin	mantenerse en forma
tranquilo	flexible
engordar	sedentario
fuerte	apurarse
estar enfermo	sufrir muchas presiones

1. activo sedentario
2. adelgazar engordar
3. aliviar el estrés sufrir muchas presiones
4. débil fuerte
5. rígido flexible
6. ir despacio apurarse
7. estar sano estar enfermo
8. con sin
9. nervioso tranquilo
10. ser teleadicto mantenerse en forma

3 Combinar Combina palabras de cada columna para formar diez frases lógicas sobre el bienestar.

1. David levanta pesas	j	a. aumentó de peso.
2. Estás en buena forma	f	b. estiramiento.
3. Felipe se lastimó	h	c. fuertes.
4. José y Rafael	g	d. presiones.
5. María y yo somos	c	e. porque quieren adelgazar.
6. Mi hermano	a	f. porque haces ejercicio.
7. Sara hace ejercicios de	b	g. sudan mucho.
8. Mis primas están a dieta	e	h. un músculo de la pierna.
9. Para llevar una vida sana	i	i. no se debe fumar.
10. Ellos sufren muchas	d	j. y corre mucho.

1 Present Check answers by reading each item individually and asking volunteers to say whether the statement is true or false. Have students change the false statements to make them true.

Tapescript
1. Se puede fumar dentro del gimnasio. (falso) **2. El teleadicto está en buena forma.** (falso) **3. Los músculos del monitor son grandes.** (cierto) **4. La mujer que está corriendo también está sudando.** (cierto) **5. Se puede recibir un masaje en el Gimnasio Sucre.** (cierto) **6. Hay cuatro hombres en la clase de ejercicios aeróbicos.** (falso) **7. El hombre que levanta pesas lleva una vida muy sedentaria.** (falso) **8. La instructora de la clase de ejercicios aeróbicos lleva una vida muy activa.** (cierto) **9. El hombre que mira televisión está a dieta.** (falso) **10. No hay nadie en el gimnasio que haga ejercicios de estiramiento.** (falso)

2 Expand Have students use each pair of opposite terms in sentences illustrating their contrasting meanings. Ex: **José está muy nervioso porque no estudió para el examen. Roberto estudió por dos horas; por eso está tranquilo.**

3 Present To check answers, ask volunteers to write each completed sentence on the board. Have the class make any necessary corrections. Discuss why any mismatches are incorrect.

3 Expand Have students create their own original endings for each of the sentence fragments in the left column.

Successful Language Learning Mention that working out to a Spanish language exercise program would be excellent listening practice.

TEACHING OPTIONS

Pairs Have pairs of students interview each other about what they do to stay in shape. Interviewers should also find out how often their partners do these things and when they did them over the past week. Ask students to write a brief report summarizing the interview.

Game Divide the class into groups of three. Ask a group to leave the room while the class chooses a vocabulary word or expression. When the group returns, they must try to guess the word by asking the class yes or no questions. If the group guesses the word within 10 questions, the group gets a point. Ex: **¿Es un lugar? ¿Describe a una persona? ¿Es una acción? ¿Es algo bueno para el bienestar?**

La nutrición
Present Project **Transparency 55.** First, ask open-ended or yes/no questions that elicit the names of the foods depicted. Ex: **¿Qué es esto? (un huevo) Y esto al lado del queso, ¿son papas fritas?** Then ask students either/or questions to elicit the vocabulary in **La nutrición**. Ex: **¿La carne es una proteína o una vitamina? ¿Las bebidas alcohólicas tienen colesterol o no?** Continue questioning, asking for information or opinions. Ex: **¿Cuáles son algunas comidas que tienen colesterol? La cafeína, ¿creen que es una droga? ¿Por qué?**

4 Expand After checking each item, ask students a personal question based on the information in that item, or have students comment on that information. Ex: **¿Comen Uds. comidas con mucha proteína después de hacer ejercicio? ¿Piensan que es buena idea comer comidas de todos los grupos alimenticios? ¿Por qué?**

5 Warm-up Present the vocabulary in **Ayuda**, using the words in sentences that describe your eating or physical activity patterns.

5 Present Have students ask each other each question, discussing it thoroughly before they move on to the next one. Also have them note opinions, ideas, and habits they have in common.

5 Expand As students share their answers with the class, have a volunteer write down any common themes that stand out. Have a class discussion about these themes and their origins.

La nutrición

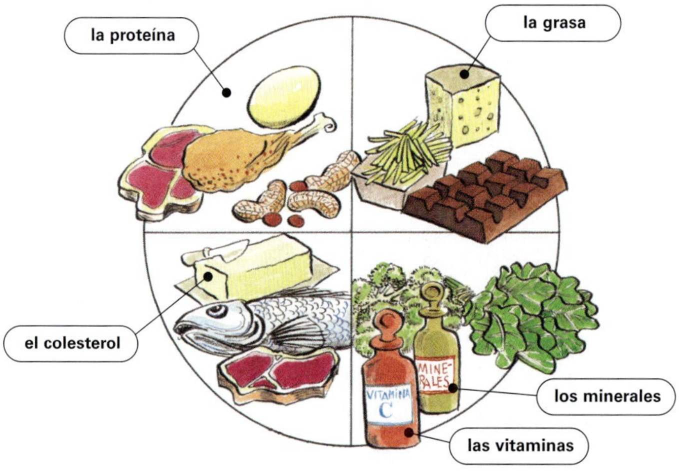

La nutrición

la bebida alcohólica	*alcoholic beverage*
la caloría	*calorie*
la merienda	*snack*
la nutrición	*nutrition*
comer una dieta equilibrada	*to eat a balanced diet*
consumir alcohol	*to consume alcohol*
merendar (e:ie)	*to have a snack in the afternoon*
descafeinado/a	*decaffeinated*

4 **Completar** Completa cada frase con la palabra adecuada.

1. Después de hacer ejercicio, como pollo o bistec porque contienen _b_.
   a. drogas b. proteínas c. grasa
2. Para _c_ es necesario consumir comidas de todos los grupos alimenticios.
   a. aliviar el estrés b. correr c. comer una dieta equilibrada
3. Claribel y Cecilia _a_ una buena comida.
   a. disfrutan de b. tratan de c. sudan
4. Juan no come chocolate ni papas fritas porque contienen _c_.
   a. dietas b. vitaminas c. mucha grasa
5. Mi padre no come mantequilla porque él necesita reducir _b_.
   a. la nutrición b. el colesterol c. el bienestar
6. Miguel cuenta _c_ porque está a dieta.
   a. las pesas b. los músculos c. las calorías

CONSÚLTALO
To review what you have learned about nutrition and food groups, see **Contextos** Lesson 8, pp. 232-235.

5 **La nutrición** En parejas, comenten los tipos de comida que comen y las consecuencias que tienen para su salud. Luego compartan la información con la clase. Answers will vary.

1. ¿Cuántas comidas con mucha grasa comes regularmente? ¿Piensas que debes comer menos comidas de este tipo? ¿Por qué?
2. ¿Compras comidas con muchos minerales y vitaminas? ¿Necesitas consumir más comidas que los contienen? ¿Por qué?
3. ¿Tiene algún miembro de tu familia problemas con el colesterol? ¿Qué haces para evitar (*avoid*) problemas con el colesterol?
4. ¿Eres vegetariano/a? ¿Conoces a alguien que sea vegetariano/a? ¿Qué piensas de la idea de no comer carne u otros productos animales? ¿Es posible comer una dieta equilibrada sin comer carne? Explica.
5. ¿Bebes cafeína en exceso? ¿Cuáles son los productos que contienen cafeína? ¿Cuáles son algunas de las ventajas (*advantages*) y problemas asociados con la cafeína?
6. ¿Crees que llevas una vida sana? ¿Y tus amigos? ¿Crees que en general los estudiantes llevan una vida sana? ¿Por qué?

AYUDA
Some useful words:
sano = saludable
en general = por lo general
estricto
normalmente
muchas veces
a veces
de vez en cuando

TEACHING OPTIONS

Extra Practice Make a series of statements about healthy and unhealthy habits. Have students call out **bueno** if the habit is healthy and **malo** if it is not. Ex: **Antes de hacer ejercicio, siempre como comidas con mucha grasa. (malo) Consumo muy poco alcohol. (bueno)**

Heritage Speakers Ask Spanish speakers to interview friends and relatives about their exercise and dietary habits. Have them also find out whether attitudes regarding diet and exercise are the same among their Spanish-speaking acquaintances as they are among their English-speaking ones. Have students report their findings to the class.

Comunicación

6 Encuesta Tu profesor(a) va a darte una hoja de actividades. Haz una encuesta en la clase para encontrar a dos personas que realicen las actividades que se mencionan en la lista. Anota sus nombres en la tabla y luego pregúntales a ellos/as por qué hacen estas cosas. Answers will vary.

Actividades	Nombre y respuesta	Nombre y respuesta
1. Entrenarse para un deporte		
2. Hacer ejercicios aeróbicos regularmente		
3. Mantenerse en forma		
4. Consumir poco alcohol		
5. No fumar		
6. Relajarse para aliviar la tensión		
7. Comer una dieta equilibrada		
8. Tomar bebidas descafeinadas		
9. Calentarse antes de hacer gimnasia		
10. Merendar frutas y verduras		

7 Un anuncio En grupos de cuatro, imaginen que son dueños/as de un gimnasio con un equipo (*equipment*) moderno, monitores cualificados y un(a) nutricionista. Preparen y presenten un anuncio para la televisión que hable del gimnasio y atraiga (*attracts*) a una gran variedad de nuevos clientes. No se olviden de presentar la siguiente información: Answers will vary.

- Las ventajas de estar en buena forma
- El equipo que tienen
- Los servicios y clases que ofrecen
- Las características únicas del gimnasio
- La dirección y el teléfono del gimnasio
- El precio para los socios (*members*) del gimnasio

8 Recomendaciones para la salud En parejas, imaginen que están preocupados con los malos hábitos de un(a) amigo/a suyo/a que no está bien últimamente (*lately*). Escriban y representen un diálogo en el cual hablan de lo que está pasando en la vida de su amigo/a y los cambios que necesita hacer para llevar una vida sana. Answers will vary.

9 El teleadicto Con un(a) compañero/a, representen los papeles (*play the roles*) de un(a) nutricionista y un(a) teleadicto/a. La persona sedentaria habla de sus malos hábitos en las comidas y de que no hace ejercicio. También dice que toma demasiado café y que siente mucho estrés. El/La nutricionista le sugiere una dieta equilibrada y una rutina para mantenerse en buena forma. El/La teleadicto/a le da las gracias por su ayuda. Answers will vary.

TEACHING OPTIONS

Pairs Have students imagine that they are personal lifestyle consultants. Have them give their partner a set of ten guidelines on how to begin a comprehensive health program. Suggestions should be made regarding diet, aerobic exercise, strength training, flexibility training, and stress management. Have students switch roles.

Extra Practice Ask students to write down five personal goals for achieving or maintaining a healthy lifestyle. Then have them write a brief paragraph explaining why they want to attain these goals and how they plan to achieve them. Call on volunteers to share their goals with the class.

6 Present Distribute **Hoja de actividades 36**. To save time, have students ask one student all of the questions before moving on to the next student.

7 Warm-up If possible, have students visit health clubs in your area to gather advertising brochures and/or fitness magazines to help them brainstorm ideas for their commercial.

7 Present Have groups write their advertisement so that each student gets to speak for an equal amount of time. Give students the option of either videotaping their ad outside of class, then showing it to their classmates, or performing it live.

8 Warm-up Suggest that students use expressions of doubt followed by the subjunctive or expressions of certainty in Activity 8. Review the verbs and expressions listed on pages 406–407 as necessary.

8 Present Have students discuss at least 5 bad habits their friend has, explain why he or she has them, and what he or she did to try to overcome them. Then, have students discuss possible ways of overcoming each habit.

9 Warm-up Review the verbs and expressions of will and influence on pages 380–381 before doing the activity.

9 Expand Have students conduct a follow-up interview which takes place one month after the initial meeting. The television addict should report on his progress. The nutritionist should applaud the addict's successes and make new suggestions for overcoming the bad habits he has not been able to change.

Section Goals

In **Fotonovela** students will:

- receive comprehensible input from free-flowing discourse
- learn functional phrases that preview lesson grammatical structures

Instructional Resources
Student Activities Manual: Video Activities 355–356
Video Program (Start: 01:22:23)

Video Synopsis Martín leads the students in some warmup stretches before the hike. During the hike, the students chat, take pictures, and admire their surroundings. Afterwards, they talk about the wonderful time they had. Don Francisco tells the group it's time to go back for dinner.

Before Presenting Fotonovela Have students read only the first statement in each numbered frame of this **Fotonovela** episode. Then have them predict the content of this **Fotonovela** episode, based only on those sentences. Write down their predictions.

Assignment Have students study **Fotonovela** and **Expresiones útiles** as homework.

Warm-up Quickly review the predictions your students made about the **Fotonovela** in the previous class. Through discussion, help the class summarize the plot.

Present Practice the pronunciation of the **Expresiones útiles** by asking for volunteers to read each expression aloud. Reinforce this active vocabulary by asking a few **¿Cómo se dice...?** questions. Ex: **¿Cómo se dice en español *It's been a pleasure?***

Continued on page 465.

¡Qué buena excursión!

NATIONAL communication cultures STANDARDS

Martín y los estudiantes van de excursión a las montañas.

PERSONAJES

MAITE

INÉS

DON FRANCISCO

ÁLEX

JAVIER

MARTÍN

1

MARTÍN Buenos días, don Francisco.

DON FRANCISCO ¡Hola, Martín!

MARTÍN Ya veo que han traído lo que necesitan. ¡Todos han venido muy bien equipados!

2

MARTÍN Muy bien. ¡Atención, chicos! Primero hagamos algunos ejercicios de estiramiento...

3

MARTÍN Es bueno que se hayan mantenido en buena forma. Entonces, jóvenes, ¿ya están listos?

JAVIER ¡Sí, listísimos! No puedo creer que finalmente haya llegado el gran día.

6

DON FRANCISCO ¡Hola! ¡Qué alegría verlos! ¿Cómo les fue en la excursión?

JAVIER Increíble, don Efe. Nunca había visto un paisaje tan espectacular. Es un lugar estupendo. Saqué mil fotos y tengo montones de escenas para dibujar.

7

MAITE Nunca había hecho una excursión. ¡Me encantó! Cuando vuelva a España, voy a tener mucho que contarle a mi familia.

8

INÉS Ha sido la mejor excursión de mi vida. Amigos, Martín, don Efe, mil gracias.

recursos

R	VIDEO Lección 15	VM pp. 355-356

TEACHING OPTIONS

Video Tips General suggestions for using video clips in the classroom can be found on page IAE-13 of the **Instructor's Annotated Edition**.

¡Qué buena excursión! To introduce the class to this video episode, play only the **Resumen** segment and have your students tell you what they saw and heard. Then play the main video episode and have your students jot down notes about the plot. Next, have the class work in small groups to compare notes and prepare summaries of the main video episode. Ask one or two groups to read their summaries to the class. Finally, discuss the plot with the entire class and correct any errors of fact or sequencing.

MARTÍN ¡Fabuloso! ¡En marcha, pues!

DON FRANCISCO ¡Adiós! ¡Cuídense!

Martín y los estudiantes pasan ocho horas caminando en las montañas. Hablan, sacan fotos y disfrutan del paisaje. Se divierten muchísimo.

ÁLEX Sí, gracias, Martín. Gracias por todo.

MARTÍN No hay de qué. Ha sido un placer.

DON FRANCISCO Chicos, pues, es hora de volver. Creo que la Sra. Vives nos ha preparado una cena muy especial.

Enfoque cultural Para estar en buena forma

Mientras a algunos hispanos les gusta ir al gimnasio para mantenerse en forma, otros prefieren practicar deportes. En Argentina, por ejemplo, se juega mucho al fútbol, en Venezuela se juega al béisbol y en Colombia y España hay muchos aficionados al ciclismo. Otro deporte conocido en el mundo hispano es el jai alai, que es un juego de pelota originario del País Vasco (España). Su nombre significa "día de fiesta" en vascuence y es un deporte que se practica también en México y en la Florida (EE.UU.).

Expresiones útiles

Getting ready to start a hike

- ▷ **Ya veo que han traído lo que necesitan.**
  I see that you have brought what you need.
- ▷ **¡Todos han venido muy bien equipados!**
  Everyone has come very well equipped!
- ▷ **Primero hagamos algunos ejercicios de estiramiento.**
  First let's do some stretching exercises.
- ▷ **No puedo creer que finalmente haya llegado el gran día.**
  I can't believe that the big day has finally arrived.
- ▶ **¿(Están) listos?**
  (Are you) ready?
- ▷ **¡En marcha, pues!**
  Let's get going, then!

Talking about an excursion

- ▶ **¿Cómo les fue en la excursión?**
  How did the hike go?
- ▷ **Nunca había visto un paisaje tan espectacular.**
  I had never seen such spectacular scenery.
- ▷ **Nunca había hecho una excursión. ¡Me encantó!**
  I had never gone on a hike before. I loved it!
- ▷ **Ha sido la mejor excursión de mi vida.**
  It's been the best hike of my life.

Courtesy expressions

- ▷ **Gracias por todo.**
  Thanks for everything.
- ▷ **Ha sido un placer.**
  It's been a pleasure.
- ▷ **¡Cuídense!**
  Take care!

To practice pronunciation, read a few lines from the **Fotonovela** aloud, having students repeat after each line. Then have the class read through the entire **Fotonovela**, with volunteers playing the various parts. See ideas for using the video in **Teaching Options**, page 464.

Comprehension Check Check comprehension of the **Fotonovela** episode by doing Activity 1, **Seleccionar**, page 466, orally with the whole class.

Suggestion Have the class look at the **Expresiones útiles**. Point out that **han traído, han venido,** and **ha sido** are examples of the present perfect, which combines a present tense form of the verb **haber** with the past participle of another verb. Explain that **había visto** and **había hecho** are examples of the past perfect, which combines an imperfect tense form of **haber** with a past participle. Finally, draw attention to the sentence **No puedo creer que finalmente haya llegado el gran día.** Tell the class that **haya llegado** is an example of the present perfect subjunctive, which combines a present subjunctive form of **haber** with a past participle. Tell your students that they will learn more about these concepts in the upcoming **Estructura** section.

Assignment Have students do Activities 2–3 in **Reacciona a la fotonovela**, page 466, as homework.

TEACHING OPTIONS

Enfoque cultural Magazines and newspapers in Spain and Latin America have picked up on the public's interest in health and often publish articles about cardiovascular fitness, maintaining a healthful diet, and avoiding stress. These topics are also frequently discussed on television and radio programs in Spain and Latin America, and on Spanish-language radio and television programs in the United States. Ask your students, especially heritage speakers, if they have read articles or tuned in to programming of this kind. Also, if you have copies of magazine or newspaper articles in Spanish about health or fitness, you may want to show them to the class.

1 Expand Have the class work in pairs or small groups to write a question that would elicit each statement.

2 Expand Give the class these additional items: **7. Bueno, chicos... hay que hacer unos ejercicios antes de empezar. (Martín) 8. ¿Qué tal les fue en la excursión? (don Francisco)**

2 Expand Have your students close their books, then give them these sentences as a dictation. Read each sentence twice slowly and then once at regular speed so that the class will have time to write. You may then want to have your students open their books and check their work.

3 Warm-up Ask your students a few questions using words from the word bank. Ex: **¿Comes mucha grasa? ¿Qué es un teleadicto? ¿Cómo te mantienes en forma? ¿Qué haces para mantenerte en forma?**

3 Expand The word **vitamina** was not used in this activity. Have your students work in pairs to write a sentence that includes this word. Ask volunteers to share their sentences with the class.

Successful Language Learning Tell your students that they will learn more efficiently if they follow good health habits, including eating well, getting enough rest, and managing their stress levels.

Reacciona a la fotonovela

1 Seleccionar Selecciona la respuesta que mejor completa cada frase.

1. Antes de salir, Martín les recomienda a los estudiantes que hagan __a__.
   a. ejercicios de estiramiento b. ejercicios aeróbicos c. gimnasia
2. Los excursionistas hablaron, __c__ en las montañas.
   a. levantaron pesas y se divirtieron b. caminaron y dibujaron
   c. sacaron fotos y disfrutaron del paisaje
3. Inés dice que ha sido la mejor excursión __c__ .
   a. del viaje b. del año c. de su vida
4. Cuando Maite vuelva a España, va a __b__.
   a. tener montones de escenas para dibujar b. tener mucho que contarle a su familia
   c. tener muchas fotos que enseñarle a su familia
5. La señora Vives les ha preparado __a__.
   a. una cena especial b. un día en las montañas muy especial
   c. una excursión espectacular

2 Identificar Identifica quién puede decir las siguientes frases.

1. Oye, muchísimas gracias por el mejor día de mi vida. ¡Fue divertidísimo! Inés
2. Parece que están todos preparados, ¿no? ¡Perfecto! Bueno, ¡vamos! Martín
3. Cuando vea a mis papás y a mis hermanos voy a tener mucho que contarles. Maite
4. Debemos volver ahora para comer. ¡Vamos a tener una cena especial! don Francisco
5. El lugar fue fenomenal, uno de los más bonitos que he visto. ¡Qué bueno que traje mi cámara! Javier
6. ¡Gracias por todo, Martín! Álex

3 Completar Selecciona algunas de las palabras que se ofrecen en la lista para completar cada frase.

grasa	aliviar el estrés	vitamina
teleadicta	un masaje	mantenerse en forma

1. A Javier le duelen los músculos después de caminar tanto. Hoy lo que necesita es __un masaje__.
2. Don Francisco a veces sufre presiones y estrés en su trabajo. Debe hacer ejercicio para __aliviar el estrés__.
3. A Inés le encanta salir con amigos o leer un buen libro. Ella nunca va a ser una __teleadicta__.
4. Álex trata de comer una dieta equilibrada. Por ejemplo, trata de llevar una dieta sin mucha __grasa__.
5. A Maite no le duelen los músculos. Cuatro veces por semana hace gimnasia para __mantenerse en forma__.

TEACHING OPTIONS

Extra Practice Ask the class a few additional questions about the **Fotonovela**. Ex: **¿Qué hicieron Martín y los chicos antes de empezar la excursión? (Hicieron unos ejercicios de estiramiento.) ¿Qué hicieron los estudiantes durante la excursión? (Caminaron, hablaron, sacaron fotos y miraron el paisaje.)**

Pairs Have your students work in pairs to prepare a television program in which a traveler is interviewed about a recent hiking trip. Give them time to prepare and rehearse; then ask for volunteers to present their programs to the class. Alternately, you may want the students to videotape their programs and play them for the class.

NATIONAL comparisons STANDARDS

Ortografía

Las letras b y v

Since there is no difference in pronunciation between the Spanish letters **b** and **v**, spelling words that contain these letters can be tricky. Here are some tips.

nombre **blusa** **absoluto** **descubrir**

The letter **b** is always used before consonants.

bonita **botella** **buscar** **bienestar**

At the beginning of words, the letter **b** is usually used when it is followed by the letter combinations **-on, -or, -ot, -u, -ur, -us, -ien,** and **-ene.**

adelgazaba **disfrutaban** **ibas** **íbamos**

The letter **b** is used in the verb endings of the imperfect tense for **–ar** verbs and **ir.**

voy **vamos** **estuvo** **tuvieron**

The letter **v** is used in the present tense forms of **ir** and in the preterite forms of **estar** and **tener.**

octavo **huevo** **activa** **grave**

The letter **v** is used in these noun and adjective endings: **-avo/a, -evo/a, -ivo/a, -ave, eve.**

Práctica Completa las palabras con las letras **b** o **v**.

1. Una _v_ez me lastimé el _b_razo cuando esta_b_a _b_uceando.
2. Manuela se ol_v_idó sus li_b_ros en el auto_b_ús.
3. Ernesto tomó el _b_orrador y se puso todo _b_lanco de tiza.
4. Para tener una _v_ida sana y saluda_b_le necesitas tomar _v_itaminas.
5. En mi pue_b_lo hay un _b_ule_v_ar que tiene muchos ár_b_oles.

El ahorcado (*Hangman*) Juega al ahorcado para adivinar las palabras.

1. n u b e s — Están en el cielo nubes
2. b u z ó n — Relacionado con el correo buzón
3. b o t e l l a — Está llena de líquido botella
4. n i e v e — Fenómeno meteorológico nieve
5. v e n t a n a s — Los "ojos" de la casa ventanas

Section Goals

In **Ortografía** students will learn about the spelling of words that contain **b** and **v**.

Present

- Ask the class if **b** or **v** is used before a consonant. Then say the words **nombre, blusa, absoluto,** and **descubrir** and have volunteers write them on the board.
- Write the words **bonita, botella, buscar,** and **bienestar** on the board. Ask the class to explain why these words are spelled with **b**.
- Ask the class if **b** or **v** is used in the endings of **–ar** verbs and the verb **ir** in the imperfect tense. Then say the words **adelgazaba, disfrutaban, ibas,** and **íbamos** and ask for volunteers to write them on the board.
- Explain that **v** is used in the present tense forms of **ir** and in the preterite forms of **estar** and **tener**. Say the words **voy, vamos, estuvo,** and **tuvieron** and ask for volunteers to write them on the board.
- Write the words **octavo, huevo, activa,** and **grave** on the board and ask the class to explain why these words are spelled with **v**.

Práctica/El ahorcado

Work through these activities with the class to practice the spelling of words that contain **b** and **v**.

TEACHING OPTIONS

Small Groups On the board, write the following sentences: **Doña __ioleta era muy acti__a y lle__aba una __ida muy sana. Siempre comía __ien y nunca toma__a __ino ni refrescos. Nunca fuma__a e i__a al gimnasio todos los días para hacer ejercicios aeró__icos.** Have your students work in groups to fill in the missing letters.

Pairs Have partners use **Vocabulario** at the back of the book to help them write five sentences that contain words with **b** and **v**. Encourage students to use as many of these words as they can. They should leave blanks in place of these letters, as in **Práctica**. Then have pairs exchange papers and complete the words.

Section Goals

In **Estructura 15.1** students will learn the use of the present perfect.

Instructional Resources
Student Activities Manual: Workbook, 175–176; Lab Manual, 307

Before Presenting Estructura 15.1 Have students turn to pages 464–465. Ask them to read the **Fotonovela** again and write down the past participles they find. Ask students if the past participles are used as adjectives or as parts of verbs. Tell students that in this lesson they will be learning to use past participles to talk about what someone has done. **Assignment** Have students study **Estructura 15.1** and do the activities on pages 469–470 as homework.

Present Go over **Ante todo** and quickly review the use and formation of the present perfect in English. Model the present perfect by making statements about what you and others in the class have done, or by asking students questions. Ex: **Yo he preparado una lección sobre el pretérito perfecto. Uds. han leído la sección de Estructura, ¿verdad? ¿Quién no la ha leído?** Explain that the present perfect is formed with the present tense of **haber** and a past participle. Model the conjugation of **haber**, having students repeat. Then, review the formation of regular past participles and quickly review the irregular past participles on page 447. Emphasize that when the past participle functions as part of a compound tense, it never changes form to agree in number and gender with an object, as it does when it acts as an adjective.

Continued on page 469.

15.1 The present perfect

NATIONAL comparisons STANDARDS

ANTE TODO In Lesson 14, you learned how to form past participles. You will now learn how to form the present perfect indicative (**el pretérito perfecto de indicativo**), a compound tense that uses the past participle. The present perfect is used to talk about what someone *has done*. In Spanish, it is formed with the present tense of the auxiliary verb **haber** and a past participle.

CONSÚLTALO

Present participles used as adjectives
To review what you have learned about participles, see Lesson 14, section 14.4, p. 447.

Ya veo que han traído todo lo que necesitan.

Present indicative of *haber*

Singular forms		Plural forms	
yo	**he**	nosotros/as	**hemos**
tú	**has**	vosotros/as	**habéis**
Ud./él/ella	**ha**	Uds./ellos/ellas	**han**

Tú no **has cerrado** la puerta.
You haven't closed the door.

¿**Ha asistido** Juan a la clase?
Has Juan attended the class?

Yo ya **he leído** esos libros.
I've already read those books.

Hemos presentado el proyecto.
We have presented the project.

▶ The past participle does not change in form when it is part of the present perfect tense. It only changes in form when it is used as an adjective.

Clara **ha abierto** la ventana.
Clara has opened the window.

Las ventanas están **abiertas.**
The windows are open.

Yo **he cerrado** la puerta.
I've closed the door.

La puerta está **cerrada.**
The door is closed.

▶ In Spanish, the present perfect indicative is generally used just as it is used in English: to talk about what someone has done or what has occurred. It usually refers to the recent past.

He trabajado cuarenta horas esta semana.
I have worked forty hours this week.

¿Cuál es el último libro que **has leído**?
What is the last book that you have read?

¡ATENCIÓN!

Remember that to say that someone has *just done something*, **acabar de** + [*infinitive*] is used, not the present perfect.

Juan acaba de llegar.
Juan has just arrived.

TEACHING OPTIONS

Extra Practice Ask students what they have done over the past week to lead a healthy lifestyle. Ask follow-up questions to elicit a variety of different conjugations of the present perfect. Ex: **¿Qué han hecho durante la semana pasada para llevar una vida sana? Y tú, ____, ¿qué has hecho? Clase, ¿qué ha hecho ____ esta semana?**

Pairs Ask students to tell their partners five things they have done in the past to stay in shape. Partners repeat back what the students have said, using the **tú** form of the present perfect. Ex: **He levantado pesas. (Muy bien. Has levantado pesas.)**

¡LENGUA VIVA!

The present perfect is being used less and less in American English. In Spanish, it continues to be used widely, especially in Spain.

▶ In English, the auxiliary verb and the past participle are often separated. In Spanish, however, these two elements—**haber** and the past participle—cannot be separated by any word.

Siempre **hemos vivido** en Bolivia. *We have always lived in Bolivia.*	Ud. nunca **ha venido** a mi oficina. *You have never come to my office.*

Creo que la Sra. Vives nos ha preparado una cena muy especial.

No hay de qué. Ha sido un placer.
Gracias, Martín.

▶ The word **no** and any object or reflexive pronouns are placed immediately before **haber.**

Yo **no he cobrado** el cheque. *I have not cashed the check.*	¿Por qué **no lo has cobrado**? *Why haven't you cashed it?*
Susana ya **lo ha hecho.** *Susana has already done it.*	Ellos **no la han arreglado.** *They haven't fixed it.*

▶ Note that *to have* can be either a main verb or an auxiliary verb in English. As a main verb, it corresponds to **tener,** while as an auxiliary, it corresponds to **haber.**

Tengo muchos amigos. *I have a lot of friends.*	**He tenido** mucho éxito. *I have had a lot of success.*

▶ To form the present perfect of **hay,** use the third person singular of haber **(ha) + habido.**

Ha habido muchos problemas con el nuevo profesor. *There have been a lot of problems with the new professor.*	**Ha habido** un accidente en la calle Central. *There has been an accident at Central Street.*

¡INTÉNTALO! Indica el pretérito perfecto de indicativo de los siguientes verbos.

1. (disfrutar, comer, vivir) yo he disfrutado, he comido, he vivido
2. (traer, adelgazar, compartir) tú has traído, has adelgazado, has compartido
3. (venir, estar, correr) Ud. ha venido, ha estado, ha corrido
4. (leer, resolver, poner) ella ha leído, ha resuelto, ha puesto
5. (decir, romper, hacer) ellos han dicho, han roto, han hecho
6. (mantenerse, dormirse) nosotros nos hemos mantenido, nos hemos dormido
7. (estar, escribir, ver) yo he estado, he escrito, he visto
8. (vivir, correr, morir) él ha vivido, ha corrido, ha muerto

Draw students' attention to **¡Atención!** Tell them that, while the present perfect is generally used in Spanish just as it is in English, the expression *to have just* done something is expressed in Spanish by **acabar de** + *infinitive.* Write the following sentences on the board and contrast them: **Acabo de venir del gimnasio.** *I have just come from the gym.* **He venido del gimnasio.** *I have come from the gym.*

Point out that, unlike in English, an adverb can never appear between **haber** and its past participle. Read the example sentences. Explain that the adverb may appear in other positions in the sentence to change emphasis. Ex: **Hemos vivido siempre en Bolivia. Hemos vivido en Bolivia siempre. Ud. no ha venido nunca a mi oficina. Ud. no ha venido a mi oficina nunca.**

Then go over the placement of *no* and direct and indirect pronouns when used with the present perfect. Point out that the placement rules are the same as the students have already learned with other verb forms. Ask students questions in the present perfect with indirect and direct objects. Ex: _____, **¿has estudiado bien la lección? (Sí, la he estudiado bien.)** _____, **¿has entendido todo lo que te he dicho? (No, no lo he entendido todo.) ¿Todos me han entregado el trabajo de hoy? (Sí, todos se lo hemos entregado a Ud.)** and so forth.

Sugerencia Check the answers to **¡Inténtalo!** just after you've reviewed present participles and how to conjugate the present perfect.

TEACHING OPTIONS

Large Groups Divide the class into three groups. Have students write down five physical activities. Then have them ask each of their group members if they have ever done those activities and record their answers. Ex: **¿Has hecho ejercicios de estiramiento alguna vez? ¿Has levantado pesas? ¿Has hecho ejercicios en un gimnasio?**

Extra Practice Draw a timeline on the board. On the far right of the line, write **el presente**. Just to the left of that point, write **el pasado muy reciente**. To the left of that, write **el pasado reciente**. Then to the far left, write **el pasado**. Make a statement using the preterite, the present perfect, or **acabar de** + *infinitive*. Have students indicate on the timeline when the action took place.

1 Present Ask volunteers to read each of the completed sentences.

1 Expand Have students write five original sentences describing their past health and that of their friends and family members.

2 Warm-up Introduce the terms in **Ayuda** using sentences that describe your and your students' lives. Ex: **He viajado a España un par de veces. Mmm... creo que he hecho tres viajes a España. ¿Quién ha viajado a España muchas veces?**

2 Present Read the **Modelo** cue and ask two volunteers to read the responses. Since answers will vary according to a student's experience, you may say each of these cues to more than one student.

2 Expand Personalize the activity by asking students questions about their responses.

2 Expand Have students work with a partner to ask each other questions about what they have done, using the activities from the exercise. Ex: **—¿Has buceado? —Sí, he buceado varias veces. ¿Y tú? —No, nunca he buceado.**

3 Warm-up Read the directions for the activity and go over the **Modelo**. Point out the information in **¡Lengua viva!** Show students how to rephrase the second part of the **Modelo**, saying *Marisela has found it, but I haven't.* **(Marisela lo ha encontrado, pero yo no.)**

3 Present Have the class as a whole read the first part of the answer, then call on a few individuals to give their version of the second part.

Práctica

1 Completar Estas oraciones describen el bienestar o los problemas de unos estudiantes. Completa las oraciones con el pretérito perfecto de indicativo de los verbos de la lista.

adelgazar	hacer	sufrir
comer	aumentar	llevar

1. Luisa ___ha sufrido___ muchas presiones este año.
2. Juan y Raúl ___han aumentado___ de peso porque no hacen ejercicio.
3. Pero María y yo ___hemos adelgazado___ porque trabajamos demasiado y nos olvidamos de comer.
4. Casi toda la vida, yo ___he llevado___ una vida muy sana.
5. Pero tú y yo no ___hemos hecho___ gimnasia este semestre.

2 ¿Qué has hecho? Indica si has hecho lo siguiente. Answers will vary.

modelo

Escalar una montaña

Sí, he escalado varias montañas./No, no he escalado nunca una montaña.

1. Jugar al baloncesto
2. Viajar a Bolivia
3. Conocer a una persona famosa
4. Levantar pesas
5. Comer un insecto
6. Ver el programa *Friends*
7. Aprender un idioma
8. Bailar salsa
9. Ver una película española
10. Escuchar música latina
11. Estar despierto 24 horas
12. Bucear

AYUDA

You may use some of these expressions in your answers:

una vez *once*
un par de veces *a couple of times*
algunas veces *a few times*
varias veces *several times*
muchas veces *many times, often*

3 La vida sana Hace poco tiempo que Marisela ha decidido cambiar su forma de vivir porque quiere llevar una vida sana. Explica lo que ha hecho según el modelo. Luego explica lo que tú has hecho al respecto (*in that regard*). Answers will vary.

modelo

Encontrar un gimnasio

Marisela ha encontrado un buen gimnasio cerca de su casa.
Yo no he encontrado un gimnasio pero sé que debo buscar uno.

1. Tratar de estar en forma
2. Estar a dieta los últimos dos meses
3. Dejar de tomar refrescos
4. Hacerse una prueba del colesterol
5. Entrenar cinco días a la semana
6. Cambiar de una vida sedentaria a una vida activa
7. Tomar vitaminas por las noches y por las mañanas
8. Hacer ejercicio para relajarse
9. Consumir mucha proteína
10. Dejar de fumar

¡LENGUA VIVA!

Spanish sentences never end with the auxiliary verb. To say *He has done it, but I haven't* you would say **Él lo ha hecho, pero yo no.**

TEACHING OPTIONS

Small Groups Divide the class into groups of four to write and perform skits in which one student plays a personal trainer, another plays a nutritionist, and the other two play clients. The personal trainer and nutritionist ask the clients whether they have or have not done the things they have recommended. The clients explain what they have done and make excuses for what they haven't done.

Pairs Have students discuss with a classmate five things they have already done today. Ex: **He estudiado la lección para esta clase. He ido al gimnasio. He hecho una clase de aeróbicos. He almorzado con unos amigos. He escrito una carta a mis abuelos. ¿Qué has hecho tú?**

Comunicación

4 **Descripción** En parejas, describan lo que ha(n) hecho y lo que no ha(n) hecho la(s) persona(s) en cada dibujo. Usen la imaginación. Answers will vary.

1. Jorge y Raúl

2. Luisa

3. Jacobo

4. Natalia y Diego

5. Ricardo

6. Carmen

5 **Describir** En parejas, identifiquen a una persona que lleva una vida muy sana. Puede ser una persona que conocen o un personaje que aparece en una película o programa de televisión. Entre los dos, escriban una descripción de lo que la persona ha hecho para llevar una vida sana. Answers will vary.

modelo

Arnold Schwarzenegger siempre ha hecho todo lo posible para mantenerse en forma. Él…

Síntesis

6 **Situación** El/La enfermero/a de la clínica de la universidad está conversando con un(a) estudiante que no se siente nada bien. El/La enfermero/a debe averiguar de dónde viene el problema e investigar los hábitos del/de la estudiante. El/La estudiante le explica lo que ha hecho en los últimos meses y cómo se ha sentido. Luego el/la enfermero/a le da recomendaciones al/a la estudiante de cómo llevar una vida más sana.
Answers will vary.

4 Warm-up Before dividing the class into pairs, have volunteers describe the people in each drawing and how they feel.

4 Present Allow pairs ten minutes to do the activity.

4 Expand Ask six volunteers to describe to the rest of the class what each of the characters in the drawings has done.

5 Present Read and expand on the **Modelo** for the whole class, then divide the class into pairs. Have them describe eight different things their chosen person has done that exemplifies a healthy lifestyle. Tell them to also include introductory and concluding statements in their descriptions.

5 Expand Have students choose someone who is the exact opposite of the healthy person they chose earlier and write a description of what that person has done that exemplifies an unhealthy lifestyle.

6 Warm-up Review the wellness (pages 298–299) and food/nutrition (pages 232–234) vocabulary with the class. Then have students work with their partners to decide what is wrong with the patient in their situation. Next, students should brainstorm a list of symptoms, activities that probably caused those symptoms, and countermeasures for each one.

6 Present Have students rehearse their situation before presenting it to the class. After presenting it once, have students switch roles.

Assignment Have students do the activities in the **Student Activities Manual: Workbook,** 175–176

TEACHING OPTIONS

Game Have students write three important things they have done over the past year on a slip of paper and put it in a box. Ex: **Este año he creado un sitio Web.** Have students draw a paper from the box, then circulate around the room, asking students if they have done the activities listed, until they find the person who wrote the slip of paper. The first person to find a match wins.

Heritage Speakers Have Spanish speakers interview someone who has immigrated from a Spanish-speaking country to the United States to find out how that person's life has changed since moving. Students should find out how the interviewee's physical activity and diet have changed. Have students present their findings in a brief written report.

Section Goals

In **Estructura 15.2** students will learn the use of the past perfect tense.

Instructional Resources *Student Activities Manual: Workbook, 177–178; Lab Manual, 308 Hoja de actividades 37*

Before Presenting Estructura 15.2 Quickly introduce the past perfect tense by making statements about the past that are true for you. Write examples of the past perfect on the board as you use them. Ex: **Esta mañana vine a la universidad montado/a en la bicicleta de mi hijo. Nunca antes había venido en bicicleta. Por lo general, vengo en carro. Muchas veces antes había caminado y también había venido en autobús cuando tenía prisa, pero nunca en bicicleta.** Tell students that they are going to learn the past perfect tense, a verb form that is similar to the present perfect. **Assignment** Have students read **Estructura 15.2** and do the exercises on pages 472–473 as homework.

Present Discuss **Ante todo** and then ask volunteers to read the captions to the video stills and point out the past perfect verb forms.

Afterward, model the pronunciation of the verbs in the chart, pointing out that **haber** is a regular **–er** verb in the imperfect.

Work through the example sentences and the discussion of **ya** and **antes de** (**¡Lengua viva!**).

Successful Language Learning Tell your students to imagine how they might use the past perfect to tell someone about their lives.

15.2 The past perfect

NATIONAL STANDARDS comparisons

ANTE TODO The past perfect indicative (**el pretérito pluscuamperfecto de indicativo**) is used to talk about what someone *had done* or what *had occurred* before another past action, event, or state. Like the present perfect, the past perfect uses a form of **haber**—in this case, the imperfect—plus the past participle.

Nunca había visto un paisaje tan espectacular.

Nunca había hecho una excursión.

Past perfect indicative

		cerrar	perder	asistir
SINGULAR FORMS	yo	**había** cerrado	**había** perdido	**había** asistido
	tú	**habías** cerrado	**habías** perdido	**habías** asistido
	Ud./él/ella	**había** cerrado	**había** perdido	**había** asistido
PLURAL FORMS	nosotros/as	**habíamos** cerrado	**habíamos** perdido	**habíamos** asistido
	vosotros/as	**habíais** cerrado	**habíais** perdido	**habíais** asistido
	Uds./ellos/ellas	**habían** cerrado	**habían** perdido	**habían** asistido

Antes de 2001, **había vivido** en California.
Before 2001, I had lived in California.

Cuando llegamos, Luis ya **había salido.**
When we arrived, Luis had already left.

▶ The past perfect is often used with the word **ya** (*already*) to indicate that an action, event, or state had already occurred before another. Remember that, unlike its English equivalent, **ya** cannot be placed between **haber** and the past participle.

Ella **ya había salido** cuando llamaron.
She had already left when they called.

Cuando llegué, Raúl **ya se había acostado.**
When I arrived, Raúl had already gone to bed.

¡LENGUA VIVA!

The past perfect is often used in conjunction with **antes de** + [*noun*] or **antes de** + [*infinitive*] to indicate that one action occurred before another.

Antes de este año, nunca había estudiado español.
Before this year, I had never studied Spanish.

Luis me había llamado antes de venir.
Luis had called me before coming.

¡INTÉNTALO! Indica el pretérito pluscuamperfecto de indicativo de cada verbo.

1. Nosotros ya <u>habíamos cenado</u> (cenar) cuando nos llamaron.
2. Antes de tomar esta clase, yo no <u>había estudiado</u> (estudiar) nunca el español.
3. Antes de ir a México, ellos nunca <u>habían ido</u> (ir) a otro país.
4. Eduardo nunca <u>se había entrenado</u> (entrenarse) antes de este año.
5. Tú siempre <u>habías llevado</u> (llevar) una vida sana antes del año pasado.
6. Antes de conocerte, yo ya te <u>había visto</u> (ver) muchas veces.

TEACHING OPTIONS

Extra Practice Have students write sentences, using the past perfect and each of following twice: **antes de** + *infinitive*, **antes de que** + *conjugated verb*, the preterite, and the imperfect. Have students peer edit their work before sharing their sentences with the class. Ex: **Nuestras bisabuelos ya habían muerto cuando éramos niños.**

TPR Make a series of statements about the past, using two different verbs. After making a statement, call out the infinitive of one of the verbs. If that action occurred before the other one, have students raise one finger. If it occurred after the other action, have them raise two fingers. Ex: **Tomás ya había bajado de la montaña cuando empezó a nevar. Empezar.** (two fingers)

Práctica

1 **Completar** Completa los minidiálogos con las formas correctas del pretérito pluscuamperfecto de indicativo.

SARA Antes de cumplir los 15 años, ¿ habías estudiado (estudiar) tú otra lengua?
JOSÉ Sí, había tomado (tomar) clases de inglés y de italiano.

DOLORES Antes de 2000, ¿ habían viajado (viajar) tú y tu familia a Europa?
TOMÁS Sí, habíamos visitado (visitar) Europa tres veces.

ANTONIO Antes de este año, ¿ había corrido (correr) Ud. en un maratón?
SRA. VERA No, nunca lo había hecho (hacer).

SOFÍA Antes de su enfermedad, ¿ había sufrido (sufrir) muchas presiones tu tío?
IRENE Sí... y mi tío nunca se había mantenido (mantenerse) en buena forma.

2 **Quehaceres** Indica lo que ya había hecho cada miembro de la familia antes de la llegada de la madre, la Sra. Ferrer. Answers will vary.

3 **Tu vida** Indica si ya habías hecho las siguientes cosas antes de cumplir los 16 años. Answers will vary.

1. Hacer un viaje en avión
2. Escalar una montaña
3. Escribir un poema
4. Leer una novela
5. Enamorarse
6. Tomar una clase de educación física
7. Montar a caballo
8. Ir de pesca
9. Manejar un carro
10. Navegar en la red

1 Present Call on pairs of volunteers to read the completed dialogues to the class.

1 Expand Have students pick one of the interchanges and expand upon it to create a dialogue with six lines.

1 Expand Have students create an original dialogue like the ones in the activity. Call on volunteers to perform their dialogues for the class.

2 Warm-up Ask questions to elicit the household activities pictured in the drawing. Ex: **¿Qué está haciendo Teresa? (Está lavando los platos.)**

2 Present Call on individuals to write their sentences on the board. Have the class suggest any corrections that are necessary and compare their own sentences with those on the board.

2 Expand Divide the class into groups of six. Have each person in a group choose the role of one of the family members. Tell students that they are cleaning the house because they want to surprise Sra. Ferrer for Mother's Day. Have students ask each other questions about what they've already done and what still needs to be done.

3 Present Ask students questions to elicit the answers for the activity. Since answers will vary, you may ask each question to more than one student. Ex: **¿Quién había hecho un viaje en avión antes de cumplir los dieciséis años?** Then, ask follow-up questions to elicit other conjugations of the past perfect. Ex: **Entonces clase, ¿quiénes habían hecho un viaje en avión antes de cumplir los dieciséis años? (Ana y Rosa habían hecho...)**

TEACHING OPTIONS

Pairs Have students imagine they have joined a gym for the first time and are telling a friend about their new experiences. Ask students to tell their partner five things they had never done before going to a gym. Ex: **Nunca había sudado tanto antes de ir al gimnasio.**

Extra Practice Ask students to write six things they had already done before the following birthdays: **los tres años, los siete años, los trece años, los dieciséis años, los dieciocho años, los veintiún años.** Ex: **Antes de los dos años ya había caminado.**

4 Present Go over the directions and ask two volunteers to read the **Modelo**. First have students work individually to complete each statement. Then divide the class into pairs and have each partner take turns making a statement and responding.

4 Expand Have pairs expand one of their exchanges into a conversation by responding to their partners' questions and elaborating on their answers.

5 Present Go over the directions and then distribute **Hoja de actividades 37**. Allow five minutes for students to write their statements. Then give them five minutes to circulate and collect reponses. After students have filled in the **Hoja de actividades**, have them tell their group members if they were right or wrong in their assumptions about what they had done.

5 Expand Call on volunteers to read their sentences to the entire class. Ask the class to react to the statements. Then, make statements about your own life and have students react to them.

6 Warm-up Have one student prepare note cards with interview questions, while the other prepares responses.

6 Present Have students rehearse their interview. Then, if possible, videotape it. Show videos to the class and have students give constructive feedback to their classmates regarding grammar usage, pronunciation, and fluency.

6 Expand Have students give a short presentation about why the audience should buy the actor's exercise video.

Assignment Have students do activities in the **Student Activities Manual: Workbook**, 177–178

Comunicación

NATIONAL communication STANDARDS

4 **Oraciones** En parejas, una persona completa las siguientes oraciones con el pretérito pluscuamperfecto de indicativo y la otra persona forma una pregunta basada en cada oración. Answers will vary.

modelo

Antes de vivir aquí, yo...
Estudiante 1: Antes de vivir aquí, yo había vivido en California.
Estudiante 2: ¿Habías vivido en otros lugares antes de vivir aquí?

1. Cuando yo llamé a mi mejor amigo/a la semana pasada, él/ella ya...
2. Antes de este año, mis amigos y yo nunca...
3. Hasta el año pasado yo siempre...
4. Antes de cumplir los veinte años, mi mejor amigo/a...
5. Antes de cumplir los treinta años, mis padres ya...
6. Hasta que cumplí los dieciocho años, yo no...
7. Antes de este semestre, el/la profesor(a) de español no...
8. Antes de tomar esta clase, yo nunca...

5 **Lo dudo** Tu profesor(a) va a darte una hoja de actividades. Escribe cinco oraciones, algunas ciertas y algunas falsas, de cosas que habías hecho antes de venir a la universidad. Luego, en grupos, túrnense para leer sus oraciones. Cada miembro del grupo debe decir "es cierto" o "lo dudo" después de cada una. Escribe la reacción de cada compañero/a en la columna apropiada. ¿Quién obtuvo más respuestas correctas? Answers will vary.

Oraciones	Miguel	Ana	Beatriz
1. Cuando tenía 10 años, ya había manejado el carro de mi papá.	Lo dudo.	Es cierto.	Lo dudo.
2.			
3.			
4.			
5.			

Síntesis

NATIONAL communication STANDARDS

6 **Entrevista** En parejas, preparen una conversación en la que un(a) reportero/a de televisión está entrevistando (*interviewing*) a un actor/una actriz famoso/a que está haciendo un video de ejercicios aeróbicos. El/La reportero/a le hace preguntas para descubrir la siguiente información: Answers will vary.

- Si siempre se había mantenido en forma antes de hacer este video
- Si había seguido una dieta especial antes de hacer este video
- Qué le recomienda a la gente que quiere mantenerse en forma
- Qué le recomienda a la gente que quiere adelgazar
- Qué va a hacer cuando termine este video

TEACHING OPTIONS

Small Groups Divide students into groups of three. Student one begins a sentence with **antes de que** + *conjugated verb*. Student two finishes the sentence with a verb in the past perfect. Student three writes the sentence down. Have students alternate their roles until they've created nine sentences. Then, have all group members check the sentences before sharing them with the class.

Large Groups Divide the class into groups of 6–8 for a game of "one-upmanship." The first student states something he had done before a certain event in his past. The second student tells what the first one had done, then counters with something even more outrageous that she had done, and so on, until everyone has participated. Ex: **Yo había... antes de (que)... _____ había..., pero yo había...**

15.3 The present perfect subjunctive

NATIONAL STANDARDS comparisons

ANTE TODO The present perfect subjunctive (**el pretérito perfecto de subjuntivo**) is equivalent to the present perfect indicative, except that it is used to talk about what *has happened* when the subjunctive tense is required in the subordinate clause. The present perfect subjunctive is formed using the present subjunctive of the auxiliary verb **haber** and a past participle.

Present perfect indicative			Present perfect subjunctive		
	PRESENT INDICATIVE OF HABER	PAST PARTICIPLE		PRESENT SUBJUNCTIVE OF HABER	PAST PARTICIPLE
yo	**he**	**hablado**	**yo**	**haya**	**hablado**

Present perfect subjunctive

		cerrar	perder	asistir
SINGULAR FORMS	yo	**haya** cerrado	**haya** perdido	**haya** asistido
	tú	**hayas** cerrado	**hayas** perdido	**hayas** asistido
	Ud./él/ella	**haya** cerrado	**haya** perdido	**haya** asistido
PLURAL FORMS	nosotros/as	**hayamos** cerrado	**hayamos** perdido	**hayamos** asistido
	vosotros/as	**hayáis** cerrado	**hayáis** perdido	**hayáis** asistido
	Uds./ellos/ellas	**hayan** cerrado	**hayan** perdido	**hayan** asistido

¡ATENCIÓN!

The perfect forms are often used with **ya** (*already*). Remember that **ya** must come either before or after **haber** and the participle, which are never separated in Spanish.

Dudo que Enrique **ya** lo **haya hecho.**

Dudo que Enrique lo **haya hecho ya.**

• • •

The present perfect subjunctive is used for a recent action even if that action would be in the past tense in English.

No creo que lo **hayas dicho** bien.
I don't think you said it right.

Espero que él **haya llegado** ayer.
I hope he arrived yesterday.

▶ The same conditions which trigger the use of the present subjunctive apply to the present perfect subjunctive.

Present subjunctive	Present perfect subjunctive
Espero que **duermas** bien. *I hope that you sleep well.*	Espero que **hayas dormido** bien. *I hope that you have slept well.*
No creo que **aumente** de peso. *I don't think he will gain weight.*	No creo que **haya aumentado** de peso. *I don't think he has gained weight.*

▶ The action expressed by the present perfect subjunctive is seen as occurring before the action expressed in the main clause.

Me alegro que Uds. **se hayan reído** tanto esta tarde.
I'm glad that you have laughed so much this afternoon.

Dudo que ella **se haya divertido** mucho con su suegra.
I doubt that she has enjoyed herself much with her mother-in-law.

¡INTÉNTALO! Indica el pretérito perfecto de subjuntivo de los verbos entre paréntesis.

1. Me gusta que Uds. hayan dicho (decir) la verdad.
2. No creo que tú hayas comido (comer) tanto.
3. Es imposible que Ud. haya podido (poder) hacer tal cosa.
4. Me alegro de que tú y yo hayamos merendado (merendar) juntas.
5. Es posible que yo haya adelgazado (adelgazar) un poco esta semana.
6. Espero que haya habido (haber) suficiente comida en la celebración.

TEACHING OPTIONS

Extra Practice Ask students to write their reactions to the following statements: **1. Ángela ha dejado de fumar. 2. Roberto ya ha estudiado ocho horas hoy. 3. Todos los teleadictos han seguido una dieta balanceada. 4. No he preparado la prueba para mañana. 5. Mi marido(a) y yo hemos estado enfermos. Ex: Martín ha perdido cinco kilos. Es bueno que Martín haya perdido cinco kilos.**

Small Groups Divide the class into groups of three. Have students take turns telling the group three wishes they hope to have fulfilled by the end of the day. Ex: **Espero que mi compañero haya limpiado el apartamento.**

Section Goals

In **Estructura 15.3** students will learn the use of the present perfect subjunctive.

Instructional Resources
Student Activities Manual: Workbook, 179–180; Lab Manual, 309

Before Presenting Estructura 15.3 Ask a volunteer to tell you something he or she has done this week. Respond with a comment using the present perfect subjunctive. Ex: **Me alegro que hayas levantado pesas. • ¡Ay, no exageres, chico/a! ¡Dudo que hayas trabajado tanto!** Write present perfect subjunctive forms on the board as you say them. Tell students that they are about to study the present perfect subjunctive. Tell them that they already know all the forms necessary for using the present perfect subjunctive. **Assignment** Have students study **Estructura 15.3** and do the exercises on pages 475–476 as homework.

Present Go over the discussion of the present perfect subjunctive point by point, reviewing as necessary the situations that trigger the subjunctive that students have learned previously. Write other examples on the board. Point out that the action expressed by the present perfect subjunctive must have occurred before the action in the main clause. Then discuss the information in **¡Atención!** Finally, as you did in **Before Presenting Estructura 15.3,** ask volunteers to tell you things they have done during the past week. Again, comment on their statements in ways that trigger the present perfect subjunctive, but this time elicit peer comments that use the present perfect subjunctive.

Close Check the answers to **¡Inténtalo!** orally with the class.

Práctica

1 Completar Laura está preocupada por su familia y sus amigos/as. Completa las oraciones con la forma correcta del pretérito perfecto de subjuntivo de los verbos entre paréntesis.

1. ¡Qué lástima que Julio ___se haya sentido___ (sentirse) tan mal! Dudo que ___se haya entrenado___ (entrenarse) lo suficiente.
2. No creo que Lourdes y su amiga ___se hayan ido___ (irse) de ese trabajo donde siempre tienen tantos problemas. Espero que Lourdes ___haya aprendido___ (aprender) a aliviar el estrés.
3. Es triste que Nuria y yo ___hayamos perdido___ (perder) el partido. Esperamos que los monitores del gimnasio nos ___hayan preparado___ (preparar) un buen programa para ponernos en forma.
4. No estoy segura de que Samuel ___haya llevado___ (llevar) una vida sana. Es bueno que él ___haya decidido___ (decidir) mejorar su dieta.
5. Me preocupa mucho que Ana y Rosa ___hayan fumado___ (fumar) tanto de jóvenes (*as young people*). Es increíble que ellas no ___se hayan enfermado___ (enfermarse).
6. Me alegro de que mi abuela ___haya disfrutado___ (disfrutar) de buena salud toda su vida. Es increíble que ella ___haya cumplido___ (cumplir) noventa años.

2 Describir Haz dos comentarios sobre la(s) persona(s) que hay en cada dibujo usando frases como **no creo que, dudo que, es probable que, me alegro de que, espero que** y **siento que.** Usa el pretérito perfecto de subjuntivo. Answers will vary.

modelo

Es probable que Javier haya levantado pesas por muchos años.
Me alegro de que Javier se haya mantenido en forma.

Javier

1. Rosa y Sandra

2. Roberto

3. Mariela

4. Lorena y su amigo

5. Sra. Matos

6. Sonia y René

CONSÚLTALO

To review verbs of will and influence, see Lesson 12, section 12.4, p. 380. To review expressions of doubt, disbelief, and denial, see Lesson 13, section 13.2, p. 406.

1 Present Call on volunteers to read each completed sentence to the class. Then call on different students to point out the verb or expression triggering the subjunctive.

1 Expand After students have read each completed item, ask them the following comprehension questions.

1. **¿Por qué crees que Julio se ha sentido mal?**
2. **¿Tiene Lourdes el mismo trabajo según la persona que habla? ¿Qué espera esa persona?**
3. **¿Por qué están tristes Nuria y su amiga? ¿Qué quieren que los monitores hagan?**
4. **¿Qué ha hecho Samuel? ¿Por qué?**
5. **¿Qué es increíble? ¿Por qué?**
6. **¿Cuántos años tiene la abuela? ¿Ha llevado una vida sana o no?**

2 Warm-up Working with the entire class, elicit descriptions of what each of the characters depicted is like and how he or she got that way.

2 Present Go over the directions, and ask two volunteers to read the **Modelo**. Have students write their comments and then exchange them with a partner for peer editing. Students should make sure their partners' sentences are logical and grammatically correct.

2 Expand For additional listening practice, call on a student to read one of her comments. Have the class indicate which person is being described.

TEACHING OPTIONS

Pairs Have students tell their partner three true things and three untrue things they have done this past year. Partners respond with an expression of doubt and the present perfect subjunctive to those things they believe are false and expression of certainty and the present perfect indicative to those they believe are true.

Video Replay the video for students. Each time they hear the present perfect indicative, have them raise their hands. Each time they hear the past perfect indicative, have them raise two hands. Each time they hear the present perfect subjunctive, have them stand.

Comunicación

3 **¿Sí o no?** En parejas, comenten estas afirmaciones (*statements*) usando frases de la lista. Answers will vary.

Es imposible que...	No creo que...	Me alegro de que (no)...
Dudo que...	Es bueno que (no)...	Espero que (no)...

modelo

Estudiante 1: Ya llegó el fin del año escolar.
Estudiante 2: Es imposible que haya llegado el fin del año escolar.

1. Recibí una A en la clase de español.
2. Tu mejor amigo aumentó de peso recientemente.
3. Madonna dio un concierto ayer con Plácido Domingo.
4. Mis padres ganaron un millón de dólares.
5. He aprendido a hablar japonés.
6. Nuestro/a profesor(a) vino aquí de Bolivia.
7. Salí anoche con...
8. El año pasado mi familia y yo fuimos de excursión a...

4 **Viaje por Bolivia** Imaginen que sus amigos, Luis y Julia, están viajando por Bolivia y que les han mandado postales a ustedes. En grupos, lean las postales y conversen de lo que les ha escrito Luis. Usen frases como **dudo que, espero que, me alegro de que, temo que, siento que** y **es posible que.** Answers will vary.

NOTA CULTURAL

Aymara is recognized as an official language of Bolivia, along with Spanish. Over half of the population speaks indigenous languages.

1° de febrero

Hola:

Estamos aprendiendo la antigua cultura aymará aquí en Tiwakanu. Julia se enfermó, quizás por algo que comió. Creo que no vamos a poder ir a la región amazónica.

Abrazos, Luis

13 de febrero

Hola:

Llegamos a Oruro justo a tiempo para el carnaval. Hemos bailado, escuchado música y disfrutado de las fiestas. ¡Todo fenomenal!

Chau, Luis

TEACHING OPTIONS

Small Groups Have students describe to groups of three or four the last time they went to the gym or engaged in an outdoor sports activity. Each group member will react appropriately using the present perfect subjunctive. Ex: **La última vez que fui al gimnasio, asistí a tres clases de aeróbicos. (No creo que hayas asistido a tres clases. Es demasiado ejercicio.)**

Pairs Have students imagine they are having a follow-up session with a nutritionist. Students should talk about five things they have done to change their diet. The nutritionist will respond appropriately using the present perfect subjunctive. Have students switch roles.

3 Warm-up Before dividing the class into pairs, go over the expressions in the word bank and ask two volunteers to read the **Modelo**. Then offer one more possible response.

3 Present Allow about ten minutes to carry out the activity. Remind students to take turns reading statements and responding to them.

3 Expand Ask pairs of students to write four additional statements about what they have done and have a second pair respond to them. Ex: **Nosotros hemos viajado a la luna. (Es imposible que ustedes hayan viajado a la luna.)**

4 Warm-up Have students read the postcards silently to themselves. Ask them to note the verbs expressing actions they might react to.

4 Present Call on volunteers to read the postcards aloud to the class. Allow pairs five minutes to write as many reactions as they can to Luis' postcards. Have students exchange their reactions with another pair for correction. After the corrected statements are returned, call on students to share some of their reactions with the class.

5 Expand Ask students to imagine they are Luis' close friends. Have them write a response to each of Luis' postcards. They should react to what Luis said in his postcards, ask questions about what Luis had done before Julia became ill or before they went to the Carnival festivities, and talk about some of the things they have done while Luis has been gone.

Assignment Have students do the activities in the **Student Activities Manual: Workbook,** 179–180

Section Goals

In **Lectura** students will:
- learn to make inferences and draw conclusions to understand a text
- read a content-rich story and practice inferential reading

Antes de leer

You may wish to introduce the terms **pista, cuento,** and **contar** before you discuss the strategy.

Introduce the strategy. Tell students that writers of fiction do not generally spell out everything for their readers. Explain that they will need to look for clues in the story to infer information that the author left unstated and draw conclusions that will help them comprehend what the author is implying.

Examinar el texto After students have scanned the text, have them work in pairs and share their lists of cognates and other clues they can use to predict about what the story is about.

¿Cierto o falso? Have volunteers tell or read aloud the clues from the story that lead them to choose **cierto** o **falso**.

Assignment Have students read **Noviembre 24, 1992** and prepare the activities in **Después de leer**, except **Preguntas**, as homework.

Lectura

NATIONAL STANDARDS communication cultures

Antes de leer

Estrategia
Making inferences

For dramatic effect and to achieve a smoother writing style, authors often do not explicitly supply the reader with all the details of a story. Clues in the text can help you infer those things the writer chooses not to state in a direct manner. You simply "read between the lines" to fill in the missing information and draw conclusions about the story. To practice making inferences, read the following statement:

A Liliana le encanta ir al gimnasio. Hace años que empezó a levantar pesas.

Based on this statement alone, what inferences can you draw about Lily?

Examinar el texto

Lee el texto brevemente y haz una lista de algunos de los cognados y de otras palabras que conoces. Según esta lista, ¿de qué trata el texto?

_______________ _______________
_______________ _______________
_______________ _______________

¿Cierto o falso?

Indica si estos comentarios sobre el texto son **ciertos** o **falsos.**

	Cierto	Falso
1. El título del cuento es una fecha.	✓	❍
2. Una narradora omnisciente narra la historia.	❍	✓
3. La narradora menciona los nombres de varias calles.	✓	❍
4. La narradora dice que va a caminar todos los días.	✓	❍

Noviembre 24, 1992

María Velázquez

María Velázquez nació en México, D.F. en 1945. Estudió antropología social en la Universidad Iberoamericana y trabajó en el Taller de Cuento de la revista Punto de Partida *de la Universidad Nacional Autónoma de México en 1978. Vivió en California, Estados Unidos, por casi diez años (1982-1991), época en la que participó en el Taller de Cuento de la Universidad de California en Irvine. El cuento que presentamos a continuación pertenece a la colección* Aun sin saber quién eres, *que se publicó en 1998.*

A los dos nos gusta mucho ir a caminar todas las mañanas, muy temprano, pues desde que ya no montas a caballo es un buen ejercicio. En cuanto mis hijos se van en el camión de la escuela, antes de las siete, me visto rápido y me pongo los tenis. Le coloco a Babar su correa, tomo las llaves y me voy volando para recogerte en la esquina de tu casa, donde me esperas. Todos los días nos vamos subiendo por Sierra Madre, felices de estar juntos y caminando a buen paso. A veces nos detenemos para ver las casas o esperamos a Babar que le ladra a cualquier ser viviente que se le acerca.

Generalmente hacemos el mismo recorrido, subimos hasta Reforma y bajamos por Prado Sur; luego subimos otra vez por Pirineos y volvemos a bajar por Sierra Madre. Muchas veces no hablamos, pero siempre me tomas la mano. Nos gusta ver las casas, fijarnos en cómo las han arreglado, recordando cómo eran antes, hace años, cuando nos cambiamos a este rumbo. Me preguntas por mis hijos y deseas saber cosas de ellos. Todos los días quieres verlos. Luego te callas y sigues caminando en silencio, siempre

TEACHING OPTIONS

Extra Practice Have students find or write healthful recipes for lowfat dishes. Encourage students to tell how the dish is made, and if possible, give a cooking demonstration. Ask students to vote on their favorite recipes. You may wish to encourage students to have an **almuerzo de baja grasa** (lowfat lunch) featuring their favorite lowfat dishes.

TPR Have students play a version of "Simón Dice" (Simon Says) in which "Simon" leads his or her classmates in pantomiming a series of warm-up exercises. For example, the leader may say: **Simón dice: —estiren los músculos del cuello. Simón dice: —flexionen los biceps. Corran 20 pasos en parada.**

a mi lado, como cuando era niña. Yo también me quedo callada, como si no hiciera falta hablar o como si ya todo estuviese dicho.

También hoy en la mañana me vestí rápido y me puse los tenis, apuré a Babar, que parecía tener flojera, y salí corriendo rumbo a tu casa. En la esquina me detuve en seco, pues sentí que me faltaba el aire. De repente, así de sopetón, me di cuenta de que hace más de dos años habías muerto y de que nunca has ido a caminar conmigo.

cuento *short story* **pertenece** *belongs* **correa** *leash*
me voy volando *I rush off* **a buen paso** *at a good clip*
que le ladra a cualquier ser viviente que se le acerca *who barks at any living being who comes near him*
hacemos el mismo recorrido *we take the same route* **fijar** *to notice*
rumbo *area* **te callas** *you fall silent* **callada** *silent*
como si no hiciera falta hablar *as if there were no need to talk*
como si ya todo estuviese dicho *as if everything had already been said*
tener flojera *to be lazy* **rumbo a** *on the way to*
me detuve en seco *I stopped suddenly* **de sopetón** *suddenly, brusquely*

Después de leer

Resumen

Lee la selección una vez más y completa este resumen con las formas correctas de las siguientes palabras. Hay dos palabras que no son necesarias.

antiguo	pasear	vivir
recorrido	morir	montar

1. En este microcuento de la mexicana María Velázquez, la narradora sale a __pasear__ todas las mañanas.
2. Ella dice que es un buen ejercicio para su compañero porque él ya no __monta__ a caballo.
3. Los protagonistas hacen generalmente el mismo __recorrido__.
4. La narradora se imagina que pasea con alguien que __murió__ hace dos años.

Inferencias

Contesta estas preguntas.

1. ¿Quién es la narradora?
2. ¿Quién es Babar?
3. ¿De quién habla la narradora? ¿Por qué lo extraña (*miss*) tanto la narradora?
4. ¿Qué siente la narradora?

Asociaciones

¿Cuáles de estos adjetivos asocias con la narradora? Explica tu respuesta.

contenta	preocupada
aburrida	nerviosa
triste	enamorada
cansada	amable
alegre	trabajadora
avergonzada	enojada

Preguntas

Contesta estas preguntas con un(a) compañero/a.

1. ¿Sales a pasear todos los días? ¿Adónde?
2. ¿Te gusta pasear con tus amigos/as o prefieres ir solo/a (*alone*)?
3. ¿Qué haces tú cuando extrañas (*you miss*) a alguien?

Después de leer

Resumen
Suggestion Ask volunteers to summarize what the story is about. Then go over Items 1–4 with the whole class.

Inferencias
Suggestion Ask the questions of the whole class. Have volunteers answer orally or write their answers on the board.

Asociaciones
Suggestion Ask volunteers to make up a sentence for each adjective they associate with the narrator.

Preguntas
Suggestion Ask pairs to work together to interview one another. Have one partner ask questions and then create a summary of his or her partner's answers. Then have them switch roles.

TEACHING OPTIONS

Variación léxica Tell students that another way to say **extrañar a alguien** (to miss someone) is **echar de menos a alguien**. For example, **La narradora echa de menos a su amigo.**

Extra Practice Ask students to read aloud the first sentence of the second paragraph. Then ask volunteers to orally describe their favorite walking, jogging, or bicycling route (**recorrido**).

Section Goals

In **Escritura** students will:
- learn to organize information logically
- integrate **Lesson 15** vocabulary and structures
- write a personal fitness plan in Spanish

Tema
Present Orally review with the whole class the suggested three categories of details to include, clarifying any unfamiliar vocabulary.

Then have volunteers make up questions or use the questions on page 480 to interview you regarding your personal fitness plan.

Estrategia
Present Have students brainstorm details of maintaining a personal fitness plan that include nutrition, exercise and stress reduction. Then have a volunteer tell about his or her plan, and guide students in organizing the information in three different ways: chronologically, sequentially, and in order of importance.

Successful Language Learning Point out to your students that this strategy will help them write better in both Spanish and English.

Assignment Have students prepare **Ideas y organización** and Primer **borrador** as homework.

Escritura

NATIONAL communication STANDARDS

Estrategia

Organizing information logically

Many times a written piece may require you to include a great deal of information. You might want to organize your information in one of three different ways:

- Chronologically (e.g., events in the history of a country)
- Sequentially (e.g., steps in a recipe)
- In order of importance

Organizing your information in this manner will make both your writing and your message clearer to your readers. If you were writing a piece on weight reduction, for example, you would need to organize your ideas about two general areas: eating right and exercise. You would need to decide which of the two is more important according to your purpose in writing the piece. If your main idea is that eating right is the key to losing weight, you might want to start your piece with a discussion of good eating habits. You might want to discuss the following aspects of eating right in order of their importance:

- Quantities of food
- Selecting appropriate foods from the food pyramid
- Healthful recipes
- Percentage of fat in each meal
- Calorie count
- Percentage of carbohydrates in each meal
- Frequency of meals

You would then complete the piece by following the same process to discuss the various aspects of the importance of getting exercise.

Tema

Escribir un plan personal de bienestar

Desarrolla un plan personal para mejorar tu bienestar, tanto físico como emocional. Tu plan debe describir:

1. Lo que has hecho para mejorar tu bienestar y llevar una vida sana
2. Lo que no has podido hacer todavía
3. Las actividades que debes hacer en los próximos meses

Considera también la siguiente lista de preguntas.

La nutrición
- ¿Comes una dieta equilibrada?
- ¿Consumes suficientes vitaminas y minerales? ¿Consumes demasiada grasa?
- ¿Quieres aumentar de peso o adelgazar?
- ¿Qué puedes hacer para mejorar tu dieta?

El ejercicio
- ¿Haces ejercicio? ¿Con qué frecuencia?
- ¿Vas al gimnasio? ¿Qué tipo de ejercicios haces allí?
- ¿Practicas algún deporte?
- ¿Qué puedes hacer para mejorar tu bienestar físico?

El estrés
- ¿Sufres muchas presiones?
- ¿Qué actividades o problemas te causan estrés?
- ¿Qué haces (o debes hacer) para aliviar el estrés y sentirte más tranquilo/a?
- ¿Qué puedes hacer para mejorar tu bienestar emocional?

TEACHING OPTIONS

Proofreading Activity Copy the following sentences containing mistakes onto the board or a transparency as a proofreading activity to do with the whole class.

1. **¿Tu padre ha tenidos problemas con el colesterol? Espero que ha dejado de comer comidas grasosas.**
2. **Ya tengo trabajado cuarenta horas esta semana y todavía no tengo terminado.**
3. **Guillermo ha un plan para aliviar el estrés. Había sufrido mucho del estrés recientemente.**
4. **Me alegro que has dejado de fumar y por fin has empezado a llevar una vida sana.**
5. **El gimnasio ya ha cerrado antes de que he llegado.**

Plan de escritura

1 Ideas y organización

Antes de escribir, piensa y anota lo que has hecho hasta ahora, lo que no has hecho, y lo que todavía tienes que hacer para conseguir tus objetivos. Organiza tus planes para el futuro según la importancia de cada actividad y/o en orden cronológico.

2 Primer borrador

Utiliza tus apuntes de **Ideas y organización** para escribir el primer borrador de tu plan personal. Haz todo lo que puedas sin la ayuda del texto o del diccionario.

3 Comentario

Intercambia tu plan personal con un(a) compañero/a y lee su borrador. Comparte tus opiniones sobre el documento, utilizando estas preguntas como guía:

a. ¿Incluye toda la información pertinente?
b. ¿Está organizada la información de una manera lógica?
c. ¿Se puede mejorar la organización de las ideas?
d. ¿Hay errores gramaticales u ortográficos?
e. ¿Qué otras sugerencias puedes darle al/a la escritor(a) para mejorar el documento?

4 Redacción

Revisa el primer borrador según las indicaciones de tu compañero/a. Antes de escribir la versión final, revisa tu trabajo según la siguiente guía:

a. Subraya cada verbo para comprobar el uso correcto de los tiempos verbales y del subjuntivo. ¡Cuidado con los verbos irregulares!
b. Revisa la concordancia entre los verbos y los sujetos.
c. Revisa la concordancia entre los sustantivos y los artículos definidos e indefinidos.
d. Revisa la concordancia entre los sustantivos y los adjetivos.
e. Revisa los pronombres para comprobar el uso correcto de cada uno.
f. Consulta tus **Anotaciones para mejorar la escritura** para evitar la repetición de errores previos.

5 Evaluación y progreso

Comparte tu descripción con tres estudiantes. Compilen las mejores ideas de cada estudiante en un nuevo plan de bienestar para presentar a la clase. Cuando recibas los comentarios y las correcciones de tu profesor(a), anota tus errores en las **Anotaciones para mejorar la escritura** en tu **Carpeta de trabajos.**

EVALUATION: Plan de negocios

Criteria	Scale
Content	1 2 3 4
Organization	1 2 3 4
Use of vocabulary	1 2 3 4
Accuracy and mechanics	1 2 3 4
Creativity	1 2 3 4

Scoring	
Excellent	18–20 points
Good	14–17 points
Satisfactory	10–13 points
Unsatisfactory	< 10 points

Comentario
Present Go over guide questions a–e with the whole class so peer readers understand their task. Then have pairs of students exchange fitness plans. **Assignment** Have students prepare **Redacción** as homework.

Evaluación y progreso
Give students five minutes to compare final drafts.

Writing Sample Here is a sample fitness plan that would constitute superior writing achievement.

Mi plan personal de bienestar
Problema: ¡He notado que es muy difícil comer cosas que no tengan azúcar! En los últimos meses he comido mucho azúcar y como resultado he aumentado de peso. Además, no siempre me siento bien. Creo que es por la cantidad de azúcar que como y la cafeína que consumo.
Solución: Voy a dejar de comer azúcar y consumir menos cafeína. Ahora tengo muchas recetas para comidas sin azúcar. Trataré de reducir la cantidad de cafeína al tomar solamente una taza de café cada día.
Hacer más ejercicio
Problema: Soy teleadicto y llevo una vida sedentaria. En el pasado, no había asistido a clases de ejercicios aeróbicos. También no caminaba más de una o dos veces por semana. Eso no es suficiente si uno quiere adelgazar.
Solución: En los próximos seis meses voy a ir al gimnasio tres o cuatro veces por semana para participar en las clases de ejercicios aeróbicos. Ahora que tengo un perro, tengo que caminar cada día. Trataré de caminar por lo menos 20 minutos dos veces al día. En adición, pienso levantar pesas y usar mi bicicleta.

¡Pronto llevaré una vida más sana!

Section Goals
In **Escuchar** students will:
- listen for the gist and for cognates
- answer questions about a radio program

Instructional Resource
Student Cassette/CD

Preparación
Warm-up Have students describe what they see.

Estrategia
Script Cuando nos casamos le prometí a Magdalena que no íbamos a residir con su familia por más de un año. Y si Dios quiere, ¡así va a ser! Magdalena y yo encontramos un condominio absolutamente perfecto. Hoy pasamos por el banco para pedir el préstamo hipotecario. ¡Espero que no haya problema con el chequeo del crédito!

Assignment Have students do **Ahora escucha** and **Comprensión** as homework.

Ahora escucha
Script Buenos días, radioyentes, y bienvenidos a *Tu bienestar*. Les habla Ofelia Cortez de Bauer. Hoy vamos a hablar de la importancia de estar en buena forma. Primero quiero que entiendan que estar en buena forma no es sólo cosa de estar delgado o ser fuerte. Para mantenerse en forma deben tener tres objetivos: condicionar el sistema cardiopulmonar, aumentar la fuerza muscular y mejorar la flexibilidad. Cada persona tiene sus propios objetivos, y también sus propias limitaciones físicas, y debe diseñar su programa con un monitor de acuerdo con éstos. Pero óiganme bien, ¡lo más importante es tener una rutina variada, con ejercicios que les gusten— porque de otro modo no lo van a hacer! Mi rutina personal es la siguiente. Dos días por semana voy a la clase de ejercicios aeróbicos, claro con un buen calentamiento al comienzo. Tres días por semana corro en el parque, o si hace mal tiempo, uso una caminadora en el gimnasio. Luego levanto pesas y termino haciendo estiramientos de los músculos. Los fines de semana me mantengo activa pero hago una variedad de cosas de acuerdo a lo que quiere hacer la familia. A veces practico la natación; otras, vamos de excursión al campo, por ejemplo. Como les había dicho la semana pasada, como unas 1.600 calorías al día, mayormente alimentos con poca grasa y sin sal. Disfruto mucho del bienestar que estos hábitos me producen.
Ahora iremos a unos anuncios de nuestros patrocinadores. Cuando regresemos, voy a contestar sus preguntas acerca del ejercicio, la dieta o el bienestar en general. El teléfono es el 43.89.76. No se vayan. Ya regresamos con mucha más información.

Escuchar

NATIONAL communication STANDARDS

Preparación

Mira la foto. ¿Qué pistas te da de lo que vas a oír?

Estrategia

Listening for the gist/ Listening for cognates

Combining these two strategies is an easy way to get a good sense of what you hear. When you listen for the gist, you get the general idea of what you're hearing, which allows you to interpret cognates and other words in a meaningful context. Similarly, the cognates give you information about the details of the story that you might not have understood when listening for the gist. To practice these strategies, you will listen to a short paragraph. Write down the gist of what you hear and jot down a few cognates. Based on the gist and the cognates, what conclusions can you draw about what you heard?

Ahora escucha

Escucha lo que dice Ofelia Cortez de Bauer. Anota algunos de los cognados que escuchas y también la idea general del discurso.

____
____
____
____

Idea general: ____________________

Ahora contesta las siguientes preguntas.

1. ¿Cuál es el género del discurso?
2. ¿Cuál es el tema?
3. ¿Cuál es el propósito?

pistas *clues* discurso *speech* género *genre* propósito *purpose* público *audience* consejos *advice* debía haber incluido *should have included*

Comprensión

¿Cierto o falso?

Indica si lo que dicen las siguentes frases es **cierto** o **falso**. Corrige las oraciones que son falsas.

	Cierto	Falso
1. La señora Bauer habla de la importancia de estar en buena forma y hace gimnasia con frecuencia.	✔	❍
2. Según ella, lo más importante es que lleves el programa sugerido por los expertos. Lo más importante es que lleves un programa variado que te guste.	❍	✔
3. La señora Bauer participa en actividades individuales y de grupo.	✔	❍
4. El único objetivo del tipo de programa que ella sugiere es adelgazar. Los objetivos de su programa son: condicionar el sistema cardiopulmonar, aumentar la fuerza muscular y mejorar la flexibilidad.	❍	✔

Preguntas Answers will vary.

1. Imagina que el programa de radio sigue. Según las pistas que ella dio, ¿qué vas a oír en la segunda parte?
2. ¿A qué tipo de público le interesa el tema del que habla la señora Bauer?
3. ¿Sigues los consejos de la señora Bauer? Explica tu respuesta.
4. ¿Qué piensas de los consejos que ella da? ¿Hay otra información que ella debía haber incluido?

communication
cultures
connections
communities

Proyecto

Promociona una excursión

Estás a cargo de promocionar una excursión por Bolivia. Este viaje no es como ningún otro porque combina ejercicio con turismo y aventura, y es sólo para personas que estén en buena forma.

1 Prepara un folleto

Crea un folleto llamativo para vender la idea de este tipo de excursión. Usa los **Recursos para la investigación** para identificar los lugares que van a visitar en Bolivia y lo que van a hacer en cada uno de esos lugares. El folleto puede incluir lo siguiente:

- Fotos y descripciones de los lugares que van a visitar
- Descripciones de las actividades que van a hacer en cada lugar, con enfoque en las actividades deportivas y de aventura
- Una explicación de las comidas y de otros aspectos de la excursión que son importantes para la salud
- Una advertencia de que las personas que participan deben estar en buena forma
- Una explicación del chequeo médico que los viajeros necesitan hacerse antes del viaje
- El costo del viaje

2 Presenta la información

Usa el folleto para crear un anuncio publicitario informativo. Explica los aspectos especiales de esta excursión, incluyendo las aventuras y las actividades deportivas que se ofrecen. Puedes presentar el anuncio informativo en vivo o filmarlo en video para después presentarlo a la clase.

En grupos pequeños, comparen las excursiones que han planeado. ¿Qué tienen en común? ¿En qué se diferencian?

Promociona *Promote* a cargo de *in charge of* folleto *brochure* llamativo *eye-catching* enfoque *focus* advertencia *warning* anuncio *commercial; announcement* en vivo *live*

recursos para la investigación

Internet Palabras clave: Bolivia, turismo, fotos, excursiones	**Comunidad** Profesores, estudiantes o personas de la comunidad que son de Bolivia o que han viajado por Bolivia
Biblioteca Guías turísticas, revistas, mapas, enciclopedias	**Otros recursos** Mapa topográfico, folletos de agencias de viajes

Section Goals

In **Proyecto** students will:
- use Spanish as they research and interact with the wider world
- write and design a brochure promoting adventure travel in Bolivia
- learn about what Bolivia has to offer the adventure traveler

Before Assigning Proyecto Students will need approximately a week to complete the project, so at the beginning of that time period, have them open their books to page 483 and glance over **Proyecto**. Explan that they are going to use their research skills to prepare a brochure for adventure travel in Bolivia. Discuss the inherent risk (**riesgo**) in adventure travel at high altitudes, and the importance of emphasizing this in the brochures.

Prepara un folleto Suggestions
- You may wish to have students include information in their brochures on vaccinations and what to do for acclimating to high altitudes. Students may find vaccination information (**información sobre vacunas**) on the Internet on the Center for Disease Control and Prevention's Website: www.cdc.gov.

Presenta la información Suggestion
- Students may want to dress the part of an adventure traveler to present their brochures. Give them time to prepare.
- You may wish to set aside sufficient class time to do a few presentations at a time until all students have had a chance to present.

The Affective Dimension Ask your students if they prefer giving their presentations live or on video, and why.

EVALUATION: Plan de negocios

Criteria	Scale
Content	1 2 3 4
Organization	1 2 3 4
Accuracy	1 2 3 4
Creativity	1 2 3 4
Oral Presentation	1 2 3 4

Scoring	
Excellent	18–20 points
Good	14–17 points
Satisfactory	10–13 points
Unsatisfactory	< 10 points

Section Goals
In **Panorama**, students will read about Bolivia.

Instructional Resources
Student Activities Manual: Workbook, 181–182
Transparency 56

Bolivia
Before Presenting Panorama Have students look at the map of Bolivia or project **Transparency 56**. Note that Bolivia is a completely land-locked country. Have students name the five countries that share its borders. Point out Bolivia's three main regions: the **Andes** region, the high plain (**altiplano**), and the Amazon basin. Ask students to read aloud the places labeled on the map, and to identify whether place names are in Spanish or in an indigenous language.

Assignment Have students read **Panorama** and write out the completed answers to the questions in **¿Qué aprendiste?** on page 485 as homework.

Present Ask volunteers to read each section of **El país en cifras**. Have volunteers create a pie chart that represents Bolivia's ethnic make-up as described in the **Población** section. As students read about the **Ciudades principales**, have them locate each city on the map. As students read about **Idiomas**, point out that **quechua** was the language of the ancient Inca empire.

Increíble pero cierto
Visitors to La Paz and other Andean cities often experience **el soroche**, or altitude sickness. Andean natives typically develop increased lung capacity and a greater capacity for diffusing oxygen to the body, helping to compensate for decreased oxygen levels at these heights.

Bolivia

El país en cifras

- **Área:** 1.098.580 km² (424.162 millas²), *equivalente al área total de Francia y España*
- **Población:** 8.705.000

Los indios quechua y aymará constituyen más de la mitad de la población de Bolivia. Estos grupos indígenas han mantenido sus culturas y lenguas tradicionales. Los mestizos, personas de descendencia indígena y europea, representan la tercera parte de la población. El 15% restante es criollo, gente de ascendencia europea nacida en América Latina. Una gran mayoría de los bolivianos, más o menos el 70%, vive en el altiplano.

- **Capital:** La Paz, sede del gobierno, capital administrativa—1.564.000; Sucre, sede del Tribunal Supremo, capital constitucional y judicial—189.000
- **Ciudades principales:** Santa Cruz de la Sierra—1.115.000, Cochabamba—794.000, Oruro—202.000, Potosí—124.000

SOURCE: Population Division, UN Secretariat

- **Moneda:** peso boliviano
- **Idiomas:** español (oficial), aymará (oficial), quechua (oficial)

Catedral de La Paz

Vista de la ciudad de Sucre

Mujer indígena con bebé

Bandera de Bolivia

Bolivianos célebres
- **Jesús Lara,** escritor (1898-1980)
- **Víctor Paz Estenssoro,** político y presidente (1907-)
- **María Luisa Pacheco,** pintora (1919-1982)
- **Matilde Casazola,** poeta (1942-)

restante *remaining* altiplano *high plateau* sede *seat* paraguas *umbrella* asciende *climbs*

recursos
R | WB pp. 181-182 | vistasonline.com

¡Increíble pero cierto!
La Paz es la capital más alta del mundo. Su aeropuerto está situado a una altitud de 3,600 m. (12,000 pies). Ah, y si viajas en carro hasta La Paz, ¡no te olvides el paraguas! En la carretera, que asciende 9.000 metros de densa selva, te encontrarás con una cascada.

TEACHING OPTIONS

Heritage Speaker Another way to become acquainted with the traditions of Bolivia's different regions is through regional dances. The **cueca collasuyo** is a traditional dance from the **altiplano** region, while the **cueca chapaca** is from the **Chaco** area. The **jiringueros del Bení** is traditionally performed by rubber tappers from the Amazon area. Invite students familiar with these traditional dances to share some of their basic steps with the class.

Worth Noting Give students the opportunity to listen to the sounds of **quechua** or **aymará**, as well as the music of the Andes, bring in recordings made by Andean musicians, such as **los Kjarkas** or **Inkuyo**. Some recordings may include lyrics in the original language and in translation.

Lugares • El Lago Titicaca

Titicaca, situado en los Andes de Bolivia y Perú, es el lago navegable más alto del mundo y está a una altitud de 3.815 metros (12.500 pies). También es el segundo lago más grande, después del Maracaibo, de América del Sur, con un área de más de 8.000 km^2 (3.000 millas^2). La mitología inca cuenta que los hijos del Dios Sol emergieron de las profundas aguas del Lago Titicaca para fundar su imperio. Los indígenas de la zona todavía hacen botes de totora a la manera antigua y los usan para navegar las claras aguas del lago.

Artes • La música andina

La música andina, compartida por Bolivia, Perú, Ecuador, Chile y Argentina, es el aspecto más conocido de su folklore. Hay muchos conjuntos profesionales que dan a conocer esta música popular de origen indígena alrededor del mundo. Uno de los grupos más importantes son los Kjarkas, que llevan más de veinticinco años actuando en los escenarios internacionales. Los instrumentos típicos que se usan son la zampoña y la quena (dos tipos de flauta), el arpa, el bombo, la guitarra y el charango, que es una pequeña guitarra andina.

Historia • Tiahuanaco

Tiahuanaco, que significa "Ciudad de los dioses", es un sitio arqueológico de ruinas preincaicas situado cerca de La Paz y el Lago Titicaca. Se piensa que los antepasados de los indígenas aymará fundaron este centro ceremonial hace unos 15.000 años. En el año 1100 la ciudad tenía más o menos 60.000 habitantes. En este sitio se pueden ver el Templo de Kalasasaya, el Monolito Ponce, el Templete Subterráneo, la Puerta del Sol y la Puerta de la Luna. La Puerta del Sol es un impresionante monumento que tiene tres metros de alto y cuatro de ancho y que pesa aproximadamente unas 10 toneladas.

¿Qué aprendiste? Responde a las preguntas con una frase completa.

1. ¿Qué idiomas se hablan en Bolivia? En Bolivia se hablan español, quechua y aymará.
2. ¿Dónde vive la mayoría de los bolivianos? La mayoría de los bolivianos vive en el altiplano.
3. ¿Cuál es la capital administrativa de Bolivia? La capital administrativa de Bolivia es La Paz.
4. ¿Cómo se llama la moneda de Bolivia? La moneda de Bolivia es el peso boliviano.
5. Según la mitología inca, ¿qué ocurrió en el lago Titicaca? Los hijos del Dios Sol emergieron del lago para fundar el imperio inca.
6. ¿Qué hacen los indios con la totora? Los indios hacen botes de totora.
7. ¿Qué es la quena? La quena es un tipo de flauta.
8. ¿Qué es el charango? El charango es una pequeña guitarra andina.
9. ¿Qué es la Puerta del Sol? La Puerta del Sol es un monumento que está en Tiahuanaco.
10. ¿Cómo se llama el sitio arqueológico situado cerca de La Paz y el Lago Titicaca? El sitio arqueológico situado cerca de La Paz y el Lago Titicaca se llama Tiahuanaco.

Conexión Internet Investiga estos temas en el sitio **www.vistasonline.com.**

1. Busca información sobre un(a) boliviano/a célebre. ¿Cuáles son algunos de los episodios más importantes de su vida? ¿Qué ha hecho esta persona? ¿Por qué es célebre?
2. Busca información sobre Tiahuanaco u otro sitio arqueológico en Bolivia. ¿Qué han descubierto los arqueólogos en ese sitio?

cuenta *tells the story* Dios *God* botes *rowboats* fundar *to found* imperio *empire* totora *reed* manera *way* conjuntos *groups* dan a conocer *make known* alrededor *around* arpa *harp* bombo *drum* antepasados *ancestors* ancho *wide* pesa *weighs*

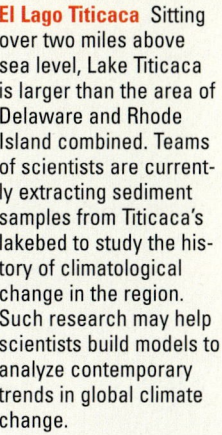

TEACHING OPTIONS

Worth Noting Ask students what they know about **Ernesto "El Che" Guevara**, the internationally reknowned revolutionary. Born and trained as a medical doctor in Argentina, Guevara gained international recognition after fighting alongside Fidel Castro in the Cuban revolution. Following his commitment to create social change and revolution worldwide, Guevara traveled to Bolivia in 1967, where he became involved with Bolivian peasants in an armed movement for social change. On October 9, 1967, Guevara was shot and killed by the Bolivian military, working with the support of the American CIA, in Villagrande, Bolivia, about 300 kilometers southeast of Santa Cruz. In October 1997, some residents of Villagrande sponsored a major international gathering to commemorate the life of Che Guevara.

El Lago Titicaca Sitting over two miles above sea level, Lake Titicaca is larger than the area of Delaware and Rhode Island combined. Teams of scientists are currently extracting sediment samples from Titicaca's lakebed to study the history of climatological change in the region. Such research may help scientists build models to analyze contemporary trends in global climate change.

La música andina Andean music is characterized by its plaintive, haunting melodies, often based in a minor or pentatonic scale. Students may like to learn this indigenous riddle about the **armadillo**, the animal whose outer shell is used to make the body of the **charango:**

Vive en el cerro, lejos del mar.
De concha el saco sin abrochar.
Cuando se muere... ¡pues a cantar!

Tiahuanaco The pre-Incan civilization that flourished at Tiahuanaco was probably a theocracy, governed by priest-kings. The primary deity was **Viracocha**, a sky and thunder god worshipped throughout much of the Andean world. The Tiahuanacan head of state was viewed as Viracocha's embodiment on earth.

¿Qué aprendiste? Go over the questions and answers with students, making sure everyone understands unfamiliar words and what the correct answers are.

Assignment Have students do activites in **Student Activities Manual: Workbook,** pages 181–182.

Conexión Internet Students will find information about Bolivia at **www.vistasonline.com,** as well as links to other sites that can help them in their research.

15 vocabulario

El bienestar

el bienestar	*well-being*
la clase de ejercicios aeróbicos	*aerobics class*
la droga	*drug*
el/la drogadicto/a	*drug addict*
el masaje	*massage*
el/la monitor(a)	*trainer*
el músculo	*muscle*
el/la teleadicto/a	*couch potato*
adelgazar	*to lose weight; to slim down*
aliviar el estrés	*to reduce stress*
aliviar la tensión	*to reduce tension*
apurarse	*to hurry; to rush*
aumentar de peso, engordar	*to gain weight*
calentarse (e:ie)	*to warm up*
disfrutar (de)	*to enjoy; to reap the benefits (of)*
entrenarse	*to practice; to train*
estar a dieta	*to be on a diet*
estar en buena forma	*to be in good shape*
(no) fumar	*(not) to smoke*
hacer ejercicio	*to exercise*
hacer ejercicios aeróbicos	*to do aerobics*
hacer ejercicios de estiramiento	*to do stretching exercises*
hacer gimnasia	*to work out*
levantar pesas	*to lift weights*
llevar una vida sana	*to lead a healthy lifestyle*
mantenerse en forma	*to stay in shape*
sudar	*to sweat*
sufrir muchas presiones	*to be under a lot of pressure*
tratar de (+ *inf.*)	*to try (to do something)*
activo/a	*active*
débil	*weak*
flexible	*flexible*
fuerte	*strong*
sedentario/a	*sedentary; related to sitting*
tranquilo/a	*calm; quiet*

La nutrición

la bebida alcohólica	*alcoholic beverage*
la caloría	*calorie*
el colesterol	*cholesterol*
la grasa	*fat*
la merienda	*afternoon snack*
el mineral	*mineral*
la nutrición	*nutrition*
la proteína	*protein*
la vitamina	*vitamin*
comer una dieta equilibrada	*to eat a balanced diet*
consumir alcohol	*to consume alcohol*
merendar (e:ie)	*to have a snack in the afternoon*
descafeinado/a	*decaffeinated*

Palabras adicionales

en exceso	*in excess; too much*
sin	*without*

Expresiones útiles	*See page 465.*

El mundo del trabajo 16

Communicative Goals

You will learn how to:

- **Talk about your future plans.**
- **Talk about and discuss work.**
- **Interview for a job.**
- **Express agreement and disagreement.**

contextos

pages 488-491

- Professions and occupations
- The work place
- Job interviews

fotonovela

pages 492-495

The students and Don Francisco talk about their plans for the future while they enjoy a delicious meal prepared by Sra. Vives. Don Francisco makes an announcement that pleases everybody.

estructura

pages 496-505

- The future tense
- The future perfect
- The past subjunctive

adelante

pages 506-511

Lectura: Read an excerpt from a novel.
Escritura: Write an essay about your plans for the future.
Escuchar: Listen to a job interview.
Proyecto: Create a plan for your professional development.

panorama

pages 512-515

Nicaragua, Dominican Republic

- Lake Nicaragua, Acahualinca
- Poet Ernesto Cardenal
- Dancing Merengue
- A passion for baseball
- Santo Domingo

Lesson Goals

In **Lesson 16** students will be introduced to the following:

- terms for professions and occupations
- work-related vocabulary
- future tense
- irregular future tense verbs
- future perfect tense
- past subjunctive tense
- recognizing similes and metaphors
- using note cards in preparation for writing
- writing a composition on personal and professional goals
- using background knowledge when listening
- listening for specific information
- developing a career plan or time line
- cultural, geographic, and historical information about Nicaragua
- cultural, geographic, and historical information about the Dominican Republic

Lesson Preview

Have students look at the photo. Ask: **¿Qué ven en la foto? ¿Qué hacen el hombre y la mujer? ¿Adónde van? ¿Tienen trabajos profesionales?**

INSTRUCTIONAL RESOURCES

Student Activities Manual: Workbook, 185–194
Student Activities Manual: Lab Manual, 311–315
Student Activities Manual: Video Activities, 357–358
Instructor's Resource Manual: Hojas de actividades, 38–39
Instructor's Resource Manual: Answer Keys
Instructor's Resource Manual: Vocabulario adicional, 58
Tapescript/Videoscript
Overhead Transparencies, 57–59

Student Cassette/CD
Lab Cassette/CD
Video Program
CD-ROM
Website: **www.vistasonline.com**
Testing Program: Prueba A, Prueba B

Section Goals

In **Contextos** students will learn and practice:
- words for professions and occupations
- labor-related terminology

Instructional Resources
Student Activities Manual: Workbook, 185–186; Lab Manual, 311
Transparency 57
Vocabulario adicional 58
Student Cassette/CD

Before Presenting Contextos Introduce active lesson vocabulary. Using pictures from your picture file, ask volunteers to identify places of business and occupations. Ex: **¿Qué tipo de negocio es? (peluquería) La persona que trabaja en una peluquería se llama peluquero/a.** and so forth. Write each job you mention on the board. Tell students they are now going to learn words associated with the world of work.

Assignment Have students study **Contextos** and prepare the activities on pages 489–490 as homework.

Note: At this point you may want to present *Más carreras y profesiones,* **Vocabulario adicional 58,** in the **Instructor's Resource Manual.**

Present Project **Transparency 57.** Ask questions that elicit the occupations. Ex: **¿Quién crea planes de edificios? (el/la arquitecto/a) Y ¿quiénes usan los planes? (los carpinteros)** and so forth. Then speak of yourself and ask students personalized questions about their career plans. Ex: **Cuando yo estudiaba, también trabajaba dos noches a la semana de cocinera en una pizzaría. • ¿Hay alguien en esta clase que estudia para arqueóloga? • ____, ¿para qué profesión estudias? • ____, ¿cuál es tu especialización?** and so forth.

16 contextos

El mundo del trabajo

Más vocabulario

el/la abogado/a	*lawyer*
el actor, la actriz	*actor*
el/la consejero/a	*counselor; advisor*
el/la contador(a)	*accountant*
el/la corredor(a) de bolsa	*stockbroker*
el/la diseñador(a)	*designer*
el/la electricista	*electrician*
el/la gerente	*manager*
el hombre/la mujer de negocios	*businessperson*
el/la jefe/a	*boss*
el/la maestro/a	*elementary school teacher*
el/la político/a	*politician*
el/la psicólogo/a	*psychologist*
el/la secretario/a	*secretary*
el/la técnico/a	*technician*
el ascenso	*promotion*
el aumento de sueldo	*raise*
la carrera	*career*
la compañía, la empresa	*company; firm*
el empleo	*job; employment*
la especialización	*field of study*
los negocios	*business; commerce*
la ocupación	*occupation*
el oficio	*trade*
la profesión	*profession*
la reunión	*meeting*
el teletrabajo	*telecommuting*
el trabajo	*job; work*
la videoconferencia	*videoconference*
dejar	*to quit; to leave behind*
despedir (e:i, i)	*to fire*
invertir (e:ie, i)	*to invest*
renunciar (a)	*to resign (from)*
tener éxito	*to be successful*
comercial	*commercial; business related*

Variación léxica

abogado/a ←→ licenciado/a (*Amér. C.*)
contador(a) ←→ contable (*Esp.*)

recursos

SCASS./CD	WB	LM	LCASS./CD
Lección 16	pp. 185-186	p. 311	Cass.8B/CD8

TEACHING OPTIONS

TPR Have students mime the work of different professionals. Write the name on a slip of paper (**actor, carpintero, arquitecto**) or whisper the name to the student. The rest of the class should guess what profession he or she is miming.

Pairs Say the Spanish term for a professional, such as **cocinero** or **bombero**. Students should write down as many words as possible that they associate with this job. Ex: **cocinero: cocina, cuchara, horno, restaurante** and so forth.

Práctica

1 **Escuchar** Escucha la descripción que hace Juan Figueres de su profesión y luego completa las frases con las palabras adecuadas.

1. Juan Figueres es un ___b___.
   a. actor b. hombre de negocios c. pintor
2. El Sr. Figueres es el ___c___ de una compañía multinacional.
   a. secretario b. técnico c. gerente
3. El Sr. Figueres quería ___a___ en la cual pudiera trabajar en otros países.
   a. una carrera b. un ascenso c. un aumento de sueldo
4. El Sr. Figueres viaja mucho porque ___a___.
   a. tiene reuniones en otros países b. prefiere el teletrabajo c. utiliza las videoconferencias

2 **Escoger** Escoge la ocupación de la lista que corresponda a cada descripción.

la arquitecta	la contadora
el corredor de bolsa	el diseñador
el bombero	la electricista
la carpintera	el maestro
el científico	la técnica

1. Desarrolla teorías de biología, química, física, etc. el científico
2. Construye (*Builds*) armarios, sillas, mesas, casas y otras cosas de madera (*wood*). la carpintera
3. Nos ayuda a iluminar nuestras casas y arregla los electrodomésticos. la electricista
4. Combate los fuegos (*fires*) que destruyen edificios. el bombero
5. Ayuda a la gente a invertir su dinero. el corredor de bolsa
6. Trabaja con números y arregla las cuentas de diferentes negocios. la contadora
7. Enseña a los niños. el maestro
8. Diseña ropa. el diseñador
9. Arregla las computadoras. la técnica
10. Diseña edificios. la arquitecta

3 **Asociaciones** ¿Qué profesiones asocias con las siguientes palabras?

modelo
emociones *psicólogo/a*

1. pinturas pintor(a)
2. consejos consejero/a
3. elecciones político/a
4. comida cocinero/a
5. leyes abogado/a
6. teatro actor/actriz
7. pirámide arqueólogo/a
8. escuela maestro/a
9. periódico reportero/a
10. pelo peluquero/a

1 Present Help students check their answers by reading the tapescript to the whole class and having volunteers give the correct choices to complete each statement.

Tapescript **Yo soy de una familia de artistas. Mi madre es diseñadora gráfica, mi padre es pintor y mi hermano es actor. Pero yo me gradué con una especialización en negocios internacionales porque quería trabajar en otros países. Ahora soy el gerente de una compañía multinacional y viajo todos los meses. Sé que a muchos hombres de negocios no les gusta viajar y prefieren utilizar el correo electrónico, el teletrabajo y la videoconferencia para hacer negocios con empresas extranjeras. Yo, sin embargo, prefiero conocer a la gente personalmente; por eso yo viajo a sus países cuando tenemos reuniones importantes.**
Student Cassette/CD

2 Present Model the activity by making a statement about a profession not listed. Ex: **Da clases en la universidad.** • **Defiende a una persona acusada de un crimen.** Have volunteers identify the occupation that corresponds to your descriptions. (**el profesor; la abogada**)

2 Expand After students finish, ask them to write job descriptions for those professions not listed in the activity. Ex: **el reportero, la cocinera, el peluquero** and so forth.

3 Present Read the **Modelo** and ask volunteers to suggest names of other associated professions. Ex: **consejero, psicólogo, artista.**

TEACHING OPTIONS

Pairs Ask students to categorize the professions according to two different paradigms. Ex: **trabajos al aire libre/trabajos en lugares cerrados; profesiones/ocupaciones; trabajos que requieren mucha fuerza/trabajos que no requieran mucha fuerza** Have each pair read their categories aloud to the class.

Game Play a modified version of Twenty Questions. Ask a volunteer to think of a profession or occupation from the vocabulary drawing or list. Other students get one chance each to ask a yes-no question until someone guesses the profession/occupation correctly. Limit attempts to 10 questions per item. Ex: **¿Es un oficio o una profesión? ¿Hay que tratarse con mucha gente?** and so forth.

Las entrevistas Introduce the vocabulary presented in **Las entrevistas** by conversing with the class about their experience with interviews. Ask: **Algunas personas se ponen muy nerviosas antes de una entrevista. ¿Eso le pasa a alguno de Uds.? ¿Cómo te preparas para una entrevista?** and so forth.

4 Suggestion If you assigned this activity as homework, go over the answers with the whole class by asking volunteers to read the completed sentences. If you did not assign it, note that it is also suitable for pairs. Each student fills in either **entrevistador** or **aspirante**. Then have them check one another's responses.

4 Expand For extra oral practice, have pairs read the completed dialogue.

5 Present Have volunteers read each completed sentence. Draw student's attention to the content of **¡Lengua viva!**

5 Expand Have pairs write logical sentences with the unused choices. Ex: **Mi hermano leyó un anuncio de trabajo en el periódico esta mañana.** Call on different pairs to read their sentences aloud.

6 Suggestion This activity may be done in pairs or in groups of three or four in round-robin fashion. Allow approximately ten minutes for completion of the activity. Afterward, call on different students to report on their group's responses.

4 Diálogo Completa la entrevista con el nuevo vocabulario que se ofrece en la lista de la derecha.

ENTREVISTADOR Recibí la _solicitud (de trabajo)_ que Ud. llenó y vi que tiene mucha experiencia.
ASPIRANTE Por eso decidí mandar una copia de mi _currículum_ cuando vi su _anuncio_ en el periódico.
ENTREVISTADOR Me alegro de que lo haya hecho. Pero dígame, ¿por qué dejó Ud. su _puesto_ anterior?
ASPIRANTE Lo dejé porque quiero un mejor _salario/sueldo_.
ENTREVISTADOR ¿Y cuánto quiere Ud. _ganar_ ?
ASPIRANTE Pues, eso depende de los _beneficios_ que me puedan ofrecer.
ENTREVISTADOR Muy bien. Pues, creo que Ud. tiene la experiencia necesaria pero tengo que _entrevistar_ a dos aspirantes más. Le vamos a llamar la semana que viene.
ASPIRANTE Hasta pronto, y gracias por la _entrevista_.

Las entrevistas

el anuncio	*advertisement*
el/la aspirante	*candidate; applicant*
los beneficios	*benefits*
el currículum	*résumé*
la entrevista	*interview*
el/la entrevistador(a)	*interviewer*
el puesto	*position; job*
el salario, el sueldo	*salary*
la solicitud (de trabajo)	*(job) application*
contratar	*to hire*
entrevistar	*to interview*
ganar	*to earn*
obtener	*to obtain; to get*
solicitar	*to apply (for a job)*

5 Completar Escoge la respuesta que completa cada frase.

1. Mi hermano dejó su _c_ porque no le gusta su jefe.
   a. anuncio b. gerente c. puesto
2. Llegué tarde a la _b_ esta mañana.
   a. profesión b. reunión c. ocupación
3. La consejera de carreras me dijo que necesito revisar mi _a_.
   a. currículum b. compañía c. aspirante
4. ¿Cuándo obtuviste _c_ más reciente?
   a. la reunión b. la videoconferencia c. el aumento de sueldo
5. Mi madre _b_ su carrera como reportera.
   a. invirtió b. tuvo éxito en c. entrevistó
6. Sara tiene la oportunidad de _a_ la empresa donde trabaja.
   a. invertir en b. entrevistar c. despedir
7. Voy a _b_ mi empleo antes de empezar mi propia empresa.
   a. tener éxito b. renunciar a c. solicitar
8. Deseo trabajar en una empresa con excelentes _a_.
   a. beneficios b. oficios c. solicitudes de trabajo

¡LENGUA VIVA!
Trabajo, **empleo**, and **puesto** all translate to *job*, but each has further meanings: **trabajo** means *work*, **empleo** means *employment*, and **puesto** means *position*.

6 Preguntas Responde a cada pregunta con una respuesta breve. Answers will vary.

1. ¿Te gusta tu especialización?
2. ¿Lees los anuncios de empleo en el periódico con regularidad?
3. ¿Piensas que una carrera que beneficia a otros es más importante que un empleo con un salario muy bueno?
4. ¿Obtienes siempre los puestos que quieres?
5. ¿Te preparas bien para las entrevistas?
6. ¿Crees que una persona debe renunciar a un puesto si no se ofrecen ascensos?
7. ¿Te gustaría más un teletrabajo o un trabajo tradicional en una oficina?
8. ¿Piensas que los jefes siempre tienen razón?
9. ¿Quieres tener tu propia empresa?
10. ¿Cuál es tu carrera ideal?

TEACHING OPTIONS

Heritage Speakers Ask Spanish speakers to describe a job that is unique to their cultural community. Ex: **gestor(a), aparejador(a), curandero/a, puestero/a.** Have them read their descriptions to the rest of the class. Write new vocabulary on the board.

Game Have students make a bingo card with the names of professions, and then ask them to exchange their boards with a classmate. Say a short description such as **Trabaja en una oficina.** If a student has a corresponding profession on his or her board, he or she makes a check mark in the corner of the box. To win, a student must have five professions in a row, read them back, and supply appropriate descriptions.

Comunicación

7 **Una entrevista** Trabaja con un(a) compañero/a para representar los papeles de un(a) aspirante a un puesto de trabajo y un(a) entrevistador(a). Answers will vary.

El/La entrevistador(a) debe describir...
- el empleo
- las responsabilidades
- el salario
- los beneficios

El/La aspirante debe...
- presentar su experiencia
- preguntar los detalles del puesto

Entonces...
- el/la entrevistador(a) debe decidir si va a contratar al/a la aspirante
- el/la aspirante debe decidir si va a aceptar el puesto

8 **Un(a) consejero/a de carreras** En parejas, representen los papeles de un(a) consejero/a de carreras y una persona que quiere saber cuál es la mejor ocupación para él/ella. El/La consejero/a debe hacerle preguntas sobre su educación, su experiencia y sus intereses y debe sugerir dos o tres profesiones posibles. Después, intercambien (*swap*) los papeles. Answers will vary.

9 **Una feria de trabajo** La clase va a celebrar una feria (*fair*) de trabajo. Unos estudiantes serán representantes de compañías que buscan empleados y otros deben ser hombres y mujeres de negocios que están buscando nuevos puestos de trabajo. Los representantes de las empresas deben preparar carteles que indiquen el nombre de su compañía y los puestos de trabajo que ofrecen. Los que buscan empleo deben circular por la clase y hablar con tres representantes. Los entrevistadores deben describir los puestos disponibles (*available*) y conseguir los nombres y las referencias de los solicitantes. Answers will vary.

7 Warm-up Give students two minutes to look at the photo and brainstorm the situation pictured. Then, ask volunteers to answer questions about the interviewing process. Ex: **En una entrevista, ¿quién explica las reponsabilidades del trabajo? ¿Quién pregunta sobre la experiencia de la otra persona?** and so forth.

7 Present Allow about ten minutes for pairs to plan and carry out the activity.

7 Expand Ask volunteers to perform their **entrevista** for the class.

8 Warm-up Have the class brainstorm questions an employment counselor might ask. Write the questions on the board.

8 Present Model the activity by providing information for an imaginary client. Ex: **Una joven busca trabajo. Le gustan mucho los niños, pero no tiene carrera universitaria. Tiene muchos hermanos y gana dinero cuidando a los niños de sus vecinos. ¿Qué trabajo le recomienda la consejera? (Ayudante de maestra; trabajadora de guardería)**

9 Present Go over the directions a second time once you have divided the class into **representantes de compañías** and **hombres/mujeres de negocios** to make sure every student understands the assignment.

9 Suggestion Videotape the **feria de trabajo** and show it during the next class, or check the tape out to students for private viewing.

TEACHING OPTIONS

Small Groups Have groups of three write a résumé for a famous person. Write a suggested format on the board for the class. Ex: **Objetivos profesionales; Formación académica; Experiencia laboral** and so forth. Circulate the résumés from group to group after they have been completed.

Game Divide the class into teams of four. Give groups five minutes to write a job announcement. Then have them take turns reading their announcements. The other teams must guess what job is being announced. Award one point for every correct guess and two points to the team who is able to stump the rest of the class.

Section goals

In **Fotonovela** students will:

- receive comprehensible input from free-flowing discourse
- learn functional phrases that preview lesson grammatical structures

Instructional Resources
Student Activities Manual: Video Activities 357–358
Video Program (Start: 01:29:11)

Video Synopsis Over dinner, don Francisco and the students discuss their career plans. Don Francisco is going to start a tourism company. Álex will start an Internet company. Maite is going to have her own interview show on TV. Javier will be a famous artist, and Inés will be an archaeologist. The group drinks to the future.

Before Presenting Fotonovela Have your class glance at the video stills and scan the **Fotonovela** for words related to career plans. Then have the class predict the content of this **Fotonovela** episode. Write down their predictions.

Assignment Have students study **Fotonovela** and **Expresiones útiles** as homework.

Warm-up Quickly review the predictions your students made about the **Fotonovela** in the previous class. Ask a few questions to help your students summarize the plot.

Present Practice the pronunciation of the **Expresiones útiles** by reading each expression and having the class repeat it. Then practice this active vocabulary by asking your students a few questions about their career plans. Ex: **¿Cuáles son tus planes para el futuro? ¿Dónde trabajarás?**

Continued on page 493.

¡Es un plan sensacional!

NATIONAL STANDARDS communication cultures

Don Francisco y los estudiantes hablan de sus ocupaciones futuras.

PERSONAJES

MAITE

INÉS

DON FRANCISCO

ÁLEX

JAVIER

1

MAITE La Sra. Vives es una cocinera magnífica.

DON FRANCISCO Me alegro de que les guste.

2

DON FRANCISCO Oigan, ¿qué me dicen del lugar donde fueron de excursión? ¿Qué les pareció?

MAITE ¡El paisaje es bellísimo!

INÉS Martín fue un guía excelente. Mostró mucho interés en que aprendiéramos sobre el medio ambiente.

3

DON FRANCISCO Sí, Martín es el mejor guía que conozco. Pero hablando de profesiones, ¿quieren saber cuáles son mis planes para el futuro?

MAITE ¡Me muero por saberlo!

DON FRANCISCO He decidido que el próximo verano voy a establecer mi propia compañía de turismo.

6

MAITE ¡Es un plan sensacional! Pero ahora escuchen el mío. Yo voy a ser periodista y tendré mi propio programa de entrevistas. Me verán en la tele entrevistando a políticos, científicos, hombres y mujeres de negocios y actores y actrices.

7

JAVIER No me cabe duda de que seré un pintor famoso. Todo el mundo querrá comprar mis cuadros y llegaré a ser más famoso que Picasso, que Dalí, que Velázquez...

8

INÉS Seré arqueóloga. Investigaré sitios arqueológicos en el Ecuador y en otros países. Escribiré libros sobre mis descubrimientos.

recursos

R	VIDEO Lección 16	VM pp. 357-358

TEACHING OPTIONS

Video Tips General suggestions for using video clips in the classroom can be found on page IAE-13 of the **Instructor's Annotated Edition**.

¡Es un plan sensacional! Play the main video episode (but not including the **Resumen** segment) and have your students jot down key words. Then have them work in groups to prepare a brief plot summary using their lists of key words. Play the main video episode again, including the **Resumen** segment, and have students return to their groups to refine their summaries. Finally, discuss the plot with the entire class and correct any errors of fact or sequencing.

JAVIER ¡Buena idea, don Efe! Con su experiencia y talento, será un gran éxito.

ÁLEX Sí, estoy completamente de acuerdo.

DON FRANCISCO ¡Qué amables son! Pero, díganme, ¿cuáles son sus planes? Supongo que también Uds. han pensado en el futuro.

ÁLEX Pues claro, don Francisco. En cinco años habré establecido una compañía especializada en el Internet.

INÉS Serás millonario, ¿eh?

ÁLEX Exactamente, porque muchísima gente habrá invertido montones de dinero en mi empresa.

MAITE ¡Fenomenal! Cuando sean famosos yo los invitaré a todos a mi programa. Y usted también vendrá, don Efe.

DON FRANCISCO ¡Enseguida! ¡Vendré conduciendo un autobús!

DON FRANCISCO ¡Por el porvenir!

ESTUDIANTES ¡Por el porvenir!

Expresiones útiles

Talking about future plans

- **¿Quieren saber cuáles son mis planes para el futuro?**
  Do you want to know what my plans for the future are?
- **Me muero por saberlo.**
  I'm dying to know.
- **¿Cuáles son tus/sus planes?**
  What are your plans?
- **Seré un(a) pintor(a) famoso/a.**
  I will be a famous painter.
- **Tendré mi propio programa.**
  I will have my own program.
- **¿Dónde trabajarás?**
  Where will you work?
- **Trabajaré en México.**
  I will work in Mexico.
- **¿Qué piensas hacer después de graduarte?**
  What do you intend to do after graduating?
- **Pienso establecer mi propia compañía.**
  I intend to start my own company.

Agreement and disagreement

- **Estoy (completamente) de acuerdo.**
  I agree (completely).
- **Claro (que sí).**
  Of course.
- **Por supuesto.**
  Of course.
- **No estoy de acuerdo.**
  I don't agree.
- **No es así.**
  That's not the way it is.
- **De ninguna manera.**
  No way.

Giving a toast

- **¡Por el porvenir!**
  Here's to the future!

Enfoque cultural Las mujeres en el mundo del trabajo

Las mujeres en los países de habla hispana están trabajando en todas las ocupaciones posibles. Aunque todavía existe en muchas ocasiones una diferencia de sueldo entre hombres y mujeres, como ocurre prácticamente en todos los países del mundo, este problema va siendo cada vez más pequeño. En Hispanoamérica muchas mujeres han ocupado altos puestos en la política, como Violeta Chamorro (Nicaragua) y Mireya Moscoso (Panamá), ambas presidentas de sus respectivos países.

To practice pronunciation, go through the **Fotonovela**, asking for volunteers to read the various parts. You may want to repeat this process with new volunteers so that more students will be able to participate. Correct any errors in pronunciation that interfere with comprehension. See ideas for using the video in **Teaching Options**, page 492.

Comprehension Check Check comprehension of the **Fotonovela** episode by doing Activity 1, **¿Cierto o falso?**, page 494, orally with the whole class.

Suggestion Have the class look at the **Expresiones útiles**. Explain that **trabajaré, trabajarás, seré,** and **tendré** are future-tense forms. Have the class scan the **Fotonovela** for more examples of the future tense (**será, serás, tendré, verán, querrá, llegaré, investigaré, escribiré, invitaré, vendrá, vendré**). Then have your students look at frame 2 of the **Fotonovela**. Tell them that **aprendiéramos** is an example of the past subjunctive. Now draw the attention of the class to frame 5. Explain that **habré establecido** and **habrá invertido** are examples of the future perfect, which is formed with a future-tense form of **haber** and a past participle. Tell your students that they will learn more about these concepts in the upcoming **Estructura** section.

Assignment Have students do activities 2–4 in **Reacciona a la fotonovela**, page 494, as homework.

TEACHING OPTIONS

Enfoque cultural Have your students work in groups to brainstorm lists of Hispanic women throughout the world who have made notable contributions in their professions. A few examples include Conchita Martínez (Spain, 1994 Wimbledon winner), Antonia Novello (former Surgeon General of the United States), Ellen Ochoa (first Hispanic female astronaut), and Rigoberta Menchú (Guatemala, winner of the Nobel Peace Prize). Have each group share its list with the class, explaining the accomplishments of each person. You may want to have your students create posters or give presentations about the some of the women on their lists.

Reacciona a la fotonovela

1 **¿Cierto o falso?** Indica si lo que dicen las siguientes frases es **cierto** o **falso**. Corrige las frases falsas.

	Cierto	Falso
1. Álex será millonario porque mucha gente invertirá en su compañía.	✓	○
2. Don Francisco preparó una comida deliciosa. La señora Vives preparó la comida.	○	✓
3. Martín insistió en que los estudiantes aprendieran sobre la historia del Ecuador. Martín insistió en que aprendieran sobre el medio ambiente.	○	✓
4. Inés será arqueóloga.	✓	○

2 **Identificar** Identifica quién puede decir las siguientes frases.

1. Con mi talento y experiencia en turismo, creo que mi compañía tendrá mucho éxito. don Francisco
2. Siempre me ha interesado mucho la historia de mi país. Inés
3. La comunicación y la tecnología me han gustado por mucho tiempo. Estableceré una empresa que se especialice en esas cosas. Álex
4. Voy a ser más famoso que Velázquez. Javier
5. ¿Mi plan para el futuro? Trabajar en televisión y hablar con gente interesante. Maite

3 **Completar** Completa las siguientes frases con la profesión correcta.

actor	científica	arquitecto
cocinera	reportera	arqueólogo

1. Maite va a entrevistar a un señor famoso que diseña casas muy bonitas de estilo mediterráneo. Él es ___arquitecto___.
2. Tendrá una entrevista con una señora que prepara platos exquisitos para el restaurante más famoso de Madrid. Ella es ___cocinera___.
3. Le gustaría tener en su programa a un hombre que trabajó en una película española buenísima. Él es ___actor___.
4. Va a hablar con una mujer que es experta en astronomía. Ella es ___científica___.

4 **Mis planes** En grupos, hablen de sus planes para el futuro. Utilicen estas frases:
Answers will vary.

- ¿Qué piensas hacer después de graduarte?
- ¿Quieres saber cuáles son mis planes para el futuro?
- ¿Cuáles son tus planes?
- ¿Dónde trabajarás?
- El próximo año/verano, voy a...
- Seré un(a)...
- Trabajaré en...

CONSÚLTALO

To see *Las Meninas* by Velázquez, one of Spain's most celebrated painters, see **Panorama** Lesson 2, p. 67.

AYUDA

Remember that the indefinite article is not used with professions unless they are modified by an adjective or other descriptor.

José es **pintor**.

José es **un buen pintor**.

NATIONAL communication STANDARDS

Reacciona a la fotonovela

1 Expand Give the class these additional items: **5. Maite dice que quiere ser actriz. (Falso. Maite quiere ser periodista.) 6. Javier dice que será un artista muy famoso. (Cierto.) 7. Inés dice que va a escribir sobre sus descubrimientos. (Cierto.) 8. Álex dice que va a establecer su propia compañía de turismo. (Falso. Don Francisco dice que va a establecer su propia compañía de turismo.)**

2 Expand Give the class these additional items: **6. Tendré mis propios autobuses. (Don Francisco) 7. Voy a hablar con todos ustedes en mi programa de entrevistas. (Maite)**

3 Expand The words **reportera** and **arqueólogo** weren't used in this activity. You may want to have your students define each of these words in Spanish and then write a sentence that uses each word.

4 Possible Response

S1: ¿Qué piensas hacer después de graduarte?

S2: Bueno, trabajaré en un colegio porque seré maestro. Voy a dar clases de inglés. Trabajaré en un colegio en el Ecuador.

S1: ¡Qué bien! ¿Quieres saber cuáles son mis planes para el futuro?

S2: Claro que sí. ¿Cuáles son tus planes?

S1: Pues, voy a ser una mujer de negocios. El próximo verano voy a trabajar en la oficina de mi tío pero pienso establecer mi propia compañía en cinco años.

TEACHING OPTIONS

Extra Practice Ask your students a few questions about the **Fotonovela**. Ex: **¿Quién es el mejor guía que conoce don Francisco? (Martín) ¿Quién quiere ser más famoso que Picasso? (Javier) ¿Quién quiere hacer investigaciones arqueológicas en Ecuador y en otros países? (Inés)**

Pairs Have your students interview each other in pairs about where they want to be and what they want to be doing in five years, in ten years, in thirty years, and so forth. Have each student take notes on his or her partner's plans. Then ask for a few volunteers to report on their partners' plans for the future.

Ortografía

Las letras y, ll y h

The letters **ll** and **y** were not pronounced alike in Old Spanish. Nowadays, however, **ll** and **y** have the same or similar pronunciations in many parts of the Spanish-speaking world. This results in frequent misspellings. The letter **h**, as you already know, is silent in Spanish, and it is often difficult to know whether words should be written with or without it. Here are some of the word groups that are spelled with each letter.

talla **sello** **botella** **amarillo**

The letter **ll** is used in these endings: **–allo/a, –ello/a, –illo/a**.

llave **llega** **llorar** **lluvia**

The letter **ll** is used at the beginning of words in these combinations: **lla-, lle-, llo-, llu-**.

cayendo **leyeron** **oye** **incluye**

The letter **y** is used in some forms of the verbs **caer**, **leer**, and **oír** and of verbs ending in **–uir**.

hiperactivo **hospital** **hipopótamo** **humor**

The letter **h** is used at the beginning of words in these combinations: **hiper-**, **hosp-**, **hidr-**, **hipo-**, **hum-**,

hiato **hierba** **hueso** **huir**

The letter **h** is also used in words that begin with these combinations: **hia-**, **hie-**, **hue-**, **hui-**.

Práctica Llena los espacios con **h, ll** o **y**. Después escribe una frase con cada una de las palabras.

1. cuchi_ll_o
2. _h_ielo
3. cue_ll_o
4. estampi_ll_a
5. estre_ll_a
6. _h_uésped
7. destru_y_ó
8. pla_y_a

Adivinanza Aquí tienes una adivinanza (*riddle*). Intenta descubrir de qué se trata.

Una cajita chiquita, blanca como la nieve: todos la saben abrir, nadie la sabe cerrar.¹
Pista: Es una comida.

1. El huevo

Section Goals

In **Ortografía** students will learn about the spelling of words that contain **y, ll,** and **h**

Present

- Write the words **talla, sello, botella,** and **amarillo** on the board. Ask the class why these words are spelled with **ll.**
- Explain that **ll** is used at the beginning of words in the combinations **lla-, lle-, llo-,** and **llu-**. Say the words **llave, llega, llorar,** and **lluvia** and ask for volunteers to spell them aloud in Spanish.
- Explain that **y** is used in some forms of the verbs **caer, leer,** and **oír,** and of verbs ending in **–uir**. Say the words **cayendo, leyeron, oye,** and **incluye** and ask for volunteers to write them on the board.
- Write the words **hiperactivo, hospital, hipopótamo,** and **humor** on the board and ask the class why these words are spelled with **h.**
- Point out that **h** is used at the beginning of words in the combinations **hia-, hie-, hue-,** and **hui-**. Say the words **hiato, hierba, hueso,** and **huir** and ask for volunteers to spell them aloud.

Práctica/Adivinanza
Work through these activities with the class to practice the spelling of words that contain **y, ll,** and **h.**

TEACHING OPTIONS

Group Work Have the class work in groups to make a list of six words that are spelled with **y, ll,** or **h** (two words for each letter). They shouldn't use the words that appear on this page. Then have them write a creative, humorous sentence that includes all six of these words. Then have a few groups share their sentences with the class.

Extra Practice Read aloud to your students a list of words that contain **y, ll,** or **h.** Each you read each word, the class will say **i griega, elle,** or **hache** to indicate which letter is used in that word. Sample words: **ayer, llegaban, oyó, llamamos, humano, huésped, millonario, cayeron, leyó.**

Section Goals

In **Estructura 16.1** students will learn:
- the future tense
- irregular verbs in the future tense
- the future tense as means of expressing conjecture or probability

Instructional Resources *Student Activities Manual: Workbook, 187–188; Lab Manual, 313 Hoja de actividades 38.*

Before Presenting Estructura 16.1 Ask students about their future activities using **ir** + **a** + *infinitive*. After they answer, repeat the information using the future tense. Ex: **¿Qué vas a hacer este fin de semana? (Ah, verás la nueva película de Brad Pitt.)** As you use a future form, write it on the board. Use examples with each form of the paradigm, ending with the **nosotros** form to talk about your own activities with family or friends. Ex: **Mis amigos y yo almorzaremos en la playa.** Tell students they are now going to learn how to form the future tense. **Assignment** Have students study **Estructura 16.1** and prepare the activities on pages 497–498 except Activity 3 as homework.

Present Review the **ir/ir** + **a** + *infinitive* constructions to express the future in Spanish using the information contained in **Ante todo**. Then work through the paradigm for the formation of the future tense. Go over regular and irregular verbs in the future point by point, calling students' attention to the information contained in **¡Atención!**Point out that there is only one set of endings for all conjugations in the future tense. Check for understanding by asking volunteers to give different forms of verbs not listed such as **renunciar, ofrecer, invertir,** and so forth.

Continued on page 497.

16.1 The future tense

NATIONAL communication STANDARDS

ANTE TODO You have already learned ways of expressing the near future in Spanish. You will now learn how to form and use the future tense. Compare the different ways of expressing the future in Spanish and English.

Present indicative

Voy al cine mañana.
I'm going to the movies tomorrow.

Present subjunctive

Ojalá **vaya al cine** mañana.
I hope I will go to the movies tomorrow.

***ir a* + infinitive**

Voy a ir al cine.
I'm going to go to the movies.

Future

Iré al cine.
I will go to the movies.

CONSÚLTALO

The present tense of ir To review **ir a** + [*infinitive*], see Lesson 4, section 4.1, p.112.

Future tense

		estudiar	aprender	recibir
SINGULAR FORMS	yo	estudiar**é**	aprender**é**	recibir**é**
	tú	estudiar**ás**	aprender**ás**	recibir**ás**
	Ud./él/ella	estudiar**á**	aprender**á**	recibir**á**
PLURAL FORMS	nosotros/as	estudiar**emos**	aprender**emos**	recibir**emos**
	vosotros/as	estudiar**éis**	aprender**éis**	recibir**éis**
	Uds./ellos/ellas	estudiar**án**	aprender**án**	recibir**án**

¡ATENCIÓN!

Note that all of the future endings have a written accent except the **nosotros/as** form.

▶ In Spanish, the future is a simple tense that consists of one word, whereas in English it is made up of the auxiliary verb *will* or *shall* and a main verb.

¿Cuándo **recibirás** el ascenso?
When will you receive the promotion?

Mañana **aprenderemos** más.
Tomorrow we will learn more.

▶ The future endings are the same for regular and irregular verbs. For regular verbs, simply add the endings to the infinitive. For irregular verbs, add the endings to the irregular stem.

Irregular verbs in the future

INFINITIVE	STEM	FUTURE FORMS
decir	dir-	diré
hacer	har-	haré
poder	podr-	podré
poner	pondr-	pondré
querer	querr-	querré
saber	sabr-	sabré
salir	saldr-	saldré
tener	tendr-	tendré
venir	vendr-	vendré

TEACHING OPTIONS

Extra Practice To provide oral practice with the future tense, create sentences that follow the pattern of the sentences in the examples. Say the sentence, have students repeat it, then change the subject. Have students then say the sentence with the new subject, changing the verb as necessary.

Game Divide the class into groups of six. Each group should have a piece of paper. When you give an infinitive in Spanish, the first group member will write the **yo** form of the verb and pass the paper to the second member, who will write the **tú** form, and so forth. The first group to finish the entire paradigm correctly wins a point.

▶ The future of **hay** (*inf.* **haber**) is **habrá** (*there will be*).

La próxima semana **habrá** dos reuniones. *Next week there will be two meetings.*	**Habrá** muchos gerentes en la videoconferencia. *There will be many managers at the videoconference.*

▶ Although the English word *will* can refer to future time, it also refers to someone's willingness to do something. In this case, Spanish uses **querer** + [*infinitive*], not the future tense.

¿Quieres llamarme, por favor? *Will you please call me?*	**¿Quieren Uds. escucharnos**, por favor? *Will you please listen to us?*

COMPARE & CONTRAST

In Spanish, the future tense has an additional use: expressing conjecture or probability. English sentences involving expressions such as *I wonder, I bet, must be, may, might,* and *probably* are often translated into Spanish using the *future of probability*.

—¿Dónde **estarán** mis llaves? *I wonder where my keys are?*	—¿Qué hora **será**? *What time can it be? (I wonder what time it is.)*
—**Estarán** en la cocina. *They're probably in the kitchen.*	—**Serán** las once o las doce. *It must be (It's probably) eleven or twelve.*

Note that although the future tense is used, these verbs express conjecture about *present* conditions, events, or actions.

CONSÚLTALO

Conjunctions followed by the subjunctive or the indicative
To review these conjunctions of time, see Lesson 14, section 14.2, p. 440.

▶ The future may also be used in the main clause of sentences in which the present subjunctive follows a conjunction of time such as **cuando, después (de) que, en cuanto, hasta que,** and **tan pronto como.**

Cuando llegues a la oficina, **hablaremos**. *When you arrive at the office, we will talk.*	**Saldremos tan pronto como termine** su trabajo. *We will leave as soon as you finish your work.*

¡INTÉNTALO! Conjuga los verbos entre paréntesis en futuro.

1. (dejar, correr, invertir) yo ___dejaré, correré, invertiré___
2. (renunciar, beber, vivir) tú ___renunciarás, beberás, vivirás___
3. (hacer, poner, venir) Lola ___hará, pondrá, vendrá___
4. (tener, decir, querer) nosotros ___tendremos, diremos, querremos___
5. (ir, ser, estar) Uds. ___irán, serán, estarán___
6. (solicitar, comer, repetir) Ud. ___solicitará, comerá, repetirá___
7. (saber, salir, poder) yo ___sabré, saldré, podré___
8. (encontrar, jugar, servir) tú ___encontrarás, jugarás, servirás___

TEACHING OPTIONS

Pairs Ask pairs to write ten academic resolutions for the upcoming semester using the future tense. Ex: **Haré dos o tres borradores de cada escritura. Practicaremos el español con los estudiantes hispanos.**

Extra Practice Ask students to finish the following sentences logically: **1. En cuanto encuentre trabajo,... 2. Tan pronto como termine mis estudios,... 3. El día que me toque ganar la lotería,... 4. Cuando lleguen las vacaciones,... 5. Hasta que tenga un puesto profesional,...**

Go over the future tense of the impersonal verb **haber**. Remind students that **hay/habrá** has only one form and does not agree with any other element in a sentence.

Then work through the explanation of **querer** + *infinitive*. Tell students that this structure functions as a softened form of a command. **¿Quieres llamarme?**, therefore, approximates the force of English *You'll call me, won't you?*

Explain to students the use of the future tense for expressing conjecture which English generally expresses with the present tense. Use images from your picture file to get students to express speculation about what characters are thinking or going to do. Ex: **¿Qué estará pensando la mujer sentada sola al bar fumando? (Estará pensando ¡ojalá pudiera dejar de fumar!) ¿Quién serán esos chicos que corren por la calle? (Estarán estudiantes que salen de la escuela.)** and so forth.

Finally, go over the use of the future in the main clause of sentences in which the present subjunctive follows a conjunction of time. Check for understanding by asking individuals to supply the main clause to prompts of present subjunctive clauses. Ex: **En cuanto pueda... ; Tan pronto como me lo digas...**

Close Have students open to **Fotonovela**, pages 492–493. Ask students to identify examples of:

- the use of the future to express upcoming actions
- the use of the future as a means of expressing conjecture or possibility

Close Do **¡Inténtalo!** on page 497 orally as a class.

Práctica

1 Planes Celia está hablando de sus planes. Repite lo que dice usando el tiempo futuro.

modelo

Voy a consultar el índice de Empresas 500 en la biblioteca.
Consultaré el índice de Empresas 500 en la biblioteca.

1. Álvaro y yo nos vamos a casar tan pronto como me gradúe. Nos casaremos...
2. Julián me va a decir dónde puedo buscar trabajo. Me dirá...
3. Voy a buscar un puesto que ofrezca ascensos. Buscaré...
4. Voy a leer los anuncios clasificados todos los días. Leeré...
5. Voy a obtener un puesto en mi especialización. Obtendré...
6. Mis amigos van a intentar obtener un teletrabajo. Intentarán...

2 Oraciones Escribe oraciones completas usando la forma correcta del verbo en futuro.

1. Sr. Moreno / renunciar / puesto de gerente / la semana que viene
   El Sr. Moreno renunciará a su puesto de gerente la semana que viene.
2. Entrevistas / para / puesto de reportero / comenzar / dentro de tres días
   Las entrevistas para el puesto de reportero comenzarán dentro de tres días.
3. En el futuro / nosotros / tener / puestos interesantes
   En el futuro, nosotros tendremos puestos interesantes.
4. La próxima semana / ellos / poner / anuncio para buscar un contador
   La próxima semana, ellos pondrán un anuncio para buscar un contador.
5. Pronto Bernardo / dejar / puesto de cocinero
   Pronto Bernardo dejará su puesto de cocinero.
6. Mariana y Felipe / tener mucho éxito / como arquitectos / en el futuro
   Mariana y Felipe tendrán mucho éxito como arquitectos en el futuro.

¡ATENCIÓN!

Useful expressions for talking about the future:

dentro de (diez años) *in/within (ten years)*
en el futuro *in the future*
el porvenir *the future*
próximo *next*

3 Preguntas En parejas, túrnense para hablar del puesto que aceptaron, basándose en los anuncios. Den todos los detalles de su futuro trabajo. Usen las preguntas de guía y hagan también sus propias preguntas. Answers will vary.

SE BUSCA DIRECTOR
de mercadeo para empresa privada. Mínimo de 5 años de experiencia en turismo y conexiones con INTUR (Instituto Nicaragüense de Turismo) y ANTUR (Asociación Nicaragüense de Turismo Receptivo). Debe hablar inglés, español y alemán. Salario anual: 306.000 córdobas. Horario flexible. Buenos beneficios. Envíe currículum por fax al 492-38-67.

MUEBLERÍA MANAGUA
busca carpintero/a. Experiencia en fabricación de muebles finos. Horario: lunes a viernes 7:30 a 11:30 y 1:30 a 5:30. Sueldo semanal: 462 córdobas (más beneficios). Comenzará inmediatamente. Solicite en persona: Calle El Lago, Managua.

1. ¿Cuál será el trabajo?
2. ¿Qué harás?
3. ¿Cuánto te pagarán?
4. ¿Sabes si te ofrecerán beneficios?
5. ¿Qué horario tendrás?
6. ¿Crees que te gustará? ¿Por qué?
7. ¿Cuándo comenzarás a trabajar?
8. ¿Qué crees que aprenderás?

AYUDA

más *plus*
mercadeo *marketing*
mueblería *furniture store/factory*

1 Warm up Briefly explain the subtle difference between expressing the future with **ir + a** + *infinitive* and the simple future. **Ir + a +** *infinitive* expresses intention to do something; the simple future is more definite.

1 Present Have two volunteers read the **Modelo**. Change the subject of the sentence and ask a volunteer for the new sentence. Ex: **Celia va a consultar el índice de Empresas 500 en la biblioteca. (Consultará el índice de Empresas 500 en la biblioteca.)**

1 Expand For further oral practice, say the following sentences: **7. Después de cinco años Álvaro y yo vamos a tener nuestro propio negocio. 8. El negocio estará en un lugar bonito. 9. Uds. van a querer comprar los productos de nuestra compañía. 10. Vamos a jubilarnos cuando tenemos cuarenta años.**

2 Present Ask volunteers to write their completed sentences on the board. Have members of the class correct grammar and spelling as necessary.

3 Warm-up Before assigning the activity, go over the expressions for constructions in the future tense in **¡Atención!** Give students a few minutes to read the two ads before assigning pairs. Refer them to the **Ayuda** section for help with new vocabulary.

3 Present Allow approximately ten minutes for the activity.

3 Expand Have students answer the same questions about the job of their dreams.

Successful Language Learning Ask your students how they could use Spanish in their present or future careers.

TEACHING OPTIONS

Large Group Tell the class that everyone will soon have a new job. Using sticky notes, place the name of a profession on each student's back. Students will circulate around the class asking closed-ended questions (yes/no) to find out what their new jobs are going to be. They should use the future tense to form their questions, and they are only allowed to ask two questions per classmate. Ex: **¿Trabajaré al aire libre? ¿Me pagarán mucho? ¿Tendré que llevar uniforme?**

Video Show the video again to give students more input about the future tense. Stop the video where appropriate to discuss the use of the future to express coming events and as a means of expressing conjecture or probability.

Comunicación

4

Conversar Tú y tu compañero/a viajarán a la República Dominicana por siete días. En parejas, indiquen lo que harán y no harán. Digan dónde, cómo, con quién o en qué fechas lo harán, usando el dibujo como guía. Pueden usar sus propias ideas también.

Answers will vary.

modelo

Estudiante 1: *¿Qué haremos el martes?*
Estudiante 2: *Visitaremos el Museo de Ámbar.*
Estudiante 1: *Pues, tu visitarás el Museo de Ámbar y yo caminaré por la Calle de las Damas.*

NOTA CULTURAL
The Dominican Republic boasts both the highest and the lowest points in the West Indies: **Pico Duarte**, at 3,175 m (10,417 ft.), and **Lago Enriquillo**, at 44 m (144 ft.) below sea level.

¡Bienvenido a la República Dominicana!

Se divertirá desde el momento en que llegue al Aeropuerto Internacional de las Américas.

- Visite la ciudad colonial de **Santo Domingo** con su interesante arquitectura.
- Vaya al **Jardín Botánico** y disfrute de nuestra abundante naturaleza.
- En el **Mercado Modelo** no va a poder resistir la tentación de comprar artesanías.
- No deje de escalar la montaña del **Pico Duarte** (se recomiendan 3 días).
- ¿Le gusta bucear? **Cabarete** tiene todo el equipo que Ud. necesita.
- ¿Desea nadar? **Punta Cana** le ofrece hermosas playas.

5

Planear En grupos pequeños, hagan planes para formar una empresa privada. Usen las preguntas como guía. Después presenten su plan a la clase. Answers will vary.

1. ¿Cómo se llamará y qué tipo de empresa será?
2. ¿Cuántos empleados tendrá y cuáles serán sus oficios o profesiones?
3. ¿Qué tipo de beneficios se ofrecerán?
4. ¿Quién será el/la gerente y quién será el jefe/la jefa? ¿Por qué?
5. ¿Permitirá su empresa el teletrabajo? ¿Por qué?
6. ¿Qué se hará para que los empleados no dejen el trabajo?
7. ¿Dónde pondrá anuncios para conseguir empleados?
8. ¿Qué harán los gerentes para que la empresa tenga éxito?

Síntesis

6

Intercambiar Tu profesor(a) te va a dar una hoja de actividades. Trabajando en parejas, imaginen que una persona es un(a) empleado/a que acaba de ser contratado/a, y la otra es el/la jefe/a. Hablen para confirmar los detalles del contrato. Túrnense para hacerse preguntas usando el tiempo futuro. Answers will vary.

modelo

Empleado: *¿Tendré una oficina con ventana?*
Jefe/a: *Eso dependerá de Ud. Si trabaja mucho, en diez años tendrá una oficina con ventana.*

4 Warm-up Go over the instructions with the whole class and have two volunteers read the **Modelo** aloud. Give pairs two minutes to review the information contained in the ad before they complete the activity.

4 Suggestion If you have any students from the Dominican Republic in your class, or if any of your students have visited the Dominican Republic, ask them to talk about the places named in the ad.

4 Expand Have several pairs of volunteers present their conversation to the class.

5 Present Allow groups ten minutes to plan and practice the activity.

5 Expand Have groups develop a visual aid to accompany their presentation to the class.

6 Present Go over the instructions with the whole class and have two volunteers read the **Modelo** aloud. Then distribute the top portion of **Hoja de actividades 38** to one member of each pair and the bottom portion to the other member.

6 Expand Have students change partners and report to one another on the details of their contract using the future tense.

Assignment Have students do activities in **Student Activities Manual: Workbook,** pages 187–188.

TEACHING OPTIONS

Game Use a ball to play a game that practices the simple future forms. Say an infinitive of a known verb followed by a subject pronoun. Ex: **tener (Uds.)** Toss the ball to a student who must give the simple future of the verb in the indicated form. **(tendrán)** When the student has given the appropritate form, he or she tosses the ball back to you. Include verbs from all conjugations and those that have irregular futures. Keep the pace rapid.

Large Groups Assign a century to each corner of the room. Ex: 2201, 2501, 2801, and so forth. Tell students they are going to go into the future in a time machine **(máquina de transporte a través del tiempo)**. They should pick which year they would like to visit and go to that corner. Once assembled, each group should develop a summary of life in their century. After groups have finished, call on a spokesperson in each group to report to the class.

Section goals

In **Estructura 16.2** students will learn the future perfect tense.

Instructional Resources
Student Activities Manual: Workbook, 189; Lab Manual, 314
Hoja de actividades 39

Before Presenting Estructura 16.2 Write a series of dates on the board, making sure the correspond to key academic events. Ex: **el 15 de diciembre; el 6 de junio.** Then model the future perfect tense by talking about what will have happened by each date. Write each future perfect form on the board as you write it. Ex: **Para el 15 de diciembre, el semestre habrá terminado. Para el 6 de junio, algunos de ustedes se habrán graduado.** and so forth. Have volunteers give information about the other dates listed. Tell students they are going to learn to talk about events that will have happened by some future point in time.

Assignment Have students study **Estructura 16.2** and prepare **¡Inténtalo!** on page 500 and Activity 1 on page 501.

Present Work through the paradigms of the future perfect tense. Then ask volunteers to read aloud the captions to the video stills and identify the future perfect verbs. Remind students that the past participle, when it is part of a compound verb, always ends in **–o**.

Discuss **para** + *time expression*. Explain that the future perfect is also used to hypothesize about a past action. Ex: **Susana ya habrá salido de la oficina.** For further explanation, refer the students to the second **¡Atención!**

Close Do **¡Inténtalo!** orally as a class.

16.2 The future perfect

NATIONAL STANDARDS comparisons

ANTE TODO Like other compound tenses you have learned, the future perfect (**el futuro perfecto**) is formed with a form of **haber** and the past participle. It is used to talk about what will have happened by some future point in time.

Future perfect

		hablar	comer	vivir
SINGULAR FORMS	yo	**habré** hablado	**habré** comido	**habré** vivido
	tú	**habrás** hablado	**habrás** comido	**habrás** vivido
	Ud./él/ella	**habrá** hablado	**habrá** comido	**habrá** vivido
PLURAL FORMS	nosotros/as	**habremos** hablado	**habremos** comido	**habremos** vivido
	vosotros/as	**habréis** hablado	**habréis** comido	**habréis** vivido
	Uds./ellos/ellas	**habrán** hablado	**habrán** comido	**habrán** vivido

¡ATENCIÓN!
As with the other compound verb tenses, in the future perfect tense the past participle never varies; it always ends in **–o**.

En cinco años habré establecido mi compañía de Internet.

Serás millonario, ¿eh?
Sí, porque mucha gente habrá invertido en mi empresa.

- The phrase **para** + [*time expression*] is used with the future perfect to talk about what will have happened by some future point in time.

Para el lunes, habré hecho todas las preparaciones.
By Monday, I will have made all the preparations.

Para el próximo año, habré renunciado a mi trabajo.
By next year, I will have resigned from my job.

¡ATENCIÓN!
The future perfect is also used like the future of probablility, except that it represents a past action.
¿Adónde habrá ido Raúl?
I wonder where Raúl went?

¡INTÉNTALO! Indica la forma apropiada del futuro perfecto.

1. Para el sábado, nosotros habremos obtenido (obtener) el dinero.
2. Yo habré terminado (terminar) el trabajo para cuando lleguen mis amigos.
3. Silvia habrá hecho (hacer) todos los planes.
4. Uds. habrán llegado (llegar) a Quito para el cinco de junio.
5. Ernesto y tú habrán recibido (recibir) muchas ofertas para esa fecha.
6. Para el ocho de octubre, nosotros ya habremos llegado (llegar) a Colombia.
7. Para entonces, yo habré vuelto (volver) de la República Dominicana.
8. Para cuando yo te llame, ¿habrás decidido (decidir) tú lo que vamos a hacer?
9. Mi hermana habrá salido (salir) para las nueve.
10. Tú y yo habremos limpiado (limpiar) el piso para las ocho.

TEACHING OPTIONS

Small Groups Divide the class into groups of three. Ask each group to work together to write a description of a classmate's future success, using the future perfect tense. The group should not include the name of their subject. Then circulate the descriptions and ask the other groups to identify the name of the classmate whose future is being predicted.

Extra Practice To provide oral practice with the future perfect, give the students oral prompts with a future date. Ex: **Para el año 2004....** Say the prompt, have students repeat it, then call on individual students to add an appropriate ending using the future perfect. (**...habremos aprendido perfectamente el español. ...Ud. se habrá jubilado.** and so forth).

Práctica

NOTA CULTURAL
In 1990, Violeta Barrios de Chamorro (1929-) became the first woman to be elected president of Nicaragua.

1 **Escoger** Juan Luis está hablando de lo que habrá ocurrido en ciertos momentos del futuro. Escoge los verbos de la lista que mejor completen cada oración y ponlos en el futuro perfecto.

comprar	solicitar	tomar
graduarse	ser	viajar
romperse	leer	casarse

1. Para mañana por la tarde yo ya _habré tomado_ mi examen de biología.
2. Para la semana que viene el profesor _habrá leído_ nuestros exámenes.
3. Dentro de tres meses Juan y Marisa _se habrán casado_ en Las Vegas.
4. Dentro de cinco meses tú y yo _nos habremos graduado_ de la universidad.
5. Para el fin de mayo, yo _habré solicitado_ un trabajo en un banco.
6. Dentro de un año tú _habrás comprado_ una casa nueva.
7. Antes de cumplir los 50 años, usted _habrá viajado_ a Europa.
8. Dentro de 25 años Emilia ya _habrá sido_ presidenta de los EE.UU.

Comunicación

NATIONAL communication STANDARDS

2 **Encuesta** Tu profesor(a) te va a dar una hoja de actividades. Pregúntales a tres compañeros/as para cuándo habrán hecho las cosas relacionadas con sus futuras carreras que se mencionan en la lista. Toma nota de las respuestas y comparte más tarde con la clase la información que obtuviste sobre tus compañeros/as. Answers will vary.

modelo

Estudiante 1: ¿Para cuándo habrás terminado tus estudios, Carla?
Estudiante 2: El año que viene habré terminado mis estudios.
Estudiante 1: Carla habrá terminado sus estudios el año que viene.

Síntesis

NATIONAL communication STANDARDS

3 **Competir** En parejas, preparen un diálogo hipotético (8 líneas o más) que ocurra en una fiesta. Una persona dice lo que habrá hecho para algún momento del futuro; la otra responde, diciendo cada vez algo más exagerado. Prepárense para representar el diálogo delante de la clase. Answers will vary.

modelo

Estudiante 1: Cuando tenga 30 años habré ganado un millón de dólares.
Estudiante 2: Y yo habré llegado a ser multimillonaria.
Estudiante 1: Para el 2020, me habrán escogido como la mejor diseñadora de París.
Estudiante 2: Pues, yo habré ganado el Premio Nobel de literatura.

TEACHING OPTIONS

Pairs Have students work in pairs to prepare skits using the future perfect and a prediction theme. One student will play the part of a fortuneteller, a psychic, or another type of expert who claims to foresee the future. The other student will be the client. Encourage the students to bring props and/or costumes for the performance of their skit to the class.

Game Divide the class into groups of three. Write a future date on the board. Ex: **el 15 de noviembre de 2008**. Groups should confer and decide what will have happened by that date. When they have their answer, one student should stand up. The quickest group to respond with a correct answer wins a point. Ex: **Para el 15 de noviembre de 2008 habremos tenido otras elecciones presidenciales.**

Suggestion Review the information in **Nota cultural.** Ask students if they know about other female politicians in Latin America.

1 Present Go over the activity with the whole class, asking volunteers to read each completed sentence.

1 Expand After you have reviewed the correct answers, use the same prepositional phrases to ask students personalized questions about their future plans. Ex: **Para mañana por la tarde, ¿qué habrás hecho? Para la semana que viene, ¿con quién habrás hablado?**

2 Present Distribute **Hoja de actividades 39**. Go over the directions with the whole class. Then have two volunteers model the activity by reading the **Modelo**, noting as they do so that the first example is the question asked, the second is the response, and the third is the rephrasing of the response by the first student.

2 Expand Assign groups of four and have each group summarize its findings in a graph or time line.

3 Present Read aloud the **Modelo** with a volunteer who takes the role of **Estudiante 2.** Model adding another exaggerated claim to the exchange. Ex: **Pues, yo ya me habré jubilado del Comité Nobel en aquel entonces.**

4 Expand After students have read their dialogues to the class, ask pairs to evaluate the claims. Ex: **La hipótesis de ____ es la más exagerada. La más ambiciosa es la de ____. La más original es la de ____.**

Assignment Have students do activities in **Student Activities Manual: Workbook,** page 189.

Section Goals

In **Estructura 16.3** students will learn the past subjunctive.

Instructional Resources
Student Activities Manual: Workbook, 190–192; Lab Manual, 315

Before Presenting Estructura 16.3
To demonstrate the use of the past subjunctive, ask volunteers to answer closed-ended questions about a recent event or popular movie. Ex: **¿Te sorprendió que la heroína se casara con el enemigo del protagonista? • ¿Esperabas que el gobernador tomara esa decisión?** As students give you short answers, write the complete sentences on the board, underlining the past subjunctive form. Ex: **A todos nos sorprendió que la heroína se casara con el enemigo del protagonista. • ____ no esperaba que el gobernador tomara esa decisión.** Tell students they are now going to learn how to use the past subjunctive in Spanish.
Assignment Have students study **Estructura 16.3** and prepare the activities on pages 503–504 as homework.

Present Begin by making sure that students understand the concept of the the imperfect subjunctive as explained in **Ante todo**. Explain that the past subjunctive is generally used in the same situations in which the present subjunctive is used, except to express past events.

Work through the paradigms of regular verbs in the past subjunctive, drawing attention to the accent on all **nosotros/as** forms. Then discuss the distinctive endings of the past subjunctive and its formation from the third-person plural preterite form.

Continued on page 503.

16.3 The past subjunctive

NATIONAL comparisons STANDARDS

ANTE TODO You will now learn how to form and use the past subjunctive (**el imperfecto de subjuntivo**), also called the imperfect subjunctive. Like the present subjunctive, the past subjunctive is used mainly in multiple-clause sentences which express states and conditions such as will, influence, emotion, commands, indefiniteness and nonexistence.

The past subjunctive

		estudiar	aprender	recibir
SINGULAR FORMS	yo	estudia**ra**	aprendie**ra**	recibie**ra**
	tú	estudia**ras**	aprendie**ras**	recibie**ras**
	Ud./él/ella	estudia**ra**	aprendie**ra**	recibie**ra**
PLURAL FORMS	nosotros/as	estudiá**ramos**	aprendié**ramos**	recibié**ramos**
	vosotros/as	estudia**rais**	aprendie**rais**	recibie**rais**
	Uds./ellos/ellas	estudia**ran**	aprendie**ran**	recibie**ran**

- The past subjunctive endings are the same for all verbs.

-ra	**-ramos**
-ras	**-rais**
-ra	**-ran**

- The past subjunctive is formed using the **Uds./ellos/ellas** form of the preterite. By dropping the **–ron** ending from this preterite form, you establish the stem of all the past subjunctive forms. To this stem you then add the past subjunctive endings.

INFINITIVE	PRETERITE FORM	STEM	PAST SUBJUNCTIVE
hablar	ellos habla~~ron~~	habla-	habla**ra,** habla**ras,** hablá**ramos**
beber	ellos bebie~~ron~~	bebie-	bebie**ra,** bebie**ras,** bebié**ramos**
escribir	ellos escribie~~ron~~	escribie-	escribie**ra,** escribie**ras,** escribié**ramos**

- Verbs with irregular preterites use the same stems and endings in the past subjunctive.

INFINITIVE	PRETERITE FORM	STEM	PAST SUBJUNCTIVE
dar	die~~ron~~	die-	die**ra,** die**ras,** dié**ramos**
decir	dije~~ron~~	dije-	dije**ra,** dije**ras,** dijé**ramos**
estar	estuvie~~ron~~	estuvie-	estuvie**ra,** estuvie**ras,** estuvié**ramos**
hacer	hicie~~ron~~	hicie-	hicie**ra,** hicie**ras,** hicié**ramos**
ir/ser	fue~~ron~~	fue-	fue**ra,** fue**ras,** fué**ramos**
poder	pudie~~ron~~	pudie-	pudie**ra,** pudie**ras,** pudié**ramos**
poner	pusie~~ron~~	pusie-	pusie**ra,** pusie**ras,** pusié**ramos**
querer	quisie~~ron~~	quisie-	quisie**ra,** quisie**ras,** quisié**ramos**
saber	supie~~ron~~	supie-	supie**ra,** supie**ras,** supié**ramos**
tener	tuvie~~ron~~	tuvie-	tuvie**ra,** tuvie**ras,** tuvié**ramos**
venir	vinie~~ron~~	vinie-	vinie**ra,** vinie**ras,** vinié**ramos**

¡ATENCIÓN!
Note that the **nosotros/as** form of the past subjunctive always has a written accent.

LENGUA VIVA
Quisiera, the past subjunctive form of **querer,** is often used to make polite requests.
Quisiera hablar con Marco, por favor.
I would like to speak to Marco, please.
¿Quisiera Ud. algo más?
Would you like anything else?

TEACHING OPTIONS

Extra Practice Write the following drill on the board. Students should change the verb according to each new subject. **1. estar: él/nosotros/tú 2. emplear: yo/ella/Ud. 3. insistir: ellos/Uds./él 4. poder: ellas/yo/nosotros 5. obtener: nosotros/tú/ella**

Heritage Speaker Ask Spanish speakers to write ten sentences that use the past subjunctive to describe their experiences during their first days at your university or college. Ex: **Me sorprendió que la biblioteca fuera tan grande. No me gustó ver que los estudiantes y profesores se vistieran con tanta indiferencia.** and so forth. Ask them to write their sentences on the board and explain any unfamiliar vocabulary.

▶ **-Ir** stem-changing verbs and other verbs with spelling changes follow a similar process to form the past subjunctive.

INFINITIVE	PRETERITE FORM	STEM	PAST SUBJUNCTIVE
preferir	prefirie~~ron~~	prefirie-	prefirie**ra**, prefirie**ras**, prefirié**ramos**
repetir	repitie~~ron~~	repitie-	repitie**ra**, repitie**ras**, repitié**ramos**
dormir	durmie~~ron~~	durmie-	durmie**ra**, durmie**ras**, durmié**ramos**
conducir	conduje~~ron~~	conduje-	conduje**ra**, conduje**ras**, condujé**ramos**
creer	creye~~ron~~	creye-	creye**ra**, creye**ras**, creyé**ramos**
destruir	destruye~~ron~~	destruye-	destruye**ra**, destruye**ras**, destruyé**ramos**
oír	oye~~ron~~	oye-	oye**ra**, oye**ras**, oyé**ramos**

CONSEJOS

Note this parallel:
main verb in present indicative → subordinate verb in present subjunctive
Espero que María **venga.**
main verb in past indicative → subordinate verb in past subjunctive
Esperaba que María **viniera.**

▶ The past subjunctive is used in the same contexts and situations as the present and present perfect subjunctive, except that it generally describes actions, events, or conditions that have already happened.

Me pidieron que no **llegara** tarde.
They asked me not to arrive late.

Me sorprendió que Uds. no **vinieran** a la cena.
It surprised me that you didn't come to the dinner.

Salió antes de que yo **pudiera** hablar contigo.
He left before I could talk to you.

Ellos querían que yo **escribiera** una novela romántica.
They wanted me to write a romantic novel.

No pensé que pudiera terminar la excursión.

Martín mostró mucho interés en que aprendiéramos sobre el medio ambiente.

¡INTÉNTALO! Indica la forma apropiada del imperfecto de subjuntivo de los verbos entre paréntesis.

1. Quería que tú ___vinieras___ (venir) más temprano.
2. Esperábamos que Uds. ___hablaran___ (hablar) mucho más en la reunión.
3. No creían que yo ___pudiera___ (poder) hacerlo.
4. ¿Dudas que nosotros ___invirtiéramos___ (invertir) el dinero ayer?
5. Siento que Ud. no ___estuviera___ (estar) con nosotros anoche.
6. No era necesario que ellas ___hicieran___ (hacer) todo.
7. Es increíble que tú ___supieras___ (saber) dónde encontrarlo.
8. No había nadie que ___creyera___ (creer) tu historia.
9. Mis padres insistieron en que yo ___fuera___ (ir) a la universidad.
10. Queríamos salir antes de que Uds. ___llegaran___ (llegar).

Check comprehension by writing on the board the infinitive of regular verbs from the three conjugations. Ask a volunteer to give the **ellos** form of the preterite. Have the class then give the three distinct past subjunctive forms.

Then, follow the same procedure with verbs that have irregular preterites or are stem-changing in the preterite.

Use pairs of examples such as the following to illustrate that the past subjunctive generally occurs in the same situations as the present subjunctive except that it deals with past events. Ex: **¿Es importante que estudies tanto? ¿Era importante que estudiaras tanto? • Me sorprendo que quieras ser político. Me sorprendió que quisieras ser político. • No hay ningún teléfono que funcione. No había ningún teléfono que funcionara.**

Ask volunteers to read the captions to the video stills and indicate the past subjunctive forms.

Draw students' attention to the **Lengua viva** sidebar on page 502. Guide students to see the usefulness of the **quisiera** form for making polite requests. Point out that the use of **quiero** instead of **quisiera** can seem rather blunt and could seem rude. Compare: **Quisiera hablar con Marco** and **Quiero hablar con Marco**, for instance, or **¿Quisiera Ud. algo?** and **¿Quiere Ud. algo?**

Close Do **¡Inténtalo!** orally as a class.

The Affective Dimension
Tell the class that some students are intimidated by the past subjunctive. Point out that its forms are fairly easy to learn and that it is used in familiar contexts.

TEACHING OPTIONS

Video Show the video again to give students more input on the use of the past subjunctive. Stop the video where appropriate to discuss how and why the past subjunctive was used.

Extra Practice Write this cloze paragraph on the board, asking students to complete it using the correct forms of the following verbs: **ser, querer, poder, estudiar, tener. Mis padres siempre querían que yo ____ (estudiara) una carrera universitaria. Nunca dudaba de que ____ (pudiera) llegar a ser lo que ____ (quisiera). Cuando ____ (tenga) hijos, espero tener la misma confianza en ellos.**

1 Present If you have not assigned this activity as homework, it can also be assigned to pairs of students. Have each partner complete the activity, exchange with his or her partner, and correct the paper he or she receives. After they have completed the activity, ask three pairs to read the dialogues aloud. Allow ten minutes for the activity.

1 Expand Assign pairs of students one of the three dialogues. Ask the partners to work together to continue the conversation using the past subjunctive. Ex: **—A mí me pasó algo igual. Me aconsejaron a que dejara un trabajo que me gustaba mucho por otro que pagaba mejor.**

2 Present Read the **Modelo** aloud. Ask volunteers to give other possible responses to the prompt. Ex: **Fue estupendo que pudieran recogerte en el aeropuerto.** Since students are likely to respond to each item differently, it is possible to have more than one student respond to each.

2 Suggestion Ask students to find a poem by Rubén Darío and bring it to class. Or have them research the poet and **modernismo**.

2 Suggestion Instead of having students compare their answers in pairs, have them do so in groups of four.

Práctica

1 Diálogos Completa los diálogos con el imperfecto de subjuntivo de los verbos entre paréntesis. Después representa los diálogos con un(a) compañero/a.

1. —¿Qué le dijo el consejero a Andrés? Quisiera saberlo.
   —Le aconsejó que ___dejara___ (dejar) los estudios de arte y que ___estudiara___ (estudiar) una carrera que ___pagara___ (pagar) mejor.
   —Siempre el dinero. ¿No se enojó Andrés de que le ___aconsejara___ (aconsejar) eso?
   —Sí, y le dijo que no creía que ninguna otra carrera le ___fuera___ (ir) a gustar más.
2. —Qué lástima que ellos no te ___ofrecieran___ (ofrecer) el puesto de gerente.
   —Querían a alguien que ___tuviera___ (tener) experiencia en el sector público.
   —Pero, ¿cómo? ¿Y tu maestría? ¿No te molestó que te ___dijeran___ (decir) eso?
   —No, no tengo experiencia en esa área pero les gustó mucho mi currículum. Me pidieron que ___volviera___ (volver) en un año y ___solicitara___ (solicitar) el puesto otra vez. Para entonces habré obtenido la experiencia que necesito y podré conseguir el puesto que quiera.
3. —Cuánto me alegro de que tus hijas ___vinieran___ (venir) ayer a visitarte. ¿Cuándo se van?
   —Bueno, yo esperaba que se ___quedaran___ (quedar) dos semanas, pero no pueden. Ojalá ___pudieran___ (poder). Hace mucho que no las veo.

2 Reaccionar Manuel acaba de llegar de Nicaragua. Reacciona a lo que te dice, usando el imperfecto de subjuntivo. Escribe las oraciones y luego compáralas con las de un(a) compañero/a. Answers will vary.

modelo

El día que llegué me esperaban mi abuela y tres primos.
¡Qué bien! Me alegro de que vieras a tu familia después de tantos años.

1. Fuimos al volcán Masaya. ¡Y vimos la lava del volcán!
2. Visitamos la Catedral de Managua, que fue dañada por el terremoto (*earthquake*) de 1972.
3. No tuvimos tiempo de ir a la playa, pero pasamos unos días en el Hotel Dariense en Granada.
4. Fui a conocer el nuevo museo de arte y también fui al Teatro Rubén Darío.
5. Nos divertimos haciendo compras en Metrocentro.
6. Eché monedas (*coins*) en la fuente (*fountain*) de la Plaza de la República y pedí un deseo.

NOTA CULTURAL

Rubén Darío (1867-1916), Nicaragua's most famous poet, was the founder of the style known as **modernismo**, which had a profound effect on poetry throughout the Spanish-speaking world.

TEACHING OPTIONS

Small Groups Ask students to write a plot summary of a movie they've seen, using the past subjunctive. Have them read their summaries in groups of five. Ex: **Su mamá no quería que se casara. Insistía en que la más joven de sus hijas se quedara soltera para cuidarla de vieja. No permitió que Tita aceptara la petición de matrimonio de Pedro. Tita tuvo que esperar hasta que se muriera su madre para tener felicidad.**

Large Groups Ask students to think of a childhood fantasy they had about another person or a fictional character and create a sentence using the past subjunctive. Ex: **Yo quería que Santa Claus fuera mi abuelo. Yo insistía que se pusiera la mesa para mis amigos imaginarios.** Then go around the room asking each person to say his/her sentence aloud, but repeating all the previous sentences first.

NATIONAL communication STANDARDS

Comunicación

3 **Escribir** Trabajen en parejas. Uno/a de Uds. ha comprado una casa; el/la otro/a es el/la gerente de la empresa responsable de las reformas (*improvements*) de la casa. El/La cliente/a llama al/a la gerente para quejarse (*to complain*) de que algunos trabajadores todavía no han hecho algunas cosas. Usen las listas y el modelo como guía.
Answers will vary.

modelo

el/la técnico/a / conectar / módem

Estudiante 1: Le pedí al técnico que conectara el módem pero todavía no ha venido.

Estudiante 2: No se preocupe. Yo también le pedí al técnico que fuera a su casa.

el/la electricista / conectar / electricidad
el/la carpintero/a / construir / balcón
el/la diseñador/a / escoger / muebles
el/la pintor(a) / pintar / paredes

4 **Oraciones** Haz cinco oraciones sobre lo que otros esperaban de ti en el pasado y cinco más sobre lo que tú esperabas de ellos. Luego, en grupos, túrnense para compartir sus propias oraciones y para transformar las oraciones de sus compañeros/as. Sigan el modelo. Answers will vary.

modelo

Estudiante 1: Mi profesora quería que yo fuera a Granada para estudiar español.

Estudiante 2: Su profesora quería que él fuera a Granada para estudiar español.

Estudiante 3: Yo deseaba que mis padres me enviaran a España.

Estudiante 4: Cecilia deseaba que sus padres la enviaran a España.

NATIONAL communication STANDARDS

Síntesis

5 **Situaciones** En grupos, escojan (*choose*) una situación y preparen un diálogo sobre ella para presentar a la clase. Answers will vary.

- Claudia dejó su puesto por la forma en que le hablaba el gerente, por el aumento que les dieron a otros empleados pero no a ella, y por el horario que no funcionaba con sus clases.
- Marcos es enfermero en una universidad y ayer tuvo un día horrible: llegaron muchos estudiantes con gripe, otros con alergias, otro con dolor de cabeza y dos atletas medio destruidos.
- Un(a) amigo/a trabaja de consejero/a para gente que busca trabajo. Ayer todos sus clientes lo/la llamaron porque querían cambiar de trabajo.

AYUDA

It may help you to remember that the first and third person forms of all regular verbs are the same in the imperfect.

yo esperaba, él/ella esperaba

yo quería, él/ella quería

3 Present Go over the directions with the whole class, then have two volunteers read the **Modelo**. Encourage students to use different verbs in their exchanges as they go along. Ex: **Yo también le insistí al técnico que resolviera el problema hoy. No se preocupe. Le dije que buscara solución hoy.**

3 Expand Call on different pairs of students to read their mini-dialogues to the class.

4 Warm-up Go over the directions with the whole class and ask four volunteers to read the **Modelo**. Give your own responses to provide another example. Ex: **Mi hijo quería que le permitiera viajar solo a México.** Then have a volunteer rephrase the corresponding statement in the third person.

4 Present Have individuals write their five sentences before dividing the class into groups of four. Allow about ten minutes for the activity.

5 Warm-up/Present Before students begin to write their dialogues, have them brainstorm different scenarios. Ex: The conversation between Claudia and her boss; a phone conversation between Claudia and a friend in which she gives an account of the event. Ask groups to brainstorm suitable verbs for both the main and subjunctive clauses as a prewriting activity.

5 Expand Call on three different groups to perform their dialogues for the class.

Assignment Have students do activities in **Student Activities Manual: Workbook,** pages 190–192.

TEACHING OPTIONS

Extra Practice Write the following sentences on the board and ask students to complete them using the past subjunctive and the preterite. **1. Cuando era pequeño/a quería que ____, pero ____. 2. Me aconsejaron que ____, pero ____. 3. Durante mucho tiempo insistía que ____, pero ____. 4. Siempre fue importante para mí que ____, pero ____.**

Game Divide the class into groups of four. Each group will write a description of a famous villain or group of villains using as many verbs in the past subjunctive as possible. Give the groups ten minutes to write their descriptions and ask the groups with the most verbs in the past subjunctive to read their descriptions aloud. The class will vote on the best description.

Section Goals

In **Lectura** students will:

- learn to recognize similes and metaphors
- read an excerpt from a Chilean novel

Antes de leer
Introduce the strategy. Review with students that similes compare one thing to another and metaphors say that one thing is another. Then write the following two sentences on the board: **Su cabello es como seda. Sus palabras son poesía.**

Ask volunteers which sentence is the simile and which is the metaphor. Ask students to make up a simile and a metaphor in Spanish and share them with the class.

Examinar el texto
Before having students scan the text, remind them that Pablo Neruda was a Chilean poet who won the Nobel Prize in Literature in 1971. Neruda had retired to his home in Isla Negra when, in 1973, a violent coup d'état sponsored by right-wing elements of the Chilean armed forces overthrew the democratically elected government of president Salvador Allende. Neruda, a long-time member of the Communist Party, died not long after the coup.

Students may note that the punctuation indicates that this excerpt is a dialogue.

Example of simile: **Pedalear con la bolsa sobre tu lomo es igual que cargar un elefante sobre los hombros.**

Contestar Go over answers with the whole class.

Assignment Have students read **El cartero de Neruda** and prepare the activities in **Después de leer** as homework.

Lectura

NATIONAL communication cultures STANDARDS

Antes de leer

Estrategia

Recognizing similes and metaphors

Similes and metaphors are figures of speech that are often used in literature to make descriptions more colorful and vivid.

In English, a simile (**símil**) makes a comparison using the words *as* or *like*. In Spanish the words **como** and **parece** are most often used in similes. Example: **Mario estaba tan contento como un niño con zapatos nuevos.** (*Mario was as happy as a kid with new shoes.*)

A metaphor (**metáfora**) is a figure of speech that identifies one thing with the attributes and qualities of another thing. Whereas a simile says one thing is like another, a metaphor says that one thing *is* another. In Spanish, **ser** is most often used in metaphors. Example: **La vida es sueño.** (*Life is a dream.*)

Examinar el texto

Lee el texto una vez usando las estrategias de lectura de las lecciones anteriores. ¿Qué te indican sobre el contenido de la lectura? Toma nota de las metáforas y los símiles que aparecen. ¿Qué significan? ¿Qué te dicen sobre el tema de la lectura?

Contestar

1. ¿Quién es Pablo Neruda? (Ve al **Panorama** de la Lección 9, página 294.)
2. ¿Cuál es el significado de las siguientes oraciones?
   a. Su corazón y sus labios dijeron al unísono. —Sí.
   b. El cartero que lo atendía se jubiló jorobado como un camello.
   c. Soy de fierro.

El cartero de Neruda
(un fragmento)

Antonio Skármeta

Antonio Skármeta nació en 1940 en Antofagasta (Chile). Estudió Humanidades en la Universidad de Chile donde trabajó como actor y director de la compañía de teatro estudiantil CADIP. En 1975, se fue a vivir a Berlín y durante esos años fue profesor en la Academia de Artes, Cine y Televisión. Hoy día, Skármeta es conocido tanto por sus novelas y cuentos como por su labor cinematográfica. El gran éxito internacional que obtuvo la película Il Postino, *basada en su novela* El cartero de Neruda (Ardiente paciencia), *le confirmó como uno de los escritores chilenos más célebres.*

Después de leer

Preguntas

Contesta las siguientes preguntas.

1. ¿Quiénes son los personajes que hablan en este fragmento de la novela?
2. ¿Cómo son los personajes?
3. ¿Cuántos clientes va a tener el cartero? ¿Por qué?
4. ¿Es bueno el sueldo del cartero?
5. ¿Le importa a Mario el sueldo?
6. ¿Te gustaría ser el cartero de Neruda? ¿Por qué?
7. ¿Con qué persona famosa quisieras trabajar?
8. ¿Cuál es tu profesión ideal?

TEACHING OPTIONS

Pairs Ask pairs to work together to write the **anuncio** that Mario responded to. Then have them write ads for other professions, such as **chófer/a, actor/a, reportero/a, científico/a, arqueólogo/a, programador/a, maestro/a, abogado/a, peluquero/a, biólogo/a, escritor/a, traductor/a, cocinero/a.** Students should include details of job duties **(funciones o responsabilidades en el trabajo)**.

Extra Practice Have students research poetry by Pablo Neruda. The University of Chile has an informative Website on the Internet with several pages on Neruda: www.uchile.cl/neruda. Students can find a timeline of his life under the section "línea de vida" and can listen to Neruda reciting some of his poetry under the section "obra." Encourage students to read his poetry, find their favorites, read them aloud, and discuss them in class.

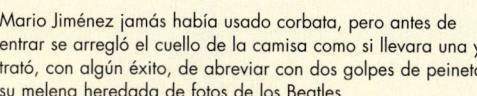

Mario Jiménez jamás había usado corbata, pero antes de entrar se arregló el cuello de la camisa como si llevara una y trató, con algún éxito, de abreviar con dos golpes de peineta su melena heredada de fotos de los Beatles.

—Vengo por el aviso —declamó al funcionario, con una sonrisa que emulaba la de Burt Lancaster.

—¿Tiene bicicleta? —preguntó aburrido el funcionario.

Su corazón y sus labios dijeron al unísono.

—Sí.

—Bueno —dijo el oficinista, limpiándose los lentes, —se trata de un puesto de cartero para isla Negra.

—Qué casualidad —dijo Mario—. Yo vivo al lado, en la caleta.

—Eso está muy bien. Pero lo que está mal es que hay un solo cliente.

—¿Uno nada más?

—Sí, pues. En la caleta todos son analfabetos. No pueden leer ni las cuentas.

—¿Y quién es el cliente?

—Pablo Neruda.

Mario Jiménez tragó lo que le pareció un litro de saliva.

—Pero eso es formidable.

—¿Formidable? Recibe kilos de correspondencia diariamente. Pedalear con la bolsa sobre tu lomo es igual que cargar un elefante sobre los hombros. El cartero que lo atendía se jubiló jorobado como un camello.

—Pero yo tengo sólo diecisiete años.

—¿Y estás sano?

—¿Yo? Soy de fierro. ¡Ni un resfrío en mi vida!

El funcionario deslizó los lentes sobre el tabique de la nariz y lo miró por encima del marco.

—El sueldo es una mierda. Los otros carteros se las arreglan con las propinas. Pero con un cliente, apenas te alcanzará para el cine una vez por semana.

—Quiero el puesto.

—Está bien. Me llamo Cosme.

—Cosme.

—Me debes decir «don Cosme».

—Sí, don Cosme.

—Soy tu jefe.

—Sí, jefe.

El hombre levantó un bolígrafo azul, le sopló su aliento para entibiar la tinta, y preguntó sin mirarlo.

—¿Nombre?

—Mario Jiménez —respondió Mario Jiménez solemnemente.

Y en cuanto terminó de emitir ese vital comunicado, fue hasta la ventana, desprendió el aviso, y lo hizo recalar en lo más profundo del bolsillo trasero de su pantalón.

abreviar *shorten* **golpes** *strokes* **peineta** *comb* **melena** *mop of hair* **heredada** *inherited* **aviso** *advertisement* **declamó** *he declaimed* **funcionario** *government employee* **sonrisa** *smile* **labios** *lips* **casualidad** *coincidence* **caleta** *cove* **analfabetos** *illiterate* **tragó** *gulped* **lomo** *back* **cargar** *to carry* **hombros** *shoulders* **jorobado** *hunchbacked* **fierro** *iron* **deslizó** *slid* **tabique** *bridge* **marco** *frame* **una mierda** *crappy* **se las arreglan** *make it up* **alcanzará** *will be enough* **sopló su aliento para entibiar la tinta** *breathed on it to warm the ink* **desprendió** *took down* **lo hizo recalar en lo más profundo del bolsillo trasero** *stuck it in the deepest part of his back pocket*

El diario de Mario

Imagina que eres Mario Jiménez. Escribe en tu diario lo que pasó el día que conseguiste el trabajo de cartero de Pablo Neruda. Incluye la siguiente información:

- Una descripción del tipo de trabajo que buscabas
- Lo que pensabas del puesto después de leer el anuncio
- Lo que hiciste antes de la entrevista
- Una descripción de la persona que te entrevistó
- Lo que pasó durante la entrevista
- Lo que pensabas
- Lo que sentías durante la entrevista
- Lo que hiciste después de la entrevista

Terminar la historia

Trabajen en grupos para escribir la continuación de la historia "El cartero de Neruda". La primera persona escribe un párrafo y lo pasa a la próxima persona. El/Ella añade un párrafo y así hasta terminar la historia. Incluyan todos los detalles posibles y asegúrense de que la historia sea coherente e interesante.

Minidrama

En parejas, preparen un minidrama basado en "El cartero de Neruda" y preséntenlo a la clase. Utilicen el diálogo que hay en el texto e inventen también una conversación más larga basada en lo que saben de la personalidad de cada personaje.

Después de leer

Preguntas
Suggestion Ask questions of the whole class. If students have trouble with the meaning of any word or phrase, help them identify corresponding context clues and explain any unfamiliar vocabulary.

El diario de Mario
Suggestion Review the suggestions about information to include in the diary entry, explaining any unfamiliar vocabulary. You may wish to have students work in pairs to write an entry.

Terminar la historia
Suggestion Have Spanish speakers work with those who are being exposed to Spanish for the first time. The Spanish speaker can write the first paragraph.

Minidrama
Suggestion Give students time to write their scripts and practice their minidramas before performing them in front of the class. You may wish to create audio or video recordings of the performances.

TEACHING OPTIONS

Heritage Speakers Ask Spanish speakers to share terms they use for *job* or *employment* and to talk briefly about how they are used and where they are used. Spanish speakers should mention that **trabajo** and **empleo** are probably the most common terms. **Oficio, ocupación,** and **profesión** are more formal. A very colloquial term used in parts of Latin America is **chamba**.

Game Have students describe the responsibilities of a particular profession. Their classmates will guess the profession they are describing.

Extra Practice Encourage students to view the video of *Il postino* (or show it in class). Encourage students to critique the film **(hacer una crítica de la película)** in Spanish.

Section Goals

In **Escritura** students will:

- learn to use note cards as a study aid
- use note cards to prepare to write a composition
- write a composition about professional and personal goals for the future

Tema

Present Go over the directions with the class, explaining that each student will write a composition on his or her plans for the future—professionally and personally. In preparation for writing about professional goals they expect to have attained, have students review the conjugation of **haber** + *past participle* to form the future perfect tense.

Estrategia

Present Explain to students that using note cards in preparation for writing a composition will help greatly in organizing the information that they may want to include. Tell them they can use note cards to prepare to write the composition about their plans for the future. Suggest they use several note cards for each of the categories **(lugar, familia, empleo, finanzas, metas profesionales).** Remind them to number the cards by category.

Assignment Have students prepare **Ideas y organización** and **Primer borrador** as homework. Tell students to keep the note cards they use to organize their first draft.

Escritura

Estrategia

Using note cards

Note cards serve as valuable study aids in many different contexts. When you write, note cards can help you organize and sequence the information you wish to present.

Let's say you are going to write a personal narrative about a trip you took. You would jot down notes about each part of the trip on a different note card. Then you could easily arrange them in chronological order or use a different organization, such as the best parts and the worst parts, traveling and staying, before and after, etc.

Here are some helpful techniques for using note cards to prepare for your writing:

- Label the top of each card with a general subject, such as **el avión** or **el hotel.**
- Number the cards in each subject category in the upper right corner to help you organize them.
- Use only the front side of each note card so that you can easily flip through them to find information.

Study the following example of a note card used to prepare a composition:

3

En el aeropuerto de Santo Domingo

Cuando llegamos al aeropuerto de Santo Domingo, después de siete horas de viajar, estábamos cansados pero felices. Hacía sol y viento.

Tema

Escribir una composición

Escribe una composición sobre tus planes profesionales y personales para el futuro. Utiliza el tiempo futuro. No te olvides de hacer planes para las siguientes áreas de tu vida:

Lugar

- ¿Dónde vivirás?
- ¿Vivirás en la misma ciudad siempre? ¿Te mudarás mucho?

Familia

- ¿Te casarás? ¿Con quién?
- ¿Tendrás hijos? ¿Cuántos?

Empleo

- ¿En qué profesión trabajarás?
- ¿Tendrás tu propia empresa?

Finanzas

- ¿Ganarás mucho dinero?
- ¿Ahorrarás mucho dinero? ¿Lo invertirás?

Termina tu composición con una lista de metas profesionales utilizando el futuro perfecto.

Por ejemplo: **Para el año 2010, habré empezado mi propio negocio. Para el año 2020, habré ganado más dinero que Bill Gates.**

TEACHING OPTIONS

Proofreading Activity Copy on the board or onto a transparency the following items containing mistakes as a proofreading activity to do with the whole class.

1. **¡A las siete! A esa hora teneré sueño. ¿Habré café en la sala de conferencias?**
2. **Ud. recibirá una yamada de parte nuestra, si decidimos ofrecerle el puesto.**
3. **Éste sará un trabajo ideal para mí. Yenaré la solicitud inmediatamente.**
4. **Me sorprendió que tú no llenaste la solicitud antes. Este proyecto le habrás interesado mucho.**
5. **El jefe izo la llamada en cuanto llegó en la oficina.**
6. **Por el año 2020 el banco haberá establecido una oficina el la luna.**

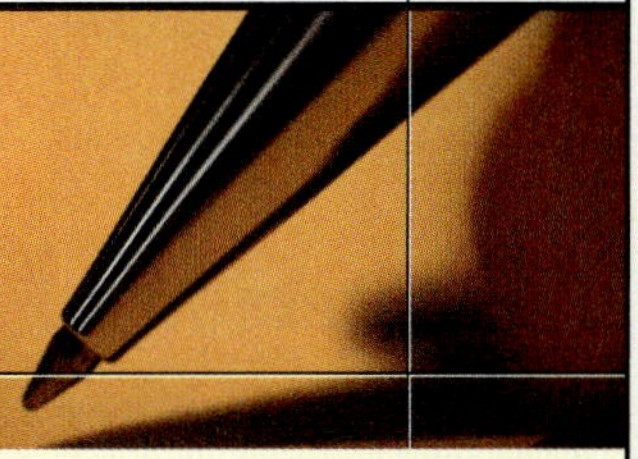

Plan de escritura

1 Ideas y organización

Utiliza unas tarjetas para apuntar tus planes y metas para el futuro. Dedica una tarjeta a cada plan o meta. No te olvides de asignar un año a cada meta.

2 Primer borrador

Utiliza tus apuntes de **Ideas y organización** para escribir el primer borrador de tu composición. Usa el diccionario sólo cómo último recurso.

3 Comentario

Intercambia tu composición con un(a) compañero/a. Lee su borrador y anota los aspectos mejor escritos de su composición. Compartan sus impresiones utilizando esta guía:

a. ¿Habla de metas específicas para su futuro?
b. ¿Ha organizado su información de una manera lógica?
c. ¿Qué sugerencias puedes darle al/a la escritor(a) para organizar mejor su descripción?
d. ¿Ves errores gramaticales u ortográficos?

4 Redacción

Revisa el primer borrador según las indicaciones de tu compañero/a. Antes de escribir tu versión final, revisa tu composición según la siguiente guía:

a. Subraya cada verbo para comprobar el modo y el tiempo. Recuerda que el tema requiere el uso del futuro y del futuro perfecto.
b. Revisa la concordancia entre los sustantivos y los adjetivos en cada oración.
c. Revisa los pronombres para comprobar el uso correcto de cada uno.
d. Consulta tus **Anotaciones para mejorar la escritura** para evitar la repetición de errores previos.

5 Evaluación y progreso

Compartan su trabajo en grupos. Cada estudiante leerá su composición al grupo. Después formulen una cronología con las metas de cada estudiante. Cuando recibas los comentarios y las correcciones de tu profesor(a), anota tus errores en las **Anotaciones para mejorar la escritura** en tu **Carpeta de trabajos.**

metas *goals* cronología *timeline* devuelva *returns*

EVALUATION: Composición

Criteria	Scale
Content	1 2 3 4
Organization	1 2 3 4
Use of vocabulary	1 2 3 4
Accuracy and mechanics	1 2 3 4
Creativity	1 2 3 4

Scoring	
Excellent	18–20 points
Good	14–17 points
Satisfactory	10–13 points
Unsatisfactory	< 10 points

Comentario

Present Go over guide questions **a–d** with the whole class so peer readers understand their task.

Assignment Have students prepare **Redacción** as homework. Ask them to rewrite their drafts, incorporating the peer comments and following the directions in **Redacción**.

Evaluación y progreso Allow sufficient time for students to read their final drafts in groups.

Writing Sample

Here is a sample composition that would constitute superior writing achievement.

MI FUTURO

Después de graduarme, me mudaré a una ciudad grande que esté cerca del mar. Viviré al lado del mar por unos diez años y después me mudaré a un sitio de las montañas.

Estudio biología marina, así que habrá ventajas en vivir al lado del mar. Trabajaré como ecóloga marina porque creo que es importante conservar los océanos, los lagos y los ríos. En cuanto pueda obtener los fondos, estableceré mi propio laboratorio donde puedo dedicarme a cualquier investigación que me interese. Habrá que hacer sacrificios, pero invertiré todo el dinero possible para que pueda jubilarme temprano.

Claro que tendré una familia también. Me casaré con mi mejor amigo. Después de cinco años, adoptaremos a dos niños.

Metas personales:
Para el año 2005, habré trabjado en tres proyectos globales. Para el año 2007, habré escrito un libro de texto sobre la ecología marina.

Para el año 2010, seré conocida como ecóloga famosa y habré conseguido mi propio laboratorio.

Section Goals

In **Escuchar** students will:
- use background knowledge and listen for specific information
- answer questions based on a recorded conversation

Instructional Resource
Student Cassette/CD

Preparación Have students say what they see in the photo.

Estrategia
Script ¿Sufre Ud. de muchas tensiones? Con sólo una semana en el hotel El Retiro, Ud. podrá aliviar su estrés. Venga y disfrute de los espectaculares bosques que lo rodean, las habitaciones modernas y elegantes y las comidas sabrosas preparadas según su dieta. Además de los maravillosos baños térmicos, se ofrecen masajes y sauna. El Retiro queda a 100 km de San José en un lugar que le traerá el descanso y la paz que Ud. necesita. Llame al 451-2356 para recibir más información.

Ahora escucha
Script Sra. Sánchez: Buenos días. Ud. es Rafael Ventura Romero, ¿no? Soy la Sra. Sánchez, la jefa de esta compañía. Siéntese, por favor. **Rafael Ventura:** Buenos días, señora. Estoy muy agradecido de tener esta oportunidad de hablar con Ud. hoy. **S:** Veo aquí que está solicitando el puesto de contador general. ¿Qué preparación tiene Ud.? **V:** En diciembre me gradúo de contador en la Universidad Politécnica de Nicaragua. Durante los últimos tres años he trabajado en Dulces González aquí en Managua como contador durante las vacaciones. Es la carrera que siempre he querido y sé que voy a tener éxito si Ud. me da la oportunidad. **S:** ¿Tiene Ud. algunas referencias? **V:** Sí, señora. El gerente de la empresa donde he trabajado, el señor Héctor Cruz, y también el Profesor Armando Carreño de la Facultad de Contaduría Pública y Finanzas. Los teléfonos y direcciones están apuntados en el currículum. **S:** Muy bien. Este puesto comienza con un salario mensual de 25.812 córdobas. Pagamos quincenal. Después de seis meses tiene la posibilidad de un aumento de sueldo. Ofrecemos beneficios excelentes. El horario es de 8:30 a 12:00 y de 2 a 6. ¿Está interesado? **V:** Estoy sumamente interesado. **S:** Pues, necesito unos días para comunicarme con las personas que Ud. ha dado de referencia. Si todo sale bien, lo llamaré antes del viernes. ¿Cuándo está dispuesto a comenzar a trabajar? Necesito a alguien lo más pronto posible. **V:** No me gradúo hasta el 15 de diciembre. Pero puedo trabajar media jornada por las siguientes 3 semanas hasta la graduación. **S:** Creo que no va a haber ningún problema con eso. Entonces hablamos en unos días. **V:** Muchas gracias por la entrevista, Sra. Sánchez. Estoy muy emocionado por la posibilidad de trabajar en esta gran empresa. Que tenga muy buen día.

Escuchar

NATIONAL communication STANDARDS

Preparación

Mira la foto. ¿De qué crees que van a hablar? Escribe una lista de la información que esperas oír en este tipo de situación.

Estrategia

Using background knowledge/ Listening for specific information

If you know the subject of something you are going to hear, your background knowledge will help you anticipate words and phrases you're going to hear and will help you identify important information that you should listen for. To practice these strategies, you will listen to a radio advertisement for the **Hotel El Retiro**. Before you listen, write down a list of the things you expect the advertisement to contain. Then make another list of important information you would listen for if you were a tourist considering staying at the hotel. After listening to the advertisement, look at your lists again. Did they help you anticipate the content of the advertisement and focus on key information? Explain your answer.

Ahora escucha

Ahora vas a oír una entrevista entre la Sra. Sánchez y Rafael Ventura Ramos. Antes de escuchar la entrevista, haz una lista de la información que esperas oír según tu conocimiento previo del tema.

1. ______
2. ______
3. ______
4. ______

Mientras escuchas la entrevista, llena el formulario con la información necesaria. Si no oyes un dato que necesitas, escribe *Buscar en el currículum*. ¿Oíste toda la información que habías anotado en tu lista?

Comprensión

Puesto solicitado contador
Nombre y apellidos del solicitante Rafael Ventura Romero
Dirección Buscar en el currículum **Tel.** Buscar en el currículum

Educación Universidad Politécnica de Nicaragua
Experiencia profesional: Puesto contado
Empresa Dulces González
¿Cuánto tiempo? 3 años durante las vacaciones de la universidad

Referencias:
Nombre Héctor Cruz
Dirección Buscar en el currículum Tel. Buscar en el currículum
Nombre Prof. Armando Carreño
Dirección Buscar en el currículum Tel. Buscar en el currículum

Preguntas

1. ¿Cuántos años hace que Rafael Ventura trabaja para Dulces González? tres años, durante las vacaciones
2. ¿Cuántas referencias tiene Rafael? dos
3. ¿Dónde trabaja Héctor Cruz? en Dulces González
4. ¿Cuál es la profesión de Armando Carreño? es profesor
5. ¿Cómo sabes si los resultados de la entrevista han sido positivos para Rafael Ventura? Los resultados fueron positivos porque la jefa quiere que él empiece a trabajar antes de que se gradúe.

conocimiento previo *prior knowledge* dato *fact*

communication cultures connections communities NATIONAL STANDARDS

Proyecto

Escribe una cronología de tu carrera

Imagina que en el futuro trabajarás para una empresa multinacional que tiene sus oficinas más importantes en Nicaragua o en la República Dominicana. Vas a crear un plan o una cronología para tu futura carrera profesional.

1 Desarrolla una cronología

Prepara una cronología con texto y fotos de tu futura carrera. Usa los **Recursos para la investigación** para buscar información sobre industrias y compañías que operen en Nicaragua o en la República Dominicana. La cronología puede incluir las siguientes cosas:

- Una descripción de la empresa y sus productos
- Fotos relacionadas con la empresa y sus productos
- Una descripción de tu carrera, desde el comienzo hasta tu jubilación, incluyendo los puestos que vas a tener en la empresa
- Fotos relacionadas con tu carrera

2 Presenta la información

Reúnete con un(a) compañero/a para explicarle tus planes para el porvenir. Usa la cronología que preparaste y muéstrale las fotos para informarle de tus planes para tu vida profesional.

cronología *timeline* **jubilación** *retirement*

recursos para la investigación

Internet Palabras clave: Nicaragua, República Dominicana, empresa, industria, compañía multinacional	**Comunidad** Personas en la comunidad que han trabajado en Centroamérica o en el Caribe
Biblioteca Revistas, periódicos, libros de economía y de comercio	**Otros recursos** Investigar las industrias y empresas principales de Nicaragua y de la República Dominicana

EVALUATION: Cronología

Criteria	Scale
Content	1 2 3 4 5
Organization	1 2 3 4 5
Accuracy	1 2 3 4 5
Creativity	1 2 3 4 5

Scoring	
Excellent	18–20 points
Good	14–17 points
Satisfactory	10–13 points
Unsatisfactory	< 10 points

Section Goals

In **Proyecto** students will:
- use Spanish as they research multinational companies
- develop a career plan or timeline for a position at a multinational company with headquarters in Nicaragua or the Dominican Republic

Before Assigning Proyecto Students will need approximately a week to complete the project, so at the beginning of that time period, have them open their books to page 511 and glance over **Proyecto**. Tell them that they are going to use their Spanish skills as they conduct research on multinational companies with headquarters (**sede**) in Nicaragua or the Dominican Republic. Tell them that when they finish their research, they will develop a career plan from start date to retirement.

Assignment Have students read page 511 and follow directions in **Desarrolla una cronología** to complete their timelines.

Desarrolla una cronología
- Students may wish to interview someone who works for a multinational company and may live in a Spanish-speaking country.
- If possible, provide students with articles or press releases written in Spanish about multinational companies and their products.

Presenta la información You may wish to have students present the time lines as though they were viewing a career history at a retirement party.

Successful Language Learning Tell students they may want to consider study-abroad programs and internship opportunities in Spanish-speaking countries. Ask them if they would feel comfortable doing so, and why.

Section Goals

In **Panorama**, students will read about the history and culture of Nicaragua.

Instructional Resources
Student Activities Manual: Workbook, 193
Transparency 58

Nicaragua

Before Presenting Panorama Have students look at the map of Nicaragua or project **Transparency 58** and talk about the physical features of the country. Point out the concentration of cities along the country's Pacific Coast, and note the sparse settlement in the eastern part of the country and along the Caribbean coast. Remind students that, before the construction of the Panama Canal, Nicaragua was the proposed site for an interoceanic canal.

Assignment Have students read Panorama and answer the questions in **¿Qué aprendiste?** on page 513 as homework.

Present Ask volunteers to read each section of **El país en cifras.** After reading about the country's varied terrain and many volcanoes, tell students that Nicaragua's national slogan is **"El país de lagos y volcanes."** After students read about the capital, ask: **¿Qué porcentaje de los nicaragüenses viven en Managua? (el 20%)** Tell students that one reason so many Nicaraguans live in the capital is due to the devastation experienced in much of the rest of the country over the past two decades due to war and natural disasters, such as Hurricane Mitch in 1998, and earthquakes and volcanic eruptions in 1999.

Increíble pero cierto Lake Nicaragua is the largest lake in Central America. Over 40 rivers drain into the lake.

Nicaragua

NATIONAL STANDARDS connections cultures

Pintada en una pared de Managua

El país en cifras

- **Área:** 129.494 km² (49.998 millas²), *aproximadamente el área de Nueva York*

Nicaragua es el país más grande de América Central. Su terreno es muy variado e incluye bosques tropicales, montañas, sabanas y marismas, además de unos 40 volcanes.

- **Población:** 5.359.000
- **Capital:** Managua—1.020.000

Managua está en una región de una notable inestabilidad geográfica, con muchos volcanes y terremotos. En décadas recientes, los nicaragüenses han decidido que no vale la pena construir rascacielos porque no resisten los terremotos.

- **Ciudades principales:** León—249.000, Masaya—149.000, Granada—113.000

SOURCE: Population Division, UN Secretariat

- **Moneda:** córdoba
- **Idiomas:** español (oficial), misquito, inglés

Bandera de Nicaragua

Nicaragüenses célebres

- Rubén Darío, poeta (1867-1916)
- Violeta Barrios de Chamorro, política y ex-presidenta (1930-)
- Daniel Ortega, político y ex-presidente (1945-)
- Gioconda Belli, poeta (1948-)

Típico hogar misquito en la costa atlántica

Pescador de langostas

recursos

R | WB pp. 193-194 | vistasonline.com

sabanas *grasslands* marismas *marshes* pulgadas *inches* no vale la pena *it's not worthwhile* rascacielos *skyscrapers* esporádicamente *sporadically* fue cercada *was closed off* tiburón *shark* agua dulce *freshwater* bahía *bay* atunes *tuna*

¡Increíble pero cierto!

En el lago Nicaragua está la única especie de tiburón de agua dulce del mundo. Los científicos creen que el lago fue antes una enorme bahía que luego fue cercada por erupciones volcánicas. Esta teoría explicaría la presencia de tiburones, atunes y otras especies de peces que sólo viven en mares y océanos.

TEACHING OPTIONS

Worth Noting Managua is a city that has been destroyed and rebuilt multiple times due to wars and natural disasters. This has contributed to the unusual method used for listing street addresses in this capital city. Many places do not have an address that includes an actual building number and street name. Instead, the address includes a reference to a local landmark, and its relationship to other permanent features of the landscape, such as Lake Nicaragua. Here's a typical Managua address: **De la Clínica Don Bosco, 2 cuadras al norte, 3 y media al sur.** Invite students who have lived in Managua to share other "typical" addresses.

Extra Practice Invite students to compare the romantic poetry of **Rubén Darío** to the contemporary work of **Ernesto Cardenal** and **Gioconda Belli.** Students can choose several poems to read aloud to the class, and then comment on differences in style and content.

Historia • Las huellas de Acahualinca

La región de Managua se caracteriza por tener un gran número de sitios prehistóricos. Las huellas de Acahualinca son uno de los restos más famosos y antiguos. Se formaron hace más de 6.000 años, a orillas del Lago Managua. Las huellas, tanto de humanos como de animales, se dirigen hacia una misma dirección, lo que ha hecho pensar a los expertos que éstos corrían hacia el lago para escapar de una erupción volcánica.

Artes • Ernesto Cardenal (1925-)

Ernesto Cardenal, poeta, escultor y sacerdote católico, es uno de los escritores más famosos de Nicaragua, país conocido por ser tierra de grandes poetas. Ha escrito más de 35 libros y se le considera uno de los principales autores de América Latina. Desde joven creyó en el poder de la poesía para mejorar la sociedad, y trabajó por establecer la igualdad y la justicia en su país. En los años 60, Cardenal estableció la comunidad artística del Archipiélago Solentiname en el Lago Nicaragua. Fue ministro de cultura del país desde 1979 hasta 1988 y también ha servido como vicepresidente de Casa de los Tres Mundos, una organización creada para el intercambio cultural.

Naturaleza • El Lago Nicaragua

El Lago Nicaragua, con un área de más de 8.000 km^2 (3.100 $millas^2$), es el segundo más grande de América Latina. Dentro del lago hay numerosas islas, formadas por las erupciones del volcán Mombacho. La Isla Zapatera, casi deshabitada ahora, fue un cementerio indígena donde todavía se encuentran estatuas prehistóricas que parecen representar dioses. En el lago se encuentran muchos peces exóticos y también más de 370 islas.

¿Qué aprendiste? Responde a las preguntas con una frase completa.

1. ¿Por qué no hay muchos rascacielos en Managua?
   No hay muchos rascacielos en Managua porque no resisten los terremotos.
2. Nombra dos ex-presidentes de Nicaragua.
   Violeta Barrios de Chamorro y Daniel Ortega son dos ex-presidentes de Nicaragua.
3. ¿Qué especie única vive en el Lago Nicaragua?
   La única especie de tiburón de agua dulce vive en el Lago Nicaragua.
4. ¿Cuál es una teoría sobre la formación de las huellas de Acahualinca?
   Una teoría dice que las personas y los animales corrían para escapar del volcán.
5. ¿Por qué es famoso el Archipiélago de Solentiname?
   El Archipiélago de Solentiname es famoso porque es el sitio de la comunidad artística establecida por Cardenal.
6. ¿Qué cree Ernesto Cardenal acerca de la poesía?
   Cardenal cree que la poesía puede mejorar la sociedad.
7. ¿Cómo se formaron las islas del Lago Nicaragua?
   Las islas se formaron por erupciones volcánicas.
8. ¿Qué hay de interés arqueológico en la Isla Zapatera?
   En la Isla Zapatera había un cementerio con estatuas prehistóricas.

Conexión Internet Investiga estos temas en el sitio **www.vistasonline.com.**

1. ¿Dónde se habla inglés en Nicaragua y por qué?
2. ¿Qué información hay ahora sobre la economía y/o los derechos humanos en Nicaragua?

pintada *political graffiti* huellas *footprints* restos *remains* antiguos *ancient* orillas *shores* se dirigen *are headed* sacerdote *priest*

La huellas de Acahualinca The **huellas de Acahualinca** were preserved in soft mud that was then covered with volcanic ash which became petrified, preserving the prints of bison, otter, deer, lizards, and birds—as well as humans.

Ernesto Cardenal After completing undergraduate studies in Nicaragua, **Ernesto Cardenal** studied in Mexico and in the United States, where he studied with religious poet Thomas Merton at the Trappist seminary in Kentucky. He later studied theology in Colombia, and was ordained in Nicaragua in 1965. It was shortly after that he founded the faith-based community of artists on **Solentiname** in **Lake Nicaragua.**

El Lago Nicaragua Environmental groups in Nicaragua have been concerned about the recent introduction of a variety of **tilapia** into Lake Nicaragua. Although **tilapia** are native to the lake, this variety is a more prolific species. Environmentalists are concerned that the Nicaraguan-Norwegian joint venture responsible for this initiative has not done an adequate environmental impact study, and that the delicate and unique ecology of the lake may be negatively impacted.

¿Qué aprendiste? Go over the questions and answers with students, making sure everyone understands unfamiliar words and what the correct answers are.

Assignment Have students do activites in **Student Activities Manual: Workbook,** page 193.

Conexión Internet Students will find more information about Nicaragua at **www.vistasonline.com.**

TEACHING OPTIONS

Worth Noting On July 19, 1979, the FSLN (Frente Sandinista de Liberación Nacional), known as the Sandinistas, came to power in Nicaragua after winning a revolutionary struggle against the dictatorship of Anastasio Somoza. The Sandinistas began a program of economic and social reform that threatened the power of Nicaragua's traditional elite, leading to a civil war known as the **Contra** war. The United States became enmeshed in this conflict, illegally providing fundings and arms to the **Contras**, who fought to oust the Sandinistas. The Sandinistas were ultimately voted out of power in 1990, and the country is now led by anti-communist president Arnoldo Alemán, elected in 1997.

Section Goals

In **Panorama**, students will read about the geography and culture of the Dominican Republic.

Instructional Resources
Student Activities Manual: Workbook, 194
Transparency 59

La República Dominicana

Before Presenting Panorama Have students look at the map of the Dominican Republic or project **Transparency 59** and talk about the physical features of the country. Ask students to note that the majority of cities are located along the coast or close to it, and that there are few cities in the center of the island. Point out that there are rugged mountains through the center of the country, with fertile valleys interspersed.

Assignment Have students read **Panorama** and write out the completed questions and anwers in **¿Qué aprendiste?** on page 515 as homework.

Present Ask volunteers to read each section of **El país en cifras.** After reading **Población**, point out to students that the neighboring country of Haiti is one of the poorest in Latin America and the Caribbean. Ask students to speculate about how that might impact the Dominican Republic. After reading **Idiomas**, the information that French Creole is widely spoken should confirm that there is a major Haitian presence in the Dominican Republic.

Increíble pero cierto The actual whereabouts of the remains of Christopher Columbus are a matter of dispute. While Santo Domingo claims to house them, the navigator died in Spain and there is an elaborate tomb said to be his in the Cathedral of Seville, the city from which his tiny fleet set sail.

La República Dominicana

El país en cifras

- **Área:** 48.730 km² (18.815 millas²), *el área combinada de New Hampshire y Vermont*
- **Población:** 8.752.000

La isla La Española, llamada así tras el primer viaje de Cristóbal Colón, estuvo bajo el completo dominio de la corona española hasta 1697, cuando la parte oeste de la isla pasó a ser propiedad francesa. Hoy día está dividida políticamente en dos países, La República Dominicana en la zona este y Haití en el oeste.

SOURCE: Population Division, UN Secretariat

- **Capital:** Santo Domingo—3.760.000

La mitad de la población de la República Dominicana vive en la capital.

- **Ciudades principales:** Santiago de los Caballeros—1.632.000, La Vega—335.000, Puerto Plata—255.000, San Pedro de Macorís—213.000
- **Moneda:** peso dominicano
- **Idiomas:** español (oficial), francés criollo

Bandera de la República Dominicana

Dominicanos célebres

- **Juan Pablo Duarte,** político y padre de la patria (1808-1876)
- **Celeste Woss y Gil,** pintora (1891-1985)
- **Juan Luis Guerra,** compositor y cantante de merengue (1956-)
- **Sammy Sosa,** beisbolista (1968-)

tras *after* corona *crown* propiedad *property* criollo *creole* mitad *half* padre de la patria *founding father* fortaleza *fortress* se construyó *was built* naufragó *wrecked* enterrado *buried*

Hombres tocando los palos en una misa en Noche Buena

Catedral de Santa María la Menor

Trabajadores del campo recogen la cosecha de ajos

recursos

R | WB pp. 193-194 | vistasonline.com

¡Increíble pero cierto!

La primera fortaleza del Nuevo Mundo se construyó en la República Dominicana en 1492 cuando la Santa María, uno de los tres barcos de Cristóbal Colón, naufragó allí. Aunque la fortaleza, hecha con los restos del barco, fue destruida por tribus indígenas, el amor de Colón por la isla nunca murió. Colón insistió en ser enterrado allí.

TEACHING OPTIONS

Variación léxica Although the Arawak and Taíno people who were indigenous to Hispaniola were virtually eliminated following the European conquest, Caribbean Spanish continues to be marked by lexical items contributed by these cultures. Invite students to learn the meaning of these words of Native American origin that have entered Spanish: **ají, cacique, canoa, hamaca, huracán** (chili pepper, political leader, canoe, hammock, hurricane).

Extra Practice Bring in recordings by **Juan Luis Guerra,** such as his 1998 release **Ni es lo mismo ni es igual.** Invite students to follow the printed lyrics as they listen to a track such as "**Mi PC**". Then, have students work together to create an English translation of the song.

Ciudades • Santo Domingo

La zona colonial de Santo Domingo, fundada en 1496, posee algunas de las construcciones más antiguas del hemisferio. La arquitectura de la ciudad es famosa no sólo por su belleza sino también por el buen estado de sus edificios, gracias a las restauraciones. Entre sus sitios más visitados se cuentan la Calle de las Damas, llamada así porque allí paseaban las señoras de la corte del Virrey; el Alcázar de Colón, un palacio construido por Diego Colón, hijo de Cristóbal, en 1509; y la Fortaleza Ozama, la más vieja de las Américas, construida en 1503.

Deportes • El béisbol

El béisbol es un deporte muy practicado en el Caribe. Los primeros países hispanos en tener una liga fueron Cuba y México, donde se empezó a jugar al béisbol en el siglo XIX. Hoy día este deporte es una afición nacional en la República Dominicana. Sammy Sosa, Pedro Martínez y Manny Ramírez son sólo tres de los muchísimos beisbolistas dominicanos que han alcanzado enorme éxito e inmensa popularidad entre los aficionados.

Artes • El merengue

El merengue, una música para bailar originaria de la República Dominicana, tiene sus raíces en el campo. Tradicionalmente, las canciones hablaban de los problemas sociales de los campesinos. Sus instrumentos eran el acordeón, el saxofón, el bajo, el guayano y la tambora, un tambor característico del lugar. Entre 1930 y 1960, el merengue se popularizó en las ciudades y adoptó un tono más urbano. En este período empezaron a formarse grandes orquestas. Uno de los cantantes más famosos y que más ha ayudado a internacionalizar esta música es Juan Luis Guerra.

¿Qué aprendiste? Responde a las preguntas con una frase completa.

1. Aproximadamente ¿qué porcentaje de la población vive en la capital?
   Aproximadamente el 50 por ciento de la población vive en la capital.
2. ¿Cuándo se fundó la ciudad de Santo Domingo?
   Santo Domingo se fundó en 1496.
3. ¿Qué es el Alcázar de Colón?
   El Alcázar de Colón es un palacio construido por Diego Colón, hijo de Cristóbal, en 1509.
4. Nombra tres beisbolistas famosos de la República Dominicana.
   Tres beisbolistas famosos de La República Dominicana son Sammy Sosa, Pedro Martínez y Manny Ramírez.
5. ¿De qué hablaban las canciones de merengue tradicionales?
   Las canciones de merengue tradicionales hablaban de los problemas sociales de los campesinos.
6. ¿Qué instrumentos se utilizaban para tocar (*play*) el merengue?
   Se utilizaban el acordeón, el saxofón, el bajo, el guayano, la tambora y el piano.
7. ¿Cuándo se transformó el merengue en un estilo urbano?
   El merengue se transformó en un estilo urbano entre los años 30 y 1960.
8. ¿Qué cantante ha ayudado a internacionalizar el merengue?
   Juan Luis Guerra ha ayudado a internacionalizar el merengue.

Conexión Internet Investiga estos temas en el sitio **www.vistasonline.com**.

1. Busca más información sobre la isla La Española. ¿Cómo son las relaciones entre la República Dominicana y Haití?
2. Busca más información sobre la zona colonial de Santo Domingo: la Catedral de Santa María, la Casa de Bastidas o el Panteón Nacional. ¿Cómo son estos edificios? ¿Te gustan? Explica tus respuestas.

posee *has* restauraciones *restorations* se cuentan *are included* siglo *century* afición *love* han alcanzado *reached* raíces *roots* campesinos *rural people* bajo *bass* guayano *metal scraper* tambor *drum*

TEACHING OPTIONS

Worth Noting Students may enjoy learning more about Latin American baseball. They can find out about the Dominican Republic's professional league at www.beisboldominicano.com. They can check out reports of Caribbean League baseball games on the Internet, with accounts of games by Dominican, Cuban, Venezuelan, and other teams. Encourage students to create a bilingual dictionary of baseball terms such as **jardinero, jardín, cuadrangular, jonrón, bateo, pitcheo, anotar carreras, ponchar, la goma, montículo** and so forth. Encourage sports fans to help you identify Latin Americans currently playing in the Major Leagues.

Santo Domingo UNESCO has declared Santo Domingo a World Heritage site because of the abundance of historical architecture. Efforts are being made to restore buildings to their original grandeur, and to "correct" restorations made in the past that were not true to original architectural styles.

El bésibol Like many other Dominicans, Sammy Sosa's first baseball glove was a milk carton, his bat was a stick, and the ball was a rolled-up sock wound with tape. Sosa has not forgotten the difficult conditions experienced by most Dominicans. After a devastating hurricane swept the island, Sosa's charitable foundation raised $700,000 for reconstruction.

El merengue The **merengue** synthesizes elements of the cultures that make up the Dominican Republic's heritage. The gourd scraper—or **güiro**—comes from the Arawak people, the **tambora**—a drum unique to the Dominican Republic— is part of the nation's African legacy, the stringed instruments were adapted from the Spanish guitar, and the accordion was introduced by German merchants. Once students hear this quick-paced music, they will understand how it came to be named after meringue—a dessert made by furiously beating egg whites!

¿Qué aprendiste? Go over the questions and answers with the whole class.

Assignment Have students do activites in Student Activities Manual: Workbook, page 194.

Conexión Internet Students will find more information about the Dominican Republic at **www.vistasonline.com.**

Ocupaciones

el/la abogado/a	*lawyer*
el actor, la actriz	*actor*
el/la arqueólogo/a	*archaeologist*
el/la arquitecto/a	*architect*
el/la bombero/a	*firefighter*
el/la carpintero/a	*carpenter*
el/la científico/a	*scientist*
el/la cocinero/a	*cook; chef*
el/la consejero/a	*counselor; advisor*
el/la contador(a)	*accountant*
el/la corredor(a) de bolsa	*stockbroker*
el/la diseñador(a)	*designer*
el/la electricista	*electrician*
el hombre/la mujer de negocios	*businessperson*
el/la maestro/a	*elementary school teacher*
el/la peluquero/a	*hairdresser*
el/la pintor(a)	*painter*
el/la político/a	*politician*
el/la psicólogo/a	*psychologist*
el/la reportero/a	*reporter; journalist*
el/la secretario/a	*secretary*
el/la técnico/a	*technician*

El mundo del trabajo

el ascenso	*promotion*
el aumento de sueldo	*raise*
la carrera	*career*
la compañía, la empresa	*company; firm*
el empleo	*job; employment*
la especialización	*field of study*
el/la gerente	*manager*
el/la jefe/a	*boss*
los negocios	*business; commerce*
la ocupación	*occupation*
el oficio	*trade*
la profesión	*profession*
la reunión	*meeting*
el teletrabajo	*telecommuting*
el trabajo	*job; work*
la videoconferencia	*videoconference*
dejar	*to quit; to leave behind*
despedir (e:i, i)	*to fire*
invertir (e:ie, i)	*to invest*
renunciar (a)	*to resign (from)*
tener éxito	*to be successful*

Entrevistas

el anuncio	*advertisement*
el/la aspirante	*candidate; applicant*
los beneficios	*benefits*
el currículum	*résumé*
la entrevista	*interview*
el/la entrevistador(a)	*interviewer*
el puesto	*position; job*
el salario, el sueldo	*salary*
la solicitud (de trabajo)	*(job) application*
contratar	*to hire*
entrevistar	*to interview*
ganar	*to earn*
obtener (*irreg.*)	*to obtain; to get*
solicitar	*to apply (for a job)*

Palabras adicionales

dentro de (diez años)	*within (ten years)*
en el futuro	*in the future*
el porvenir	*the future*
próximo/a	*next*

Expresiones útiles

Expresiones útiles	*See page 493.*

Un festival de arte 17

Communicative Goals

You will learn how to:

- Talk about and discuss the arts.
- Express what you would like to do.
- Express hesitation.

Lesson Goals

In **Lesson 17** students will be introduced to the following:

- fine arts terms
- vocabulary for television and film
- conditional tense
- conditional perfect tense
- past perfect subjunctive tense
- summarizing a text in their own words
- finding biographical information
- writing a composition
- listening for key words and using context
- writing a report on Salvadoran and Honduran artists
- cultural and geographic information about El Salvador
- cultural, economic, and historical information about Honduras

Lesson Preview

Have students look at the photo. Say: **En la foto el joven toca la guitarra.** Then ask: **¿Al joven le gusta la música? ¿Qué tipo de música le gustará? ¿Tocan Uds. instrumentos?**

INSTRUCTIONAL RESOURCES

Student Activities Manual: Workbook, 195–204
Student Activities Manual: Lab Manual, 317–321
Student Activities Manual: Video Activities, 359–360
Instructor's Resource Manual: Hojas de actividades, 40–43
Instructor's Resource Manual: Answer Keys
Tapescript/Videoscript
Overhead Transparencies, 60–62
Student Cassette/CD
Lab Cassette/CD
Video Program
CD-ROM
Website: **www.vistasonline.com**
Testing Program: Prueba A, Prueba B

Section Goals

In **Contextos**, students will learn vocabulary related to
- fine arts
- television and film

Instructional Resources
Student Activities Manual: Workbook, 195–196; Lab Manual, 317
Hoja de actividades 40
Transparency 60
Student Cassette/CD

Before Presenting Contextos Begin a conversation by telling the class about some of your favorite artists and why you like them. Write unfamiliar vocabulary on the board as you use it. Ex: **¿Tienen Uds. un pintor favorito? Para mí, Pablo Picasso me fascina. Pintó de una manera muy original.** and so forth. Be sure to mention singers, bands, and actors in the conversation. Tell students that they are going to learn vocabulary related to the arts.

Assignment Have students study **Contextos** and do the exercises on pages 519–520 as homework.

Present Project **Transparency 60**. Point to an object or person on the transparency and ask students to name it. When you point to a person, ask what he or she is doing. As you go through the items depicted ask students about their opinions and feelings, eliciting the words in **Más vocabulario**. Ex: **¿Saben cuánto costó un boleto al último concierto de U2? Me escandalizó al saberlo, pero lo pagué. ¿Cuánto pagaría tu por una entrada, ____?** and so forth. Also ask students who are studying the arts about their opinions. Ex: ____, **estudias el baile, ¿no? Para tí, ¿qué es la fascinación del baile? Tienes que practicar muchísimo, ¿no?**

Un festival de arte

Más vocabulario

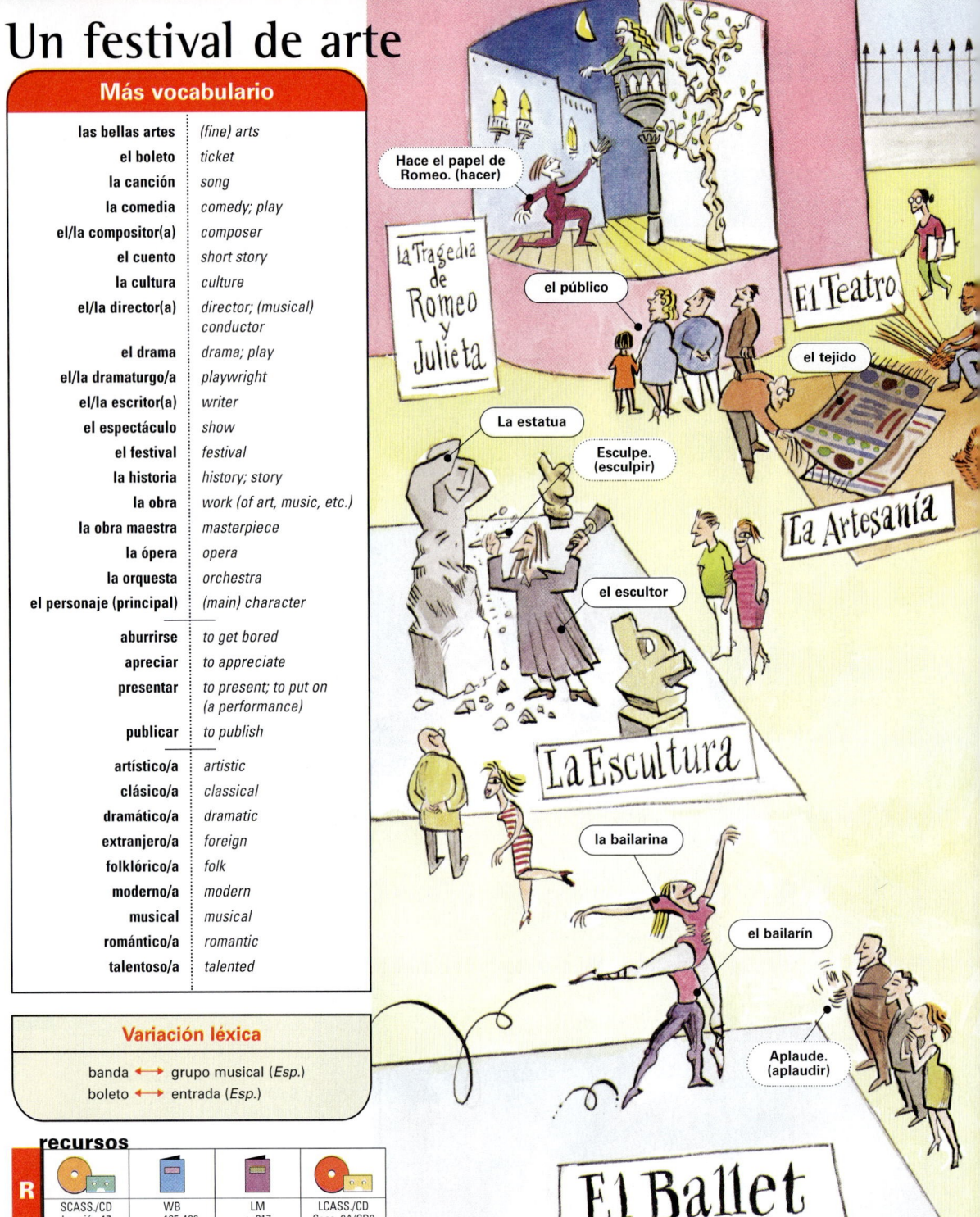

las bellas artes	*(fine) arts*
el boleto	*ticket*
la canción	*song*
la comedia	*comedy; play*
el/la compositor(a)	*composer*
el cuento	*short story*
la cultura	*culture*
el/la director(a)	*director; (musical) conductor*
el drama	*drama; play*
el/la dramaturgo/a	*playwright*
el/la escritor(a)	*writer*
el espectáculo	*show*
el festival	*festival*
la historia	*history; story*
la obra	*work (of art, music, etc.)*
la obra maestra	*masterpiece*
la ópera	*opera*
la orquesta	*orchestra*
el personaje (principal)	*(main) character*
aburrirse	*to get bored*
apreciar	*to appreciate*
presentar	*to present; to put on (a performance)*
publicar	*to publish*
artístico/a	*artistic*
clásico/a	*classical*
dramático/a	*dramatic*
extranjero/a	*foreign*
folklórico/a	*folk*
moderno/a	*modern*
musical	*musical*
romántico/a	*romantic*
talentoso/a	*talented*

Variación léxica

banda ⟷ grupo musical (*Esp.*)
boleto ⟷ entrada (*Esp.*)

recursos

R	SCASS./CD Lección 17	WB pp. 195-196	LM p. 317	LCASS./CD Cass. 9A/CD9

TEACHING OPTIONS

Variación Léxica Tell students that, as well as **boleto** and **entrada**, they may also hear the word **billete** used to name a ticket for admission to a concert or museum. The ticket window where you buy your ticket is called **taquilla** in Spain, while in most of Latin America it is called the **boletería**.

Extra Practice Have students finish your statements with the vocabulary words from **Un festival de arte**. Ex: **Miguel Ángel esculpió muchas ____ importantes. *Carmen* es una ____ de Georges Bizet. Federico García Lorca es el ____ que escribió *Romancero gitano*.** and so forth.

Práctica

1 **Escuchar** Escucha la conversación y contesta las preguntas.

1. ¿Adónde fueron Ricardo y Juanita?
   Ellos fueron a un festival de arte.
2. ¿Cuál fue el espectáculo que más le gustó a Ricardo?
   Le gustó más la tragedia de Romeo y Julieta.
3. ¿Qué le gustó más a Juanita?
   A Juanita le gustó la banda.
4. ¿Qué dijo Ricardo del actor?
   Ricardo dijo que él era excelente.
5. ¿Qué dijo Juanita del actor?
   Ella dijo que él era guapo.
6. ¿Qué compró Juanita en el festival?
   Ella compró un disco compacto.
7. ¿Qué compró Ricardo?
   Ricardo compró dos libros de poesía.
8. ¿Qué poetas le interesaron a Ricardo?
   A Ricardo le interesaron Claribel Alegría y Roque Dalton.

2 **¿Cierto o falso?** Indica si lo que se afirma en las siguientes oraciones es **cierto** o **falso.**

	Cierto	Falso
1. Las bellas artes incluyen la pintura, la escultura, la música, el baile y el drama.	✓	○
2. Un boleto es un tipo de instrumento musical que se usa mucho en las óperas.	○	✓
3. El tejido es un tipo de música.	○	✓
4. La comedia es un tipo de orquesta.	○	✓
5. "Hacer un papel" quiere decir usar materiales como papel y pinturas de muchos colores.	○	✓
6. Un cuento es una narración corta que puede ser oral o escrita.	✓	○
7. Una obra maestra es un ejemplo del mejor trabajo de un(a) artista.	✓	○
8. Un compositor es el personaje principal de una obra de teatro.	○	✓
9. Publicar es la acción de hablar al público en grandes grupos.	○	✓
10. Los personajes principales de una ópera cantan.	✓	○

3 **Artistas** Indica la especialidad de cada uno de estos artistas.

1. Antonio Banderas actor
2. Frida Kahlo pintora
3. Gloria Estefan cantante
4. Octavio Paz poeta, escritor
5. William Shakespeare dramaturgo, poeta
6. Miguel de Cervantes escritor
7. Joan Miró pintor, escultor
8. Leonard Bernstein compositor
9. Toni Morrison escritora
10. Mikhail Baryshnikov bailarín

1 Warm-up Remind students to read the questions before listening to the audio. This will help them to know what information to listen for.

1 Present Check answers orally with the class.

Tapescript
Juanita: Me encantó el festival de arte. Fue maravilloso, ¿verdad, Ricardo?
Ricardo: Sí. Me divertí mucho.
J: ¿Qué espectáculo te gustó más?
R: Pues, pienso que me gustó más la tragedia de *Romeo y Julieta.* El actor que hizo el papel principal fue excelente.
J: Y guapo.
R: Supongo que sí. Y tú, Juanita, ¿cuál fue tu favorito?
J: Sin duda alguna la banda. La cantante era magnífica.
R: Sí. Y los músicos tocaron con mucha pasión. Después, vendieron discos compactos. ¿Compraste uno?
J: Sí. Y tú, ¿compraste algo?
R: Sí, compré dos libros de poesía. Uno es de Claribel Alegría y el otro es de Roque Dalton.
J: Bueno, espero que el festival regrese el próximo año.
R: ¡Ojalá!
Student Cassette/CD

2 Present Ask volunteers to read each statement and say whether it is true or false. Have them correct any false statements.

2 Expand Ask students to write 6 more statements, three true and three false. Have students read their statements to a partner who decides which are true or false.

3 Expand After students have stated the profession of each person, ask them if they know the name of one of their works.

TEACHING OPTIONS

Heritage Speakers Have Spanish speakers choose a Hispanic artist and research his or her life and works. Have students then present their findings in a short oral report. If the subject works in a visual medium, encourage the speaker to bring reproductions of his or her work, if possible.

TPR Play a game of charades. Ask volunteers to choose a vocabulary word. Students act out the word for the class to guess.

Large Groups Write the names of well known artists on sticky notes and attach them to the backs of students, who then circulate around the room asking their classmates yes/no questions to determine their identity. Ex: **¿Soy escritor? ¿Escribo comedias? ¿Escribo novelas?**

4 Warm-up Use information about programing in your area to introduce vocabulary by talking and asking questions about today's programs. Ex: **En el canal 5, la programación del día comienza con los dibujos animados. A las 2 de la tarde, habrá la telenovela *En carne viva* con María Conchita Alonzo. ¡Qué lástima que no la puedo ver! Tengo una clase a esta hora. ¿Alguien de Uds. mira *En carne viva*? A las 2, hay un programa de entrevistas muy famoso, *Oprah*.**

4 Present Read the **Modelo** aloud, correcting it if necessary. Then ask individuals each of the items. Since answers will vary, be sure to ask more than one student to respond to each item. Express your reactions to students' opinions.

4 Suggestion You might make the activity more humorous by asking the class to respond to their classmates' preferences with thumbs up or thumbs down.

5 Present You may either call on volunteers to read the completed sentences orally to the class or have pairs of students work together to correct each other's sentences.

6 Present Ask students to explain the relationship between the first set of words. Then, have them share their answers for the second set.

6 Expand Ask students if they can think of any other words that belong to the same "family" for these word sets:
pintura ↔ pintor (pintar)
• **cantante ↔ cantar (canción)**
• **drama ↔ dramaturgo (dramático/a)**
• **escultor ↔ escultura (esculpir)**

4 **Mis gustos** Da un ejemplo de cada tipo de programa. Comparte tus ejemplos con la clase. Answers will vary.

modelo
una película musical
Mi película musical favorita es Brigadoon.

1. una película de ciencia ficción ______
2. un programa de entrevistas ______
3. una telenovela ______
4. una película de horror ______
5. una película de acción ______
6. un concurso ______
7. una película de vaqueros ______
8. una película de aventuras ______
9. un documental ______
10. un programa de dibujos animados ______

El cine y la televisión

el canal	*channel*
el concurso	*game show; contest*
los dibujos animados	*cartoons*
el documental	*documentary*
la estrella (*m., f.*) de cine	*movie star*
el premio	*prize; award*
el programa de entrevistas	*talk show*
la telenovela	*soap opera*
...de acción	*action*
...de aventuras	*adventure*
...de ciencia ficción	*science fiction*
...de horror	*horror*
...de vaqueros	*western*

5 **Completar** Completa las siguientes frases con las palabras adecuadas.

artística	musical	canal	extranjera
estrella	de vaqueros	aburrirse	folklórica
talentosa	aplauden	director	romántica

1. Una película que fue hecha en otro país es una película... extranjera.
2. Si las personas que asisten a un espectáculo lo aprecian, ellos... aplauden.
3. Una persona que puede hacer muchas cosas muy bien es una persona... talentosa.
4. Una película que trata del amor y de las emociones es una película... romántica.
5. Una persona que pinta, esculpe y/o hace artesanía es una persona... artística.
6. La música que refleja la historia de una región o de un país es música... folklórica.
7. Si la acción tiene lugar en el oeste de los EE.UU. durante los años 1800 probablemente es una película... de vaqueros.
8. Una obra en la cual los actores presentan la historia por medio de (*by means of*) canciones y bailes es un drama... musical.
9. Cuando una película no tiene una buena historia el público empieza a... aburrirse.
10. Si quieres ver un programa de televisión diferente, es necesario que cambies de... canal.

¡ATENCIÓN!

Apreciar means *to appreciate* only in the sense of *to enjoy*, not in the sense of *to be thankful for*. To express this meaning **agradecer** is used.

Le **agradezco** mucho su ayuda.
I thank you for your help.

6 **Analogías** Completa las analogías con las palabras adecuadas.

1. alegre ↔ triste = comedia ↔ tragedia
2. escultor ↔ escultora = bailarín ↔ bailarina
3. drama ↔ dramaturgo = pintura ↔ pintor
4. *Los Simpson* ↔ dibujos animados = *Jeopardy* ↔ concurso
5. de entrevistas ↔ programa = de vaqueros ↔ película
6. aplaudir ↔ público = hacer el papel ↔ actor/actriz
7. poema ↔ literatura = tejido ↔ artesanía
8. músico ↔ tocar = cantante ↔ cantar

¡LENGUA VIVA!

Remember that last names are never pluralized; instead, **los** is used with the name.

Los Simpson
The Simpsons

TEACHING OPTIONS

Game Divide the class into two teams. Have each team list a work that fits each of the nine categories in **El cine y la televisión** (i.e. **dibujos animados, documental, película/programa de acción** and so forth). The first member of Team A calls out a work from his team's list. Ex: **la película *Braveheart*.** The first member of Team B must name its category. Ex: **una película de acción.** Next, the second member of Team B calls out a work and the second member of Team A must name its category. Continue until all eighteen works have been mentioned. The team with the most correct answers wins.

Small Groups Have groups of three role-play a situation in which there is only one television and no one can agree on which shows to watch. Students should discuss what shows are on that night, which are better and why, and so forth.

Comunicación

NATIONAL communication STANDARDS

7 **Encuesta** Tu profesor(a) te dará una hoja de actividades. Pregúntales a tus compañeros/as de clase si han participado en las actividades culturales que se mencionan en la lista. Answers will vary.

Actividades	Número de estudiantes
1. Asistir a un concierto de música clásica	
2. Asistir a la ópera	
3. Hacer un papel en un drama	
4. Hacer cerámica	
5. Tocar un instrumento	
6. Esculpir estatuas u otras cosas	
7. Componer (to compose) una canción	
8. Recibir un premio por sus obras de arte	
9. Escribir un poema o un cuento	
10. Bailar en un ballet	

8 **Preguntas** Contesta las siguientes preguntas sobre el arte en tu vida. Comparte tus respuestas con un(a) compañero/a. Answers will vary.

La música

1. ¿Qué tipo de música prefieres? ¿Por qué?
2. ¿Con qué frecuencia la escuchas y en qué situaciones y/o lugares?
3. ¿Tocas un instrumento? ¿Cuál?
4. ¿Qué instrumento quisieras aprender a tocar?

El cine

5. ¿Con qué frecuencia vas al cine?
6. ¿Qué tipos de películas prefieres?
7. ¿Qué opinión tienes del papel de las películas en nuestra sociedad?

Las bellas artes

8. ¿Qué haces que se puede considerar artístico? ¿Pintas, dibujas, esculpes, haces artesanías, haces papeles en dramas, tocas un instrumento, cantas o escribes?
9. ¿Con qué frecuencia vas a un museo de arte o asistes a conciertos, al teatro o a lecturas públicas de poesía?
10. ¿Es el arte una parte importante de tu vida? ¿Por qué?

9 **Programa** Trabajen en grupos pequeños para crear un programa de televisión o un corto (*short film*) para el canal de televisión de la universidad. Answers will vary.

- Primero decidan el género y el propósito del programa o del corto. Cada grupo debe escoger un género distinto. Algunos de los géneros posibles: documental, concurso, programa de entrevistas, película de acción.
- Después escriban el programa o el corto y preséntenlo a la clase.

AYUDA

género *genre*
propósito *purpose*

TEACHING OPTIONS

Pairs Have pairs of students create a poster advertising an artistic event in the community. Students should use 5–8 vocabulary words in their poster. Then, have students exchange their posters with another pair who will talk about the event, one student trying to convince the other to go to the event with him or her and the other resisting.

Extra Practice Ask students to imagine that they've just returned from an arts festival. Have them write a paragraph consisting of at eight to ten sentences describing what they did, saw, and heard. Students should use as many vocabulary words as possible in their paragraphs. Have students exchange their papers for peer editing.

7 Warm-up Briefly review past participles and how to form the present perfect tense.

7 Present Distribute copies of **Hoja de actividades 40**. Have students read the items and form corresponding questions. Then allow ten minutes for students to circulate and ask questions.

7 Expand Have students create two follow-up questions for each item. Ex: **¿Cómo fue la orquesta? ¿Te gustó la selección de música?** Ask students to interview 2–3 of their classmates again, asking their follow-up questions when applicable.

8 Warm-up Ask students to read the questions silently to themselves and think about the answers they would give.

8 Present Allow pairs ten minutes to ask and answer questions. Ask each partner to take notes as the other partner answers a question. Then, have students select one category and summarize their partners' responses. Students read the summaries to their partners to check for accuracy before turning them in.

9 Warm-up Introduce the terms **género** and **propósito** in **Ayuda**.

9 Present Have students work as a group to write an outline. Then have students divide up the scenes to be written. Students should make sure that each person has about the same number of lines. When they have finished their drafts students should exchange scenes for peer editing. Next, the group puts all the scenes together, making any final corrections. Finally, students rehearse and present their program or film to the class.

Assignment Have students do **Student Activities Manual: Workbook**, 195–196.

Section goals

In **Fotonovela** students will:

- receive comprehensible input from free-flowing discourse
- learn functional phrases that preview lesson grammatical structures

Instructional Resources
Student Activities Manual: Video Activities 359–360
Video Program (Start 01:35:56)

Video Synopsis Outside the theater, Álex and Maite chat about their artistic interests. After the theater performance, Álex and Maite return to the house. Javier and Inés catch them in the middle of a romantic moment.

Before Presenting Fotonovela Have your students predict the plot of this **Fotonovela** episode, based on its title and the video stills. Write down their predictions.

Assignment Have students study **Fotonovela** and **Expresiones útiles** as homework.

Warm-up Quickly review the predictions your students made about the **Fotonovela**. Through discussion, help the class summarize the plot.

Present Work through the active vocabulary in **Expresiones útiles** by pronouncing each phrase or expression and having the class repeat. Then ask students what they would like to be in the future. Ex: **¿Te gustaría ser profesor(a) de español? ¿Qué te gustaría hacer?**

¡Ahí vienen Romeo y Julieta!

NATIONAL STANDARDS communication cultures

Álex y Maite van a ver una obra de teatro.

PERSONAJES

MAITE

ÁLEX

JAVIER

INÉS

ÁLEX Oye, ¿qué clase de películas te gustan? ¿las de acción? ¿las de horror? Para mí las mejores son las de ciencia ficción.

MAITE Eso no me sorprende. Mis películas favoritas son las películas románticas. ¿Pero sabes lo que me fascina?

ÁLEX No. Pero dime, querida, ¿qué es lo que más te fascina?

MAITE La poesía. Ahora estoy leyendo una colección de García Lorca... Es fenomenal...

ÁLEX ¡No me digas! A mí también me gusta la poesía. ¿Conoces a Octavio Paz, el poeta mexicano?

MAITE Pues, claro. Fue Premio Nobel de Literatura en 1990...

MAITE Oye, Álex, ¿te gustaría ser escritor?

ÁLEX Pues, creo que me gustaría ser poeta, pero publicaría todos mis poemas en el Internet. ¿Te gustaría ser poeta?

MAITE Pues, no. Pero sí creo que me gustaría ser cantante. De no ser periodista, habría sido cantante de ópera.

ÁLEX ¿Cantante de ópera? Odio la ópera.

JAVIER Mira, ahí vienen Romeo y Julieta. ¡Míralos qué contentos! Ven conmigo... Vamos a sorprenderlos antes de que abran la puerta.

recursos

R	VIDEO Lección 17	VM pp. 359-360

Pedro Almodóvar

TEACHING OPTIONS

Video Tips General suggestions for using video clips in the classroom can be found on page IAE-13 of the **Instructor's Annotated Edition**.

¡Ahí vienen Romeo y Julieta! Make copies of the script of the **¡Ahí vienen Romeo y Julieta!** segment of this lesson's video module and distribute them to your students. After your students have skimmed the script for the gist, ask them what this segment is about. Next, show the **¡Ahí vienen Romeo y Julieta!** segment and have your students circle all words related to music and the arts. Finally, ask your students to summarize this segment in their own words. You may want to ask a few questions to lead the class toward a correct plot summary.

ÁLEX ¡Uuuuyy! ¡Eres una experta en literatura!

MAITE Sí, leo de todo. Ahora en la mesita de noche tengo una colección de cuentos de Carme Riera, una española que también es periodista. En cuanto la termine te la dejo.

ÁLEX ¡Trato hecho!

Álex y Maite se besan.

JAVIER ¿Qué? ¿Les gustó la obra de teatro?

Expresiones útiles

Accepting an offer

- **¡Trato hecho!**
  You've got a deal!

Talking about things you would like to do

- **¿Te gustaría ser escritor(a)?**
  Would you (fam.) *like to be a writer?*
- **Creo que me gustaría ser poeta/cantante.**
  I think I would like to be a poet/singer.
- **De no ser periodista, habría sido cantante de ópera.**
  If I weren't a journalist I would have been an opera singer.

Hesitating

- **Bueno...**
  Well...
- **Pues...**
  Well...
- **Este...**
  Umm...

Enfoque cultural El cine hispano

El cine hispano siempre se ha distinguido por su excelencia. El español Luis Buñuel fue uno de los primeros directores del cine de vanguardia (*avant-garde*). Su película *El perro andaluz* de 1929 es una obra maestra de este género. Pedro Almodóvar, otro español de gran éxito, consiguió un Oscar en 2000 con su película *Todo sobre mi madre.* En la generación más joven hay directores como el estadounidense de origen mexicano Robert Rodríguez, que ha hecho películas de éxito como *El mariachi* y *Desperado.*

Have the class work in groups of three to read the **Fotonovela** aloud. Each group member should play a different role (Álex, Maite, or Javier). Circulate around the classroom and correct pronunciation problems as needed, focusing on errors that would interfere with comprehension. You may want volunteers to ad-lib this **Fotonovela** episode for the class. See ideas for using the video in **Teaching Options**, page 522.

Comprehension Check Check comprehension of the **Fotonovela** episode by doing Activity 1, **Seleccionar**, page 524, orally with the whole class.

Suggestion Have the class look at frame 6 of the **Fotonovela**. Tell them that **gustaría** and **publicaría** are examples of the conditional tense, which is used to talk about what *would* happen. Draw the attention of the class to frame 7, and explain that **habría sido** is an example of the conditional perfect, which is used to talk about what *would have happened.* Tell your students that they will learn more about these concepts in the upcoming **Estructura** section.

Assignment Have students do activities 2-4 in **Reacciona a la fotonovela**, page 524, as homework.

TEACHING OPTIONS

Enfoque cultural Point out to the class that many Hispanics made significant contributions to the arts in the twentieth century, including Carme Riera (Spanish writer), Camilo José Cela (Spanish writer), Gabriel García Márquez (Colombian writer), Pablo Casals (Spanish cellist), Andrés Segovia (Spanish guitarist), Pablo Picasso (Spanish painter), Federico García Lorca (Spanish poet and playwright), Mario Vargas Llosa (Peruvian writer), Octavio Paz (Mexican writer), Jorge Luis Borges (Argentinian writer), Gabriela Mistral (Chilean poet), Diego Rivera (Mexican painter), and Frida Kahlo (Mexican painter), to name just a few. Ask your students if they know of other Hispanics who have distinguished themselves in the arts. You may want to have your students create posters or prepare presentations about the some of these famous Hispanics.

Reacciona a la fotonovela

1 Warm-Up Have the class work through a few **cierto/falso** items before doing this activity. Ex: **1. A Maite no le gusta la ópera. (Falso) 2. Maite quiere ser actriz. (Falso) 3. A Álex le gustaría publicar poemas en el Internet. (Cierto)**

2 Expand Give these additional items to the class: **7. ¿Has leído las obras de Octavio Paz? Es un escritor fascinante. (Álex) 8. Tengo un libro de cuentos en mi habitación. (Maite) 9. Sí, me gustaría mucho leer ese libro de cuentos. (Álex)**

3 Expand Have your students write definitions in Spanish of the words **exposición, concierto, telenovela, ópera,** and **tragedia**. Have volunteers share their definitions with the class.

4 Possible Response

S1: ¿Qué te gustaría hacer este fin de semana?

S2: Pues, como a mí me gusta la música, creo que me gustaría ver una ópera.

S1: ¡Uy, odio la ópera! Además, es muy caro ir.

S2: Ay, sí, es cierto. Este... ¿te gustaría asistir a un concierto de la orquesta nacional?

S1: Buena idea. Me gusta la música clásica.

S2: Y a ti, ¿qué te gustaría hacer?

S1: Bueno, como me gusta el arte tanto, me gustaría ver una exposición de arte moderno.

S2: ¡Trato hecho!

Reacciona a la fotonovela

1 Seleccionar Selecciona la respuesta correcta.

1. Maite está leyendo ahora a los autores __a__.
   a. Riera y García Lorca b. Octavio Paz y García Lorca c. Octavio Paz y Riera
2. __c__ ganó el Premio Nobel de Literatura en 1990.
   a. García Lorca b. Carme Riera c. Octavio Paz
3. __b__ dice que le gustaría ser poeta, porque le gusta mucho la poesía.
   a. Maite b. Álex c. Javier
4. Si no estudiara periodismo, Maite sería __a__.
   a. cantante de ópera b. escritora de novelas románticas c. poeta
5. "Romeo y Julieta" hace referencia a __c__.
   a. Javier e Inés b. el espectáculo que vieron Álex y Maite c. Álex y Maite

2 Identificar Identifica quién puede decir las siguientes frases.

1. Me encantan los cuentos de Riera. ¿Te interesa leer sus libros? Maite
2. Ya llegaron los románticos. ¿Por qué no los sorprendemos? Javier
3. ¡Parece que sabes muchísimo de poesía y de novelas! Álex
4. Oye, ¿qué tal la obra que vieron? ¿Me la recomiendan o no? Javier
5. Me gusta mucho la ópera. A veces creo que me gustaría cantar profesionalmente. Maite
6. Prefiero las películas de ciencia ficción a las de horror o de acción. Álex

ÁLEX

JAVIER

MAITE

3 Correspondencias ¿A qué eventos culturales asistirán Álex y Maite juntos?

una exposición de cerámica precolombina	un concierto	una ópera
una exposición de pintura española	una telenovela	una tragedia

1. Escucharán música clásica y conocerán a un director muy famoso. un concierto
2. El público aplaudirá mucho a la señora que es soprano. una ópera
3. Como a Inés le gusta la historia, la llevarán a ver esto. una exposición de cerámica precolombina
4. Como a Javier le gustaría ver esto, entonces irán con él. una exposición de pintura española

4 El fin de semana Vas a asistir a dos eventos culturales el próximo fin de semana con un(a) compañero/a de clase. Comenten entre Uds. por qué les gustan o les disgustan algunas de las actividades que van sugiriendo. Escojan al final dos actividades que puedan realizar juntos. Usen las siguientes frases y expresiones en su conversación.

Answers will vary.

- ¿Qué te gustaría ver/hacer este fin de semana?
- ¿Te gustaría asistir a...?
- ¡Trato hecho!
- Este.../Pues.../Bueno...

NATIONAL communication STANDARDS

TEACHING OPTIONS

Small Groups Have your students work in small groups to write a paragraph about the future of Maite's and Álex's relationship. Give your students time to prepare, and ask a few groups to read their paragraphs to the class.

Pairs Have your students chat in pairs about what they would like to do or be in the future and why. Tell them to use **te gustaría** and **me gustaría** if possible. Then ask a few students to summarize what their partners told them.

comparisons NATIONAL STANDARDS

Ortografía

Las trampas ortográficas

Some of the most common spelling mistakes in Spanish occur when two or more words have very similar spellings. This section reviews some of those words.

compro **compró** **hablo** **habló**

There is no accent mark in the **yo** form of **–ar** verbs in the present tense. There is, however, an accent mark in the **él/ella/Ud.** form of **–ar** verbs in the preterite.

este (adjective) **éste** (pronoun) **esté** (verb)

The demonstrative adjectives **esta** and **este** do not have an accent mark. The demonstrative pronouns **ésta** and **éste** have an accent mark on the first syllable. The verb forms **está** (*indicative*) and **esté** (*subjunctive*) have an accent mark on the last syllable.

jo-ven **jó-ve-nes** **bai-la-rín** **bai-la-ri-na**

The location of the stressed syllable in a word determines whether or not a written accent mark is needed. When a plural or feminine form has more syllables than the singular or masculine form, an accent mark must sometimes be added or deleted to maintain the correct stress.

No me gusta la ópera, sino el teatro.
No quiero ir al festival si no vienes conmigo.

The conjunction **sino** (*but rather*) should not be confused with **si no** (*if not*). Note also the difference between **mediodía** (*noon*) and **medio día** (*half a day*) and between **por qué** (*why*) and **porque** (*because*).

Práctica Completa las frases con las palabras adecuadas para cada ocasión.

1. Javier me explicó que ___si no___ lo invitabas, él no iba a venir. (sino/si no)
2. Me gustan mucho las ___canciones___ folklóricas. (canciones/canciónes)
3. Marina ___presentó___ su espectáculo en El Salvador. (presento/presentó)
4. Yo prefiero ___éste___. (éste/esté)

Palabras desordenadas Ordena las letras para descubrir de qué palabras se trata. Después ordena las letras indicadas para descubrir la respuesta a la pregunta.

¿Adónde va Manuel?[1]

yunasedó _ ◯ _ ◯ _ _ _ _
querop _ _ ◯ _ _ _
zogadela ◯ _ _ ◯ _ _ _ _
áset _ _ ◯ _
haitesabonci _ _ _ _ ◯ _ _ _ ◯ _ _ _

Manuel va _ _ _ _ _ _ _ _.[1]

Respuestas: desayunó, porque, adelgazo, está, habitaciones
[1]Manuel va al teatro.

Section Goals

In **Ortografía** students will learn about Spanish words that have similar spellings.

Present

- Point out that the **yo** forms of **–ar** verbs in the present tense have no accent. Say the words **compro** and **hablo** and have volunteers write them on the board. Then explain that the **él/ella/Ud.** form of **–ar** verbs in the preterite requires an accent. Write the words **compró** and **habló** on the board and have volunteers pronounce them.
- Write the words **este, éste,** and **esté** on the board and have volunteers explain how the words are different. You may want to have the class create a sentence that uses each word.
- Write the words **joven, jóvenes, bailarín,** and **bailarina** on the board and have the class explain why a written accent is needed in **jóvenes** but not in **bailarina**.
- Write the words **sino, si no, medio día, mediodía, por qué,** and **porque** on the board. Have volunteers explain what each word means. You may want to have the class create a sentence that uses each word.

Práctica/Palabras desordenadas
Work through these activities with the class to practice the correct spelling of words that are written in similar ways.

TEACHING OPTIONS

Small Groups Have your students work in groups to write an amusing example sentence or two for each of the spelling rules presented on this page. Circulate around the class to verify correct spellings. Then ask for a few volunteers to write their sentences on the board.

Extra Practice Read aloud a few sentences that contain words presented on this page and have your students write them down. Then write the sentences on the board so that your students can check their work. Ex: **Si no compro la comida hoy, la compraré mañana. ¿Prefieres este vestido o éste? La Sra. Pardo no es vieja, sino joven.**

Section Goals

In **Estructura 17.1** students will learn:

- to use the conditional tense
- to make polite requests and hypothesize about past conditions

Instructional Resources
Student Activities Manual: Workbook, 197–198; Lab Manual, 319
Hojas de actividades 41–43

Before Presenting Estructura 17.1 Ask students to imagine they are attending an arts festival. Ask students about what they would like to do there. Ex: **¿Qué te gustaría hacer o ver en el festival de arte? A mí me gustaría ver las comedias que se dan. ¿Y a ti?** Tell students that **gustaría** is a conditional form of **gustar** that they have already learned to use to make polite requests. They are now going to learn all the forms and more uses of the conditional tense.

Assignment Have students study **Estructura 17.1** and do the activities on pages 527–528 as homework.

Present Discuss the grammatical explanation in **Ante todo** and then model the pronunciation of the conditional forms of **visitar, comer,** and **aplaudir.** Ask volunteers to read the captions to the video stills and indicate which verbs are in the conditional tense. Point out that in the conditional tense, as in the future, there is only one set of endings for **-ar, -er,** and **-ir** verbs. Then go through the list of verbs with irregular stems in the conditional. Guide students to see that these are the same verbs that have irregular stems in the future. Quickly, have students say with you a complete conjugation in the conditional of several of these verbs with irregular stems.

Continued on page 527.

17.1 The conditional tense

NATIONAL STANDARDS comparisons

ANTE TODO The conditional tense in Spanish expresses what you *would do* or what *would happen* under certain circumstances. In Lesson 7, you learned the polite expression **Me gustaría...** (*I would like...*), which uses a conditional form of **gustar**.

The conditional tense

		visitar	comer	aplaudir
SINGULAR FORMS	yo	visitar**ía**	comer**ía**	aplaudir**ía**
	tú	visitar**ías**	comer**ías**	aplaudir**ías**
	Ud./él/ella	visitar**ía**	comer**ía**	aplaudir**ía**
PLURAL FORMS	nosotros/as	visitar**íamos**	comer**íamos**	aplaudir**íamos**
	vosotros/as	visitar**íais**	comer**íais**	aplaudir**íais**
	Uds./ellos/ellas	visitar**ían**	comer**ían**	aplaudir**ían**

Oye, Álex, ¿te gustaría ser escritor?

Pues creo que me gustaría ser poeta, pero publicaría todos mis poemas en el Internet.

- The conditional tense is formed like the future tense. The endings are the same for all verbs, both regular and irregular. For regular verbs, you simply add the appropriate endings to the infinitive.

- For irregular verbs add the conditional endings to the irregular stems.

INFINITIVE	STEM	CONDITIONAL	INFINITIVE	STEM	CONDITIONAL
decir	dir-	dir**ía**	querer	querr-	querr**ía**
hacer	har-	har**ía**	saber	sabr-	sabr**ía**
poder	podr-	podr**ía**	salir	saldr-	saldr**ía**
poner	pondr-	pondr**ía**	tener	tendr-	tendr**ía**
haber	habr-	habr**ía**	venir	vendr-	vendr**ía**

¡ATENCIÓN!
All forms of the conditional have an accent mark.
•••
The infinitive of **hay** is **haber**, so its conditional form is **habría**.

- While in English the conditional is a compound verb form made up of the auxiliary verb *would* and a main verb, in Spanish it is a simple verb form that consists of one word.

Miguel **iría** al concierto.
Miguel would go to the concert.

¿**Vivirían** Uds. en otro país?
Would you live in another country?

TEACHING OPTIONS

Game Line students up in teams of six several feet from the board. Write an infinitive on the board and call out **¡Empieza!** The first team members race to the board and write the **yo** form of the verb in the conditional, then pass the chalk to the next team members, who write the **tú** form, and so on. The team that finishes first and has all the forms correct wins the round.

Extra Practice Ask students what they would or would not do over the next 6 months if they could do anything their hearts desired and money and time were no object. Ex: **Yo viajaría por todo el mundo.** Call on volunteers to read their sentences, then ask the class comprehension questions about what was said. Ex: **Clase, ¿qué harían Alicia y Tomás?**

- The conditional is commonly used to make polite requests.

¿**Podrías** abrir la ventana, por favor?
Would you open the window, please?

¿**Sería** tan amable de venir a mi oficina?
Would you be so kind as to come to my office?

- In Spanish, as in English, the conditional expresses the future in relation to a past action or state of being. In other words, the future indicates what *will happen* whereas the conditional indicates what *would happen*.

Creo que mañana **hará** sol.
I think it will be sunny tomorrow.

Creía que hoy **haría** sol.
I thought it would be sunny today.

- The English *would* is often used with a verb to express the conditional, but it can also mean *used to*, in the sense of past habitual action. To express past habitual actions, Spanish uses the imperfect, not the conditional.

Íbamos al parque los sábados.
We would go to the park on Saturdays.

De adolescentes, **comíamos** mucho.
As teenagers, we used to eat a lot.

CONSEJOS

Keep in mind the two parallel combinations shown in these sentences:

1) present tense in main clause → future tense in subordinate clause
2) past tense in main clause → conditional in subordinate clause

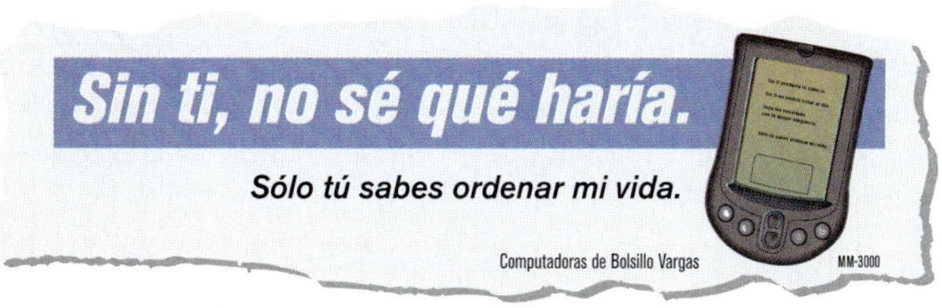

Sin ti, no sé qué haría.
Sólo tú sabes ordenar mi vida.
Computadoras de Bolsillo Vargas
MM-3000

COMPARE & CONTRAST

In Lesson 16, you learned the *future of probability*. Spanish also has the *conditional of probability*, which expresses conjecture or probability about a past condition, event, or action. Compare these Spanish and English sentences.

Serían las once de la noche cuando Elvira me llamó.
It must have been (It was probably) 11 p.m. when Elvira called me.

Sonó el teléfono. ¿**Llamaría** Emilio para cancelar nuestra cita?
The phone rang. I wondered if it was Emilio calling to cancel our date.

Note that English conveys conjecture or probability with phrases such as *I wondered if*, *probably*, and *must have been*. In contrast, Spanish gets these same ideas across with conditional forms.

¡INTÉNTALO!

Indica la forma apropiada del condicional de los verbos que están entre paréntesis.

1. Yo escucharía, leería, esculpiría (escuchar, leer, esculpir)
2. Tú apreciarías, comprenderías, compartirías (apreciar, comprender, compartir)
3. Marcos pondría, vendría, querría (poner, venir, querer)
4. Nosotras seríamos, sabríamos, iríamos (ser, saber, ir)
5. Uds. presentarían, deberían, aplaudirían (presentar, deber, aplaudir)
6. Ella saldría, podría, haría (salir, poder, hacer)
7. Yo tendría, tocaría, me aburriría (tener, tocar, aburrirse)
8. Tú dirías, verías, publicarías (decir, ver, publicar)

TEACHING OPTIONS

Extra Practice Tell students to imagine that their family has come into a great deal of money. Ask them to write ten sentences describing what they and their family members would do with the money. Students should try to use as many different verbs and conjugations as possible. Ex: **Mi familia y yo les ayudaríamos a los artistas de nuestra ciudad.**

Pairs Have students work together to role-play a reporter interviewing a candidate running for a place on the arts council in their state. Reporters should ask the candidate about what he or she would do to help all artists statewide. Have students switch roles.

Ask what the future tense form of **hay** is. Then ask: If the future of **hay** is **habrá**, what would you expect the conditional form to be? **(habría)** Point out the information in **¡Atención!.**

Then, discuss the use of the conditional in polite requests. Remind students of the forms **me gustaría** and **te gustaría,** which they have already learned. You might point out that usage tends to occur in set expressions, such as **¿Podrías...?. ¿Sería Ud. tan amable de...?, ¿Tendrían Uds. la bondad de...? ¿Me harías el favor de...?** and so forth.

Point out that the conditional is sometimes called the *future of the past.* Explain that the conditional is used to express some action that was yet to occur at some past time and illustrate with the examples in the book and others. Ex: **Sé que el concierto será fabuloso. Sabía que el concierto sería fabuloso. • No creo que el público pagará una entrada tan alta. No creía que el público pagaría una entrada tan alta.** and so forth.

Remind students that a habitual action in the past is not expressed with the conditional in Spanish, but with the imperfect.

Compare and Contrast Present Remind students of the future of probability and of the fact that the conditional is sometimes called *the future of the past.* Point out that the conditional of probability functions just as the future of probability but in a past context. Compare the second example to the following: **Suena el teléfono. ¿Estará Emilio para cancelar nuestra cita?**

Close Go over **¡Inténtalo!** orally with the whole class, asking volunteers to read each item aloud.

1 Present Ask six volunteers to write the completed sentences on the board. Then go over all items with the whole class, asking volunteers to correct spelling and grammar as necessary.

2 Present Ask two volunteers to read the **Modelo**. Read the dehydrated question. Have a volunteer read the "rehydrated" question and another read the response. Finally, have five volunteers write their "rehydrated" questions and responses on the board. Ask volunteers to correct spelling and grammar as necessary.

3 Warm-up Work with the class to brainstorm a list of steps to take when looking for a job. Next, draw attention to the expressions **Si yo fuera tú...** and **Yo en tú lugar...** modeling the use of each. Ex: **Si yo fuera tú, haría una lista y buscaría en los anuncios clasificados. Yo en tu lugar iría a una agencia de trabajo.**

3 Present If you haven't assigned this activity as homework, before you divide the class into pairs, allow individuals sufficient time to plan their eight pieces of advice to Matilde. Then have students work with a partner to give advice. Tell them to take turns making suggestions.

3 Expand Have partners choose their three best suggestions to present to the class. Write the different suggestions on the board, then ask the class to vote on which are the most helpful.

3 Expand Have students write a cover letter for a job, explaining why they have the necessary skills. Students should include at least five things they would do to improve the company's performance.

Práctica

1 De viaje A un grupo de artistas le gustaría hacer un viaje a Honduras. En las siguientes oraciones nos cuentan sus planes de viaje. Complétalas con el condicional del verbo entre paréntesis.

1. Me ___gustaría___ (gustar) llevar algunos libros de poesía de Leticia de Oyuela.
2. Ana ___querría___ (querer) ir primero a Copán para conocer las ruinas mayas.
3. Yo ___diría___ (decir) que fuéramos a Tegucigalpa primero.
4. Nosotras ___preferiríamos___ (preferir) ver una obra del Grupo Dramático de Tegucigalpa. Luego ___podríamos___ (poder) tomarnos un café.
5. Y nosotros, ___veríamos___ (ver) los cuadros del pintor José Antonio Velásquez. Y tú, Luisa, ¿qué ___harías___ (hacer)?
6. Yo ___tendría___ (tener) interés en ver o comprar cerámica de José Arturo Machado. Y a ti, Carlos, ¿te ___interesaría___ (interesar) ver la arquitectura colonial?

NOTA CULTURAL

Leticia de Oyuela, author and historian, has been for years one of the intellectual leaders of Honduras. To learn more about the painter **José Antonio Velásquez** and the Mayan city of **Copán**, see **Panorama,** p. 545.

2 Preguntas Forma preguntas con las palabras que se dan en cada ocasión. Inventa luego las respuestas para esas preguntas. Usa el condicional.

modelo

hacer (Uds.) / documental / sobre objetos indígenas de El Salvador
—¿Harían Uds. un documental sobre objetos indígenas de El Salvador?
—No, haríamos un documental sobre la arquitectura colonial.

1. asistir (tú) / todos conciertos / orquesta filarmónica
   ¿Asistirías a todos los conciertos de la orquesta filarmónica? / Answers will vary.
2. comprar (ellos) / escultura / Botero
   ¿Comprarían una escultura de Botero? / Answers will vary.
3. creer (tú) que / poder / hacer / papel / personaje principal / ópera italiana
   ¿Crees que podrías hacer el papel del personaje principal en una ópera italiana? / Answers will vary.
4. tener (nosotros) / dinero / para publicar / periódico en español
   ¿Tendríamos el dinero para publicar un periódico en español? / Answers will vary.
5. saber (ella) / apreciar más / cuadro / arte moderno o uno impresionista
   ¿Sabría apreciar más un cuadro de arte moderno o uno impresionista? / Answers will vary.

NOTA CULTURAL

Fernando Botero, a Colombian, is one of South America's most popular artists. He is famous for his paintings and sculptures of exaggeratedly obese figures.

3 Sugerencias Matilde busca trabajo. Dile ocho cosas que tú harías si fueras ella. Usa el condicional. Luego compara tus sugerencias con las de un(a) compañero/a.
Answers will vary.

AYUDA

Here are two ways of saying *If I were you:*
Si yo fuera tú...
Yo en tu lugar...

TEACHING OPTIONS

Pairs Have students take turns asking each other to do favors, using the conditional for courtesy. Partners respond by either saying they will do the favor or not. If partners can't do the favor, they should make an excuse. Ex: **¿Me podrías buscar al gimnasio a las cinco de la tarde? (Lo siento, pero no puedo. Tengo una clase de escultura hasta las cinco y media.)**

Heritage Speakers Ask Spanish speakers to think of a Spanish-speaking writer or artist that they would like to meet. Have students give a short presentation describing what the meeting would be like, where they would meet, and what they would talk about with their celebrity.

Comunicación

4 **Diálogos** Tu profesor(a) te dará una hoja de actividades. En ella se presentan dos listas con diferentes problemas que supuestamente tienen los estudiantes. En parejas, túrnense para explicar los problemas de su lista; uno cuenta lo que le pasa y el/la otro/a dice lo que haría en esa situación usando la frase "Yo en tu lugar..." (*If I were you...*)

Answers will vary.

modelo

Estudiante 1: ¡Qué problema! Mi novio/a no me habla desde el domingo.
Estudiante 2: Yo en tu lugar no le diría nada por unos días para ver qué pasa.

5 **Escribir** En grupos, miren los apuntes (*notes*) del jefe sobre la última tira cómica (*comic strip*) que hizo Carlos. Preparen el memorándum que el jefe le va a enviar, pidiéndole algunos cambios. Usen los tiempos verbales que sean necesarios, incluyendo el condicional. Answers will vary.

modelo

(apuntes) Los dibujos son demasiado serios.
(memo) Me gustaría que la tira cómica fuera más divertida. ¿Podrías usar un estilo más humorístico?

- La historia está bien, pero es demasiado dramática.
- No hay suficiente acción.
- No me gustó que el personaje principal fuera tan agresivo.
- Necesitamos más variedad.
- Los personajes son un poco aburridos.

Síntesis

6 **Encuesta** Tu profesor(a) te dará una hoja de actividades. Circula por la clase y pregúntales a tres compañeros/as qué actividad relacionada con las artes les gustaría realizar. Usa el condicional de los verbos. Anota las respuestas e informa a la clase de los resultados de la encuesta. Answers will vary.

modelo

Estudiante 1: ¿Harías el papel de un loco en una obra de teatro?
Estudiante 2: Sí, lo haría. Sería un papel muy interesante.

TEACHING OPTIONS

Small Groups Divide the class into groups of four. Have each group brainstorm a list of professions, both artistic and non-artistic. Each group member then chooses a different profession. Students take turns being interviewed by a three-person board about what they would do for their community in their chosen profession. Each board member should ask the interviewee at least two questions.

Extra Practice Ask students to write a short paragraph answering this question: **¿Si pudieras cambiar tu vida, que harías?** Call on volunteers to write their paragraphs on the board. Ask the class to check the paragraphs for correct usage and spelling.

4 Warm-up Go over the directions with the whole class. Explain that the class is going to work in pairs. Partners will alternate describing problems found on their **Hojas de actividades** and proposing solutions. When the directions are clear, ask two volunteers to read the **Modelo**. Ask several volunteers to suggest other solutions.

4 Present Distribute **Hoja de actividades 41** to one member of a pair and **42** to the other. Allow 10 minutes for partners to complete the activity. Have students note the suggestions they receive.

4 Expand Working with the class as a whole, name a problem from one of the lists and ask several volunteers to share the suggestions they received. Encourage other students to comment on the suggestions. Go through several problems in this way.

5 Warm-up Go over the directions with the whole class and ask volunteers to read aloud each of the handwritten notes. Then write the following model for a memorandum on the board:

SERVICIO INTERNO
A:
DE:
FECHA:

5 Present Read the **Modelo** aloud. The allow five to seven minutes for students to write their memos. You may have students hand in their memos to you or exchange them with a partner for peer editing.

6 Present Distrubute **Hoja de actividades 43**. Allow ten minutes for students to circulate. Afterward discuss the suggestions with the class.

Assignment Have students do the activities in the **Student Activities Manual,** Workbook, 197–198.

Section Goals

In **Estructura 17.2** students will learn the use of the conditional perfect tense.

Instructional Resources
Student Activities Manual: Workbook, 199; Lab Manual, 320

Before Presenting Estructura 17.2 Briefly review the **yo** forms of the present, past, and future perfect tenses. Point out that all these tenses are formed by a conjugated form of ***haber*** + *past participle.* Tell students they are now going to learn another compound tense, one that describes *what would have happened* (but didn't). Make a true statement about yourself, using the conditional perfect tense. Ex: **A no ser profesor(a), yo habría sido periodista.** Ask a volunteer to identify the conditional perfect he or she heard in your statement. **Assignment** Have students study the **Estructura** and prepare the activities on pages 530–531 as homework.

Present Work through **Ante todo** and the paradigms of the conditional perfect. Point out that the conditional tense of **haber** is formed on the future stem, **habr-**. Ask a volunteer to read aloud the captions to the video stills, pointing out the conditional perfect form. Then engage students in a conversation about what students might have done last night if they hadn't been studying. Ask: **A no haber estudiado para la clase de español anoche, ¿qué habrían hecho Uds.? ¿Habrían ido al cine? ¿Habrían salido con los amigos?** and so forth.

Close Go over **¡Inténtalo!** orally with the whole class.

17.2 The conditional perfect

NATIONAL STANDARDS comparisons

ANTE TODO Like other compound tenses you have learned—the present perfect, the past perfect, and the future perfect—the conditional perfect (**el condicional perfecto**) is formed with **haber** + [*past participle*].

Y a ti, Maite, ¿te gustaría ser poeta?

Me gustaría ser cantante. De no ser periodista, habría sido cantante de ópera.

The conditional perfect

		pintar	comer	vivir
SINGULAR FORMS	yo	**habría** pintado	**habría** comido	**habría** vivido
	tú	**habrías** pintado	**habrías** comido	**habrías** vivido
	Ud./él/ella	**habría** pintado	**habría** comido	**habría** vivido
PLURAL FORMS	nosotros/as	**habríamos** pintado	**habríamos** comido	**habríamos** vivido
	vosotros/as	**habríais** pintado	**habríais** comido	**habríais** vivido
	Uds./ellos/ellas	**habrían** pintado	**habrían** comido	**habrían** vivido

▶ The conditional perfect is used to express an action that would have occurred, but didn't.

¿No fuiste al espectáculo? ¡Te **habrías divertido**!
You didn't go to the show? You would have had a good time!

Maite **habría preferido** ir a la ópera, pero Álex prefirió ir al cine.
Maite would have preferred to go to the opera, but Álex preferred to see a movie.

¡INTÉNTALO! Indica las formas apropiadas del condicional perfecto de los verbos entre paréntesis.

1. Nosotros habríamos hecho (hacer) todos los quehaceres.
2. Tú habrías apreciado (apreciar) mi poesía.
3. Ellos habrían pintado (pintar) un mural.
4. Ud. habría tocado (tocar) el piano.
5. Ellas habrían puesto (poner) la mesa.
6. Tú y yo habríamos resuelto (resolver) los problemas.
7. Silvia y Alberto habrían esculpido (esculpir) una estatua.
8. Yo habría presentado (presentar) el informe.
9. Uds. habrían vivido (vivir) en el campo.
10. Tú habrías abierto (abrir) la puerta.

TEACHING OPTIONS

Extra Practice Ask students to write five sentences describing how the life of their favorite writer or artist would have been different if the writer had lived in another century. Ex: **Stephen King habría escrito sus novelas con una pluma de cuervo.**

Small Groups Give students five minutes to work in groups of three to describe what would have happened to Cinderella had she not lost her glass slipper. Tell students that the translations for Cinderella, prince, and glass slipper in Spanish are **Cenicientas, príncipe,** and **zapatilla de vidrio.**

Práctica

1 **Completar** Completa los diálogos con la forma apropiada del condicional perfecto de los verbos de la lista. Luego, en parejas, representen los diálogos.

querer	divertirse	presentar	tener
venir	hacer	sentir	tocar

1. —Tú <u>habrías hecho</u> el papel de Aída mejor que ella. ¡Qué lástima!
   —Sí, mis padres <u>habrían venido</u> desde California sólo para oírme cantar en Aída.
2. —Olga, yo esperaba algo más. Con un poco de dedicación y práctica la orquesta <u>habría tocado</u> mejor y los músicos <u>habrían tenido</u> más éxito.
   —Menos mal que la compositora no los escuchó. Se <u>habría sentido</u> avergonzada.
3. —Tania <u>habría presentado</u> la comedia pero no pudo porque cerraron el teatro.
   —¡Qué lástima! Mi esposa y yo <u>habríamos querido</u> ir a la presentación de la obra. Siempre veo tragedias y sé que <u>me habría divertido</u>.

¡LENGUA VIVA!
The common expression **Menos mal que...** means *It's a good thing that...* or *It's just as well that...* . It is followed by a verb in the indicative.

2 **Combinar** Combina elementos de las tres columnas para formar oraciones usando el condicional perfecto. Answers will vary.

con talento artístico	yo	estudiar...
con más tiempo libre	tú	pintar...
en otra especialización	la gente	esculpir...
con más aprecio de las artes	mis compañeros y yo	viajar...
con más dinero	los artistas	escribir...

3 **¿Qué habrías hecho?** Los siguientes dibujos muestran situaciones poco comunes. No sabemos qué hicieron estas personas, pero tú, ¿qué habrías hecho? Comparte tus respuestas con un(a) compañero/a. Answers will vary.

AYUDA
Some possible answers are:
Habría llevado el dinero a....
Yo habría atacado al oso (bear) con....
Yo habría...

1 Warm-up Discuss the information in **¡Lengua viva!** and model the use of **Menos mal que...** Ex: **¿No estudiaron anoche? Menos mal que no tenemos examen hoy.**

1 Present First check answers by going over the activity orally with the whole class, then divide the class into pairs to act out the dialogues.

1 Expand Have students choose one of the three dialogues and write four more lines to extend it. Call on volunteers to perform their expanded dialogues for the class.

2 Present Model the activity with a sentence about yourself. Ex: **Con talento artístico, yo habría estudiado piano.** If you assigned this activity as homework, have students put their papers away before combining the elements orally. Ask volunteers to call out sentences using elements from the three columns. Ask other volunteers to act as secretaries, writing examples on the board. Ask the class to help you correct grammar and spelling as necessary.

3 Warm-up Ask the class as a whole to describe each of the drawings. Write useful vocabulary on the board, including the expressions in **Ayuda**.

3 Present Have students write at least two sentences for each drawing. After students share sentences with their partners, ask pairs to read their best sentences to the class.

3 Expand Have students work with their partners to write a short story based on one of the drawings in the activity.

TEACHING OPTIONS

Pairs Ask students to tell their partner about the most embarrassing moment in their life. Partners respond to the students' stories by telling them what they would have done in their place. Ex: **En tu lugar, yo habría...**

Extra Practice Ask students to state what the following people would have done had they had more money: **mis padres, yo, mi mejor amigo, los estudiantes de la universidad, mi profesor/a de español** Ex: **Con más dinero, mis padres habrían comprado una casa más grande.**

4 Warm-up Have students figure out what year it will be when they are fifty. Ask two volunteers to help you read the **Modelo** aloud. You read the cue.

4 Present Allow ten minutes to complete the activity. Remind students to take turns asking and answering each question. Then call on individual students to report what their partners said.

4 Expand Have students create four more original questions to ask their partner.

5 Warm-up Go over the directions, divide the class into pairs, and have the pairs read the letter. When they have finished reading, ask a volunteer to read the **Modelo** aloud.

5 Suggestion Discuss the information in **¡Lengua viva!** Use **de haber tenido la oportunidad** and related forms in example sentences.

5 Present Allow five minutes for pairs to come up with five things Mario would have done differently. Then have students work with another pair and compare their sentences. Have students share some of their sentences with the class.

5 Expand Ask students to respond to Mario's letter. Students should commiserate with Mario's difficulties and state what they would have done differently.

6 Warm-up Have students think of eight errors they've made in their lives and write them down. Help students with any new vocabulary they may need to complete the activity.

Assignment Have students do the activities in the **Student Activities Manual: Workbook,** 199.

Comunicación

4 Preguntas En parejas, imaginen que tienen cincuenta años y están hablando de sus años de juventud. ¿Qué habrían hecho de manera diferente? Answers will vary.

modelo

¿Te (interesar) aprender a tocar un instrumento?
Estudiante 1: ¿Te habría interesado aprender a tocar un instrumento?
Estudiante 2: Sí, habría aprendido a tocar el piano.

1. ¿Te (gustar) viajar por América Latina?
2. ¿Qué escritores (leer)?
3. ¿Qué clases (tomar)?
4. ¿Qué tipo de música (escuchar)?
5. ¿Qué tipo de amigos/as (tener)?
6. ¿A qué fiestas o viajes no (ir)?
7. ¿Con qué tipo de persona (salir)?
8. ¿Qué tipo de ropa (llevar)?

5 Una carta En parejas, lean la carta que Mario le escribió a Ángela. Digan qué cosas Mario habría hecho de una manera diferente de haber tenido la oportunidad.

Answers will vary.

modelo

Mario se habría quedado más tiempo en la isla de Roatán.

Querida Ángela:

Regresé ayer de mi viaje a Honduras. Fui con un grupo de personas que no conocía y viajamos en autobús. Comenzamos en Tegucigalpa, donde fuimos tres días seguidos al museo. Viajamos por una carretera muy mala hasta La Mosquitia, donde pasamos cuatro días. ¡No me gustó nada! Luego fuimos a la isla de Roatán, que es un lugar bellísimo, a bucear por un día. No tuve cuidado con el agua y me enfermé del estómago después del segundo día.

Un abrazo,
Mario

¡LENGUA VIVA!

The useful expression **de haber tenido la oportunidad** means *if I/he/you/etc. had had the opportunity.* You can make many similar sentences, such as **De haberlo sabido ayer, te habría llamado.**

Síntesis

6 Yo en tu lugar Háblale a un(a) compañero/a de algunos de los errores que has cometido en tu vida. Tu compañero/a te dirá lo que habría hecho en esa situación.

Answers will vary.

modelo

Estudiante 1: El año pasado saqué una mala nota en biología.
Estudiante 2: Yo no habría sacado una mala nota. Habría estudiado mucho más.

TEACHING OPTIONS

Pairs Have students make a list of everything they did last weekend. Then, ask students to tell their partners what they did, when they did it, and how they did it. Partners will counter with how they would have done each thing. Ex: **Bailé por cinco horas durante una fiesta el sábado pasado. (Yo no habría bailado por tanto tiempo. Yo habría bailado por sólo dos horas.)**

Large Groups Divide the class into three groups. Have each student answer the following question: **Con más oportunidad en el colegio, ¿qué habrías hecho de una manera diferente?** After everyone has spoken, have the group discuss which missed opportunities would have been the most important in making a difference in their lives.

17.3 The past perfect subjunctive

NATIONAL comparisons STANDARDS

CONSÚLTALO

The past perfect
To review the past perfect indicative, see Lesson 15, section 15.2, p. 472. To review the **present perfect subjunctive**, see Lesson 15, section 15.3, p. 475.

ANTE TODO The past perfect subjunctive (**el pluscuamperfecto de subjuntivo**), also called the pluperfect subjunctive, is formed with the past subjunctive of **haber** + [*past participle*]. Compare the following subjunctive forms.

Present subjunctive	Present perfect subjunctive
yo trabaje	yo haya trabajado
Past subjunctive	**Past perfect subjunctive**
yo trabajara	yo hubiera trabajado

Past perfect subjunctive

		pintar	comer	vivir
SINGULAR FORMS	yo	**hubiera** pintado	**hubiera** comido	**hubiera** vivido
	tú	**hubieras** pintado	**hubieras** comido	**hubieras** vivido
	Ud./él/ella	**hubiera** pintado	**hubiera** comido	**hubiera** vivido
PLURAL FORMS	nosotros/as	**hubiéramos** pintado	**hubiéramos** comido	**hubiéramos** vivido
	vosotros/as	**hubierais** pintado	**hubierais** comido	**hubierais** vivido
	Uds./ellos/ellas	**hubieran** pintado	**hubieran** comido	**hubieran** vivido

▶ The past perfect subjunctive is used in subordinate clauses under the same conditions that you have learned for other subjunctive forms, and in the same way the past perfect is used in English (*I had talked, you had spoken,* etc.). It refers to actions or conditions that had taken place before another action or condition in the past.

No había nadie que **hubiera dormido**.
There wasn't anyone who had slept.

Dudaba que Juan **hubiera ganado** el partido.
I doubted that Juan had won the game.

Dudaba que ellos **hubieran llegado**.
I doubted that they had arrived.

Llegué antes de que la clase **hubiera comenzado**.
I arrived before the class had begun.

¡INTÉNTALO! Indica la forma apropiada del pretérito pluscuamperfecto de subjuntivo de cada verbo entre paréntesis.

1. Esperaba que Uds. hubieran hecho (hacer) eso.
2. Dudaba que tú hubieras dicho (decir) eso.
3. No estaba seguro de que ellos hubieran ido (ir).
4. No creían que nosotros hubiéramos hablado (hablar) con Ricardo.
5. ¿Conoces a alguien que hubiera podido (poder) comer tanto como él?
6. No había nadie que hubiera visto (ver) el espectáculo.
7. Ojalá que tú me hubieras llamado (llamar) antes.
8. ¿Había alguien que no hubiera visto (ver) esa película?
9. No creían que nosotras hubiéramos bailado (bailar) en el festival.
10. No era cierto que yo hubiera ido (ir) con él al concierto.

TEACHING OPTIONS

Extra Practice Make a series of statements using the past perfect indicative, then begin reactions to the statements that call for the subjunctive. Have students complete the reactions. Ex: **Jorge había esculpido una estatua para el festival. Era maravilloso que... (Jorge hubiera esculpido una estatua para el festival.**

TPR Make a series of statements using either the present perfect or the past perfect subjunctive. If students hear a statement using the present perfect subjunctive, they raise one hand. If they hear one with the past perfect subjunctive, they raise two hands.

Section Goals

In **Estructura 17.3**, students will learn the use of the past perfect subjunctive.

Instructional Resources
Student Activities Manual: Workbook, 200–202; Lab Manual, 321

Before Presenting Estructura 17.3 Briefly review the past perfect indicative and the present perfect subjunctive. Ask volunteers what the cues that trigger the subjunctive mood in a subordinate clause are. (verbs of emotion; doubt, disbelief, denial; certain conjunctions; reference to persons or things not know to exist; and so forth) Then tell students that they are now going to learn the past perfect subjunctive. Ask them to write predictions about how the past perfect subjunctive is conjugated and used. **Assignment** Have students study **Estructura 17.3** and do the activities on pages 533–534 as homework.

Present Briefly check student predictions. Ask a volunteer to explain how to conjugate the past perfect subjunctive. Then go over the paradigms of **pintar, comer,** and **vivir**. Then discuss the use of the past perfect subjunctive and examine the example sentences. Ask volunteers to identify the cue that triggered the subjunctive mood in each example. Then ask them to suggest other sentences that follow the patterns of the example sentences. Ex: **No conozco a nadie que hubiera dormido mientras tocaba aquella banda. El cantante empezó a cantar antes de que hubiera entrado el teatro.** and so forth.

Close Go over **¡Inténtalo!** orally with the whole class.

1 Present Have students exchange their work with a partner for correction. If students disagree on whether an item is correct or not, suggest they consult a third person.

1 Expand For oral practice, ask students comprehension questions about the information in the activity. Ex: **¿Por qué se alegró la persona de la primera oración? ¿Qué le molestó a la persona de la segunda oración?** and so forth.

2 Warm-up Have students read **¡Lengua viva!** before completing the activity. Tell them that they will need to decide whether the verb in the main clause should be changed to the imperfect or preterite as well as changing the verb in the subordinate clause to the past perfect subjunctive.

2 Present Have volunteers write the answers to the activity on the board. Review tenses and spelling with the entire class.

2 Expand To illustrate time relationships among verbs, have students rewrite Item 6 using the present subjunctive and the past subjunctive. Then, have them translate the four versions (the two from the activity as written and the two new ones). **Dudo que cierren el museo. Dudaba que cerraran el museo. Dudo que hayan cerrado el museo. Dudaba que hubieran cerrado el museo.**

3 Present Read the **Modelo** aloud then go over the items, asking volunteers to call out each completed sentence.

3 Expand Ask students to imagine that they have been on the same spaceship as Emilio Hernández. Have them write six statements about what they hoped had changed over the past 30 years.

Práctica

1 Completar Completa las oraciones con el pluscuamperfecto de subjuntivo de los verbos entre paréntesis.

1. Me alegré de que mi familia ___se hubiera ido___ (irse) de viaje.
2. Me molestaba que Carlos y Miguel no ___hubieran venido___ (venir) a visitarme.
3. Dudaba que la música que yo escuchaba ___hubiera sido___ (ser) la misma que escuchaban mis padres.
4. No creían que nosotros ___hubiéramos podido___ (poder) aprender tanto español en un año.
5. Los músicos se alegraban de que su programa le ___hubiera gustado___ (gustar) tanto al público.
6. La profesora se sorprendió de que nosotros ___hubiéramos hecho___ (hacer) la tarea antes de venir a clase.

2 Transformar María está hablando de las emociones que ha sentido ante ciertos acontecimientos (*events*). Transforma sus oraciones según el modelo.

modelo

Me alegro de que hayan venido los padres de Micaela.
Me alegré de que hubieran venido los padres de Micaela.

1. Es muy triste que haya muerto la tía de Miguel.
   Fue muy triste que hubiera muerto la tía de Miguel.
2. Dudo que Guillermo haya comprado una casa tan grande.
   Dudaba que Guillermo hubiera comprado una casa tan grande.
3. No puedo creer que nuestro equipo haya perdido el partido.
   No podía creer que nuestro equipo hubiera perdido el partido.
4. Me alegro de que mi novio me haya llamado.
   Me alegré de que mi novio me hubiera llamado.
5. Me molesta que el periódico no haya llegado.
   Me molestó que el periódico no hubiera llegado.
6. Dudo que hayan cerrado el Museo de Arte.
   Dudaba que hubieran cerrado el Museo de Arte.

¡LENGUA VIVA!

Both the preterite and the imperfect can be used to describe past thoughts or emotions. In general, the imperfect describes a particular mental state without reference to its beginning or end, while the preterite refers to the occurrence of a thought or emotion at a specific moment.

Pensaba que mi vida era aburrida.

Pensé que había dicho algo malo.

3 El regreso Usa el pluscuamperfecto de subjuntivo para indicar lo que el astronauta Emilio Hernández esperaba que hubiera pasado en su familia y en el mundo durante los 30 años que había estado en el espacio sin tener noticias del exterior.

modelo

su esposa / no casarse con otro hombre
Esperaba que su esposa no se hubiera casado con otro hombre.

1. su hija Diana / conseguir ser una pintora famosa
   Esperaba que su hija Diana hubiera conseguido ser una pintora famosa.
2. los políticos / acabar con todas las guerras (*wars*)
   Esperaba que los políticos hubieran acabado con todas las guerras.
3. su suegra / irse a vivir a la Florida
   Esperaba que su suegra se hubiera ido a vivir a la Florida.
4. su hermano Ramón / tener un empleo más de dos meses
   Esperaba que su hermano Ramón hubiera tenido un empleo más de dos meses.
5. todos los países / resolver sus problemas económicos
   Esperaba que todos los países hubieran resuelto sus problemas económicos.
6. su esposa / ya pagar el préstamo de la casa
   Esperaba que su esposa ya hubiera pagado el préstamo de la casa.

TEACHING OPTIONS

Pairs Have students make six statements about something that happened last year. Partners counter with statements declaring that the action had not really occurred. Ex: **El poeta Arturo Cruz se murió mientras leía su poesía. (No es cierto que Arturo Cruz se hubiera muerto mientras leía su poesía.)**

Small Groups Divide the class into groups of three. Have students take turns telling their group about things they wish had happened over the course of their lives. Ex: **¡Ojalá que hubiera aprendido a tocar el piano!**

Comunicación

4 **Mentiras** Rita y Andrés dijeron muchas mentiras la semana pasada. En parejas, túrnense para decir que no creyeron sus mentiras. Answers will vary.

Rita

Andrés

modelo

Rita dijo que había tocado el violín en una orquesta.
Dudaba que Rita hubiera tocado el violín en una orquesta.

1. Rita dijo que había vivido en París.
2. Andrés dijo que su hermana había conocido al presidente de los EE.UU.
3. Andrés dijo que su tía había comprado una pintura famosa.
4. Rita dijo que había salido con Leonardo DiCaprio.
5. Rita y Andrés dijeron que habían visto una erupción volcánica en El Salvador.
6. Rita dijo que había ayudado a Martha Stewart a decorar una casa.

NOTA CULTURAL

El Salvador still has several active volcanoes. The volcano **Izalco**, which was active until 1957, was known for its constant production of smoke and lava. Sailors called it "The Lighthouse of the Pacific."

5 **Reacciones** Imagina que los siguientes acontecimientos (*events*) ocurrieron la semana pasada. En parejas, indiquen cuáles fueron sus reacciones ante cada uno de ellos. Answers will vary.

modelo

Vino a visitarte tu tía.
Me alegré de que hubiera venido a visitarte.

1. Se murió la abuela de un(a) amigo/a.
2. Tu mejor amigo/a compró un coche.
3. Tu ex novio/a se casó con un(a) amigo/a.
4. Tu tío favorito te mandó mil dólares.
5. Tus amigos/as te hicieron una fiesta.
6. Tu universidad te dio una beca (*scholarship*).

Síntesis

6 **Titulares** En grupos, lean los siguientes titulares (*headlines*) e indiquen cuáles fueron sus reacciones ante cada uno de ellos. Luego, cada estudiante escribe tres titulares más y los comparte con su grupo. Answers will vary.

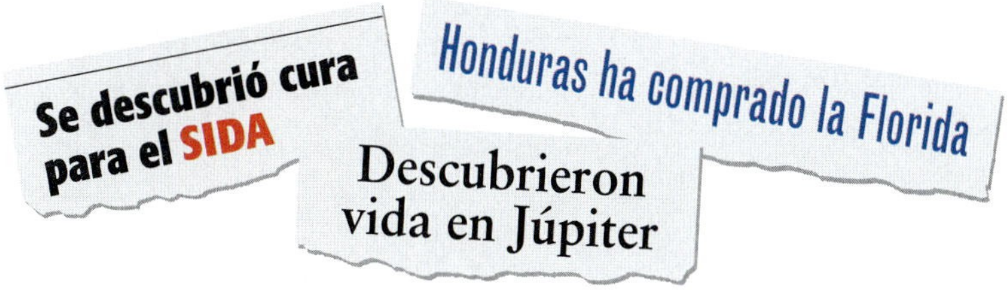
Se descubrió cura para el SIDA
Honduras ha comprado la Florida
Descubrieron vida en Júpiter

AYUDA

El SIDA (Síndrome de Imunodeficiencia Adquirida) is the Spanish term for the AIDS virus.

TEACHING OPTIONS

Extra Practice Tell students to write six sentences describing how they felt about what happened at an arts festival held last weekend. Ex: **Estaba triste que mi cantante favorito no hubiera cantado en el festival.**

Small Groups Divide students into groups of three. Student one picks an event, such as final exams or a concert. Student two begins a statement in the past that triggers the subjunctive. Student three completes the sentence with a verb in the past perfect subjunctive. Ex: **el concierto de Ricky Martin/No había nadie que... / ...no se hubiera divertido.**

4 Present Have a volunteer read the **Modelo** before dividing the class into pairs.

Sugerencia Read the **Nota cultural** with students. Have students find the volcano Izalco on the map on page 542. Then ask them where else in Latin America volcanoes can be found. You might suggest that students research the roles volcanoes have played in the myths and legends of Latin America.

5 Warm-up Review expressions of emotion that trigger the subjunctive in subordinate clauses.

5 Present Read the **Modelo** aloud. Then have students write their responses individually. Then call on volunteers to read their sentences to the class. Ask the class to listen for correct use of the past perfect subjunctive and the preterite or imperfect tense in the main clause.

6 Present Divide the class into groups of four. After having written their original headlines, have students take turns reading them to the group. Each group member responds to a different headline written by the same student.

6 Expand Have students find a Spanish language newspaper online and copy down five different headlines. Then have students respond to each headline using the past perfect subjunctive.

Assignment Have students do the activities in the **Student Activities Manual: Workbook,** 200–202.

The Affective Dimension Reassure students, who may be feeling overwhelmed, that many tenses are made up of forms they have already learned. Encourage them to review previously learned tenses regularly.

Section Goals

In **Lectura** students will:
- learn to summarize a text in their own words
- read a poem in Spanish

Antes de leer

Tell students that summarizing a text in their own words will greatly increase their comprehension of it. Explain that they may want to develop the habit of scanning a text, summarizing what they have read, taking notes, and then rereading the text. Tell them this strategy can help them understand any text they read.

Examinar el texto First, ask students to look at the format of the text and tell you what genre the text is. Then have students skim the poem. Read the poem aloud for the class. Ask students to say what the poem means to them.

Resumen Ask pairs to work together to complete the sentences. When pairs are finished, go over the answers orally with the whole class.

Preguntas Ask questions of the whole class. Ask volunteers to answer orally or to write their answers on the board.

Assignment Have students read **Escribir** and prepare the activities in **Después de leer** as homework.

Lectura

NATIONAL STANDARDS communication cultures

Antes de leer

Estrategia

Summarizing a text in your own words

Summarizing a text in your own words can help you comprehend it better. Before summarizing a text, you may find it helpful to skim it and jot down a few notes about its general meaning. You can then read the text again, writing down the important details. Your notes will help you summarize what you have read. If the text is particularly long, you may want to subdivide it into smaller segments so that you can summarize it more easily.

Examinar el texto

Lee la selección rápidamente. ¿Qué tipo de documento es? ¿De qué trata? Luego lee el texto una segunda vez para comprenderlo mejor. Resume el texto con tus propias palabras.

Resumen

Después de leer, completa el siguiente resumen del texto usando las siguientes palabras.

amor	poeta	poesía
ira	atención	

La ___poeta___ describe su rutina diaria. Pone mucha ___atención___ en su trabajo porque espera que su ___poesía___ se publique un día. Para la poeta las cosas más importantes en la vida son la ___ira___, la hermandad y el ___amor___.

Preguntas

1. ¿Quién es la poeta? ¿De dónde es?
2. ¿Quién es José Coronel Urtecho?
3. ¿Quién puede ser la persona que habla al final del poema?

¿De qué trata? *What is it about?*

Escribir

(A José Coronel Urtecho)

Claribel Alegría

Claribel Alegría, una de las poetas hispanoamericanas más reconocidas, nació en Nicaragua en 1924. Siendo niña fue a vivir a El Salvador por lo que se considera a sí misma salvadoreña. Su poesía trata tanto de temas personales como de los problemas sociales y políticos de Hispanoamérica. Entre su obra se encuentran Sobrevivo *(1978), que obtuvo el Premio poesía de las Américas,* Suma y sigue *(1981) y* Luisa en el país de la realidad *(1987). El poema "Escribir" es de la colección* Y este poema río *(1988). Este poema está dedicado a José Coronel Urtecho (1906-1994), un prestigioso poeta nicaragüense que apoyó la insurrección popular contra la dictadura de Somoza.*

TEACHING OPTIONS

Heritage Speakers Ask Spanish speakers to prepare a brief presentation on their favorite Spanish-language poet. Students should include a short biography of the poet and be prepared to read for the class their favorite poem by him or her.

Small Groups Have groups of three select a country they would like to visit in Central America. Ask students to research cultural information about the country. Students should compile the information into a brief report and be prepared to present it to the class.

Extra Practice Ask students to write a biography of Claribel Alegría. Have them research the reason she calls El Salvador home and tell about the major themes in her writing. Students should include a bibliography of her works.

Mientras escribo a diario
me concentro
sueño tener un día
el libro entre mis manos
acariciar su lomo
abrir sus hojas
ver en letra de molde
mis poemas
que lleguen a otros ojos
a otras manos
mientras digo
repito
trato de convencerme
que es motivo de vida
el escribir
como lo es el amor
la ira
la hermandad
toco mi hombro izquierdo
me lo tocas
se me erizan los pelos
de la nuca
me susurras:
te estás jugando
la vida.

apoyó *supported* **acariciar** *to caress* **lomo** *spine* **hojas** *pages* **letra de molde** *printed letters* **ira** *rage* **hermandad** *brotherhood* **hombro** *shoulder* **se me erizan los pelos de la nuca** *the hairs on the back of my neck stand on end* **susurras** *you whisper*

Después de leer

Contestar

Contesta las siguientes preguntas sobre el poema.

1. ¿Con qué frecuencia escribe la poeta?
2. ¿Qué imagina mientras escribe?
3. ¿Qué crees que quiere decir la poeta en los siguientes versos: trato de convencerme / que es motivo de vida / el escribir?
4. Explica qué significan para ti los últimos versos del poema.

Poema redactado

Utilizando partes del poema "Escribir", escribe un poema sobre una actividad que te gusta. Usa un infinitivo como título del poema. Utiliza el siguiente esquema.

____

Mientras __________ a diario
me concentro
sueño un día __________
____
____
trato de convencerme
que es motivo de vida
el __________
como lo es __________
____
____
Tú __________
te estás
jugando la vida.

Tú eres el/la poeta

En grupos, un(a) estudiante asume el papel del/de la poeta de "Escribir". Los otros estudiantes le harán preguntas sobre las ideas y los sentimientos expresados en su poema.

Un grupo de poetas

En grupos, elijan un tema personal o social que sea importante para Uds. y escriban un poema sobre ese tema. Altérnense para escribir un verso cada vez que sea su turno. Compartan su obra maestra con la clase cuando cada poeta del grupo haya escrito tres versos.

redactado *rewritten* **esquema** *outline* **verso** *line (of poetry)*

TEACHING OPTIONS

Extra Practice Ask students to research Central American arts and crafts. (**artesanías**) Ask them to prepare a brief presentation that includes bringing in a sample or pictures of the craft. Students should explain what materials are used and how the craft is made.

TPR Ask students to work in groups and to research folk music and traditional dance(s) native to a Central American country. Ex.: **el baile de la marimba de Nicaragua.** Encourage them to learn the dance(s) and to perform it for their classmates.

Después de leer

Contestar
Suggestion Ask students to work in pairs and ask the questions of one another. When pairs have finished, go over the answers orally with the whole class.

Poema redactado
Suggestion Write the first five lines from the poem frame on the board. Brainstorm with students other activities the poem could be about. (Possible responses: **cantar, bailar, pintar, esculpir, dibujar,** and so on.) Ask students to think of other details to add to the poem that correspond to the activity.
Ex.: **Tocar guitarra**

Mientras toco a diario
me concentro
sueño un día
tener la guitarra entre mis brazos
tocando las cuerdas
oír las notas
mi música
que lleguen a otros oídos
a otros corazones
mientras toco

Tú eres el/la poeta
Suggestion Have groups brainstorm questions. Give groups time to practice questions and answers. Students conduct a panel discussion in which the poets sit at a table facing the rest of the class and answer questions from all groups.

Un grupo de poetas
Suggestion You may wish to provide samples of simple free verse poems to use as models.

The Affective Dimension
Tell your students that reading poetry can be daunting, even in one's native tongue, because poetry is often written in very symbolic language. Point out that reading Spanish poetry will be less anxiety-provoking if students use the reading strategies they have learned so far in **Vistas**.

Section Goals

In **Escritura** students will:

- learn to find biographical information
- integrate vocabulary and structures taught in **Lesson 17**
- write a composition

Tema
Present Working with the whole class, brainstorm several artists, musicians, movie stars, scientists, historians, politicians, athletes, and others whom they would like to invite for dinner. Then have them brainstorm questions they may wish to ask their dinner guests. Then model the pronunciation of the phrases on page 538, asking students to suggest verbs in the conditional tense to complete them.

Estrategia
Present Explain to students that when they research biographical information, they may wish to start with general resources and work their way toward specific sources. Guide students in suggesting where to look for biographical information on the Mexican muralist Diego Rivera. Students should mention resources similar to the following: the Website www.diegorivera.com, books on Mexican muralists or books specifically about Rivera such as *Dreaming With His Eyes Open*, by Patrick Marnham, and *Diego Rivera: A Retrospective* by Cynthia Newman Helms, et al.

Assignment Have students prepare **Ideas y organización** and **Primer borrador** as homework.

Escritura

Estrategia

Finding biographical information

Biographical information can be useful for a great variety of writing topics. Whether you are writing about a famous person, a period in history, or even a particular career or industry, you will be able to make your writing both more accurate and more interesting when you provide detailed information about the people who are related to your topic.

To research biographical information, you may wish to start with general reference sources, such as encyclopedias and periodicals. Additional background information on people can be found in biographies or in nonfiction books about the person's field or industry. For example, if you wanted to write about Jennifer López, you could find background information from periodicals, including magazine interviews and movie or concert reviews. You might also find information in books or articles related to contemporary film and music.

Biographical information may also be available on the Internet, and depending on your writing topic, you may even be able to conduct interviews to get the information you need. Make sure to confirm the reliability of your sources whenever your writing includes information about other people.

You might want to look for the following kinds of information:

- Date of birth
- Date of death
- Childhood experiences
- Education
- Family life
- Place of residence
- Life-changing events
- Personal and professional accomplishments

Tema

¿A quién te gustaría conocer?

Si pudieras invitar a cinco personas famosas a cenar en tu casa, ¿a quiénes invitarías? Pueden ser de cualquier época de la historia y de cualquier profesión. Algunas posibilidades incluyen:

- el arte
- la música
- el cine
- las ciencias
- la historia
- la política

Escribe una composición breve sobre la cena. Explica por qué invitarías a estas personas y describe lo que harías, lo que preguntarías y lo que dirías si tuvieras la oportunidad de conocerlas. Utiliza algunas de las siguientes frases:

Si conociera a	*If I met...*
Si tuviera la oportunidad de hablar con...	*If I had the opportunity to speak with...*
Si un día me encontrara con...	*If one day I found myself with...*
Si pudiera hablar con...	*If I could speak to...*

cualquier *any*

TEACHING OPTIONS

Proofreading Activity Copy the following sentences containing mistakes onto the board or a transparency as a proofreading activity to do with the whole class.

1. **Creíamos que un artista tan famoso haría pintado más cuadros esté año.**
2. **Luis compro un libro de poemas de Ernesto Cardenal por qué le gusta mucho a su obra.**
3. **La bailarína siguió bailando, pero dijo que se jubilara dentro de un mes.**
4. **De haberme preguntando a mí, había recomendado que la orquesta había tocado otro tipo de música.**
5. **Los dos jovenes habrían asistido al concierto en el parque sino hubiera llovido.**
6. **Miguel dijo que el querería ser autor de no ficción algun día.**

Plan de escritura

1 Ideas y organización

Busca información en el Internet y en la biblioteca sobre las personas que escogiste. Organiza la información de una manera lógica.

2 Primer borrador

Utiliza tus notas de **Ideas y organización** para escribir el primer borrador de tu composición.

3 Comentario

Comparte tu párrafo y los datos recogidos en **Ideas y organización** con un(a) compañero/a de clase. Lee su información y su composición y ofrécele consejos basados en esta guía:

- **a.** ¿Es interesante la composición?
- **b.** ¿Contiene suficientes detalles?
- **c.** ¿Está bien organizada?
- **d.** ¿Hay errores ortográficos o gramaticales?

4 Redacción

Revisa el primer borrador según las indicaciones de tu compañero/a. Antes de escribir tu versión final, revisa tu trabajo según esta guía:

- **a.** Busca los verbos en condicional. ¿Están escritos correctamente?
- **b.** Revisa la concordancia entre los sustantivos y los adjetivos en cada oración.
- **c.** Subraya los pronombres para comprobar el uso correcto de cada uno.
- **d.** Consulta tus **Anotaciones para mejorar la escritura** para evitar la repetición de errores previos.

5 Evaluación y progreso

En grupos, compartan sus composiciones. Luego túrnense para crear diálogos basados en las cenas. Para cada diálogo, un(a) estudiante hará el papel del/de la entrevistador(a) y los/las otros/as estudiantes representarán a las personas famosas. Cuando el/la profesor(a) te devuelva tu trabajo, lee sus observaciones para mejorar tu próxima composición. Anota como siempre tus errores en las **Anotaciones para mejorar la escritura** en tu **Carpeta de trabajos.**

escogiste *you chose* datos *pieces of information* recogidos *collected* Subraya *Underline* devuelva *returns*

Comentario
Present Go over guide questions **a–d** with the class and allow a few minutes for students to exchange their compositions.

Assignment Have students prepare **Redacción** as homework.

Evaluación y progreso
Give groups sufficient time to read the compositions and role play dialogues based on them.

Writing Sample Below is a brief composition that would constitute superior writing achievement.

LA CENA FAMOSA

Si yo tuviera la oportunidad de invitar a cinco personas famosas a cenar en mi casa, invitaría a las siguientes personas: Frida Kahlo, Pedro Almodóvar, Tim Berners-Lee, Pete Sampras y Albert Einstein.

Si una noche me encontrara con Frida Kahlo sentada en mi comedor, le preguntaría sobre los temas de su arte y que me contara algo interesante sobre cada cuadro.

Si pudiera cenar y charlar con Pedro Almodóvar, le diría que me encanta sus películas y le preguntaría sobre sus fuentes de inspiración.

Si conociera a Tim Berners-Lee, el inventor del Internet, le preguntaría sobre los planes futuros para el Internet y si le gusta la rapidez con la cual está desarrollando.

Si pudiera hablar con Pete Sampras, campeón de tenis, le preguntaría sobre sus estrategias para controlar los nervios bajo presión.

Si me tocara la oportunidad de cenar con Albert Einstein, el famoso científico, le pediría una explicación de la teoría de relatividad.

En fin, ¡sería una cena inolvidable!

EVALUATION: Composición

Criteria	Scale
Content	1 2 3 4
Organization	1 2 3 4
Use of vocabulary	1 2 3 4
Grammatical accuracy	1 2 3 4
Creativity	1 2 3 4

Scoring	
Excellent	18–20 points
Good	14–17 points
Satisfactory	10–13 points
Unsatisfactory	< 10 points

Section Goals

In **Escuchar** students will:
- listen to a letter sent to a job applicant
- practice the strategies of listening for key words and using context
- listen to a film review

Preparación
Warm-up Guide students to see that the art is a poster for a horror movie.

Estrategia
Script Estimada Srta. Negrón: Es un gran placer ofrecerle un puesto en el bufete de abogados Chirinos y Alemán. Como se mencionó durante su entrevista la semana pasada, el sueldo comenzará en $52.500 anuales. Los beneficios incluirán un seguro de salud, tres semanas de vacaciones pagadas y un seguro de vida. Quisiéramos que comenzara a trabajar el lunes, 17 de mayo. Favor de presentarse a las ocho en punto ese día. Si no le es posible comenzar ese día, favor de comunicarse conmigo lo más pronto posible.
Assignment Have the students do **Ahora escucha** and **Comprensión** as homework.

Ahora escucha
Script Hoy viernes, como siempre les vamos a ayudar a hacer sus planes para el fin de semana. Les traemos una reseña de la película que estrenó esta semana, *El fantasma del lago Enriquillo*. Esta película, en la cual regresa a la pantalla el famoso Jorge Verdoso, se anuncia como una película de ciencia ficción.
Es una lástima ver al talentoso Verdoso en esta película. Generalmente lo hemos visto en comedias románticas y su arte tanto como su apariencia se prestan más a ese tipo de obra que a *El fantasma del lago Enriquillo*. La trama es tan exagerada que acaba siendo una sátira.

La película tiene sus momentos especiales a pesar de sus limitaciones. Las escenas que Jorge Verdoso comparte con la estrella Lourdes del Río son fascinantes. Hay una energía fabulosa entre estos artistas.
Los efectos especiales no son lo que hoy día esperamos ver; parecen ser algo de una película de hace quince años. Pero la música del gran compositor Jaime Rebelde es espectacular.

Recomiendo la película pero con reservas. Los aficionados a las películas de Verdoso y del Río no se la van a querer perder. Pero vayan con el conocimiento de que algunos momentos supuestamente dramáticos son cómicos.

Escuchar

Preparación

Basándote en el dibujo, ¿qué palabras crees que usaría un crítico en una reseña de esta película?

Estrategia

Listening for key words/ Using the context

The comprehension of key words is vital to understanding spoken Spanish. Use your background knowledge of the subject to help you anticipate what the key words might be. When you hear unfamiliar words, remember that you can use context to figure out their meaning. To practice these strategies, you will now listen to a paragraph from a letter sent to a job applicant. Jot down key words, as well as any other words you figured out from the context.

Ahora escucha

Ahora vas a escuchar la reseña de la película. Mientras escuches al crítico, recuerda que las críticas de cine son principalmente descriptivas. La primera vez que escuches, identifica las palabras clave que se asocian con las palabras y frases en la columna A. Luego, escucha otra vez la reseña e identifica el significado de las palabras en la coumna B mediante el contexto.

A

1. película de ciencia ficción
2. famoso, talentoso Verdoso
3. trama exagerada
4. escenas fascinantes
5. energía fabulosa entre los artistas
6. música espectacular

B

1. estrenar
2. a pesar de
3. con reservas
4. supuestamente
5. la trama
6. conocimiento

recursos
R SCASS./CD Lección17

reseña *review* clave *key*

Comprensión

Cierto o falso

	Cierto	Falso
1. El fantasma del lago Enriquillo es una película de ciencia ficción.	✓	❍
2. Los efectos especiales son espectaculares.	❍	✓
3. Generalmente se ha visto a Jorge Verdoso en comedias románticas.	✓	❍
4. Jaime Rebelde es un actor espectacular.	❍	✓

Preguntas Answers will vary.

1. ¿Qué aspectos de la película le gustaron al crítico?
2. ¿Qué no le gustó al crítico de la película?
3. Si a ti te gustaran los actores, ¿irías a ver esta película? ¿Por qué?
4. Para ti, ¿cuáles son los aspectos más importantes de una película? Explica tu respuesta.

Ahora Uds. Answers will vary.

Trabaja con un grupo de compañeros/as. Escojan una película con actores muy famosos que no fue lo que esperaban. Escriban una reseña que describa el papel de los actores, la trama, los efectos especiales, la cinematografía u otros aspectos importantes de la película.

communication cultures connections communities

NATIONAL STANDARDS

Proyecto

Escribe un informe

Imagina que estás escribiendo un informe sobre los mejores y más famosos artistas de América Central. Tu informe debe incluir información sobre los artistas de El Salvador y de Honduras.

1 Escribe una sección del informe

Usa los **Recursos para la investigación** para buscar información de la historia del arte en Honduras y en El Salvador. Escoge tres o cuatro de los artistas más famosos de cada país. El informe debe incluir la siguiente información:

- Una descripción de las obras de cada artista
- Una explicación de por qué el artista fue escogido para aparecer en el informe
- Una foto de cada artista
- Fotos de las obras de cada artista (si no hay fotos disponibles debes describir las obras más detalladamente)

2 Presenta la información

Presenta el informe a la clase. Resume lo que escribiste y muéstrales a tus compañeros/as las fotos que encontraste de los artistas y de su arte. Describe las obras y da tus opiniones sobre ellas.

Iglesia con mural, El Salvador

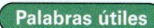

Palabras útiles

el tema	*subject*
colorido/a	*colorful*
abstracto/a	*abstract*
informe	*report*

Escoge *Choose* disponibles *available* más detalladamene *in greater detail* Resume *Summarize* conservador(a) *curator*

recursos para la investigación

Internet Palabras clave: Honduras, El Salvador, arte, museo, galería	**Comunidad** Profesores, estudiantes o personas en la comunidad que son de Honduras o El Salvador; profesores o estudiantes de arte
Biblioteca Libros, enciclopedias	**Otros recursos** El/La conservador(a) del museo local o del museo de la universidad

Section Goals

In **Proyecto** students will:

- write a report on Salvadoran and Honduran artists
- use Spanish as they research and interact with the wider world

Before Assigning Proyecto Students will need approximately a week to complete the project, so at the beginning of that time period, have them open their books to page 541 and glance over **Proyecto**. Explain that they are going to write a report about the most famous artists in El Salvador and Honduras.

Assignment Have students read page 541 and follow directions in **Escribe una sección del informe** to complete their composition.

Escribe una sección del informe Suggestions

- You may wish to have students work in small groups. Have them determine what they will say about each artist and decide how to split up the work.
- Students can seek information on artist in El Salvador and Honduras by using the Spanish key words and phrases **arte el salvador, arte honduras, artistas salvadoreños, artistas hondureños,** and **artistas reconocidos de El Salvador y Honduras.**

Presenta la información Suggestions

- Students will present their reports in small groups. You may wish to have groups display samples or pictures of the artists' work on tables or desks.
- You may wish to set aside sufficient class time to do a few presentations at a time until all students have had a chance to present.

EVALUATION: Informe

Criteria	Scale
Content	1 2 3 4
Organization	1 2 3 4
Grammatical accuracy	1 2 3 4
Creativity	1 2 3 4
Oral presentation	1 2 3 4

Scoring	
Excellent	18–20 points
Good	14–17 points
Satisfactory	10–13 points
Unsatisfactory	< 10 points

Section Goals

In **Panorama**, students will read about the geography and culture of El Salvador.

Instructional Resources
Student Activities Manual: Workbook, 203
Transparency 61

El Salvador

Before Presenting Panorama Have students look at the map of El Salvador or project **Transparency 61**. Model the pronunciation of the main cities and natural features of the country. Draw students' attention to the number of active volcanoes in El Salvador. Tell students that because of the fertility of El Salvador's volcanic soil, the country has a strong agricultural sector which, in turn, has promoted a large population. Have students look at the inset map as you point out that El Salvador is the only Central American country without a Caribbean coast. Look at the call-out photos and ask volunteers to read the captions. **Assignment** Have students read **Panorama** and answer the questions in **¿Qué aprendiste?** on page 543 as homework.

Present Ask volunteers to read aloud each of the sections of **El país en cifras,** pausing as necessary to clarify unfamiliar vocabulary and concepts.

Increíble pero cierto
Of course, the soccer game that gave the conflict its name was only the spark that set a long-simmering problem ablaze. The causes of the war lie in El Salvador's small size and large population. Salvadoran squatters had been settling in larger and sparsely settled Honduras for nearly a decade. By 1967 some 300,000 Salvadorans had settled on Honduran territory and their existence became a sore spot for Honduras.

El Salvador

NATIONAL STANDARDS connections cultures

El país en cifras

- **Área:** 21.040 km² (8.124 millas²), *el tamaño de Massachusetts*
- **Población:** 6.519.000

El Salvador es el país centroamericano más pequeño y el más densamente poblado. Su población, al igual que la de Honduras, es muy homogénea: casi el 95 por ciento de la población es mestiza.

- **Capital:** San Salvador—1.490.000
- **Ciudades principales:** Soyapango—252.000, Santa Ana—202.000, San Miguel—183.000, Mejicanos—145.000

SOURCE: Population Division, UN Secretariat

- **Moneda:** colón
- **Idiomas:** español (oficial), náhuatl, lenca

Bandera de El Salvador

Salvadoreños célebres

- **Óscar Romero,** arzobispo y activista por los derechos humanos (1917-1980)
- **Claribel Alegría,** poeta, novelista y cuentista (1924-)
- **Roque Dalton,** poeta, ensayista y novelista (1935-1975)
- **María Eugenia Brizuela,** política (1956-)

Óscar Romero

densamente *densely* arzobispo *archbishop*
derechos humanos *human rights*

Ruinas de Tazumal

Salvadoreña muestra huevos de pato en El Jocotal.

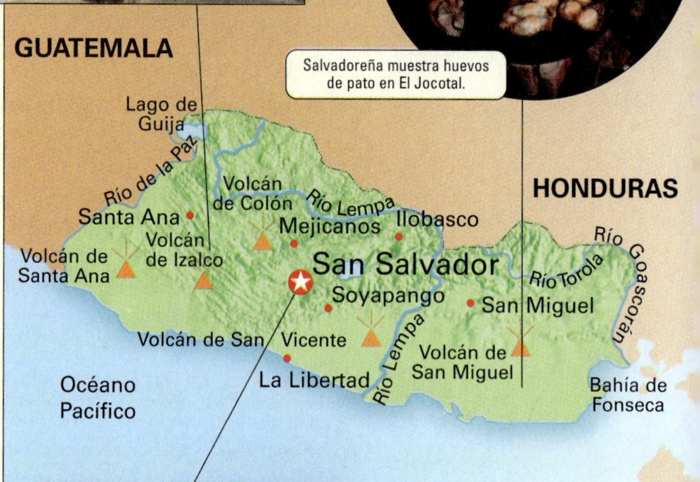

Aeropuerto Ilopango en San Salvador

recursos

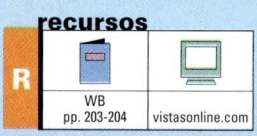

R | WB pp. 203-204 | vistasonline.com

¡Increíble pero cierto!

En 1969, cuando El Salvador perdió contra Honduras en un partido de clasificación para la Copa Mundial de Fútbol, estalló una terrible guerra entre los dos países. Aunque la famosa "Guerra del Fútbol" duró sólo 100 días, las relaciones entre los dos países fueron tensas por casi una década.

TEACHING OPTIONS

Worth Noting El Salvador's overpopulation, chronic economic problems, and lack of social justice resulted, in the early 1970s, in social disturbances which the government put down with brutal force. Such repression intensified resistance, and by the mid-1970s a civil war was being fought between government forces and the FMLN, an armed guerrilla movement. Among the many martyrs of the war was the Archbishop of San Salvador, Óscar Romero. A descendent of the privileged class in El Salvador, Romero came to champion the cause of peace and social justice for the poor. This position made him the target of reactionary elements. On March 24, 1980, Archbishop Romero was assassinated while saying mass in the Cathedral of San Salvador. His life and death became an inspiration for those seeking social justice. Still, it was only in 1991 that a cease fire brought an end to the civil war.

Deportes • El *surfing*

El Salvador, con unos 300 kilómetros de costa en el océano Pacífico, se ha convertido en un gran centro de *surfing* por la calidad y consistencia de sus olas. La Libertad es la playa que está más cerca de la capital, y allí las condiciones son perfectas para el *surfing*. Por eso vienen surfistas de todo el mundo a este pequeño pueblo salvadoreño. Los fines de semana hay muchísima gente en La Libertad y por eso muchos surfistas van al oeste, por la Costa del Bálsamo, donde las olas son buenas y hay menos gente.

Naturaleza • El Parque Nacional Montecristo

El bosque nuboso Montecristo se encuentra en el norte del país. Es conocido también como El Trifinio porque es el punto donde se unen Guatemala, Honduras y El Salvador. Este bosque está a una altitud de 2.400 metros (7.900 pies). Recibe 200 centímetros (80 pulgadas) de lluvia al año y con frecuencia tiene una humedad relativa de 100 por ciento. Sus altísimos árboles forman una bóveda que la luz del sol no puede traspasar. Allí hay muchas especies interesantes de plantas y animales, como orquídeas, hongos, monos araña, pumas, quetzales y tucanes.

Artes • La artesanía de Ilobasco

Ilobasco es un pueblo de grandes artesanos. Es famoso por sus objetos de arcilla y por los artículos de cerámica pintados a mano. Los productos más tradicionales de Ilobasco son los juguetes, los adornos y los utensilios de cocina y se ofrecen excursiones en las que se puede observar su fabricación paso a paso. Las "sorpresas" de Ilobasco, pequeñas piezas de cerámica en cuyo interior están representadas escenas de la vida diaria, son especialmente populares.

¿Qué aprendiste? Responde a las preguntas con una frase completa.

1. ¿Qué es el náhuatl? El náhuatl es un idioma que se habla en El Salvador.
2. ¿Quien es María Eugenia Brizuela? María Eugenia Brizuela es una política salvadoreña.
3. Hay muchos lugares ideales para el *surfing* en El Salvador. ¿Por qué? Hay muchos lugares ideales para el *surfing* porque El Salvador recibe algunas de las mejores olas del océano Pacífico.
4. ¿A qué altitud se encuentra el bosque nuboso? El bosque nuboso se encuentra a una altitud de 2.400 metros.
5. ¿Cuáles son algunos de los animales y las plantas que se encuentran en el bosque nuboso? En el bosque nuboso hay orquídeas, hongos, monos araña, pumas, quetzales y tucanes.
6. ¿Por qué al Parque Nacional Montecristo se le llama también El Trifinio? Al Parque Nacional Montecristo también se le llama El Trifinio porque es el punto donde se unen Guatemala, Honduras y El Salvador.
7. ¿Por qué es famoso el pueblo de Ilobasco? El pueblo de Ilobasco es famoso por los objetos de arcilla y por los artículos de cerámica pintados a mano.
8. ¿Qué se puede ver en una excursión en Ilobasco? En una excursión en Ilobasco se puede ver la fabricación de los artículos de cerámica paso a paso.
9. ¿Qué son las "sorpresas" de Ilobasco? Las "sorpresas" son pequeñas piezas de cerámica en cuyo interior están representadas escenas de la vida diaria.

Conexión Internet Investiga estos temas en el sitio **www.vistasonline.com.**

1. El Parque Nacional Montecristo es una reserva natural; busca información sobre otros parques o zonas protegidas en El Salvador. ¿Cómo son estos lugares? ¿Qué tipos de plantas y animales se encuentran allí?
2. Busca información sobre museos u otros lugares turísticos en San Salvador (u otra ciudad de El Salvador).

calidad *quality* olas *waves* El bosque nuboso *cloud forest* se unen *come together* pulgadas *inches* humedad *humidity* bóveda *canopy* traspasar *pierce* hongos *fungi* monos araña *spider monkeys* arcilla *clay* a mano *by hand* juguetes *toys* adornos *ornaments* paso a paso *step by step* pieza *piece*

El *surfing* Tell students that La Libertad is a relatively small town that sees a large influx of beach-goers, not just surfers during the weekends and holidays. Black, volcanic sand covers the beach of La Libertad. About five miles east lies Zunzal beach, which, during Holy Week (**Semana Santa**) each year, is the site of International surfing competitions.

El Parque Nacional Montecristo Montecristo cloud forest (**bosque nuboso**) is a protected area at the point where El Salvador, Honduras, and Guatemala meet. The point, at the summit of Montecristo, is called **El Trifinio**. The cloud forest receives an average of 78 inches of rain per year and the average relative humidity is 100%. Visitors have access to Montecristo only between October and March. The rest of the year it is closed to visitors.

La artesanía de Ilobasco Ilobasco is a crafts village that specializes in ceramic ware. **Sorpresas** are one of the most famous items. They are miniscule, intricate scenes and figures inside egg-shaped shells about the size of a walnut. Every year on September 29th a crafts fair drawing thousands of visitors from around the world is held.

¿Qué aprendiste? Go over the questions and answers orally with the whole class.

Assignment Have students do activites in **Student Activities Manual: Workbook,** page 203.

Conexión Internet Students will find information about Honduras at **www.vistasonline.com,** as well as links to other sites that can help them in their research.

TEACHING OPTIONS

Variación léxica Pupusa is the name given to the Salvadoran version of the **tortilla**. In fact, pupusas are made by putting a filling such as red beans, onions, garlic, and cheese on one uncooked tortilla, laying another tortilla over it and pressing the two together so they adhere, and then frying both in hot oil until the pupusa is golden and crunchy. Served sizzling from the fryer, **pupusas** are delicious. They are so popular that in El Salvador there are many stores, called **pupuserías**, that specialize in them. And if you visit a neighborhood in the United States where Salvadorans have settled, you will inevitably find a **pupusería**.

Section Goals
In **Panorama**, students will read about the economy and culture of Honduras.

Instructional Resources
Student Activities Manual: Workbook, 204
Transparency 62

Honduras
Before Presenting Panorama Have students look at the map of Honduras or project **Transparency 62** and talk about the physical features of the country. Hills and mountains cover three quarters of Honduras, with lowlands found only along coastal areas and in major river valleys. Deforestation is a major environmental challenge in Honduras. If deforestation continues at the current rate of 300 square kilometers per year, Honduras will have no trees left by 2020.
Assignment Have students read **Panorama** and answer the questions in **¿Qué aprendiste?** on page 545.

Present Ask volunteers to read each section of **El país en cifras**. After reading about the indigenous populations of Honduras, tell students that the **miskito** people are also found along the Caribbean coast of Nicaragua. After students read about **Idiomas**, point out that **garífuna** speakers are descendants of indigenous **caribs** who intermarried with African slaves following the shipwreck of a slaving ship some 300 years ago.

Increíble pero cierto Honduras is not known for the fairness of its justice system. Many prisoners of the **Penitenciaría Central de Tegucigalpa** have never been officially sentenced for the crimes that landed them in prison! Severe overcrowding is another problem. Given these conditions, the works of the prison artisans of Tegucigalpa are all the more impressive.

Honduras

NATIONAL STANDARDS connections cultures

El país en cifras

- **Área:** 112.492 km² (43.870 millas²), *un poco más grande que Tennessee*
- **Población:** 6.828.000

Cerca del 90 por ciento de la población de Honduras es mestiza. Todavía hay pequeños grupos indígenas como los jicaque, los miskito y los paya que han mantenido su cultura sin influencias exteriores y que no hablan español.

- **Capital:** Tegucigalpa—1.016.000

Tegucigalpa

- **Ciudades principales:** San Pedro Sula—470.000, El Progreso—81.000, La Ceiba—72.000

SOURCE: Population Division, UN Secretariat

- **Moneda:** lempira
- **Idiomas:** español (oficial), miskito, garífuna

Bandera de Honduras

Hondureños célebres
- José Antonio Velásquez, pintor (1906-1983)
- Argentina Díaz Lozano, escritora (1909-)
- Carlos Roberto Reina, juez y presidente del país (1926-)
- Roberto Sosa, escritor (1930-)

juez *judge* presos *prisoners*

Guacamayo en vuelo

Hombres garífuna en Santa Fe

Niños pescando en el lago de Yojoa.

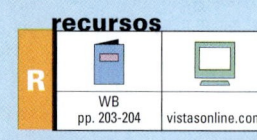

recursos
R — WB pp. 203-204 | vistasonline.com

¡Increíble pero cierto!

Los presos de la Penitenciaría Central de Tegucigalpa hacen objetos de madera, hamacas y hasta instrumentos musicales. Sus artesanías son tan populares que los funcionarios de la prisión han abierto una pequeña tienda donde los turistas pueden regatear con este especial grupo de artesanos.

TEACHING OPTIONS

Worth Noting It was in Honduras, on his fourth voyage of discovery, that Christopher Columbus first set foot on the mainland of the continent that would become the Americas. On August 14, 1502, the navigator landed at a site near Trujillo and named the country **Honduras** (depths) because of the deep waters along the northern Caribbean coast.

Extra Practice At this point in their studies, your students should be able to read and understand the poem **"La casa de la justicia,"** by Roberto Sosa, without difficulty. (You can find the text online at http://www.poesia.com/forum/Forum1/HTML/000544.html.) Discuss the poem with your students, asking them what they think the poet's impression of the Honduran justice system is.

Lugares • Copán

Copán es el sitio arqueológico más importante de Honduras, y para los que estudian la cultura maya es uno de los más fascinantes de la región. Aproximadamente en 400 d.C., la ciudad era muy grande, con más de 150 edificios y plazas, patios, templos y canchas para el juego de pelota. Copán es famoso por las esculturas pintadas que adornan sus edificios; por los "excéntricos", que son cetros ceremoniales de piedra finamente esculpidos; y por el templo llamado Rosalila.

Economía • Las plantaciones de bananas

Hoy día las bananas son la exportación principal de Honduras. Hace más de cien años que tienen un papel fundamental en la historia económica y política del país. En 1889, la Standard Fruit Company empezó a exportar bananas a Nueva Orleans y la fruta resultó tan popular que rápidamente empezó a generar grandes beneficios para la Standard Fruit y otras compañías norteamericanas. Debido al enorme poder económico que tenía en el país, la Standard Fruit Company intervino muchas veces en la política hondureña.

Artes • José Antonio Velásquez, (1906-1983)

José Antonio Velásquez fue uno de los pintores primitivistas más famosos de su tiempo. Se le compara a pintores europeos del mismo género, como Paul Gauguin o Emil Nolde, porque en sus obras representaba lo más concreto de la vida diaria que lo rodeaba. Se nota fácilmente el énfasis del pintor en los detalles de la escena. En su pintura desaparecen casi totalmente los juegos de perspectiva, y los colores utilizados en los paisajes son puros.

¿Qué aprendiste? Responde a las preguntas con una frase completa.

1. ¿Qué es la lempira?
   La lempira es la moneda nacional de Honduras.
2. ¿Qué es un "excéntrico"?
   Un "excéntrico" es un cetro ceremonial de piedra.
3. ¿Dónde está el templo Rosalila?
   El templo Rosalila está en Copán.
4. ¿Cuál es la exportación principal de Honduras?
   Las bananas son la exportación principal de Honduras.
5. ¿Qué es la Standard Fruit Company? La Standard Fruit Company es una compañía norteamericana que exportaba bananas de Honduras e intervino muchas veces en la política hondureña.
6. ¿Cómo es el estilo de José Antonio Velásquez?
   El estilo de Velásquez es primitivista.
7. ¿Qué temas trataba Velásquez en su pintura?
   Velásquez pintaba la vida diaria que lo rodeaba.

Conexión Internet Investiga estos temas en el sitio **www.vistasonline.com**.

1. ¿Cuáles son algunas de las exportaciones principales de Honduras, además de las bananas? ¿A qué países exporta Honduras sus productos?
2. Busca información sobre Copán u otro sitio arqueológico en Honduras. En tu opinión, ¿cuáles son los aspectos más interesantes del sitio?

canchas *courts* pelota *jai-alai* cetros *scepters* finamente *in a refined way* generar *to generate* beneficios *profits* Debido al *Due to* poder *power* intervino *intervened* primitivistas *primitivist* género *genre* rodeaba *surrounded* detalles *details* escena *scene* desaparecen *disappear*

TEACHING OPTIONS

Worth Noting Honduras was among the hardest hit of the Central American nations when Hurricane Mitch struck in November 1998. Major roadways and bridges were destroyed, entire communities were covered in mud, and an air of hopelessness and desperation pervaded the country. With one of the lowest per capita income levels and one of the highest illiteracy rates in Central America, Hondurans were already struggling before the devastation of Mitch. Despite international aid, reconstruction is slow and the level of desperation in Honduras has been reflected in the increase in violent crime.

Heritage Speakers Ask Spanish speakers to research one of the Honduran topics mentioned in **Panorama** and write a three-paragraph essay about it. Heritage speakers may then present their findings orally to the whole class.

Copán Recent archaeological studies have focused on the abrupt disappearance of the Maya from Copán around the 9th Century C.E. Findings indicate that the Mayan dynasty suffered a sudden collapse that left the Copán valley virtually depopulated within a century.

Las plantaciones de bananas When Hurricane Mitch struck Central America in November 1998, it not only wiped out much of the infrastructure of Honduras, but also destroyed 60% of the projected agricultural exports. Instead of the 33 million boxes of bananas projected for export in 1999, only 4 million boxes were exported. The banana industry is still trying to recover from this major setback.

José Antonio Velásquez The primitive style established by José Antonio Velásquez is now being carried on by his son, Tulio Velásquez. Tulio was taught by his father, and had his first exhibition in 1959. Since then, his primitive art has been exhibited throughout the Americas, in Europe, and in Asia. Have students view works by each artist and then write a brief comparison of their styles.

¿Qué aprendiste? Go over the questions and answers with the whole class.

Assignment Have students do activites in **Student Activities Manual: Workbook,** page 204.

Conexión Internet Students will find information about Honduras at **www.vistasonline.com,** as well as links to other sites that can help them in their research.

Las bellas artes

el baile, la danza	*dance*
el ballet	*ballet*
la banda	*band*
las bellas artes	*(fine) arts*
el boleto	*ticket*
la canción	*song*
la comedia	*comedy; play*
el concierto	*concert*
el cuento	*short story*
la cultura	*culture*
el drama	*drama; play*
la escultura	*sculpture*
el espectáculo	*show*
la estatua	*statue*
el festival	*festival*
la historia	*history; story*
la música	*music*
la obra	*work (of art, music, etc.)*
la obra maestra	*masterpiece*
la ópera	*opera*
la orquesta	*orchestra*
el personaje (principal)	*(main) character*
la pintura	*painting*
el poema	*poem*
la poesía	*poetry*
el público	*audience*
el teatro	*theater*
la tragedia	*tragedy*
aburrirse	*to get bored*
aplaudir	*to applaud*
apreciar	*to appreciate*
esculpir	*to sculpt*
hacer el papel (de)	*to play the role (of)*
pintar	*to paint*
presentar	*to present; to put on (a performance)*
publicar	*to publish*
tocar	*to touch; to play (a musical instrument)*
artístico/a	*artistic*
clásico/a	*classical*
dramático/a	*dramatic*
extranjero/a	*foreign*
folklórico/a	*folk*
moderno/a	*modern*
musical	*musical*
romántico/a	*romantic*
talentoso/a	*talented*

Artistas

el bailarín, la bailarina	*dancer*
el/la cantante	*singer*
el/la compositor(a)	*composer*
el/la director(a)	*director; (musical) conductor*
el/la dramaturgo/a	*playwright*
el/la escritor(a)	*writer*
el/la escultor(a)	*sculptor*
la estrella (*m., f.*) de cine	*movie star*
el/la músico/a	*musician*
el/la poeta	*poet*

El cine y la televisión

el canal	*channel*
el concurso	*game show; contest*
los dibujos animados	*cartoons*
el documental	*documentary*
el premio	*prize; award*
el programa de entrevistas	*talk show*
la telenovela	*soap opera*
...de acción	*action*
...de aventuras	*adventure*
...de ciencia ficción	*science fiction*
...de horror	*horror*
...de vaqueros	*western*

Artesanía

la artesanía	*craftsmanship; crafts*
la cerámica	*pottery*
el tejido	*weaving*

Expresiones útiles	*See page 523.*

Las actualidades

18

Communicative Goals

You will learn how to:

- **Talk about and describe your travel experiences.**
- **Discuss current events and issues.**
- **Talk about and discuss the media.**

Lesson Goals

In **Lesson 18** students will be introduced to the following:

- terms for current events
- political terms
- words for social issues
- **si** clauses in the subjunctive mood
- **si** clauses with verbs in the indicative mood
- review of subjunctive forms
- using the subjunctive, indicative, and infinitive in complex sentences
- recognizing chronological order
- writing strong introductions and conclusions
- writing a composition about improving the world
- recognizing genre and taking notes while listening
- writing a news article on currents events in Uruguay and Paraguay
- cultural and geographic information about Paraguay
- cultural and geographic information about Uruguay

Lesson Preview

Have students look at the photo. Ask: **¿Qué ven en la foto? ¿Qué hace el hombre? ¿Qué tipo de revistas leen Uds.? ¿Qué aprenden de las revistas?**

INSTRUCTIONAL RESOURCES

Student Activities Manual: Workbook, 205–214
Student Activities Manual: Lab Manual, 323–326
Student Activities Manual: Video Activities, 361–362
Instructor's Resource Manual: Hojas de actividades, 44–45
Instructor's Resource Manual: Answer Keys
Tapescript/Videoscript
Overhead Transparencies, 63–65
Student Cassette/CD
Lab Cassette/CD
Video Program
CD-ROM
Website: **www.vistasonline.com**
Testing Program: Prueba A, Prueba B

Section Goals

In **Contextos**, students will learn and practice terminology related to:

- current events
- politics
- social issues

Instructional Resources
Student Activities Manual: Workbook, 205–206; Lab Manual, 323
Transparency 63
Student Cassette/CD

Before Presenting Contextos Introduce active lesson vocabulary. Bring in a current newspaper (Spanish-language if possible) and talk to the students about the headlines and/or main stories. Ex: **¿Qué dice la prensa hoy? ¿Cuál es el reportaje principal? Anoche hubo un terremoto en…** and so forth. Show other headlines and ask volunteers to tell the class what they know about the story and what their opinions are.
Assignment Have students study **Contextos** and prepare the activities on pages 549–550 as homework.

Present Give students two minutes to review the picture on pages 548–549. Then project **Transparency 63**. Have students refer to the picture to answer questions about news-making events. Ex: **¿Qué tiempo hace? ¿Quién se presenta como candidato en las elecciones? ¿Qué hace la Sra. sentada delante del banco? ¿y el hombre que sale corriendo del banco?** As you continue, introduce personalized questions about student opinions and current events. Ask: **¿Cuál es su opinión de los candidatos para ____? ¿Por qué creen eso? ¿Quién de Uds. ha participado alguna vez en una huelga? ¿Cuál fue el resultado? ¿Cuántos leen el diario cada mañana? ¿Cuántos escuchan las noticias por la radio?** and so forth.

Las actualidades

Más vocabulario

el acontecimiento	*event*
las actualidades	*news; current events*
el artículo	*article*
el desastre (natural)	*(natural) disaster*
el desempleo	*unemployment*
la (des)igualdad	*(in)equality*
la discriminación	*discrimination*
la encuesta	*poll; survey*
la experiencia	*experience*
la guerra	*war*
el huracán	*hurricane*
el informe	*report; paper (written work)*
la inundación	*flood*
la libertad	*liberty; freedom*
los medios de comunicación	*means of communication; media*
las noticias	*news*
la paz	*peace*
la prensa	*press*
el racismo	*racism*
el reportaje	*report*
el sexismo	*sexism*
el SIDA	*AIDS*
el terremoto	*earthquake*
anunciar	*to announce; to advertise*
comunicarse (con)	*to communicate (with)*
durar	*to last*
informar	*to inform*
luchar (por/contra)	*to fight; to struggle (for/against)*
ocurrir	*to occur; to happen*
transmitir, emitir	*to broadcast*
(inter)nacional	*(inter)national*
peligroso/a	*dangerous*

Variación léxica

informe ⟷ trabajo (*Esp.*)
noticiero ⟷ informativo (*Esp.*)

recursos

R	SCASS./CD Lección 18	WB pp. 205-206	LM p. 323	LCASS./CD Cass. 9B/CD9

TEACHING OPTIONS

Heritage Speakers Ask Spanish-speakers to watch a news broadcast on a Spanish station or surf the Internet for the latest news in their home communities. Have them summarize the report to the rest of the class.
Variación léxica Common newspaper terms: **titular** (headline), **artículo regular** (column), **sección de deportes** (sports page), **editorial** (editorial), **carta al/a la director(a)** (letter to the editor)

Extra Practice Write the following groups of words on the board and have students indicate which word doesn't belong in the group. **1. discurso elecciones política choque (choque) 2. televisión prensa locutora radio (locutora) 3. lluvia terremoto inundación tormenta (terremoto) 4. guerra desastre militar ejército (desastre) 5. peligroso huelga trabajador sueldo (peligroso)**

La política

el/la ciudadano/a	*citizen*
el deber	*responsibility; obligation*
los derechos	*rights*
la dictadura	*dictatorship*
las elecciones	*election*
el impuesto	*tax*
la política	*politics*
el/la representante	*representative*
declarar	*to declare; to say*
elegir	*to elect*
obedecer	*to obey*
votar	*to vote*
político/a	*political*

Práctica

1 Escuchar Escucha las noticias y selecciona la frase que mejor completa las siguientes oraciones.

1. Los ciudadanos creen que __b__.
   a. hay un huracán en el Caribe
   b. hay discriminación en la imposición de los impuestos
   c. hay una encuesta en el Caribe
2. Los ciudadanos creen que los candidatos tienen __a__.
   a. el deber de asegurar la igualdad en los impuestos
   b. el deber de hacer las encuestas
   c. los impuestos
3. La encuesta muestra que los ciudadanos __c__.
   a. quieren desigualdad en las elecciones
   b. quieren hacer otra encuesta
   c. quieren igualdad en los impuestos
4. Hay __b__ en el Caribe.
   a. un incendio grande b. una tormenta peligrosa c. un tornado
5. Los servicios de Puerto Rico predijeron anoche que __c__ podrían destruir edificios y playas.
   a. los vientos b. los terremotos c. las inundaciones
6. La tormenta ha durado __b__.
   a. dos semanas b. muchos días c. muchos años

2 Categorías Mira la lista e indica la categoría de cada uno de los siguientes términos. Las categorías son: **desastres naturales, política, medios de comunicación.**

1. reportaje — medios de comunicación
2. inundación — desastres naturales
3. incendio — desastres naturales
4. candidato/a — política
5. informe — medios de comunicación
6. ciudadano — política
7. encuesta — política
8. tornado — desastres naturales
9. noticiero — medios de comunicación
10. prensa — medios de comunicación
11. elecciones — política
12. terremoto — desastres naturales

3 Definir Trabaja con un(a) compañero/a para definir las siguientes palabras. Answers will vary.

1. guerra
2. crimen
3. ejército
4. desempleo
5. discurso
6. acontecimiento
7. sexismo
8. SIDA
9. huelga
10. racismo
11. locutor(a)
12. libertad

TEACHING OPTIONS

Pairs Ask students to categorize all the nouns using different paradigms than those given. Ex: **fenómenos del tiempo relacionados con el agua: tormenta, huracán, inundación. Conceptos democráticos: huelga, elecciones, derechos.** Have each pair read their categories aloud to the class.

Extra Practice Have the students complete the following analogies. **1. locutora : ____ :: candidato : discurso (reportaje) 2. SIDA : salud :: ____ : libertad (dictadura) 3. pagar : impuesto :: ____ : candidato (votar) 4. lluvia ____ :: viento : huracán (inundación/tormenta) 5. terminar : ____ :: desobedecer : obedecer (durar)**

1 Present Help students check their answers by reading the tapescript to the whole class and asking volunteers to read the correctly completed sentences.

Tapescript Las noticias de hoy de Montevideo y de todo el mundo... En noticias políticas... Ahora que se acercan las elecciones, una encuesta nacional muestra que los ciudadanos creen que hay discriminación en la imposición de los impuestos. Se cree que los candidatos tienen el deber de asegurar la igualdad de los impuestos para todos o, por lo menos, de explicar claramente por qué la desigualdad en ciertos impuestos ayuda a mejorar el bienestar nacional. En noticias internacionales... Esta noche una peligrosa tormenta se acerca a las islas del Caribe, con vientos de más de 120 kilómetros por hora. Esta tormenta es casi un huracán. Los servicios meteorológicos de Puerto Rico y de la República Dominicana pronosticaron que las inundaciones podrían destruir edificios, playas y productos agrícolas. *Student Cassette/CD*

2 Present Model the activity by naming the term not listed. Ex: **huracán, impuesto, diario.** Have volunteers identify the category.

3 Present Allow 10 minutes for pairs to come up with definitions. Then have each pair join two other pairs and compare their definitions.

3 Expand Ask students to give antonyms for the first column of words. Possible answers: **paz, obediencia a las leyes, población civil, empleo, silencio, rutina**

4 Completar Completa la siguiente noticia con los verbos adecuados para cada frase. Conjuga los verbos en el tiempo verbal correspondiente.

1. El grupo ___anunció___ a todos los medios de comunicación que iba a organizar una huelga general de los trabajadores.
   a. durar b. votar c. anunciar
2. El presidente del país ha sugerido algunas soluciones para evitar que eso ___ocurra___.
   a. ocurrir b. luchar c. elegir
3. Todos los representantes políticos les pidieron a los ciudadanos que ___obedecieran___ al presidente.
   a. comer b. obedecer c. aburrir
4. La oposición, por otro lado, ___eligió___ a un líder para promover la huelga.
   a. publicar b. emitir c. elegir
5. El líder de la oposición dijo que si el gobierno ignoraba sus opiniones, la huelga iba a ___durar___ mucho tiempo.
   a. transmitir b. obedecer c. durar
6. Hoy día, el líder de la oposición declaró que los ciudadanos estaban listos para ___luchar___ por sus derechos.
   a. informar b. comunicarse c. luchar

5 Diálogo Completa el siguiente diálogo con las palabras adecuadas.

derechos	declarar	artículo
choque	violencia	dictaduras
paz	transmitir	peligrosa

RAÚL Oye, Agustín, ¿leíste el ___artículo___ del diario *El País*?
AGUSTÍN ¿Cuál? ¿El del ___choque___ entre dos autobuses?
RAÚL No, el otro, sobre...
AGUSTÍN ¿Sobre la tormenta ___peligrosa___ que viene mañana?
RAÚL No, hombre, el artículo sobre política...
AGUSTÍN ¡Ay, claro! Un análisis de las peores ___dictaduras___ de la historia.
RAÚL ¡Agustín! Deja de interrumpir. Te quería hablar del artículo sobre la organización que lucha por los ___derechos___ humanos y la ___paz___.
AGUSTÍN Ah, no lo leí.
RAÚL Parece que te interesan más las noticias sobre la ___violencia___, ¿eh?

6 La vida civil ¿Estás de acuerdo con las siguientes afirmaciones? Comparte tus respuestas con la clase. Answers will vary.

1. Los medios de comunicación nos informan bien de las noticias.
2. Los medios de comunicación nos dan una visión global del mundo.
3. Los candidatos para las elecciones deben aparecer en todos los medios de comunicación.
4. Nosotros y nuestros representantes nos comunicamos bien.
5. Es importante que todos obedezcamos las leyes.
6. Es importante leer el diario todos los días.
7. Es importante mirar o escuchar un noticiero todos los días.
8. Es importante votar.

AYUDA

You might want to use these expressions when you do activity 6.

En mi opinión...
Está claro que...
(No) Estoy de acuerdo.
Según mis padres...
Sería ideal que...

4 Present If you assigned this activity as homework, go over it with the whole class, asking volunteers to read the completed sentences.

4 Suggestion This activity is also suited for pair work. Have partners complete alternate sentences. Then ask them to check the other's responses.

4 Expand Ask students to write a summary of a current news event using this activity as a model.

5 Present Go over the answers with the whole class by asking two volunteers to read the completed dialogue.

5 Expand Have pairs convert the dialogue into a summary of events as reported by **El País.** Ex: **Hay cuatro artículos de interés en El País hoy. Agustín ha leído todos los artículos sobre los acontecimientos violentos, pero a Raúl le interesa el reportaje sobre los derechos humanos y la paz. Agustín no le deja hablar a Raúl.**

6 Warm-up Go over the information contained in **Ayuda** before assigning this activity.

6 Suggestion This activity can also be done in small groups of three or four in round robin fashion. Call on different students to report on their group's responses.

6 Expand Assign students to groups of five, and ask them to develop a survey based on these questions. Have them survey students for the next class and present the results.

Successful Language Learning Tell students that watching or listening to the news in Spanish is a good way to practice their comprehension skills. Point out that many of the words used in news broadcasts are cognates.

TEACHING OPTIONS

TPR Have students stand. Say an expression at random **(Eres locutor.)** and point at a student who should perform an appropriate gesture. Keep the pace rapid. Vary by pointing to more than one student **(Uds. están en un huracán).**

Game Have students write in Spanish five trivia questions and answers concerning news events. Ask them to number their questions from 1 **(al más fácil)** to 5 **(al más difícil).** Use these questions and the format of any popular television game show, but have the students compete in teams rather than as individual contestants.

Comunicación

7 **Las actualidades** En parejas, describan lo que ven en las fotos. Luego, escriban una historia para explicar qué pasó en cada foto. Answers will vary.

8 **Un noticiero** En grupos, trabajen para presentar un noticiero de la tarde. Presenten por lo menos cuatro reportajes, incluyendo desastres naturales, política, crimen y temas sociales. Answers will vary.

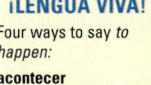

¡LENGUA VIVA!
Four ways to say *to happen:*
acontecer
ocurrir
pasar
suceder

9 **Las elecciones** Trabajen en parejas para representar una entrevista entre un(a) reportero/a de la televisión y un(a) político/a que va a ser candidato/a en las próximas elecciones. Antes de la entrevista, hagan una lista de los temas de los que el/la candidato/a va a hablar. Durante la entrevista, la clase va a hacer el papel del público y, después de la entrevista, el/la reportero/a va a hacerle preguntas y pedirle comentarios al público. Answers will vary.

7 Warm-up Allow the class two minutes to note details in the photos and think of scenarios for the events.

7 Present Ask volunteers to answer closed-ended questions about each picture. Ex: **¿Ocurrió en la ciudad o en el campo? ¿Fue un acontecimiento político o un desastre natural? ¿Hubo muchas víctimas? ¿Fue reciente o distante el acontecimiento?** and so forth.

7 Expand With the whole class, ask volunteers to summarize one of their descriptions.

8 Warm-up Give example sentences of the four ways to say *happen* in Spanish. Then have groups of four work together using idea maps to brainstorm different ideas for their four news reports.

8 Expand Ask groups to choose one of their reports and present it to the class. Alternatively, have all groups present their news report during the next class meeting, encouraging them to bring props and/or visuals to enrich their presentations.

9 Present Pick a prominent politician and ask students what questions they would ask him/her. Write their suggestions on the board.

9 Suggestion Videotape the **entrevistas** and show parts during the next class or check the tape out to students for private viewing.

Assignment Have students do activities in **Student Activities Manual: Workbook,** pages 205–206.

TEACHING OPTIONS

Small Groups Assign groups of three for a debate on a current campus issue. Give the teams some time in class to prepare their strategy, but ask each team member to prepare his/her argument of two to three minutes as homework. Have the rest of the class judge the debate.

Game Divide the class into teams of four. Give groups five minutes to write a job announcement. Then have them take turns reading their announcements. The other teams must guess what job is being announced. Award one point for every correct guess and two points to the team who is able to stump the rest of the class.

Section goals

In **Fotonovela** students will:

- receive comprehensible input from free-flowing discourse
- learn functional phrases that preview lesson grammatical structures

Instructional Resources
Student Activities Manual: Video Activities 361–362
Video Program (Start: 01:42:43)

Video Synopsis Upon the students' return to the university, Maite's friend Roberto interviews the group about their experiences on the excursion. Then don Francisco and the students say good-bye to each other.

Before Presenting Fotonovela Have the class read the title, scan the captions for cognates, and look at the stills. Ask them to predict what they think the episode will be about.
Assignment Have students study **Fotonovela** and **Expresiones útiles** as homework.

Warm-up Quickly review the predictions your students made about the **Fotonovela**. Ask a few questions to help them summarize the plot.

Present Work through the **Expresiones útiles** by having the class repeat each expression after you. Then practice this active vocabulary by asking your students a few questions about recent vacations they have taken. Ex: **¿Adónde fuiste de vacaciones el verano pasado? ¿Cuál fue tu experiencia favorita?**

Continued on page 553.

¡Hasta la próxima!

NATIONAL STANDARDS connections cultures

Los estudiantes comparten con Roberto sus recuerdos (*memories*) favoritos de la aventura.

PERSONAJES

MAITE

INÉS

DON FRANCISCO

ÁLEX

JAVIER

SRA. RAMOS

ROBERTO

1

SRA. RAMOS ¡Hola! Espero que todos hayan tenido un magnífico viaje.

JAVIER ¡Lo hemos pasado maravillosamente!

SRA. RAMOS ¿Qué tal, don Francisco? ¡Qué gusto volver a verlo!

2

MAITE ¡Roberto! ¿Cómo estás?

3

MAITE Álex, ven... es mi amigo Roberto. Nos conocimos en clase de periodismo. Es reportero del periódico de la universidad. Roberto, éste es mi novio, Álex.

ROBERTO Mucho gusto, Álex.

ÁLEX El gusto es mío.

6

ROBERTO A ver... Inés. ¿Cuál fue tu experiencia favorita?

INÉS Para mí lo mejor fue la excursión que hicimos a las montañas.

ROBERTO ¿Fue peligroso?

JAVIER No... Pero si nuestro guía no hubiera estado allí con nosotros, ¡seguro que nos habríamos perdido!

7

ROBERTO ¿Qué más ocurrió durante el viaje?

MAITE Pues figúrate que un día fuimos a comer al restaurante El Cráter. A la hora del postre la señora Perales, la dueña, me sorprendió con un pastel y un flan para mi cumpleaños.

8

JAVIER También tuvimos un problema con el autobús, pero Inés resolvió el problema con la ayuda de un mecánico. Ahora la llamamos La Mujer Mecánica.

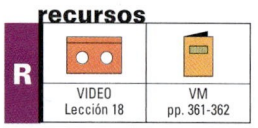

recursos

R	VIDEO Lección 18	VM pp. 361-362

TEACHING OPTIONS

Video Tips General suggestions for using video clips in the classroom can be found on page IAE-13 of the **Instructor's Annotated Edition**.

¡Hasta la próxima! Before you play the **¡Hasta la próxima!** segment of this video module, give your students a list of questions about it. Tell them to read the questions and listen for the answers as they watch the video. After playing the **¡Hasta la próxima!** segment, go over the questions with the class. If necessary, replay the segment. Sample questions: **¿Quiénes esperan a los estudiantes en la universidad? (Sra. Ramos, Roberto) ¿Quién es Roberto? (un amigo que Maite conoció en la clase de periodismo)**

4

MAITE Y éstos son mis amigos. Inés... Javier...

JAVIER & INÉS ¡Hola!

5

MAITE Pero, ¿qué estás haciendo tú aquí?

ROBERTO Ay, Maite, es que estoy cansado de escribir sobre el crimen y la política. Me gustaría hacerles una entrevista sobre las experiencias del viaje.

MAITE ¡Fenomenal!

9

ROBERTO Si pudieran hacer el viaje otra vez, ¿lo harían?

ÁLEX Sin pensarlo dos veces. Viajar es una buena manera de conocer mejor a las personas y de hacer amigos.

10

DON FRANCISCO ¡Adiós, chicos!

ESTUDIANTES ¡Adiós! ¡Adiós, don Efe! ¡Hasta luego!

DON FRANCISCO ¡Hasta la próxima, Sra. Ramos!

Expresiones útiles

Saying you're happy to see someone

- **¡Qué gusto volver a verte!**
  I'm happy to see you (fam.) *again!*
- **¡Qué gusto volver a verlo/la!**
  I'm happy to see you (form.) *again!*
- **Gusto de verte.**
  It's nice to see you (fam.).
- **Gusto de verlo/la.**
  It's nice to see you (form.).

Saying you had a good time

- **¡Lo hemos pasado maravillosamente!**
  We've had a great time!
- **¡Lo hemos pasado de película!**
  We've had a great time!
- **Lo pasamos muy bien.**
  We had a good time.
- **Nos divertimos mucho.**
  We had a lot of fun.

Talking about your trip

- **¿Cuál fue tu experiencia favorita?**
  What was your favorite experience?
  - **Lo mejor fue la excursión que hicimos a las montañas.**
    The best thing was the hike we went on in the mountains.
- **¿Qué más ocurrió durante el viaje?**
  What else happened on the trip?
  - **Lo peor fue cuando tuvimos un problema con el autobús.**
    The worst thing was when we had a problem with the bus.
- **Si pudieran hacer el viaje otra vez, ¿lo harían?**
  If you could make the trip again, would you do it?
  - **Sin pensarlo dos veces.**
    I wouldn't give it a second thought.

Enfoque cultural Los medios de comunicación

Entre los medios de comunicación más importantes en los países hispanos están la radio, la televisión, los periódicos y las revistas. El periódico en español que más se vende en el mundo es *El País*, de Madrid. Se venden más de un millón de ejemplares (*copies*) cada día. En cuanto a la televisión, una de las cadenas (*networks*) más importantes es Univisión, de gran popularidad en los Estados Unidos. Además, las publicaciones en el Internet van siendo cada vez más importantes y desarrolladas.

Work through the **Fotonovela** by having volunteers read the various parts aloud. You may want to ask a few volunteers to ad-lib the interview portion of the **Fotonovela**. See ideas for using the video in **Teaching Options**, page 552.

Comprehension Check Do Activity 1, **¿Cierto o falso?**, page 554, orally with the whole class.

Suggestion Have the class look at the **Expresiones útiles** and locate the sentence **Si pudieran hacer el viaje otra vez, ¿lo harían?** Tell them that this sentence contains an *if* clause that uses the past subjunctive, followed by a clause containing a conditional form. Have the class identify the two verb forms. Then have the class look at the caption for frame 6 of the **Fotonovela** and find the sentence **Pero si nuestro guía no hubiera estado con nosotros, ¡seguro que nos habríamos perdido!** Explain that this sentence contains an if-clause that uses the past perfect subjunctive, followed by a clause containing a conditional perfect form. Have the class tell you which verb is in the past perfect subjunctive and which is in the conditional perfect. Tell your students that they will learn more about these concepts in the upcoming **Estructura** section.

Assignment Have students do Activities 2–4 in **Reacciona a la fotonovela,** page 554.

The Affective Dimension Ask students if they feel more comfortable watching the video now than when they started the course. You may recommend that they view all the episodes again to help them realize how much their proficiency has increased.

TEACHING OPTIONS

Enfoque cultural Tell the class that there is a substantial Spanish-language media presence in the United States. Have the class work in small groups to brainstorm lists of the specific Spanish-language media that they are aware of, including local, regional, and national television networks, radio stations, magazines, and newspapers. Ask a few groups to tell the class about the media outlets on their lists. If possible, have your students bring examples of Spanish-language newspapers and magazines to class. They should be prepared to tell their classmates where each one is published and what audience it hopes to reach.

Reacciona a la fotonovela

1 Expand Give the class these additional items: **6. Roberto es el novio de Inés. (Falso. Roberto es un amigo de Maite.) 7. Javier se divirtió mucho durante el viaje. (Cierto.) 8. Roberto quiere hablar con los estudiantes sobre el viaje. (Cierto.)**

2 Warm-Up Have your students skim the **Fotonovela** before completing this activity.

3 Expand Give this additional item to the class: **6. ¿Tuvieron experiencias interesantes durante el viaje? (Roberto)**

3 Present Have your students work in pairs to complete this activity. They should take turns reading the questions and giving the answers.

4 Possible Response

S1: ¡Hola! ¡Qué gusto volver a verte!
S2: Sí, gusto de verte. ¿Cómo has estado?
S1: Muy bien, gracias. Hice un viaje a Asia en junio.
S2: ¿Te divertiste?
S1: Sí, lo pasé de película.
S2: ¿Cuál fue tu experiencia favorita?
S1: Para mí lo mejor fue el viaje que hice a Tailandia. Vi muchas cosas fascinantes y comí muy bien.
S2: ¿Y cuál fue la peor experiencia?
S1: Lo peor fue cuando nos quedamos sin gasolina en una carretera en la China. Oye, ¿qué has hecho tú este verano?
S2: Yo acabo de volver de Europa…

Reacciona a la fotonovela

1 ¿Cierto o falso? Decide si lo que se afirma en las siguientes frases es cierto o falso. Corrige las frases que sean falsas.

	Cierto	Falso
1. Roberto es reportero; escribe artículos para el periódico de la universidad.	✓	❍
2. Los artículos sobre el crimen y la política ya no le interesan tanto a Roberto.	✓	❍
3. Para Inés, la mejor experiencia fue cuando cenaron en el restaurante El Cráter. Para Inés, la mejor experiencia fue la excursión que hicieron a las montañas.	❍	✓
4. La señora Ramos sabe mucho de autobuses; por eso la llaman La Mujer Mecánica. Inés sabe mucho de autobuses; ella es "La Mujer Mecánica".	❍	✓
5. A Álex le encantó el viaje pero es algo que sólo haría una vez en su vida. Álex haría el viaje otra vez, sin pensarlo dos veces.	❍	✓

2 Identificar Identifica quién puede hacer las siguientes afirmaciones.

1. ¿Te acuerdas del problema mecánico con el autobús? Qué bueno que estaba Inés allí, ¿no? Javier
2. Si quieres hacer amigos y conocer mejor un país, tienes que viajar. Álex
3. ¡Hola! Qué bueno volver a verlos. Me imagino que tuvieron un viaje maravilloso. Sra. Ramos
4. Creo que el mejor día fue cuando fuimos a un restaurante y me prepararon un pastel. Maite
5. Ya no quiero escribir sobre cosas negativas. Prefiero hacer entrevistas sobre experiencias interesantes. Roberto

3 Preguntas Responde a las siguientes preguntas.

1. ¿Dónde se conocieron Maite y Roberto?
   Se conocieron en la universidad, en la clase de periodismo.
2. Normalmente, ¿sobre qué cosas escribe Roberto?
   Escribe sobre el crimen y la política.
3. ¿Piensa Javier que el viaje fue peligroso? ¿Qué habría pasado si Martín no hubiera estado con ellos?
   No. Si Martín no hubiera estado con ellos, se habrían perdido.
4. ¿Cuál fue la mejor experiencia de Maite? ¿Por qué? Fue cuando comieron en el restaurante El Cráter porque la sorprendieron con un pastel para su cumpleaños.
5. ¿Qué piensa Álex sobre viajar?
   Viajar es una buena forma de conocer mejor a las personas y de hacer amigos.

4 Mis experiencias Tú y un(a) compañero/a de clase son unos amigos que no se han visto en algunos años. Hablen de las experiencias buenas y malas que tuvieron durante ese tiempo. Utilicen estas frases en la conversación: Answers will vary.

- ¡Qué gusto volver a verte!
- Gusto de verte.
- Lo pasé de película/maravillosamente/muy bien.
- Me divertí mucho.
- Lo mejor fue…
- Lo peor fue…

NATIONAL communication STANDARDS

TEACHING OPTIONS

Extra Practice Scramble the order of these events from the **Fotonovela** and have the class put them back in order: **1. El autobús llega a la universidad. 2. Roberto le pregunta a Inés sobre el viaje. 3. Maite habla de su fiesta de cumpleaños. 4. Javier recuerda el problema con el autobús. 5. Don Francisco se va.**

Pairs Have your students write a short paragraph about a memorable trip, real or imaginary. Tell them to be sure to describe the best and worst parts of the trip. You may want to have your students share their paragraphs with the class, along with photographs, if possible.

comparisons
NATIONAL STANDARDS

Ortografía

Neologismos y anglicismos

As societies develop and interact, new words are needed to refer to inventions and discoveries, as well as to objects and ideas introduced by other cultures. In Spanish, many new terms have been invented to refer to such developments, and additional words have been "borrowed" from other languages.

bajar un programa *download*	**borrar** *to delete*	**correo basura** *junk mail*
en línea *online*	**enlace** *link*	**herramienta** *tool*
navegador *browser*	**pirata** *hacker*	**sistema operativo** *operating system*

Many Spanish neologisms, or "new words," refer to computers and technology. Due to the newness of these words, more than one term may be considered acceptable.

cederrón, CD-ROM **escáner** **fax** **zoom**

In Spanish, many anglicisms, or words borrowed from English, refer to computers and technology. Note that the spelling of these words is often adapted to the sounds of the Spanish language.

jazz, yaz **rap** **rock** **walkman**

Music and music technology are another common source of anglicisms.

gángster **hippy, jipi** **póquer** **whisky, güisqui**

Other borrowed words refer to people or things that are strongly associated with another culture.

chárter	**esnob**	**estrés**	**flirtear**
gol	**hall**	**hobby**	**iceberg**
jersey	**júnior**	**récord**	**yogur**

There are many other sources of borrowed words. Over time, some anglicisms are replaced by new terms in Spanish, while others are accepted as standard usage.

Práctica Completa el diálogo usando las siguientes palabras.

borrar	chárter	correo basura
en línea	esnob	estrés

GUSTAVO Voy a leer el correo electrónico.
REBECA Bah, yo sólo recibo __correo basura__. Lo único que hago con la computadora es __borrar__ mensajes.
GUSTAVO Mira, cariño, hay un anuncio en el Internet—un viaje barato a Punta del Este. Es un vuelo __chárter__.
REBECA Últimamente tengo tanto __estrés__. Sería buena idea que fuéramos de vacaciones. Pero busca un hotel muy bueno.
GUSTAVO Rebeca, no seas __esnob__, lo importante es ir y disfrutar. Voy a comprar los boletos ahora mismo __en línea__.

Dibujo Describe el dibujo utilizando por lo menos cinco anglicismos.

TEACHING OPTIONS

Small Groups Have the class work in groups of three or four to write a humorous paragraph using as many neologisms and anglicisms as possible. Circulate around the class, checking grammar and spelling as necessary. Then have a few volunteers to read their paragraphs to the class.

Extra Practice Have your students write a few questions using neologisms and/or anglicisms. Have a few volunteers write their questions on the board. Then work through the questions with the whole class.

Worth Noting New technology has long been the source of neologisms and cross-cultural borrowings. Most of the words of Arabic origin in Spanish, for instance, named "new technology" or products of their day. Ex: **azúcar** (sugar), **zafra** (harvest of sugar cane), **alberca** (artificial pond, swimming pool), **algodón** (cotton), **alquiler** (rent), **almohada** (pillow), **aduana** (customs)

Section Goals

In **Ortografía** students will learn about
- recently invented Spanish words
- anglicisms

Present
- Ask the class to give you a few neologisms that refer to computers and technology. Then have the class invent a few sentences that use these words. Write a few of their sentences on the board.
- Write the words **CD-ROM, escáner, fax,** and **zoom** on the board. Ask the class what each word means and what language it came from.
- Ask the class to give you a few anglicisms that refer to music and music technology. Ask the class to create a few sentences that use these words, and have volunteers write a few of their sentences on the board.
- Write the words **gángster, hipi, póquer,** and **whisky** on the board. Ask for volunteers to explain what each word means and use it in a sentence.
- Have the class work in pairs to write sentences using the words **gol, yogur, récord,** and **esnob**. Ask for a few volunteers to share their sentences with the class.

Práctica/Dibujo
Work through these activities with the class to practice the usage and spelling of new words and anglicisms.

Section Goals

In **Estructura 18.1** students will learn:

- **si** clauses in the subjunctive mood
- **si** clauses with verbs in the indicative

Instructional Resources. *Student Activities Manual: Workbook, 207–208; Lab Manual, 325*

Before Presenting Estructura 18.1 Ask students to look at the caption to the first video still on this page. Ask a volunteer to identify the tense and mood of the verb in the first clause (**pudieran**—past subjunctive) and the verb in the second clause (**harían**–conditional). Ask another volunteer to translate the sentence into English. Tell students they are now going to learn how to express hypotheses about the future and contrary-to-fact situations in the past. **Assignment** Have students study **Estructura 18.1** and prepare **¡Inténtalo!** on page 557 and Activities 1 and 2 on page 558 as homework.

Present Introduce the concept of a **si** clause by going over **Ante todo.** Then work through hypothetical and contrary-to-fact statements that have a dependent clause that begins with **si**. Check understanding by providing main clauses and having volunteers finish the sentence with a si clause. Ex: *Hypothetical* **No lo haría... (si fuera tú.) El huracán habría destruido tu casa... (si no hubieras tomado precauciones.) Iré contigo... (si vas a participar en la huelga.)** *Contrary-to-fact* **No lo hubiera hecho... (si habría sido tú.)** and so forth.

Continued on page 557.

18.1 Si clauses

NATIONAL comparisons STANDARDS

ANTE TODO **Si** *(if)* clauses describe a condition or event upon which another condition or event depends. Sentences with **si** clauses consist of a **si** clause and a main (or result) clause.

Si pudieran hacer el viaje otra vez, ¿lo harían?

Sin pensarlo dos veces.

▶ **Si** clauses are used to speculate or hypothesize about a current event or condition. In other words, they express what *would happen* if an event or condition *were to occur.* This is called a contrary-to-fact situation. In such instances, the verb in the **si** clause is in the past subjunctive while the verb in the main clause is in the conditional.

Si **cambiaras de empleo, serías** más feliz.
If you changed jobs, you would be happier.

Iría de viaje a América del Sur si **tuviera** dinero.
I would travel to South America if I had money.

¡ATENCIÓN!
Remember the difference between **si** (*if*) and **sí** (*yes*).

▶ **Si** clauses can also describe a contrary-to-fact situation in the past. They can express what *would have happened* if an event or condition *had occurred.* In these sentences, the verb in the **si** clause is in the past perfect subjunctive while the verb in the main clause is in the conditional perfect.

Si **hubiera sido** estrella de cine, **habría sido** rico.
If I had been a movie star, I would have been rich.

No **habrías tenido** hambre si **hubieras desayunado.**
You wouldn't have been hungry if you had eaten breakfast.

▶ **Si** clauses can also express conditions or events that are possible or likely to occur. In such instances, the **si** clause is in the present indicative while the main clause uses a present, near future, future, or command form.

Si **puedes** venir, **llámame.**
If you can come, call me.

Si **puedo** venir, **te llamo.**
If I can come, I'll call you.

Si **terminas** la tarea, **tendrás** tiempo para mirar la televisión.
If you finish your homework, you will have time to watch TV.

Si **terminas** la tarea, **vas a tener** tiempo para mirar la televisión.
If you finish your homework, you are going to have time to watch TV.

¡LENGUA VIVA!
Note that while in English *would* is sometimes used after *if* (*If you would call me...*), in Spanish the conditional is never used immediately following **si.**

TEACHING OPTIONS

Extra Practice To provide oral practice with hypothetical **si** clauses, create sentences that follow the pattern of the example sentences. Say the main clause, then have the students suggest different **si** clauses. Ex: **...tendría que caminar a las clases. (Si no tuviera bicicleta...) • ...hablaríamos español todo el día. (Si estuviéramos en México...) • ...pondría el noticiero de la tarde. (Si estuviera en casa...)**

Heritage Speakers Ask Spanish speakers to write a composition entitled **"Si yo no hablara español..."** The piece should describe how the student's life would have been different if he or she had not been born into a Spanish-speaking family. The compositions should have at least five hypothetical and five contrary-to-fact complex sentences with **si** clauses. Have students present their compositions to the rest of the class.

- When the **si** clause expresses habitual past conditions or events, *not* a contrary-to-fact situation, the imperfect is used in both the **si** clause and the main (or result) clause.

Si Alicia me **invitaba** a una fiesta, yo siempre **iba**. *If (Whenever) Alicia invited me to a party, I would (used to) go.*	Mis padres siempre **iban** a la playa si **hacía** buen tiempo. *My parents always went to the beach if the weather was good.*

- The **si** clause may be the first or second clause in a sentence. Note that a comma is used only when the **si** clause comes first.

Si tuviera tiempo, iría contigo. *If I had time, I would go with you.*	Iría contigo **si tuviera tiempo.** *I would go with you if I had time.*

Summary of *si* clause sequences

Condition	*Si* clause	Main clause
Possible or likely	**Si** + present	Present
Possible or likely	**Si** + present	Near future (**ir a** + infinitive)
Possible or likely	**Si** + present	Future
Possible or likely	**Si** + present	Command
Habitual in the past	**Si** + imperfect	Imperfect
Contrary-to-fact (present)	**Si** + past (imperfect) subjunctive	Conditional
Contrary-to-fact (past)	**Si** + past perfect (pluperfect) subjunctive	Conditional perfect

¡INTÉNTALO! Cambia los tiempos y modos de los verbos que aparecen entre paréntesis para practicar todos los tipos de oraciones con **si** que se muestran en la tabla anterior.

1. Si Ud. ___va___ (ir) a la playa, tenga cuidado con el sol.
2. Si tú ___quieres___ (querer), te preparo la merienda.
3. Si mis amigos ___iban___ (ir) de viaje, sacaban muchas fotos.
4. Si ___hace___ (hacer) buen tiempo, voy a ir al parque.
5. Si ella me ___llama___ (llamar), la invitaré a la fiesta.
6. Si yo ___fuera___ (ser) astronauta, iría a la luna.
7. Si nosotros ___queremos___ (querer) ir al teatro, compraremos los boletos antes.
8. Si yo ___me levanto___ (levantarse) temprano, desayuno antes de ir a clase.
9. Si ellos ___hubieran trabajado___ (trabajar) más, habrían tenido más éxito.
10. Si tú ___tienes___ (tener) tiempo, cómprame un helado.
11. Si él ___ganara___ (ganar) un millón de dólares, compraría una casa en la playa.
12. Si Uds. me ___hubieran dicho___ (decir) la verdad, no habríamos tenido este problema.

TEACHING OPTIONS

Pairs Ask students to reflect on the past semester(s) studying Spanish. Then assign them partners to write a list of eight complex sentences to express what they wish they had done and why. Ex: **Si hubiera hablado español con mi amiga puertorriqueña, podría hablar mejor.**

Extra Practice Ask students to finish the following sentences logically: **1. Si tomas español otra vez el año próximo... 2. Si hubieras estudiado periodismo.... 3. Si la tormenta no pasa pronto... 4. Si no hubiera llegado el ejército... 5. Si quieres ser locutor/a de televisión...**

Then have students open to **Fotonovela**, page 552, and read Javier's remark under Frame 6. Make a question from his statement. Ex: **Si la guía no hubiera estado con ellos en las montañas, ¿qué habría pasado?** Have a volunteer state the mood and tense of the verbs and translate the sentence.

Next, go over the use of the indicative in a **si** clause when it expresses something that is likely to happen or habitual past conditions or events. Give more examples.

Also point out that a **si** clause can begin or end a sentence, but that its position does not effect the mood or tense of the verb.

Then go over the summary of **si** clause sequences. Give the students a complex sentence in the indicative, and have them work in pairs to form seven sentences using **si** clauses as per the chart. Ex: **Cuando viene un tornado, bajamos al sótano. (Si viene un tornado, bajamos al sótano/bajaremos al sótano. Si viniera un tornado, bajaríamos al sótano. Si hubiera venido un tornado, habríamos bajado al sótano.** and so forth.

The Affective Dimension Ask your students if they feel intimidated by the variety of **si** clauses that can be created in Spanish. Tell them that the chart on this page will help them sort out the possibilities and that they will feel more comfortable with **si** clauses with time and practice.

Close Do **¡Inténtalo!** orally as a class.

1 Present Go over the activity with the whole class, asking volunteers to read each completed sentence.

1 Expand Change the tense/mood in the **si** clauses, and have the students change the main clause accordingly. Ex: **Si hubiera habido un terremoto aquí… (…no habrían permitido edificios altos) • Si me informara bien… (…podría explicar el desempleo) • Si me hubiera dado el uniforme… (…se lo habría mostrado al director.** and so forth.

2 Present If you have assigned this activity as homework, go over it with the whole class, asking two volunteers to read each mini-dialogue.

2 Suggestion This activity is also suitable for work in pairs. One student fills in the answers in Teresa's part of the dialogue and the other Anita's.

2 Expand Ask questions about the mini-dialogues and have students answer in complete sentences. Ex: **¿Cuándo visitará Teresa a sus parientes? ¿Qué haría Teresa si tuviera tiempo?**

3 Present Model the activity by having three or four volunteers complete the first sentence in different ways.

3 Suggestion To vary the final phase of the activity, ask some students to read their sentences to the class, and others to report on their partner's responses.

Práctica

1 Emparejar Empareja frases de la columna A con las de la columna B para crear oraciones lógicas.

A	B
1. Si aquí hubiera terremotos, __e__	a. se lo muestro al director.
2. Si me informo bien, __d__	b. habrían muerto muchos más.
3. Si me das el informe, __a__	c. muchos van a pasar hambre.
4. Si la guerra hubiera continuado, __b__	d. podré explicar el desempleo.
5. Si la huelga dura más de un mes, __c__	e. no permitiríamos edificios altos.

AYUDA
Remember these forms of **haber**:
(si) hubiera
(if) there were
habría
there would be

2 Minidiálogos Completa los minidiálogos entre Teresa y Anita.

TERESA ¿Qué __habrías__ hecho tú si tu papá te __hubiera__ regalado un carro?
ANITA No __habría__ podido creérmelo.

ANITA Si __viajas__ (viajar) a Paraguay, ¿qué vas a hacer?
TERESA __Voy__ a visitar a mis parientes.

TERESA Si tú y tu familia __tuvieran__ un millón de dólares, ¿qué comprarían?
ANITA Si nosotros tuviéramos un millón de dólares, __compraríamos__ tres casas nuevas.

ANITA Si tú __tuvieras__ tiempo, ¿irías al cine con más frecuencia?
TERESA Sí, yo __iría__ con más frecuencia si tuviera tiempo.

3 Completar En parejas, completen las frases de una manera lógica. Luego lean sus oraciones a sus compañeros. Answers will vary.

1. Si tuviera un accidente de carro…
2. Me volvería loco/a (*I would go crazy*) si mi familia…
3. Me habría ido al Cuerpo de Paz (*Peace Corps*) si…
4. No volveré a ver las noticias en ese canal si…
5. Habría menos problemas si los medios de comunicación…
6. Si mis padres hubieran insistido en que fuera al ejército…
7. Si oigo una expresión racista…
8. Me habría enojado mucho si…
9. Si hubiera un desastre natural en mi pueblo…
10. Yo habría votado en las elecciones pasadas si…

TEACHING OPTIONS

Pairs Have students work with a partner to write ten sentences about things they would do to improve their community or the wider society. First, ask pairs to list the problems they would change and how they would do so. Then have them form their sentences as contrary-to-fact statements. Ex: **Si no se permitiera contribuciones grandes a los candidatos, habría menos corrupción en el gobierno. • Habría menos delincuencia si hubiera más lugares donde los jóvenes podrían entretenerse. • Si la universidad edificara más residencias, los alquileres no serían tan altas en nuestra comundiad.**

Video Show the video again to give students more input about **si** clauses. Ask students to write each one down as they hear it. Afterwards, have students compare their notes in groups of four.

NATIONAL communication STANDARDS

Comunicación

4 **Situaciones** Trabajen en grupos para contestar las siguientes preguntas. Después deben comunicar sus respuestas a la clase. Answers will vary.

1. ¿Qué harías si fueras de vacaciones a Uruguay y al llegar no hubiera habitaciones en ninguno de los hoteles?
2. ¿Qué haces si encuentras dinero en la calle?
3. Imagina que estuviste en Montevideo por tres semanas. ¿Qué habrías hecho si hubieras observado un crimen allí?
4. ¿Qué harías tú si fueras de viaje y las líneas aéreas estuvieran en huelga?
5. Si alguien entrara en los Estados Unidos sin pasaporte, ¿qué le pasaría?
6. Si tomas otra clase de español, ¿qué harás diferente?
7. ¿Qué haces si estás en la calle y alguien te pide dinero?
8. ¿Qué harías si estuvieras en un país extranjero y un reportero te confundiera (*confused*) con un actor o una actriz de Hollywood?

NOTA CULTURAL

Uruguay has a long tradition of providing for the welfare of its population. It has free health care, free education, pensions and social security. Uruguay boasts the highest life expectancy and the highest literacy rate in South America.

5 **Oraciones** En parejas, túrnense para hablar de lo que hacen, harían o habrían hecho bajo estas circunstancias. Answers will vary.

1. Si ves a tu novio/a con otro/a en el cine
2. Si hubieras estudiado para ser experto/a en huesos de dinosaurios
3. Si fueras médico/a
4. Si te hubieras ganado un viaje al Uruguay
5. Si mañana tuvieras el día libre
6. Si te casaras y tuvieras ocho hijos
7. Si tuvieras que cuidar a tus padres cuando sean mayores
8. Si no tuvieras que preocuparte por el dinero

NATIONAL communication STANDARDS

Síntesis

6 **Entrevista** En grupos, preparen cinco preguntas para hacerle a un(a) candidato/a a la presidencia de Estados Unidos. Luego, túrnense para hacer el papel de entrevistador(a) y de candidato/a. El/La entrevistador(a) reacciona a cada una de las respuestas del/de la candidato/a. Answers will vary.

modelo

Entrevistador(a): *¿Qué haría Ud. sobre el sexismo en el ejército?*
Candidato/a: *Pues, dudo que las mujeres puedan servir en una guerra. Creo que deben hacer trabajos menos peligrosos.*
Entrevistador(a): *¿Entonces usted no haría nada para eliminar el sexismo en el ejército?*
Candidato/a: *Si yo fuera presidente/a…*

4 Warm-up Review the information contained in **Nota cultural**. Ask any students who have been to Uruguay to talk about their experience.

4 Present Model the activity by doing the first sentence yourself.

4 Expansion Ask groups to write a short description of what they would do if they took a group trip to Uruguay. Write a prompt on the board to get them started. Ex: **Si nosotros hiciéramos un viaje al Uruguay…**

5 Suggestion Ask students to formulate a multiple-choice survey with the sentence fragments given. Then have them survey one another and record the answers. Ex: **Si ves a tu novio/a con otro/a en el cine… 1. empiezas a llorar 2. haces un escándalo 3. los ignoras**

6 Warm-up Ask students to identify different political issues. Ex: **problemas sociales, la preparación del ejército, el sexismo en el trabajo** and so forth. Write these general categories on the board.

6 Present Go over the directions with the whole class and ask two volunteers to read the **Modelo**.

6 Expand Ask groups to develop an assessment tool for the evaluation of the **entrevista**. Then have each group present their interviews to the class. The other groups will evaluate each presentation on the basis of their assessment tool.

Assignment Have students do activities in **Student Activities Manual: Workbook,** pages 207–208

TEACHING OPTIONS

Large Group Ask each student to write a question that contains a **si** clause. Then have students walk around the room until you signal them to stop. At your cue each student should turn to the nearest classmate. Give students three minutes to ask and answer one another's question before having them begin walking around the room again. Each time you say stop, they ask their question of a new partner.

Small groups Ask students to bring in the most outlandish news report they can find. Assign students to groups of four and have them write a list of statements that use **si** clauses about each report. Ex: **Si los extraterrestres vuelven a reunirse con el Presidente, deben entrevistarles personalmente.**

Section Goals

In **Estructura 18.2** students will review:

- the forms of the subjunctive
- the use of the subjunctive, indicative, and infinitive in complex sentences

Instructional Resources
Student Activities Manual: Workbook, 209–212; Lab Manual 326
Hojas de actividades 44–45

Before presenting Estructura 18.2 Review the subjunctive by summing up the year's activities in statements that use the subjunctive. Ex: **En cuanto pasen unas semanas, habrá terminado el semestre. Espero que todos Uds. hayan aprendido mucho español. Antes de que nos despidamos, quisiera desearlos a todos buena suerte.** and so forth. Ask volunteers to identify the subjunctive form in each statement. Then tell them that they are about to review the uses of the subjunctive.
Assignment Have students study **Estructura 18.2** and prepare Activities 1 and 2 on page 562.

Present Ask volunteers to read the captions to the video stills and identify the verbs in the subjunctive.

Summary of subjunctive forms Before working through the summary of subjunctive forms, review the three tenses of the subjunctive with the students, using the same sentence stated in each tense. Ex: **Cuando termine la discriminación, habrá la justicia. • Si terminara la discriminación, habría la justicia. • Si hubiera terminado la discriminación, habría habido ya la justicia.**

Continued on page 561.

18.2 Summary of the uses of the subjunctive

NATIONAL comparisons STANDARDS

ANTE TODO Since Lesson 12, you have been learning about subjunctive verb forms and practicing their uses. The following chart summarizes the subjunctive forms you have studied. The chart on page 561 summarizes the uses of the subjunctive you have seen and contrasts them with uses of the indicative and the infinitive. These charts will help you review and synthesize what you have learned about the subjunctive in this book.

CONSÚLTALO

The subjunctive
You will find the various forms of the subjunctive in the following sections:
Present subjunctive 12.3, p. 376
Present perfect subjunctive 15.3, p. 475
Past subjunctive 16.3, p. 502
Past perfect subjunctive 17.3, p. 533

¡Hola! Espero que todos hayan tenido un magnífico viaje.

Si nuestro guía no hubiera estado allí con nosotros, ¡seguro que nos habríamos perdido!

Summary of subjunctive forms

–ar verbs: PRESENT SUBJUNCTIVE	–ar verbs: PAST SUBJUNCTIVE	–er verbs: PRESENT SUBJUNCTIVE	–er verbs: PAST SUBJUNCTIVE	–ir verbs: PRESENT SUBJUNCTIVE	–ir verbs: PAST SUBJUNCTIVE
hable	hablara	beba	bebiera	viva	viviera
hables	hablaras	bebas	bebieras	vivas	vivieras
hable	hablara	beba	bebiera	viva	viviera
hablemos	habláramos	bebamos	bebiéramos	vivamos	viviéramos
habléis	hablarais	bebáis	bebierais	viváis	vivierais
hablen	hablaran	beban	bebieran	vivan	vivieran

–ar verbs	–er verbs	–ir verbs
PRESENT PERFECT SUBJUNCTIVE	**PRESENT PERFECT SUBJUNCTIVE**	**PRESENT PERFECT SUBJUNCTIVE**
haya hablado	haya bebido	haya vivido
hayas hablado	hayas bebido	hayas vivido
haya hablado	haya bebido	haya vivido
hayamos hablado	hayamos bebido	hayamos vivido
hayáis hablado	hayáis bebido	hayáis vivido
hayan hablado	hayan bebido	hayan vivido
PAST PERFECT SUBJUNCTIVE	**PAST PERFECT SUBJUNCTIVE**	**PAST PERFECT SUBJUNCTIVE**
hubiera hablado	hubiera bebido	hubiera vivido
hubieras hablado	hubieras bebido	hubieras vivido
hubiera hablado	hubiera bebido	hubiera vivido
hubiéramos hablado	hubiéramos bebido	hubiéramos vivido
hubierais hablado	hubierais bebido	hubierais vivido
hubieran hablado	hubieran bebido	hubieran vivido

TEACHING OPTIONS

Small Groups Bring in or prepare a news report in Spanish about a recent natural disaster. Go over it with the whole class, clarifying any unfamiliar vocabulary. Then ask small groups to write a summary of the article in which they use at least three sentences in the subjunctive.
Game Divide the class into groups of three. Ask groups to think of an important historical event such as the assassination of Martin Luther King Jr., the Cuban Missile Crisis, D-Day, the Iranian Revolution. Have them write two contrary-to-fact statements about the event without naming it. Each group will read their statements and the others will try to guess the event. Award one point for every correct guess. Ex: **Si el Norte no hubiera atacado el Sur, no habríamos entrado en la guerra. Si Nixon no hubiera sido presidente, la guerra habría terminado antes. (la guerra de Vietnam)**

The subjunctive is used...

After verbs and/or expressions of will and influence when the subject of the subordinate clause is different from the subject of the main clause	Los ciudadanos **desean** que el candidato presidencial los **escuche.**
After verbs and/or expressions of emotion when the subject of the subordinate clause is different from the subject of the main clause	Alejandra **se alegró** mucho de que le **dieran** el trabajo.
After verbs and/or expressions of doubt, disbelief, and denial	**Dudo** que **vaya** a tener problemas para encontrar su maleta.
After the conjunctions **a menos que, antes (de) que, con tal (de) que, en caso (de) que, para que,** and **sin que**	Cierra las ventanas **antes de que empiece** la tormenta.
After **cuando, después (de) que, en cuanto, hasta que,** and **tan pronto como** when they refer to future actions	**Tan pronto como haga** la tarea, podrá salir con sus amigos.
To refer to an indefinite or nonexistent antecedent mentioned in the main clause	Busco un empleado que **haya estudiado** computación.
After **si** to express something impossible, improbable, or contrary to fact	**Si hubieras escuchado** el noticiero, te habrías informado sobre el terremoto.

The indicative is used...

After verbs and/or expressions of certainty and belief	**Es cierto** que Uruguay **tiene** unas playas espectaculares.
After the conjunctions **cuando, después (de) que, en cuanto, hasta que,** and **tan pronto como** when they do not refer to future actions	Hay más violencia **cuando hay** desigualdad social.
To refer to a definite or specific antecedent mentioned in the main clause	Busco a la señora que me **informó** del crimen que ocurrió ayer.
After **si** to express something possible, probable, or not contrary to fact	Pronto habrá más igualdad **si luchamos** contra la discriminación.

The infinitive is used...

After expressions of will and influence when there is no change of subject from the main clause to the subordinate clause	Martín **desea ir** a Montevideo este año.
After expressions of emotion when there is no change of subject from the main clause to the subordinate clause	**Me alegro de conocer** a tu esposo.

TEACHING OPTIONS

Large Group Prepare sentences based on the example sentences. Break each sentence into two clauses or fragments and write each one on an index card. Distribute the index cards and have students form sentences by finding a partner. Ex: **Me alegro mucho de que... /...hayan publicado tu artículo sobre el SIDA. • Quisiera... /...visitar Montevideo algún día.** Remember, there will be various logical combinations of some sentence parts.

Extra Practice To provide oral practice, create sentences that follow the pattern of the sentences in the examples. Say the sentence, have students repeat it, then change the tense of the main clause. Have students then say the sentence, changing the subordianate clause as necessary. Ex: **Dudo que terminemos el proyecto luego. Dudaba que... (...termináramos el proyecto luego.)**

Ask students to look over the simple forms of the subjunctive of regular verbs. Ask them which verb form the present subjunctive is based on (present tense **yo** form) and which the past subjunctive is based on (preterite **ellos/ellas/Uds.** form). Then, ask them to give you the past or present subjunctive of common irregular verbs such as **decir, traer, introducir, conocer, and tener.** Finally, review the completely irregular verbs: **dar, estar, haber, ir, saber,** and **ser.**

Finally, review the formation of the compound forms.

Uses of the subjunctive Before working through the summary of subjunctive usage, review the concepts of indicative and subjunctive with students. Explain that in most discourse the verbs are in the indicative, the mood used for making statements and asking question. Then ask volunteers to tell you when the subjunctive is used. Write their statements on the board, revising them for clarity and correctness.

Then work through the summaries of the use of the subjunctive, indicative, and infinitive comparatively. After you have discussed the subjunctive after expressions of influence, emotion, or doubt, for instance, discuss the indicative after expressions of certainty. After you discuss the subjunctive after certain conjunctions, discuss the indicative after conjunctives. After you have worked through the comparison of subjunctive vs. indicative, discuss cases where the infinitive is used after expressions of influence or emotion.

As you work through each of the points, provide further example sentences or ask volunteers to provide them.

1 Warm-up Go over the information in **Nota Cultural.** Point out that virtually from independence (1811) to the ouster of Stroessner, Paraguay has been a police state. In 1814 the sinister Dr. Francia took power and ruled through terror and oppression as **El Supremo** until 1840.

1 Present Go over the activity with the whole class. Ask volunteers to read the completed sentences and state their reason for choosing either the subjunctive or the indicative form.

1 Expand Have students summarize the dialogue in the third person.

2 Warm-up/Present After you have reviewed the instructions, give students two minutes to study the twelve phrases given. Then have them write down the main idea of their piece and three supporting ideas on the basis of the sentence fragments.

2 Present Model the activity orally by completing the first item. Ex: **Yo votaré por Woodrow Wilson con tal de que no nos mezcle en guerras europeas.**

2 Expand Have students read and comment on one another's paragraphs in groups of three.

3 Warm-up Go over the expressions listed in **Ayuda,** asking volunteers to give example sentences using each expression.

3 Present With the whole class, have two volunteers read the **Modelo** aloud. Provide a second response using an infinitive. Ex: **No pienso preocuparme de eso.** Divide the class into pairs, allowing 10 minutes for completion of the activity.

3 Expand Call on two or three pairs to read their dialogue to the class.

Práctica

NOTA CULTURAL

Paraguay's General Alfredo Stroessner was South America's longest-ruling dictator. He was in power from 1954 to 1989.

1 Conversación Completa la conversación con el tiempo verbal adecuado.

EMA Busco al reportero que __publicó__ (publicar) el libro sobre la dictadura de Stroessner.

ROSA Ah, Ud. busca a Miguel Pérez. Ha salido.

EMA Le había dicho que yo vendría a verlo el martes, pero él me dijo que __viniera__ (venir) hoy.

ROSA No creo que a Miguel se le __olvidara__ (olvidar) la cita. Si Ud. __hubiera pedido__ (pedir) una cita, él me lo habría mencionado.

EMA Pues no, no pedí cita, pero si él me hubiera dicho que era necesario yo lo __habría hecho__ (hacer).

ROSA Creo que Miguel __fue__ (ir) a cubrir un incendio hace media hora. No pensaba que nadie __fuera__ (ir) a venir esta tarde. Si quiere le digo que la __llame__ (llamar) tan pronto como __llegue__ (llegar). A menos que Ud. __quiera__ (querer) dejar un recado... *(Entra Miguel)*

EMA ¡Miguel! Amor, si hubieras llegado cinco minutos más tarde, no me __habrías visto__ (ver).

MIGUEL ¡Ema! ¿Qué haces aquí?

EMA Me dijiste que viniera hoy para que __tuviéramos__ (tener) más tiempo.

ROSA *(En voz baja)* ¿Cómo? ¿Serán novios?

2 Escribir Escribe uno o dos párrafos sobre tu participación en las próximas elecciones. Usa por lo menos cuatro de las frases que siguen. Answers will vary.

- Votaré por... con tal de que...
- Quisiera saber...
- Si gana mi candidato/a...
- Espero que la economía...
- Estoy seguro de que...
- A menos que...
- Mis padres siempre me dijeron que...
- Si a la gente realmente le importara la familia...
- No habría escogido a ese/a candidato/a si...
- Si le preocuparan más los impuestos...
- Dudo que el/la otro/a candidato/a...
- En las próximas elecciones espero que...

3 Explicar En parejas, escriban un diálogo breve sobre cada tema de la lista. Usen por lo menos un verbo en el subjuntivo y otro en el indicativo o en el infinitivo. Sigan el modelo. Answers will vary.

modelo

tornado

Estudiante 1: *Temo que este año haya tornados por nuestra zona.*

Estudiante 2: *No te preocupes. Creo que este año no va a haber tornados fuertes.*

una guerra	unas elecciones	un terremoto	la libertad
un incendio	una inundación	una huelga	la prensa

AYUDA

Some useful expressions:

Espero que...
Ojalá que...
Es posible que...
Es terrible que...
Es importante que...

TEACHING OPTIONS

Heritage Speakers Have Spanish speakers write a description of a particular news event that impacted their cultural community. Remind them to use complex sentences. Check for correct verb forms in the independent clauses before asking them to read their accounts to the class.

Pairs Have students create an informative bulletin in Spanish with a description and emergency instructions in case of a natural disaster. Focus on problems typical in your region, such as earthquakes on the West Coast, tornados in the Great Plains, and hurricanes on the East Coast. Remind students to use complex sentences with various subjunctive, indicative, and infinitive verb forms.

Comunicación

4 **Preguntas** Entrevista a un(a) compañero/a usando las siguientes preguntas. Answers will vary.

1. ¿Te irías a vivir a un lugar donde pudiera ocurrir un desastre natural? ¿Pensarías lo mismo si el desastre fuera un tornado? ¿Un huracán? ¿Un terremoto? ¿Una inundación?
2. ¿Es probable que algún desastre natural te afecte en el futuro?
3. ¿Te gustaría que tu vida fuera como la de tus padres? ¿Por qué? Y tus hijos, ¿preferirías que tuvieran experiencias diferentes a las tuyas? ¿Cuáles?
4. ¿Te parece importante que se elija a una mujer para presidente? ¿Por qué?
5. ¿Qué harías si hubiera una dictadura en tu país? ¿Lucharías en su contra? ¿Qué riesgos (*risks*) correrías?
6. Si hubiera una guerra y te llamaran para entrar en el ejército, ¿obedecerías? ¿Lo considerarías tu deber? ¿Qué sentirías? ¿Qué pensarías?

5 **Consejos** En parejas, lean la guía turística. Luego túrnense para representar los papeles de un cliente y de un agente de viajes. El/La agente le da consejos al/a la cliente/a sobre los lugares que debe visitar y el/la cliente/a da su opinión sobre los consejos. Answers will vary.

NOTA CULTURAL

Uruguay has one of the most moderate climates in world: the average temperature is 22°C (72°F) in the summer and 13°C (55°F) in the winter. Most days are sunny, rainfall is moderate, and it never snows.

¡Conozca Uruguay!

La **Plaza Independencia** en **Montevideo,** con su **Puerta de la Ciudadela,** forma el límite entre la ciudad antigua y la nueva. Si le interesan las compras, desde este lugar puede comenzar su paseo por la **Avenida 18 de Julio,** la principal arteria comercial de la capital.

No deje de ir a **Punta del Este.** Conocerá uno de los lugares turísticos más fascinantes del mundo. No se pierda las maravillosas playas, el **Museo de Arte Americano** y la **Catedral Maldonado** (1895) con su famoso altar, obra del escultor **Antonio Veiga.**

Sin duda, querrá conocer la famosa ciudad vacacional de **Piriápolis,** con su puerto que atrae barcos cruceros, y disfrutar de sus playas y lindos paseos.

Tampoco se debe perder la **Costa de Oro**, junto al **Río de la Plata.** Para

aquellos interesados en la historia, dos lugares favoritos son la conocida iglesia **Nuestra Señora de Lourdes** y el chalet de **Pablo Neruda.**

Síntesis

6 **Dos artículos** Su profesor(a) les va a dar una hoja de actividades que incluye dos artículos: uno sobre una huelga de trabajadores, y otro sobre la violencia en las escuelas. Trabajando en parejas, cada uno escoge y lee un artículo. Luego, háganse preguntas sobre los artículos. Answers will vary.

4 Present Remind pairs that they should take turns asking each other these questions. Tell them to take notes on what their partner says. Allow 10 minutes for completion of the activity.

4 Expand Ask students to create two more questions for the interview, keeping within the framework of natural disasters and sociopolitical issues.

4 Expand Ask students to report to the class on their partner's responses. Survey responses to find those on which there is general agreement and those on which there is not.

5 Warm-up Go over the information provided in **Nota cultural**.

5 Present Give pairs about ten minutes to read the tourist guide, prepare their parts, and carry out the activity.

5 Expand Have the "clients" sit on one side of the room, and the "travel agents" on the other. Then ask individual students about the advice they gave/were given. Ex: **¿Qué monumentos te aconsejó que visite? • ¿Qué consejos le diste sobre los museos?**

6 Present Go over directions with the whole class before dividing into pairs. Distribute a copy of **Hojas de actividad 44** and **45** to each pair. Have partners skim the articles and choose the one they want to work with. Allow 10 minutes for pairs to read the articles and ask each other the questions.

6 Expand Have partners develop three more questions they would ask about each article.

TEACHING OPTIONS

Pairs Have students write a news article about the end of the semester. The article should highlight the positive points of the class as well as the contributions of the students. Tell them to use the articles from the **Hojas de actividades 44** and **45** as a guide.

Extra Practice Write this cloze paragraph on the board, asking students to complete it with the correct forms of **ver, llegar, creer, hacer, aprender, ser.**

Es difícil ____ (creer) que ____ (lleguemos/hayamos llegado) al final del semestre. Espero que todos Uds. ____ (hayan aprendido) mucho, no sólo del español, sino del lenguaje en general. Si deciden seguir con el español, ____ (van a ver/verán) que se ____ (hace/hará) más fácil con el tiempo.

Section Goals

In **Lectura** students will:
- learn to recognize chronological order
- read an excerpt from a Spanish novel

Antes de leer

Introduce the strategy Tell students that understanding the order of events allows a reader to follow what is happening in the narrative.

Successful Language Learning Tell your students to look for connecting words and transitions, because they are helpful in following a chain of events.

Examinar el texto If students are unfamiliar with the character don Quijote, explain that his creator, Miguel de Cervantes Saavedra, is thought to be Spain's greatest writer and that the novel *El ingenioso hidalgo don Quijote de la Mancha* is considered his masterpiece. Ask volunteers to tell what they know about the plot. Students should mention that the story is about an elderly gentleman who has read so many stories of chivalry that he goes mad and imagines that he is a knight errant. Seeking adventure, he travels through late medieval Spain, getting mixed up in all sorts of mad encounters. On his journey he is accompanied by his neighbor Sancho Panza, a skeptical peasant who provides a continual ironic commentary on don Quijote's madness.

Have students scan the text. Explain any unfamiliar vocabulary. You may wish to have students read the excerpt aloud to aid comprehension.

Continued on page 565.

Lectura

NATIONAL STANDARDS communication cultures

Antes de leer

Estrategia

Recognizing chronological order

Recognizing the chronological order of events in a narrative is key to understanding the cause and effect relationship between them. When you are able to establish the chronological chain of events, you will easily be able to follow the plot. In order to be more aware of the order of events in a narrative, you may find it helpful to prepare a numbered list of the events as you read.

Examinar el texto

Lee el texto usando las estrategias de lectura que has aprendido.
- ¿Ves palabras nuevas o cognados? ¿Qué significan?
- ¿Qué te dice el dibujo sobre el contenido?
- ¿Tienes algún conocimiento previo sobre don Quijote?
- ¿Cuál es el propósito del texto?
- ¿Cuál es el punto de vista del narrador?
- ¿De qué trata la lectura?

Ordenar

Lee el texto otra vez para establecer el orden cronológico de los eventos. Luego ordena los siguientes eventos cronológicamente según van ocurriendo en la historia.

__3__ Don Quijote lucha contra los molinos de viento pensando que son gigantes.
__5__ Don Quijote y Sancho toman el camino hacia Puerto Lápice.
__2__ Don Quijote y Sancho descubren unos molinos de viento en un campo.
__4__ El primer molino da un mal golpe a don Quijote, a su lanza y a su caballo.
__1__ Don Quijote y Sancho Panza salen de su pueblo en busca de aventuras.

Don Quijote y los molinos de viento

Miguel de Cervantes

Fragmento adaptado de
El ingenioso hidalgo don Quijote de la Mancha

Miguel de Cervantes y Saavedra, el escritor más universal de la literatura española, nació en Alcalá de Henares en 1547 y murió en Madrid en 1616, tras haber vivido una vida llena de momentos difíciles, llegando a estar en la cárcel más de una vez. Su obra, sin embargo, ha disfrutado a través de los siglos de todo el éxito que se merece. Don Quijote representa no sólo la locura sino también la búsqueda del ideal. En esta ocasión presentamos el famoso episodio de los molinos de viento.

Entonces descubrieron treinta o cuarenta molinos de viento que había en aquel campo. Cuando don Quijote los vio, dijo a su escudero:

—La fortuna va guiando nuestras cosas mejor de lo que deseamos; porque allí, amigo Sancho Panza, se ven treinta, o pocos más, enormes gigantes con los que pienso hacer batalla y quitarles a todos las vidas, y comenzaremos a ser ricos; que ésta es buena guerra, y es gran servicio de Dios quitar tan malos seres de la tierra.

—¿Qué gigantes?

—Aquellos que ves allí —respondió su amo— de los brazos largos, que algunos normalmente los tienen de casi dos leguas.

Después de leer

¿Realidad o fantasía?

Indica si las siguientes afirmaciones sobre la lectura pertenecen a la realidad o la fantasía.

1. Don Quijote desea matar a los enemigos. realidad
2. Su escudero no ve a ningún ser sobrenatural. realidad
3. El caballero ataca a unas criaturas cobardes y viles. fantasía
4. Don Quijote no ganó la batalla porque los gigantes fueron transformados en molinos de viento. fantasía
5. El sabio Frestón transformó los gigantes en molinos de viento. fantasía

conocimiento previo *prior knowledge* propósito *purpose*
¿De qué trata...? *What is it about...?* matar *to kill* ser *being*

TEACHING OPTIONS

Variación léxica Explain to students that **Quijote** has an alternative, older spelling, **Quixote**. In addition, point out that Quijote's eccentric behavior became emblematic, so that several terms derived from his name have entered the Spanish language. Among them are **quijote** (a dreamer, hopelessly unrealistic person), **quijotada** (quixotic act), **quijotesco** (quixotic), **quijotismo** (quixotism).

Extra Practice Ask students to research Miguel de Cervantes and to write a brief biography on the literary figure. Students should include a bibliography of his works.

Game Ask students to give clues about characters in *Don Quijote* **(don Quijote, Rocinante, Dulcinea, Sancho Panza, los gigantes, Frestón)** Ex. **el amigo que trata de convencer a don Quijote que los molinos no son gigantes (Frestón).** Others guess which character they are describing.

—Mire Ud. —respondió Sancho— que aquéllos que allí están no son gigantes, sino molinos de viento, y lo que parecen brazos son las aspas, que movidas por el viento, hacen andar la piedra del molino.

—Bien veo —respondió don Quijote— que no estás acostumbrado a las aventuras: ellos son gigantes; y si tienes miedo, quítate de ahí y reza mientras yo voy a combatir con ellos en fiera batalla.

Y diciendo esto, dio de espuelas a su caballo Rocinante, sin oír las voces que su escudero Sancho le daba, diciéndole que, sin duda alguna, eran molinos de viento, y no gigantes, aquellos que iba a atacar. Pero él iba tan convencido de que eran gigantes, que ni oía las voces de su escudero Sancho, ni se daba cuenta, aunque estaba ya muy cerca, de lo que eran; antes iba diciendo en voz alta:

—No huyáis, cobardes y viles criaturas, que sólo os ataca un caballero.

Se levantó entonces un poco de viento, y las grandes aspas comenzaron a moverse, y cuando don Quijote vio esto, dijo:

—Pues aunque mováis más brazos que los del gigante Briareo, me lo vais a pagar.

Y diciendo esto, y encomendándose de todo corazón a su señora Dulcinea, pidiéndole que le ayudase en esta difícil situación, bien cubierto de su rodela, con la lanza en posición de ataque, fue a todo el galope de Rocinante y embistió el primer molino que estaba delante: y dándole con la lanza en el aspa, el viento la giró con tanta furia, que la rompió en pequeños fragmentos, llevándose con ella al caballo y al caballero, que fue dando vueltas por el campo. Fue rápidamente Sancho Panza a ayudarle, todo lo rápido que podía correr su asno, y cuando llegó encontró que no se podía mover: tan grande fue el golpe que se dio con Rocinante.

—¡Por Dios! —dijo Sancho—. ¿No le dije yo que mirase bien lo que hacía, que sólo eran molinos de viento, y la única persona que podía equivocarse era alguien que tuviese otros molinos en la cabeza?

—Calla, amigo Sancho —respondió don Quijote—, que las cosas de la guerra, más que otras, cambian continuamente; estoy pensando que aquel sabio Frestón, que me robó el estudio y los libros, ha convertido estos gigantes en molinos por quitarme la gloria de su vencimiento: tan grande es la enemistad que me tiene; pero al final, sus malas artes no van a poder nada contra la bondad de mi espada.

—Dios lo haga como pueda —respondió Sancho Panza.

Y ayudándole a levantarse, volvió a subir sobre Rocinante, que medio despaldado estaba. Y hablando de la pasada aventura, siguieron el camino del Puerto Lápice.

tras *after* **cárcel** *jail* **locura** *insanity* **búsqueda** *search* **campo** *field* **molinos de viento** *windmills* **escudero** *squire* **amo** *master* **leguas** *leagues (measure of distance)* **aspas** *sails* **reza** *pray* **fiera** *vicious* **dio de espuelas** *he spurred* **No huyáis** *Do not flee* **cobardes** *cowards* **caballero** *knight* **encomendándose de todo corazón** *commending himself with all his heart* **rodela** *round shield* **embistió** *charged* **asno** *donkey* **golpe** *knock* **Calla** *Be quiet* **sabio** *magician* **vencimiento** *defeat* **espada** *sword* **que medio despaldado estaba** *whose back was half-broken*

Personajes

1. En este fragmento, se mencionan los siguientes personajes. ¿Quiénes son?
   - don Quijote
   - Rocinante
   - Dulcinea
   - Sancho Panza
   - los gigantes
   - Frestón
2. ¿Qué puedes deducir de los personajes según la información que se da en este episodio?
3. ¿Quiénes son los personajes principales?
4. ¿Cuáles son las diferencias entre don Quijote y Sancho Panza? ¿Qué tienen en común?

¿Un loco o un héroe?

En un párrafo da tu opinión del personaje de don Quijote, basándote en la aventura de los molinos de viento. Ten en cuenta las acciones, los motivos y los sentimientos de don Quijote en su batalla contra los molinos de viento.

Una entrevista

Trabajen en grupos de tres para preparar una entrevista sobre los acontecimientos de este fragmento de la novela de Cervantes. Un(a) estudiante representará el papel del/de la entrevistador(a) y los otros dos asumirán los papeles de don Quijote y de Sancho Panza, quienes comentarán el episodio desde su punto de vista.

TEACHING OPTIONS

Extra Practice Ask students to write a paragraph about someone they consider to be a hero or heroine **(héroe, heroína)**. Students should explain why they think that person is a hero and describe at least one heroic act **(acto heroico)** carried out by him or her.

Heritage Speaker Ask Spanish speakers to write five contrary-to-fact statements about the episode. Ex: **Si don Quijote no hubiera leído tantos libros no se habría vuelto loco.** Have them share their statements with the class.

Ordenar If students have trouble putting the events in order, have them refer to portions of the text and help them find the passages that contain the information. Then go over the items in **Ordenar** orally with the whole class.

Assignment Have students read **Don Quijote y los molinos de viento** and prepare the exercises in **Después de leer** for the next class.

Después de leer

¿Realidad o fantasía?
Suggestion You may wish to have pairs work together to complete this activity. Have partners take turns reading the statements aloud and deciding whether the statement is **realidad** or **fantasía**.

Personajes
Suggestion Ask the questions of the whole class. Have volunteers answer orally or write their answers on the board.

¿Un loco o un héroe?
Suggestion You may wish to have Spanish-speakers work with those who are being exposed to Spanish for the first time. When students are finished writing, ask them to read their paragraphs aloud.

Una entrevista
Suggestion Have groups brainstorm their questions and write them out on cards. Ask groups to practice asking and answering questions and to perform their interviews for the class.

Successful Language Learning Ask your students if they approach reading in Spanish or English in a different way after learning the strategies presented in ***Vistas***.

Section Goals

In **Escritura** students will:
- learn to write strong introductions and conclusions
- write a composition

Tema
Present Read through the list of possible topics with the students and have them choose one. Then go over the instructions. You may wish to have students who have chosen the same topic get together and brainstorm ideas about the changes they would make.

Estrategia
Present Explain to students that to write a strong introduction **(introducción)**, they should briefly outline the topic and tell readers of the important points that will be addressed in the composition. Ask students to tell why an introduction to a biography of Miguel de Cervantes that does not mention *Don Quijote* is not a strong introduction. Explain that a strong conclusion **(conclusión)** summarizes the information in the body of the composition and inspires the reader to find out more about the topic. Ask students to tell how the following conclusion could be stronger: **Cervantes fue gran escritor**.

Introducciones y conclusiones
Write weak introductions and conclusions for each of the three topics on the board. Discuss these with the whole class, calling on volunteers to give suggestions and to change or edit the introductions and conclusions to make them stronger.

Assignment Have students prepare **Ideas y organización** and **Primer borrador** as homework.

Escritura

NATIONAL communication STANDARDS

Estrategia

Writing strong introductions and conclusions

Introductions and conclusions serve a similar purpose: both are intended to focus the reader's attention on the topic being covered. The introduction presents a brief preview of the topic. In addition, it informs your reader of the important points that will be covered in the body of your writing. The conclusion reaffirms those points and concisely sums up the information that has been provided. A compelling fact or statistic, a humorous anecdote, or a question directed to the reader are all interesting ways to begin or end your writing.

For example, if you were writing a biographical report on Miguel de Cervantes, you might begin your essay with the fact that his most famous work, *Don Quijote de La Mancha,* is the second most widely published book ever. The rest of your introductory paragraph would outline the areas you would cover in the body of your paper, such as Cervantes' life, his works, and the impact of the *Quijote* on world literature. In your conclusion, you would sum up the most important information in the report and tie this information together in a way that would make your reader want to learn even more about the topic. You could write, for example: "Cervantes, with his wit and profound understanding of human nature, is without peer in the history of world literature."

Introducciones y conclusiones

Trabajen en parejas para escribir una frase de introducción y otra de conclusión sobre los siguientes temas.

1. El episodio de *Don Quijote de la Mancha*
2. La definición de la locura
3. La realidad y la fantasía en la literatura

Tema

Escribir una composición

Si tuvieras la oportunidad, ¿qué harías para mejorar el mundo? Escribe una composición sobre los cambios que harías en el mundo si tuvieras el poder y los recursos necesarios. Piensa en lo que puedes hacer ahora y en lo que podrás hacer en el futuro. Considera estas preguntas:

- ¿Pondrías fin a todas las guerras? ¿Cómo?
- ¿Protegerías el medio ambiente? ¿Cómo?
- ¿Promoverías la igualdad y eliminarías el sexismo y el racismo? ¿Cómo?
- ¿Eliminarías la corrupción en la política? ¿Cómo?
- ¿Eliminarías la falta de vivienda y el hambre?
- ¿Promoverías el fin de la violencia entre las personas?
- ¿Promoverías tu causa en la prensa? ¿Cómo?
- ¿Te dedicarías a alguna causa específica dentro de tu comunidad? ¿Cuál?
- ¿Te dedicarías a solucionar problemas nacionales o internacionales? ¿Cuáles?

poder *power* **Promoverías** *Would you promote* **falta de vivienda** *homelessness*

TEACHING OPTIONS

Proofreading Activity Copy on the board or onto a transparency the following items containing mistakes as a proofreading activity to do with the whole class.
1. **Si el periodista podría escribir sobre este tema otra vez, ¿lo hiciera?**
2. **Si sería Ud. periodista con una agencia internacional, viajara por todo el mundo.**
3. **El presidente aceptaría recibir la prensa si tuviera tiempo suficiente.**
4. **Si tenía que hacer reportajes sobre violencia, no me gustara hacerlo.**
5. **Espero que me das un libro que me explica la política.**
6. **A menos que acaban las inundaciones, los agricultores no podían plantar sus campos.**

Plan de escritura

1 Ideas y organización

Antes de escribir, organiza de una manera lógica la lista de los cambios que efectuarías para mejorar el mundo.

2 Primer borrador

Utiliza tus apuntes de **Ideas y organización** para escribir el primer borrador de tu composición. Empieza y concluye con un hecho o una pregunta que despierte el interés de tu lector(a). Utiliza el diccionario sólo como último recurso.

3 Comentario

Intercambia tu composición con un(a) compañero/a. Lee su borrador y coméntalo, usando estas preguntas como guía:

a. ¿Es interesante la introducción? ¿Cómo se puede mejorar?
b. ¿Es interesante la conclusión? ¿Cómo se puede mejorar?
c. ¿Hay errores gramaticales u ortográficos?
d. ¿Está organizada de una manera lógica?

4 Redacción

Revisa el primer borrador según las indicaciones de tu compañero/a. Antes de escribir tu versión final, revisa tu trabajo según la siguiente guía:

a. Subraya los verbos para comprobar que están en el modo y el tiempo adecuados. ¿Has utilizado el subjuntivo y el condicional correctamente?
b. Revisa la concordancia entre el sujeto y el verbo en cada oración.
c. Revisa la concordancia entre los sustantivos y los adjetivos en cada oración.
d. Subraya los pronombres para comprobar el uso correcto de cada uno.
e. Consulta tus **Anotaciones para mejorar la escritura** para evitar la repetición de errores previos.

5 Evaluación y progreso

En grupos de tres o cuatro estudiantes, intercambien sus composiciones. Cada persona debe leer la composición de un(a) compañero/a y resumirla oralmente en tres o cuatro oraciones. Cuando tu profesor(a) te devuelva sus comentarios, léelos con cuidado. Repasa tu **Carpeta de trabajos** para poder apreciar tu progreso en la escritura. No te olvides de mirar tus **Anotaciones para mejorar la escritura.** Seguramente te sorprenderás de ver que hoy parece fácil lo que hace unos meses parecía tan difícil.

efectuarías *you would put into effect* apuntes *notes* hecho *fact* Subraya *Underline* comprobar *to confirm* concordancia *agreement* devuelva *returns*

EVALUATION: Composición

Criteria	Scale
Content	1 2 3 4 5
Use of vocabulary	1 2 3 4 5
Grammatical accuracy	1 2 3 4 5
Use of introductions/conclusions	1 2 3 4 5

Scoring	
Excellent	18–20 points
Good	14–17 points
Satisfactory	10–13 points
Unsatisfactory	< 10 points

Comentario
Present Go over guide questions **a–d** with the whole class. Then have pairs exchange compositions. Allow five minutes for comments.
Assignment Have students prepare **Redacción** as homework.

Writing Sample
This composition would constitute superior writing achievement.

¡Comida y casas para todos!

Cada 3,6 segundos una persona muere de hambre. El 75% de estas personas son niños. ¿Cómo es posible que se permita que cualquier persona vive sin suficiente comida? El hambre crea graves problemas con la salud y el bienestar. También puede causar problemas en la sociedad como el crimen, la violencia y la desigualdad. Si hay suficiente comida para alimentar a toda la gente, ¿por qué no se lo hace?

También es un problema la falta de viviendas. Sólo en los Estados Unidos hay más o menos 600.000 personas que no tienen donde vivir. La cifra sube en el resto del mundo. ¿Por qué los ricos viven en mansiones y los pobres viven en sus carros o en la calle? Tenemos que construir más casas y apartamentos para nuestra gente.

Si podría dar a todos una vivienda y comida yo, lo haría sin pensarlo dos veces. ¡Qué injusticia! Tenemos que trabajar juntos para eliminar el hambre y la falta de viviendas. Hay que mandar cartas a los políticos y votar para aquellos que tengan soluciones a estos problemas.¡Si trabajamos juntos podemos lograr las metas!

Successful Language Learning Ask your students if they approach writing in Spanish or English in a different way after using the strategies presented in ***Vistas***.

Section Goals

In **Escuchar** students will:

- practice the strategies of recognizing genre and taking notes as they listen
- jot down the types of information they hear in a news broadcast

Instructional Resource
Student Cassette/CD

Preparación
Warm-up Have students look at the photo and guess who the woman depicted is. Guide them to recognize that she is a news reader. Have them list the types of information they would expect to hear about in a news broadcast.

Successful Language Learning Ask your students if they approach listening to Spanish or English in a different way after using the strategies presented in ***Vistas***.

Estrategia
Script **Con la nueva pasta de dientes BrillaBoca, usted gozará de dientes blancos y una boca fresca. Este producto le cambiará la vida. Nunca más estará solo en casa un sábado por la noche. ¡Disfrute de su vida! ¡Use pasta de dientes BrillaBoca!**

Assignment Have students do the activities in **Ahora escucha** and **Comprensión** as homework.

Ahora escucha
Script **Buenas tardes. Les habla Sonia Hernández, dándoles la bienvenida al Noticiero del Mediodía. Y ahora las actualidades del miércoles, 21 de abril. El candidato presidencial Jaime Pantufla del Partido Colorado anunció ayer en su discurso ante los ciudadanos de Salto un plan para mejorar la recaudación de impuestos con el fin de mejorar la situación económica del país.**

Escuchar

Preparación

Según la foto, anticipa qué es lo que vas a escuchar en el siguiente fragmento y haz una lista en la que indiques los diferentes tipos de información que crees que vas a oír.

Estrategia

Recognizing genre/ Taking notes as you listen

If you know the genre or type of discourse you are going to encounter, you can use your background knowledge to write down a few notes about what you expect to hear. You can then make additions and changes to your notes as you listen. To practice these strategies, you will now listen to a short toothpaste commercial. Before listening to the commercial, write down the information you expect it to contain. Then update your notes as you listen.

Ahora escucha

Mira la lista de los tipos de información que apuntaste en **Preparación.** Luego escucha el noticiero presentado por Sonia Hernández. Mientras escuchas, apunta los tipos de información que anticipaste y los que no anticipaste.

Tipos de información que anticipaste

1. Answers will vary.
2. Answers will vary.
3. Answers will vary.

Tipos de información que no anticipaste

1. Answers will vary.
2. Answers will vary.
3. Answers will vary.

Comprensión

Preguntas

1. ¿Dónde está Sonia Hernández?
   Está en una estación de televisión en Montevideo, Uruguay.
2. ¿Quién es Jaime Pantuflo?
   Es un candidato presidencial.
3. ¿Dónde hubo una tormenta?
   Hubo una tormenta en las Filipinas.
4. ¿Qué tipo de música toca el grupo Maná?
   Toca música rock.
5. ¿Qué tipo de artista es Ugo Nespolo?
   Es un pintor.
6. Además de lo que Sonia menciona, ¿de qué piensas que va a hablar en la próxima sección del programa?
   Answers will vary.

Ahora Uds.

En parejas, usen la presentación de Sonia Hernández como modelo para escribir un breve noticiero para la ciudad donde viven. Incluyan noticias locales, nacionales e internacionales. Luego compartan el papel de locutor(a) y presenten el noticiero a la clase. Pueden grabar el noticiero si quieren.

recursos
R SCASS./CD Lección 18

Ahora la noticias internacionales. La tormenta que ha dejado más de 17 centímetros de lluvia sobre las Filipinas ha causado desastrosas inundaciones. Se informó que aproximadamente 12.000 personas han perdido sus casas. Las inundaciones también han traído gran peligro de enfermedades.
Seguimos con los más importantes acontecimientos de arte y cultura. Pasado mañana, el conocido grupo de rock, Maná, presentará un concierto en el estacionamiento del Centro Comercial Portones en Montevideo. Hoy comienza la nueva exposición del pintor Ugo Nespolo en el Museo Nacional de Artes Visuales de Montevideo.
Regresaremos después de unas breves noticias con el pronóstico del tiempo de Montevideo y sus alrededores.

National Standards: communication, cultures, connections, communities

Proyecto

Prepara un reportaje

Imagina que eres un(a) reportero/a que está cubriendo el Cono Sur para una emisora de radio y un diario. Te han pedido un reportaje de noticias sobre Paraguay y/o Uruguay.

1 Escribe un artículo periodístico

Escribe un artículo sobre las últimas noticias de Uruguay y/o de Paraguay. Usa los **Recursos para la investigación** para informarte de lo que está pasando en esos países. El artículo puede incluir las siguientes cosas:

- Un titular
- Una descripción del/de los acontecimiento(s), con una explicación de cuándo y dónde tuvieron lugar, quiénes participaron, etc.
- Un pequeño mapa que indique dónde tuvo lugar el acontecimiento
- Fotos de los acontecimientos

2 Presenta la información

El locutor de la emisora de radio está enfermo y te toca a ti presentar el noticiero. Usa el artículo que escribiste para hacer un reportaje radial. Recuerda que el reportaje debe ser más corto que el artículo. Presenta el noticiero a la clase en vivo o en una grabación.

34F

Comienza el Carnaval

Hoy viernes, comienzan las grandes fiestas del Carnaval en Encarnación, capital del departamento de Itapúa, Paraguay. Esta ciudad es famosa por la música, los desfiles y las bailarinas de su Carnaval. Es tan popular que vienen muchas personas de otras partes del país y del extranjero. Todos los hoteles y pensiones están llenos en esta época del año.

¡Se prohíbe tirar agua a los participantes de los desfiles! La policía estará pendiente.

emisora de radio *radio station* titular *headline* te toca a ti *it is up to you* en vivo *live* grabación *tape recording* embajadas *embassies* consulados *consulates*

recursos para la investigación

Internet Palabras clave: Uruguay, Paraguay, periódico, diario, noticias	**Comunidad** Profesores, estudiantes o personas en la comunidad que son de Uruguay o Paraguay
Biblioteca Periódicos, revistas, mapas	**Otros recursos** Profesores de la Facultad de Asuntos Internacionales o de Estudios Latinoamericanos; embajadas o consulados

EVALUATION: Reportaje

Criteria	Scale
Content	1 2 3 4
Organization	1 2 3 4
Grammatical accuracy	1 2 3 4
Creativity	1 2 3 4
Oral presentation	1 2 3 4

Scoring	
Excellent	18–20 points
Good	14–17 points
Satisfactory	10–13 points
Unsatisfactory	< 10 points

Section Goals

In **Proyecto** students will:
- use Spanish as they research current events in Uruguay and/or Paraguay
- write a news article on current events in Uruguay and/or Paraguay

Before Assigning Proyecto Students will need approximately a week to complete the project, so at the beginning of that time period, have them open their books to page 569 and glance over **Proyecto**. Tell them that they are going to use their Spanish skills as they carry out research on current events in Uruguay and Paraguay. Tell them that when they finish their research, they will write a newspaper article on current events.

Assignment Have students read page 569 and follow directions in **Prepara un reportaje** to complete their article.

Escribe un artículo periodístico

Suggestions
- Provide students with examples of articles written in Spanish about current events. Many Spanish-language newspapers can be found on the Internet. Tell students the abbreviations in URLs for Uruguay and Paraguay are **uy** and **py**, respectively.
- Students can seek information on Uruguay or Paraguay by using the Spanish key words and phrases **Cono Sur, actualidades Uruguay o Paraguay, noticias del Uruguay o Paraguay.**

Presenta la información

Suggestion You may wish to set aside sufficient class time to do a few presentations at a time until all students have had a chance to present.

Paraguay

NATIONAL STANDARDS connections cultures

El país en cifras

- **Área:** 406.750 km^2 (157.046 millas^2), *el tamaño de California*
- **Población:** 5.778.000
- **Capital:** Asunción—1.343.000
- **Ciudades principales:** Ciudad del Este—134.000, San Lorenzo—133.000, Lambaré—100.000, Fernando de la Mora—95.000

SOURCE: Population Division, UN Secretariat

- **Moneda:** guaraní
- **Idiomas:** español (oficial), guaraní (oficial)

Las tribus indígenas que habitaban la zona antes de la llegada de los españoles hablaban guaraní. Ahora el 90 por ciento de los paraguayos habla esta lengua, que se usa con frecuencia en canciones, poemas, periódicos y libros. Varios institutos y asociaciones como el Teatro Guaraní se dedican a preservar la cultura y la lengua guaraníes.

Bandera de Paraguay

Paraguayos célebres

- **Agustín Barrios,** guitarrista y compositor (1885-1944)
- **Josefina Plá,** escritora y ceramista (1909-1999)
- **Augusto Roa Bastos,** escritor (1918-)
- **Olga Blinder,** pintora (1921-)

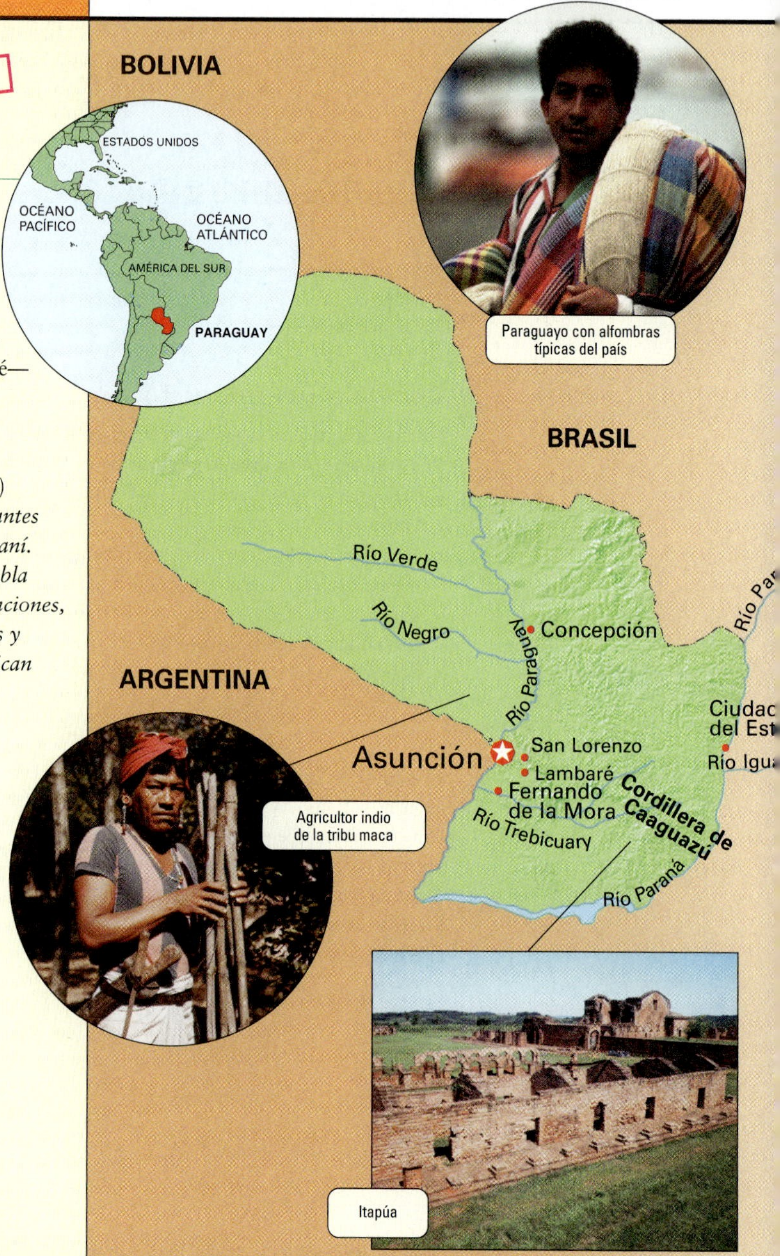

Paraguayo con alfombras típicas del país

Agricultor indio de la tribu maca

Itapúa

sin parar *nonstop* Aunque *Although* lugareños *local residents*

¡Increíble pero cierto!

En Paraguay, hay una pequeña zona cerca del río Paraná en la que llueve tanto que, según cuenta la leyenda, ha llovido sin parar por un millón de años. Aunque esto pueda ser difícil verificarlo, una cosa sí es cierta: los lugareños no han visto en su vida un día sin lluvia.

recursos

R | WB pp. 213-214 | vistasonline.com

Section Goals

In **Panorama**, students will read about the geography and culture of Paraguay.

Instructional Resources
Student Activities Manual: Workbook, 213
Transparency 64

Paraguay
Before Presenting Panorama Have students look at the map of Paraguay or project **Transparency 64**. Note that the major population centers lie east of the Paraguay River, which divides the country in two. West of the river is the **Gran Chaco,** a sparsely populated and largely infertile region. Model the pronunciation of place names. Have volunteers read aloud the call-out captions.

Assignment Have students read **Panorama** and answer the questions in **¿Qué aprendiste?** on page 571 as homework.

Present Ask volunteers to read aloud each section of **El país en cifras.** As you read about **Idiomas**, point out that **guaraní** is also spoken in neighboring Bolivia, Brazil, and Argentina. However, as an officially bilingual nation, Paraguay has the largest concentration of guaraní speakers. As students read about **Paraguayos célebres**, let them know that writer **Augusto Roa Bastos** is well-known throughout Latin America as both a poet and novelist. His novels *El Supremo* and *Hijo de Hombre* deal with the turbulent and difficult history of Paraguay.

Increíble pero cierto
Rainfall is heaviest in Paraguay during **verano**, October through March. About four-fifths of the annual precipitation occurs during this period, and often takes the form of drenching downpours accompanied by hailstorms.

TEACHING OPTIONS

Worth Noting Students can get some flavor of the guaraní language by reading aloud the names of these typical Paraguayan dishes: **chipa** (a baked good flavored with **anís**), **kiveve** (a stew made from **andaí**, a type of squash), and **pastel mandi'o** (turnovers made with the South American staple, manioc flour, and filled with **so'o ku'í**, chopped meat). Invite students who have visited or lived in Paraguay to share other information about traditional Paraguayan fare. Don't forget to have them mention the national drink of Paraguay (as well as of Uruguay, Argentina, and Rio Grande do Sul in Brazil), **yerba mate. Yerba mate** is a caffein-rich infusion made from the leaves of a tree native to Paraguay and is sometimes called Paraguay tea in English.

Artesanía • El ñandutí

El ñandutí es la forma artesanal más conocida de Paraguay. Es un fino encaje hecho a mano que generalmente tiene forma circular. En guaraní, su nombre significa telaraña y se llama así porque imita su trazado. Estos encajes suelen ser blancos, pero también los hay de colores, y sus diseños pueden tener formas geométricas o florales. Aunque el ñandutí es originario de Itaguá, con el tiempo ha llegado a ser muy conocido en toda Sudamérica.

Ciencias • La represa Itaipú

La represa Itaipú, la obra hidroeléctrica más ambiciosa hasta nuestros días, se encuentra en la frontera entre Paraguay y Brasil. Su construcción se inició en 1974 y duró once años. Durante los primeros cinco años, se usó suficiente concreto como para construir un edificio de 350 pisos. El proyecto dio trabajo a 100.000 paraguayos. En 1984 se puso en funcionamiento la Central Hidroeléctrica de Itaipú, la mayor del mundo. Gracias a su cercanía a las famosas Cataratas de Iguazú, muchos turistas visitan la central atraídos por lo imponente de su construcción.

Naturaleza • Los ríos Paraguay y Paraná

Los ríos Paraguay y Paraná sirven de frontera natural entre Paraguay y Argentina y son las principales rutas de transporte dentro de Paraguay. El río Paraná tiene unos 3.200 km navegables, y por esta ruta pasan barcos de más de 5.000 toneladas que pueden ir desde el estuario del Río de la Plata hasta la ciudad de Asunción. El río Paraguay divide el Gran Chaco, una zona poco poblada, de la meseta Paraná, donde vive la mayoría de los paraguayos.

¿Qué aprendiste? Responde a las preguntas con una frase completa.

1. ¿Quién es Augusto Roa Bastos?
   Augusto Roa Bastos es un escritor paraguayo.
2. ¿Cómo se llama la moneda de Paraguay?
   La moneda de Paraguay se llama guaraní.
3. ¿Qué es el ñandutí?
   El ñandutí es un tipo de encaje.
4. ¿De dónde es originario el ñandutí?
   El ñandutí es originario de Itaguá.
5. ¿Qué forma imita el ñandutí?
   Imita la forma de una telaraña.
6. En total, ¿cuántos años tomó la construcción de la represa Itaipú?
   La construcción de la represa Itaipú tomó 11 años.
7. ¿A cuántos paraguayos dio trabajo la construcción de la represa?
   La construcción de la represa dio trabajo a 100.000 paraguayos.
8. ¿Qué países separan los ríos Paraguay y Paraná? Los ríos Paraguay y Paraná separan Argentina y Paraguay.
9. ¿Qué distancia se puede navegar por el Paraná?
   Se pueden navegar 3.200 km.

Conexión Internet Investiga estos temas en el sitio **www.vistasonline.com.**

1. Busca información sobre Alfredo Stroessner, el ex-presidente de Paraguay. ¿Por qué se le considera un dictador?
2. Busca información sobre la historia de Paraguay. En tu opinión, ¿cuáles fueron los episodios decisivos en su historia?

encaje *lace* telaraña *spiderweb* trazado *outline; design* represa *dam* meseta *plateau*

TEACHING OPTIONS

Worth Noting Paraguay has eight national parks, encompassing over 11,000 square miles. In addition, there are eight other ecological preserves, dedicated to the preservation of endangered flora and fauna. The rich diversity of plant and animal life, and the government's commitment to preserving these natural wonders, have made Paraguay a popular destination for ecotourists. These parks cover a wide spectrum of ecology. The **Parque Nacional Defensores del Chaco** and **Parque Nacional Teniente Enciso** are located in the semi-arid Chaco. Other parks, like **Parque Nacional Caaguazú** southeast of Asunción are covered with sub-tropical rainforest.

El ñandutí In recent years, the number of traditional **ñandutí** makers has been in serious decline. The artisans of **Itaguá** grew tired of the low levels of compensation they received, and many have turned to other more profitable sources of income. Formal instruction in the skill of making **ñandutí** has even been incorporated in the curriculum of local handicraft schools in an effort to keep this traditional art alive.

La represa Itaipú The **Itaipú** dam project is a joint venture between Brazil and Paraguay, and has been remarkably successful. By 1995, 4 years after it went into production, the dam generated 25% of Brazil's energy supply, and 78% of that of Paraguay. Annual electrical output continues to increase yearly.

Los ríos Paraguay y Paraná The Paraná River in particular was a highway for the settlement of Paraguay. Along its banks, between the 16th and late 18th centuries, the Jesuits organized their Guaraní-speaking parishioners into small, self-supporting city states built around mission settlements, similar to the Franciscan mission system in California during the same period.

¿Qué aprendiste? Go over the questions and answers with students, making sure everyone understands unfamiliar words and what the correct answers are.

Assignment Have students do activites in **Student Activities Manual: Workbook,** page 213.

Conexión Internet Students will find information about Paraguay at **www.vistasonline.com,** as well as links to other sites that can help them in their research.

Section Goals

In **Panorama**, students will read about the geography and culture of Uruguay.

Instructional Resources
Student Activities Manual: Workbook, 214
Transparency 65

Uruguay

Before Presenting Panorama Have students look at the map of Uruguay or project **Transparency 65** and talk about the physical features of the country. Point out the long coastline that runs along the Río de la Plata, separating Uruguay from neighboring Argentina. Point out that Uruguay and Argentina have a great deal in common culturally. **Assignment** Have students read **Panorama** and answer the questions in **¿Qué aprendiste?** on page 573 as homework.

Present Ask volunteers to read each section of **El país en cifras**. After reading the text in italics, you may wish to tell students that at the time of European contact, the area from Punta del Este northward up the coast of Brazil to Río Grande do Sul was one enormous, uninterrupted beach. Early explorers were awestruck by the natural beauty of the Uruguayan landscape, which had rich and varied wildlife, including the ostrich-like **ñandú**, the jaguar, and many marine mammals. After reading about **Uruguayos célebres**, point out that **Horacio Quiroga's** ***Cuentos de la selva*** are set amidst Uruguay's natural flora and fauna.

Increíble pero cierto Uruguayans also consume many other sorts of meat. Beef makes up over 65% of meat consumption, while lamb makes up 13.9%, chicken is 11.5% and pork just 7%. Uruguayans also enjoy rabbit and other wild game.

Uruguay

NATIONAL STANDARDS connections cultures

El país en cifras

- **Área:** 176.220 km^2 (68.039 $millas^2$) *el tamaño del estado de Washington*
- **Población:** 3.385.000
- **Capital:** Montevideo—1.238.000

Casi la mitad de la población de Uruguay vive en Montevideo. Situada en la desembocadura del famoso Río de la Plata, esta ciudad cosmopolita e intelectual es también un destino popular para las vacaciones, debido a sus numerosas playas de arena blanca que se extienden hasta la ciudad de Punta del Este.

- **Ciudades principales:** Salto—77.000, Paysandú—75.000, Las Piedras—61.000, Rivera—55.000

SOURCE: Population Division, UN Secretariat

- **Moneda:** peso uruguayo
- **Idiomas:** español (oficial)

Bandera de Uruguay

Gaucho uruguayo

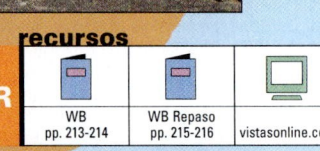

Entrada a la Ciudad Vieja, Colonia del Sacramento

Uruguayos célebres

- Horacio Quiroga, escritor (1878-1937)
- Juana de Ibarbourou, escritora (1895-1979)
- Mario Benedetti, escritor (1920-)
- Cristina Peri Rossi, escritora y profesora (1941-)

recursos

R	WB pp. 213-214	WB Repaso pp. 215-216	vistasonline.com

¡Increíble pero cierto!

¡Uruguay es el país más carnívoro del planeta! Los uruguayos poseen el récord mundial de consumo de carne de res per cápita. Cada año, cada uruguayo consume 80 kilogramos de carne de res o, lo que es lo mismo, ¡¡MEDIA VACA!!

TEACHING OPTIONS

Variación léxica Montevideo looks out across the wide estuary of the Río de la Plata at Buenos Aires, Argentina, and the Spanish of Uruguay's major city has much in common with the **Porteño** Spanish of its neighbor. When speaking, Uruguayans tend to use **vos** as frequently as **tú,** as well as all the accompanying verb forms. The plural of both forms is **Uds.**, as in the rest of Latin America. In the northern part of Uruguay, along the border with Brazil, the majority of residents are bilingual in Portuguese and Spanish.

Extra Practice To taste the flavor of popular culture in the carnivore nation, encourage students to translate these Uruguayan sayings: **Todo bicho** *(animal)* **que camina va a parar al asador. • Comida que mucho hierve, sabor pierde.**

Costumbres • La carne y el mate

La gran importancia de la producción ganadera en las economías de Uruguay y Argentina se refleja en sus hábitos culinarios. Para los uruguayos, como para los argentinos, la carne de res es un elemento esencial de la dieta diaria. Algunos platos representativos son el asado, la parrillada y el chivito. El mate, una infusión similar al té, es también muy típico de esta región. Es una bebida de origen indígena que está muy presente en la vida social y familiar de estos países aunque, curiosamente, no se puede consumir en bares o restaurantes.

Deportes • El fútbol

El fútbol es, sin lugar a dudas, el deporte nacional de Uruguay. La afición a este deporte se inició muy pronto en Uruguay. En 1891, se formó el primer equipo de fútbol uruguayo y, en 1930, el país fue la sede de la primera copa mundial. A partir de los años treinta se inició el período profesional del fútbol uruguayo. El equipo nacional ha conseguido grandes éxitos a lo largo de los años: dos campeonatos olímpicos en 1923 y 1928, y dos campeonatos mundiales: en 1930 y 1950. De hecho, los uruguayos ya están trabajando para que la Copa Mundial de 2030 se celebre en su país.

Costumbres • El Carnaval

El Carnaval de Montevideo es el más largo del mundo y uno de los mejores de Sudamérica. Dura unos cuarenta días y cuenta con la participación de casi todos los habitantes de la ciudad. Durante el Carnaval, los uruguayos disfrutan de desfiles, bailes y música en las calles de su capital. La celebración más conocida es el Desfile de las Llamadas, en el que participan bailarines que desfilan al ritmo del candombe, un colorido baile de tradición africana.

¿Qué aprendiste? Responde a las preguntas con una frase completa.

1. ¿Qué tienen en común los uruguayos célebres mencionados en la página 572? Son escritores.
2. ¿Cuál es el elemento esencial de la dieta uruguaya? La carne de res es esencial en la dieta uruguaya.
3. ¿En qué países es importante la producción ganadera? La producción ganadera es importante en Uruguay y Argentina.
4. ¿Qué es el mate? El mate es una bebida indígena que es similar al té.
5. ¿Cuándo se formó el primer equipo uruguayo de fútbol? En 1891 se formó el primer equipo de fútbol uruguayo.
6. ¿Cuándo se celebró la primera Copa Mundial de fútbol? La primera Copa Mundial se celebró en 1930.
7. ¿Cómo se llama la celebración más conocida del Carnaval de Montevideo? La celebración más conocida del Carnaval de Montevideo se llama El Desfile de las Llamadas.
8. ¿Cuántos días dura el Carnaval de Montevideo? El Carnaval de Montevideo dura unos cuarenta días.

Edificio del Parlamento en Montevideo

Conexión Internet Investiga estos temas en el sitio **www.vistasonline.com.**

1. Uruguay es conocido como un país de muchos escritores. Busca información sobre uno de ellos y escribe una biografía.
2. Investiga cuáles son las comidas y bebidas favoritas de los uruguayos. Descríbelas e indica cuáles te gustaría probar y por qué.

ganadera *cattle (adj.)* asado *barbecue* parrillada *beef platter* chivito *goat* sede *site* Desfile *Parade*

La carne y el mate A legend from the **guaraní** people of Uruguay says that **yerba mate** was a gift from the god **Pa-i Shume.** Traditionally, the **yerba mate** leaves are packed into a **mate**—a cup made from a gourd—and hot water is poured over them. The infusion is sipped through a **bombilla**—a metal straw with a built-in tea strainer. The **mate** is refilled and drained several times, passing from hand to hand among a group of friends or family.

El fútbol Uruguayan women have begun to make their mark in soccer. Although the International Federation of Association Football (FIFA) established a women's league in 1982, it wasn't until 1985 that the first women's league—from Brazil—was formally established. The women's league of Uruguay now participates in international soccer play, showing that Uruguayan women can be just as fanatical as the men when it comes to **fútbol**.

El carnaval Like the rest of Latin America, Uruguay also imported slaves from Africa during the colonial period. The music of the African-influenced **candombe** culture is popular with Uruguayans from all sectors of society.

¿Qué aprendiste? Go over the questions and answers with students, making sure everyone understands unfamiliar words and what the correct answers are.

Assignment Have students do activites in **Student Activities Manual: Workbook,** page 214.

Conexión Internet Students will find information about Uruguay at **www.vistasonline.com,** as well as links to other sites that can help them in their research.

TEACHING OPTIONS

Worth Noting Uruguay is similar to its larger, more powerful neighbor, Argentina, in many ways: the Uruguayans also love the **tango** and **yerba mate**, they play the Argentine card game **truco**, and they are devoted carnivores. Historically cattle ranching, the culture of the **gaucho**, and the great cattle ranches called **estancias** have been an important element in the Uruguayan national fabric. Another, less pleasant, similarity was in the Dirty War **(Guerra sucia)** waged by an Uruguayan military dictatorship against domestic dissidents during the 70s and 80s. In 1984 the military allowed the election of a civilian government. In 1989 that government was peacefully succeeded by another. Democratic government seems to be well on the mend in today's Uruguay.

Successful Language Learning Tell your students that they may want to review all the end-of-lesson vocabulary lists at this time. Tell them to imagine how they would use each lesson's vocabulary in everyday life.

The Affective Dimension Tell your students to consider their feelings about speaking Spanish at the beginning of the course and think about how they feel about speaking Spanish now. Tell them that this is a good time to consider their motivations and set new goals as they continue learning the language.

18 vocabulario

Los medios de comunicación

el acontecimiento	*event*
las actualidades	*news; current events*
el artículo	*article*
el diario	*newspaper*
el informe	*report; paper (written work)*
el/la locutor(a)	*(TV or radio) announcer*
los medios de comunicación	*means of communication; media*
las noticias	*news*
el noticiero	*newscast*
la prensa	*press*
el reportaje	*report*
anunciar	*to announce; to advertise*
comunicarse (con)	*to communicate (with)*
durar	*to last*
informar	*to inform*
ocurrir	*to occur; to happen*
transmitir, emitir	*to broadcast*
(inter)nacional	*(inter)national*
peligroso/a	*dangerous*

Las noticias

el choque	*collision*
el crimen	*crime; murder*
el desastre (natural)	*(natural) disaster*
el desempleo	*unemployment*
la (des)igualdad	*(in)equality*
la discriminación	*discrimination*
el ejército	*army*
la experiencia	*experience*
la guerra	*war*
la huelga	*strike*
el huracán	*hurricane*
el incendio	*fire*
la inundación	*flood*
la libertad	*liberty; freedom*
la paz	*peace*
el racismo	*racism*
el sexismo	*sexism*
el SIDA	*AIDS*
el terremoto	*earthquake*
la tormenta	*storm*
el tornado	*tornado*
la violencia	*violence*
luchar (por/contra)	*to fight; to struggle (for/against)*

La política

el/la candidato/a	*candidate*
el/la ciudadano/a	*citizen*
el deber	*responsibility; obligation*
los derechos	*rights*
la dictadura	*dictatorship*
el discurso	*speech*
las elecciones	*election*
la encuesta	*poll; survey*
el impuesto	*tax*
la política	*politics*
el/la representante	*representative*
declarar	*to declare; to say*
elegir	*to elect*
obedecer	*to obey*
votar	*to vote*
político/a	*political*

Expresiones útiles	*See page 553.*

English Translations of the Fotonovela Conversations

Lesson 1

All Aboard!

The four tourists, don Francisco, and Mrs. Ramos meet at the university.

1 SRA. RAMOS Good morning, everybody. I am Isabel Ramos from the Ecuatur agency.
DON FRANCISCO And I'm don Francisco, the driver.

2 SRA. RAMOS Well, who is María Teresa Fuentes de Alba?
MAITE That's me!
SRA. RAMOS Oh, good. Here are your travel documents.
MAITE Thank you.

3 SRA. RAMOS Javier Gómez Lozano?
JAVIER Here . . . that's me.

4 SRA. RAMOS And you are Inés Ayala Loor, right?
INÉS Yes, I'm Inés.
SRA. RAMOS And you are Alejandro Morales Paredes, right?
ÁLEX Yes, ma'am.

5 INÉS Hi. I'm Inés.
MAITE Pleased to meet you. My name is Maite. Where are you from?
INÉS I'm from Portoviejo, Ecuador. And you?
MAITE From Spain. I'm from Madrid, the capital. Listen, what time is it?
INÉS It's 10:03.

6 JAVIER How are you? My name is Javier.
ÁLEX Pleased to meet you. I'm Alex. Where are you from?
JAVIER From Puerto Rico. And you?
ÁLEX I'm from Mexico.

7 DON FRANCISCO Well, everybody, all aboard!

8 INÉS Excuse me.

9 ÁLEX Pardon me.

10 DON FRANCISCO And the others?
SRA. RAMOS That's it.
DON FRANCISCO Okay.

Lesson 2

What classes are you taking?

Maite, Inés, Javier, and Álex talk about their classes.

1 ÁLEX Hi, Ricardo . . . Here we are in the middle of the world. How are classes going at UNAM?

2 MAITE It's exactly like the photographs in geography books.
INÉS Yes! Are you also taking geography?
MAITE Not me. I'm taking English and literature. I'm also taking a journalism class.

3 MAITE Good morning. María Teresa Fuentes, of Radio Andina FM 93. Today I'm with students from San Francisco University in Quito. Let's see. The young woman who's near the window . . . What is your name and where are you from?

4 INÉS Hi. My name is Inés Ayala Loor, and I'm from Ecuador . . . from Portoviejo.
MAITE Delighted to meet you. What classes are you taking at the university?
INÉS I'm taking geography, English, history, sociology, and art.

5 MAITE You're taking lots of classes, aren't you?
INÉS Well, yes, I enjoy studying a lot.

6 MAITE In which class are there more guys?
INÉS Well, um . . . in history class.
MAITE And more girls?
INÉS There are more girls in sociology class, almost 85%.

7 MAITE And you, young man, what is your name and where are you from?
JAVIER My name is Javier Gómez, and I'm from San Juan, Puerto Rico.
MAITE Are you taking lots of classes this semester?
JAVIER Yes, I'm taking three: history and art on Mondays, Wednesdays, and Fridays, and computer science on Tuesdays and Thursdays.

8 MAITE Do you like computers, Javier?
JAVIER I don't like them at all. I like art much better . . . but most of all, I like drawing.
ÁLEX What do you mean? You don't like computers?

9 ÁLEX But they're so interesting, man.

10 JAVIER Yes, really interesting!

Lesson 3

Do you have a large family?

The boys and girls talk about their families on the bus.

1 MAITE Inés, do you have a large family?
INÉS Well, yes . . . my parents, my grandparents, four sisters, and many aunts, uncles, and cousins.

2 INÉS I only have an older brother, Pablo. His wife Francesca is a doctor. She is not Ecuadorian; she's Italian. Her parents live in Rome, I think. They come to visit every year. Ah . . . and Pablo is a journalist.
MAITE How interesting!

3 INÉS And you, Javier, do you have siblings?
JAVIER No, but I have some photographs of my family.

INÉS Oh, great, let's see!

4 **JAVIER** Here they are!
INÉS Your father is so tall! And your mother, how pretty!

5 **JAVIER** Look, here I am. And this is my grandfather. He is my mother's father.
INÉS How old is your grandfather?
JAVIER Ninety-two.

6 **INÉS** And what's he like?
JAVIER He's very nice. He's old, but he's a very hard-working man.

7 **MAITE** Hey, Javier, what are you drawing?
JAVIER Huh? Who? Me? Nothing!
MAITE Come on! Don't be silly!

8 **MAITE** Jaaavieeer . . . Listen, but . . . you really draw well!
JAVIER This . . . well . . . Yes, thanks!

9 **MAITE** Álex, look, do you like it?
ÁLEX Yes, very much. It's really pretty.

10 **DON FRANCISCO** Hey, what's going on between Inés and Javier?

Lesson 4

Let's go to the park!

The students explore the city and talk about their pastimes.

1 **DON FRANCISCO** It's three o'clock. You have one hour free. You can explore the city, if you want. We have to go to the cabins at four.

2 **JAVIER** Inés, do you want to take a walk around the city?
INÉS Yes, let's go.

3 **ÁLEX** Why don't we go to the park, Maite? We can talk and get some sun.
MAITE Good idea! It's very sunny today. I also want to write some postcards.

4 **MAITE** Are you a sports fan, Álex?
ÁLEX Yes, I like soccer a lot. I also like swimming, running, and hiking in the mountains.
MAITE I run a lot, too.

5 **ÁLEX** Listen, Maite, why don't we play soccer with him?
MAITE Hmm... I don't want to. I'm going to finish writing some postcards.

6 **ÁLEX** Maite!
MAITE Oh my goodness!

7 **YOUNG MAN** Please forgive me. I'm really sorry.
MAITE Oh, it's nothing, I'm fine!

8 **ÁLEX** It's already two-thirty. We should get back to the bus, don't you think?
MAITE You're right.
ÁLEX Listen, Maite, what are you going to do tonight?
MAITE I don't have any plans. Why?

9 **ÁLEX** Listen, . . . sometimes I go run at night. Do you want to go running with me?
MAITE Yes, let's go. At what time?
ÁLEX At six?
MAITE Perfect.

10 **DON FRANCISCO** Tonight they're going to run. And I don't have energy to take a walk!

Lesson 5

We have a reservation.

Don Francisco and the students arrive at the hotel.

1 **EMPLOYEE** How can I help you?
DON FRANCISCO I'm Francisco Castillo Moreno, and we have a reservation in my name.
EMPLOYEE Hmm . . . I don't see your name. It's not here.

2 **DON FRANCISCO** Are you sure, miss? Maybe the reservation is under the name of the Ecuatur travel agency.
EMPLOYEE Oh yes, here it is . . . two double rooms, and one single, from 101 to 103 . . . all in the first cabins.
DON FRANCISCO Thank you. That's very kind of you.

3 **BELLHOP** Here's room number 101 . . . After you.

4 **ÁLEX** Hi, girls. What are you doing?
MAITE We're resting.

5 **JAVIER** Listen, the cabins aren't bad at all, are they?
INÉS Everything is very clean and orderly.
ÁLEX Yes, it's excellent.
MAITE And the beds are so comfortable.

6 **INÉS** Listen, I'm bored. Do you want to do something?
JAVIER Why don't we go and explore the city a bit more?
INÉS Great idea! Let's go!

7 **MAITE** No, I'm not going. I'm tired, and I want to rest a little because at six I'm going running with Álex.
ÁLEX And I want to write an e-mail message before going for the run.

8 **JAVIER** Well, we're ready, right, Inés?
INÉS Yes, let's go.
MAITE Good-bye.
INÉS & JAVIER Bye!

9 **ÁLEX** Well, see you at six.
MAITE Yes, so long.
ÁLEX Bye.

10 **MAITE** Inés and Javier? Together again?

Lesson 6

What pretty clothes!

Javier and Inés go shopping at the market.

1. **INÉS** Javier, what pretty clothes! I like this white shirt with black stripes. It must be cotton. Do you like it?
   JAVIER I prefer the shirt on the left . . . the gray one with red stripes. It goes well with my brown boots.

2. **INÉS** Okay, Javier. Look, I need to buy my sister Graciela a present. She just started a new job . . .
   JAVIER Maybe a purse?

3. **SALESPERSON** These bags are typical of the mountains. Do you like them?
   INÉS Yes. I want to buy one for my sister.

4. **INÉS** I like that one. How much does it cost?

5. **SALESPERSON** This one costs one hundred twenty thousand sucres. It's very good quality!
   INÉS Ugh, too expensive. Maybe another day.

6. **SALESPERSON** Good afternoon, young man. May I help you with something?
   JAVIER Yes. I'm going hiking in the mountains, and I need a good sweater.
   SALESPERSON What size do you wear?
   JAVIER I wear a large.

7. **SALESPERSON** These ones are large.
   JAVIER What is the price of that one?
   SALESPERSON Do you like this sweater? It only costs a hundred and fifty thousand sucres.
   JAVIER Hmm . . . I want to buy it. But, I'm not rich. A hundred and twenty thousand sucres?

8. **SALESPERSON** Well, for you . . . only eighty thousand sucres.
   JAVIER Okay.

9. **JAVIER** I've just bought myself a sweater. And you, what did you buy?
   INÉS I bought this bag for my sister.

10. **INÉS** I also bought myself a blouse and a hat. How do I look?
    JAVIER Good-looking, very good-looking!

Lesson 7

I never get up early!

Álex and Javier talk about their daily routines.

1. **JAVIER** Hi, Álex. What are you doing?
   ÁLEX Nothing . . . I'm just reading my e-mail. Where did you go?

2. **JAVIER** Inés and I went to a market. It was a lot of fun. Look, I bought this sweater. I love it. It wasn't cheap, but it's great, isn't it?
   ÁLEX Yes, it's perfect for the mountains.

3. **JAVIER** Outdoor markets are so interesting! I'd like to go back, but it's already late. Listen, Álex, you know that tomorrow we have to get up early.
   ÁLEX No problem.

4. **JAVIER** Are you sure? Well, I never get up early. I never hear the alarm clock when I'm home, and my mom gets mad.
   ÁLEX Relax, Javier. I have a solution.

5. **ÁLEX** When I'm home in Mexico City, I always wake up at 6:00 on the dot. I take a shower in five minutes, and then I brush my teeth. Then, I shave, I get dressed, and, as soon as I'm ready, I'm off!

6. **JAVIER** Incredible! Álex, the superman!
   ÁLEX Listen, Javier, why can't you get up early?
   JAVIER It's just that at night I don't want to sleep, I want to draw and listen to music. That's why it's hard for me to wake up in the morning.

7. **JAVIER** The bus doesn't leave until 8:30. Are you going to get up at 6:00 tomorrow too?
   ÁLEX No, but I have to get up at a quarter to seven because I'm going running.

8. **JAVIER** Oh, okay... Can you wake me up after running?
   ÁLEX This is the plan for tomorrow. I'll wake up at a quarter to seven and run for thirty minutes. I'll come back, take a shower, get dressed, and at seven thirty I'll wake you up. Agreed?
   JAVIER Absolutely! No objection!

9. **DON FRANCISCO** Hi, guys. Tomorrow we leave early, at 8:30 . . . not a minute earlier and not a minute later.
   ÁLEX Don't worry, don Francisco. Everything is under control.
   DON FRANCISCO Well, then, see you tomorrow.

10. **DON FRANCISCO** Ah, these students! They always go to bed late. What a life!

Lesson 8

How's the food?

Don Francisco and the students go to the El Cráter restaurant.

1. **JAVIER** Do you know where we are?
   INÉS Hmm, I don't know. Listen, don Francisco, do you know where we are?
   DON FRANCISCO We're near Cotacachi.

2. **ÁLEX** Where are we going to eat lunch, don Francisco? Do you know a good restaurant in Cotocahi?
   DON FRANCISCO Well, I know doña Rita Perales, the owner of the best restaurant in town, the El Cráter restaurant.

3. **DOÑA RITA** Hey, don Paco, you're here?
   DON FRANCISCO Yes, doña Rita . . . and today I'm bringing you customers. I would like to introduce you to Maite, Inés, Álex, and Javier. I'm taking them to the mountains to go on a hike.

(4) **DOÑA RITA** Welcome to El Cráter! You are in very good hands. . . . don Francisco is the best driver in the country. And there's nothing prettier than our mountains. But if you're going to go hiking, you need to eat well. Come with me, kids, through here.

(5) **JAVIER** What do you recommend?
DOÑA RITA Well, the corn tortillas are delicious. The house special is beef soup. . . . You have to try it! The grilled flank steak is a little more expensive than the soup, but it is delicious. I also recommend the lemon-marinated shrimp and the mixed grill.

(6) **MAITE** I'm going to have the beef soup and grilled flank steak.
JAVIER Corn tortillas and lemon-marinated shrimp for me.
ÁLEX I would like the corn tortillas and lemon-marinated shrimp, too, please.
INÉS I'm going to order the beef soup and grilled flank steak.

(7) **DON FRANCISCO** I want corn tortillas and a platter of mixed grill.
DOÑA RITA And to drink, I recommend the pineapple, strawberry, and blackberry juice. Should I bring it for everybody?
ALL Yes, perfect.

(8) **WAITER** What dish did you order?
MAITE A beef soup and a grilled flank steak.

(9) **DOÑA RITA** How was the food? Tasty?
JAVIER Not just tasty, super tasty!
ÁLEX Yes, and the service was quick.
MAITE A delicious meal, thanks.

(10) **DON FRANCISCO** Today is Maite's birthday . . .
DOÑA RITA Ah, we have cakes that are to die for . . .

Lesson 9

Happy birthday, Maite!

In the El Cráter restaurant, don Francisco and the students celebrate Maite's birthday.

(1) **INÉS** I love sweets. Maite, what are you going to order?
MAITE Oh, I don't know. Everything looks so delicious. Maybe the chocolate cake.

(2) **JAVIER** The chocolate cake with ice cream for me. I love chocolate. Álex, and you, what are you going to have?
ÁLEX I usually prefer fruit, but today I think I will try the chocolate cake.
DON FRANCISCO I always order baked custard and coffee.

(3) **DOÑA RITA & WAITER** Happy Birthday, Maite!
INÉS Is today your birthday, Maite?
MAITE Yes, June 22nd. And it seems like we're going to celebrate it.
ALL BUT MAITE Congratulations!

(4) **MAITE** Thank you, but who told you that it's my birthday?
DOÑA RITA I found it out through don Francisco.

(5) **ÁLEX** Yesterday I asked you, and you didn't want to tell me. Hey! You're terrible.
JAVIER How old are you?
MAITE Twenty-three.

(6) **ÁLEX** I also just turned twenty-three.
MAITE When?
ÁLEX May fourth.

(7) **DOÑA RITA** Here is the baked custard, the chocolate cake with ice cream . . . and a bottle of wine to celebrate.
MAITE What a surprise! I don't know what to say! Thank you very, very much.

(8) **DON FRANCISCO** The driver can't drink wine. Doña Rita, thanks for everything. Can you bring us the bill?
DOÑA RITA Right away, Paco.

(9) **INÉS** I think we should leave a good tip. What do you guys think?
MAITE Yes, let's leave Mrs. Perales a good tip. She's extremely nice.

(10) **DON FRANCISCO** Thanks again. I always have a good time here.
MAITE Thanks so much, Mrs. Perales. For the food, for the surprise, and for being so nice to us.

Lesson 10

Ow! It hurts!

Don Francisco and Javier go to Dr. Márquez's clinic.

(1) **JAVIER** I'm bored . . . I feel like drawing. Excuse me.

(2) **INÉS** Javier! What happened?
JAVIER Oh, ugh, it hurts! I think I broke my ankle!

(3) **DON FRANCISCO** Don't worry, Javier. We're near the clinic where my friend, Dr. Márquez, works.

(4) **JAVIER** Does it hurt? Yes, very much. Where? In the ankle. Do I have fever? I don't think so. Am I dizzy? A little bit. Am I allergic to any medication? No. Pregnant? Definitely NOT.

(5) **DR. MÁRQUEZ** How did you hurt your foot?
JAVIER I fell while I was on the bus.

(6) **DR. MÁRQUEZ** How long ago did you fall?
JAVIER I already forgot . . . let me see . . . umm . . . it was more or less 2:00 or 2:30 when I fell . . . in other words, more than an hour. It hurts a lot!
DR. MÁRQUEZ Well, we're going to take an x-ray. We want to see if you broke any bones in your foot.

(7) **DON FRANCISCO** You know, Javier, when I was young, I was very scared of doctors. I used to go to the doctor often because I used to get sick a lot, and I used to get a lot of throat infections. I didn't like injections or pills. One time, I broke my leg playing soccer . . .

(8) **JAVIER** Doctor! What is it? Is my ankle broken?
DR. MÁRQUEZ Relax, I have good news, Javier. Your ankle isn't broken. It's just sprained.

(9) **JAVIER** But will I be able to go hiking with my friends?
DR. MÁRQUEZ I think so. But you should rest and not walk too much for a couple of days. I will prescribe some pills for the pain.

(10) **DR. MÁRQUEZ** Goodbye, Francisco. Goodbye, Javier. Be careful! Good luck in the mountains!

Lesson 11

Technoman, my hero!

The bus breaks down.

(1) **ÁLEX** Hello? . . . This is he . . . Oh, how are you? . . . I'm very good. We're going to Ibarra. Do you know what happened? This afternoon we were going to Ibarra when Javier had an accident on the bus. He fell, and we had to take him to a clinic.

(2) **JAVIER** Episode twenty-one: Technoman and his superfriends save the world one more time.
INÉS Oh, Technoman, my hero.
MAITE What comedians! One of these days, you're going to see . . .

(3) **ÁLEX** You're going to see who Technoman really is. My superfriends and I talk everyday through the Internet, working to save the world. But for now, with your permission, I'd like to write an e-mail to my mom and surf the Web for a while.

(4) **DON FRANCISCO** Kids, I think we have a problem with the bus. Why don't you get off?

(5) **DON FRANCISCO** Hmm, I don't see the problem.
INÉS When I was in high school, I worked in my uncle's auto shop. He taught me a lot about mechanics. Luckily, I got to fix some buses like this one.
DON FRANCISCO You don't say! Well, what do you think?

(6) **INÉS** Well . . . I don't know . . . I think it's the alternator. Let's see . . . yes . . . Look, don Francisco... the alternator is burned out.
DON FRANCISCO Oh, yes. But we can't fix it here. I know a mechanic, but he's in Ibarra, twenty kilometers from here.

(7) **ÁLEX** Technoman, at your service.
DON FRANCISCO You're our savior, Álex! Call Mr. Fonseca at 532-4791. We know each other very well. I'm sure he'll help us.

(8) **ÁLEX** Good afternoon. May I please speak with Mr. Fonseca? . . . I'm Álex Morales, a client of Ecuatur. I'm speaking to you on behalf of Francisco Castillo . . . We were on our way to Ibarra, and our bus broke down . . . We think it's the . . . the alternator . . . We're twenty kilometers from the city . . .

(9) **MR. FONSECA** I think it will be better to fix the bus right there. Relax, I'll leave right away.

(10) **ÁLEX** Good news. Mr. Fonseca is coming right away. He thinks he can fix the bus right here.
MAITE Mechanicwoman and Technoman, my heroes!
DON FRANCISCO And mine too!

Lesson 12

You'll love the house!

Don Francisco and the students arrive in Ibarra.

(1) **MRS. VIVES** Hi, welcome!
DON FRANCISCO Mrs. Vives, let me introduce the boys and girls. Kids, this is Mrs. Vives, the housekeeper.

(2) **MRS. VIVES** Delighted. Come with me . . . I want to show you the house. You're going to love it!

(3) **MRS. VIVES** This bedroom is for the boys. You have two beds, a night table, a chest of drawers . . . In the closet there are more blankets and pillows if you need them.

(4) **MRS. VIVES** Javier, don't put the suitcases on the bed. Put them on the floor, please.

(5) **MRS. VIVES** Take this bedroom, girls.

(6) **MRS. VIVES** This is the living room. The sofa and the armchairs are very comfortable. But please, don't get them dirty!

(7) **MRS. VIVES** The kitchen and dining room are over there. At the end of the hall there is a bathroom.

(8) **DON FRANCISCO** Kids, let's see . . . attention! Mrs. Vives will prepare your meals. But I want you to help her with the household chores. I want you to straighten your rooms, make the beds, and set the table . . . understood?
JAVIER Don't worry . . . we'll help however we can.
ÁLEX Yes, you can count on us.

(9) **INÉS** We insist that you let us help you make the food.
MRS. VIVES No, kids, it's no big deal, but thanks for the offer. Rest awhile; I'm sure you're tired.
ÁLEX Thanks. I would like to take a walk around the city.

(10) **INÉS** Excuse me, don Francisco, what time is the guide coming tomorrow?
DON FRANCISCO Martín? He's coming early, at seven in the morning. I recommend that you go to bed early tonight. No television or long conversations, either!
STUDENTS Oh, don Francisco!

Lesson 13

What a beautiful landscape!

Martín and the students visit the trailhead in the mountains.

(1) **DON FRANCISCO** Everybody, I want to introduce Martín Dávalos, your hiking guide. Martín, our passengers—Maite, Javier, Inés, and Álex.

(2) **MARTÍN** Pleased to meet you. I'm going to take you to the area where we'll go hiking tomorrow. How does that sound?
STUDENTS Yes, let's go!

(3) **MAITE** What beautiful countryside!
INÉS I don't think there is a prettier place in all the world!

(4) **MARTÍN** We hope you have a lot of fun, but you have to take care of nature.
JAVIER We can take photos, can't we?
MARTÍN Yes, as long as you don't touch the flowers or the plants.

(5) **ÁLEX** Are there problems with pollution in this region?
MARTÍN Pollution is a problem throughout the world. But here we have a recycling program. If you see bottles, papers, or cans along the trail, pick them up.

(6) **JAVIER** I understand that tomorrow we're going to cross a river. Is it polluted?
MARTÍN In the mountains, the river does not seem to be affected by pollution. Near the cities, however, the river is pretty polluted.

(7) **ÁLEX** How clean the air is to breathe here! It isn't like in Mexico City. We have a severe pollution problem.
MARTÍN Unless you resolve that problem, the population will suffer from many illnesses in the future.

(8) **INÉS** I think we should all do something to protect the environment.
MAITE I think all countries should make laws controlling the automobiles use.

(9) **JAVIER** But Maite, are you going to stop using your car in Madrid?
MAITE I guess I'm going to have to use the subway . . . But you know that my car is so small . . . it hardly pollutes anything at all.

(10) **INÉS** Come on, Javier!
JAVIER I'm going!!

Lesson 14

We're lost.

Maite and Álex run errands downtown.

(1) **MARTÍN & DON FRANCISCO** Good afternoon.
JAVIER Hi. How are you? We're talking about the hike tomorrow.

(2) **DON FRANCISCO** Do you have everything you need? I always recommend to hikers that they wear comfortable shoes, a backpack, sunglasses, and a sweater, in case it's cold.
JAVIER All set, don Francisco.

(3) **MARTÍN** I recommend you to bring something to eat.
ÁLEX Hmm . . . we didn't think of that.
MAITE Stop worrying so much, Álex! We can buy something at the supermarket right now. Want to go?

(4) **ÁLEX** Excellent idea! As soon as I finish my coffee, I'll go with you.
MAITE I need to go by the bank and by the post office to send some letters.
ÁLEX That's fine.

(5) **ÁLEX** Do you need anything from downtown?
INÉS Yes! !hen you go to the post office, can you put these postcards in the mailbox? I also need some stamps.
ÁLEX Of course.

(6) **YOUNG MAN** Hi! Can I help you with something?
MAITE Yes, we're lost. Is there a bank around here with an ATM?
YOUNG MAN Hmm . . . There are no banks on this block that have an ATM.

(7) **YOUNG MAN** But I know one on Pedro Moncayo Street that does have an ATM. Cross this street and then turn left. Go straight ahead, and before you get to the Crespo Jewelry Store you're going to see a big sign for Pacific Bank.

(8) **MAITE** We're also looking for a supermarket.
YOUNG MAN Well, right there, facing the bank is a small supermarket. Easy, isn't it?
MAITE I think so. Thanks a lot for your help.

(9) **MAITE** Take your stamps, sweetie.
INÉS Thanks, Maite. How did it go downtown?
MAITE Really great! We went to the bank and to the post office. Then in the supermarket we bought food for the hike. And before we came back, we stopped at an ice cream shop.

(10) **MAITE** Oh! Another thing. When we arrived downtown, we met a very nice young man who gave us directions. He was very friendly . . . and very good-looking!

Lesson 15

What a great hike!

Martín and the students go hiking in the mountains.

1 **MARTÍN** Good morning, don Francisco.
DON FRANCISCO Hi, Martin.
MARTÍN I see that you have brought what you need. Everyone has come very well-equipped.

2 **MARTÍN** Very well. Attention, everybody! First let's do some stretching exercises . . .

3 **MARTÍN** It's good that you've stayed in shape. Well, kids, are you ready?
JAVIER Yes, very ready! I can't believe that the big day has finally arrived.

4 **MARTÍN** Fabulous! Let's get going, then!
DON FRANCISCO Bye! Take care!

5 **Martín and the students spend eight hours hiking in the mountains. They have a lot of fun talking, looking at the countryside, and taking photos.**

6 **DON FRANCISCO** Hi. I'm so happy to see you! How did the hike go?
JAVIER Incredible, don F. I hadn't ever seen such spectacular scenery. It's a stupendous place. I took a thousand photos and I have a lot of scenes to draw.

7 **MAITE** I hadn't ever gone on a hike before. I loved it! When I return to Spain, I'm going to have a lot to tell my family.

8 **INÉS** It's been the hike of my life. Friends, Martín, don F., thanks so much.

9 **ÁLEX** Yes, thanks, Martín. Thanks for everything.
MARTÍN You're welcome. It's been a pleasure.

10 **DON FRANCISCO** Well, everyone, it's time to return. I think that Mrs. Vives has prepared a very special meal for us.

Lesson 16

That's a sensational plan!

Don Francisco and the students talk about their future occupations.

1 **MAITE** Mrs. Vives is a magnificent cook.
DON FRANCISCO I'm glad you like it.

2 **DON FRANCISCO** Listen, what can you tell me about the place where you went on the hike? What did you think of it?
MAITE The landscape is really beautiful!
INÉS Martín was an excellent guide. He showed a lot of interest in us learning about the environment.

3 **DON FRANCISCO** Yes, Martín is the best guide I know. But speaking of professions, do you want to know what my plans for the future are?
MAITE I'm dying to know!
DON FRANCISCO I've decided that next summer I'm going to establish my own tour package company.

4 **JAVIER** Good idea, don F.! With your experience and talent, you'll be a great success.
ÁLEX Yes, I completely agree.
DON FRANCISCO How kind you are! But, tell me, what are your plans? I suppose you've also thought about the future.

5 **ÁLEX** But of course, don Francisco. In five years I will have established a company specializing in the Internet.
INÉS You'll be a millionaire, right?
ÁLEX Exactly, because a lot of people will have invested loads of money in my firm.

6 **MAITE** It's a sensational plan! But now listen to mine. I'm going to be a journalist, and I will have my own talk show. You'll see me on TV interviewing politicians, scientists, businessmen and women, and actors and actresses.

7 **JAVIER** I have no doubt that I will be a famous painter. Everybody will want to buy my paintings, and I'll be even more famous than Picasso, than Dalí, than Velázquez . . .

8 **INÉS** I will be an archeologist. I will explore archeological sites in Ecuador and in other countries. I'll write books about my discoveries.

9 **MAITE** Phenomenal! When you're famous, I'll invite all of you to my program. And you too will come, don F.
DON FRANCISCO Right away! I'll come driving a bus!

10 **DON FRANCISCO** Here's to the future!
STUDENTS Here's to the future!

Lesson 17

Here come Romeo and Juliet.

Álex and Maite go to see a play.

1 **ÁLEX** Listen, what kind of movies do you like? Action? Horror? As far as I'm concerned, the best are science fiction.
MAITE That doesn't surprise me. My favorite movies are romantic ones. But do you know what fascinates me?

2 **ÁLEX** No, but tell me, dear, what fascinates you most?
MAITE Poetry. Right now I'm reading a collection by García Lorca . . . It's phenomenal . . .

3 **ÁLEX** Don't tell me! I like poetry too. Do you know Octavio Paz, the Mexican poet?

MAITE Of course. He won the Nobel prize in literature in 1990 . . .

4 **ÁLEX** Wow! You're an expert on literature!

5 **MAITE** Yes, I read everything. Right now on my night table, I have a collection of stories by Carme Riera, a Spaniard who is also a journalist. As soon as I finish it, I'll give it to you.
ÁLEX You've got a deal!

6 **MAITE** Listen, Álex, would you like to be a writer?
ÁLEX Well, I think I would like to be a poet, but I would publish all my poetry on the Internet. Would you like to be a poet?

7 **MAITE** Well, no. But I do think I'd like to be a singer. If I hadn't chosen to be a journalist, I would have been an opera singer.
ÁLEX Opera singer? I hate opera.

8 **JAVIER** Look, Romeo and Juliet are coming. Look how happy they are! Come with me . . . let's surprise them before they open the door.

9 **Álex and Maite kiss.**

10 **JAVIER** What? Did you like the play?

Lesson 18

Until the next time!

The students share their favorite memories of the adventure with Roberto.

1 **MRS. RAMOS** Hello! I hope you've had a magnificent trip.
JAVIER We've had a great time! Thanks a lot!
MRS. RAMOS How are you, don Francisco? I'm happy to see you again!

2 **MAITE** ¡Roberto! How are you?

3 **MAITE** Álex, come . . . this is my friend Roberto. We met in journalism class. He's a reporter for the university newspaper. Roberto, this is my boyfriend, Álex.
ROBERTO Pleased to meet you, Álex.
ÁLEX The pleasure is mine.

4 **MAITE** And these are my friends, Inés and Javier.
JAVIER & INÉS Hi!

5 **MAITE** But, what are you doing here?
ROBERTO Oh, Maite, I'm tired of writing about crime and politics. I'd like to do an interview of your experiences on the trip.
MAITE ¡Phenomenal!

6 **ROBERTO** Let's see . . . let's start with you, Inés. What was your favorite experience?
INÉS For me the best thing was the hike we took to the mountains. How can I describe so much beauty?
ROBERTO Was it dangerous?
JAVIER No, not at all . . . But if our guide hadn't been with us, we would have gotten lost for sure!

7 **ROBERTO** What else happened during the trip?
MAITE Well, one day we went to eat in the restaurant El Cráter. When it was time for dessert, Mrs. Perales, the owner, surprised me with a cake and baked custard for my birthday.

8 **JAVIER** We also had a mechanical problem with the bus, but Inés solved the problem with the help of a mechanic. Now we call her Mechanicwoman.

9 **ROBERTO** If you could take the trip again, would you do it?
ÁLEX Without a second thought. Traveling is a good way to get to know people better and to make friends.

10 **DON FRANCISCO** Goodbye, everybody!
STUDENTS Goodbye! Bye, don F.! See you later!
DON FRANCISCO Until next time, Mrs. Ramos!

Glossary of Grammatical Terms

ADJECTIVE A word that modifies, or describes, a noun or pronoun.

muchos libros
many books

un hombre **rico**
*a **rich** man*

las mujeres **altas**
*the **tall** women*

Demonstrative adjective An adjective that points out a specific noun.

esta fiesta
***this** party*

ese chico
***that** boy*

aquellas flores
***those** flowers*

Possessive adjective An adjective that indicates ownership or possession.

mi mejor vestido
***my** best dress*

Éste es **mi** hermano.
*This is **my** brother*

Stressed possessive adjective A possessive adjective that emphasizes the owner or possessor.

Es un libro **mío**.
*It's **my book**./It's a book **of mine**.*

Es amiga **tuya**; yo no la conozco.
*She's a friend **of yours**; I don't know her.*

ADVERB A word that modifies, or describes, a verb, adjective, or other adverb.

Pancho escribe **rápidamente**.
*Pancho writes **quickly**.*

Este cuadro es **muy** bonito.
*This picture is **very** pretty.*

ARTICLE A word that points out either a specific (definite) noun or a non-specific (indefinite) noun.

Definite article An article that points out a specific noun.

el libro
***the** book*

la maleta
***the** suitcase*

los diccionarios
***the** dictionaries*

las palabras
***the** words*

Indefinite article An article that points out a noun in a general, non-specific way.

un lápiz
***a** pencil*

una computadora
***a** computer*

unos pájaros
***some** birds*

unas escuelas
***some** schools*

CLAUSE A group of words that contains both a conjugated verb and a subject, either expressed or implied.

Main (or Independent) clause A clause that can stand alone as a complete sentence.

Pienso ir a cenar pronto.
I plan to go to dinner soon.

Subordinate (or Dependent) clause A clause that does not express a complete thought and therefore cannot stand alone as a sentence.

Trabajo en la cafetería **porque necesito dinero para la escuela.**
*I work in the cafeteria **because I need money for school.***

COMPARATIVE A word or construction used with an adjective or adverb to express a comparison between two people, places, or things.

Este programa es **más interesante** que el otro.
*This program is **more interesting** than the other one.*

Tomás no es **tan alto como** Alberto.
*Tomás is not **as tall as** Alberto.*

CONJUGATION A set of the forms of a verb for a specific tense or mood or the process by which these verb forms are presented.

Preterite conjugation of cantar

canté	cant**amos**
cant**aste**	cant**asteis**
cant**ó**	cant**aron**

CONJUNCTION A word or phrase used to connect words, clauses, or phrases.

Susana es de Cuba, **y** Pedro es de España.
*Susana is from Cuba, **and** Pedro is from Spain.*

No quiero estudiar, **pero** tengo que hacerlo.
*I don't want to study, **but** I have to.*

CONTRACTION The joining of two words into one. The only contractions in Spanish are **al** and **del**.

Mi hermano fue **al** concierto ayer.
*My brother went **to the** concert yesterday.*

Saqué dinero **del** banco.
*I took money **from the** bank.*

DIRECT OBJECT A noun or pronoun that directly receives the action of the verb.

Tomás lee **el libro.** — *Tomás reads **the book**.*
La pagó ayer. — *She paid **it** yesterday.*

GENDER The grammatical categorizing of certain kinds of words, such as nouns and pronouns, as masculine, feminine, or neuter.

Masculine
articles **el, uno**
pronouns **él, lo, mío, este, ese, aquello**
adjective **simpático**

Feminine
articles **la, una**
pronouns **ella, la, mía, esta, esa, aquella**
adjective **simpática**

IMPERSONAL EXPRESSION A third-person expression with no expressed or specific subject.

Es muy importante. — *It's **very important.***
Llueve mucho. — ***It's raining** hard.*

Aquí **se habla** español.
*Spanish **is spoken** here.*

INDIRECT OBJECT A noun or pronoun that receives the action of the verb indirectly; the object, often a living being, to or for whom an action is performed.

Eduardo **le** dio un libro **a Linda.**
*Eduardo gave a book **to Linda.***

La profesora **me** dio una C en el examen.
*The professor gave **me** a C on the test.*

INFINITIVE The basic form of a verb. Infinitives in Spanish end in **-ar**, **-er**, or **-ir**.

hablar	**correr**	**abrir**
to speak	*to run*	*to open*

INTERROGATIVE An adjective or pronoun used to ask a question.

¿**Quién** habla? — ***Who** is speaking?*
¿**Cuántos** compraste? — ***How many** did you buy?*

¿**Qué** piensas hacer hoy?
***What** do you plan to do today?*

INVERSION Changing the word order of a sentence, often to form a question.

Statement: Elena pagó la cuenta del restaurante.

Inversion: ¿Pagó Elena la cuenta del restaurante?

MOOD A grammatical distinction of verbs that indicates whether the verb is intended to make a statement or command or to express a doubt, emotion, or condition contrary to fact.

Imperative mood Verb forms used to make commands.

Di **la verdad.** — *Tell **the truth.***
Caminen **Uds. conmigo.** — *Walk **with me.***

¡Comamos **ahora!**
*Let's eat **now!***

Indicative mood Verb forms used to state facts, actions, and states considered to be real.

Sé que **tienes** el dinero.
***I know** that **you have** the money*

Subjunctive mood Verb forms used principally in subordinate (or dependent) clauses to express wishes, desires, emotions, doubts, and certain conditions, such as contrary-to-fact situations.

Prefieren que **hables** en español.
*They prefer that **you speak** in Spanish.*

Dudo que Luis **tenga** el dinero necesario.
*I doubt that Luis **has** the necessary money.*

NOUN A word that identifies people, animals, places, things, and ideas.

hombre / *man*	**gato** / *cat*
México / *Mexico*	**casa** / *house*
libertad / *freedom*	

NUMBER A grammatical term that refers to singular or plural. Nouns in Spanish and English have number. Other parts of a sentence, such as adjectives, articles, and verbs, can also have number.

Singular	Plural
una cosa *a thing*	**unas** cosas *some things*
el profesor ***the** professor*	**los** profesores ***the** professors*

NUMBERS Words that represent amounts.

Cardinal numbers Words that show specific amounts.

cinco minutos
***five** minutes*

el año **dos mil y dos**
the year 2002

Ordinal numbers Words that indicate the order of a noun in a series.

el **cuarto** jugador
*the **fourth** player*

la **décima** hora
*the **tenth** hour*

PAST PARTICIPLE A past form of the verb used in compound tenses. The past participle may also be used as an adjective, but it must then agree in number and gender with the word it modifies.

Han **buscado** por todas partes.
*They have **searched** everywhere.*

Yo no había **estudiado** para el examen.
*I hadn't **studied** for the exam.*

Hay una **ventana abierta** en la sala.
*There is an **open window** in the living room.*

PERSON The form of the verb or pronoun that indicates the speaker, the one spoken to, or the one spoken about. In Spanish, as in English, there are three persons: first, second, and third.

Person	Singular	Plural
1st	**yo** I	**nosotros/as** we
2nd	**tú, Ud.** you	**vosotros/as, Uds.** you
3rd	**él, ella** *he/she*	**ellos, ellas** *they*

PREPOSITION A word that describes the relationship, most often in time or space, between two other words.

Anita es **de** California.
*Anita is **from** California.*

La chaqueta está **en** el carro.
*The jacket is **in** the car.*

Marta se peinó **antes** de salir.
*Marta combed her hair **before** going out.*

PRESENT PARTICIPLE In English, a verb form that ends in *-ing*. In Spanish, the present participle ends in **-ndo**, and is often used with **estar** to form a progressive tense.

Mi hermana está **hablando** por teléfono ahora mismo.
*My sister is **talking** on the phone right now.*

PRONOUN A word that takes the place of a noun or nouns.

Demonstrative pronoun A pronoun that takes the place of a specific noun.

Quiero **ésta**.
*I want **this one**.*

¿Vas a comprar **ése**?
*Are you going to buy **that one**?*

Juan prefirió **aquéllos**.
*Juan preferred **those** (over there).*

Object pronoun A pronoun that functions as a direct or indirect object of the verb.

Te digo la verdad.
*I'm telling **you** the truth.*

Me lo trajo Juan.
*Juan brought **it** to **me**.*

Reflexive pronoun A pronoun that indicates that the action of a verb is performed by the subject on itself. These pronouns are often expressed in English with *-self: myself, yourself*, etc.

Yo **me bañé** antes de salir.
***I bathed (myself)** before going out.*

Elena **se acostó** a las once y media.
*Elena **went to bed** at eleven-thirty.*

Relative pronoun A pronoun that connects a subordinate clause to a main clause.

El chico **que** nos escribió viene a visitar mañana.
*The boy **who** wrote us is coming to visit tomorrow.*

Ya sé **lo que** tenemos que hacer.
*I already know **what** we have to do.*

Subject pronoun A subject pronoun that replaces the name or title of a person or thing and acts as the subject of a verb.

Tú debes estudiar más.
***You** should study more.*

Él llegó primero.
***He** arrived first.*

SUBJECT A noun or pronoun that performs the action of a verb and is often implied by the verb.

María va al supermercado.
***María** goes to the supermarket.*

(**Ellos**) Trabajan mucho.
***They** work hard.*

Esos **libros** son muy caros.
*Those **books** are very expensive.*

SUPERLATIVE A word or construction used with an adjective or adverb to express the highest or lowest degree of a specific quality among three or more people, places, or things.

Entre todas mis clases, ésta es la **más interesante**.
*Among all my classes, this is the **most interesting**.*

Raúl es el **menos simpático** de los chicos.
*Raúl is the **least nice** of the boys.*

TENSE A set of verb forms that indicates the time of an action or state: past, present, or future.

Compound tense A two-word tense made up of an auxiliary verb and a present or past participle. In Spanish, there are two auxiliary verbs: **estar** and **haber**.

En este momento, **estoy estudiando**.
*At this time, **I am studying**.*

El paquete no **ha llegado** todavía.
*The package **has** not **arrived** yet.*

Simple tense A tense expressed by a single verb form.

María **estaba** mal anoche.
*María **was** ill last night.*

Juana **hablará** con su mamá mañana.
*Juana **will** speak with her mom tomorrow.*

VERB A word that expresses actions or states-of-being.

Auxiliary verb A verb used with a present or past participle to form a compound tense. **Haber** is the most commonly used auxiliary verb in Spanish.

Los chicos **han** visto los elefantes.
*The children **have** seen the elephants.*

Espero que **hayas** comido.
*I hope you **have** eaten.*

Reflexive verb A verb that describes an action performed by the subject on itself and is always used with a reflexive pronoun.

Me compré un carro nuevo.
I bought myself *a new car.*

Pedro y Adela **se levantan** muy temprano.
*Pedro and Adela **get (themselves) up** very early.*

Spelling change verb A verb that undergoes a predictable change in spelling in order to reflect its actual pronunciation in the various conjugations.

practicar	practico	practi**qué**
dirigir	diri**j**o	dirigí
almorzar	almorzó	almor**c**é

Stem-changing verb A verb whose stem vowel undergoes one or more predictable changes in the various conjugations.

entender (i:ie)	ent**ie**ndo
pedir (e:i)	p**i**den
dormir (o:ue, u)	d**ue**rmo, d**u**rmieron

Verb conjugation tables

The verb lists

The list of verbs below and the model-verb tables that start on page 588 show you how to conjugate every verb taught in **VISTAS**. Each verb in the list is followed by a model verb that is conjugated according to the same pattern. The number in parentheses indicates where in the tables you can find the conjugated forms of the model verb. If you want to find out how to conjugate **divertirse**, for example, look up number 33, **sentir**, the model for verbs that follow the **i:ie** stem-change pattern.

How to use the verb tables

In the tables you will find the infinitive, past and present participles, and all the simple forms of each model verb. The formation of the compound tenses of any verb can be inferred from the table of compound tenses, pages 590–597, either by combining the past participle of the verb with a conjugated form of **haber** or combining the present participle with a conjugated form of **estar**.

abrazar (c) like cruzar (37)
abrir like vivir (3)
aburrir(se) like vivir (3)
acabar de like hablar (1)
acampar like hablar (1)
acompañar like hablar (1)
aconsejar like hablar (1)
acordarse (o:ue) like contar (24)
acostarse (o:ue) like contar (24)
adelgazar (c) like cruzar (37)
afeitarse like hablar (1)
ahorrar like hablar (1)
alegrarse like hablar (1)
aliviar like hablar (1)
almorzar (o:ue) like contar (24) *except* (z:c)
alquilar like hablar (1)
anunciar like hablar (1)
apagar (gu) like llegar (41)
aplaudir like vivir (3)
apreciar like hablar (1)
aprender like comer (2)
apurarse like hablar (1)
arrancar (qu) like tocar (43)
arreglar like hablar (1)
asistir like vivir (3)
aumentar like hablar (1)
ayudar(se) like hablar (1)
bailar like hablar (1)
bajar(se) like hablar (1)
bañarse like hablar (1)
barrer like comer (2)
beber like comer (2)
besar(se) like hablar (1)
brindar like hablar (1)
bucear like hablar (1)
buscar (qu) like tocar (43)
caber (4)
caer(se) (5)
calentarse (e:ie) like pensar (30)
calzar (c) like cruzar (37)
cambiar like hablar (1)
caminar like hablar (1)
cantar like hablar (1)
casarse like hablar (1)
celebrar like hablar (1)
cenar like hablar (1)
cepillarse like hablar (1)
cerrar (e:ie) like pensar (30)
chocar (qu) like tocar (43)
cobrar like hablar (1)
cocinar like hablar (1)
comenzar (e:ie) like empezar (26)
comer (2)
compartir like vivir (3)
comprar like hablar (1)
comprender like comer (2)
comprometerse like comer (2)
comunicarse (qu) like tocar (43)
conducir (c:zc) (6)
confirmar like hablar (1)
conocer (c:zc) (35)
conseguir (e:i) like seguir (32)
conservar like hablar (1)
consumir like vivir (3)
contaminar like hablar (1)
contar (o:ue) (24)
controlar like hablar (1)
correr like comer (2)
costar (o:ue) like contar (24)
creer (y) (36)
cruzar (c) (37)
cubrir like vivir (3)
cuidar like hablar (1)
cumplir like vivir (3)
dañar like hablar (1)
dar(se) (7)
deber like comer (2)
decidir like vivir (3)
decir (e:i) (8)
declarar like hablar (1)
dejar like hablar (1)
depositar like hablar (1)
desarrollar like hablar (1)
desayunar like hablar (1)
descansar like hablar (1)
describir like vivir (3)
descubrir like vivir (3)
desear like hablar (1)
despedirse (e:i) like pedir (29)
despertarse (e:ie) like pensar (30)
destruir (y) (38)
dibujar like hablar (1)
disfrutar like hablar (1)
divertirse (e:ie) like sentir (33)
divorciarse like hablar (1)
doblar like hablar (1)
doler (o:ue) like volver (34) *except* past participle is regular
dormir(se) (o:ue) (25)
ducharse like hablar (1)
dudar like hablar (1)
durar like hablar (1)
echar like hablar (1)
elegir (e:i) like pedir (29) *except* (g:j)
emitir like vivir (3)
empezar (e:ie) (26)
enamorarse like hablar (1)

encantar like hablar (1)
encontrar(se) (o:ue) like contar (24)
enfermarse like hablar (1)
engordar like hablar (1)
enojarse like hablar (1)
enseñar like hablar (1)
ensuciar like hablar (1)
entender (e:ie) (27)
entrenarse like hablar (1)
entrevistar like hablar (1)
enviar (envío) (39)
escalar like hablar (1)
escribir like vivir (3)
escuchar like hablar (1)
esculpir like vivir (3)
esperar like hablar (1)
esquiar (esquío) like enviar (39)
establecer (c:zc) like conocer (35)
estacionar like hablar (1)
estar (9)
estornudar like hablar (1)
estudiar like hablar (1)
evitar like hablar (1)
explicar (qu) like tocar (43)
explorar like hablar (1)
faltar like hablar (1)
fascinar like hablar (1)
firmar like hablar (1)
fumar like hablar (1)
funcionar like hablar (1)
ganar like hablar (1)
gastar like hablar (1)
graduarse (gradúo) (40)
guardar like hablar (1)
gustar like hablar (1)
haber (hay) (10)
hablar (1)
hacer (11)
importar like hablar (1)
imprimir like vivir (3)
informar like hablar (1)
insistir like vivir (3)
interesar like hablar (1)
invertir (e:ie) like sentir (33)
invitar like hablar (1)
ir(se) (12)
jubilarse like hablar (1)
jugar (u:ue) (28)
lastimarse like hablar (1)
lavar(se) like hablar (1)
leer (y) like creer (36)
levantar(se) like hablar (1)
limpiar like hablar (1)
llamar(se) like hablar (1)
llegar (41) (gu)
llenar like hablar (1)
llevar(se) like hablar (1)
llover (o:ue) like volver (34) *except* past participle is regular
luchar like hablar (1)
mandar like hablar (1)
manejar like hablar (1)
mantener(se) (e:ie) like **tener** (20)
maquillarse like hablar (1)
mejorar like hablar (1)
merendar (e:ie) like pensar (30)
mirar like hablar (1)
molestar like hablar (1)
montar like hablar (1)
morir (o:ue) like dormir (25)
mostrar (o:ue) like contar (24)
mudarse like hablar (1)
nacer (c:zc) like conocer (35)
nadar like hablar (1)
navegar (gu) like llegar (41)
necesitar like hablar (1)
negar (e:ie) like pensar (30) *except* (g:gu)
nevar (e:ie) like pensar (30)
obedecer (c:zc) like conocer (35)
obtener (e:ie) like tener (20)
ocurrir like vivir (3)
odiar like hablar (1)
ofrecer (c:zc) like conocer (35)
oír (13)
olvidar like hablar (1)
pagar (gu) like llegar (41)
parar like hablar (1)
parecer (c:zc) like conocer (35)
pasar like hablar (1)
pasear like hablar (1)
patinar like hablar (1)
pedir (e:i) (29)
peinarse like hablar (1)
pensar (e:ie) (30)
perder (e:ie) like entender (27)
pescar (qu) like tocar (43)
pintar like hablar (1)
planchar like hablar (1)
poder (o:ue) (14)
ponchar like hablar (1)
poner(se) (15)
practicar (qu) like tocar (43)
preferir (e:ie) like sentir (33)
preguntar like hablar (1)
preocuparse like hablar (1)
preparar like hablar (1)
presentar like hablar (1)
prestar like hablar (1)
probar(se) (o:ue) like contar (24)
prohibir like vivir (3)
proteger (42)
publicar (qu) like tocar (43)
quedar(se) like hablar (1)
querer (e:ie) (16)
quitar(se) like hablar (1)
recetar like hablar (1)
recibir like vivir (3)
reciclar like hablar (1)
recoger like proteger (42)
recomendar (e:ie) like pensar (30)
recordar (o:ue) like contar (24)
reducir (c:zc) like conducir (6)
regalar like hablar (1)
regatear like hablar (1)
regresar like hablar (1)
reír(se) (e:i) (31)
relajarse like hablar (1)
renunciar like hablar (1)
repetir (e:i) like pedir (29)
resolver (o:ue) like volver (34)
respirar like hablar (1)
revisar like hablar (1)
rogar (o:ue) like contar (24) *except* (g:gu)
romper(se) like comer (2)
saber (17)
sacar (qu) like tocar (43)
sacudir like vivir (3)
salir (18)
saludar(se) like hablar (1)
seguir (e:i) (32)
sentarse (e:ie) like pensar (30)
sentir(se) (e:ie) (33)
separarse like hablar (1)
ser (19)
servir (e:i) like pedir (29)
solicitar like hablar (1)
sonar (o:ue) like contar (24)
sonreír (e:i) like reír(se) (31)
sorprender like comer (2)
subir like vivir (3)
sudar like hablar (1)
sufrir like vivir (3)
sugerir (e:ie) like sentir (33)
suponer like poner (15)
temer like comer (2)
tener (e:ie) (20)
terminar like hablar (1)
tocar (43) (qu)
tomar like hablar (1)
torcerse (o:ue) like volver (34) *except* (c:z)
toser like comer (2)
trabajar like hablar (1)
traducir (c:zc) like conducir (6)
traer (21)
transmitir like vivir (3)
tratar like hablar (1)
usar like hablar (1)
vender like comer (2)
venir (e:ie) (22)
ver (23)
vestirse (e:i) like pedir (29)
viajar like hablar (1)
visitar like hablar (1)
vivir (3)
volver (o:ue) (34)

Regular verbs: simple tenses

		INDICATIVE					SUBJUNCTIVE		IMPERATIVE
	Infinitive	Present	Imperfect	Preterite	Future	Conditional	Present	Past	
1	hablar	hablo	hablaba	hablé	hablaré	hablaría	hable	hablara	habla tú (no hables)
		hablas	hablabas	hablaste	hablarás	hablarías	hables	hablaras	hable Ud. (no hable)
	Participles:	habla	hablaba	habló	hablará	hablaría	hable	hablara	hablen Uds. (no hablen)
	hablando	hablamos	hablábamos	hablamos	hablaremos	hablaríamos	hablemos	hablámos	hablemos
	hablado	habláis	hablabais	hablabais	hablaréis	hablaríais	habléis	hablarais	
		hablan	hablaban	hablaban	hablarán	hablarían	hablen	hablaran	
2	comer	como	comía	comí	comeré	comería	coma	comiera	come tú (no comas)
		comes	comías	comiste	comerás	comerías	comas	comieras	coma Ud. (no coma)
	Participles:	come	comía	comió	comerá	comería	coma	comiera	coman Uds. (no coman)
	comiendo	comemos	comíamos	comimos	comeremos	comeríamos	comamos	comiéramos	comamos
	comido	coméis	comíais	comisteis	comeréis	comeríais	comáis	comierais	
		comen	comían	comieron	comerán	comerían	coman	comieran	
3	vivir	vivo	vivía	viví	viviré	viviría	viva	viviera	vive tú (no vivas)
		vives	vivías	viviste	vivirás	vivirías	vivas	vivieras	viva Ud. (no viva)
	Participles:	vive	vivía	vivió	vivirá	viviría	viva	viviera	vivan Uds. (no vivan)
	viviendo	vivimos	vivíamos	vivimos	viviremos	viviríamos	vivamos	viviéramos	vivamos
	vivido	vivís	vivíais	vivisteis	viviréis	viviríais	viváis	vivierais	
		viven	vivían	vivieron	vivirán	vivirían	vivan	vivieran	

All verbs: compound tenses

PERFECT TENSES											
INDICATIVE								SUBJUNCTIVE			
Present Perfect		Past Perfect		Future Perfect		Conditional Perfect		Present Perfect		Past Perfect	
he has ha hemos habéis han	hablado comido vivido	había habías había habíamos habíais habían	hablado comido vivido	habré habrás habrá habremos habréis habrán	hablado comido vivido	habría habrías habría habríamos habríais habrían	hablado comido vivido	haya hayas haya hayamos hayáis hayan	hablado comido vivido	hubiera hubieras hubiera hubiéramos hubierais hubieran	hablado comido vivido

PROGRESSIVE TENSES											
INDICATIVE								SUBJUNCTIVE			
Present Progressive		Past Progressive		Future Progressive		Conditional Progressive		Present Progressive		Past Progressive	
estoy		estaba		estaré		estaría		esté		estuviera	
estás	hablando	estabas	hablando	estarás	hablando	estarías	hablando	estés	hablando	estuvieras	hablando
está	comiendo	estaba	comendo	estará	comiendo	estaría	comiendo	esté	comiendo	estuviera	comiendo
estamos	viviendo	estábamos	viviendo	estaremos	viviendo	estaríamos	viviendo	estémos	viviendo	estuviéramos	viviendo
estáis		estabais		estaréis		estaríais		estéis		estuvierais	
estan		estaban		estarán		estarán		estén		estuvieran	

Irregular verbs

	Infinitive	INDICATIVE Present	Imperfect	Preterite	Future	Conditional	SUBJUNCTIVE Present	Past	IMPERATIVE
4	caber	**quepo**	cabía	**cupe**	**cabré**	**cabría**	quepa	**cupiera**	cabe tú (no **quepas**)
		cabes	cabías	**cupiste**	**cabrás**	**cabrías**	**quepas**	**cupieras**	quepa Ud. (no **quepa**)
	Participles:	cabe	cabía	**cupo**	**cabrá**	**cabría**	**quepa**	**cupiera**	**quepan** Uds. (no **quepan**)
	cabiendo	cabemos	cabíamos	**cupimos**	**cabremos**	**cabríamos**	**quepamos**	**cupiéramos**	**quepamos**
	cabido	cabéis	cabíais	**cupisteis**	**cabréis**	**cabríais**	**quepáis**	**cupierais**	
		caben	cabían	**cupieron**	**cabrán**	**cabrían**	**quepan**	**cupieran**	
5	caer(se)	**caigo**	caía	**caí**	caeré	caería	**caiga**	**cayera**	cae tú (no **caigas**)
		caes	caías	**caíste**	caerás	caerías	**caigas**	**cayeras**	**caiga** Ud. (no **caiga**)
	Participles:	cae	caía	**cayó**	caerá	caería	**caiga**	**cayera**	**caigan** Uds. (no **caigan**)
	cayendo	caemos	caíamos	**caímos**	caeremos	caeríamos	**caigamos**	**cayéramos**	**caigamos**
	caído	caéis	caíais	**caísteis**	caeréis	caeríais	**caigáis**	**cayerais**	
		caen	caían	**cayeron**	caerán	caerían	**caigan**	**cayeran**	
6	conducir	conduzco	conducía	**conduje**	conduciré	conduciría	**conduzca**	**condujera**	conduce tú (no **conduzcas**)
	(c:zc)	conduces	conducías	**condujiste**	conducirás	conducirías	**conduzcas**	**condujeras**	**conduzca** Ud. (no **conduzca**)
	Participles:	conduce	conducía	**condujo**	conducirá	conduciría	**conduzca**	**condujera**	**conduzcan** Uds.
	conduciendo	conducimos	conducíamos	**condujimos**	conduciremos	conduciríamos	**conduzcamos**	**condujéramos**	(no **conduzcan**)
	conducido	conducís	conducíais	**condujisteis**	conduciréis	conduciríais	**conduzcáis**	**condujerais**	**conduzcamos**
		conducen	conducían	**condujeron**	conducirán	conducirían	**conduzcan**	**condujeran**	

	Infinitive	INDICATIVE					SUBJUNCTIVE		IMPERATIVE
		Present	Imperfect	Preterite	Future	Conditional	Present	Past	
7	dar	**doy**	daba	**di**	daré	daría	**dé**	**diera**	da tú (no des)
		das	dabas	**diste**	darás	darías	des	**dieras**	**dé** Ud. (no **dé**)
	Participles:	da	daba	**dio**	dará	daría	**dé**	**diera**	den Uds. (no den)
	dando	damos	dábamos	**dimos**	daremos	daríamos	demos	**diéramos**	demos
	dado	dais	dabais	**disteis**	daréis	daríais	deis	**dierais**	
		dan	daban	**dieron**	darán	darían	den	**dieran**	
8	decir (e:i)	**digo**	decía	**dije**	**diré**	**diría**	**diga**	**dijera**	**di** tú (no **digas**)
		dices	decías	**dijiste**	**dirás**	**dirías**	**digas**	**dijeras**	**diga** Ud. (no **diga**)
	Participles:	**dice**	decía	**dijo**	**dirá**	**diría**	**diga**	**dijera**	**digan** Uds. (no **digan**)
	diciendo	decimos	decíamos	**dijimos**	**diremos**	**diríamos**	**digamos**	**dijéramos**	**digamos**
	dicho	decís	decíais	**dijisteis**	**diréis**	**diríais**	**digáis**	**dijerais**	
		dicen	decían	**dijeron**	**dirán**	**dirían**	**digan**	**dijeran**	
9	estar	**estoy**	estaba	**estuve**	estaré	estaría	**esté**	**estuviera**	**está** tú (no **estés**)
		estás	estabas	**estuviste**	estarás	estarías	**estés**	**estuvieras**	**esté** Ud. (no **esté**)
	Participles:	está	estaba	**estuvo**	estará	estaría	**esté**	**estuviera**	**estén** Uds. (no **estén**)
	estando	estamos	estábamos	**estuvimos**	estaremos	estaríamos	estemos	**estuviéramos**	**estemos**
	estado	estáis	estabais	**estuvisteis**	estaréis	estaríais	estéis	**estuvierais**	
		están	estaban	**estuvieron**	estarán	estarían	**estén**	**estuvieran**	
10	haber	**he**	había	**hube**	**habré**	**habría**	**haya**	**hubiera**	**he** tú (no **hayas**)
		has	habías	**hubiste**	**habrás**	**habrías**	**hayas**	**hubieras**	**haya** Ud. (no **haya**)
	Participles:	**ha**	había	**hubo**	**habrá**	**habría**	**haya**	**hubiera**	**hayan** Uds. (no **hayan**)
	habiendo	**hemos**	habíamos	**hubimos**	**habremos**	**habríamos**	**hayamos**	**hubiéramos**	**hayamos**
	habido	**habéis**	habíais	**hubisteis**	**habréis**	**habríais**	**hayáis**	**hubierais**	
		han	habían	**hubieron**	**habrán**	**habrían**	**hayan**	**hubieran**	
11	hacer	**hago**	hacía	**hice**	**haré**	**haría**	**haga**	**hiciera**	**haz** tú (no **hagas**)
		haces	hacías	**hiciste**	**harás**	**harías**	**hagas**	**hicieras**	**haga** Ud. (no **haga**)
	Participles:	hace	hacía	**hizo**	**hará**	**haría**	**haga**	**hiciera**	**hagan** Uds. (no **hagan**)
	haciendo	hacemos	hacíamos	**hicimos**	**haremos**	**haríamos**	**hagamos**	**hiciéramos**	**hagamos**
	hecho	hacéis	hacíais	**hicisteis**	**haréis**	**haríais**	**hagáis**	**hicierais**	
		hacen	hacían	**hicieron**	**harán**	**harían**	**hagan**	**hicieran**	
12	ir	**voy**	**iba**	**fui**	iré	iría	**vaya**	**fuera**	**ve** tú (no **vayas**)
		vas	**ibas**	**fuiste**	irás	irías	**vayas**	**fueras**	**vaya** Ud. (no **vaya**)
	Participles:	va	**iba**	**fue**	irá	iría	**vaya**	**fuera**	**vayan** Uds. (no **vayan**)
	yendo	vamos	**íbamos**	**fuimos**	iremos	iríamos	**vayamos**	**fuéramos**	**vayamos**
	ido	vais	**ibais**	**fuisteis**	iréis	iríais	**vayáis**	**fuerais**	
		van	**iban**	**fueron**	irán	irían	**vayan**	**fueran**	
13	oír (y)	**oigo**	oía	**oí**	oiré	oiría	**oiga**	**oyera**	**oye** tú (no **oigas**)
		oyes	oías	**oíste**	oirás	oirías	**oigas**	**oyeras**	**oiga** Ud. (no **oiga**)
	Participles:	**oye**	oía	**oyó**	oirá	oiría	**oiga**	**oyera**	**oigan** Uds. (no **oigan**)
	oyendo	**oímos**	oíamos	**oímos**	oiremos	oiríamos	**oigamos**	**oyéramos**	**oigamos**
	oído	**oís**	oíais	**oísteis**	oiréis	oiríais	**oigáis**	**oyerais**	
		oyen	oían	**oyeron**	oirán	oirían	**oigan**	**oyeran**	

		INDICATIVE					SUBJUNCTIVE		IMPERATIVE
	Infinitive	**Present**	**Imperfect**	**Preterite**	**Future**	**Conditional**	**Present**	**Past**	
14	poder (o:ue)	**puedo**	podía	**pude**	**podré**	**podría**	**pueda**	**pudiera**	**puede** tú (no **puedas**)
		puedes	podías	**pudiste**	**podrás**	**podrías**	**puedas**	**pudieras**	**pueda** Ud. (no **pueda**)
	Participles:	**puede**	podía	**pudo**	**podrá**	**podría**	**pueda**	**pudiera**	**puedan** Uds. (no **puedan**)
	pudiendo	podemos	podíamos	**pudimos**	**podremos**	**podríamos**	podamos	**pudiéramos**	podamos
	podido	podéis	podíais	**pudisteis**	**podréis**	**podríais**	podáis	**pudierais**	
		pueden	podían	**pudieron**	**podrán**	**podrían**	**puedan**	**pudieran**	
15	poner	**pongo**	ponía	**puse**	**pondré**	**pondría**	**ponga**	**pusiera**	**pon** tú (no **pongas**)
		pones	ponías	**pusiste**	**pondrás**	**pondrías**	**pongas**	**pusieras**	**ponga** Ud. (no **ponga**)
	Participles:	pone	ponía	**puso**	**pondrá**	**pondría**	**ponga**	**pusiera**	**pongan** Uds. (no **pongan**)
	poniendo	ponemos	poníamos	**pusimos**	**pondremos**	**pondríamos**	**pongamos**	**pusiéramos**	**pongamos**
	puesto	ponéis	poníais	**pusisteis**	**pondréis**	**pondríais**	**pongáis**	**pusierais**	
		ponen	ponían	**pusieron**	**pondrán**	**pondrían**	**pongan**	**pusieran**	
16	querer (e:ie)	**quiero**	quería	**quise**	**querré**	**querría**	**quiera**	**quisiera**	**quiere tú** (no **quieras**)
		quieres	querías	**quisiste**	**querrás**	**querrías**	**quieras**	**quisieras**	**quiera** Ud. (no **quiera**)
	Participles:	**quiere**	quería	**quiso**	**querrá**	**querría**	**quiera**	**quisiera**	**quieran** Uds. (no **quieran**)
	queriendo	queremos	queríamos	**quisimos**	**querremos**	**querríamos**	queramos	**quisiéramos**	**queramos**
	querido	queréis	queríais	**quisisteis**	**querréis**	**querríais**	queráis	**quisierais**	
		quieren	querían	**quisieron**	**querrán**	**querrían**	**quieran**	**quisieran**	
17	saber	**sé**	sabía	**supe**	**sabré**	**sabría**	**sepa**	**supiera**	sabe tú (no **sepas**)
		sabes	sabías	**supiste**	**sabrás**	**sabrías**	**sepas**	**supieras**	**sepa** Ud. (no **sepa**)
	Participles:	sabe	sabía	**supo**	**sabrá**	**sabría**	**sepa**	**supiera**	**sepan** Uds. (no **sepan**)
	sabiendo	sabemos	sabíamos	**supimos**	**sabremos**	**sabríamos**	**sepamos**	**supiéramos**	**sepamos**
	sabido	sabéis	sabíais	**supisteis**	**sabréis**	**sabríais**	**sepáis**	**supierais**	
		saben	sabían	**supieron**	**sabrán**	**sabrían**	**sepan**	**supieran**	
18	salir	**salgo**	salía	salí	**saldré**	**saldría**	**salga**	saliera	**sal** tú (no **salgas**)
		sales	salías	saliste	**saldrás**	**saldrías**	**salgas**	salieras	**salga** Ud. (no **salga**)
	Participles:	sale	salía	salió	**saldrá**	**saldría**	**salga**	saliera	**salgan** Uds. (no **salgan**)
	saliendo	salimos	salíamos	salimos	**saldremos**	**saldríamos**	**salgamos**	saliéramos	**salgamos**
	salido	salís	salíais	salisteis	**saldréis**	**saldríais**	**salgáis**	salierais	
		salen	salían	salieron	**saldrán**	**saldrían**	**salgan**	salieran	
19	ser	**soy**	**era**	**fui**	seré	sería	**sea**	**fuera**	**sé** tú (no **seas**)
		eres	**eras**	**fuiste**	serás	serías	**seas**	**fueras**	**sea** Ud. (no **sea**)
	Participles:	**es**	**era**	**fue**	será	sería	**sea**	**fuera**	**sean** Uds. (no **sean**)
	siendo	**somos**	**éramos**	**fuimos**	seremos	seríamos	**seamos**	**fuéramos**	**seamos**
	sido	**sois**	**erais**	**fuisteis**	seréis	seríais	**seáis**	**fuerais**	
		son	**eran**	**fueron**	serán	serían	**sean**	**fueran**	
20	tener (e:ie)	**tengo**	**tenía**	**tuve**	**tendré**	**tendría**	**tenga**	**tuviera**	**ten** tú (no **tengas**)
		tienes	**tenías**	**tuviste**	**tendrás**	**tendrías**	**tengas**	**tuvieras**	**tenga** Ud. (no **tenga**)
	Participles:	**tiene**	**tenía**	**tuvo**	**tendrá**	**tendría**	**tenga**	**tuviera**	**tengan** Uds. (no **tengan**)
	teniendo	tenemos	**teníamos**	**tuvimos**	**tendremos**	**tendríamos**	**tengamos**	**tuviéramos**	**tengamos**
	tenido	tenéis	**teníais**	**tuvisteis**	**tendréis**	**tendríais**	**tengáis**	**tuvierais**	
		tienen	**tenían**	**tuvieron**	**tendrán**	**tendrían**	**tengan**	**tuvieran**	

	Infinitive	INDICATIVE					SUBJUNCTIVE		IMPERATIVE
		Present	Imperfect	Preterite	Future	Conditional	Present	Past	
21	traer	**traigo**	traía	**traje**	traeré	traería	**traiga**	**trajera**	trae tú (no **traigas**)
		traes	traías	**trajiste**	traerás	traerías	**traigas**	**trajeras**	**traiga** Ud. (no **traiga**)
	Participles:	trae	traía	**trajo**	traerá	traería	**traiga**	**trajera**	**traigan** Uds. (no **traigan**)
	trayendo	traemos	traíamos	**trajimos**	traeremos	traeríamos	**traigamos**	**trajéramos**	**traigamos**
	traído	traéis	traíais	**trajisteis**	traeréis	traeríais	**traigáis**	**trajerais**	
		traen	traían	**trajeron**	traerán	traerían	**traigan**	**trajeran**	
22	venir (e:ie)	**vengo**	venía	**vine**	**vendré**	**vendría**	**venga**	**viniera**	**ven** tú (no **vengas**)
		vienes	venías	**viniste**	**vendrás**	**vendrías**	**vengas**	**vinieras**	**venga** Ud. (no **venga**)
	Participles:	**viene**	venía	**vino**	**vendrá**	**vendría**	**venga**	**viniera**	**vengan** Uds. (no **vengan**)
	viniendo	venimos	veníamos	**vinimos**	**vendremos**	**vendríamos**	**vengamos**	**viniéramos**	**vengamos**
	venido	venís	veníais	**vinisteis**	**vendréis**	**vendríais**	**vengáis**	**vinierais**	
		vienen	venían	**vinieron**	**vendrán**	**vendrían**	**vengan**	**vinieran**	
23	ver	**veo**	**veía**	vi	veré	vería	**vea**	viera	**ve** tú (no **veas**)
		ves	**veías**	viste	verás	verías	**veas**	vieras	**vea** Ud. (no **vea**)
	Participles:	ve	**veía**	vio	verá	vería	**vea**	viera	**vean** Uds. (no **vean**)
	viendo	vemos	**veíamos**	vimos	veremos	veríamos	**veamos**	viéramos	**veamos**
	visto	veis	**veíais**	visteis	veréis	veríais	**veáis**	vierais	
		ven	**veían**	vieron	verán	verían	**vean**	vieran	

Stem changing verbs

	Infinitive	INDICATIVE					SUBJUNCTIVE		IMPERATIVE
		Present	Imperfect	Preterite	Future	Conditional	Present	Past	
24	contar (o:ue)	**cuento**	contaba	conté	contaré	contaría	**cuente**	contara	**cuenta** tú (no **cuentes**)
		cuentas	contabas	contaste	contarás	contarías	**cuentes**	contaras	**cuente** Ud. (no **cuente**)
	Participles:	**cuenta**	contaba	contó	contará	contaría	**cuente**	contara	**cuenten** Uds. (no **cuenten**)
	contando	contamos	contábamos	contamos	contaremos	contaríamos	contemos	contáramos	contemos
	contado	contáis	contabais	contasteis	contaréis	contaríais	contéis	contarais	
		cuentan	contaban	contaron	contarán	contarían	**cuenten**	contaran	
25	dormir (o:ue)	**duermo**	dormía	dormí	dormiré	dormiría	**duerma**	**durmiera**	**duerme** tú (no **duermas**)
		duermes	dormías	dormiste	dormirás	dormirías	**duermas**	**durmieras**	**duerma** Ud. (no **duerma**)
	Participles:	**duerme**	dormía	**durmió**	dormirá	dormiría	**duerma**	**durmiera**	**duerman** Uds. (no **duerman**)
	durmiendo	dormimos	dormíamos	dormimos	dormiremos	dormiríamos	**durmamos**	**durmiéramos**	**durmamos**
	dormido	dormís	dormíais	dormisteis	dormiréis	dormiríais	**durmáis**	**durmierais**	
		duermen	dormían	**durmieron**	dormirán	dormirían	**duerman**	**durmieran**	
26	empezar (e:ie) (c)	**empiezo**	empezaba	**empecé**	empezaré	empezaría	**empiece**	empezara	**empieza** tú (no **empieces**)
		empiezas	empezabas	empezaste	empezarás	empezarías	**empieces**	empezaras	**empiece** Ud. (no **empiece**)
		empieza	empezaba	empezó	empezará	empezaría	**empiece**	empezara	**empiecen** Uds. (no **empiecen**)
	Participles:	empezamos	empezábamos	empezamos	empezaremos	empezaríamos	**empecemos**	empezáramos	**empecemos**
	empezando	empezáis	empezabais	empezasteis	empezaréis	empezaríais	**empecéis**	empezarais	
	empezado	**empiezan**	empezaban	empezaron	empezarán	empezarían	**empiecen**	empezaran	

	Infinitive	INDICATIVE					SUBJUNCTIVE		IMPERATIVE
		Present	Imperfect	Preterite	Future	Conditional	Present	Past	
27	entender (e:ie) **Participles:** entendiendo entendido	**entiendo** **entiendes** **entiende** entendemos entendéis **entienden**	entendía entendías entendía entendíamos entendíais entendían	entendí entendiste entendió entendimos entendisteis entendieron	entenderé entenderás entenderá entenderemos entenderéis entenderán	entendería entenderías entendería entenderíamos entenderíais entenderían	**entienda** **entiendas** **entienda** entendamos entendáis **entiendan**	entendiera entendieras entendiera entendiéramos entendierais entendieran	**entiende** tú (no **entiendas**) **entienda** Ud. (no **entienda**) **entiendan** Uds. (no **entiendan**) **entendamos**
28	jugar (u:ue) (gu) **Participles:** jugando jugado	**juego** **juegas** **juega** jugamos jugáis **juegan**	jugaba jugabas jugaba jugábamos jugabais jugaban	**jugué** jugaste jugó jugamos jugasteis jugaron	jugaré jugarás jugará jugaremos jugaréis jugarán	jugaría jugarías jugaría jugaríamos jugaríais jugarían	**juegue** **juegues** **juegue** **juguemos** **juguéis** **jueguen**	jugara jugaras jugara jugáramos jugarais jugaran	**juega** tú (no **juegues**) **juegue** Ud. (no **juegue**) **jueguen** Uds. (no **jueguen**) **juguemos**
29	pedir (e:i) **Participles:** **pidiendo** pedido	**pido** **pides** **pide** pedimos pedís **piden**	pedía pedías pedía pedíamos pedíais pedían	pedí pediste **pidió** pedimos pedisteis **pidieron**	pediré pedirás pedirá pediremos pediréis pedirán	pediría pedirías pediría pediríamos pediríais pedirían	**pida** **pidas** **pida** **pidamos** **pidáis** **pidan**	**pidiera** **pidieras** **pidiera** **pidiéramos** **pidierais** **pidieran**	**pide** tú (no **pidas**) **pida** Ud. (no **pida**) **pidan** Uds. (no **pidan**) **pidamos**
30	pensar (e:ie) **Participles:** pensando pensado	**pienso** **piensas** **piensa** pensamos pensáis **piensan**	pensaba pensabas pensaba pensábamos pensabais pensaban	pensé pensaste pensó pensamos pensasteis pensaron	pensaré pensarás pensará pensaremos pensaréis pensarán	pensaría pensarías pensaría pensaríamos pensaríais pensarían	**piense** **pienses** **piense** pensemos penséis **piensen**	pensara pensaras pensara pensáramos pensarais pensaran	**piensa** tú (no **pienses**) **piense** Ud. (no **piense**) **piensen** Uds. (no **piensen**) pensemos
31	reír(se) (e:i) **Participles:** **riendo** **reído**	**río** **ríes** **ríe** **reímos** **reís** **ríen**	reía reías reía reíamos reíais reían	**reí** **reíste** **rió** **reímos** **reísteis** **rieron**	reiré reirás reirá reiremos reiréis reirán	reiría reirías reiría reiríamos reiríais reirían	**ría** **rías** **ría** **riamos** **riáis** **rían**	**riera** **rieras** **riera** **riéramos** **rierais** **rieran**	**ríe** tú (no **rías**) **ría** Ud. (no **ría**) **rían** Uds. (no **rían**) **riamos**
32	seguir (e:i) (gu) **Participles:** **siguiendo** seguido	**sigo** **sigues** **sigue** seguimos seguís **siguen**	seguía seguías seguía seguíamos seguíais seguían	seguí seguiste **siguió** seguimos seguisteis **siguieron**	seguiré seguirás seguirá seguiremos seguiréis seguirán	seguiría seguirías seguiría seguiríamos seguiríais seguirían	**siga** **sigas** **siga** **sigamos** **sigáis** **sigan**	**siguiera** **siguieras** **siguiera** **siguiéramos** **siguierais** **siguieran**	**sigue** tú (no **sigas**) **siga** Ud. (no **siga**) **sigan** Uds. (no **sigan**) **sigamos**
33	sentir (e:ie) **Participles:** **sintiendo** sentido	**siento** **sientes** **siente** sentimos sentís **sienten**	sentía sentías sentía sentíamos sentíais sentían	sentí sentiste **sintió** sentimos sentisteis **sintieron**	sentiré sentirás sentirá sentiremos sentiréis sentirán	sentiría sentirías sentiría sentiríamos sentiríais sentirían	**sienta** **sientas** **sienta** **sintamos** **sintáis** **sientan**	**sintiera** **sintieras** **sintiera** **sintiéramos** **sintierais** **sintieran**	**siente** tú (no **sientas**) **sienta** Ud. (no **sienta**) **sientan** Uds. (no **sientan**) **sintamos**

	INDICATIVE					SUBJUNCTIVE		IMPERATIVE
Infinitive	**Present**	**Imperfect**	**Preterite**	**Future**	**Conditional**	**Present**	**Past**	
34 volver (o:ue)	**vuelvo**	volvía	volví	volveré	volvería	**vuelva**	volviera	**vuelve** tú (no **vuelvas**)
	vuelves	volvías	volviste	volverás	volverías	**vuelvas**	volvieras	**vuelva** Ud. (no **vuelva**)
Participles:	**vuelve**	volvía	volvió	volverá	volvería	**vuelva**	volviera	**vuelvan** Uds. (no **vuelvan**)
volviendo	volvemos	volvíamos	volvimos	volveremos	volveríamos	volvamos	volviéramos	volvamos
vuelto	volvéis	volvíais	volvisteis	volveréis	volveríais	volváis	volvierais	
	vuelven	volvían	volvieron	volverán	volverían	**vuelvan**	volvieran	

Verbs with spelling changes only

	INDICATIVE					SUBJUNCTIVE		IMPERATIVE
Infinitive	**Present**	**Imperfect**	**Preterite**	**Future**	**Conditional**	**Present**	**Past**	
35 conocer	**conozco**	conocía	conocí	conoceré	conocería	**conozca**	conociera	conoce tú (no **conozcas**)
(c:zc)	conoces	conocías	conociste	conocerás	conocerías	**conozcas**	conocieras	**conozca** Ud. (no **conozca**)
	conoce	conocía	conoció	conocerá	conocería	**conozca**	conociera	**conozcan** Uds. (no **conozcan**)
Participles:	conocemos	conocíamos	conocimos	conoceremos	conoceríamos	**conozcamos**	conociéramos	**conozcamos**
conociendo	conocéis	conocíais	conocisteis	conoceréis	conoceríais	**conozcáis**	conocierais	
conocido	conocen	conocían	conocieron	conocerán	conocerían	**conozcan**	conocieran	
36 creer (y)	creo	creía	**creí**	creeré	creería	crea	**creyera**	cree tú (no creas)
	crees	creías	**creíste**	creerás	creerías	creas	**creyeras**	crea Ud. (no crea)
Participles:	cree	creía	**creyó**	creerá	creería	crea	**creyera**	crean Uds. (no crean)
creyendo	creemos	creíamos	**creímos**	creeremos	creeríamos	creamos	**creyéramos**	creamos
creído	creéis	creíais	**creísteis**	creeréis	creeríais	creáis	**creyerais**	
	creen	creían	**creyeron**	creerán	creerían	crean	**creyeran**	
37 cruzar (c)	cruzo	cruzaba	**crucé**	cruzaré	cruzaría	**cruce**	cruzara	cruza tú (no **cruces**)
	cruzas	cruzabas	cruzaste	cruzarás	cruzarías	**cruces**	cruzaras	**cruce** Ud. (no **cruce**)
Participles:	cruza	cruzaba	cruzó	cruzará	cruzaría	**cruce**	cruzara	**crucen** Uds. (no **crucen**)
cruzando	cruzamos	cruzábamos	cruzamos	cruzaremos	cruzaríamos	**crucemos**	cruzáramos	**crucemos**
cruzado	cruzáis	cruzabais	cruzasteis	cruzaréis	cruzaríais	**crucéis**	cruzarais	
	cruzan	cruzaban	cruzaron	cruzarán	cruzarían	**crucen**	cruzaran	
38 destruir (y)	**destruyo**	destruía	destruí	destruiré	destruiría	**destruya**	**destruyera**	**destruye** tú (no **destruyas**)
	destruyes	destruías	destruiste	destruirás	destruirías	**destruyas**	**destruyeras**	**destruya** Ud. (no **destruya**)
Participles:	**destruye**	destruía	**destruyó**	destruirá	destruiría	**destruya**	**destruyera**	**destruyan** Uds. (no **destruyan**)
destruyendo	destruimos	destruíamos	destruimos	destruiremos	destruiríamos	**destruyamos**	**destruyéramos**	**destruyamos**
destruido	destruís	destruíais	destruisteis	destruiréis	destruiríais	**destruyáis**	**destruyerais**	
	destruyen	destruían	**destruyeron**	destruirán	destruirían	**destruyan**	**destruyeran**	
39 enviar	**envío**	enviaba	envié	enviaré	enviaría	**envíe**	enviara	**envía** tú (no **envíes**)
(envío)	**envías**	enviabas	enviaste	enviarás	enviarías	**envíes**	enviaras	**envíe** Ud. (no **envíe**)
	envía	enviaba	envió	enviará	enviaría	**envíe**	enviara	**envíen** Uds. (no **envíen**)
Participles:	enviamos	enviábamos	enviamos	enviaremos	enviaríamos	**enviemos**	enviáramos	enviemos
enviando	enviáis	enviabais	enviasteis	enviaréis	enviaríais	**enviéis**	enviarais	
enviado	**envían**	enviaban	enviaron	enviarán	enviarían	**envíen**	enviaran	

	Infinitive	INDICATIVE Present	Imperfect	Preterite	Future	Conditional	SUBJUNCTIVE Present	Past	IMPERATIVE
40	graduarse (gradúo) **Participles:** graduando graduado	**gradúo** **gradúas** **gradúa** **graduamos** **graduáis** **gradúan**	graduaba graduabas graduaba graduábamos graduabais graduaban	gradué graduaste graduó graduamos graduasteis graduaron	graduaré graduarás graduará graduaremos graduaréis graduarán	graduaría graduarías graduaría graduaríamos graduaríais graduarían	**gradúe** **gradúes** **gradúe** **graduemos** **graduéis** **gradúen**	graduara graduaras graduara graduáramos graduarais graduaran	**gradúa** tú (no **gradúes**) **gradúe** Ud. (no **gradúe**) **gradúen** Uds. (no **gradúen**) graduemos
41	llegar (gu) **Participles:** llegando llegado	llego llegas llega llegamos llegáis llegan	llegaba llegabas llegaba llegábamos llegabais llegaban	**llegué** llegaste llegó llegamos llegasteis llegaron	llegaré llegarás llegará llegaremos llegaréis llegarán	llegaría llegarías llegaría llegaríamos llegaríais llegarían	**llegue** **llegues** **llegue** **lleguemos** **lleguéis** **lleguen**	llegara llegaras llegara llegáramos llegarais llegaran	llega tú (no **llegues**) **llegue** Ud. (no **llegue**) **lleguen** Uds. (no **lleguen**) **lleguemos**
42	proteger (j) **Participles:** protegiendo protegido	**protejo** proteges protege protegemos protegéis protegen	protegía protegías protegía protegíamos protegíais protegían	protegí protegiste protegió protegimos protegisteis protegieron	protegeré protegerás protegerá protegeremos protegeréis protegerán	protegería protegerías protegería protegeríamos protegeríais protegerían	**proteja** **protejas** **proteja** **protejamos** **protejáis** **protejan**	protegiera protegieras protegiera protegiéramos protegierais protegieran	protege tú (no **protejas**) **proteja** Ud. (no **proteja**) **protejan** Uds. (no **protejan**) **protejamos**
43	tocar (qu) **Participles:** tocando tocado	toco tocas toca tocamos tocáis tocan	tocaba tocabas tocaba tocábamos tocabais tocaban	**toqué** tocaste tocó tocamos tocasteis tocaron	tocaré tocará tocarás tocaremos tocaréis tocarán	tocaría tocarías tocaría tocaríamos tocaríais tocarían	**toque** **toques** **toque** **toquemos** **toquéis** **toquen**	tocara tocaras tocara tocáramos tocarais tocaran	toca tú (no **toques**) **toque** Ud. (no **toque**) **toquen** Uds. (no **toquen**) **toquemos**

Guide to Vocabulary

Note on alphabetization

Formerly, **ch**, **ll**, and **ñ** were considered separate letters in the Spanish alphabet, **ch** appearing after **c**, **ll** after **l**, and **ñ** after **n**. In current practice, for purposes of alphabetization, **ch** and **ll** are not treated as separate letters, but **ñ**, still follows **n**. Therefore, in this glossary you will find that **año**, for example, appears after **anuncio**.

Abbreviations used in this glossary

adj.	adjective	*i.o.*	inderect object	*prep.*	preposition
adv.	adverb	*m.*	masculine	*pron.*	pronoun
conj.	conjunction	*n.*	noun	*ref.*	reflexive
d.o.	direct object	*obj.*	object	*sing.*	singular
f.	feminine	*p.p.*	past participle	*sub.*	subject
fam.	familiar	*pl.*	plural	*v.*	verb
form.	formal	*poss.*	possessive		

Spanish-English

A

a *prep.* at; to 1
¿A qué hora...? At what time . . . ? 1
a bordo aboard 1
a dieta on a diet 15
a la derecha to the right 2
a la izquierda to the left 2
a la plancha grilled 8
a la(s) + *time* at + *time* 1
a menos que unless 13
a menudo often 10
a nombre de in the name of 5
a plazos in installments 14
A sus órdenes. At your service. 11
a tiempo on time 10
a veces sometimes 10
a ver let's see 2
¡Abajo! *adv.* Down! 15
abeja *f.* bee 6
abierto/a *p.p.* open 5
abogado/a lawyer 16
abrazar(se) *v.* to hug; to embrace (each other) 11
abrigo *m.* coat 6
abril *m.* April 5
abrir *v.* to open 3
abuelo/a *m., f.* grandfather; grandmother 3
abuelos *pl.* grandparents 3
aburrido/a *adj.* bored; boring 5
aburrir *v.* to bore 7
aburrirse *v.* to get bored 17
acabar de (+ *inf.***)** *v.* to have just (*done something*) 6
acampar *v.* to camp 5
accidente *m.* accident 10
acción *f.* action 17
aceite *m.* oil 8
ácido/a *adj.* acid 13
acompañar *v.* to go with; to accompany 14
acondicionado *adj.* conditioned 5
aconsejar *v.* to advise 12
acontecimiento *m.* event 18
acordarse (de) (o:ue) *v.* to remember 7
acostarse (o:ue) *v.* to go to bed 7
activo/a *adj.* active 15
actor *m.* actor 16
actriz *f.* actor 16
actualidades *f., pl.* news; current events 18
acuático/a *adj.* aquatic 4
acuerdo *m.* agreement 16
adelgazar *v.* to lose weight; to slim down 15
además (de) *adv.* furthermore; besides; in addition (to) 10
adicional *adj.* additional 2
adiós *m.* good-bye 1
adjetivo *m.* adjective 3
administración de empresas *f.* business administration 2
adolescencia *f.* adolescence 9
¿adónde? *adv.* where? (destination) 2
aduana *f.* customs 5
aeróbico/a *adj.*, aerobic 15
aeropuerto *m.* airport 5
afectado/a *adj.* affected 13
afeitarse *v.* to shave 7
aficionado/a *adj.* fan 4
afirmativo/a *adj.* affirmative 7
afueras *f., pl.* suburbs; outskirts 12
agencia de viajes *f.* travel agency 5
agente de viajes *m., f.* travel agent 5
agosto *m.* August 5
agradable *adj.* pleasant 5
agrícola *adj.* agricultural 6
agua *f.* water 8
agua mineral mineral water 8
águila *f.* eagle 1
ahora *adv.* now 5
ahora mismo right now 5
ahorrador(a) *adj.*frugal 6
ahorrar *v.* to save money 14
ahorros *m.* savings 14
aire *m.* air 13
ajo *m.* garlic 8
al (*contraction of* **a + el**) 2
al aire libre open-air 6
al contado in cash 14
al este to the east 14
al fondo (de) at the end (of) 12
al lado de beside 2
al norte to the north 14
al oeste to the west 14
al sur to the south 14
alberca *f.* swimming pool 4
albergue juvenil *m.* youth hostel 5
alcoba *f.* bedroom 12
alcohol *m.* alcohol 15
alcohólico/a *adj.* alcoholic 15
alegrarse (de) *v.* to be happy 13
alegre *adj.* happy; joyful 5
alegría *f.* joy 9
alemán, alemana *adj.* German 3
alérgico/a *adj.* allergic 10
alfombra *f.* carpet; rug 12
algo *pron.* something; anything 7
algodón *m.* cotton 6
alguien *pron.* someone; somebody; anyone 7
algún, alguno/a(s) *adj.* any; some 7
aliviar *v.* to ease; alleviate 15
aliviar el estrés/la tensión to reduce stress/tension 15
allí *adv.* there 5
allí mismo right there 14
almacén *m.* department store 6
almohada *f.* pillow 12

almorzar (o:ue) *v.* to have lunch 8
almuerzo *m.* lunch 8
aló hello (*on the telephone*) 11
alojamiento *m.* lodging 5
alquilar *v.* to rent 12
alquiler *m.* rent 12
alternador *m.* alternator 11
altillo *m.* attic 12
alto/a *adj.* tall 3
altura *f.* height 3
aluminio *m.* aluminum 13
amable *adj.* nice; friendly 5
ama de casa *f.* housekeeper; caretaker; housewife 12
amarillo/a yellow 6
amigo/a friend 3
amistad *f.* friendship 9
amor *m.* love 9
anaranjado/a *adj.* orange 6
animal *m.* animal 13
aniversario (de bodas) (wedding) anniversary 9
anoche last night 6
anteayer the day before yesterday 6
antes *adv.* before 7
antes (de) que *conj.* before 13
antes de *prep.* before 7
antibiótico *m.* antibiotic 10
antiguo/a *adj.* old 2
antipático/a *adj.* unpleasant 3
anunciar *v.* to announce; to advertise 18
anuncio *m.* advertisement 16
año *m.* year 2
apagar *v.* to turn off 11
aparato *m.* appliance 12
aparato doméstico domestic appliance 12
apartamento *m.* apartment 12
apellido *m.* last name 9
apenas *adv.* hardly; scarcely; just 10
aplaudir *v.* to applaud 17
apoyar *v.* support 8
apreciar *v.* to appreciate 17
aprender *v.* to learn 3
apurarse *v.* to hurry; to rush 15
aquel, aquella *adj.* that; those (over there) 6
aquél, aquélla *pron.* that; those (over there) 6
aquello *neuter, pron.* that; that thing; that fact 6
aquí *adv.* here 1
Aquí está... Here it is . . . 5
Aquí estamos en... Here we are in . . . 2
aquí mismo right here 11
árbol *m.* tree 13
archivo *m.* file 11
armario *m.* closet 12
arqueólogo/a *m., f.* archaeologist 16
arquitecto/a *m., f.* architect 16
arrancar *v.* to start (*a car*) 11
arrecife *m.* reef 5
arreglar *v.* to fix; to arrange 11
arriba *adv.* up 15
arroz *m.* rice 8
arte *m.* art 2
artes *f., pl.* arts 17
artesanía *f.* craftsmanship; crafts 17
artículo *m.* article 18
artista *m., f.* artist 3
artístico/a *adj.* artistic 17
arveja *m.* pea 8
asado/a *p.p.* roasted 8
ascenso *m.* promotion 16
ascensor *m.* elevator 5
así *adj.* thus; so (*in such a way*) 10
así así so so 1
asignación *f.* homework 2
asistir (a) *v.* to attend 3
aspiradora *f.* vacuum cleaner 12
aspirante *m. f.* candidate 16
aspirina *f.* aspirin 10
atletismo *m.* track and field 4
atraer *v.* attract 4
atún *m.* tuna 8
aumentar de peso to gain weight 15
aumento *m.* increase 16
aumento de sueldo pay raise 16
aunque although 3
autobús *m.* bus 1
automático/a *adj.* automatic 14
automóvil *m.* automobile 5
autopista *f.* highway 11
autorretrato *m.* selfportrait 4
ave *f.* bird 13
avenida *f.* avenue 11
aventura *f.* adventure 17
avergonzado/a *adj.* embarrassed 5
avión *m.* airplane 5
¡Ay! Oh! 10
¡Ay, qué dolor! Oh, what pain! 10
ayer *adv.* yesterday 6
ayudar (a) *v.* to help 12
ayudarse *v.* to help each other 11
azafrán *m.* saffran 2
azúcar *m.* sugar 8
azul *m.* blue 6

B

bahía *f.* bay 5
bailar *v.* to dance 2
bailarín/bailarina *m., f.* dancer 17
baile *m.* dance 17
bajar(se) *v.* to go down; to get off (of) 11
bajo/a *adj.* short (*in height*) 3
bajo/a *prep.* under 7
balcón *m.* balcony 12
ballet *m.* ballet 17
baloncesto *m.* basketball 4
banana *f.* banana 8
banco *m.* bank 14
banda *f.* band 17
bandera *f.* flag 1
bañarse *v.* to bathe take a bath 7
baño *m.* bathroom 7
barato/a *adj.* cheap 6
barco *m.* ship 5
barrer *v.* to sweep 12
barrer el suelo *v.* to sweep the floor 12
barrio *m.* neighborhood 12
bastante *adj.* enough sufficient 10
basura *f.* trash 12
baúl *m.* trunk 11
beber *v.* to drink 3
bebida *f.* drink 8
béisbol *m.* baseball 4
bellas artes *f., pl.* fine arts 17
belleza *f.* beauty 14
beneficio *m.* benefit 16
besar(se) *v.* to kiss (each other) 11
beso *m.* kiss 9
biblioteca *f.* library 2
bicicleta *f.* bicycle 4
bien *adj.* good well 1
bienestar *m.* well-being 15
bienvenido/a *adj.* welcome 12
billete *m.* paper money 8
biología *f.* biology 2
bistec *m.* steak 8
blanco/a *adj.* white 6
bluejeans *m., pl.* jeans 6
blusa *f.* blouse 6
boca *f.* mouth 10
boda *f.* wedding 9
boleto *m.* ticket 17
bolígrafo *m.* pen 2
bolsa *f.* purse, bag 6
bolsista *m., f.* stock broker 16
bombero/a *m., f.* firefighter 16
bonito/a *adj.* pretty 3
borrador *m.* eraser 2
bosque *m.* forest 13
bosque tropical tropical forest, rainforest 13
bota *f.* boot 6
botella *f.* bottle 9
botella de vino bottle of wine 9
botones *m., sing.* bellhop 5
brazo *m.* arm 10
brindar *v.* to toast (*drink*) 9
bucear *v.* to dive 4
bueno *adv.* well 2
bueno/a, buen *adj.* good 1
Buen viaje. Have a good trip. 1
buena forma good shape (*physical*) 15

Buenas noches Good evening; Good night. 1
Buenas tardes. Good afternoon. 1
buenísimo extremely good 8
¿Bueno? Hello. (*on telephone*) 11
Buenos días. Good morning. 1
bulevar *m.* boulevard 11
buscar *v.* to look for 2
buzón *m.* mailbox 14

C

caballo *m.* horse 5
cabaña *f.* cabin 5
cabe: no cabe duda que... there's no doubt that . . . 13
cabeza *f.* head 10
cable *m.* cable 11
cada *adj.* each 6
cadena *f.* channel (TV) 17
caerse *v.* to fall (down) 10
café *m.* café 4; brown 6; coffee 8
cafetera *f.* coffee maker 12
cafetería *f.* cafeteria 2
caído *p.p.* fallen 14
caja *f.* cash register 6
cajero/a *m., f.* cashier 14
cajero automático *m.* automatic teller machine (ATM) 14
calavera *m.* skull 4
calcetín *m.* sock 6
calculadora *f.* calculator 11
caldo *m.* soup 8
caldo de patas *m.* beef soup 8
calentarse *v.* to warm up 15
calidad *f.* quality 6
calle *m.* street 11
calor *m.* heat 4
caloría *f.* calorie 15
calzar *v.* to take size ... shoes 6
cama *f.* bed 5
cámara de video *f.*videocamera 11
cámara *f.* camera 11
camarero/a *m., f.* waiter 8
camarón *m.* shrimp 8
cambiar (de) *v.* to change 9
cambio de moneda currency exchange 8
caminar *v.* to walk 2
camino *m.* road 11
camión *m* truck, bus 5
camisa *f.* shirt 6
camiseta *f.* t-shirt 6
campo *m.* countryside 5
canadiense *adj.* Canadian 3
canal *m.* channel (TV) 11
canción *f.* song 17
candidato/a *m., f.* candidate 18
cansado/a *adj.* tired 5
cantante *m., f.* singer 17
cantar *v.* to sing 2
caña *f.* cane 6
capital *f.* capital (city) 1
capó *m.* hood 11
cara *f.* face 7
carne *f.* meat 8
carne de res *f.* beef 8
carnicería *f.* butcher shop 14
caro/a *adj.* expensive 6
carpintero/a *m., f.* carpenter 16
carrera *f.* career 16
carretera *f.* highway 11
carro *m.* car; automobile 11
carroza *f.* float 1
carta *f.* letter 4; (playing) card 5
cartel *m.* poster 12
cartera *f.* wallet 6
cartero *m.* mail carrier 14
casa *f.* house; home 4
casa de apartamentos *f.* apartment building 12
casado/a *adj.* married 9
casarse (con) *v.* to get married (to) 9
casi *adv.* almost 10
catarro *m.* cold (*disease*) 10
catorce *adj.* fourteen 1
cazar *v.* to hunt 4
cebolla *f.* onion 8
celebrar *v.* to celebrate 9
celular *adj.* cellular 11
cena *f.* dinner 8
cenar *v.* to have dinner 8
centro *m.* downtown 4
centro comercial *m.* shopping mall 6
cepillarse los dientes/el pelo *v.* to brush one's teeth/one's hair 7
cerámica *f.* pottery 17
cerca de *adv.* near 2
cerdo *m.* pork 8
cereales *m., pl.* cereal; grains 8
cero *m.* zero 1
cerrado/a *p.p.* closed 5
cerrar (e:ie) *v.* to close 4
cerveza *f.* beer 8
césped *m.* grass 13
ceviche *m.* marinated fish dish 8
ceviche de camarón *m.* marinated shrimp 8
chaleco *m.* vest 6
champiñón *m.* mushroom 8
champú *m.* shampoo 7
chaqueta *f.* jacket 6
chau *fam.* bye 1
cheque *m.* (bank) check 14
cheque de viajero *m.* traveler's check 14
chequeo *m.* physical exam 10
chévere *adj., fam.* terrific 1
chicle *m.* chewing gum 6
chico/a *adj.* boy girl 1
chino/a *adj.* Chinese 3
chocar (con) *v.* to run into 11
chocolate *m.* chocolate 9
choque *m.* collision 18
chuleta *f.* chop (*food*) 8
chuleta de cerdo *f.* pork chop 8
ciclismo *m.* cycling 4
cielo *m.* sky 13
cien(to) one hundred 5
ciencia *f.* science 2
ciencia ficción *f.* science fiction 17
científico/a *m., f.* scientist 16
cierto *m.* certain; true 13
cifra *f.* figure 1
cinco five 1
cincuenta fifty 2
cine *m.* movie theater 4
cinta *f.* (audio)tape 11
cinturón *m.* belt 6
circulación *f.* traffic 11
cita *f.* date; appointment 9
ciudad *f.* city 4
ciudadano/a *adj.* citizen 18
claro que sí *fam.* of course 16
clase *f.* class 2
clase de ejercicios aeróbicos *f.* aerobics class 15
clásico/a *adj.* classical 17
cliente *m., f.* customer 6
clínica *f.* clinic 10
cobrar *v.* to cash a check 14
coche *m.* car 11
cocina *f.* kitchen; stove 12
cocinar *v.* to cook 12
cocinero/a *m., f.* cook, chef 16
cola *f.* line 14
colesterol *m.* cholesterol 15
colibrí *m.* humming bird 6
color *m.* color 6
comedia *f.* comedy 17
comedor *m.* dining room 12
comenzar (e:ie) *v.* to begin 4
comer *v.* to eat 3
comercial *adj.* commercial; business-related 16
comida *f.* food; meal 8
como like as 8
¿cómo? what; how 1
¿Cómo es...? What's... like? 3
¿Cómo está Ud.? *form.* How are you? 1
¿Cómo estás? *fam.* How are you? 1
¿Cómo les fue...? *pl.* How did . . . go for you? 15
¿Cómo se llama (Ud.)? *(form.)* What's your name? 1
¿Cómo te llamas (tú)? *(fam.)* What's your name? 1
cómoda *f.* chest of drawers 12
cómodo/a *adj.* comfortable 5
compañero/a de clase *m., f.* classmate 2
compañero/a de cuarto *m., f.* roommate 2
compañía *f.* company; firm 16
comparación *f.* comparison 8
compartir *v.* to share 3

competir *v.* to compete 4
complejo/a *adj.* complex 8
completamente *adv.* completely 16
compositor(a) *m., f.* composer 17
comprar *v.* to buy 2
compras *f., pl.* purchases 5
ir de compras go shopping
comprender *v.* to understand 3
comprobar *v.* to check 8
comprometerse (con) *v.* to get engaged (to) 9
computación *f.* computer science 2
computadora *f.* computer 1
computadora portátil *f.* portable computer; laptop 11
común *adj.* common, shared 2
comunicación *f.* communication 18
comunicarse (con) *v.* to communicate (with) 18
con *prep.* with 2
Con él/ella habla. This is he/she. (*on telephone*) 11
con frecuencia frequently 10
Con permiso. Pardon me., Excuse me. 1
con tal (de) que provided (that) 13
concierto *m.* concert 17
concordar *v.* to agree 8
concurso *m.* contest; game show 17
condicionado/a *adj.* determined 4
conducir *v.* to drive 8
conductor(a) *m., f.* chauffeur; driver 1
conejo *m.* rabbit 2
confirmar la reservación *v.* to confirm the reservation 5
confirmar *v.* to confirm 5
congelador *m.* freezer 12
congestionado/a *adj.* congested; stuffed-up 10
conmigo *pron.* with me 4
conocer *v.* to know; to be acquainted with 8
conocido *adj.* known 2
conseguir (e:i) *v.* to get; to obtain 4
consejero/a *m., f.* counselor; advisor 16
consejo *m.* advice 9
conservar *v.* to conserve 13
construir *v.* build 4
consultorio *m.* doctor's office 10
consumir *v.* consume 15
contabilidad *f.* accounting 2
contador(a) *m., f.* accountant 16
contaminación *f.* pollution; contamination 4
contaminación del aire/del agua air/water pollution 13
contaminado/a *m., f.* polluted 13
contaminar *v.* to pollute 13
contar (con) *v.* to count (on) 12
contento/a *adj.* happy; content 5
contestadora *f.* answering machine 11
contestar *v.* to answer
contigo *fam.* with you 8
control *m.* control 7
control remoto remote control 11
controlar *v.* to control 13
conversar *v.* to talk 8
convertirse *v.* to become 6
copa *f.* wineglass; goblet 12
corazón *m.* heart 10
corbata *f.* tie 6
correa *m.* belt 6
correo *m.* post office; mail 14
correo electrónico *m.* e-mail 4
correr *v.* to run; to jog 3
corrida de toros *f.* bullfights 4
corte *f.* court 2
cortesía *f.* courtesy 1
cortinas *f., pl.* curtains 12
corto/a *adj.* short (*in length*) 6
cosa *f.* thing 1
costar (o:ue) *f.* to cost 6
costumbres *f.* customs 1
cráter *m.* crater 13
crear *v.* to create 4
crecimiento *m.* growth 4
crédito *m.* credit 6
creer (en) *v.* to believe (in); to think 3
creído *p.p.* believed 14
crema de afeitar *f.* shaving cream 7
crimen *m.* crime; murder 18
cruzar *v.* to cross 14
cuaderno *m.* notebook 1
cuadra *f.* city block 14
¿cuál(es)? which?; which ones?; what? 2
¿Cuál es la fecha (de hoy)? What is the date (today)? 5
cuadro *m.* picture 12
cuando when 7
¿cuándo? when? 2
¿cuánto/a(s)? how much?, how many? 1
¿Cuánto cuesta...? How much does . . . cost? 6
¿Cuántos años tienes? How old are you? 3
cuarenta forty 2
cuarto de baño *m.* bathroom 7
cuarto *m.* room 7
cuarto/a *adj.* fourth 5
cuatro four 1
cuatrocientos/as *m., f.* four hundred 5
cubiertos *m./pl.* silverware 12
cubierto *p.p.* covered 14
cubrir *v.* to cover 14
cuchara *f.* tablespoon 12
cuchillo *m.* knife 12
cuello *m.* neck 10
cuenta *f.* bill 9; account 14
cuenta corriente *f.* checking account 14
cuenta de ahorros *f.* savings account 14
cuento *m.* story 17
cuerpo *m.* body 10
cuidado *m.* care 3
cuidar *v.* to take care of 13
cultivar *v.* to grow 6
cultura culture 17
cumpleaños *m., sing.* birthday 9
cumplir años *v.* to have a birthday 9
cuñado/a *m., f.* brother-in-law; sister-in-law 3
currículum *m.* résumé; curriculum vitae 16
curso *m.* course 2
custodiar *v.* to guard 5

D

danza *f.* dance 17
dañar *v.* to damage 11
dar *v.* to give 9
dar un consejo *v.* to give advice 9
darse con *v.* to bump into; to run into 10
de *prep.* of; from 1
¿De dónde eres (tú)? *fam.* Where are you from? 1
¿De dónde es (Ud.)? *form.* Where are you from? 1
¿De parte de quién? Who is calling? (*on telephone*) 11
¿de quién? whose (*sing.*) 1
¿de quiénes? whose (*pl.*) 1
de acuerdo a according to 4
de algodón (made of) cotton 6
de aluminio made of aluminum 13
de compras shopping 5
de cuadros plaid 6
de excursión hiking 4
de hecho in fact 5
de ida y vuelta roundtrip 5
de la mañana in the morning; A.M. 1
de la noche in the evening; at night; P.M. 1
de la tarde in the afternoon; in the early evening; P.M. 1
de lana (made of) wool 6
de lunares polka-dotted 6
de mi vida in my life 15
de moda in fashion 6
De nada. You're welcome. 1
de ninguna manera no way 16
de niño as a child 10
de nuevo new 1
de parte de on behalf of 11

de plástico (made of) plastic 13
de rayas striped 6
de repente suddenly 6
de seda (made of) silk 6
de tomar to drink (I'll have) 8
de vaqueros western (genre) 17
de vez en cuando from time to time 10
de vidrio made of glass 13
debajo de *prep.* below; under 2
debe ser *v.* it must be 6
deber (+ *infin.*) *v.* to have to (*do something*), should (*do something*) 3
deber *v.* responsibility; obligation 18
deberes *m.* homework 2
debido a due to; the fact that 3
débil *adj.* weak 15
decidido *adj.* decided 14
decidir *v.* to decide 3
décimo/a *adj.* tenth 5
decir *v.* to say; to tell 9
declarar *v.* to declare; to say 18
dedo *m.* finger 10
dejar *v.* to let 12; to quit; to leave behind 16
dejar de (*+ inf.*) *v.* to stop (*doing something*)
dejar una propina *v.* to leave a tip 9
del (*contraction of* **de + el**) of the; from the 1
delante de *prep.* in front of 2
delgado/a *adj.* thin; slender 3
delicioso/a *adj.* delicious 8
demás *pron.* the rest 5
demasiado *adv.* too much 6
dentista *m., f.* dentist 10
dentro de within 16
dependiente/a *m., f.* clerk 6
deporte *m.* sport 4
deportista *m.* sports person 1
deportivo/a *adj.* sports-loving 4
depositar *v.* to deposit 14
derecha *f.* right 2
derecho/a *adj.* straight 14
derechos *m.* rights 18
desarrollar *v.* to develop 13
desastre natural *m.* natural disaster 18
desayunar *v.* to have breakfast 8
desayuno *m.* breakfast 8
descafeinado/a *adj.* decaffeinated 15
descansar *v.* to rest 2
descompuesto/a *adj.* not working; out-of-order 11
describir *v.* to describe 18
descubierto *p.p.* discovered 14
descubrir *v.* to discover 13
desde *prep.* from; since 6
desear *v.* to wish; to desire 2
desempleo *m.* unemployment 18
desfile *m.* parade 1
deforestación *f.* deforestation 13
desierto *m.* desert 13
desigualdad *f.* equality 18
desordenado/a *adj.* disorderly 5
despacio *adj.* slowly 8
despedida *f.* farewell; good-bye 1
despedirse (de) (e:i) *v.* to say good-bye (to) 7
despejado/a *adj.* clear (*weather*) 4
despertador *m.* alarm clock 7
despertarse (e:ie) *v.* to wake up 7
después *adv.* afterwards; then 7
después de after 7
destruir *v.* to destroy 13
detrás de *adv.* behind 2
día de fiesta holiday 9
día *m.* day 1
diario *m.* diary 1; newspaper 18
diario/a *adj.* daily 7
dibujar *v.* to draw 2
dibujo *m.* drawing 17
dibujos animados *m., pl.* cartoons 17
diccionario *m.* dictionary 1
dicho *p.p.* said 14
diciembre *m.* December 5
dictadura *f.* dictatorship 18
diecinueve nineteen 1
dieciocho eighteen 1
dieciséis sixteen 1
diecisiete seventeen 1
diente *m.* tooth 7
dieta *f.* diet 15
dieta equilibrada balanced diet 15
diez ten 1
difícil *adj.* hard; difficult 3
difuntos *m. f.* deceased 4
Diga. Hello. (*on telephone*) 11
diligencia *f.* errand 14
dinero *m.* money 6
dirección *f.* address 14
direcciones *f., pl.* directions 14
director(a) *m., f.* director; (*musical*) conductor 17
disco compacto compact disc (CD) 11
disco *m.* (computer) disk 11
discriminación *f.* discrimination 18
disculpar *v.* to excuse 8
discurso *m.* speech 18
diseñador(a) *m., f.* designer 16
diseño *m.* design 3
disfrutar (de) *v.* to enjoy; to reap the benefits (of) 15
diversión *f.* fun activity 4
divertido/a *adj.* fun 7
divertirse (e:ie) *v.* to have fun 9
divorciado/a *adj.* divorced 9
divorciarse (de) *v.* to get divorced (from) 9
divorcio *m.* divorce 9
doblar *v.* to turn 14
doble *adj.* double **5**
doce twelve 1
doctor(a) *m., f.* doctor 10
documental *m.* documentary 17
documento de viaje *m.* travel documents 1
doler (o:ue) *v.* to hurt 10
dolor de cabeza *m.* headache 10
dolor *m.* ache; pain 10
doméstico/a *adj.* domestic 18
dominar *v.* dominate 4
domingo *m.* Sunday 2
don/doña *title of respect used with a person's first name* 1
donde *prep.* where
¿Dónde está...? Where is . . . ? 2
¿dónde? where? 1
dormir (o:ue) *v.* to sleep 4
dormirse (o:ue) *v.* to go to sleep; to fall asleep 7
dos two 1
dos veces *f.* twice; two times 6
doscientos/as *m.* two hundred 5
drama *m.* drama; play 17
dramático/a *adj.* dramatic 17
dramaturgo/a *m., f.* playwright 17
droga *f.* drug 15
drogadicto/a *adj.* drug addict 15
ducha *f.* shower 7
ducharse *v.* to shower; to take a shower 7
duda *f.* doubt 13
dudar *v.* to doubt 13
dueño/a *m., f* owner; landlord 8
dulces *m., pl.* sweets; candy 9
durante *prep.* during 7
durar *v.* to last 18

E

e *conj.* (*used instead of* **y** *before words beginning with* **i** *and* **hi**) and 4
echar *v.* to throw 14
echar una carta al buzón *v.* to throw a letter in the mailbox 14
ecología *f.* ecology 13
economía *f.* economics 2
ecoturismo *m.* ecotourism 13
Ecuador *m.* Ecuador 1
ecuatoriano/a *adj.* Ecuadorian 3
edad *f.* age 8
edificio *m.* building 14
efectivo *m.* cash 14
eficaz *adj.* 8
ejercicios *m.* exercise 15
ejercicios aeróbicos *m.* aerobic exercises 15
ejercicios de estiramiento stretching exercises 15
ejército *m.* army 18
el *m., sing,* the 1
él *pron.* he; him 1
elección *f.* election 18
electricista *m., f.* electrician 16
elegante *adj.* elegant 6
elegir *v.* to elect 18

ella *pron.* she; her 1
ellos/as *pron.* them 1
embarazada *adj.* pregnant 10
emergencia *f.* emergency 10
emitir *v.* to broadcast 18
emocionante *f.* exciting 15
empezar (e:ie) *v.* to begin 4
empleado/a *m., f.* employee 5
empleo *m.* job; employment 16
empresa *f.* company; firm 16
en *prep.* in; on 2
en casa at home 7
en caso (de) que in case (that) 13
en cuanto as soon as 14
en efectivo in cash 14
en exceso in excess; too much 15
en línea in-line 4
¡En marcha! Forward ho! 15
en mi nombre in my name 5
en punto on the dot; exactly; sharp (*time*) 1
en qué in what; how 2
¿En qué puedo servirles? How may I help you? 5
enamorado/a *adj.* in love; beloved 5
enamorarse (de) *v.* to fall in love (with) 9
encantado/a *adj.* delighted; pleased to meet you 1
encantar *v.* to like very much; to love (*inanimate things*) 7
encima de *adv.* on top of 2
encontrar (o:ue) *v.* to find 4
encontrar(se) *v.* to meet (each other); to find (each other) 11
encuesta *f.* poll; survey 18
energía *f.* energy 13
enero *m.* January 5
enfermarse *v.* to get sick 10
enfermedad *f.* illness 10
enfermero/a *m., f.* nurse 10
enfermo/a *adj.* sick 10
enfrente de *adv.* opposite; facing 14
engordar *v.* to gain weight 15
enojado/a *adj.* mad; angry 5
enojarse (con) *v.* to get angry (with) 7
ensalada *f.* salad 8
enseguida *adv.* right away 9
enseñar *v.* to teach 2
ensuciar *v.* to dirty; to get dirty 12
entender (e:ie) *v.* to understand 4
entonces *adv.* then 7
entrada *f.* entrance 12; ticket 17
entre *prep.* between; among 2
entremeses *m., pl.* hors d'oeuvres; appetizers 8
entrenarse *v.* to practice; to train 15
entrevista *f.* interview 16
entrevistador(a) *m., f.* interviewer 16
entrevistar *v.* to interview 16
envase *m.* container 13
enviar *v.* to send 14
equilibrado/a *adj.* balanced 15
equipado/a *adj.* equipped 15
equipaje *m.* luggage 5
equipo *m.* team 4
equivocado/a *adj.* mistaken; wrong 5
eres *fam.* you are 1
es he/she/it is 1
Es (una) lástima que... It's a shame that . . . 13
Es bueno que... It's good that . . . 12
Es de... He/She is from . . . 1
Es extraño que... It's strange that . . . 13
Es importante que... It's important that . . . 12
Es imposible que... It's impossible that . . . 13
Es improbable que... It's improbable that . . . 13
Es la una. It's one o'clock. 1
Es malo que... It's bad that . . . 12
Es mejor que... It's better that . . . 12
Es necesario que... It's necessary that . . . 12
Es ridículo que... It's ridiculous that . . . 13
Es seguro que... It's sure that . . . 13
Es terrible que... It's terrible that . . . 13
Es triste que... It's sad that . . . 13
Es urgente que... It's urgent that . . . 12
Es verdad que... It's true that . . . 13
esa(s) *f., adj.* that; those 6
ésa(s) *f., pron.* those (ones) 6
escalar *v.* to climb 4
escalar montañas *v.* to climb mountains 4
escalera *f.* stairs; stairway 12
escoger *v.* choose 8
escribir *v.* to write 3
escribir un mensaje electrónico to write an e-mail message 4
escribir una (tarjeta) postal to write a postcard 4
escribir una carta to write a letter 4
escrito *p.p.* written 14
escritor(a) *m., f* writer 17
escritorio *m.* desk 2
escuchar *v.* to listen to 2
escuchar la radio to listen to the radio 2
escuchar música to listen to music 2
escuela *f.* school 1
esculpir *v.* to sculpt 17
escultor(a) *m., f.* sculptor 17
escultura *f.* sculpture 17
ese *m., sing., adj.* that 6
ése *m., sing., pron.* that (one) 6
eso *neuter, pron.* that 6
esos *m., pl., adj.* those 6
ésos *m., pl., pron.* those (ones) 6
España *f.* Spain 1
español *m.* Spanish (*language*) 2
español(a) *m., f., adj.* Spanish 3
espárragos *m., pl* asparagus 8
especialización *f.* major field of study or interest; specialization 16
espectacular *adj.* spectacular 15
espectáculo *m.* show 17
espejo *m.* mirror 7
esperar *v.* to wait for to hope 2; to wish 13
esposo/a *m., f.* husband/wife; spouse 3
esquema *m.* outline 8
esquí (acuático) *m.* (water) skiing 4
esquiar *v.* to ski 4
esquina *m.* corner 14
está he, she, it is, you are 1
Está (muy) despejado. It's (very) clear. (*weather*) 4
Está (muy) nublado. It's (very) cloudy. (*weather*) 4
Está bien. That's fine. It's okay. 11
esta(s) *f., adj.* this these 4
esta noche tonight 4
ésta(s) *f., pron.* this (one); these (ones) 6
Ésta es... *f.* This is . . . (*introducting someone*) 1
establecer to establish 16
estación *f.* station; season 5
estación de autobuses bus station 5
estación del metro subway station 5
estacionar to park 11
estadio *m.* stadium 2
estado *m.* state 5
estado civil *m.* marital status 9
Estados Unidos *m.* (EE.UU.; E.U.) United States 1
estadounidense *adj.* from the United States 3
estampado/a *adj.* print 6
estampilla *f.* stamp 14
estante *m.* bookcase; bookshelf 12
estar *v.* to be 2
estar a (veinte kilómetros) de aquí. to be (20 kilometers) from here 11
estar a dieta to be on a diet 15
estar aburrido/a to be bored 5
estar afectado/a por to be affected by 13

estar bajo control to be under control 7
estar cansado/a to be tired 5
estar contaminado/a to be polluted 13
estar de acuerdo to agree 16
estar de moda to be in fashion 6
estar de vacaciones *f., pl.* to be on vacation 5
estar en buena forma to be in good shape 15
estar enfermo/a to be sick 10
estar perdido/a to be lost 14
estar roto/a to be broken 10
estar seguro/a to be sure 5
estar torcido/a to be twisted; to be sprained 10
(no) está nada mal it's not at all bad 5
estatua *f.* statue 17
este *m.* east 14
este *m., sing., adj.* this 6
éste *m., sing., pron.* this (one) 6
Éste es... *m.* This is . . . (introducing someone) 1
estéreo *m.* stereo 11
estilo *m.* style 5
estiramiento *m.* stretching 15
esto *neuter pron.* this; this thing 6
estómago *m.* stomach 10
estornudar *v.* to sneeze 10
estos *m., pl., adj.* these 6
éstos *m., pl., pron.* these (ones) 6
estrella *f.* star 13
estrella de cine *m., f.* movie star 17
estrés *m.* stress 15
estudiante *m., f.* student 1
estudiantil *adj.* student 2
estudiar *v.* to study 2
estufa *f.* stove 12
estupendo/a *adj.* stupendous 5
etapa *f.* stage; step 9
evitar *v.* to avoid 13
evolucionar *v.* evolve 3
examen *m.* test; examination 2
excelente *adj.* excellent 5
exceso *m.* excess too much 15
excursión *f.* hike; tour; excursion 4
excursionista *m., f.* hiker 4
éxito *m.* success 16
experiencia *f.* experience 18
explicar *v.* to explain 18
explorar to explore 4
explorar un pueblo to explore a town 4
explorar una ciudad to explore a city 4
expresión *f.* expression 1
extinción *f.* extinction 13
extranjero/a *adj.* foreign 17
extraño/a *adj.* strange 13

F

fabuloso/a *adj* fabulous 5
fácil *adj.* easy 3
falda *f.* skirt 6
faltar *v.* to lack to need 7
familia *f.* family 3
famoso/a *adj.* famous 16
farmacia *f.* pharmacy 10
fascinar *v.* to fascinate 7
favorito/a *adj.* favorite 4
fax *m.* fax (machine) 11
febrero *m.* February 5
fecha *f.* date 5
feliz *adj.* happy 5
¡Felicidades! Congratulations! (*for an event such as a birthday or anniversary*) 9
¡Felicitaciones! Congratulations! (*for an event such as an engagement or a good grade on a test*) 9
¡Feliz cumpleaños! Happy birthday! 9
fenomenal *adj.* phenomenal; great 5
feo/a *adj.* ugly 3
festival *m.* festival 17
fiebre *f.* fever 10
fiesta *f.* party 9
fijo/a *adj.* set, fixed 6
fin *m.* end 4
fin de semana weekend 4
finalmente *adv.* finally *15*
firmar *v.* to sign (*a document*) 14
física *f.* physics 2
flan *m.* baked custard 9
flexible *adj.* flexible 15
flor *f.* flower 13
folklórico/a *adj.* folk folkloric 17
folleto *m.* brochure 5
fondo *m.* end 12
forma *f.* shape 15
formulario *m.* form 14
foto(grafía) *f.* photograph 1
francés, francesa *m., f.* French 3
frecuentemente *adv.* frequently 10
frenos *m., pl.* brakes 11
fresco/a *adj.* cool 4
frijoles *m., pl.* beans 8
frío/a *m.* cold 4
fritada *f.* fried dish (pork, fish, etc.) 8
frito/a *adj.* fried 8
fruta *f.* fruit 8
frutería *f.* fruit store 14
frutilla *f.* strawberry 8
fuente de fritada *f.* platter of fried food 8
fuente *f.* platter 8
fuera *adv.* outside 8
fuerte *adj.* strong 15
fumar *v.* to smoke 15
funcionar *v.* to work; to function 11
fútbol *m.* soccer 4
fútbol americano *m.* football 4
futuro/a *adj.* future 16

G

gafas (oscuras) *f., pl.* (sun)glasses 6
galleta *f.* cookie 9
ganar *v.* to win 4; to earn (money) 16
ganga *f.* bargain 6
garaje *m.* garage 12
garganta *f.* throat 10
gasolina *f.* gasoline 11
gasolinera *f.* gas station 11
gastar *v.* to spend (*money*) 6
gato/a *m., f.* cat 13
gente *f.* people 3
geografía *f.* geography 2
gerente *m., f.* manager 16
gimnasio *m.* gymnasium 4
gobierno *m.* government 13
golf *m.* golf 4
gordo/a *adj.* fat 3
grabadora *f.* tape recorder 1
gracias *f., pl.* thank you; thanks 1
Gracias por todo. Thanks for everything. 9
Gracias una vez más. Thanks again. 9
graduarse (en) *v.* to graduate (from) 9
gran, grande *adj.* big 3
grasa *f.* fat 15
gratis *adj.* free of charge 14
grave *adj.* grave serious 10
gravísimo/a *adj.* extremely serious 13
grillo *m.* cricket 4
gripe *f.* flu 10
gris *f.* gray 6
gritar *v.* to scream 7
guagua *f.* bus 5
guantes *m., pl.* gloves 6
guapo/a *adj.* handsome; good-looking 3
guardar *v.* to save (on a computer) 11
guerra *f.* war 18
guía *m., f.* guide 12
guisantes *m.* peas 8
gustar *v.* to be pleasing to; to like 7
gusto *m.* pleasure 1
El gusto es mío. The pleasure is mine. 1
Gusto de *(+ inf.).* It's a pleasure to . . . 18

H

haber *(aux.) v.* to have (*done something*) 15
ha sido un placer it's been a pleasure 15
habitación *f.* room 5
habitación doble double room 5
habitación individual single room 5

hablar *v.* to talk; to speak 2
hacer *v.* to do; to make; to be 4
Hace (mucho) viento. It's (very) windy. (*weather*) 4
Hace buen tiempo. The weather is good ; It's good weather. 4
Hace calor. It's hot. (*weather*) 4
Hace fresco. It's cool. (*weather*) 4
Hace frío. It's cold. (*weather*) 4
Hace mal tiempo. The weather is bad; It's bad weather. 4
Hace sol. It's sunny. (*weather*) 4
hacer cola to stand in line 14
hacer diligencias to do errands; to run errands 14
hacer ejercicio to exercise 15
hacer ejercicios aeróbicos to do aerobics 15
hacer ejercicios de estiramiento to do stretching exercises 15
hacer el papel to play a role 17
hacer gimnasia to work out 15
hacer juego (con) to match 6
hacer la cama to make the bed 12
hacer las maletas to pack the suitcases 5
hacer quehaceres domésticos to do household chores 12
hacer turismo to go sightsee ing 5
hacer un viaje to go on a trip 5
hacer una excursión to go on a hike; to go on a tour 5
hacha *f.* ax 1
hacia *prep.* toward 14
hambre *f.* hunger 3
hamburguesa *f.* hamburger 8
hasta *prep.* until, toward 1
Hasta la vista. See you later. 1
Hasta luego. See you later. 1
Hasta mañana. See you tomor row. 1
hasta que until 14
Hasta pronto. See you soon. 1
hay there is; there are 1
Hay (mucha) contaminación. It's (very) smoggy. 4
Hay (mucha) niebla. It's (very) foggy. 4
No hay duda que... there's no doubt that . . . 13
No hay de qué. You're welcome. 1
hay que it is necessary that 14
hecho *p. p.* done 14
heladería *f.* ice cream shop 14
helado/a *adj.* iced 8
helado *m.* ice cream 9
hermanastro/a *m., f.* stepbrother, stepsister 3
hermano/a *m., f.* brother/sister 3
hermano/a mayor/menor *m., f.* older/younger brother/sister 3
hermanos *m., pl.* brothers and sisters 3
hermoso/a *adj.* beautiful 6
hierba *f.* grass 13
hijastro/a *m., f.* stepson; stepdaughter 3
hijo/a *m., f.* son; daughter 3
hijo/a único/a *m., f.* only child 3
hijos *m., pl.* children 3
historia *f.* history 2; story 17
hockey *m.* hockey 4
hola hello; hi 1
hombre *m.* man 1
hombre de negocios *m.* businessman 16
hora *f.* hour 1
horario *m.* schedule 2
horno *m.* oven 12
horno de microondas *m.* microwave oven 12
horror *m.* horror 17
hospital *m.* hospital 10
hostal *m.* inn 5
hotel *m.* hotel 5
hoy *adv.* today 2
hoy día *adv.* nowadays 5
Hoy es... Today is . . . 2
huelga *f.* strike (labor) 18
hueso *m.* bone 10
huésped(a) *m., f.* guest 5
huevo *m.* egg 8
humanidades *f., pl.* humanities 2
huracán *m.* hurricane 18

I

ida *f.* one way (*travel*) 5
idea *f.* idea 4
igualdad *f.* equality 18
igualmente *adv.* likewise 1
imperio *m.* empire 6
impermeable *m.* raincoat 6
importante *adj.* important 3
importar *v.* to be important to; to matter 7
imposible *adj.* impossible 13
impresora *f.* printer 11
imprimir *v.* to print 11
improbable *adj.* improbable 13
impuesto *m.* tax 18
incendio *m.* fire 18
increíble *adj.* incredible 5
indicio *m.* evidence 5
individual *adj.* private (*room*) 5
infección *f.* infection 10
influír *v.* influence 4
informar *v.* to inform 18
informe *m.* report; paper (*written work*) 18
ingeniero/a *m., f.* engineer 3
inglés *m.* English (*language*) 2
inglés, inglesa *adj.* English 3
inolvidable *adj.* unforgettable 7
insistir (en) *v.* to insist (on) 12
inspector(a) de aduanas *m.* customs inspector 5
inspirar *v.* inspire 3
inteligente *adj.* intelligent 3
intentar *v.* to try 8
intercambiar *v.* exchange 8
interesante *adj.* interesting 3
interesar *v.* to be interesting to; to interest 7
internacional *adj.* international 18
Internet *m.* Internet 11
interpretar *v.* to perform 6
inundación *f.* flood 18
invertir (i:ie) *v.* to invest 16
invierno *m.* winter 5
invitado/a *m., f.* guest (*at a function*) 9
invitar *v.* to invite 9
inyección *f.* injection 10
ir *v.* to go 4
ir a (+ *inf.*) to be going to do something 4
ir de compras to go shopping 5
ir de excursión (a las montañas) to go for a hike (in the mountains) 4
ir de pesca to go fishing 5
ir de vacaciones to go on vacation 5
ir en auto(móvil) to go by auto(mobile); to go by car 5
ir en autobús to go by bus 5
ir en barco to go by ship 5
ir en metro to go by subway 5
ir en motocicleta to go by motorcycle 5
ir en taxi to go by taxi 5
ir en tren to go by train 5
ir en avión to go by plane 5
irse to go away; to leave 7
italiano/a *adj.* Italian 3
izquierdo/a *adj.* left 2
a la izquierda de to the left of 2

J

jabón *m.* soap 7
jamás *adv.* never not ever 7
jamón *m.* ham 8
japonés, japonesa *adj.* Japanese 3
jardín *m.* garden, yard 12
jefe, jefa *m., f.* boss 16
joven *adj.* young 3
joven *m., f.* youth, young person 1
joyas *f.* jewels 1
joyería *f.* jewelry store 14
jubilarse *v.* to retire (*from work*) 9
juegos *m.* games 5
jueves *m., sing.* Thursday 2
jugador(a) *m., f.* player 4
jugar (u:ue) *v.* to play 4
jugar a las cartas *v.* to play cards 5

jugo *m.* juice 8
jugo de fruta *m.* fruit juice 8
julio *m.* July 5
junio *m.* June 5
juntos/as *adj.* together 9
juvenil *adj.* youthful 1
juventud *f.* youth 9

K

kilómetro *m.* kilometer 11

L

la *f., sing., d.o. pron.* her, it, you 5
la *f., sing.* the 1
laboratorio *m.* laboratory 2
lago *m.* lake 5
lámpara *f.* lamp 12
lana *f.* wool 6
langosta *f.* lobster 8
lápiz *m.* pencil 1
largo/a *m.* long (*in length*) 6
las *f., pl.* the 1
las *f., pl., d.o.pron.* them 5
lástima *f.* shame 13
lastimarse *v.* to injure oneself 10
lastimarse el pie to injure one's foot 10
lata *f.* (*tin*) can 13
lavabo *m.* sink 7
lavadora *f.* washing machine 12
lavandería *f.* laundromat 14
lavaplatos *m., sing.* dishwasher 12
lavar *v.* to wash 12
lavarse *v.* to wash oneself 7
lavarse la cara to wash one's face 7
lavarse las manos to wash one's hands 7
lazos *m.* ties 4
le *sing., i.o. pron.* to/for him, her, *form.* you 6
Le presento a... *form.* I would like to introduce . . . to you. 1
lección *f.* lesson 1
leche *f.* milk 8
lechuga *f.* lettuce 8
lector *m., f.* reader 8
leer *v.* to read 3
leer el correo electrónico *v.* to read e-mail 4
leer el periódico to read the newspaper 4
leer la revista to read the magazine 4
leído *p.p.* read 14
lejos de *adv.* far from 2
lengua *f.* language 2
lenguas extranjeras *f., pl.* foreign languages 2
lentes de contacto *m., pl.* contact lenses 6
lentes de sol/oscuros/negros *f.* sunglasses 6
lento/a *adj.* slow 11
les *pl., i.o. pron.* to/for them, *form* you 5
letrero *m.* sign 14
levantar *v.* to lift 15
levantar pesas *v.* to lift weights 15
levantarse *v.* to get up 7
ley *f.* law 13
libertad *f.* liberty, freedom 18
libre *adj.* free 4
librería *f.* bookstore 2
libro *m.* book 2
licencia de conducir *f.* driver's license 11
limón *m.* lemon 8
limpiar la casa *v.* to clean the house 12
limpiar *v.* to clean 12
limpio/a *adj.* clean 5
línea *f.* line 4
listo/a *adj.* smart 5; ready 15
literatura *f.* literature 2
liviano/a *adj.* light 6
llamar *v.* to call 7
llamar por teléfono to call on the phone 11
llamarse *v.* to be called; to be named 7
llanta *f.* tire 11
llave *f.* key 5
llegada *f.* arrival 5
llegar *v.* to arrive 2
llenar *v.* to fill 11; *v.* to fill out a form 14
llenar el tanque to fill the tank 11
llenar un formulario to fill out a form 14
lleno/a *adj.* full 11
llevar *v.* to carry, to take 2; *v.* to wear 6
llevar una vida sana to lead a healthy lifestyle 15
llevarse bien/mal con to get along well/badly with 9
llover (o:ue) *v.* to rain 4
Llueve. It's raining. 4
lluvia *f.* rain 13
lluvia ácida acid rain 13
lo *d.o. pronoun.* it, him, *form.* you 5
lo mejor the best (thing) 18
lo pasamos de película we had a great time 18
lo peor the worst (thing) 18
lo que what that which 12
lo siento I'm sorry 1
loco/a *adj.* crazy 6
locutor(a) *m., f.* TV or radio announcer 18
lomo a la plancha grilled flank steak 8
lomo *m.* flank steak 8
los *m.pl.d.o.pron.* them, *form.* you 5
los *m., pl.* the 1
luchar (por) *v.* to fight struggle (for) 18
luego *adv.* afterwards, then 7; *adv.* later 1
lugar *m.* place 4
luna *f.* moon 13
luna de miel *f.* honeymoon 5
lunar *m.* polka dot 6
lunes *m., sing.* Monday 2
luz *f.* light, electricity 12

M

madrastra *f.* stepmother 3
madre *f.* mother 3
madurez *f.* maturity; middle age 9
maestro/a teacher (*elementary school*)
magnífico/a *adj.* magnificent 6
maíz *m.* corn 5
mal, malo, mala *adj.* bad 8
maleta *f.* suitcase 3
mamá *f.* mom 1
mami *f.* mom 3
mañana *f.* morning, A.M. 1; *f.* tomorrow 1
mandar *v.* to order 3
manejar *v.* to drive 11
manera *v.* way 16
mano *f.* hand 1
¡Manos arriba! Hands up! 15
manta *f.* blanket 12
mantener *v.* to maintain 15
mantenerse en forma to stay in shape 15
mantequilla *f.* butter 8
manzana *f.* apple 8
mapa *m.* map 1
maquillaje *m.* make-up 7
maquillarse *v.* to put on makeup 7
mar *m.* sea, ocean 5
maravillosamente *adv.* marvelously 18
maravilloso/a *adj.* marvelous 5
mareado/a *adj.* dizzy; nauseated 10
margarina *f.* margarine 8
mariscos *m., pl.* shellfish 8
marrón *adj.* brown 6
martes *m., sing.* Tuesday 2
marzo *m.* March 5
más *pron.* more 1
más de (+ *number*) more than (+ *number*) 8
más tarde later 7
más... que more . . . than 8
masaje *m.* massage 15
matemáticas *f., pl.* mathematics 2
materia *f.* course 2
matrimonio *m.* marriage 9

máximo/a *m.* maximum 11
mayo *m.* May 5
mayonesa *f.* mayonnaise 8
mayor *adj.* older 3
el/la mayor *adj.* oldest 8
mazmorra *f.* dungeon 5
me *pron.* me 5
Me duele mucho. It hurts me a lot. 10
Me gusta... I like . . . 2
No me gustan nada. I don't like . . . at all. 2
Me gustaría(n)... I would like . . . 7
Me llamo... My name is . . . 1
Me muero por... I'm dying to (for) . . . 1
mecánico/a *m., f.* mechanic 11
mediano/a *adj.* medium 6
medianoche *f.* midnight 1
medias *f.,pl.* pantyhose, stockings 6
medicamento *m.* medication 10
medicina *f.* medicine 10
médico/a *adj.* medical 10
médico/a *m., f.* doctor 3
medio/a *m.* half 3
medio ambiente *m.* environment 13
medio/a hermano/a *m., f.* half-brother; half-sister 3
mediodía *m.* noon 1
medios de comunicación *m., pl.* means of communication media 18
medir *v.* to measure 8
mejor *adj.* better best 8
el/la mejor *m., f.* the best 8
mejorar *v.* to improve 13
melocotón *m.* peach 8
menor *adj.* younger 3
el/la menor *m., f.* youngest 8
menos *adv.* less 10
menos cuarto... menos quince... quarter to . . . (*time*) 1
menos de + ***number*** less than + ***number*** 8
menos... que less . . . than 8
mensaje electrónico *m.* e-mail message 4
menú *m.* menu 8
mercado *m.* market 6
mercado al aire libre open-air market 6
merendar *v.* to snack to have a snack 15
merienda *f.* snack 15
mes *m.* month 5
mesa *f.* table 2
mesita *f.* end table 12
mesita de noche night stand 12
metro *m.* subway 5
mexicano/a *adj.* Mexican 3
México *m.* Mexico 1
mí *pron.* me 8
mi(s) *poss.* my 3
microonda *f.* microwave 12
horno de microondas *m.* microwave oven 12
miedo *m.* fear 3
mientras *adv.* while 10
miércoles *m., sing.* Wednesday 2
mil *m.* one thousand 4
Mil perdones. I'm extremely sorry. (*lit.* A thousand pardons.) 4
milla *f.* mile 11
millón *m.* million 5
millones (de) *m.* a billion (of) 5
mineral *m.* mineral 15
minuto *m.* minute 1
mío/a(s) *poss.* my (of) mine 11
mirar *v.* to watch 2
mirar (la) televisión to watch television 2
mismo/a *adj.* same 3
mochila *f.* backpack 2
moda *f.* fashion 6
módem *m.* modem 11
moderno/a *adj.* modern 17
molestar *v.* to bother to annoy 7
monitor *m.* (computer) monitor 11
monitor(a) *m., f.* trainer 15
montaña *f.* mountain 4
montar a caballo *v.* to ride a horse 5
monumento *m.* monument 4
mora *f.* blackberry 8
morado/a *adj.* purple 6
moreno/a *adj.* brunet(te) 3
morir (o:ue) *v.* to die 8
mostrar (o:ue) *v.* to show 4
moto *f.* motorcycle 5
motocicleta *f.* motorcycle 5
motor *m.* motor 11
muchacho/a *m., f.* boy, girl 3
mucho/a *adj.* many a lot of 2; *adj.* much 2
muchas veces many times 10
Muchísimas gracias. Thank you very much. 9
Mucho gusto. Pleased to meet you. 1
(Muchas) gracias. Thank you (very much). Thanks (a lot). 1
muchísimo very much 2
mudarse *v.* to move (from one house to another) 12
muebles *m., pl.* furniture 12
muela *f.* tooth 10
muerte *f.* death 9
muerto/a *p.p.* died 14
mujer *f.* woman 1
mujer de negocios *f.* business woman 16
mujer policía *f.* female police officer 11
multa *f.* fine 11
mundial *adj.* worldwide 5
mundo *m.* world 11
municipal *m.* municipal 4
músculo *m.* muscle 15
museo *m.* museum 4
música *f.* music 17
musical *adj.* musical 17
músico/a *m., f.* musician 17
muy *adv.* very 1
Muy amable. That's very kind of you. 5
Muy bien gracias. Very well, thank you. 1

N

nacer *v.* to be born 9
nacimiento *m.* birth 9
nacional *m., f.* national 18
nacionalidad *f.* nationality 1
nada nothing 1
nada mal not bad at all 5
nadar *v.* to swim 4
nadie *pron.* no one, nobody, not anyone 7
naranja *m.* orange 8
nariz *f.* nose 10
narradora *f.* narrator 4
natación *f.* swimming 4
natural *adj.* natural 13
naturaleza *f.* nature 13
navegar (en) *v.* to surf (*the Web*) 11
Navidad *f.* Christmas 9
necesario/a *adj.* necessary 12
necesitar *v.* to need 2
negar (e:ie) *v.* to deny 13
negativo/a *m.* negative 7
negocios *m., pl.* business commerce 16
negro/a *m., f.* black 6
nervioso/a *adj.* nervous 5
nevar (e:ie) *v.* to snow 4
Nieva. It's snowing. 4
ni nor 10
ni... neither... nor 7
niebla *f.* fog 4
nieto/a *m., f.* grandson; granddaughter 3
nieve *f.*snow 8
niñez *f.* childhood 9
ningún problema no problem 7
ningún, ninguno/a(s) *adj.* no; none; not; any 7
niño/a *m., f.* child 3
no no; not 1
No cabe duda que... There is no doubt that . . . 13
No es para tanto. It's no big deal. 12
No es seguro que... It's not sure that . . . 13
No es verdad que... It's not true that . . . 13
No está nada mal. It's not bad at all. 5

no estar de acuerdo to disagree 16
No estoy seguro. I'm not sure. 1
No hay de qué. You're welcome. 1
No hay duda. There is not doubt 13
no hay there is not, there are not 1
¡No me diga(s)! You don't say! 11
No me gustan nada. I don't like them at all. 2
no muy bien not very well 1
¿no? right? 1
no quiero I don't want to 4
no sé I don't know 1
No se preocupe. Don't worry. 7
no tener razón to be wrong 3
noche *f.* night 1
nombre *m.* name 5
norte *m.* north 14
norteamericano/a *m., f.* (North) American 3
nos *pron.* us 5
Nos vemos. See you. 1
nosotros/as *ob. pron.* us 8
nosotros/as *sub. pron.* we 1
notar *v.* to notice 4
noticias *f., pl.* news 18
noticiero *m.* newscast 18
novecientos/as *adj.* nine hundred 5
noveno/a *adj.* ninth 5
noventa ninety 2
noviembre *m.* November 5
novio/a *m., f.* boyfriend, girlfriend 3
nube *f.* cloud 13
nublado/a *adj.* cloudy 4
Está (muy) nublado. It's very cloudy. 4
nuera *f.* daughter-in-law 3
nuestro/a(s) *poss.* our 3
nueve. nine 1
nuevo/a *adj.* new 6
número *m.* number 1
número (shoe) size 6
nunca *adj.* never, not ever 7
nutrición *f.* nutrition 15

O

o or 7
o... o; either . . . or 7
obedecer (c:zc) *v.* to obey 18
obra *f.* work (*of art, literature, music, etc.*) 17
obra maestra *f.* masterpiece 17
obtener *v.* to obtain; to get 16
océano *m.* ocean; sea 5
ochenta eighty 2
ocho *m.* eight 1
ochocientos/as *adj.* eight hundred 5
octavo/a *adj.* eighth 5
octubre *m.* October 5
ocupación *f.* occupation 16
ocupado/a *adj.* busy 5
ocurrir *v.* to occur; to happen 18
odiar *v.* to hate 9
oeste *m.* west 14
oferta *f.* offer 12
oficina *f.* office 12
oficio *m.* trade 16
ofrecer (c:zc) *v.* to offer 8
ofrenda *f.* offering 4
oído *m.* sense of hearing; inner ear 10
oído *p.p.* heard 14
oír *v.* to hear 4
oigan *form., pl.* listen (*in conversation*) 5
oye *fam., sing.* listen (*in conversation*) 1
ojalá (que) I hope (that); I wish (that) 13
ojo *m.* eye 10
olvidar *v.* to forget 10
once eleven 1
ópera *f.* opera 17
operación *f.* operation 10
ordenado/a *adj.* orderly; well organized 5
ordinal *adj.* ordinal (*number*) 5
oreja *f.* (outer) ear 10
orgullo *m.* pride 1
orquesta *f.* orchestra 17
ortográfico *adj.* spellling 8
os *fam., pl.* you
otoño *m.* autumn 5
otro/a *adj.* other; another 6
otra vez again 15
oyentes *m. f.* listeners 6

P

paciente *m., f.* patient 10
padrastro *m.* stepfather 3
padre *m.* father 3
padres *m., pl.* parents 3
pagar *v.* in installments 14
pagar al contado to pay in cash 14
pagar en efectivo to pay in cash 14
pagar la cuenta to pay the bill 9
página *f.* page 11
página principal *f.* home page 11
país *m.* country 1
paisaje *m.* landscape; countryside 5
pájaro *m.* bird 13
palabra *f.* word 1
pan *m.* bread 8
pan tostado *m.* toasted bread; toast 8
panadería *f.* bakery 14
pantalla *f.* screen 11
pantalones *m., pl.* pants 6
pantalones cortos *m., pl.* shorts 6
papa *f.* potato 8
papas fritas *f., pl* fried potatoes; french fries 8
papá *m.* dad 3
papás *m., pl.* parents 3
papel *m.* paper 2; *m.* role 17
papi *m.* daddy 3
paquete *m.* package 14
par *m.* pair 6
un par de días *m.* a couple of days 10
para *prep.* for; in order to 11
para que so that 13
parabrisas *m., sing.* windshield 11
parador *m.* lodging 5
parar *v.* to stop 11
parecer *v.* to seem; to appear 8
pared *f.* wall 12
pareja (married) couple; partner 9
parientes *m., pl.* relatives 3
parque *m.* park 4
párrafo *m.* paragraph 5
parte: de parte de on behalf of 11
partido *m.* game; match (*sports*) 4
pasado/a *adj.* last; past 6
pasado *p.p.* passed 15
pasaje *m.* ticket 5
pasaje de ida y vuelta *m.* roundtrip ticket 5
pasajero/a *m., f.* passenger 1
pasaporte *m.* passport 5
pasar *v.* to go by 5; to pass 12; to spend time 4
pasar la aspiradora to vacuum 12
pasar por el banco to go by the bank 14
pasar por la aduana to go through customs 5
pasar tiempo to spend time 4
pasarlo bien/mal to have a good/bad time 9
pasatiempo *m.* pastime 4
pasear *v.* to take a walk; to stroll 4
pasear en bicicleta to ride a bicycle 4
pasillo *m.* hallway 12
pastel *m.* cake; pie 9
pastel de chocolate *m.* chocolate cake 9
pastel de cumpleaños *m.* birthday cake 9
pastelería *f.* pastry shop 14
pastilla *f.* pill; tablet 10
patata *f.* potato 8

patatas fritas *f.* fried potatoes 8
patinar (en línea) *v.* to skate (in-line) 4
patio *m.* patio; yard 12
patrimonio *m.* heritage 6
pavo *m.* turkey 8
paz *f.* peace 18
pedir (e:i) *v.* to ask for; to request 4; to order (*food*) 8
pedir prestado *v.* to borrow 14
pedir préstamo *v.* to apply for a loan 14
peinarse *v.* to comb one's hair 7
película *f.* movie 4
peligro *m.* danger 13
peligroso/a *adj.* dangerous 18
pelirrojo/a *adj.* red-headed 3
pelo *m.* hair 7
pelota *f.* ball 4; baseball
peluquería *f.* beauty salon 14
peluquero/a *m., f.* hairdresser 16
penicilina *f.* penicillin 10
pensar (e:ie) *v.* to think 4
pensar (+ *inf.*) *v.* to intend to; to plan to (*do something*) 4
pensar en *v.* to think about 4
pensión *f.* boardinghouse 5
peor *adj.* worse; worst 8
(el/la) peor *adj.* the worst 8
pequeño/a *adj.* small 3
pera *f.* pear 8
perder (e:ie) *v.* to lose 4
perdido/a *adj.* lost 14
Perdón. Pardon me.; Excuse me. 1
perezoso/a *adj.* lazy 3
perfecto/a *adj.* perfect 5
periódico *m.* newspaper 4
periodismo *m.* journalism 2
periodista *m., f.* journalist 3
permiso *m.* permission 1
pero but 2
perro *m.* dog 13
persona *f.* person 1
personaje *m.* character 17
personaje principal *m.* main character 17
pesa *f.* weight 15
pesca *f.* fishing 5
pescadería *f.* fish market 14
pescado *m.* fish (*cooked*) 8
pescador *m.* fisherman 5
pescar *v.* to fish 5
pez *m.* fish (*live*) 13
pico *m.* beak 6
pie *m.* foot 10
piedra *f.* stone 13
pierna *f.* leg 10
pimienta *f.* black pepper 8
piña *f.* pineapple 8
pintar *v.* to paint 17
pintor(a) *m., f.* painter 16
pintoresca *adj.* picturesque 2
pintura *f.* painting 12
piscina *f.* swimming pool 4
piso *m.* floor (*of a building*) 5
pizarra *f.* blackboard 2
placer *m.* pleasure 15
planchar la ropa *v.* to iron clothes 12
planes *m., pl.* plans 4
planta *f.* plant 13
planta baja *f.* ground floor 5
plástico *m.* plastic 13
plátano *m.* plantain 8
plato *m.* dish (*in a meal*) 8; *m.* plate 12
plato principal *m.* main dish 8
playa *f.* beach 5
plazos *m., pl.* periods; time 14
pluma *f.* pen 2
población *f.* population 13
pobre *adj.* poor 6
pobreza *f.* poverty 3
poco/a *adj.* little; few 5
poder (o:ue) *v.* to be able to; can 4
poema *m.* poem 17
poesía *f.* poetry 17
poeta *m., f.* poet 17
policía *f.* police (force) 11; *m.* (male) police officer 11
política *f.* politics 18
político/a *m., f.* politician 16
pollo *m.* chicken 8
pollo asado *m.* roast chicken 8
ponchar *v.* to go flat 11
poner *v.* to put; to place 4; *v.* to turn on (*electrical appliances*) 11
poner la mesa *v.* to set the table 12
poner una inyección *v.* to give an injection 10
ponerse (+ *adj.*) *v.* to become (+ *adj.*) 7; *v.* to put on clothing 7
por due to; in exchange for; for the sake of 11; for; by; in; through 11
por aquí around here 11
por avión by; plane 5
por ejemplo for example 11
por eso that's why; therefore 11
Por favor. Please. 1
por fin finally 11
por la mañana in the morning 7
por la noche at night 7
por la tarde in the afternoon 7
por lo menos at least 10
por supuesto of course 16
por teléfono by phone; on the phone 7
¿por qué? why? 2
por último finally 7
porque because 2
portátil *m.* portable 11
porvenir *m.* future 16
posesivo/a *adj.* possessive 3
posible *adj.* possible 13
postal *f.* postcard 4
postre *m.* dessert 9
practicar *v.* to practice 2
practicar deportes *m., pl.* to play sports 4
precio (fijo) *m.* (fixed; set) price 6
preferir (e:ie) *v.* to prefer 4
pregunta *f.* question **2**
preguntar *v.* to ask (*a question*) 2
premio *m.* prize; award 17
prensa *f.* press 18
preocupado/a *adj.* worried 5
preocuparse (por) *v.* to worry (about) 7
preparar *v.* to prepare 2
preposición *f.* preposition 2
presentación *f.* introduction 1
presentar *v.* to introduce 1; to put on (*a performance*) 17
presiones *f., pl.* pressures 15
prestado/a *adj.* borrowed 14
préstamo *m.* loan 14
prestar *v.* to lend 6
primavera *f.* spring 5
primer, primero/a *adj.* first 5
primo/a *m., f.* cousin 3
principal *adj.* main 8
prisa *f.* haste 3
probable *adj.* probable 13
probar (o:ue) *v.* to taste; to try 8
probarse (o:ue) *v.* to try on 7
problema *m.* problem 1
profesión *f.* profession 3
profesor(a) *m., f.* teacher; professor 1
programa *m.* 1
programa de computación *m.* software 11
programa de entrevistas *m.* talk show 17
programador(a) *m., f.* programmer 3
prohibir *v.* to prohibit; to forbid 10
pronombre *m.* pronoun 8
pronto *adj.* soon 10
propina *f.* tip 9
propio/a *adj.* own 16
proteger *v.* to protect 13
proteína *f.* protein 15
próximo/a *adj.* next 16
prueba *f.* test; quiz 2
psicología *f.* psychology 2
psicólogo/a *m., f.* psychologist 16
publicar *v.* to publish 17
público *m.* audience 17
pueblo *m.* town 4
puente *m.* bridge 2
puerta *f.* door 2
Puerto Rico *m.* Puerto Rico 1
puertorriqueño/a *adj.* Puerto Rican 3
pues well 2

puesto *m.* position; job 16; *p.p.* put 14
punto *m.* point 1
puro/a *adj.* pure 13

Q

que *pron.* that; who 12
¡Qué...! How . . . ! 3
¡Qué dolor! What pain! 10
¡Qué gusto + *inf.*! What a pleasure to . . . ! 18
¡Qué ropa más bonita! What pretty clothes! 6
¡Qué sorpresa! What a surprise! 9
¿Qué día es hoy? What day is it? 2
¿Qué hay de nuevo? What's new? 1
¿Qué hora es? What time is it? 1
¿Qué les parece? What do you (*pl.*) think? 9
¿Qué pasa? What's happening?; What's going on? 1
¿Qué pasó? What happened?; What's wrong? 11
¿Qué precio tiene? What is the price? 6
¿Qué tal...? How is/are . . . ? 2
¿Qué tal? How are you?; How is it going? 1
¿Qué talla lleva/usa? What size do you take? 6
¿Qué tiempo hace? What's the weather like? 4
¿qué? what? 1
quedar *v.* to be left over; to fit (*clothing*) 7
quedar *v.* to be located 14
quedarse *v.* to stay; to remain 7
quehaceres domésticos *m., pl.* household chores 12
quemado/a *adj.* burned (out) 11
querer (e:ie) *v.* to want; to love 4
querido/a *adj.* beloved 17
queso *m.* cheese 8
quien *pron.* who; whom 12
¿Quién es...? Who is . . . ? 1
¿Quién habla? Who is speaking? (*telephone*) 11
¿quién(es)? who?; whom? 1
química *f.* chemistry 2
quince *adj.* fifteen 1
quinceañera *f.* young woman's fifteenth birthday celebration 9
quinientos/as *adj.* five hundred 5
quinto/a *adj.* fifth 5
quisiera *v.* I would like 8
quitar la mesa *v.* to clear the table 12
quitarse *v.* to take off 7
quizás *adv.* perhaps 5

R

racismo *m.* racism 18
radio *f.* radio (*medium*) 2
radio *m.* radio (set) 2
radiografía *f.* X-ray 10
radioyente *m.* radio listener 4
raíz *f.* root 5
rápido/a *adj.* fast 8
ratón *m.* mouse 11
ratos libres *m., pl.* spare time 4
raya *f.* stripe 6
razón *f.* reason 3
real *adj.* royal 2
realizar *v.* to occur 4
rebaja *f.* sale 6
recado *m.* (telephone) message 11
receta *f.* prescription 10
recetar *v.* to prescribe 10
recibir *v.* to receive 3
reciclaje *m.* recycling 13
reciclar *v.* to recycle 13
recién casado/a *m., f.* newlywed 9
recoger *v.* to pick up 13
recomendar (e:ie) *v.* to recommend 8
recordar (o:ue) *v.* to remember 4
recorrer *v.* to tour around an area 5
recurso *m.* resource 13
recurso natural *m.* natural resource 13
red *f.* network; Internet 11
reducir *v.* to reduce 13
refresco *m.* soft drink 8
refrigerador *m.* refrigerator 12
regalar *v.* to give (*as a gift*) 9
regalo *m.* gift; present 6
regatear *v.* to bargain 6
región *f.* region; area 13
regresar *v.* to return 2
regular *adj.* so so.; OK 1
reído *p.p.* laughed 14
reina *f.* queen 6
reírse (e:i) *v.* to laugh 9
relaciones *f., pl.* relationships 9
relajarse *v.* to relax 9
reloj *m.* clock; watch 2
renunciar (a) *v.* to resign (from) 16
repetir (e:i) *v.* to repeat 4
reportaje *m.* report 18
reportero/a *m., f.* reporter; journalist 16
reservación *f.* reservation 5
resfriado *m.* cold (*illness*) 10
residencia estudiantil *f.* dormitory 2
resolver (o:ue) *v.* to resolve; to solve 13
respirar *v.* to breathe 13
respuesta *f.* answer **5**
restaurante *m.* restaurant 4
resuelto *p.p.* resolved 14
reunión *f.* meeting 16
revisar *v.* to check 11
revisar el aceite *v.* to check the oil 11
revista *f.* magazine 4
rico/a *adj.* rich 6; *adj.* tasty; delicious 8
ridículo *adj.* ridiculous 13
río *m.* river 13
riquísima *adj.* extremely delicious 8
rodilla *f.* knee 10
rogar (o:ue) *v.* to beg; to plead 12
rojo/a *m., f.* red 6
romántico/a *adj.* romantic 17
romper (con) *v.* to break up (with) 9
romperse *v.* to break 10
romperse la pierna *v.* to break one's leg 10
ropa *f.* clothing; clothes 6
ropa interior *f.* underwear 6
rosado/a *adj.* pink 6
roto/a *adj.* broken 10
rubio/a *m., f.* blond(e) 3
rutina *f.* routine 7
rutina diaria *f.* daily routine 7

S

sábado *m.* Saturday 2
saber *v.* to know; to know how to 8
sabores *m.* flavors 1
sabrosísimo/a *adj.* extremely delicious 8
sabroso/a *adj.* tasty; delicious 8
sacar *v.* to take out 10
sacar fotos *v.* to take pictures 5
sacar la basura to take out the trash 12
sacar una muela to extract a tooth; to pull a tooth 10
sacudir *v.* to dust 12
sacudir los muebles dust the furniture **12**
sal *f.* salt 8
sala *f.* living room; room 12
sala de emergencia emergency room 10
salario *m.* salary 16
salchicha *f.* sausage 8
salida *f.* departure; exit 5
salir *v.* to leave; to go out 4
salir con to go out with; to date (*someone*) 9
salir de to leave from 4
salir para to leave for (*a place*) 4
salmón *m.* salmon 8
salón de belleza *m.* beauty; salon 14
salsa *f.* sauce 5
salud *f.* health 10

saludable *adj.* healthy 10
saludar(se) *v.* to greet (each other) 11
saludo *m.* greeting 1
saludos a... greetings to . . . 1
sandalia *f.* sandal 6
sándwich *m.* sandwich 8
sano/a *adj.* healthy 10
se *ref.pron.* himself, herself, itself, *form.* yourself, themselves, yourselves 7
se *impersonal* one 10
Se nos dañó... The . . . broke down on us. 11
Se hizo... He/she/it became . . . 5
Se nos pinchó una llanta. We had a flat tire. 11
secadora *f.* clothes dryer 12
sección de (no) fumar *f.* (no) smoking section 8
secretario/a *m., f.* secretary 16
secuencia *f.* sequence 7
sed *f.* thirst 3
seda *f.* silk 6
sedentario/a *adj.* sedentary; related to sitting 15
seguir (e:i) *v.* to follow; to continue 4
según according to 8
segundo/a *adj.* second 5
seguro/a *adj.* sure 5
seis six 1
seiscientos/as *adj.* six hundred 5
sello *m.* stamp 14
selva *f.* jungle 13
semáforo *m.* traffic signal 11
semana *f.* week 2
semana santa holy week 8
semestre *m.* semester 2
sendero *m.* trail; trailhead 13
sentarse (e:ie) *v.* to sit down 7
sentido *m.* sense 8
sentido del orden sense of the order 8
sentimental *adj.* sentimental 9
sentir(se) (e:ie) *v.* to be sorry; to regret 13
señor (Sr.) *m.* Mr.; sir 1
señora (Sra.) *f.* Mrs.; ma'am 1
señorita (Srta.) *f.* Miss 1
separarse (de) *v.* to separate (from) 9
septiembre *m.* September 5
séptimo/a *adj.* seventh 5
ser *v.* to be 1
ser aficionado/a (a) to be a fan (of) 4
ser alérgico/a (a) to be allergic (to) 10
ser gratis to be free of charge 14
serio/a *adj.* serious 3
servilleta *f.* napkin 12
servir (e:i) *v.* to serve; to help 5
sesenta sixty 2
setecientos/as *adj.* seven hundred 5
setenta seventy 2
sexismo *m.* sexism 18
sexto/a *adj.* sixth 5
sí *adv.* yes 1
si if 4
SIDA *m.* AIDS 18
sido *p.p.* been 15
siempre *adv.* always 7
siete seven 1
siglo *m.* century 6
silla *f.* seat 2
sillón *m.* armchair 12
simbolizar *v.* symbolize 8
similar *adj.* similar 7
simpático/a *adj.* nice; likeable 3
sin *prep.* without 15
sin duda whitout a dobut 6
sin embargo however 5
sin que *conj.* without 13
sino but 7
síntoma *m.* symptom 10
sitio *m.* Web; Web site 11
situado/a *p.p.* located 14
sobre *m.* envelope 14; *prep.* on; over 2
sobresaliente *adj.* outstanding 8
sobrino/a *m., f.* nephew; niece 3
sociología *f.* sociology 2
sofá *m.* couch; sofa 12
sol *m.* sun 4
solicitar *v.* to apply (*for a job*) 16
solicitud (de trabajo) *f.* (job) application 16
solo *adj.* alone 8
sólo *adv.* only 3
soltero/a *adj.* single; unmarried 9
solución *f.* solution 13
sombrero *m.* hat 6
son las... It's . . . o'clock 1
sonar (o:ue) *v.* to ring 11_
sonreído *p.p.* smiled 14
sonreír (e:i) *v.* to smile 9
sopa *f.* soup 8
sorprender *v.* to surprise 9
sorpresa *f.* surprise 9
sostener *v.* support 8
sótano *m.* basement; cellar 12
soy I am 1
Soy yo. That's me. 1
soy de... I'm from . . . 1
su(s) *poss.* his; her; *form.* your; their; 3
subir *v.* to go up; to get on/in (*a vehicle*) 11
subrayado *adj.* 8
sucio/a *adj.* dirty 5
sucre *m.* Ecuadorian currency 6
sudar *v.* to sweat 15
suegro/a *m., f.* father-in-law; mother-in-law 3
sueldo *m.* salary 16
suelo *m.* floor 12
sueño *n.* sleep 3
suerte *f.* luck 3
suéter *m.* sweater 6
sufrir *v.* to suffer 10
sufrir muchas presiones to be under a lot of pressure 15
sufrir una enfermedad to suffer an illness 10
sugerencia *f.* suggestion 8
sugerir (e:ie) *v.* to suggest 12
sumamente *adv.* extremely 5
supermercado *m.* supermarket 14
suponer *v.* to suppose; to assume 4
sur *m.* south 14
sustantivo *m.* noun 1
suyo/a(s) *poss.* (of) his, her, (of) hers, (of) its, *form.* your, (of) yours, their (of) 11
sentir *v.* to feel 7

T

tablero *m.* blackboard 2
tal vez *adv.* maybe 5
talentoso/a *adj.* talented 17
tales como such as 4
talla *f.* size 6
talla grande *f.* large 6
tallar *v.* to carve 6
taller *m.* workshop 11
taller de mecánica *m.* mechanic's workshop 11
también *adv.* also; too 2
tampoco *adv.* neither; not either 7
tan *adv.* so 8
tan pronto como as soon as 14
tan... como as . . . as 8
tanque *m.* tank 11
tanto *adv.* so much 12
tanto... como as much . . . as 8
tantos/as... como as many . . . as 8
tapices *m., pl.* tapestries 3
tarde *adv.* late 7
tarde *f.* afternoon; evening; P.M. 1
tarea *f.* homework 2
tarjeta *f.* card 4
tarjeta de crédito *f.* credit card 6
tarjeta postal *f.* postcard 4
taxi *m.* taxi(cab) 5
taza *f.* cup 12
te *fam.* you 6
Te presento a... *fam.* Let me introduce you to . . . 1
¿Te gustaría? Would you like to? 4
¿Te gusta(n)... ? Do you like . . . ? 2
té *m.* tea 8

té helado *m.* iced tea 8
teatro *m.* theater 17
teclado *m.* keyboard 11
técnico/a *m., f.* technician 16
tejido *m.* weaving 17
teleadicto/a *m., f.* couch potato 15
teléfono (celular) *m.* (cell) telephone 11
telenovela *f.* soap opera 17
teletrabajo *m.* telecommuting 16
televisión *f.* television 11
televisión por cable *f.* cable television 11
televisor *m.* television set 11
temer *v.* to fear 13
temperatura *f.* temperature 10
temprano *adj.* early 7
tenedor *m.* fork 12
tener *v.* to have 3
  tener calor to be hot 3
  tener cuidado to be careful 3
  tener dolor de to have a pain in 10
  tener éxito to be successful 16
  tener fiebre to have a fever 10
  tener frío to be cold 3
  tener ganas de (+ *inf.*) to feel like (*doing something*) 3
  tener hambre *f.* to be hungry 3
  tener miedo de to be afraid of; scared of 3
  tener miedo (de) que to be afraid that 13
  tener planes *m., pl.* to have plans 4
  tener prisa to be in a hurry 3
  tener que (+ *inf.*) *v.* to have to (*do something*) 3
  tener razón *f.* to be right 3
  tener sed *f.* to be thirsty 3
  tener sueño *v.* to be sleepy 3
  tener suerte to be lucky 3
  tener una cita to have a date, an appointment 9
  tener... años to be . . . years old 3
  tengo I have 3
  Tengo... años. I'm . . . years old. 3
tenis *m.* tennis 4
tensión *f.* tension 15
tercero/a *adj.* third 5
terminar *v.* to end; to finish 2
  terminar de (+*inf.*) *v.* to finish (*doing something*) 4
terremoto *m.* earthquake 18
terrible *adj.* terrible 13
tesoro *m.* treasure 3
ti *obj. of prep., fam.* you 8
tiempo *m.* time; weather 4
tiempo libre free time 4
tienda *f.* shop; store 6
tienda *f.* tent 5
  tienda de campaña tent 5
tierra *f.* land; soil 13
tinto *m.* red (wine) 8
tío/a *m., f.* uncle; aunt 3
tíos *m.* aunts and uncles 3
título *m.* title 1
tiza *f.* chalk 2
toalla *f.* towel 7
tobillo *m.* ankle 10
tocadiscos compacto *m.* compact-disk player 11
tocar *v.* to play (*a musical instrument*) 17
tocar *v.* to touch 13
todavía *adv.* yet; still 5
todo *m.* everything 5
  todo el mundo the whole world; all over the world 13
  Todo está bajo control. Everything is under control. 7
  (todo) derecho straight ahead 14
  ¡Todos a bordo! All aboard! 1
todo/a *adj.* whole; all 4
todos *m., pl.* all of us 1
todos *m., pl.* everybody; everyone 13
todos los días every day 10
tomar *v.* to take; to drink 2
  tomar clases *f., pl.* to take classes 2
  tomar el sol to sunbathe 4
  tomar en cuenta take into account 8
  tomar fotos *f., pl.* to take photos 5
  tomar la temperatura to take someone's temperature 10
tomate *m.* tomato 8
tonto/a *adj.* silly; foolish 3
torcerse (el tobillo) *v.* to sprain (one's ankle) 10
torcido/a *adj.* twisted; sprained 10
tormenta *f.* storm 18
tornado *m.* tornado 18
tortilla *f.* kind of flat bread 8
  tortillas de maíz flat bread made of corn flour 8
tortuga *f.* turtle 3
tos *f., sing.* cough 10
toser *v.* to cough 10
tostado/a *adj.* toasted 8
tostadora *f.* toaster 12
trabajador(a) *m., f.* hard-working 3
trabajar *v.* to work 2
trabajo *m.* job; work; written work 16
traducir *v.* to translate 8
traer *v.* to bring 4
tragedia *f.* tragedy 17
traído *p.p.* brought 14
traje *m.* suit 6
  traje de baño *m.* bathing suit 6
tranquilo/a *adj.* calm; quiet 15
  ¡Tranquilo! Stay calm! 7
transmitir to broadcast 18
tratar de (+ *inf.*) *v.* to try to (*do something*) 15
trato *m.* deal 17
  Trato hecho. It's a deal. 17
trece thirteen 1
treinta thirty 1
tren *m.* train 5
tres three 1
trescientos/as *adj.* three hundred 5
trimestre *m.* trimester; quarter 2
triste *adj.* sad 5
trozo *m.* slice 1
tú *fam. pron.* you 1
  Tú eres... You are . . . 1
tu(s) *fam. poss.* your 3
turismo *m.* tourism 5
turista *m., f.* tourist 1
turístico/a *adj.* touristic 5
turno *m.* turn 9
tuyo/a(s) *fam.poss.* your; (of) yours 11

U

Ud. *form. sing.* you 1
Uds. *form., pl.* you 8
último/a *adj.* last 15
un, uno/a *art.* a; one 1
  una vez más one more time 9
  una vez once; one time 6
único/a *adj.* only 3
unido/a *adj.* close 3
universidad *f.* university; college 2
unos/as *pron.* some 1
urgente *adj.* urgent 12
usar *v.* to wear; to use 6
usted *form. sing.* you 1
  ustedes *form., pl.* you 1
utensilio *m.* utensil 12
útil *adj.* useful 1
uva *f.* grape 8

V

vaca *f.* cow 13
vacaciones *f. pl.* vacation 5
valer la pena to be worthy 8
valle *m.* valley 13
vamos let's go 4
vaquero *m.* cowboy 17
varios/as *pron.* various 8
vaso *m.* glass 12
veces *f., pl.* times 4
vecino/a *m., f.* neighbor 12
veinte twenty 1

veinticinco twenty-five 1
veinticuatro twenty-four 1
veintidós twenty-two 1
veintinueve twenty-nine 1
veintiocho twenty-eight 1
veintiséis twenty-six 1
veintisiete twenty-seven 1
veintitrés twenty-three 1
veintiún, veintiuno/a *adj.* twenty-one 1
vejez *f.* old age 9
velocidad *f.* speed 11
  velocidad máxima *f.* speed limit 11
vendedor(a) *m., f.* salesperson 6
vender *v.* to sell 6
venido *p.p.* come; arrived 15
venir *v.* to come 3
ventana *f.* window 2
ver *v.* to see 4
ver películas *f., pl.* to see movies 4
verano *m.* summer 5
verbo *m.* verb 2
verdad *f.* truth 13
  ¿verdad? right? 1
verdadero *adj.* true 1
verde *m.* green 6
verduras *pl., f.* vegetables 8
vestido *m.* dress 6
vestirse (e:i) *v.* to get dressed 7
vez *f.* time 6
viajar *v.* to travel 2
viaje *m.* trip 5
viajero/a *m., f.* traveler 5
vida *f.* life 9
video(casete) *m.* video (cassette) 11
videocasetera *f.* VCR 11
videoconferencia *f.* teleconference; video conference 16
vidrio *m.* glass 13
viejo/a *adj.* old 3
viento *m.* wind 4
viernes *m., sing.* Friday 2
vinagre *m.* vinegar 8
vino *m.* wine 8
  vino blanco *m.* white wine 8
  vino tinto *m.* red wine 8
violencia *f.* violence 18
visitar *v.* to visit 4
  visitar monumentos *m., pl.* to visit monuments 4
visto/a *p.p.* seen 15
vitamina *f.* vitamin 15
viudo/a *adj.* widowed 9
vivienda *f.* housing 12
vivir *v.* to live 3
vivo/a *adj.* bright; lively; living 4
volante *m.* steering wheel 11
volcán *m.* volcano 13
voleibol *m.* volleyball 4
volver (o:ue) *v.* to return 4
volver a ver(te, lo, la) *v.* to see (you) again 18
vos *pron.* you 1
vosotros/as *form., pl.* you 1
votar *v.* to vote 18
vuelta *f.* return trip 5
vuelto *p.p.* returned 14
vuestro/a(s) *poss.* your 3

W

walkman *m.* Walkman 11

Y

y and 1
  y cuarto quarter after (time) 1
  y media half-past (time) 1
  y quince quarter after (time) 1
  y treinta thirty (minutes past the hour) 1
  ¿Y tú? *fam.* And you? 1
  ¿Y Ud.? *form.* And you? 1
ya *adv.* already 6
yerno *m.* son-in-law 3
yo *pron.* I 1
  Yo soy... I'm . . . 1
yogur *m.* yogurt 8

Z

zanahoria *f.* carrot 8
zapatería *f.* shoe store 14
zapatillas de deportes *f.* tennis shoes 6
zapatos (de tenis) *m., pl.* (tennis) shoes 6

English-Spanish

A

A.M. **mañana** *f.*1
able: be able to **poder (o:ue)** *v.* 4
aboard **a bordo** 1
accident **accidente** *m.* 10
accompany **acompañar** *v.* 14
according to **de acuerdo a** 4; **según** 8
account **cuenta** *f.*14
accountant **contador(a)** *m., f.* 16
accounting **contabilidad** *f.*2
ache **dolor** *m.* 10
acid **ácido/a** *adj.* 13
  acid rain **lluvia ácida** 13
acquainted: be acquainted with **conocer** *v.* 8
action **acción** *f.* 17
active **activo/a** *adj.* 15
actor **actor** *m.*, **actriz** *f.* 16
addict (*drug*) **drogadicto/a** *adj.* 15
additional **adicional** 2
address **dirección** *f.* 14
adjective **adjetivo** *m.* 3
adolescence **adolescencia** *f.* 9
adventure **aventura** *f.* 17
advertise **anunciar** *v.* 18
advertisement **anuncio** *m.* 16
advice **consejo** *m.* 9
  give advice **dar un consejo** 9
advise **aconsejar** *v.* 12
advisor **consejero/a** *m., f.* 16
aerobic **aeróbico/a** *adj.* 15
  aerobic exercises **ejercicios aeróbicos** 15
  aerobics class **clase de ejercicios aeróbicos** 15
affected **afectado/a** *adj.* 13
  be affected by **estar afectado/a por** 13
affirmative **afirmativo/a** *adj.* 7
afraid: be afraid (of) **tener miedo (de)** 3
  be afraid that **tener miedo (de) que** 13
after **después de** *prep.* 7
afternoon **tarde** *f.* 1
afterward **después** *adv.* 7; **luego** *adv.*7
again **otra vez** 15
age **edad** *f.* 8
agree **concordar** *v.* 8
agree **estar de acuerdo** 16
agreement **acuerdo** *m.* 16
agricultural **agrícola** *adj.* 6
AIDS **SIDA** *m.* 18
air **aire** *m.* 13
air pollution **contaminación del aire** 13
airplane **avión** *m.* 5
airport **aeropuerto** *m.* 5
alarm clock **despertador** *m.* 7
alcohol **alcohol** *m.* 15
alcoholic **alcohólico/a** *adj.* 15
all **todo/a** *adj.* 4
  All aboard! **¡Todos a bordo!** 1
  all of us *m., pl.* **todos** 1
  all over the world **en todo el mundo** 13
allergic **alérgico/a** *adj.* 10
  be allergic (to) **ser alérgico/a (a)** 10
alleviate **aliviar** *v.* 15
almost **casi** *adv.* 10
alone **solo/a** *adj.* 8
along **por** *prep.* 11
already **ya** *adv.* 6
also **también** *adv.* 2
alternator **alternador** *m.* 11
although **aunque** 3
aluminum **aluminio** *m.* 13
  made of aluminum **de aluminio** 13
always **siempre** *adv.*7
American (*North*) **norteamericano/a** *adj.* 3
among **entre** *prep.* 2
and **y** 1, **e** (*before words beginning with i or hi*) 4
  And you?**¿Y tú?** *fam.* 1; **¿Y Ud.?** *form.* 1
angry **enojado/a** *adj.* 5
  get angry (with) **enojarse** *v.* **(con)** 7
animal **animal** *m.* 13
ankle **tobillo** *m.* 10
anniversary **aniversario** *m.* 9
  (wedding) anniversary **aniversario** *m.* **(de bodas)** 9
announce **anunciar** *v.* 18
announcer (*TV/radio*) **locutor(a)** *m., f.* 18
annoy **molestar** *v.* 7
another **otro/a** *adj.* 6
answer **contestar** *v.* 2; **respuesta** *f.* 5
answering machine **contestadora** *f.* 11
antibiotic **antibiótico** *m.* 10
any **algún, alguno/a(s)** *adj.* 7
anyone **alguien** *pron.* 7
anything **algo** *pron.* 7
apartment **apartamento** *m.*12
apartment building **casa de apartamentos** 12
appear **parecer** *v.* 8
appetizers **entremeses** *m., pl.* 8
applaud **aplaudir** *v.* 17
apple **manzana** *f.* 8
appliance **aparato** *m.* 12
application **solicitud** *f.* 16
  job application **solicitud de trabajo** 16
apply (*for a job*) **solicitar** *v.* 16
  apply for a loan **pedir** *v.* **préstamo** 14
appointment **cita** *f.* 9
  have an appointment **tener una cita** 9
appreciate **apreciar** *v.* 17
April **abril** *m.* 5
aquatic **acuático/a** *adj.* 4
archaeologist **arqueólogo/a** *m., f.* 16
architect **arquitecto/a** *m., f.* 16
area **región** *f.* 13
arm **brazo** *m.* 10
armchair **sillón** *m.* 12
army **ejército** *m.* 18
around here **por aquí** 11
arrival **llegada** *f.* 5
arrive **llegar** *v.* 2
art **arte** *m.* 2
  fine arts **bellas artes** *f., pl.* 17
article *m.* **artículo** 18
artist **artista** *m., f.* 3
artistic **artístico/a** *adj.* 17
arts **artes** *f., pl.* 17
as **como** 8
  as . . . as **tan... como** 8
  as a child **de niño** 10
  as many . . . as **tantos/as... como** 8
  as much . . . as **tanto... como** 8
  as soon as **en cuanto** 14; **tan pronto como** 14
ask (*a question*) *v.* **preguntar** 2
  ask for **pedir (e:i)** *v.* 4
asparagus **espárragos** *m., pl.* 8
aspirin **aspirina** *f.* 10
assume **suponer** *v.* 4
at **a** *prep.* 1
  at + *time* **a la(s)** + *time* 1
  at home **en casa** 7
  at least **por lo menos** 10
  at night **por la noche** 7
  at the end (of) **al fondo (de)** 12
  At what time . . . ? **¿A qué hora...?** 1
  At your service. **A sus órdenes.** 11
attend **asistir (a)** *v.* 3
attic **altillo** *m.* 12
attract **atraer** *v.* 4
audience **público** *m.* 17
August **agosto** *m.* 5
aunt **tía** *f.* 3
  aunts and uncles **tíos** *m.* 3
automatic **automático/a** *adj.* 14
  automatic teller machine (ATM) **cajero automático** 14
automobile **automóvil** *m.* 5; *m.* **carro** 11
autumn **otoño** *m.* 5
avenue **avenida** *f.* 11
avoid **evitar** *v.* 13
award **premio** *m.* 17
ax **hacha** *f.* 1

B

backpack **mochila** *f.* 2
bad **mal, malo/a** *adj.* 8
It's bad that . . . **Es malo que...** 12
It's not at all bad. **No está nada mal.** 5
bag **bolsa** *f.* 6
bakery **panadería** *f.* 14
balanced **equilibrado/a** *adj.* 15
balanced diet **dieta equilibrada** 15
balcony **balcón** *m.*12
ball **pelota** *f.* 4
ballet **ballet** *m.* 17
banana **banana** *f.* 8
band **banda** *f.* 17
bank **banco** *m.* 14
bargain **ganga** *f.* 6; **regatear** *v.* 6
baseball **pelota** *f.*4; (*game*) **béisbol** *m.*4
basement **sótano** *m.* 12
basketball (*game*) **baloncesto** *m.*4
bathe **bañarse** *v.* 7
bathing suit **traje** *m.***de baño** 6
bathroom **baño** *m.*7; **cuarto de baño** *m.* 7
bay **bahía** *f.* 5
be . . . years old **tener... años** 3
be **ser** *v.* 1; **estar** *v.* 2
beach **playa** *f.* 5
beak **pico** *m.* 6
beans **frijoles** *m., pl.* 8
beautiful **hermoso/a** *adj.* 6
beauty **belleza** *f.* 14
beauty salon **peluquería** *f.* 14; **salón** *m.***de belleza** 14
because **porque** *conj.* 2
because of **por** *prep.* 11
become (+ *adj.*) **ponerse (+ *adj.*)** 7; **convertirse** *v.* 6
bed **cama** *f.* 5
go to bed **acostarse (o:ue)** *v.* 7
bedroom **alcoba** *f.* 12; **recámara** *f.* 12; **cuarto** *m.* 12
bee **abeja** *f.* 6
beef **carne de res** *f.* 8
beef soup **caldo de patas** 8
been **sido** *p.p.* 15
beer **cerveza** *f* .8
before **antes** *adv.* 7; **antes de** *prep.* 7; **antes (de) que** *conj.* 13
beg **rogar (o:ue)** *v.* 12
begin **comenzar (e:ie)** *v.* 4; **empezar (e:ie)** *v.* 4
behalf: on behalf of **de parte de** 11
behind **detrás de** *prep.* 2
believe (in) **creer** *v.* **(en)** 3
bellhop **botones** *m., sing.* 5
beloved **enamorado/a** *adj.* 5
beloved **querido/a** *adj.* 17
below **debajo de** *prep.* 2
belt **correa** *m.* 6; **cinturón** *m.* 6
benefit **beneficio** *m.* 16
beside **al lado de** *prep.* 2
best **mejor** *adj.* 8
the best **el/la mejor** *m., f.* 8 **lo mejor** *neuter* 18
better **mejor** *adj.* 8
It's better that . . . **Es mejor que...** 12
between **entre** *prep.* 2
bicycle **bicicleta** *f.* 4
big **gran, grande** *adj.* 3
bill **cuenta** *f.* 14
billion: a billion (of) **millones (de)** 5
biology **biología** *f* . 2
bird **ave** *f.* 13; **pájaro** *m.* 13
birth **nacimiento** *m.* 9
birthday **cumpleaños** *m., sing.* 9
birthday cake **pastel de cumpleaños** 9
have a birthday **cumplir** *v.* **años** 9
black **negro/a** *adj.* 6
blackberry **mora** *f.* 8
blackboard **pizarra** *f.* 2
blanket **manta** *f.* 12
block (city) **cuadra** *f.* 14
blond(e) **rubio/a** *adj.* 3
blouse **blusa** *f.* 6
blue **azul** *adj.* 6
boardinghouse **pensión** *f.* 5
body **cuerpo** *m.* 10
bone **hueso** *m.* 10
book **libro** *m.* 2
bookcase **estante** *m.* 12
bookstore **librería** *f.* 2
boot **bota** *f.* 6
bore **aburrir** *v.* 7
bored **aburrido/a** *adj.* 5
be bored **estar aburrido/a** 5
get bored **aburrirse** *v.* 17
boring **aburrido/a** *adj.* 5
born: be born **nacer** *v.* 9
borrow **pedir prestado** 14
borrowed **prestado/a** *adj.* 14
boss **jefe** *m.*, **jefa** *f.* 16
bottle **botella** *f.* 9
bottle of wine **botella de vino** 9
bother **molestar** *v.* 7
bottom **fondo** *m.* 12
boulevard **bulevar** *m.* 11
boy **chico** *m.* 1; **muchacho** *m.* 3
boyfriend **novio** *m.* 3
brakes **frenos** *m., pl.* 11
bread **pan** *m.* 8
break **romperse** *v.* 10
break a leg **romperse la pierna** 10
break down: The . . . broke down on us. **Se nos dañó el/la...** 11
break up (with) **romper** *v.* **(con)** 9
breakfast **desayuno** *m.* 8
have breakfast **desayunar** *v.* 8
breathe **respirar** *v.* 13
bridge **puente** *m.* 2
bright **vivo/a** *adj.* 4
bring **traer** *v.* 4
broadcast **transmitir** *v.* 18; **emitir** *v.* 18
brochure **folleto** *m.* 5
broken **roto/a** *adj.* 10
be broken **estar roto/a** 10
brother **hermano** *m.* 3
brother-in-law **cuñado** *m., f.* 3
brothers and sisters **hermanos** *m., pl.* 3
brought **traído** *p.p.* 14
brown **café** *adj.* 6; **marrón** *adj.*6
brunet(te) **moreno/a** *adj.* 3
brush **cepillar** *v.* 7
brush one's hair **cepillarse el pelo** 7
brush one's teeth **cepillarse los dientes** 7
build **construir** *v.* 4
building **edificio** *m.* 14
bullfight **corrida** *f.* **de toros** 4
bump into (*meet accidentally*) **darse con** 10
burned (out) **quemado/a** *adj.* 11
bus **autobús** *m.* 1
bus station **estación** *f.* **de autobuses** 5
business **negocios** *m. pl.* 16
business administration **administración** *f.* **de empresas** 2
business-related **comercial** *adj.* 16
businessman **hombre** *m.* **de negocios** 16
businesswoman **mujer** *f.* **de negocios** 16
busy **ocupado/a** *adj.* 5
but **pero** *conj.* 2; **sino** *conj.* (*in negative sentences*) 7
butcher shop **carnicería** *f.* 14
butter **mantequilla** *f.* 8
buy **comprar** *v.* 2
by **por** *conj.* 11
by phone **por teléfono** 7
by plane **en avión** 5
bye **chau** *fam.* 1

C

cabin **cabaña** *f.* 5
cable **cable** *m.* 11
cable television **televisión** *f.* **por cable** 11
café **café** *m.* 4
cafeteria **cafetería** *f.* 2
cake **pastel** *m.* 9
calculator **calculadora** *f.* 11
call **llamar** *v.* 7

call on the phone **llamar por teléfono** 11
be called **llamarse** *v.* 7
calm **tranquilo/a** *adj.* 15
Stay calm! **¡Tranquilo!** *adj.* 7
calorie **caloría** *f.* 15
camera **cámara** *f.* 11
camp **acampar** *v.* 5
can **lata** *f.* 13
can **poder (o:ue)** *v.* 4
Canadian **canadiense** *adj.* 3
candidate **aspirante** *m. f.* 16; candidate **candidato/a** *m., f.* 18
candy **dulces** *m., pl.* 9
cane **caña** *f.* 6
capital (city) **capital** *f.* 1
car **coche** *m.* 11; **carro** *m.* 11; **automóvil** *m.* 11
card **tarjeta** *f.* 4; (*playing*) **carta** *f.* 5
care **cuidado** *m.* 3
take care of **cuidar** *v.* 13
career **carrera** *f.* 16
careful: be careful **tener cuidado** 3
carpenter **carpintero/a** *m., f.* 16
carpet **alfombra** *f.* 12
carrot **zanahoria** *f.* 8
carry **llevar** *v.* 2
cartoons **dibujos** *m, pl.* **animados** 17
carve **tallar** *v.* 6
case: in case (that) **en caso (de) que** 13
cash (a check) **cobrar** *v.* 14; **efectivo** *m.* 14
cash register **caja** *f.* 6
pay in cash **pagar al contado** 14; **pagar en efectivo** 14
cashier **cajero/a** *m., f.* 14
cat **gato/a** *m., f.* 13
celebrate **celebrar** *v.* 9
cellar **sótano** *m.* 12
cellular **celular** *adj.* 11
cellular telephone **teléfono celular** *m.* 11
century **siglo** *m.* 2
cereal **cereales** *m., pl.* 8
certain **cierto** *m.* 13
chalk **tiza** *f.* 2
change **cambiar** *v.* **(de)** 9
channel (*TV*) **cadena** *f.* 17; **canal** *m.* 11
character (*fictional*) **personaje** *m.* 17
main character *m.* **personaje principal** 17
chauffeur **conductor(a)** *m., f.* 1
cheap **barato/a** *adj.* 6
check. **comprobar** *v.* 8; **revisar** *v.* 11; (*bank*) **cheque** *m.* 14
check the oil **revisar el aceite** 11
checking account **cuenta** *f.* **corriente** 14
cheese **queso** *m.* 8
chef **cocinero/a** *m., f.* 16
chemistry **química** *f.* 2
chest of drawers **cómoda** *f.* 12
chewing gum **chicle** *m.* 6
chicken **pollo** *m.* 8
child **niño/a** *m., f.* 3
childhood **niñez** *f.* 9
children **hijos** *m., pl.* 3
Chinese **chino/a** *adj.* 3
chocolate **chocolate** *m.* 9
chocolate cake **pastel** *m.* **de chocolate** 9
cholesterol **colesterol** *m.* 15
choose **escoger** *v.* 8
chop (*food*) **chuleta** *f.* 8
Christmas **Navidad** *f.* 9
citizen **ciudadano/a** *adj.* 18
city **ciudad** *f.* 4
class **clase** *f.* 2
take classes **tomar clases** 2
classical **clásico/a** *adj.* 17
classmate **compañero/a** *m., f.* **de clase** 2
clean **limpio/a** *adj.* 5; **limpiar** *v.* 12
clean the house *v.* **limpiar la casa** 12
clear (*weather*) **despejado/a** *adj.* 4
clear the table **quitar la mesa** 12
It's (very) clear. (*weather*) **Está (muy) despejado.** 4
clerk **dependiente/a** *m., f.* 6
climb **escalar** *v.* 4
climb mountains **escalar montañas** 4
clinic **clínica** *f.* 10
clock **reloj** *m.* 2
close **cerrar (e:ie)** *v.* 4
close **unido/a** *adj.* 3
closed **cerrado/a** *adj.* 5
closet **armario** *m.* 12
clothes **ropa** *f.* 6
clothes dryer **secadora** *f.* 12
cloud **nube** *f.* 13
cloudy **nublado/a** *adj.* 4
It's (very) cloudy. **Está (muy) nublado.** 4
coat **abrigo** *m.* 6
coffee **café** *m.* 8
coffee maker **cafetera** *f.* 12
cold **frío** *m.* 4; (*disease*) **catarro** *m.* 10; **resfriado** *m.* 10
be (*feel*) cold **tener frío** 3
It's cold. (*weather*) **Hace frío.** 4
college **universidad** *f.* 2
collision **choque** *m.* 18
color **color** *m.* 6
comb one's hair **peinarse** *v.* 7
come **venir** *v.* 3
comedy **comedia** *f.* 17.
comfortable **cómodo/a** *adj.* 5
commerce **negocios** *m., pl.* 16
commercial **comercial** *adj.* 16
common **común** *adj.*2
communicate (with) **comunicarse** *v.* **(con)** 18
communication **comunicación** *f.* 18
means of communication **medios** *m. pl.* **de comunicación** 18
compact disc (CD) **disco** *m.* **compacto** 11
compact disk player **tocadiscos** *m. sing.* **compacto** 11
company **compañía** *f.* 16; **empresa** *f.* 16
comparison **comparación** *f.* 8
compete **competir** *v.* 4
completely **completamente** *adv.* 16
complex **complejo** *adj.* 8
composer **compositor(a)** *m., f.* 17
computer **computadora** *f.* 1
computer disk **disco** *m.* 11
computer monitor **monitor** *m.* 11
computer science **computación** *f.* 2
concert **concierto** *m.* 17
conditioned **acondicionado** *adj.* 5
conductor (*musical*) **director(a)** *m., f.* 17
confirm **confirmar** *v.* 5
confirm the reservation **confirmar la reservación** 5
congested **congestionado/a** *adj.* 10
Congratulations! (*for an event such as a birthday or anniversary*) **¡Felicidades!** 9; (*for an event such as an engagement or a good grade on a test*) *f., pl.* **¡Felicitaciones!** 9
conserve **conservar** *v.* 13
consume **consumir** *v.* 15
contact lenses **lentes** *m. pl.* **de contacto** 6
container **envase** *m.* 13
contamination **contaminación** *f.* 4
content **contento/a** *adj.* 5
contest **concurso** *m.* 17
continue **seguir (e:i)** *v.* 4
control **control** *m.* 7; control **controlar** *v.* 13
be under control **estar bajo control** 7
cook **cocinar** *v.* 12; **cocinero/a** *m., f.* 16
cookie **galleta** *f.* 9
cool **fresco/a** *adj.* 4
It's cool. (*weather*) **Hace fresco.** 4
corn **maíz** *m.* 5

corner **esquina** *m.* 14
cost **costar (o:ue)** *v.* 6
cotton **algodón** *m.* 6
made of cotton **de algoldón** 6
couch potato **teleadicto/a** *m., f.* 15
couch **sofá** *m.* 12
cough **tos** *f.* 10; cough **toser** *v.* 10
counselor **consejero/a** *m., f.* 16
count (on) **contar** *v.* **(con)** 12
country (*nation*) **país** *m.* 1
countryside **campo** *m.* 5; **paisaje** *m.* 5
couple: a couple of days **un par de días** 10
course **curso** *m.* 2; course **materia** *f.* 2
court **corte** *f.* 2
courtesy **cortesía** *f.* 1
cousin **primo/a** *m., f.* 3
cover **cubrir** *v.* 14
covered **cubierto** *p.p.* 14
cow **vaca** *f.* 13
cowboy **vaquero** *m.* 17
crafts **artesanía** *f.* 17
craftsmanship **artesanía** *f.* 17
crater **cráter** *m.* 13
crazy **loco/a** *adj.* 6
create **crear** *v.* 4
credit **crédito** *m.* 6
credit card **tarjeta** *f.* **de crédito** 6
cricket **grillo** *m.* 4
crime **crimen** *m.* 18
cross **cruzar** *v.* 14
culture **cultura** *f.* 17
cup **taza** *f.* 12
currency exchange **cambio de moneda** 8
current events **actualidades** *f., pl.* 18
curriculum vitae **currículum** *m.* 16
curtains **cortinas** *f., pl.* 12
custard (*baked*) **flan** *m.* 9
custom **costumbre** *f.* 1
customer **cliente** *m., f.* 6
customs **aduana** *f.* 5
customs inspector **inspector(a)** *m., f.* **de aduanas** 5
cycling **ciclismo** *m.* 4

D

dad **papá** *m.* 3
daily **diario/a** *adj.* 7
daily routine **rutina** *f.* **diaria** 7
damage **dañar** *v.* 11
dance **bailar** *v.* 2; **danza** *f.* 17; **baile** *m.* 17
dancer **bailarín/bailarina** *m. f.* 17
danger **peligro** *m.* 13
dangerous **peligroso/a** *adj.* 18
date (*appointment*) **cita** *f.* 9; (*calendar*) **fecha** *f.* 5; (*someone*) **salir** *v.* **con (alguien)** 9
date: have a date **tener una cita** 9
daughter **hija** *f.* 3
daughter-in-law **nuera** *f.* 3
day **día** *m.* 1
day before yesterday *adv.* **anteayer** 6
deal **trato** *m.* 17
It's a deal. **Trato hecho.** 17
It's no big deal. **No es para tanto.** 12
death **muerte** *f.* 9
decaffeinated **descafeinado/a** *adj.* 15
December **diciembre** *m.* 5
decide **decidir** *v.* 3
decided **decidido/a** *adj.* 14
declare **declarar** *v.* 18
deforestation **deforestación** *f.* 13
delicious **delicioso/a** *adj.* 8; **rico/a** *adj.* 8; **sabroso/a** *adj.* 8
delighted **encantado/a** *adj.* 1
dentist **dentista** *m., f.* 10
deny **negar (e: ie)** *v.* 13
department store **almacén** *m.* 6
departure **salida** *f.* 5
deposit **depositar** *v.* 14
describe **describir** *v.* 18
desert **desierto** *m.* 13
design **diseño** *m.*3
designer **diseñador(a)** *m., f.* 16
desk **escritorio** *m.*2
dessert **postre** *m.* 9
destroy **destruir** *v.* 13
determined **condicionado** *adj.* 4
develop **desarrollar** *v.* 13
diary **diario** *m.* 1
dictatorship **dictadura** *f.* 18
dictionary **diccionario** *m.* 1
die **morir (o:ue)** *v.* 8
died **muerto** *p.p.* 14
diet **dieta** *f.* 15
be on a diet **estar a dieta** 15
difficult **difícil** *adj.* 3
dining room **comedor** *m.* 12
dinner **cena** *f.* 8
have dinner **cenar** *v.* 8
directions **direcciones** *f., pl.* 14
give directions **dar direcciones** 14
director **director(a)** *m., f.* 17
dirty **ensuciar** *v.* 12; **sucio/a** *adj.* 5
get dirty **ensuciar** *v.* 12
disagree **no estar de acuerdo** 16
discover **descubrir** *v.* 13
discovered **descubierto** *p.p.* 14
discrimination **discriminación** *f.* 18
dish **plato** *m.* 8
main dish *m.* **plato principal** 8
dishwasher **lavaplatos** *m., sing.* 12
disk **disco** *m.* 11
disorderly **desordenado/a** *adj.* 5
dive **bucear** *v.* 4
divorce **divorcio** *m.* 9
divorced **divorciado/a** *adj.* 9
get divorced (from) **divorciarse** *v.* **(de)** 9
dizzy **mareado/a** *adj.* 10
do **hacer** *v.* 4
do aerobics **hacer ejercicios aeróbicos** 15
do errands **hacer diligencias** 14
do household chores **hacer quehaceres domésticos** 12
do stretching exercises **hacer ejercicios de estiramiento** 15
doctor **doctor(a)** *m., f.* 10; **médico/a** *m., f.* 3
documentary (*film*) **documental** *m.* 17
dog **perro/a** *m., f.* 13
domestic **doméstico/a** *adj.* 18
domestic appliance **aparato** *m.* **doméstico** 12
dominate **dominar** *v.* 4
done **hecho** *p.p.* 14
door **puerta** *f.* 2
dormitory **residencia** *f.* **estudiantil** 2
double **doble** *adj.* 5
double room **habitación** *f.* **doble** 5
doubt **duda** *f.* 13; **dudar** *v.* 13
There is no doubt that . . . **No cabe duda que...** 13; **No hay duda que...** 13
Down with . . . ! **¡Abajo el/la...!** 15
downtown **centro** *m.* 4
drama **drama** *m.* 17
dramatic **dramático/a** *adj.* 17
draw **dibujar** *v.* 2
drawing **dibujo** *m.* 17
dress **vestido** *m.* 6
get dressed **vestirse (e:i)** *v.* 7
drink **beber** *v.* 3; **bebida** *f.*8; **tomar** *v.* 2
Do you want something to drink? **¿Quieres algo de tomar?** 8
drive **conducir** *v.* 8; **manejar** *v.* 11
driver **conductor(a)** *m., f.* 1
drug *f.* **droga** 15
drug addict **drogadicto/a** *adj.* 15
due to **por** *prep.* 11
due to the fact that **debido a** 3
dungeon **mazmorra** *f.* 5
during **durante** *prep.* 7; **por** *prep.* 11

dust **sacudir** *v.* 12
dust the furniture **sacudir los muebles** 12
dying: I'm dying to (for) . . . **me muero por...** 1

E

each **cada** *adj.* 6
eagle **águila** *f.* 1
ear **oreja** *f.* 10
early **temprano** *adj.* 7
earn **ganar** *v.* 16
earthquake **terremoto** *m.* 18
ease **aliviar** *v.* 15
east **este** *m.* 14
to the east **al este** 14
easy **fácil** *adj.* 3
eat **comer** *v.* 3
ecology **ecología** *f.* 13
economics **economía** *f.* 2
ecotourism **ecoturismo** *m.* 13
Ecuadorian **ecuatoriano/a** *adj.* 3
effective **eficaz** *adj.* 8
egg **huevo** *m.* 8
eight hundred **ochocientos/as** 5
eight **ocho** 1
eighteen **dieciocho** 1
eighth **octavo/a** 5
eighty **ochenta** 2
either . . . or **o... o** *conj.* 7
elect **elegir** *v.* 18
election **elección** *f.* 18
electrician **electricista** *m., f.* 16
electricity **luz** *f.* 12
elegant **elegante** *adj.* 6
elevator **ascensor** *m.* 5
eleven **once** 1
e-mail **correo** *m.* **electrónico** 4
e-mail message **mensaje** *m.* **electrónico** 4
read e-mail **leer el correo electrónico** 4
embarrassed **avergonzado/a** *adj.* 5
embrace (each other) **abrazar(se)** *v.* 11
emergency **emergencia** *f.* 10
emergency room **sala** *f.* **de emergencia** 10
empire **imperio** *m.*6
employee **empleado/a** *m., f.* 5
employment **empleo** *m.* 16
end **fin** *m.* 4; **terminar** *v.* 2
end table **mesita** *f.*12
energy **energía** *f.*13
engaged: get engaged (to) **comprometerse** *v.* **(con)** 9
engineer **ingeniero/a** *m., f.* 3
English (*language*) **inglés** *m.*2; **inglés, inglesa** *adj.*3
enjoy **disfrutar** *v.* **(de)** 15
enough **bastante** *adj.* 10
entrance **entrada** *f.* 12
envelope **sobre** *m.*14
environment **medio ambiente** *m.* 13
equality **igualdad** *f.* 18
equipped **equipado/a** *adj.* 15
eraser **borrador** *m.* 2
errand *f.* **diligencia** 14
establish **establecer** *v.* 16
evening **tarde** *f.* 1
event **acontecimiento** *m.* 18
every day **todos los días** 10
everybody **todos** *m., pl.* 13
everything **todo** *m.* 5
Everything is under control. **Todo está bajo control.** 7
evidence **indicio** *m.* 5
evolve **evolucionar** *v.* 3
exactly **en punto** 1
exam **examen** *m.* 2
excellent **excelente** *adj.* 5
excess **exceso** *m.* 15
in excess **en exceso** 15
exchange **intercambiar** *v.* 8
in exchange for **por** 11
exciting **emocionante** *f.* 15
excursion **excursión** *f.* 4
excuse **disculpar** *v.* 8
Excuse me. (*May I?*) **Con permiso.** 1; (*I beg your pardon.*) **Perdón.** 1
exercise **ejercicio** *m.* 15
hacer ejercicio 15
exit **salida** *f.* 5
expensive **caro/a** *adj.* 6
experience **experiencia** *f.* 18
explain **explicar** *v.* 18
explore **explorar** *v.* 4
explore a city/town **explorar una ciudad/pueblo** 4
expression **expresión** *f.*1
extinction **extinción** *f.* 13
extremely **sumamente** *adv.* 5
eye **ojo** *m.* 10

F

fabulous **fabuloso/a** *adj* 5
face **cara** *f.* 7
facing **enfrente de** *prep.* 14
fact: in fact **de hecho** 5
fall (down) **caerse** *v.* 10
fall asleep **dormirse (o:ue)** *v.* 7
fall in love (with) **enamorarse** *v.* **(de)** 9
fallen **caído** *p.p.*14
family **familia** *f.* 3
famous **famoso/a** *adj.* 16
fan **aficionado/a** *adj.* 4
be a fan of **ser aficionado/a a** 4
far from **lejos de** *adv.* 2
farewell **despedida** *f.* 1
fascinate **fascinar** *v.* 7
fashion **moda** *f.* 6
be in fashion **estar de moda** 6
fast **rápido/a** *adj.* 8
fat **gordo/a** *adj.* 3; **grasa** *f.* 15
father **padre** *m.* 3
father-in-law **suegro** *m.* 3
favorite **favorito/a** *adj.* 4
fax (machine) **fax** *m.* 11
fear **miedo** *m.* 3; fear **temer** *v.* 13
February **febrero** *m.* 5
feel *v.* **sentir** 7
feel like (*doing something*) **tener ganas de (+ *inf.*)** 3
festival **festival** *m.* 17
fever **fiebre** *f.* 10
have a fever **tener fiebre** 10
few **pocos/as** *adj. pl.* 5
field: major field of study **especialización** *f.* 16
fifteen **quince** 1
fifth **quinto/a** 5
fifty **cincuenta** 2
fight **luchar** *v.* **(por)** 18
figure (*number*) **cifra** *f.* 1
file **archivo** *m.* 11
fill **llenar** *v.* 11
fill out a form **llenar un formulario** 14
fill the tank **llenar el tanque** 11
finally **finalmente** *adv.* 15; **por último** 7; **por fin** 11
find **encontrar (o:ue)** *v.* 4
find (each other) **encontrar(se)** *v.* 11
fine arts **bellas artes** *f., pl.* 17
fine **multa** *f.* 11
That's fine. **Está bien.** 11
finger **dedo** *m.* 10
finish *v.* **terminar** 2
finish (*doing something*) **terminar** *v.* **de (+*inf.*)** 4
fire **incendio** *m.*18
firefighter **bombero/a** *m., f.* 16
firm **compañía** *f.* 16; **empresa** *f.* 16
first **primer, primero/a** *adj.* 5
fish(*food*) **pescado** *m.* 8; **pescar** *v.* 5; (*live*) **pez** *m.* 13
fish market **pescadería** *f.* 14
fisherman **pescador** *m.* 5
fishing **pesca** *f.* 5
fit (*clothing*) **quedar** *v.* 7
five **cinco** 1
five hundred **quinientos/as** 5
fix (*put in working order*) **arreglar** *v.* 11
fixed **fijo/a** *adj.* 6
flag **bandera** *f.* 1
flank steak **lomo** *m.* 8
flat tire: We had a flat tire. **Se nos pinchó una llanta.** 11
go flat *v.* **ponchar** 11
flavor **sabor** *m.* 1
flexible **flexible** *adj.* 15

float **carroza** *f.* 1
flood **inundación** *f.*18
floor (*story in a building*) **piso** *m.* 5; **suelo** *m.*12
ground floor **planta** *f.* **baja** 5
top floor **planta** *f.* **alta** 5
flower **flor** *f.* 13
flu **gripe** *f.* 10
fog **niebla** *f.* 4
foggy: It's (very) foggy. **Hay (mucha) niebla.** 4
folk **folklórico/a** *adj.* 17
follow **seguir (e:i)** *v.* 4
food **comida** *f.* 8
foolish **tonto/a** *adj.* 3
foot **pie** *m.* 10
football **fútbol** *m.* **americano** 4
for **para** *prep.* 11; **por** *prep.* 11
for example **por ejemplo** 11
forbid **prohibir** *v.* 10
foreign **extranjero/a** *adj.* 17
foreign languages **lenguas** *f. pl.* **extranjeras** 2
forest **bosque** *m.* 13
forget **olvidar** *v.* 10
fork **tenedor** *m.* 12
form **formulario** *m.* 14
forty **cuarenta** *m.* 2
forward **en marcha** 15
four **cuatro** 1
four hundred **cuatrocientos/as** 5
fourteen **catorce** 1
fourth **cuarto/a** *m., f.* 5
free **libre** *adj.* 4
be free (of charge) **ser gratis** 14
free time **tiempo libre** 4; **ratos libres** 4
freedom **libertad** *f.* 18
freezer **congelador** *m.* 12
French **francés, francesa** *m., f.* 3
french fries **papas** *f., pl* **fritas** 8
frequently **frecuentemente** 10; **con frecuencia** 10
Friday **viernes** *m., sing.* 2
fried **frito/a** *adj.*8
fried food *f.* **fritada** 8
fried potatoes **papas** *f., pl.* **fritas** 8; **patatas** *f., pl.* **fritas** 8
friend **amigo/a** *m., f.* 3
friendly **amable** *adj.* 5
friendship **amistad** *f.* 9
from **desde** *prep.* 6; **de** 1
from the United States *adj.* **estadounidense** 3
from time to time **de vez en cuando** 10
He/She/It is from . . . **Es de...** 1
frugal **ahorrador** *adj.* 6
fruit **fruta** *f.* 8
fruit juice **jugo** *m.* **de fruta** 8
fruit store **frutería** *f.* 14
full **lleno/a** *adj.*11
fun **divertido/a** *adj.* 7
fun activity **diversión** *f.* 4
have fun **divertirse (e:ie)** *v.* 9
function **funcionar** *v.* 11
furniture **muebles** *m., pl.*12
furthermore **además (de)** *adv.* 10
future **futuro** *adj.* 16; **porvenir** *m.* 16

G

gain weight **aumentar de peso** 15; **engordar** 15
game **juego** *m.* 5; (*match*) **partido** *m.* 4
game show **concurso** *m.* 17
garage **garaje** *m.* 12
garden **jardín** *m.* 12
garlic **ajo** *m.* 8
gas station **gasolinera** *f.* 11
gasoline **gasolina** *f.* 11
geography **geografía** *f.* 2
German **alemán, alemana** *adj.* 3
get **conseguir (e:i)** *v.* 4; **obtener** *v.* 16
get along well/badly with **llevarse bien/mal con** 9
get off (a vehicle) **bajar** *v.* **(de)** 11
get on/in (a vehicle) **subir a** 11
get up **levantarse** *v.* 7
gift **regalo** *m.* 6
girl **chica** *f.* 1; **muchacha** *f.* 3
girlfriend **novia** *f.* 3
give **dar** *v.* 9; (*as a gift*) **regalar** 9
give a kiss **dar un beso** 9
glass (*drinking*) **vaso** *m.* 12; **vidrio** *m.* 13
made of glass **de vidrio** 13
glasses **gafas** *f., pl.* 6
sunglasses **gafas** *f., pl.* **oscuras** 6
gloves **guantes** *m., pl.* 6
go *v.* **ir** 4
go away **irse** 7
go by bus **ir en autobús** 5
go by car **ir en auto(móvil)** 5
go by motorcycle **ir en motocicleta** 5
go by plane **ir en avión** 5
go by ship **ir en barco** 5
go by subway **ir en metro** 5
go by taxi **ir en taxi** 5
go by the bank **pasar por el banco** 14
go by train **ir en tren** 5
go by *v.* **pasar por** 5
go down; *v.* **bajar(se)** 11
go fishing **ir de pesca** 5
go for a hike (in the mountains) **ir de excursión (a las montañas)** 4
go out *v.* **salir** 4
go out with **salir con** 9
go through customs **pasar por la aduana** 5
go up **subir** *v.* 11
go with **acompañar** *v.* 14
Let's go. **Vamos.** 4
goblet **copa** *f.* 12
going to: be going to (*do something*) **ir a (+ *inf.*)** 4
golf **golf** *m.* 4
good **buen, bueno/a** *adj.* 1
Good afternoon. **Buenas tardes.** 1
Good evening. **Buenas noches.** 1
Good morning. **Buenos días.** 1
Good night. **Buenas noches.** 1
I'm good, thanks. **Bien, gracias.** 1
It's good that . . . **es bueno que...** 12
good-bye *m.* **adiós** 1
say good-bye (to) *v.* **despedirse (de) (e:i)** 7
good-looking **guapo/a** *adj.* 3
government **gobierno** *m.* 13
graduate (from) **graduarse** *v.* **(en)** 9
grains **cereales** *m., pl.* 8
granddaughter **nieta** *f.* 3
grandfather **abuelo** *m.* 3
grandmother **abuela** *f.* 3
grandparents **abuelos** *m. pl.* 3
grandson **nieto** *m.* 3
grape **uva** *f.*8
grass **césped** *m.* 13; **hierba** *f.* 13
grave **grave** *adj.* 10
gray **gris** *f.* 6
great **fenomenal** *adj.* 5
green **verde** *m.* 6
greet (each other) **saludar(se)** *v.* 11
greeting **saludo** *m.* 1
Greetings to . . . **Saludos a...** 1
grilled (*food*) **a la plancha** 8
grilled flank steak **lomo a la plancha** 8
ground floor **planta baja** *f.* 5
grow **cultivar** *v.* 6
growth **crecimiento** *m.* 4
guard **custodiar** *v.* 5
guest (*at a house/hotel*) **huésped(a)** *m., f.* 5 (*invited to a function*) **invitado/a** *m., f.* 9
guide **guía** *m., f.* 12
gymnasium **gimnasio** *m.* 4

H

hair **pelo** *m.* 7
hairdresser **peluquero/a** *m., f.* 16
half **medio/a** *adj.* 3
half-brother **medio hermano** 3; half-sister **media hermana** 3
half-past . . . (*time*) **...y media** 1
hallway **pasillo** *m.* 12
ham **jamón** *m.* 8
hamburger **hamburguesa** *f.* 8

hand **mano** *f.* 1
Hands up! **¡Manos arriba!** 15
handsome **guapo** *adj.* 3
happen **ocurrir** *v.* 18
Happy birthday! **¡Feliz cumpleaños!** 9
happy **alegre** *adj.* 5; **contento/a** *adj.* 5; **feliz** *adj.* 5
be happy **alegrarse (de)** 13
hard **difícil** *adj.* 3
hard-working **trabajador(a)** *adj.* 3
hardly **apenas** *adv.* 10
haste **prisa** *f.* 3
hat **sombrero** *m.* 6
hate **odiar** *v.* 9
have **tener** *v.* 3
have to (*do something*) **tener que (+** ***inf.*****)** 3; **deber (+** ***inf.*****)** 3
head **cabeza** *f.* 10
headache **dolor de cabeza** *m.* 10
health **salud** *f.* 10
healthful **saludable** *adj.* 10
healthy **sano/a** *adj.* 10
hear **oír** *v.* 4
heard **oído** *p.p.* 14
hearing: sense of hearing **oído** *m.* 10
heart **corazón** *m.* 10
heat **calor** *m.*4
height *f.* **altura** 3
Hello. **Hola.** 1; (*on the telephone*) **Aló.**; 11 **¿Bueno?** 11; **Diga.** 11
help (to) **ayudar** *v.* **(a)** 12; **servir (e:i)** *v.* 5
help each other **ayudarse** *v.* 11
her **su(s)** *poss.* 3; hers **suyo/a(s)** *poss.* 11
here *adv.* **aquí** 1
Here it is. **Aquí está.** 5
Here we are in . . . **Aquí estamos en...** 2
heritage **patrimonio** *m.* 6
Hi. **Hola.** 1
highway **autopista** *f.* 11; **carretera** *f.*11
hike **excursión** *f.* 4
go on a hike **hacer una excursión** 5
hiking **de excursión** 4
hiker *m., f.* **excursionista** 4
his **su(s)** *poss.* 3; **suyo/a(s)** *poss.* 11
history **historia** *f.* 2
hockey **hockey** *m.* 4
holiday **día** *m.* **de fiesta** 9
holy week **semana** *f.* **santa** 8
home **casa** *f.* 4
home page **página** *f.* **principal** 11
homework **asignación** *f.* 2; **tarea** *f.* 2; **deberes** *m. pl.* 2
honeymoon **luna** *f.* **de miel** 5
hood **capó** *m.* 11
hope **esperar** *v.* 2
horror **horror** *m.* 17
hors d'oeuvres **entremeses** *m., pl.* 8
horse **caballo** *m.* 5
hospital **hospital** *m.* 10
hot: be hot (*weather*) **hacer calor** 4; (*feel*) **tener calor** 3
hotel **hotel** *m.* 5
hour **hora** *f.* 1
house **casa** *f.* 4
household chores **quehaceres** *m. pl.* **domésticos** 12
housewife **ama** *f.***de casa** 12
housing **vivienda** *f.* 12
How . . . ! **¡Qué...!** 3
how **¿cómo?** *adv.* 1
How are you? **¿Qué tal?** 1
How are you?**¿Cómo estás?** *fam.* 1
How are you?**¿Cómo está usted?** *form.* 1
How did it go for you . . .? **¿Cómo le/les fue...?** 15
How is it going? **¿Qué tal?** 1
How is/are . . . ? **¿Qué tal...?** 2
How many?**¿Cuánto/a(s) ?** 1
How may I help you **¿En qué puedo servirles?** 5
How much does it cost? **¿Cuánto cuesta...?** 6
How old are you? **¿Cuántos años tienes?** 3
however **sin embargo** 5
hug (each other) **abrazar(se)** *v.* 11
humanities **humanidades** *f., pl.*2
humming bird **colibrí** *m.* 6
hunger **hambre** *f.* 3
hungry: be hungry **tener hambre** 3
hunt **cazar** *v.* 4
hurricane **huracán** *m.* 18
hurry **apurarse** *v.* 15
be in a hurry **tener prisa** 3
hurt **doler (o:ue)** *v.* 10
It hurts me a lot . . . **Me duele mucho...** 10
husband **esposo** *m.*3

I

I am . . . **Yo soy...** 1
I hope (that) *interj.* **ojalá (que)** 13
I wish (that) *interj.* **ojalá (que)** 13
ice cream **helado** *m.*9
ice cream shop **heladería** *f.* 14
iced **helado/a** *adj.* 9
iced tea *m.* **té helado** 8
idea **idea** *f.* 4
if **si** *conj.* 4
illness **enfermedad** *f.*10
important **importante** *adj.*3
be important to **importar** *v.* 7
impossible **imposible** *adj.* 13
improbable **improbable** *adj.*13
improve **mejorar** *v.*13
in **en** *prep.* 2
in the afternoon **de la tarde** 1; **por la tarde** 7
in the evening **de la noche** 1; **por la noche** 7
in the morning **de la mañana** 1; **por la mañana** 7
in front of **delante de** *prep.* 2
increase **aumento** *m.* 16
incredible **increíble** *adj.* 5
inequality **desigualdad** *f.* 18
infection **infección** *f.* 10
influence **influir en** *v.* 4
inform **informar** *v.* 18
injection **inyección** *f.* 10
give an injection *v.* **poner una inyección** 10
injure (oneself) **lastimarse** 10
injure (one's foot) **lastimarse (el pie)** 10
in-line (skates) **(patinas) en línea** 4
inn **hostal** *m.* 5
inner ear **oído** *m.* 10
insist (on) **insistir** *v.* **(en)** 12
inspire **inspirar** *v.* 3
installments: pay in installments **pagar a plazos** 14
intelligent **inteligente** *adj.* 3
intend to **pensar** *v.* **(+** ***inf.*****)** 4
interest **interesar** *v.* 7
interesting **interesante** *adj.*3
be interesting to **interesar** *v.* 7
international **internacional** *adj.* 18
Internet **red** *f.* 11; **Internet** *m.* 11
interview **entrevista** *f.* 16; interview **entrevistar** *v.* 16
interviewer **entrevistador(a)** *m., f.* 16
introduction **presentación** *f.* 1
invest **invertir (i:ie)** *v.* 16
invite **invitar** *v.* 9
iron (clothes) **planchar la ropa** 12
Italian **italiano/a** *adj.* 3
its **su(s)** *poss.*3 , **suyo/a(s)** *poss.* 11

J

jacket **chaqueta** *f.* 6
January **enero** *m.* 5
Japanese **japonés, japonesa** *adj.* 3
jeans **bluejeans** *m., pl.* 6
jewelry store **joyería** *f.* 14
jewels **joyas** *f.* 1
job **empleo** *m.* 16; **puesto** *m.* 16; **trabajo** *m.* 16
job application **solicitud** *f.* **de trabajo** 16

jog **correr** *v.* 3
journalism **periodismo** *m.* 2
journalist **periodista** *m., f.* 3; **reportero/a** *m., f.* 16
joy **alegría** *f.* 9
give joy **dar alegría** 9
joyful **alegre** *adj.* 5
juice **jugo** *m.* 8
July **julio** *m.* 5
June **junio** *m.* 5
jungle **selva** *f.* 13
just **apenas** *adv.* 10
have just (*done something*) **acabar de (+ *inf.*)** 6

K

key **llave** *f.* 5
keyboard **teclado** *m.* 11
kilometer **kilómetro** *m.* 11
kind: That's very kind of you. **Muy amable.** 5
kiss (each other) **besar(se)** *v.* 11; **beso** *m.* 9
kitchen **cocina** *f.* 12
knee **rodilla** *f.* 10
knife **cuchillo** *m.* 12
know **saber** *v.* 8; **conocer** *v.* 8
known **conocido/a** *adj.* 2

L

laboratory **laboratorio** *m.* 2
lack **faltar** *v.* 7
lake **lago** *m.* 5
lamp **lámpara** *f.* 12
land **tierra** *f.* 13
landlord **dueño/a** *m., f.* 8
landscape **paisaje** *m.* 5
language **lengua** *f.* 2
laptop (computer) **computadora** *f.* **portátil** 11
large (*clothing size*) **talla grande** 6
last **durar** *v.* 18; **pasado/a** *adj.* 6; **último/a** *adj.* 15
last name **apellido** *m.* 9
last night **anoche** *adv.* 6
late **tarde** *adv.* 7
later **más tarde** 7
See you later. **Hasta la vista.** 1; **Hasta luego.** 1
laugh **reírse (e:i)** *v.* 9
laughed **reído** *p.p.* 14
laundromat **lavandería** *f.* 14
law **ley** *f.* 13
lawyer **abogado/a** *m., f.* 16
lazy **perezoso/a** *adj.* 3
learn **aprender** *v.* 3
leave **salir** *v.* 4; **irse** *v.* 7
leave a tip **dejar una propina** 9
leave for (*a place*) **salir para** 4
leave from **salir de** 4
leave behind **dejar** *v.* 16
left **izquierdo/a** *adj.* 2
be left over **quedar** *v.* 7
to the left (of) **a la izquierda (de)** 2
leg **pierna** *f.* 10
lemon **limón** *m.*8
lend **prestar** *v.* 6
less **menos** *adv.* 10
less . . . than **menos... que** 8
less than + *number* **menos de +** *number* 8
lesson **lección** *f.* 1
let **dejar** *v.* 12
let's see **a ver** 2
letter **carta** *f.* 4
lettuce **lechuga** *f.* 8
liberty **libertad** *f.* 18
library **biblioteca** *f.* 2
license (*driver's*) **licencia** *f.* **de conducir** 11
life **vida** *f.* 9
in my life **de mi vida** 15
lifestyle: lead a healthy lifestyle **llevar una vida sana** 15
lift **levantar** *v.* 15
lift weights **levantar pesas** 15
light **liviano** *adj.* 6; **luz** 12
like **como** *prep.* 8; **gustar** *v.* 7
I like . . . very much *v.* **Me encanta...** 7
Do you like . . . ? **¿Te gusta(n)...?** 2
likeable **simpático/a** *adj.* 3
likewise **igualmente** *adv.* 1
line **línea** *f.* 4; **cola** (*queue*) *f.* 14
listen to **escuchar** *v.* 2
Listen! (*command*) **¡Oye!** *fam., sing.*1; **¡Oigan!** *form., pl.* 5
listen to music **escuchar música** 2
listen to the radio **escuchar la radio** 2
listener *m.* **radioyente** *m., f.* 4; **oyente** *m., f.* 6
literature **literatura** *f.* 2
little **poco/a** *adj.* 5
live **vivir** *v.* 3
lively **vivo/a** *adj.* 4
living room **sala** *f.* 12
loan **préstamo** *m.* 14
lobster **langosta** *f.* 8
located **situado/a** *adj.* 14
be located **quedar** *v.* 14
lodging **alojamiento** *m.* 5; **parador** *m.* 5
long **largo/a** *adj.* 6
look for **buscar** *v.* 2
lose **perder (e:ie)** *v.* 4
lose weight **adelgazar** *v.* 15
lost **perdido/a** *adj.* 14
be lost **estar perdido/a** 14
lot of, a **mucho/a** *adj.* 2
love (*another person*) **querer (e:ie)** *v.* 4; (*things*) **encantar** *v.* 7 ; **amor** *m.* 9
in love **enamorado/a** *adj.* 5
luck **suerte** *f.* 3
lucky: be lucky **tener suerte** 3
luggage **equipaje** *m.* 5
lunch **almuerzo** *m.* 8
have lunch **almorzar (o:ue)** *v.* 8

M

ma'am **señora (Sra.)** *f.* 1
mad **enojado/a** *adj.* 5
magazine **revista** *f.* 4
magnificent **magnífico/a** *adj.* 6
mail **correo** *m.* 14
mail carrier **cartero** *m.* 14
mailbox **buzón** *m.* 14
main **principal** *adj.* 8
maintain **mantener** *v.* 15
make **hacer** *v.* 4
make the bed **hacer la cama** 12
make-up **maquillaje** *m.* 7
man **hombre** *m.* 1
manager **gerente** *m., f.* 16
many **mucho/a** *adj.* 2
many times **muchas veces** 10
map **mapa** *m.* 1
March **marzo** *m.* 5
margarine **margarina** *f.* 8
marinated fish **ceviche** *m.* 8
marinated shrimp **ceviche** *m.* **de camarón** 8
marital status **estado civil** 9
market **mercado** *m.* 6
marriage **matrimonio** *m.* 9
married **casado/a** *adj.* 9
get married (to) **casarse** *v.* **(con)** 9
marvelous **maravilloso/a** *adj.* 5
marvelously **maravillosamente** *adv.* 18
massage **masaje** *m.* 15
masterpiece **obra maestra** *f.* 17
match (*sports*) **partido** *m.* 4
match **hacer juego (con)** 6
mathematics **matemáticas** *f., pl.* 2
matter **importar** *v.* 7
maturity **madurez** *f.* 9
maximum **máximo/a** *m.* 11
May **mayo** *m.* 5
maybe **tal vez** 5; **quizás** 5
mayonnaise **mayonesa** *f.* 8
meal **comida** *f.* 8
means of communication **medios** *m. pl.* **de comunicación** 18
measure **medir** *v.* 8
meat **carne** *f.* 8
mechanic **mecánico/a** *m., f.* 11

mechanic's workshop **taller de mecánica** 11
media **medios** *m., pl.* **de comunicación** 18
medical **médico/a** *adj.* 10
medication **medicamento** *m.* 10
medicine **medicina** *f.* 10
medium **mediano/a** *adj.* 6
meet (each other) **encontrar(se)** *v.* 11
meeting **reunión** *f.* 16
menu **menú** *m.* 8
message (*telephone*) **recado** *m.* 11
Mexican **mexicano/a** *adj.* 3
Mexico **México** *m.* 1
microwave **microonda** *f.*12
microwave oven **horno** *m.***de microondas** 12
middle age **madurez** *f.* 9
midnight **medianoche** *f.* 1
mile **milla** *f.*11
milk **leche** *f.*8
million **millón** *m.* 5
mine **mío/a(s)** *poss.*11
mineral **mineral** *m.* 15
mineral water **agua** *f.* **mineral** 8
minute **minuto** *m.* 1
mirror **espejo** *m.* 7
Miss **señorita (Srta.)** *f.* 1
mistaken **equivocado/a** *adj.* 5
modem **módem** *m.* 11
modern **moderno/a** *adj.* 17
mom **mamá** *f.*1; **mami** *f.* 3
Monday **lunes** *m., sing.* 2
money **dinero** *m.* 6
monitor **monitor** *m.* 11
month **mes** *m.* 5
monument **monumento** *m.* 4
moon **luna** *f.* 13
more **más**
more . . . than **más... que** 8
more than (+ *number*) **más de (+ *number*)** 8
morning **mañana** *f.* 1
mother **madre** *f.* 3
mother-in-law **suegra** *f.* 3
motor **motor** *m.* 11
motorcycle **moto** *f.* 5; **motocicleta** *f.* 5
mountain **montaña** *f.* 4
mouse **ratón** *m.* 11
mouth **boca** *f.* 10
move (*to another house/city/country*) **mudarse** *v.* 12
movie **película** *f.* 4
movie star **estrella** *f.* **de cine** 17
movie theater **cine** *m.* 4
Mr. **señor (Sr.)** *m.* 1
Mrs. **señora (Sra.)** *f.*1
much **mucho/a** *adj.* 2
municipal **municipal** *m.* 4
murder **crimen** *m.* 18
muscle **músculo** *m.* 15
museum **museo** *m.* 4
mushroom **champiñón** *m.* 8
music **música** *f.* 17
musical **musical** *adj.* 17
musician **músico/a** *m., f.* 17
must: It must be . . . **Debe ser...**6
my **mi(s)** *poss.* 3; **mío/a(s)** *poss.* 11

N

name **nombre** *m.* 5
in the name of **a nombre de** 5
last name *m.* **apellido** 9
My name is . . . **Me llamo...** 1
be named **llamarse** *v.* 7
napkin **servilleta** *f.* 12
narrator **narradora** *f.* 4
national **nacional** *adj.* 18
nationality **nacionalidad** *f.* 1
natural **natural** *adj.* 13
natural disaster **desastre** *m.* **natural** 18
natural resource **recurso** *m.* **natural** 13
nature **naturaleza** *f.* 13
nauseated **mareado/a** *adj.* 10
near **cerca de** *prep.* 2
necessary **necesario/a** *adj.* 12
It is necessary that . . . **Hay que...** 14
neck **cuello** *m.* 10
need **faltar** *v.* 7; **necesitar** *v.* 2
negative **negativo/a** *m.* 7
neighbor **vecino/a** *m., f.* 12
neighborhood **barrio** *m.* 12
neither . . . nor **ni... ni** *conj.* 7;
neither **tampoco** *adv.* 7
nephew **sobrino** *m.* 3
nervous **nervioso/a** *adj.* 5
network **red** *f.* 11
never **nunca** *adj.* 7; **jamás** 7
new **nuevo/a** *adj.* 6
newlywed **recién casado/a** *m., f.* 9
news **noticias** *f., pl.* 18; **actualidades** *f., pl.* 18
newscast **noticiero** *m.* 18
newspaper **periódico** 4; **diario** *m.* 18
next **próximo/a** *adj.* 16
nice **simpático/a** *adj.* 3; **amable** *adj.* 5
niece **sobrina** *f.* 3
night **noche** *f.* 1
night stand **mesita** *f.* **de noche** 12
nine **nueve** 1
nine hundred **novecientos/as** 5
nineteen **diecinueve** 1
ninety **noventa** 2
ninth **noveno/a** 5
no **no** 1; **ningún, ninguno/a(s)** *adj.* 7
no one **nadie** *pron.* 7
No problem. **Ningún problema.** 7
no way **de ninguna manera** 16
none **ningún, ninguno/a(s)** *adj.* 7
noon **mediodía** *m.* 1
nor **ni** *conj.* 7
north **norte** *m.* 14
to the north **al norte** 14
nose **nariz** *f.* 10
not **no** 1
not any **ningún, ninguno/a(s)** *adj.* 7
not anyone **nadie** *pron.* 7
not anything **nada** *pron.* 7
not bad at all **nada mal** 5
not either **tampoco** *adv.* 7
not ever **nunca** *adv.* 7; **jamás** *adv.* 7
not very well **no muy bien** 1
not working **descompuesto/a** *adj.* 11
notebook **cuaderno** *m.* 1
nothing **nada** *f.* 1
notice **notar** *v.* 4
noun **sustantivo** *m.* 1
November **noviembre** *m.* 5
now **ahora** *adv.* 5
nowadays **hoy día** *adv.* 5
number **número** 1 *adv.*
nurse **enfermero/a** *m., f.* 10
nutrition **nutrición** *f.* 15

O

o'clock: It's . . . o'clock **Son las...** 1
It's one o'clock. **Es la una.** 1
obey **obedecer (c:zc)** *v.* 18
obtain **conseguir (e:i)** *v.* 4; **obtener** *v.* 16
occupation **ocupación** *f.* 16
occur **realizar** *v.* 4; **ocurrir** *v.* 18
ocean **mar** *m.* 5; **océano** *m.* 5
October **octubre** *m.* 5
of **de** *prep.* 1
of course **claro que sí** 16; **por supuesto** 16
offer **oferta** *f.* 12; **ofrecer (c:cz)** *v.* 8
offering **ofrenda** *f.* 4
office (*medical*) **consultorio** *m.* 10; **oficina** *f.* 12
often **a menudo** *adv.* 10
Oh! **¡Ay!** 10
oil **aceite** *m.* 8
okay **regular** *adj.* 1
It's okay. **Está bien.** 11
old **antigua** *adj.* 2; **viejo/a** *adj.* 3
old age **vejez** *f.* 9
older **mayor** *adj.* 3

olderbrother, sister **hermano/a mayor** *m., f.* 3
oldest **el/la mayor** 8
on **en** *prep.* 2: **sobre** *prep.* 2
on behalf of **por** *prep.* 11
on the dot **en punto** 1
on time **a tiempo** 10
on top of **encima de** 2
once **una vez** 6
one **un, uno/a** 1
one hundred **cien(to)** 5
one more time **una vez más** 9
one thousand **mil** 4
one time **una vez** 6
one way (*travel*) **ida** *f.* 5
onion **cebolla** *f.* 8
only **sólo** *adv.* 3; **único/a** *adj.* 3
only child **hijo/a único/a** *m., f.* 3
open **abierto/a** *adj.* 5; **abrir** *v.* 3
open-air **al aire libre** 6
opera **ópera** *f.* 17
operation **operación** *f.* 10
opposite **en frente de** *prep.* 14
or **o** *conj.* 7
orange **anaranjado/a** *adj.* 6; **naranja** *f.* 8
orchestra **orquesta** *f.* 17
order **mandar** 3; (*food*) **pedir (e:i)** *v.* 8
in order to **para** *prep.* 11
orderly **ordenado/a** *adj.* 5
ordinal (*numbers*) **ordinal** *adj.* 5
other **otro/a** *adj.* 6
our **nuestro/a(s)** *pron.* 3
out of order **descompuesto/a** *adj.* 11
outside **fuera** *adv.* 8
outskirts **afueras** *f., pl.* 12
outstanding **sobresaliente** *adj.* 8
oven **horno** *m.* 12
over **sobre** *prep.* 2
own **propio/a** *adj.* 16
owner **dueño/a** *m., f* 8

P

P.M. **tarde** *f.* 1
pack the suitcases **hacer** *v.* **las maletas** 5
package **paquete** *m.* 14
page **página** *f.* 11
pain **dolor** *m.* 10
have a pain in the (knee) **tener dolor de (rodilla)** 10
paint **pintar** *v.* 17
painter **pintor(a)** *m., f.* 16
painting **pintura** *f.* 12
pair **par** *m.* 6
pants **pantalones** *m., pl.* 6
pantyhose **medias** *f.,pl.* 6
paper **papel** *m.* 2; (*report*) **informe** *m.* 18
paper money **billete** *m.* 8
parade **desfile** *m.* 1
paragraph **párrafo** *m.* 5
Pardon me. (*May I?*) **con permiso** 1; (*Excuse me.*) Pardon me. **Perdón.** 1
parents **padres** *m., pl.* 3; **papás** *m., pl.* 3
park **estacionar** *v.* 11; **parque** *m.* 4
partner (*one of a married couple*) **pareja** *f.* 9
party **fiesta** *f.* 9
pass **pasar** *v.* 12
passed **pasado/a** *p.p.* 15
passenger **pasajero/a** *m., f.* 1
passport **pasaporte** *m.* 5
past **pasado/a** *adj.* 6
pastime **pasatiempo** *m.* 4
pastry shop **pastelería** *f.* 14
patient **paciente** *m., f.* 10
patio **patio** *m.* 12
pay the bill **pagar la cuenta** 9
pea **arveja** *m.* 8; **chícharo** *m.* 8; **guisante** *m.* 8
peace **paz** *f.* 18
peach **melocotón** *m.* 8
pear **pera** *f.* 8
pen **bolígrafo** *m.* 2; **pluma** *f.* 2
pencil **lápiz** *m.* 1
penicillin **penicilina** *f.* 10
people **gente** *f.* 3
pepper (*black*) **pimienta** *f.* 8
perfect **perfecto/a** *adj.* 5
perform (*act*) **interpretar** *v.* 6
perhaps **quizás** 5; **tal vez** 5
periods **plazos** *m., pl.* 14
permission **permiso** *m.* 1
person **persona** *f.* 3
pharmacy **farmacia** *f.* 10
phenomenal **fenomenal** *adj.* 5
photograph **foto(grafía)** *f.* 1
physical (*medical examination*) **chequeo** *m.* 10
physics **física** *f.* 2
pick up **recoger** *v.* 13
picture **cuadro** *m.* 12
picturesque **pintoresca** *adj.* 2
pie **pastel** *m.* 9
pill **pastilla** *f.* 10
pillow **almohada** *f.* 12
pineapple **piña** *f.* 8
pink **rosado/a** *adj.* 6
place **lugar** *m.* 4; **poner** *v.* 4
plaid **de cuadros** 6
plan *(to do something)* **pensar** *v.* **(+ *inf.*)** 4
plans **planes** *m., pl.* 4
have plans **tener planes** 4
plant **planta** *f.* 13
plantain **plátano** *m.* 8
plastic **plástico** *m.* 13
made of plastic **de plástico** 13
plate **plato** *m.* 12
platter **fuente** *f.* 8
platter of fried food **fuente** *f.* **de fritada** 8
play **drama** *m.* 17; **jugar (u:ue)** *v.* 4; (*a musical instrument*) **tocar** *v.* 17; (*a role*) **hacer el papel** 17; (*cards*) **jugar a (las cartas)** 5; (*sports*) **practicar deportes** 4
player **jugador(a)** *m., f.* 4
playwright **dramaturgo/a** *m., f.* 17
plead **rogar (o:ue)** *v.* 12
pleasant **agradable** *adj.* 5
Please. **Por favor.** 1
Pleased to meet you. **Mucho gusto.** 1; **Encantado/a.** *adj.* 1
pleasing: be pleasing to **gustar** *v.* 7
pleasure **gusto** *m.* 1; **placer** *m.* 15
It's a pleasure to . . . **Gusto de (+ *inf.*)** 18
It's been a pleasure. **Ha sido un placer.** 15
The pleasure is mine. **El gusto es mío.** 1
poem **poema** *m.* 17
poet **poeta** *m., f.* 17
poetry **poesía** *f.* 17
point **punto** *m.* 1
police (force) **policía** *f.* 11
police officer **policía** *m.*, **mujer policía,** *f.* 11
politician **político/a** *m., f.* 16
politics **política** *f.* 18
polka-dot **de lunares** 6; **lunar** *m.* 6
poll **encuesta** *f.* 18
pollute **contaminar** *v.* 13
polluted **contaminado/a** *m., f.* 13
be polluted **estar contaminado/a** 13
pollution **contaminación** *f.* 4
poor **pobre** *adj.* 6
population **población** *f.* 13
pork **cerdo** *m.* 8
pork chop **chuleta** *f.* **de cerdo** 8
portable **portátil** *adj.* 11
portable computer **computadora** *f.* **portátil** 11
position **puesto** *m.* 16
possessive **posesivo/a** *adj.* 3
possible **posible** *adj.* 13
post office **correo** *m.* 14
postcard **postal** *f.* 4; **tarjeta postal** *f.* 4
poster **cartel** *m.* 12
potato **papa** *f.* 8; **patata** *f.* 8
pottery **cerámica** *f.* 17
poverty **pobreza** *f.* 3
practice **entrenarse** *v.* 15; **practicar** *v.* 2
prefer **preferir (e:ie)** *v.* 4
pregnant **embarazada** *adj.* 10
prepare **preparar** *v.* 2

preposition **preposición** *f.* 2
prescribe (*medicine*) **recetar** *v.* 10
prescription **receta** *f.* 10
present **regalo** *m.* 6
press **prensa** *f.* 18
pressure: be under a lot of pressure **sufrir muchas presiones** 15
pretty **bonito/a** *adj.* 3
price **precio** *m.* 6
fixed price **precio** *m.* **fijo** 6
pride **orgullo** *m.* 1
print **estampado/a** *adj.* 6; **imprimir** *v.* 11
printer **impresora** *f.* 11
private (*room*) **individual** *adj.* 5
prize **premio** *m.* 17
probable **probable** *adj.* 13
problem **problema** *m.* 1
profession **profesión** *f.* 3
professor **profesor(a)** *m., f.* 1
program **programa** *m.* 1
programmer **programador(a)** *m., f.* 3
prohibit **prohibir** *v.* 10
promotion (*career*) **ascenso** *m.* 16
pronoun **pronombre** *m.* 8
protect **proteger** *v.* 13
protein **proteína** *f.* 15
provided that **con tal (de) que** *conj.* 13
psychologist **psicólogo/a** *m., f.* 16
psychology **psicología** *f.* 2
publish **publicar** *v.* 17
Puerto Rican **puertorriqueño/a** *adj.* 3
Puerto Rico **Puerto Rico** *m.* 1
pull a tooth **sacar una muela** 10
purchases **compras** *f., pl.* 5
pure **puro/a** *adj.* 13
purple **morado/a** *adj.* 6
purse **bolsa** *f.* 6
put **poner** *v.* 4; **puesto** *p.p.* 14
put a letter in the mailbox **echar una carta al buzón** 14
put on (*a performance*) **presentar** *v.* 17
put on (*clothing*) **ponerse** *v.* 7
put on makeup **maquillarse** *v.* 7

Q

quality **calidad** *f.* 6
quarter *m.* **trimestre** 2
quarter after (*time*) **y cuarto** 1; **y quince** 1
quarter to (*time*) **menos cuarto** 1; **menos quince** 1
queen **reina** *f.* 6
questions **preguntas** *f.* 2
quiet **tranquilo/a** *adj.* 15
quit **dejar** *v.* 16
quiz **prueba** *f.* 2

R

rabbit **conejo** *m.* 2
racism **racismo** *m.* 18
radio (*medium*) **radio** *f.* 2; radio (*receiver*) **radio** *m.* 2
rain **llover o:ue** *v.* 4; rain **lluvia** *f.* 13
It's raining. **Llueve.** 4
raincoat **impermeable** *m.* 6
rainforest **bosque** *m.* **tropical** 13
raise (*salary*) **aumento de sueldo** 16
read **leer** *v.* 3; read **leído** *p.p.* 14
reader **lector** *m., f.* 8
ready **listo/a** *adj.* 15
reap the benefits (of) *v.* **disfrutar (de)** 15
reason **razón** *f.* 3
receive **recibir** *v.* 3
recommend **recomendar (e:ie)** *v.* 8
recycle **reciclar** *v.* 13
recycling **reciclaje** *m.* 13
red **rojo/a** *adj.* 6
red-headed **pelirrojo/a** *adj.* 3
reduce **reducir** *v.* 13
reduce stress/tension **aliviar el estrés/la tensión** 15
reef **arrecife** *m.* 5
refrigerator **refrigerador** *m.* 12
region **región** *f.* 13
regret **sentir(se) (e:ie)** *v.* 13
related to sitting **sedentario/a** *adj.* 15
relationships **relaciones** *f., pl.* 9
relatives **parientes** *m., pl.* 3
relax **relajarse** *v.* 9
remain **quedarse** *v.* 7
remember **acordarse (o:ue)** *v.* **(de)** 7; **recordar (o:ue)** *v.* 4
remote control **control remoto** *m.* 11
rent **alquilar** *v.* 12; **alquiler** *m.* 12
repeat **repetir (e:i)** *v.* 4
report **informe** *m.* 18; **reportaje** *m.* 18
reporter **reportero/a** *m., f.* 16
request **pedir (e:i)** *v.* 4
reservation **reservación** *f.* 5
resign (from) **renunciar (a)** *v.* 16
resolve **resolver (o:ue)** *v.* 13
resolved **resuelto** *p.p.* 14
resource **recurso** *m.* 13
responsibility **deber** *v.* 18
rest **descansar** *v.* 2
the rest **lo/los/las demás** *pron.* 5
restaurant **restaurante** *m.* 4
résumé **currículum** *m.* 16
retire (from work) **jubilarse** *v.* 9
return **regresar** *v.* 2; **volver (o:ue)** *v.* 4
return trip **vuelta** *f.* 5
returned **vuelto** *p.p.* 14
rice **arroz** *m.* 8
rich **rico/a** *adj.* 6
ride a bicycle **pasear en bicicleta** 4
ride a horse **montar a caballo** 5
ridiculous **ridículo/a** *adj.* 13
right **derecha** *f.* 2; (*intensifier*) **mismo/a** *adj.* 5
right here **aquí mismo** 11
right now **ahora mismo** 5
right there **allí mismo** 14
right away **enseguida** *adv.* 9
be right *f.* **tener razón** 3
to the right **a la derecha** 2
right? (*question tag*) **¿no?** 1; **¿verdad?** 1
rights **derechos** *m.* 18
ring (*a doorbell*) **sonar (o:ue)** *v.* 11
river **río** *m.* 13
road **camino** *m.* 11
roast chicken **pollo** *m.* **asado** 8
roasted **asado/a** *p.p.* 8
role **papel** *m.* 17
romantic **romántico/a** *adj.* 17
room **habitación** *f.* 5; **cuarto** *m.* 7; (*large, living*) **sala** *f.* 12
roommate **compañero/a** *m., f.* **de cuarto** 2
root **raíz** *f.* 5
roundtrip **de ida y vuelta** 5
roundtrip ticket **pasaje** *m.* **de ida y vuelta** 5
routine **rutina** *f.* 7
royal **real** *adj.* 2
rug **alfombra** *f.* 12
run **correr** *v.* 3
run errands **hacer diligencias** 14
run into (*have an accident*) **chocar (con)** *v.* 11; (*meet accidentally*) **darse con** 10
rush **apurarse** *v.* 15

S

sad **triste** *adj.* 5
saffran **azafrán** *m.* 2
said **dicho** *p.p.* 14
sake: for the sake of **por** 11
salad **ensalada** *f.* 8
salary **salario** *m.* 16; **sueldo** *m.* 16
sale **rebaja** *f.* 6
salesperson **vendedor(a)** *m., f.* 6
salmon **salmón** *m.* 8
salt **sal** *f.* 8
same **mismo/a** *adj.* 3
sandal **sandalia** *f.* 6
sandwich **sándwich** *m.* 8
Saturday **sábado** *m.* 2
sauce **salsa** *f.* 5
sausage **salchicha** *f.* 8

save (*on a computer*) **guardar** *v.* 11; save (money) **ahorrar** *v.* 14
savings **ahorros** *m.* 14
  savings account **cuenta** *f.* **de ahorros** 14
say **decir** *v.* 9
scarcely **apenas** *adv.* 10
schedule **horario** *m.* 2
school **escuela** *f.* 1
science *f.* **ciencia** 2
  science fiction **ciencia ficción** *f.* 17
scientist **científico/a** *m., f.* 16
scream **gritar** *v.* 7
screen **pantalla** *f.* 11
sculpt **esculpir** *v.* 17
sculptor **escultor(a)** *m., f.* 17
sculpture **escultura** *f.* 17
sea **mar** *m.* 5; **océano** *m.* 5
season **estación** *f.* 5
seat **silla** *f.* 2
second **segundo/a** *adj.* 5
secretary **secretario/a** *m., f.* 16
sedentary **sedentario/a** *adj.* 15
see **ver** *v.* 4
  see (you) again **volver a ver(te, lo, la)** 18
  see movies **ver películas** 4
  See you. **Nos vemos.** 1
  See you later. **Hasta la vista.** 1; **Hasta luego.** 1
  See you soon. **Hasta pronto.** 1
  See you tomorrow. **Hasta mañana.** 1
seem **parecer** *v.* 8
seen *p.p.* **visto/a** 15
selfportrait **autorretrato** *m.* 4
sell **vender** *v.* 6
semester **semestre** *m.* 2
send **enviar** *v.* 14
sense **sentido** *m.* 8
  sense of the order **sentido** *m.* **del orden** 8
sentimental **sentimental** *adj.* 9
separate (from) **separarse** *v.* **(de)** 9
September **septiembre** *m.* 5
sequence **secuencia** *f.* 7
serious **grave** *adj.* 10; **serio/a** *adj.* 3
serve **servir (e:i)** *v.* 5
set (*fixed*) **fijo** *adj.* 6
  set the table **poner la mesa** 12
seven **siete** 1
seven hundred **setecientos/as** 5
seventeen **diecisiete** 1
seventh **séptimo/a** 5
seventy **setenta** 2
sexism **sexismo** *m.* 18
shame **lástima** *f.* 13
  It's a shame that . . . **Es (una) lástima que...** 13
shampoo **champú** *m.* 7
shape **forma** *f.* 15
  be in good shape **estar en buena forma** 15
share **compartir** *v.* 3
sharp (*time*) **en punto** 1
shave **afeitarse** *v.* 7
shaving cream **crema** *f.* **de afeitar** 7
shellfish **mariscos** *m., pl.* 8
ship **barco** *m.* 5
shirt **camisa** *f.* 6
shoe **zapato** *m.* 6
  shoe size **número** *m.* 6
  shoe store **zapatería** *f.* 14
  tennis shoes **zapatos** *m., pl.* **de tenis** 6
shop **tienda** *f.* 6
shopping, to go **ir de compras** 5
  shopping mall **centro comercial** *m.* 6
short (*in height*) **bajo/a** *adj.* 3; **corto/a** *adj.* 6
shorts **pantalones cortos** *m., pl.* 6
should (*do something*) **deber (+ *infin.*)** 3
show **espectáculo** *m.* 17; **mostrar (o:ue)** *v.* 4
shower **ducha** *f.* 7; shower **ducharse** *v.* 7
shrimp **camarón** *m.* 8
sick **enfermo/a** *adj.* 10
  be sick **estar enfermo/a** 10
  get sick **enfermarse** *v.* 10
sightseeing: go sightseeing **hacer turismo** 5
sign **firmar** *v.* 14; **letrero** *m.* 14
silk **seda** *f.* 6; (*made of*) **de seda** 6
silly **tonto/a** *adj.* 3
silverware **cubierto** *m.* 12
similar **similar** *adj.* 7
since **desde** *prep.* 6
sing **cantar** *v.* 2
singer **cantante** *m., f.* 17
single **soltero/a** *adj.* 9
  single room **habitación** *f.* **individual** 5
sink **lavabo** *m.* 7; **lavamanos** *m.* 7
sir **señor (Sr.)** *m.* 1
sister **hermana** *f.* 3
sister-in-law **cuñada** *f.* 3
sit down **sentarse (e:ie)** *v.* 7
six **seis** 1
six hundred **seiscientos/as** 5
sixteen **dieciséis** 1
sixth **sexto/a** 5
sixty **sesenta** 2
size **talla** *f.* 6
  shoe size *m.* **número** 6
skate (in-line) **patinar (en línea)** 4
ski **esquiar** *v.* 4
skiing **esquí** *m.* 4
  water-skiing **esquí** *m.* **acuático** 4
skirt **falda** *f.* 6
skull **calavera** *m.* 4
sky **cielo** *m.* 13
sleep **dormir (o:ue)** *v.* 4; sleep **sueño** *m.* 3
  go to sleep **dormirse (o:ue)** *v.* 7
sleepy: be sleepy **tener sueño** 3
slice **trozo** *m.* 1
slim down **adelgazar** *v.* 15
slow **despacio** *adj.* 8; **lento/a** *adj.* 11
small **pequeño/a** *adj.* 3
smart **listo/a** *adj.* 5
smile **sonreír (e:i)** *v.* 9
smiled **sonreído** *p.p.* 14
smoggy: It's (very) smoggy. **Hay (mucha) contaminación.** 4
smoke **fumar** 15 *v.*
smoking section **sección** *f.* **de fumar** 8
  (no) smoking section *f.* **sección de (no) fumar** 8
snack **merendar** *v.* 15; snack **merienda** *f.* 15
  have a snack **merendar** *v.* 15
sneeze **estornudar** *v.* 10
snow **nevar (e:ie)** *v.* 4; **nieve** *f.* 8
snowing: It's snowing. **Nieva.** 4
so (*in such a way*) **así** *adj.* 10; **tan** *adv.* 8
  so much **tanto** *adv.* 12
  so so **así así** 1, **regular** 1
  so that **para que** 13
soap **jabón** *m.* 7
  soap opera **telenovela** *f.* 17
soccer **fútbol** *m.* 4
sociology *f.* **sociología** 2
sock **calcetín** *m.* 6
sofa **sofá** *m.* 12
soft drink **refresco** *m.* 8
software **programa** *m.* **de computación** 11
soil **tierra** *f.* 13
solution **solución** *f.* 13
solve **resolver (o:ue)** *v.* 13
some **algún, alguno/a(s)** *adj.* 7; **unos/as** *pron.* 1
somebody **alguien** *pron.* 7
someone **alguien** *pron.* 7
something **algo** *pron.* 7
sometimes **a veces** 10
son **hijo** *m.* 3
song **canción** *f.* 17
son-in-law **yerno** *m.* 3
soon **pronto** *adj.* 10
  See you soon. **Hasta pronto.** 1
sorry: be sorry **sentir(se) (e:ie)** *v.* 13
  I'm sorry **lo siento** 1
  I'm extremely sorry. **Mil perdones.** 4
soup **caldo** *m.* 8; **sopa** *f.* 8
south **sur** *m.* 14
  to the south **al sur** 14
Spain **España** *f.* 1

Spanish (*language*) **español** *m.* 2; **español(a)** *adj.* 3
spare time **ratos libres** 4
speak **hablar** *v.* 2
specialization **especialización** *f.* 16
spectacular **espectacular** *adj.* 15
speech **discurso** *m.* 18
speed **velocidad** *f.* 11
speed limit **velocidad** *f.* **máxima** 11
spelling **ortográfico** *adj.* 8
spend (*money*) **gastar** *v.* 6
spend time **pasar tiempo** 4
spoon (*table or large*) **cuchara** *f.* 12
sport **deporte** *m.* 4
sporting **deportista** *adj.* 1
sports-loving **deportivo/a** *adj.* 4
spouse **esposo/a** *m., f.* 3
sprain (an ankle) **torcerse (el tobillo)** 10
sprained **torcido/a** *adj.* 10
be sprained **estar torcido/a** 10
spring **primavera** *f.* 5
stadium **estadio** *m.* 2
stage **etapa** *f.* 9
stairs **escalera** *f.* 12
stairway **escalera** *f.* 12
stamp **estampilla** *f.* 14; **sello** *m.* 14
stand on line **hacer cola** 14
star **estrella** *f.* 13
start (*a vehicle*) **arrancar** *v.* 11
state **estado** *m.* 5
station **estación** *f.* 5
statue **estatua** *f.* 17
status: marital status **estado civil** 9
stay **quedarse** *v.* 7
Stay calm! **¡Tranquilo!** *adj.* 7
stay in shape **mantenerse en forma** 15
steak **bistec** *m.* 8
steering wheel **volante** *m.* 11
step **etapa** *f.* 9
stepbrother **hermanastro** *m.* 3
stepdaughter **hijastra** *f.* 3
stepfather **padrastro** *m.* 3
stepmother **madrastra** *f.* 3
stepsister **hermanastra** *f.* 3
stepson **hijastro** *m.* 3
stereo **estéreo** *m.* 11
still **todavía** *adv.* 5
stock broker **bolsista** *m., f.* 16
stomach **estómago** *m.* 10
stone **piedra** *f.* 13
stop **parar** *v.* 11
stop (*doing something*) **dejar de (+ *inf.*)** 13
store **tienda** *f.* 6
storm **tormenta** *f.* 18
story **cuento** *m.* 17; **historia** *f.* 17
stove **estufa** *f.* 12
straight **derecho** *adj.* 14
straight ahead **(todo) derecho** 14
strange **extraño/a** *adj.* 13
It's strange that . . . **Es extraño que...** 13
strawberry **frutilla** *f.*; fresa *f.* 8
street **calle** *m.* 11
stress **estrés** *m.* 15
stretching **estiramiento** *m.* 15
stretching exercises **ejercicios** *m. pl.* **de estiramiento** 15
strike (*labor*) **huelga** *f.* 18
stripe **raya** *f.* 6
striped **de rayas** 6
stroll **pasear** *v.* 4
strong **fuerte** *adj.* 15
struggle (for) **luchar** *v.* **(por)** 18
student **estudiante** *m., f.* 1; **estudiantil** *adj.* 2
study **estudiar** *v.* 2
stuffed-up (*sinuses*) **congestionado/a** *adj.* 10
stupendous **estupendo/a** *adj.* 5
style **estilo** *m.* 5
suburbs **afueras** *f., pl.* 12
subway **metro** *m.* 5
subway station **estación** *f.* **del metro** 5
success **éxito** *m.* 16
successful: be successful **tener éxito** 16
such as **tales como** 4
suddenly **de repente** 6
suffer *v.* **sufrir** 10
suffer from an illness **sufrir una enfermedad** 10
sufficient **bastante** *adj.* 10
sugar **azúcar** *m.* 8
suggest **sugerir (e:ie)** *v.* 12
suggestion **sugerencia** *f.* 8
suit **traje** *m.* 6
suitcase **maleta** *f.* 3
summer **verano** *m.* 5
sun **sol** *m.* 4
sunbathe **tomar el sol** 4
Sunday **domingo** *m.* 2
sunglasses **gafas** *f., pl.* **oscuras/negras** 6; **lentes** *m. pl.* **de sol** 6
sunny: It's sunny. **Hace sol.** 4
supermarket **supermercado** *m.* 14
support **apoyar** *v.* 8; **sostener** *v.* 8
suppose **suponer** *v.* 4
sure **seguro/a** *adj.* 5
be sure **estar seguro/a** 5
surf (*Internet*) **navegar** *v.* **(en)** 11
surprise **sorprender** *v.* 9; **sorpresa** *f.* 9
survey **encuesta** *f.* 18
sweat **sudar** *v.* 15
sweater **suéter** *m.* 6
sweep (the floor) **barrer (el suelo)** 12
sweets **dulces** *m., pl.* 9
swim **nadar** *v.* 4
swimming **natación** *f.* 4
swimming pool **piscina** 4 *f.* 4; **alberca** *f.* 4
symbolize **simbolizar** *v.* 8
symptom **síntoma** *m.* 10

T

table **mesa** *f.* 2
tablespoon **cuchara** *f.* 12
tablet (*pill*) **pastilla** *f.* 10
take **llevar** *v.* 2; **tomar** *v.* 8
take (someone's) temperature **tomar la temperatura (a alguien)** 10
take (*wear*) a shoe size *v.* **calzar** 6
take a bath **bañarse** *v.* 7
take into account **tomar en cuenta** 8
take off **quitarse** *v.* 7
take out (the trash) *v.* **sacar (la basura)** 10
take photos **tomar fotos** 5; **sacar fotos** 5
talented **talentoso/a** *adj.* 17
talk *v.* **hablar** 2; **conversar** *v.* 8
talk show **programa** *m.* **de entrevistas** 17
tall **alto/a** *adj.* 3
tank **tanque** *m.* 11
tape (audio) **cinta** *f.* 11
tape recorder **grabadora** *f.* 1
tapestries **tapices** *m., pl.* 3
taste **probar (o:ue)** *v.* 8
tasty **rico/a** *adj.* 8; **sabroso/a** *adj.* 8
tax **impuesto** *m.* 18
taxi(cab) **taxi** *m.* 5
tea **té** *m.* 8
teach **enseñar** *v.* 2
teacher **profesor(a)** *m., f.* 1; (*elementary school*) **maestro/a** *m., f.* 16
team **equipo** *m.* 4
technician **técnico/a** *m., f.* 16
telecommuting **teletrabajo** *n.* 16
teleconference **videoconferencia** *f.* 16
telephone **teléfono** *m.* 11
cellular telephone **teléfono** *m.* **celular** 11
television **televisión** *f.* 11
television set **televisor** *m.* 11
temperature **temperatura** *f.* 10
ten **diez** 1
tennis **tenis** *m.* 4
tennis shoes **zapatillas** *f. pl.* **de deporte** 6; **zapatos** *m., pl.***de tenis** 6

tension **tensión** *f.* 15
tent **tienda** *f.* **(de campaña)** 5
tenth **décimo/a** 5
terrible **terrible** *adj.* 13
terrific **chévere** *adj.* 1
test **prueba** *f.* 2; **examen** *m.* 2
Thank you. *f., pl.* **Gracias.** 1
Thank you (very much). **(Muchas) gracias.** 1
Thank you very much. **Muchísimas gracias.** 9
Thanks (a lot). **(Muchas) gracias.** 1
Thanks again. **Gracias una vez más.** 9
Thanks for everything. **Gracias por todo.** 9
that **que** *conj.* 12
that (one) **ése, ésa, eso** *pron.* 6; **ese, esa,** *adj.* 6
that (*over there*) **aquél, aquélla, aquello** *pron.* 6; **aquel, aquella** *adj.* 6
that which **lo que** *conj.* 12
that's why **por eso** 11
theater **teatro** *m.* 17
their **su(s)** *poss.* 3; **suyo/a(s)** *poss.* 11
then **después** (*afterward*) *adv.* 7; **entonces** (*as a result*) *adv.* 7; (*next*) **luego** *adv.*1; **pues** *adv.* 15
there **allí** *adv.* 5
There is/are . . . **Hay...** 1;
There is/are no . . . **No hay...** 1
therefore **por eso** 11
thin **delgado/a** *adj.* 3
thing **cosa** *f.* 1
think **pensar (e:ie)** *v.* 4; (believe) **creer** *v.* 3
think about **pensar en** *v.* 4
third **tercero/a** 5
thirst **sed** *f.* 3
thirsty: be thirsty **tener sed** 3
thirteen **trece** 1
thirty **treinta** 1; thirty (*minutes past the hour*) **y treinta** 1
this **este, esta** *adj.*; **éste, ésta, esto** *pron.* 6
This is . . . (*introduction*) **Éste/a es...** 1
This is he/she. (*on telephone*) **Con él/ella habla.** 11
three **tres** 1
three hundred **trescientos/as** 5
throat **garganta** *f.* 10
through **por** *prep.* 11
throw **echar** *v.* 14
Thursday **jueves** *m., sing.* 2
thus (*in such a way*) **así** *adj.* 10
ticket **boleto** *m.* 17; **entrada** *f.* 17; **pasaje** *m.* 5
tie **corbata** *f.* 6
ties **lazos** *m.* 4
time **vez** *f.* 6; time **tiempo** *m.* 4
buy on time **comprar a plazos** *m., pl.* 14
have a good/bad time **pasarlo bien/mal** 9
We had a great time. **Lo pasamos de película.** 18
times **veces** *f., pl.* 4
many times **muchas veces** 10
tip **propina** *f.* 9
tire **llanta** *f.* 11
tired **cansado/a** *adj.* 5
be tired **estar cansado/a** 5
title **título** *m.* 1
to **a** *prep.* 1
toast (*drink*) **brindar** *v.* 9
toast **pan;** *m.* **tostado** 8
toasted **tostado/a** *adj.* 8
toaster **tostadora** *f.* 12
today **hoy** *adv.* 2
Today is . . . **Hoy es...** 2
together **juntos/as** *adj.* 9
tomato **tomate** *m.* 8
tomorrow **mañana** *f.* 1
See you tomorrow. **Hasta mañana.** 1
tonight **esta noche** *adv.* 4
too **también** *adv.* 2
too much **demasiado** *adv.* 6; **en exceso** 15
tooth **diente** *m.* 7; tooth **muela** *f.* 10
tornado **tornado** *m.* 18
tortilla **tortilla** *f.* 8
touch **tocar** *v.* 13
tour around an area **recorrer** *v.* 5; **excursión** *f.* 4
go on a tour **hacer una excursión** 5
tourism **turismo** *m.* 5
tourist **turista** *m., f.* 1; **turístico/a** *adj.* 5
toward **hacia** *prep.* 14
towel **toalla** *f.* 7
town **pueblo** *m.* 4
track and field **atletismo** *m.* 4
trade **oficio** *m.* 16
traffic **circulación** *f.* 11
traffic signal **semáforo** *m.* 11
tragedy **tragedia** *f.* 17
trail **sendero** *m.* 13
trailhead **sendero** *m.* 13
train **entrenarse** *v.* 15; **tren** *m.* 5
trainer **monitor** *m., f.* 15
translate **traducir** *v.* 8
trash **basura** *f.* 12
travel **viajar** *v.* 2
travel agency **agencia** *f.* **de viajes** 5
travel agent **agente** *m., f.* **de viajes** 5
travel documents **documento** *m.* **de viaje** 1
traveler **viajero/a** *m., f.* 5
traveler's check **cheque de viajero** 14
treasure **tesoro** *m.* 3
tree **árbol** *m.* 13
trimester **trimestre** *m.* 2
trip **viaje** *m.* 5
go on a trip **hacer un viaje** 5
tropical forest **bosque** *m.* **tropical** 13
truck bus **camión** *m.* 5
true **cierto** *m.* 13; **verdadero/a** *adj.* 1
trunk **baúl** *m.* 11
truth **verdad** *f.* 13
try **intentar** *v.* 8; **probar (o:ue)** *v.* 8
try (*to do something*) **tratar de (+ *inf.*)** 15
try on **probarse (o:ue)** *v.* 7
t-shirt **camiseta** *f.* 6
Tuesday **martes** *m., sing.* 2
tuna **atún** *m.* 8
turkey *m.* **pavo** 8
turn **doblar** *v.* 14; **turno** *m.* 9
turn off (*electricity/appliance*) **apagar** *v.* 11
turn on (*electricity/appliance*) **poner** *v.* 11
turtle **tortuga** *f.* 3
twelve **doce** 1
twenty **veinte** 1
twenty-eight **veintiocho** 1
twenty-five **veinticinco** 1
twenty-four **veinticuatro** 1
twenty-nine **veintinueve** 1
twenty-one **veintiún, veintiuno/a** 1
twenty-seven **veintisiete** 1
twenty-six **veintiséis** 1
twenty-three **veintitrés** 1
twenty-two **veintidós** 1
twice **dos veces** 6
twisted **torcido/a** *adj.* 10; be twisted **estar torcido/a** 10
two **dos** 1
two hundred **doscientos/as** 5
two times **doce veces** 1

U

ugly **feo/a** *adj.* 3
uncle **tío** *m.* 3
under **bajo** *adv.* 7
underlined **subrayado/a** *adj.* 8
understand **comprender** *v.* 3; **entender (e:ie)** *v.* 4
underwear **ropa interior** 6
unemployment **desempleo** *m.* 18
unforgettable **inolvidable** *adj.*7
United States **Estados Unidos** *m. pl.* 1
university **universidad** *f.* 2
unless **a menos que** *adv.* 13
unmarried **soltero/a** *adj.* 9
unpleasant **antipático/a** *adj.* 3

until **hasta** *prep.* 1; **hasta que** *adv.* 14
up **arriba** *adv.* 15
urgent **urgente** *adj.* 12
use **usar** *v.* 6
useful **útil** *adj.* 1
utensil **utensilio** *m.* 12

V

vacation **vacaciones** *f. pl.* 5
be on vacation **estar de vacaciones** 5
go on vacation **ir de vacaciones** 5
vacuum **pasar la aspiradora** 12
vacuum cleaner **aspiradora** *f.* 12
valley **valle** *m.* 13
various **varios/as** *adj. pl.* 8
VCR **videocasetera** *f.* 11
vegetables **verduras** *pl., f.* 8
verb **verbo** *m.* 2
very **muy** *adv.* 1
very much **muchísimo** *adv.* 2
Very good, thank you. **Muy bien gracias.** 1
vest **chaleco** *m.* 6
video **video** *m.* 11
video(cassette) **video(casete)** *m.* 11
video conference **videoconferencia** *f.* 16
videocamera **cámara** *f.* **de video** 11
vinegar **vinagre** *m.* 8
violence **violencia** *f.* 18
visit **visitar** *v.* 4
visit monuments **visitar monumentos** 4
vitamin **vitamina** *f.* 15
volcano **volcán** *m.* 13
volleyball **vóleibol** *m.* 4
vote **votar** *v.* 18

W

wait for **esperar** *v.* 13
waiter **camarero/a** *m., f.* 8
wake up **despertarse (e:ie)** *v.* 7
walk **caminar** *v.* 2
take a walk **pasear** *v.* 4
Walkman **walkman** *m.* 11
wall **pared** *f.* 12
wallet **cartera** *f.* 6
want **querer (e:ie)** *v.* 4
war **guerra** *f.* 18
warm (oneself) up **calentarse** *v.* 15
wash **lavar** *v.* 12
wash one's face/hands **lavarse la cara/las manos** 7
wash oneself *v.* **lavarse** 7
washing machine **lavadora** *f.* 12
watch **mirar** *v.* 2; **reloj** *m.* 2
watch television **mirar (la) televisión** 2
water **agua** *f.* 8
water pollution **contaminación del agua** 13
water-skiing *m.* **esquí acuático** 4
way **manera** *f.* 16
weak **débil** *adj.* 15
wear **llevar** *v.* 6; **usar** 6
weather **tiempo** *m.* 4
It's bad weather. **Hace mal tiempo.** 4
It's good weather. **Hace buen tiempo.** 4
It's hot. (*weather*) **Hace calor.** 4
weaving **tejido** *m.* 17
Web site **sitio** *m.* 11
wedding **boda** *f.* 9
Wednesday **miércoles** *m., sing.* 2
week **semana** *f.* 2
weekend **fin** *m.* **de semana** 4
weight **pesa** *f.* 15
welcome **bienvenido/a(s)** *adj.* 12
well-being **bienestar** *m.* 15
well organized **ordenado/a** *adj.* 5
west **oeste** *m.* 14
to the west **al oeste** 14
western (*genre*) **de vaqueros** 17
what **lo que** 12
what? **¿qué?** 1;
At what time . . . ? **¿A qué hora...?** 1
What a . . . ! **¡Qué...!** 1
What a pleasure to . . . ! **¡Qué gusto (+ *inf.*)...** 18
What a surprise! **¡Qué sorpresa!** 9
What day is it? **¿Qué día es hoy?** 2
What did you say? **¿Cómo?** 1
What do you think? **¿Qué le/les** *form.* **parece?** 9
What happened? **¿Qué pasó?** 11
What is the date (today)? **¿Cuál es la fecha (de hoy)?** 5
What is the price? **¿Qué precio tiene?** 6
What pain! **¡Qué dolor!** 10
What pretty clothes! **¡Qué ropa más bonita!** 6
What size do you take? **¿Qué talla lleva (usa)?** 6
What time is it? **¿Qué hora es?** 1
What's going on? **¿Qué pasa?** 1
What's happening? **¿Qué pasa?** 1
What's like? **¿Cómo es...?** 3
What's new? **¿Qué hay de nuevo?** 1
What's the weather like? **¿Qué tiempo hace?** 4
What's wrong? **¿Qué pasó?** 11
What's your name? **¿Cómo se llama(usted)?** 1 *form.*
What's your name? **¿Cómo te llamas(tú)?** *fam.* 1
when **cuando** *conj.*7
When? **¿Cuándo?** 2
where **donde** *prep.*
where? (*destination*) **¿adónde?** 2; (*location*)**¿dónde?** 1
Where are you from? (*fam.*) **¿De dónde eres (tú)?** 1; (*form.*) **¿De dónde es (Ud.)?** 1
Where is . . .? **¿Dónde está...?** 2
which? **¿cuál(es)?** 2; **¿qué?** 2
while **mientras** *adv.* 10
white **blanco/a** *adj.* 6
white wine **vino blanco** 8
Who is . . . ? **¿Quién es...?** 1
Who is calling? (*on telephone*) **¿De parte de quién?** 11
Who is speaking? (*on telephone*) **¿Quién habla?** 11
who **que** *pron.* 12; **quien(es)** *pron.* 12
who? **¿quién(es)?** 1
whole **todo/a** *adj.* 4
whose **¿de quién(es)?** 1
why? **¿por qué?** 2
widower/widow **viudo/a** *adj.* 9
wife **esposa** *f.*3
win **ganar** *v.* 4; **vencer** 15
wind **viento** *m.* 4
window **ventana** *f.* 2
windshield **parabrisas** *m., sing.* 11
windy: It's (very) windy. **Hace (mucho) viento.** 4
wine **vino** *m.* 8
red wine **vino tinto** 8
white wine **vino blanco** 8
wineglass **copa** *f.* 12
winter **invierno** *m.*5
wish *v.* **desear** 2; **esperar** 13
with **con** *prep.*2
with me **conmigo** 4
with you **contigo** *fam.* 8
within **dentro de** *prep.* 16
without **sin** *prep.* 15; **sin que** *conj.* 13
without a doubt **sin duda** 6
woman **mujer** *f.* 1; **esposa** *f.* 3
wool **lana** *f.*6
made of wool **de lana** 6
word **palabra** *f.* 1
work **trabajar** *v.* 2; **funcionar** *v.* 11; **trabajo** *m.* 16
work (*of art, literature, music, etc.*) **obra** *f.* 17
work out **hacer gimnasia** 15
workshop *m.* **taller** 1; (*mechanic's*) **taller de mecánica** 11

world **mundo** *m.* 11
worldwide **mundial** *adj.* 5
worried **preocupado/a** *adj.* 5
worry (about) **preocuparse** *v.* **(por)** 7
  Don't worry. **No se preocupe** *form.* 7
worse **peor** *adj.* 8
worst **el/la peor, lo peor** 8
worst: the worst **el/la peor** *m., f.* 8 **lo peor** *neuter* 18
worthy: be worthy **valer la pena** 8
Would you like to? **¿Te gustaría?** 4
write **escribir** *v.* 3
  write a letter/post card/e-mail message **escribir una carta/(tarjeta) postal/ mensaje electrónico** 4
writer **escritor(a)** *m., f* 17
written **escrito/a** *p.p.* 14
wrong **equivocado/a** *adj.* 5
  be wrong **no tener razón** 3

X

X-ray **radiografía** *f.* 10

Y

yard **jardín** *m.* 12; **patio** *m.* 12
year **año** *m.* 2
yellow **amarillo/a** *adj.* 6
yes **sí** 1
yesterday **ayer** *adv.* 6
yet **todavía** *adv.* 5
yogurt **yogur** *m.* 8
You don't say! **¡No me diga(s)!** 11
You're welcome. **De nada.** 1; **No hay de que.** 1
young **joven** *adj.* 3
  young person **joven** *m., f.* 1
younger **menor** *adj.* 3
younger: younger brother, sister *m., f.* **hermano/a menor** 3
youngest **el/la menor** *m., f.* 8
your **su(s)** *poss. form.* 3
  your **tu(s)** *poss. fam. sing.* 3
  your **vuestro/a(s)** *poss. form. pl.* 3
  your(s) *form.* **suyo/a(s)** *poss. form.* 11
  your(s) **tuyo/a(s)** *poss. fam. sing.* 11
youth *f.* **juventud** 9; (young person) **joven** *m., f.* 1
  youth hostel **albergue juvenil** *m.* 5
  youthful **juvenil** *adj.* 1

Z

zero **cero** *m.* 1

Índice

G

H

I

J

L

M

N

Ñ

O

P

Text Credits

450-451 © Marco Denevi, *Falsificaciones*, Buenos Aires, Corregidor, 1999, pág. 52, reprinted by permission of Ediciones Corregidor.
478-479 © María Velázquez, "Noviembre 24, 1992" from *Aun sin saber quién eres*, 1998, reprinted by permission of the author.
506-507 © Antonio Skármeta, un fragmento de *Ardiente Paciencia. El cartero de Neruda*, 1985, reprinted by permission of the author.
536-537 © Claribel Alegría, "Escribir", 1988, reprinted by permission of the author.

Illustration Credits

Cover Illustration: José Ortega
Herman Mejía: 5, 12, 13, 15, 16, 20, 21, 48, 55, 59, 73, 81 (b), 84, 92, 93, 113, 117, 120, 145, 148, 152, 153, 157, 173, 189, 202, 210, 215, 220, 243, 272, 282, 301, 312, 313, 342, 345, 348, 374, 383, 388, 408, 422, 448, 471, 473, 476, 478-479, 508, 531, 540, 565.
Pere Virgili: 2-3, 36-37, 56, 70-71, 81 (t), 104-106, 122, 123, 136-138, 149, 164, 170-172, 200-201, 222, 223, 232-234, 270-271, 298-299, 328-330, 360-362, 394-396, 428-430, 460-462, 488-489, 518-519, 548-549.
Yayo: 9, 43, 77, 111, 143, 177, 207, 241, 277, 305, 335, 367, 401, 418-419, 435, 450-451, 467, 495, 518-519, 525, 555.

Photography Credits

AP: **513** (r) Wide World. **542** (ml).
Martin Bernetti: 1, 2, 6 (b), 10, 14, 17, 28, 30, 31 (b), 32 (b), 35, 38, 40 (b), 46, 51, 52, 60, 61, 62, 64, 65 (b), 69, 71, 72, 74 (b), 80, 82, 85, 87, 88, 94, 95, 96, 98, 99 (ml, mr, bl, br), 100, 101 (ml, bmr, b), 103, 105, 108 (b), 121, 127, 128, 130, 131 (b), 135, 147, 162, 169, 181, 184-187, 192, 194, 195 (b), 199 204 (b), 209, 211, 214, 224, 226, 227, 228 (tl, tr, m,,mr), 229, 231, 237, 244, 262, 264, 269, 273, 297, 302 (b), 309, 320, 322, 327, 332 (b), 339, 344, 352, 354, 359, 363, 386, 393, 395 (tl, bl), 404, 409, 427, 432 (b), 442, 445, 452, 454, 455 (b), 459, 480, 482, 484-485, 487, 491, 492 (b), 510, 511 (b), 517, 528, 535, 538, 547, 558, 564-565, 568.
Corbis Images: **32** (tr), (tl) Robert Holmes, (m) Phil Schermeister. **33** (mr) Tony Arruza, (ml) Qwen Franken, (b) Patrick Ward. **66** (tl, tr) Patrick Ward, (m) Elke Stolzenberg, (b) Reuters New Media Inc. **67** (tl) Paul Almasy, (tr) Jean-Pierre Lescourret, (ml) Francis G. Mayer, (mr) Tony Arruza, (b) Dave G. Houser. **126** **132** (tl) George Lepp. **133** (tr) Bettmann, (br) Sergio Dorantes. **139** (b) David Lees. **140** (b) Davis Less. **166** (b) Dave G. Houser. **167** (tr) Steve Chenn. **197** (br) Ariel Ramerez. **228** (fl) Colita, (b) Yann Arthus-Bertrand. **238** (b) Macduff Everton. **266** (t) Bob Winsett, (ml, mr, b) Dave G. Houser. **267** (tl) Craig Lovell, (tr) Michael and Patricia Fogden, (bl) Jan Butchofsky-Houser, (br) Qwen Franken. **288** (b) Pablo Corral. **289** Patrick Ward. **293** Hubert Stadler. **294** (tl) Dave G. Houser, (ml) Pablo Carral, (bl) Bettmann, (tr, mr) Macduff Everton, (bmr) Charles O'Rear, (br). **295** (tl) Wolfgang Kaehler, (bl) Roger Ressmeyer, (tr) Duomo, (br) Charles O'Rear. **319** Galen Rowell. **323** Stephanie Maze. **324** (tl) Martin Rogers, (tr) Dave G. Houser, (ml) Jan Butchofsky-Houser, (mr) Buddy Mays, (bl) Bill Gentile, (br) Bob Winsett. **325** (t) Wolfgang Kaehler, (mr) Dave G. Houser, (ml) Jacques M. Chenet, (b) Martin Rogers. **355** (b) Kevin Fleming. **356** (t) Stephanie Maze, (ml) Arvind Garg, (mtr, mbr) Galen Rowell, (b) Pablo Corral. **357** (t, r, b) Pablo Corral, (ml) Owen Franken. **364** (b) José F. Poblete. **384** Danny Lehman. **388** **389** (b) Tony Arruza. **390** (tl) Kevin Schafer, (tr, b) Danny Lehman. **391** (tl) Amos Nachoum, (mr) Bettman, (ml) Ralph A. Clevenger, (b) Danny Lehman. **395** (tr) Stephanie Maze, (br) Roger Tidman. **398** (b) Wolfgang Kaehler. **420** Ric Ergenbright. **423** (b) Kennan Ward. **425** (r) **456** (t) Pablo Corral, (ml) Paul A. Souders, (mr) Neil Rabinowitz. **457** (t) Caroline Penn, (mr, ml, b) Pablo Corral. **464** (b) Pablo San Juan. **483** (b) Robert Weight. **504** Bill Gentile. **512** (tl) Jeremy Horner, (tr) Bill Gentile, (m) Kevin Schafer, (b) Stephen Frink. **513** (tl) Brian Vikander, (bl) Gary Braasch. **514** (tl) Tony Arruza, (tr) Reinhard Eisele, (m) Richard Bickel, (b) Francis G. Mayer. **515** (tl) Jeremy Horner, (mr) AFP, (bl) Tony Arruza. **522** (b) Anna Clopet. **541** (b) Carmen Redondo. **542** (tl) Lynda Richardson, (tr) José F. Poblete, (mr) Lake County Museum, (b) AFP. **543** (l) Guy Motil, (r) Frank Lane Picture Agency. **544** (tl) Tom Brakefield, (tr) Macduff Everton, (ml) Owen Franken, (mr) Tony Arruza. **545** (l) Kevin Schafer, (r) Owen Franken. **551** (t) Nik Wheeler, (b) Bill Gentile. **552** (b) Shelley Gazin. **563** (l) Dave G. Houser. **566** Archivo Iconografico, S. A. **570** (t) Peter Guttman, (m) Paul Ammasy, (b) Archivo Iconografico, S. A. **571** (mr) Joel Creed. **572** (tr) Wolfgang Kaehler, (tl) Dave G. Houser, (m) Diego Lezama Orezzoli, (b) Miki Kraftsman. **573** (tl) Dave G. Houser, (mr) Temp Sport, (b) Wolfgang Kaehler.
DDB Stock: **571** (tl) Chris R. Sharp, (bl) Francis E. Caldwell.
Carlos Gaudier: **160-161**, **165** (b), **166** (tl, tr, ml, mr), **167** (tl, bl)
Lenin Martell: **290**
Odyssey/Chicago: **196** (tl, mrb) Robert Frerck. **197** (tl, bl) Robert Frerck, (tr) Barry W. Baker.
PhotoDisc: **29** **31** (t) **33** (tl) **167** (br) **196** (t, b), **563** (r)
Tony Stone Images: **274** (b) Bertrand Rieger. **456** (b) Ken Fisher.
The Viesti Collection: **573** (ml) Joe Viesti.

About the Authors

Philip M. Donley received his M.A. in Hispanic Literature from the University of Texas at Austin in 1986 and his Ph.D. in Foreign Language Education from the University of Texas at Austin in 1997. Dr. Donley has taught Spanish at Austin Community College, Southwestern University, and the University of Texas at Austin. He has published articles and conducted workshops about language anxiety, language anxiety management, and the development of critical thinking skills.

Mary Ann Dellinger is an instructor of Spanish and Second Language methodology at the University of Phoenix (Tucson Campus), as well as the Faculty Curriculum Coordinator for Continuing Education. She has taught Spanish at the secondary and college levels both in the United States and in Spain since 1982. She is currently finishing her doctoral studies in Peninsular Literature at Arizona State University with a specialty in twentieth-century essay. Ms. Dellinger is also the author of several ancillary texts for Spanish for Native Speakers of Spanish at the secondary level, as well as co-author of *Sendas literarias,* Second Edition.

María Isabel García received her degree in Hispanic Philology at the *Universidad de Alicante* (Spain) in 1992 and her M.A. in Hispanic Language and Literature at the University of Rhode Island in 1996. She is currently finishing her doctoral dissertation in Peninsular Literature at Boston University. Ms. García has taught Spanish at the college level both in the United States and overseas since 1994.

José A. Blanco is the President and founder of Hispanex, Inc., a company that has been developing Spanish language materials since 1989. A native of Barranquilla, Colombia, Mr. Blanco holds degrees in literature and Hispanic Studies from Brown University and the University of California, Santa Cruz. He has worked as a writer, editor, and translator for Houghton Mifflin and D.C. Heath and has taught Spanish at the secondary and university levels.

About the Senior Consulting editor

Elaine K. Horwitz is director of the Foreign Language Education Program at the University of Texas at Austin. Professor Horwitz is the author of numerous pedagogical articles and chapters and is particularly well known for her work in foreign language anxiety and learner beliefs about language learning. She has taught foreign languages at the secondary and university levels, as well as undergraduate and graduate methods courses. Professor Horwitz has supervised over forty doctoral students in foreign language education. She received her Ph.D. in Second Language Acquisition and Teaching from the University of Illinois at Urbana-Champaign.